WESTERN CANADA
82

EASTERN CANADA
84

SOUTHEASTERN
CANADA
86

NORTHERN
ROCKIES, U.S.A.
72

UPPER
MIDWEST,
U.S.A.
66

GREAT LAKES,
U.S.A.
64

NORTHEASTERN
U.S.A
58

THE
FAR WEST,
U.S.A.
76

SOUTHWESTERN
U.S.A.
74

LOWER
MIDWEST,
U.S.A.
68

SOUTH ATLANTIC
U.S.A
60

TEXAS, U.S.A.
70

SOUTHEASTERN
U.S.A.
62

THE
BRITISH
ISLES
124

SOUTHERN
GREAT
BRITAIN
126

THE
LOW
COUNTRIES
132

NORTHEASTERN
EUROPE
148

NORTHERN
EUROPEAN
RUSSIA
154

SOUTHERN
EUROPEAN
RUSSIA
156

GERMANY
136

NORTHERN
CENTRAL
EUROPE
142

CENTRAL
EASTERN
EUROPE
150

FRANCE
128

THE ALPINE
NATIONS
138

WESTERN
BALKANS
144

THE IBERIAN
PENINSULA
130

ITALY
AND
MALTA
140

EASTERN
BALKANS
146

THE MEDITERRANEAN SEA
158

P9-DVF-947

THE ARCTIC OCEAN
44

THE RUSSIAN FEDERATION
152

CENTRAL ASIA
178

NORTHEASTERN CHINA
AND KOREA
186

EASTERN ASIA
184

JAPAN
198

TURKEY, CYPRUS,
AND TRANSCAUCASIA
170

A S I A

NORTHERN
MIDDLE EAST
172

AFGHANISTAN, IRAN,
AND PAKISTAN
176

SOUTHEASTERN CHINA
AND TAIWAN
188

Ryuku Islands
198

Sakishima-shotō
198

THE HIMALAYA AND
THE GANGETIC PLAIN
182

THE ARABIAN
PENINSULA
174

SOUTHERN ASIA
180

MAINLAND
SOUTHEAST
ASIA
190

THE PHILIPPINES
196

NORTHEASTERN
AFRICA
212

MICRONESIA
AND POLYNESIA
236

Maldives
180

BRUNEI, MALAYSIA,
AND SINGAPORE
194

Seychelles
38

MARITIME SOUTHEAST ASIA
192

MICRONESIA
AND POLYNESIA
236

CENTRAL AND EAST
AFRICA
216

Cocos Islands
38

MELANESIA
234

Mauritius
38

Rodrigues
38

SOUTHERN
AFRICA
218

Réunion
38

O C E A N I A

AUSTRALIA
230

THE INDIAN OCEAN
38

NEW ZEALAND
232

ANTARCTICA
240

the **illustrated**
WORLD ATLAS

the **illustrated**

WORLD ATLAS

Color reproduction by Colourscan Overseas Co Pte Ltd.
Printed in Singapore by Tien Wah Press (Pte) Limited.

3 5 7 9 10 8 6 4 2 1

CARTOGRAPHIC CONSULTANTS

Dr William Cartwright
Associate Professor in Multimedia Cartography
School of Mathematical and Geospatial Sciences
RMIT University, Melbourne, Australia
Vice-President, International
Cartographic Association

Professor Michael P. Peterson
Department of Geography/Geology
University of Nebraska at Omaha, U.S.A.
Chair, International Cartographic Association
Commission on Maps and the Internet

REGIONAL MAPPING CONSULTANTS

Imran Ali
Cartographer, Pakistan

M. (John) Balodis
FMSIA Adjunct Professor
Curtin University, Perth, Australia

Professor Jean Carrière
Professeur titulaire
Directeur du Département de géographie
Université du Québec à Montréal, Canada

Dr Prem Chetri
School of Mathematical and Geospatial Sciences
RMIT University, Melbourne, Australia

Professor Benjamin Cohen
Department of Photogrammetry
and Cartography
University of Architecture, Civil Engineering
and Geodesy, Sofia, Bulgaria

Igor Drecki
Geographics Unit Manager
School of Geography and Environmental Science
University of Auckland, Auckland, New Zealand

Dr Francisco Escobar
Profesor Titular de Análisis Geográfico Regional
Departamento de Geografía
Universidad de Alcalá de Henares, Spain

Dr David Fairbairn
School of Civil Engineering and Geosciences
University of Newcastle, Newcastle, U.K.

Steve Foldi
Cartographer, Windsor, Australia

Scott Furey
School of Mathematical and Geospatial Sciences
RMIT University, Melbourne, Australia

Professor Dr Georg Gartner
Institut für Kartographie und Geo-Medientechnik
Technische Universitat Wien, Vienna, Austria

Ibrahim Hanna
Hydrogeologist, Syria

Hashim al Hashimi
Geo-Information Analyst
Environmental Research and Wildlife
Development Agency, United Arab Emirates

Dr Stephen Hutchinson
Southampton Oceanography Centre
University of Southampton, Southampton, U.K.

Dr Simon Jones
School of Mathematical and Geospatial Sciences
RMIT University, Melbourne, Australia

Professor Milan Konecny
Department of Geography, Faculty of Science
Masaryk University, Brno, Czech Republic

Professor Alexandra Koussoulakou
Department of Cadastre, Photogrammetry
and Cartography
The Aristotle University, Thessaloniki, Greece

Colin Kropman
Geographic Consultant, Sydney, Australia

Hyun Jong (David) Lee
Sung Kyun Kwan University, Seoul, South Korea

Antonio Hernández Navarro
Geodetic Coordinator
National Institute of Statistics,
Geography and Informatics (INEGI)
National Mapping Agency of Mexico,
Aguascaliente, Mexico

Professor Ferjan Ormeling,
University of Utrecht, Netherlands
Secretary-General, International
Cartographic Association

Will Pringle
Cartographic Director
Australian Geographic Pty Ltd,
Sydney, Australia

Professor Patrick Quilty
Honorary Research Professor
School of Earth Sciences
University of Tasmania, Hobart, Australia

Cristhiane da Silva Ramos
School of Mathematical and Geospatial Sciences
RMIT University, Melbourne, Australia

Rushan Gul Rozi
School of Mathematical and Geospatial Sciences
RMIT University, Melbourne, Australia

Afshin Alizadeh Shabini
University of Tehran, Tehran, Iran

Hussein Tawansi
Fellow Member, Institute of Quarrying
Sydney, Australia

Professor Dr Theodor Wintges
Munich University of Applied Sciences,
Munich, Germany

Assistant Professor Hiroyuki Yoshida
Faculty of Policy Management
SFC, Keio University, Endo, Japan

Jason Zhang
School of Mathematical and Geospatial Sciences
RMIT University, Melbourne, Australia

THEMATIC MAPPING CONSULTANTS

Dr Colin Arrowsmith
Senior Lecturer
School of Mathematical and Geospatial Sciences
RMIT University, Melbourne, Australia

Dr Paul Bahn
Archaeologist/author, Hull, U.K.

Robert Burnham
Senior Editor, *Astronomy* Magazine
Hales Corner, U.S.A

Dr Susan Canney
Department of Zoology
University of Oxford, Oxford, U.K.

Professor Bernard Comrie
Director, Department of Linguistics
Max Planck Institute for Evolutionary
Anthropology, Leipzig, Germany

Professor John Connell
School of Geosciences
University of Sydney, Sydney, Australia

Associate Professor Jim Forrest
Head, Department of Human Geography
Macquarie University, Sydney, Australia

Dr Stephen Gale
School of Geoscience
University of Sydney, Sydney, Australia

Dr Stephen Hutchinson
Southampton Oceanography Centre
University of Southampton, Southampton, U.K.

Dorothy F. Prescott
Senior Fellow
School of Anthropology, Geography
and Environmental Science
University of Melbourne, Melbourne, Australia

Professor John Robert Victor Prescott
Professor Emeritus and Professorial Fellow
School of Anthropology, Geography
and Environmental Studies
University of Melbourne, Melbourne, Australia

Professor Patrick Quilty
Honorary Research Professor
School of Earth Sciences
University of Tasmania, Hobart, Australia

Dr Anne I. Thackeray
Honorary Research Associate
Archaeology Division, School of Geography,
Archaeology and Environmental Studies
University of the Witwatersrand,
Johannesburg, South Africa

Richard Whitaker
Weathersmart Meteorological Services
Sydney, Australia

Associate Professor Charles Zika
Head, Department of History
University of Melbourne, Melbourne, Australia

Below: The dark-red Namib Desert is
clearly visible at bottom center in this
satellite photo of the southwestern
coast of Africa.

Below left: These abstract patterns are
sand beds in The Bahamas that have been
carved by the tides and currents.

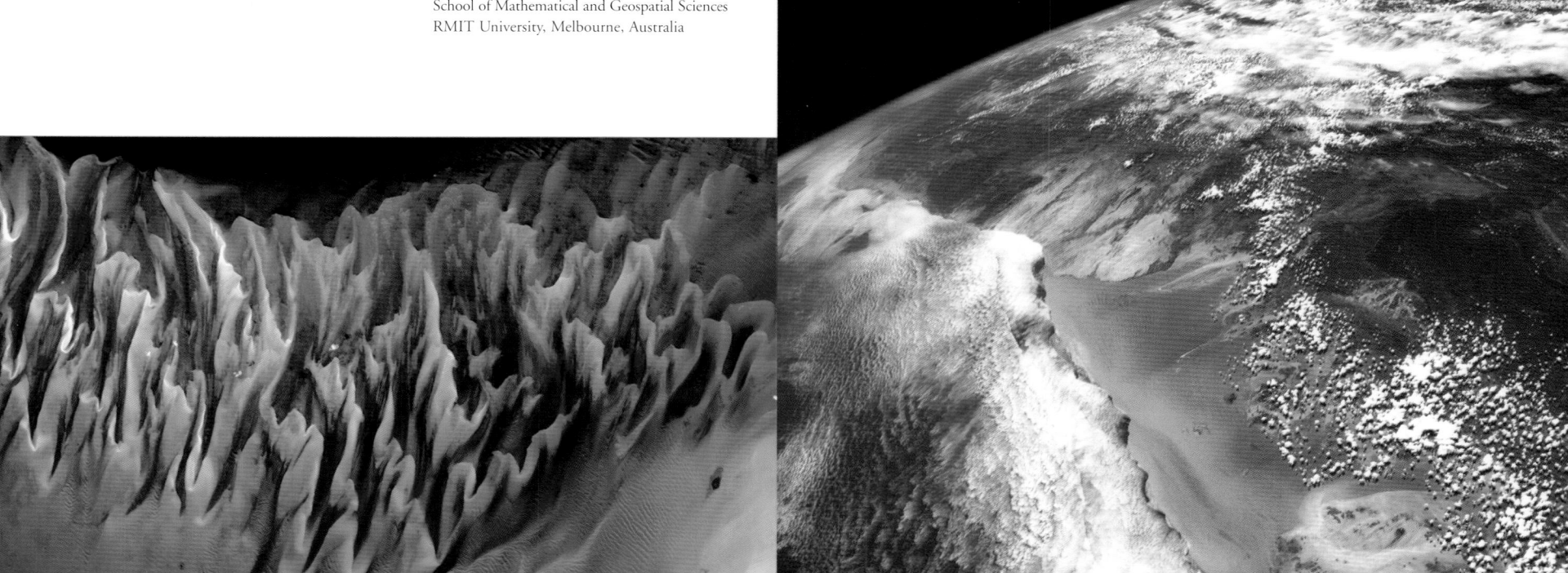

CONTENTS

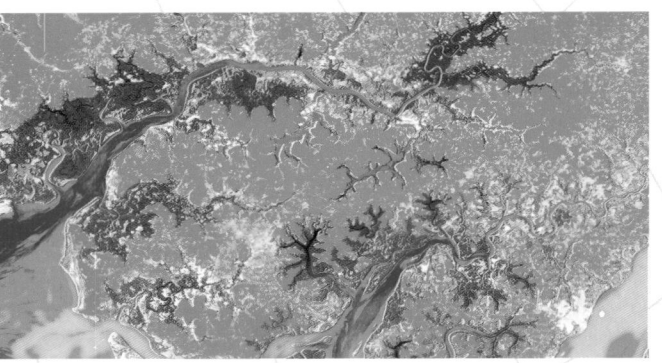
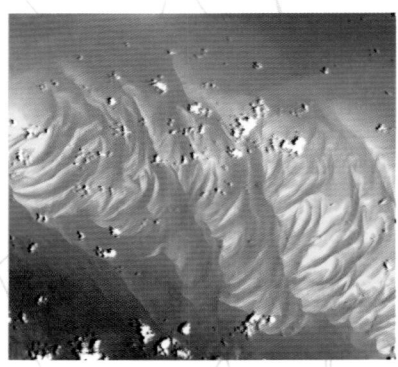
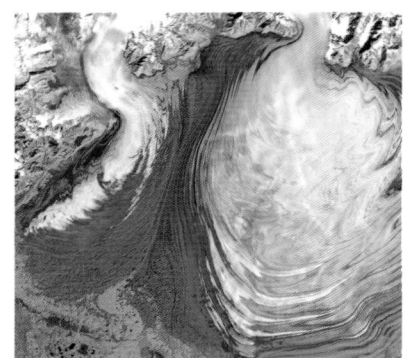
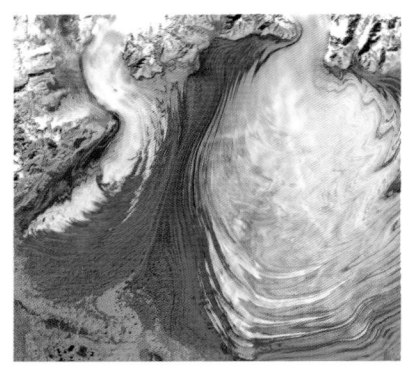
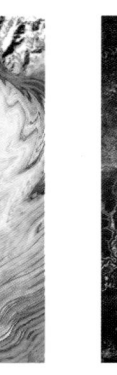

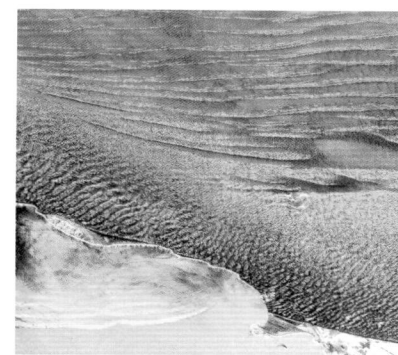

HOW TO USE THIS ATLAS

The atlas is organized into two major sections. The first, World View, provides an introductory survey of the physical, human, and economic geography of planet Earth. The second section, Mapping the World, contains detailed regional maps, arranged by continent, and includes physical, political, and human impact maps for the six largest continents. A reference section completes the atlas. It includes geographical comparisons, a fact file of the world's nations, a glossary, and a complete gazetteer.

REGIONAL MAPS

Each central map is accompanied by economic profile and population pattern maps. Included for selected regions are three-dimensional terrain maps and illustrations of significant cities. Annotated photographs of regional features support the central maps.

Grid reference
The location of each place, as listed in the gazetteer, is referenced against the grid frame.

Regional map
Each regional map includes detailed information on the physical landscape of a region, as well as its human geography.

Photographs
Photographs of natural features and human structures are included, with captions.

Locator map
This map indicates the location of the region within its continent.

Illustration
Illustrations highlight significant areas within a major city.

Population Patterns key

Population Patterns map
The population distribution of the area is plotted on this map.

Economic Profile key

Economic Profile map
The regional land use and economic activity are displayed on this map.

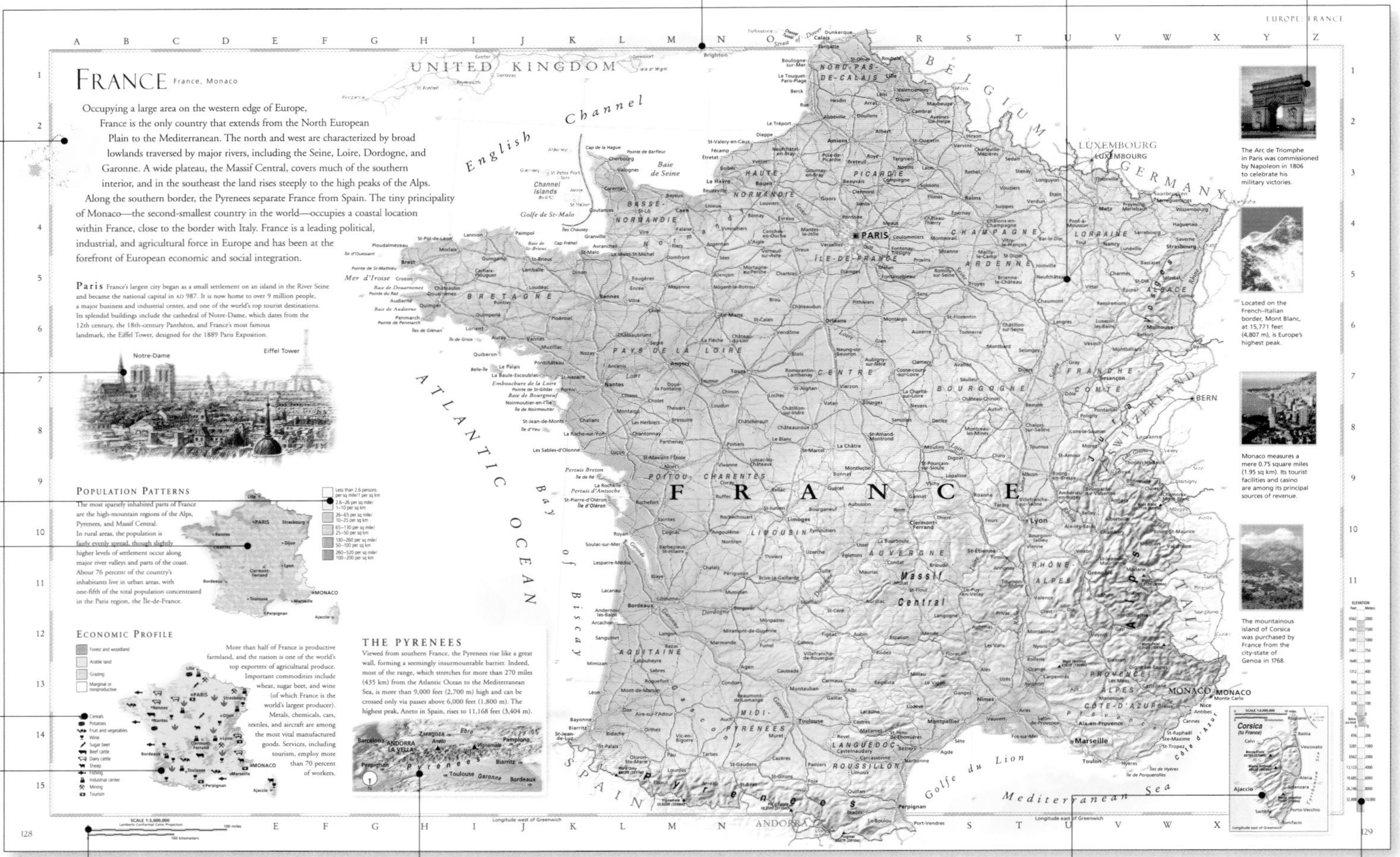

Scale
The scale of the main map, plus a scale bar and projection information, are included here.

Three-dimensional terrain map
This computer-generated map focuses on a specific physical feature.

Inset map
Associated regions that fall outside the area are included as detailed inset maps.

Elevation chart
This chart indicates elevation, the height above sea level, as well as ocean depths.

THEMATIC MAPS

These pages include detailed world maps accompanied by illustrations, diagrams, charts, graphs, and photographs. They cover topics as diverse as our place in space, climate, wildlife, natural resources, exploration, population, religions, languages, indigenous peoples, transport and communications, economics, and governments.

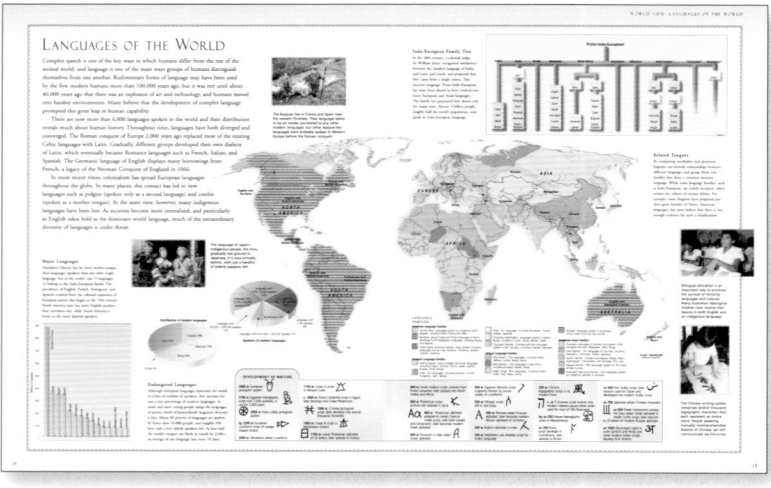

SATELLITE VIEWS

Included for the six largest continents are double-page spreads featuring images obtained from the satellites that orbit the globe. The photos reveal the diversity of population patterns, agricultural areas, and concentrations of industry across the continents. From space, the details of landscapes and the impact of human activity are often startlingly clear.

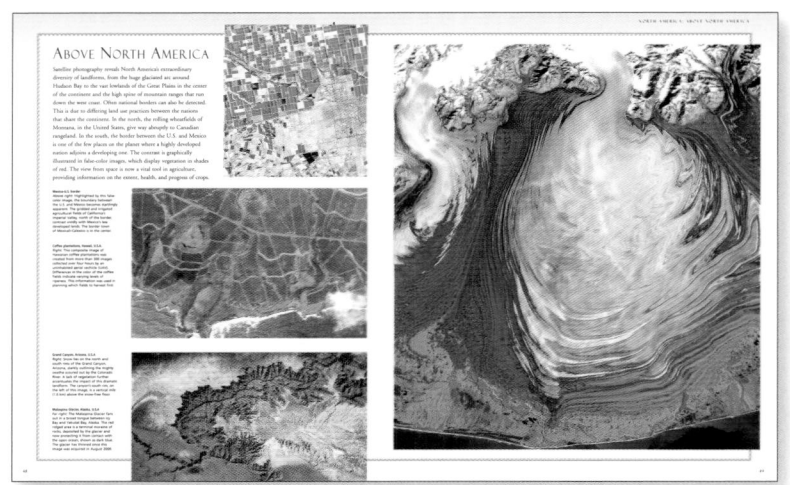

PHYSICAL CONTINENT MAPS

The central map displays the landform of each continent, including major waterways, mountain ranges, and geographical features. Smaller maps reveal the continental climate and vegetation zones. A side panel, containing a map, diagram, and photograph, reviews a significant natural hazard that occurs on the continent. Satellite photographs highlight major physical features of the continent.

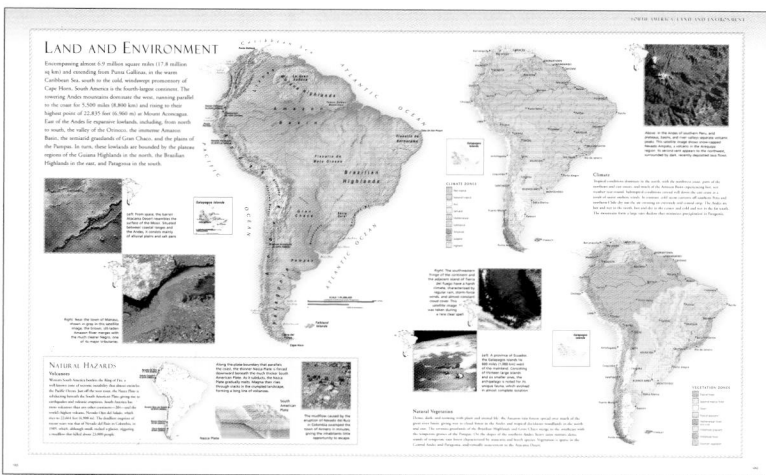

POLITICAL CONTINENT MAPS

The large political map displays the human geography of the continent. Supporting maps reveal the continental population distribution, and trade or political organizations. A series of historical maps highlight major political and social changes over time. A side panel includes flashpoint maps that focus on areas of current dispute and conflict. The maps are accompanied by a graph indicating the population of the largest cities.

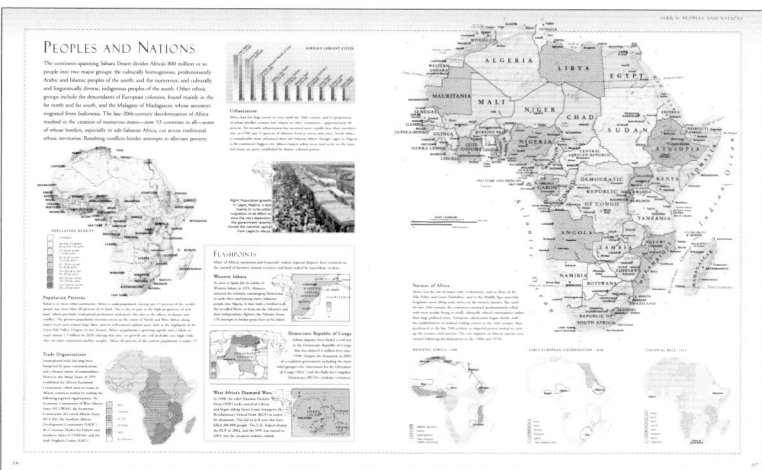

HUMAN IMPACT CONTINENT MAPS

The main map indicates land use and significant economic activities across the continent. A supporting map, accompanied by photographs, underlines the threats to the continent's environment. A side panel focuses on a dramatic environmental change as a result of human activity. A graph showing protected land illustrates the efforts of selected countries to reverse environmental damage.

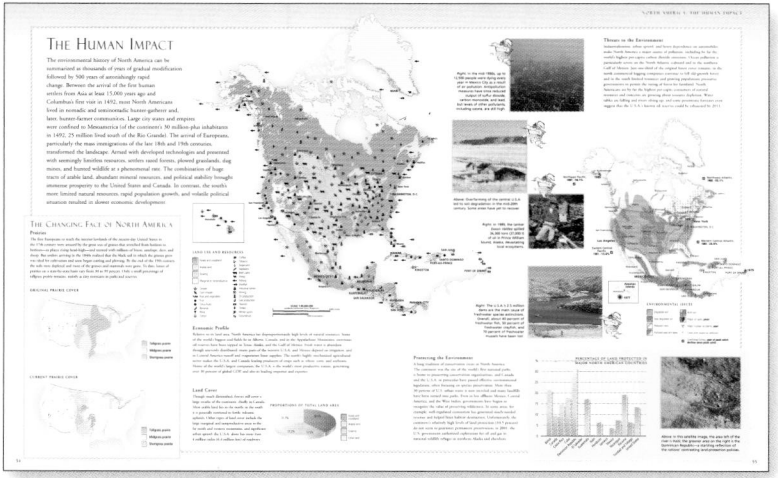

KEY TO REGIONAL MAPS

PHYSICAL FEATURES

ELEVATION

Feet	Meters
6562	2000
4921	1500
3281	1000
2461	750
1640	500
1312	400
984	300
656	200
328	100
Below sea level	0
0	0
656	200
3281	1000
6562	2000
13,123	4000
19,685	6000
26,246	8000
32,808	10,000

Ice cap
Ice shelf

▲ Mountain peak/volcano
Height, feet (meters)
+ Pole
△ Geomagnetic Pole
▲ Seamount
▼ Sea trench
Depth, feet (meters)

WATER FEATURES

Lake
Salt pan/Dry/Intermittent lake
Coastline
~ Major river
~ Minor river
✖ River source
▼ Waterfall

TRANSPORT

Major road
Main road
Minor road
Railway

GRATICULE FEATURE

125° Graticule number
Graticule line
Tropics/polar circle
Equator

BORDERS

International border
Defined maritime boundary
Equidistant lines
Disputed border
Demarcation/line of control/ceasefire line
State/territory border (Australia, Canada, U.S.A.)
International Date Line

NATIONAL/DEPENDENT TERRITORY CAPITAL CITIES

Over 5 million	▣	**LONDON**
1–5 million	◉	**OTTAWA**
100,000–1 million	✴	**HELSINKI**
100,000–1 million	✴	**KINGSTON**
0–100,000	✴	**HONIARA**
0–100,000	✴	**BELMOPAN**

STATE/TERRITORY CAPITAL CITIES (Australia, Canada, U.S.A.)

Over 5 million	▣	**Toronto**
1–5 million	◉	Sydney
100,000–1 million	✴	Québec
0–100,000	✴	Columbia

OTHER CITIES OR TOWNS

Over 5 million	■	**São Paulo**
1–5 million	●	Calicut
100,000–1 million	○	Luxor
0–100,000	○	Lillehammer

□ Research base

Built-up area

TYPOGRAPHIC KEY

POLITICAL FEATURES

Country	**BELIZE**
Dependent territory with parent state	VIRGIN ISLANDS *(to U.S.A.)*
Internal administrative region	UMBRIA
State/Territory (Australia, Canada, U.S.A.)	VICTORIA

PHYSICAL FEATURES

Mountain range	*Allegheny Mountains*
Mountain peak	*Mt Davis*
Geographic feature	*Nullarbor Plain*
Peninsula	*Cape York Peninsula*
Headland/point/cape	*Cabo de São Vincent*
Island group	*Solomon Islands*
Island	*New Caledonia*
Pole	*North Pole*

WATER FEATURES

Ocean	*PACIFIC OCEAN*
Sea	*Irish Sea*
Bay/gulf	*Gulf of Mexico*
Channel/strait	*Bass Strait*
Undersea ridge	*Carlsberg Ridge*
Seamount/Sea trench	*Golden Dragon Seamount*
Lake/Salt pan/Dry/Intermittent lake	*Lake Titicaca*
Major river	*Nile*
Minor river	*Salween*
River source	*Source of the Amazon*
Waterfall	*Angel Falls*

GRATICULE FEATURES

| Tropics/polar circle/equator | Tropic of Capricorn |
| Date line | International Date Line |

INDEX TO MAP PAGES

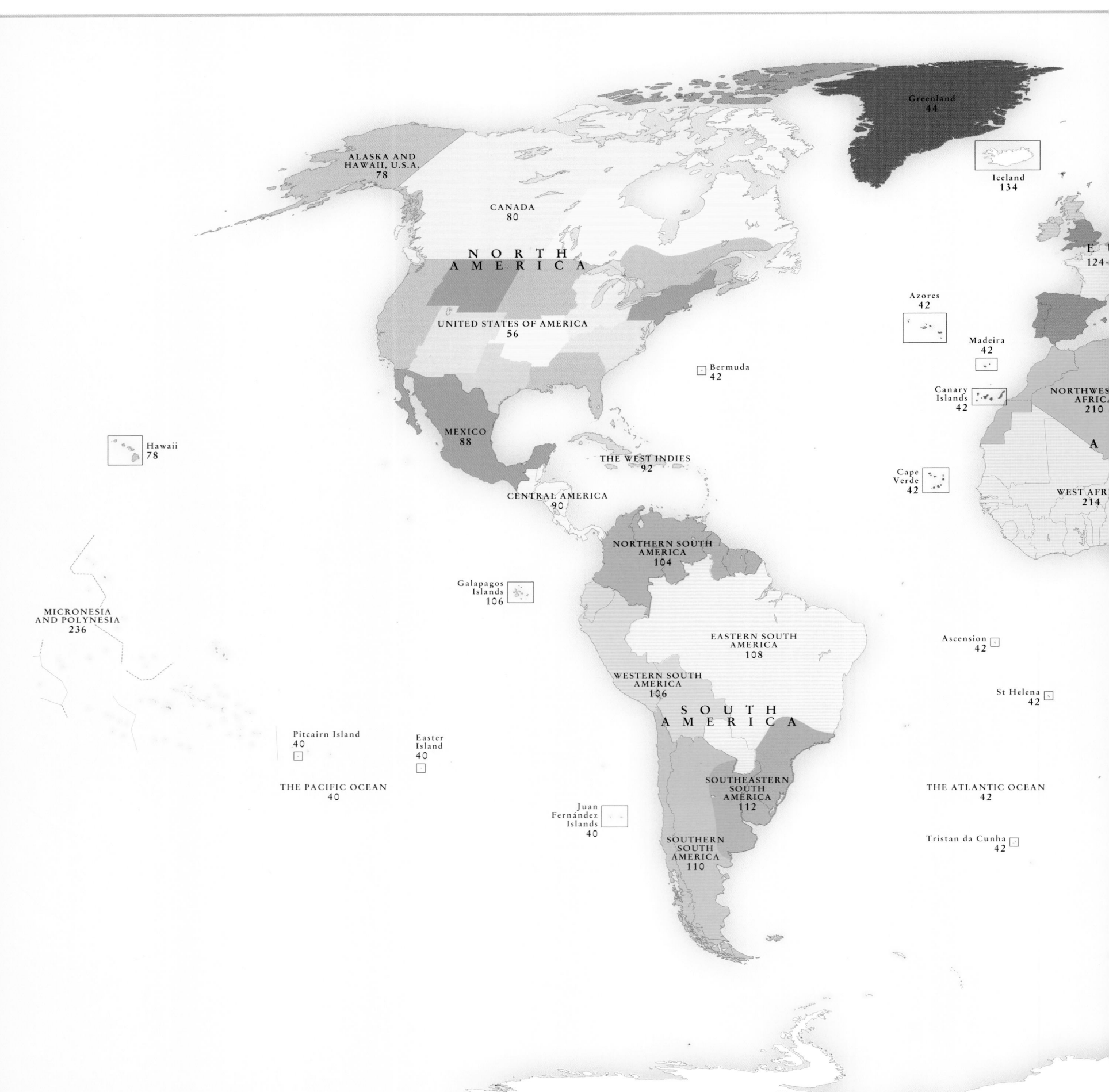

Greenland
44

Iceland
134

ALASKA AND
HAWAII, U.S.A.
78

CANADA
80

NORTH
AMERICA

E
124-

UNITED STATES OF AMERICA
56

Azores
42

Madeira
42

Bermuda
42

Canary
Islands
42

NORTHWES
AFRIC.
210

Hawaii
78

MEXICO
88

THE WEST INDIES
92

Cape
Verde
42

WEST AFR
214

A

CENTRAL AMERICA
90

NORTHERN SOUTH
AMERICA
104

Galapagos
Islands
106

MICRONESIA
AND POLYNESIA
236

EASTERN SOUTH
AMERICA
108

Ascension
42

WESTERN SOUTH
AMERICA
106

SOUTH
AMERICA

St Helena
42

Pitcairn Island
40

Easter
Island
40

THE PACIFIC OCEAN
40

SOUTHEASTERN
SOUTH
AMERICA
112

THE ATLANTIC OCEAN
42

Juan
Fernández
Islands
40

Tristan da Cunha
42

SOUTHERN
SOUTH
AMERICA
110

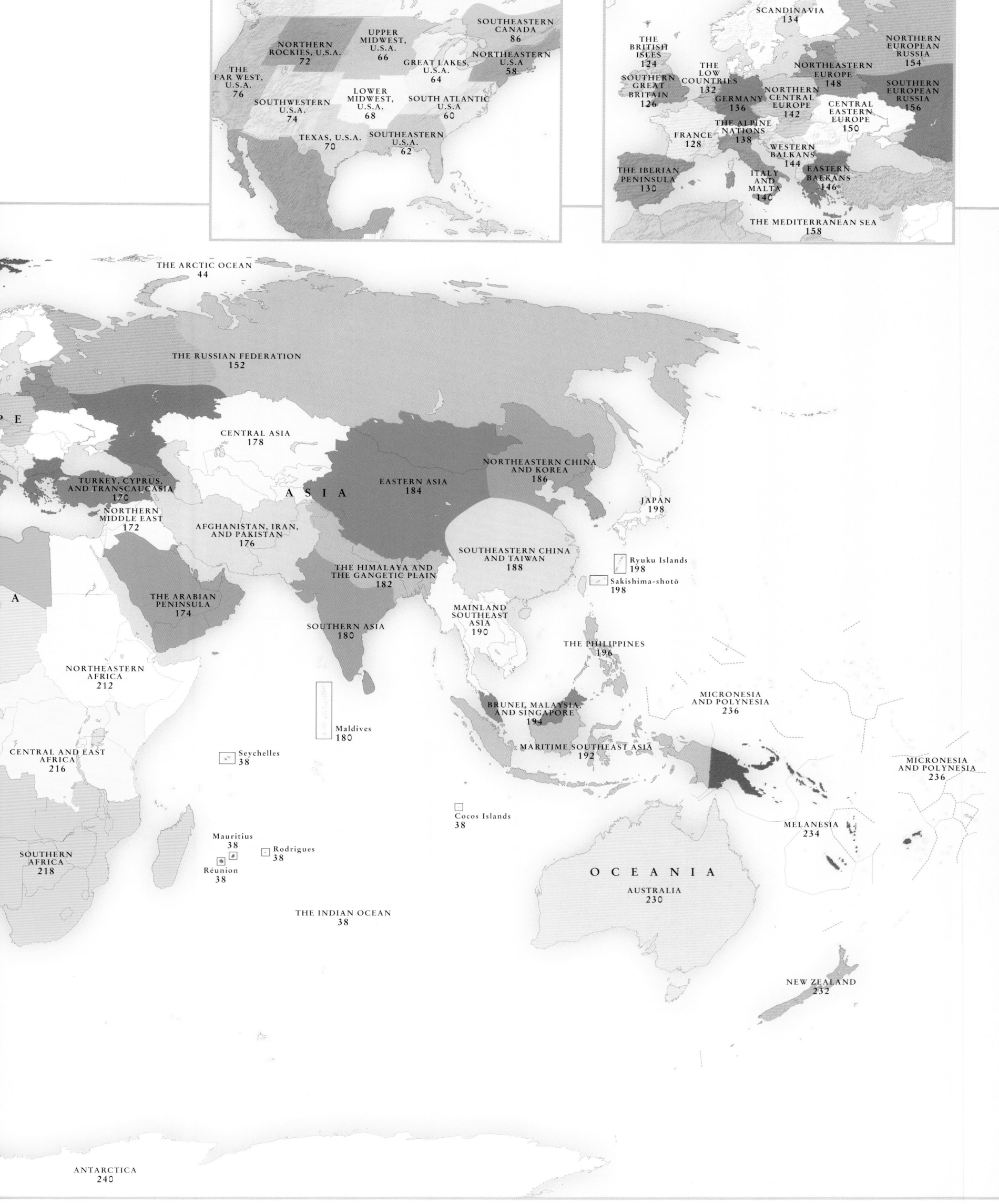

WESTERN CANADA
82

EASTERN CANADA
84

SOUTHEASTERN
CANADA
86

NORTHERN
ROCKIES, U.S.A.
72

UPPER
MIDWEST, U.S.A.
66

NORTHEASTERN
U.S.A
58

THE
FAR WEST,
U.S.A.
76

GREAT LAKES,
U.S.A.
64

SOUTHWESTERN
U.S.A.
74

LOWER
MIDWEST,
U.S.A.
68

SOUTH ATLANTIC
U.S.A
60

TEXAS, U.S.A.
70

SOUTHEASTERN
U.S.A.
62

SCANDINAVIA
134

THE
BRITISH
ISLES
124

NORTHERN
EUROPEAN
RUSSIA
154

SOUTHERN
GREAT
BRITAIN
126

THE
LOW
COUNTRIES
132

NORTHEASTERN
EUROPE
148

GERMANY
136

NORTHERN
CENTRAL
EUROPE
142

SOUTHERN
EUROPEAN
RUSSIA
156

CENTRAL
EASTERN
EUROPE
150

FRANCE
128

THE ALPINE
NATIONS
138

WESTERN
BALKANS
144

THE IBERIAN
PENINSULA
130

ITALY
AND
MALTA
140

EASTERN
BALKANS
146

THE MEDITERRANEAN SEA
158

THE ARCTIC OCEAN
44

THE RUSSIAN FEDERATION
152

CENTRAL ASIA
178

NORTHEASTERN CHINA
AND KOREA
186

PE

TURKEY, CYPRUS,
AND TRANSCAUCASIA
170

EASTERN ASIA
184

A S I A

JAPAN
198

NORTHERN
MIDDLE EAST
172

AFGHANISTAN, IRAN,
AND PAKISTAN
176

A

SOUTHEASTERN CHINA
AND TAIWAN
188

Ryuku Islands
198

THE HIMALAYA AND
THE GANGETIC PLAIN
182

Sakishima-shotō
198

THE ARABIAN
PENINSULA
174

MAINLAND
SOUTHEAST
ASIA
190

NORTHEASTERN
AFRICA
212

SOUTHERN ASIA
180

THE PHILIPPINES
196

MICRONESIA
AND POLYNESIA
236

Maldives
180

BRUNEI, MALAYSIA,
AND SINGAPORE
194

CENTRAL AND EAST
AFRICA
216

Seychelles
38

MICRONESIA
AND POLYNESIA
236

MARITIME SOUTHEAST ASIA
192

Cocos Islands
38

MELANESIA
234

Mauritius
38

Rodrigues
38

Réunion
38

O C E A N I A

SOUTHERN
AFRICA
218

AUSTRALIA
230

THE INDIAN OCEAN
38

NEW ZEALAND
232

ANTARCTICA
240

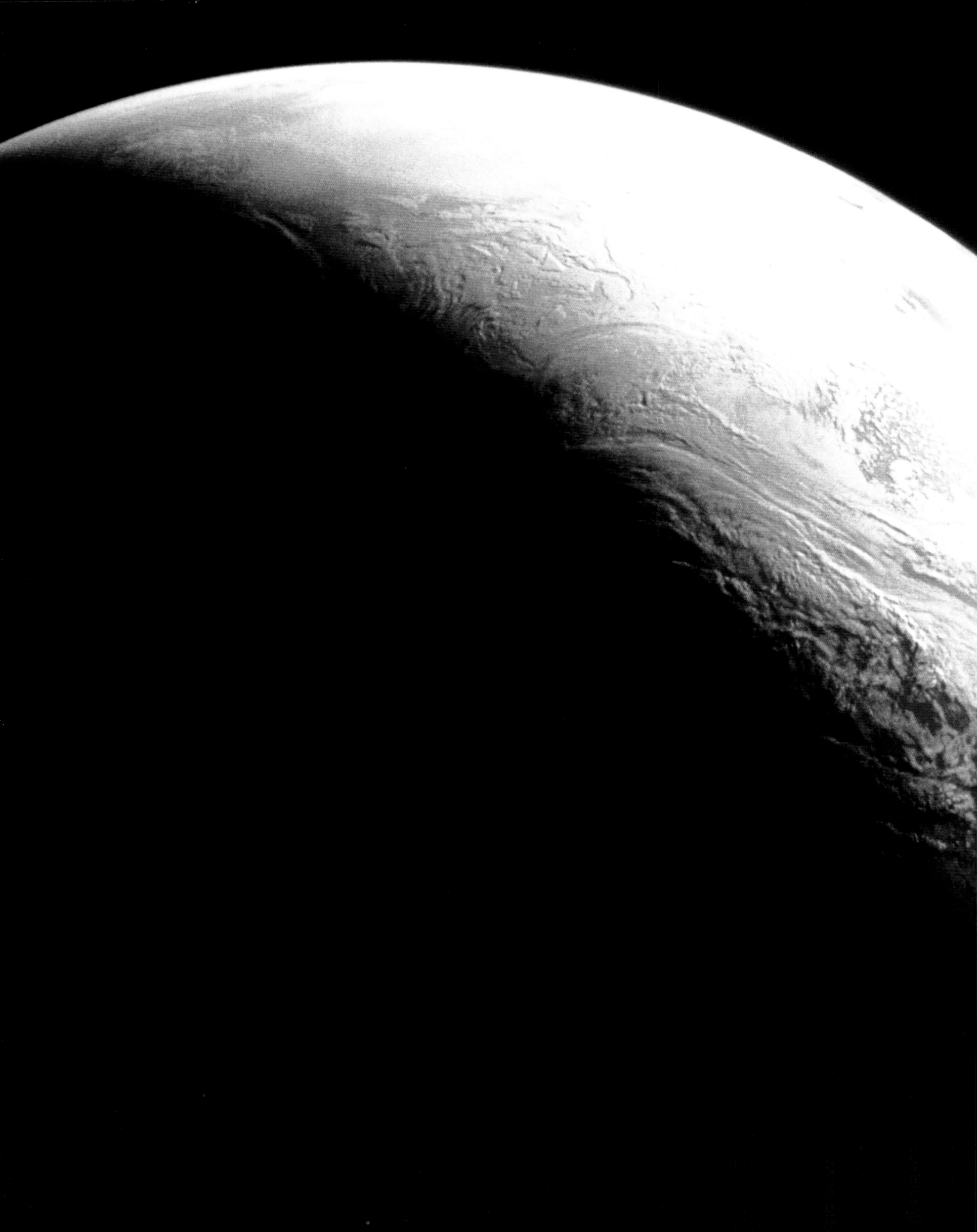

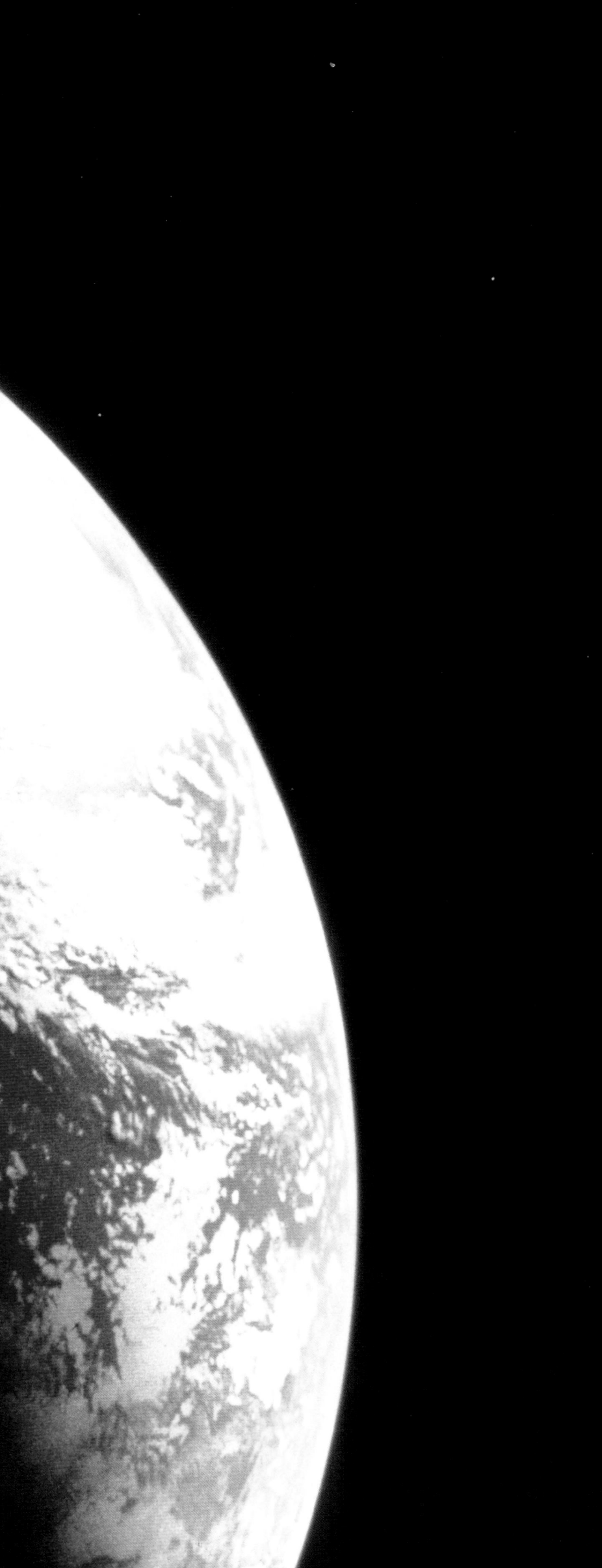

WORLD VIEW

This image of Earth was taken from the Apollo 4 spacecraft, which was launched on November 9, 1967. It is one of the earliest photographs of Earth taken from space. The dramatic distinction between day and night is clearly visible, and the side of the planet in daylight appears to form a crescent. It is difficult to distinguish any physical features on the sunlit side of Earth due to the significant amount of cloud cover.

Our Place in Space

As vast as our planet may seem when we map and describe its features, it is a mere speck compared to the immensity of the universe. Earth is the third of nine planets orbiting the Sun, which is just one of 200 billion stars in the Milky Way galaxy. The Milky Way, in turn, is simply one of perhaps 50 billion galaxies that populate space.

The solar system forms Earth's local neighborhood. At its center is the Sun, a giant ball of hydrogen and helium. Like other stars, the Sun shines because nuclear reactions in its core release tremendous amounts of energy. The planets fall into two main groups—the inner rocky planets of Mercury, Venus, Earth, and Mars, and the outer gas giants of Jupiter, Saturn, Uranus, and Neptune. The ninth planet, Pluto, fits into neither group and is probably an icy planetesimal. Other icy planetesimals orbit beyond Pluto, some traveling inward to become comets. Smaller, rocky bodies known as asteroids orbit in a loose band between Mars and Jupiter or occasionally pass near Earth. Meteoroids are pieces of rocky debris scattered through the solar system. We see them as meteors, or "shooting stars," when they burn up after entering Earth's atmosphere.

Beyond the solar system are other stars, some with their own planets. The Sun, other stars, and clouds of gas and dust make up the Milky Way galaxy, part of a cluster of galaxies known as the Local Group. This cluster belongs to the Local Supercluster, one of the many collections of galaxies thought to make up the honeycomb structure of the universe.

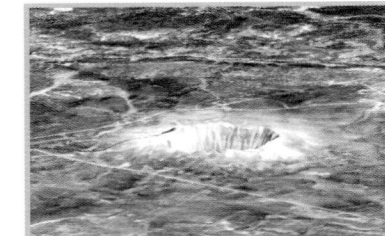

Earth rises over the Moon's dusty surface in this image captured by Apollo astronauts. Our planet's only natural satellite, the Moon is 2,160 miles (3,476 km) in diameter.

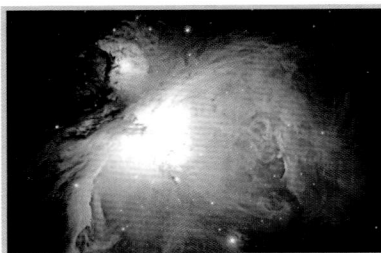

Erosion has erased most of Earth's impact scars, but a few can still be seen. A house-size meteorite that struck 50,000 years ago created Meteor Crater in Arizona, U.S.A.

Throughout space, new stars are being born in clouds of gas and dust known as nebulas. The Orion nebula is one of many star-producing regions in the Milky Way galaxy.

Neptune
- 30,775 miles (49,528 km) wide
- 17.1 x Earth's mass
- 2,793 million miles (4,495 million km) from Sun
- 164.8 year orbit
- 16h 7m rotation
- 13 moons

Pluto
- 1,485 miles (2,390 km) wide
- 0.002 x Earth's mass
- 3,647 million miles (5,870 million km) from Sun
- 248 year orbit
- 6.4 day rotation
- 1 moon

Where Space Begins

No sharp line separates space from Earth's atmosphere—the air just gradually becomes thinner with altitude. The atmosphere's last traces can be detected roughly 600 miles (1,000 km) above the ground.

Exosphere

Thermosphere

Mesosphere

Stratosphere

Troposphere

120 miles (190 km)

50 miles (80 km)

30 miles (50 km)

6 miles (10 km)

Sea level

To the Edge of the Universe

One light-year is the distance that light travels in a year, or 5.9 trillion miles (9.5 trillion km). On this scale, the Moon is just 1.3 light-seconds from Earth, while Pluto, the most distant planet, is 6 light-hours away. The Milky Way galaxy is 100,000 light-years across, and the nearest large galaxy, Andromeda, lies at a distance of 2.8 million light-years. The edge of the visible universe lies more than 13 billion light-years away.

The Local Group
With about 40 members, the Local Group is a cluster of galaxies held together by their mutual gravity. It features three large spiral galaxies—our own Milky Way, the Andromeda galaxy, and the Pinwheel.

The solar system
The Sun makes up 99.9 percent of the solar system's mass. Its powerful gravity keeps Earth and eight other planets in orbit, along with countless smaller bodies—more than 135 moons, millions of asteroids, and maybe trillions of comets.

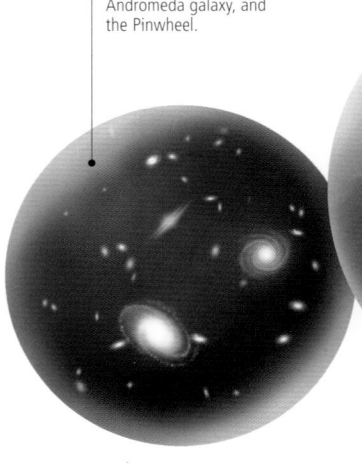

The Milky Way
Our galaxy is made up of the Sun and about 200 billion other stars. The spiral is slowly turning, with the Sun taking 226 million years to complete one revolution.

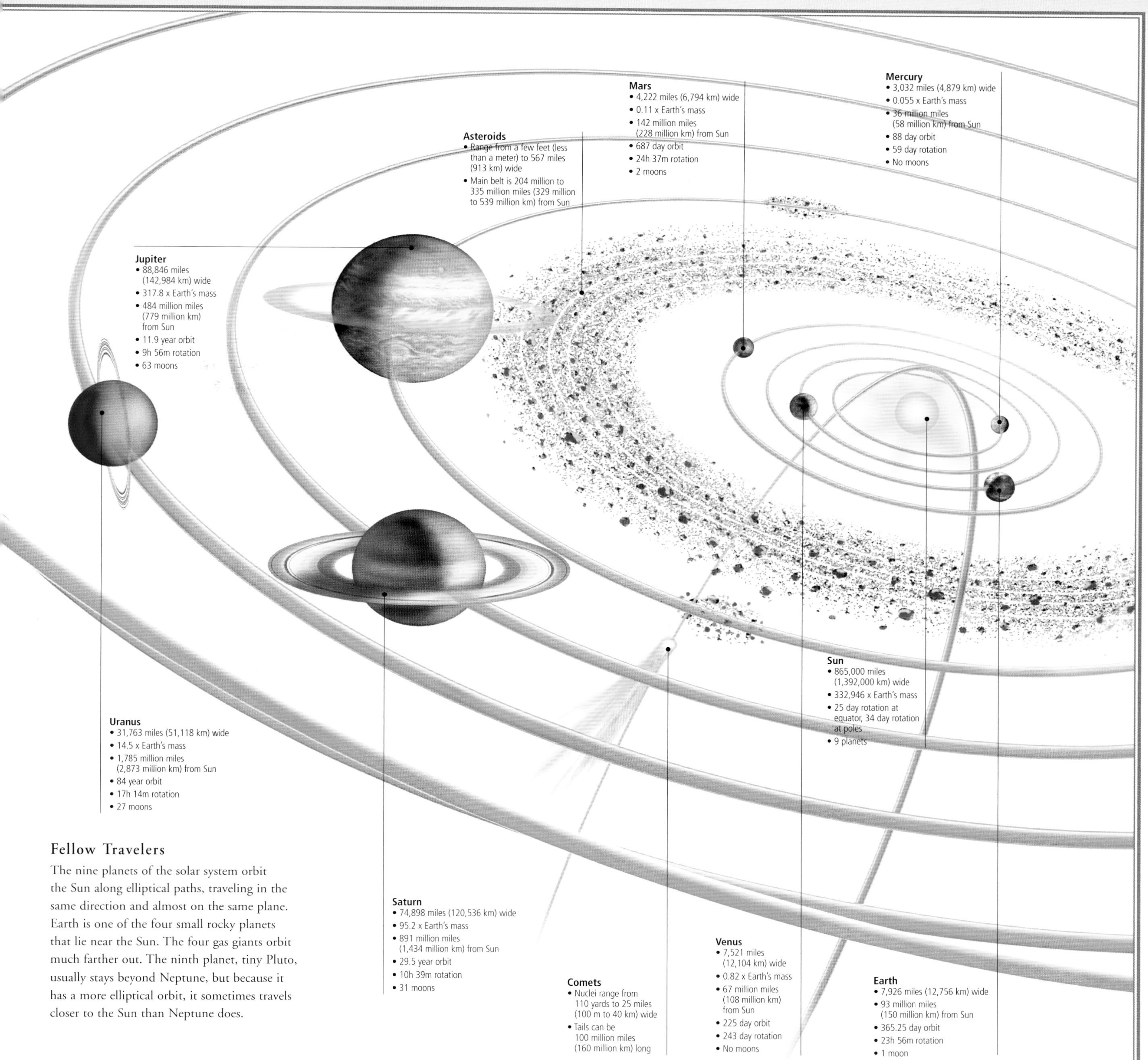

Mars
- 4,222 miles (6,794 km) wide
- 0.11 x Earth's mass
- 142 million miles (228 million km) from Sun
- 687 day orbit
- 24h 37m rotation
- 2 moons

Mercury
- 3,032 miles (4,879 km) wide
- 0.055 x Earth's mass
- 36 million miles (58 million km) from Sun
- 88 day orbit
- 59 day rotation
- No moons

Asteroids
- Range from a few feet (less than a meter) to 567 miles (913 km) wide
- Main belt is 204 million to 335 million miles (329 million to 539 million km) from Sun

Jupiter
- 88,846 miles (142,984 km) wide
- 317.8 x Earth's mass
- 484 million miles (779 million km) from Sun
- 11.9 year orbit
- 9h 56m rotation
- 63 moons

Uranus
- 31,763 miles (51,118 km) wide
- 14.5 x Earth's mass
- 1,785 million miles (2,873 million km) from Sun
- 84 year orbit
- 17h 14m rotation
- 27 moons

Sun
- 865,000 miles (1,392,000 km) wide
- 332,946 x Earth's mass
- 25 day rotation at equator, 34 day rotation at poles
- 9 planets

Fellow Travelers

The nine planets of the solar system orbit the Sun along elliptical paths, traveling in the same direction and almost on the same plane. Earth is one of the four small rocky planets that lie near the Sun. The four gas giants orbit much farther out. The ninth planet, tiny Pluto, usually stays beyond Neptune, but because it has a more elliptical orbit, it sometimes travels closer to the Sun than Neptune does.

Saturn
- 74,898 miles (120,536 km) wide
- 95.2 x Earth's mass
- 891 million miles (1,434 million km) from Sun
- 29.5 year orbit
- 10h 39m rotation
- 31 moons

Comets
- Nuclei range from 110 yards to 25 miles (100 m to 40 km) wide
- Tails can be 100 million miles (160 million km) long

Venus
- 7,521 miles (12,104 km) wide
- 0.82 x Earth's mass
- 67 million miles (108 million km) from Sun
- 225 day orbit
- 243 day rotation
- No moons

Earth
- 7,926 miles (12,756 km) wide
- 93 million miles (150 million km) from Sun
- 365.25 day orbit
- 23h 56m rotation
- 1 moon

SOLAR SYSTEM BIRTH

Most scientists believe that the solar system formed about 4.6 billion years ago, when a large cloud of dust and gas began to collapse. The densest part of the cloud formed a core that grew hotter and larger, eventually becoming the infant Sun. Meanwhile, some of the cloud formed a broad disk around the hot core. As dust particles in the disk collided, they formed solid bodies, which continued to grow through further collisions. Near the heat of the young Sun, the bodies were rocky and would become the small inner planets, while farther out they remained water- and gas-rich and ended up as the gas giant planets.

Spinning Disk
A cloud of dust and gas collapses and forms the solar nebula, a broad, thin disk rotating around a dense core.

Colliding Bodies
The core becomes the hot infant Sun, as lumps of dust in the disk collide and form solid bodies called planetesimals.

Sun and Planets
The Sun becomes a star and, through violent collisions, the planetesimals gradually grow and form the planets.

EARTH'S STRUCTURE

Beneath our feet, planet Earth is restless. The continents slowly drift, mountains are gradually built, earthquakes shake the ground, and volcanoes spectacularly erupt. Meanwhile, on the surface, wind and water sculpt intricate shapes from the land.

Deep inside Earth, the heat of its iron–nickel core stirs the rocks of the mantle above it. Like slowly boiling water, mantle rocks circulate in convection currents, rising as they heat up and forming a soft layer called the asthenosphere. As they move toward the thin rocky crust at the surface, the mantle rocks cool and become solid. Together, the crust and the solid upper mantle form Earth's outer layer, the lithosphere, which carries the continents and oceans.

The movements of the mantle cracked the lithosphere of the young Earth, splitting it into tectonic plates. Today, the convection currents continue to shift the plates, slowly but surely. Plates sliding past each other can rattle the ground in an earthquake. Plates moving apart can widen an ocean or create a new sea. And colliding plates may form mountains, volcanoes, or ocean trenches. Over millions of years, tectonic activity also alters the shape and position of the continents.

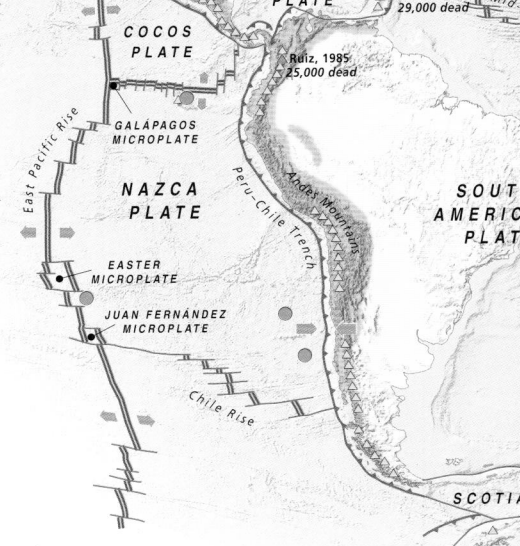

Tectonic Boundaries

The movements of the seven large and many small tectonic plates that make up Earth's surface have shaped much of the land and ocean floor. This map shows how the distribution of volcanoes and earthquakes relates closely to the plate boundaries.

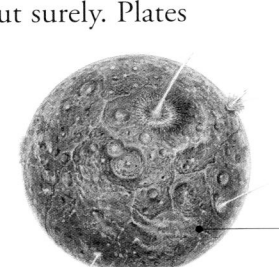

4.6–4.2 billion years ago
The infant Earth's surface is bombarded by meteorites and comets, as the interior starts to heat up and heavier elements sink to the core.

4.2–3.8 billion years ago
Bombardment slows. Lava flows released by the impacts cool and form the crust. Water from volcanoes and comets slowly forms the oceans.

SCALE 1:109,600,000
Robinson Projection

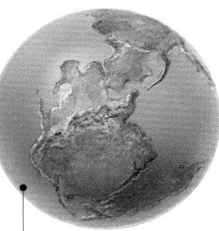

200 million years ago
The landmasses of the Northern and Southern hemispheres are joined in the single supercontinent of Pangaea, surrounded by one large ocean.

90 million years ago
Pangaea has broken up and the South Atlantic Ocean has opened, but North America remains close to Europe, and Australia remains joined to Antarctica.

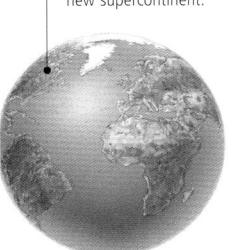

Today
The continents had reached their present positions by roughly 12 million years ago. Continental collisions will eventually result in a new supercontinent.

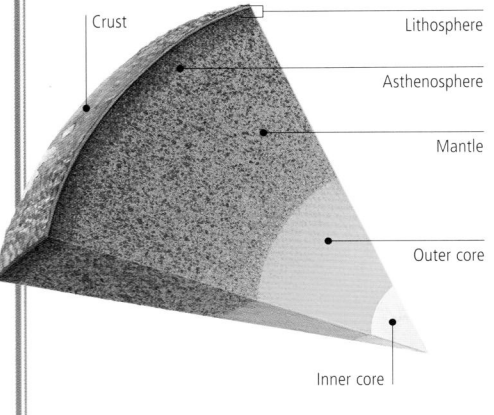

Crust — Lithosphere
Asthenosphere
Mantle
Outer core
Inner core

Inside Earth

Earth's core has two layers of iron and nickel—solid in the inner core, and liquid in the outer core. The mantle is made of layers of rock—solid in the lower mantle, soft in the asthenosphere, and solid in the upper mantle. The upper mantle and the rocky crust make up the lithosphere.

Moving Plates

Powered by convection currents in the mantle, Earth's tectonic plates are always on the move. Plate boundaries can be divergent (two plates pulling away from each other); convergent (two plates colliding); or transform (two plates sliding past each other).

Undersea collision
When two oceanic plates meet at a convergent boundary, one plate is subducted beneath the other, creating a trench such as the Mariana Trench. An arc of volcanic islands may appear parallel to the trench.

Mid-ocean ridge
Magma rising where two oceanic plates meet forces them apart, making a divergent boundary. It also creates new seafloor, forming an undersea mountain chain such as the Mid-Atlantic Ridge.

Hot-spot volcanoes
Volcanoes can appear when a powerful plume of magma pushes up from the mantle and bursts through the crust. The Hawaiian Islands formed at a volcanic hot spot.

Coastal collision
When oceanic and continental plates converge, the thinner oceanic plate is subducted, creating a deep trench in the ocean. Mountains such as the Andes may form on the land.

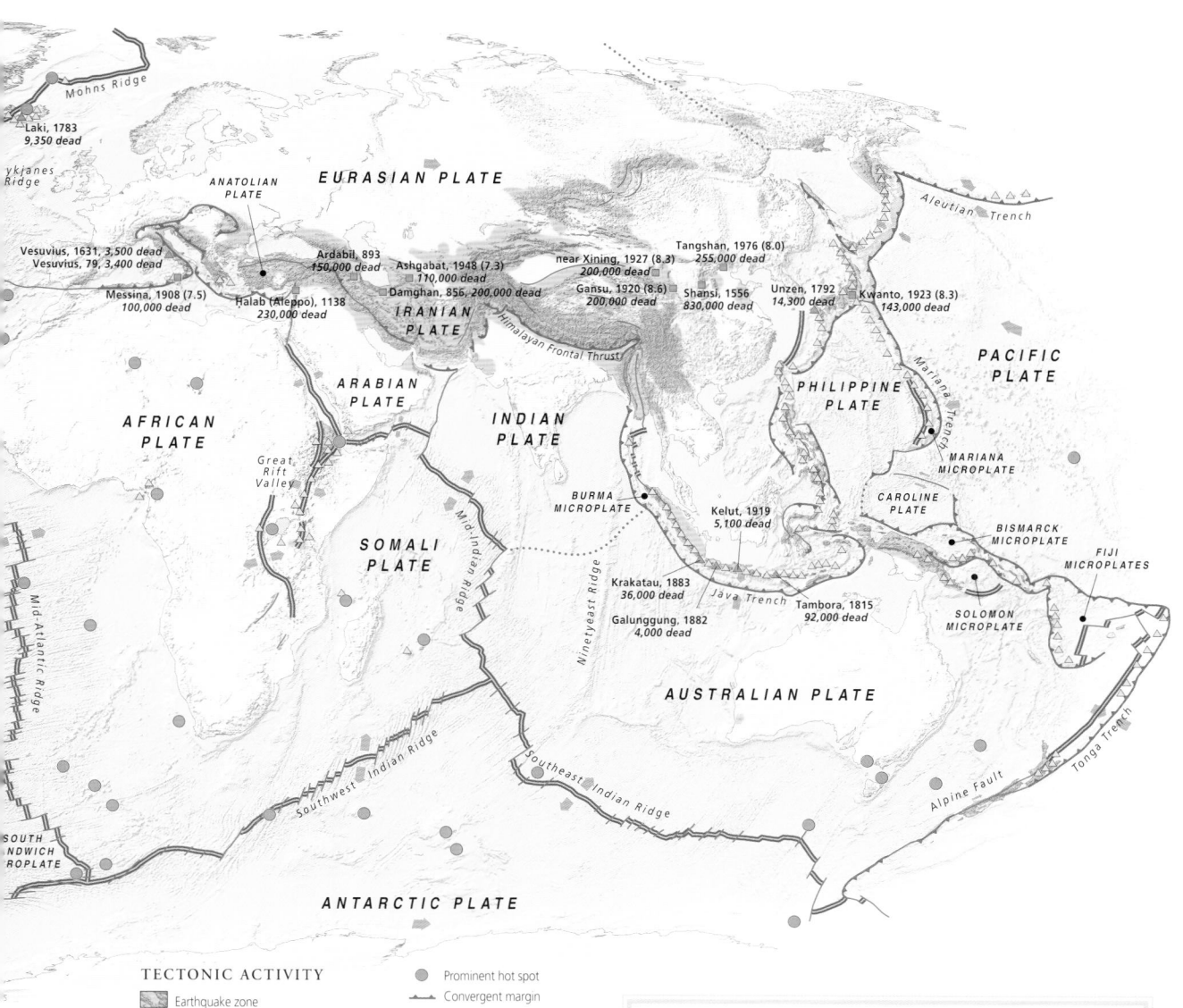

Laki, 1783
9,350 dead

ykjanes
Ridge

Vesuvius, 1631, 3,500 dead
Vesuvius, 79, 3,400 dead

ANATOLIAN
PLATE

EURASIAN PLATE

Ardabil, 893
150,000 dead

Ashgabat, 1948 (7.3)
110,000 dead

near Xining, 1927 (8.3)
200,000 dead

Tangshan, 1976 (8.0)
255,000 dead

Aleutian Trench

Messina, 1908 (7.5)
100,000 dead

Halab (Aleppo), 1138
230,000 dead

Damghan, 856, 200,000 dead

Gansu, 1920 (8.6)
200,000 dead

Shansi, 1556
830,000 dead

Unzen, 1792
14,300 dead

Kwanto, 1923 (8.3)
143,000 dead

IRANIAN
PLATE

Himalayan Frontal Thrust

PACIFIC
PLATE

ARABIAN
PLATE

INDIAN
PLATE

PHILIPPINE
PLATE

Mariana Trench

AFRICAN
PLATE

Great
Rift
Valley

MARIANA
MICROPLATE

SOMALI
PLATE

Mid-Indian Ridge

BURMA
MICROPLATE

Kelut, 1919
5,100 dead

CAROLINE
PLATE

BISMARCK
MICROPLATE

FIJI
MICROPLATES

Mid-Atlantic Ridge

Ninetyeast Ridge

Krakatau, 1883
36,000 dead

Java Trench

Tambora, 1815
92,000 dead

SOLOMON
MICROPLATE

Galunggung, 1882
4,000 dead

AUSTRALIAN PLATE

Southeast Indian Ridge

Alpine Fault

Tonga Trench

SOUTH
SANDWICH
MICROPLATE

Southwest Indian Ridge

ANTARCTIC PLATE

TECTONIC ACTIVITY

- Earthquake zone
- Deadliest earthquakes: Location, year (magnitude, where known), *number dead*
- Volcanic zone
- Deadliest volcanoes: Location, year, *number dead*
- Prominent hot spot
- Convergent margin
- Divergent margin
- Transform fault
- Diffuse or uncertain
- Direction of movement

50 million years from now
The Atlantic widens, the Mediterranean vanishes as Africa and Europe join up, Australia and Southeast Asia collide, and California slides up to Alaska.

The Story of Earth

About 4.6 billion years ago, Earth formed with the rest of the solar system from a swirling cloud of dust and gas. Since then, our planet has been in a state of flux. The theory of plate tectonics explains how the continents have drifted and altered over millions of years to reach their present state, and how they will continue to change in the future.

THE ROCK CYCLE

Earth's crust features three kinds of rock. Igneous rocks, such as granite and basalt, form when molten magma either cools below ground, or erupts as lava and cools at the surface. Sedimentary rocks, such as sandstone and limestone, are made from mud, silt, or sand broken down from other rocks, or from organic matter such as shells. Metamorphic rocks, such as marble and slate, are rocks that have been altered by heat or pressure. Earth's rocks constantly transform as they are processed through the rock cycle.

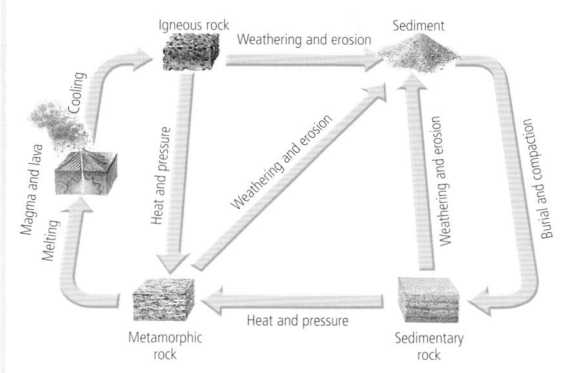

Igneous rock — Weathering and erosion — Sediment

Cooling

Magma and lava

Melting

Heat and pressure

Weathering and erosion

Weathering and erosion

Burial and compaction

Metamorphic rock — Heat and pressure — Sedimentary rock

Sliding plates
At transform boundaries, two plates slide horizontally past each other. California's San Andreas Fault is a transform boundary on land, but most such faults are in the ocean.

Continental rift
When two continental plates move apart at a divergent boundary, a wide valley, such as Africa's Great Rift Valley, is formed. Eventually, such a rift may be flooded by water from a nearby ocean and become a new sea.

Folding crust
When two continental plates collide, neither is subducted. Instead, the crusts buckle, forming high mountains such as the Himalayas.

The Forces of Erosion

As wind and water move across the landscape, they wear down rocks and carry away the sediment, gradually reshaping Earth's surface. Water can flow through the terrain in rivers, seep underground through rocks, inch downhill in frozen form as glaciers, or crash along the coast as ocean waves. Winds can pick up loose rock particles, carry them long distances, and blast them at the surface. Temperature can also have a dramatic effect, with extremes of heat and cold both causing rocks to crack and split.

Ruth Glacier is one of many glaciers on North America's highest peak, Mount McKinley in Alaska. The ice has gouged out a U-shaped valley as gravity slowly drags it downhill.

The Goosenecks of the San Juan River in Utah, U.S.A., formed when the region was uplifted, boosting the meandering river's ability to carve its path into the rocks.

Off the coast of Victoria, Australia, ocean waves have carved the Twelve Apostles. These impressive rock stacks are islands of hard limestone that have resisted erosion.

The volcanic landscape of Cappadocia in Turkey has been shaped by the wind. The bizarre formations were created when the soft pumice layers eroded at a different rate to the harder tuff layers.

CLIMATE AND WEATHER

The atmosphere that surrounds Earth is in a constant state of flux, subject to variations in temperature, wind, pressure, humidity, and precipitation that collectively create our weather. The long-term pattern of weather in a particular region is known as its climate and depends on three main factors: latitude, altitude, and proximity to the sea.

The world's weather is fueled by the Sun's uneven heating. Because Earth is a sphere, sunlight is more intense and the air is warmer at the Equator than at the poles. Warm air expands and rises, creating an area of low atmospheric pressure. As it rises, the air cools and its water vapor condenses into clouds, often bringing rain. Cold air is heavier and sinks, forming a high-pressure area with clear skies and settled weather. Wind is created when air flows from areas of high pressure to lower-pressure zones. Sometimes "wedges" of cold air, known as cold fronts, push under existing air, forcing it to rise rapidly and resulting in towering clouds and dramatic storms.

Constantly working toward equilibrium, the atmosphere carries warm air from the Equator toward the poles, and cold air toward the Equator. Earth's rotation deflects these air masses, creating complex patterns that are matched by the warm and cold currents in the ocean. The large-scale air and ocean currents determine the world's various climates, while smaller circulations and individual clouds within them bring our day-to-day weather.

Lightning is an electrical discharge created within a thunderstorm. The heat of the discharge makes the air expand explosively, causing a dramatic clap of thunder.

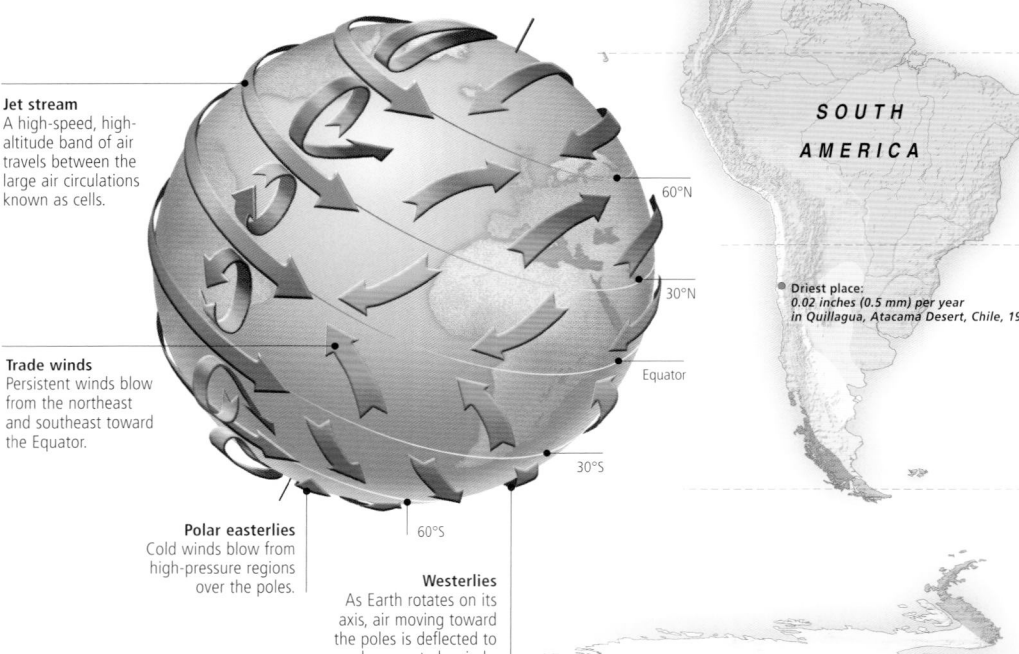

Churchill

Greatest temperature change in a day:
100°F (56°C), from 44°F (6.7°C) to –56°F (–49°C),
at Browning, Montana, U.S.A., 1916

Most snow in one year:
1,224 inches (31,102 mm)
on Mt Rainier, Washington, U.S.A., 1971/72

Windiest place:
231 mph (372 km/h)
on Mt Washington, U.S.A., 1934

NORTH AMERICA

SOUTH AMERICA

Driest place:
0.02 inches (0.5 mm) per year
in Quillagua, Atacama Desert, Chile, 1964–2

60°N

30°N

Equator

30°S

60°S

A tornado is a spinning column of air that extends from a thundercloud to the ground. Its powerful winds can exceed speeds of 300 mph (480 km/h).

Global Circulation

The Sun strikes Earth more directly near the Equator than at the poles. The warm air of the tropics rises and moves toward the colder polar regions, then cools and sinks at about 30 degrees north and south latitude. Most of it travels back toward the Equator, but some continues to move poleward until it meets cold polar air at about 60 degrees north and south.

Jet stream
A high-speed, high-altitude band of air travels between the large air circulations known as cells.

Trade winds
Persistent winds blow from the northeast and southeast toward the Equator.

Polar easterlies
Cold winds blow from high-pressure regions over the poles.

Westerlies
As Earth rotates on its axis, air moving toward the poles is deflected to produce westerly winds.

The heat of the tropics can be dispersed to the middle latitudes by tropical storm systems known as cyclones, typhoons, or hurricanes. Hurricane Fran (pictured) hit North Carolina in 1996.

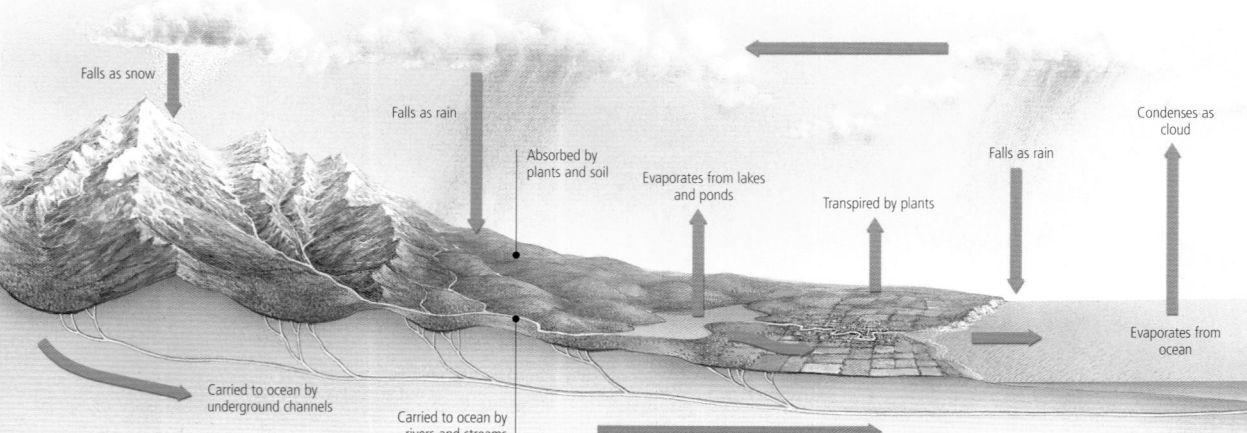

Falls as snow

Falls as rain

Absorbed by plants and soil

Evaporates from lakes and ponds

Transpired by plants

Falls as rain

Condenses as cloud

Evaporates from ocean

Carried to ocean by underground channels

Carried to ocean by rivers and streams

The Water Cycle

Much of our weather is generated by the water cycle, the continuous interchange of moisture between oceans, land, plants, and clouds. Moisture enters the atmosphere when water in oceans, rivers, and lakes is heated by the Sun and evaporates, and when plants exude water as part of photosynthesis. It condenses as clouds and returns to Earth's surface when it falls as rain, hail, or snow.

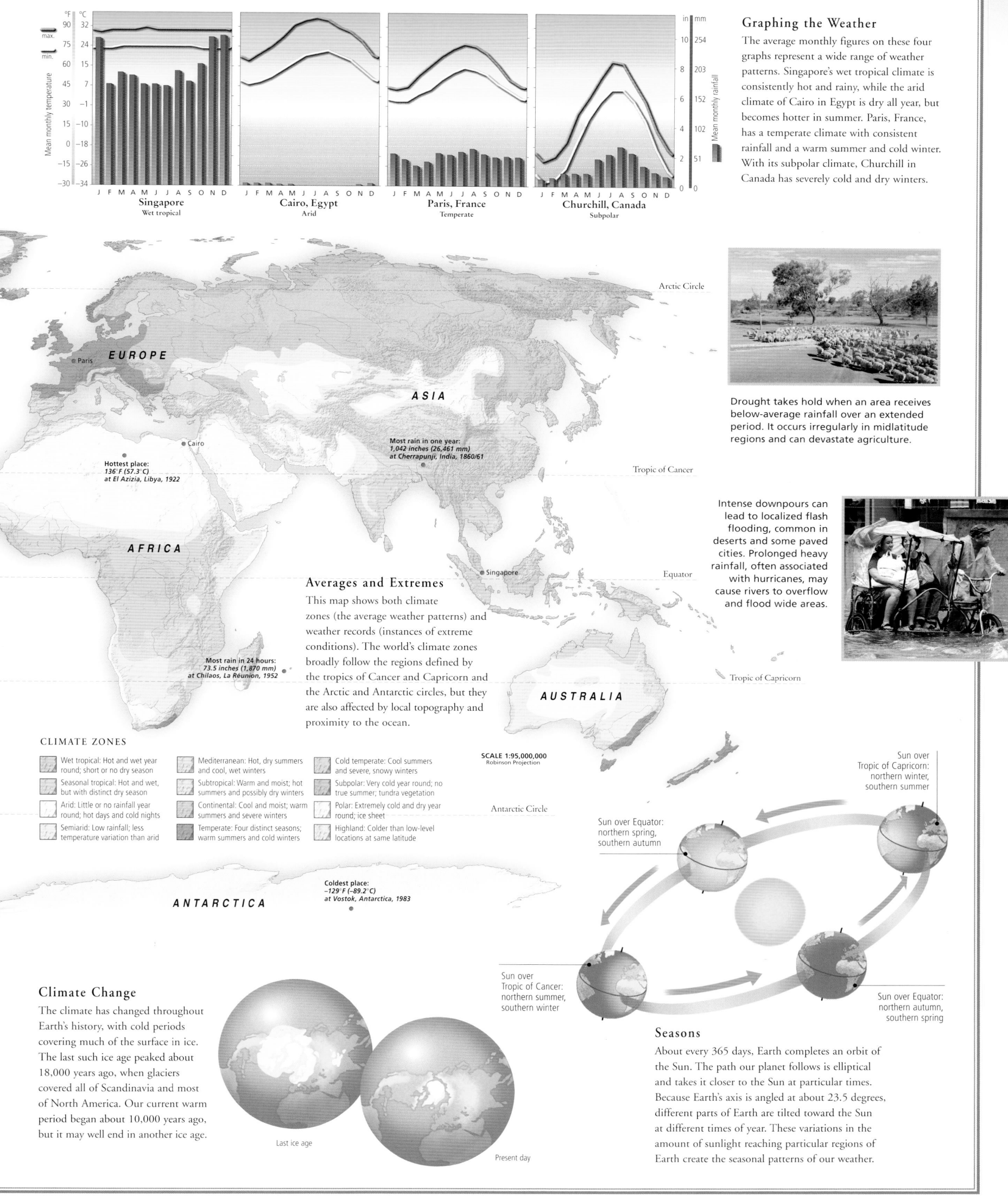

Graphing the Weather

The average monthly figures on these four graphs represent a wide range of weather patterns. Singapore's wet tropical climate is consistently hot and rainy, while the arid climate of Cairo in Egypt is dry all year, but becomes hotter in summer. Paris, France, has a temperate climate with consistent rainfall and a warm summer and cold winter. With its subpolar climate, Churchill in Canada has severely cold and dry winters.

Singapore
Wet tropical

Cairo, Egypt
Arid

Paris, France
Temperate

Churchill, Canada
Subpolar

Drought takes hold when an area receives below-average rainfall over an extended period. It occurs irregularly in midlatitude regions and can devastate agriculture.

Intense downpours can lead to localized flash flooding, common in deserts and some paved cities. Prolonged heavy rainfall, often associated with hurricanes, may cause rivers to overflow and flood wide areas.

EUROPE

ASIA

Paris

Cairo

Most rain in one year:
1,042 inches (26,461 mm)
at Cherrapunji, India, 1860/61

Arctic Circle

Tropic of Cancer

Hottest place:
136°F (57.3°C)
at El Azizia, Libya, 1922

AFRICA

Singapore

Equator

Most rain in 24 hours:
73.5 inches (1,870 mm)
at Chilaos, La Réunion, 1952

Averages and Extremes

This map shows both climate zones (the average weather patterns) and weather records (instances of extreme conditions). The world's climate zones broadly follow the regions defined by the tropics of Cancer and Capricorn and the Arctic and Antarctic circles, but they are also affected by local topography and proximity to the ocean.

AUSTRALIA

Tropic of Capricorn

CLIMATE ZONES

- Wet tropical: Hot and wet year round; short or no dry season
- Seasonal tropical: Hot and wet, but with distinct dry season
- Arid: Little or no rainfall year round; hot days and cold nights
- Semiarid: Low rainfall; less temperature variation than arid

- Mediterranean: Hot, dry summers and cool, wet winters
- Subtropical: Warm and moist; hot summers and possibly dry winters
- Continental: Cool and moist; warm summers and severe winters
- Temperate: Four distinct seasons; warm summers and cold winters

- Cold temperate: Cool summers and severe, snowy winters
- Subpolar: Very cold year round; no true summer; tundra vegetation
- Polar: Extremely cold and dry year round; ice sheet
- Highland: Colder than low-level locations at same latitude

SCALE 1:95,000,000
Robinson Projection

Antarctic Circle

ANTARCTICA

Coldest place:
–129°F (–89.2°C)
at Vostok, Antarctica, 1983

Sun over Tropic of Capricorn:
northern winter,
southern summer

Sun over Equator:
northern spring,
southern autumn

Sun over Tropic of Cancer:
northern summer,
southern winter

Sun over Equator:
northern autumn,
southern spring

Climate Change

The climate has changed throughout Earth's history, with cold periods covering much of the surface in ice. The last such ice age peaked about 18,000 years ago, when glaciers covered all of Scandinavia and most of North America. Our current warm period began about 10,000 years ago, but it may well end in another ice age.

Last ice age

Present day

Seasons

About every 365 days, Earth completes an orbit of the Sun. The path our planet follows is elliptical and takes it closer to the Sun at particular times. Because Earth's axis is angled at about 23.5 degrees, different parts of Earth are tilted toward the Sun at different times of year. These variations in the amount of sunlight reaching particular regions of Earth create the seasonal patterns of our weather.

THE IMPACT OF GEOGRAPHY

The history of humankind and the societies we live in today have been profoundly influenced by geography. The concentration of wealth and power in the hands of people of Eurasian origin is largely a legacy of the European empire-building that began in about AD 1500. When Europeans arrived to colonize the Americas, Africa, and Australasia, they brought with them military superiority provided by their steel weapons, guns, and cavalry horses; new, deadly diseases to which the local people had little resistance; better communication through writing; and centralized political organization. The fact that these critical advantages belonged to Europeans rather than to the colonized peoples can be largely explained by Earth's geography.

Until the end of the last ice age, about 13,000 years ago, all the world's peoples were hunter-gatherers. Following the change in climate, a transition to settled life and the adoption of agriculture occurred in many places, allowing populations to grow and, eventually, cities and states to form. In some regions of the world, such as Australia, farming was not developed because the land offered few plants and animals that could be domesticated. Eurasia, on the other hand, had more domesticable plant and animal species than any other continent. In the Americas and Africa, a north–south orientation gives the continents a highly varied climate and environment, which impeded the spread of agricultural and technological innovations. The east–west orientation of Eurasia produces a broadly similar climate throughout the extensive land mass. Innovations could spread relatively easily and quickly, yielding increased food production and allowing large, stratified societies to develop.

The crops of Southwest Asia took only a few hundred years to spread to Egypt (grain harvest depicted above), Europe, and India.

The Maya and Aztecs of Mesoamerica built great cities such as Tikal, but the region was isolated by desert to the north and the narrow Isthmus of Panama to the south.

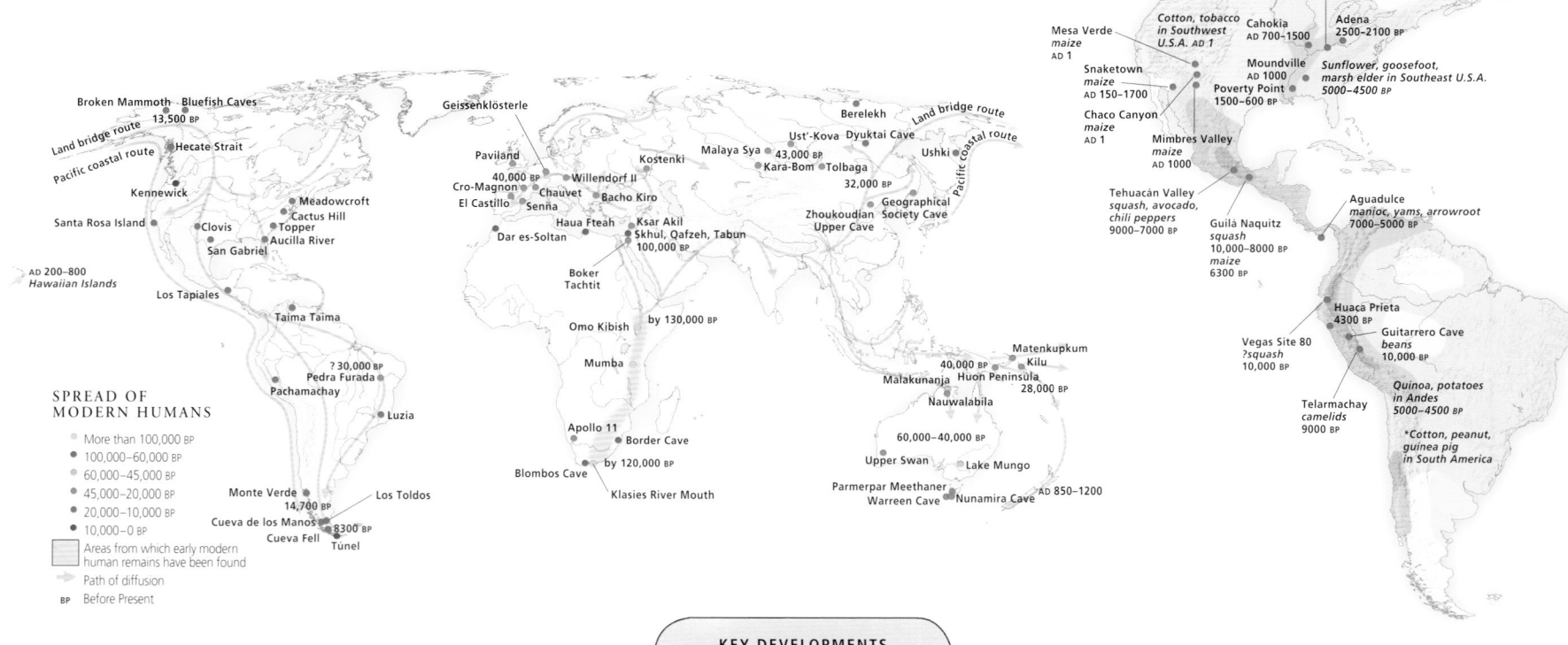

SPREAD OF MODERN HUMANS

- More than 100,000 BP
- 100,000–60,000 BP
- 60,000–45,000 BP
- 45,000–20,000 BP
- 20,000–10,000 BP
- 10,000–0 BP
- Areas from which early modern human remains have been found
- Path of diffusion

BP Before Present

Colonizing the Globe

Advanced stone tools and social flexibility allowed anatomically modern humans to flourish in a wide range of habitats. By about 100,000 years ago, they had moved into Southwest Asia from Africa, and sometime between 60,000 and 40,000 years ago, they traveled to Australia by boat. Europe was colonized by 40,000 years ago, after which evidence of art, ritual, and symbolism begins to accumulate. By 15,000 years ago, humans had reached the Americas, either by crossing the Bering Land Bridge that existed during the ice age or by boat along a Pacific route. Far-flung islands such as New Zealand and Hawaii have been settled only in the last 2,000 years.

KEY DEVELOPMENTS

130,000 BP Modern humans (*Homo sapiens*) in Africa

100,000 BP Modern humans (*Homo sapiens*) in Southwest Asia; first evidence of deliberate burials (Israel)

77,000 BP Rare examples of art (Blombos Cave, South Africa)

70,000 BP Composite tools in Africa (Howieson's Poort industry)

60,000 BP Modern humans in East Asia and Australia—first sea voyages

40,000 BP Modern humans (Cro-Magnon) in Europe, associated with early evidence of burials, art, and music

37,000 BP Ivory carvings of animals in southwestern Germany

28,000 BP Female statuettes known as "Venus" figurines in Europe

"Venus of Willendorf"
26,000–24,000 BP

26,000 BP First cremation (Australia)

16,000 BP First fired clay pottery (Japan)

15,000 BP Modern humans spread into America (possibly earlier)

13,000 BP Domesticated plants in Southwest Asia

12,500 BP Settled villages of hunter-gatherers in Southwest Asia

12,000 BP First animal domestication (dogs in the Levant)

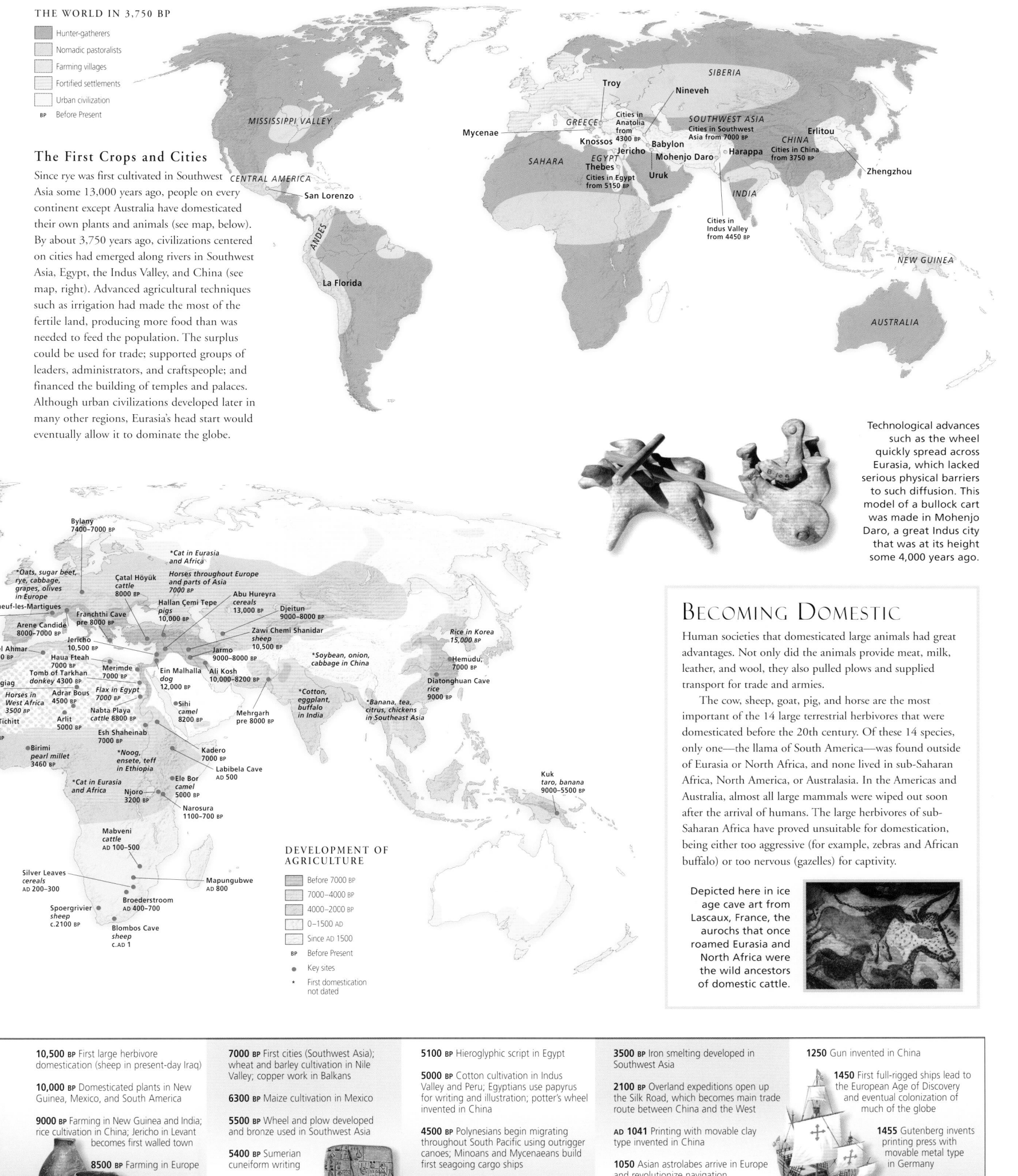

THE WORLD IN 3,750 BP

- Hunter-gatherers
- Nomadic pastoralists
- Farming villages
- Fortified settlements
- Urban civilization
- **BP** Before Present

The First Crops and Cities

Since rye was first cultivated in Southwest Asia some 13,000 years ago, people on every continent except Australia have domesticated their own plants and animals (see map, below). By about 3,750 years ago, civilizations centered on cities had emerged along rivers in Southwest Asia, Egypt, the Indus Valley, and China (see map, right). Advanced agricultural techniques such as irrigation had made the most of the fertile land, producing more food than was needed to feed the population. The surplus could be used for trade; supported groups of leaders, administrators, and craftspeople; and financed the building of temples and palaces. Although urban civilizations developed later in many other regions, Eurasia's head start would eventually allow it to dominate the globe.

Map labels (top map)

MISSISSIPPI VALLEY
CENTRAL AMERICA
San Lorenzo
ANDES
La Florida
SAHARA
GREECE
Mycenae
Knossos
Troy
Nineveh
SIBERIA
SOUTHWEST ASIA
Cities in Anatolia from 4300 BP
Jericho
Babylon
Cities in Southwest Asia from 7000 BP
CHINA
Erlitou
Cities in China from 3750 BP
Zhengzhou
EGYPT
Thebes
Cities in Egypt from 5150 BP
Uruk
Mohenjo Daro
Harappa
Cities in Indus Valley from 4450 BP
INDIA
NEW GUINEA
AUSTRALIA

Technological advances such as the wheel quickly spread across Eurasia, which lacked serious physical barriers to such diffusion. This model of a bullock cart was made in Mohenjo Daro, a great Indus city that was at its height some 4,000 years ago.

Development of Agriculture map labels

Bylany 7400–7000 BP
*Oats, sugar beet, rye, cabbage, grapes, olives in Europe
auneuf-les-Martigues
Arene Candide 8000–7000 BP
*Cat in Eurasia and Africa
Çatal Höyük cattle 8000 BP
Horses throughout Europe and parts of Asia 7000 BP
Hallan Çemi Tepe pigs 10,000 BP
Abu Hureyra cereals 13,000 BP
Franchthi Cave pre 8000 BP
Djeitun 9000–8000 BP
us el Ahmar 000 BP
Jericho 10,500 BP
Zawi Chemi Shanidar sheep 10,500 BP
Jarmo 9000–8000 BP
Rice in Korea 15,000 BP
Haua Fteah 7000 BP
Tomb of Tarkhan donkey 4300 BP
Merimde 7000 BP
Ein Malhalla dog 12,000 BP
Ali Kosh 10,000–8200 BP
*Soybean, onion, cabbage in China
Hemudu, 7000 BP
uggiag
Horses in West Africa 3500 BP
Adrar Bous 4500 BP
Flax in Egypt 7000 BP
Sihi camel
Mehrgarh pre 8000 BP
*Cotton, eggplant, buffalo in India
*Banana, tea, citrus, chickens in Southeast Asia
Diatonghuan Cave rice 9000 BP
ar Tichitt ins 0 BP
Nabta Playa cattle 8800 BP
Arlit 5000 BP
Esh Shaheinab 7000 BP
Birimi pearl millet 3460 BP
*Noog, ensete, teff in Ethiopia
Kadero 7000 BP
Labibela Cave AD 500
Ele Bor camel 5000 BP
Kuk taro, banana 9000–5500 BP
*Cat in Eurasia and Africa
Njoro 3200 BP
Narosura 1100–700 BP
Mabveni cattle AD 100–500
Silver Leaves cereals AD 200–300
Mapungubwe AD 800
Broederstroom AD 400–700
Spoergrivier sheep c.2100 BP
Blombos Cave sheep c.AD 1

DEVELOPMENT OF AGRICULTURE

- Before 7000 BP
- 7000–4000 BP
- 4000–2000 BP
- 0–1500 AD
- Since AD 1500
- **BP** Before Present
- • Key sites
- * First domestication not dated

BECOMING DOMESTIC

Human societies that domesticated large animals had great advantages. Not only did the animals provide meat, milk, leather, and wool, they also pulled plows and supplied transport for trade and armies.

The cow, sheep, goat, pig, and horse are the most important of the 14 large terrestrial herbivores that were domesticated before the 20th century. Of these 14 species, only one—the llama of South America—was found outside of Eurasia or North Africa, and none lived in sub-Saharan Africa, North America, or Australasia. In the Americas and Australia, almost all large mammals were wiped out soon after the arrival of humans. The large herbivores of sub-Saharan Africa have proved unsuitable for domestication, being either too aggressive (for example, zebras and African buffalo) or too nervous (gazelles) for captivity.

Depicted here in ice age cave art from Lascaux, France, the aurochs that once roamed Eurasia and North Africa were the wild ancestors of domestic cattle.

Timeline (bottom)

10,500 BP First large herbivore domestication (sheep in present-day Iraq)

10,000 BP Domesticated plants in New Guinea, Mexico, and South America

9000 BP Farming in New Guinea and India; rice cultivation in China; Jericho in Levant becomes first walled town

8500 BP Farming in Europe

Grain pots from Swiss Alps 6000 BP

7000 BP First cities (Southwest Asia); wheat and barley cultivation in Nile Valley; copper work in Balkans

6300 BP Maize cultivation in Mexico

5500 BP Wheel and plow developed and bronze used in Southwest Asia

5400 BP Sumerian cuneiform writing

Sumerian tablet c. 5000 BP

5100 BP Hieroglyphic script in Egypt

5000 BP Cotton cultivation in Indus Valley and Peru; Egyptians use papyrus for writing and illustration; potter's wheel invented in China

4500 BP Polynesians begin migrating throughout South Pacific using outrigger canoes; Minoans and Mycenaeans build first seagoing cargo ships

3700 BP The world's first codified laws are recorded in Babylon in Code of Hammurabi

3500 BP Iron smelting developed in Southwest Asia

2100 BP Overland expeditions open up the Silk Road, which becomes main trade route between China and the West

AD 1041 Printing with movable clay type invented in China

1050 Asian astrolabes arrive in Europe and revolutionize navigation

1183 Magnetic compass invented in China

1250 Gun invented in China

1450 First full-rigged ships lead to the European Age of Discovery and eventual colonization of much of the globe

1455 Gutenberg invents printing press with movable metal type in Germany

Columbus's ship *Santa Maria*

POPULATION

The number of people in the world has increased tenfold in the past 400 years, but such explosive growth is a very recent phenomenon. World population can expand only when there are more births than deaths, and for most of human history, birth and death rates both remained at high levels. The introduction of farming from around 8000 BC led to the first significant growth in human numbers, but the increase was gradual and it took until AD 1500 to move from 10 million to 500 million people.

In the developed regions, such as Europe and North America, death rates began to decline during the 18th century as revolutions in both agriculture and industry led to improved living conditions and health care. Birth rates stayed high, however, because people had not yet adjusted to the idea that all their children were likely to reach adulthood. Over the next 200 years, population figures exploded, but gradually birth rates started to drop and growth in these regions slowed. Today, some European populations are actually shrinking.

The developing parts of the world, however, are at an earlier stage in the process and are experiencing even more rapid growth. Although the birth rates in much of Asia, Africa, and South America are now falling, it will be many decades before their populations stabilize. Most experts believe that at this point there will be more than 10 billion people on Earth, but nobody knows whether our planet has the capacity to sustain such enormous numbers.

Where People Live

Earth's total population of 6 billion or so is distributed very unevenly. People have tended to live along river valleys or near the coast, with the largest concentrations being in China, India, and Europe. Rural-to-urban migration has led to about half the world's population now living in cities. Combined with explosive growth, it has also caused the proliferation of megacities in the developing world.

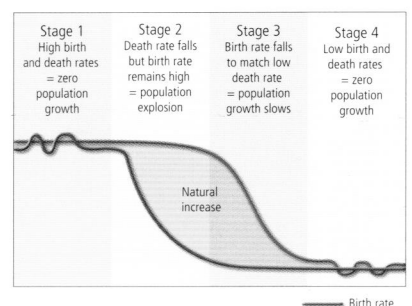

Stages of Growth

In Stage 1, birth and death rates are both high and there is little population growth. When health care and living conditions improve, death rates drop but birth rates initially remain high, leading to a natural increase in the population. During Stage 3, the birth rate gradually falls, eventually leading to the zero growth of Stage 4.

Urbanization

In the developed countries, the Industrial Revolution was followed by a massive shift of population from rural to urban areas. With later but more rapid industrialization, developing countries are experiencing a sudden increase in city dwellers. In the coming years, almost all the world's population growth will be in urban areas.

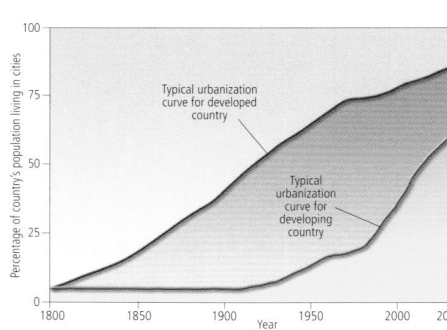

The walled towns of Europe, such as Albarracín, in Spain, reflect a time before technology allowed vast, sprawling cities to become a feature of the modern landscape.

In the Philippines and many other developing countries, extensive shantytowns have grown up, as millions have erected makeshift shelters on the outskirts of cities.

Top Ten Countries

The population of a country can be assessed in various ways, including the total number of inhabitants, the ratio of inhabitants to land, and the rate at which it is growing. Many of today's most populous countries are in Asia, but Africa and the Middle East are seeing the highest rates of growth. Apart from Bangladesh, the most densely populated countries listed here all have small land areas.

LARGEST POPULATIONS		MOST CROWDED COUNTRIES		FASTEST GROWING COUNTRIES*	
COUNTRY	POPULATION	COUNTRY	POPULATION DENSITY	COUNTRY	ANNUAL GROWTH
China	1,302,207,990	Monaco	26,784 per sq mile (16,620 per sq km)	Liberia	5.53%
India	1,080,264,390	Singapore	11,629 per sq mile (7,219 per sq km)	Sierra Leone	4.54%
United States	295,734,130	Vatican City	5,015 per sq mile (3,111 per sq km)	Eritrea	4.22%
Indonesia	241,973,880	Malta	2,073 per sq mile (1,286 per sq km)	Somalia	4.21%
Brazil	186,112,790	Maldives	1,877 per sq mile (1,164 per sq km)	Yemen	4.07%
Pakistan	156,689,150	Bangladesh	1,735 per sq mile (1,078 per sq km)	Afghanistan	3.68%
Bangladesh	144,319,630	Bahrain	1,667 per sq mile (1,035 per sq km)	Niger	3.63%
Russia	143,736,790	Taiwan	1,143 per sq mile (710 per sq km)	Democratic Republic of Congo	3.34%
Nigeria	140,601,620	Barbados	1,042 per sq mile (648 per sq km)	Oman	3.27%
Japan	127,417,240	Nauru	1,004 per sq mile (621 per sq km)	Uganda	3.11%

Countries with more than 1 million inhabitants

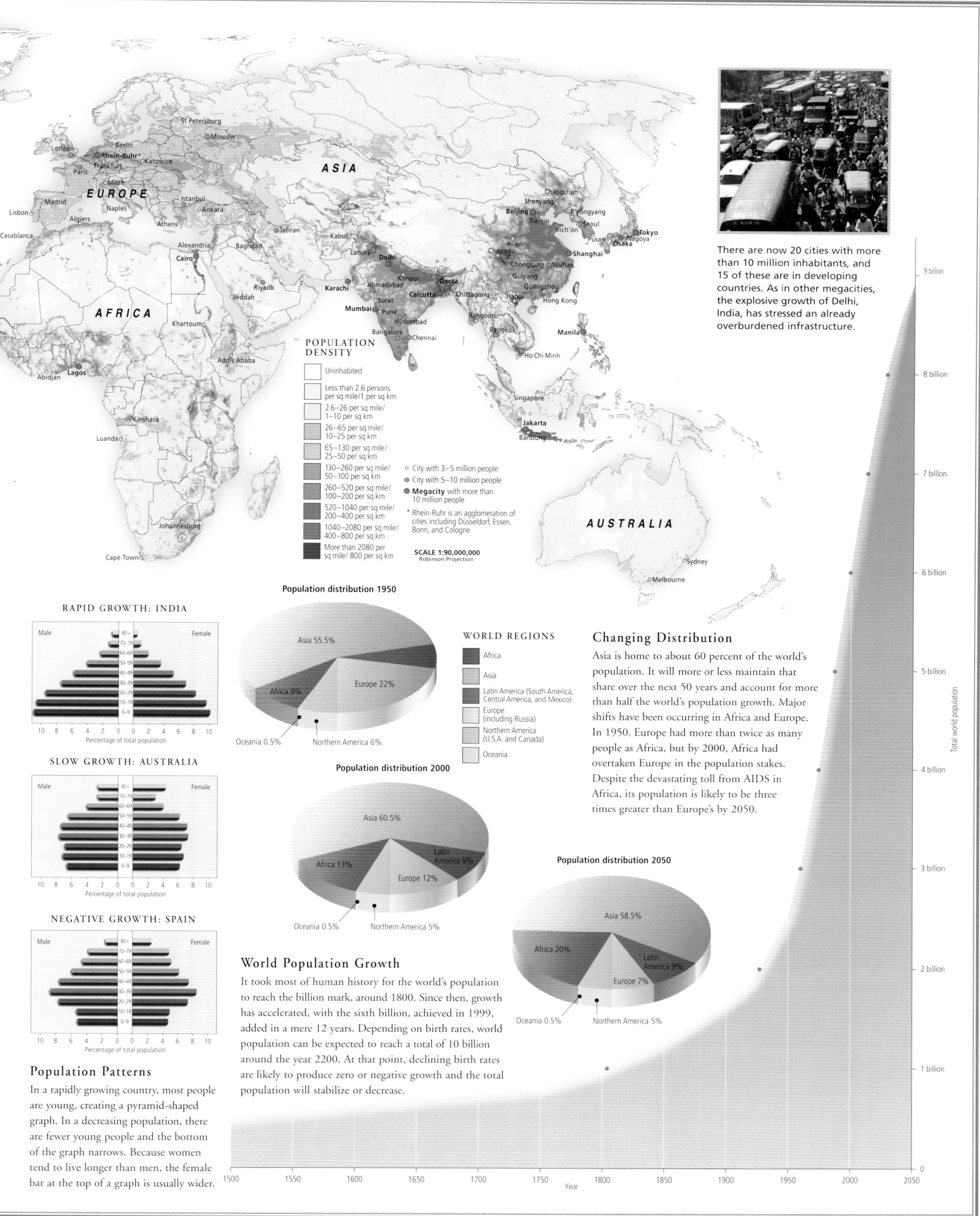

POPULATION DENSITY

Uninhabited

Less than 2.6 persons per sq mile/1 per sq km

2.6–26 per sq mile/ 1–10 per sq km

26–65 per sq mile/ 10–25 per sq km

65–130 per sq mile/ 25–50 per sq km

130–260 per sq mile/ 50–100 per sq km

260–520 per sq mile/ 100–200 per sq km

520–1040 per sq mile/ 200–400 per sq km

1040–2080 per sq mile/ 400–800 per sq km

More than 2080 per sq mile/ 800 per sq km

○ City with 3–5 million people

○ City with 5–10 million people

● **Megacity** with more than 10 million people

* Rhein-Ruhr is an agglomeration of cities including Düsseldorf, Essen, Bonn, and Cologne

SCALE 1:90,000,000
Robinson Projection

There are now 20 cities with more than 10 million inhabitants, and 15 of these are in developing countries. As in other megacities, the explosive growth of Delhi, India, has stressed an already overburdened infrastructure.

Population distribution 1950

Asia 55.5%
Europe 22%
Africa 9%
Northern America 6%
Oceania 0.5%

WORLD REGIONS

Africa

Asia

Latin America (South America, Central America, and Mexico)

Europe (including Russia)

Northern America (U.S.A. and Canada)

Oceania

Changing Distribution

Asia is home to about 60 percent of the world's population. It will more or less maintain that share over the next 50 years and account for more than half the world's population growth. Major shifts have been occurring in Africa and Europe. In 1950, Europe had more than twice as many people as Africa, but by 2000, Africa had overtaken Europe in the population stakes. Despite the devastating toll from AIDS in Africa, its population is likely to be three times greater than Europe's by 2050.

RAPID GROWTH: INDIA

Male | Female
80+
70–79
60–69
50–59
40–49
30–39
20–29
10–19
0–9
10 8 6 4 2 0 0 2 4 6 8 10
Percentage of total population

SLOW GROWTH: AUSTRALIA

Male | Female
80+
70–79
60–69
50–59
40–49
30–39
20–29
10–19
0–9
10 8 6 4 2 0 0 2 4 6 8 10
Percentage of total population

NEGATIVE GROWTH: SPAIN

Male | Female
80+
70–79
60–69
50–59
40–49
30–39
20–29
10–19
0–9
10 8 6 4 2 0 0 2 4 6 8 10
Percentage of total population

Population Patterns

In a rapidly growing country, most people are young, creating a pyramid-shaped graph. In a decreasing population, there are fewer young people and the bottom of the graph narrows. Because women tend to live longer than men, the female bar at the top of a graph is usually wider.

Population distribution 2000

Asia 60.5%
Latin America 9%
Europe 12%
Africa 13%
Oceania 0.5%
Northern America 5%

World Population Growth

It took most of human history for the world's population to reach the billion mark, around 1800. Since then, growth has accelerated, with the sixth billion, achieved in 1999, added in a mere 12 years. Depending on birth rates, world population can be expected to reach a total of 10 billion around the year 2200. At that point, declining birth rates are likely to produce zero or negative growth and the total population will stabilize or decrease.

Population distribution 2050

Asia 58.5%
Latin America 9%
Europe 7%
Africa 20%
Oceania 0.5%
Northern America 5%

Total world population

9 billion
8 billion
7 billion
6 billion
5 billion
4 billion
3 billion
2 billion
1 billion
0

1500 1550 1600 1650 1700 1750 1800 1850 1900 1950 2000 2050
Year

LANGUAGES OF THE WORLD

Complex speech is one of the key ways in which humans differ from the rest of the animal world, and language is one of the main ways groups of humans distinguish themselves from one another. Rudimentary forms of language may have been used by the first modern humans more than 100,000 years ago, but it was not until about 40,000 years ago that there was an explosion of art and technology, and humans moved into harsher environments. Many believe that the development of complex language prompted this great leap in human capability.

There are now more than 6,000 languages spoken in the world and their distribution reveals much about human history. Throughout time, languages have both diverged and converged. The Roman conquest of Europe 2,000 years ago replaced most of the existing Celtic languages with Latin. Gradually, different groups developed their own dialects of Latin, which eventually became Romance languages such as French, Italian, and Spanish. The Germanic language of English displays many borrowings from French, a legacy of the Norman Conquest of England in 1066.

In more recent times, colonialism has spread European languages throughout the globe. In many places, this contact has led to new languages such as pidgins (spoken only as a second language) and creoles (spoken as a mother tongue). At the same time, however, many indigenous languages have been lost. As societies become more centralized, and particularly as English takes hold as the dominant world language, much of the extraordinary diversity of languages is under threat.

The Basques live in France and Spain near the western Pyrenees. Their language seems to be an isolate (unrelated to any other modern language), but other Basque-like languages were probably spoken in Western Europe before the Roman conquest.

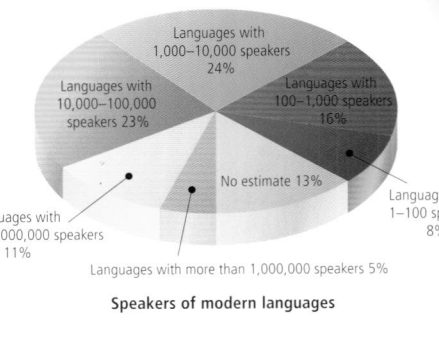

French and Native American

English and Na-Dene

English and Native American

NORTH AMERICA

Spanish and Native American

Spanish and Native American

Portuguese and Native American

SOUTH AMERICA

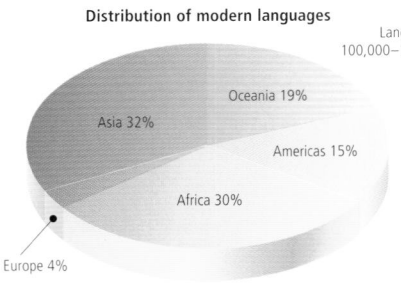

The language of Japan's indigenous people, the Ainu, gradually lost ground to Japanese. It is now virtually extinct, with just a handful of elderly speakers left.

Major Languages

Mandarin Chinese has far more mother-tongue (first-language) speakers than any other single language, but of the world's top 15 languages, 12 belong to the Indo-European family. The prevalence of English, French, Portuguese, and Spanish resulted from the colonial expansion of European power that began in the 15th century. North America now has more English speakers than anywhere else, while South America is home to the most Spanish speakers.

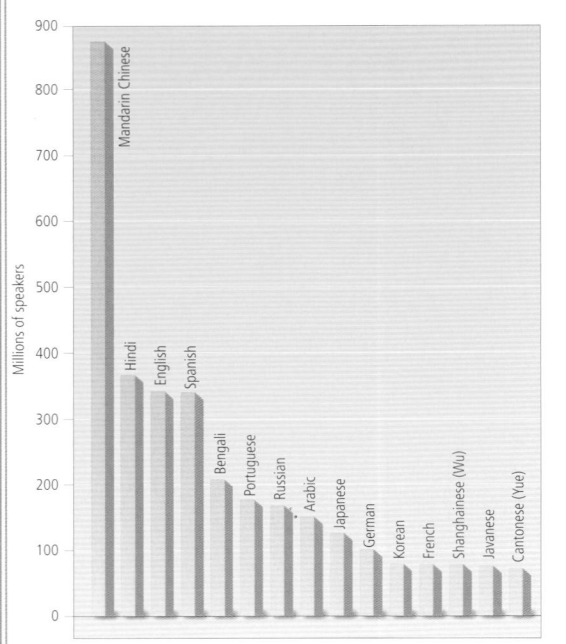

Millions of speakers — bar chart:
Mandarin Chinese, Hindi, English, Spanish, Bengali, Portuguese, Russian, Arabic, Japanese, German, Korean, French, Shanghainese (Wu), Javanese, Cantonese (Yue)

Distribution of modern languages

- Oceania 19%
- Asia 32%
- Americas 15%
- Africa 30%
- Europe 4%

Speakers of modern languages

- Languages with 1,000–10,000 speakers 24%
- Languages with 100–1,000 speakers 16%
- Languages with 10,000–100,000 speakers 23%
- No estimate 13%
- Languages with 100,000–1,000,000 speakers 11%
- Languages with 1–100 speakers 8%
- Languages with more than 1,000,000 speakers 5%

Endangered Languages

Although European languages dominate the world in terms of number of speakers, they account for just a tiny percentage of modern languages. As more and more young people adopt the languages of power, much of humankind's linguistic diversity is lost. About 40 percent of languages are spoken by fewer than 10,000 people, and roughly 450 have only a few elderly speakers left. At least half the world's tongues are likely to vanish by 2100—an average of one language lost every 10 days.

DEVELOPMENT OF WRITING

3400 BC Sumerian pictogram system

3100 BC Egyptian hieroglyphs, script with 2,500 symbols, in use for 3,500 years

2500 BC Indus Valley pictogram system

by 2500 BC Sumerian cuneiform script of wedge-shaped strokes

2400 BC Akkadians adopt cuneiform

1750 BC Linear A script in Minoan Crete

c. 1600 BC Proto-Canaanite script in Egypt, later develops into Linear Phoenician

1500 BC Chinese pictogram script, later develops into several thousand characters

1400 BC Linear B script in Mycenaean Greece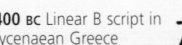

1100 BC Linear Phoenician alphabet of 22 letters, later spreads to Greece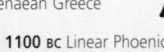

Indo-European Family Tree

In the 18th century, a colonial judge, Sir William Jones, recognized similarities between the Sanskrit language of India, and Latin and Greek, and proposed that they came from a single source. This ancestor language, Proto-Indo-European, has since been shown to have evolved into many European and Asian languages. The family tree presented here shows only the major ones. Almost 3 billion people, roughly half the world's population, now speak an Indo-European language.

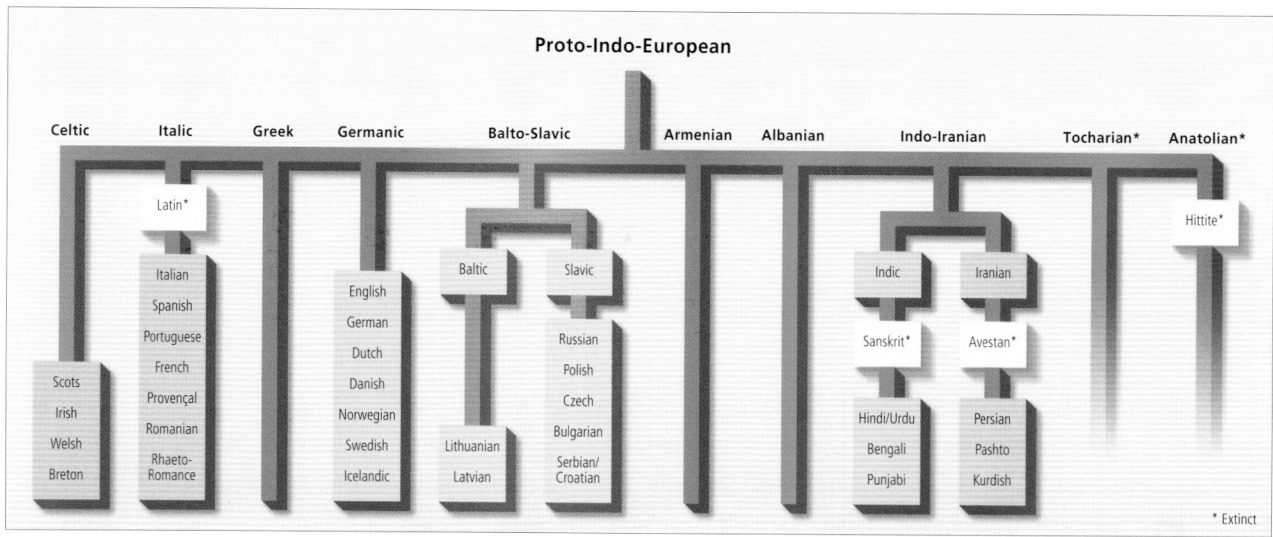

Proto-Indo-European

Celtic | Italic | Greek | Germanic | Balto-Slavic | Armenian | Albanian | Indo-Iranian | Tocharian* | Anatolian*

Latin*

Italian, Spanish, Portuguese, French, Provençal, Romanian, Rhaeto-Romance

Scots, Irish, Welsh, Breton

English, German, Dutch, Danish, Norwegian, Swedish, Icelandic

Baltic — Lithuanian, Latvian

Slavic — Russian, Polish, Czech, Bulgarian, Serbian/Croatian

Indic — Sanskrit*, Hindi/Urdu, Bengali, Punjabi

Iranian — Avestan*, Persian, Pashto, Kurdish

Hittite*

* Extinct

Related Tongues

By comparing vocabulary and grammar, linguists can identify relationships between different languages and group them into families that share a common ancestor language. While some language families, such as Indo-European, are widely accepted, others remain the subject of intense debate. For example, some linguists have proposed just three great families of Native American languages, but most believe that there is not enough evidence for such a classification.

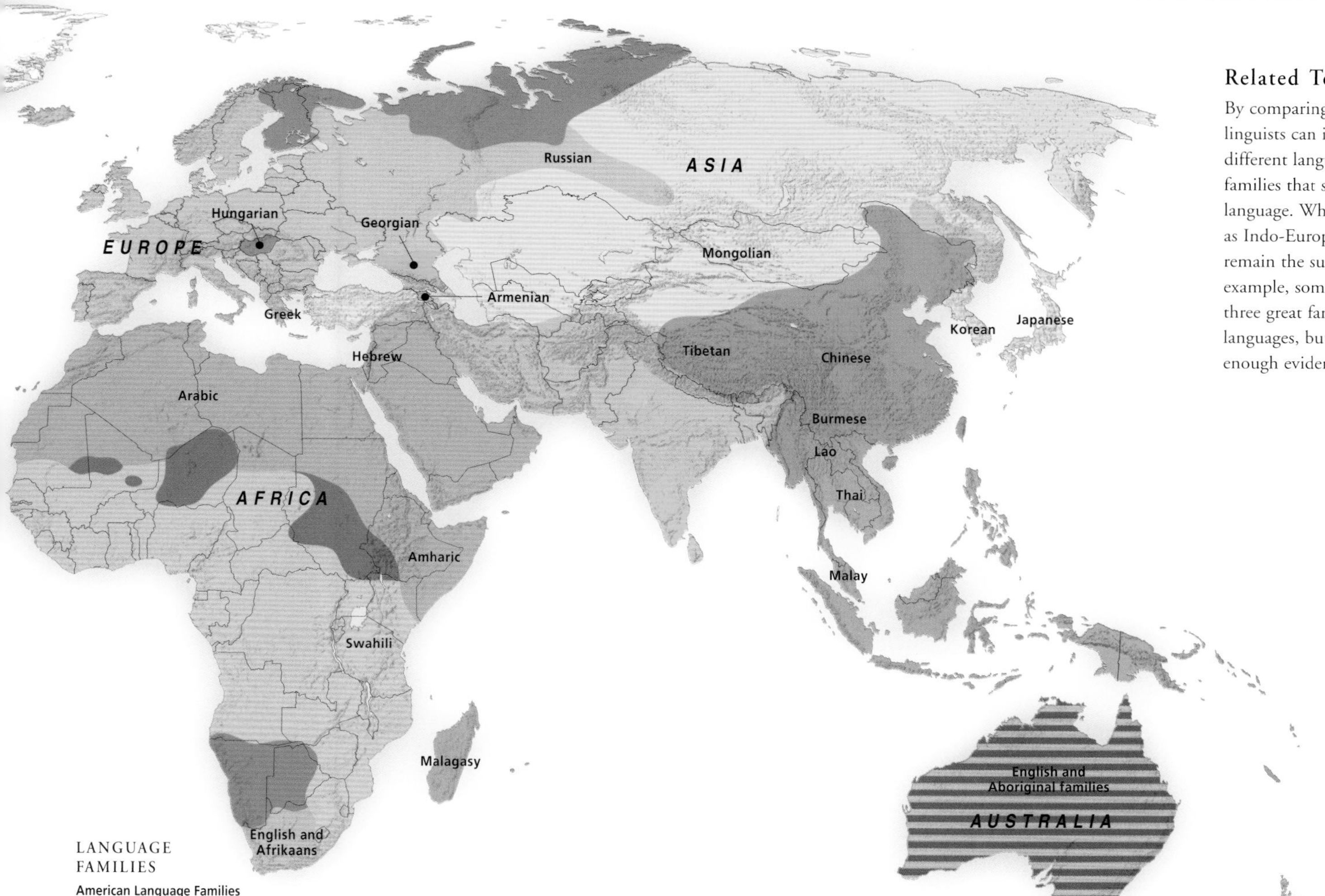

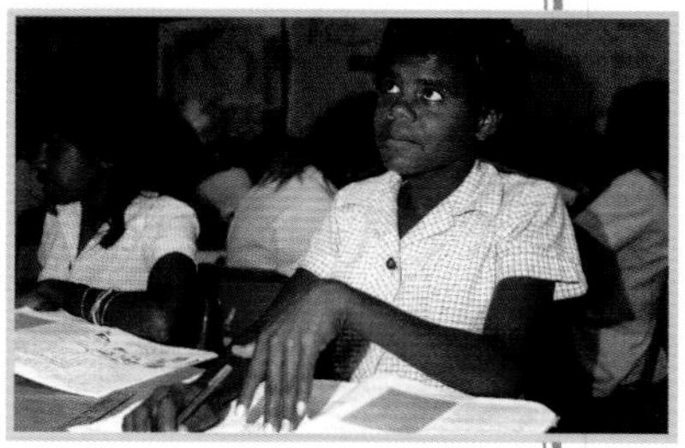

Bilingual education is an important way to promote the survival of minority languages and cultures. Many Australian Aboriginal children now receive their lessons in both English and an indigenous language.

The Chinese writing system comprises several thousand logographs, characters that each represent an entire word. People speaking mutually incomprehensible dialects of Chinese can still communicate via this script.

LANGUAGE FAMILIES

American Language Families

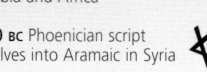 Eskimo-Aleut: languages spoken by indigenous arctic peoples, including Asiatic Eskimo and Aleut

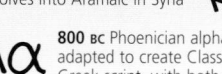 Na-Dene: groups Haida and Tlingit languages of Pacific Northwest with Athabaskan languages, including Navajo and Apache

Other Native American families: many families including languages such as Cree, Mohawk, Shoshone, Jacaltec, Guarani, Quechua

Eurasian Language Families

Indo-European: many European and Asian languages, including English, German, French, Italian, Spanish, Russian, Hindi, Persian

Uralic: 20+ languages, including Estonian, Finnish, Hungarian, Sami, Nenets

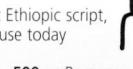 Altaic: 50+ languages, including Mongolian, Turkish, Korean, Japanese

Chukotko-Kamchatkan: languages spoken in eastern Russia, including Chukchi, Alutor, Itelmen, Kerek

Caucasian families: 3 families with 40+ languages spoken in the Caucasus, including Chechen, Georgian

African Language Families

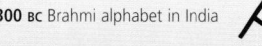 Afro-Asiatic: 370+ languages, including Arabic, Hebrew, Somali, Berber, Hausa

Nilo-Saharan: 100+ languages in East Africa, including Songhai, Nubian, Masai

Niger-Congo: 900+ languages, including Swahili, Fulani, Zulu, Mossi, Shona

Khoisan: languages spoken in southwest Africa, many featuring click sounds

Southeast Asian Families

 Dravidian: languages of southern and eastern India, including Kannada, Malayalam, Tamil, Telugu

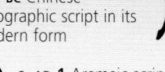 Sino-Tibetan: 130+ languages of East Asia, including Mandarin, Cantonese, Tibetan, Burmese

Austric families: includes Austronesian (Malay, Maori), Austroasiatic (Vietnamese), and Tai-Kadai (Thai, Lao)

Papuan families: 700+ languages spoken on the island of New Guinea

 Australian Aboriginal families: 250+ languages spoken by indigenous peoples of Australia

English and Maori

 SCALE 1:90,000,000
Robinson Projection

---

800 BC South Arabian script, evolved from Proto-Canaanite, later spreads into North Arabia and Africa

800 BC Phoenician script evolves into Aramaic in Syria

800 BC Phoenician alphabet adapted to create Classical Greek script, with both vowels and consonants; later becomes modern Greek alphabet

600 BC Etruscans in Italy adapt Greek alphabet

600 BC Egyptian demotic script supplants hieratic (a cursive variety of cuneiform)

500 BC Ethiopic script, still in use today

500 BC Romans adapt Etruscan alphabet, later becomes modern Roman alphabet of 26 letters

300 BC Brahmi alphabet in India

200 BC Nabateans use Aramaic script for Arabic language

200 BC Chinese logographic script in its modern form

c. AD 1 Aramaic script evolves into modern Hebrew square letter script, used for most of Old Testament

by AD 250 Mayan hieroglyphic script in Mesoamerica

AD 250 Runic script develops in Scandinavia, later spreads to Britain

AD 400 First Arabic script, later versions used for Koran and developed into modern Arabic script

AD 700 Japanese adopt Chinese characters

AD 900 Greek missionaries among the Slavs adapt Greek alphabet to create Cyrillic script, later reduced to 33 letters of modern Russian alphabet

AD 1000 Devanagari (used to write Sanskrit and Hindi) and other modern Indian scripts develop from Brahmi

THE GLOBAL ECONOMY

Global industrial output increased 50-fold during the 20th century. The wealth this generated, however, was shared by relatively few and led to an ever greater gap between rich and poor, both within countries and across the world. The richest 1 percent of the world's people receive as much income as the poorest 57 percent. More than 1.2 billion people live on less than US$1 a day, and 2.8 billion live on less than US$2 a day. Developing countries (ones yet to achieve effective industrial production levels) make up much of Asia, Africa, South America, and the Pacific; account for about 75 percent of world population; and share just 20 percent of world income.

During the 1990s, more than 50 developing countries became poorer and many others stagnated, victims of failed economic growth, declining aid from rich countries, rising debt repayments, and falling prices for the raw materials that make up the bulk of their export revenue. The HIV/AIDS epidemic has also been devastating, especially in sub-Saharan Africa, which has 70 percent of the world's 42 million cases.

Even within prosperous countries there can be great disparities in wealth, and in poor countries the brunt of the hardship is borne by disadvantaged groups. On average, men have a larger share of resources than women do, and urban dwellers are far better off than people in rural areas, with greater access to income, education, safe water and sanitation, and health services. On both a national and global level, future stability depends on a fairer distribution of the world's wealth.

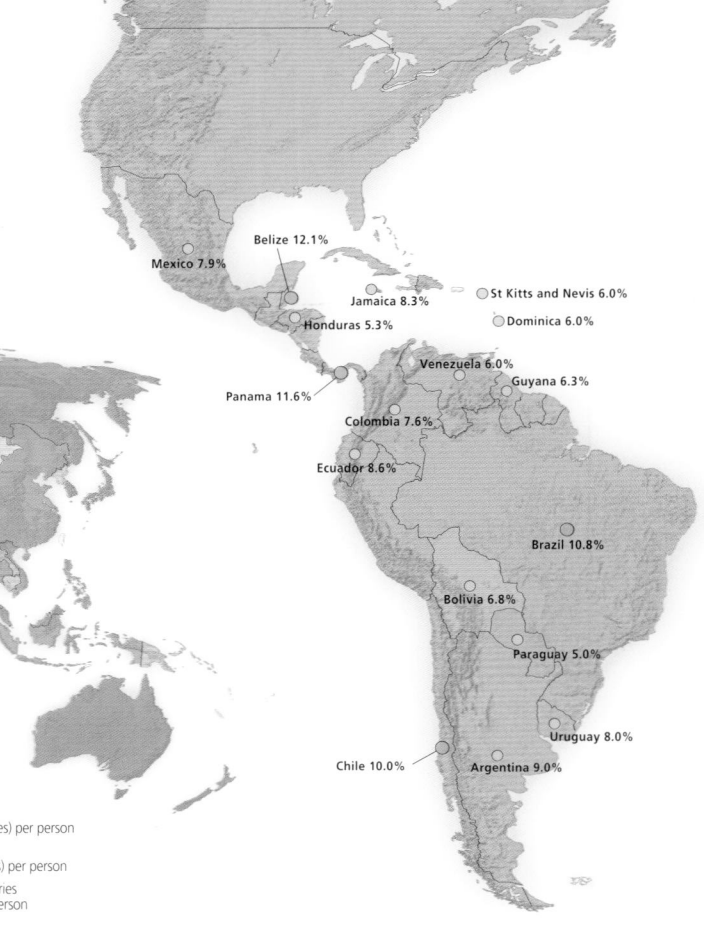

Famine can be both a cause and an effect of armed conflict, which prevents farmers from producing and distributing food. While essential during a crisis, food aid does not provide a long-term solution.

Food Supply

More than 800 million people do not have enough to eat. The Dietary Energy Supply (DES) estimates the energy that is available for human consumption in the total food supply of each country. An adequate daily DES is 2,600 Calories (10,900 kilojoules) per person. A daily DES of fewer than 2,300 Calories (9,600 kilojoules) indicates widespread hunger and malnutrition.

Belize 12.1%
Mexico 7.9%
Jamaica 8.3%
Honduras 5.3%
St Kitts and Nevis 6.0%
Dominica 6.0%
Venezuela 6.0%
Guyana 6.3%
Panama 11.6%
Colombia 7.6%
Ecuador 8.6%
Brazil 10.8%
Bolivia 6.8%
Paraguay 5.0%
Uruguay 8.0%
Chile 10.0%
Argentina 9.0%

DAILY DIETARY ENERGY SUPPLY (DES)

- More than 3,200 Calories (13,400 kilojoules) per person
- 2,900–3,200 Calories (12,000–13,400 kilojoules) per person
- 2,600–2,900 Calories (10,900–12,000 kilojoules) per person
- 2,300–2,600 Calories (9,600–10,900 kilojoules) per person
- 2,000–2,300 Calories (8,400–9,600 kilojoules) per person
- Fewer than 2,000 Calories (8,400 kilojoules) per person
- Insufficient data

HEALTH INDICATORS

The gulf between the haves and have-nots is reflected most keenly in a comparison of key health indicators. Most of the risk factors that contribute to the world's major health problems are related to patterns of consumption. Poor countries are home to 170 million underweight children, 3 million of whom die each year. At the same time, obesity contributes to about half a million deaths every year in North America and Western Europe. Unsafe water, sanitation, and hygiene lead to 1.7 million deaths every year. Other leading risk factors in Africa and Asia include unsafe sex, iron deficiency, and indoor smoke from solid fuels.

COUNTRY COMPARISON

- Norway (HDI 0.942)*
- Mexico (HDI 0.796)
- Indonesia (HDI 0.684)
- Pakistan (HDI 0.499)
- Sierra Leone (HDI 0.275)

* HDI Human Development Index

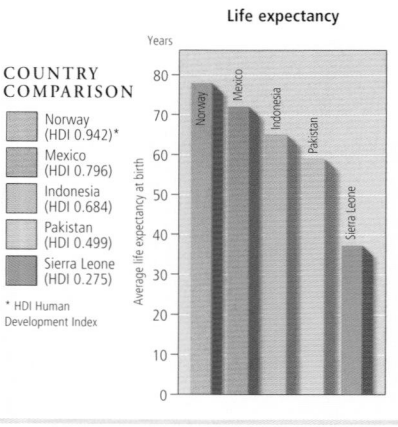

Life expectancy

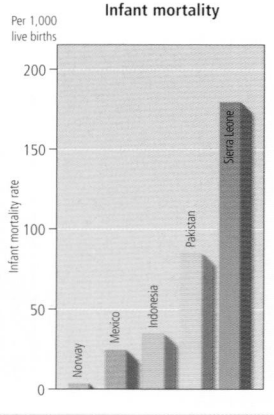

Infant mortality

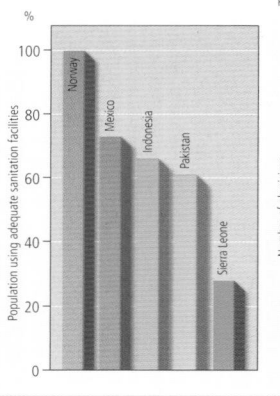

Sanitation

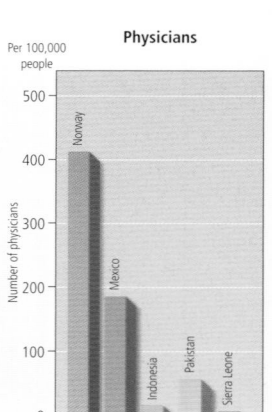

Physicians

RICHEST COUNTRIES: GDP PER CAPITA*

Luxembourg	US$44,000
United States	US$37,600
San Marino	US$34,600
Norway	US$31,800
Switzerland	US$31,700
Ireland	US$30,500
Canada	US$29,400
Belgium	US$29,000
Denmark	US$29,000
Japan	US$28,000

POOREST COUNTRIES: GDP PER CAPITA*

East Timor	US$500
Somalia	US$550
Sierra Leone	US$580
Burundi	US$600
Democratic Republic of Congo	US$610
Tanzania	US$630
Malawi	US$670
Afghanistan	US$700
Comoros	US$720
Eritrea	US$740

All GDP figures are in PPP (Purchasing Power Parity), which takes into account price differences between countries.

In developed countries, computers are now a feature of classrooms. With only 8 percent of the world connected to the Internet, the "digital divide" is likely to further disadvantage the poorest people.

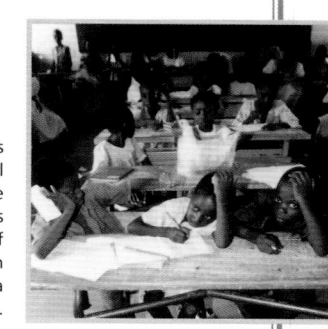

Although the 1990s saw primary school enrollments increase in every region, less than 60 percent of young children in sub-Saharan Africa attend school.

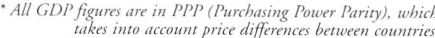

LOWEST ADULT LITERACY RATES**

COUNTRY	1990	2001
Niger	11.4%	16.5%
Burkina Faso	16.3%	24.8%
Mali	18.8%	26.4%
Gambia	25.6%	37.8%
Senegal	28.4%	38.3%
Benin	26.4%	38.6%
Guinea-Bissau	27.2%	39.6%
Ethiopia	28.6%	40.3%
Bangladesh	34.2%	40.6%
Mauritania	34.8%	40.7%

** Comparable statistics for several poor countries are not available, but some estimates put Somalia's adult literacy rate at about 25%, Sierra Leone's at about 30%, Guinea's and Afghanistan's at about 35%, and Angola's and Iraq's at about 40%.

Map labels

Estonia 6.9%
Latvia 6.8%
Lithuania 16.1%
Slovakia 12.8%
Poland 8.7%
Czech Republic 8.4%
Ukraine 6.0%
Russian Federation 5.6%
Hungary 26.4%
Moldova 12.8%
Croatia 14.6%
Romania 6.7%
Kazakhstan 14.9%
Bosnia and Herzegovina 6.3%
Bulgaria 10.1%
Macedonia 5.7%
Turkey 15.2%
Uzbekistan 7.4%
Kyrgyzstan 11.6%
South Korea 6.2%
Lebanon 8.7%
Tajikistan 7.6%
Morocco 7.7%
Tunisia 6.8%
Jordan 7.6%
Algeria 8.0%
Pakistan 5.0%
Mauritania 8.9%
Guinea-Bissau 11.7%
Sierra Leone 12.8%
Nigeria 6.2%
Philippines 10.9%
Côte d'Ivoire 5.9%
Ghana 6.0%
Thailand 17.5%
São Tomé and Principe 8.5%
Gabon 10.5%
Malaysia 7.1%
Angola 19.7%
Indonesia 10.7%
Papua New Guinea 9.1%
Lesotho 8.6%

DEBT REPAYMENTS

○ Countries in which debt repayments are 5–10% of the GDP
○ Countries in which debt repayments are 10–15% of the GDP
● Countries in which debt repayments are above 15% of the GDP

SCALE 1:90,000,000
Robinson Projection

HUMAN DEVELOPMENT INDEX (HDI) VALUES

High 0.9–1.0
High 0.8–0.9
Medium 0.7–0.8
Medium 0.6–0.7
Medium 0.5–0.6
Low 0.4–0.5
Low 0.3–0.4
Low 0.2–0.3
Insufficient data

Assessing Development

A country's average standard of living can be measured by its Gross Domestic Product (GDP), the total value of all goods and services produced in a year. For a broader assessment of achievement, the Human Development Index (HDI) also takes into account life expectancy, adult literacy, and education enrollments. Many disadvantaged countries are trapped in poverty by the unsustainable debts they owe to wealthier countries, often paying more to service their foreign loans than they receive in foreign aid. In an attempt to address this problem, the United Nations has initiated debt relief schemes.

Adults with HIV/AIDS

%
7.00
1.00
0.50
0.00

Adult population (age 15–49) living with HIV/AIDS

Norway
Mexico
Indonesia
Pakistan
Sierra Leone

Leading causes of death

Infectious and parasitic diseases
Cancers
Cardiovascular diseases
Childbirth-related
Injuries
Other*

Developed world
Leading causes of death in Europe

5%
19%
15%
8%
1%
52%

Developing world
Leading causes of death in Africa

62%
9%
5%
9%
8%
7%

* Other causes of death include: nutritional deficiencies, nervous disorders, diabetes, cirrhosis of the liver, pulmonary disease, kidney conditions.

WOMEN'S SHARE

Throughout the world, women are poorer than their male compatriots, and three-fifths of the world's 1 billion poorest people are women. Ethiopian women, for example, earn an average of US$550 per year, compared to an average of US$1,074 for men. Education is an important factor—of the nearly 1 billion people who cannot read, two-thirds are women. Even in a country with well-educated women, such as Sweden, the average female income is less than 70 percent of the male income. Other causes of gender inequality include the poor pay that traditionally female work attracts and the lack of women in positions of power in politics and business.

In developed and developing countries alike, women earn significantly less than men.

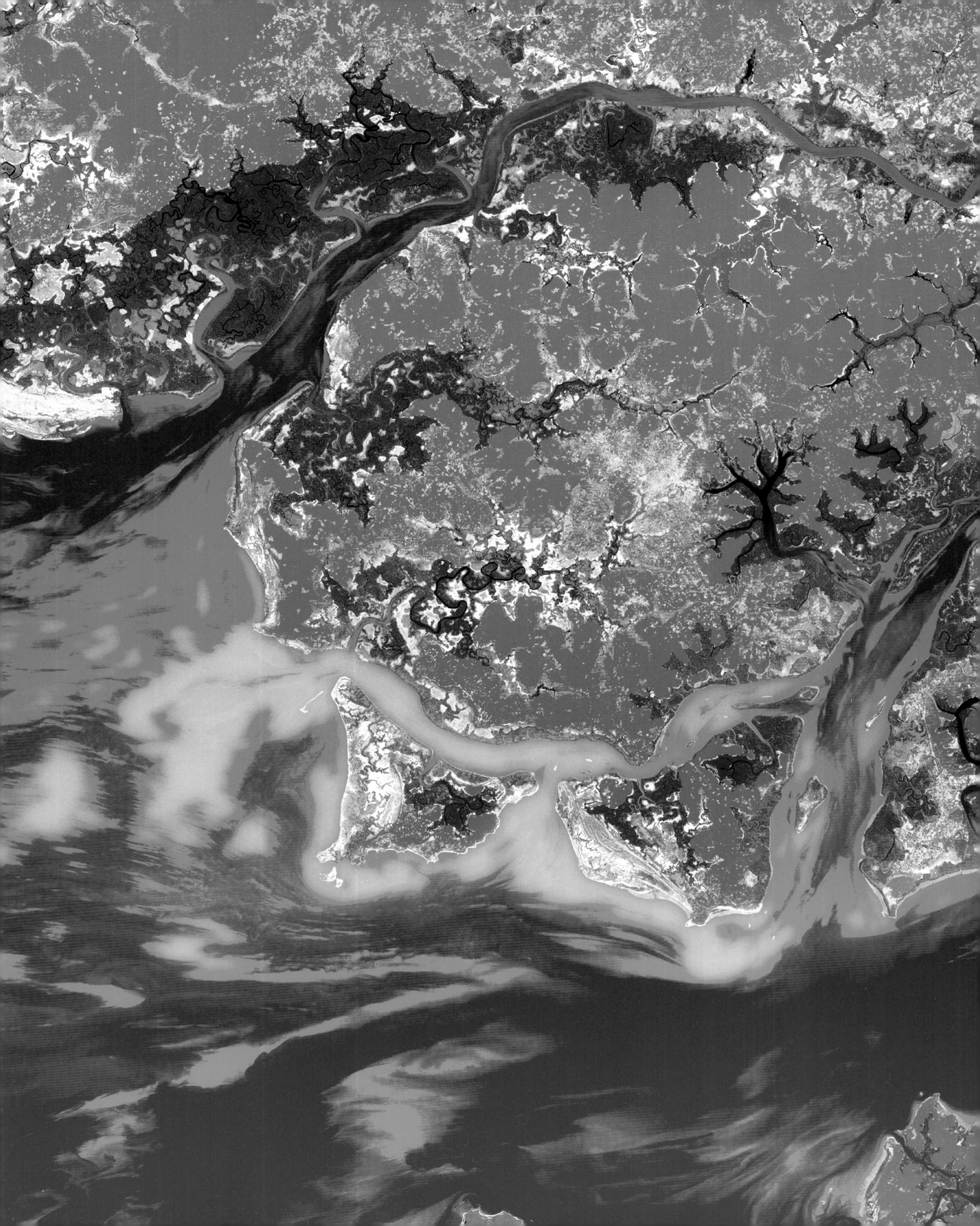

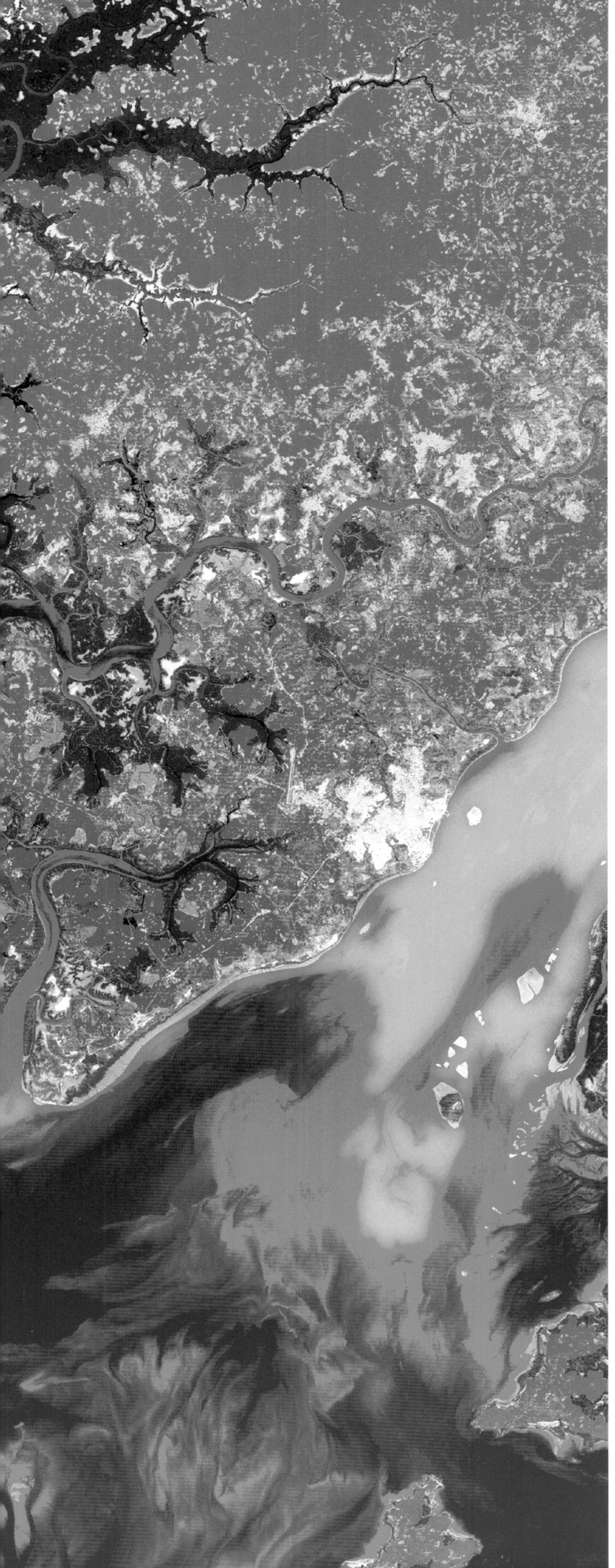

MAPPING THE WORLD

Part of the coastline of Guinea-Bissau in western Africa is visible in this color-enhanced satellite image. It was photographed from Landsat 7 using infrared, red and blue wavelengths. The blue ribbons are river systems; at center right is the River Geba. The light blue areas are silt that has been deposited as rivers flow into the Atlantic Ocean at the bottom of the image.

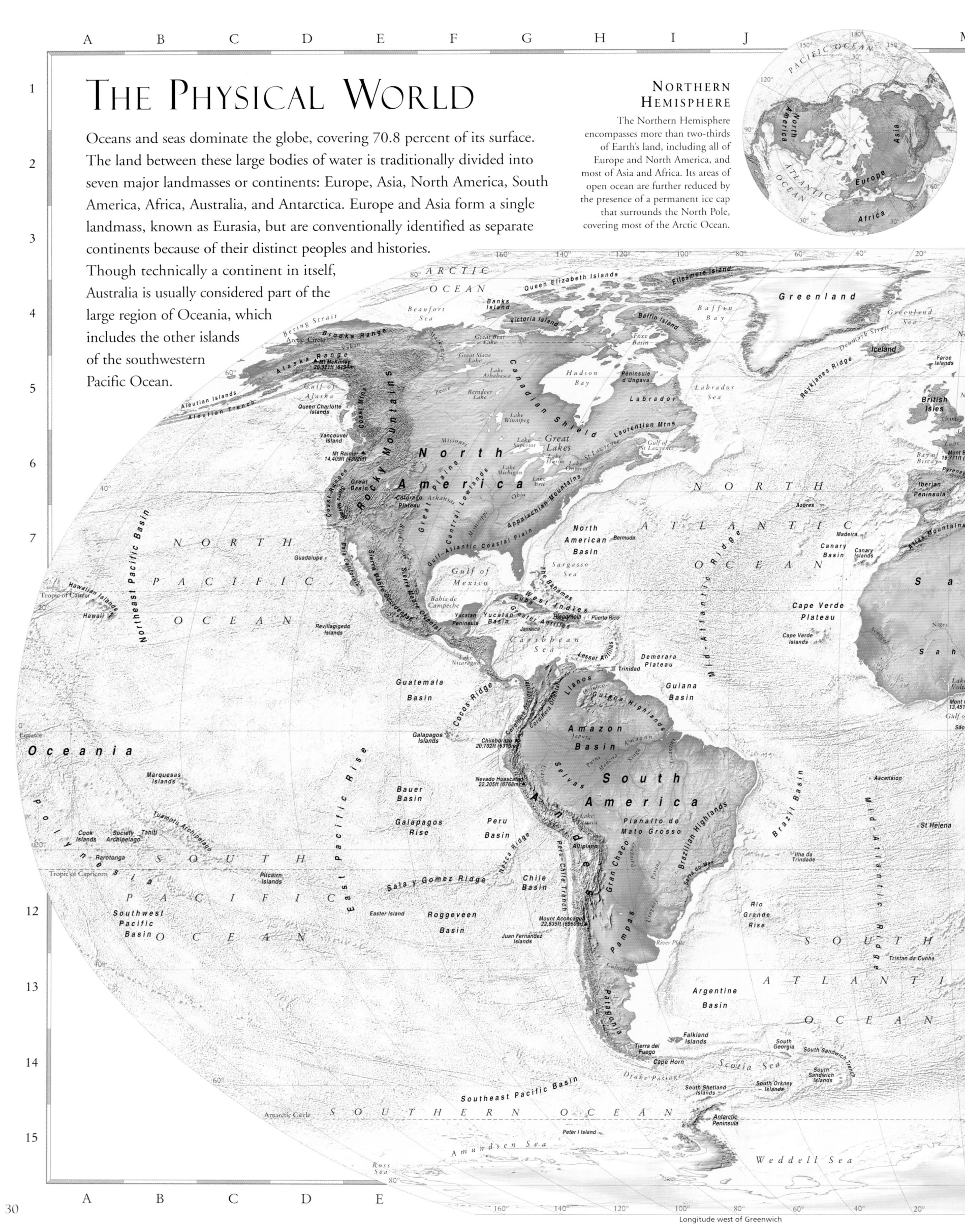

THE PHYSICAL WORLD

Oceans and seas dominate the globe, covering 70.8 percent of its surface. The land between these large bodies of water is traditionally divided into seven major landmasses or continents: Europe, Asia, North America, South America, Africa, Australia, and Antarctica. Europe and Asia form a single landmass, known as Eurasia, but are conventionally identified as separate continents because of their distinct peoples and histories. Though technically a continent in itself, Australia is usually considered part of the large region of Oceania, which includes the other islands of the southwestern Pacific Ocean.

NORTHERN HEMISPHERE

The Northern Hemisphere encompasses more than two-thirds of Earth's land, including all of Europe and North America, and most of Asia and Africa. Its areas of open ocean are further reduced by the presence of a permanent ice cap that surrounds the North Pole, covering most of the Arctic Ocean.

Longitude west of Greenwich

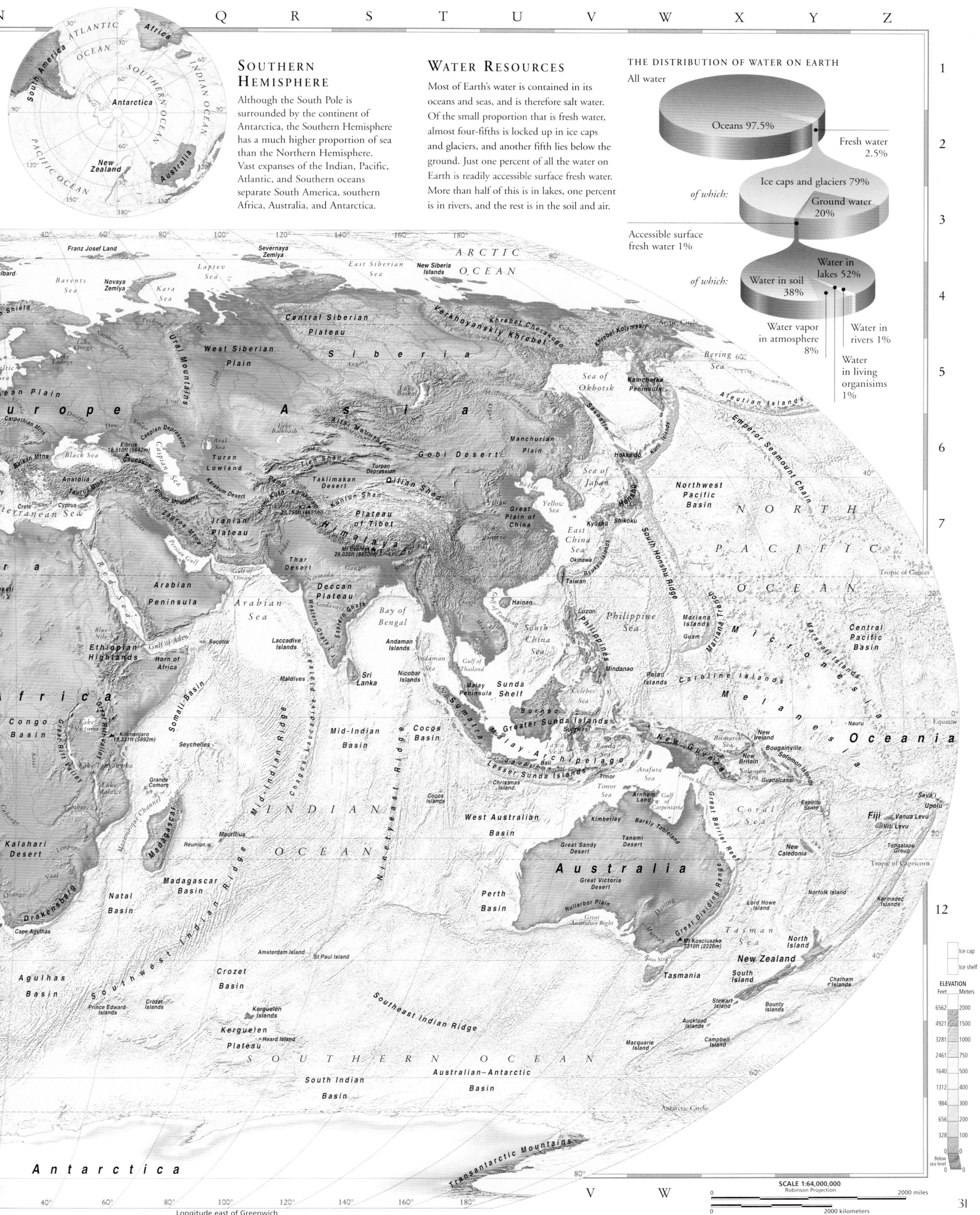

SOUTHERN HEMISPHERE

Although the South Pole is surrounded by the continent of Antarctica, the Southern Hemisphere has a much higher proportion of sea than the Northern Hemisphere. Vast expanses of the Indian, Pacific, Atlantic, and Southern oceans separate South America, southern Africa, Australia, and Antarctica.

WATER RESOURCES

Most of Earth's water is contained in its oceans and seas, and is therefore salt water. Of the small proportion that is fresh water, almost four-fifths is locked up in ice caps and glaciers, and another fifth lies below the ground. Just one percent of all the water on Earth is readily accessible surface fresh water. More than half of this is in lakes, one percent is in rivers, and the rest is in the soil and air.

THE DISTRIBUTION OF WATER ON EARTH

All water

Oceans 97.5%

Fresh water 2.5%

of which:

Ice caps and glaciers 79%

Ground water 20%

Accessible surface fresh water 1%

of which:

Water in soil 38%

Water in lakes 52%

Water vapor in atmosphere 8%

Water in rivers 1%

Water in living organisims 1%

SCALE 1:64,000,000
Robinson Projection

2000 miles

2000 kilometers

Ice cap

Ice shelf

ELEVATION

Feet	Meters
6562	2000
4921	1500
3281	1000
2461	750
1640	500
1312	400
984	300
656	200
328	100
0	0
	Below sea level

Longitude east of Greenwich

THE POLITICAL WORLD

With the exception of Antarctica, where territorial claims have been suspended, all the land on Earth is divided into 192 independent countries and about 60 dependent territories. The countries range in size from the largest, the vast Russian Federation, to the smallest, the Vatican City, which lies entirely within the city of Rome in Italy. Most dependent territories came about as the result of colonization and belong to a few, mainly European nations. Some areas of land, usually on the fringes of countries, are the focus of territorial disputes.

Dividing the World

About 150,000 miles (250,000 km) of land boundaries separate the world's countries and territories. These borders may follow landforms, waterways, the margins of traditional ethnic territories, lines of latitude or longitude, or arbitrary lines plotted by colonial administrators. Many seaboard nations have also established maritime boundaries. A nation's maritime territorial claim extends 12 nautical miles offshore, but exclusive fishing and economic zones are generally recognized up to 200 nautical miles offshore.

PACIFIC OCEAN
Yap Caroline Islands Pohnpei
Chuuk Kosrae
Islands
FEDERATED STATES OF MICRONESIA

The Exclusive Economic Zone (EEZ) of the Federated States of Micronesia encompasses over 1.3 million square miles (3 million sq km) of ocean.

The Vatican City covers less than a fifth of a square mile (0.5 sq km) of the city of Rome.

ARCTIC OCEAN
Beaufort Sea
Ellesmere Island
Greenland (to Denmark)
Jan Mayen (to Norway)
Baffin Island
Baffin Bay
Victoria Island
Arctic Circle
U.S.A. (Alaska)
Gulf of Alaska
ICELAND
REYKJAVÍK
Faroe Islands (to Denmark)
Aleutian Islands (U.S.A.)
Hudson Bay
CANADA
UNITED KINGDOM
DUBLIN LONDON
REPUBLIC OF IRELAND BRUSSELS
PARIS
NORTH
OTTAWA
St Pierre and Miquelon (to France)
FRANCE
MONACO
ANDORRA
PORTUGAL MADRID
UNITED STATES OF AMERICA
WASHINGTON, D.C.
NORTH
Azores (to Portugal)
LISBON
SPAIN
ALG
PACIFIC
ATLANTIC
Madeira (to Portugal)
RABAT
MOROCCO
OCEAN
Bermuda (to U.K.)
Canary Islands (to Spain)
ALGER
Tropic of Cancer
Guadalupe (to Mexico)
Gulf of Mexico
THE BAHAMAS
NASSAU
OCEAN
LAÂYOUNE
WESTERN SAHARA (occupied by Morocco)
Hawaii (U.S.A.)
MEXICO
HAVANA
CUBA
DOMINICAN REPUBLIC
SANTO DOMINGO
MAURITANIA
NOUAKCHOTT
Revillagigedo Islands (to Mexico)
MEXICO CITY
Cayman Is (to U.K.)
BELIZE KINGSTON
BELMOPAN JAMAICA
HAITI PORT-AU-PRINCE
Puerto Rico (to U.S.A.)
ST KITTS AND NEVIS
ANTIGUA AND BARBUDA
DOMINICA
MALI
CAPE VERDE
PRAIA
SENEGAL
DAKAR BANJUL
GAMBIA
BISSAU BAMAKO
GUATEMALA
GUATEMALA HONDURAS
SAN SALVADOR TEGUCIGALPA
EL SALVADOR NICARAGUA
MANAGUA
ST LUCIA
ST VINCENT AND THE GRENADINES BARBADOS
GRENADA
GUINEA-BISSAU CONAKRY GUINEA
OUAGADOU
BURKINA FASO
CÔTE D'IVOIRE
NIA
COSTA RICA PANAMA CITY
SAN JOSÉ PANAMA
TRINIDAD AND TOBAGO
PORT OF SPAIN
FREETOWN
SIERRA LEONE
YAMOUSSOUKRO
MONROVIA
ACCRA LOME
Clipperton Island (to France)
CARACAS
VENEZUELA
GEORGETOWN
GUYANA CAYENNE
LIBERIA
EQUA GUI
BOGOTÁ
PARAMARIBO
SURINAME FRENCH GUIANA (to France)
COLOMBIA
SÃO TO
SÃO TOMÉ AND PRÍNC
Galapagos Islands (to Ecuador)
QUITO
ECUADOR
KIRIBATI
Fernando de Noronha (to Brazil)
SOUTH
PERU
BRAZIL
Ascension (to U.K.)
PACIFIC
LIMA
BOLIVIA
LA PAZ
BRASÍLIA
American Samoa (to U.S.A.)
SUCRE
St Helena (to U.K.)
Cook Islands (to N.Z.)
PAPEETE Tahiti
French Polynesia (to France)
OCEAN
PARAGUAY
Ilha da Trindade (to Brazil)
AVARUA
Tropic of Capricorn
ADAMSTOWN
Pitcairn Islands (to U.K.)
Sala y Gómez (to Chile)
ASUNCIÓN
SOUTH
Easter Island (to Chile)
ARGENTINA
Juan Fernández Islands (to Chile)
URUGUAY
ATLANTIC
SANTIAGO CHILE
MONTEVIDEO
BUENOS AIRES
Tristan da Cunha (to U.K.)
OCEAN
Falkland Islands (to U.K.)
South Georgia (to U.K.)
Gough Island (to U.K.)
South Sandwich Islands (to U.K.)
South Shetland Islands
South Orkney Islands
Antarctic Circle
SOUTHERN OCEAN
Peter I Island (to Norway)
Antarctic Peninsula
Weddell Sea
AN N
International Date Line
Equator
NORTH
0°
Longitude west of Greenwich

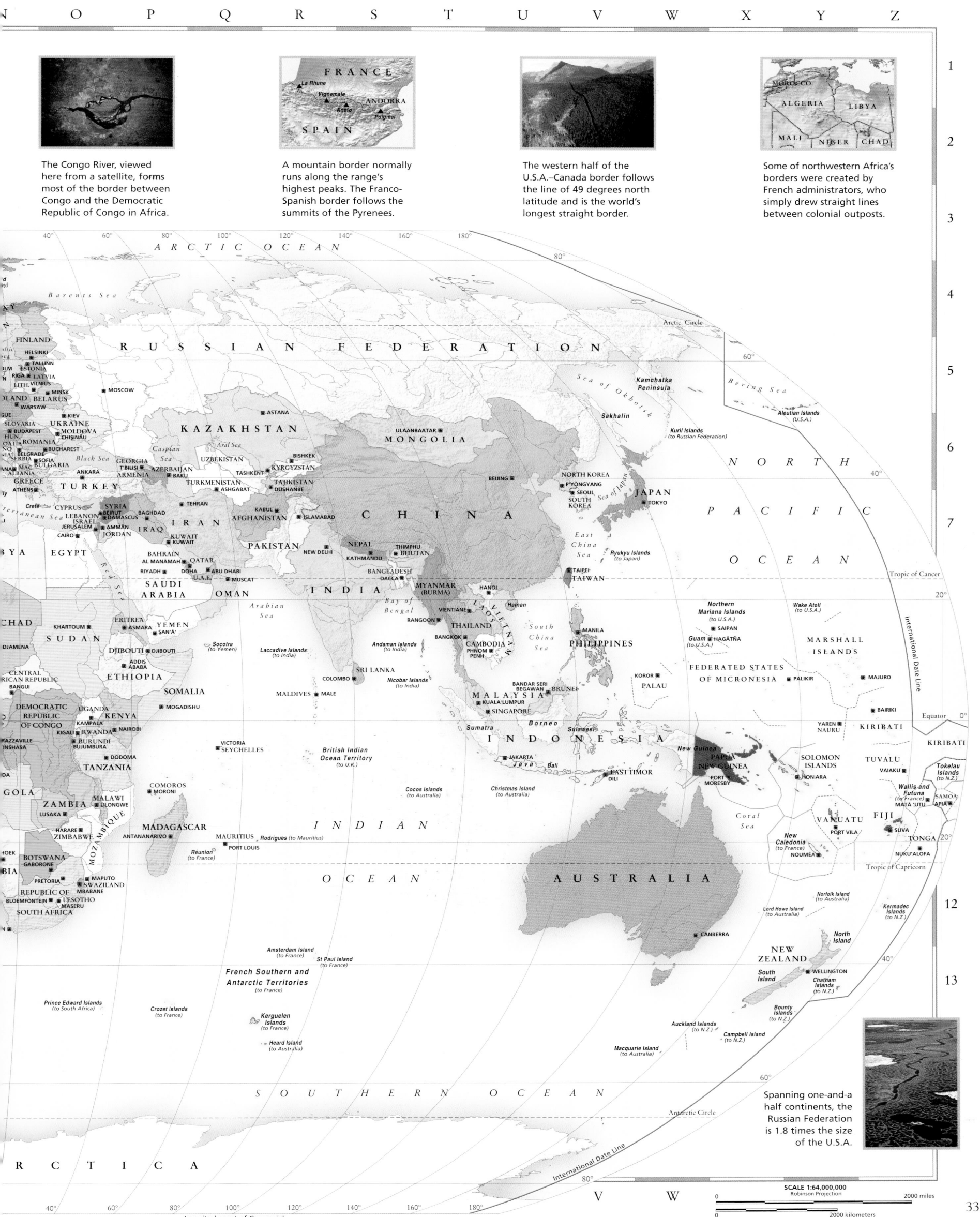

The Congo River, viewed here from a satellite, forms most of the border between Congo and the Democratic Republic of Congo in Africa.

A mountain border normally runs along the range's highest peaks. The Franco-Spanish border follows the summits of the Pyrenees.

The western half of the U.S.A.–Canada border follows the line of 49 degrees north latitude and is the world's longest straight border.

Some of northwestern Africa's borders were created by French administrators, who simply drew straight lines between colonial outposts.

Spanning one-and-a half continents, the Russian Federation is 1.8 times the size of the U.S.A.

SCALE 1:64,000,000
Robinson Projection

Longitude east of Greenwich

33

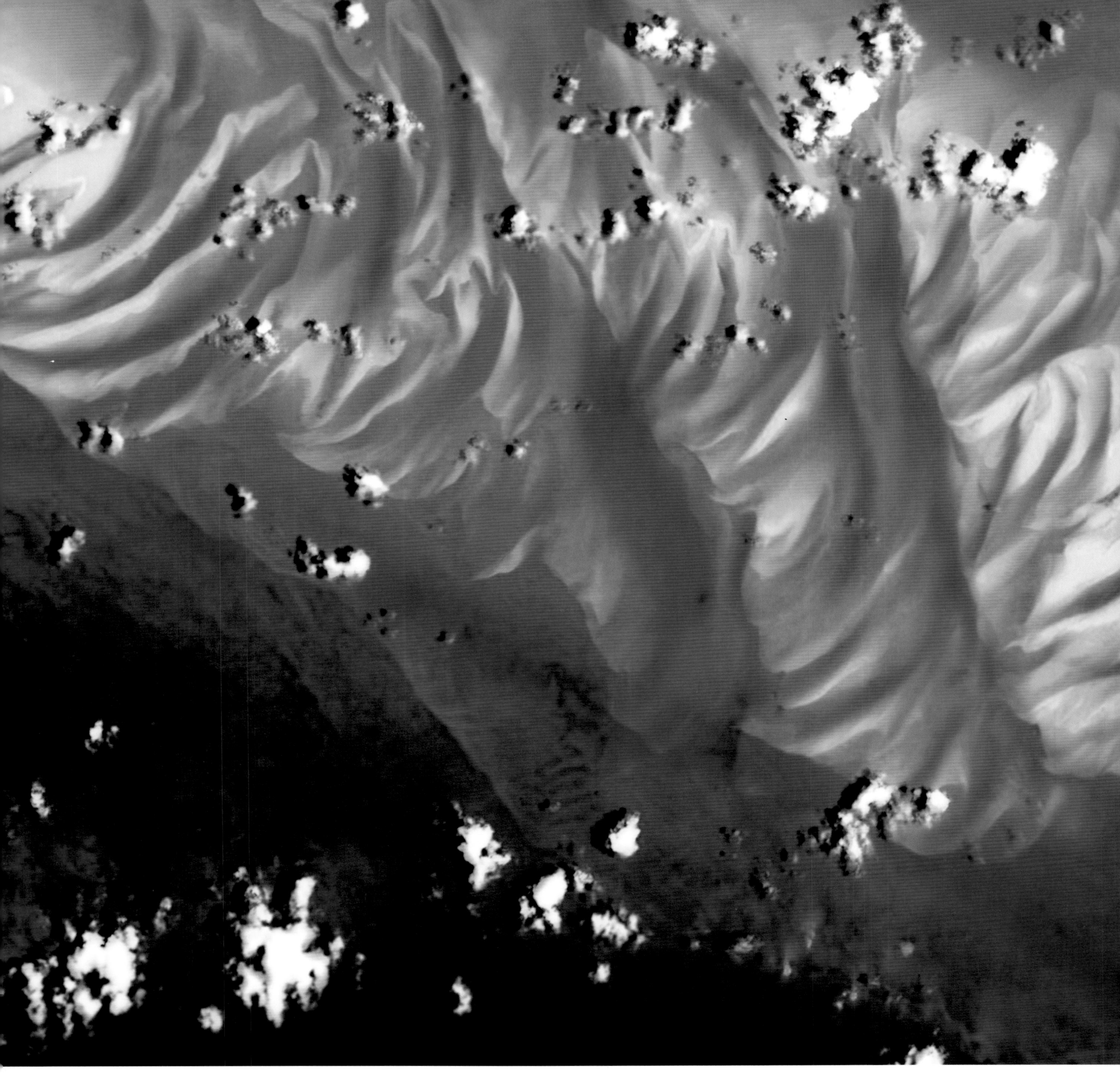

Taken from NASA's Terra satellite, this image shows underwater sand dunes in the waters of Tarpum Bay, southwest of Eleuthera Island in The Bahamas. These dunes, shaped by ocean currents, are made of sand eroded from limestone coral reefs.

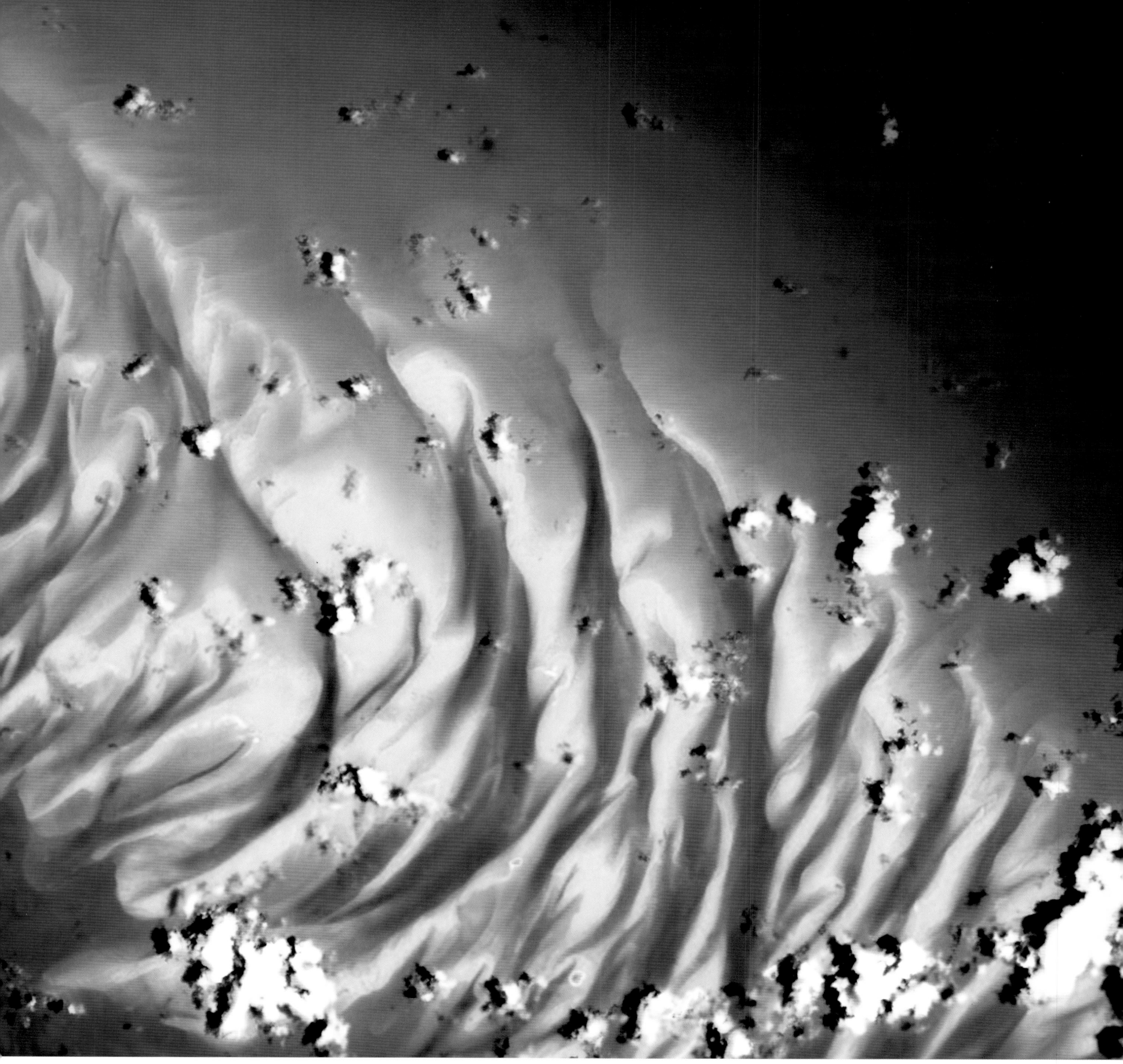

THE OCEANS

THE OCEANS

More than two-thirds of Earth's surface is covered by its five connected oceans. The Pacific, Atlantic, Indian, and Arctic have been recognized for centuries. The fifth ocean, the Southern, was demarcated by the International Hydrographic Organization only in the year 2000. It encompasses all the waters surrounding Antarctica up to 60 degrees south latitude, taking in areas formerly considered part of the Pacific, Atlantic, and Indian oceans. A region known as the Antarctic Polar Frontal Zone separates the icy waters of the Southern Ocean from the warmer waters to the north.

The oceans absorb more than 80 percent of the solar radiation that reaches Earth, and water has a remarkable capacity for storing heat. Consequently, the uppermost 10 percent of the oceans contains more heat than the entire atmosphere. As ocean currents carry immense quantities of heat around the globe, they modify the climate. The Gulf Stream, for example, carries warm water from the Caribbean past the eastern United States to northern Europe, making northern Europe significantly warmer than northern Canada at the same latitudes.

Recent technologies such as satellites, submersibles, and sounding equipment have dramatically enhanced our understanding of the sea. The underwater landscape contains Earth's greatest canyons and longest mountain chains. Bizarre lifeforms adapted to the cold, dark depths have been discovered. Even so, more than 90 percent of Earth's oceans are still to be explored.

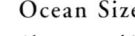

SCALE 1:115,000,000
Robinson Projection

Tidal Forces

Every day as Earth rotates, the Moon's gravity pulls on its oceans, creating high tide on the side facing the Moon. Centrifugal force produced by Earth's rotation creates high tide on the opposite side as well. When the Sun and Moon line up, their combined gravitational pull creates especially high tides, known as spring tides. When the Sun and Moon are at right angles to each other, the tidal range is small and neap tides occur.

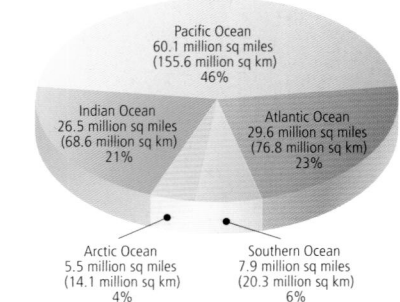

Ocean Size

Almost equal in size to the Indian, Atlantic, and Arctic combined, the Pacific is by far the largest ocean. Together, the five oceans cover about 130 million square miles (335 million sq km). They contain 335 million cubic miles (1,400 million cubic km) of water, which makes up 97 percent of all Earth's water and is 18 times greater than the volume of Earth's land.

In warm, shallow seas, vast reefs can be built by coral polyps, tiny animals that produce casings of limestone. Referred to as "the rain forests of the sea," coral reefs harbor a rich diversity of life.

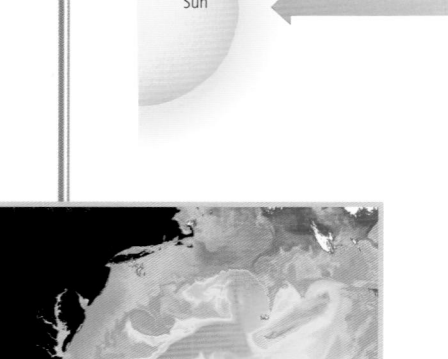

The Gulf Stream is a warm surface current in the Atlantic Ocean off the east coast of the United States. In this false-color satellite image, warmer waters are shown as red, and cooler waters are shown as blue.

Great Ocean Conveyor Belt

A "great ocean conveyor belt" transports heat around the globe. As surface currents carry warm water from the Pacific through the Indian and into the Atlantic, the water cools and evaporation increases its salinity. In the North Atlantic, this denser, colder water sinks, creating a deep current that carries it back to the Indian, Southern, and Pacific oceans. Changes in precipitation and ice melt may affect the belt's strength, which in turn may alter the global climate.

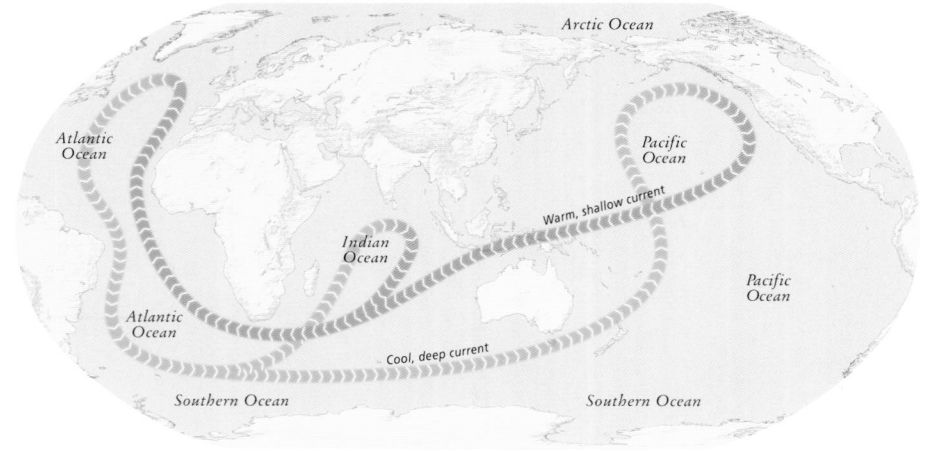

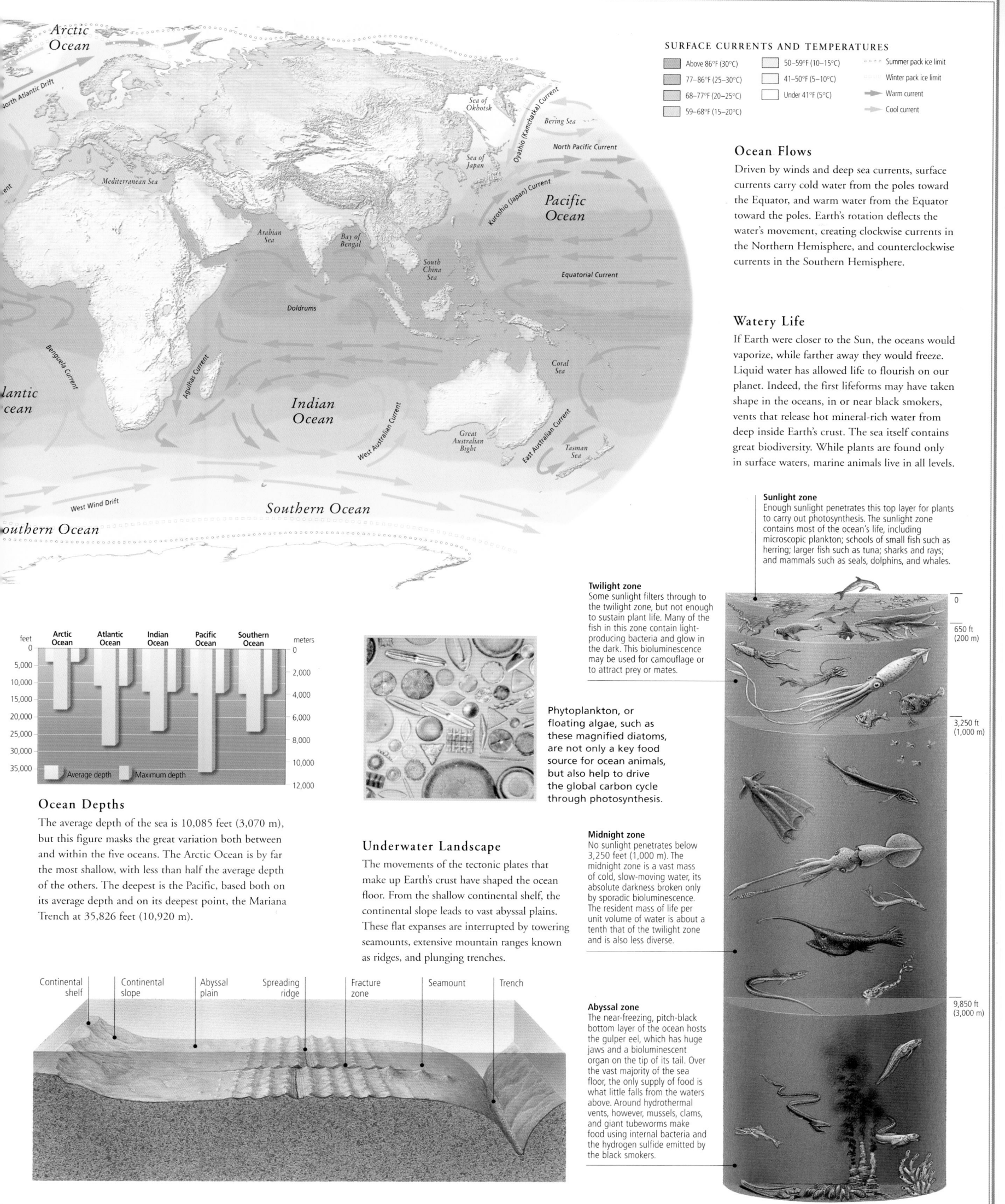

SURFACE CURRENTS AND TEMPERATURES

Above 86°F (30°C)	50–59°F (10–15°C)	···· Summer pack ice limit
77–86°F (25–30°C)	41–50°F (5–10°C)	---- Winter pack ice limit
68–77°F (20–25°C)	Under 41°F (5°C)	→ Warm current
59–68°F (15–20°C)		→ Cool current

Map labels: Arctic Ocean; North Atlantic Drift; Mediterranean Sea; Sea of Okhotsk; Bering Sea; Oyashio (Kamchatka) Current; North Pacific Current; Sea of Japan; Kuroshio (Japan) Current; Pacific Ocean; Arabian Sea; Bay of Bengal; South China Sea; Equatorial Current; Doldrums; Coral Sea; Benguela Current; Agulhas Current; Indian Ocean; Great Australian Bight; West Australian Current; East Australian Current; Tasman Sea; Atlantic Ocean; Southern Ocean; West Wind Drift; Southern Ocean

Ocean Flows

Driven by winds and deep sea currents, surface currents carry cold water from the poles toward the Equator, and warm water from the Equator toward the poles. Earth's rotation deflects the water's movement, creating clockwise currents in the Northern Hemisphere, and counterclockwise currents in the Southern Hemisphere.

Watery Life

If Earth were closer to the Sun, the oceans would vaporize, while farther away they would freeze. Liquid water has allowed life to flourish on our planet. Indeed, the first lifeforms may have taken shape in the oceans, in or near black smokers, vents that release hot mineral-rich water from deep inside Earth's crust. The sea itself contains great biodiversity. While plants are found only in surface waters, marine animals live in all levels.

Sunlight zone
Enough sunlight penetrates this top layer for plants to carry out photosynthesis. The sunlight zone contains most of the ocean's life, including microscopic plankton; schools of small fish such as herring; larger fish such as tuna; sharks and rays; and mammals such as seals, dolphins, and whales.

Twilight zone
Some sunlight filters through to the twilight zone, but not enough to sustain plant life. Many of the fish in this zone contain light-producing bacteria and glow in the dark. This bioluminescence may be used for camouflage or to attract prey or mates.

0

650 ft (200 m)

3,250 ft (1,000 m)

Phytoplankton, or floating algae, such as these magnified diatoms, are not only a key food source for ocean animals, but also help to drive the global carbon cycle through photosynthesis.

Midnight zone
No sunlight penetrates below 3,250 feet (1,000 m). The midnight zone is a vast mass of cold, slow-moving water, its absolute darkness broken only by sporadic bioluminescence. The resident mass of life per unit volume of water is about a tenth that of the twilight zone and is also less diverse.

Ocean Depths

The average depth of the sea is 10,085 feet (3,070 m), but this figure masks the great variation both between and within the five oceans. The Arctic Ocean is by far the most shallow, with less than half the average depth of the others. The deepest is the Pacific, based both on its average depth and on its deepest point, the Mariana Trench at 35,826 feet (10,920 m).

Ocean Depths chart:

feet	Arctic Ocean	Atlantic Ocean	Indian Ocean	Pacific Ocean	Southern Ocean	meters
						0
5,000						2,000
10,000						4,000
15,000						6,000
20,000						8,000
25,000						10,000
30,000						
35,000						12,000

Average depth   Maximum depth

Underwater Landscape

The movements of the tectonic plates that make up Earth's crust have shaped the ocean floor. From the shallow continental shelf, the continental slope leads to vast abyssal plains. These flat expanses are interrupted by towering seamounts, extensive mountain ranges known as ridges, and plunging trenches.

Underwater landscape labels: Continental shelf; Continental slope; Abyssal plain; Spreading ridge; Fracture zone; Seamount; Trench

Abyssal zone
The near-freezing, pitch-black bottom layer of the ocean hosts the gulper eel, which has huge jaws and a bioluminescent organ on the tip of its tail. Over the vast majority of the sea floor, the only supply of food is what little falls from the waters above. Around hydrothermal vents, however, mussels, clams, and giant tubeworms make food using internal bacteria and the hydrogen sulfide emitted by the black smokers.

9,850 ft (3,000 m)

THE INDIAN OCEAN

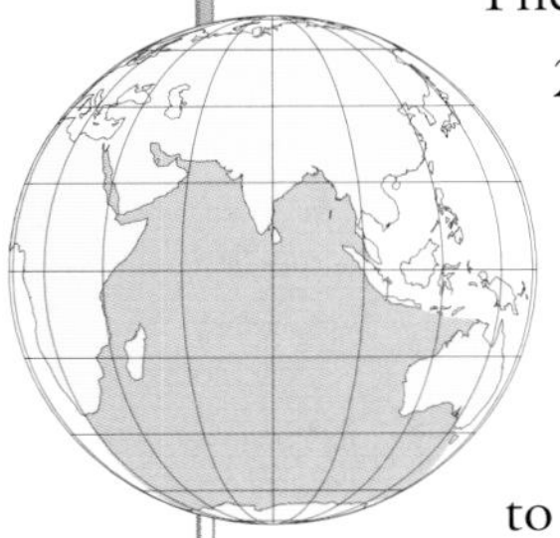

The third-largest ocean on Earth, the Indian Ocean covers 26.5 million square miles (68.6 million sq km), extending from the east coast of Africa to the west coast of Australia, and from the southern shore of Asia to the Southern Ocean. A series of major spreading ridges, including the Mid-Indian Ridge, runs southeast from the Arabian Sea to the center of the ocean, forking to form the Southwest Indian and Southeast Indian ridges. South of these two plate boundaries, broad basins are interrupted by the massive Kerguelen Plateau. To the north lie numerous plateaus and subsidiary, stable ridges, including the Ninetyeast Ridge, the longest straight ridge in the world, named for its location along the 90 degrees east meridian. The deepest part of the Indian Ocean is the Java Trench, south of the Indonesian island of Java, where the ocean floor drops to 23,376 feet (7,125 m) below sea level.

Residents watch a fiery lava flow from Piton de la Fournaise, an active volcano on the island of Réunion.

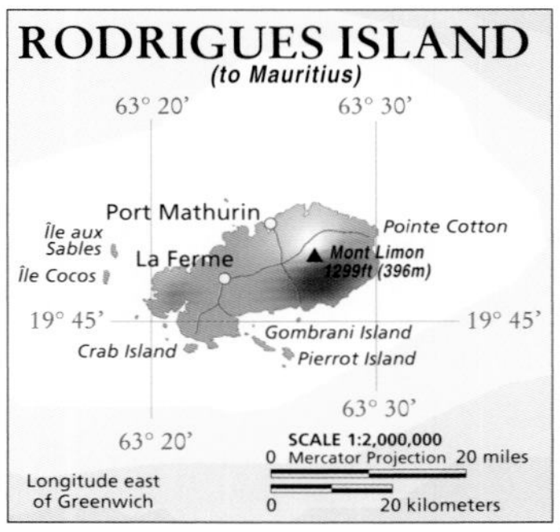

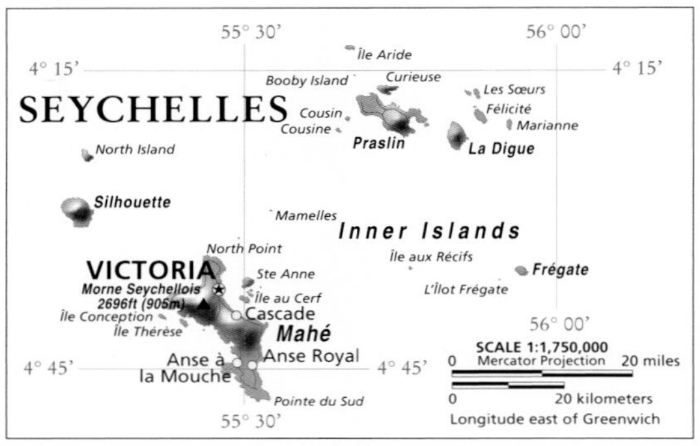

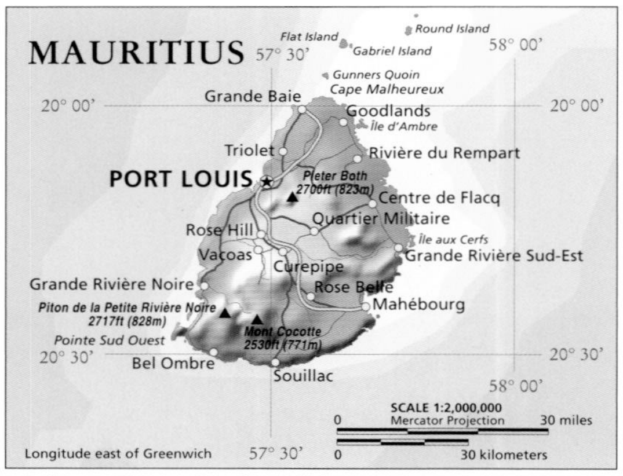

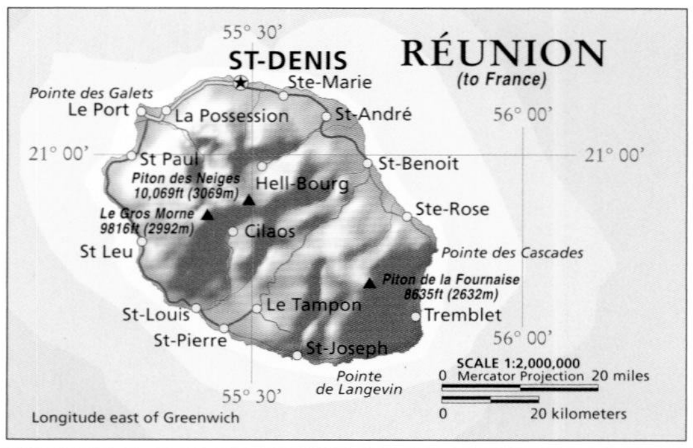

RODRIGUES ISLAND
(to Mauritius)

63° 20'   63° 30'

Port Mathurin
Île aux Sables   Pointe Cotton
Île Cocos   La Ferme   ▲ Mont Limon 1299ft (396m)

19° 45'   19° 45'
Crab Island   Gombrani Island
Pierrot Island

63° 20'   63° 30'
SCALE 1:2,000,000
0   Mercator Projection   20 miles
Longitude east of Greenwich
0   20 kilometers

SEYCHELLES

55° 30'   56° 00'
                      Île Aride
4° 15'   Booby Island   Curieuse   Les Sœurs   4° 15'
          Cousin   Félicité
          Cousine Praslin   Marianne
North Island   La Digue
Silhouette
                    Mamelles
VICTORIA   Inner Islands
Morne Seychellois   Île aux Récifs
2696ft (905m) North Point   Frégate
Île Conception Ste Anne
Île Thérèse Île au Cerf   L'Îlot Frégate
          Cascade
          Mahé   56° 00'
4° 45'   Anse Royal   4° 45'
Anse à   SCALE 1:1,750,000
la Mouche   0   Mercator Projection   20 miles
Pointe du Sud
55° 30'   0   20 kilometers
                    Longitude east of Greenwich

MAURITIUS

                Flat Island Round Island
57° 30'   Gabriel Island 58° 00'
              Gunners Quoin
          Cape Malheureux
20° 00' Grande Baie Île d'Ambre 20° 00'
          Goodlands
Triolet   Rivière du Rempart
PORT LOUIS Pieter Both
              2706ft (823m)
          Centre de Flacq
          Quartier Militaire
Rose Hill   Île aux Cerfs
Vacoas   Grande Rivière Sud-Est
        Curepipe
Grande Rivière Noire Rose Belle
Piton de la Petite Rivière Noire Mahébourg
2717ft (828m) ▲ Mont Cocotte
Pointe Sud Ouest 2530ft (771m)
Bel Ombre
          Souillac
20° 30'   20° 30'
              58° 00'
          SCALE 1:2,000,000
          0 Mercator Projection 30 miles
Longitude east of Greenwich 57° 30'
          0   30 kilometers

NATURAL RESOURCES

Busy shipping routes crisscross the ocean, with much of the traffic originating in the Persian Gulf oil fields. Other major oil reserves lie off Saudi Arabia, Iran, India, and Australia; in total, the Indian Ocean generates 40 percent of world offshore production. Sands and placer deposits are mined along the shoreline, and potentially valuable manganese nodules litter the ocean floor, though these have not yet been successfully exploited. Fish stocks, especially shrimps along the coast and tuna in the open ocean, are vital to many seaboard nations. Commercial harvesting occurs on only a modest scale, though fleets come from as far afield as Russia and Japan.

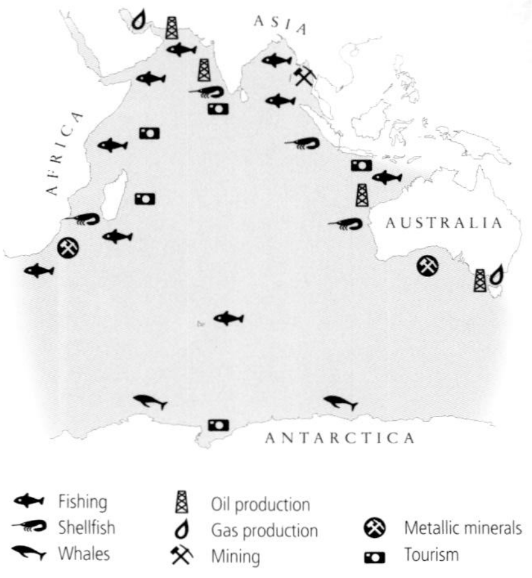

Fishing
Shellfish
Whales
Oil production
Gas production
Mining
Metallic minerals
Tourism

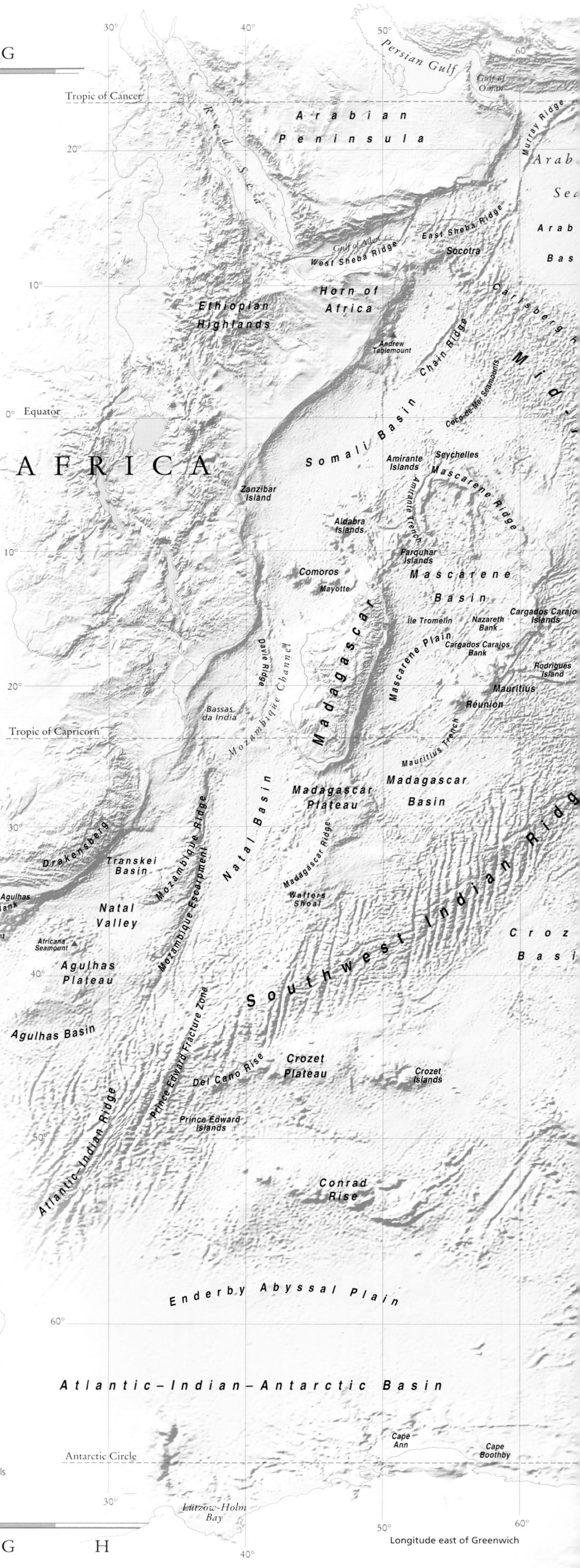

RÉUNION
(to France)

55° 30'
ST-DENIS Ste-Marie
Pointe des Galets
Le Port   La Possession St-André   56° 00'
21° 00'   St-Paul   21° 00'
        Piton des Neiges
        10,069ft (3069m)   St-Benoit
        Le Gros Morne   Hell-Bourg
        9816ft (2992m)
St-Leu   Cilaos   Ste-Rose
                    Pointe des Cascades
              ▲ Piton de la Fournaise
              8635ft (2632m)
St-Louis   Le Tampon   Tremblet
St-Pierre   56° 00'
          St-Joseph
              Pointe
              de Langevin
          SCALE 1:2,000,000
55° 30'   0 Mercator Projection 20 miles
Longitude east of Greenwich
          0   20 kilometers

Main map labels

30°   40°   50°   60°
Persian Gulf
Gulf of Oman
Tropic of Cancer
Red Sea
Arabian Peninsula
Arabian Sea
Arabian Basin
Murray Ridge
Gulf of Aden   East Sheba Ridge
West Sheba Ridge   Socotra
Horn of Africa   Carlsberg Ridge
Ethiopian Highlands
Andrew Tablemount   Mid-Indian Ridge
Equator   0°
Somali Basin
AFRICA   Cocos-Keeling Seamounts
Amirante Islands   Seychelles
Amirante Trench   Mascarene Ridge
Zanzibar Island
Aldabra Islands
Comoros   Farquhar Islands
Mayotte   Mascarene Basin
Île Tromelin   Nazareth Bank
Cargados Carajos Islands
Cargados Carajos Bank
Rodrigues Island
Mauritius
Réunion
10°
Davie Ridge
Madagascar
Mascarene Plain
Bassas da India
Mozambique Channel
Tropic of Capricorn
20°
Madagascar Plateau   Madagascar Basin
Mozambique Escarpment
Drakensberg   Mozambique Ridge
Transkei Basin   Natal Basin   Madagascar Ridge
Cape Agulhas   Walters Shoal
Agulhas Bank   Natal Valley
▲ Protea Seamount
Africana Seamount
Crozet Basin
Agulhas Plateau   Prince Edward Fracture Zone
Southwest Indian Ridge
Del Cano Rise   Crozet Plateau   Crozet Islands
Agulhas Basin   Prince Edward Islands
Atlantic-Indian Ridge
30°
Conrad Rise
Enderby Abyssal Plain
60°
Atlantic-Indian-Antarctic Basin
Antarctic Circle
Cape Ann   Cape Boothby
Lützow-Holm Bay
Pointe de Langevin
50°   60°
Longitude east of Greenwich

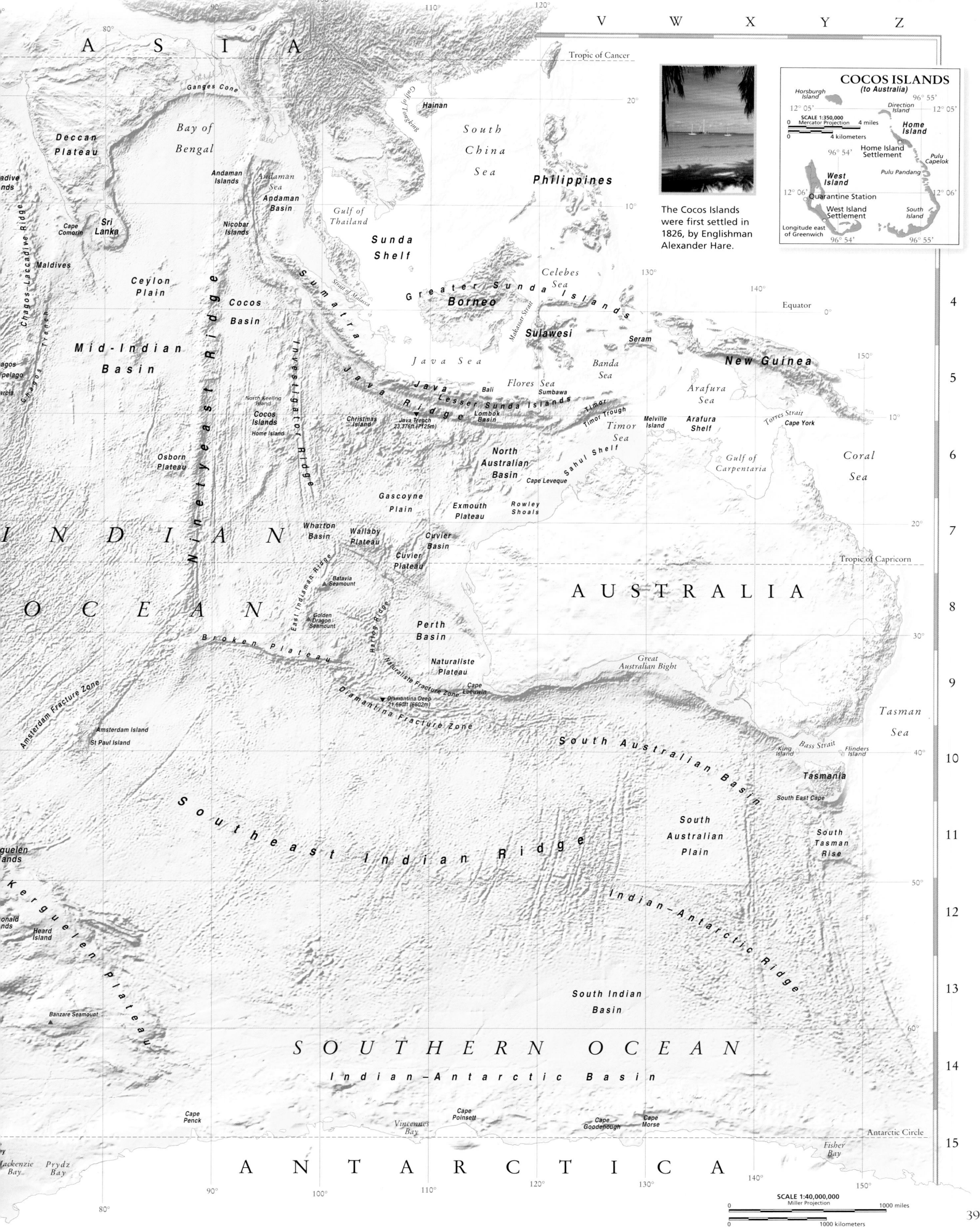

The Cocos Islands were first settled in 1826, by Englishman Alexander Hare.

THE PACIFIC OCEAN

Not only is the Pacific the largest of the oceans, it is twice as large and holds twice as much water as the Atlantic Ocean, and exceeds the combined area of all of Earth's landmasses. Spanning 60.1 million square miles (155.6 million sq km), it separates the continents of Asia and Australia from the Americas. A divergent plate boundary running south from Mexico forms the East Pacific Rise, part of the great chain of mid-ocean ridges that winds round the globe. Trenches formed by subduction border the eastern continental shelves, and volcanic peaks line the shores above. In the west, a complex series of mainly convergent plate boundaries forms a number of deep trenches bordered by volcanic archipelagoes. These zones of volcanic and seismic activity that almost encircle the Pacific Ocean are known as the Ring of Fire. In contrast, the floor of the central Pacific is relatively stable, consisting mainly of wide basins scarred by long, west–east-trending fractures and studded with myriad seamounts, thousands of which breach the sea surface to form islands and atolls.

The Pacific Ocean yields approximately 50 percent of the world's tuna catch.

In the kelp forests off the west coast of North America, the diversity of species rivals that of tropical rain forests.

NATURAL RESOURCES

The Pacific yields 60 percent of the world's fish catch, with the Northwest Pacific alone providing one-quarter of the entire global catch in recent years. Offshore oil and gas reserves are especially important for China, the U.S.A., Australia, and New Zealand. Sand and gravel are mined in most seaboard nations, and phosphates are extracted off the coasts of Australia, California, and Peru. Metallic nodules are common on the ocean floor, but the high cost of retrieval means that they are not yet mined commercially. The Pacific has by far the most extensive coral reefs of any ocean, which in many regions generate significant revenue from tourism.

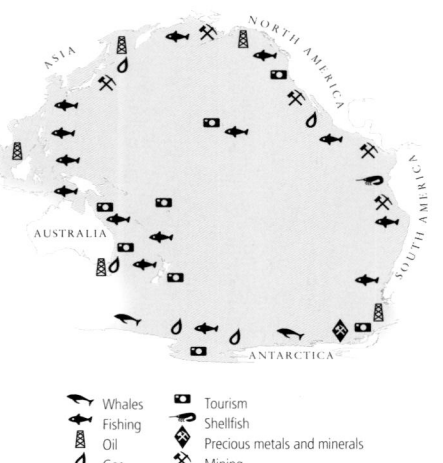

Whales
Fishing
Oil
Gas
Tourism
Shellfish
Precious metals and minerals
Mining

THE MARIANA TRENCH

Arcing for 1,580 miles (2,550 km) around the Mariana Islands, the Mariana Trench is the deepest part of the Pacific Ocean and the world's deepest ocean trench. Formed as a result of the Pacific Plate being forced beneath the Philippine Plate—the Mariana Islands are the tips of volcanoes created by this subduction—it reaches 35,826 feet (10,920 m) below sea level at Challenger Deep. This site was named for the British survey ship *Challenger II*, the first vessel to survey the trench, in 1951. In 1960, Jacques Piccard and Donald Walsh descended here in the U.S. bathyscaph *Trieste* to a depth of 35,797 feet (10,911 m), a record that remains unsurpassed.

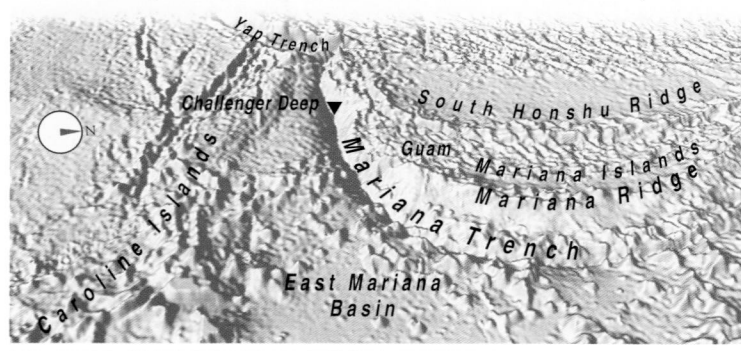

In May 2000, Kavachi, an undersea volcano in the Solomon Islands, erupted, giving birth to a new island.

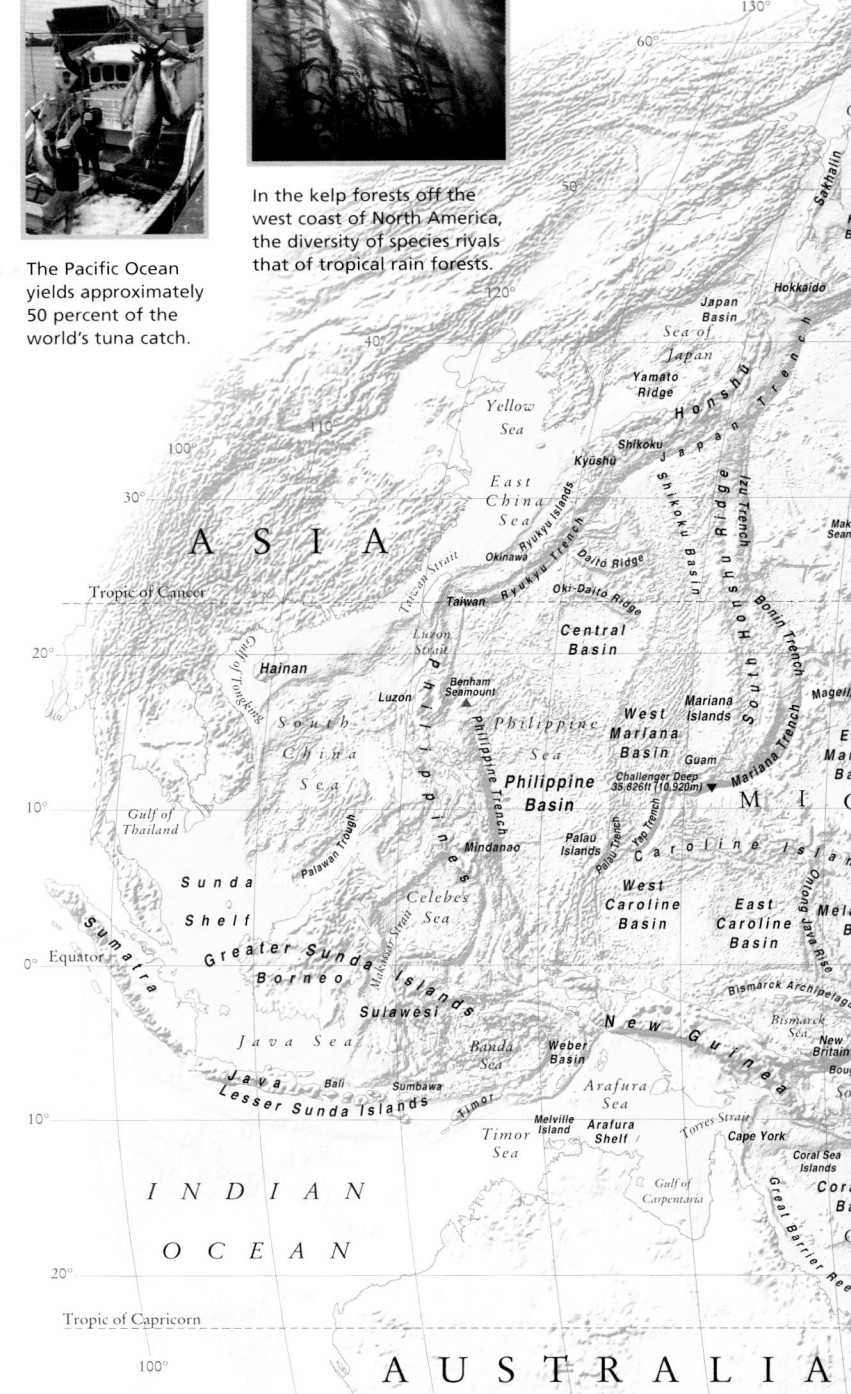

The humpback whales residing in Alaska in summer migrate to lower latitudes in winter.

The Pacific's coral reefs have six times as many fish species as those of the Caribbean Sea.

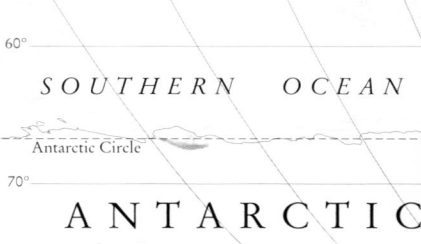

SCALE 1:50,000,000
Robinson Projection

0 — 1500 miles
0 — 1500 kilometers

Longitude east of Greenwich

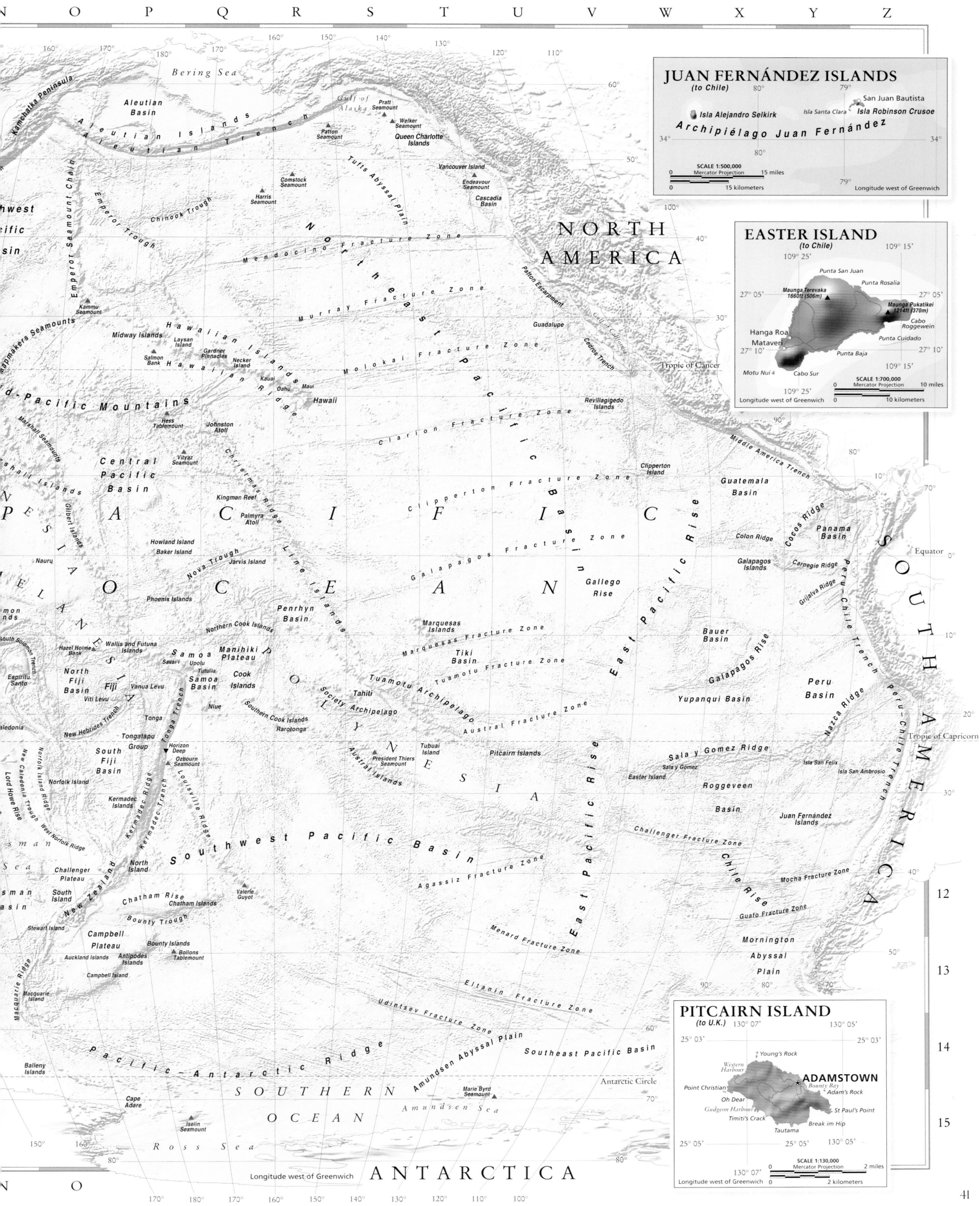

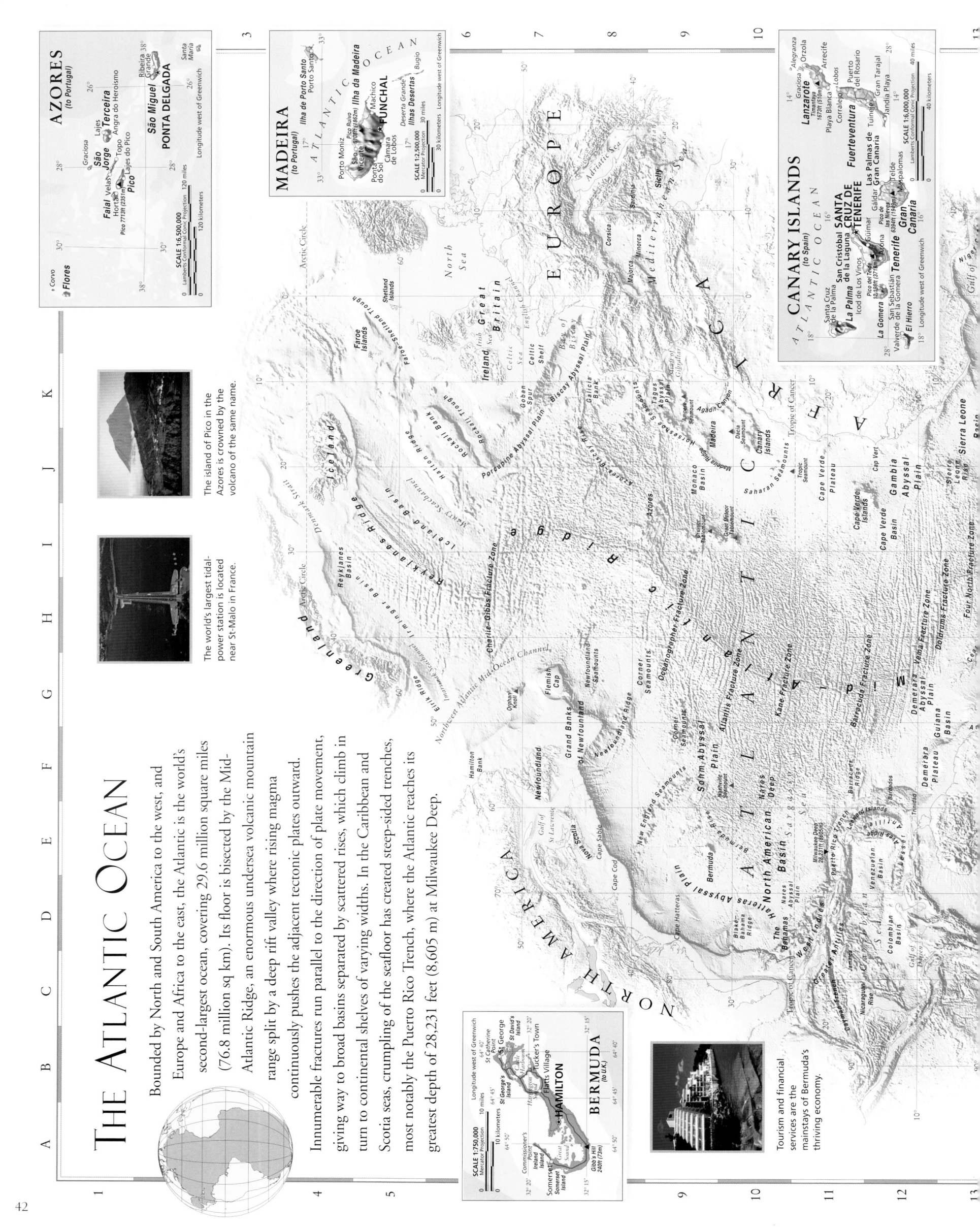

AZORES
(to Portugal)

Corvo
Flores
Graciosa
São Jorge
Terceira
Lajes
Velas
Angra do Heroísmo
Topo
Faial
Horta
Lajes do Pico
Pico
Pico 7713ft (2351m)
São Miguel
PONTA DELGADA
Ribeira Grande
Santa Maria

SCALE 1:6,500,000
Lamberts Conformal Conic Projection
0 120 kilometers
0 120 miles
Longitude west of Greenwich

MADEIRA
(to Portugal)

Porto Moniz
São Vicente
Pico Ruivo 6107ft (1862m)
Ilha da Madeira
Machico
FUNCHAL
Câmara de Lobos
Ponta do Sol
Ilha de Porto Santo
Porto Santo
Deserta Grande
Ilhas Desertas
Bugio
ATLANTIC OCEAN

SCALE 1:2,500,000
Mercator Projection
0 30 kilometers
0 30 miles
Longitude west of Greenwich

CANARY ISLANDS
(to Spain)

ATLANTIC OCEAN
Graciosa
Alegranza
Orzola
Lanzarote
Timanfaya 1673ft (510m)
Arrecife
Playa Blanca
Corralejo
Lobos
Puerto del Rosario
Fuerteventura
Gran Tarajal
Jandía Playa
Santa Cruz de la Palma
La Palma
Icod de los Vinos
Pico del Teide 12,198ft (3718m)
San Cristóbal de la Laguna
SANTA CRUZ DE TENERIFE
Las Palmas de Gran Canaria
Guímar
Galdar
Las Nieves
Telde
Teror
Pico de las Nieves 6394ft (1949m)
Gran Canaria
Mospalomas
Tenerife
San Sebastián de la Gomera
Valverde de la Gomera
La Gomera
El Hierro

SCALE 1:5,000,000
Lamberts Conformal Conic Projection
0 40 kilometers
0 40 miles
Longitude west of Greenwich

THE ATLANTIC OCEAN

Bounded by North and South America to the west, and Europe and Africa to the east, the Atlantic is the world's second-largest ocean, covering 29.6 million square miles (76.8 million sq km). Its floor is bisected by the Mid-Atlantic Ridge, an enormous undersea volcanic mountain range split by a deep rift valley where rising magma continuously pushes the adjacent tectonic plates outward.

Innumerable fractures run parallel to the direction of plate movement, giving way to broad basins separated by scattered rises, which climb in turn to continental shelves of varying widths. In the Caribbean and Scotia seas, crumpling of the seafloor has created steep-sided trenches, most notably the Puerto Rico Trench, where the Atlantic reaches its greatest depth of 28,231 feet (8,605 m) at Milwaukee Deep.

The island of Pico in the Azores is crowned by the volcano of the same name.

The world's largest tidal-power station is located near St-Malo in France.

Tourism and financial services are the mainstays of Bermuda's thriving economy.

BERMUDA
(to U.K.)

Commissioner's Point
Ireland Island
Somerset Island
Great Sound
Flatts Village
Tucker's Town
St Catherine Point
St George's Island
St George
St David's Island
HAMILTON
Gibb's Hill 240ft (73m)
Longitude west of Greenwich

SCALE 1:750,000
Mercator Projection
0 10 kilometers
0 10 miles

Map labels (main map)

Arctic Circle
Denmark Strait
Greenland
Iceland
Reykjanes Basin
Reykjanes Ridge
Iceland Basin
Kolbeinsey Ridge
Jan Mayen Fracture Zone
Mohns Ridge
Norwegian Basin
Faroe-Shetland Trough
Shetland Islands
Faroe Islands
North Sea
Great Britain
Ireland
Irish Sea
Celtic Shelf
English Channel
Bay of Biscay
EUROPE
Adriatic Sea
Corsica
Sardinia
Sicily
Mediterranean Sea
Majorca
Minorca
Tyrrhenian Sea
Gibraltar
Monaco Basin
AFRICA
Gulf of Nigeria
Hatton Ridge
Rockall Bank
Rockall Trough
Porcupine Abyssal Plain
Goban Spur
Biscay Abyssal Plain
Galicia Bank
Tagus Abyssal Plain
Iberian Abyssal Plain
Agadir Canyon
Horseshoe Seamounts
Azores-Biscay Rise
Josephine Seamount
Ampère Seamount
Madeira
Madeira Ridge
Dacia Seamount
Canary Islands
Saharan Seamounts
Tropic of Cancer
Tropic Seamount
Cape Verde Plateau
Cape Verde
Cape Verde Islands
Cape Verde Basin
Gambia Abyssal Plain
Sierra Leone Rise
Sierra Leone Basin
Azores
Great Meteor Tablemount
King's Trough
Charlie-Gibbs Fracture Zone
Maxwell Seamount
Mid-Atlantic Ridge
Oceanographer Fracture Zone
Atlantis Fracture Zone
Kane Fracture Zone
Barracuda Ridge
Barbados
Lesser Antilles
Vema Fracture Zone
Doldrums Fracture Zone
Four North Fracture Zone
Demerara Abyssal Plain
Demerara Plateau
Guiana Basin
Northwest Atlantic Mid-Ocean Channel
Milne Seamounts
Tagus Abyssal Plain
Orphan Knoll
Flemish Cap
Grand Banks of Newfoundland
Newfoundland
Newfoundland Ridge
Newfoundland Seamounts
Corner Seamounts
Milne Seamounts
Hamilton Bank
Labrador Sea
Gulf of St Lawrence
Nova Scotia
Cape Sable
Cape Cod
Cape Hatteras
New England Seamounts
Sohm Abyssal Plain
Nashville Seamount
Nares Abyssal Plain
Nares Deep
North American Basin
Bermuda
Bermuda Rise
NORTH AMERICA
Blake-Bahama Ridge
The Bahamas
Hatteras Abyssal Plain
Sargasso Sea
Puerto Rico Trench
Milwaukee Deep 28,231ft (8605m)
Leeward Islands
Barbuda
Antilles
Windward Islands
Trinidad
West Indies
Florida
Gulf of Mexico
Tropic of Cancer
Cuba
Jamaica
Greater Antilles
Cayman Trench
Nicaragua Rise
Gulf of Darién
Venezuelan Basin
Colombian Basin
Aves Ridge
Caribbean Sea
Grenada Basin
ATLANTIC OCEAN

A B C D E F G H I J K
1 2 3 4 5 6 7 8 9 10 11 12 13

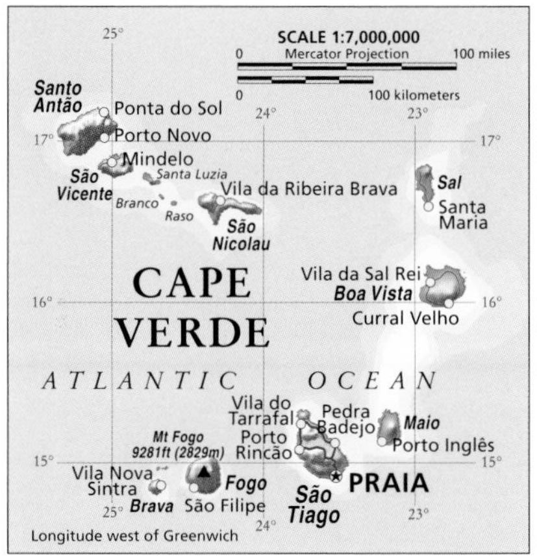

TRISTAN DA CUNHA
(to U.K.)

SETTLEMENT OF EDINBURGH

Queen Mary's Peak
708ft (2160m)

Tristan da Cunha

Rookery Point
Stonyhill Point
Nodl Bay

Inaccessible Island
Middle Island
Nightingale Island

Stoltenhoff Island

North Point
East Point

SCALE 1:1,250,000
Mercator Projection

0   15 kilometers
0   15 miles

Longitude west of Greenwich

ST HELENA
(to U.K.)

JAMESTOWN

Sugar Loaf Point
Barn Long Point
Prosperous Bay
Longwood
Gill Island
George Island
Diana's Peak
2700ft (823m)
Flagstaff Bay
Bennett's Point
Egg Island
South West Point
Manati Bay
Sandy Bay
Speery Island
Castle Rock Point

SCALE 1:750,000
Mercator Projection

0   10 kilometers
0   10 miles

Longitude west of Greenwich

ASCENSION
(to U.K.)

GEORGETOWN

North Point
Porpoise Point
Two Boats Village
The Peak
2816ft (859m)
English Bay
South East Bay
Unicorn Point
Main Base
Clarence Bay
South West Bay
Portland Point
Pillar Bay
South Point

SCALE 1:750,000
Mercator Projection

0   10 kilometers
0   10 miles

Longitude west of Greenwich

CAPE VERDE

PRAIA

Santo Antão
Mindelo
São Vicente
Santa Luzia
Branco
Raso
Sal
Santa Maria
Ponta do Sol
Porto Novo
São Nicolau
Vila da Ribeira Brava
Vila do Sal Rei
Boa Vista
Curral Velho
Porto Inglês
Maio
Pedra Badejo
São Tiago
Vila do Tarrafal
Porto Rincão
Fogo
928m (2829m)
Vila Nova
Sintra
São Filipe
Brava

ATLANTIC OCEAN

SCALE 1:7,000,000
Mercator Projection

0   100 kilometers
0   100 miles

Longitude west of Greenwich

The Atlantic's busiest shipping routes connect Western Europe with the U.S.A.

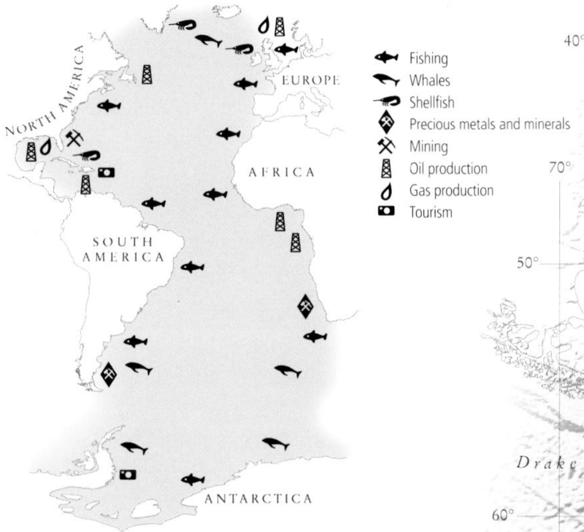

NATURAL RESOURCES

Upwellings of cold, nutrient-rich water on continental shelves give rise to huge plankton blooms that support large fish stocks, notably of cod and haddock in the north, and hake and tuna in the south. But the formerly productive Atlantic fisheries have been overexploited and many species are depleted. As much as one-third of the world's oil and gas may lie under the Atlantic coastal shelves; large deposits are being exploited in the North Sea and Gulf of Mexico, and off Newfoundland and West Africa. Sand and gravels are mined in U.S. and U.K. waters, and placer deposits of gemstones and other minerals are retrieved from many river mouths. Huge tides in Canada and France are harnessed to generate electricity.

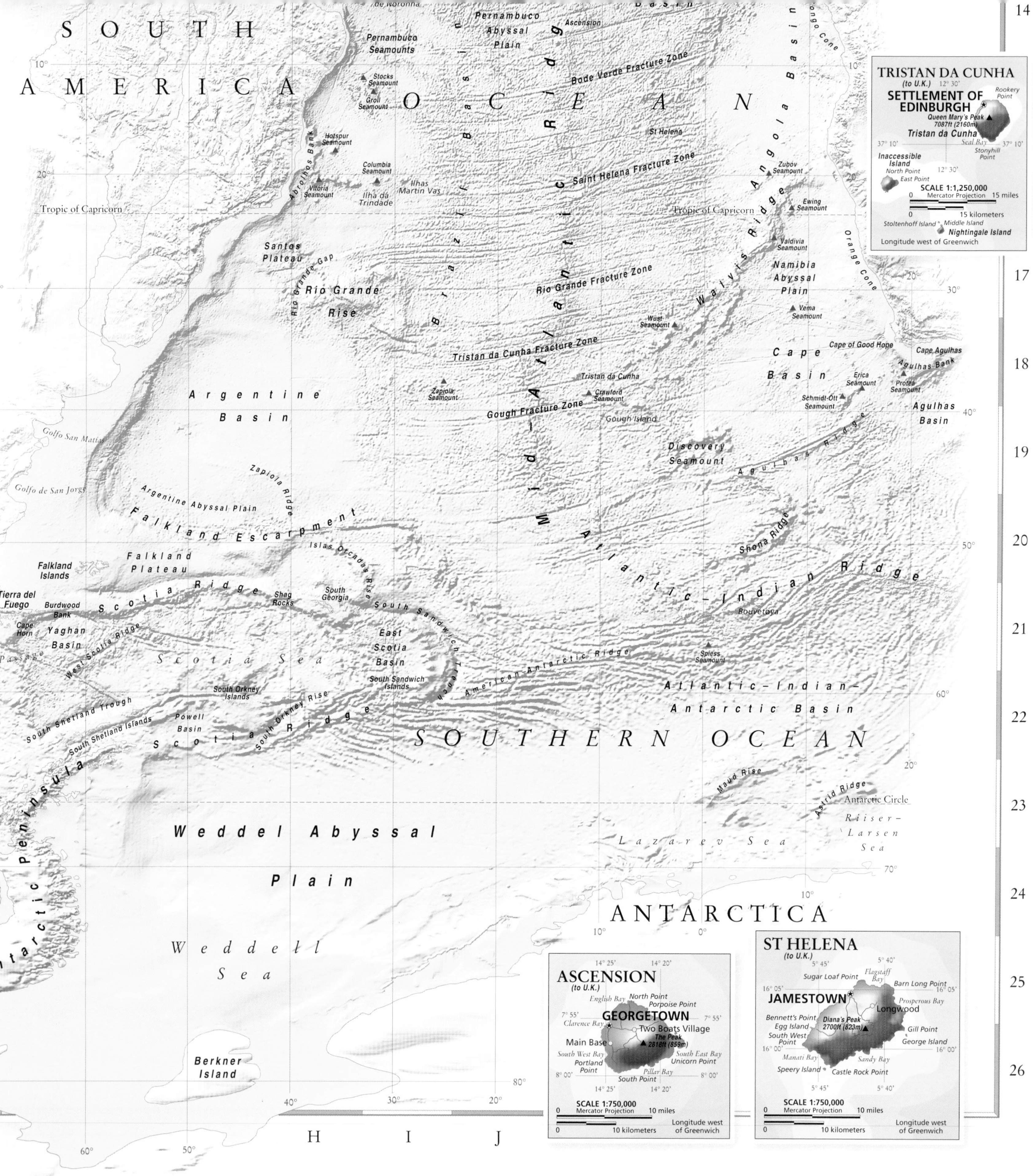

Fishing
Whales
Shellfish
Precious metals and minerals
Mining
Oil production
Gas production
Tourism

EUROPE
AFRICA
NORTH AMERICA
SOUTH AMERICA
ANTARCTICA

SCALE 1:48,000,000
Miller Projection

0   1000 miles
0   1000 kilometers

Longitude west of Greenwich

Main map labels:

SOUTH AMERICA

ATLANTIC OCEAN

SOUTHERN OCEAN

ANTARCTICA

Mid-Atlantic Ridge

Walvis Ridge

Cape Verde Fracture Zone

Bode Verde Fracture Zone

Saint Helena Fracture Zone

Rio Grande Fracture Zone

Tristan da Cunha Fracture Zone

Gough Fracture Zone

Agulhas Basin

Cape Basin

Angola Basin

Namibia Abyssal Plain

Pernambuco Abyssal Plain

Argentine Basin

Argentine Abyssal Plain

Rio Grande Rise

Santos Plateau

Abrolhos Bank

Zapiola Ridge

Atlantic-Indian Basin

Atlantic-Indian Ridge

Antarctic Basin

Weddell Abyssal Plain

Weddell Plain

Weddell Sea

Lazarev Sea

Larsen Sea

Riiser-Larsen Sea

Berkner Island

Falkland Islands

Falkland Plateau

Falkland Escarpment

Burdwood Bank

Scotia Sea

Scotia Ridge

South Georgia

South Sandwich Islands

South Sandwich Trench

South Orkney Islands

South Shetland Islands

East Scotia Basin

Islas Orcadas Rise

American-Antarctic Ridge

Antarctic Peninsula

Alexander Island

Tierra del Fuego

Cape Horn

Drake Passage

Golfo San Matías

Golfo de San Jorge

Tropic of Capricorn

Antarctic Circle

Cape Agulhas

Agulhas Bank

Cape of Good Hope

St Helena

Ascension

Tristan da Cunha

Gough Island

Ilha da Trindade

Ilhas Martin Vaz

Discovery Seamount

Meteor Rise

Herdman Seamount

Stocks Seamount

Groll Seamount

Columbia Seamount

Vitória Seamount

Vema Seamount

West Seamount

Valdivia Seamount

Zubov Seamount

Ewing Seamount

Schmidt-Ott Seamount

Erica Seamount

Protea Seamount

Zapiola Seamount

Crawford Seamount

Spiess Seamount

Bouvetøya

Maud Rise

Astrid Ridge

Gunnerus Ridge

Kaiser-Wilhelm II Ridge

Powell Basin

Jane Basin

Protector Basin

Shag Rocks

Yaghan Basin

Orange Cone

Congo Cone

THE ARCTIC OCEAN

Covering 5.5 million square miles (14.1 million sq km), the Arctic Ocean is the world's smallest ocean. It is ringed by the continental fringes of North America, Europe, and Asia, as well as associated islands, including the largest island on Earth, Greenland. The ocean reaches depths of over 18,000 feet (5,500 m) and is divided into major basins by extensive undersea ranges, the largest of which, the Lomonosov Ridge, surpasses 10,000 feet (3,000 m) in height. Pack ice covers most of the sea surface year-round, expanding to reach most surrounding landmasses in winter. This shoreline has been inhabited by indigenous groups such as the North American Inuit, Asian Yakut, and European Saami for thousands of years. They have learned to cope with the Arctic's extreme climate, including months of darkness in winter, and exploit its restricted range of biological resources. Europeans first explored the Arctic Ocean in the 16th century, searching for a shortcut between Europe and Asia. More recently, outsiders have been lured here by the discovery of potentially vast undersea mineral reserves.

The polar ice pack is 10 feet (3 m) thick on average, but ridges form that may be up to three times that depth.

Directly beneath the North Pole, the ocean is 13,410 feet (4,087 m) deep.

NATURAL RESOURCES

The Arctic Ocean's pack ice blocks sunlight, inhibiting photosynthetic processes and limiting marine life, but rich fisheries exist in areas of open ocean such as the Barents, Greenland, and Bering seas. Seals and whales were long a valuable resource for native peoples and, from the late 17th century, the basis of lucrative commercial trades operated by Europeans. Whaling is now banned, but sealing still takes place in Newfoundland and the White Sea. Sparse grazing lands fringe the ocean, providing food for wild caribou in North America and about 3 million domesticated reindeer in Scandinavia and Russia. Huge reserves of oil, coal, and gas have been tapped in northern Siberia and Alaska; even larger supplies are thought to lie offshore, but so far remain inaccessible.

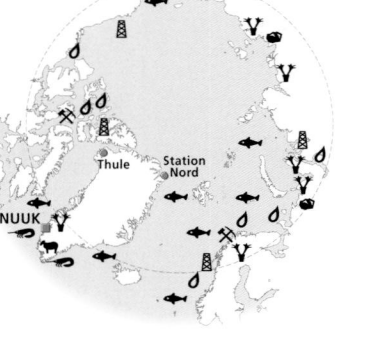
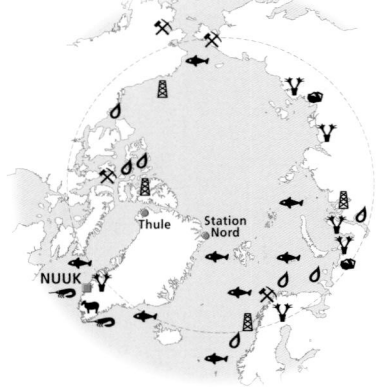

Thule · Station Nord · NUUK

- Sheep
- Fishing
- Shellfish
- Mining
- Oil
- Gas
- Reindeer
- Coal

GREENLAND AND ICELAND

At the boundary between the Arctic and Atlantic oceans, the narrow Denmark Strait divides Greenland from the much smaller island of Iceland. About two-thirds of Greenland lies within the Arctic Circle, and the northern tip of the island lies just 500 miles (800 km) from the North Pole. More than 80 percent of the landmass is blanketed by the world's second-largest ice sheet. Cupped within a basin encircled by coastal peaks, it has an average thickness of about 5,000 feet (1,500 m). Iceland sits astride the Reykjanes Ridge, part of the Mid-Atlantic Ridge. Divergence of tectonic plates along this boundary steadily tears the island apart, giving rise to great faults as well as volcanoes and geysers.

In winter, the Arctic fox grows a white coat to blend in with the snow.

Baffin Island · Davis Strait · NUUK · Greenland · Ammassalik · Ittoqqortoormiit · Denmark Strait · Iceland · Reykjanes Ridge

About 3,000 people live on Svalbard, working mainly in coal extraction.

Yakut hunters in the Siberian Arctic employ modern means to catch traditional prey, including seals and walruses.

NORTH AM... · Mackenzie · Great Slave Lake · King William Island · Hudson Bay · Southampton Island · Coats Island · Mansel Island · Melville Peninsula · Foxe Basin · Foxe Peninsula · Prince Charles Island · Baffin Island · Hudson Strait · Ungava Bay · Cape Chidley · Labrador Sea · Labrador Basin · NUUK · J.A.D. Jenson Nunatak 5472ft (1668m) · Ivittuut · Narsarsuaq · Apostolens Tommel 7510ft (2289m) · Nanortalik

X Y Z

1

2

3

4

5

6

7

8

9

10

11

12

13

14

15

Bering Sea

Gulf of Anadyr

St Lawrence Island

Norton Sound

Seward Peninsula

Kotzebue Sound

Bering Strait

Arctic Circle

Cook Inlet

I C A

Brooks Range

Proliv Longa

Chukchi Sea

Wrangel Island

Beaufort Sea

Northwind Plain

Chukchi Abyssal Plain

Chukchi Plateau

Canada Abyssal Plain

Canadian Basin

Limit of permanent ice cap

Mendeleyev Ridge

East Siberian Sea

Wrangel Sea

Ostrov Novaya Sibir'

Lyakhovskiye Ostrova

New Siberia Islands

Ostrov Kotel'nyy

Limit of permanent ice cap

A S I A

Kolyma

Indigirka

Yana

Lena

Prolix Dmitriya Lapteva

Buorkhaya Guba

Olenek

Laptev Sea

Khatangskiy Zaliv

Ozero Taymyr

Banks Island

oria and

McClure Strait

Prince Patrick Island

Melville Island

Viscount Melville Sound

Mackenzie King Island

Lougheed Island

Ellef Ringnes Island

Amund Ringnes Island

Queen Elizabeth Islands

Parry Islands

Bathurst Island

Axel Heiberg Island

Devon Island

Ellesmere Island

A R C T I C   O C E A N

Alpha Ridge

Makarov Basin

Lomonosov Ridge

North Pole

Pole Plain

Fram Basin

Nansen Cordillera

Nansen Basin

Severnaya Zemlya

Ostrov Bol'shevik

Ostrov Oktyabr'skoy Revolyutsii

Kara Sea

Yenisey

Yeniseyskiy Zaliv

Taz

Cape Columbia

Nares Strait

Kap Morris Jesup

Wandel Sea

Limit of permanent ice cap

Franz Josef Land

Barents Plain

Ostrov Belyy

Obskaya Guba

Novaya Zemlya

Baydaratskaya Guba

Ostrov Vaygach

Proliv Karskiye Vorota

Ob'

Baffin Basin

Ummannaq · Thule

Knud Rasmussen Land

Peary Land

Independence Fjord

Station Nord

aff in

Bay

Nuussuaq

Tasiusaq

Sigguup Nunaa

Kangersuatsiaq

Nuugaatsiaq

uussuaq

GREENLAND
(to Denmark)

Kong Frederik VIII Land

Ymer Nunatak 3596ft (1096m)

Kong Frederik IX Land

ng Ingrid

Kong Christian X Land

Petermann Bjerg 9646ft (2940m)

Daneborg

SVALBARD
(to Norway)

Nordaustlandet

Spitsbergen

Longyearbyen

Edgeoya

Bjørnøya (to Norway)

Murmansk Rise

Barents Sea

Ostrov Kolguyev

Cheshskaya Guba

angerlussaq

Kong Christian IX Land

Mont Forel 11,024ft (3360m)

Guenbjorn Fjeld 12,139ft (3700m)

Ittoqqortoormiit

Kap Brewster

Greenland Plain

Greenland Sea

Mohns Ridge

Barents Trough

Nordkapp

Fugløya Bank

Kola Peninsula

White Sea

Gulf of Bothnia

Ammassalik

Denmark Strait

Kap Brewster

Jan Mayen (to Norway)

Icelandic Plateau

Norwegian Sea

Arctic Circle

Voring Plateau

E U R O P E

ykjanes

Basin

I C E L A N D

Iceland Basin

Reykjanes Ridge

Faroe-Iceland Ridge

Faroe Islands (to Denmark)

Norwegian Basin

X Y Z

45

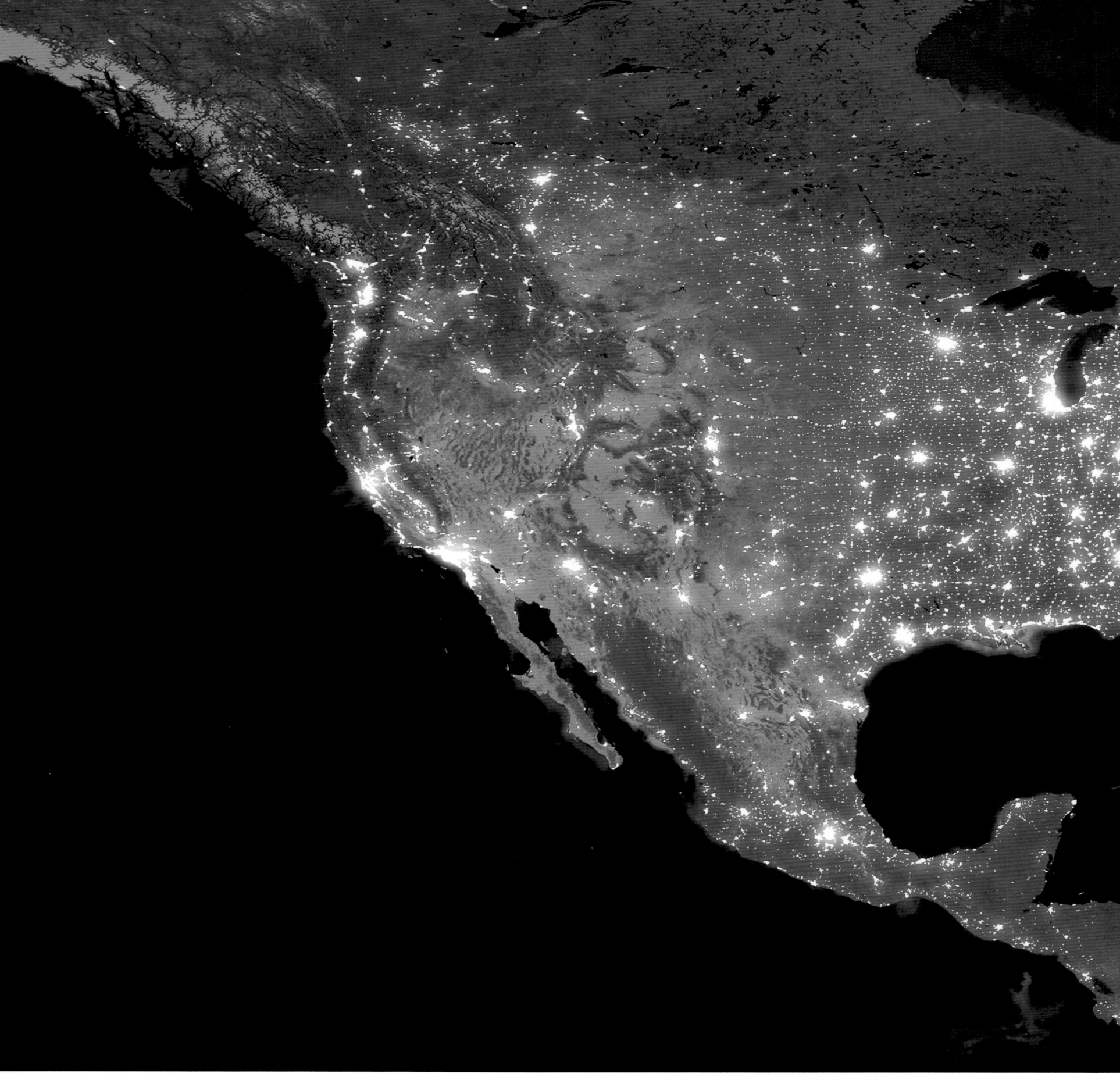

This image from space reveals the concentration of people and infrastructure in the eastern part of the North American continent. The interstate highways create a lattice pattern across the United States, connecting the bright areas of the city centers.

NORTH AMERICA

ABOVE NORTH AMERICA

Satellite photography reveals North America's extraordinary diversity of landforms, from the huge glaciated arc around Hudson Bay to the vast lowlands of the Great Plains in the center of the continent and the high spine of mountain ranges that run down the west coast. Often national borders can also be detected. This is due to differing land use practices between the nations that share the continent. In the north, the rolling wheatfields of Montana, in the United States, give way abruptly to Canadian rangeland. In the south, the border between the U.S. and Mexico is one of the few places on the planet where a highly developed nation adjoins a developing one. The contrast is graphically illustrated in false-color images, which display vegetation in shades of red. The view from space is now a vital tool in agriculture, providing information on the extent, health, and progress of crops.

Mexico-U.S. border
Above right: Highlighted by this false-color image, the boundary between the U.S. and Mexico becomes startlingly apparent. The gridded and irrigated agricultural fields of California's Imperial Valley, north of the border, contrast vividly with Mexico's less developed lands. The border town of Mexicali-Calexico is in the center.

Coffee plantations, Hawaii, U.S.A.
Right: This composite image of Hawaiian coffee plantations was created from more than 300 images collected over four hours by an uninhabited aerial vechicle (UAV). Differences in the color of the coffee fields indicate varying levels of ripeness. This information was used in planning which fields to harvest first.

Grand Canyon, Arizona, U.S.A
Right: Snow lies on the north and south rims of the Grand Canyon, Arizona, starkly outlining the mighty swathe scoured out by the Colorado River. A lack of vegetation further accentuates the impact of this dramatic landform. The canyon's south rim, on the left of this image, is a vertical mile (1.6 km) above the snow-free floor.

Malaspina Glacier, Alaska, U.S.A
Far right: The Malaspina Glacier fans out in a broad tongue between Icy Bay and Yakutat Bay, Alaska. The red ridged area is a terminal moraine of rocks, deposited by the glacier and now protecting it from contact with the open ocean, shown as dark blue. The glacier has thinned since this image was acquired in August 2000.

LAND AND ENVIRONMENT

Stretching from the Arctic Circle almost to the Equator, North America covers 9.5 million square miles (24.6 million sq km) and is the third-largest continent. It is bounded by ocean on all sides and linked to South America only by the slender Isthmus of Panama. As well as the mainland, it includes Greenland, the islands of the Caribbean (the West Indies), and the Hawaiian Islands, which lie 2,500 miles (4,000 km) away, in the middle of the Pacific Ocean. Mountains dominate the west and south of the mainland, coastal ranges running from Alaska to Panama and the Rocky Mountains arcing through Canada and the United States. East of the Rockies lie the plateau of the Great Plains and the lowlands of the Canadian Shield and U.S. Midwest. The lowlands extend to the Gulf of Mexico in the south; in the east and north, they are bounded by ancient mountains, including the Appalachian Mountains, the Laurentian Mountains, and the uplands of Labrador.

NATURAL HAZARDS

Tornadoes

Tornadoes occur in many parts of the world but are most strongly associated with and most common in the United States—about 1,000 are recorded there each year. At certain times of the year, cold air from the Arctic meets warm, moist air from the tropics over the central and eastern U.S.A., fueling atmospheric instability and thunderstorms. On occasions, wind patterns cause a storm to rotate, creating a spinning column of air, or tornado. Generating powerful updrafts and fearsome winds of up to 300 mph (480 km/h), a tornado can obliterate almost anything in its path.

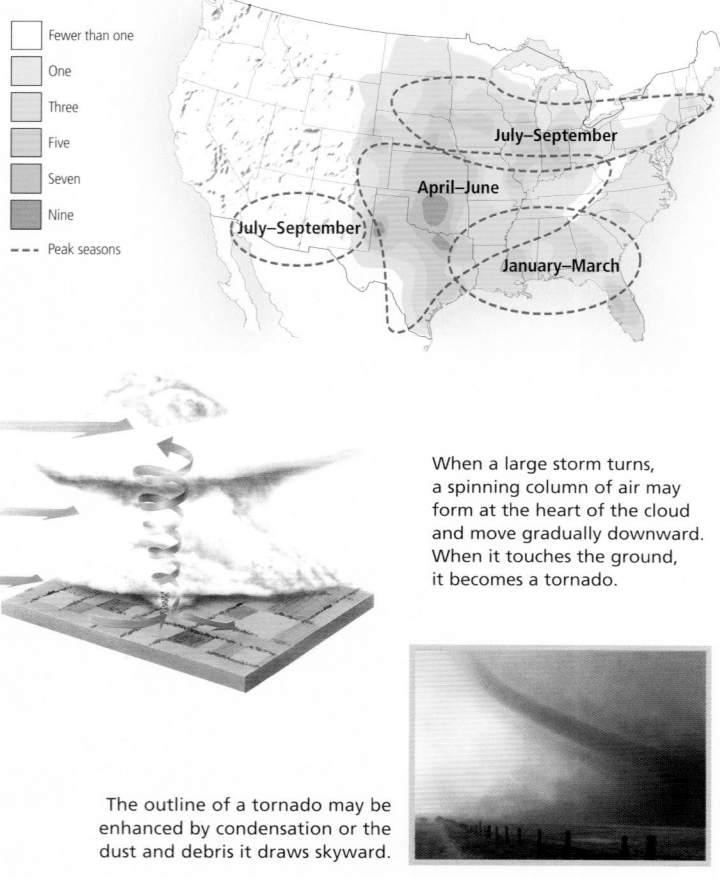

AVERAGE NUMBER OF TORNADOES PER YEAR
PER 10,000 SQUARE MILES (26,000 SQ KM)

- Fewer than one
- One
- Three
- Five
- Seven
- Nine
- --- Peak seasons

July–September
April–June
July–September
January–March

When a large storm turns, a spinning column of air may form at the heart of the cloud and move gradually downward. When it touches the ground, it becomes a tornado.

The outline of a tornado may be enhanced by condensation or the dust and debris it draws skyward.

Map labels

ASIA · Chukchi Sea · Bering Strait · Bering Sea · Beaufort Sea · Queen Elizabeth Islands · Axel Heiberg Island · Ellef Ringnes Island · Ellesmere Island · Parry Islands · Melville Island · Bathurst Island · Devon Island · Baffin Bay · Banks Island · Somerset Island · Prince of Wales Island · Boothia Peninsula · Baffin Island · Victoria Island · Melville Peninsula · Foxe Basin

Aleutian Islands · Aleutian Range · Alaska Range · Mt McKinley 20,321ft (6194m) · Brooks Range · Yukon · Mackenzie Mountains · Great Bear Lake · Hudson Bay · PACIFIC OCEAN · Gulf of Alaska · Coast Mountains · Great Slave Lake · Reindeer Lake · Lake Athabasca · Peace · Athabasca · Canadian Shield

Mt Logan 19,551ft · Cascade Range · Columbia · Mt Hood 11,239ft (3426m) · Snake · Great Salt Lake · North Saskatchewan · South Saskatchewan · Lake Winnipeg · Lake Manitoba · Lake Nipigon · Lake Superior · Great Lakes · Lake Michigan · Rocky Mountains · Great Plains · Central Lowlands · Missouri · Mississippi · Arkansas

Sierra Nevada · Mt Whitney 14,495ft (4418m) · Great Basin · Mt Elbert 14,432ft (4399m) · Colorado Plateau · Grand Canyon · Colorado · Mojave Desert · Sonoran Desert · Sierra Madre Occidental · Sierra Madre Oriental · Rio Grande · Gulf-Atlantic Coastal · Mississippi Delta · Gulf of Mexico · Baja California · Gulf of California · Yucatán Peninsula

Volcán Popocatépetl 17,887ft (5452m) · Pico de Orizaba 18,405ft (5610m) · Sierra Madre del Sur

Hawaiian Islands inset

Hawaiian Islands · Kauai · Niihau · Oahu · Molokai · Lanai · Maui · Kahoolawe · Mauna Kea 13,796ft (4205m) · Mauna Loa 13,678ft (4169m) · Hawaii · SCALE 1:12,000,000 · 150 miles · 150 kilometers

Left: The world's second-largest ice sheet covers 80 percent of Greenland, shown at the bottom of this satellite image. Ellesmere Island appears at top left.

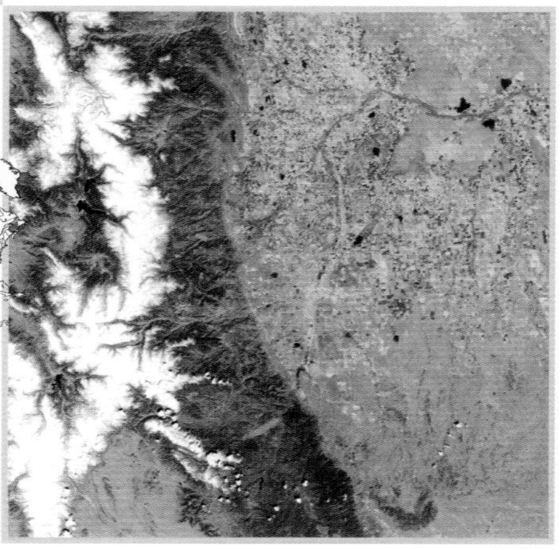

Right: The peaks of the Front Range, the tallest part of the Rockies, rise abruptly from the plains west of Denver, which appears here as a pale gray patch.

CLIMATE ZONES

	Wet tropical			Continental
	Seasonal tropical			Temperate
	Arid			Cold temperate
	Semiarid			Subpolar
	Mediterranean			Highland
	Subtropical			Polar

Climate

North America's remarkably varied climates encompass most extremes of weather. In the far north, low temperatures and polar winds keep sea and land frozen for much of the year. To the south, the cold temperate zone experiences heavy winter snowfalls and short summers. Winter snow is also abundant in the northeastern U.S.A., where summers are hot and humid. The greatest aridity occurs in the southwestern U.S.A. and northwestern Mexico. Humidity increases to the southeast, giving rise to regular rains and seasonal storms, including hurricanes in the Caribbean Sea.

Left: The Baja California peninsula extends for 760 miles (1,220 km) along the Gulf of California.

SCALE 1:35,000,000
Lamberts Conformal Conic Projection
0 — 1000 miles
0 — 1000 kilometers

VEGETATION ZONES

	Tropical forest
	Seasonal tropical forest
	Desert
	Tropical grassland
	Mediterranean forest and scrub
	Midlatitude grassland
	Midlatitude forest
	Boreal forest
	Tundra
	Mountain vegetation
	Ice sheet

Left: Channels mark the sediments deposited by the Mississippi River as it enters the sea.

Natural Vegetation

A permanent cover of ice swathes most of Greenland. South of the arctic tundra—a barren region of bogs, mosses, and scattered conifers—a huge belt of boreal forest blankets most of Canada and reaches southward along the western ranges. Grasslands flank the Rocky Mountains, stretching across the interior to the broadleaved forests of the east, and merging with Mediterranean scrub near the west coast. Deserts extend from the southwestern U.S.A. across much of northern Mexico. In the far south, high rainfall supports dense tropical forests in Central America and the West Indies.

51

PEOPLES AND NATIONS

North America has a population of about 500 million and includes 23 nations and 16 dependencies and territories. These can be divided broadly between the large, affluent, industrialized, predominantly English-speaking nations of Canada and the United States of America (U.S.A.), and the smaller, less affluent, mainly agricultural and Spanish-speaking countries and territories to the south. More than three-quarters of Americans and Canadians are descended from European immigrants, and one-eighth from African slaves; another eighth is of Hispanic origin. Native peoples now account for less than one percent of the population. In the south, Amerindian peoples are significantly outnumbered by mestizos—people of mixed Spanish and Amerindian descent—and also, in the West Indies, by people of African and mixed African–Spanish origin.

The population of Mexico City expanded dramatically in the second half of the 20th century, increasing sixfold between 1950 and 2000. In comparison, New York's population grew by just 25 percent in the same period. Mexico City overtook New York as North America's largest urban center in the mid-1990s and is now the world's third-biggest city.

FLASHPOINTS

Central America and the Caribbean have experienced frequent political instability, often as a result of uprisings or military coups. On several occasions, the United States has intervened, overtly and covertly, to protect its interests in the region.

Belize–Guatemala Border

Since 1821, when it became independent, Guatemala has laid claim to a large area of southern Belize and refused to recognize the latter's western boundary (though it finally recognized its independence in 1991). In recent years, incidents involving alleged illegal settlers and armed forces have led to a number of deaths and increased tension between the two countries.

South Cay

Honduras and Nicaragua have been in dispute over the tiny and uninhabited but potentially oil-rich island of South Cay (Cayo Sur) in the Caribbean Sea since 1999, when Honduras asserted its claim to the island by ratifying the 1986 Caribbean Sea Maritime Limits Treaty with Colombia. This has led to increased military activity on both sides of the common land border.

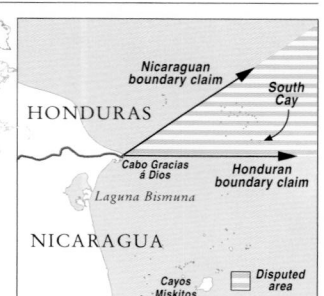

Guantanamo Bay, Cuba

Cuba achieved independence from Spain in 1898, following U.S. military intervention. Despite the 1959 communist revolution that brought Fidel Castro to power, the subsequent imposition by the U.S.A. of an embargo on trade with Cuba, and strong Cuban opposition to its presence, an American naval base still operates at Guantanamo Bay.

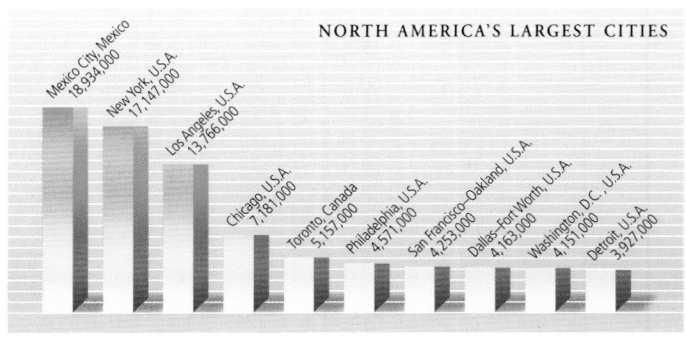

NORTH AMERICA'S LARGEST CITIES

Urbanization

Most of North America's largest urban areas are located in the highly industrialized United States and Canada, where four-fifths of inhabitants live in towns and cities. Even in the traditionally agricultural regions of Mexico, Central America, and the West Indies, urbanization has increased dramatically, rising to approximately 65 percent. Many cities in these regions have struggled to cope with the enormous influx of new residents, resulting in widespread social deprivation, most prominent in the form of slums and shanty towns on city fringes.

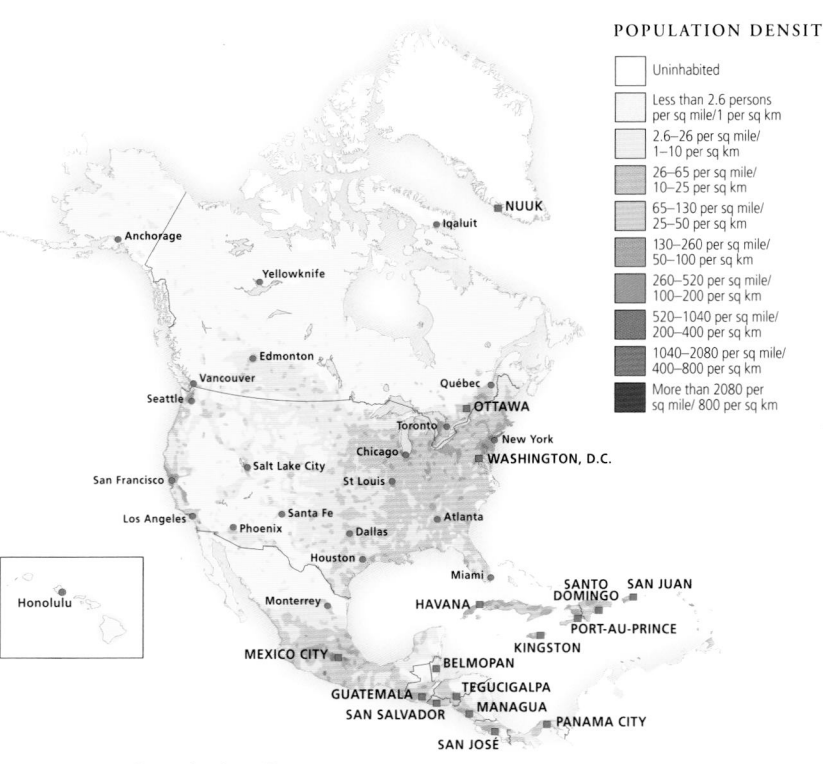

POPULATION DENSITY

- Uninhabited
- Less than 2.6 persons per sq mile/1 per sq km
- 2.6–26 per sq mile/ 1–10 per sq km
- 26–65 per sq mile/ 10–25 per sq km
- 65–130 per sq mile/ 25–50 per sq km
- 130–260 per sq mile/ 50–100 per sq km
- 260–520 per sq mile/ 100–200 per sq km
- 520–1040 per sq mile/ 200–400 per sq km
- 1040–2080 per sq mile/ 400–800 per sq km
- More than 2080 per sq mile/ 800 per sq km

Population Patterns

Rugged terrain, a harsh climate, and poor soil make the far north one of the world's most sparsely inhabited regions. Canada occupies two-fifths of the continent but, with 35 million inhabitants, has just 7 percent of its population. The U.S.A. has almost ten times as many people, who are heavily concentrated in the northeast and on the west coast. Both countries have low population growth by world standards. In contrast, growth is high in Mexico, Central America, and the West Indies, where the most densely settled areas are the uplands of the mainland and the Caribbean islands.

North American Trade Organizations

Signed by the U.S.A., Canada, and Mexico, the North American Free Trade Agreement (NAFTA) came into effect in 1994, creating the world's largest free-trade zone. The Central American Free Trade Zone (CAFTZ) includes El Salvador, Guatemala, Honduras, and Nicaragua. Mexico also belongs to the Latin American Integration Association (LAIA).

- North American Free Trade Agreement (NAFTA)
- Latin American Integration Association (LAIA)
- Central American Free Trade Zone (CAFTZ)

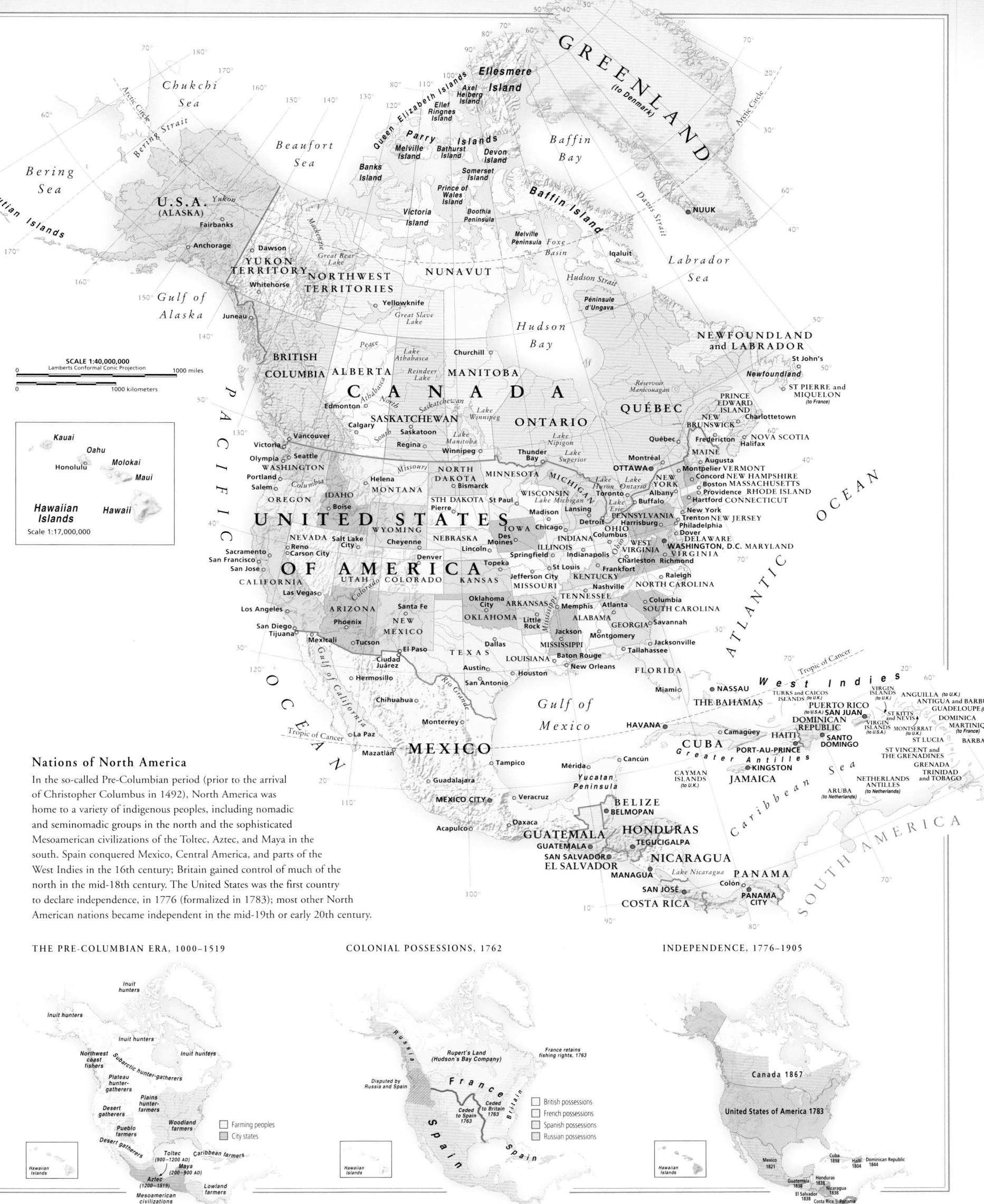

GREENLAND (to Denmark)

Nations of North America

In the so-called Pre-Columbian period (prior to the arrival
of Christopher Columbus in 1492), North America was
home to a variety of indigenous peoples, including nomadic
and seminomadic groups in the north and the sophisticated
Mesoamerican civilizations of the Toltec, Aztec, and Maya in the
south. Spain conquered Mexico, Central America, and parts of the
West Indies in the 16th century; Britain gained control of much of the
north in the mid-18th century. The United States was the first country
to declare independence, in 1776 (formalized in 1783); most other North
American nations became independent in the mid-19th or early 20th century.

SCALE 1:40,000,000
Lamberts Conformal Conic Projection
1000 miles
1000 kilometers

Hawaiian Islands
Scale 1:17,000,000
Kauai
Oahu
Honolulu
Molokai
Maui
Hawaii

THE PRE-COLUMBIAN ERA, 1000–1519

Inuit hunters
Northwest coast fishers
Subarctic hunter-gatherers
Plateau hunter-gatherers
Plains hunter-farmers
Desert gatherers
Pueblo farmers
Desert Gatherers
Woodland farmers
Caribbean farmers
Toltec (900–1200 AD)
Maya (200–900 AD)
Aztec (1200–1519)
Mesoamerican civilizations
Lowland farmers

☐ Farming peoples
◼ City states

Hawaiian Islands

COLONIAL POSSESSIONS, 1762

Russia
France
Spain
Britain
Rupert's Land (Hudson's Bay Company)
France retains fishing rights, 1763
Disputed by Russia and Spain
Ceded to Spain 1763
Ceded to Britain 1763

☐ British possessions
☐ French possessions
☐ Spanish possessions
☐ Russian possessions

Hawaiian Islands

INDEPENDENCE, 1776–1905

Canada 1867
United States of America 1783
Mexico 1821
Cuba 1898
Haiti 1804
Dominican Republic 1844
Guatemala 1838
Honduras 1838
Nicaragua 1838
El Salvador 1838
Costa Rica 1838
Panama 1903

Hawaiian Islands

THE HUMAN IMPACT

The environmental history of North America can be summarized as thousands of years of gradual modification followed by 500 years of astonishingly rapid change. Between the arrival of the first human settlers from Asia at least 15,000 years ago and Columbus's first visit in 1492, most North Americans lived in nomadic and seminomadic hunter-gatherer and, later, hunter-farmer communities. Large city states and empires were confined to Mesoamerica (of the continent's 30 million-plus inhabitants in 1492, 25 million lived south of the Rio Grande). The arrival of Europeans, particularly the mass immigrations of the late 18th and 19th centuries, transformed the landscape. Armed with developed technologies and presented with seemingly limitless resources, settlers razed forests, plowed grasslands, dug mines, and hunted wildlife at a phenomenal rate. The combination of huge tracts of arable land, abundant mineral resources, and political stability brought immense prosperity to the United States and Canada. In contrast, the south's more limited natural resources, rapid population growth, and volatile political situation resulted in slower economic development.

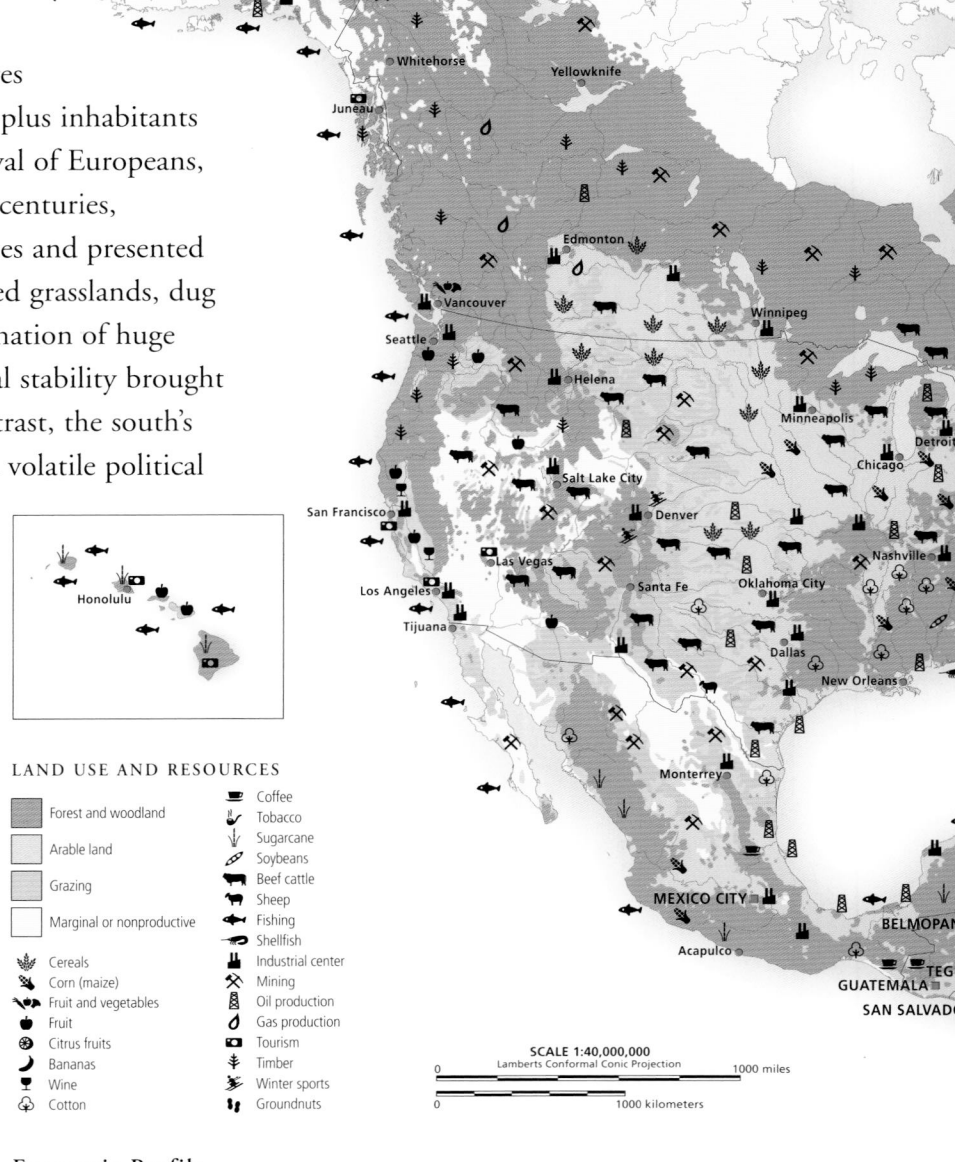

THE CHANGING FACE OF NORTH AMERICA

Prairies

The first Europeans to reach the interior lowlands of the present-day United States in the 17th century were amazed by the great seas of grasses that stretched from horizon to horizon—in places rising head-high—and teemed with millions of bison, antelope, deer, and sheep. But settlers arriving in the 1840s realized that the black soil in which the grasses grew was ideal for cultivation and soon began cutting and plowing. By the end of the 19th century, the soils were depleted and most of the grasses and mammals were gone. To date, losses of prairies on a state-by-state basis vary from 30 to 99 percent. Only a small percentage of tallgrass prairie remains, mainly as tiny remnants in parks and reserves.

ORIGINAL PRAIRIE COVER

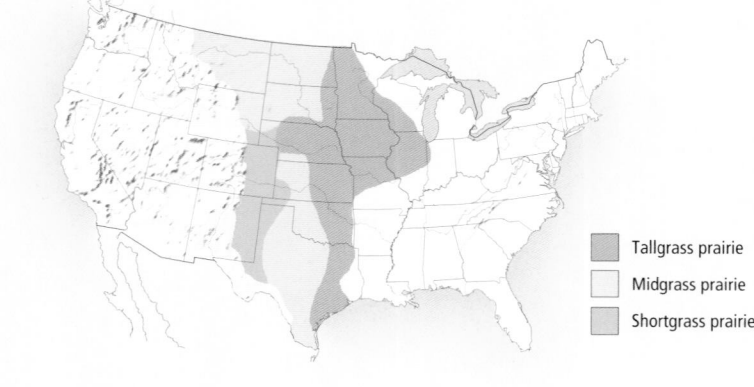

- Tallgrass prairie
- Midgrass prairie
- Shortgrass prairie

CURRENT PRAIRIE COVER

- Tallgrass prairie
- Midgrass prairie
- Shortgrass prairie

LAND USE AND RESOURCES

- Forest and woodland
- Arable land
- Grazing
- Marginal or nonproductive

- Cereals
- Corn (maize)
- Fruit and vegetables
- Fruit
- Citrus fruits
- Bananas
- Wine
- Cotton

- Coffee
- Tobacco
- Sugarcane
- Soybeans
- Beef cattle
- Sheep
- Fishing
- Shellfish
- Industrial center
- Mining
- Oil production
- Gas production
- Tourism
- Timber
- Winter sports
- Groundnuts

SCALE 1:40,000,000
Lamberts Conformal Conic Projection

Economic Profile

Relative to its land area, North America has disproportionately high levels of natural resources. Some of the world's biggest coal fields lie in Alberta, Canada, and in the Appalachian Mountains; enormous oil reserves have been tapped in Texas, Alaska, and the Gulf of Mexico. Fresh water is abundant, though unevenly distributed: many parts of the western U.S.A. and Mexico depend on irrigation, and in Central America runoff and evaporation limit supplies. The north's highly mechanized agricultural sector makes the U.S.A. and Canada leading producers of crops such as wheat, corn, and soybeans. Home of the world's largest companies, the U.S.A. is the world's most productive nation, generating over 30 percent of global GDP, and also its leading importer and exporter.

Land Cover

Though much diminished, forests still cover a large swathe of the continent, chiefly in Canada. Most arable land lies in the north; in the south it is generally restricted to fertile volcanic uplands. Other types of land cover include the large marginal and nonproductive areas in the far north and western mountains, and significant urban sprawl: the U.S.A. alone has more than 4 million miles (6.4 million km) of roadways.

PROPORTIONS OF TOTAL LAND AREA

- 38.6%
- 31.7%
- 17.2%
- 12.5%

- Forest and woodland
- Arable land
- Grazing
- Other land

Right: In the mid-1990s, up to 12,500 people were dying every year in Mexico City as a result of air pollution. Antipollution measures have since reduced output of sulfur dioxide, carbon monoxide, and lead, but levels of other pollutants, including ozone, are still high.

Threats to the Environment

Industrialization, urban sprawl, and heavy dependence on automobiles make North America a major source of pollution, including by far the world's highest per-capita carbon dioxide emissions. Ocean pollution is particularly severe on the North Atlantic seaboard and in the northern Gulf of Mexico. Just one-third of the original forest cover remains; in the north commercial logging companies continue to fell old-growth forest, and in the south limited resources and growing populations pressurize governments to permit the razing of forest for farmland. North Americans are by far the highest per-capita consumers of natural resources and concerns are growing about resource depletion. Water tables are falling and rivers silting up, and some pessimistic forecasts even suggest that the U.S.A.'s known oil reserves could be exhausted by 2011.

Above: Overfarming of the central U.S.A. led to soil degradation in the mid-20th century. Some areas have yet to recover.

Right: In 1989, the tanker *Exxon Valdez* spilled 36,300 tons (37,000 t) of oil in Prince William Sound, Alaska, devastating local ecosystems.

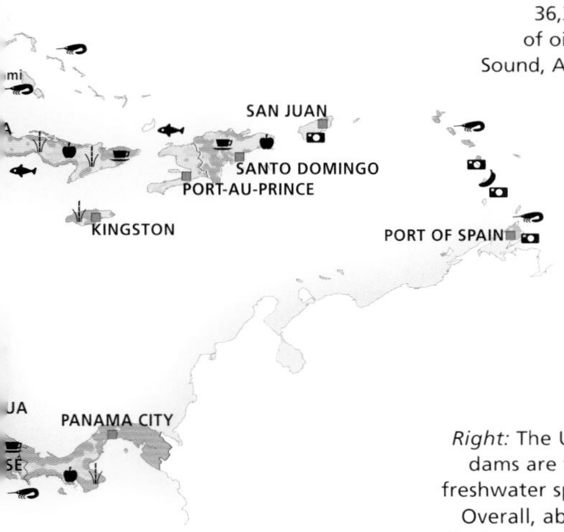

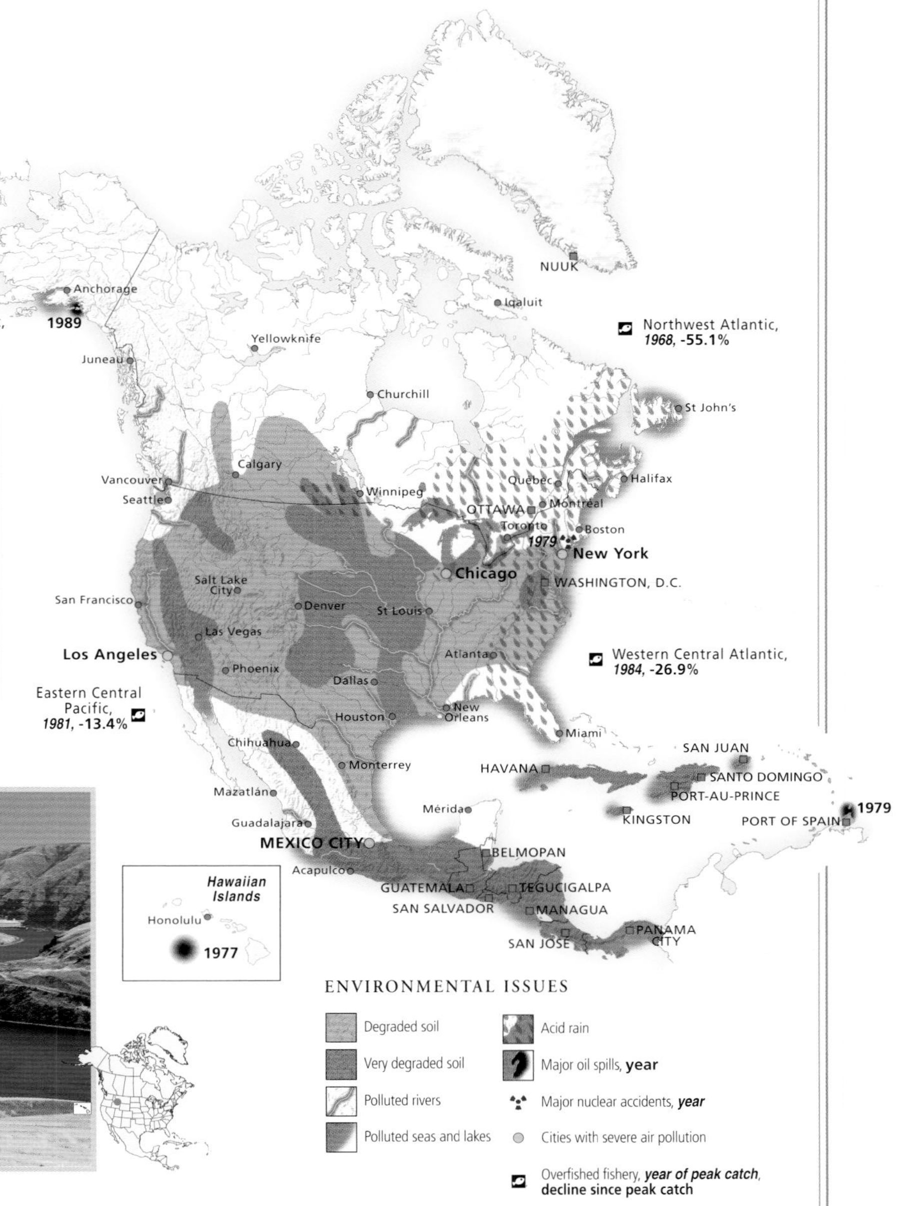

Right: The U.S.A.'s 2.5 million dams are the main cause of freshwater species extinctions. Overall, about 40 percent of freshwater fish, 50 percent of freshwater crayfish, and 70 percent of freshwater mussels have been lost.

Northeast Pacific, *1987, -18.1%*

Northwest Atlantic, *1968, -55.1%*

Western Central Atlantic, *1984, -26.9%*

Eastern Central Pacific, *1981, -13.4%*

Hawaiian Islands
1977

ENVIRONMENTAL ISSUES

- Degraded soil
- Very degraded soil
- Polluted rivers
- Polluted seas and lakes
- Acid rain
- Major oil spills, **year**
- Major nuclear accidents, **year**
- Cities with severe air pollution
- Overfished fishery, **year of peak catch**, decline since peak catch

Protecting the Environment

A long tradition of conservation exists in North America. The continent was the site of the world's first national parks, is home to pioneering conservation organizations, and Canada and the U.S.A. in particular have passed effective environmental legislation, often focusing on species preservation. More than 30 percent of U.S. urban waste is now recycled and many landfills have been turned into parks. Even in less affluent Mexico, Central America, and the West Indies, governments have begun to recognize the value of preserving wilderness. In some areas, for example, well-regulated ecotourism has generated much-needed revenue and helped limit habitat destruction. Unfortunately, the continent's relatively high levels of land protection (10.5 percent) do not seem to guarantee permanent preservation: in 2001, the U.S. government authorized exploration for oil and gas in national wildlife refuges in northern Alaska and elsewhere.

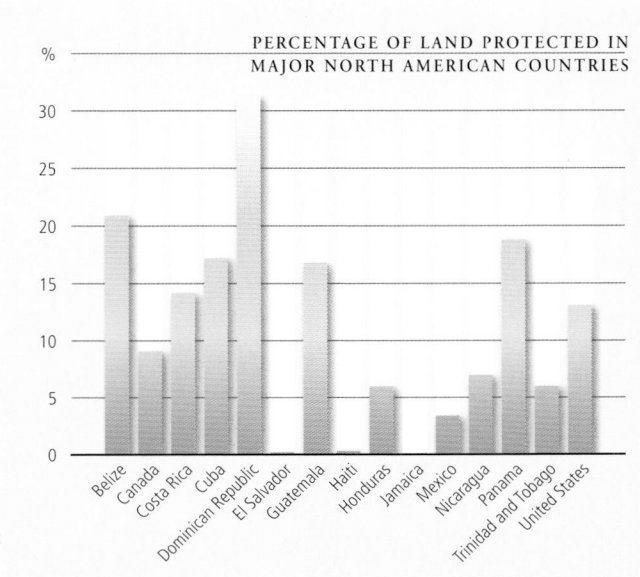

PERCENTAGE OF LAND PROTECTED IN MAJOR NORTH AMERICAN COUNTRIES

(Belize, Canada, Costa Rica, Cuba, Dominican Republic, El Salvador, Guatemala, Haiti, Honduras, Jamaica, Mexico, Nicaragua, Panama, Trinidad and Tobago, United States)

Above: In this satellite image, the area left of the river is Haiti; the greener area on the right is the Dominican Republic—a startling reflection of the nations' contrasting land-protection policies.

UNITED STATES OF AMERICA

A federal republic made up of 50 states, the United States of America (U.S.A.) is the world's third-largest country by size and population. Its contiguous 48 states span the center of North America, from the Pacific Ocean to the Atlantic shoreline. The other two states are Alaska, in the far northwest of the continent, and the island state of Hawaii, in the central Pacific Ocean. On the western side of the lower 48, coastal ranges and the central Rocky Mountains enclose a series of high, arid plateaus and peaks. Plains predominate in the center and east, the much-eroded Appalachian Mountains dividing the vast Mississippi River Basin from the Atlantic Coastal Plain. The U.S.A. declared independence from British rule in 1776 and, with help from France, defeated Britain in the Revolutionary War. It has since flourished to become the world's leading economic and political power.

POPULATION PATTERNS

The U.S.A. has a large population, but it is distributed over a wide area. Density is higher in the eastern half of the country, especially on the northeastern seaboard, but California is the most populous state. Although the western interior is the least densely inhabited area, it has the fastest-growing state populations. The majority of Americans, 69.1 percent, are non-Hispanic whites; Hispanics make up 12.5 percent of the population, blacks 12.3 percent, Asians 3.6 percent, and Native Americans 0.9 percent.

Less than 2.6 persons per sq mile/1 per sq km
2.6–26 per sq mile/ 1–10 per sq km
26–65 per sq mile/ 10–25 per sq km
65–130 per sq mile/ 25–50 per sq km
130–260 per sq mile/ 50–100 per sq km
260–520 per sq mile/ 100–200 per sq km
520–1040 per sq mile/ 200–400 per sq km
1040–2080 per sq mile/ 400–800 per sq km

ECONOMIC PROFILE

The U.S.A. is the most productive nation on Earth. It has the world's largest coal reserves and generates 40 percent of its oil. Intensive farming of rich agricultural lands yields half of the world's corn, one-fifth of its meat, and one-tenth of its wheat. The U.S.A. is also the top producer of soybeans and the biggest source of timber. Forestry, mining, and agriculture are far surpassed, however, in terms of contribution to GDP, by manufacturing—led by transport equipment, industrial machinery, electronic components, and computers—and services, which employ 73.5 percent of workers, primarily in the financial and health sectors.

The Rockies attain their highest elevations in Colorado, which has 53 peaks above 14,000 feet (4,270 m).

The Mississippi River nears the end of its 2,339-mile (3,765-km) journey at New Orleans in Louisiana.

Corn (maize)
Cereals
Fruit
Citrus fruits
Cotton
Tobacco
Soybeans
Groundnuts
Beef cattle
Sheep
Fishing
Shellfish
Industrial center
Mining
Oil production
Tourism
Timber
Winter sports
Potatoes
Wine
Forest and woodland
Arable land
Grazing
Marginal or nonproductive

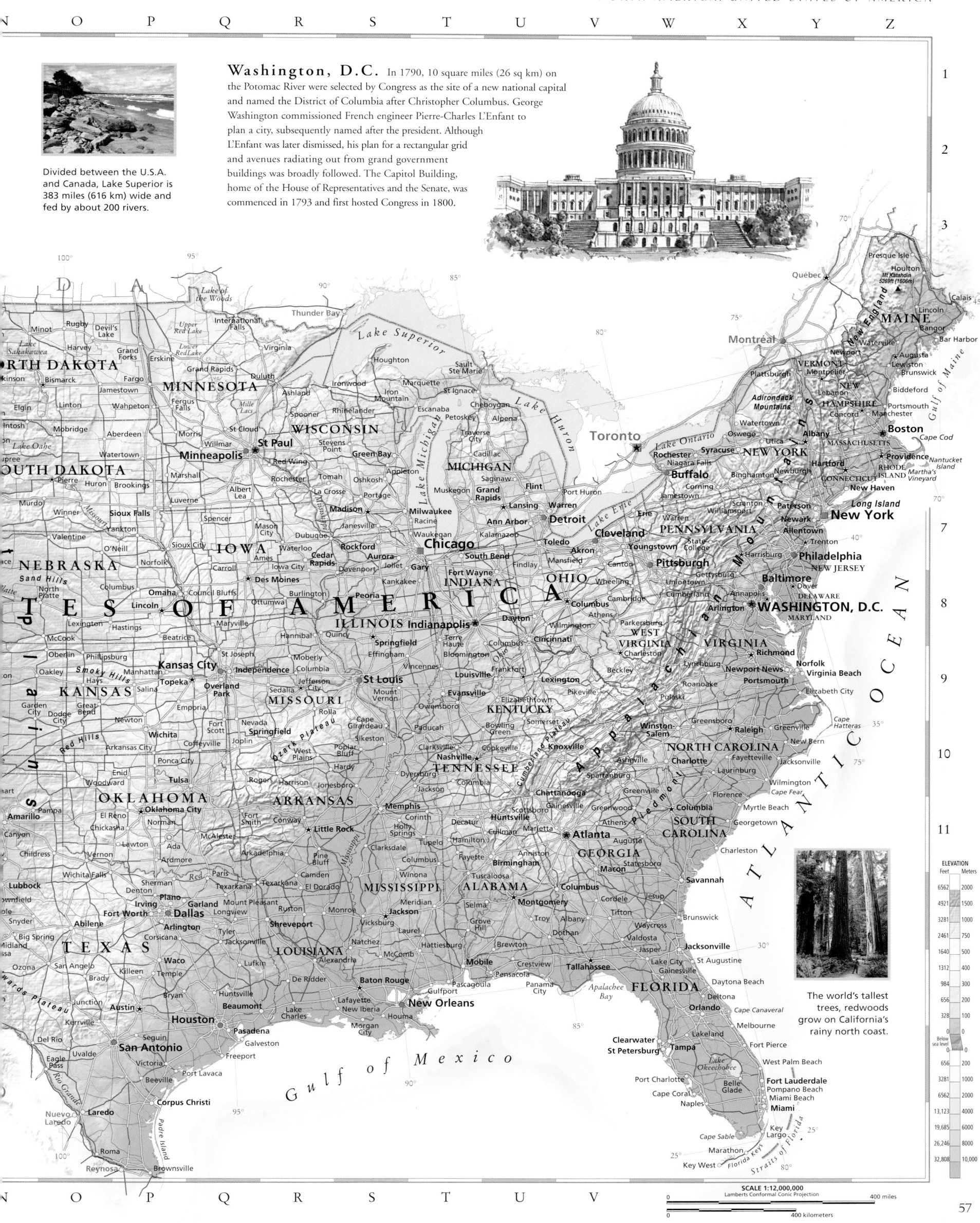

Divided between the U.S.A. and Canada, Lake Superior is 383 miles (616 km) wide and fed by about 200 rivers.

Washington, D.C. In 1790, 10 square miles (26 sq km) on the Potomac River were selected by Congress as the site of a new national capital and named the District of Columbia after Christopher Columbus. George Washington commissioned French engineer Pierre-Charles L'Enfant to plan a city, subsequently named after the president. Although L'Enfant was later dismissed, his plan for a rectangular grid and avenues radiating out from grand government buildings was broadly followed. The Capitol Building, home of the House of Representatives and the Senate, was commenced in 1793 and first hosted Congress in 1800.

The world's tallest trees, redwoods grow on California's rainy north coast.

ELEVATION

Feet	Meters
32,808	10,000
26,246	
19,685	
13,123	
6562	2000
4921	1500
3281	1000
2461	750
1640	500
1312	400
984	300
656	200
328	100
0	0
Below sea level	
656	200
3281	1000
6562	2000
13,123	
19,685	
26,246	
32,808	

SCALE 1:12,000,000
Lamberts Conformal Conic Projection
0   400 miles
0   400 kilometers

NORTHEASTERN U.S.A.

Connecticut, Maine, Massachusetts, New Hampshire, New Jersey, New York, Pennsylvania, Rhode Island, Vermont

The site of some of the continent's earliest European settlements and subsequently the entry point to North America for millions of immigrants, the northeastern seaboard is the most densely populated part of the U.S.A. On the southern half of the coastal plain lies a string of cities that have merged to form one massive, almost continuous urban area. Running from Boston south to Washington, D.C., it is sometimes referred to as the megalopolis or BosWash corridor.

In the north, the shoreline is less developed and more rugged, deep bays and promontories lining southern Maine. To the west, the coastal plain is hemmed in by the ancient, forested peaks of the Appalachian Mountains. Studded with lakes and breached by rivers, including the Hudson, Delaware, and Connecticut, the Appalachians reach west to the shores of the Great Lakes, to the Adirondack Mountains, and north into Canada.

Measuring 3,500 miles (5,630 km) in length, the heavily indented Maine coast is fringed by rocky inlets and 1,200 islands.

The strongest winds ever measured were recorded on top of Mount Washington in New Hampshire's White Mountains.

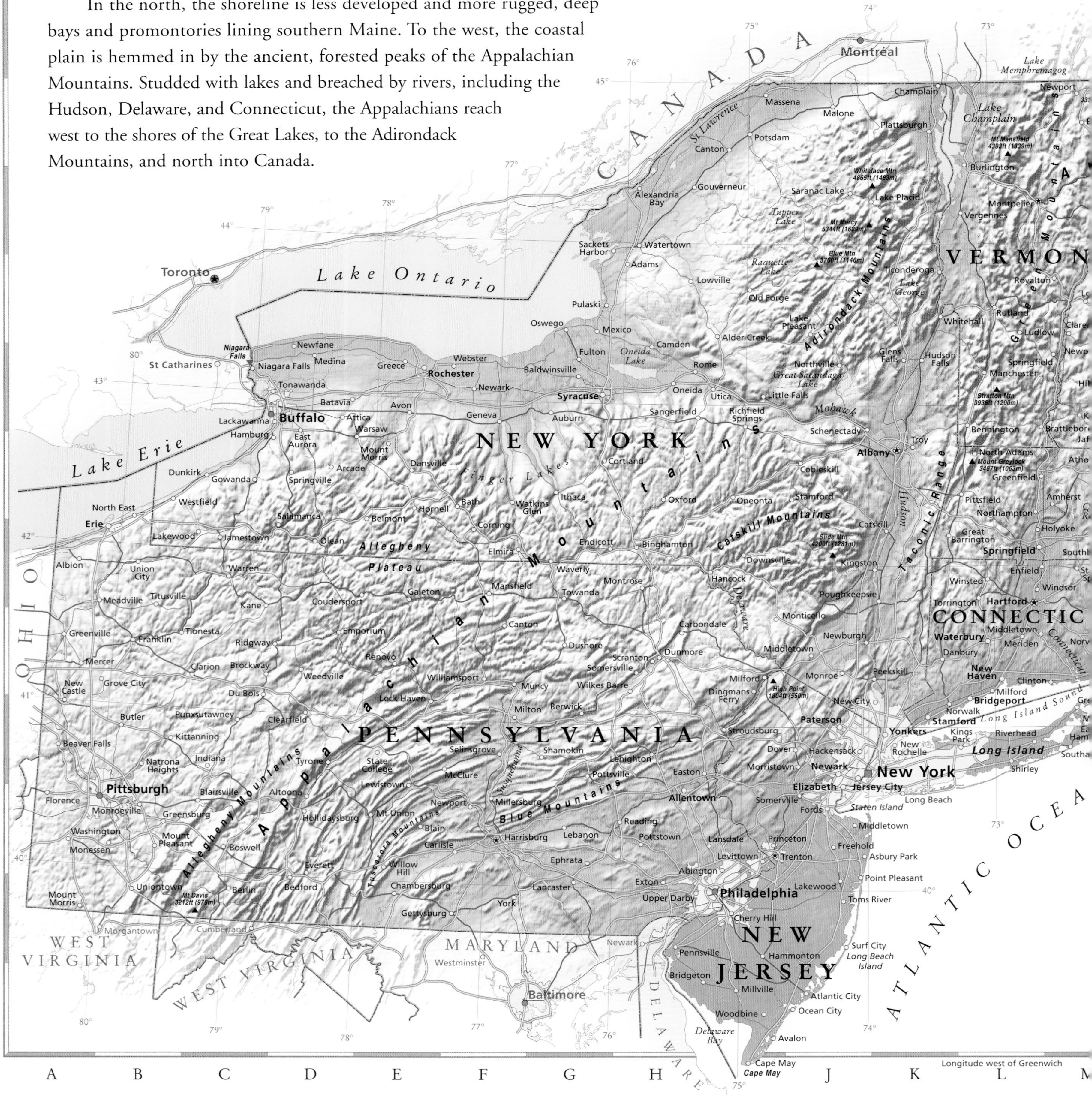

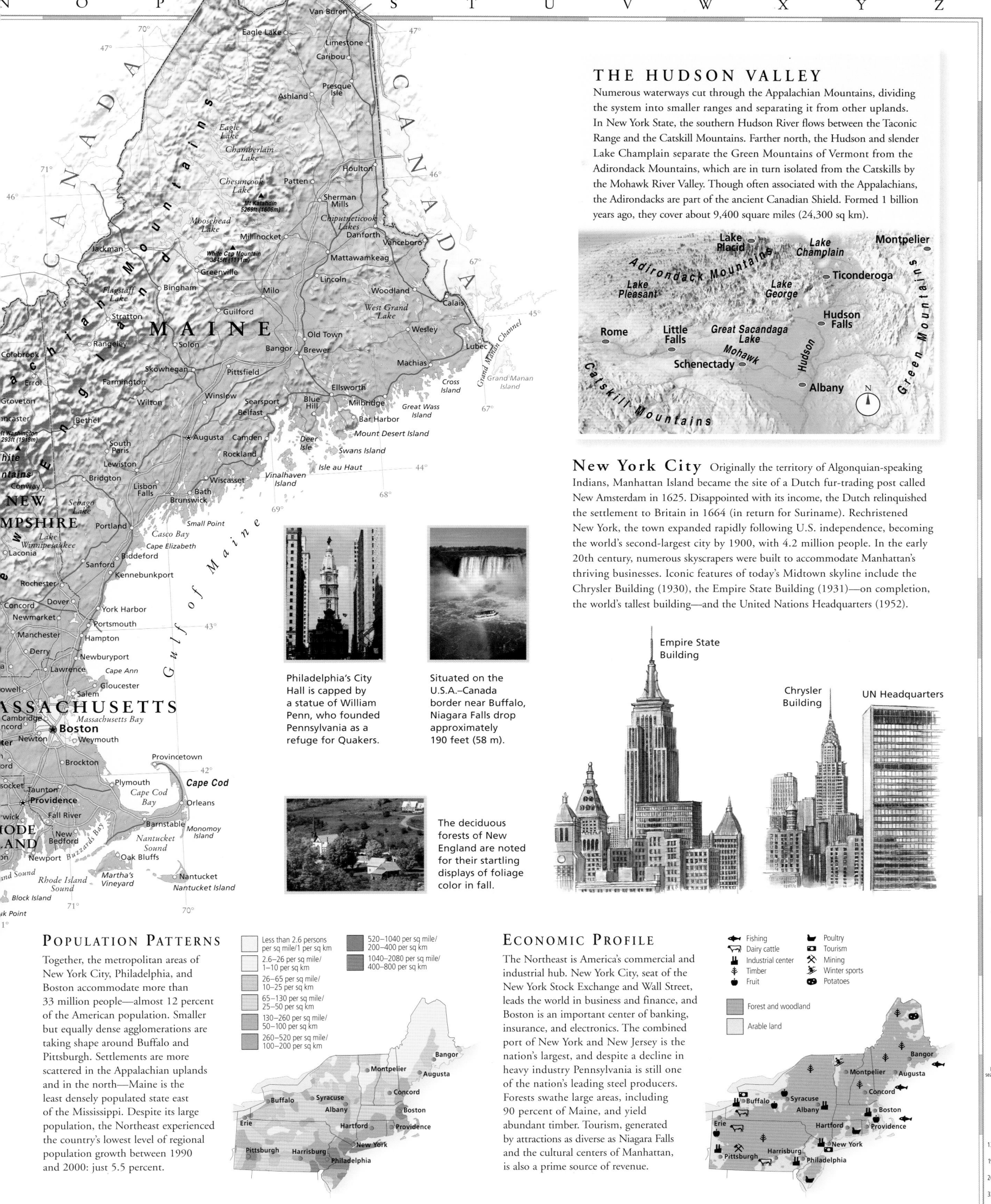

THE HUDSON VALLEY

Numerous waterways cut through the Appalachian Mountains, dividing the system into smaller ranges and separating it from other uplands. In New York State, the southern Hudson River flows between the Taconic Range and the Catskill Mountains. Farther north, the Hudson and slender Lake Champlain separate the Green Mountains of Vermont from the Adirondack Mountains, which are in turn isolated from the Catskills by the Mohawk River Valley. Though often associated with the Appalachians, the Adirondacks are part of the ancient Canadian Shield. Formed 1 billion years ago, they cover about 9,400 square miles (24,300 sq km).

New York City Originally the territory of Algonquian-speaking Indians, Manhattan Island became the site of a Dutch fur-trading post called New Amsterdam in 1625. Disappointed with its income, the Dutch relinquished the settlement to Britain in 1664 (in return for Suriname). Rechristened New York, the town expanded rapidly following U.S. independence, becoming the world's second-largest city by 1900, with 4.2 million people. In the early 20th century, numerous skyscrapers were built to accommodate Manhattan's thriving businesses. Iconic features of today's Midtown skyline include the Chrysler Building (1930), the Empire State Building (1931)—on completion, the world's tallest building—and the United Nations Headquarters (1952).

Philadelphia's City Hall is capped by a statue of William Penn, who founded Pennsylvania as a refuge for Quakers.

Situated on the U.S.A.–Canada border near Buffalo, Niagara Falls drop approximately 190 feet (58 m).

Empire State Building

Chrysler Building

UN Headquarters

The deciduous forests of New England are noted for their startling displays of foliage color in fall.

POPULATION PATTERNS

Together, the metropolitan areas of New York City, Philadelphia, and Boston accommodate more than 33 million people—almost 12 percent of the American population. Smaller but equally dense agglomerations are taking shape around Buffalo and Pittsburgh. Settlements are more scattered in the Appalachian uplands and in the north—Maine is the least densely populated state east of the Mississippi. Despite its large population, the Northeast experienced the country's lowest level of regional population growth between 1990 and 2000: just 5.5 percent.

Less than 2.6 persons per sq mile/1 per sq km
2.6–26 per sq mile/1–10 per sq km
26–65 per sq mile/10–25 per sq km
65–130 per sq mile/25–50 per sq km
130–260 per sq mile/50–100 per sq km
260–520 per sq mile/100–200 per sq km
520–1040 per sq mile/200–400 per sq km
1040–2080 per sq mile/400–800 per sq km

ECONOMIC PROFILE

The Northeast is America's commercial and industrial hub. New York City, seat of the New York Stock Exchange and Wall Street, leads the world in business and finance, and Boston is an important center of banking, insurance, and electronics. The combined port of New York and New Jersey is the nation's largest, and despite a decline in heavy industry Pennsylvania is still one of the nation's leading steel producers. Forests swathe large areas, including 90 percent of Maine, and yield abundant timber. Tourism, generated by attractions as diverse as Niagara Falls and the cultural centers of Manhattan, is also a prime source of revenue.

Fishing
Dairy cattle
Industrial center
Timber
Fruit
Poultry
Tourism
Mining
Winter sports
Potatoes

Forest and woodland
Arable land

ELEVATION	
Feet	Meters
6562	2000
4921	1500
3281	1000
2461	750
1640	500
1312	400
984	300
656	200
328	100
Below sea level	0
0	0
656	200
3281	1000
6562	2000
13,123	4000
19,685	6000
26,246	8000
32,808	10,000

SCALE 1:3,000,000
Lamberts Conformal Conic Projection
0   100 miles
0   100 kilometers

SOUTH ATLANTIC U.S.A.

Delaware, District of Columbia, Kentucky, Maryland, North Carolina, South Carolina, Tennessee, Virginia, West Virginia

The northern perimeter of this region, formed by the Ohio River and the southern border of Pennsylvania—the so-called Mason and Dixon Line—is the traditional divide between North and South: prior to the Civil War it separated slave-owning states from abolitionists. History and terrain have created other regional distinctions. The thickly forested ridges of the Appalachian Mountains form a sparsely populated enclave of mining and timber towns.

To the west lie the pastoral hills of central Tennessee and Kentucky's Bluegrass region, and the heavily cultivated lowlands of the Mississippi and Ohio rivers. In the east, the wooded Appalachian foothills, known as the Piedmont, descend to a broad coastal plain bordered by historic ports and barrier islands.

POPULATION PATTERNS

In the northeast, the population is heavily urbanized and concentrated in the Washington–Baltimore area, home to 7.6 million people. Elsewhere the proportion of rural dwellers is high, rising from 27 percent in Virginia to 51 percent in West Virginia. In Virginia and the Carolinas, people cluster in the Piedmont, but the cities here are relatively small; the largest urban centers outside the northeast are Nashville and Memphis in Tennessee. Population growth between 1990 and 2000 varied markedly, from –5.7 percent in the District of Columbia to 21.4 percent in North Carolina.

Less than 2.6 persons per sq mile/1 per sq km
2.6–26 per sq mile/1–10 per sq km
26–65 per sq mile/10–25 per sq km
65–130 per sq mile/25–50 per sq km
130–260 per sq mile/50–100 per sq km
260–520 per sq mile/100–200 per sq km
520–1040 per sq mile/200–400 per sq km
1040–2080 per sq mile/400–800 per sq km

ECONOMIC PROFILE

Farming has declined in importance, though this is still the country's main source of tobacco and yields sizable crops of soybeans, corn, and vegetables. Kentucky is also renowned for horse-breeding. Manufacturing industries include whiskey in Kentucky and Tennessee; chemicals in Tennessee, Virginia, and Delaware; and textiles and high-tech goods in North Carolina. Service industries predominate in the northeast, with the government being a major employer. Appalachia has some of America's most productive coal fields. Fishing, mainly of shellfish, remains important around Chesapeake Bay.

Corn (maize)
Cotton
Shellfish
Tobacco
Fishing
Industrial center
Timber
Beef cattle
Mining
Fruit
Poultry
Soybeans
Pigs

Forest and woodland
Arable land
Grazing

Longitude west of Greenwich

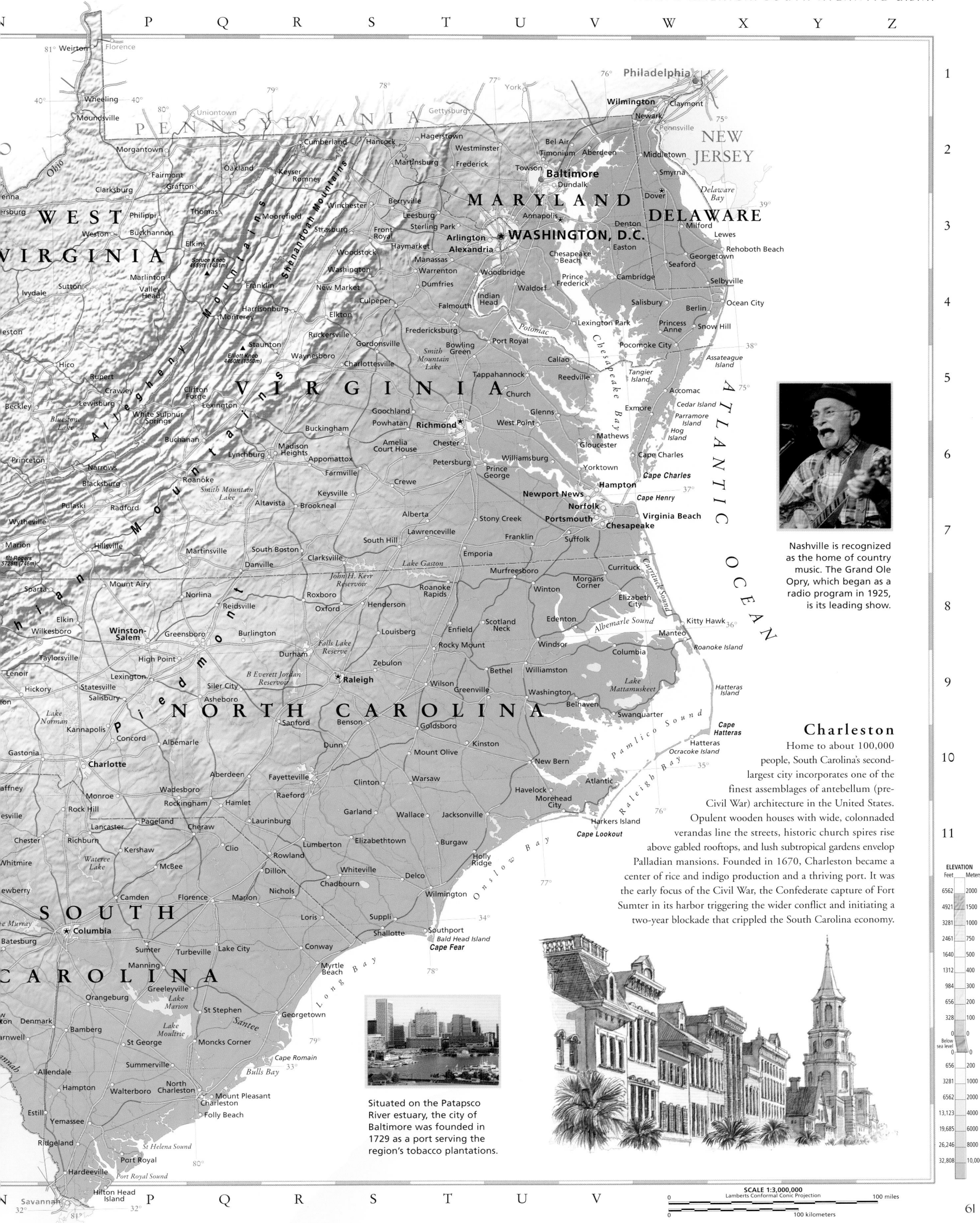

Nashville is recognized as the home of country music. The Grand Ole Opry, which began as a radio program in 1925, is its leading show.

Charleston

Home to about 100,000 people, South Carolina's second-largest city incorporates one of the finest assemblages of antebellum (pre-Civil War) architecture in the United States. Opulent wooden houses with wide, colonnaded verandas line the streets, historic church spires rise above gabled rooftops, and lush subtropical gardens envelop Palladian mansions. Founded in 1670, Charleston became a center of rice and indigo production and a thriving port. It was the early focus of the Civil War, the Confederate capture of Fort Sumter in its harbor triggering the wider conflict and initiating a two-year blockade that crippled the South Carolina economy.

Situated on the Patapsco River estuary, the city of Baltimore was founded in 1729 as a port serving the region's tobacco plantations.

ELEVATION

Feet	Meters
6562	2000
4921	1500
3281	1000
2461	750
1640	500
1312	400
984	300
656	200
328	100
Below sea level	0
0	0
656	200
3281	1000
6562	2000
13,123	4000
19,685	6000
26,246	8000
32,808	10,000

SCALE 1:3,000,000
Lamberts Conformal Conic Projection
100 miles
100 kilometers

SOUTHEASTERN U.S.A.
Alabama, Florida, Georgia, Louisiana, Mississippi

In the southeastern corner of the United States, rolling hills and low plateaus cover much of the interior, rising in northern Alabama and Georgia to the southern edge of the Appalachian Mountains and descending along a broad sweep to the alluvial plain of the Mississippi River, the Gulf and Atlantic coastal plains, and the broad, flat Florida Peninsula. In the 16th century, Spanish explorers became the first Europeans to visit this predominantly swampy coastline, then home to various Indian groups. The Spanish founded the settlement of St Augustine, Florida, in 1565, now the oldest city in the country. In the late 17th century, French traders took control of the Mississippi Basin, establishing a port at New Orleans. Under the Treaty of Paris of 1763, New Orleans and the western Mississippi Valley passed to Spain, while the land to the east of the Mississippi, including Spanish Florida, came under British control. After the Civil War, continuing discrimination against the African-American population made the Southeast the focus of civil-rights protests, which reached a peak in the 1960s with mass demonstrations in Montgomery and Birmingham, Alabama, and the 1963 March on Washington for Jobs and Freedom.

Hurricanes regularly strike the Southeast. In August 1992, Hurricane Andrew caused US$25 billion worth of damage and 23 deaths.

The distinctive architecture of New Orleans reflects the origins of its early inhabitants. Founded by the French in 1718, it was ceded to Spain in 1763.

POPULATION PATTERNS

The Southeast's inhabitants are fairly evenly spread, though coastal wetlands limit settlement in parts of the Gulf Coast (notably the Mississippi Delta) and Florida. Population density and urbanization are lower in the three western states, particularly in Mississippi. In contrast, Georgia and Florida have large urban populations, with settlement focused on cities such as Atlanta (home to half of Georgia's people), Tampa, and Miami. The populations of these two states are growing rapidly, with Florida's projected to reach 20 million by 2010, due in part to its popularity as a retirement destination.

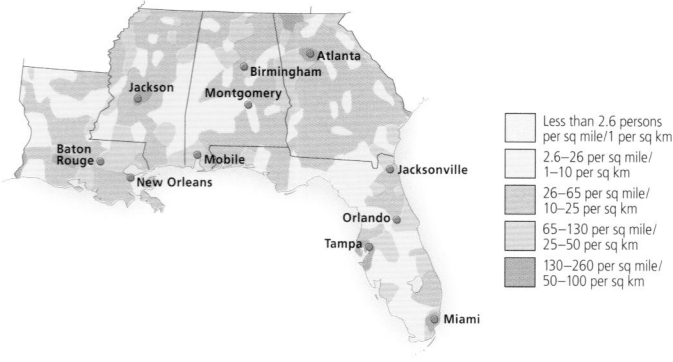

	Less than 2.6 persons per sq mile/1 per sq km
	2.6–26 per sq mile/1–10 per sq km
	26–65 per sq mile/10–25 per sq km
	65–130 per sq mile/25–50 per sq km
	130–260 per sq mile/50–100 per sq km

ECONOMIC PROFILE

Until the early 20th century, the Southeast was dependent on agriculture, especially the cultivation of cotton and tobacco. These crops remain significant, but farmers have diversified into soybeans, corn, peanuts, and, in Florida, citrus fruits. Extensive forests provide abundant timber, and the industrial sector has expanded to include textiles, transportation equipment, electronics, and the aerospace industry. Louisiana is one of the nation's leading producers of oil and gas, Georgia is home to major corporations—Atlanta is the headquarters of Coca-Cola and CNN (Cable News Network)—and Florida has a thriving tourist industry.

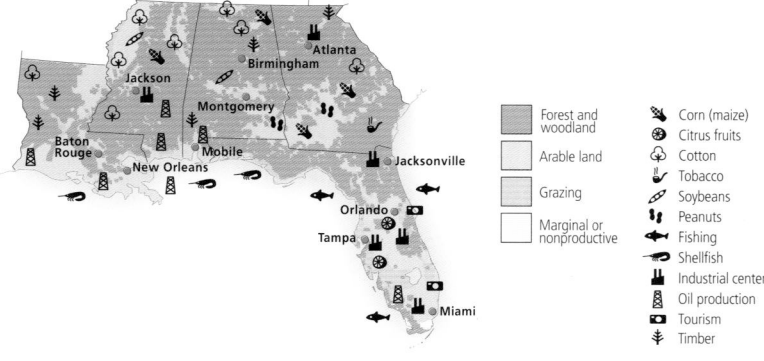

	Forest and woodland
	Arable land
	Grazing
	Marginal or nonproductive

- Corn (maize)
- Citrus fruits
- Cotton
- Tobacco
- Soybeans
- Peanuts
- Fishing
- Shellfish
- Industrial center
- Oil production
- Tourism
- Timber

Longitude west of Greenwich

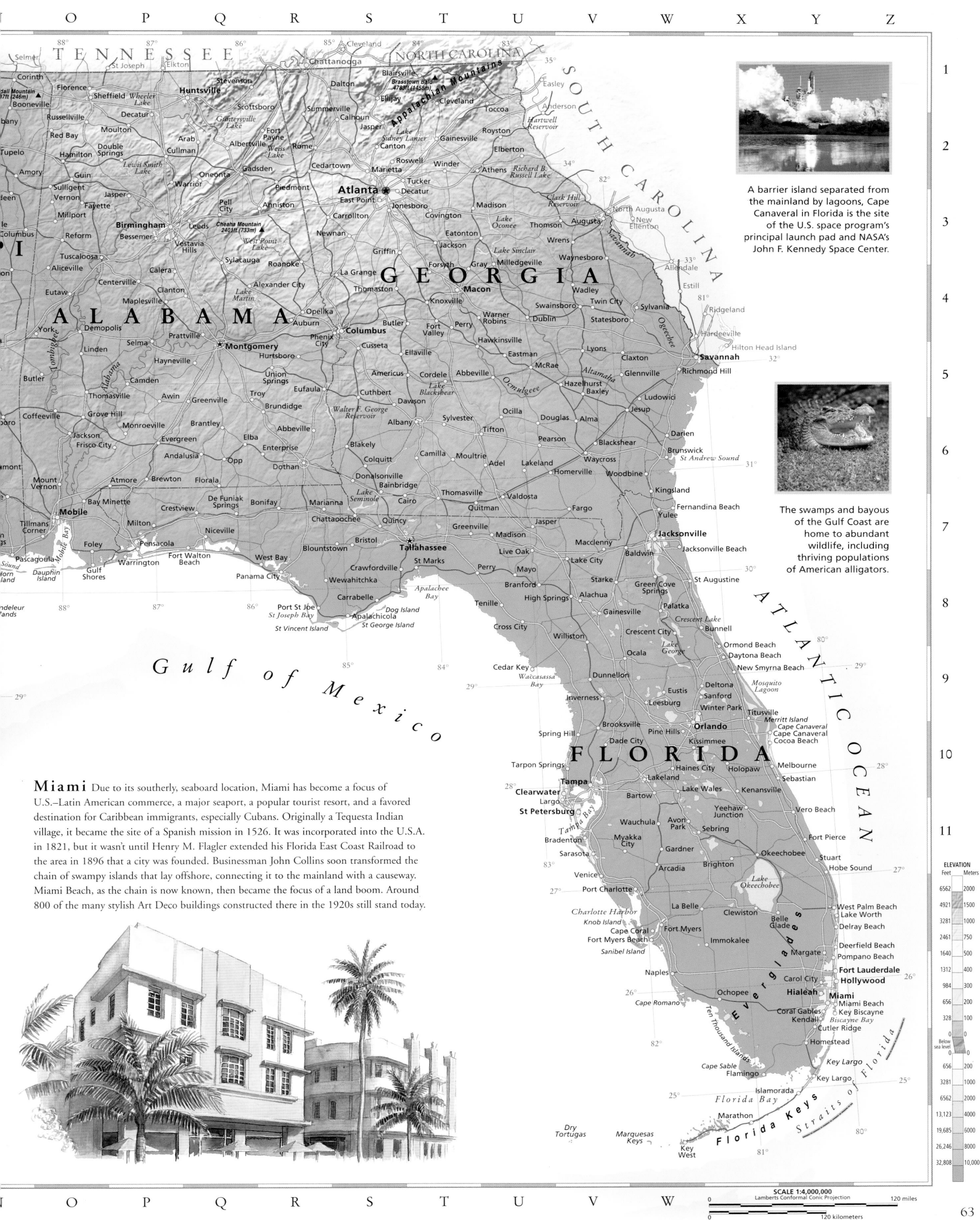

A barrier island separated from the mainland by lagoons, Cape Canaveral in Florida is the site of the U.S. space program's principal launch pad and NASA's John F. Kennedy Space Center.

The swamps and bayous of the Gulf Coast are home to abundant wildlife, including thriving populations of American alligators.

Miami Due to its southerly, seaboard location, Miami has become a focus of U.S.–Latin American commerce, a major seaport, a popular tourist resort, and a favored destination for Caribbean immigrants, especially Cubans. Originally a Tequesta Indian village, it became the site of a Spanish mission in 1526. It was incorporated into the U.S.A. in 1821, but it wasn't until Henry M. Flagler extended his Florida East Coast Railroad to the area in 1896 that a city was founded. Businessman John Collins soon transformed the chain of swampy islands that lay offshore, connecting it to the mainland with a causeway. Miami Beach, as the chain is now known, then became the focus of a land boom. Around 800 of the many stylish Art Deco buildings constructed there in the 1920s still stand today.

ELEVATION	
Feet	Meters
32,808	10,000
26,246	8000
19,685	6000
13,123	4000
6562	2000
3281	1000
656	200
0	0
Below sea level	
0	0
328	100
656	200
984	300
1312	400
1640	500
2461	750
3281	1000
4921	1500
6562	2000

SCALE 1:4,000,000
Lamberts Conformal Conic Projection

0 — 120 miles
0 — 120 kilometers

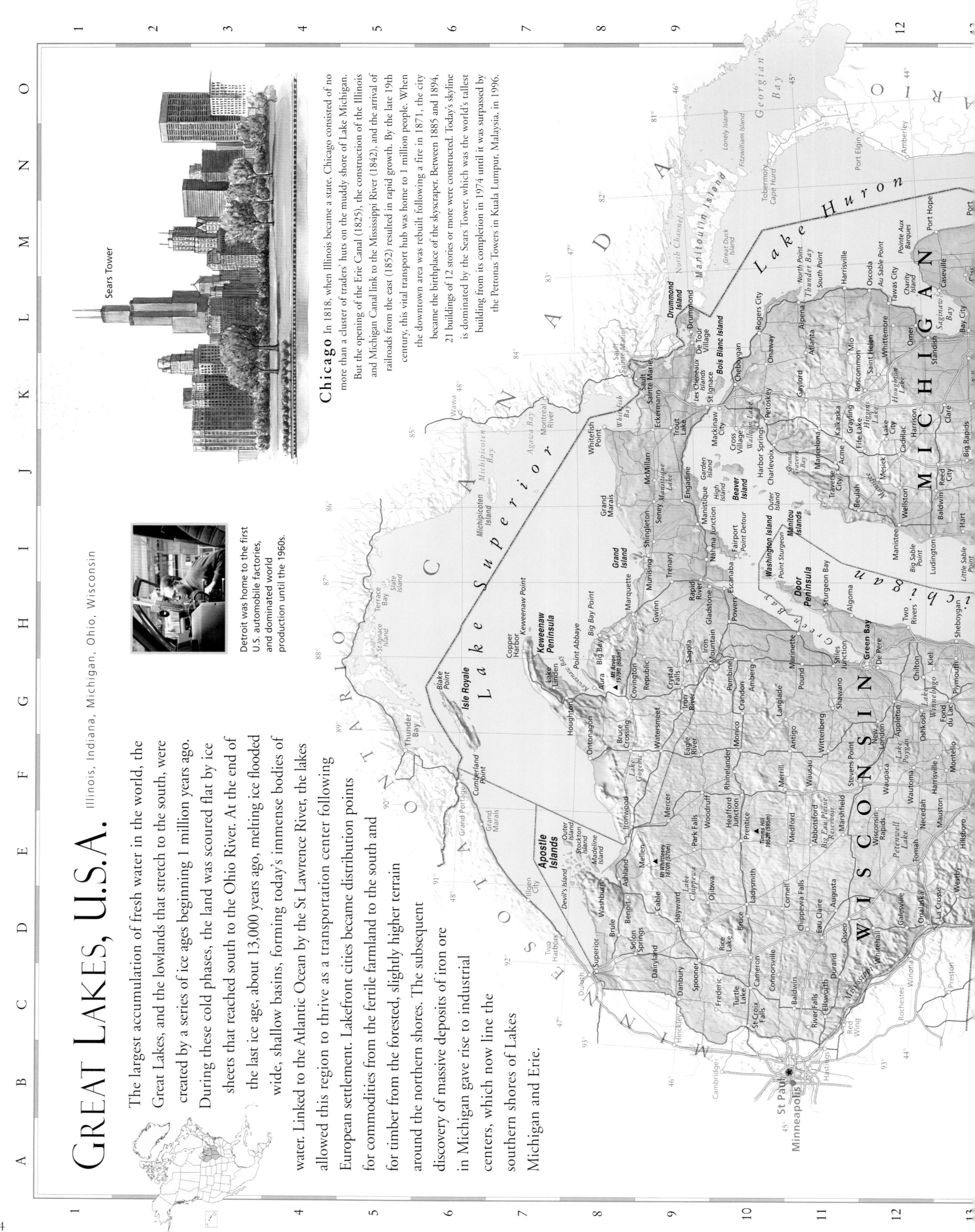

GREAT LAKES, U.S.A.

Illinois, Indiana, Michigan, Ohio, Wisconsin

The largest accumulation of fresh water in the world, the Great Lakes, and the lowlands that stretch to the south, were created by a series of ice ages beginning 1 million years ago. During these cold phases, the land was scoured flat by ice sheets that reached south to the Ohio River. At the end of the last ice age, about 13,000 years ago, melting ice flooded wide, shallow basins, forming today's immense bodies of water. Linked to the Atlantic Ocean by the St Lawrence River, the lakes allowed this region to thrive as a transportation center following European settlement. Lakefront cities became distribution points for commodities from the fertile farmland to the south and for timber from the forested, slightly higher terrain around the northern shores. The subsequent discovery of massive deposits of iron ore in Michigan gave rise to industrial centers, which now line the southern shores of Lakes Michigan and Erie.

Sears Tower

Detroit was home to the first U.S. automobile factories, and dominated world production until the 1960s.

Chicago In 1818, when Illinois became a state, Chicago consisted of no more than a cluster of traders' huts on the muddy shore of Lake Michigan. But the opening of the Erie Canal (1825), the construction of the Illinois and Michigan Canal link to the Mississippi River (1842), and the arrival of railroads from the east (1852) resulted in rapid growth. By the late 19th century, this vital transport hub was home to 1 million people. When the downtown area was rebuilt following a fire in 1871, the city became the birthplace of the skyscraper. Between 1885 and 1894, 21 buildings of 12 stories or more were constructed. Today's skyline is dominated by the Sears Tower, which was the world's tallest building from its completion in 1974 until it was surpassed by the Petronas Towers in Kuala Lumpur, Malaysia, in 1996.

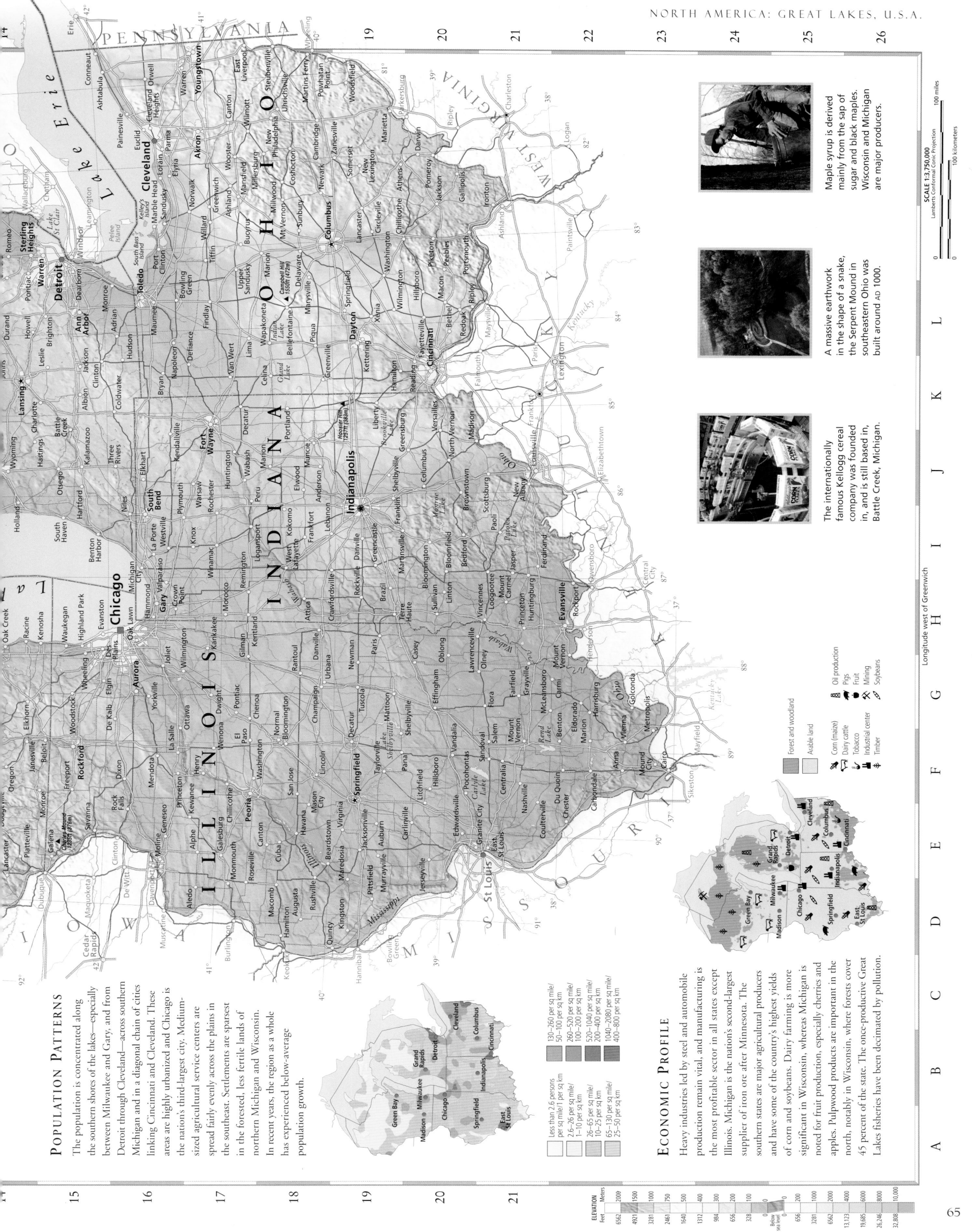

POPULATION PATTERNS

The population is concentrated along the southern shores of the lakes—especially between Milwaukee and Gary, and from Detroit through Cleveland—across southern Michigan and in a diagonal chain of cities linking Cincinnati and Cleveland. These areas are highly urbanized and Chicago is the nation's third-largest city. Medium-sized agricultural service centers are spread fairly evenly across the plains in the southeast. Settlements are sparsest in the forested, less fertile lands of northern Michigan and Wisconsin. In recent years, the region as a whole has experienced below-average population growth.

Less than 2.6 persons per sq mile/1 per sq km
2.6–26 per sq mile/1–10 per sq km
26–65 per sq mile/10–25 per sq km
65–130 per sq mile/25–50 per sq km
130–260 per sq mile/50–100 per sq km
260–520 per sq mile/100–200 per sq km
520–1040 per sq mile/200–400 per sq km
1040–2080 per sq mile/400–800 per sq km

ECONOMIC PROFILE

Heavy industries led by steel and automobile production remain vital, and manufacturing is the most profitable sector in all states except Illinois. Michigan is the nation's second-largest supplier of iron ore after Minnesota. The southern states are major agricultural producers and have some of the country's highest yields of corn and soybeans. Dairy farming is more significant in Wisconsin, whereas Michigan is noted for fruit production, especially cherries and apples. Pulpwood products are important in the north, notably in Wisconsin, where forests cover 45 percent of the state. The once-productive Great Lakes fisheries have been decimated by pollution.

Forest and woodland
Arable land

Corn (maize)
Dairy cattle
Tobacco
Timber

Oil production
Pigs
Fruit
Mining
Soybeans

Industrial center

The internationally famous Kellogg cereal company was founded in, and is still based in, Battle Creek, Michigan.

A massive earthwork in the shape of a snake, the Serpent Mound in southeastern Ohio was built around AD 1000.

Maple syrup is derived mainly from the sap of sugar and black maples. Wisconsin and Michigan are major producers.

SCALE 1:3,750,000
Lambert's Conformal Conic Projection

0   100 miles
0   100 kilometers

Longitude west of Greenwich

ELEVATION
Feet	Meters
32,808	10,000
26,246	8000
19,685	6000
13,123	4000
6562	2000
3281	1000
1640	500
656	200
328	100
0	0 Below sea level
656	200
3281	1000
6562	2000
9843	3000

Upper Midwest, U.S.A.

Iowa, Minnesota, Nebraska,
North Dakota, South Dakota

A seemingly boundless sea of crops is the image most strongly associated with the Upper Midwest, and indeed more than half of the land is used for cultivation and agriculture dominates the economy. Wheat fields swathe much of the Great Plains plateau on the western side of the region. Myriad streams and rivers follow the plateau's gentle eastward inclination, carving gullies and channels through hills and badlands, and feeding for the most part into the Missouri River. Undulating farmland—mainly fields of corn and soybeans—also covers most of Iowa and southern Minnesota. In the northeast, the plains are studded with lakes and marshes formed by the retreat of glaciers at the end of last ice age. The upper Mississippi and Missouri were vital transportation routes for Native Americans and early European explorers and trappers, but widespread intensive settlement did not take place until after the arrival of the railroads around 1870.

POPULATION PATTERNS

The western part of this region is one of the most sparsely inhabited parts of the lower 48, and North and South Dakota are, respectively, the second and fourth least populous states. The east has larger settlements, especially along major rivers. The Upper Midwest generally experiences lower than average population growth: between 1990 and 2000, North Dakota had the country's lowest rate of growth, a mere 0.5 percent. The overall proportion of rural dwellers is significantly higher than average, reaching almost half in South Dakota.

Less than 2.6 persons per sq mile/1 per sq km
2.6–26 per sq mile/1–10 per sq km
26–65 per sq mile/10–25 per sq km
65–130 per sq mile/25–50 per sq km
130–260 per sq mile/50–100 per sq km

ECONOMIC PROFILE

These states are among the nation's largest agricultural producers. The west forms part of the Great Plains Wheat Belt; the so-called Corn Belt encompasses eastern Nebraska, Iowa, and southern Minnesota. Grazing of cattle and pigs occurs throughout the region. Minnesota is the nation's largest producer of iron ore, Nebraska and North Dakota have modest supplies of petroleum, and South Dakota's Black Hills are a prime source of gold. Farming is the basis of most manufacturing and services, though tourism and the insurance industry are also important.

Forest and woodland
Arable land
Grazing
Cereals
Corn (maize)
Beef cattle
Industrial center
Mining
Oil production
Soybeans
Pigs

CANADA

MONTANA

WYOMING

COLORADO

NORTH DAKOTA

SOUTH DAKOTA

NEBRASKA

Melita
Boissevain
Manitou
Westhope
Rocklake
Langdon
Dunseith
Cando
Fortuna
Bowbells
Kenmare
Rugby
Tioga
Ray
Stanley
Minot
Towner
Devil's Lake
Williston
New Town
Velva
Devil's Lake
Watford City
Lake Sakakawea
Max
Harvey
New Rockford
Sheye
McClusky
Fessenden
Grassy Butte
Killdeer
Underwood
Wilton
Tuttle
Carrington
Pingree
Manning
Halliday
Beach
Hebron
Medina
Sentinel Butte
3428ft (1045m)
Belfield
Dickinson
Mandan
Bismarck
Sterling
Dawson
Jamestown
Badlands
White Butte
3530ft (1076m)
Mott
Elgin
Napoleon
Linton
Edgeley
Baker
Cannonball
Breien
Wishek
Bowman
Reeder
Eller
Hettinger
Lemmon
McIntosh
McLaughlin
Ashley
Selfridge
Buffalo
Reva
Bison
Grand
Mobridge
Selby
Roscoe
Isabel
Moreau
Mud Butte
Faith
Dupree
La Plant
Gettysburg
Redfield
Belle Fourche
Howes
Lake Oahe
Blunt
Spearfish
Cheyenne
Hayes
Pierre
Highmore
Wolsey
Sturgis
Billsburg
Black Hills
Mt Rushmore
5725ft (1745m)
Rapid City
Wall
Murdo
Chamberlain
Plankito
Custer
Kadoka
Winner
Hot Springs
White
Mission
Gregory
Pickstown
Edgemont
Oelrichs
Pine Ridge
Martin
Lusk
Chadron
Merriman
Niobrara
Valentine
Harrison
Crawford
Hay Springs
Ainsworth
Bassett
Hemingford
Sand Hills
Alliance
Scottsbluff
Hyannis
Thedford
Taylor
Bartlett
Hogback Mtn
5082ft (1549m)
Bridgeport
Dunning
Ansley
North Platte
Arthur
Tryon
Stapleton
Kimball
Oshkosh
Lake McConaughy
Sidney
Ogallala
North Platte
St Pa
Holyoke
Grant
Gothenburg
Lexington
Kearney
Imperial
Maywood
Holdrege
McCook
Arapahoe
Alma
Has
104°
102°
100°
48°
46°
44°
42°
40°

KANSAS

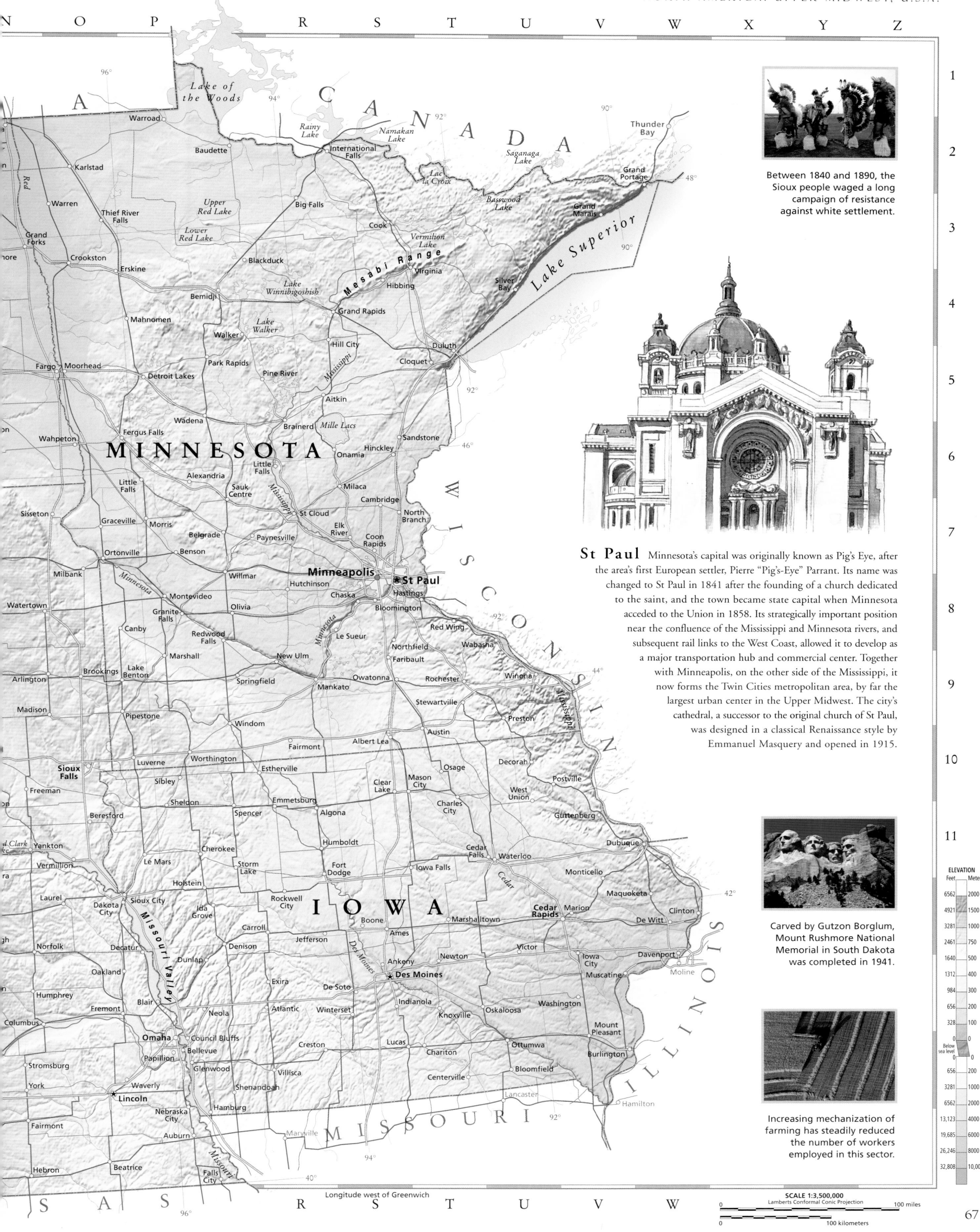

Between 1840 and 1890, the Sioux people waged a long campaign of resistance against white settlement.

St Paul Minnesota's capital was originally known as Pig's Eye, after the area's first European settler, Pierre "Pig's-Eye" Parrant. Its name was changed to St Paul in 1841 after the founding of a church dedicated to the saint, and the town became state capital when Minnesota acceded to the Union in 1858. Its strategically important position near the confluence of the Mississippi and Minnesota rivers, and subsequent rail links to the West Coast, allowed it to develop as a major transportation hub and commercial center. Together with Minneapolis, on the other side of the Mississippi, it now forms the Twin Cities metropolitan area, by far the largest urban center in the Upper Midwest. The city's cathedral, a successor to the original church of St Paul, was designed in a classical Renaissance style by Emmanuel Masquery and opened in 1915.

Carved by Gutzon Borglum, Mount Rushmore National Memorial in South Dakota was completed in 1941.

Increasing mechanization of farming has steadily reduced the number of workers employed in this sector.

SCALE 1:3,500,000
Lamberts Conformal Conic Projection

67

LOWER MIDWEST, U.S.A.

Arkansas, Kansas, Missouri, Oklahoma

From the central Mississippi River, pioneers launched the great wave of westward expansion that began in the 1840s, turning this region into the "Gateway to the West." Most traveled along the Missouri River, over the hills of present-day Kansas and across the treeless plateau of the Great Plains. But the rugged, densely forested terrain of the Ozark Plateau and Ouachita Mountains in the east, the presence of large groups of displaced Native Americans in the so-called Indian Territory of the west, and early reports that the plains were a desert meant that the majority simply passed through. It wasn't until the end of the century that farmers turned the western plains into the major agricultural region that, despite occasional droughts such as those that created the Dust Bowl of the 1930s, it remains today.

Thermal springs are among the attractions that have made the Ozark Plateau a popular tourist center.

St Louis Sited at the heart of the mainland U.S.A., just south of the confluence of the Missouri and Mississippi rivers, St Louis was ideally placed to become a major transportation hub. It was founded by the French as a fur-trading post in 1764, came briefly under Spanish control, and was acquired by the U.S.A. as part of the Louisiana Purchase of 1803. Not only did St Louis cater to trappers and traders traveling north, northwest, and south along the rivers, it also became a major supply depot and departure point for exploratory parties venturing west and for thousands of pioneers setting off along the Santa Fe, Oregon, and California trails. The massive Gateway Arch commemorates the city's historic role in U.S. expansion. Standing almost 630 feet (192 m) high, it was designed by Eero Saarinen and erected in 1965.

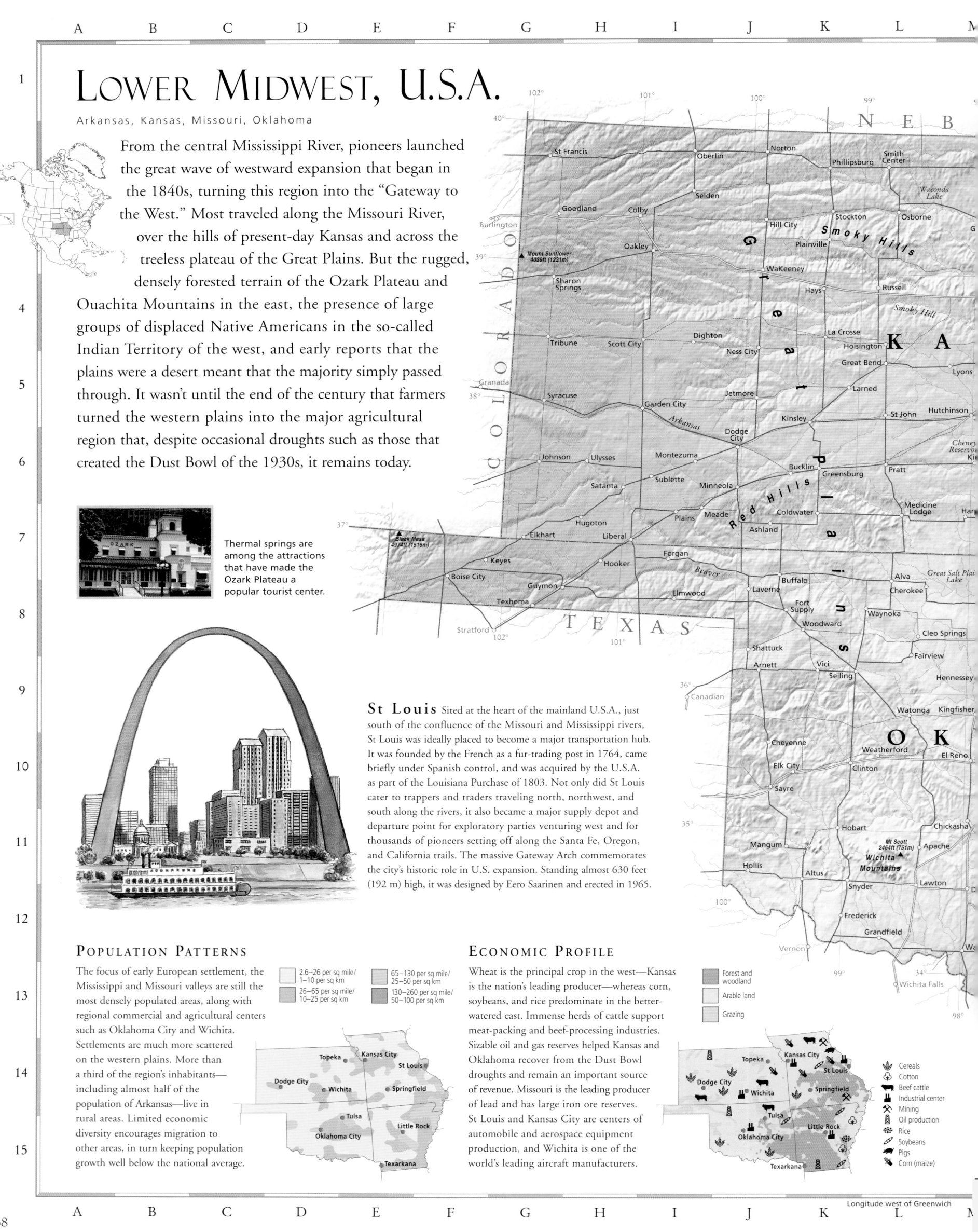

POPULATION PATTERNS

The focus of early European settlement, the Mississippi and Missouri valleys are still the most densely populated areas, along with regional commercial and agricultural centers such as Oklahoma City and Wichita. Settlements are much more scattered on the western plains. More than a third of the region's inhabitants—including almost half of the population of Arkansas—live in rural areas. Limited economic diversity encourages migration to other areas, in turn keeping population growth well below the national average.

2.6–26 per sq mile/ 1–10 per sq km
26–65 per sq mile/ 10–25 per sq km
65–130 per sq mile/ 25–50 per sq km
130–260 per sq mile/ 50–100 per sq km

ECONOMIC PROFILE

Wheat is the principal crop in the west—Kansas is the nation's leading producer—whereas corn, soybeans, and rice predominate in the better-watered east. Immense herds of cattle support meat-packing and beef-processing industries. Sizable oil and gas reserves helped Kansas and Oklahoma recover from the Dust Bowl droughts and remain an important source of revenue. Missouri is the leading producer of lead and has large iron ore reserves. St Louis and Kansas City are centers of automobile and aerospace equipment production, and Wichita is one of the world's leading aircraft manufacturers.

Forest and woodland
Arable land
Grazing

Cereals
Cotton
Beef cattle
Industrial center
Mining
Oil production
Rice
Soybeans
Pigs
Corn (maize)

Longitude west of Greenwich

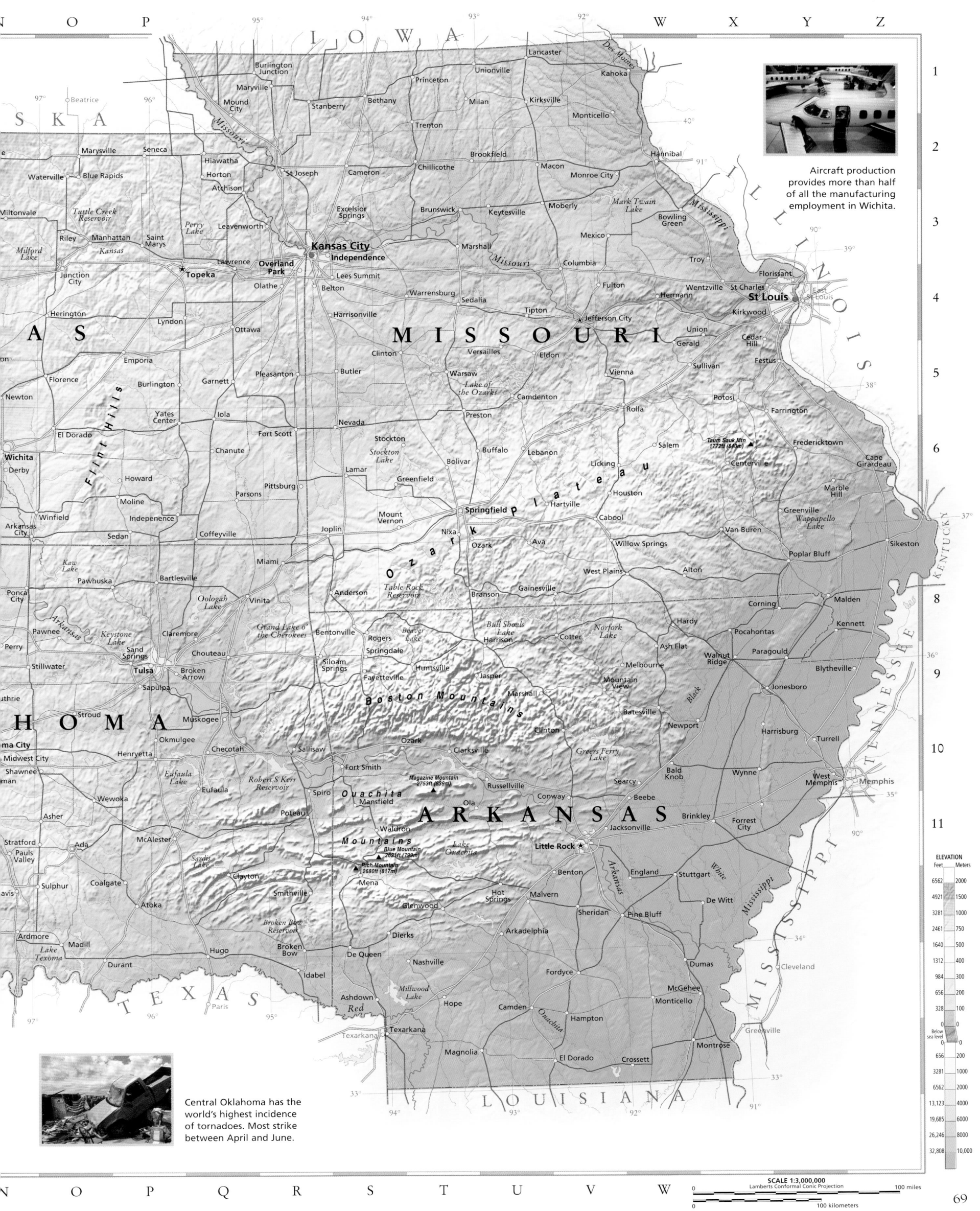

Aircraft production provides more than half of all the manufacturing employment in Wichita.

Central Oklahoma has the world's highest incidence of tornadoes. Most strike between April and June.

SCALE 1:3,000,000
Lamberts Conformal Conic Projection

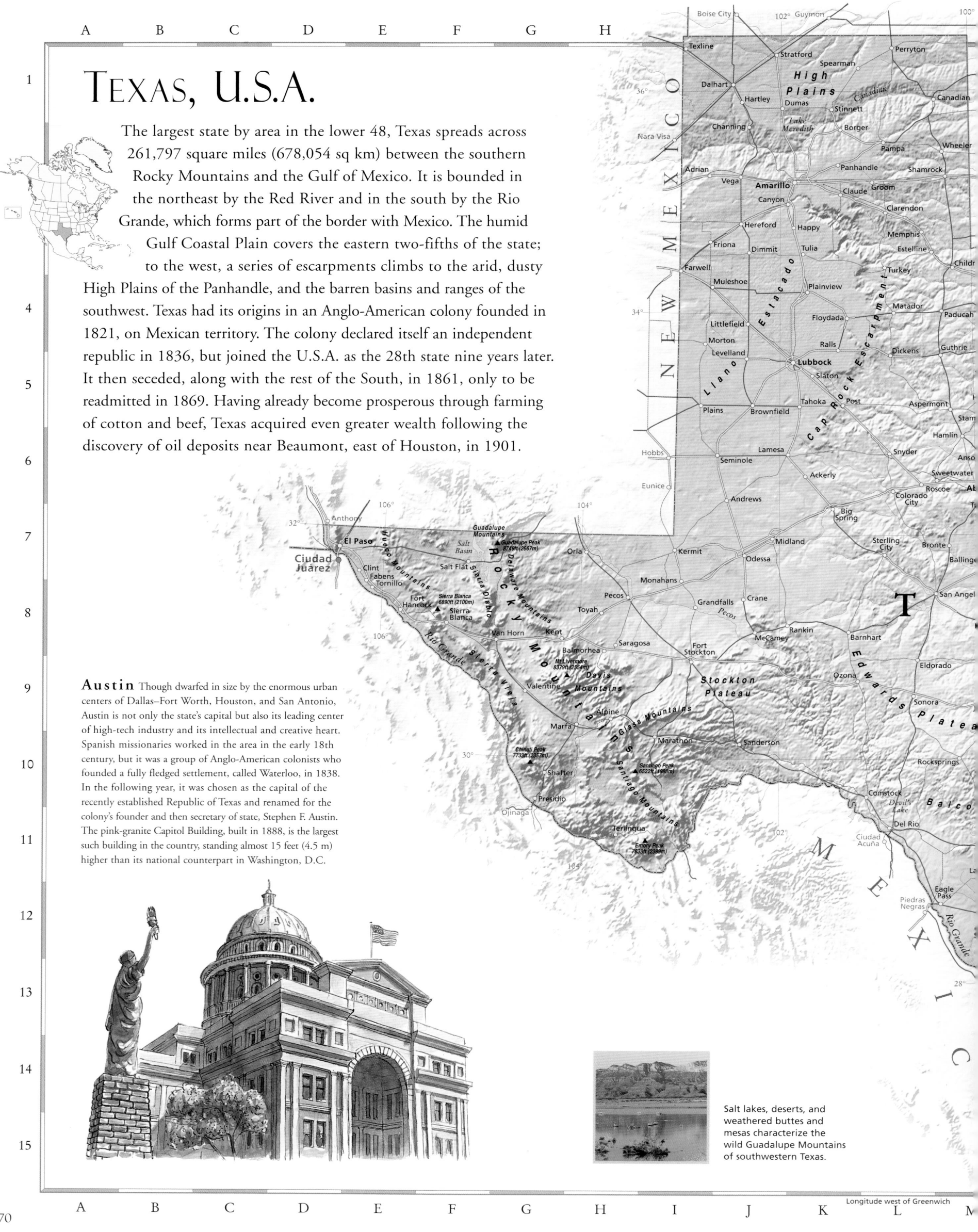

TEXAS, U.S.A.

The largest state by area in the lower 48, Texas spreads across 261,797 square miles (678,054 sq km) between the southern Rocky Mountains and the Gulf of Mexico. It is bounded in the northeast by the Red River and in the south by the Rio Grande, which forms part of the border with Mexico. The humid Gulf Coastal Plain covers the eastern two-fifths of the state; to the west, a series of escarpments climbs to the arid, dusty High Plains of the Panhandle, and the barren basins and ranges of the southwest. Texas had its origins in an Anglo-American colony founded in 1821, on Mexican territory. The colony declared itself an independent republic in 1836, but joined the U.S.A. as the 28th state nine years later. It then seceded, along with the rest of the South, in 1861, only to be readmitted in 1869. Having already become prosperous through farming of cotton and beef, Texas acquired even greater wealth following the discovery of oil deposits near Beaumont, east of Houston, in 1901.

Austin Though dwarfed in size by the enormous urban centers of Dallas–Fort Worth, Houston, and San Antonio, Austin is not only the state's capital but also its leading center of high-tech industry and its intellectual and creative heart. Spanish missionaries worked in the area in the early 18th century, but it was a group of Anglo-American colonists who founded a fully fledged settlement, called Waterloo, in 1838. In the following year, it was chosen as the capital of the recently established Republic of Texas and renamed for the colony's founder and then secretary of state, Stephen F. Austin. The pink-granite Capitol Building, built in 1888, is the largest such building in the country, standing almost 15 feet (4.5 m) higher than its national counterpart in Washington, D.C.

Salt lakes, deserts, and weathered buttes and mesas characterize the wild Guadalupe Mountains of southwestern Texas.

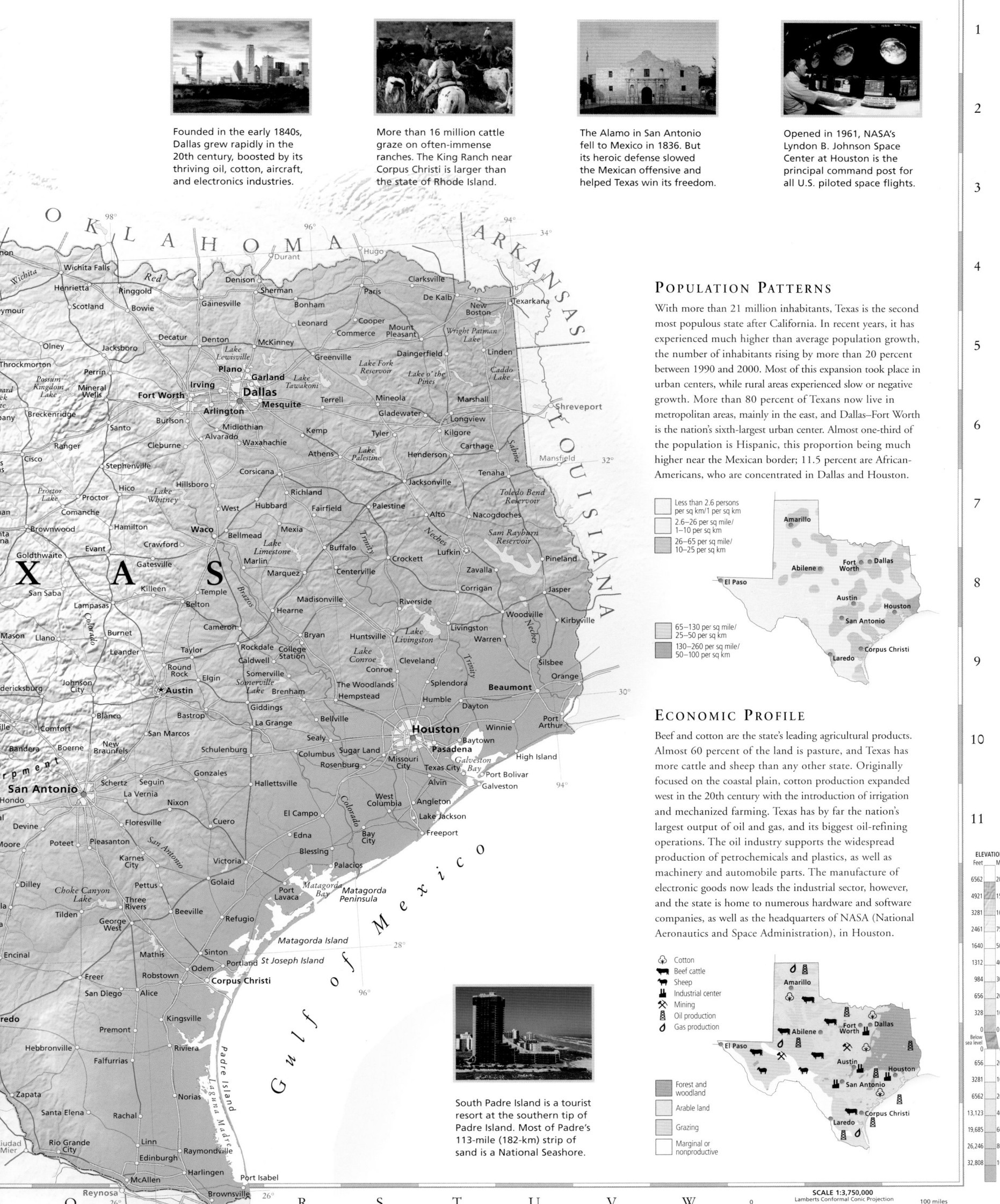

Founded in the early 1840s, Dallas grew rapidly in the 20th century, boosted by its thriving oil, cotton, aircraft, and electronics industries.

More than 16 million cattle graze on often-immense ranches. The King Ranch near Corpus Christi is larger than the state of Rhode Island.

The Alamo in San Antonio fell to Mexico in 1836. But its heroic defense slowed the Mexican offensive and helped Texas win its freedom.

Opened in 1961, NASA's Lyndon B. Johnson Space Center at Houston is the principal command post for all U.S. piloted space flights.

POPULATION PATTERNS

With more than 21 million inhabitants, Texas is the second most populous state after California. In recent years, it has experienced much higher than average population growth, the number of inhabitants rising by more than 20 percent between 1990 and 2000. Most of this expansion took place in urban centers, while rural areas experienced slow or negative growth. More than 80 percent of Texans now live in metropolitan areas, mainly in the east, and Dallas–Fort Worth is the nation's sixth-largest urban center. Almost one-third of the population is Hispanic, this proportion being much higher near the Mexican border; 11.5 percent are African-Americans, who are concentrated in Dallas and Houston.

Less than 2.6 persons per sq km/1 per sq mile
2.6–26 per sq mile/ 1–10 per sq km
26–65 per sq mile/ 10–25 per sq km
65–130 per sq mile/ 25–50 per sq km
130–260 per sq mile/ 50–100 per sq km

ECONOMIC PROFILE

Beef and cotton are the state's leading agricultural products. Almost 60 percent of the land is pasture, and Texas has more cattle and sheep than any other state. Originally focused on the coastal plain, cotton production expanded west in the 20th century with the introduction of irrigation and mechanized farming. Texas has by far the nation's largest output of oil and gas, and its biggest oil-refining operations. The oil industry supports the widespread production of petrochemicals and plastics, as well as machinery and automobile parts. The manufacture of electronic goods now leads the industrial sector, however, and the state is home to numerous hardware and software companies, as well as the headquarters of NASA (National Aeronautics and Space Administration), in Houston.

Cotton
Beef cattle
Sheep
Industrial center
Mining
Oil production
Gas production

Forest and woodland
Arable land
Grazing
Marginal or nonproductive

South Padre Island is a tourist resort at the southern tip of Padre Island. Most of Padre's 113-mile (182-km) strip of sand is a National Seashore.

ELEVATION

Feet	Meters
6562	2000
4921	1500
3281	1000
2461	750
1640	500
1312	400
984	300
656	200
328	100
Below sea level	0
656	200
3281	1000
6562	2000
13,123	4000
19,685	6000
26,246	8000
32,808	10,000

SCALE 1:3,750,000
Lambert's Conformal Conic Projection
0   100 miles
0   100 kilometers

NORTHERN ROCKIES, U.S.A.

Idaho, Montana, Wyoming

The Rocky Mountains form a broad diagonal band across northern Idaho and western Montana and Wyoming. In southern Idaho, the Columbia Plateau and Snake River Plain skirt the mountains. On their eastern flank, the Rockies level out on the Great Plains, an expanse of rolling pastures and wheat fields. Still little developed, the Northern Rockies are the traditional homeland of native peoples such as the Nez Perce, Shoshone, Cheyenne, and Sioux. The first Europeans to visit were Lewis and Clark, during their momentous expedition of 1804–06. Only a trickle of traders and trappers followed, until a gold rush in the early 1860s. Once the boom was over, prospectors turned their hands to mining other minerals, and to forestry and farming—still the foundations of the economy.

POPULATION PATTERNS

Population density is low—Wyoming is the nation's least populous state, despite being the ninth biggest by area—and there are few large cities, with only Boise's population surpassing 100,000. Towns line the major river valleys, and half of Wyoming's population is concentrated in the southeastern quarter of the state. Wide open spaces separate settlements elsewhere. The population is overwhelmingly white, but includes a much higher than average proportion of Native Americans. In 1990–2000, Idaho was the fifth fastest-growing state and Boise was the nation's seventh fastest-growing metropolitan area.

Less than 2.6 persons per sq mile/1 per sq km
2.6–26 per sq mile/1–10 per sq km
26–65 per sq mile/10–25 per sq km
65–130 per sq mile/25–50 per sq km

ECONOMIC PROFILE

Coal, oil, and gas are major sources of revenue in Montana and especially Wyoming (the nation's top coal producer), whereas mining in Idaho is focused on silver, lead, and molybdenum. Irrigation supports the cultivation of a range of crops, most notably potatoes in Idaho and wheat in the east. Huge numbers of cattle and sheep roam the plateaus and prairies. Forests are extensive, covering one-third of Idaho; timber is a vital resource there and in Montana. Most manufacturing involves the processing of raw materials. Tourism is a leading employer and revenue source.

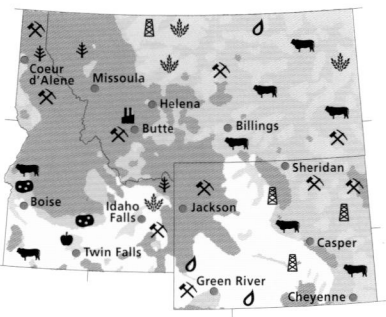

Forest and woodland
Arable land
Grazing
Marginal or nonproductive

Cereals
Potatoes
Gas production
Beef cattle
Timber
Industrial center
Mining
Oil production
Fruit

THE TETON RANGE

Extending for 40 miles (64 km) across northwestern Wyoming, the Teton Range is one of the youngest and most imposing mountain ranges in the Rockies. Its jagged peaks began to form more than 1 million years ago when the land to the east dropped downward along a 50-mile (80-km) fault line. Today, 13,770-foot (4,197-m) Grand Teton, the highest peak in the range, rises 7,000 feet (2,135 m) above the valley of Jackson Hole.

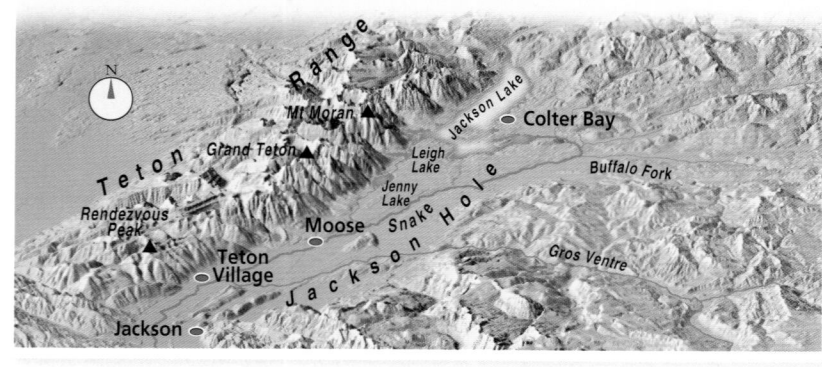

ELEVATION

Feet	Meters
6562	2000
4921	1500
3281	1000
2461	750
1640	500
1312	400
984	300
656	200
328	100
0 Below sea level	0
656	200
3281	1000
6562	2000
13,123	4000
19,685	6000
26,246	8000
32,808	10,000

Old Faithful is one of 200 or so geysers in Yellowstone National Park, Wyoming. A major tourist destination, Yellowstone also encompasses 10,000 hot springs.

The Northern Rockies harbor the country's largest bison populations.

The Capitol Building in Boise was completed in 1920, 30 years after Idaho became a state.

Longitude west of Greenwich

SOUTHWESTERN U.S.A.

Arizona, Colorado, New Mexico, Utah

The immense Colorado Plateau constitutes the core of this arid region. Bounded to the west by basin and range country, to the north and east by the southern Rockies, and to the south by the Sonoran Desert, it is characterized by ancient, eroded landscapes where barren plateaus sit beneath forested, snow-capped peaks, and rivers have carved deep chasms between broad mesas and towering buttes. Scattered cliff-dwellings and pueblos testify to thousands of years of Native American habitation. Historic missions and adobe architecture recall Spanish occupation between the 16th and early 19th centuries, and subsequent Mexican rule over much of the Southwest until 1848. Today, the region's dry, sunny climate, thriving high-tech industries, and astounding scenery make it one of the most-visited and fastest-growing parts of the country.

THE GRAND CANYON

A deep gash in the southwestern corner of the Colorado Plateau, the Grand Canyon was carved over millennia by the Colorado River. Extending 277 miles (446 km) and measuring 15 miles (24 km) across at its widest point, it is up to 6,000 feet (1,800 m) deep. Erosion has exposed rocks at the bottom of the canyon that are about 2 billion years old. Now encompassed by the national park of the same name, the canyon attracts up to 5 million visitors annually.

Salt Lake City In 1846, fleeing persecution in Illinois, 148 Mormons migrated more than 1,000 miles (1,600 km) to present-day Utah. Settling in the Valley of the Great Salt Lake in 1847, they founded a new settlement, initially called Great Salt Lake City. By the late 19th century, it had become, and remains, one of the most important commercial centers in the western U.S.A. Its focal point, and the heart of the Mormon faith, is Temple Square, site of the six-towered Mormon Temple, begun in 1853 and completed 40 years later.

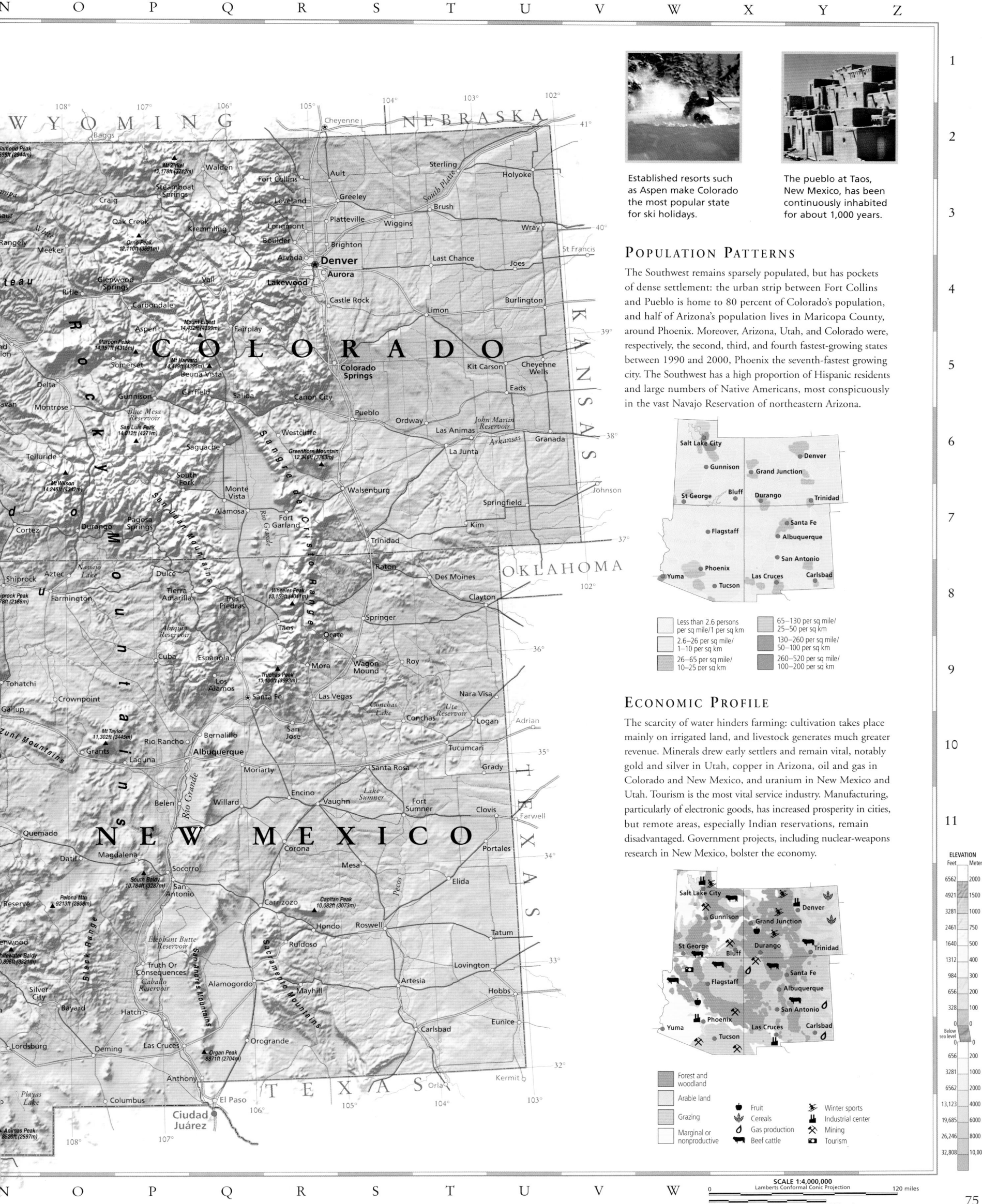

Established resorts such as Aspen make Colorado the most popular state for ski holidays.

The pueblo at Taos, New Mexico, has been continuously inhabited for about 1,000 years.

POPULATION PATTERNS

The Southwest remains sparsely populated, but has pockets of dense settlement: the urban strip between Fort Collins and Pueblo is home to 80 percent of Colorado's population, and half of Arizona's population lives in Maricopa County, around Phoenix. Moreover, Arizona, Utah, and Colorado were, respectively, the second, third, and fourth fastest-growing states between 1990 and 2000, Phoenix the seventh-fastest growing city. The Southwest has a high proportion of Hispanic residents and large numbers of Native Americans, most conspicuously in the vast Navajo Reservation of northeastern Arizona.

Less than 2.6 persons per sq mile/1 per sq km

2.6–26 per sq mile/ 1–10 per sq km

26–65 per sq mile/ 10–25 per sq km

65–130 per sq mile/ 25–50 per sq km

130–260 per sq mile/ 50–100 per sq km

260–520 per sq mile/ 100–200 per sq km

ECONOMIC PROFILE

The scarcity of water hinders farming: cultivation takes place mainly on irrigated land, and livestock generates much greater revenue. Minerals drew early settlers and remain vital, notably gold and silver in Utah, copper in Arizona, oil and gas in Colorado and New Mexico, and uranium in New Mexico and Utah. Tourism is the most vital service industry. Manufacturing, particularly of electronic goods, has increased prosperity in cities, but remote areas, especially Indian reservations, remain disadvantaged. Government projects, including nuclear-weapons research in New Mexico, bolster the economy.

Forest and woodland

Arable land

Grazing

Marginal or nonproductive

Fruit

Cereals

Gas production

Beef cattle

Winter sports

Industrial center

Mining

Tourism

ELEVATION

Feet	Meters
6562	2000
4921	1500
3281	1000
2461	750
1640	500
1312	400
984	300
656	200
328	100
0	0
Below sea level	
656	200
3281	1000
6562	2000
13,123	4000
19,685	6000
26,246	8000
32,808	10,000

SCALE 1:4,000,000
Lamberts Conformal Conic Projection

0 — 120 miles

0 — 120 kilometers

THE FAR WEST, U.S.A.

California, Nevada, Oregon, Washington

Geologically, the U.S. mainland's western fringe is its youngest and most active region. Plate movements here cause regular earthquakes in California and occasional volcanic eruptions in the Pacific Northwest. They have also given rise, over millions of years, to the two long mountain chains that parallel the shoreline. The Coast Ranges climb steeply from the sea, falling to sheltered lowlands, including the Central and Willamette valleys, which are enclosed in turn by the loftier peaks of the Cascade Range and Sierra Nevada. Farther east lies a jumble of arid landforms, including volcanic plateaus in the north, rows of north–south-trending basins and ranges in Nevada, and low-lying deserts in southeastern California. This intimidating terrain deterred early European immigrants, who clustered in coastal settlements and threaded their way along river valleys before being lured into the uplands by the discovery of gold and other minerals in the mid-19th century. In the 20th century, southern California's warm climate, available land, and thriving ports drew millions west, making it one of the nation's most populous regions.

POPULATION PATTERNS

California has the largest state population, of more than 34 million. More than 90 percent of these people live in urban areas, mainly around Los Angeles and San Diego, and San Francisco and Oakland. One-third of Californians are Hispanic or Latino. In the Pacific Northwest, densely populated areas include the shores of Puget Sound and Oregon's Willamette Valley. In the east, settlements are small and scattered; an exception is Las Vegas, a desert metropolis founded on gambling and tourism. Between 1990 and 2000, Nevada grew faster than any other state, increasing its population by 66 percent.

less than 2.6 persons per sq mile/1 per sq km
2.6–26 per sq mile/1–10 per sq km
26–65 per sq mile/10–25 per sq km
65–130 per sq mile/25–50 per sq km
130–260 per sq mile/50–100 per sq km
260–520 per sq mile/100–200 per sq km
520–1040 per sq mile/200–400 per sq km

ECONOMIC PROFILE

The region has just a few pockets of arable land, most of which require irrigation, but they include California's productive Central Valley and its Napa Valley vineyards, and the fertile Columbia Basin. The Pacific Northwest has enormous stands of timber and abundant hydroelectric power—Washington generates one-third of U.S. supplies. Nevada benefits from reserves of gold and mercury, and hosts major military test sites—85 percent of the land is government-owned. Seattle and San Francisco's famed Silicon Valley are world leaders in new technologies, and Seattle is also a major aircraft manufacturer. As well as the Hollywood film industry, Los Angeles is home to major TV and music corporations. Tourism is a vital industry throughout the region.

Forest and woodland
Arable land
Grazing
Marginal or nonproductive

Fruit and vegetables
Fruit
Wine
Beef cattle
Fishing
Industrial center
Mining
Tourism
Timber
Cereal
Citrus fruits
Dairy cattle

Washington's Mount Rainier is crowned by the largest glacier system in the lower 48 states.

Crater Lake, Oregon, fills a caldera that was once part of an enormous volcano, Mount Mazama.

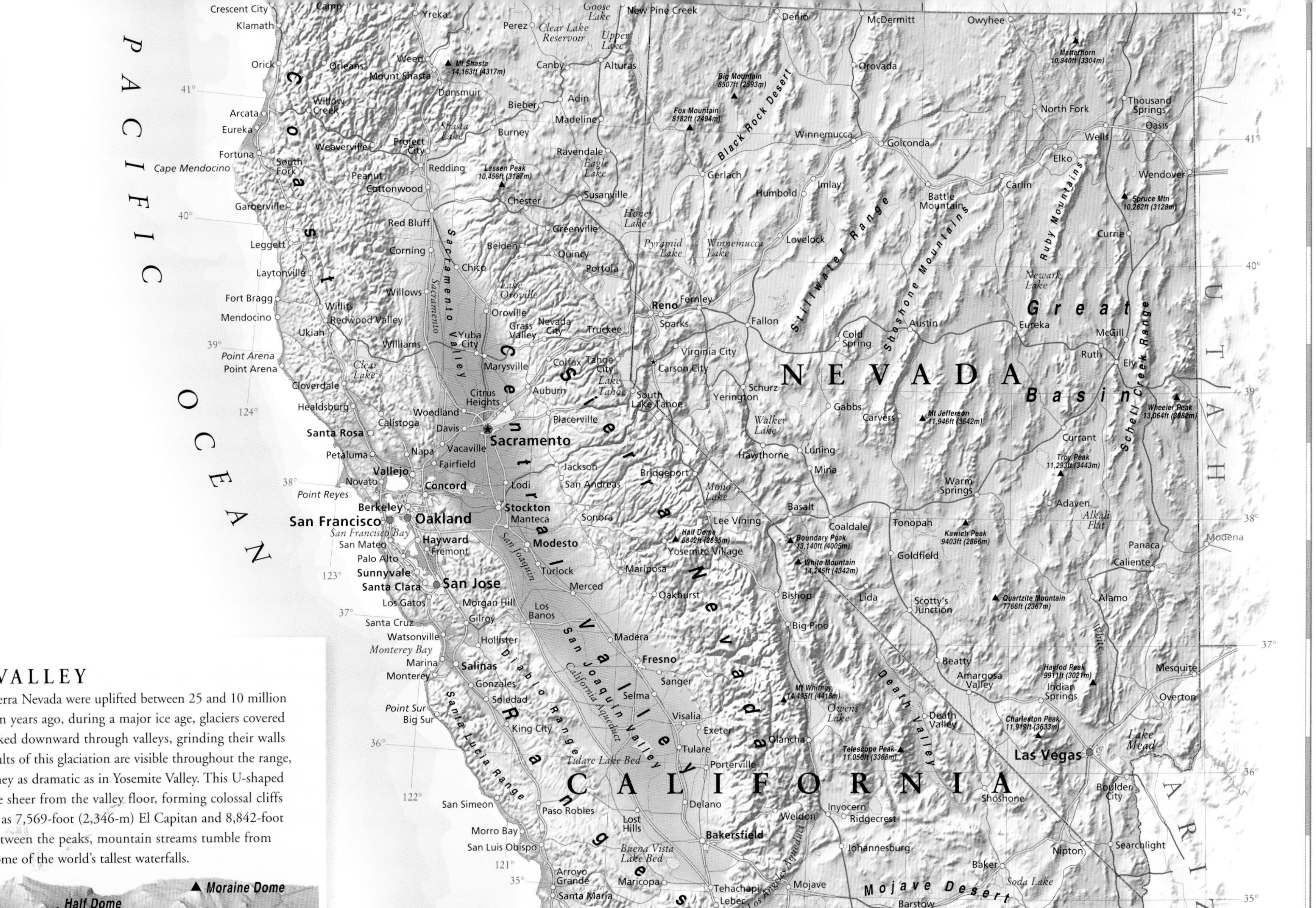

PACIFIC OCEAN

U T A H

A R I Z O N A

N E V A D A

C A L I F O R N I A

M E X I C O

Great Basin

Sierra Nevada

Central Valley

Sacramento Valley

San Joaquin Valley

Coast Ranges

Coast

Mojave Desert

Colorado Desert

Sonoran Desert

Death Valley

Diablo Range

Santa Lucia Range

Channel Islands

Los Angeles

Las Vegas

San Diego

Sacramento

San Francisco

YOSEMITE VALLEY

The granite peaks of the Sierra Nevada were uplifted between 25 and 10 million years ago. Around 1 million years ago, during a major ice age, glaciers covered the highest slopes and snaked downward through valleys, grinding their walls smooth and steep. The results of this glaciation are visible throughout the range, but perhaps nowhere are they as dramatic as in Yosemite Valley. This U-shaped canyon's polished walls rise sheer from the valley floor, forming colossal cliffs surmounted by peaks such as 7,569-foot (2,346-m) El Capitan and 8,842-foot (2,695-m) Half Dome. Between the peaks, mountain streams tumble from hanging valleys, creating some of the world's tallest waterfalls.

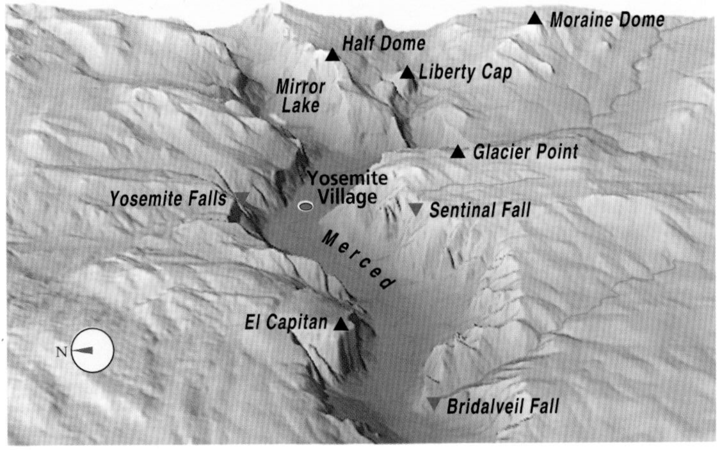

Moraine Dome
Liberty Cap
Half Dome
Glacier Point
Sentinal Fall
Mirror Lake
Yosemite Village
Yosemite Falls
Merced
El Capitan
Bridalveil Fall

N

Founded by Spanish settlers in 1781, Los Angeles became part of the U.S.A. in 1846. It is now its second-largest city.

In Death Valley, California, the land drops to 282 feet (86 m) below sea level, North America's lowest point.

The construction of the Hoover Dam across the Colorado River created Lake Mead in Nevada.

SCALE 1:4,500,000
Lambert's Conformal Conic Projection

0   120 miles
0   120 kilometers

ELEVATION
Feet / Meters

77

ALASKA AND HAWAII, U.S.A.

Alaska and Hawaii are the only two states that are not part of the lower 48, and both became states—the 49th and 50th, respectively—in the same year, 1959. Their territories, however, could hardly be more different. Separated from the rest of the country by western Canada, Alaska is by far the largest state and about 95 times the size of Hawaii—though it has only half as many inhabitants. Its huge, oblong landmass is mountainous, little developed, and mostly inhospitable: winters are severe across most of the state and one-third of the land is barren tundra. Hawaii is a chain of 137 volcanic islands, measuring 1,500 miles (2,400 km) in length and including eight major islands, located in the middle of the Pacific Ocean, about 2,400 miles (3,860 km) west of San Francisco. Cloaked with tracts of tropical forest and fringed by golden beaches, the Hawaiian Islands have fertile soils and are warm and, for the most part, well-watered year-round.

In summer, herds of caribou migrate to Alaska's Arctic tundra to breed.

The Trans-Alaska Oil Pipeline extends from Prudhoe Bay to the port of Valdez.

HAWAII

SCALE 1:5,750,000
Lamberts Conformal Conic Projection
0   100 miles
0   100 kilometers

Longitude west of Greenwich

Named Denali by local Native American people, Mount McKinley is the tallest peak in North America, rising to 20,321 feet (6,194 m).

Kilauea, on the island of Hawaii, is the world's largest active volcanic crater. Its regular eruptions generate extensive lava flows.

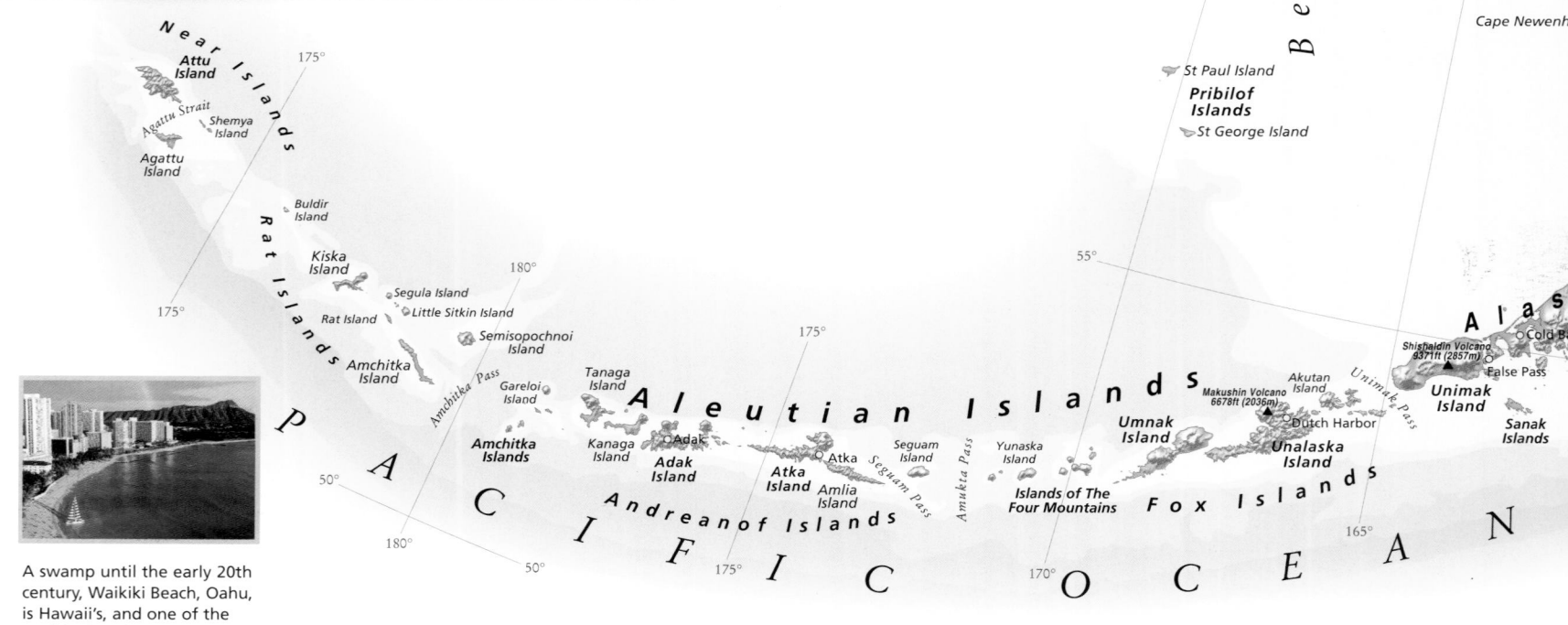

ELEVATION
Feet   Meters
6562   2000
4921   1500
3281   1000
2461   750
1640   500
1312   400
984   300
656   200
328   100
0   0
Below   Below
sea level   sea level
656   200
3281   1000
6562   2000
13,123   4000
19,685   6000
26,246   8000
32,808   10,000

A swamp until the early 20th century, Waikiki Beach, Oahu, is Hawaii's, and one of the world's, best-known beaches.

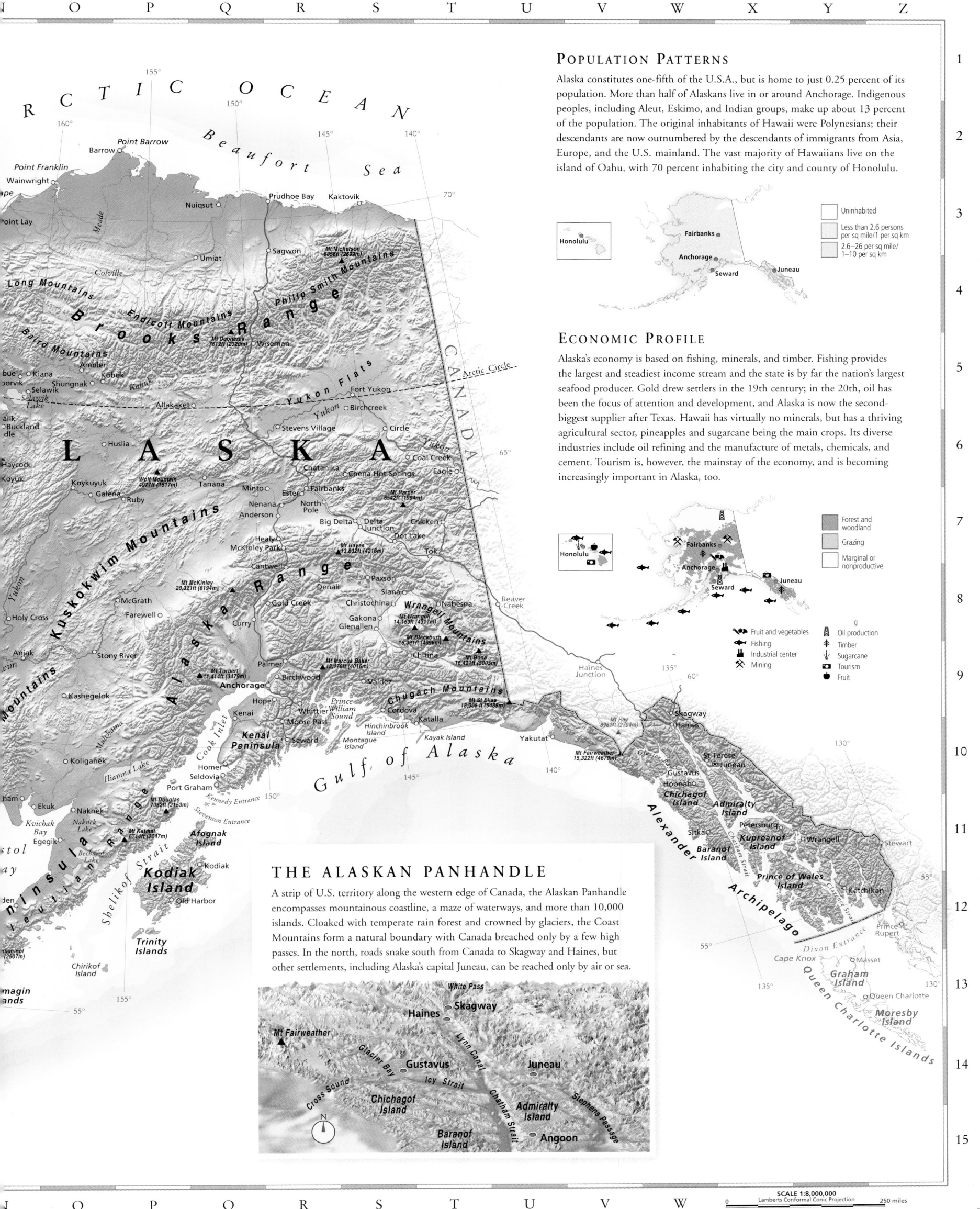

POPULATION PATTERNS

Alaska constitutes one-fifth of the U.S.A., but is home to just 0.25 percent of its population. More than half of Alaskans live in or around Anchorage. Indigenous peoples, including Aleut, Eskimo, and Indian groups, make up about 13 percent of the population. The original inhabitants of Hawaii were Polynesians; their descendants are now outnumbered by the descendants of immigrants from Asia, Europe, and the U.S. mainland. The vast majority of Hawaiians live on the island of Oahu, with 70 percent inhabiting the city and county of Honolulu.

Uninhabited
Less than 2.6 persons per sq mile/1 per sq km
2.6–26 per sq mile/ 1–10 per sq km

ECONOMIC PROFILE

Alaska's economy is based on fishing, minerals, and timber. Fishing provides the largest and steadiest income stream and the state is by far the nation's largest seafood producer. Gold drew settlers in the 19th century; in the 20th, oil has been the focus of attention and development, and Alaska is now the second-biggest supplier after Texas. Hawaii has virtually no minerals, but has a thriving agricultural sector, pineapples and sugarcane being the main crops. Its diverse industries include oil refining and the manufacture of metals, chemicals, and cement. Tourism is, however, the mainstay of the economy, and is becoming increasingly important in Alaska, too.

Forest and woodland
Grazing
Marginal or nonproductive

Fruit and vegetables
Fishing
Industrial center
Mining
Oil production
Timber
Sugarcane
Tourism
Fruit

THE ALASKAN PANHANDLE

A strip of U.S. territory along the western edge of Canada, the Alaskan Panhandle encompasses mountainous coastline, a maze of waterways, and more than 10,000 islands. Cloaked with temperate rain forest and crowned by glaciers, the Coast Mountains form a natural boundary with Canada breached only by a few high passes. In the north, roads snake south from Canada to Skagway and Haines, but other settlements, including Alaska's capital Juneau, can be reached only by air or sea.

SCALE 1:8,000,000
Lamberts Conformal Conic Projection
250 miles
250 kilometers

CANADA

Occupying most of the northern third of North America, Canada is the world's second-largest country by area, but also one of its most sparsely inhabited. A band of western ranges, including the Coast and Rocky mountains, and a number of lower, much older mountain chains in the east, enclose the vast Canadian Shield, an ancient, low, bowl-shaped plateau. Originally home to scattered Indian and Inuit peoples, Canada was visited in the 11th century by Viking explorers, who founded a short-lived settlement in Newfoundland. The French laid claim to the St Lawrence River Valley in the 16th century, but by 1763 most of North America was under British control. The self-governing British dominion of Canada was created in 1867. Initially, it included only Ontario, Québec, New Brunswick, and Nova Scotia, but other areas were gradually absorbed into the confederation, which now consists of ten provinces and three territories.

Mostly uninhabited, mountainous Baffin Island is Canada's largest island.

Waterlogged boreal forest, of spruce, fir, and birch, spans the entire country.

Toronto Canada's most populous city, with around 5 million inhabitants, and its leading commercial and financial center, Toronto originated in the 17th century as a trading post founded at the intersection of several Indian trails (Toronto is a Huron word meaning "meeting place"). Despite being chosen as the site for the capital of Ontario in 1793, the settlement remained undeveloped until the arrival of the Grand Trunk and Great Western railways in the 1850s, after which its population rose to more than half a million by 1921. The modern skyline is dominated by the CN Tower, which rises to 1,815 feet (553 m) and is the world's tallest self-supporting structure.

CN Tower

POPULATION PATTERNS

Vast areas of northern Canada are virtually uninhabited: Nunavut and the Yukon and Northwest territories encompass 41 percent of the land, but have just 0.3 percent of the population. Nunavut has no roads. About 80 percent of Canadians live in the temperate south, within 100 miles (160 km) of the U.S. border. The population is highly urbanized, with four-fifths living in towns and cities. It is also ethnically diverse, one-third of Canadians being of mixed descent. Most, however, are of European, especially British or French, origin. Indigenous peoples make up just 3 percent of the population. Both English and French are official languages and bilingualism is encouraged: 17 percent of Canadians can use both languages.

Uninhabited

Less than 2.6 persons per sq mile/1 per sq km

2.6–26 per sq mile/ 1–10 per sq km

26–65 per sq mile/ 10–25 per sq km

65–130 per sq mile/ 25–50 per sq km

130–260 per sq mile/ 50–100 per sq km

260–520 per sq mile/ 100–200 per sq km

520–1040 per sq mile/ 200–400 per sq km

1040–2080 per sq mile/ 400–800 per sq km

More than 2080 per sq mile/800 per sq km

ECONOMIC PROFILE

Almost half of the country is forested and Canada is the world's leading producer of pulp, paper, and wood. Ample fresh water is harnessed by hydroelectric plants to provide 60 percent of energy needs. Canada is among the world's top sources of zinc, uranium, nickel, bauxite, copper, and gold, and produces far more oil and gas than it uses. Arable land is limited in extent, covering just 7 percent of the country, but productive. Manufacturing is led by transportation equipment, food, machinery, and wood products. Services employ three-quarters of Canadians and generate two-thirds of GDP.

Cereals
Fruit and vegetables
Fruit
Beef cattle
Fishing
Industrial center
Mining
Oil production
Gas production
Timber

Forest and woodland
Arable land
Grazing
Marginal or nonproductive

Longitude west of Greenwich

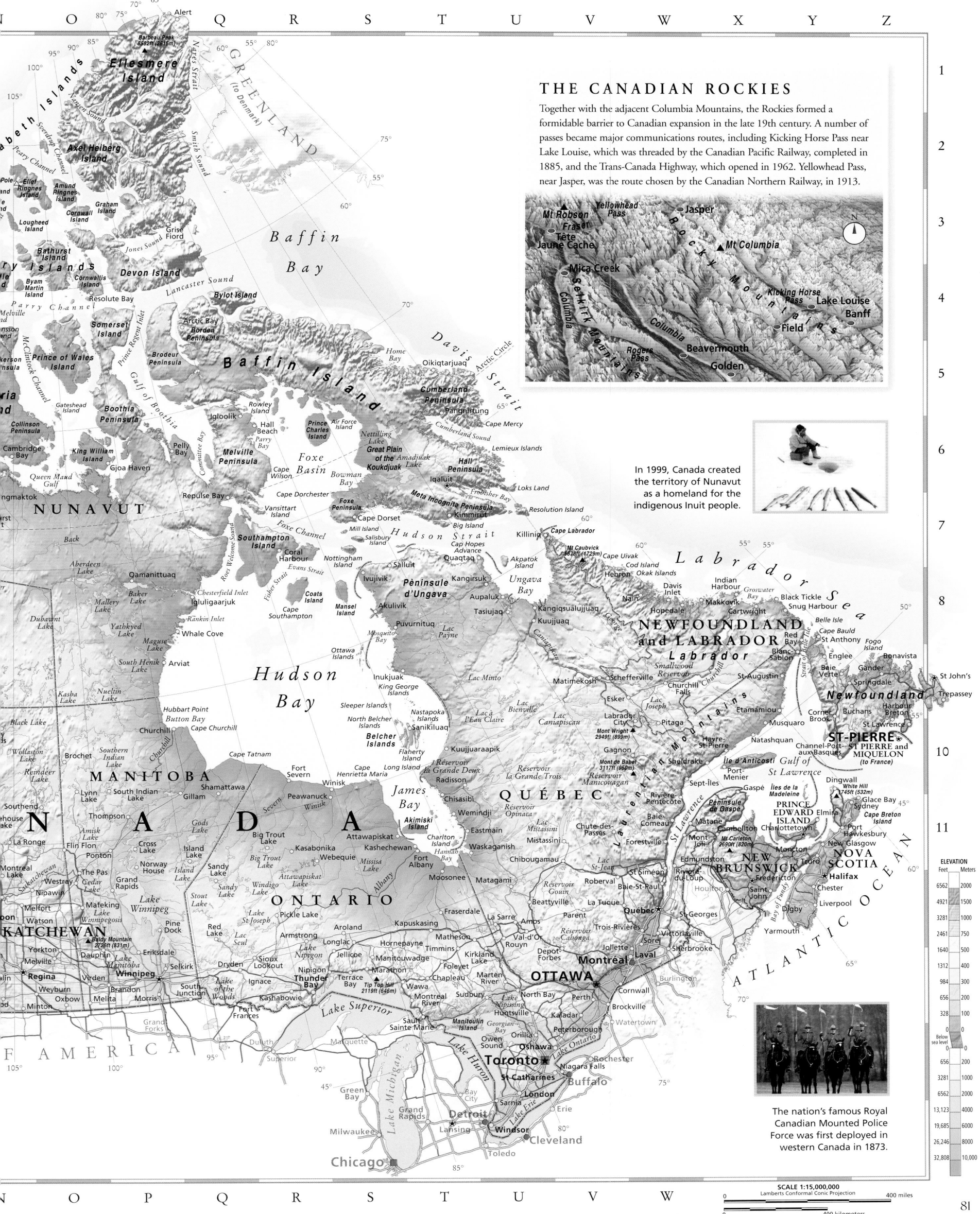

THE CANADIAN ROCKIES

Together with the adjacent Columbia Mountains, the Rockies formed a formidable barrier to Canadian expansion in the late 19th century. A number of passes became major communications routes, including Kicking Horse Pass near Lake Louise, which was threaded by the Canadian Pacific Railway, completed in 1885, and the Trans-Canada Highway, which opened in 1962. Yellowhead Pass, near Jasper, was the route chosen by the Canadian Northern Railway, in 1913.

In 1999, Canada created the territory of Nunavut as a homeland for the indigenous Inuit people.

The nation's famous Royal Canadian Mounted Police Force was first deployed in western Canada in 1873.

SCALE 1:15,000,000
Lamberts Conformal Conic Projection

WESTERN CANADA

Alberta, British Columbia, Northwest Territories, Nunavut, Saskatchewan, Yukon Territory

The broad belt of mountains that parallels Canada's Pacific shoreline spreads up to 500 miles (800 km) inland. It is bounded in the east by the Coast Mountains, site of the country's highest peaks, and in the west by the Canadian Rockies. On their eastern flank, the Rockies drop to the flatlands of the interior. The Great Plains plateau extends into southern Alberta and Saskatchewan; to the north, immense boreal forests, broken by lakes, gradually yield to swamp and tundra. Settlement of this still relatively undeveloped region was stimulated by gold rushes in British Columbia in 1858 and the Klondike in 1897, as well as the completion of the Canadian Pacific Railway in 1885, which drew hundreds of thousands of immigrants to the fertile plains of Alberta and Saskatchewan.

British Columbia's largest city, Vancouver was founded as a sawmilling town in the 1870s.

Glaciers fashioned Moraine Lake and the dramatic Valley of Ten Peaks near Banff.

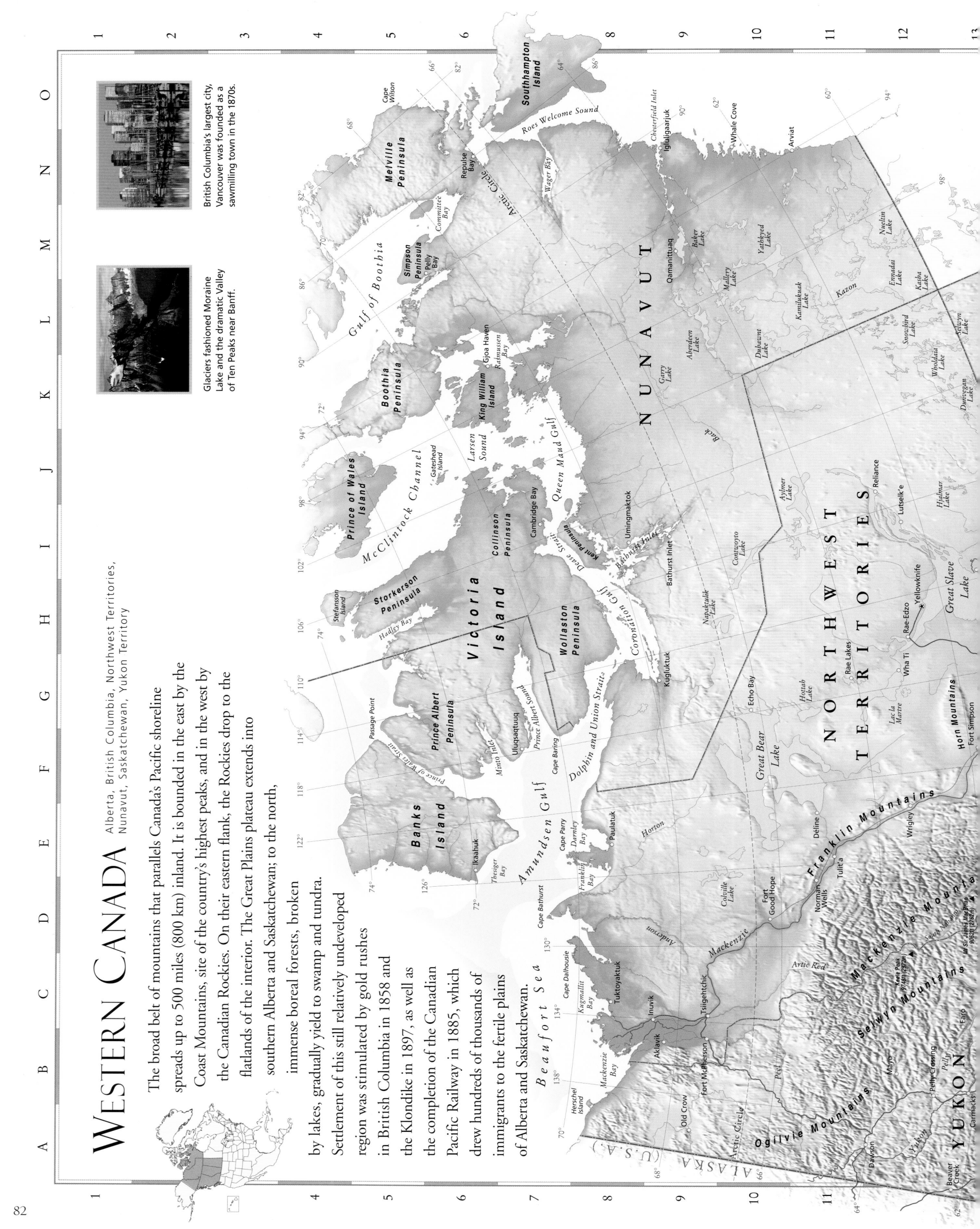

Cape Wilson

Southampton Island

Roes Welcome Sound

Melville Peninsula

Gulf of Boothia

Repulse Bay

Committee Bay

Wager Bay

Arctic Circle

Chesterfield Inlet

Igluligaarjuk

Whale Cove

Arviat

Simpson Peninsula

Pelly Bay

Baker Lake

Qamanittuaq

Naujaat Lake

Boothia Peninsula

Gjoa Haven

Rasmussen Bay

King William Island

N U N A V U T

Mallery Lake

Yathkyed Lake

Emmdai Lake

Katha Lake

Prince of Wales Island

Larsen Sound

Garry Lake

Aberdeen Lake

Kazon

Dubawnt Lake

Kamilukuak Lake

Selwyn Lake

Wholdaia Lake

Snowbird Lake

McClintock Channel

Gateshead Island

Queen Maud Gulf

Back

Dunvegan Lake

Collinson Peninsula

Cambridge Bay

Kent Peninsula

Dease Strait

Aylmer Lake

Reliance

Lutselk'e

Hjalmar Lake

Storkerson Peninsula

Victoria Island

Bathurst Inlet

Umingmaktok

Contwoyto Lake

Echo Bay

Lac la Martre

Rae Lakes

Rae-Edzo

Yellowknife

Great Slave Lake

Stefansson Island

Hadley Bay

Wollaston Peninsula

Coronation Gulf

Kugluktuk

Napaktulik Lake

Hottah Lake

Wha Ti

Horn Mountains

Passage Point

Prince Albert Peninsula

Prince Albert Sound

Dolphin and Union Straits

Great Bear Lake

Déline

Fort Simpson

Minto Inlet

Uluqsaqtuuq

Cape Baring

N O R T H W E S T   T E R R I T O R I E S

Wrigley

Franklin Mountains

Banks Island

Prince of Wales Strait

Amundsen Gulf

Cape Parry

Paulatuk

Horton

Coville Lake

Fort Good Hope

Norman Wells

Tulita

Kcaahuk

Thesiger Bay

Cape Darnley

Franklin Bay

Anderson

Mackenzie

Kerr Peak 9718ft (2762m)

Mackenzie Mountains

Cape Bathurst

Arctic Red

Selwyn Mountains

Beaufort Sea

Cape Dalhousie

Tuktoyaktuk

Tsiigehtchic

Norman Wells

Mt Sir James MacBrien 9062ft (2762m)

Kugmallit Bay

Inuvik

Peel

Ogilvie Mountains

Mackenzie Bay

Aklavik

Fort McPherson

Old Crow

Arctic Circle

Pelly Crossing

Pelly

Mayo

Herschel Island

A L A S K A   (U.S.A.)

Arctic Circle

Dawson

Yukon

Y U K O N

Faro

Beaver Creek

Carmacks

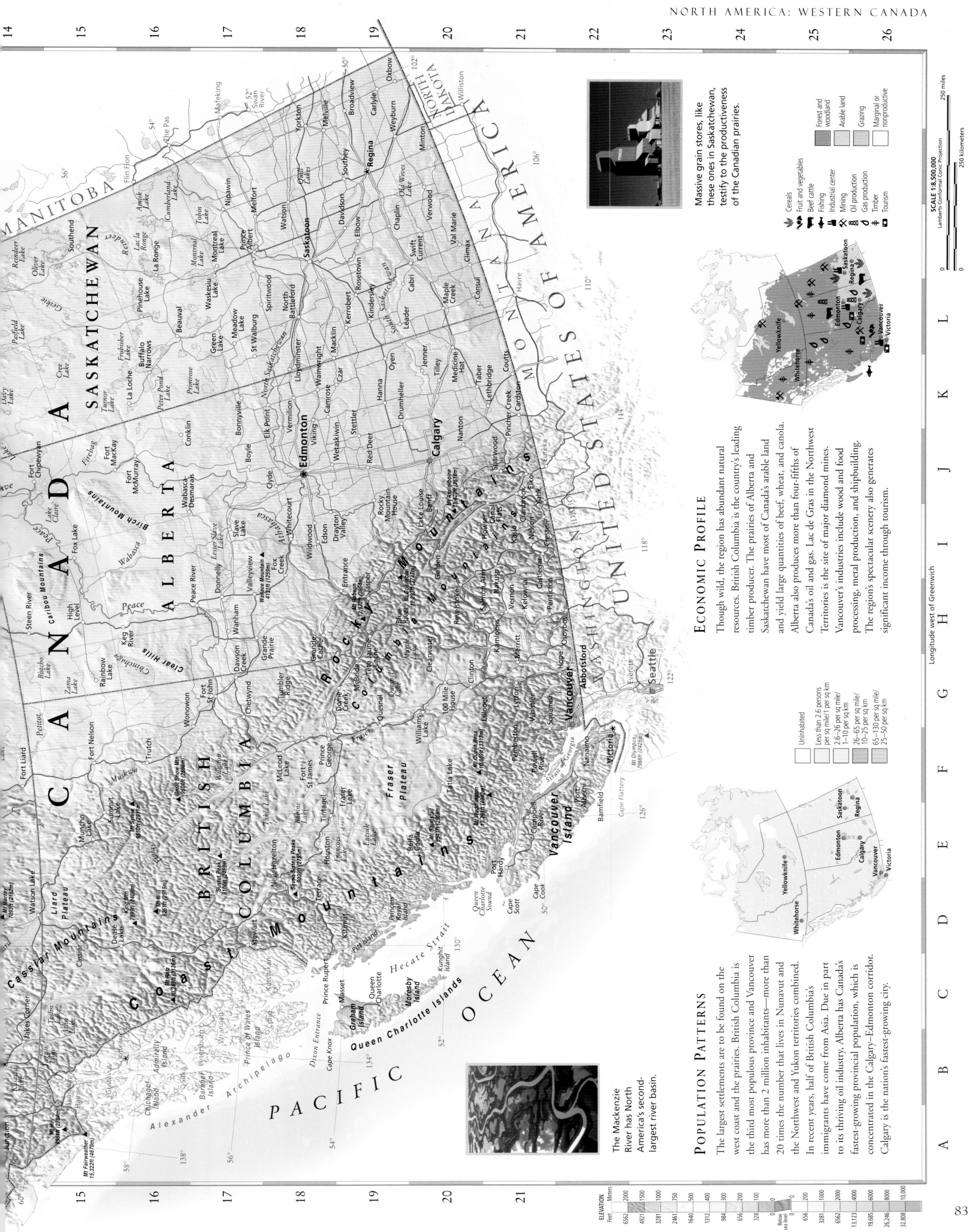

Massive grain stores, like these ones in Saskatchewan, testify to the productiveness of the Canadian prairies.

The Mackenzie River has North America's second-largest river basin.

ECONOMIC PROFILE

Though wild, the region has abundant natural resources. British Columbia is the country's leading timber producer. The prairies of Alberta and Saskatchewan have most of Canada's arable land and yield large quantities of beef, wheat, and canola. Alberta also produces more than four-fifths of Canada's oil and gas. Lac de Gras in the Northwest Territories is the site of major diamond mines. Vancouver's industries include wood and food processing, metal production, and shipbuilding. The region's spectacular scenery also generates significant income through tourism.

POPULATION PATTERNS

The largest settlements are to be found on the west coast and the prairies. British Columbia is the third most populous province and Vancouver has more than 2 million inhabitants—more than 20 times the number that lives in Nunavut and the Northwest and Yukon territories combined.

In recent years, half of British Columbia's immigrants have come from Asia. Due in part to its thriving oil industry, Alberta has Canada's fastest-growing provincial population, which is concentrated in the Calgary–Edmonton corridor. Calgary is the nation's fastest-growing city.

SCALE 1:8,500,000
Lamberts Conformal Conic Projection

Longitude west of Greenwich

Legend — land use

Forest and woodland
Arable land
Grazing
Marginal or nonproductive

Cereals
Fruit and vegetables
Beef cattle
Fishing
Industrial center
Mining
Oil production
Gas production
Timber
Tourism

Population density

Uninhabited
Less than 2.6 persons per sq mile/1 per sq km
2.6–26 per sq mile/1–10 per sq km
26–65 per sq mile/10–25 per sq km
65–130 per sq mile/25–50 per sq km

ELEVATION

Feet	Meters
6562	2000
4921	1500
3281	1000
2461	750
1640	500
1312	400
984	300
656	200
328	100
0	0
Below sea level	
656	200
3281	1000
13,123	4000
19,685	6000
26,246	8000
32,808	10,000

EASTERN CANADA

Manitoba, New Brunswick, Newfoundland and Labrador, Nova Scotia, Nunavut, Ontario, Prince Edward Island, Québec, St Pierre and Miquelon

Underpinned by the ancient Canadian Shield, Eastern Canada consists of a horseshoe-shaped swathe of mostly low-lying land that curls around and inclines gently toward the shores of Hudson Bay. Mountains rise along the eastern fringes of the shield, on Baffin Island, and in Labrador, New Brunswick, and eastern Québec. North America's great belt of lake-studded boreal forest blankets much of Manitoba, Ontario, and Québec, separating the windswept northern tundra from a narrow temperate zone in the south that is home to most of Canada's cities, businesses, and industries, as well as its capital. Before coming under British control in the 18th century, this region was settled by groups of French immigrants. Many remained, and the province of Québec is still culturally distinct from the rest of Canada in that the vast majority of its inhabitants are of French descent and French-speaking. Its demands for greater autonomy constitute Canada's most problematic and potentially disruptive political issue.

In Hudson Bay, polar bears live onshore in summer but hunt seals across the pack ice throughout winter.

Founded in 1642 on an island in the St Lawrence River, Montréal is Canada's second-largest city.

POPULATION PATTERNS

Six out of every ten Canadians live in the provinces of Ontario and Québec, which also encompass 15 of the country's 25 largest cities. Ontario has been the focus of recent immigration to Canada, absorbing half of all incomers in the 1990s. By far the densest settlement occurs along the Great Lakes–St Lawrence lowlands. In Manitoba, the population is concentrated in the productive southern prairies, but mechanization of agricultural processes has kept numbers low. Newfoundland and Labrador's population has dropped sharply in recent years, mainly as a result of migration to other provinces. The north is the site of far-flung indigenous communities and outposts founded on resource exploitation.

Uninhabited

Less than 2.6 persons per sq mile/1 per sq km

2.6–26 per sq mile/ 1–10 per sq km

26–65 per sq mile/ 10–25 per sq km

65–130 per sq mile/ 25–50 per sq km

130–260 per sq mile/ 50–100 per sq km

260–520 per sq mile/ 100–200 per sq km

520–1040 per sq mile/ 200–400 per sq km

1040–2080 per sq mile/ 400–800 per sq km

More than 2080 per sq mile/ 800 per sq km

ECONOMIC PROFILE

Ontario and Québec supply most of Canada's gold, and Sudbury in Ontario produces 20 percent of the world's nickel as well as large amounts of copper, silver, gold, and iron ore. Large gas reserves lie off Cape Sable Island in Nova Scotia, and oil platforms operate off the coast of Newfoundland. Almost all of the energy requirements of Newfoundland and Labrador, Québec, and Manitoba are met by hydroelectric power. Newfoundland's Grand Banks are Canada's richest fisheries, although overfishing has significantly reduced catches since the mid-1970s. Southern Ontario and Québec form the country's industrial and commercial heartland.

Forest and woodland

Arable land

Marginal or nonproductive

Cereals
Fruit
Beef cattle
Fishing
Industrial center
Mining
Timber

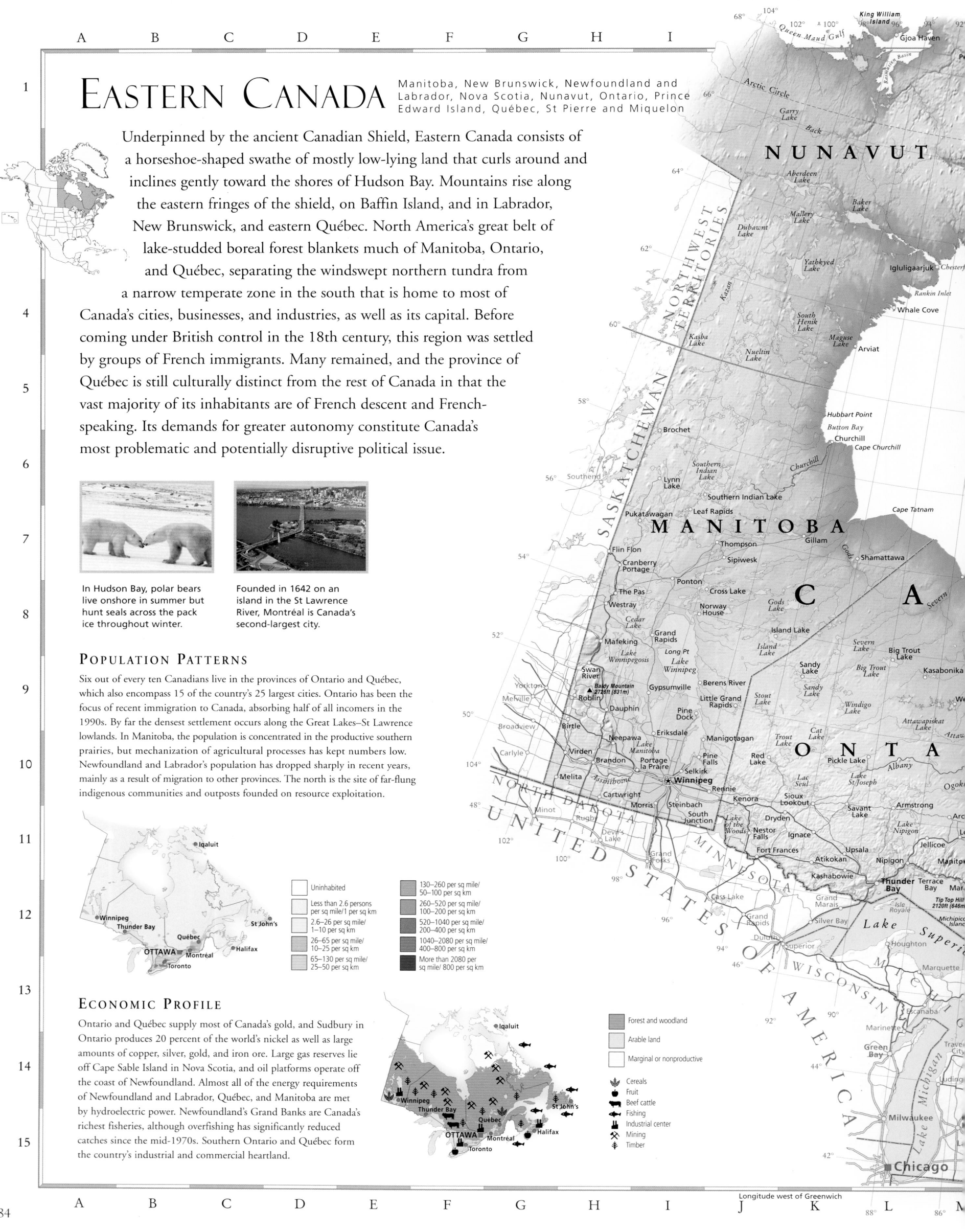

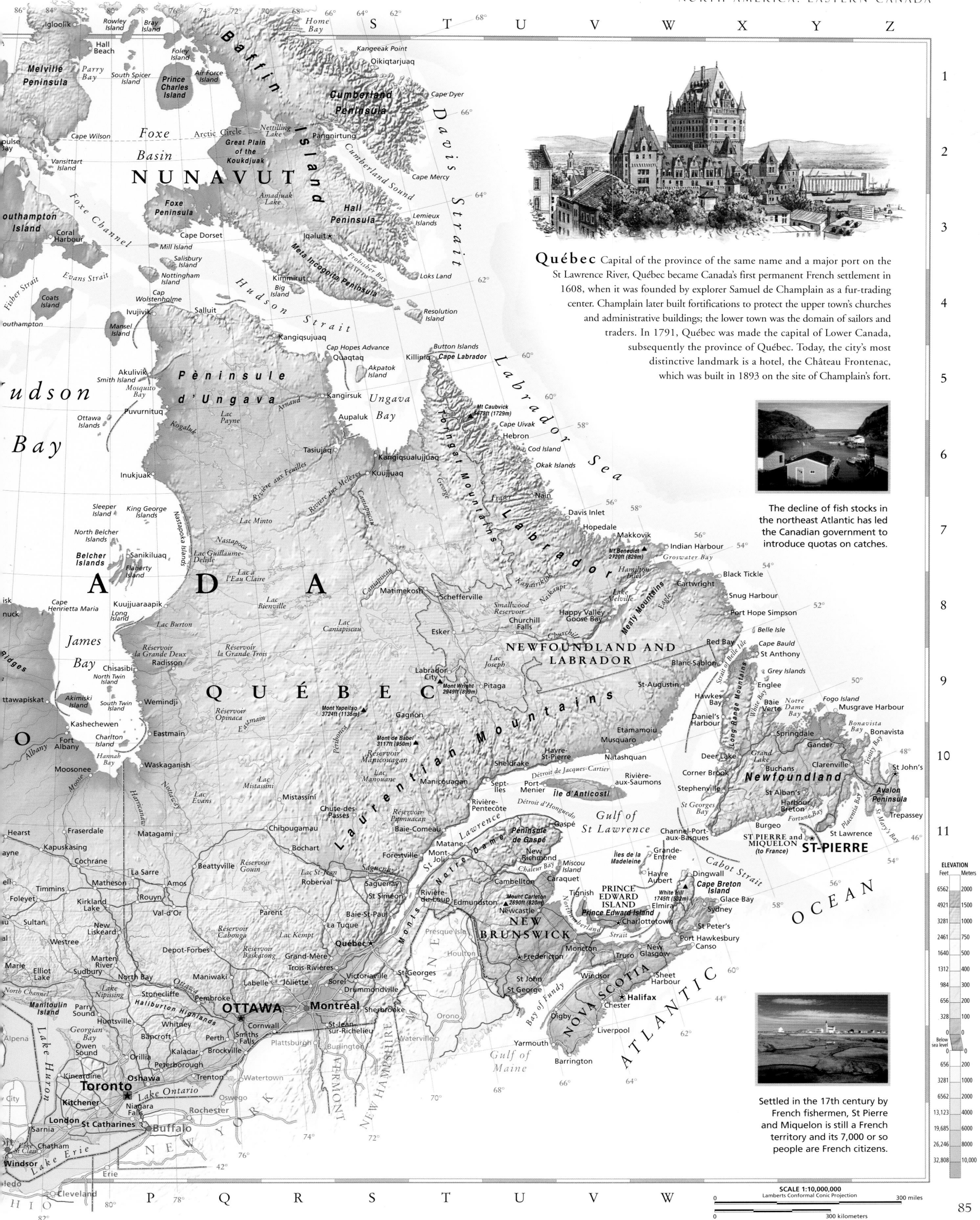

Québec Capital of the province of the same name and a major port on the St Lawrence River, Québec became Canada's first permanent French settlement in 1608, when it was founded by explorer Samuel de Champlain as a fur-trading center. Champlain later built fortifications to protect the upper town's churches and administrative buildings; the lower town was the domain of sailors and traders. In 1791, Québec was made the capital of Lower Canada, subsequently the province of Québec. Today, the city's most distinctive landmark is a hotel, the Château Frontenac, which was built in 1893 on the site of Champlain's fort.

The decline of fish stocks in the northeast Atlantic has led the Canadian government to introduce quotas on catches.

Settled in the 17th century by French fishermen, St Pierre and Miquelon is still a French territory and its 7,000 or so people are French citizens.

SCALE 1:10,000,000
Lamberts Conformal Conic Projection

0   300 miles

0   300 kilometers

ELEVATION

Feet	Meters
6562	2000
4921	1500
3281	1000
2461	750
1640	500
1312	400
984	300
656	200
328	100
0	0
Below sea level	
656	200
3281	1000
6562	2000
13,123	4000
19,685	6000
26,246	8000
32,808	10,000

SOUTHEASTERN CANADA

New Brunswick, Nova Scotia, Ontario, Prince Edward Island, Québec

Flowing northeast out of Lake Ontario, the St Lawrence River courses for almost 800 miles (1,300 km) to the wide Gulf of St Lawrence and the Atlantic Ocean. The river was the main entry point to the interior for early European adventurers, and in the 17th century the country's first ports were founded on its banks by French explorers. The temperate climate and fertile soils of the river valley and the northern shores of Lakes Ontario and Erie form a stark contrast to the cold, waterlogged plateaus to the north and the wet, precipitous terrain of the Appalachian Mountains to the south. Settlers consequently clustered on these lowlands, and today this is Canada's most populous region, the site of its largest cities, and the home of its national capital, Ottawa.

The commercial center and capital of Nova Scotia, Halifax began as a French fishing port in the 18th century.

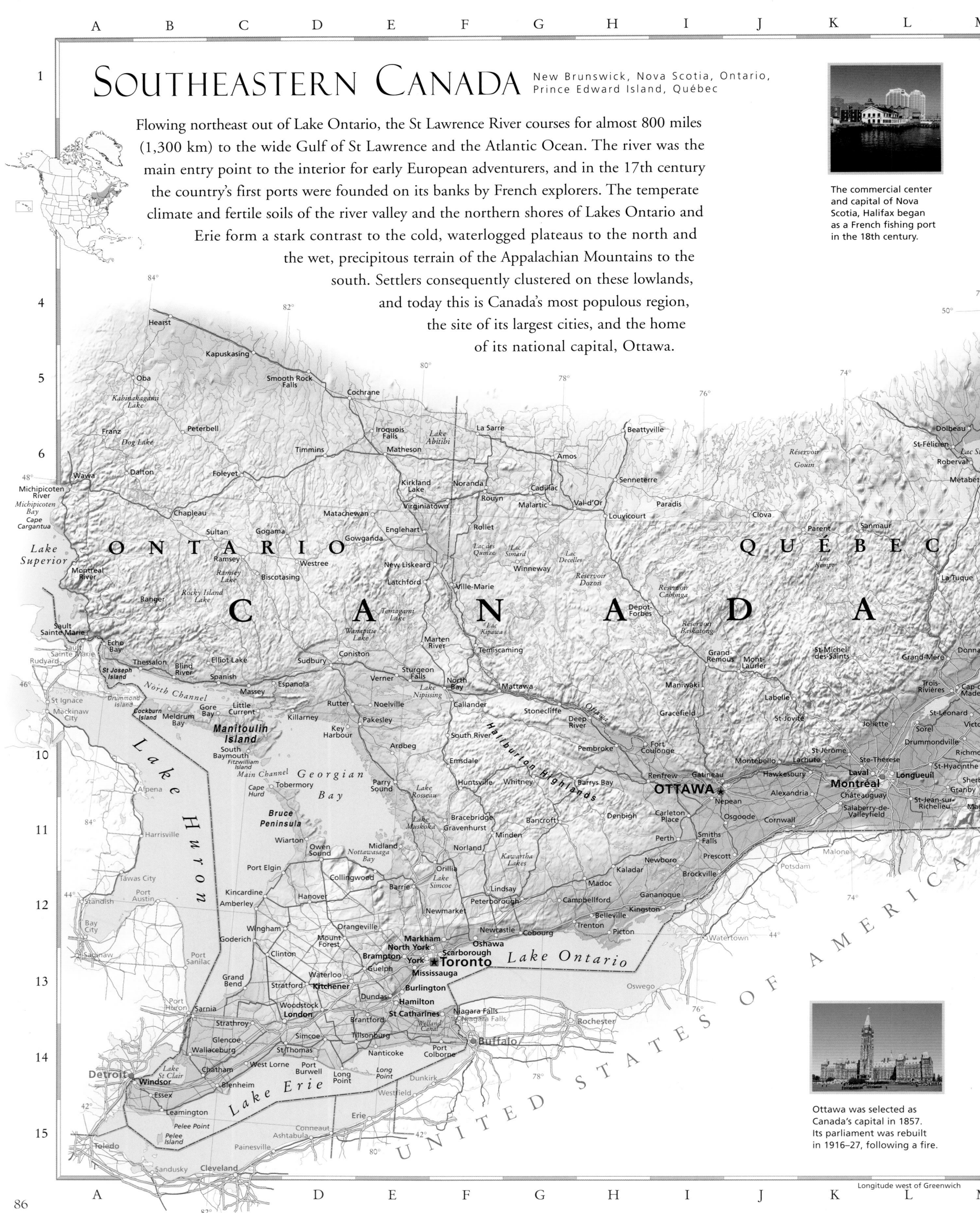

Ottawa was selected as Canada's capital in 1857. Its parliament was rebuilt in 1916–27, following a fire.

Longitude west of Greenwich

86

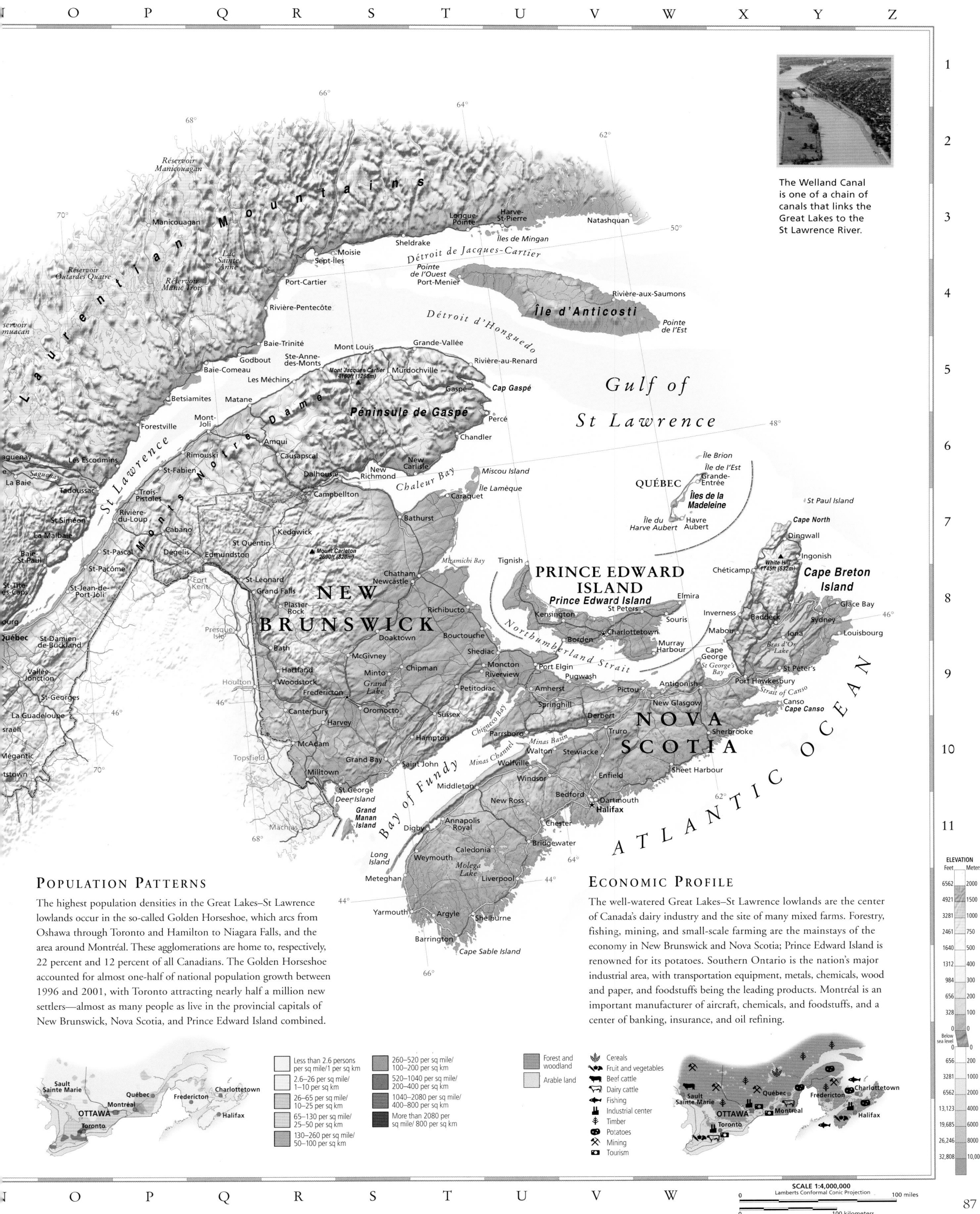

The Welland Canal is one of a chain of canals that links the Great Lakes to the St Lawrence River.

POPULATION PATTERNS

The highest population densities in the Great Lakes–St Lawrence lowlands occur in the so-called Golden Horseshoe, which arcs from Oshawa through Toronto and Hamilton to Niagara Falls, and the area around Montréal. These agglomerations are home to, respectively, 22 percent and 12 percent of all Canadians. The Golden Horseshoe accounted for almost one-half of national population growth between 1996 and 2001, with Toronto attracting nearly half a million new settlers—almost as many people as live in the provincial capitals of New Brunswick, Nova Scotia, and Prince Edward Island combined.

ECONOMIC PROFILE

The well-watered Great Lakes–St Lawrence lowlands are the center of Canada's dairy industry and the site of many mixed farms. Forestry, fishing, mining, and small-scale farming are the mainstays of the economy in New Brunswick and Nova Scotia; Prince Edward Island is renowned for its potatoes. Southern Ontario is the nation's major industrial area, with transportation equipment, metals, chemicals, wood and paper, and foodstuffs being the leading products. Montréal is an important manufacturer of aircraft, chemicals, and foodstuffs, and a center of banking, insurance, and oil refining.

Population density

| Less than 2.6 persons per sq mile/1 per sq km |
| 2.6–26 per sq mile/1–10 per sq km |
| 26–65 per sq mile/10–25 per sq km |
| 65–130 per sq mile/25–50 per sq km |
| 130–260 per sq mile/50–100 per sq km |
| 260–520 per sq mile/100–200 per sq km |
| 520–1040 per sq mile/200–400 per sq km |
| 1040–2080 per sq mile/400–800 per sq km |
| More than 2080 per sq mile/800 per sq km |

Forest and woodland
Arable land

Cereals
Fruit and vegetables
Beef cattle
Dairy cattle
Fishing
Industrial center
Timber
Potatoes
Mining
Tourism

ELEVATION

Feet	Meters
6562	2000
4921	1500
3281	1000
2461	750
1640	500
1312	400
984	300
656	200
328	100
0 Below sea level	0
656	200
3281	1000
6562	2000
13,123	4000
19,685	6000
26,246	8000
32,808	10,000

SCALE 1:4,000,000
Lamberts Conformal Conic Projection
0 — 100 miles
0 — 100 kilometers

MEXICO

Mexico's interior is dominated by a vast, V-shaped plateau known as the Mesa Central. Extending from the U.S. border southward beyond Mexico City, it is edged by two major mountain ranges, the Sierra Madre Occidental and the Sierra Madre Oriental. A slender, broken coastal plain runs along the Pacific shore, converging in the far northwest with the long, rugged, and extremely arid arm of Baja California. At the southern end of the wide, humid east-coast lowlands, the Yucatan Peninsula, a flat, low swathe of limestone, juts into the Gulf of Mexico. In the early 16th century, Spain rapidly conquered the prosperous native civilizations of the Aztec and the Maya. Its subsequent colonization of the entire region resulted in the eradication of many Amerindian communities. Mexico shook off Spanish rule in 1821 and became a republic two years later, though it experienced revolutions and civil wars for the next 100 years. In the 20th century, explosive population growth limited the benefits of genuine social and economic progress.

POPULATION PATTERNS

Mexico's population has increased by 500 percent since 1915 and has become highly urbanized in recent decades—75 percent of Mexicans live in towns and cities. By far the most densely populated area is the southern belt linking Guadalajara, Mexico City, Puebla, and Veracruz. Fueled by U.S.-backed industrial expansion, the northern border towns are also growing rapidly. Population density is lowest in the arid north and in Chiapas and eastern Yucatan. About 60 percent of Mexicans are mestizos, 30 percent Amerindian, and 9 percent of European origin.

Less than 2.6 persons per sq mile/1 per sq km
2.6–26 per sq mile/1–10 per sq km
26–65 per sq mile/10–25 per sq km
65–130 per sq mile/25–50 per sq km
130–260 per sq mile/50–100 per sq km
260–520 per sq mile/100–200 per sq km
520–1040 per sq mile/200–400 per sq km

ECONOMIC PROFILE

Mexico has enormous mineral resources, limited arable land, and expanding industries. It is one of the world's largest producers of oil—its main source of income—and the largest supplier of silver; it also has sizable gas and coal reserves. Industries, led by the processing of oil, food, and metals and the manufacture of machinery, chemicals, and textiles, are concentrated in Mexico City. Only about one-fifth of the country is arable; half of this area is given over to corn cultivation. Cattle ranching is the main agricultural activity in the arid north. Tourism is now the nation's second-biggest source of revenue.

Forest and woodland
Arable land
Grazing
Marginal or nonproductive

Corn (maize)
Cotton
Coffee
Sugarcane
Industrial center
Mining
Oil production
Fishing
Beef cattle
Tourism

ELEVATION
Feet / Meters
32,808 / 10,000
26,246 / 8000
19,685 / 6000
13,123 / 4000
6562 / 2000
3281 / 1000
656 / 200
0 / 0
Below sea level / 0
0 / 0
656 / 200
1312 / 400
1640 / 500
2461 / 750
3281 / 1000
4921 / 1500
6562 / 2000

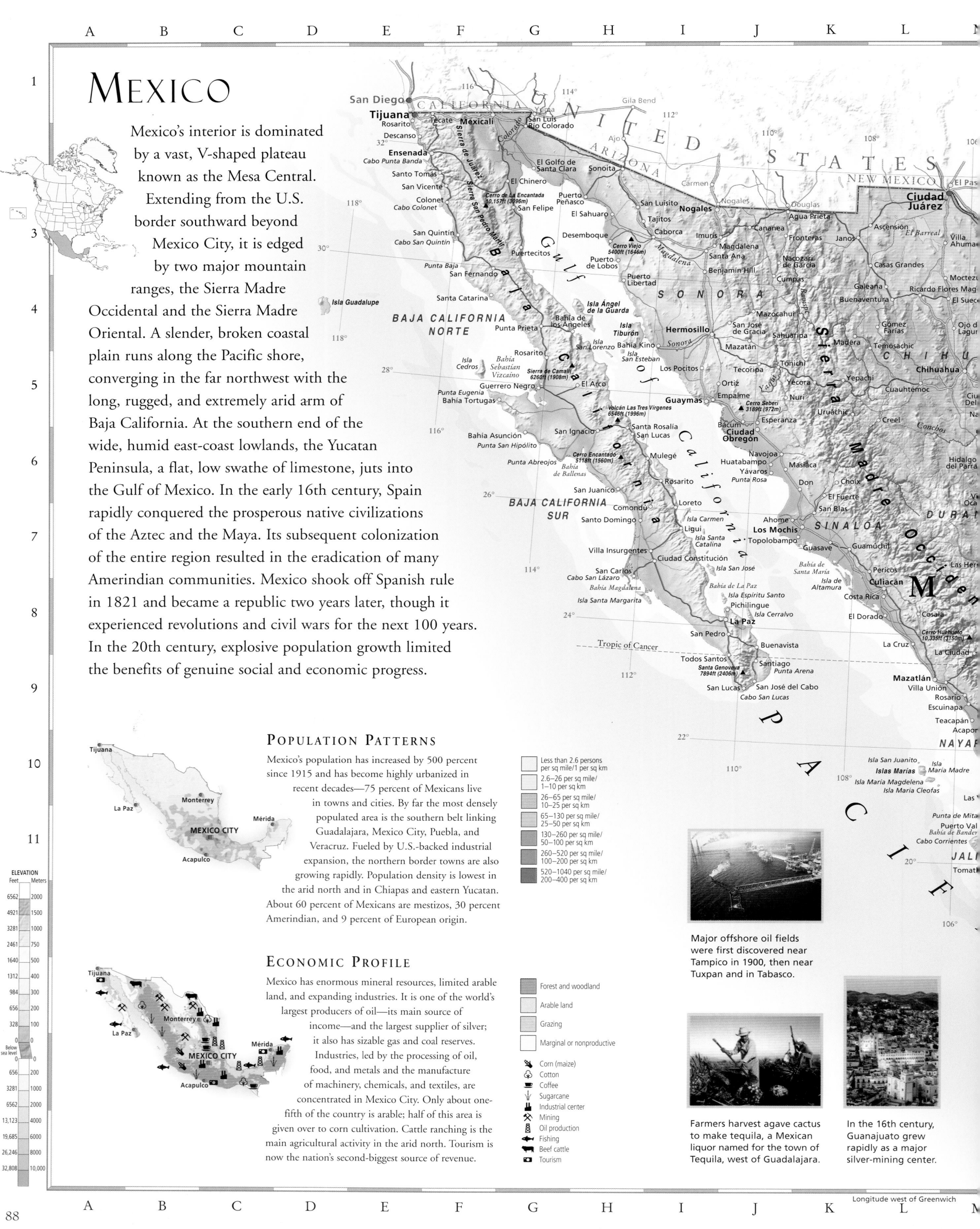

Major offshore oil fields were first discovered near Tampico in 1900, then near Tuxpan and in Tabasco.

Farmers harvest agave cactus to make tequila, a Mexican liquor named for the town of Tequila, west of Guadalajara.

In the 16th century, Guanajuato grew rapidly as a major silver-mining center.

Longitude west of Greenwich

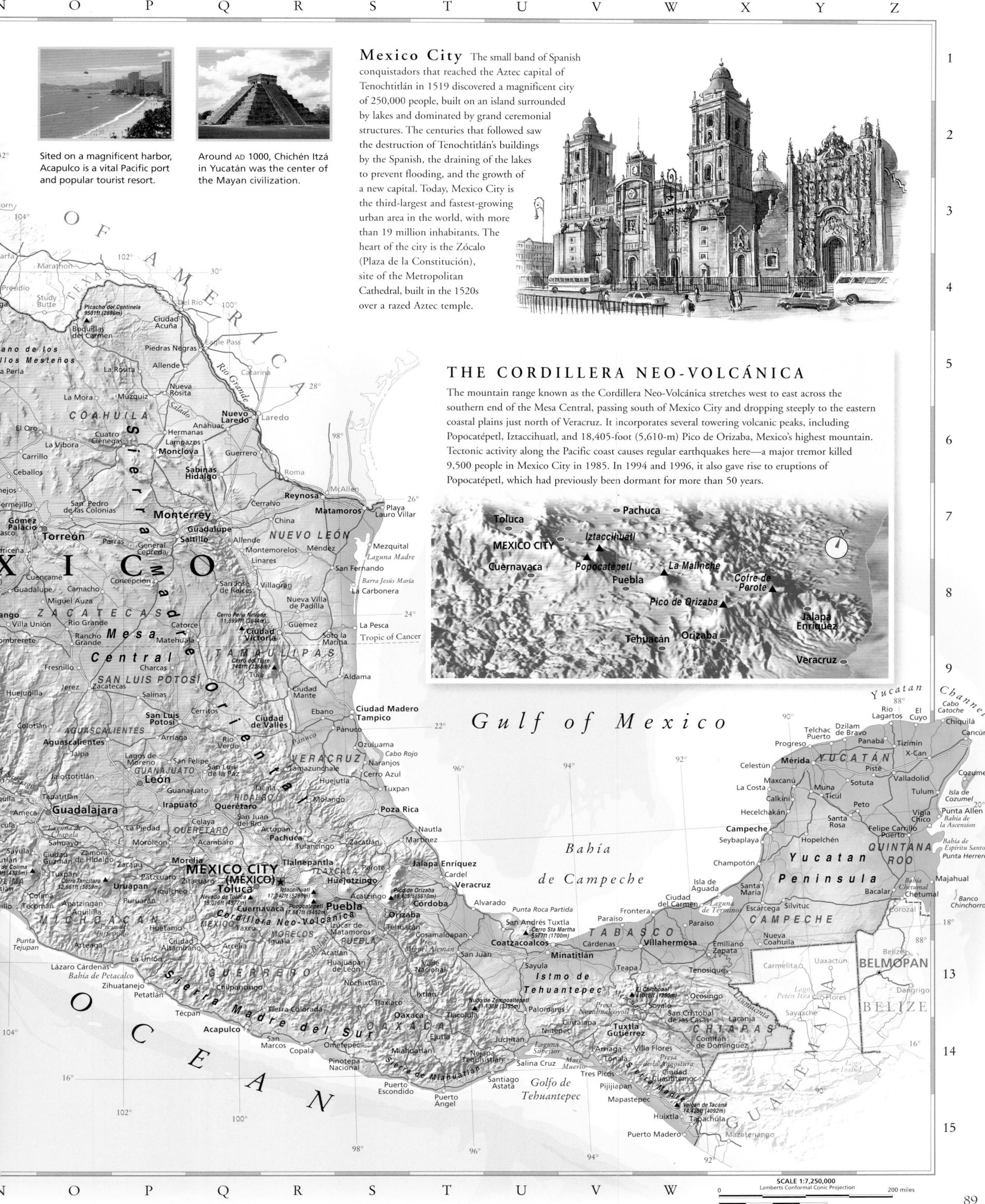

Sited on a magnificent harbor, Acapulco is a vital Pacific port and popular tourist resort.

Around AD 1000, Chichén Itzá in Yucatán was the center of the Mayan civilization.

Mexico City The small band of Spanish conquistadors that reached the Aztec capital of Tenochtitlán in 1519 discovered a magnificent city of 250,000 people, built on an island surrounded by lakes and dominated by grand ceremonial structures. The centuries that followed saw the destruction of Tenochtitlán's buildings by the Spanish, the draining of the lakes to prevent flooding, and the growth of a new capital. Today, Mexico City is the third-largest and fastest-growing urban area in the world, with more than 19 million inhabitants. The heart of the city is the Zócalo (Plaza de la Constitución), site of the Metropolitan Cathedral, built in the 1520s over a razed Aztec temple.

THE CORDILLERA NEO-VOLCÁNICA

The mountain range known as the Cordillera Neo-Volcánica stretches west to east across the southern end of the Mesa Central, passing south of Mexico City and dropping steeply to the eastern coastal plains just north of Veracruz. It incorporates several towering volcanic peaks, including Popocatépetl, Iztaccihuatl, and 18,405-foot (5,610-m) Pico de Orizaba, Mexico's highest mountain. Tectonic activity along the Pacific coast causes regular earthquakes here—a major tremor killed 9,500 people in Mexico City in 1985. In 1994 and 1996, it also gave rise to eruptions of Popocatépetl, which had previously been dormant for more than 50 years.

SCALE 1:7,250,000
Lamberts Conformal Conic Projection

200 miles

200 kilometers

89

CENTRAL AMERICA

Belize, Costa Rica, El Salvador, Guatemala, Honduras, Nicaragua, Panama

From the Mexican border, Central America dog-legs and tapers southeastward, connecting with Colombia in South America at the eastern end of the Isthmus of Panama. Forested mountain ranges parallel the Pacific coast, spreading east across Honduras and northern Nicaragua, and covering four-fifths of the entire landmass. Narrow coastal plains line the Pacific shore; wider, swampy lowlands border the Caribbean Sea. With the exception of the former British colony of Belize, the nations of Central America share a predominantly Hispanic culture stemming from a long period of Spanish domination and shaped to varying degrees by other imported and indigenous cultures. Central America's recent history has been clouded by coups, periods of repressive military rule, and guerilla warfare, especially in the north. The southern nations of Costa Rica and Panama have the highest standards of living and have been more stable, although the U.S.A. invaded Panama in 1989 to remove a corrupt military regime.

POPULATION PATTERNS

Most of the population is mestizo, though the ethnic makeup varies from country to country. Almost one-third of people in Belize are of African origin, and most Costa Ricans are of European descent. Indigenous peoples are in a small minority in most countries except Guatemala, where they form almost half of the population. Settlement has favored the west, especially the cool, fertile uplands, over the humid Caribbean plains, and the north is more populous—one-third of Central Americans live in Guatemala. Urbanization ranges from just over 40 percent in Guatemala to almost 66 percent in El Salvador.

	Less than 2.6 persons per sq mile/1 per sq km
	2.6–26 per sq mile/1–10 per sq km
	26–65 per sq mile/10–25 per sq km
	65–130 per sq mile/25–50 per sq km
	130–260 per sq mile/50–100 per sq km

ECONOMIC PROFILE

Development is hampered by political unrest, poor infrastructure, and inequitable distribution of land. Many people grow corn, beans, squashes, and fruit for their own consumption, but much of the best farmland has been turned into large, often foreign-owned, cattle ranches and plantations producing sugar, bananas, and coffee. Mineral resources are, for the most part, scanty or undeveloped. Forests provide timber and chicle (used in chewing gum), but are not harvested sustainably. Industries are limited mainly to food processing and textiles. Services are most significant in Panama, where a free-trade zone is centered on Colón.

- Fruit
- Bananas
- Cotton
- Coffee
- Sugarcane
- Shellfish
- Beef cattle
- Timber
- Industrial center

- Forest and woodland
- Arable land
- Grazing
- Marginal or nonproductive

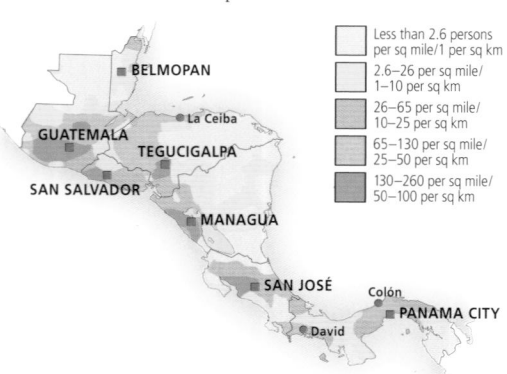

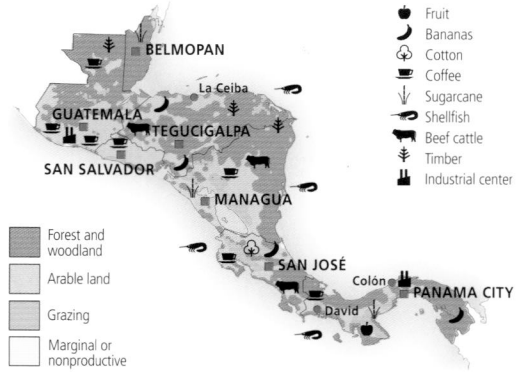

Wildlife-rich rain forests are among the attractions that draw over 1 million overseas visitors a year to Costa Rica.

Lake Nicaragua is the world's only freshwater lake that is home to saltwater fish such as sharks and swordfish.

SCALE 1:4,000,000
Lamberts Conformal Conic Projection
100 miles
100 kilometers

Longitude west of Greenwich

Tegucigalpa Cathedral, a baroque, 18th-century construction, is the focal point of Honduras's capital.

The ruined city of Tikal, in northern Guatemala, was a ceremonial center of Mayan culture from 300 BC to AD 900.

Guatemala The National Palace stands on Plaza Mayor (also known as Parque Central), a popular gathering place at the heart of Guatemala, the capital of the country of the same name and the largest city in Central America, with close to 4 million inhabitants. Guatemala became the capital of Spanish-ruled Guatemala after the first capital, Antigua Guatemala, was flattened by an earthquake in 1773. Much of the modern capital, including the National Palace (completed in 1943), dates from a period of reconstruction following a series of violent tremors in 1917–18, which lasted for six weeks and razed large areas of the city center.

Honduras and Costa Rica are among the world's leading banana producers.

THE ISTHMUS OF PANAMA

The narrowest and one of the lowest points in Central America, the Isthmus of Panama was an obvious choice for the site of a canal linking the Pacific and Atlantic oceans. The idea was first proposed by the Spanish in the 16th century; work began in 1881 and was completed with U.S. assistance in 1914. Measuring 51 miles (82 km) in length, the canal can save ships traveling from the east to west coasts of the U.S.A. up to 8,000 miles (12,900 km) of sailing.

THE WEST INDIES

Antigua and Barbuda, The Bahamas, Barbados, Cuba, Dominica,
Dominican Republic, Grenada, Haiti, Jamaica, St Kitts and Nevis,
St Lucia, St Vincent and the Grenadines, Trinidad and Tobago

Forming the northern boundary of the Caribbean Sea, the islands
of the West Indies arc east then south from Florida in the U.S.A.
to the north coast of South America. They include two
major island groups: the Greater Antilles, consisting
of the large islands of Cuba, Hispaniola,
Jamaica, and Puerto Rico, and the
Lesser Antilles, a string of small,
high, chiefly volcanic islands. Following
the arrival of Christopher Columbus in
1492 at San Salvador in The Bahamas
(his belief that he had reached Asia led to the
region being called the "West" Indies), the islands were
fought over by various imperial powers, who imported huge
numbers of African slaves to work on plantations. Today, this
history is reflected in the region's cultural diversity and large
number of dependencies, including French Guadeloupe,
British Montserrat, and the Netherlands Antilles.

The twin volcanic peaks of
the Pitons rise almost sheer
from the sea near Soufrière
on the island of St Lucia.

Over 100 million tourists visit
the West Indies each year.
Tourism generates two-fifths
of the region's GNP.

ELEVATION

Feet	Meters
6562	2000
4921	1500
3281	1000
2461	750
1640	500
1312	400
984	300
656	200
328	100
0	0
Below sea level	
0	0
656	200
1312	1000
6562	2000
13,123	4000
19,685	6000
26,246	8000
32,808	10,000

UNITED STATES OF AMERICA

THE BAHAMAS

Grand Bahama
Freeport
Pelican Point
Cooper's Town
Marsh Harbour
Great Abaco
Cornwall
Bimini Islands
Alice Town
Mastic Point
New Providence
★ NASSAU
Andros Town
Eleuthera
Tarpum
Andros Island
Mangrove Cay
Cat Island
Kemp's Bay
Exuma Cays
Great Exuma Island
Long
Deadman

Straits of Florida
Santaren Channel
Great Bahama Bank
Cay Sal
Anguilla Cay

Tropic of Cancer

HAVANA (LA HABANA) ★
Guanabacoa
Matanzas
Cárdenas
Archipiélago de Sabana
Mariel
Artemisa
Güines
Colón
Sagua la Grande
Archipiélago de Camagüey
Minas de Matahambre
Los Palacios
Surgidero de Batabanó
Jagüey Grande
Santa Clara
Caibarién
Cayo Romano
Guane
Pinar del Río
Golfo de Batabanó
Cienfuegos
Pico San Juan 3793ft (1156m) ▲
Esmeralda
Cayo Sabinal
Lafé
Cabo San Antonio
Cabo Corrientes
Nueva Gerona
Santa Fé
Archipiélago de los Canarreros
Cayo del Rosario
Cayo Largo
Trinidad
Sancti Spíritus
Ciego de Ávila
Minas
Nuevitas
Isla de la Juventud

CUBA

Greater
Vertientes
Camagüey
Puerto Padre
Las Tunas
Holguín
Archipiélago de los Jardines de la Reina
Santa Cruz del Sur
Cueto
Golfo de Guacanayabo
Bayamo
Sierra Maestra
Pico Turquino 6378ft (1944m) ▲
Guantá
Guantánamo Naval (to U.S
Cabo Cruz
Pilón

GEORGE TOWN
Little Cayman
Cayman Brac
Grand Cayman
CAYMAN ISLANDS (to U.K.)

Cayman Trench

Jamaica Cha

Montego Bay
Falmouth
Ocho Rios
South Negril Point
Savanna-la-Mar
Port Antonio
Mandeville
JAMAICA
★ KINGSTON

Pedro Bank

Rosalind Bank

Misteriosa Bank

Rosario Bank

BELIZE
★ BELMOPAN
Dangriga

Swan Islands (to Honduras)

Alice Shoal

Serranilla Bank

Gulf of Honduras
Islas de la Bahía
Isla de Utila
Isla de Guanaja
Isla de Roatán
Puerto Barrios
La Ceiba
Cabo Camarón
Punta Patuca

Banco Gorda

HONDURAS

Cabo Gracias á Dios
South Cay

Cayos Miskitos

Mosquito Coast

Isla de Providencia (to Colombia)

Ca ri b

NICARAGUA

Punta de Perlas
Rama
Laguna de Perlas
Bluefields
Islas del Maíz (to Nicaragua)
Isla de San Andrés (to Colombia)
Cayos de Albuquerque (to Colombia)
Punta del Mono
San Carlos
Bahía de San Juan del Norte
San Juan del Norte

COSTA RICA
Acoyapa
Limón
★ SAN JOSÉ
Almirante
Golfo de los Mosquitos
Colón
Gulf of Darién
Isthmus of Panama
PANAMA CITY (PANAMÁ) ★
Cartagena
Golfo de Uraba

PANAMA

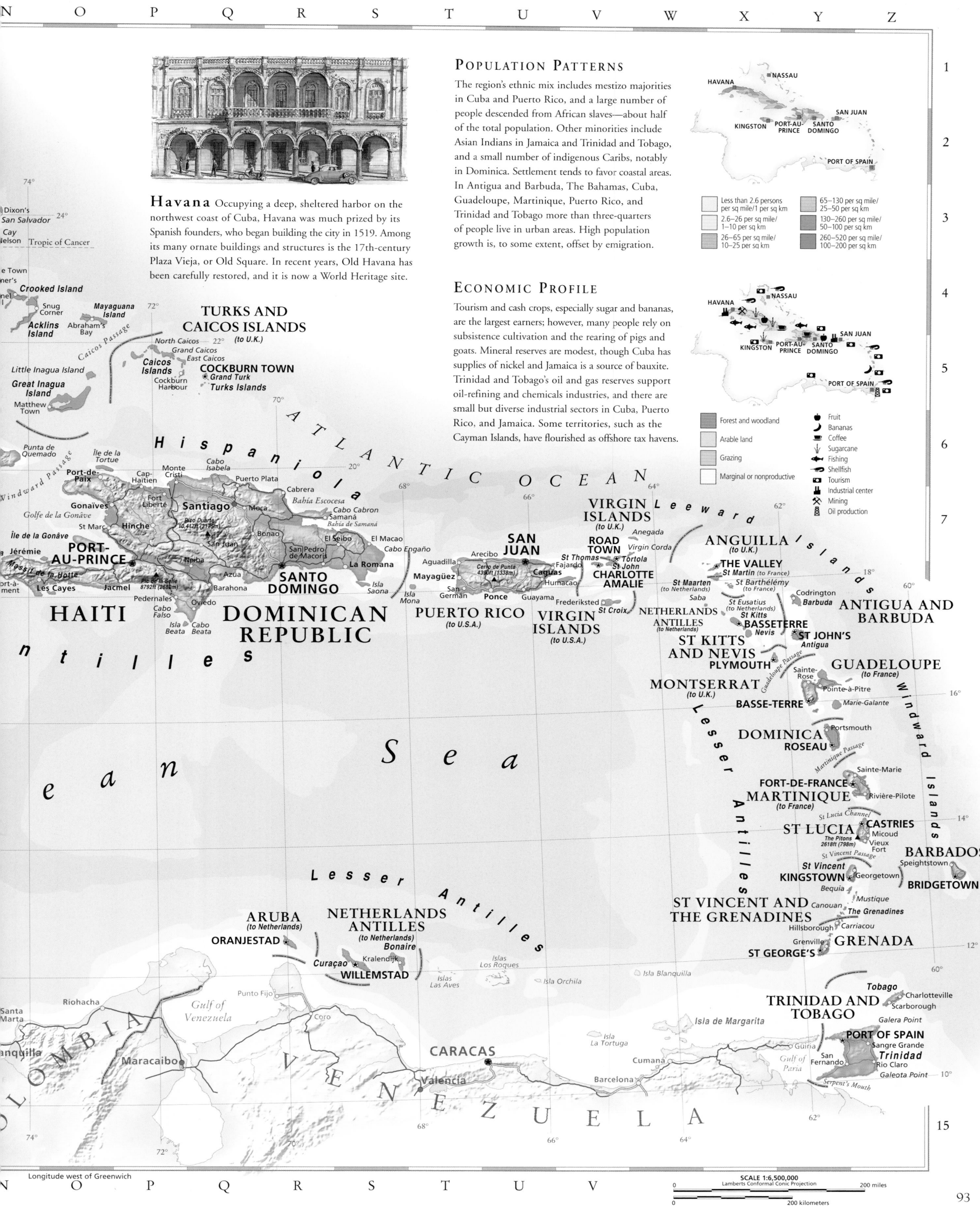

Havana Occupying a deep, sheltered harbor on the northwest coast of Cuba, Havana was much prized by its Spanish founders, who began building the city in 1519. Among its many ornate buildings and structures is the 17th-century Plaza Vieja, or Old Square. In recent years, Old Havana has been carefully restored, and it is now a World Heritage site.

POPULATION PATTERNS

The region's ethnic mix includes mestizo majorities in Cuba and Puerto Rico, and a large number of people descended from African slaves—about half of the total population. Other minorities include Asian Indians in Jamaica and Trinidad and Tobago, and a small number of indigenous Caribs, notably in Dominica. Settlement tends to favor coastal areas. In Antigua and Barbuda, The Bahamas, Cuba, Guadeloupe, Martinique, Puerto Rico, and Trinidad and Tobago more than three-quarters of people live in urban areas. High population growth is, to some extent, offset by emigration.

HAVANA · NASSAU · KINGSTON · PORT-AU-PRINCE · SANTO DOMINGO · SAN JUAN · PORT OF SPAIN

Less than 2.6 persons per sq mile/1 per sq km
2.6–26 per sq mile/1–10 per sq km
26–65 per sq mile/10–25 per sq km
65–130 per sq mile/25–50 per sq km
130–260 per sq mile/50–100 per sq km
260–520 per sq mile/100–200 per sq km

ECONOMIC PROFILE

Tourism and cash crops, especially sugar and bananas, are the largest earners; however, many people rely on subsistence cultivation and the rearing of pigs and goats. Mineral reserves are modest, though Cuba has supplies of nickel and Jamaica is a source of bauxite. Trinidad and Tobago's oil and gas reserves support oil-refining and chemicals industries, and there are small but diverse industrial sectors in Cuba, Puerto Rico, and Jamaica. Some territories, such as the Cayman Islands, have flourished as offshore tax havens.

HAVANA · NASSAU · KINGSTON · PORT-AU-PRINCE · SANTO DOMINGO · SAN JUAN · PORT OF SPAIN

Forest and woodland
Arable land
Grazing
Marginal or nonproductive

Fruit
Bananas
Coffee
Sugarcane
Fishing
Shellfish
Tourism
Industrial center
Mining
Oil production

Map labels

Dixon's · San Salvador · Cay Nelson · Tropic of Cancer · 74° · 24°

Crooked Island · Snug Corner · Acklins Island · Abraham's Bay · Mayaguana Island · 72°

TURKS AND CAICOS ISLANDS (to U.K.)

North Caicos · Grand Caicos · East Caicos · 22° · Caicos Islands · Cockburn Harbour · **COCKBURN TOWN** · Grand Turk · Turks Islands · 70°

Little Inagua Island · Great Inagua Island · Matthew Town

Punta de Quemado · Île de la Tortue · Monte Cristi · Cabo Isabela · 20° · Puerto Plata · Cabrera · Bahía Escocesa · Cabo Cabron · Samaná · Bahía de Samaná

Hispaniola

ATLANTIC OCEAN · 68° · 66° · 64°

Port-de-Paix · Cap-Haïtien · Fort Liberté · **Santiago** · Moca · Bonao · San Juan · El Seibo · El Macao · Cabo Engaño · 62°

Windward Passage · Gonaïves · Golfe de la Gonâve · St Marc · Hinche · Pico Duarte 10,417ft (3175m) ▲

Île de la Gonâve · Jérémie · Massif de la Hotte · **PORT-AU-PRINCE** · Neiba · Azua · San Pedro de Macorís · La Romana · Isla Saona

Les Cayes · Jacmel · Pic de la Selle 8792ft (2680m) ▲ · Pedernales · Cabo Falso · Barahona · Oviedo · Isla Beata · Cabo Beata · **SANTO DOMINGO**

HAITI · **DOMINICAN REPUBLIC**

Aguadilla · Arecibo · **SAN JUAN** · St Thomas · Virgin Gorda · Anegada · 18°

VIRGIN ISLANDS (to U.K.) · **ROAD TOWN** · Virgin Corda · Tortola

Mayagüez · Fajardo · St John · **CHARLOTTE AMALIE** · St Martin (to France) · **THE VALLEY** · **ANGUILLA** (to U.K.)

San German · Caguas · Cerro de Punta 4390ft (1338m) ▲ · Humacao · St Croix · St Barthélemy (to France)

Ponce · Guayama · Frederiksted · St Maarten (to Netherlands) · St Eustatius (to Netherlands) · Saba · Codrington · Barbuda

Isla Mona · **PUERTO RICO** (to U.S.A.) · **VIRGIN ISLANDS** (to U.S.A.) · **NETHERLANDS ANTILLES** (to Netherlands) · St Kitts · Nevis · **BASSETERRE** · **ST JOHN'S** · Antigua

ANTIGUA AND BARBUDA

Leeward Islands · 60°

ntilles · **St KITTS AND NEVIS** · **PLYMOUTH** · Sainte-Rose · **GUADELOUPE** (to France) · Guadeloupe Passage

MONTSERRAT (to U.K.) · Pointe-à-Pitre · **BASSE-TERRE** · Marie-Galante · 16°

Windward Islands

DOMINICA · Portsmouth · **ROSEAU** · Martinique Passage

e a n · Sainte-Marie · **Lesser** · **S e a** · **FORT-DE-FRANCE** · **MARTINIQUE** (to France) · Rivière-Pilote

St Lucia Channel · **CASTRIES** · Micoud · **ST LUCIA** · The Pitons 2618ft (798m) ▲ · Vieux Fort · **BARBADOS** · Speightstown

St Vincent Passage · **St Vincent** · **KINGSTOWN** · Georgetown · **BRIDGETOWN**

Bequia · Mustique · **ST VINCENT AND THE GRENADINES** · Canouan · The Grenadines

Hillsborough · Carriacou · Grenville · **GRENADA** · 12°

ARUBA (to Netherlands) · **NETHERLANDS ANTILLES** (to Netherlands) · Bonaire · Islas Los Roques · **ST GEORGE'S**

ORANJESTAD · Curaçao · Kralendijk · Islas Las Aves · Isla Orchila · Isla Blanquilla · Tobago · Charlotteville

WILLEMSTAD · Scarborough · **TRINIDAD AND TOBAGO** · Galera Point

Riohacha · Punto Fijo · Gulf of Venezuela · Coro · Isla La Tortuga · Isla de Margarita · Isla · **PORT OF SPAIN** · Sangre Grande

Santa Marta · Maracaibo · **CARACAS** · Cumana · Gulf of Paria · San Fernando · *Trinidad* · Rio Claro

anquilla · **COLOMBIA** · Valencia · Barcelona · Güiria · Serpent's Mouth · Galeota Point · 10°

VENEZUELA

74° · 72° · 70° · 68° · 66° · 64° · 62°

SCALE 1:6,500,000
Lamberts Conformal Conic Projection
0 — 200 miles
0 — 200 kilometers

The lights of South America reveal the focus of development around the continent's edges while the interior jungle remains mostly dark. The three brightest areas on the east coast are the sprawling cities of Rio de Janeiro, São Paulo, and Buenos Aires.

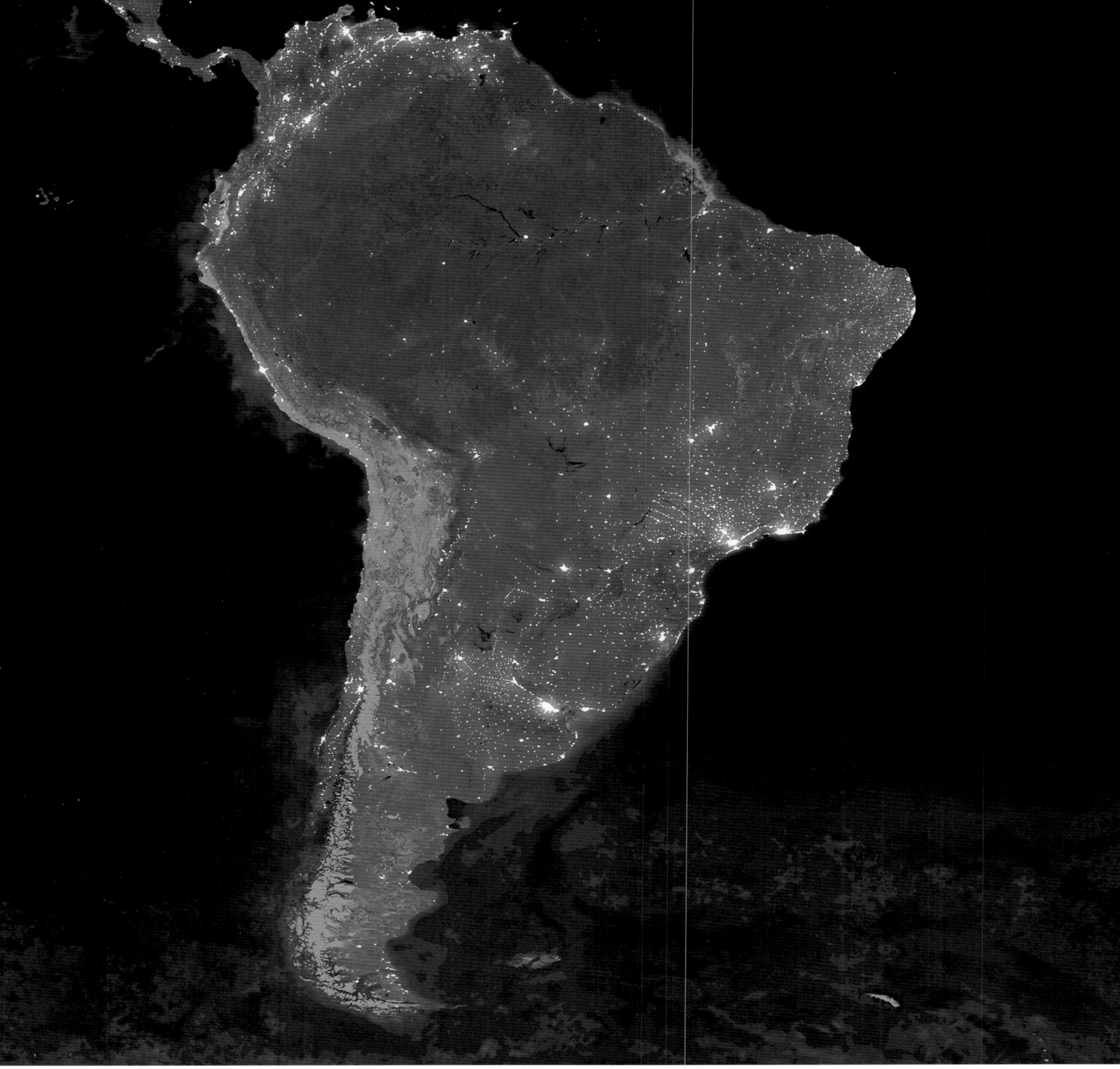

SOUTH AMERICA

ABOVE SOUTH AMERICA

From space, the details of South America's landscapes are revealed. The human impact is startling: many photographs record the scars of logging and burning in the vast tropical rain forests of Brazil; others are dominated by artificial features such as the enormous dams and reservoirs created for irrigation and hydroelectric power. Satellite photography can also help explain natural phenomena. The Andes Mountains run like a spine down the west coast of South America, creating what is known as a rain-shadow effect. Tradewinds from the east carry warm, moist tropical air over the forested interior. As the air climbs the high eastern slopes of the Andes, it cools, condenses, and falls as rain or snow, which runs into the Amazon River and Basin. The air warms again as it descends the western slopes and so holds its moisture as it crosses the Atacama Desert to the coast. This effect contributes to both the extreme dryness of the Atacama Desert, in the rain-shadow area, and the lushness of the Amazon Basin, which dominates the continent's interior and is one of the wettest places on the planet.

Atacama Desert, Chile
Below: Two banks of clouds flank Chile's Atacama Desert. Those on the left stop at the coast because the cold waters of the Humboldt (Peru) Current, just off shore, cause rain to fall over the ocean. On the right, the Andes stop a line of clouds, forcing rain to fall on the eastern slopes. Parts of the Atacama Desert have never recorded rain.

Rain forest, Brazil
Below right: The destruction of Brazil's forests is dramatically illustrated in this false-color image. The remaining tropical forest appears as bright red, while darker areas represent cleared land, and black and gray patches are recently burned areas. The vertical lines indicate land cleared along transportation routes.

Represa Três Marias, Brazil
Above: The serpentine Represa Três Marias winds across this true-color image of southeastern Brazil. This reservoir was built in 1960 to generate hydroelectric power for the state of Minas Gerais. It occupies some 60 miles (95 km) of the São Francisco River, which can be seen carrying sediment into the reservoir's southern end.

River Plate, Argentina
Right: In this satellite view of Argentina, the sediment-laden waters filling the bay of the River Plate reflect light and so appear bright. In contrast, the waters stretching north along the coast have absorbed light, perhaps because of a phytoplankton bloom, and so look very dark. Buenos Aires is the gray-green area at the bay's western end.

LAND AND ENVIRONMENT

Encompassing almost 6.9 million square miles (17.8 million sq km) and extending from Punta Gallinas, in the warm Caribbean Sea, south to the cold, windswept promontory of Cape Horn, South America is the fourth-largest continent. The towering Andes mountains dominate the west, running parallel to the coast for 5,500 miles (8,800 km) and rising to their highest point of 22,835 feet (6,960 m) at Mount Aconcagua. East of the Andes lie expansive lowlands, including, from north to south, the valley of the Orinoco, the immense Amazon Basin, the semiarid grasslands of Gran Chaco, and the plains of the Pampas. In turn, these lowlands are bounded by the plateau regions of the Guiana Highlands in the north, the Brazilian Highlands in the east, and Patagonia in the south.

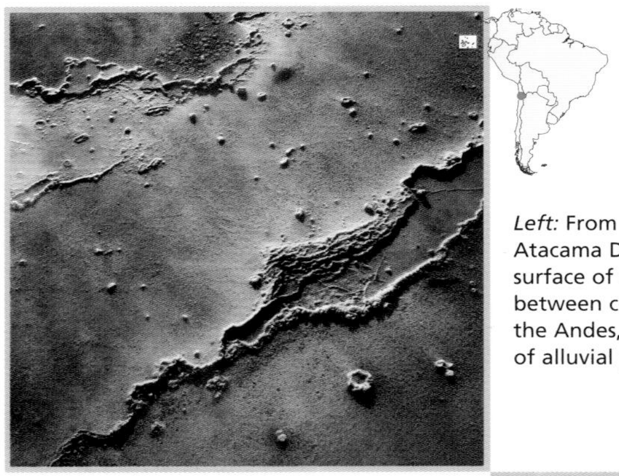

Left: From space, the barren Atacama Desert resembles the surface of the Moon. Situated between coastal ranges and the Andes, it consists mainly of alluvial plains and salt pans.

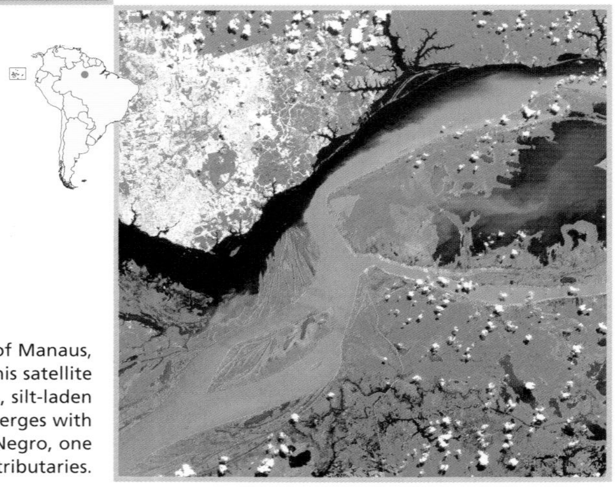

Galapagos Islands

Fernandina
Isla Isabela
Isla San Salvador
Isla Santa Cruz
Isla San Cristobal

SCALE 1:12,500,000   100 miles
100 kilometres

Right: Near the town of Manaus, shown in gray in this satellite image, the brown, silt-laden Amazon River merges with the much clearer Negro, one of its major tributaries.

SCALE 1:35,000,000
Lamberts Conformal Conic Projection
1000 kilometers

NATURAL HAZARDS

Volcanoes

Western South America borders the Ring of Fire, a well-known zone of tectonic instability that almost encircles the Pacific Ocean. Just off the west coast, the Nazca Plate is subducting beneath the South American Plate, giving rise to earthquakes and volcanic eruptions. South America has more volcanoes than any other continent—204—and the world's highest volcano, Nevado Ojos del Salado, which rises to 22,664 feet (6,908 m). The deadliest eruption of recent years was that of Nevado del Ruiz in Colombia, in 1985, which, although small, melted a glacier, triggering a mudflow that killed about 23,000 people.

Nevado del Ruiz
17,716ft (5400m)
Volcán Cotopaxi
19,344ft (5896m)
Nevado Ojos del Salado
22,664ft (6908m)
Volcán Villarrica
9318ft (2840m)
Cerro Hudson
8530ft (2600m)

Along the plate boundary that parallels the coast, the thinner Nazca Plate is forced downward beneath the much thicker South American Plate. As it subducts, the Nazca Plate gradually melts. Magma then rises through cracks in the crumpled landscape, forming a long line of volcanoes.

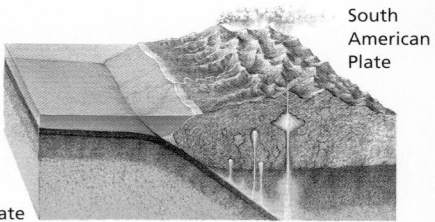
Nazca Plate
South American Plate

The mudflow caused by the eruption of Nevado del Ruiz in Colombia swamped the town of Armero in minutes, giving the inhabitants little opportunity to escape.

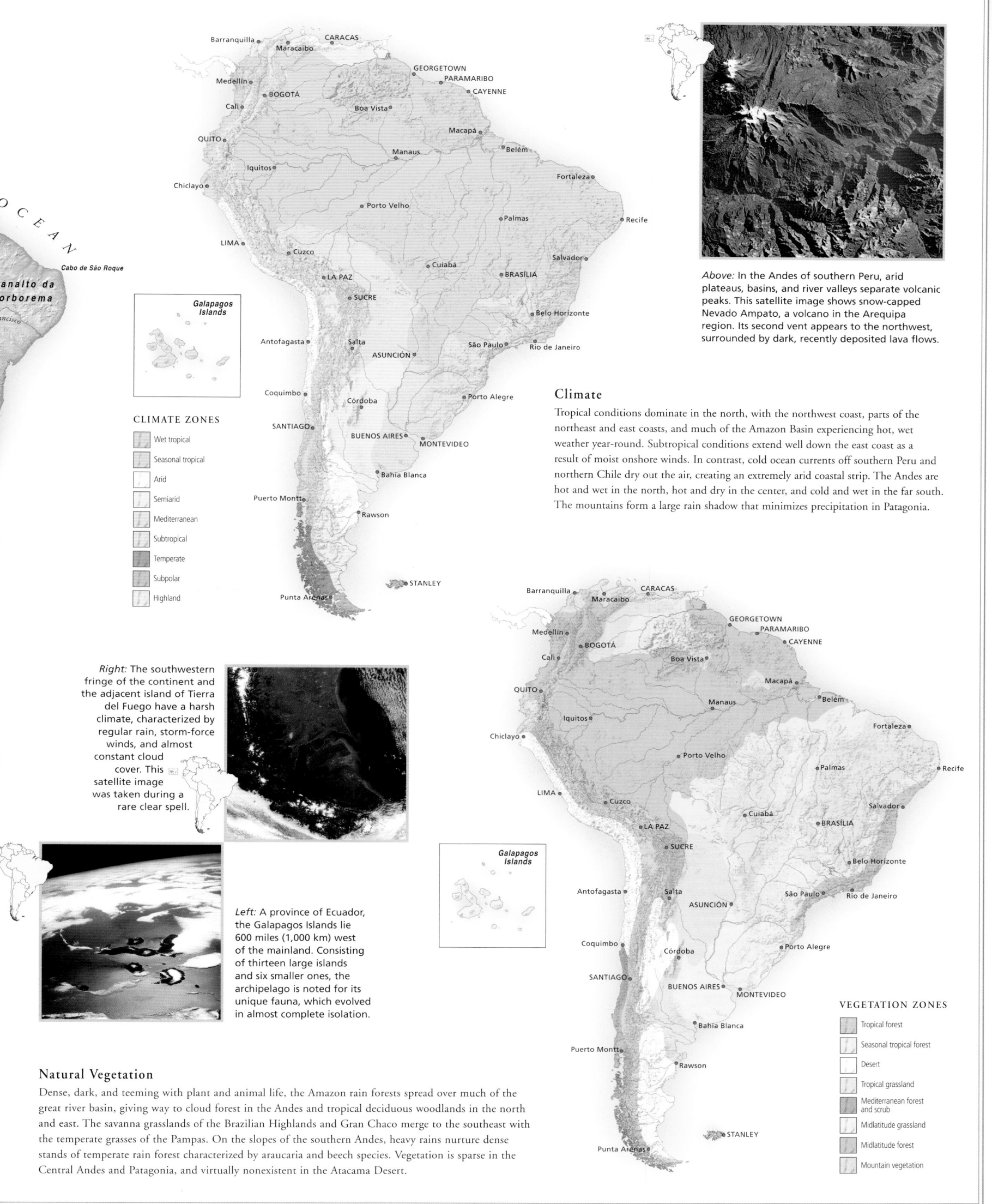

Above: In the Andes of southern Peru, arid plateaus, basins, and river valleys separate volcanic peaks. This satellite image shows snow-capped Nevado Ampato, a volcano in the Arequipa region. Its second vent appears to the northwest, surrounded by dark, recently deposited lava flows.

Climate

Tropical conditions dominate in the north, with the northwest coast, parts of the northeast and east coasts, and much of the Amazon Basin experiencing hot, wet weather year-round. Subtropical conditions extend well down the east coast as a result of moist onshore winds. In contrast, cold ocean currents off southern Peru and northern Chile dry out the air, creating an extremely arid coastal strip. The Andes are hot and wet in the north, hot and dry in the center, and cold and wet in the far south. The mountains form a large rain shadow that minimizes precipitation in Patagonia.

CLIMATE ZONES

- Wet tropical
- Seasonal tropical
- Arid
- Semiarid
- Mediterranean
- Subtropical
- Temperate
- Subpolar
- Highland

Right: The southwestern fringe of the continent and the adjacent island of Tierra del Fuego have a harsh climate, characterized by regular rain, storm-force winds, and almost constant cloud cover. This satellite image was taken during a rare clear spell.

Left: A province of Ecuador, the Galapagos Islands lie 600 miles (1,000 km) west of the mainland. Consisting of thirteen large islands and six smaller ones, the archipelago is noted for its unique fauna, which evolved in almost complete isolation.

Natural Vegetation

Dense, dark, and teeming with plant and animal life, the Amazon rain forests spread over much of the great river basin, giving way to cloud forest in the Andes and tropical deciduous woodlands in the north and east. The savanna grasslands of the Brazilian Highlands and Gran Chaco merge to the southeast with the temperate grasses of the Pampas. On the slopes of the southern Andes, heavy rains nurture dense stands of temperate rain forest characterized by araucaria and beech species. Vegetation is sparse in the Central Andes and Patagonia, and virtually nonexistent in the Atacama Desert.

VEGETATION ZONES

- Tropical forest
- Seasonal tropical forest
- Desert
- Tropical grassland
- Mediterranean forest and scrub
- Midlatitude grassland
- Midlatitude forest
- Mountain vegetation

PEOPLES AND NATIONS

Relative to its size, South America has a modest population of about 350 million. These people inhabit twelve nations and two overseas territories. Their dominant cultures and languages are those of the European colonial powers that, from the early 16th century onward, seized large parts of the continent. Portuguese is the official language in Brazil; Spanish predominates in most other areas. English, Dutch, and French are spoken in, respectively, the Falkland Islands and the former British colony of Guyana; the former Dutch colony of Suriname; and French Guiana, a French territory. Amerindian languages are restricted mainly to the Amazon Basin, the central Andes, and western Paraguay.

Left: São Paulo is the continent's largest city and the second-biggest urban agglomeration in the world after Tokyo in Japan. In 1947, São Paulo's city center had just three high-rise buildings; now it bristles with skyscrapers.

POPULATION DENSITY

- Uninhabited
- Less than 2.6 persons per sq mile/1 per sq km
- 2.6–26 per sq mile/ 1–10 per sq km
- 26–65 per sq mile/ 10–25 per sq km
- 65–130 per sq mile/ 25–50 per sq km
- 130–260 per sq mile/ 50–100 per sq km
- 260–520 per sq mile/ 100–200 per sq km

FLASHPOINTS

Though it has been relatively stable since the mid-19th century, South America has recently experienced conflict between guerilla groups and governments, as well as several border disputes.

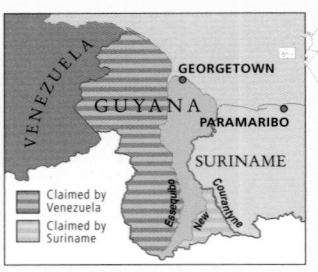

Claimed by Venezuela
Claimed by Suriname

Guyana

Guyana has long faced significant territorial claims from its western and eastern neighbors, which, if realized, would see its territory drastically reduced. Venezuela disputes ownership of the entire area west of the Essequibo River, asserting that it inherited the land from Spain. Suriname claims the triangular region between the New (Upper Courantyne) and Courantyne rivers.

Northern Chile

In 1879–83, Chile defeated Bolivia and Peru in the War of the Pacific. As a result, it gained much of the Atacama region including southern Peru and coastal Bolivia. Peru regained some territory in 1929 as a result of negotiation, but Chile has refused to consider regular requests from Bolivia for sovereign access to the sea. This has led to repeated breakdowns in diplomatic relations.

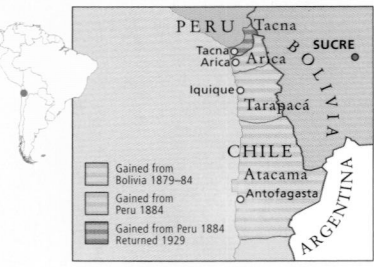

Gained from Bolivia 1879–84
Gained from Peru 1884
Gained from Peru 1884 Returned 1929

Colombia

Since the mid-1960s, guerillas belonging to the Revolutionary Armed Forces of Colombia (FARC) and the National Liberation Army (ELN) have been attempting to install a socialist government by force, a conflict that has cost 38,000 lives. Although the current government is supported by right-wing paramilitaries and the U.S.A., the guerilla groups control more than half of the country, and have formed alliances with drug traffickers.

Main Areas of Activity
FARC
ELN
Paramilitaries

Population Patterns

Sometimes referred to as "the hollow continent," South America has a sparsely populated interior ringed by areas of heavy coastal settlement. Among the most densely inhabited areas are the northeast and south coasts of Brazil, the Andean plateaus, and the River Plate region of Argentina and Uruguay. Most South Americans are descended from one or more of four main groups: native Amerindian peoples; early Spanish or Portuguese colonists; African slaves brought to the continent between the 16th and early 19th centuries; and more recent immigrants, especially from Italy, Spain, Portugal, Eastern Europe, and Japan.

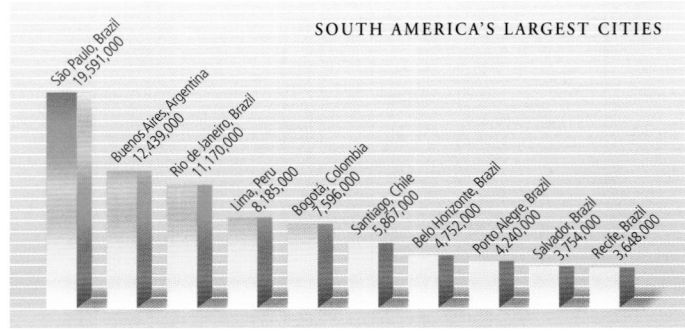

SOUTH AMERICA'S LARGEST CITIES

São Paulo, Brazil 19,591,000
Buenos Aires, Argentina 12,439,000
Rio de Janeiro, Brazil 11,170,000
Lima, Peru 8,185,000
Bogotá, Colombia 7,596,000
Santiago, Chile 5,867,000
Belo Horizonte, Brazil 4,752,000
Porto Alegre, Brazil 4,240,000
Salvador, Brazil 3,754,000
Recife, Brazil 3,648,000

Urbanization

Prior to the early 16th century, major population centers lay on the Pacific Coast, in the Andes, and along the waterways of the Amazon Basin. The arrival by sea of Spanish and Portuguese colonists and traders caused a shift of settlement to seaboard towns. In the mid-20th century, rapid industrialization of these centers, combined with a lack of development, communications, and infrastructure in the interior, spurred large-scale migration to coastal cities. Continent-wide, urbanization has risen from less than 50 percent in 1950 to a current level of around 82 percent.

Nations of South America

Prior to the 16th century, South America was inhabited by about 20 million people living in diverse communities. Under the Treaty of Tordesillas of 1494, Spain and Portugal agreed to divide the world along a line of demarcation at roughly 46° west. Portugal colonized eastern South America and Spain laid claim to the west. Following the collapse of the Spanish and Portuguese empires in the early 19th century, their South American territories rapidly achieved independence. Guyana and Suriname attained political autonomy only in the late 20th century.

PRIOR TO IBERIAN
CONQUEST, 1525

Farming peoples
Hunter-gatherers
Inca Empire
Chiefdoms

COLONIAL
POSSESSIONS, 1750–63

INDEPENDENCE,
1810–33

South American Trade Organizations

All South American nations except Guyana and Suriname are members of the Latin American Integration Association (LAIA), which also includes Mexico. Established by the Treaty of Montevideo in 1980, it aims to facilitate economic cooperation throughout Central and South America. Other important regional organizations include Mercosur (the Southern Common Market), a free trade zone formed by Argentina, Brazil, Paraguay, and Uruguay; and the Andean Group, which aims to establish a common market between Bolivia, Colombia, Ecuador, Peru, and Venezuela by 2005.

Mercosur
(Southern Common Market)

Andean Group

Latin American Integration
Association (LAIA)

THE HUMAN IMPACT

By the time of European colonization, human modification of the South American landscape was already widespread, though uneven. Hunter-gatherer lifestyles still predominated in some areas, but many of the continent's estimated 6 to 9 million inhabitants practiced agriculture, cultivating crops that would become staples worldwide, such as corn, potatoes, and beans. From 1800 BC, large settlements incorporating ceremonial buildings and irrigation systems took shape on the west coast. In the 15th century, the Inca expanded the practice of building terraces to increase agricultural output and constructed a road network covering 13,000 miles (21,000 km). After 1532, the pace of change accelerated. The Portuguese cleared huge swathes of tropical forest on the east coast to make way for sugar and, later, coffee plantations; less than 8 percent of that forest remains. The Andes, too, were stripped of timber, and the woodlands that covered the Pampas were cleared and planted with grasses to feed introduced livestock. Rapid population growth in the second half of the 20th century increased pressure on remaining wilderness areas, and has given rise to overcrowding and severe pollution and waste problems in cities.

Economic Profile

Though unevenly distributed, South America's abundant natural resources help make it a major exporter of primary produce. The continent provides one-quarter of the world's copper and one-fifth of its iron ore, as well as large supplies of tin and bauxite. Oil reserves have been located in areas such as Lake Maracaibo in Venezuela, the western Amazon Basin, and southern Patagonia. The immense pastures of the east and southeast support massive beef-cattle herds, and tropical plantations generate enormous cash crops of sugar, coffee, citrus fruits, and rubber. The southeastern Pacific Ocean is the world's second-most productive fishery. Plentiful metals and hydroelectric power have aided the development of industries, but most remain resource-based and South America is dependent on imports of many manufactured goods.

Land Cover

Forests still swathe more than half of the continent and account for 25 percent of global forest cover. South America has extensive reserves of cultivable land, though most is used as pasture. Other types of land cover include sprawling coastal settlements, wetlands, and the barren Andean uplands and western and southern deserts.

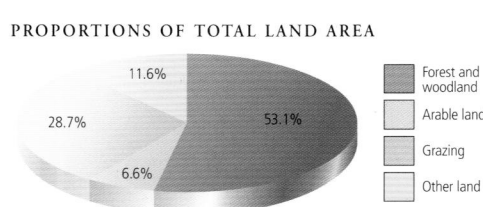

PROPORTIONS OF TOTAL LAND AREA

- 53.1% Forest and woodland
- 11.6% Arable land
- 6.6% Grazing
- 28.7% Other land

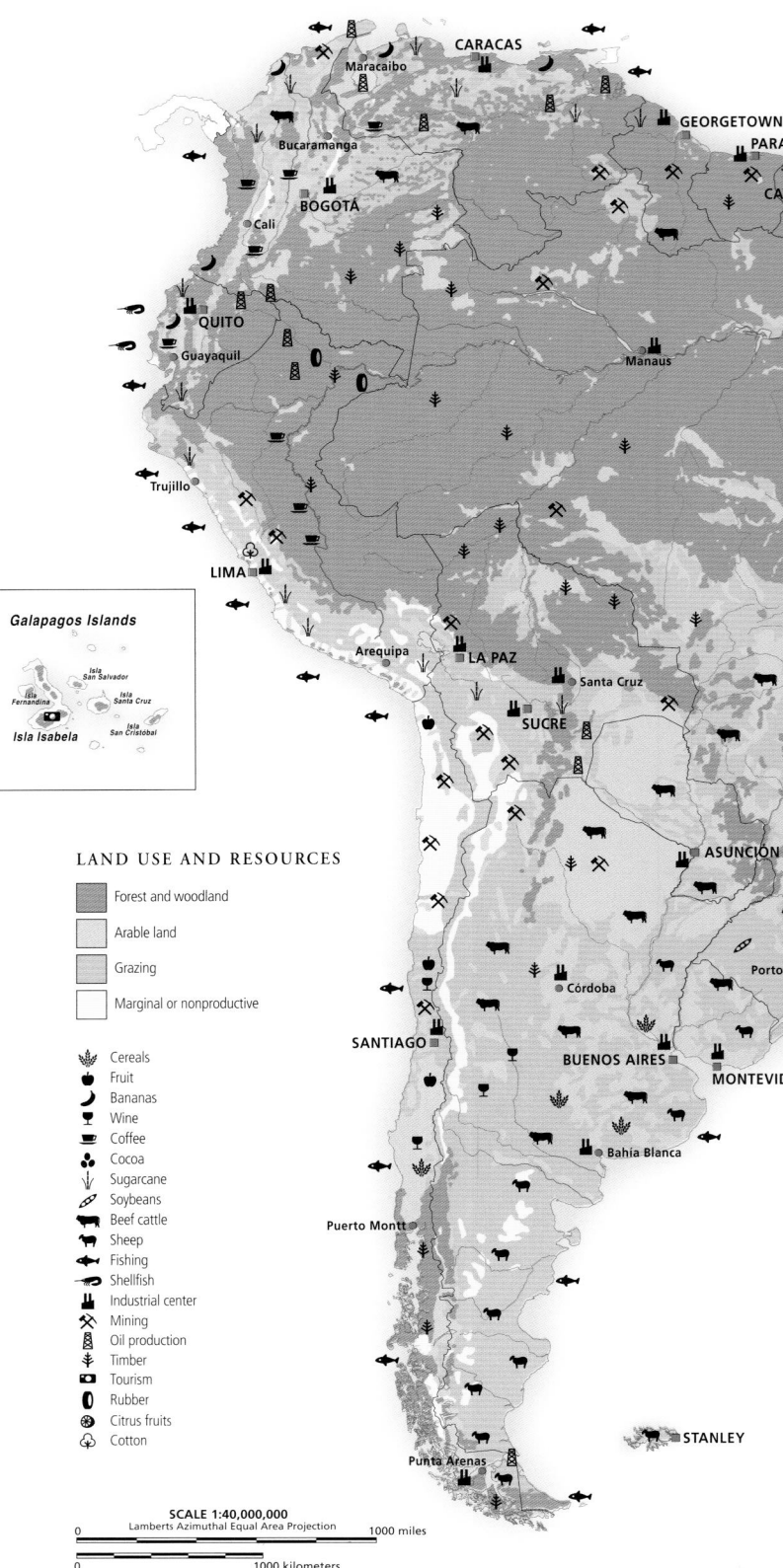

LAND USE AND RESOURCES

- Forest and woodland
- Arable land
- Grazing
- Marginal or nonproductive

- Cereals
- Fruit
- Bananas
- Wine
- Coffee
- Cocoa
- Sugarcane
- Soybeans
- Beef cattle
- Sheep
- Fishing
- Shellfish
- Industrial center
- Mining
- Oil production
- Timber
- Tourism
- Rubber
- Citrus fruits
- Cotton

SCALE 1:40,000,000
Lamberts Azimuthal Equal Area Projection
0   1000 miles

0   1000 kilometers

THE CHANGING FACE OF SOUTH AMERICA

The Amazon Rain Forest

The Amazon rain forest covers an area as large as the United States and harbors at least 40 percent of the world's plant and animal species, as well as 180,000 indigenous people; it also recycles 10 percent of the world's airborne carbon. Since the mid-20th century, this ecologically vital and once-remote environment has come increasingly under threat. In 1960, faced with mounting pressure from a land-hungry citizenry, the Brazilian government adopted the vote-winning policy of populating the region. Ten percent of the rain forest was cleared within seven years. Currently, an area the size of New Jersey disappears every year and total losses now amount to an area as large as France. Despite this, Brazil recently announced another plan to cover the region with dams, settlements, and thousands of miles of roads. Conservation groups estimate this could result in the loss of between 33 and 42 percent of the remaining Amazon rain forest.

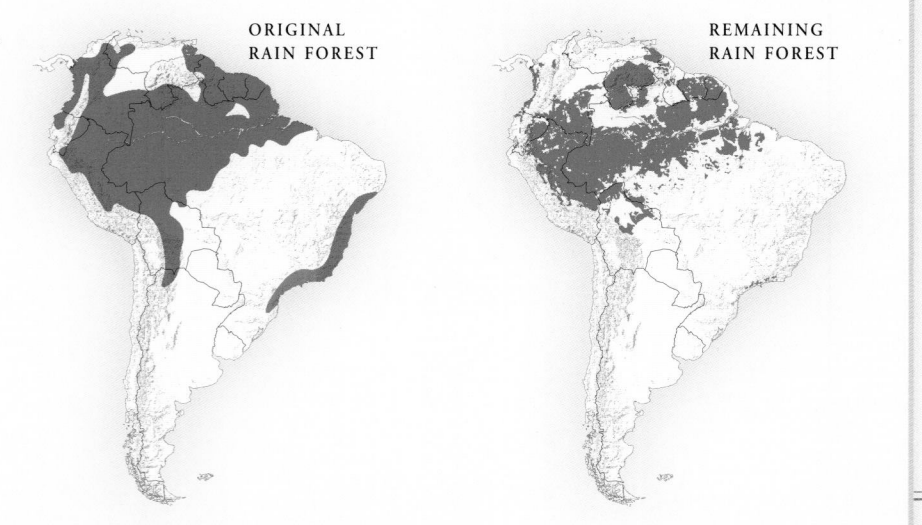

ORIGINAL RAIN FOREST

REMAINING RAIN FOREST

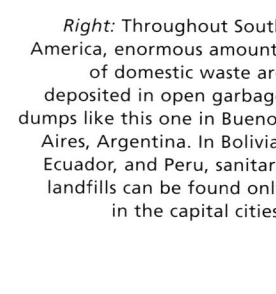

Right: Throughout South America, enormous amounts of domestic waste are deposited in open garbage dumps like this one in Buenos Aires, Argentina. In Bolivia, Ecuador, and Peru, sanitary landfills can be found only in the capital cities.

Right: Hydroelectricity provides much of South America's energy, but it has an environmental cost. Construction of the Itaipu dam, on the Brazil–Paraguay border, the world's largest, destroyed 270 square miles (700 sq km) of forest and wiped out several rare plant species.

Below: In 1980, the Brazilian industrial city of Cubatão was so polluted that it reportedly had no birds or insects and one-third of infants died in their first year.

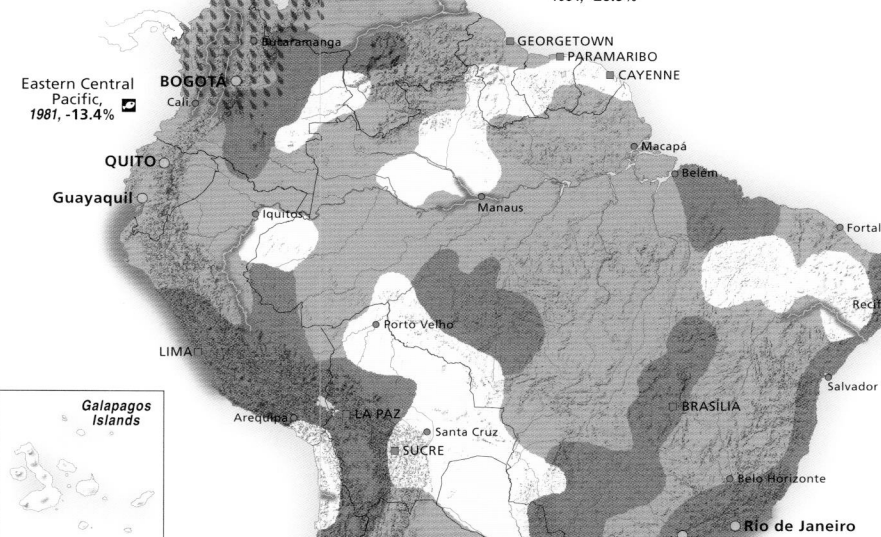

CARACAS 1979
Maracaibo
Bucaramanga
Western Central Atlantic, *1984, -26.9%*
GEORGETOWN
PARAMARIBO
CAYENNE
Eastern Central Pacific, *1981, -13.4%*
BOGOTÁ
Cali
Macapá
QUITO
Belém
Guayaquil
Iquitos
Manaus
Fortaleza
Porto Velho
LIMA
Recife
Galapagos Islands
Arequipa
BRASÍLIA
Salvador
LA PAZ
Santa Cruz
SUCRE
Belo Horizonte
Southeast Pacific, *1994, -28.5%*
ASUNCIÓN
Rio de Janeiro
São Paulo
Córdoba
Porto Alegre
SANTIAGO
BUENOS AIRES
MONTEVIDEO
Bahía Blanca
Puerto Montt
STANLEY
Punta Arenas

Above: In 1972 in Peru, a combination of overfishing and an El Niño episode saw fish stocks plummet by two-thirds for the next 15 years. More than 80 percent of stocks in South American waters are now fully fished, overfished, or depleted.

Threats to the Environment

Over the past century, rapid population growth and widespread poverty, the concentration of land and power in the hands of wealthy individuals and corporations, corruption, and a lack of government control have contributed to widespread overexploitation of resources. Deforestation proceeds apace, from the rain forests of Guyana to the conifer forests of Chile, with logging, mining, and road-building being the main causes. Soil degradation resulting from deforestation, grazing, and overuse of chemicals affects about 15 percent of the continent. Massive hydroelectric projects threaten vital wetlands and continuing urbanization has exacerbated air and water pollution as well as waste-disposal problems.

ENVIRONMENTAL ISSUES

Degraded soil

Very degraded soil

Polluted rivers

Polluted seas and lakes

Acid rain

Major oil spills, **year**

Cities with severe air pollution

Overfished fishery, *year of peak catch,* **decline since peak catch**

Protecting the Environment

Air pollution has been reduced in several cities, most notably Santiago, and Argentina has led the way in setting voluntary greenhouse-gas emission targets. South America's carbon dioxide emissions per capita are now below the world average. Modest reductions in deforestation rates have been recorded in some countries and government incentives for the creation of plantations have stimulated reforestation (although plantations do not fully compensate for the loss of natural forests, which support specialized ecosystems). Approximately 7.4 percent of the continent is now protected and Ecuador and Venezuela have, respectively, the highest and second-highest proportions of protected areas in the world. However, many South American preserves lack the funds and personnel to prevent degradation.

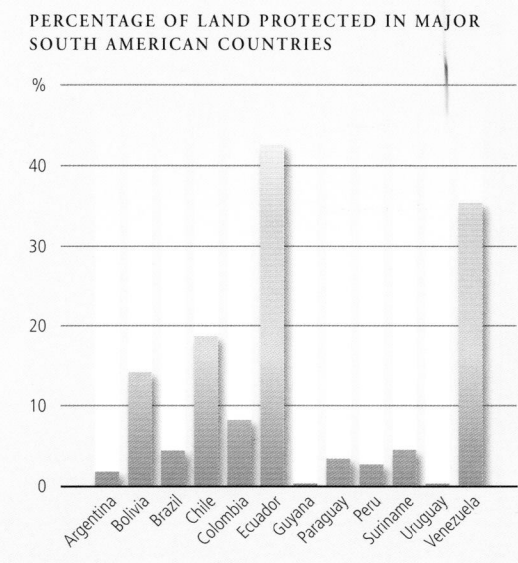

PERCENTAGE OF LAND PROTECTED IN MAJOR SOUTH AMERICAN COUNTRIES

%

40

30

20

10

0

Argentina
Bolivia
Brazil
Chile
Colombia
Ecuador
Guyana
Paraguay
Peru
Suriname
Uruguay
Venezuela

Skillful town planning has made Curitiba in Brazil a model of sustainability. It has dozens of parks, a traffic-free downtown zone, highly efficient public transport, and an effective recycling program.

NORTHERN SOUTH AMERICA

Colombia, Guyana, Suriname, Venezuela

Nearing their northern limit in southern Colombia, the Andes Mountains divide into three separate chains, forming a rugged hinterland of valleys and ranges. This is paralleled to the east by a broad sweep of low land, including part of the heavily forested Amazon Basin in the south and, in the north, the Llanos, humid savanna grasslands drained by the Orinoco River. Beyond the Orinoco, the flat-topped Guiana Highlands sprawl across southern Venezuela, Guyana, Suriname, and French Guiana, descending in the north to densely forested lowlands and swampy coastal plains. Despite significant natural resources, and for a variety of reasons, the countries in this region have struggled to attain stability and prosperity. Colombia's government has fought a draining struggle against armed guerillas and powerful drug-traffickers; oil-rich Venezuela's progress has been hindered by inefficient economic management and inequitable distribution of wealth; and the less-developed Guyana, Suriname, and French Guiana still lack infrastructure.

THE COLOMBIAN CORDILLERAS

The three northern branches of the Andes—the Cordillera Occidental, Cordillera Central, and Cordillera Oriental—are separated by the fertile valleys of the Cauca and Magdalena rivers. These valleys and adjacent slopes are the site of Colombia's largest cities (including the capital Bogotá) and most productive coffee and sugar plantations. They also contain vital natural resources, including oil, emeralds, and gold. In the north, the Cordillera Oriental splits again, its two arms enclosing the wide ocean inlet of Lake Maracaibo, site of Venezuela's second-largest city, Maracaibo, and the principal source of the country's enormous oil reserves.

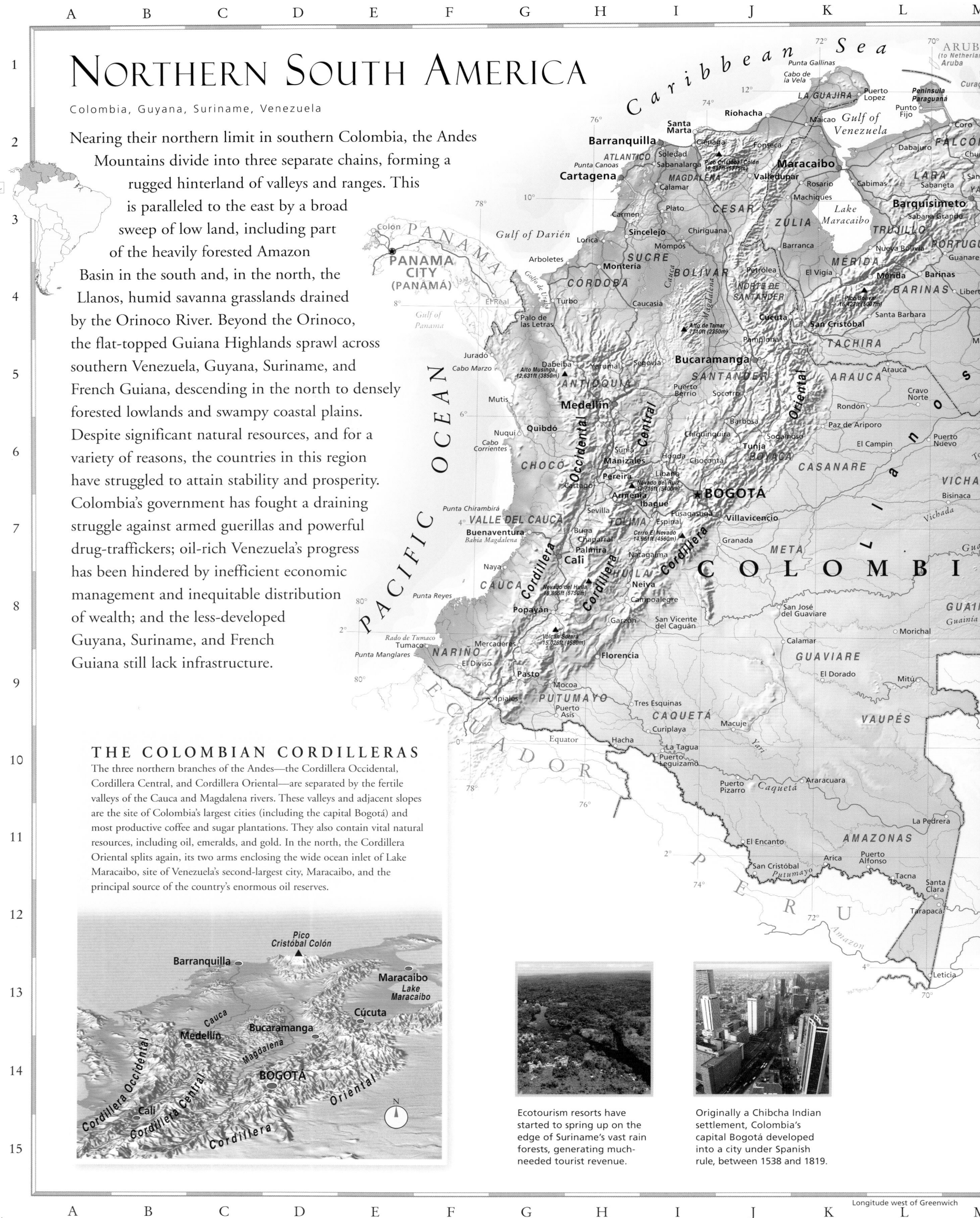

Ecotourism resorts have started to spring up on the edge of Suriname's vast rain forests, generating much-needed tourist revenue.

Originally a Chibcha Indian settlement, Colombia's capital Bogotá developed into a city under Spanish rule, between 1538 and 1819.

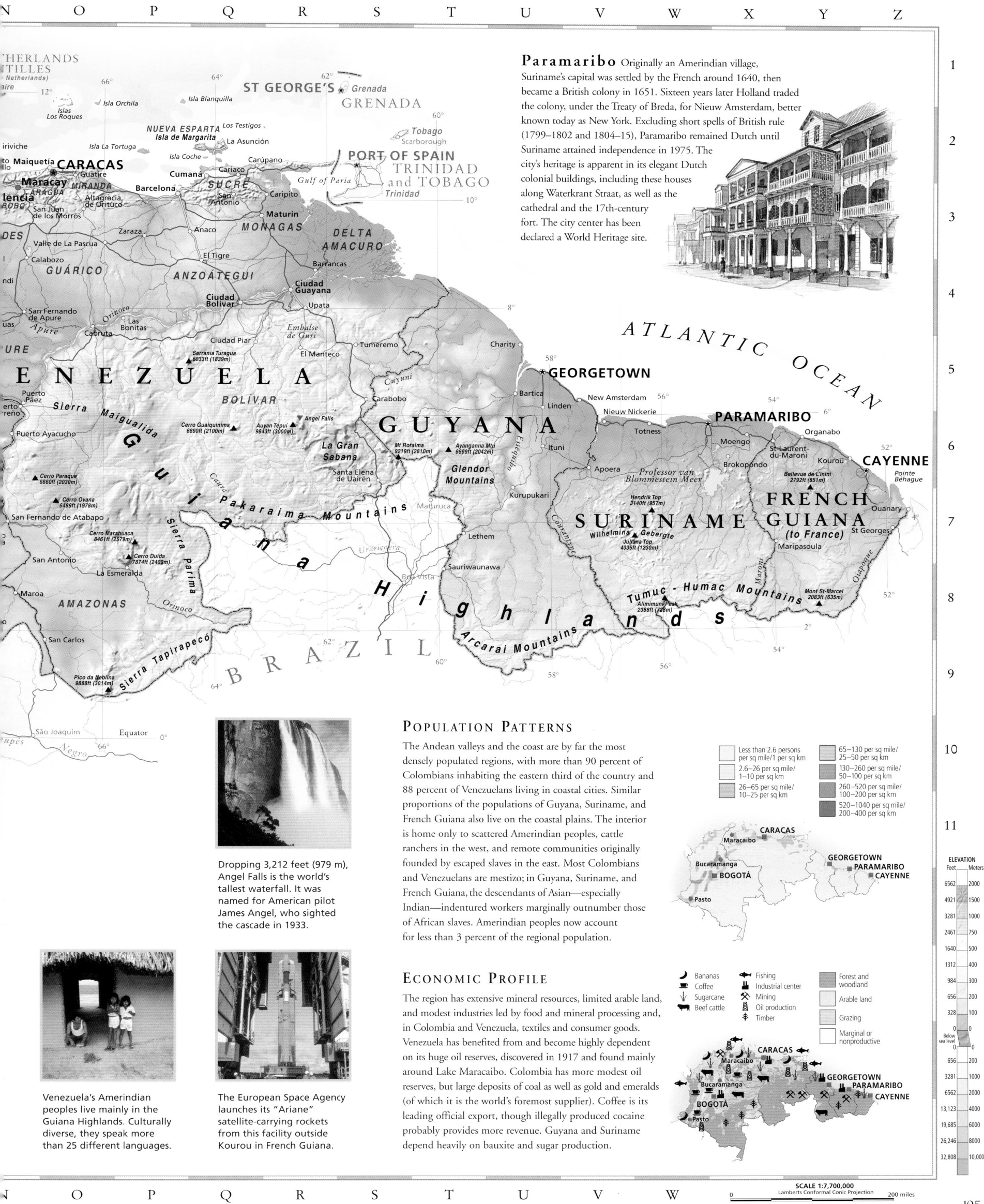

Map labels

NETHERLANDS ... TILLES (Netherlands)

St GEORGE'S — Grenada — GRENADA

Isla Orchila, Isla Blanquilla, Isla La Tortuga, Isla Coche

NUEVA ESPARTA — Los Testigos — Isla de Margarita — La Asunción

Tobago — Scarborough

PORT OF SPAIN — TRINIDAD and TOBAGO — Trinidad — Gulf of Paria

Islas Los Roques — Bonaire

Maiquetía — CARACAS — Maracay — Guatire — MIRANDA — Valencia — ARAGUA — Cariaco — Carúpano — Cumaná — Barcelona — SUCRE — San Antonio — Caripito — Anaco — MONAGAS — Maturín

San Juan de los Morros — GUÁRICO — Zaraza — El Tigre — ANZOÁTEGUI — DELTA AMACURO

Valle de La Pasca — Calabozo — Las Bonitas — Cabruta — Ciudad Bolívar — Ciudad Guayana — Upata — Barrancas

San Fernando de Apure — Apure — Orinoco — Ciudad Piar — Embalse de Guri — Tumeremo — Charity

VENEZUELA — BOLÍVAR — Serranía Turagua 6033ft (1839m) — El Manteco

Puerto Páez — Puerto Ayacucho — Sierra Maigualida — Cerro Guaiquinima 6890ft (2100m) — Auyán Tepui 9843ft (3000m) — Angel Falls — La Gran Sabana — GEORGETOWN — GUYANA — New Amsterdam — Bartica — Linden — Nieuw Nickerie — PARAMARIBO

Cerro Paraque 6660ft (2030m) — Cerro Ovana 6489ft (1978m) — Cerro Marahuaca 8461ft (2579m) — Cerro Duida 7874ft (2400m) — Santa Elena de Uairén — Mt Roraima 9219ft (2810m) — Ayangganna Mtn 6699ft (2042m) — Glendor Mountains — Pakaraima Mountains — Sierra Parima — Kurupukari — Totness — Moengo — St-Laurent-du-Maroni — Kourou — CAYENNE — Organabo — Brokopondo — Professor van Blommestein Meer — Bellevue de L'Inini 2792ft (851m) — Pointe Béhague

La Esmeralda — AMAZONAS — San Antonio — Lethem — Maturuca — Uraricoera — Boa Vista — Saurimaunawa — Wilhelmina Gebergte — Juliana Top 4035ft (1230m) — Hendrik Top 3140ft (957m) — SURINAME — FRENCH GUIANA (to France) — St Georges — Mariposula — Mont St-Marcel 2083ft (635m)

Maroa — Sauriwaunawa — Tumuc-Humac Mountains — Alimmimun Peak 2388ft (728m) — Coppename — Marowijne

San Carlos — Pico da Neblina 9888ft (3014m) — Sierra Tapirapecó — BRAZIL — Arcarai Mountains — Guiana Highlands

São Joaquim — Equator — Negro — Uaupés

ATLANTIC OCEAN

Paramaribo

Paramaribo Originally an Amerindian village, Suriname's capital was settled by the French around 1640, then became a British colony in 1651. Sixteen years later Holland traded the colony, under the Treaty of Breda, for Nieuw Amsterdam, better known today as New York. Excluding short spells of British rule (1799–1802 and 1804–15), Paramaribo remained Dutch until Suriname attained independence in 1975. The city's heritage is apparent in its elegant Dutch colonial buildings, including these houses along Waterkrant Straat, as well as the cathedral and the 17th-century fort. The city center has been declared a World Heritage site.

Dropping 3,212 feet (979 m), Angel Falls is the world's tallest waterfall. It was named for American pilot James Angel, who sighted the cascade in 1933.

Venezuela's Amerindian peoples live mainly in the Guiana Highlands. Culturally diverse, they speak more than 25 different languages.

The European Space Agency launches its "Ariane" satellite-carrying rockets from this facility outside Kourou in French Guiana.

POPULATION PATTERNS

The Andean valleys and the coast are by far the most densely populated regions, with more than 90 percent of Colombians inhabiting the eastern third of the country and 88 percent of Venezuelans living in coastal cities. Similar proportions of the populations of Guyana, Suriname, and French Guiana also live on the coastal plains. The interior is home only to scattered Amerindian peoples, cattle ranchers in the west, and remote communities originally founded by escaped slaves in the east. Most Colombians and Venezuelans are mestizo; in Guyana, Suriname, and French Guiana, the descendants of Asian—especially Indian—indentured workers marginally outnumber those of African slaves. Amerindian peoples now account for less than 3 percent of the regional population.

Population density legend:
- Less than 2.6 persons per sq mile/1 per sq km
- 2.6–26 per sq mile/1–10 per sq km
- 26–65 per sq mile/10–25 per sq km
- 65–130 per sq mile/25–50 per sq km
- 130–260 per sq mile/50–100 per sq km
- 260–520 per sq mile/100–200 per sq km
- 520–1040 per sq mile/200–400 per sq km

CARACAS — Maracaibo — Bucaramanga — BOGOTÁ — Pasto — GEORGETOWN — PARAMARIBO — CAYENNE

ECONOMIC PROFILE

The region has extensive mineral resources, limited arable land, and modest industries led by food and mineral processing and, in Colombia and Venezuela, textiles and consumer goods. Venezuela has benefited from and become highly dependent on its huge oil reserves, discovered in 1917 and found mainly around Lake Maracaibo. Colombia has more modest oil reserves, but large deposits of coal as well as gold and emeralds (of which it is the world's foremost supplier). Coffee is its leading official export, though illegally produced cocaine probably provides more revenue. Guyana and Suriname depend heavily on bauxite and sugar production.

Economic profile legend:
- Bananas
- Coffee
- Sugarcane
- Beef cattle
- Fishing
- Industrial center
- Mining
- Oil production
- Timber
- Forest and woodland
- Arable land
- Grazing
- Marginal or nonproductive

CARACAS — Maracaibo — Bucaramanga — BOGOTÁ — Pasto — GEORGETOWN — PARAMARIBO — CAYENNE

ELEVATION
Feet	Meters
6562	2000
4921	1500
3281	1000
2461	750
1640	500
1312	400
984	300
656	200
328	100
Below sea level	0
656	200
3281	1000
6562	2000
13,123	4000
19,685	6000
26,246	8000
32,808	10,000

SCALE 1:7,700,000
Lamberts Conformal Conic Projection
200 miles
200 kilometers

WESTERN SOUTH AMERICA
Bolivia, Ecuador, Peru

Separated from the Pacific Ocean by a slender coastal plain, the towering peaks of the Andes dominate the entire western side of this region, yielding in the east to well-watered, forest-cloaked lowlands, most of which drain into the vast Amazon Basin. Narrower in the north, the Andes broaden in southern Peru and Bolivia, splitting into two parallel chains, the Cordillera Occidental and the Cordillera Oriental. In the south, these ranges enclose an expansive, arid plateau known as the Altiplano. From around 1200 until shortly after the arrival of the Spanish conquistadors, Cuzco in the northern Altiplano was the capital of the Inca empire, which encompassed virtually the entire Andean sector of this region. Spanish rule left most of the region's wealth and resources in the hands of European-dominated elites. Dissatisfaction with this state of affairs has since fueled indigenous uprisings, labor unrest, Maoist guerilla activity in Peru, and repeated changes of government. In turn, this has hampered economic development, especially in Bolivia, South America's poorest nation.

Quito The world's second-highest capital city after La Paz in Bolivia, Ecuador's capital occupies a narrow valley on the slopes of spectacular Pichincha volcano in the Andes. Little trace remains of the Amerindian and Inca settlements that once stood here, but the city's rich array of buildings from the early period of Spanish settlement in the 16th and 17th centuries, including the elegant Monastery of San Francisco, Ecuador's oldest church, make it the best-preserved capital city in South America.

In the 16th century, the silver-mining center of Potosí in Bolivia was the New World's largest city, with 120,000 inhabitants.

The Galapagos Islands' wildlife includes a host of species unique to the archipelago, including the land iguana.

POPULATION PATTERNS

In Ecuador and Peru, the population is split evenly between coastal and mountain dwellers, with only a minority inhabiting the interior. One-third of Peruvians live in Lima. In Bolivia, the Altiplano is by far the most densely populated region, despite attempts in the late 20th century to encourage people to settle in the east. Relative to other South American nations, all three countries have high proportions of indigenous peoples—25 percent in Ecuador, 45 percent in Peru, and more than 50 percent in Bolivia. They live mainly in the Andean uplands.

	persons per sq mile/1 per sq km
	Less than 2.6 per sq mile/1 per sq km
	2.6–26 per sq mile/1–10 per sq km
	26–65 per sq mile/10–25 per sq km
	65–130 per sq mile/25–50 per sq km
	130–260 per sq mile/50–100 per sq km

ECONOMIC PROFILE

Subsistence farming involving the cultivation of corn and potatoes and grazing of sheep and llamas takes place in the uplands. On the coast, Ecuador's fertile lowlands yield bananas (of which Ecuador is the world's largest exporter), coffee, and sugar; Peru's irrigated plains produce sugar, cotton, and rice. Peru and Bolivia are the leading producers of coca, the source of cocaine, an illegal but profitable crop. Metals, especially silver, copper, and tin, have long been mainstays of the economy; oil and gas have also become vital. Industries are mainly resource-based and include smelting, oil refining, food processing, and textiles.

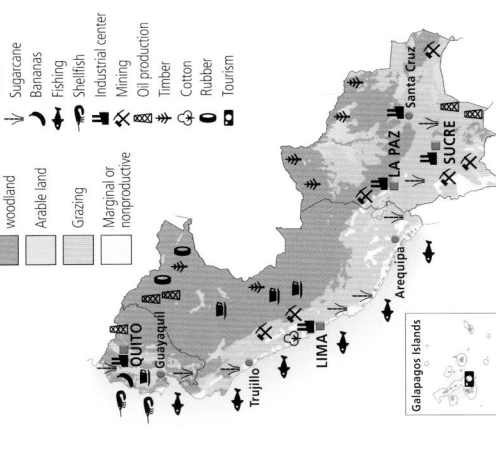

Coffee
Sugarcane
Bananas
Fishing
Shellfish
Industrial center
Mining
Oil production
Timber
Cotton
Rubber
Tourism

Forest and woodland
Arable land
Grazing
Marginal or nonproductive

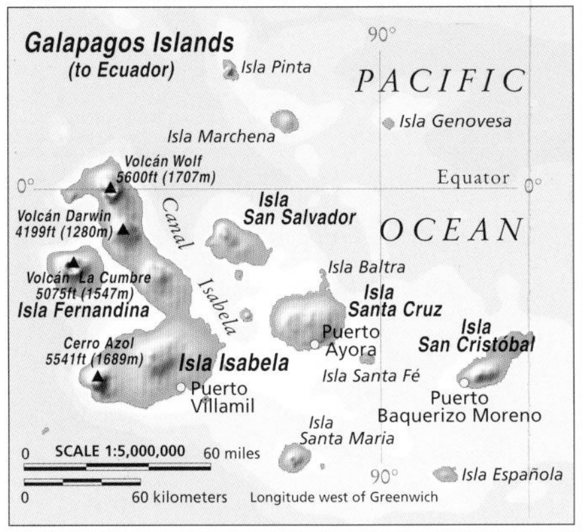

The mountaintop citadel of Machu Picchu, near Cuzco in southern Peru, was built by the Inca in the mid-15th century.

The Aymara people are native to the Altiplano. Aymara women wear distinctive derby hats and woollen shawls.

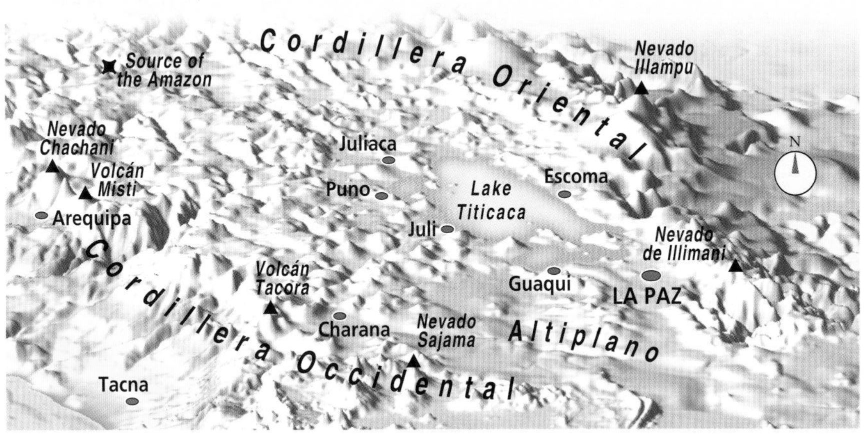

La Paz (left) is Bolivia's administrative capital and seat of national government. Sucre is the constitutional capital and home of the supreme court.

THE ALTIPLANO

Consisting of a series of basins located at around 12,000 feet (3,650 m) between the Cordillera Occidental and the Cordillera Oriental, the Altiplano extends for 600 miles (965 km) from southeastern Peru to southwestern Bolivia. Its northernmost basin, situated on the border between Peru and Bolivia, is the site of Lake Titicaca, at an altitude of 12,500 feet (3,810 m) the highest navigable body of water on Earth, and La Paz, the world's highest capital city, which climbs from 10,650 feet (3,250 m) to 13,250 feet (4,050 m). Many of the surrounding mountains, including Nevado de Illimani near La Paz and Bolivia's highest peak Nevado Sajama, rise above 20,000 feet (6,100 m). Just to the northwest of the Altiplano, in the Peruvian Andes, the Amazon River begins its long, transcontinental journey of over 4,000 miles (6,400 km) to the Atlantic Ocean.

Galapagos Islands
(to Ecuador)
SCALE 1:5,000,000
60 miles
60 kilometers

EASTERN SOUTH AMERICA
Brazil, Paraguay

Encompassing more than 2.3 million square miles (6 million sq km) between the Andes and the eastern seaboard, the Amazon Basin is the world's largest drainage system. Cloaked with dense tropical rain forest embroidered by more than 1,000 tributaries, it dominates western and northern Brazil, its great river draining into the Atlantic Ocean near the town of Macapá. To the south rises the extensive plateau region of the Brazilian Highlands, which falls steeply to the coast in the east but descends more gently in the west to the swamps of the Pantanal, the low hills of eastern Paraguay, and the plains of Argentina. Here, the main drainage outlets are the Paraná River, and the plains of Argentina. Here, the main drainage outlets are the Paraná River, which forms Paraguay's eastern boundary, and its major tributary, the Paraguay, which bisects the nation of the same name, dividing its eastern uplands from its semiarid western plains. Relatively small and landlocked, Paraguay has modest natural resources and a predominantly agricultural economy. In contrast, Brazil is South America's biggest and the world's fifth-largest country, with 5,400 miles (8,700 km) of coastline, the continent's largest population, and immense natural resources.

POPULATION PATTERNS

Brazil's population is concentrated on the coast, especially around São Paulo and Rio de Janeiro. About half of Brazilians are of European origin, 6 percent are of African descent, and 38 percent are of mixed African-European or African-Amerindian descent (so-called mulatos or pardos). Just 0.1 percent are Amerindian. These diverse groups are united by the Portuguese language. In Spanish-speaking Paraguay, 95 percent of the population is mestizo. Many Paraguayans also speak the indigenous Guaraní language. Paraguay is sparsely inhabited, and only 5 percent of the population lives west of the Paraguay River.

Population density legend:
- Less than 2.6 persons per sq mile/1 per sq km
- 2.6–26 per sq mile/1–10 per sq km
- 26–65 per sq mile/10–25 per sq km
- 65–130 per sq mile/25–50 per sq km
- 130–260 per sq mile/50–100 per sq km
- 260–520 per sq mile/100–200 per sq km

ECONOMIC PROFILE

Though hyperinflation, inequitable wealth distribution, and social problems have hampered development, Brazil has enormous economic potential. It is the world's second-largest iron-ore producer and third-biggest bauxite producer and it has the world's second-largest forests. Self-sufficient in food, it is the world's third-biggest meat producer and leading supplier of coffee, sugar, and oranges. Almost 90 percent of its energy comes from hydroelectric power. Industries include the manufacture of automobiles, petrochemicals, steel, shoes and textiles, and wood products. Paraguay generates all of its energy from hydroelectricity. It has a large "informal" or cash economy involving the resale of imported goods, often at street stalls.

Economic legend:
- Coffee
- Cocoa
- Sugarcane
- Soybeans
- Beef cattle
- Fishing
- Industrial center
- Mining
- Timber
- Citrus fruits

Land use legend:
- Forest and woodland
- Arable land
- Grazing
- Marginal or nonproductive

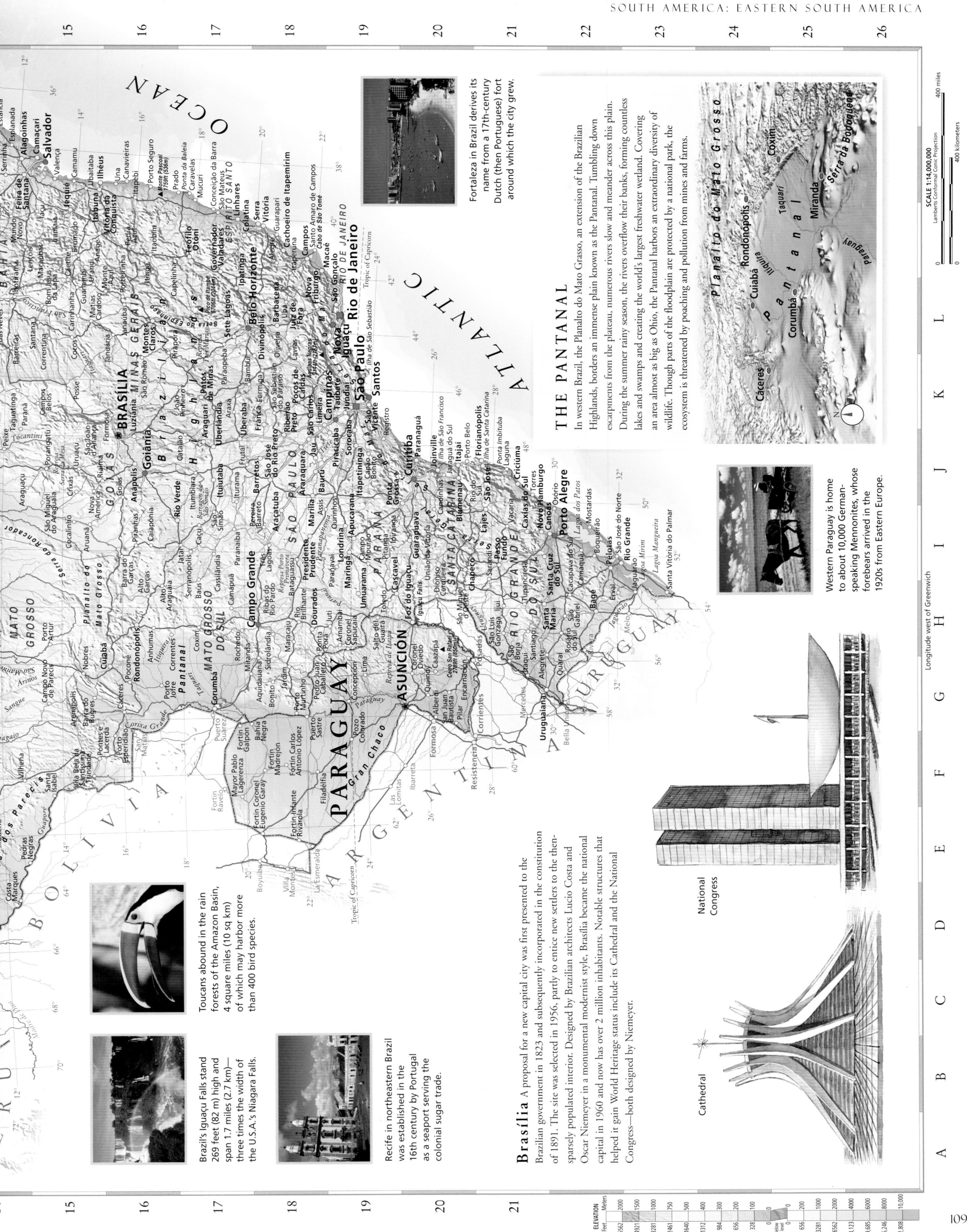

Fortaleza in Brazil derives its name from a 17th-century Dutch (then Portuguese) fort around which the city grew.

THE PANTANAL

In western Brazil, the Planalto do Mato Grosso, an extension of the Brazilian Highlands, borders an immense plain known as the Pantanal. Tumbling down escarpments from the plateau, numerous rivers slow and meander across this plain. During the summer rainy season, the rivers overflow their banks, forming countless lakes and swamps and creating the world's largest freshwater wetland. Covering an area almost as big as Ohio, the Pantanal harbors an extraordinary diversity of wildlife. Though parts of the floodplain are protected by a national park, the ecosystem is threatened by poaching and pollution from mines and farms.

Western Paraguay is home to about 10,000 German-speaking Mennonites, whose forebears arrived in the 1920s from Eastern Europe.

Toucans abound in the rain forests of the Amazon Basin, 4 square miles (10 sq km) of which may harbor more than 400 bird species.

Brazil's Iguaçu Falls stand 269 feet (82 m) high and span 1.7 miles (2.7 km)—three times the width of the U.S.A.'s Niagara Falls.

Recife in northeastern Brazil was established in the 16th century by Portugal as a seaport serving the colonial sugar trade.

Brasília A proposal for a new capital city was first presented to the Brazilian government in 1823 and subsequently incorporated in the constitution of 1891. The site was selected in 1956, partly to entice new settlers to the then-sparsely populated interior. Designed by Brazilian architects Lúcio Costa and Oscar Niemeyer in a monumental modernist style, Brasília became the national capital in 1960 and now has over 2 million inhabitants. Notable structures that helped it gain World Heritage status include its Cathedral and the National Congress—both designed by Niemeyer.

National Congress

Cathedral

Longitude west of Greenwich

SCALE 1:14,000,000
Lambert's Conformal Conic Projection
400 miles
400 kilometers

ELEVATION

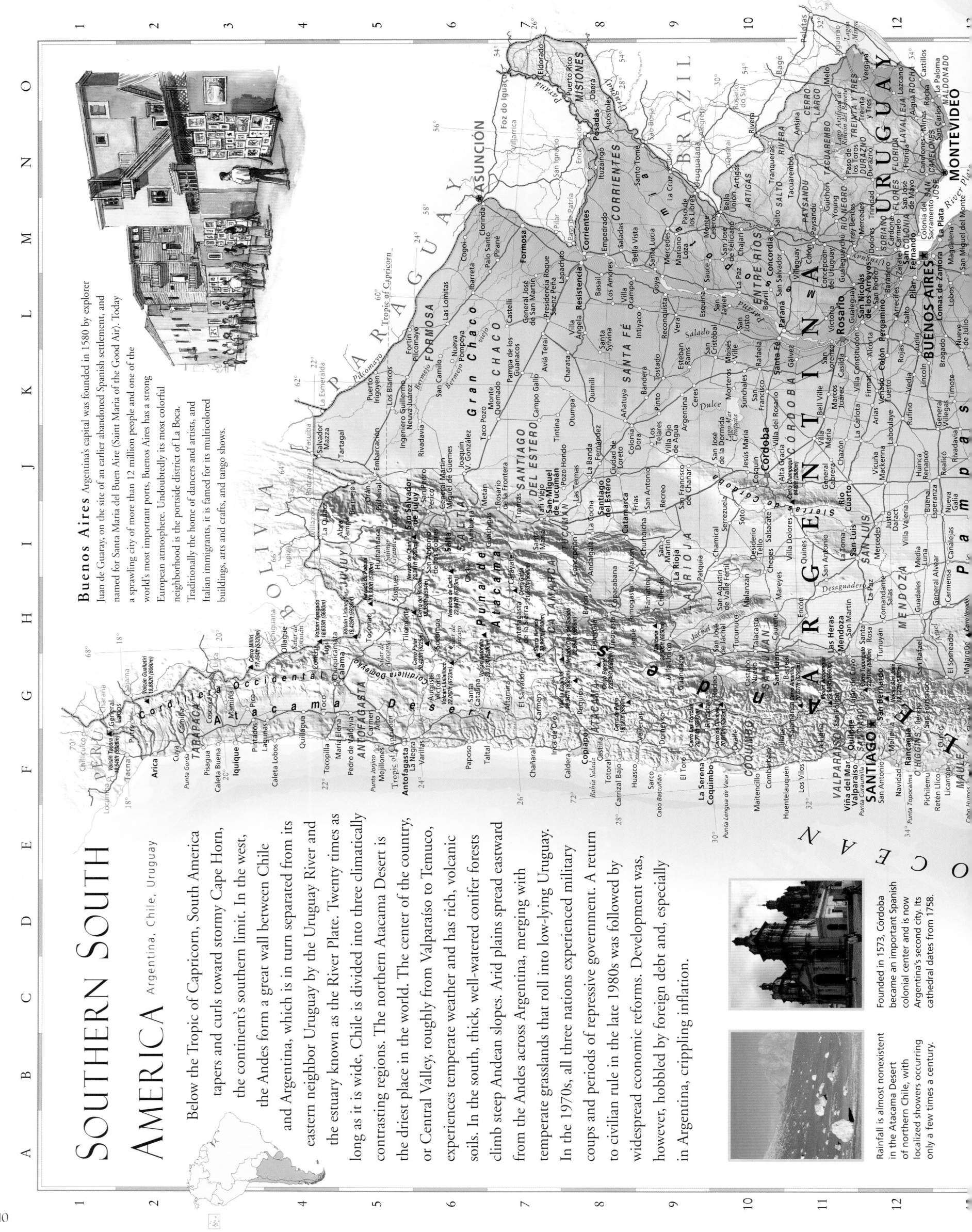

SOUTHERN SOUTH AMERICA Argentina, Chile, Uruguay

Below the Tropic of Capricorn, South America tapers and curls toward stormy Cape Horn, the continent's southern limit. In the west, the Andes form a great wall between Chile and Argentina, which is in turn separated from its eastern neighbor Uruguay by the Uruguay River and the estuary known as the River Plate. Twenty times as long as it is wide, Chile is divided into three climatically contrasting regions. The northern Atacama Desert is the driest place in the world. The center of the country, or Central Valley, roughly from Valparaíso to Temuco, experiences temperate weather and has rich, volcanic soils. In the south, thick, well-watered conifer forests climb steep Andean slopes. Arid plains spread eastward from the Andes across Argentina, merging with temperate grasslands that roll into low-lying Uruguay. In the 1970s, all three nations experienced military coups and periods of repressive government. A return to civilian rule in the late 1980s was followed by widespread economic reforms. Development was, however, hobbled by foreign debt and, especially in Argentina, crippling inflation.

Buenos Aires Argentina's capital was founded in 1580 by explorer Juan de Garay, on the site of an earlier abandoned Spanish settlement, and named for Santa Maria del Buen Aire (Saint Maria of the Good Air). Today a sprawling city of more than 12 million people and one of the world's most important ports, Buenos Aires has a strong European atmosphere. Undoubtedly its most colorful neighborhood is the portside district of La Boca. Traditionally the home of dancers and artists, and Italian immigrants, it is famed for its multicolored buildings, arts and crafts, and tango shows.

Founded in 1573, Córdoba became an important Spanish colonial center and is now Argentina's second city. Its cathedral dates from 1758.

Rainfall is almost nonexistent in the Atacama Desert in northern Chile, with localized showers occurring only a few times a century.

110

SOUTHERN PATAGONIA

On the southern Chile–Argentina border, extensive icefields crown Andean peaks such as Cerro Murallón and Cerro Fitz Roy. Glaciers snake down from these summits, plowing through expansive conifer forests. In the west, they reach the ragged, island-studded coast. In the east, they fall to lakes such as Argentino—site of the huge Moreno Glacier—and Viedma, and fuel mountain streams that drain across the barren Patagonian plateau and feed in turn into major rivers such as the Chico and Gallegos.

The Moreno Glacier forms a 200-foot (60-m) wall of ice across an arm of Lago Argentino in the foothills of the Argentine Andes.

Argentina has long claimed ownership of the British-ruled Falkland Islands. An Argentine invasion in 1982 led to defeat in a brief war with the U.K.

POPULATION PATTERNS

Almost 90 percent of the region's inhabitants live in cities, mainly in the central temperate belt, in and around the cities of Santiago in Chile, Buenos Aires and Córdoba in Argentina, and Montevideo in Uruguay. Settlements are sparse on Andean peaks, and in the cold, wet southwest. Chile's population is predominantly mestizo, with a small residual population of mainly Mapuche Indians. Argentina and Uruguay have more varied cultures, influenced by the large numbers of Spanish, Italian, and German immigrants who arrived after 1870. Indigenous groups still inhabit remote parts of Argentina but have almost vanished from Uruguay.

Uninhabited
Less than 2.6 persons per sq mile/1 per sq km
2.6–26 per sq mile/1–10 per sq km
26–65 per sq mile/10–25 per sq km
65–130 per sq mile/25–50 per sq km
130–260 per sq mile/50–100 per sq km
260–520 per sq mile/100–200 per sq km

ECONOMIC PROFILE

All three countries are strong exporters of primary goods. Chile is the world's leading supplier of copper and in the top five fish producers. Its forests provide abundant timber and the Central Valley yields large quantities of wheat, rice, fruit, and vegetables. Beef and wool from livestock grazed on the Pampas are the traditional mainstays of the Argentine and Uruguayan economies. Uruguay has few mineral resources, but Argentina has sizable oil reserves. Chile and Argentina have thriving wine industries, and Argentina is now the world's fifth-largest producer. All three capital cities are important commercial centers.

Leading industries include food processing, chemicals, and textiles.

Cereals
Fruit
Wine
Beef cattle
Sheep
Fishing
Industrial center
Mining
Timber
Oil production

Forest and woodland
Arable land
Grazing
Marginal or nonproductive

SCALE 1:9,000,000
Lambert's Conformal Conic Projection

ELEVATION
Feet | Meters
6562 | 2000
4921 | 1500
3281 | 1000
2461 | 750
1640 | 500
1312 | 400
984 | 300
656 | 200
328 | 100
0 | Below sea level
655 | 200
3281 | 1000
6562 | 2000
13,123 | 4000
19,685 | 6000
26,246 | 8000
32,808 | 10,000

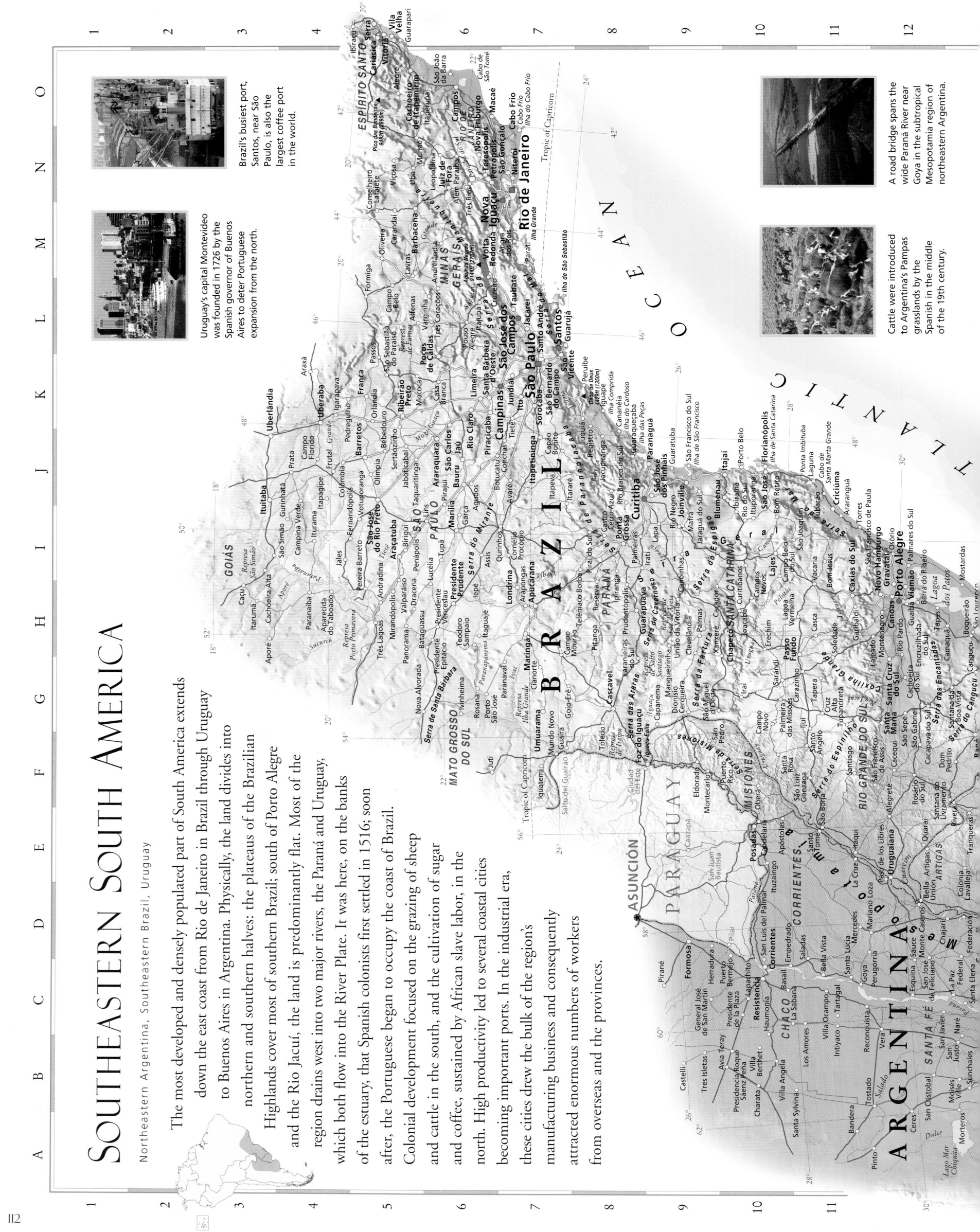

SOUTHEASTERN SOUTH AMERICA

Northeastern Argentina, Southeastern Brazil, Uruguay

The most developed and densely populated part of South America extends down the east coast from Rio de Janeiro in Brazil through Uruguay to Buenos Aires in Argentina. Physically, the land divides into northern and southern halves: the plateaus of the Brazilian Highlands cover most of southern Brazil; south of Porto Alegre and the Rio Jacuí, the land is predominantly flat. Most of the region drains west into two major rivers, the Paraná and Uruguay, which both flow into the River Plate. It was here, on the banks of the estuary, that Spanish colonists first settled in 1516; soon after, the Portuguese began to occupy the coast of Brazil. Colonial development focused on the grazing of sheep and cattle in the south, and the cultivation of sugar and coffee, sustained by African slave labor, in the north. High productivity led to several coastal cities becoming important ports. In the industrial era, these cities drew the bulk of the region's manufacturing business and consequently attracted enormous numbers of workers from overseas and the provinces.

Brazil's busiest port, Santos, near São Paulo, is also the largest coffee port in the world.

Uruguay's capital Montevideo was founded in 1726 by the Spanish governor of Buenos Aires to deter Portuguese expansion from the north.

A road bridge spans the wide Paraná River near Goya in the subtropical Mesopotamia region of northeastern Argentina.

Cattle were introduced to Argentina's Pampas grasslands by the Spanish in the middle of the 19th century.

POPULATION PATTERNS

The overwhelming majority of the region's inhabitants live in cities. Metropolitan Buenos Aires has more than 12 million people, almost one-third of the national population. Over 1.3 million Uruguayans, 40 percent of the country's inhabitants, live in Montevideo. Elsewhere, Uruguay is sparsely populated: the next largest city, Salto, is less than one-tenth the size of the capital. Southern Brazil includes the country's most populous urban centers, São Paulo and Rio de Janeiro (which accommodate about 17 percent of Brazil's huge population), as well as several other cities, including Curitiba and Porto Alegre. The state of São Paulo is home to 37 million people. Its capital's vast citizenry includes the biggest Japanese population outside Japan and South America's largest Jewish community.

ECONOMIC PROFILE

The southern lowlands are used chiefly for raising beef cattle and sheep, though wheat is also cultivated on the Pampas. Fruit, including oranges and bananas, and rice are grown along the Brazilian coast; sugarcane, soybeans, and coffee are planted across the uplands. Livestock exports and food processing underpin the industrial sector in Montevideo and Buenos Aires, though the latter is also a center of automobile production, oil refining, and printing. São Paulo is South America's industrial powerhouse. It generates 40 percent of Brazil's GDP and its factories employ 15 percent of the national population. Its major industries are the manufacture of automobiles, textiles, chemicals, and metals, and oil refining. Services are more significant in Rio de Janeiro, the headquarters of many large businesses.

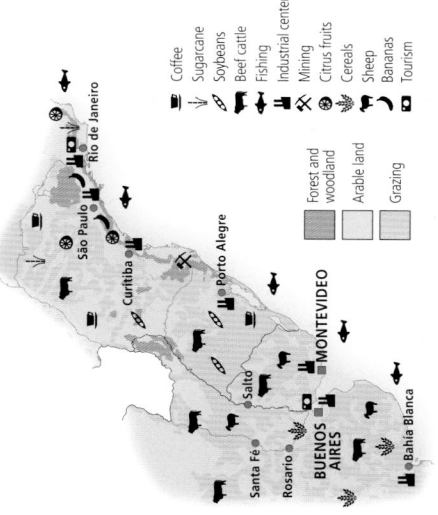

Uruguay has over 15 million sheep, and wool is one of the country's most valuable exports.

THE SERRA DO MAR

On their eastern flank, the Brazilian Highlands abut the coast along a 1,600-mile (2,600-km) escarpment, the southern part of which is known as the Serra do Mar (Sea Range). Averaging 3,000 feet (1,000 m) in height, this range rises almost sheer from the sea at several points. The precipitous slopes provide a mountainous backdrop to Rio de Janeiro and other coastal cities. Associated outcrops have created islands, such as Ilha de São Sebastião and Ilha Grande, and other coastal formations including Rio's famous Sugar Loaf Mountain.

Rio de Janeiro

One of the most distinctive landmarks in South America, the 100-foot (30-m) statue of Christ the Redeemer in Rio de Janeiro was built by engineer Heitor da Silva Costa and completed in 1931. From its site atop 2,428-foot (740-m) Mount Corcovado, it overlooks Guanabara Bay and the city of 11 million that spreads inland from the bay's northern and western shores. The name Rio de Janeiro, meaning "January River," was coined by the area's first Portuguese explorers: arriving in January, 1502, they assumed the bay was the mouth of a river. Portuguese settlers returned to occupy the bay in 1565, and a burgeoning sugar trade soon gave rise to a town. In 1763, Rio became the colonial capital, and in 1822, when Brazil achieved independence, it became the national capital, remaining so until 1960, when the country's seat of government was transferred to Brasília.

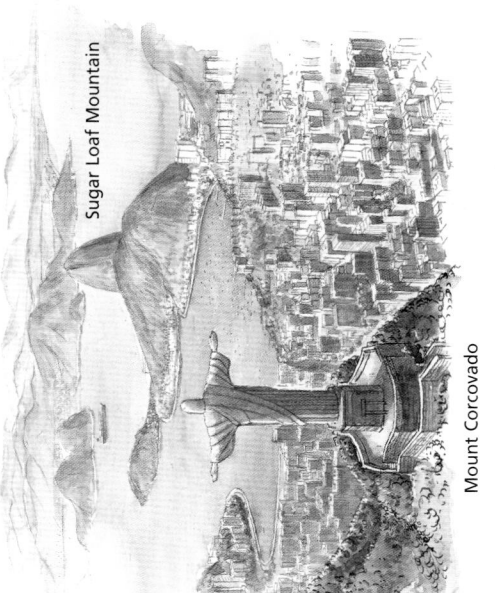

Sugar Loaf Mountain

Mount Corcovado

Longitude east of Greenwich

SCALE 1:7,500,000
Lambert's Conformal Conic Projection

0   250 miles

0   250 kilometers

113

Seen from a satellite, the bright lights of Europe reveal a highly urbanized continent. The pattern of human settlement along the coasts ensures that the outline of much of western Europe is clearly visible from space.

EUROPE

ABOVE EUROPE

Satellites and space shuttles have been collecting images of our planet from space for more than 40 years. These images are sometimes assigned "false colors" to emphasize particular elements. From above, the patterns of dense populations, concentrations of industry, and vast agricultural areas of Europe emerge in astonishing detail. Revealed also is a surprising amount of natural environment, including the high lands of the Alps and the icy plains that stretch east from the jagged Norwegian coast to the Ural Mountains. Satellites have tracked oil slicks off the Atlantic coasts, captured the eruptions of Mount Etna and Mount Vesuvius, and followed wildfires through the forests of France, Spain, and Portugal. Observations such as these can help civil defense authorities to plan disaster responses. Glaciers, sensitive indicators of global climate change, have also been monitored over decades.

Volga delta, The Russian Federation
Below: The Volga flows 2,291 miles (3,688 km) from near Moscow south to the landlocked Caspian Sea, where it empties its waters through a delta of about 500 outlets. In this false-color image the delta wetlands are shown as bright green. The long thin lines just offshore indicate artificially maintained shipping channels.

Aletsch Glacier, Switzerland
Right: Climate change can be measured by the varying rates of retreat of glaciers such as Switzerland's Aletsch Glacier, seen here curving across the center and upper right of the image. Glacial ice is shown as pale blue, and, from above, the moraine lines that mark its slow-moving path look almost like vehicle tracks.

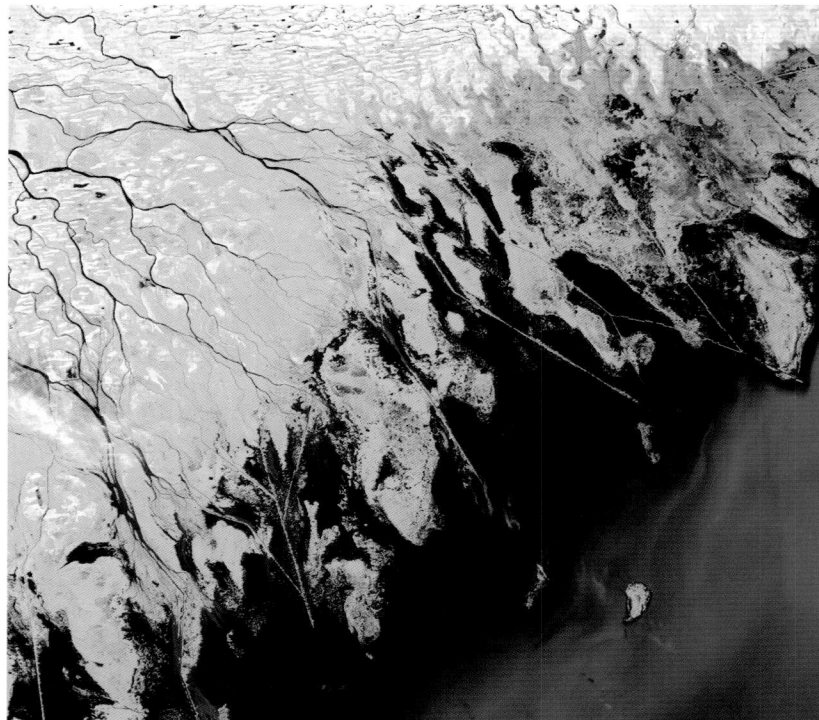

Nordrhein-Westfalen, Germany
Below: Coal mines fan into farmlands in this simulated natural color view of a 19 by 22 mile (30 by 36 km) region of Nordrhein-Westfalen, Germany. The white and dark blue patterns on the right are huge opencast coal mines. The myriad patches are agricultural fields; light green indicates crops, gray is bare soil. The thin dark lines are roads.

Mount Etna, Italy
Below right: Mount Etna, on the Italian island of Sicily, is Europe's largest and most active volcano. Here a dark, thick plume of smoke and ash from its November 2002 eruption is shown blowing southeast toward the city and airport of Catania. The white smoke is from forest fires sparked by ash fall on the slopes of the volcano.

LAND AND ENVIRONMENT

Covering over 3.8 million square miles (9.8 million sq km), Europe is the second-smallest continent. It is separated from Asia by the Ural Mountains of Russia and bounded by sea to the north, west, and south. A chain of mountain ranges, including the Pyrenees, Alps, and Carpathian Mountains, stretches across the continent from west to east. It separates the rugged lands that fringe the island-studded Mediterranean Sea from the North European Plain, a belt of flat land that extends from the English Channel to the Urals. Farther north lie the broad, glacier-carved Scandinavian Peninsula and the large islands of Great Britain, Ireland, and Iceland.

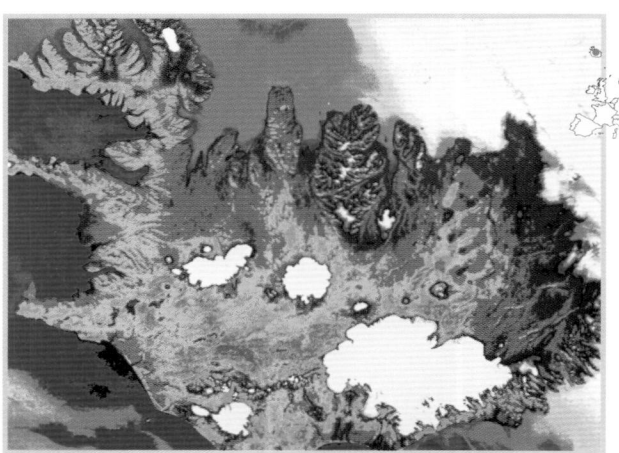

Above: As its name suggests, much of the isolated volcanic island of Iceland is covered by ice. The island's largest ice sheet, Vatnajökull, clearly visible at the bottom right of this satellite image, is bigger than all of mainland Europe's glaciers combined.
Below: The Alps stretch for 650 miles (1,000 km) from southeastern France, through Italy, Switzerland, and Austria to Slovenia. This satellite photograph shows the western end of the chain.

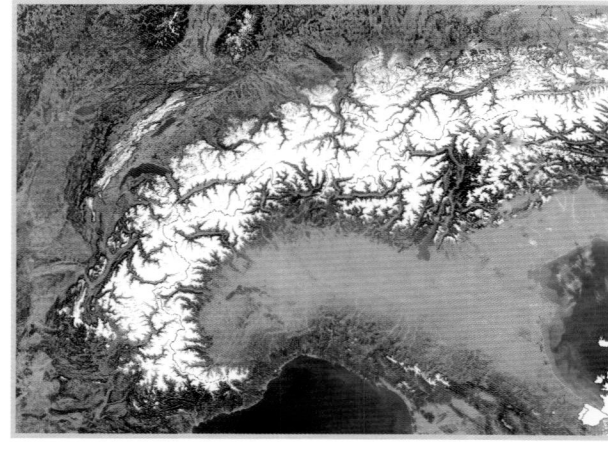

SCALE 1:20,000,000
Lamberts Conformal Conic Projection

NATURAL HAZARDS

Earthquakes

Europe is located on the western side of the Eurasian Plate. Beneath the Mediterranean Sea, this plate is colliding with the African Plate and the smaller Anatolian Plate. Sudden movements along the plate boundaries create shock waves that are felt regularly in parts of southern Europe as earthquakes. Over the centuries, earthquakes have caused massive destruction and many deaths.

A woman salvages belongings from the remains of her home following the 1980 earthquake in southern Italy.

Along the plate boundaries that run through the Mediterranean, the thinner African Plate is forced under the thicker Eurasian Plate, buckling the land above and forcing magma to the surface. This creates volcanoes such as Mounts Etna and Vesuvius in Italy.

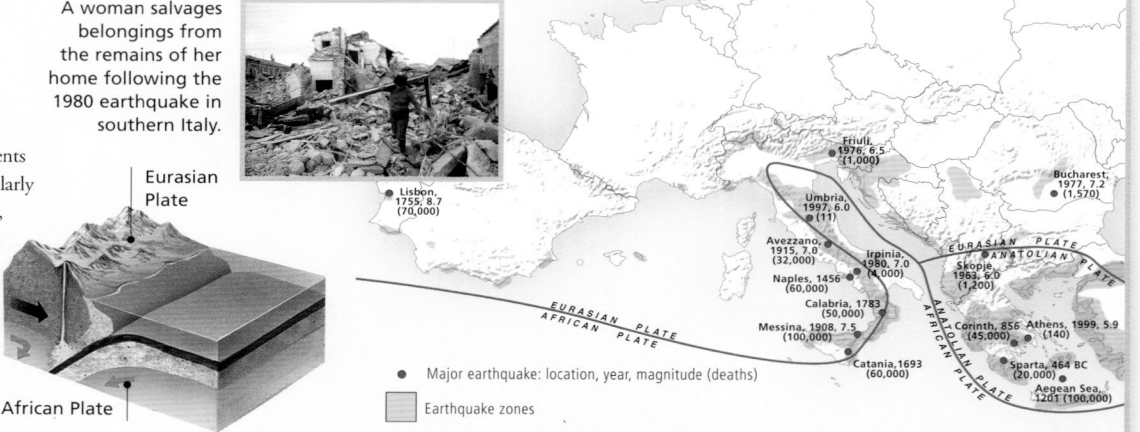

● Major earthquake: location, year, magnitude (deaths)

▢ Earthquake zones

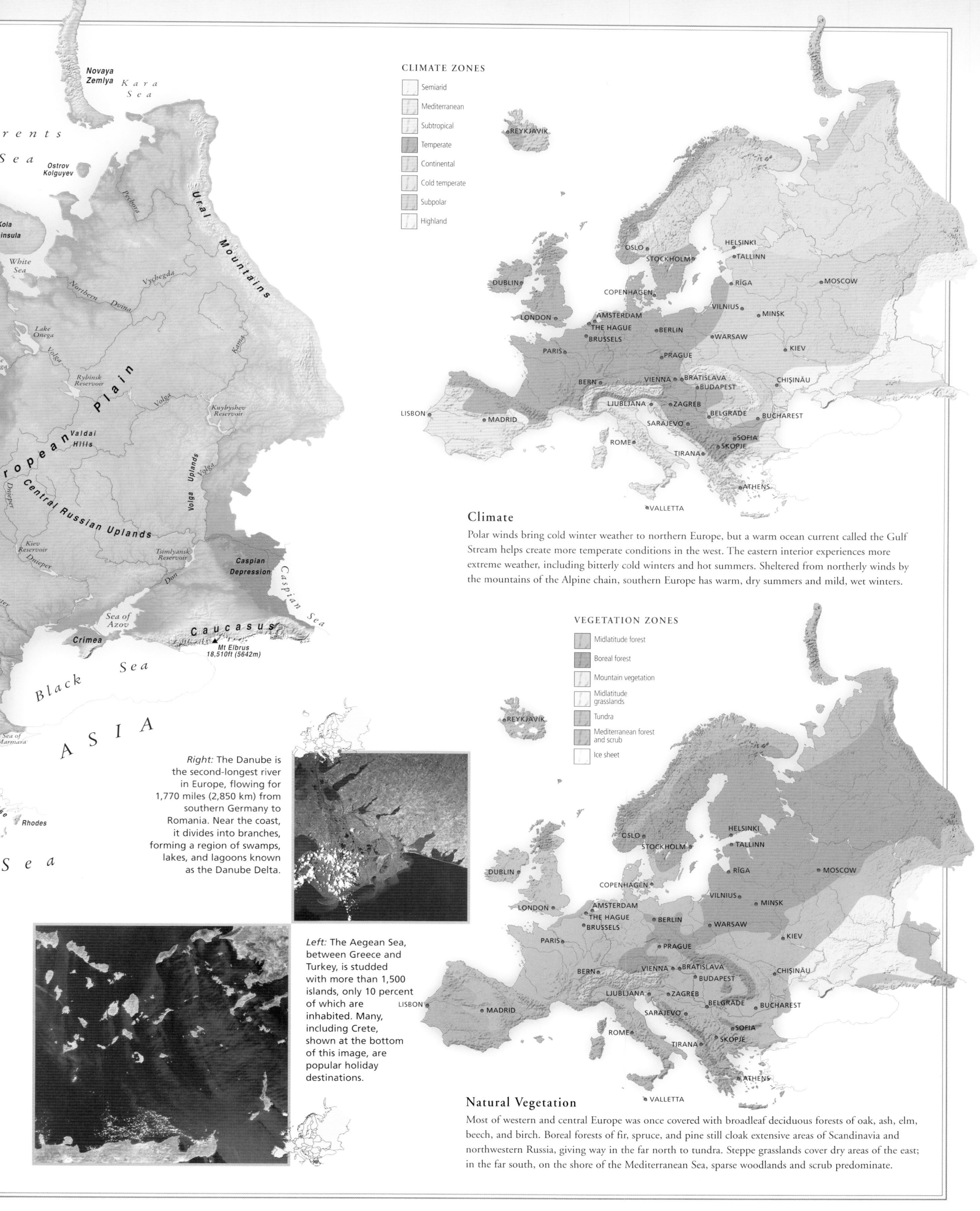

CLIMATE ZONES

- Semiarid
- Mediterranean
- Subtropical
- Temperate
- Continental
- Cold temperate
- Subpolar
- Highland

Map labels (land and sea features): Novaya Zemlya, Kara Sea, Barents Sea, Ostrov Kolguyev, Pechora, Ural Mountains, Kola Peninsula, White Sea, Northern Dvina, Vychegda, Lake Onega, Volga, Kama, Rybinsk Reservoir, Kuybyshev Reservoir, European Plain, Valdai Hills, Volga Uplands, Volga, Central Russian Uplands, Dnieper, Kiev Reservoir, Dnieper, Don, Tsimlyansk Reservoir, Caspian Depression, Caspian Sea, Sea of Azov, Crimea, Caucasus, Mt Elbrus 18,510ft (5642m), Black Sea, Sea of Marmara, ASIA, Rhodes, Sea

City labels (climate map): REYKJAVÍK, OSLO, STOCKHOLM, HELSINKI, TALLINN, MOSCOW, DUBLIN, COPENHAGEN, RĪGA, VILNIUS, MINSK, LONDON, AMSTERDAM, THE HAGUE, BRUSSELS, BERLIN, WARSAW, KIEV, PARIS, PRAGUE, BERN, VIENNA, BRATISLAVA, BUDAPEST, CHIŞINĂU, LISBON, MADRID, LJUBLJANA, ZAGREB, BELGRADE, BUCHAREST, SARAJEVO, ROME, SOFIA, SKOPJE, TIRANA, ATHENS, VALLETTA

Climate

Polar winds bring cold winter weather to northern Europe, but a warm ocean current called the Gulf Stream helps create more temperate conditions in the west. The eastern interior experiences more extreme weather, including bitterly cold winters and hot summers. Sheltered from northerly winds by the mountains of the Alpine chain, southern Europe has warm, dry summers and mild, wet winters.

VEGETATION ZONES

- Midlatitude forest
- Boreal forest
- Mountain vegetation
- Midlatitude grasslands
- Tundra
- Mediterranean forest and scrub
- Ice sheet

Right: The Danube is the second-longest river in Europe, flowing for 1,770 miles (2,850 km) from southern Germany to Romania. Near the coast, it divides into branches, forming a region of swamps, lakes, and lagoons known as the Danube Delta.

Left: The Aegean Sea, between Greece and Turkey, is studded with more than 1,500 islands, only 10 percent of which are inhabited. Many, including Crete, shown at the bottom of this image, are popular holiday destinations.

City labels (vegetation map): REYKJAVÍK, OSLO, STOCKHOLM, HELSINKI, TALLINN, MOSCOW, DUBLIN, COPENHAGEN, RĪGA, VILNIUS, MINSK, LONDON, AMSTERDAM, THE HAGUE, BERLIN, WARSAW, KIEV, PARIS, BRUSSELS, PRAGUE, BERN, VIENNA, BRATISLAVA, BUDAPEST, CHIŞINĂU, LISBON, MADRID, LJUBLJANA, ZAGREB, BELGRADE, BUCHAREST, SARAJEVO, ROME, SOFIA, SKOPJE, TIRANA, ATHENS, VALLETTA

Natural Vegetation

Most of western and central Europe was once covered with broadleaf deciduous forests of oak, ash, elm, beech, and birch. Boreal forests of fir, spruce, and pine still cloak extensive areas of Scandinavia and northwestern Russia, giving way in the far north to tundra. Steppe grasslands cover dry areas of the east; in the far south, on the shore of the Mediterranean Sea, sparse woodlands and scrub predominate.

PEOPLES AND NATIONS

Europe has a population of about 720 million and has long been one of the most densely inhabited parts of the world. It is home to a great diversity of peoples, languages, and cultures—the result of thousands of years of migrations, invasions, wars, and changing allegiances—and its cities are rich in historical, architectural, and artistic treasures. Today, Europe encompasses 42 nations as well as the Eastern Thrace region of Turkey and the eastern part of the Russian Federation, which are sometimes referred to as European Turkey and European Russia. Most European nations have substantial natural resources, and the inhabitants of northwestern Europe, especially, enjoy a high standard of living.

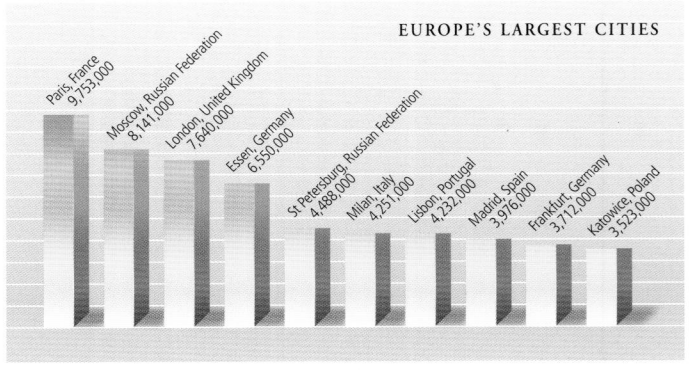

EUROPE'S LARGEST CITIES

Paris, France 9,753,000
Moscow, Russian Federation 8,141,000
London, United Kingdom 7,640,000
Essen, Germany 6,550,000
St Petersburg, Russian Federation 4,488,000
Milan, Italy 4,251,000
Lisbon, Portugal 4,232,000
Madrid, Spain 3,976,000
Frankfurt, Germany 3,712,000
Katowice, Poland 3,523,000

Urbanization

Until the 18th century, relatively few Europeans lived in cities. Following the Industrial Revolution, however, urban areas expanded rapidly. Toward the end of the 18th century, London became the first city in the world to reach a population of 1 million, a figure attained by nine other cities by 1900. Today, approximately 74 percent of Europeans live in urban areas.

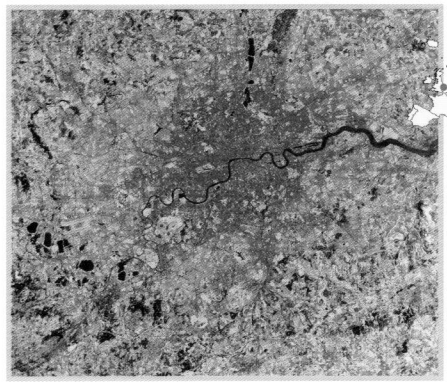

Right: In this false-color satellite image of London, urban areas appear blue, with commercial areas darker than the lighter residential areas. Pale green and orange areas are parklands, and dark orange and red areas indicate arable land. The River Thames is clearly visible as a dark, snaking line.

POPULATION DENSITY

- Uninhabited
- Less than 2.6 persons per sq mile/1 per sq km
- 2.6–26 per sq mile/ 1–10 per sq km
- 26–65 per sq mile/ 10–25 per sq km
- 65–130 per sq mile/ 25–50 per sq km
- 130–260 per sq mile/ 50–100 per sq km
- 260–520 per sq mile/ 100–200 per sq km

Population Patterns

Europe's early population growth centered on strategically important ports and major rivers. Industrial development in the 19th century attracted large numbers of workers to major manufacturing centers, such as central England, Germany's Ruhr Valley, and northern Italy, and these urban areas are still the most densely populated regions. The least densely populated parts of Europe are the high peaks of the central mountain ranges and the far north, most notably northern Scandinavia, and the Scottish Highlands.

The European Union

Twenty-five European nations belong to the European Union (EU), which seeks to establish common economic, social, and judicial policies across the continent. The EU began to take shape in the early 1950s, when Belgium, France, Germany, Italy, Luxembourg, and the Netherlands agreed to establish a common trading market, the European Economic Community (EEC). Its success led other countries to apply for membership. The EU's major institutions include the Council of the EU, the principal decision-making body located in Brussels, Belgium, and the European Parliament, based in Strasbourg, France.

- EU members
- Applicant members
- Seeking membership

FLASHPOINTS

With so many nations, peoples, and cultures living in close proximity to each other, it is not surprising that Europe is the site of several longstanding disputes.

Basqueland

The Basque people of northern Spain and southwestern France have a distinct culture and unique language. Since the 1970s, in an attempt to gain independence for their homeland from Spain, Basques belonging to a group called ETA, or Euzkada Ta Askatasuna (Basque Homeland and Liberty), have resorted to terrorism.

Northern Ireland

In 1921, Ireland became self-governing and the six counties of Northern Ireland were incorporated into the United Kingdom (U.K.). Since then, Northern Ireland has been the site of violent conflict between Protestants, who want to remain part of the U.K., and Catholics, who wish to unite with Ireland.

Percentage of Total Population
Catholic 100 80 60 40 20 0
Protestant 0 20 40 60 80 100

Kosovo

About 90 percent of the inhabitants of the Serbian province of Kosovo are ethnic Albanians, most of whom would like their region to be autonomous or independent. Serbia has violently resisted Kosovar moves toward independence, partly because it fears the unification of Kosovo with neighboring Albania.

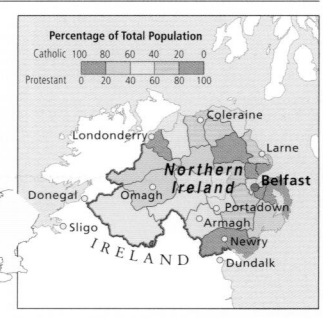

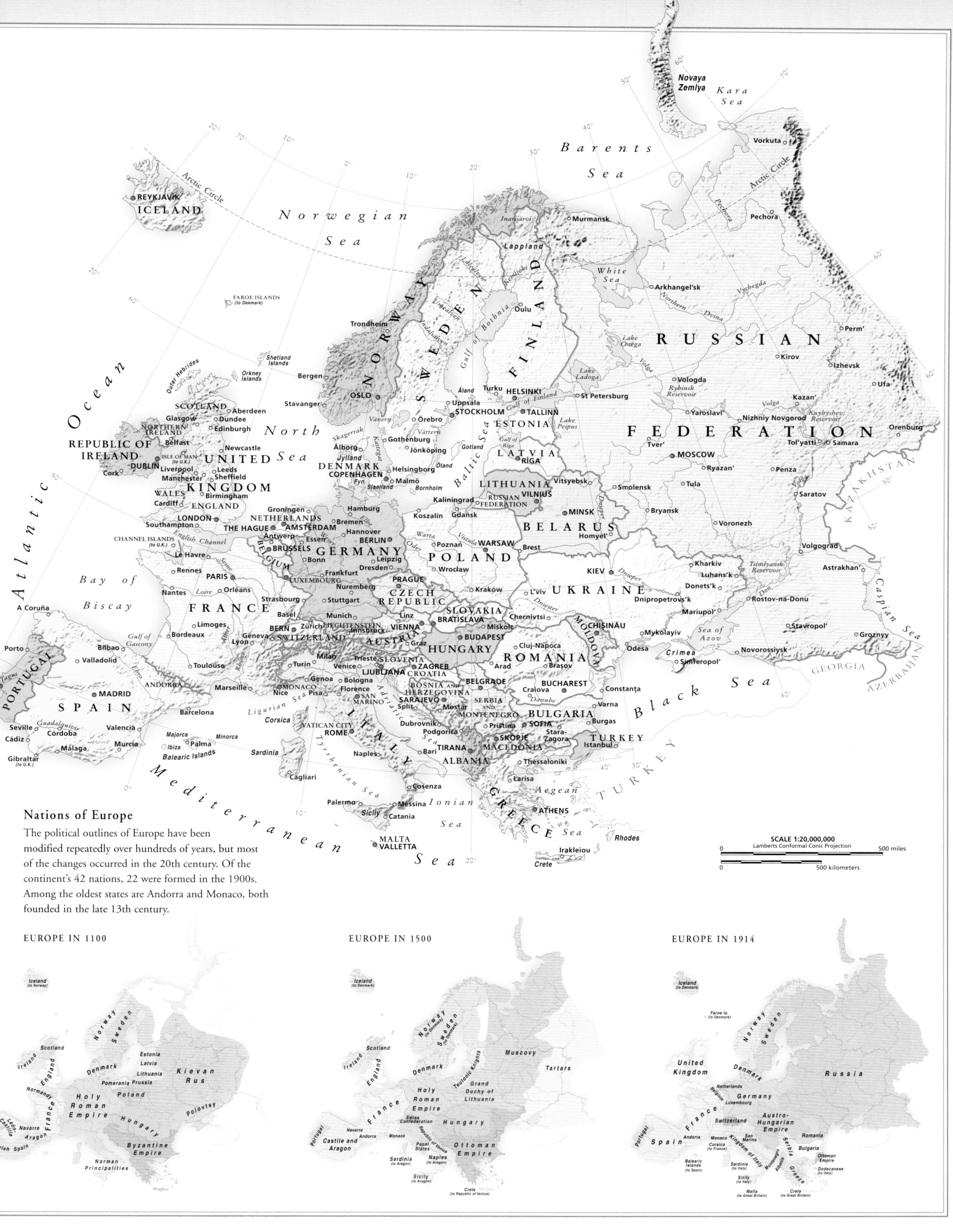

Nations of Europe

The political outlines of Europe have been modified repeatedly over hundreds of years, but most of the changes occurred in the 20th century. Of the continent's 42 nations, 22 were formed in the 1900s. Among the oldest states are Andorra and Monaco, both founded in the late 13th century.

EUROPE IN 1100

EUROPE IN 1500

EUROPE IN 1914

SCALE 1:20,000,000
Lamberts Conformal Conic Projection

THE HUMAN IMPACT

Along with eastern and southern Asia, Europe was the focus of early population growth. Large-scale modification of the landscape began with the development of subsistence farming around 4000 BC, increased with the introduction of the iron plow and commercial farming in the Middle Ages, then accelerated rapidly with the advent of industry in the 18th century. Humans have now removed more than half of the continent's original forest, along with large areas of natural steppe grasslands. Urban areas, roadways, and railways form a tangled web of concrete, tarmac, and steel covering thousands of square miles. Mines have been excavated, rivers dammed, and swamps drained. Overall, humans are thought to have modified about 65 percent of Europe's surface—double the proportion of any other continent. These transformations have brought significant benefits and enabled Europeans to enjoy a high standard of living. But continuing prosperity could be undermined by damage to the environment caused by depletion of resources and the polluting effects of waste.

THE CHANGING FACE OF EUROPE

Forests

About 8,000 years ago, forests covered about 70 percent of Europe, flourishing almost everywhere except for especially high, exposed, or poorly drained land. As populations expanded and technology developed, Europeans cleared ever-larger numbers of trees to provide farmland, fuel, and building materials. Today, excluding Russia, 68 percent of the original forest has disappeared and only one percent of old-growth trees survive. Large stands of forest remain only in northern Europe, European Russia, and subalpine regions. On a more positive note, Europe has increased its forest cover in recent years by 4 percent—more than any other continent.

ORIGINAL FOREST COVER

CURRENT FOREST COVER

LAND USE AND RESOURCES

- Forest and woodland
- Arable land
- Grazing
- Marginal or nonproductive

Cereals	Oilseed rape	Pigs
Rice	Tobacco	Fishing
Flax	Sugar beet	Shellfish
Potatoes	Flowers	Industrial center
Fruit and vegetables	Olives	Mining
Fruit	Reindeer	Oil production
Vegetables	Beef cattle	Gas production
Citrus fruits	Dairy cattle	Tourism
Wine	Sheep	Timber
		Winter sports

Economic Profile

Europe's abundant resources include major reserves of fossil fuels, reliable supplies of fresh water, and sizable swathes of arable land. The fertile west, center, and southeast produce large amounts of cereals (20 percent of the world's supply), root crops (including two-thirds of the world's potatoes), fruit, and livestock products. Dairy and beef cattle predominate in the north; the south is better suited to the farming of olives, grapes, citrus fruits, sheep, and goats. European industries make half of the world's steel, one-third of its chemicals, and a plethora of consumer goods, the continent also accounts for half of the world's exports and imports.

Land Cover

Most of Europe's forests and woodlands lie in European Russia and Scandinavia. Western Europe has much higher proportions of arable land and pasture. Large parts of Europe are covered by urban and industrial areas, roads, and railways.

PROPORTIONS OF TOTAL LAND AREA

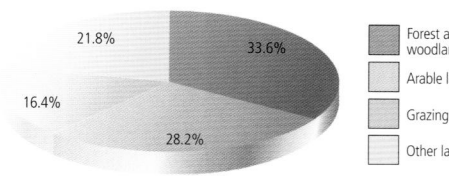

- 21.8%
- 33.6%
- 16.4%
- 28.2%

- Forest and woodland
- Arable land
- Grazing
- Other land

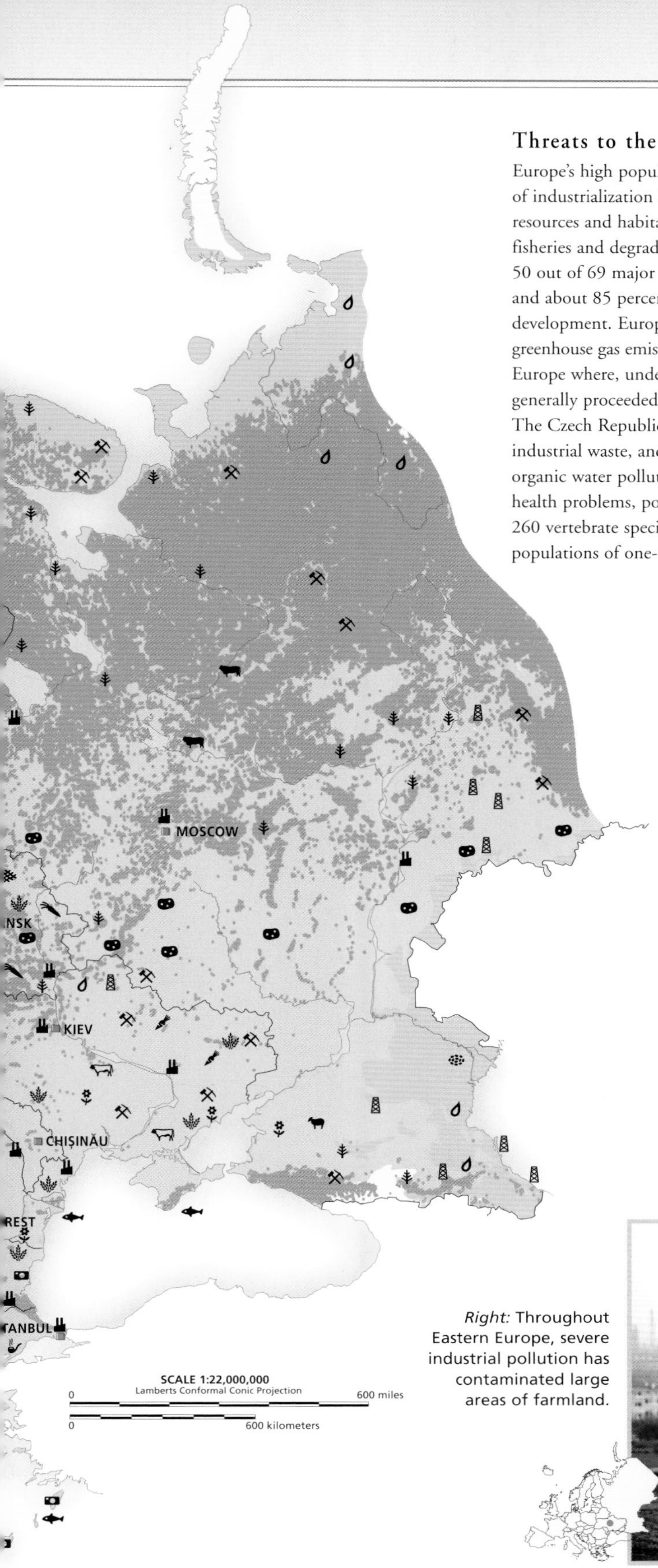

Threats to the Environment

Europe's high population density and high level of industrialization have placed great strain on its natural resources and habitats. Overexploitation has depleted fisheries and degraded soils. A recent assessment found 50 out of 69 major rivers to be of poor ecological quality, and about 85 percent of the coastline is threatened by development. Europe is responsible for one-third of global greenhouse gas emissions; pollution is especially bad in Eastern Europe where, under Soviet control, industrialization generally proceeded unchecked by environmental restrictions. The Czech Republic now has the continent's highest levels of industrial waste, and Moldova has the highest levels of organic water pollutants. As well as giving rise to human health problems, pollution has decimated wildlife—about 260 vertebrate species are on the brink of extinction and the populations of one-third of bird species are in decline.

Right: On November 19, 2002, the *Prestige* oil tanker ran aground off the northwest coast of Spain, releasing 24,500 tons (25,000 t) of oil. The spill decimated wildlife and local fishing industries.

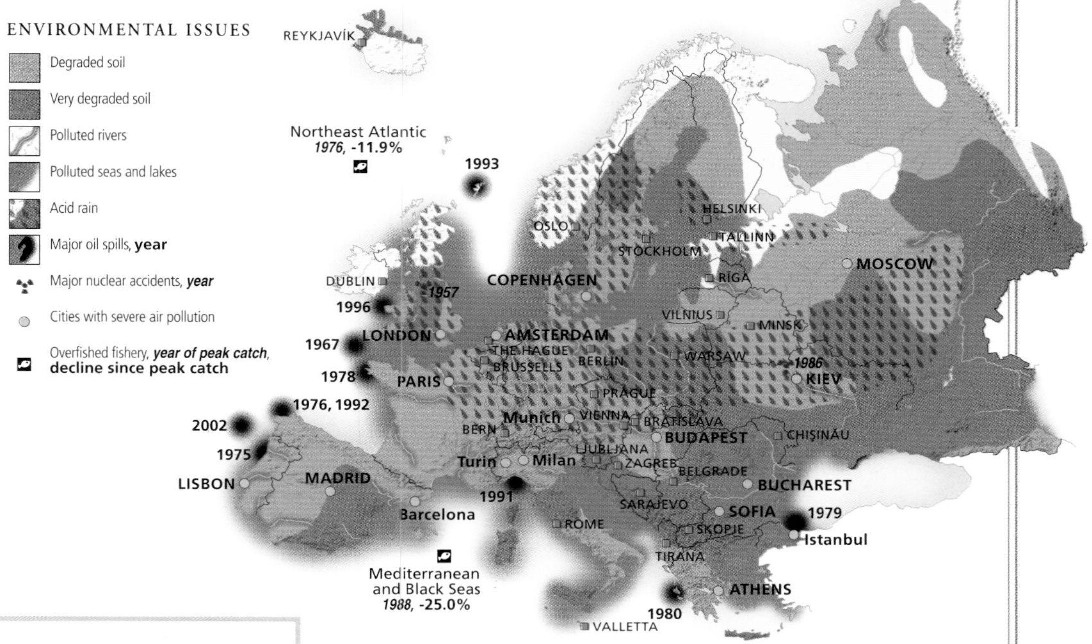

ENVIRONMENTAL ISSUES

- Degraded soil
- Very degraded soil
- Polluted rivers
- Polluted seas and lakes
- Acid rain
- Major oil spills, **year**
- Major nuclear accidents, **year**
- Cities with severe air pollution
- Overfished fishery, *year of peak catch*, **decline since peak catch**

Northeast Atlantic
1976, -11.9%

Mediterranean and Black Seas
1988, -25.0%

SCALE 1:22,000,000
Lamberts Conformal Conic Projection
0 — 600 miles
0 — 600 kilometers

Right: Throughout Eastern Europe, severe industrial pollution has contaminated large areas of farmland.

Right: Chernobyl in the Soviet Union (now Ukraine) was the site of the worst-ever nuclear disaster, in April 1986. It killed 32 people and spread radioactive fallout throughout Europe.

Protecting the Environment

The implementation of recent international legislation has resulted in significant progress in reducing pollution, with greenhouse-gas emissions falling 2 percent between 1990 and 1998, and carbon dioxide emissions declining 8 percent in Eastern Europe between 1990 and 2000. The use of pesticides has dwindled in Eastern Europe, and phosphorous discharges have dropped by 50 to 80 percent in Western Europe in the past 20 years. Levels of the heavy metals cadmium, lindane, and mercury in seas fell by 80 percent in the 1990s. The number of protected areas grows every year and in Western Europe legislation designed to protect biodiversity now covers over 54 million acres (22 million ha) of farmland. However, environmental groups fear that the level of protection offered by many preserves is inadequate.

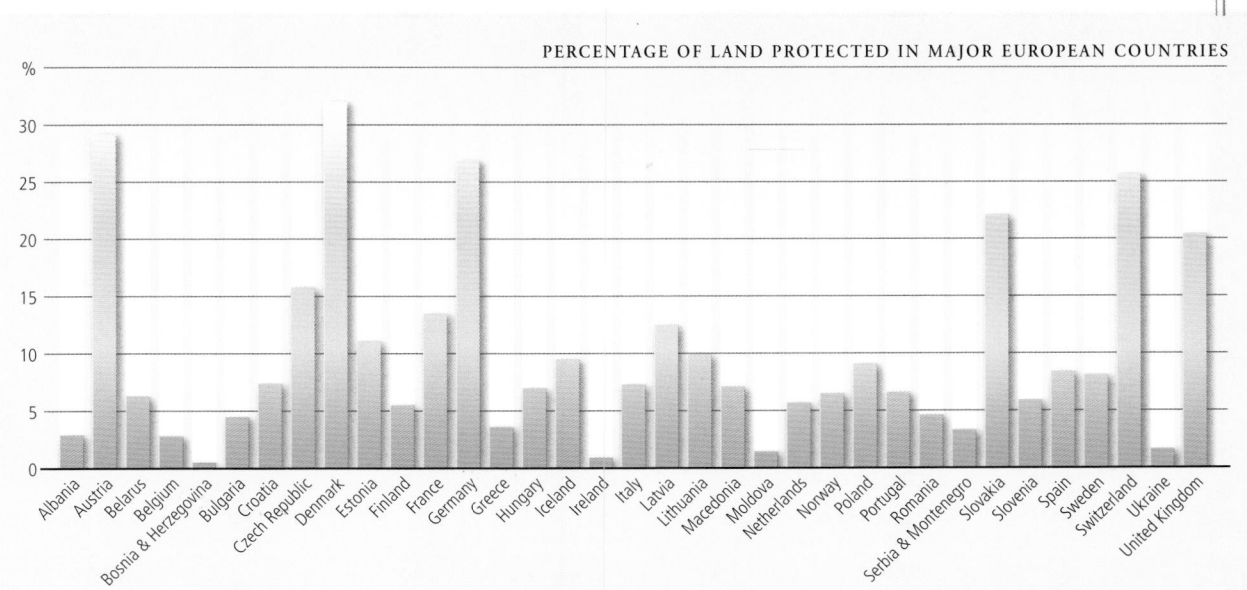

PERCENTAGE OF LAND PROTECTED IN MAJOR EUROPEAN COUNTRIES

THE BRITISH ISLES
Republic of Ireland, United Kingdom

The British Isles consist of two large islands, Great Britain and Ireland, and numerous smaller islands located off the northwest coast of mainland Europe.

Together with the troubled province of Northern Ireland, the once-independent nations of England, Scotland, and Wales make up the United Kingdom (U.K.).

The southern part of the island of Ireland became self-governing in 1921, becoming almost entirely flat in the east-coast Fens region. To the north and west, the land is more rugged, with hills and mountains dominating central northern England, much of Wales, southern and northern Scotland, and parts of Northern Ireland. In southern Ireland, a well-watered central plain is studded with lakes and peat bogs and ringed by coastal uplands. Both the U.K. and Ireland have recently developed closer social and economic ties with other European nations, and a physical link between Britain and the rest of the continent was forged in 1994 with the completion of the Channel Tunnel.

Oxford, England, is a manufacturing center, noted for automobile production. But it is best known as the site of the U.K.'s oldest university, founded in the 12th century.

On the west coast of Ireland, uplands abut the Atlantic Ocean, forming dramatic coastal landforms such as the spectacular Cliffs of Moher, near Hag's Head.

POPULATION PATTERNS

The U.K. is highly urbanized population—about 90 percent inhabit towns and cities—is heavily concentrated in the southeast and around the industrial centers of Birmingham, Manchester, Leeds, Glasgow, and Belfast. The least densely populated areas are the Scottish Highlands, where sheep far outnumber people, and the uplands of northwest England and Wales. Ireland's population is more evenly distributed, with about 60 percent living in urban areas.

Less than 2.6 persons per sq mile/1 per sq km
2.6–26 per sq mile/1–10 per sq km
26–65 per sq mile/10–25 per sq km
65–130 per sq mile/25–50 per sq km
130–260 per sq mile/50–100 per sq km
260–520 per sq mile/100–200 per sq km

ECONOMIC PROFILE

The decline of the U.K.'s manufacturing industries has been paralleled by the growth in services, which now employ three-quarters of workers. Still-important industries include engineering, chemicals and chemical products, metals, and food and beverages. The nation's most abundant food crops are cereals (especially wheat and barley), potatoes, sugar beet, and oilseed rape. Ireland's farming sector is more dependent on livestock. Its industries experienced a boom in the late 20th century, led by textiles, chemicals, machinery, and computer hardware and software.

Cereals
Potatoes
Sugar beet
Oilseed rape
Beef cattle
Dairy cattle
Sheep

Industrial center
Fishing
Oil production
Gas production
Shellfish
Timber

Forest and woodland
Arable land
Grazing

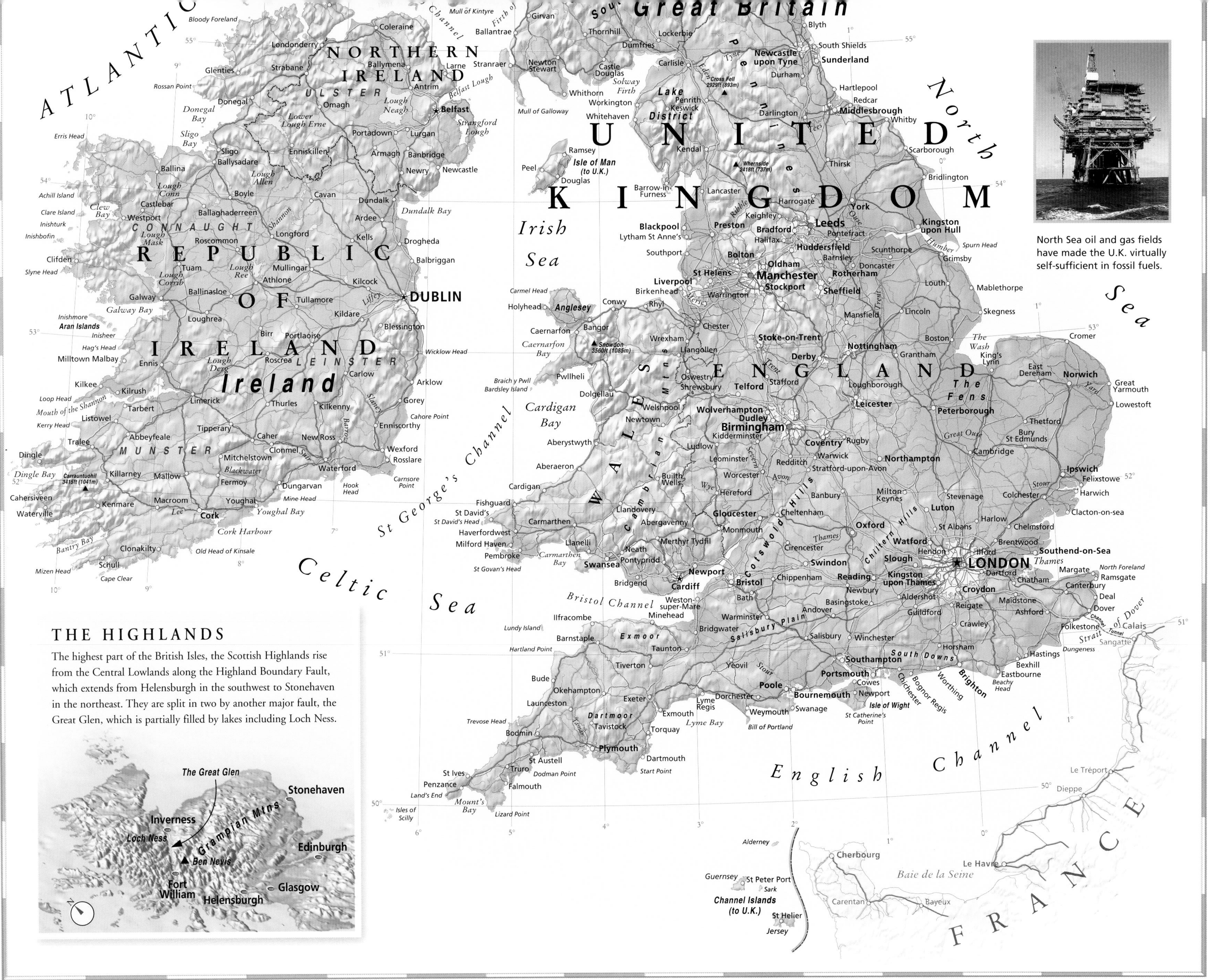

North Sea oil and gas fields have made the U.K. virtually self-sufficient in fossil fuels.

THE HIGHLANDS

The highest part of the British Isles, the Scottish Highlands rise from the Central Lowlands along the Highland Boundary Fault, which extends from Helensburgh in the southwest to Stonehaven in the northeast. They are split in two by another major fault, the Great Glen, which is partially filled by lakes including Loch Ness.

Stonehaven

Edinburgh

Glasgow

Grampian Mtns

Ben Nevis

The Great Glen

Inverness

Loch Ness

Fort William

Helensburgh

SCALE 1:3,000,000
Lamberts Conformal Conic Projection

100 miles

100 kilometers

Longitude west of Greenwich

ELEVATION

Feet	Meters
6562	2000
4921	1500
3281	1000
2461	750
1640	500
1312	400
984	300
656	200
328	100
0	0
	Below sea level

Feet	Meters
656	200
3281	1000
6562	2000
13,123	4000
19,685	6000
26,246	8000
32,808	10,000

UNITED KINGDOM

ENGLAND

WALES

Great Britain

NORTHERN IRELAND

REPUBLIC OF IRELAND

ULSTER

CONNAUGHT

LEINSTER

MUNSTER

Ireland

FRANCE

North Sea

Irish Sea

Celtic Sea

ATLANTIC

English Channel

Bristol Channel

St George's Channel

LONDON

DUBLIN

Belfast

SOUTHERN GREAT BRITAIN

From the southern flanks of the Pennines, a broad belt of roads, towns, and cities runs southeastward through the low-lying heart of England, the region known as the Midlands, to London, the capital of the U.K. and its largest city. This corridor is by far the most developed part of the country, encompassing the majority of its industrial and commercial centers, the bulk of its freeways, and more than half of its population.

The urban sprawl is, however, broken by sizable tracts of fertile farmland—most notably in the East Midlands—remnants of forests, and scenic ranges of hills, including the Cotswolds and the Chilterns. On the eastern and western fringes lie quieter, culturally and geographically distinctive areas. The Cambrian Mountains dominate the interior of the Celtic nation of Wales, descending to a long, heavily indented coastline. In the east, the formerly swampy Fens isolate the tranquil agricultural plains of East Anglia, and in the far southwest, a picturesque, rocky coastline bounds the narrow, traditionally Celtic enclave of Cornwall and the rolling pastures and moorlands of Devon.

Made of chalk, the famous white cliffs of Dover border the English Channel.

The Royal Liver Building, a Liverpool landmark, was completed in 1911.

Snowdon in northwest Wales has five peaks. The tallest, Yr Wyddfa, is the highest point in England and Wales.

POPULATION PATTERNS

This region has more than two-thirds of the U.K. population, with the highest concentrations occurring in London (home to 7.6 million people), Birmingham, and the cluster of cities between Liverpool and Leeds. Population growth is relatively low and due mainly to natural increase. In the late 20th century, the demise of heavy industry and coal mining in the northwest, Wales, and Scotland accelerated migration to London. However, a concurrent trend saw many people and businesses move out of the capital to peripheral areas such as the East Midlands, East Anglia, and the southwest. One-quarter of people in Wales speak Welsh; the region's other Celtic language, Cornish, has all but died out.

ECONOMIC PROFILE

The economy is dominated by services, particularly finance, retailing, health care, and tourism. While the northwest and Wales have suffered due to the collapse of coal mining and heavy industries, the east and southeast have thrived due to the boom in services and success in attracting light, high-tech industries to areas such as Cambridge and Reading. Southern England has most of the U.K.'s best farmland. The highly mechanized cultivation of wheat, oilseed rape, and sugar beet takes place in the east; dairy and beef cattle are reared in the west; and market gardening (the small-scale cultivation of fruit and vegetables) predominates in the southeast.

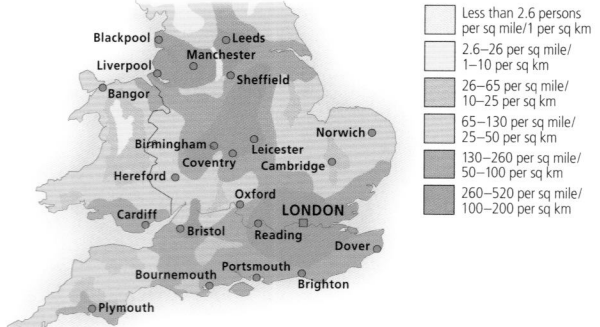

Less than 2.6 persons per sq mile/1 per sq km
2.6–26 per sq mile/1–10 per sq km
26–65 per sq mile/10–25 per sq km
65–130 per sq mile/25–50 per sq km
130–260 per sq mile/50–100 per sq km
260–520 per sq mile/100–200 per sq km

Forest and woodland
Arable land
Grazing
Cereals
Sugar beet
Oilseed rape
Beef cattle
Dairy cattle
Sheep
Industrial center
Fishing
Tourism
Mining
Fruit and vegetables

London The Romans founded Londinium, as they named it, on the banks of the Thames in the first century AD. After being all but abandoned in the fifth century, the town flourished again under the Saxons and the Normans, whose king, William I (the Conqueror), built a fortress to control local trade. Known as the White Fort and later the Tower of London, it was expanded by several monarchs over the following centuries, becoming a royal residence and, notoriously, a prison and place of execution. The city grew with it, attaining a population of 1 million by 1800 and 6.5 million a century later. Now a popular tourist attraction, the tower still hosts a military garrison and is patrolled by guards, known as "beefeaters," who dress in distinctive Tudor uniforms.

ELEVATION
Feet / Meters

6562	2000
4921	1500
3281	1000
2461	750
1640	500
1312	400
984	300
656	200
328	100
0 Below sea level	0
656	200
3281	1000
6562	2000
13,123	4000
19,685	6000
26,246	8000
32,808	10,000

SCALE 1:1,500,000
Lamberts Conformal Conic Projection
0   50 miles
0   50 kilometers

W X Y Z

From the early 18th century, windmills like this one near Holt, Norfolk, were used to drain marshes in East Anglia.

Irish Sea

North Sea

Liverpool Bay

Morecambe Bay

ENGLAND

UNITED KINGDOM

East Anglia

The Wash

The Fens

The Broads

Coniston · Windermere · Kendal · Sedbergh · Hawes · Northallerton · Scarborough
Lake District · Newby Bridge · Kirkby Lonsdale · Whernside 2418ft (737m) · Yorkshire Dales · Bedale · Thirsk · Helmsley · Kirkbymoorside · Filey Head · Filey
Ulverston · Milnthorpe · Ingleborough 2372ft (724m) · Ripon · Easingwold · Malton · Pickering · Hunmanby · Flamborough · Flamborough Head
Dalton-in-Furness · Carnforth · Ingleton · Pen-y-ghent 2274ft (693m) · Boroughbridge · Stillington · Wharram le Street · Bridlington · Bridlington Bay
Barrow-in-Furness · Isle of Walney · Morecambe · Lancaster · Settle · Long Preston · Knaresborough · Stamford Bridge · Skipsea
Heysham · Forest of Bowland · Newton · Skipton · Ilkley · Harrogate · Pateley Bridge · Spofforth · York · Holme-upon-Spalding-Moor · Leven · Hornsea
Fleetwood · Cockerham · Clitheroe · Keighley · Otley · Wetherby · Pocklington · Market Weighton · Beverley · Holderness
Garstang · Great Harwood · Shipley · Tadcaster · Selby · Howden · Kingston upon Hull · Tunstall · Withernsea
Poulton-le-Fylde · Blackpool · Kirkham · Preston · Leyland · Chorley · Blackburn · Burnley · Halifax · Bradford · Leeds · Garforth · Castleford · Pontefract · Snaith · Askern · Barton-upon-Humber · Immingham · Grimsby · Spurn Head
Lytham St Anne's · Southport · Ormskirk · Formby · Wigan · Bolton · Oldham · Huddersfield · Wakefield · Barnsley · Hatfield · Scunthorpe · Cleethorpes · Tetney · North Somercotes
Liverpool · Bootle · St Helens · Salford · Manchester · Holmfirth · Stocksbridge · Doncaster · Epworth · Brigg · Caistor · Louth · Mablethorpe
Birkenhead · Heswall · Warrington · Widnes · Runcorn · Altrincham · Stockport · Glossop · Rotherham · Sheffield · Maltby · Bawtry · Blyton · Market Rasen · Wragby · Maltby le Marsh · Alford
Prestatyn · Rhyl · Holywell · Flint · Ellesmere Port · Chapel-en-le-Frith · Aston · Blyth · Retford · Gainsborough · Lincoln · Horncastle · Coningsby · Ingoldmells · Skegness
Colwyn Bay · St Asaph · Chester · Northwich · Middlewich · Macclesfield · Buxton · Chesterfield · Bolsover · Worksop · Saxilby · Billinghay · Wainfleet All Saints
Denbigh · Hope · Wrexham · Sandbach · Congleton · Bakewell · Matlock · Alfreton · Mansfield · Ollerton · Sherwood Forest · Newark-on-Trent · Leadenham · Sleaford · Sibsey · Wrangle
Rhosllanerchrugog · Ruabon · Nantwich · Crewe · Kidsgrove · Leek · Ashbourne · Ripley · Sutton in Ashfield · Eastwood · Stapleford · Nottingham · Grantham · Swineshead · Fosdyke · Hunstanton · Blakeney Point · Blakeney · Cromer
Llangollen · Llanddulas · Oswestry · Whitchurch · Newcastle-under-Lyme · Stoke-on-Trent · Derby · West Bridgford · Loughborough · Bourne · Spalding · Holbeach · Terrington St Clement · King's Lynn · Snettisham · Dersingham · Wells-next-the-Sea · Holt · North Walsham · Aylsham · Coltishall · The Hoveton Broads · Hemsby
Bala · Market Drayton · Stafford · Burton upon Trent · Castle Donington · Waltham on the Wolds · Melton Mowbray · Pinchbeck · Wisbech · Downham Market · East Dereham · Fakenham · Guist · Taverham · Norwich · Acle · Great Yarmouth
Welshpool · Shrewsbury · Newport · Wellington · Penkridge · Cannock · Lichfield · Tamworth · Leicester · Oakham · Stamford · March · Whittlesey · Chatteris · Littleport · Ely · Mildenhall · Brandon · Thetford · Mundford · Swaffham · Attleborough · Long Stratton · Bungay · Beccles · Kessingland · Lowestoft
Montgomery · Church Stretton · Telford · Wolverhampton · Walsall · Sutton Coldfield · Hinckley · Wigston · Market Harborough · Corby · Oundle · Stilton · Warboys · St Ives · Soham · Newmarket · Bury St Edmunds · Stanton · Ixworth · Diss · Scole · Eye · Halesworth · Southwold
Newtown · Bridgnorth · Dudley · West Bromwich · Birmingham · Nuneaton · Lutterworth · Rothwell · Kettering · Wellingborough · Huntingdon · Cambridge · Stowmarket · Dennington · Yoxford · Saxmundham · Aldeburgh
Llangurig · Clun · Craven Arms · Kidderminster · Stourbridge · Halesowen · Solihull · Coventry · Rugby · Husbands Bosworth · Northampton · Rushden · St Neots · Sandy · Sawston · Haverhill · Lavenham · Wickham Market · Claydon · Woodbridge
Knighton · Ludlow · Tenbury Wells · Bromsgrove · Redditch · Studley · Kenilworth · Warwick · Royal Leamington Spa · Daventry · Wellingborough · Bedford · Biggleswade · Royston · Saffron Walden · Sudbury · Hadleigh · Ipswich · Felixstowe
Penybont · Llandrindod Wells · Presteigne · Leominster · Worcester · Alcester · Stratford-upon-Avon · Towcester · Silverstone · Newport Pagnell · Ampthill · Hitchin · Halstead · Colchester · Harwich · The Naze · Walton-on-the-Naze
Builth Wells · Kington · Bodenham · Hereford · Great Malvern · Evesham · Chipping Campden · Banbury · Brackley · Milton Keynes · Bletchley · Stevenage · Bishop's Stortford · Braintree · Coggeshall · Clacton-on-Sea
Garth · Talgarth · Hay-on-Wye · Glasbury · Ledbury · Broadway · Moreton-in-Marsh · Stow-on-the-Wold · Bicester · Leighton Buzzard · Dunstable · Luton · Great Dunmow · Witham · Maldon · Mersea Island · Blackwater
Brecon · Black Mountains · Crickhowell · Ross-on-Wye · Cheltenham · Chipping Norton · Woodstock · Aylesbury · Hemel Hempstead · St Albans · Waltham Abbey · Harlow · Chipping Ongar · Billericay · Rayleigh · Foulness Point · Foulness Island
Pen y Fan 2907ft (886m) · Abergavenny · Gloucester · Burford · Witney · Thame · Wendover · Amersham · Watford · Barnet · Enfield · Romford · Brentwood · Basildon · Southend-on-Sea · Canvey Island
Ebbw Vale · Abertillery · Monmouth · Raglan · Forest of Dean · Cirencester · Kidlington · Oxford · High Wycombe · Beaconsfield · Slough · LONDON · Ilford · Tilbury · Gravesend · Canterbury
Merthyr Tydfil · Aberdare · Pontypool · Chepstow · Caldicot · Stroud · Nailsworth · Lechlade · Faringdon · Abingdon · Marlow · Maidenhead · Windsor · Richmond upon Thames · Greenwich · Bromley · Rochester · Gillingham · Chatham · Sittingbourne · Faversham · Margate · North Foreland · Broadstairs · Ramsgate · Pegwell Bay · Sandwich · Deal
Rhondda · Pontypridd · Caerphilly · Newport · Portishead · Thornbury · Chipping Sodbury · Tetbury · Malmesbury · Swindon · Wantage · Didcot · Reading · Wokingham · Bracknell · Bagshot · Staines · Kingston upon Thames · Croydon · Dartford · Herne Bay · Isle of Sheppey
Porth · Llantrisant · Bridgend · Patchway · Kingswood · Corsham · Chippenham · Marlborough Downs · Lambourn · Newbury · Camberley · Woking · Epsom · Sevenoaks · Maidstone · Chilham · Barham
Caerphilly · Cardiff · Roath · Penarth · Bristol · Long Ashton · Bath · Bradford-on-Avon · Melksham · Devizes · Marlborough · Hungerford · Burbage · Highclere · Kingsclere · Basingstoke · Hook · Farnborough · Aldershot · Guildford · Godalming · Reigate · Oxted · Tonbridge · Royal Tunbridge Wells · Wye · Ashford · Dover
Bridgend · Barry · Weston-super-Mare · Burnham-on-Sea · Cheddar · Wells · Shepton Mallet · Frome · Warminster · Salisbury Plain · Amesbury · Andover · Whitchurch · Alton · New Alresford · Winchester · Haslemere · Hindhead · Crawley · East Grinstead · Crowborough · Cranbrook · Tenterden · Hythe · Folkestone
Bristol Channel · Bridgwater Bay · Minehead · Williton · Bridgwater · Glastonbury · Castle Cary · Wincanton · Gillingham · Shaftesbury · Wilton · Salisbury · Romsey · Eastleigh · Petersfield · Midhurst · Petworth · Pulborough · Billingshurst · Horsham · Haywards Heath · Uckfield · Battle · Hailsham · Rye · Winchelsea · Dungeness · New Romney · Dymchurch
Porlock · Exmoor · Bishop's Lydeard · Taunton · Ilchester · Sherborne · Sturminster Newton · King's Worthy · New Alresford · North Downs · Arundel · Worthing · Brighton · Hove · Lewes · Newhaven · Eastbourne · Bexhill · Hastings · Rye Bay · The Weald · South Downs · Beachy Head
Bampton · Ilminster · Crewkerne · Yeovil · Blandford Forum · Ringwood · Southampton · Fareham · Portchester · Chichester · Bognor Regis · Littlehampton
Dulverton · Cullompton · Honiton · Axminster · Chard · Beaminster · Fordingbridge · Wimborne Minster · Lymington · Lyndhurst · New Forest · Waterlooville · Havant · Hayling Island · Selsey
Crediton · Pinhoe · Topsham · Sidmouth · Bridport · Dorchester · Wareham · Poole · Bournemouth · Christchurch · Gosport · Portsmouth · Ryde · Bembridge
Teignmouth · Newton Abbot · Babbacombe Bay · Seaton · Lyme Regis · Abbotsbury · Weymouth · Corfe Castle · Swanage · The Needles · Freshwater · Cowes · Newport · Sandown · Shanklin
Torquay · Tor Bay · Paignton · Brixham · Weymouth Bay · Isle of Portland · Fortuneswell · Easton · Bill of Portland · Poole Bay · Studland · Chale · Ventnor · Isle of Wight · The Solent
Dartmouth · Start Bay · Start Point · St Alban's Head · St Catherine's Point

English Channel

Strait of Dover · Channel Tunnel

Lyme Bay

The precise function of the stone circles at Stonehenge, near Salisbury, begun around 2700 BC, remains uncertain.

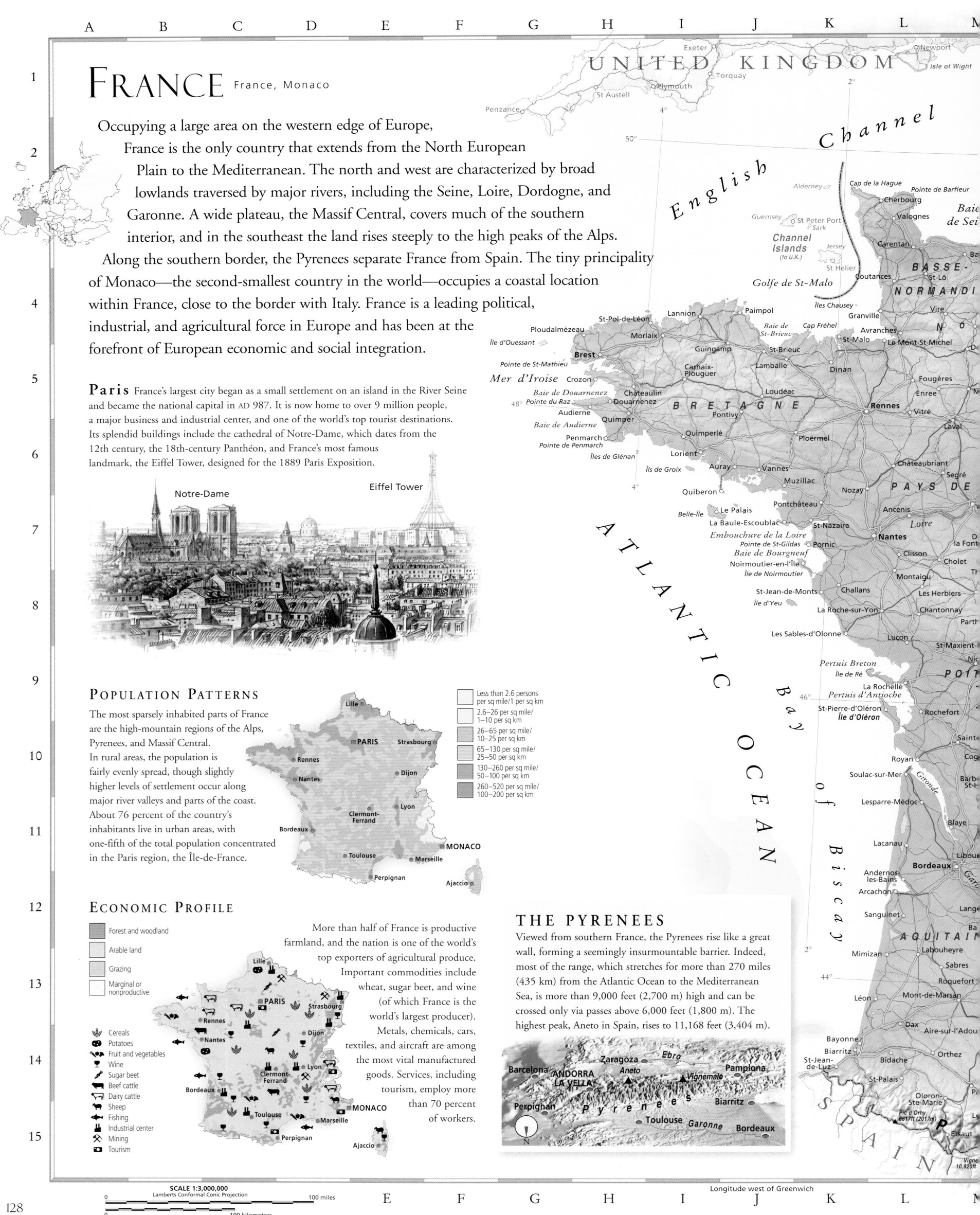

FRANCE France, Monaco

Occupying a large area on the western edge of Europe,
France is the only country that extends from the North European
Plain to the Mediterranean. The north and west are characterized by broad
lowlands traversed by major rivers, including the Seine, Loire, Dordogne, and
Garonne. A wide plateau, the Massif Central, covers much of the southern
interior, and in the southeast the land rises steeply to the high peaks of the Alps.
Along the southern border, the Pyrenees separate France from Spain. The tiny principality
of Monaco—the second-smallest country in the world—occupies a coastal location
within France, close to the border with Italy. France is a leading political,
industrial, and agricultural force in Europe and has been at the
forefront of European economic and social integration.

Paris France's largest city began as a small settlement on an island in the River Seine
and became the national capital in AD 987. It is now home to over 9 million people,
a major business and industrial center, and one of the world's top tourist destinations.
Its splendid buildings include the cathedral of Notre-Dame, which dates from the
12th century, the 18th-century Panthéon, and France's most famous
landmark, the Eiffel Tower, designed for the 1889 Paris Exposition.

Notre-Dame

Eiffel Tower

POPULATION PATTERNS

The most sparsely inhabited parts of France
are the high-mountain regions of the Alps,
Pyrenees, and Massif Central.
In rural areas, the population is
fairly evenly spread, though slightly
higher levels of settlement occur along
major river valleys and parts of the coast.
About 76 percent of the country's
inhabitants live in urban areas, with
one-fifth of the total population concentrated
in the Paris region, the Île-de-France.

Less than 2.6 persons per sq mile/1 per sq km
2.6–26 per sq mile/ 1–10 per sq km
26–65 per sq mile/ 10–25 per sq km
65–130 per sq mile/ 25–50 per sq km
130–260 per sq mile/ 50–100 per sq km
260–520 per sq mile/ 100–200 per sq km

ECONOMIC PROFILE

Forest and woodland
Arable land
Grazing
Marginal or nonproductive

Cereals
Potatoes
Fruit and vegetables
Wine
Sugar beet
Beef cattle
Dairy cattle
Sheep
Fishing
Industrial center
Mining
Tourism

More than half of France is productive
farmland, and the nation is one of the world's
top exporters of agricultural produce.
Important commodities include
wheat, sugar beet, and wine
(of which France is the
world's largest producer).
Metals, chemicals, cars,
textiles, and aircraft are among
the most vital manufactured
goods. Services, including
tourism, employ more
than 70 percent
of workers.

THE PYRENEES

Viewed from southern France, the Pyrenees rise like a great
wall, forming a seemingly insurmountable barrier. Indeed,
most of the range, which stretches for more than 270 miles
(435 km) from the Atlantic Ocean to the Mediterranean
Sea, is more than 9,000 feet (2,700 m) high and can be
crossed only via passes above 6,000 feet (1,800 m). The
highest peak, Aneto in Spain, rises to 11,168 feet (3,404 m).

SCALE 1:3,000,000
Lamberts Conformal Conic Projection
0   100 miles
0   100 kilometers

Longitude west of Greenwich

The Arc de Triomphe in Paris was commissioned by Napoleon in 1806 to celebrate his military victories.

Located on the French–Italian border, Mont Blanc, at 15,771 feet (4,807 m), is the Alps' highest peak.

Monaco measures a mere 0.75 square miles (1.95 sq km). Its tourist facilities and casino are among its principal sources of revenue.

The mountainous island of Corsica was purchased by France from the city-state of Genoa in 1768.

THE IBERIAN PENINSULA

Andorra, Portugal, Spain

Located at the southwestern edge of Europe, the wide, almost square-shaped Iberian Peninsula is flanked by the Atlantic Ocean to the west and by the Mediterranean Sea to the east. It is separated from France by the Pyrenees, and from Africa by the Strait of Gibraltar, which is just 8 miles (12.8 km) wide at its narrowest point. Spain occupies more than 80 percent of the landmass, Portugal almost all of the remainder; the tiny principality of Andorra nestles in the eastern Pyrenees. A large plateau, the Meseta, extends across much of the peninsula. It is bisected by the Sistema Central mountain chain and fringed by other ranges. Between the 15th and 17th centuries, Spain and Portugal ruled vast empires. But their 20th-century histories were marred by war and repressive regimes, and their economies are still recovering.

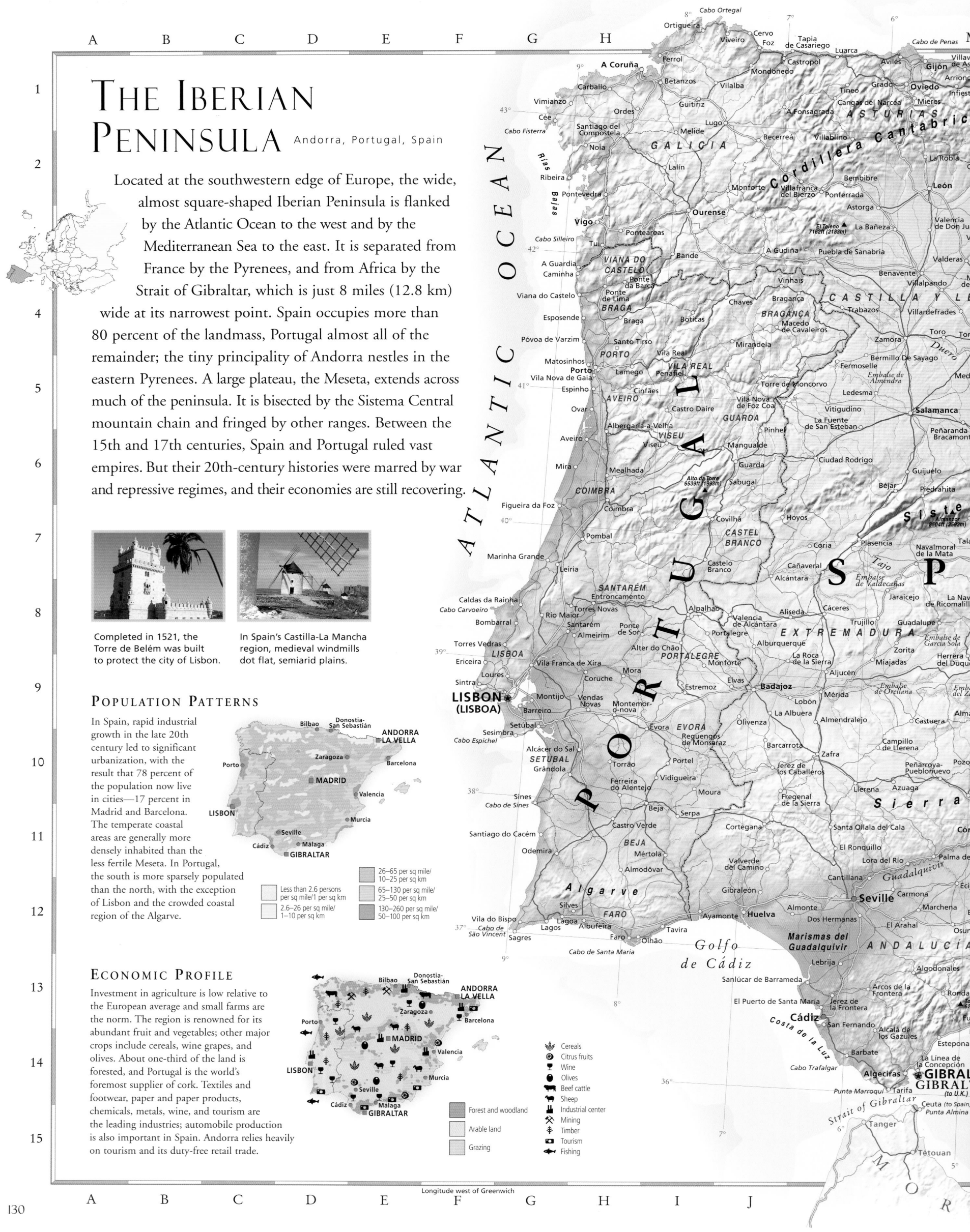

Completed in 1521, the Torre de Belém was built to protect the city of Lisbon.

In Spain's Castilla-La Mancha region, medieval windmills dot flat, semiarid plains.

POPULATION PATTERNS

In Spain, rapid industrial growth in the late 20th century led to significant urbanization, with the result that 78 percent of the population now live in cities—17 percent in Madrid and Barcelona. The temperate coastal areas are generally more densely inhabited than the less fertile Meseta. In Portugal, the south is more sparsely populated than the north, with the exception of Lisbon and the crowded coastal region of the Algarve.

Less than 2.6 persons per sq mile/1 per sq km

2.6–26 per sq mile/ 1–10 per sq km

26–65 per sq mile/ 10–25 per sq km

65–130 per sq mile/ 25–50 per sq km

130–260 per sq mile/ 50–100 per sq km

ECONOMIC PROFILE

Investment in agriculture is low relative to the European average and small farms are the norm. The region is renowned for its abundant fruit and vegetables; other major crops include cereals, wine grapes, and olives. About one-third of the land is forested, and Portugal is the world's foremost supplier of cork. Textiles and footwear, paper and paper products, chemicals, metals, wine, and tourism are the leading industries; automobile production is also important in Spain. Andorra relies heavily on tourism and its duty-free retail trade.

Cereals
Citrus fruits
Wine
Olives
Beef cattle
Sheep
Industrial center
Mining
Timber
Tourism
Fishing

Forest and woodland
Arable land
Grazing

THE SISTEMAS BÉTICOS

In southeastern Spain, a mountain chain, known as the Sistemas Béticos or Baetic Cordillera, extends from Punta Marroquí on the Strait of Gibraltar to Cabo de la Nao on the Costa Blanca. Incorporating numerous small ranges, it rises to its highest point of 11,421 feet (3,481 m) at Mulhacén, northwest of Almería. East of Cabo de la Nao, the chain continues beneath the Mediterranean Sea—the Balearic Islands of Ibiza, Majorca, and Minorca are the summits of its submerged slopes.

SCALE 1:3,000,000
Lamberts Conformal Conic Projection
Longitude east of Greenwich

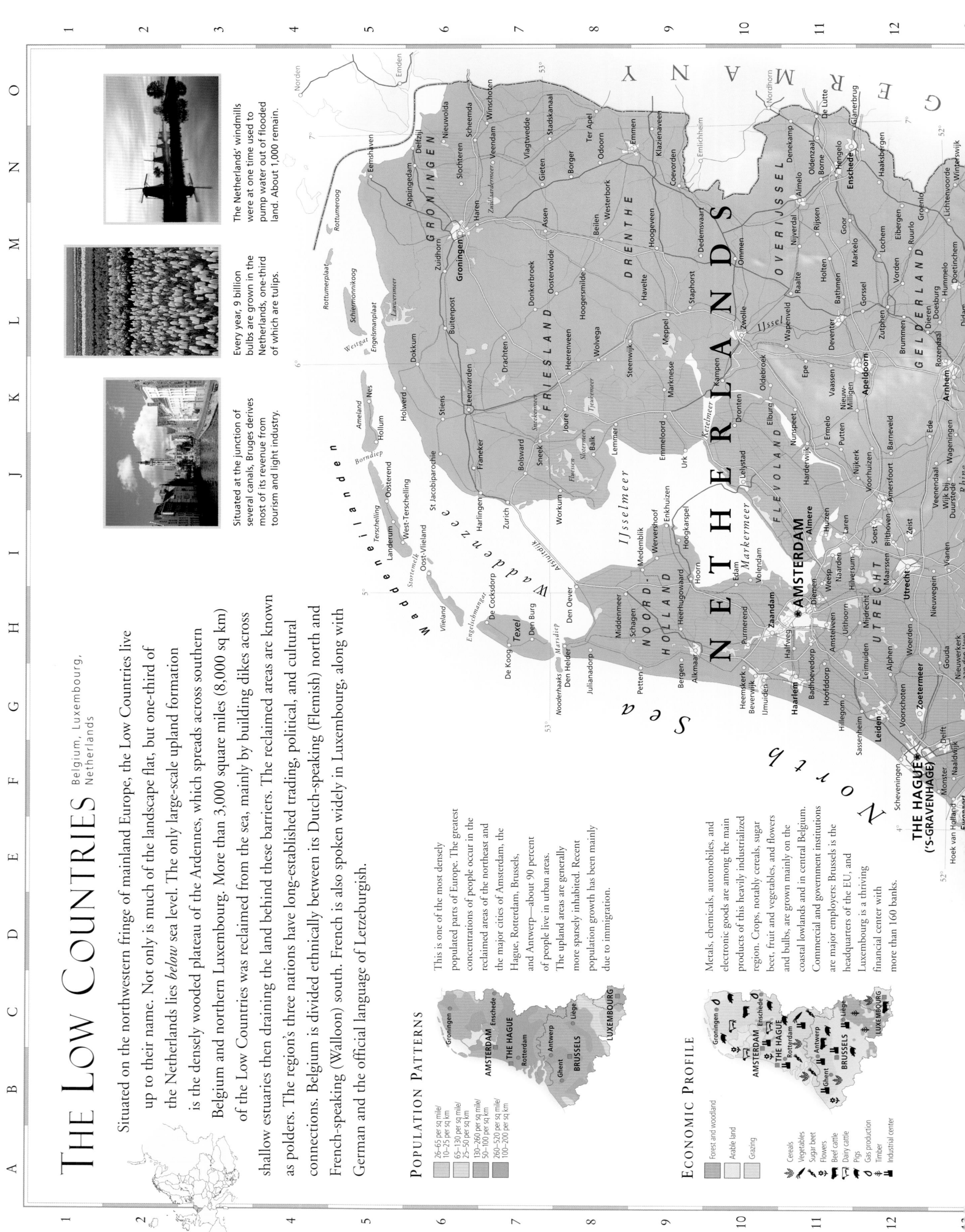

THE LOW COUNTRIES

Belgium, Luxembourg, Netherlands

Situated on the northwestern fringe of mainland Europe, the Low Countries live up to their name. Not only is much of the landscape flat, but one-third of the Netherlands lies *below* sea level. The only large-scale upland formation is the densely wooded plateau of the Ardennes, which spreads across southern Belgium and northern Luxembourg. More than 3,000 square miles (8,000 sq km) of the Low Countries was reclaimed from the sea, mainly by building dikes across shallow estuaries then draining the land behind these barriers. The reclaimed areas are known as polders. The region's three nations have long-established trading, political, and cultural connections. Belgium is divided ethnically between its Dutch-speaking (Flemish) north and French-speaking (Walloon) south. French is also spoken widely in Luxembourg, along with German and the official language of Letzeburgish.

POPULATION PATTERNS

This is one of the most densely populated parts of Europe. The greatest concentrations of people occur in the reclaimed areas of the northeast and the major cities of Amsterdam, the Hague, Rotterdam, Brussels, and Antwerp—about 90 percent of people live in urban areas. The upland areas are generally more sparsely inhabited. Recent population growth has been mainly due to immigration.

- 26–65 per sq mile / 10–25 per sq km
- 65–130 per sq mile / 25–50 per sq km
- 130–260 per sq mile / 50–100 per sq km
- 260–520 per sq mile / 100–200 per sq km

ECONOMIC PROFILE

Metals, chemicals, automobiles, and electronic goods are among the main products of this heavily industrialized region. Crops, notably cereals, sugar beet, fruit and vegetables, and flowers and bulbs, are grown mainly on the coastal lowlands and in central Belgium. Commercial and government institutions are major employers: Brussels is the headquarters of the EU, and Luxembourg is a thriving financial center with more than 160 banks.

- Forest and woodland
- Arable land
- Grazing
- Cereals
- Vegetables
- Sugar beet
- Flowers
- Beef cattle
- Dairy cattle
- Pigs
- Gas production
- Timber
- Industrial center

The Netherlands' windmills were at one time used to pump water out of flooded land. About 1,000 remain.

Every year, 9 billion bulbs are grown in the Netherlands, one-third of which are tulips.

Situated at the junction of several canals, Bruges derives most of its revenue from tourism and light industry.

BELGIUM
GERMANY
FRANCE
LUXEMBOURG
BRUSSELS
(BRUSSEL/BRUXELLES)
LUXEMBOURG
Flanders
Ardennes
WEST-VLAANDEREN
OOST-VLAANDEREN
ANTWERPEN
LIMBURG
VLAAMS BRABANT
BRABANT WALLON
HAINAUT
NAMUR
LIÈGE
LUXEMBOURG
DIEKIRCH
GREVENMACHER
ZEELAND
NOORD-BRABANT
Antwerp
Ghent
Bruges
Liège
Charleroi
Namur
Mons
Maastricht
Eindhoven
Tilburg
Breda
Aachen
Oostende
Kortrijk
Leuven
Mechelen
Hasselt
Arlon
Bastogne
Esch-sur-Alzette
Escaut
Meuse
Sambre
Maas
Ourthe
Semois
Lys
IJzer
Westerschelde
Oosterschelde
Signal de Botrange 2277ft (694m)
Baraque de Fraiture 2139ft (652m)
Longitude east of Greenwich
ELEVATION
Feet
Meters
6562 2000
4921 1500
3281 1000
2461 750
1640 500
1312 400
984 300
656 200
328 100
0 0
Below sea level
0
656 200
3281 1000
6562 2000
13,123 4000
19,685 6000
26,246 8000
32,808 10,000
SCALE 1:1,100,000
Lamberts Conformal Conic Projection
30 miles
30 kilometers

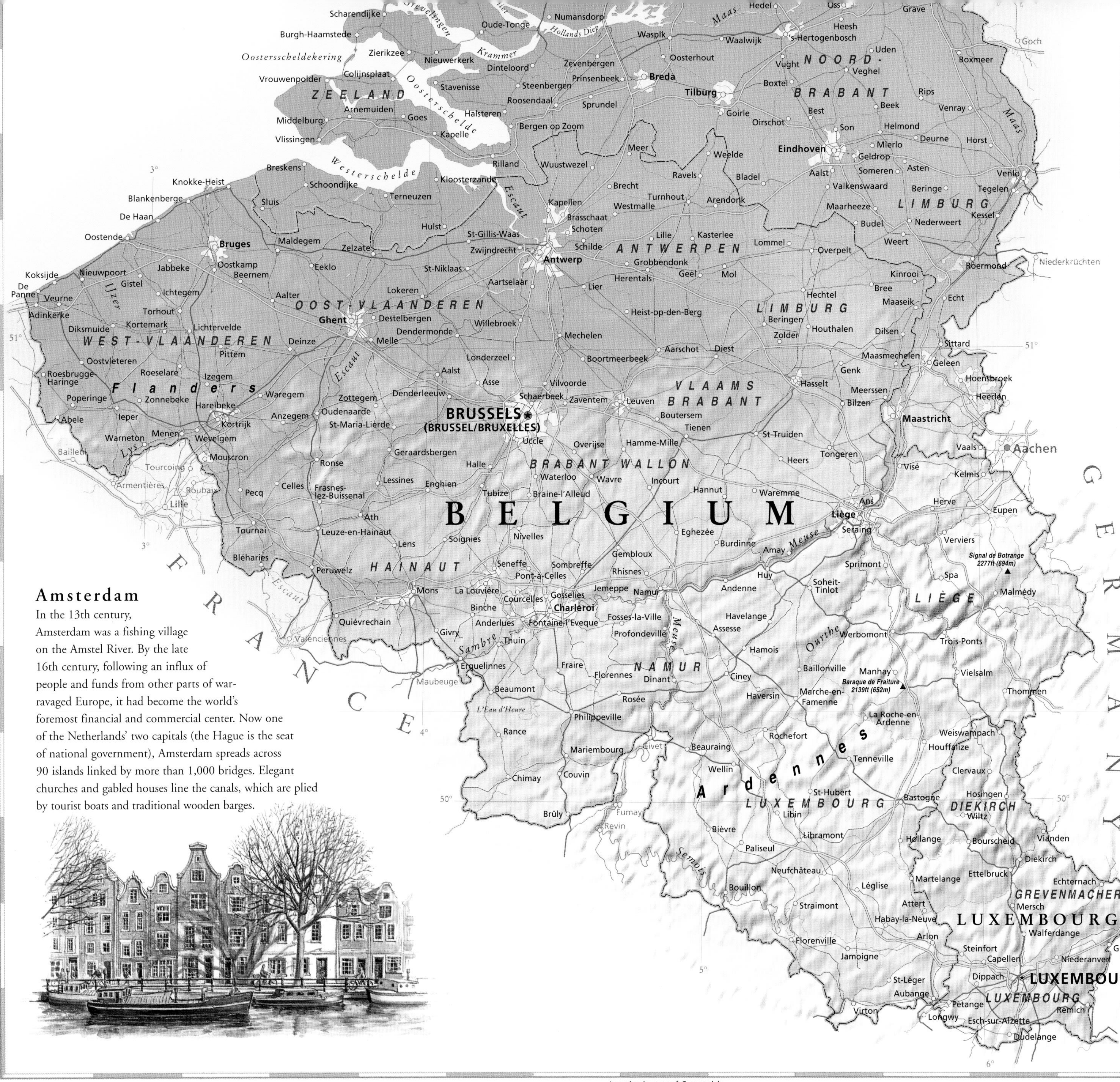

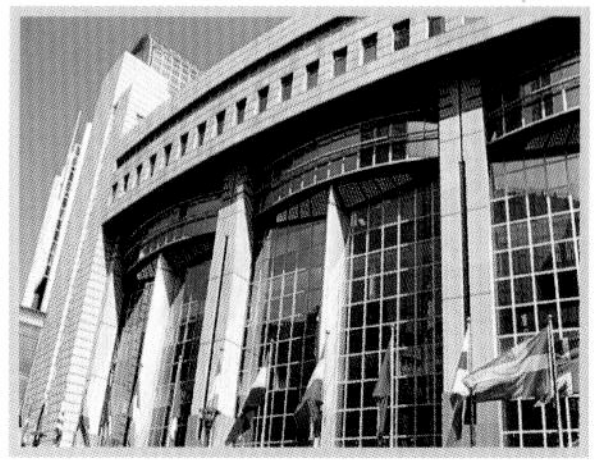

The European Parliament meets at this building in Brussels, as well as others in Luxembourg and in Strasbourg, France.

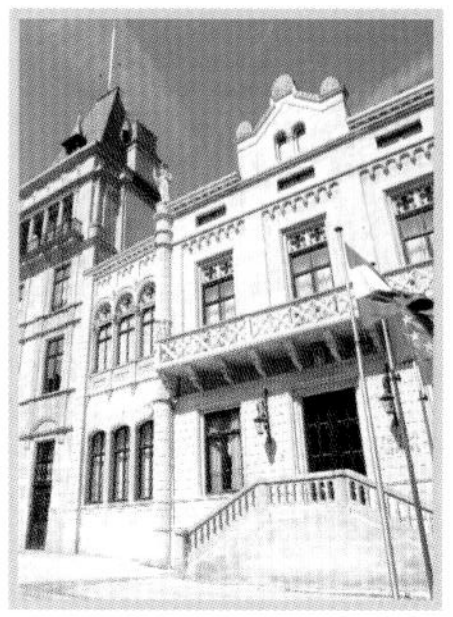

Luxembourg's Grand Ducal Palace has been the home of the head of state (the Grand Duke) since the 1890s.

Amsterdam

In the 13th century, Amsterdam was a fishing village on the Amstel River. By the late 16th century, following an influx of people and funds from other parts of war-ravaged Europe, it had become the world's foremost financial and commercial center. Now one of the Netherlands' two capitals (the Hague is the seat of national government), Amsterdam spreads across 90 islands linked by more than 1,000 bridges. Elegant churches and gabled houses line the canals, which are plied by tourist boats and traditional wooden barges.

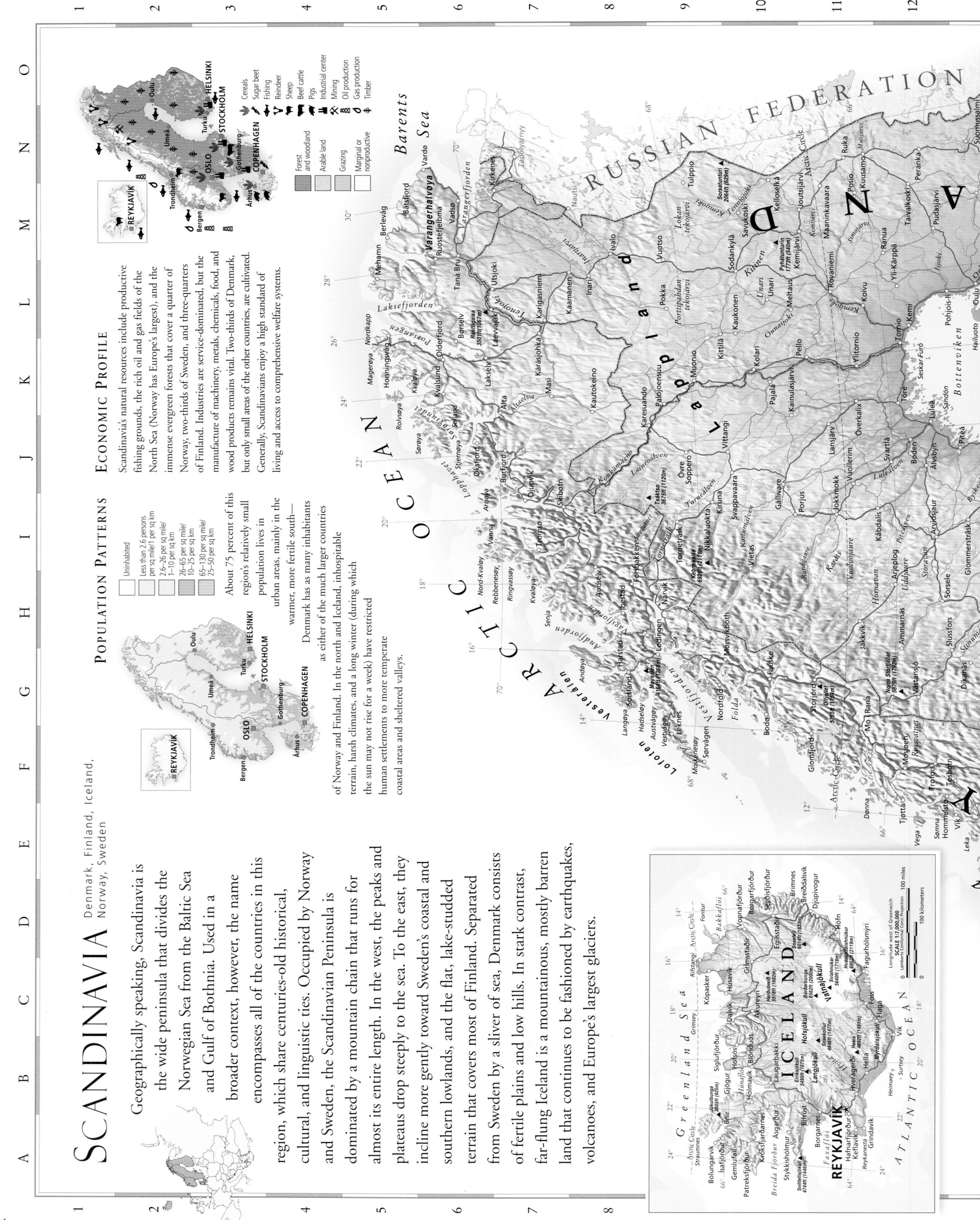

SCANDINAVIA
Denmark, Finland, Iceland, Norway, Sweden

Geographically speaking, Scandinavia is the wide peninsula that divides the Norwegian Sea from the Baltic Sea and Gulf of Bothnia. Used in a broader context, however, the name encompasses all of the countries in this region, which share centuries-old historical, cultural, and linguistic ties. Occupied by Norway and Sweden, the Scandinavian Peninsula is dominated by a mountain chain that runs for almost its entire length. In the west, the peaks and plateaus drop steeply to the sea. To the east, they incline more gently toward Sweden's coastal and southern lowlands, and the flat, lake-studded terrain that covers most of Finland. Separated from Sweden by a sliver of sea, Denmark consists of fertile plains and low hills. In stark contrast, far-flung Iceland is a mountainous, mostly barren land that continues to be fashioned by earthquakes, volcanoes, and Europe's largest glaciers.

ECONOMIC PROFILE

Scandinavia's natural resources include productive fishing grounds, the rich oil and gas fields of the North Sea (Norway has Europe's largest), and the immense evergreen forests that cover a quarter of Norway, two-thirds of Sweden, and three-quarters of Finland. Industries are service-dominated, but the manufacture of machinery, metals, chemicals, food, and wood products remains vital. Two-thirds of Denmark, but only small areas of the other countries, are cultivated. Generally, Scandinavians enjoy a high standard of living and access to comprehensive welfare systems.

Cereals
Sugar beet
Fishing
Reindeer
Sheep
Beef cattle
Pigs
Industrial center
Mining
Oil production
Gas production
Timber

Forest and woodland
Arable land
Grazing
Marginal or nonproductive

POPULATION PATTERNS

Uninhabited
Less than 2.6 persons per sq mile/1 per sq km
2.6–26 per sq mile/1–10 per sq km
26–65 per sq mile/10–25 per sq km
65–130 per sq mile/25–50 per sq km

About 75 percent of this region's relatively small population lives in urban areas, mainly in the warmer, more fertile south—Denmark has as many inhabitants as either of the much larger countries of Norway and Iceland. In the north and Iceland, inhospitable terrain, harsh climates, and a long winter (during which the sun may not rise for a week) have restricted human settlements to more temperate coastal areas and sheltered valleys.

134

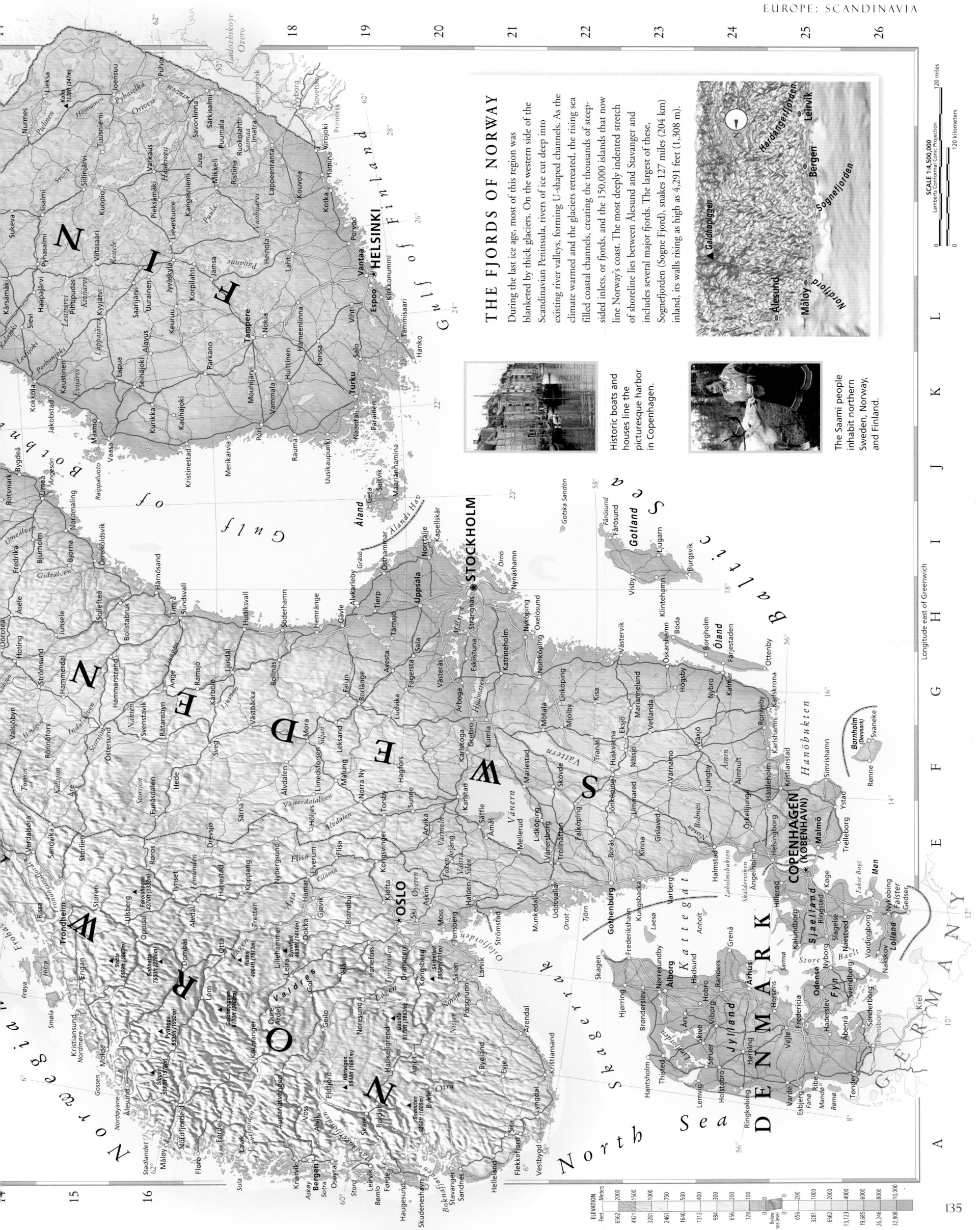

THE FJORDS OF NORWAY

During the last ice age, most of this region was blanketed by thick glaciers. On the western side of the Scandinavian Peninsula, rivers of ice cut deep into existing river valleys, forming U-shaped channels. As the climate warmed and the glaciers retreated, the rising sea filled coastal channels, creating the thousands of steep-sided inlets, or fjords, and the 150,000 islands that now line Norway's coast. The most deeply indented stretch of shoreline lies between Ålesund and Stavanger and includes several major fjords. The largest of these, Sognefjorden (Sogne Fjord), snakes 127 miles (204 km) inland, its walls rising as high as 4,291 feet (1,308 m).

Historic boats and houses line the picturesque harbor in Copenhagen.

The Saami people inhabit northern Sweden, Norway, and Finland.

SCALE 1:4,500,000
Lamberts Conformal Conic Projection

Longitude east of Greenwich

ELEVATION

135

GERMANY

When East Germany and West Germany merged in October 1990, the reunified nation became the most populous country in Europe. More than 80 million people dwell in this broad land, which stretches south from the North and Baltic seas to the northern flank of the Alps. Germany can be divided into three main physical regions. In the northern lowlands, wide rivers, including the Elbe and Weser, meander seaward across expansive, sandy plains.

A complex series of basins, partially wooded plateaus, and mountains extends across the center of the country. In the south, beyond the valley of the Main, stand the nation's highest ranges: the Black Forest, Swabian Alp, and Bavarian Alps. The great Rhine River, a historic artery of trade, defines the nation's southwestern boundaries. Continuing north, it cuts through the central uplands before veering westward across the plains to the Netherlands. Despite the economic and social challenges posed by reunification, Germany has retained its position as Europe's leading industrial power.

POPULATION PATTERNS

Until the 19th century, Germany was divided into numerous small states with their own capitals and trading centers. As a result, its population is highly urbanized but fairly evenly distributed. Dense concentrations of inhabitants occur at the confluence of the Rhine and Ruhr rivers—the industrial heartland—and around Leipzig and Dresden in the east. Immigration has been the main contributor to recent population growth—10 million incomers settled in West Germany between 1950 and 1990.

- 2.6–26 per sq mile / 1–10 per sq km
- 26–65 per sq mile / 10–25 per sq km
- 65–130 per sq mile / 25–50 per sq km
- 130–260 per sq mile / 50–100 per sq km
- 260–520 per sq mile / 100–200 per sq km

ECONOMIC PROFILE

West Germany staged a remarkable economic recovery after the Second World War, and Germany is now the third-largest industrial power after the U.S.A. and Japan. The mainstays of manufacturing are machinery, automobiles, iron and steel, chemicals, electrical goods, and food and beverages. Two of the most significant agricultural products are wine and beer; cereals, potatoes, and sugar beet are also grown widely. The largest pastures are in the northwest, but dairying takes place throughout the country.

- Cereals
- Potatoes
- Sugar beet
- Wine
- Beef cattle
- Dairy cattle
- Sheep
- Pigs
- Industrial center
- Mining
- Timber

- Forest and woodland
- Arable land
- Grazing

Construction of Cologne Cathedral, the largest Gothic church in Northern Europe, began in 1248 but was not completed until 1880.

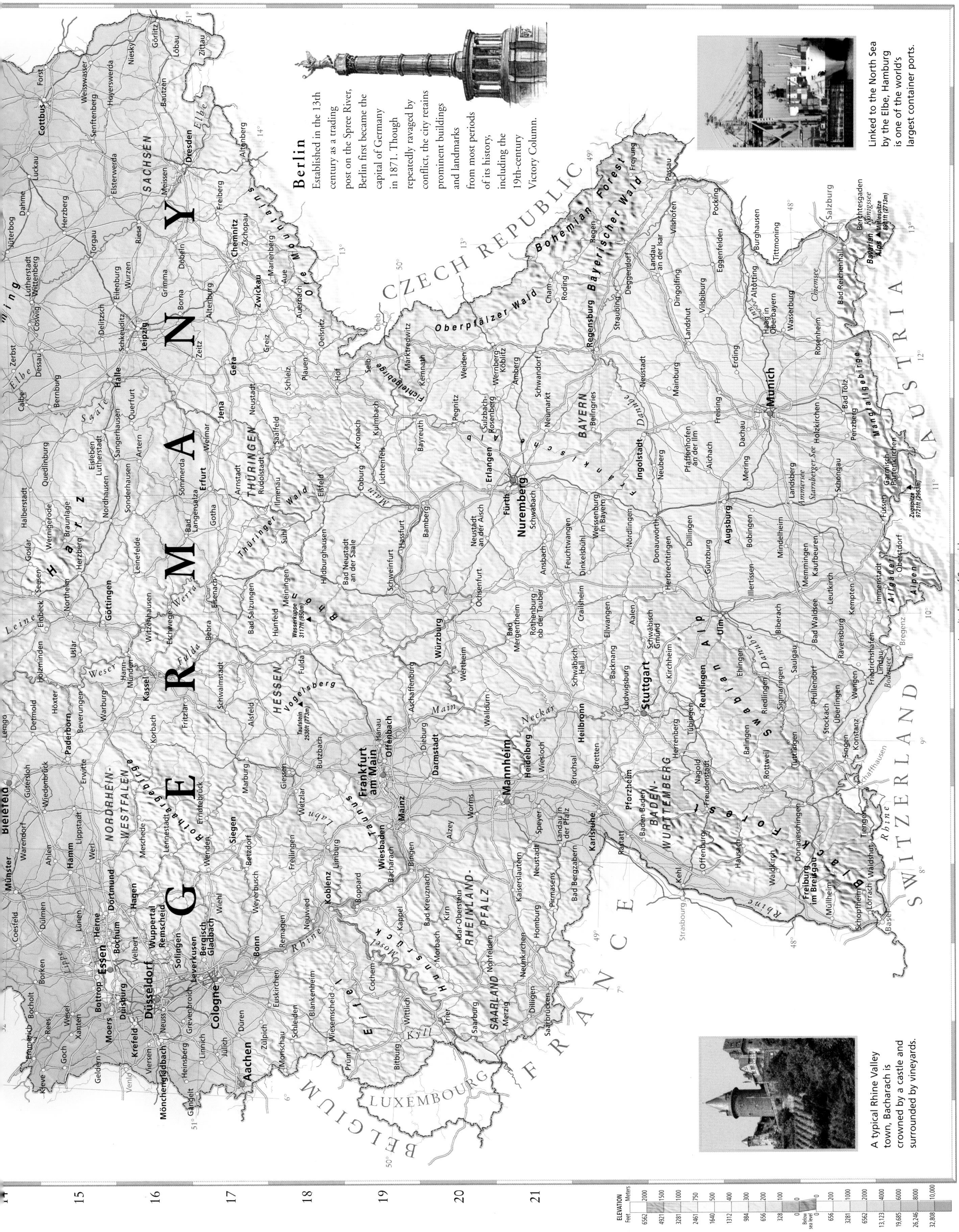

Berlin

Established in the 13th century as a trading post on the Spree River, Berlin first became the capital of Germany in 1871. Though repeatedly ravaged by conflict, the city retains prominent buildings and landmarks from most periods of its history, including the 19th-century Victory Column.

Linked to the North Sea by the Elbe, Hamburg is one of the world's largest container ports.

A typical Rhine Valley town, Bacharach is crowned by a castle and surrounded by vineyards.

SCALE 1:2,250,000
Lamberts Conformal Conic Projection

0   60 miles

0   60 kilometers

Longitude east of Greenwich

ELEVATION

feet	Meters
32,808	10,000
26,246	8000
19,685	6000
13,123	4000
6562	2000
3281	1000
1640	500
656	200
328	100
0	Sea level
0	Below sea level
656	200
984	300
1312	400
1640	500
2461	750
3281	1000
4921	1500
6562	2000

THE ALPINE NATIONS
Austria, Liechtenstein, Switzerland

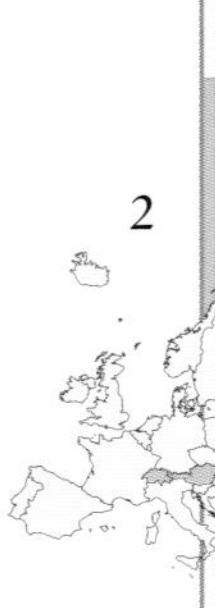

Arcing northeastward from France, the countless peaks and valleys of the Alps sprawl across more than half of Switzerland, the tiny monarchy of Liechtenstein, and two-thirds of Austria. These nations occupy a continental crossroads, their mountain passes permitting the flow of people and goods between north and south, the Danube Valley forming a natural corridor between eastern and western Europe. Despite its strategic importance, Switzerland has remained politically neutral for almost 200 years. This, along with its prosperity and secretive banking practices, has made it a haven for international organizations, businesses, and funds. Austria's more tempestuous past includes periods as the heart of the powerful Holy Roman and Austro-Hungarian empires; its present boundaries were defined after the First World War. Liechtenstein established its independence, and neutrality, in 1866.

Millions of people visit the Alps each year to holiday at winter-sports resorts.

The spectacular Jet d'Eau, a 460-foot (140-m) fountain, is Geneva's best-known landmark.

THE CENTRAL ALPS

The Central Alps extend from Lake Geneva in the west to the Rhine Valley in the east. They encompass several ranges including the Bernese Alps—Switzerland's highest—and the valleys of two of Europe's great rivers, the Rhône and Rhine, which form a deep, straight, almost continuous gouge through the mountains. The northern flank of the Central Alps descends to Switzerland's Central Plateau, which is hemmed in to the north by the peaks of the Jura.

POPULATION PATTERNS

Rugged terrain has always limited the settlement of mountainous areas, so most of the population is concentrated in valleys and lowlands, most notably Switzerland's Central Plateau, site of the nation's major urban centers, and the Danube Valley, where Vienna accommodates one-fifth of the Austrian population. Postindustrial depopulation of upland areas has been slowed by the boom in tourism, which has brought jobs and funds to remote communities.

	Less than 2.6 persons per sq mile/1 per sq km
	2.6–26 per sq mile/1–10 per sq km
	26–65 per sq mile/10–25 per sq km
	65–130 per sq mile/25–50 per sq km
	130–260 per sq mile/50–100 per sq km

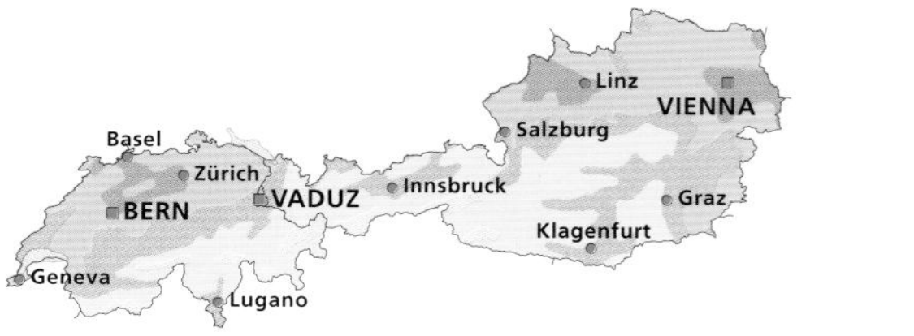

Longitude east of Green

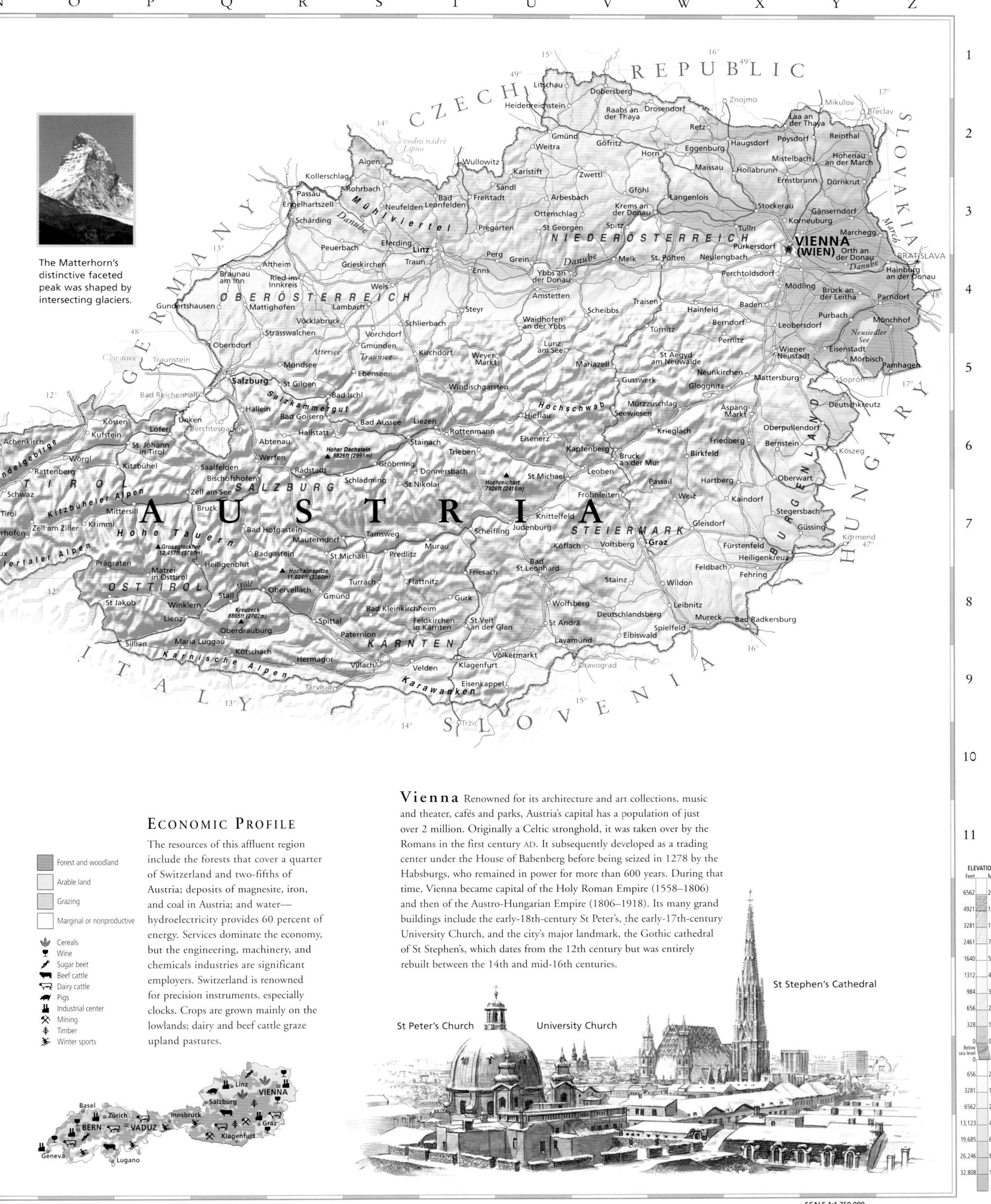

The Matterhorn's distinctive faceted peak was shaped by intersecting glaciers.

ECONOMIC PROFILE

The resources of this affluent region include the forests that cover a quarter of Switzerland and two-fifths of Austria; deposits of magnesite, iron, and coal in Austria; and water—hydroelectricity provides 60 percent of energy. Services dominate the economy, but the engineering, machinery, and chemicals industries are significant employers. Switzerland is renowned for precision instruments, especially clocks. Crops are grown mainly on the lowlands; dairy and beef cattle graze upland pastures.

Forest and woodland
Arable land
Grazing
Marginal or nonproductive

Cereals
Wine
Sugar beet
Beef cattle
Dairy cattle
Pigs
Industrial center
Mining
Timber
Winter sports

Vienna Renowned for its architecture and art collections, music and theater, cafés and parks, Austria's capital has a population of just over 2 million. Originally a Celtic stronghold, it was taken over by the Romans in the first century AD. It subsequently developed as a trading center under the House of Babenberg before being seized in 1278 by the Habsburgs, who remained in power for more than 600 years. During that time, Vienna became capital of the Holy Roman Empire (1558–1806) and then of the Austro-Hungarian Empire (1806–1918). Its many grand buildings include the early-18th-century St Peter's, the early-17th-century University Church, and the city's major landmark, the Gothic cathedral of St Stephen's, which dates from the 12th century but was entirely rebuilt between the 14th and mid-16th centuries.

St Peter's Church   University Church   St Stephen's Cathedral

ELEVATION

Feet	Meters
6562	2000
4921	1500
3281	1000
2461	750
1640	500
1312	400
984	300
656	200
328	100
0 Below sea level	0
656	200
3281	1000
6562	2000
13,123	4000
19,685	6000
26,246	8000
32,808	10,000

SCALE 1:1,750,000
Lamberts Conformal Conic Projection
0   50 miles
0   50 kilometers

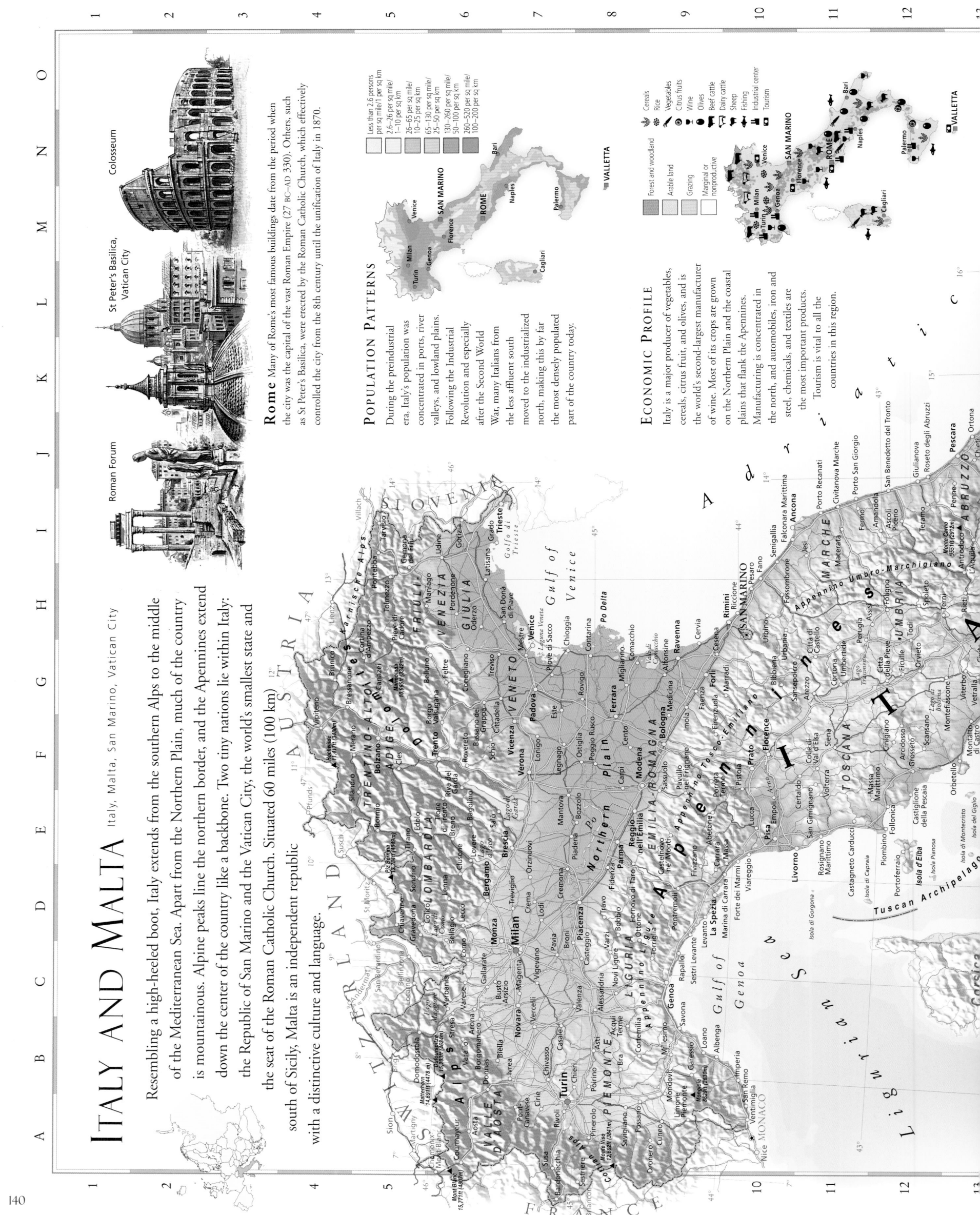

ITALY AND MALTA

Italy, Malta, San Marino, Vatican City

Resembling a high-heeled boot, Italy extends from the southern Alps to the middle of the Mediterranean Sea. Apart from the Northern Plain, much of the country is mountainous. Alpine peaks line the northern border, and the Apennines extend down the center of the country like a backbone. Two tiny nations lie within Italy: the Republic of San Marino and the Vatican City, the world's smallest state and the seat of the Roman Catholic Church. Situated 60 miles (100 km) south of Sicily, Malta is an independent republic with a distinctive culture and language.

Rome Many of Rome's most famous buildings date from the period when the city was the capital of the vast Roman Empire (27 BC–AD 330). Others, such as St Peter's Basilica, were erected by the Roman Catholic Church, which effectively controlled the city from the 8th century until the unification of Italy in 1870.

Colosseum

St Peter's Basilica, Vatican City

Roman Forum

POPULATION PATTERNS

During the preindustrial era, Italy's population was concentrated in ports, river valleys, and lowland plains. Following the Industrial Revolution and especially after the Second World War, many Italians from the less affluent south moved to the industrialized north, making this by far the most densely populated part of the country today.

Less than 2.6 persons per sq mile/1 per sq km
2.6–26 per sq mile/ 1–10 per sq km
26–65 per sq mile/ 10–25 per sq km
65–130 per sq mile/ 25–50 per sq km
130–260 per sq mile/ 50–100 per sq km
260–520 per sq mile/ 100–200 per sq km

ECONOMIC PROFILE

Italy is a major producer of vegetables, cereals, citrus fruit, and olives, and is the world's second-largest manufacturer of wine. Most of its crops are grown on the Northern Plain and the coastal plains that flank the Apennines. Manufacturing is concentrated in the north, and automobiles, iron and steel, chemicals, and textiles are the most important products. Tourism is vital to all the countries in this region.

Cereals
Rice
Vegetables
Citrus fruits
Wine
Olives
Beef cattle
Dairy cattle
Sheep
Fishing
Industrial center
Tourism

Forest and woodland
Arable land
Grazing
Marginal or nonproductive

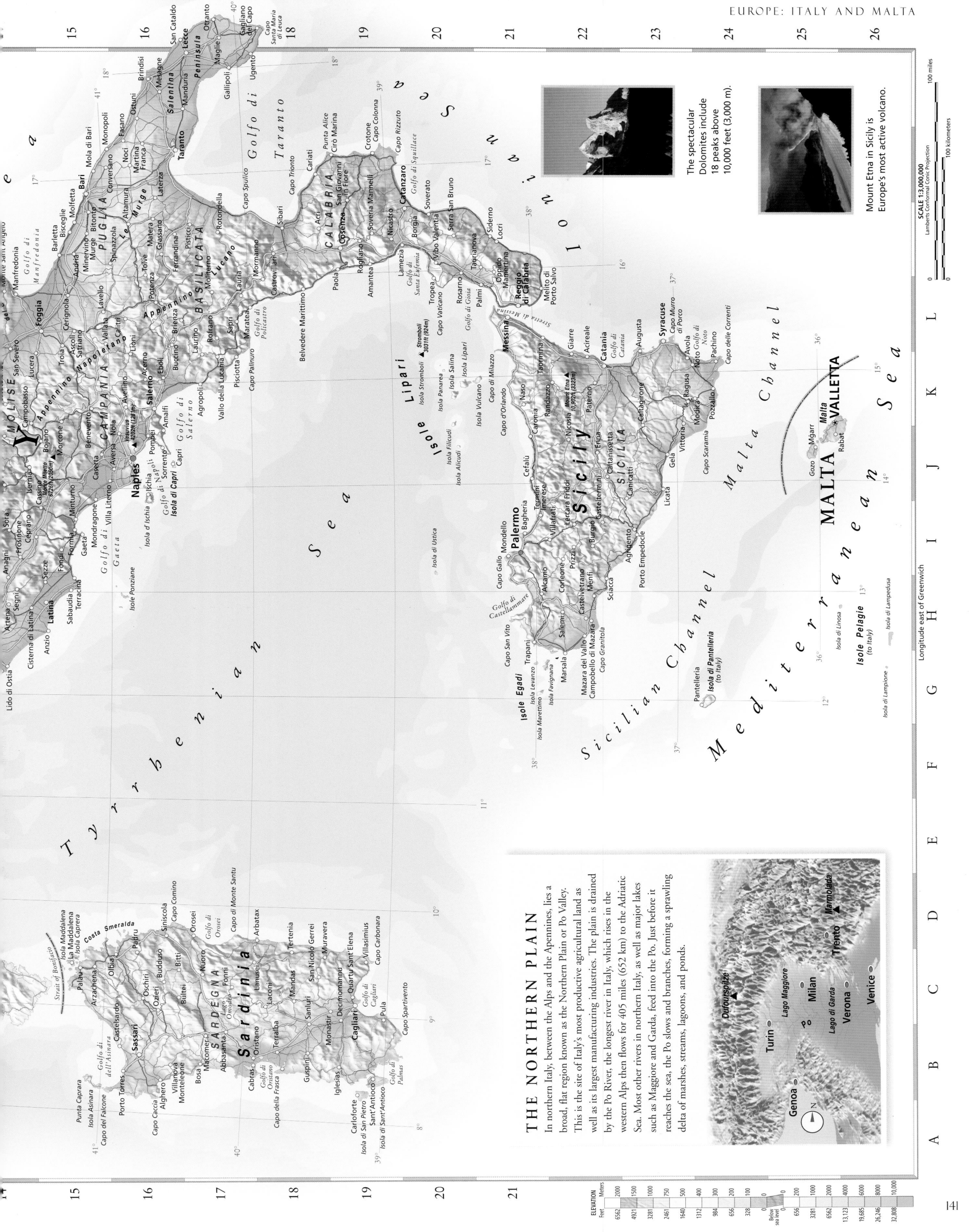

THE NORTHERN PLAIN

In northern Italy, between the Alps and the Apennines, lies a broad, flat region known as the Northern Plain or Po Valley. This is the site of Italy's most productive agricultural land as well as its largest manufacturing industries. The plain is drained by the Po River, the longest river in Italy, which rises in the western Alps then flows for 405 miles (652 km) to the Adriatic Sea. Most other rivers in northern Italy, as well as major lakes such as Maggiore and Garda, feed into the Po. Just before it reaches the sea, the Po slows and branches, forming a sprawling delta of marshes, streams, lagoons, and ponds.

The spectacular Dolomites include 18 peaks above 10,000 feet (3,000 m).

Mount Etna in Sicily is Europe's most active volcano.

SCALE 1:3,000,000
Lamberts Conformal Conic Projection

Longitude east of Greenwich

141

Northern Central Europe

Czech Republic, Hungary, Poland, Slovakia

The Bohemian Massif and the Carpathian Mountains bisect this region from west to east, separating the flatlands of the North European Plain from those of the Great Hungarian Plain in the south. A ring of mountain ranges around a broad central basin, the Bohemian Massif covers most of the Czech Republic. The heavily forested Carpathians—a continuation of the Alps—occupy northern and central Slovakia, giving way to plains in the south and east. Separated from these two nations by the peaks that line its southern border, Poland otherwise has little high land. Rivers meander across its central lowlands and lake-studded coastal plains, many, notably the Oder and Vistula, flowing all the way to the Baltic Sea. Hungary, too, is mostly flat, the Great Hungarian Plain spreading across more than half of its territory. All of these independent, democratic nations were part of the Eastern bloc until the collapse of communism in 1989. In 1992, Czechoslovakia split into two nations, the Czech Republic and Slovakia.

Population Patterns

2.6–26 per sq mile/ 1–10 per sq km	
26–65 per sq mile/ 10–25 per sq km	
65–130 per sq mile/ 25–50 per sq km	
130–260 per sq mile/ 50–100 per sq km	
260–520 per sq mile/ 100–200 per sq km	

About 65 percent of the region's inhabitants are urban dwellers, with the highest levels in the Czech Republic and the lowest in less-developed Slovakia (which has half the population of its northwestern neighbor). The most densely populated areas are Poland's industrialized south and its capital Warsaw, the northern Czech Republic, and the Budapest region, home to one-quarter of Hungary's people. Settlements are more scattered in the Slovakian mountains and on the windswept and relatively infertile Baltic Sea coast. More than 5 percent of Hungary's population are ethnic Roma (Gypsy) people.

Economic Profile

Forest and woodland	
Arable land	
Grazing	

Significant natural resources in this region include Poland's rich Silesian coal fields, the more modest but vital mineral reserves of Slovakia's Ore Mountains, and Hungary's large swathes of arable land. Cereals and potatoes are the major crops, along with sugar beet in Poland and Hungary. Leading industries include engineering and the production of automobiles, chemicals, textiles, and food and beverages—the Czech Republic is renowned for its beer and Hungary has a thriving wine industry.

Economic Profile legend: Cereals, Potatoes, Dairy cattle, Pigs, Mining, Industrial center, Timber, Wine, Sugar beet

In the mid-18th century, Gdańsk was the largest city in Eastern Europe. Still Poland's main port, it is also a center of shipbuilding.

The jagged Tatra Mountains of northern Slovakia and southern Poland are a refuge for rare animals such as bears and wolves.

Prague Undoubtedly the most famous of the many bridges that cross the Vltava River in the city of Prague, the Charles Bridge dates from 1357. At that time, Prague was the capital of Bohemia and the Holy Roman Empire under Charles IV, and a major trading center. Merchants remained central to the development of the economy until the Industrial Revolution, and were responsible for commissioning many of the magnificent Gothic and Baroque buildings and monuments that today attract a steady influx of visitors. Prague became capital of the nation of Czechoslovakia in 1918 and capital of the newly formed Czech Republic in 1992.

Situated on the east bank of the Danube, Budapest's Parliament was completed in 1902.

SCALE 1:2,750,000
Lambert's Conformal Conic Projection

100 miles

100 kilometers

Longitude east of Greenwich

UKRAINE

SLOVAKIA

HUNGARY

CZECH REPUBLIC

GERMANY

AUSTRIA

CROATIA

SLOVENIA

SERBIA and MONTENEGRO

ROMANIA

ELEVATION

Feet	Meters
6562	2000
4921	1500
3281	1000
2461	750
1640	500
1312	400
984	300
656	200
328	100
0	0
	Below sea level
656	200
1312	400
3281	1000
6562	2000
13,123	4000
19,685	6000
26,246	8000
32,808	10,000

143

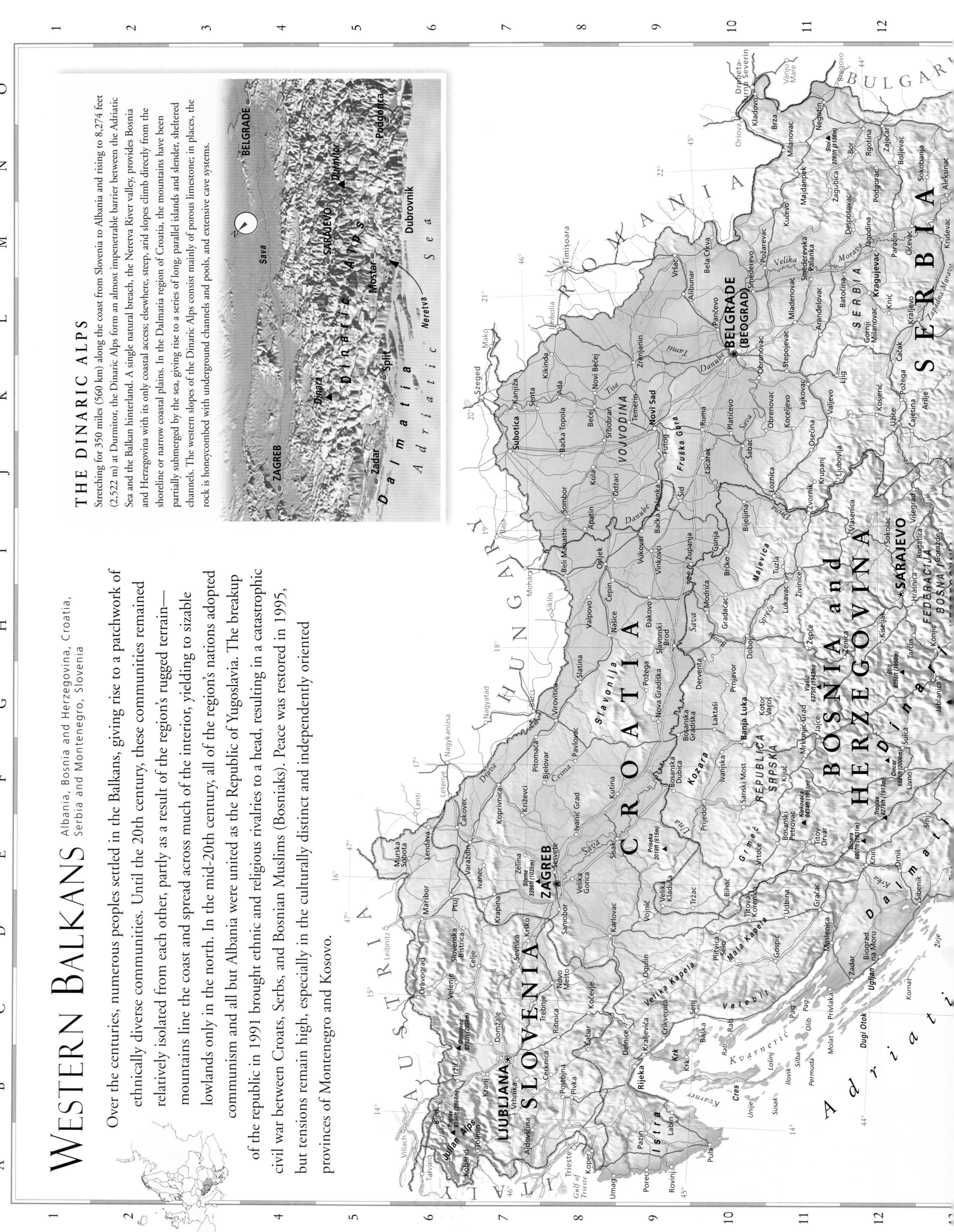

WESTERN BALKANS

Albania, Bosnia and Herzegovina, Croatia, Serbia and Montenegro, Slovenia

Over the centuries, numerous peoples settled in the Balkans, giving rise to a patchwork of ethnically diverse communities. Until the 20th century, these communities remained relatively isolated from each other, partly as a result of the region's rugged terrain—mountains line the coast and spread across much of the interior, yielding to sizable lowlands only in the north. In the mid-20th century, all of the region's nations adopted communism and all but Albania were united as the Republic of Yugoslavia. The breakup of the republic in 1991 brought ethnic and religious rivalries to a head, resulting in a catastrophic civil war between Croats, Serbs, and Bosnian Muslims (Bosniaks). Peace was restored in 1995, but tensions remain high, especially in the culturally distinct and independently oriented provinces of Montenegro and Kosovo.

THE DINARIC ALPS

Stretching for 350 miles (560 km) along the coast from Slovenia to Albania and rising to 8,274 feet (2,522 m) at Durmitor, the Dinaric Alps form an almost impenetrable barrier between the Adriatic Sea and the Balkan hinterland. A single natural breach, the Neretva River valley, provides Bosnia and Herzegovina with its only coastal access; elsewhere, steep, arid slopes climb directly from the shoreline or narrow coastal plains. In the Dalmatia region of Croatia, the mountains have been partially submerged by the sea, giving rise to a series of long, parallel islands and slender, sheltered channels. The western slopes of the Dinaric Alps consist mainly of porous limestone; in places, the rock is honeycombed with underground channels and pools, and extensive cave systems.

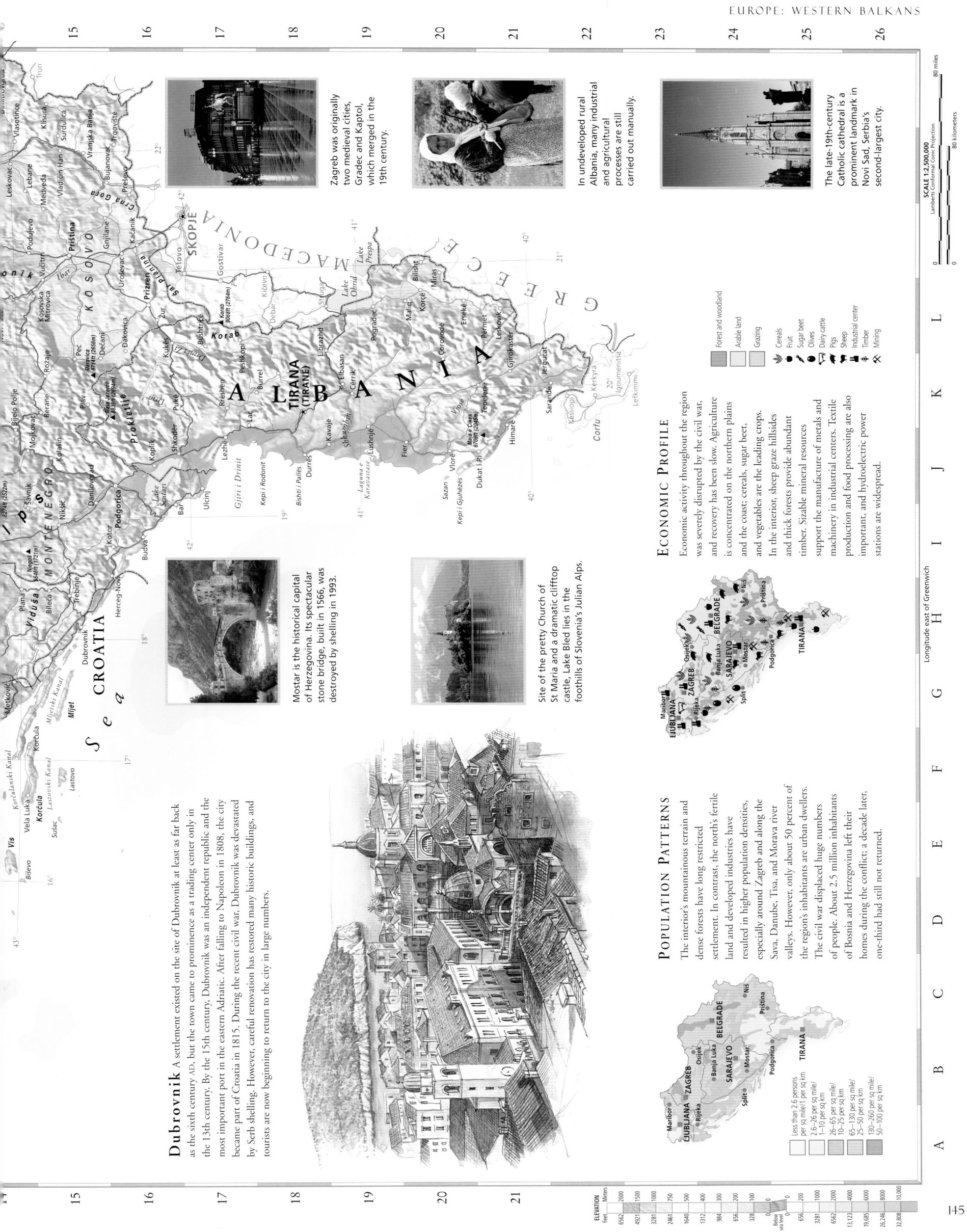

Zagreb was originally two medieval cities, Gradec and Kaptol, which merged in the 19th century.

In undeveloped rural Albania, many industrial and agricultural processes are still carried out manually.

The late-19th-century Catholic cathedral is a prominent landmark in Novi Sad, Serbia's second-largest city.

Mostar is the historical capital of Herzegovina. Its spectacular stone bridge, built in 1566, was destroyed by shelling in 1993.

Site of the pretty Church of St Maria and a dramatic clifftop castle, Lake Bled lies in the foothills of Slovenia's Julian Alps.

Dubrovnik

A settlement existed on the site of Dubrovnik at least as far back as the sixth century AD, but the town came to prominence as a trading center only in the 13th century. By the 15th century, Dubrovnik was an independent republic and the most important port in the eastern Adriatic. After falling to Napoleon in 1808, the city became part of Croatia in 1815. During the recent civil war, Dubrovnik was devastated by Serb shelling. However, careful renovation has restored many historic buildings, and tourists are now beginning to return to the city in large numbers.

Economic Profile

Economic activity throughout the region was severely disrupted by the civil war, and recovery has been slow. Agriculture is concentrated on the northern plains and the coast; cereals, sugar beet, and vegetables are the leading crops. In the interior, sheep graze hillsides and thick forests provide abundant timber. Sizable mineral resources support the manufacture of metals and machinery in industrial centers. Textile production and food processing are also important, and hydroelectric power stations are widespread.

Forest and woodland
Arable land
Grazing

Cereals
Fruit
Sugar beet
Olives
Pigs
Dairy cattle
Sheep
Timber
Industrial center
Mining

Population Patterns

The interior's mountainous terrain and dense forests have long restricted settlement. In contrast, the north's fertile land and developed industries have resulted in higher population densities, especially around Zagreb and along the Sava, Danube, Tisa, and Morava river valleys. However, only about 50 percent of the region's inhabitants are urban dwellers. The civil war displaced huge numbers of people. About 2.5 million inhabitants of Bosnia and Herzegovina left their homes during the conflict; a decade later, one-third had still not returned.

Less than 2.6 persons per sq mile/1 per sq km
2.6–26 per sq mile/1–10 per sq km
26–65 per sq mile/10–25 per sq km
65–130 per sq mile/25–50 per sq km
130–260 per sq mile/50–100 per sq km

Longitude east of Greenwich

SCALE 1:2,500,000
Lambert's Conformal Conic Projection

ELEVATION
Feet / Meters
32,808 / 10,000
26,246 / 8000
19,685 / 6000
13,123 / 4000
6562 / 2000
3281 / 1000
1640 / 500
984 / 300
656 / 200
328 / 100
Below sea level

145

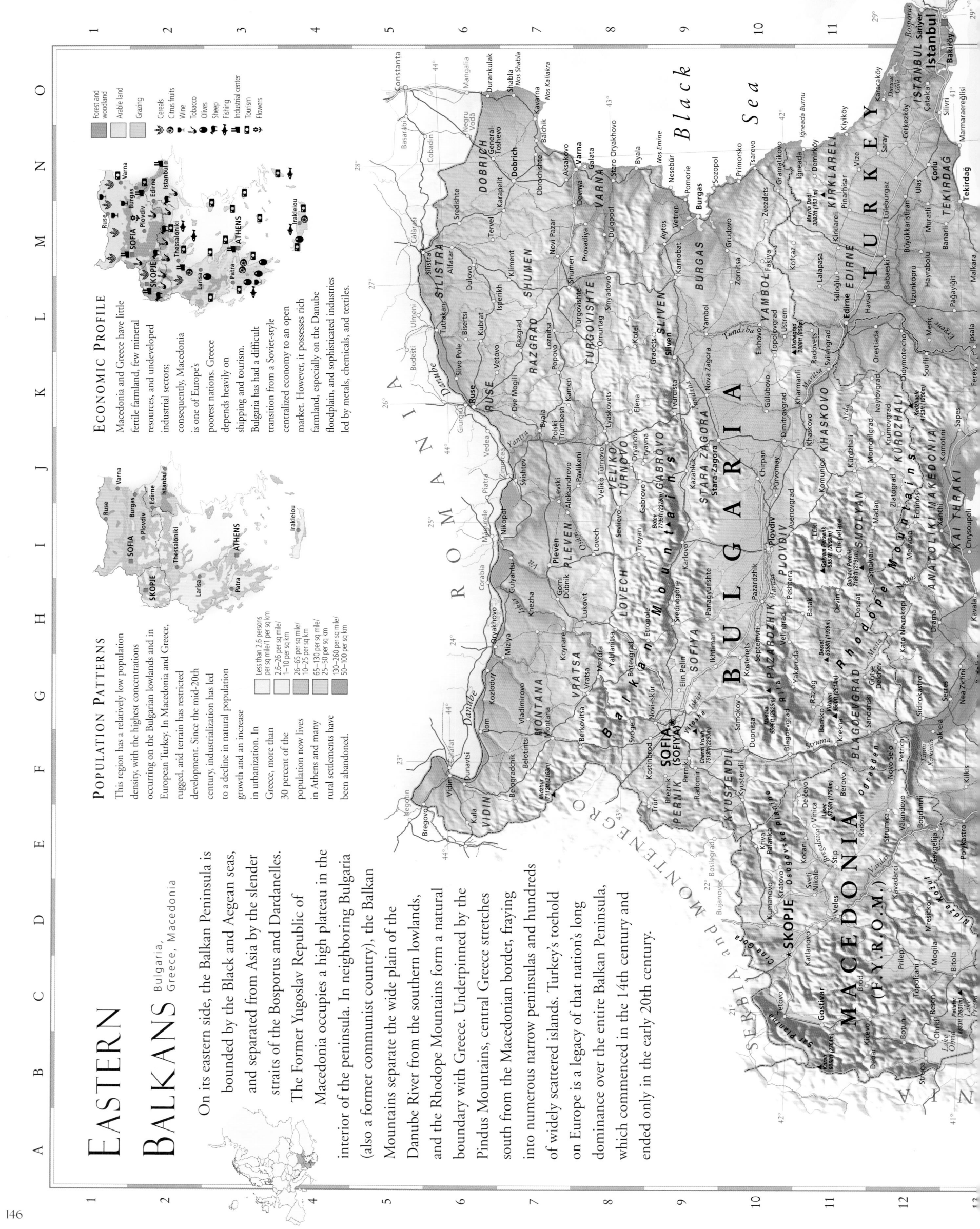

EASTERN BALKANS

Bulgaria,
Greece, Macedonia

On its eastern side, the Balkan Peninsula is bounded by the Black and Aegean seas, and separated from Asia by the slender straits of the Bosporus and Dardanelles. The Former Yugoslav Republic of Macedonia occupies a high plateau in the interior of the peninsula. In neighboring Bulgaria (also a former communist country), the Balkan Mountains separate the wide plain of the Danube River from the southern lowlands, and the Rhodope Mountains form a natural boundary with Greece. Underpinned by the Pindus Mountains, central Greece stretches south from the Macedonian border, fraying into numerous narrow peninsulas and hundreds of widely scattered islands. Turkey's toehold on Europe is a legacy of that nation's long dominance over the entire Balkan Peninsula, which commenced in the 14th century and ended only in the early 20th century.

ECONOMIC PROFILE

Macedonia and Greece have little fertile farmland, few mineral resources, and undeveloped industrial sectors; consequently, Macedonia is one of Europe's poorest nations. Greece depends heavily on shipping and tourism. Bulgaria has had a difficult transition from a Soviet-style centralized economy to an open market. However, it possesses rich farmland, especially on the Danube floodplain, and sophisticated industries led by metals, chemicals, and textiles.

POPULATION PATTERNS

This region has a relatively low population density, with the highest concentrations occurring on the Bulgarian lowlands and in European Turkey. In Macedonia and Greece, rugged, arid terrain has restricted development. Since the mid-20th century, industrialization has led to a decline in natural population growth and an increase in urbanization. In Greece, more than 30 percent of the population now lives in Athens and many rural settlements have been abandoned.

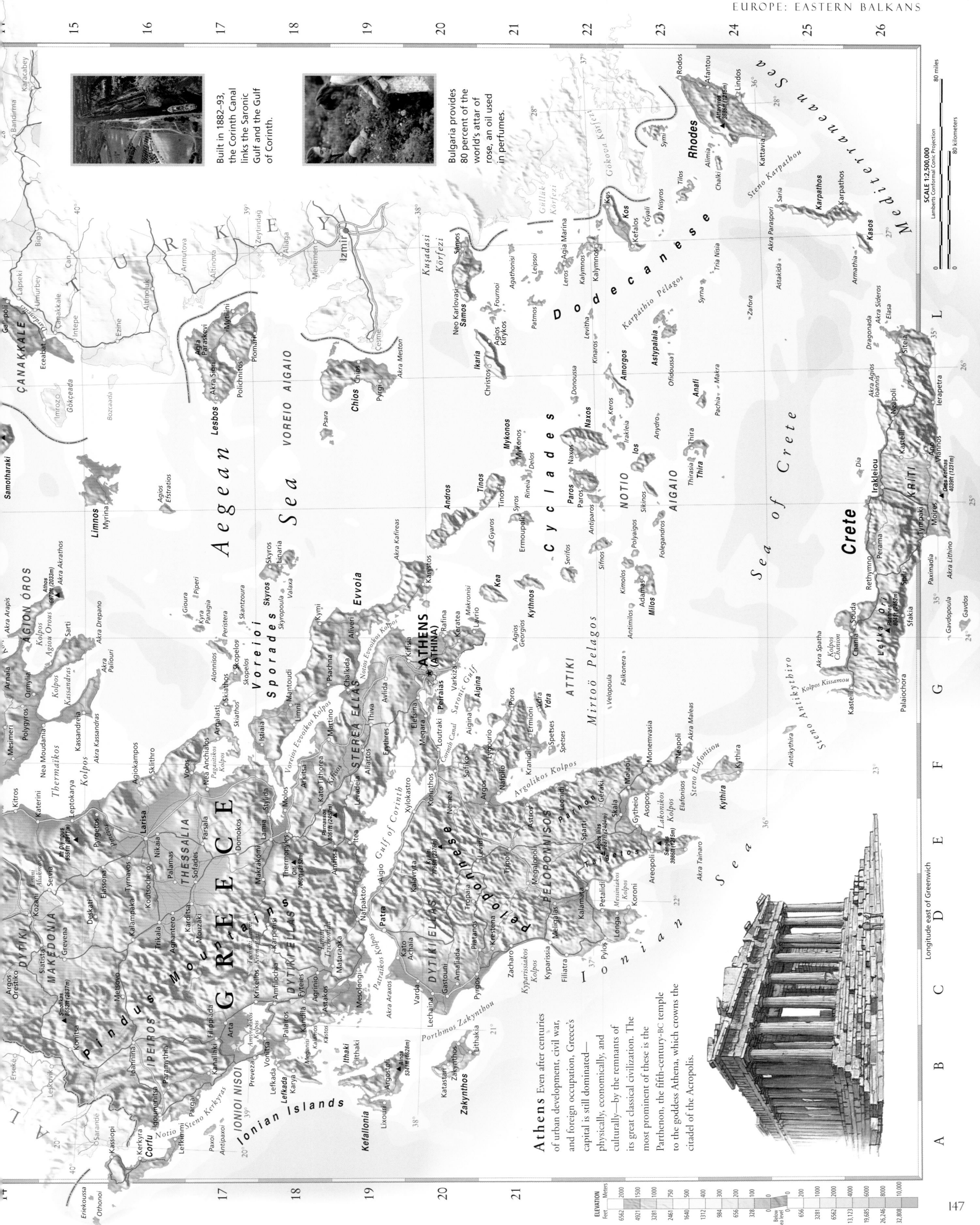

Built in 1882–93, the Corinth Canal links the Saronic Gulf and the Gulf of Corinth.

Bulgaria provides 80 percent of the world's attar of rose, an oil used in perfumes.

Athens Even after centuries of urban development, civil war, and foreign occupation, Greece's capital is still dominated—physically, economically, and culturally—by the remnants of its great classical civilization. The most prominent of these is the Parthenon, the fifth-century-BC temple to the goddess Athena, which crowns the citadel of the Acropolis.

NORTHEASTERN EUROPE
Belarus, Estonia, Latvia, Lithuania

Much of Northeastern Europe's low-lying landscape was fashioned during the last ice age. Across the region, extensive plains, scoured flat by ice, are separated by hills and ridges originally deposited by the wide snouts of glaciers. Innumerable lakes fill hollows, and winding rivers have given rise to some of Europe's largest wetlands. Due to their proximity to the Baltic Sea, the nations of Estonia, Latvia, and Lithuania are often referred to as the Baltic States, even though the three countries are ethnically and linguistically distinct. In common with their southern neighbor Belarus, the Baltic States were, for long periods of their histories, controlled by more powerful nations, including Poland, Russia, Germany, Denmark, and Sweden. In the mid-20th century, all four countries became part of the Soviet Union, but all reasserted their independence soon after the collapse of the Eastern bloc in 1989. The Russian enclave around Kaliningrad is a remnant of the Soviet empire, and a vital Baltic port for the Russian Federation.

POPULATION PATTERNS

Northeastern Europe's population is fairly evenly spread, though it thins out in northern Latvia and on Estonia's chilly Baltic coast—only 14 of Estonia's 1,541 islands are inhabited. About 60 percent of people in Latvia and 70 percent in the other countries are urban dwellers; in both Estonia and Latvia roughly one-third inhabit the capital city. People of Russian origin live throughout the region, but make up 30 percent of the population in Estonia and Latvia, the result of a Soviet policy of encouraging workers from the U.S.S.R. to settle in these states.

2.6–26 per sq mile/ 1–10 per sq km	
26–65 per sq mile/ 10–25 per sq km	
65–130 per sq mile/ 25–50 per sq km	
130–260 per sq mile/ 50–100 per sq km	

ECONOMIC PROFILE

These nations are still dealing with the transition to a market economy, and are still dependent to some extent (especially Belarus) on Russian raw materials and sales. Much of Belarus's arable land was contaminated by fallout from Chernobyl, but it remains a significant supplier of flax as well as potash (widely used for fertilizers), and peat (from its marshlands); its heavy industries produce machinery, tools, tractors, and trucks. Estonia's oil-shale provides much of the Baltic States' energy. The Baltic States are also noted for wood products and textiles, and Lithuania is a major source of amber.

Forest and woodland
Arable land

Cereals
Flax
Potatoes
Vegetables
Dairy cattle
Sugar beet
Pigs
Industrial center
Timber

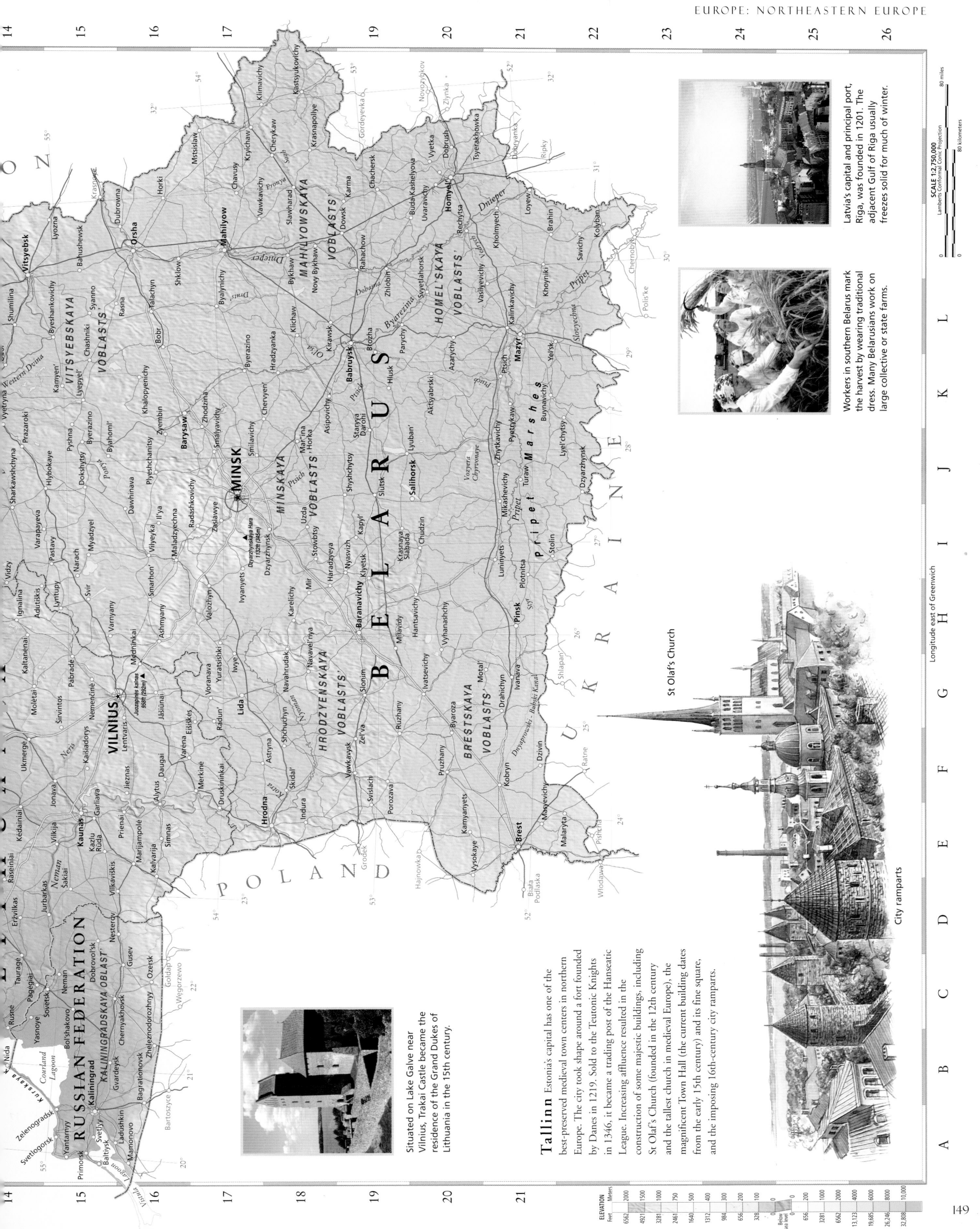

Situated on Lake Galve near Vilnius, Trakai Castle became the residence of the Grand Dukes of Lithuania in the 15th century.

Tallinn Estonia's capital has one of the best-preserved medieval town centers in northern Europe. The city took shape around a fort founded by Danes in 1219. Sold to the Teutonic Knights in 1346, it became a trading post of the Hanseatic League. Increasing affluence resulted in the construction of some majestic buildings, including St Olaf's Church (founded in the 12th century and the tallest church in medieval Europe), the magnificent Town Hall (the current building dates from the early 15th century) and its fine square, and the imposing 16th-century city ramparts.

St Olaf's Church

City ramparts

Latvia's capital and principal port, Riga, was founded in 1201. The adjacent Gulf of Riga usually freezes solid for much of winter.

Workers in southern Belarus mark the harvest by wearing traditional dress. Many Belarusians work on large collective or state farms.

SCALE 1:2,750,000
Lamberts Conformal Conic Projection

80 miles

80 kilometers

Longitude east of Greenwich

ELEVATION

Feet	Meters
6562	2000
4921	1500
3281	1000
2461	750
1640	500
1312	400
984	300
656	200
328	100
	Below sea level
656	200
3281	1000
6562	2000
13,123	4000
19,685	6000
26,246	8000
32,808	10,000

CENTRAL EASTERN EUROPE Moldova, Romania, Ukraine

Three major rivers flow through Central Eastern Europe to the north shore of the Black Sea. The Danube courses along Romania's southern border, its vast floodplain contrasting with the mountains of the interior. The Dniester runs from the uplands of western Ukraine along the eastern edge of Moldova; in western Moldova, hundreds of other, mainly short, rivers have carved steep ravines and gorges amid low hills. Flowing first south, then east and west in a great S-shape, the Dnieper River snakes through the immense steppe grasslands that cover most of Ukraine. Formerly part of the Soviet Union, Ukraine is now Europe's largest country. Romania and Moldova share strong linguistic and ethnic links, and most of Moldova was incorporated into Romania from 1918 to 1940. In the mid-20th century, both nations were part of the Eastern bloc; like Ukraine, they are now independent fledgling democracies.

POPULATION PATTERNS

	Less than 2.6 persons per sq mile/1 per sq km
	2.6–26 per sq mile/ 1–10 per sq km
	26–65 per sq mile/ 10–25 per sq km
	65–130 per sq mile/ 25–50 per sq km
	130–260 per sq mile/ 50–100 per sq km
	260–520 per sq mile/ 100–200 per sq km

Moldova is the most densely populated of the former Soviet republics, yet the majority of its inhabitants still live in rural areas; one-third of the urban population dwells in the capital. More than half of Romanians and Ukrainians live in towns and cities. Romania has areas of low population density in the mountains and swampy Danube Delta; Ukraine's population is a little more evenly spread, with the highest concentrations in the industrial southeast—home to one-third of the population—and the fertile belt that runs eastward from the Dniester. Ukraine and Moldova have many inhabitants of Russian origin, whereas Romania's largest minorities are ethnic Roma (Gypsy) people and Hungarians.

ECONOMIC PROFILE

	Forest and woodland
	Arable land
	Grazing

Cereals		Mining	
Sugar beet		Oil production	
Flowers		Gas production	
Dairy cattle		Wine	
Industrial center		Fishing	

All three countries have productive farmland. Cereals are grown widely in lowland areas, especially on the fertile black-soil plains of Ukraine, formerly known as "the breadbasket of the Soviet Union." Sugar beet (Ukraine is the world's largest producer) and sunflowers are also vital crops, and Romania and Moldova are significant wine producers. Moldova has few mineral resources and remains dependent on agriculture. Romania and Ukraine's reserves of oil, coal, and gas support major industries including the manufacture of metals, machinery, and chemicals. Textiles and footwear are important in Romania. Despite some economic progress, these nations remain among Europe's poorest.

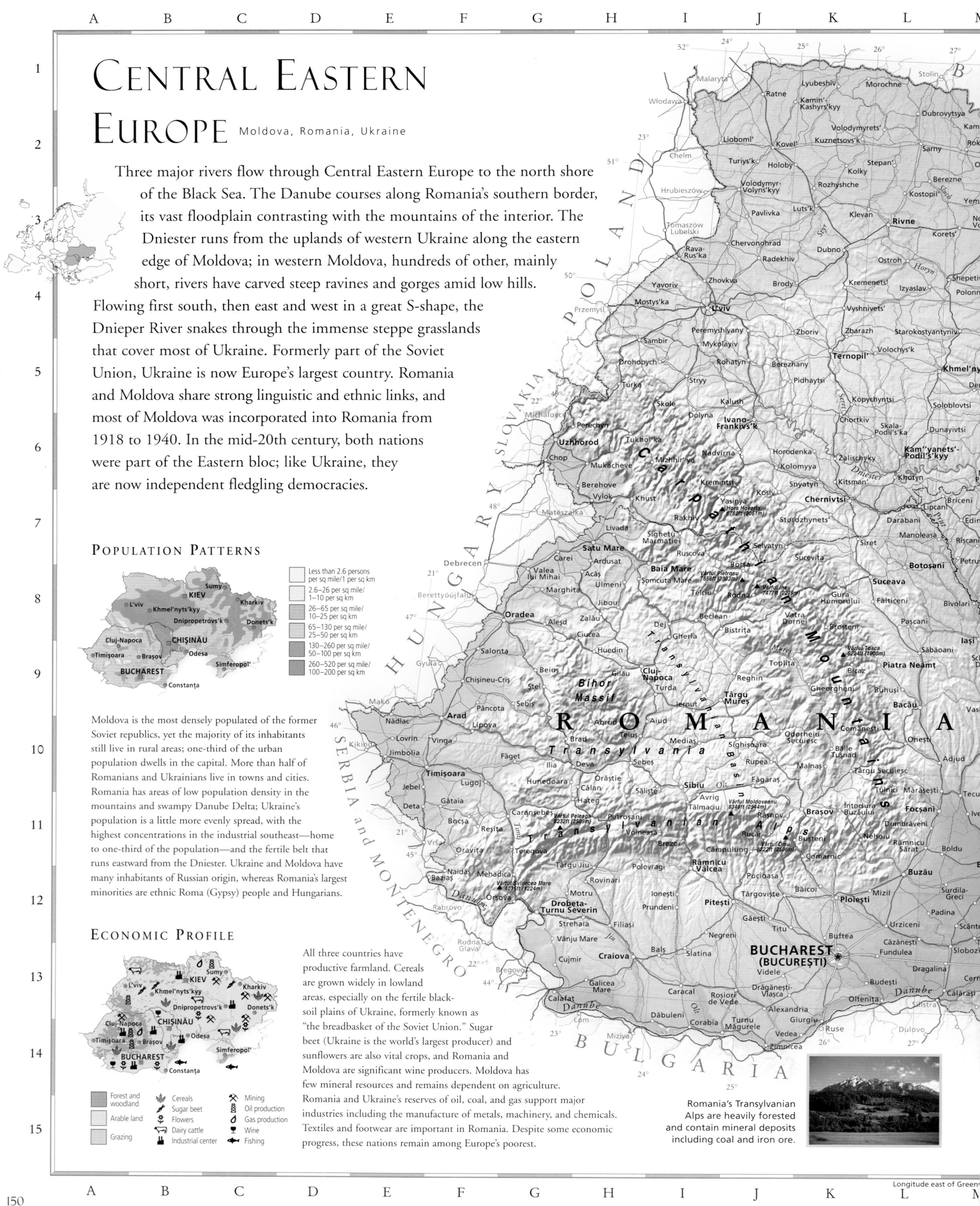

Romania's Transylvanian Alps are heavily forested and contain mineral deposits including coal and iron ore.

Longitude east of Green

In the Soviet era, Ukraine produced one-fifth of the U.S.S.R.'s agricultural goods.

Chișinău's buildings reflect Turkish and Soviet influences.

Kiev The Ukrainian capital's best-known landmark is golden-domed St Sophia Cathedral, which dates from 1037. At that time Kiev was the center of the powerful independent state of Kievan Rus. The city was razed by Mongol invaders in the 13th century and subsequently ruled by Poland, Lithuania, and Russia. It became the capital of newly independent Ukraine in 1991.

TRANSYLVANIA

Viewed from Romania's western border, the Carpathian Mountains and Transylvanian Alps form a vast amphitheater of mountains encompassing the region of Transylvania. Formerly autonomous but also ruled by Hungary for long periods, Transylvania was entirely ceded to Romania only in 1947.

ELEVATION

Feet	Meters
32,808	10,000
26,246	8000
19,685	6000
13,123	4000
6562	2000
3281	1000
656	200
328	100
0 Below sea level	0
656	200
3281	1000
6562	2000
1640	500
1312	400
984	300
2461	750
4921	1500
6562	2000

SCALE 1:3,500,000
Lamberts Conformal Conic Projection
0   100 miles
0   100 kilometers

THE RUSSIAN FEDERATION

Spanning 11 time zones and most of the Eastern Hemisphere, the Russian Federation is the largest country on Earth. It is divided into European Russia and Asian Russia, or Siberia, by the Ural Mountains, which stretch from the shore of the Kara Sea to Kazakhstan. In European Russia, the site of the nation's largest cities, major rivers divide plains and ranges of low, rolling hills. East of the Urals, an immense, swampy plain stretches to the Yenisey River, where the land climbs to the wide Central Siberian Plateau. High mountains line the Mongolian border and skirt the east coast. An almost unbroken band of boreal forest crosses the entire country, dividing the tundra of the far north from the woodlands and steppe grasslands of the south.

In 1917, after a bloody revolution, Russia became a communist state known as the Soviet Union, or Union of Soviet Socialist Republics (U.S.S.R.). Following the collapse of communism in 1991, ten Soviet republics declared independence. The remainder of the union, about 75 percent of its land area, became the Russian Federation.

St Petersburg's Winter Palace is one of a series of buildings constructed in the mid-18th century by Peter the Great.

Local fishermen harvest more than 50 species of fish from Lake Baikal, the deepest lake in the world.

The Chukchi of northeastern Russia live mainly by herding reindeer, fishing, and hunting whales, seals, and walruses.

MOSCOW The focal point of Russia's capital city, Red Square, dates from the late 15th century and acquired its present name —the Russian word for "red" also means "beautiful"—in the 17th century. It is the site of some of the nation's most important buildings, including the Kremlin, Lenin's Tomb, and the 12-domed Cathedral of St Basil the Blessed (below). The cathedral was built between 1554 and 1560 by Ivan IV ("the Terrible") to celebrate his victory over the Mongols. Legend has it that Ivan had the architect blinded to prevent him ever building anything to surpass this extraordinary work.

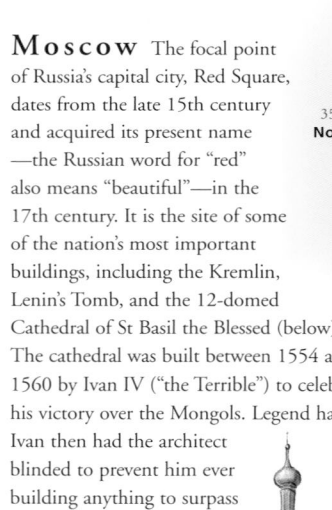
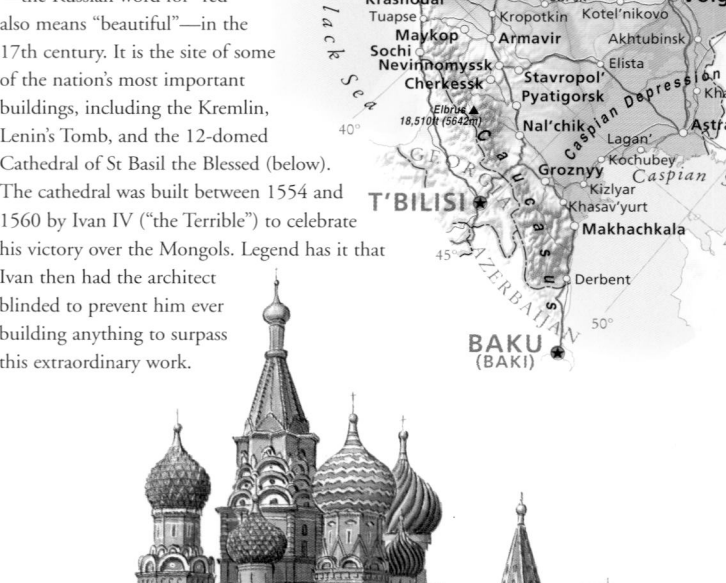

THE KAMCHATKA PENINSULA

Remote, cold, and desolate, the Kamchatka Peninsula extends for 750 miles (1,200 km) southwestward from the eastern edge of Russia, dividing the Sea of Okhotsk from the Bering Sea. Its forbidding landscape is characterized by forest-studded tundra, few towns or roads, hot springs, and more than 120 steep-sided volcanic peaks, including 15,584-foot (4,750-m) Sopka Klyuchevskaya, Siberia's highest mountain. No fewer than 22 of these volcanoes are still active.

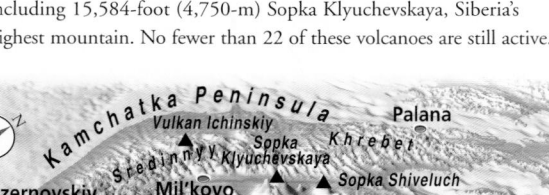

Longitude east of Greenwich

POPULATION PATTERNS

European Russia constitutes one-quarter of the country but is home to four-fifths of its inhabitants. Settlement is especially dense around Moscow, along the River Volga, and in the southwest. East of the Urals, Russians cluster around the industrial centers of Omsk and Novosibirsk, the towns strung along the Trans-Siberian railway, and far-flung northern ports and mining centers. Over the past century, Russians have steadily abandoned the countryside for cities; 73 percent now live in urban areas. More than four-fifths are ethnic Russians; the remainder consists of a large number of other ethnic groups, including Ukrainians, Tatars, and Bashkirs.

Uninhabited
Less than 2.6 persons per sq mile/1 per sq km
2.6–26 per sq mile/1–10 per sq km
26–65 per sq mile/10–25 per sq km
65–130 per sq mile/25–50 per sq km
130–260 per sq mile/50–100 per sq km
260–520 per sq mile/100–200 per sq km

ECONOMIC PROFILE

Much of the Soviet Union's best arable land was located in the now-independent republics of Ukraine and Belarus. Less than one-sixth of the Russian Federation is farmland; wheat, barley, and sugar beet are among the major crops. Russia has the world's largest forests and plentiful supplies of minerals, including coal, oil, gas, gold, copper, and nickel. These support the processing of metals and fossil fuels, and the manufacturing of chemicals and machinery. Communist rule accelerated industrialization, but ultimately stifled development. A shift toward privatization and a more open market is under way.

Forest and woodland
Arable land
Grazing
Marginal or nonproductive

Potatoes
Beef cattle
Industrial center
Mining
Oil production
Gas production
Timber
Reindeer
Fishing

ELEVATION

Feet	Meters
6562	2000
4921	1500
3281	1000
2461	750
1640	500
1312	400
984	300
656	200
328	100
Below sea level	
656	200
1312	400
3281	1000
6562	2000
13,123	4000
19,685	6000
26,246	8000
32,808	10,000

SCALE 1:18,500,000
Lamberts Conformal Conic Projection

0 — 500 miles
0 — 500 kilometers

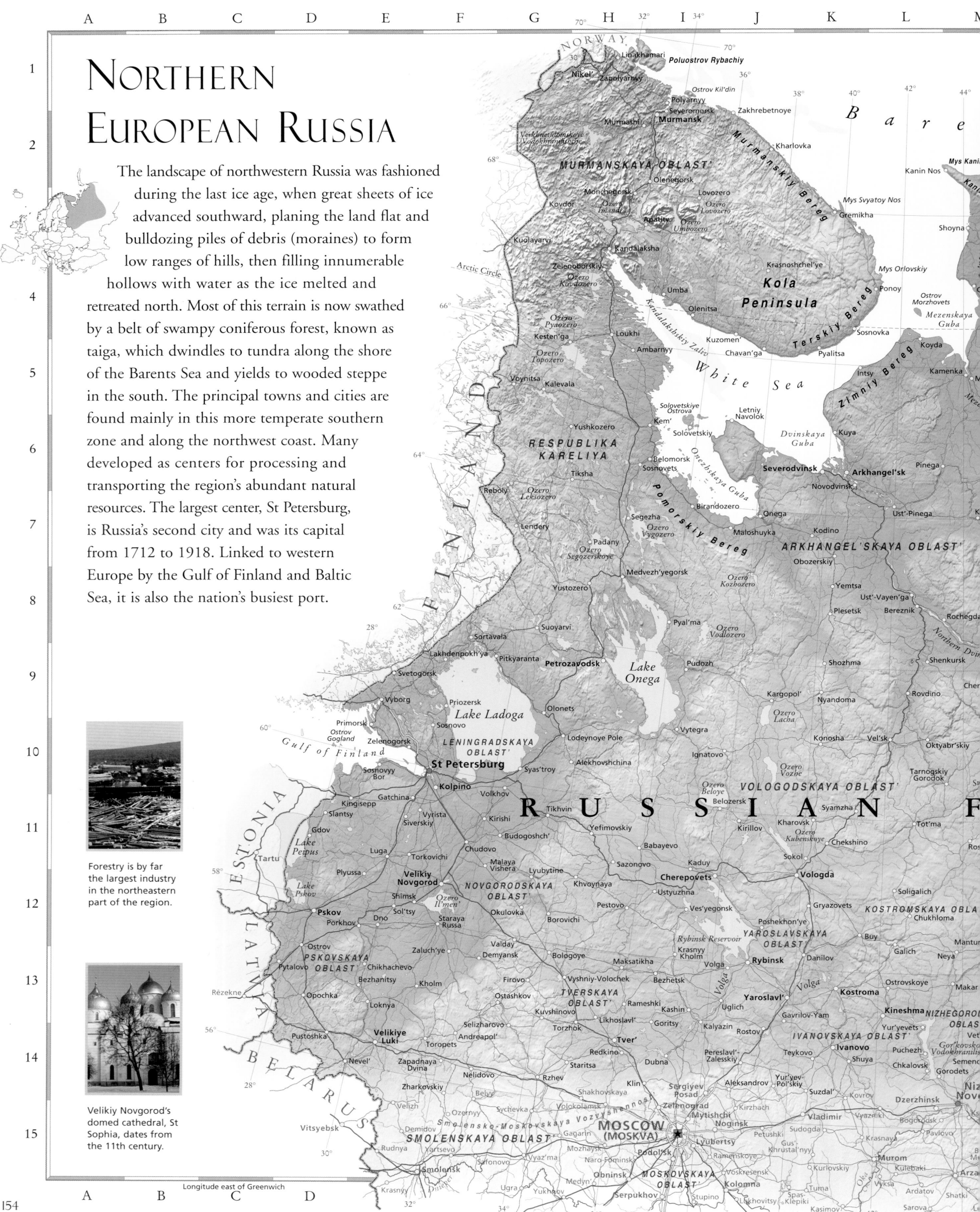

Northern European Russia

The landscape of northwestern Russia was fashioned during the last ice age, when great sheets of ice advanced southward, planing the land flat and bulldozing piles of debris (moraines) to form low ranges of hills, then filling innumerable hollows with water as the ice melted and retreated north. Most of this terrain is now swathed by a belt of swampy coniferous forest, known as taiga, which dwindles to tundra along the shore of the Barents Sea and yields to wooded steppe in the south. The principal towns and cities are found mainly in this more temperate southern zone and along the northwest coast. Many developed as centers for processing and transporting the region's abundant natural resources. The largest center, St Petersburg, is Russia's second city and was its capital from 1712 to 1918. Linked to western Europe by the Gulf of Finland and Baltic Sea, it is also the nation's busiest port.

Forestry is by far the largest industry in the northeastern part of the region.

Velikiy Novgorod's domed cathedral, St Sophia, dates from the 11th century.

Longitude east of Greenwich

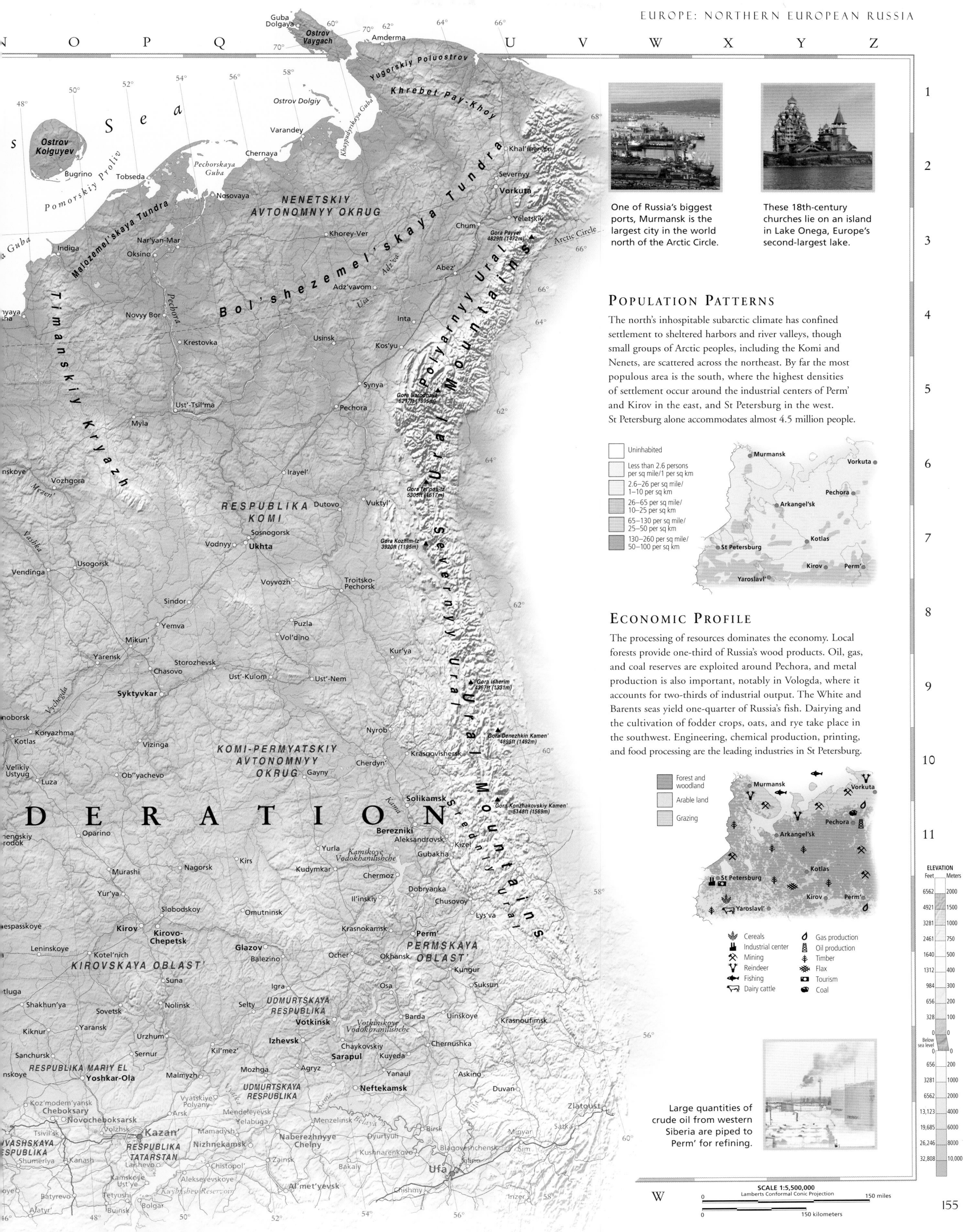

One of Russia's biggest ports, Murmansk is the largest city in the world north of the Arctic Circle.

These 18th-century churches lie on an island in Lake Onega, Europe's second-largest lake.

POPULATION PATTERNS

The north's inhospitable subarctic climate has confined settlement to sheltered harbors and river valleys, though small groups of Arctic peoples, including the Komi and Nenets, are scattered across the northeast. By far the most populous area is the south, where the highest densities of settlement occur around the industrial centers of Perm' and Kirov in the east, and St Petersburg in the west. St Petersburg alone accommodates almost 4.5 million people.

Uninhabited

Less than 2.6 persons per sq mile/1 per sq km

2.6–26 per sq mile/1–10 per sq km

26–65 per sq mile/10–25 per sq km

65–130 per sq mile/25–50 per sq km

130–260 per sq mile/50–100 per sq km

ECONOMIC PROFILE

The processing of resources dominates the economy. Local forests provide one-third of Russia's wood products. Oil, gas, and coal reserves are exploited around Pechora, and metal production is also important, notably in Vologda, where it accounts for two-thirds of industrial output. The White and Barents seas yield one-quarter of Russia's fish. Dairying and the cultivation of fodder crops, oats, and rye take place in the southwest. Engineering, chemical production, printing, and food processing are the leading industries in St Petersburg.

Forest and woodland

Arable land

Grazing

Cereals
Industrial center
Mining
Reindeer
Fishing
Dairy cattle
Gas production
Oil production
Timber
Flax
Tourism
Coal

Large quantities of crude oil from western Siberia are piped to Perm' for refining.

ELEVATION

Feet	Meters
6562	2000
4921	1500
3281	1000
2461	750
1640	500
1312	400
984	300
656	200
328	100
0 Below sea level	0
656	200
3281	1000
6562	2000
13,123	4000
19,685	6000
26,246	8000
32,808	10,000

SCALE 1:5,500,000
Lamberts Conformal Conic Projection
0   150 miles
0   150 kilometers

Southern European Russia

Europe's second-largest urban center, Moscow is not only the capital of the Russian Federation, but the heart of its most densely populated, developed, and productive region. The city lies on the wide valley of the Moskva River, a tributary of the Oka, which in turn flows east into the Volga, Europe's longest river. A chain of cities lines these waterways, running eastward and veering south with the Volga through Samara to Volgograd. West of the river, the Volga Hills roll down to the banks of the Don, Europe's fifth-longest waterway, which forms the eastern boundary of the Central Russian Uplands, a low plateau. Near Volgograd, the two rivers almost meet and are linked by the Volga–Don Canal. Turning away from each other, the Don and the Volga then drain across arid lowlands into, respectively, the Sea of Azov and the Caspian Sea. In the far south, where the mighty Caucasus range forms Russia's southern frontier and a natural boundary with Asia, a mere 200 miles (320 km) or so divides Europe's lowest point, in the Caspian Depression, from its highest, the towering summit of Elbrus.

THE CASPIAN DEPRESSION

Covering 77,000 square miles (200,000 sq km), the Caspian Depression is a vast lowland on the northwestern edge of the Caspian Sea. Part of an immense downward fold caused by crumpling of Earth's crust, it descends to 92 feet (28 m) below sea level at the shoreline. In the north, the depression is traversed by the Volga River, which forms Russia's largest delta. Elsewhere, the depression is mainly barren, although beneath its surface lie large deposits of oil and salt.

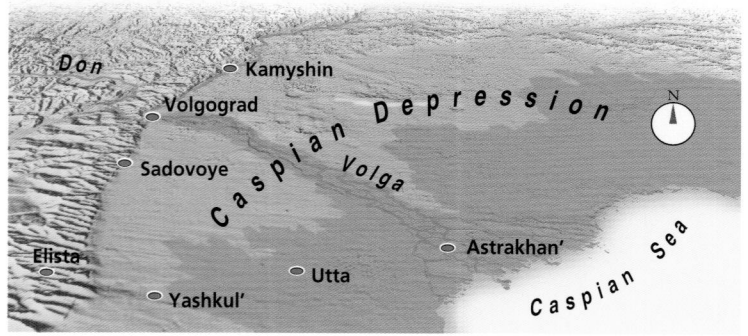

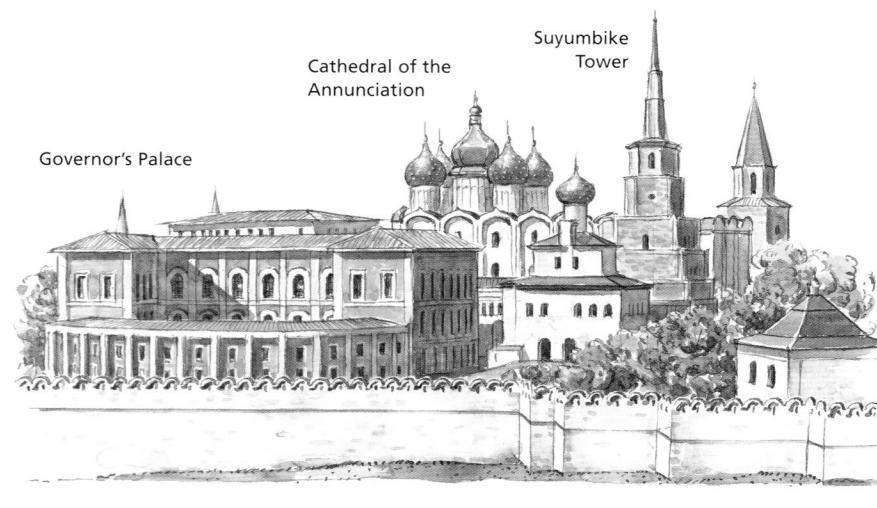

Governor's Palace

Cathedral of the Annunciation

Suyumbike Tower

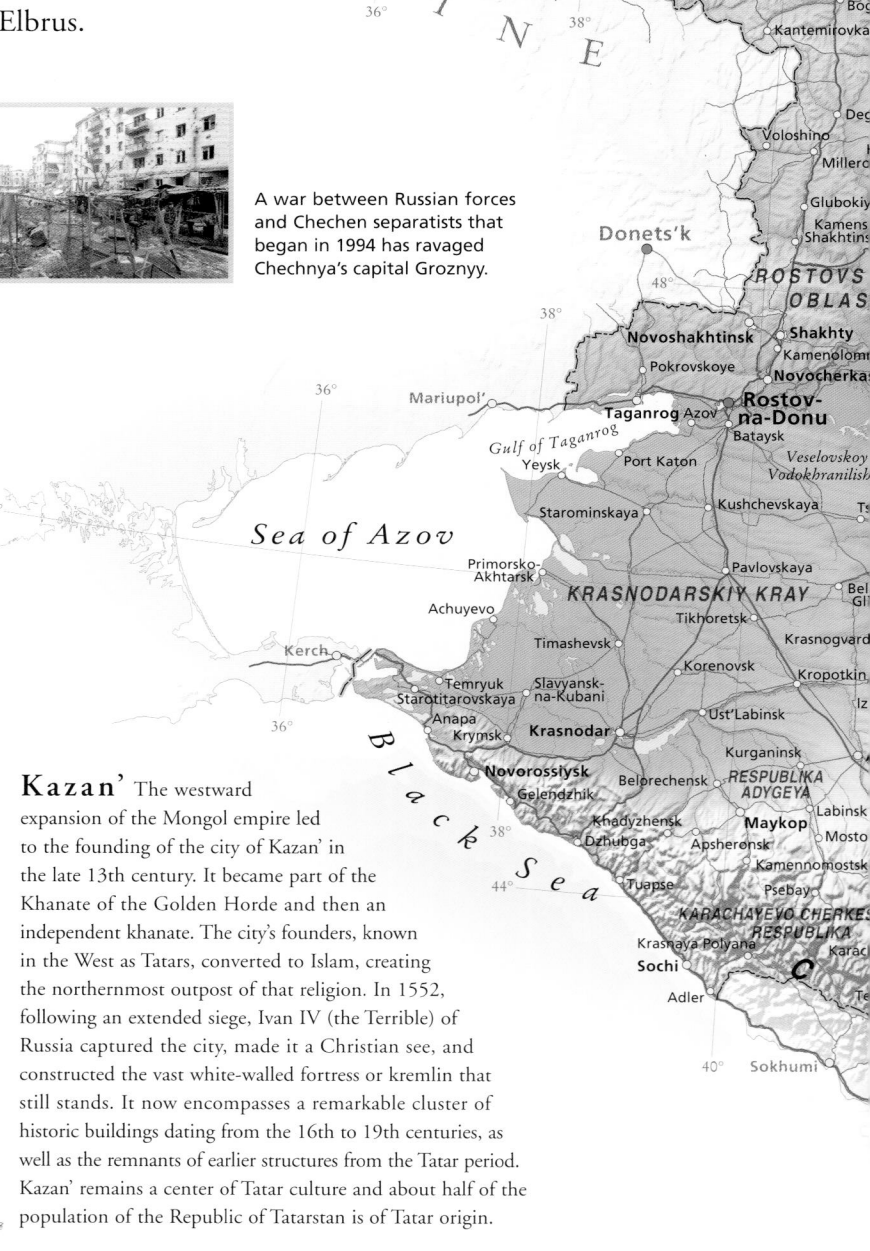

A war between Russian forces and Chechen separatists that began in 1994 has ravaged Chechnya's capital Groznyy.

Kazan' The westward expansion of the Mongol empire led to the founding of the city of Kazan' in the late 13th century. It became part of the Khanate of the Golden Horde and then an independent khanate. The city's founders, known in the West as Tatars, converted to Islam, creating the northernmost outpost of that religion. In 1552, following an extended siege, Ivan IV (the Terrible) of Russia captured the city, made it a Christian see, and constructed the vast white-walled fortress or kremlin that still stands. It now encompasses a remarkable cluster of historic buildings dating from the 16th to 19th centuries, as well as the remnants of earlier structures from the Tatar period. Kazan' remains a center of Tatar culture and about half of the population of the Republic of Tatarstan is of Tatar origin.

Longitude east of Greenwich

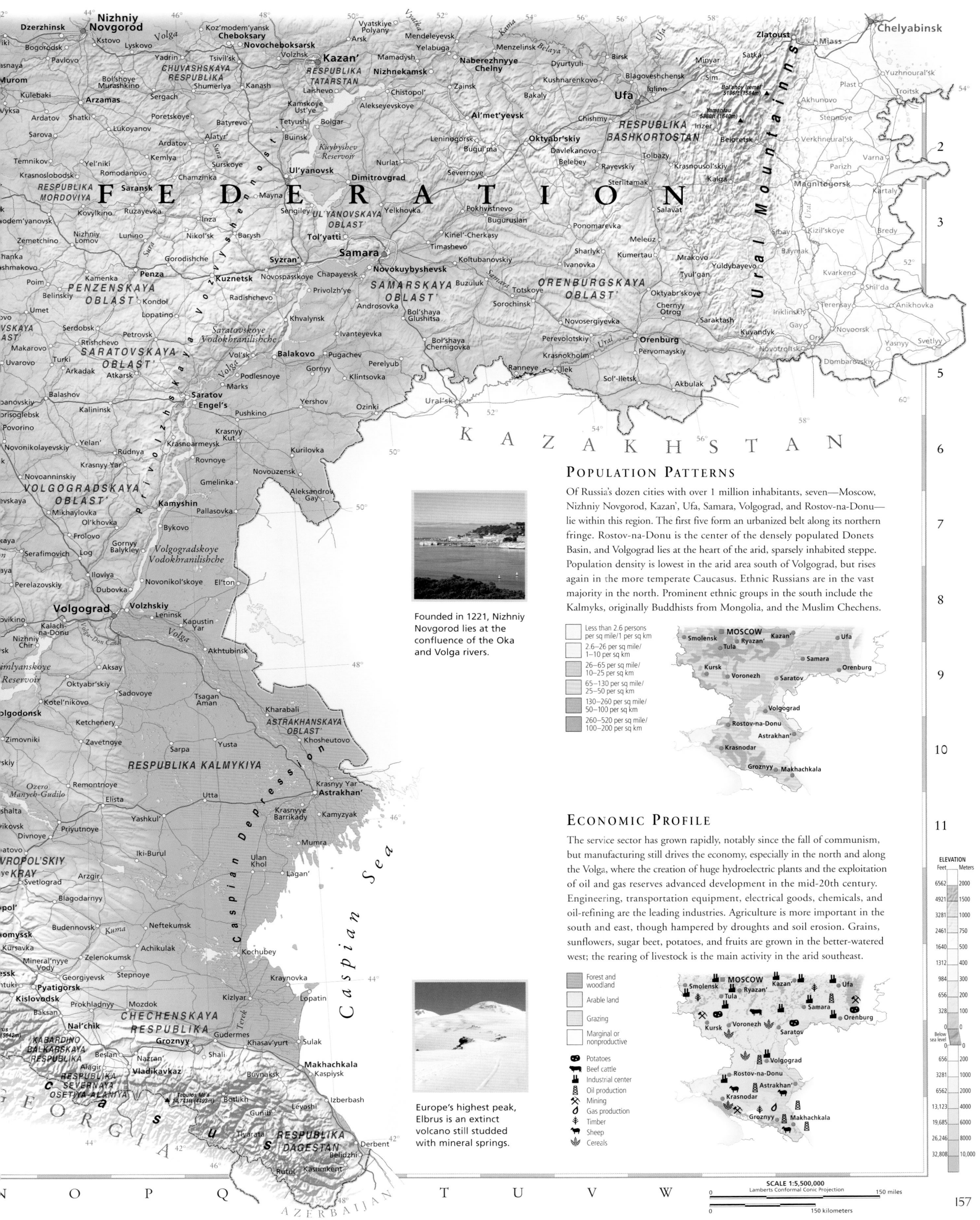

Founded in 1221, Nizhniy Novgorod lies at the confluence of the Oka and Volga rivers.

POPULATION PATTERNS

Of Russia's dozen cities with over 1 million inhabitants, seven—Moscow, Nizhniy Novgorod, Kazan', Ufa, Samara, Volgograd, and Rostov-na-Donu—lie within this region. The first five form an urbanized belt along its northern fringe. Rostov-na-Donu is the center of the densely populated Donets Basin, and Volgograd lies at the heart of the arid, sparsely inhabited steppe. Population density is lowest in the arid area south of Volgograd, but rises again in the more temperate Caucasus. Ethnic Russians are in the vast majority in the north. Prominent ethnic groups in the south include the Kalmyks, originally Buddhists from Mongolia, and the Muslim Chechens.

Less than 2.6 persons per sq mile/1 per sq km
2.6–26 per sq mile/ 1–10 per sq km
26–65 per sq mile/ 10–25 per sq km
65–130 per sq mile/ 25–50 per sq km
130–260 per sq mile/ 50–100 per sq km
260–520 per sq mile/ 100–200 per sq km

ECONOMIC PROFILE

The service sector has grown rapidly, notably since the fall of communism, but manufacturing still drives the economy, especially in the north and along the Volga, where the creation of huge hydroelectric plants and the exploitation of oil and gas reserves advanced development in the mid-20th century. Engineering, transportation equipment, electrical goods, chemicals, and oil-refining are the leading industries. Agriculture is more important in the south and east, though hampered by droughts and soil erosion. Grains, sunflowers, sugar beet, potatoes, and fruits are grown in the better-watered west; the rearing of livestock is the main activity in the arid southeast.

Forest and woodland
Arable land
Grazing
Marginal or nonproductive

Potatoes
Beef cattle
Industrial center
Oil production
Mining
Gas production
Timber
Sheep
Cereals

Europe's highest peak, Elbrus is an extinct volcano still studded with mineral springs.

ELEVATION	
Feet	Meters
6562	2000
4921	1500
3281	1000
2461	750
1640	500
1312	400
984	300
656	200
328	100
Below sea level	0
656	200
3281	1000
6562	2000
13,123	4000
19,685	6000
26,246	8000
32,808	10,000

SCALE 1:5,500,000
Lambert Conformal Conic Projection
0   150 miles
0   150 kilometers

THE MEDITERRANEAN SEA

Part of the Atlantic Ocean, to which it is connected by the narrow Strait of Gibraltar, the Mediterranean Sea spans 969,000 square miles (2,510,000 sq km). It separates Europe from Africa, and borders Asia to the east. The strait of the Bosporus links it to the Black Sea, the Suez Canal to the Red Sea. The seafloor is divided into two parts by a shelf running between Tunisia and Sicily. The western side consists mainly of large basins; to the east, parallel trenches and ridges curve around southern Greece. Twice as much water evaporates from the Mediterranean as is replenished by rivers; consequently, there is a steady inflow of sea water from the Atlantic. The Mediterranean's diverse peoples created some of the most powerful civilizations in history, including those of ancient Egypt, Greece, Carthage, and Rome, and the Ottoman Empire, which, in 1700, extended from present-day Morocco around the southern and eastern Mediterranean to the Balkans.

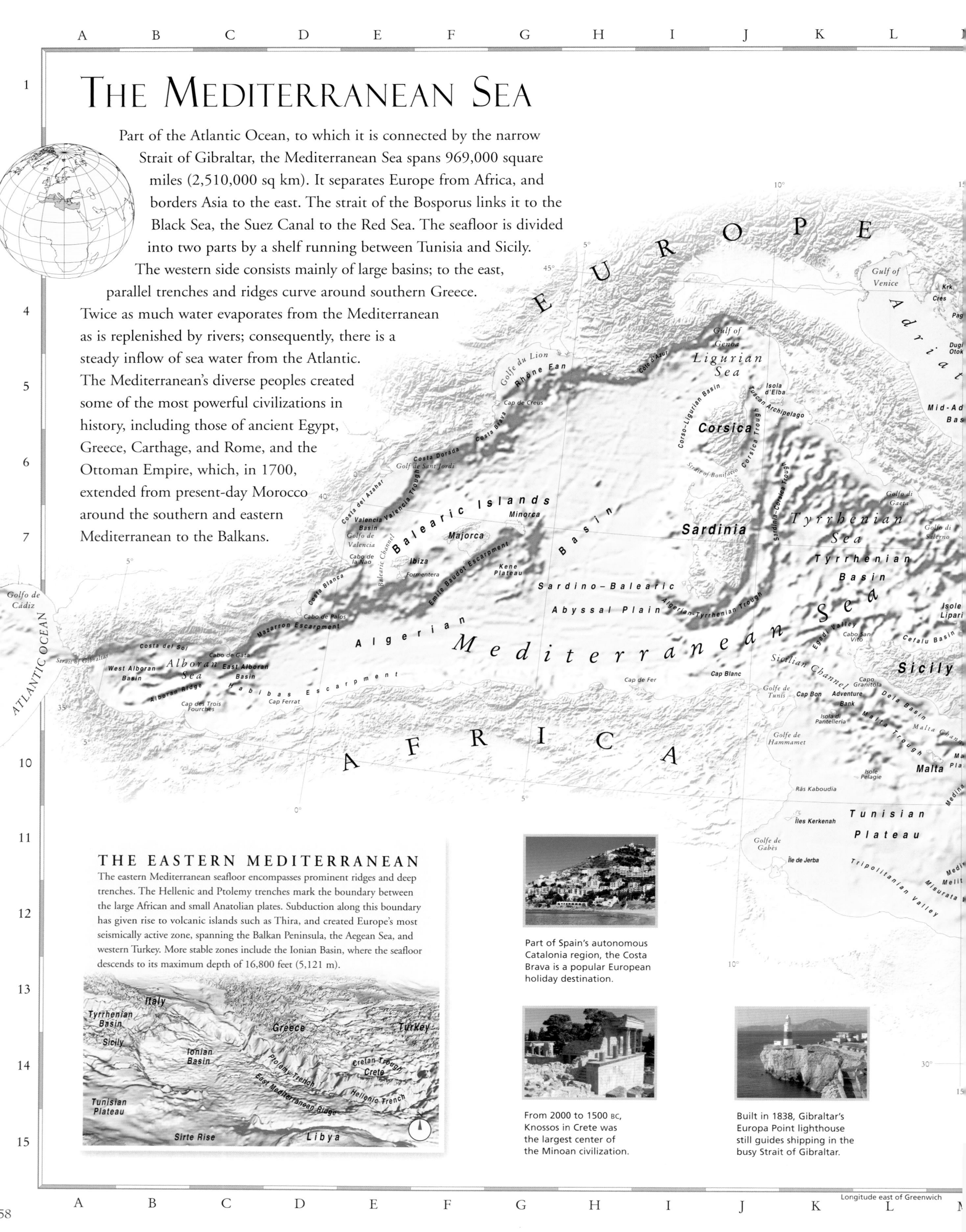

THE EASTERN MEDITERRANEAN

The eastern Mediterranean seafloor encompasses prominent ridges and deep trenches. The Hellenic and Ptolemy trenches mark the boundary between the large African and small Anatolian plates. Subduction along this boundary has given rise to volcanic islands such as Thira, and created Europe's most seismically active zone, spanning the Balkan Peninsula, the Aegean Sea, and western Turkey. More stable zones include the Ionian Basin, where the seafloor descends to its maximum depth of 16,800 feet (5,121 m).

Part of Spain's autonomous Catalonia region, the Costa Brava is a popular European holiday destination.

From 2000 to 1500 BC, Knossos in Crete was the largest center of the Minoan civilization.

Built in 1838, Gibraltar's Europa Point lighthouse still guides shipping in the busy Strait of Gibraltar.

Longitude east of Greenwich

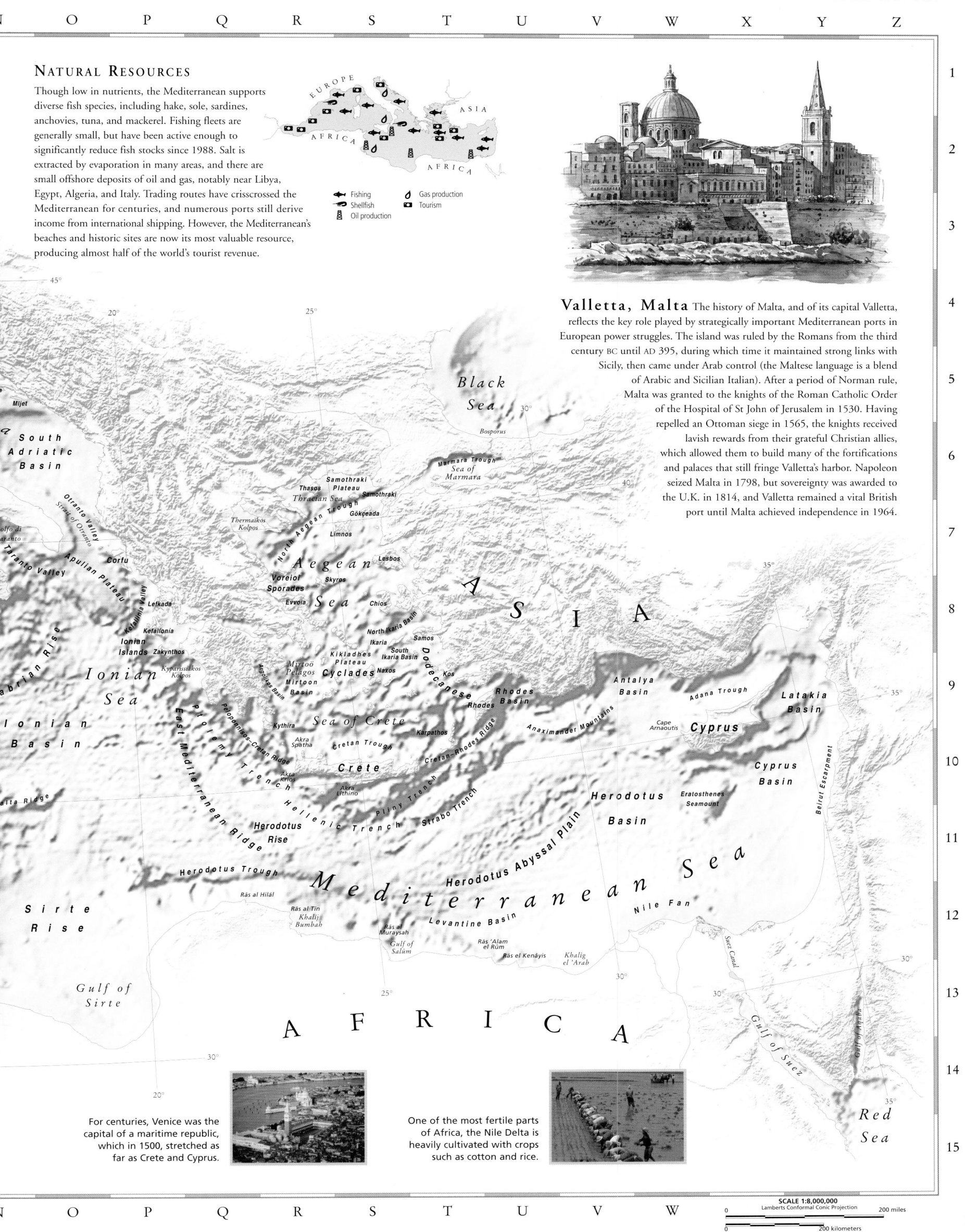

N O P Q R S T U V W X Y Z

NATURAL RESOURCES

Though low in nutrients, the Mediterranean supports diverse fish species, including hake, sole, sardines, anchovies, tuna, and mackerel. Fishing fleets are generally small, but have been active enough to significantly reduce fish stocks since 1988. Salt is extracted by evaporation in many areas, and there are small offshore deposits of oil and gas, notably near Libya, Egypt, Algeria, and Italy. Trading routes have crisscrossed the Mediterranean for centuries, and numerous ports still derive income from international shipping. However, the Mediterranean's beaches and historic sites are now its most valuable resource, producing almost half of the world's tourist revenue.

EUROPE

ASIA

AFRICA

AFRICA

Fishing

Shellfish

Oil production

Gas production

Tourism

Valletta, Malta The history of Malta, and of its capital Valletta, reflects the key role played by strategically important Mediterranean ports in European power struggles. The island was ruled by the Romans from the third century BC until AD 395, during which time it maintained strong links with Sicily, then came under Arab control (the Maltese language is a blend of Arabic and Sicilian Italian). After a period of Norman rule, Malta was granted to the knights of the Roman Catholic Order of the Hospital of St John of Jerusalem in 1530. Having repelled an Ottoman siege in 1565, the knights received lavish rewards from their grateful Christian allies, which allowed them to build many of the fortifications and palaces that still fringe Valletta's harbor. Napoleon seized Malta in 1798, but sovereignty was awarded to the U.K. in 1814, and Valletta remained a vital British port until Malta achieved independence in 1964.

For centuries, Venice was the capital of a maritime republic, which in 1500, stretched as far as Crete and Cyprus.

One of the most fertile parts of Africa, the Nile Delta is heavily cultivated with crops such as cotton and rice.

SCALE 1:8,000,000
Lamberts Conformal Conic Projection
0 — 200 miles
0 — 200 kilometers

159

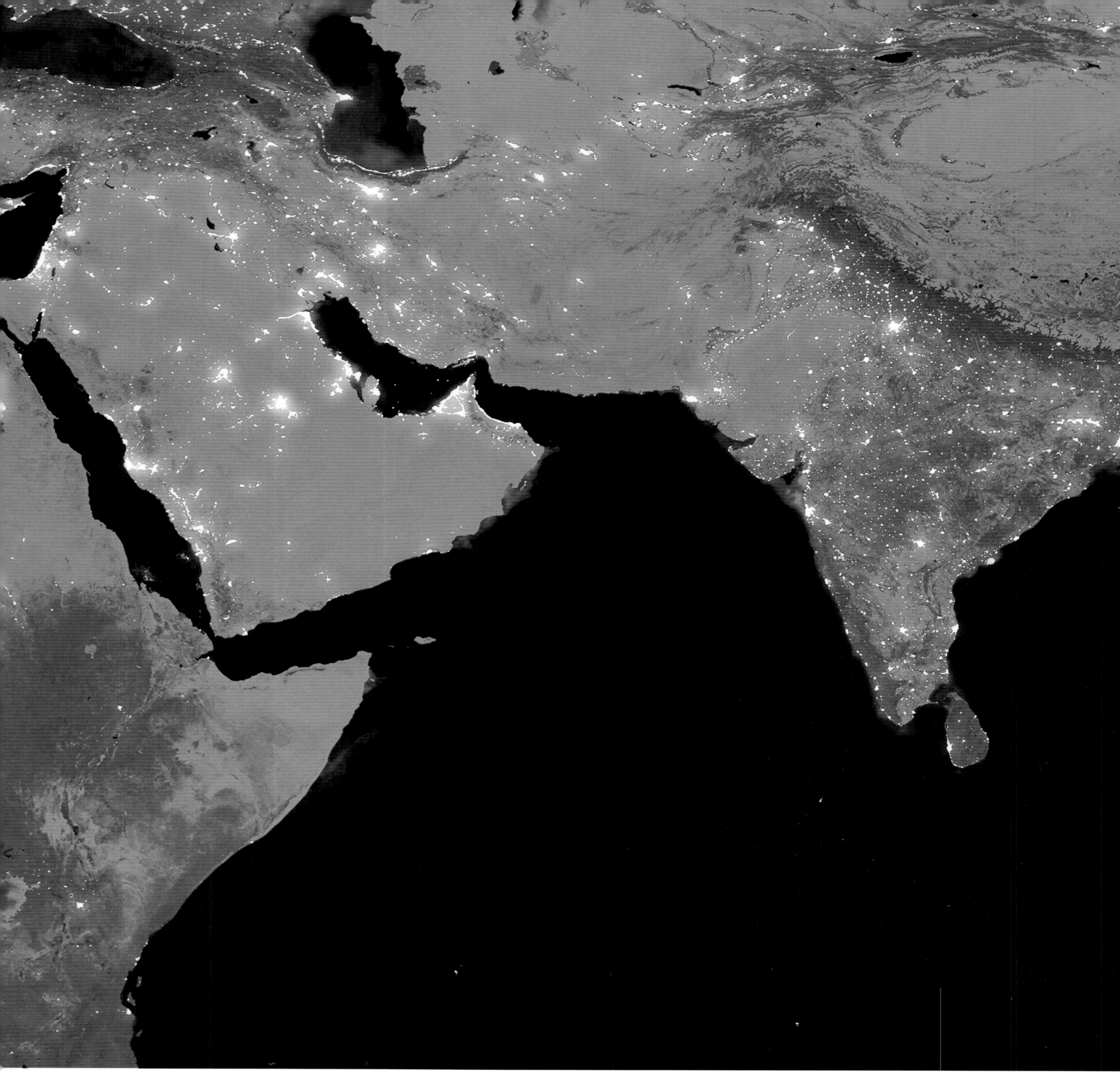

The intensity of light from Japan reflects that nation's high population density and considerable urbanization. The Indian subcontinent and eastern China stand out at night. The Himalayan mountains and the Gobi Desert remain mostly dark.

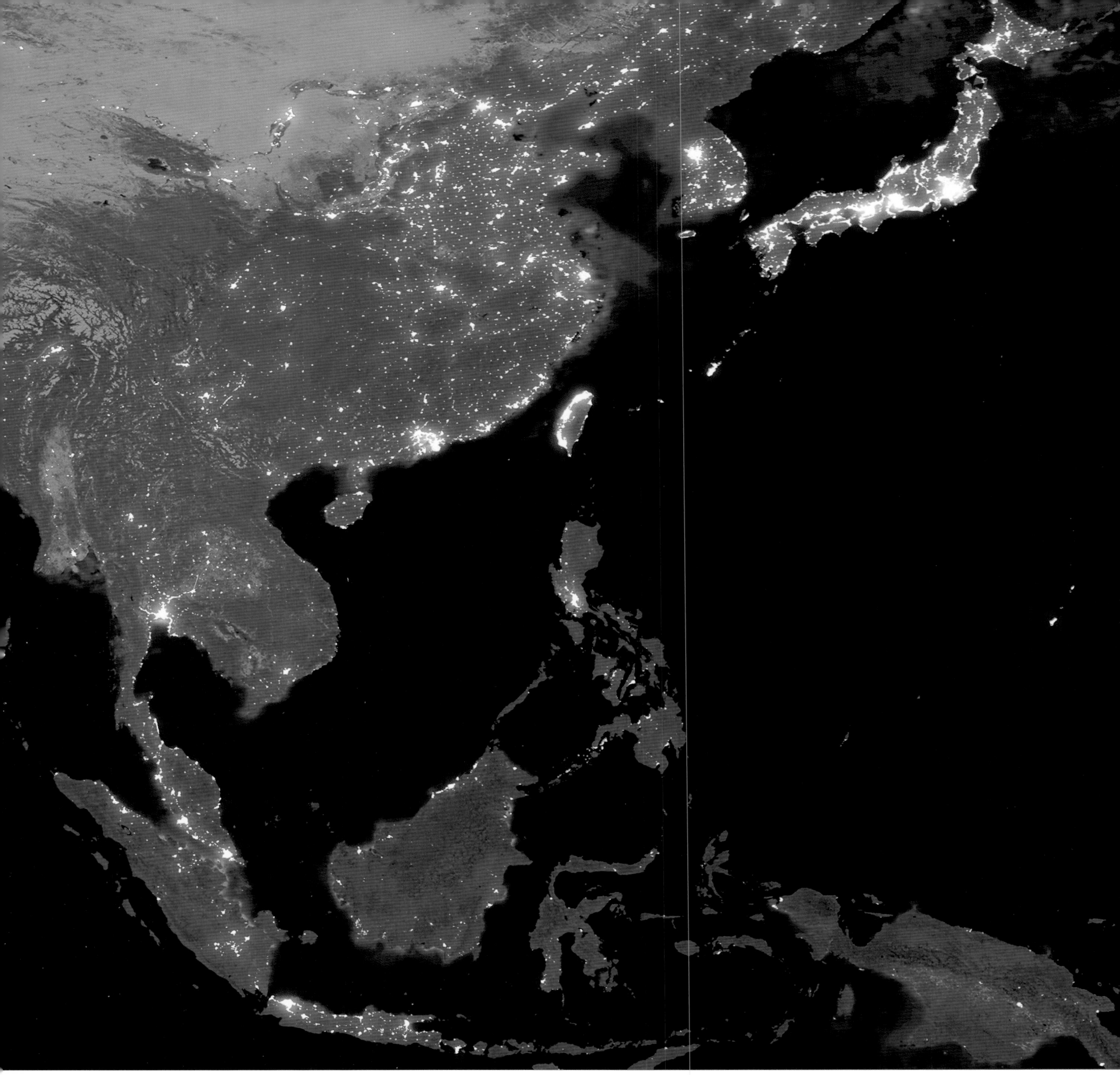

ASIA

ABOVE ASIA

Asia's eastern and southern fringes lie near the edge of a mighty tectonic plate called the Eurasian plate. It is one of the constantly shifting pieces of Earth's crust that make up the surface of the planet. The collision zone where the Eurasian plate converges with other plates is marked by the upthrust of massive mountain ranges such as the Himalayas, recurring earthquakes, and numerous active volcanoes, including the chain that runs from Sumatra through Java and north to Japan. Satellites have captured dramatic images of both current activity and the results of past upheavals. Also visible is evidence of climate change. Radar images of China's Taklimakan Desert reveal ancient alluvial fans laid down in wetter times, and changed landforms caused by the Kunlun Shan on the edge of the desert being pushed north by the continuing collision of the Eurasian plate with the Indian plate.

Gunung Merbabu and Merapi, Indonesia
Below: This false-color image shows part of the volcanic chain that crosses the Indonesian island of Java. Old lava flows appear in shades of yellow and green on Gunung Merbabu, center, and Gunung Merapi, lower right. In November 1994, six weeks after this image was collected, Gunung Merapi erupted, killing more than 60 people.

Taklimakan Desert, China
Bottom: The veined patterns in the center of this radar image of China's Taklimakan Desert are gravel deposits that accumulated at the base of the Kunlun Shan when the climate was wetter. They mark ancient alluvial fans. The large lavender triangles are the modern fans. Yellow areas on the modern fans are vegetated oases.

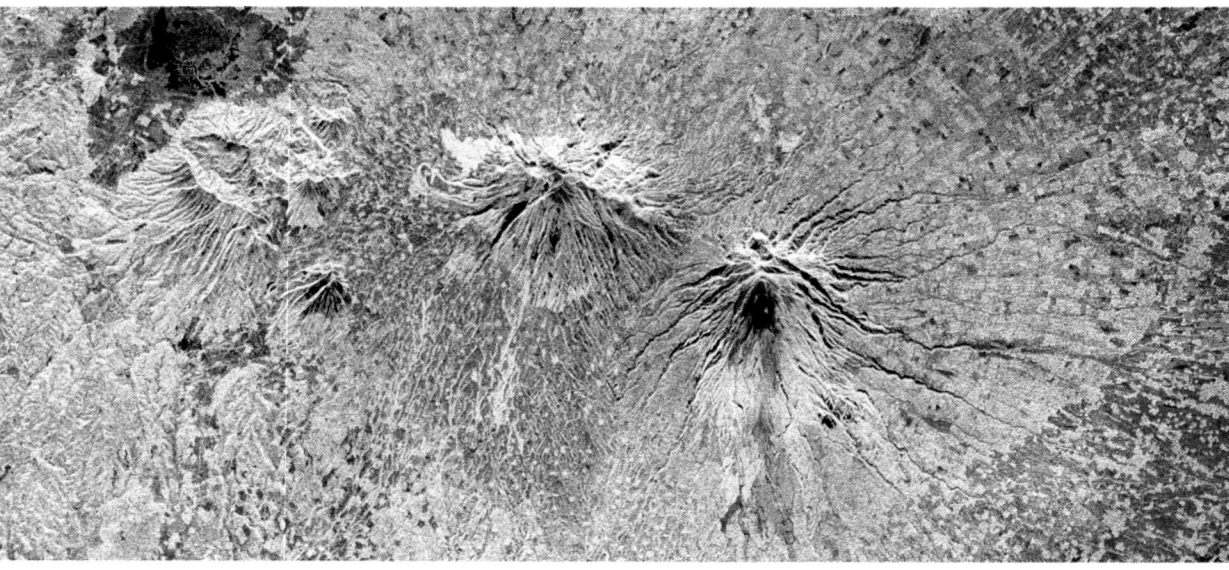

The Bosporus, Istanbul, Turkey
Left: This false-color view of the Turkish city of Istanbul displays urban areas as blue-green and vegetation as red. The busy shipping channel of the Bosporus divides the city and links the Black Sea in the north with the Sea of Marmara in the south. This image also indicates water temperature, with colder waters shown in deeper shades of blue.

Desert, northern Oman
Below: This radar image of a desert area in northern Oman, on the Arabian Peninsula, was collected by the space shuttle Endeavour in 1994. The bright arcs are limestone, formed on the bed of a shallow sea, and worn away into hills after sea levels dropped. The branching patterns are ancient drainage channels cut in wetter times.

LAND AND ENVIRONMENT

Asia covers 17.4 million square miles (45 million sq km), one-third of the world's landmass. The mainland is separated from Europe by Russia's Ural and Caucasus mountains and the narrow straits of the Bosporus in Turkey, from Africa by the Red Sea and Suez Canal, and from North America by the Bering Strait. Its center is dominated by an immense plateau region ringed by high mountain ranges. The northern ranges ripple across eastern Siberia to the Bering Sea. To the west, the uplands stretch through Afghanistan, Iran, and Turkey, dividing the arid Arabian Peninsula from the plains bordering the Caspian sea. The southern peaks are crowned by the world's highest mountain chain, the Himalaya, which falls steeply to the Gangetic Plain of the Indian Subcontinent but slopes more gently toward the Indochina Peninsula. Islands and archipelagoes fringe Asia's south and east coasts, including Sri Lanka, Japan, and the sprawling Malay Archipelago.

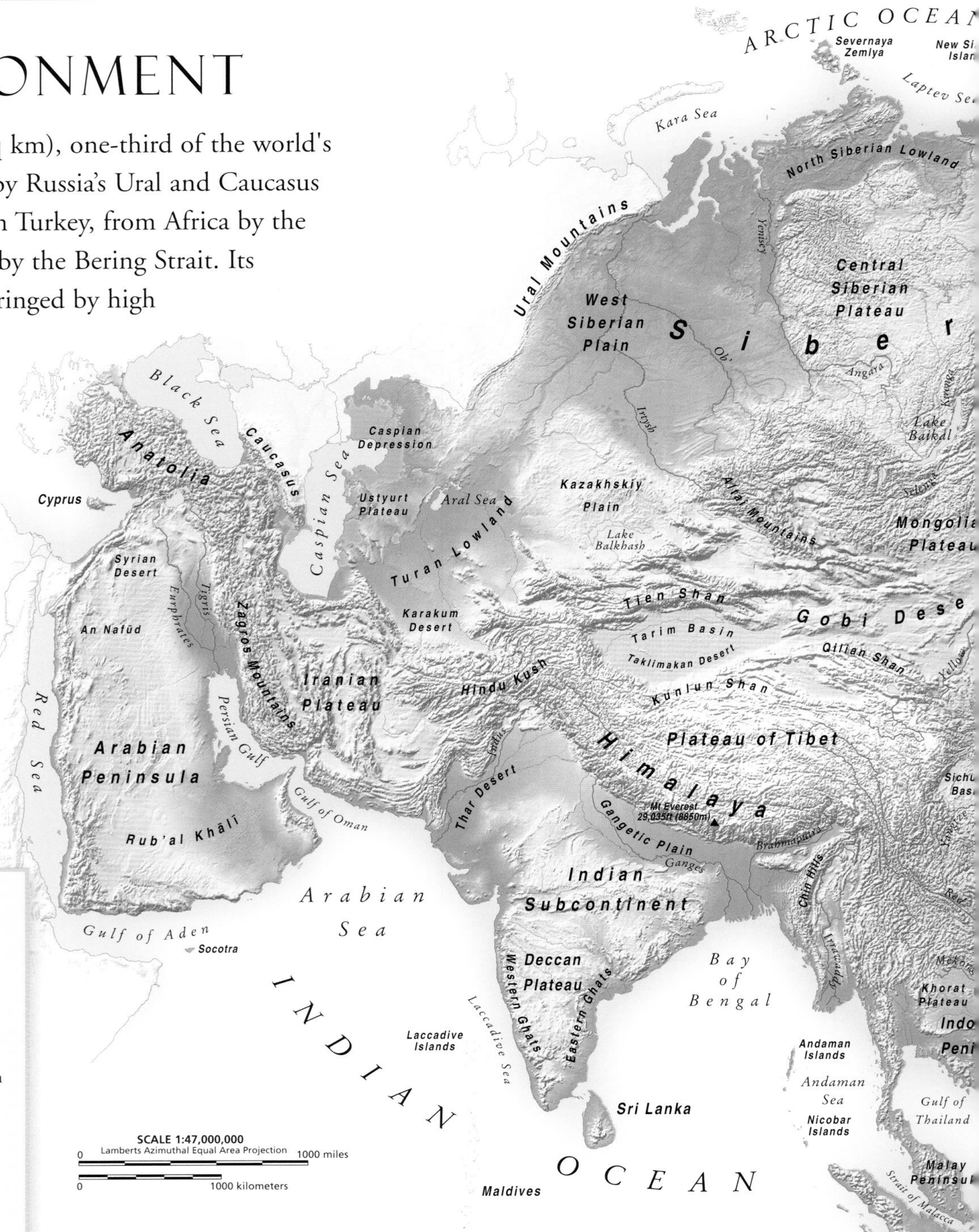

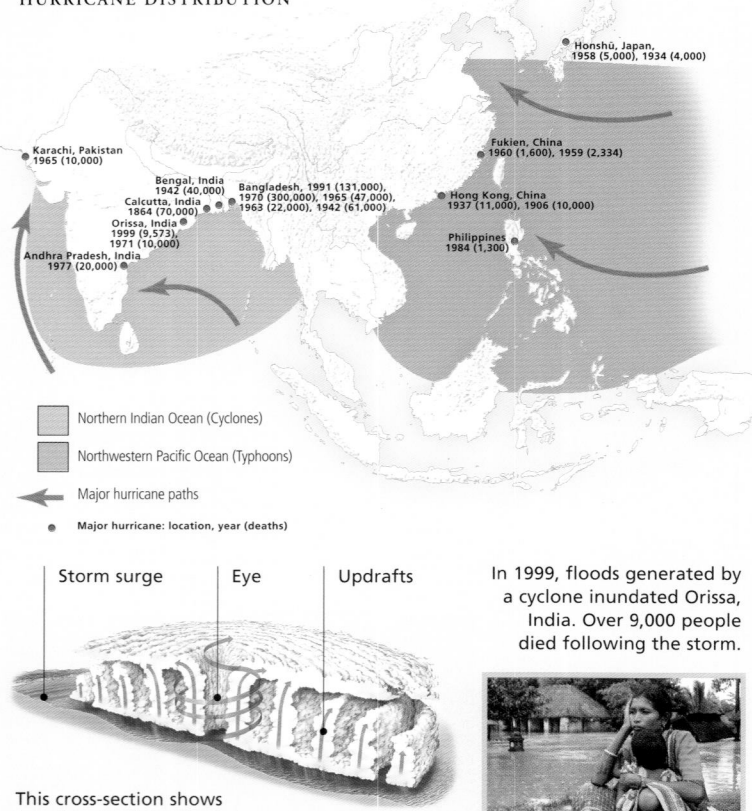

NATURAL HAZARDS

Hurricanes

Known in the western Pacific as typhoons (from the Cantonese *tai-fung*, meaning "great wind") and around the Indian Ocean as tropical cyclones, hurricanes regularly bring devastation to many parts of southern and eastern Asia. They occur when a large cluster of thunderstorms forms over open ocean and begins to spin as a result of Earth's rotation—something that occurs only if the storm system is more than five degrees from the Equator. Once the system starts spinning, it may intensify and grow. It qualifies as a hurricane when its wind speeds reach 74 mph (119 km/h), and it can generate wind gusts of up to 190 mph (305 km/h). One of its most destructive side-effects is a storm surge, a huge wave that can swamp low-lying areas.

HURRICANE DISTRIBUTION

Honshū, Japan, 1958 (5,000), 1934 (4,000)

Karachi, Pakistan 1965 (10,000)

Bengal, India 1942 (40,000)
Calcutta, India 1864 (70,000)
Orissa, India 1999 (9,573), 1971 (10,000)

Bangladesh, 1991 (131,000), 1970 (300,000), 1965 (47,000), 1963 (22,000), 1942 (61,000)

Fukien, China 1960 (1,600), 1959 (2,334)

Hong Kong, China 1937 (11,000), 1906 (10,000)

Philippines 1984 (1,300)

Andhra Pradesh, India 1977 (20,000)

Northern Indian Ocean (Cyclones)

Northwestern Pacific Ocean (Typhoons)

Major hurricane paths

Major hurricane: location, year (deaths)

| Storm surge | Eye | Updrafts |

This cross-section shows how bands of cloud spiral around the eye of the hurricane.

In 1999, floods generated by a cyclone inundated Orissa, India. Over 9,000 people died following the storm.

Right: The Himalaya divides the vast Plateau of Tibet from the low-lying Gangetic Plain. The gray veil that covers most of the plain in this image is air pollution.

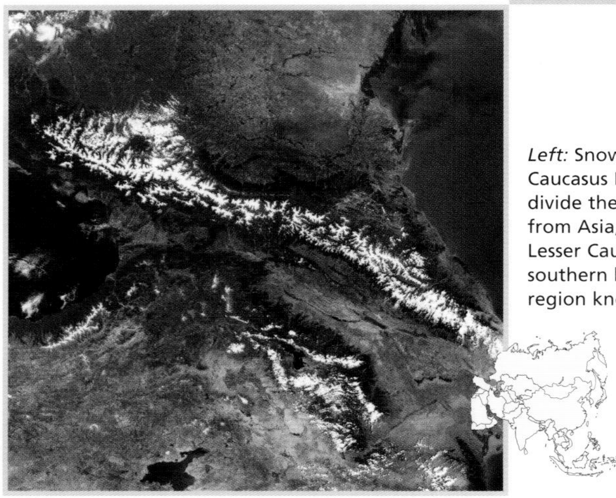

Left: Snow cover highlights the Caucasus Mountains, which divide the Russian Federation from Asia, and the associated Lesser Caucasus, which form the southern boundary of the region known as Transcaucasia.

SCALE 1:47,000,000
Lamberts Azimuthal Equal Area Projection
0   1000 miles
0   1000 kilometers

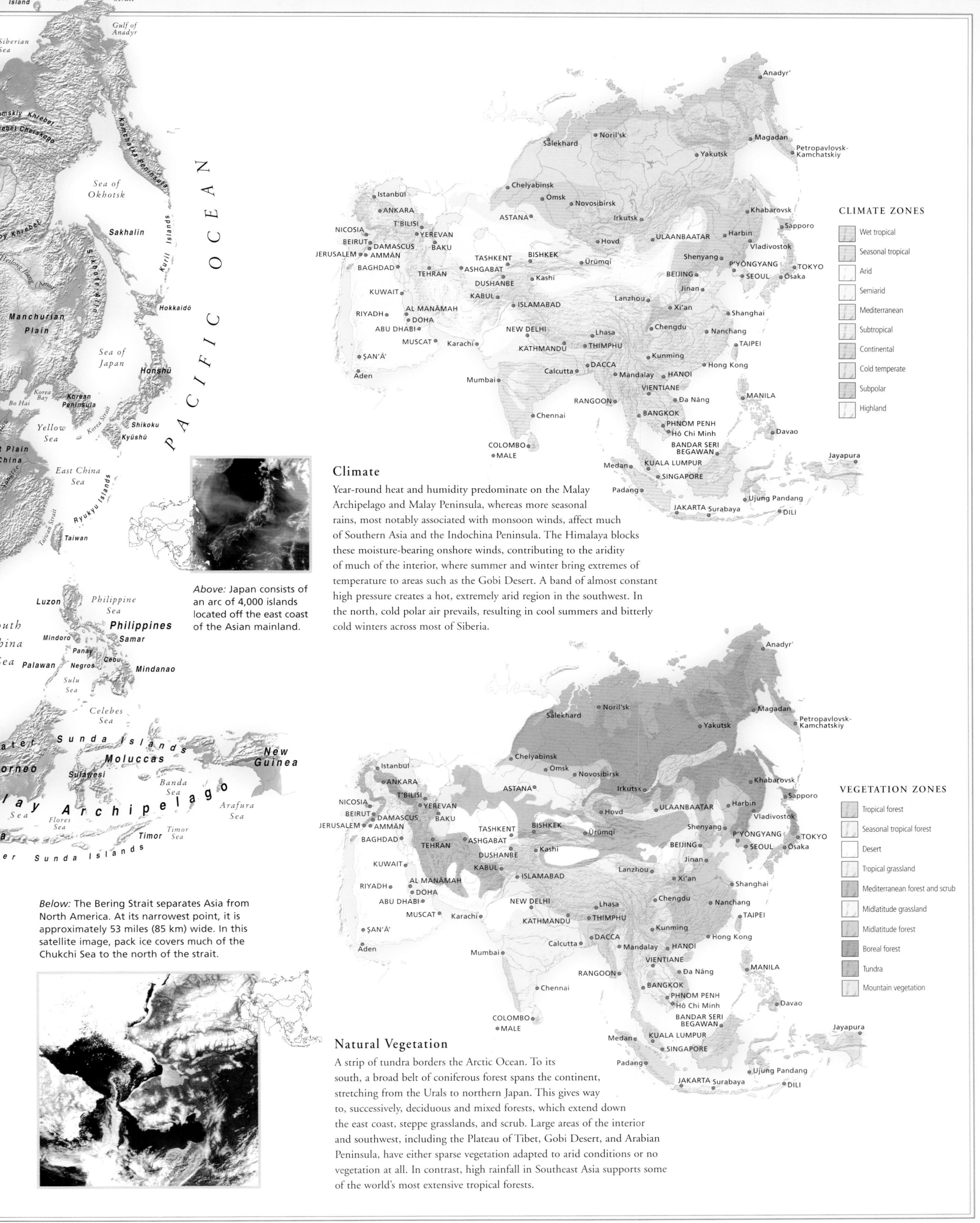

Climate

Year-round heat and humidity predominate on the Malay Archipelago and Malay Peninsula, whereas more seasonal rains, most notably associated with monsoon winds, affect much of Southern Asia and the Indochina Peninsula. The Himalaya blocks these moisture-bearing onshore winds, contributing to the aridity of much of the interior, where summer and winter bring extremes of temperature to areas such as the Gobi Desert. A band of almost constant high pressure creates a hot, extremely arid region in the southwest. In the north, cold polar air prevails, resulting in cool summers and bitterly cold winters across most of Siberia.

CLIMATE ZONES
- Wet tropical
- Seasonal tropical
- Arid
- Semiarid
- Mediterranean
- Subtropical
- Continental
- Cold temperate
- Subpolar
- Highland

Above: Japan consists of an arc of 4,000 islands located off the east coast of the Asian mainland.

Below: The Bering Strait separates Asia from North America. At its narrowest point, it is approximately 53 miles (85 km) wide. In this satellite image, pack ice covers much of the Chukchi Sea to the north of the strait.

Natural Vegetation

A strip of tundra borders the Arctic Ocean. To its south, a broad belt of coniferous forest spans the continent, stretching from the Urals to northern Japan. This gives way to, successively, deciduous and mixed forests, which extend down the east coast, steppe grasslands, and scrub. Large areas of the interior and southwest, including the Plateau of Tibet, Gobi Desert, and Arabian Peninsula, have either sparse vegetation adapted to arid conditions or no vegetation at all. In contrast, high rainfall in Southeast Asia supports some of the world's most extensive tropical forests.

VEGETATION ZONES
- Tropical forest
- Seasonal tropical forest
- Desert
- Tropical grassland
- Mediterranean forest and scrub
- Midlatitude grassland
- Midlatitude forest
- Boreal forest
- Tundra
- Mountain vegetation

PEOPLES AND NATIONS

In Asia, more than three-fifths of Earth's population—3.7 billion people—occupy one-third of its land. They inhabit 50 nations, ranging in size from the tiny city-state of Singapore to the world's largest country, the Russian Federation. The majority of these are developing nations, and many people lack ready access to clean water, reliable food supplies, and adequate health services. However, several nations, including Japan, South Korea, Singapore, Brunei, the Russian Federation, and Israel, have advanced economies and a relatively high standard of living. Asia has a great diversity of ethnic groups, and was the birthplace of all the world's major religions.

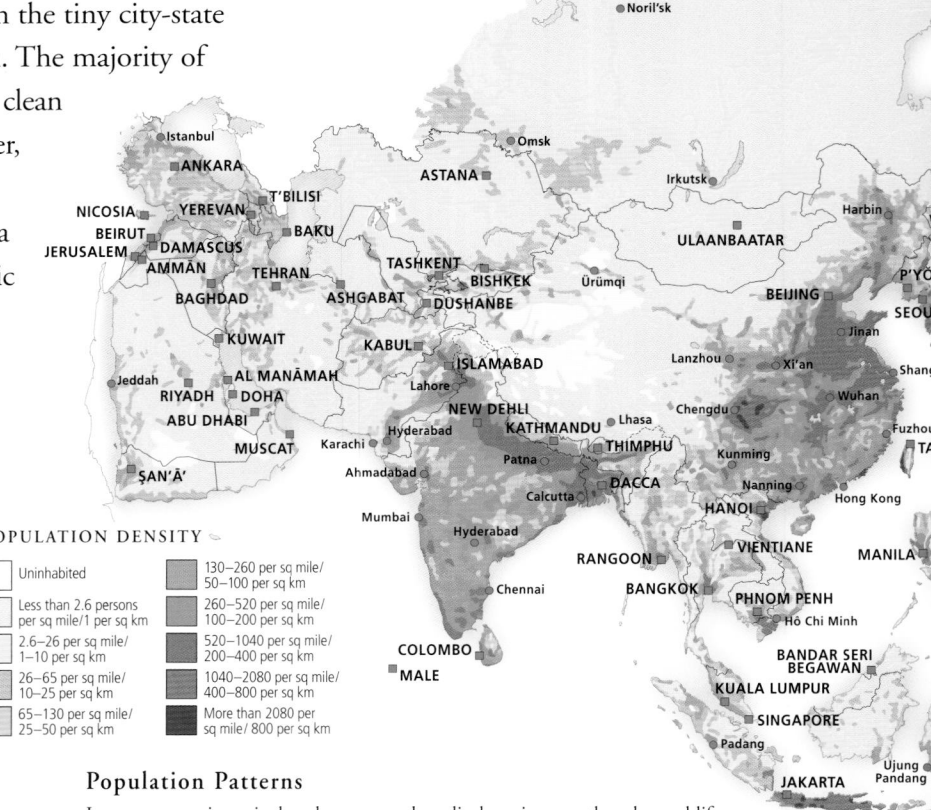

POPULATION DENSITY

☐ Uninhabited	☐ 130–260 per sq mile/ 50–100 per sq km
☐ Less than 2.6 persons per sq mile/1 per sq km	☐ 260–520 per sq mile/ 100–200 per sq km
☐ 2.6–26 per sq mile/ 1–10 per sq km	☐ 520–1040 per sq mile/ 200–400 per sq km
☐ 26–65 per sq mile/ 10–25 per sq km	☐ 1040–2080 per sq mile/ 400–800 per sq km
☐ 65–130 per sq mile/ 25–50 per sq km	☐ More than 2080 per sq mile/ 800 per sq km

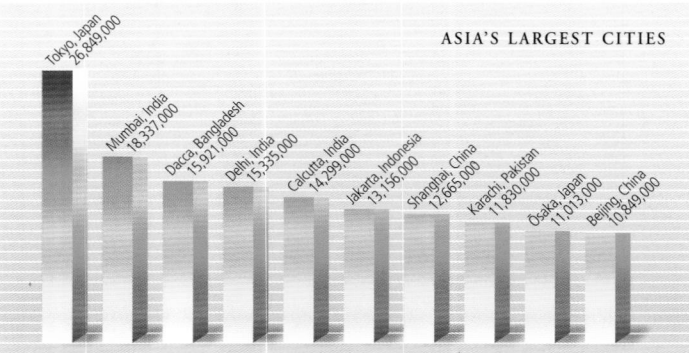

ASIA'S LARGEST CITIES

Urbanization

Most Asians are still dependent on subsistence farming and three-fifths live in rural areas. But many regions are becoming rapidly urbanized and industrialized. Singapore, Japan, and Israel are already among the world's most urbanized nations; South Korea's urban population was 21 percent in 1950, has passed 80 percent, and may reach 90 percent around 2025. By then, over half of all Asians are likely to be city dwellers. Already, six of the world's ten largest cities are located in Asia, three of them in India.

Population Patterns

Improvements in agricultural output and medical services greatly enhanced life expectancy in Asia during the 20th century, resulting in a population explosion. Between 1950 and the beginning of the 21st century, the population almost tripled, and it is expected to reach close to 5 billion by 2030. Despite this, great swathes of Asia remain virtually uninhabited, including Siberia, the barren Plateau of Tibet, and the deserts of Central Asia and the Arabian Peninsula. The bulk of the population is concentrated in the south and east, with especially high densities occurring along major rivers such as the Ganges, Yangtze, and Yellow, along the south and east coasts, and on the principal islands of the Japanese and Indonesian archipelagoes. Populations are also dense in fertile pockets of the southwest.

FLASHPOINTS

Religious rivalries underpin many conflicts in Asia. Other causes include ideological schisms, such as the one that divides Korea in two; territorial disputes; independence movements; and internal rebellions against authoritarian governments.

Palestine

Proclaimed in 1948 in predominantly Arab Palestine, the Jewish state of Israel expanded as a result of territorial gains made in a series of wars (in 1948, 1967, and 1973). This displaced thousands of Palestinian people and has led to almost continuous conflict. Palestinians seek restoration of occupied territories and the creation of their own state. Israel has used military might to quash uprisings and often-violent protests.

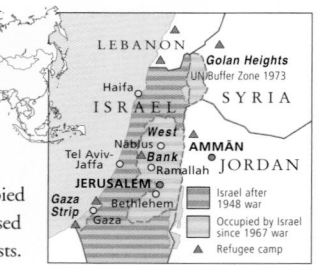

Kashmir

In 1947, the partition of British India created the Islamic state of Pakistan and the predominantly Hindu nation of India. The mainly Muslim state of Kashmir became part of India, but has been claimed by Pakistan ever since, resulting in two wars (1947–48 and 1967) and regular border skirmishes. A Kashmiri separatist movement, opposed by both India and Pakistan, has also conducted a guerilla campaign in recent years.

Korea

The Korean War of 1950–53 led to the creation of communist North Korea and democratic South Korea, and the demilitarized zone (DMZ) that separates them. About 151 miles (243 km) long and 2.5 miles (4 km) wide, it is guarded by 1.1 million soldiers on the North Korean side and, to the south, by 650,000 South Korean and 37,000 U.S. troops. Regular military exercises in the area keep tensions high.

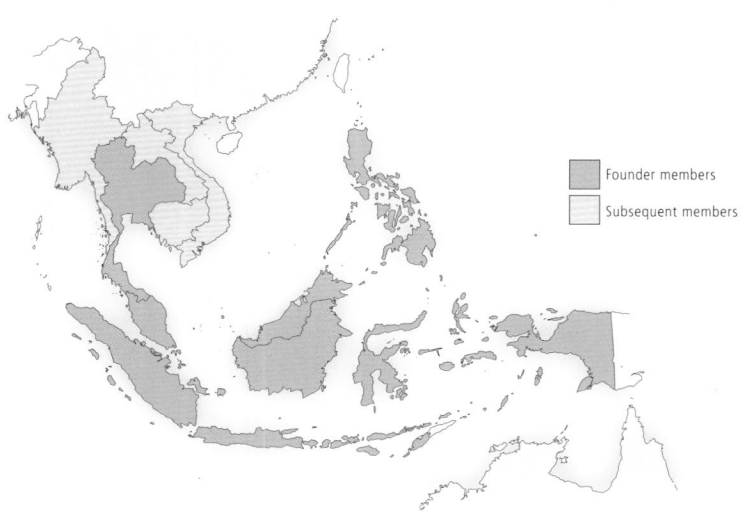

☐ Founder members	
☐ Subsequent members	

Association of Southeast Asian Nations

Since the mid-19th century, Asian countries have been heavily reliant on exports to Western nations and have often competed for lucrative markets. Greater intraregional economic cooperation has developed only since the 1960s. Aside from international associations formed by traders in the same commodities, few formal bodies have emerged. By far the most significant is the Association of Southeast Asian Nations, or ASEAN. Founded in 1967, it now has ten members—Indonesia, Thailand, Malaysia, the Philippines, Singapore, Brunei, Vietnam, Laos, Myanmar (Burma), and Cambodia. It aims to promote trade between members in order to strengthen economic growth and political stability.

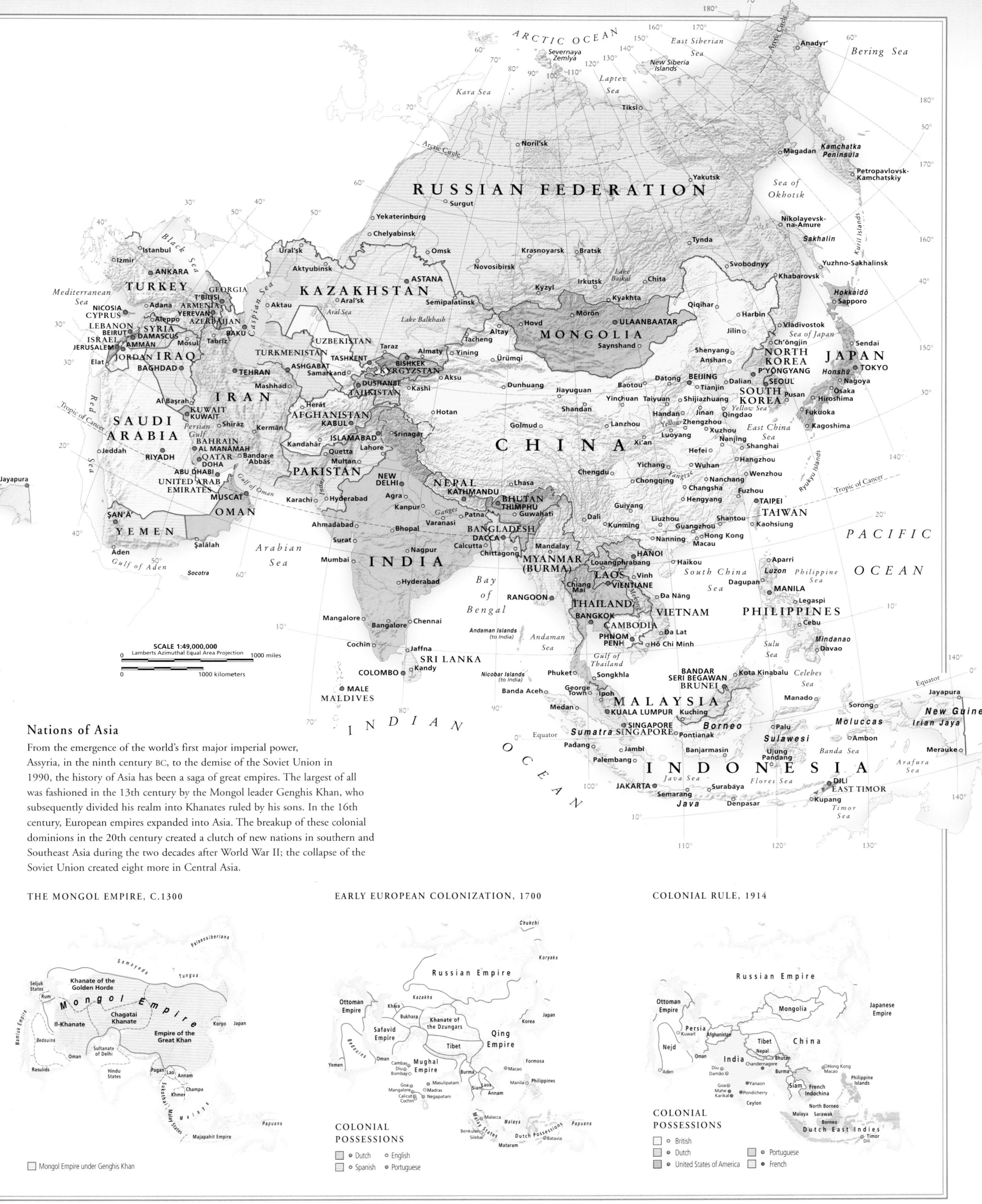

Nations of Asia

From the emergence of the world's first major imperial power, Assyria, in the ninth century BC, to the demise of the Soviet Union in 1990, the history of Asia has been a saga of great empires. The largest of all was fashioned in the 13th century by the Mongol leader Genghis Khan, who subsequently divided his realm into Khanates ruled by his sons. In the 16th century, European empires expanded into Asia. The breakup of these colonial dominions in the 20th century created a clutch of new nations in southern and Southeast Asia during the two decades after World War II; the collapse of the Soviet Union created eight more in Central Asia.

THE MONGOL EMPIRE, C.1300

EARLY EUROPEAN COLONIZATION, 1700

COLONIAL RULE, 1914

THE HUMAN IMPACT

Human transformation of the landscape and harnessing of natural resources first occurred on a large scale in Asia. The world's earliest agricultural settlements evolved in the Fertile Crescent region of Southwest Asia, where wheat, olives, peas, goats, and sheep were domesticated more than 10,000 years ago. About 9,000 years ago, farmers in eastern China began to cultivate rice and millet and rear pigs and silkworms. In turn, these settlements became the world's first cities. Southwest Asia and China remained centers of innovation, and from antiquity until the 15th century the flow of ideas and technology was mainly from Asia to Europe. Western interest in Asian technology led to the establishment of arteries of trade such as the Silk Road and the eventual European colonization of much of the continent. The colonial rulers accelerated land clearance, principally to permit the cultivation of plantation crops for export to the West. Steady industrialization and explosive population growth in the 20th century exerted even greater pressure on land and resources, resulting in widespread deforestation, land degradation, and pollution.

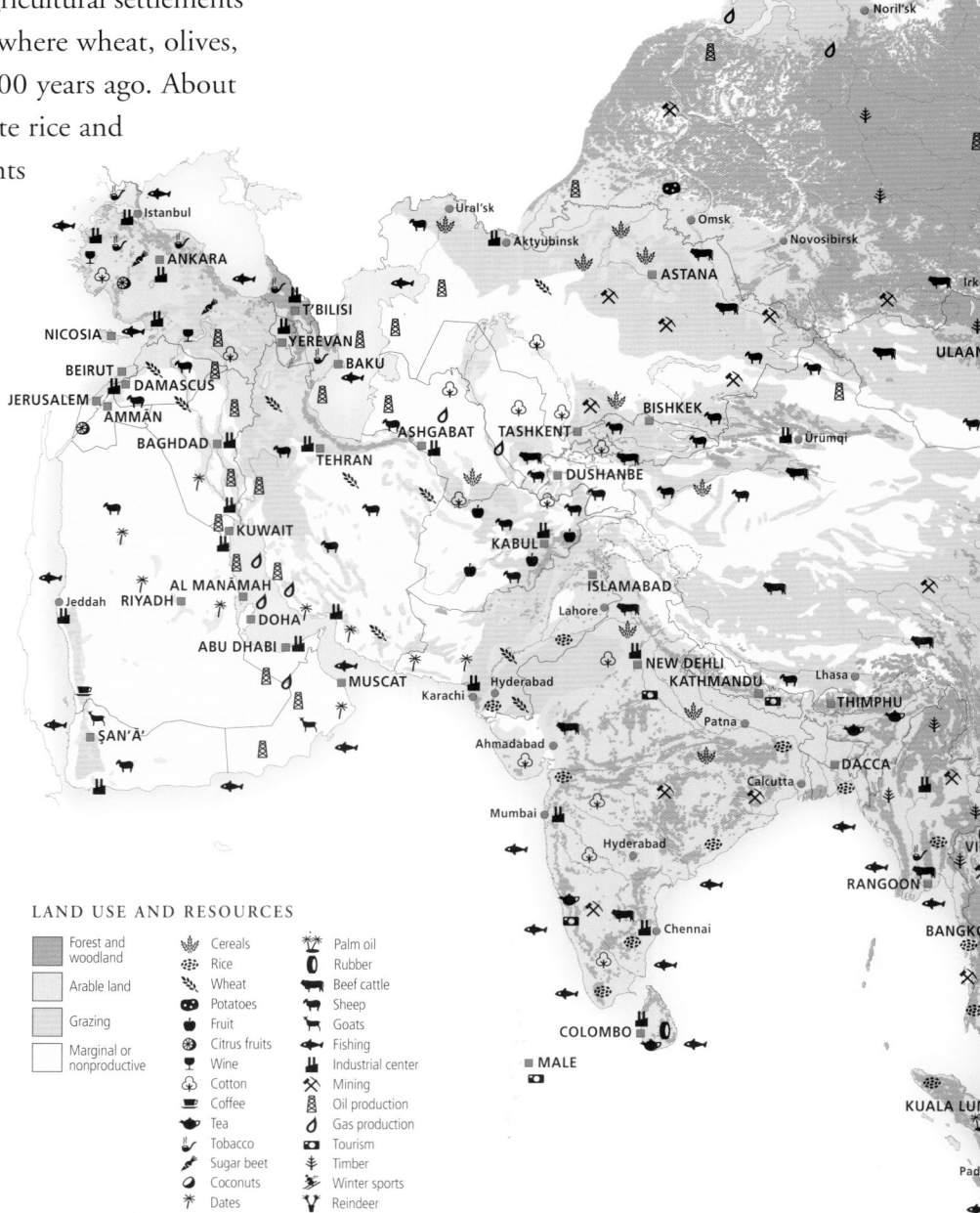

THE CHANGING FACE OF ASIA

The Aral Sea

About 85 percent of Asia's water is used for farming and the continent has two-thirds of all irrigated land. The creation of vast irrigation systems has had a catastrophic effect on river basins, most notably in Central Asia. The Aral Sea was once the world's fourth-largest inland sea and had a thriving fishing industry. In the 1960s, the Soviet Union began diverting the rivers that fed the sea, the Amudar'ya and Syrdar'ya, to irrigate cotton fields. Since then, the sea has shrunk to 15 percent of its former volume. Evaporation has raised salinity levels, and pesticides used by farmers have contaminated the remaining waters, decimating marine life. Salt- and chemical-laden sands from the shore have been blown across surrounding land, poisoning plants, animals, and humans. Efforts have been made to raise the sea's water level, but the damage is thought to be irreversible.

DEPLETION OF THE ARAL SEA, 1960–2002

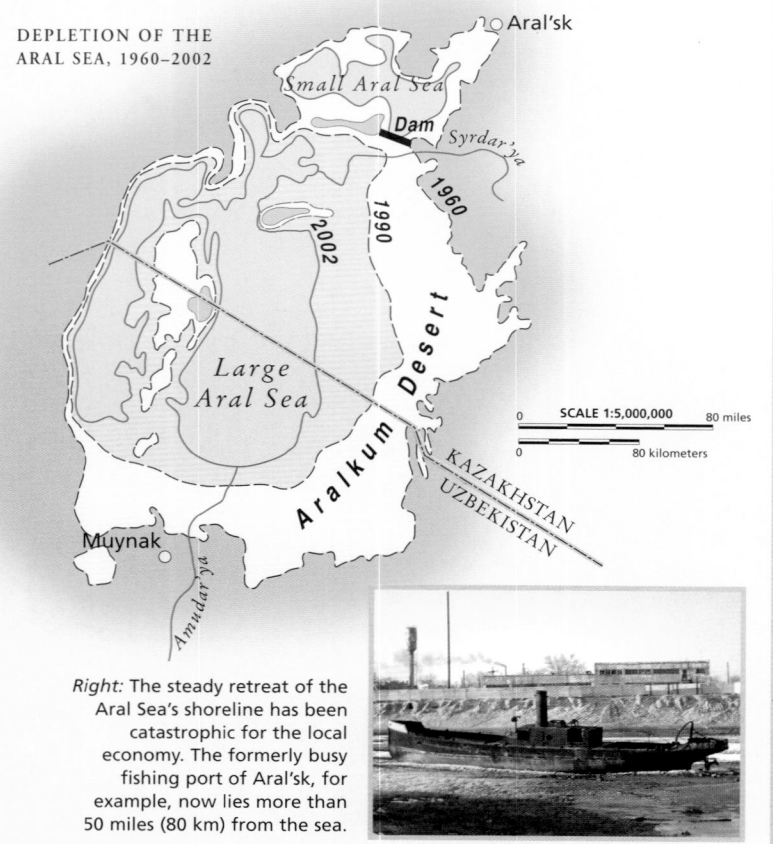

Right: The steady retreat of the Aral Sea's shoreline has been catastrophic for the local economy. The formerly busy fishing port of Aral'sk, for example, now lies more than 50 miles (80 km) from the sea.

LAND USE AND RESOURCES

▓ Forest and woodland	🌾 Cereals		🌴 Palm oil
░ Arable land	🌾 Rice		○ Rubber
░ Grazing	🌾 Wheat		🐄 Beef cattle
□ Marginal or nonproductive	🥔 Potatoes		🐑 Sheep
	🍐 Fruit		🐐 Goats
	🍊 Citrus fruits		🐟 Fishing
	🍷 Wine		⚒ Industrial center
	🌿 Cotton		⚒ Mining
	☕ Coffee		🛢 Oil production
	🍃 Tea		🔥 Gas production
	🌿 Tobacco		☂ Tourism
	🌱 Sugar beet		⚓ Timber
	🥥 Coconuts		⛷ Winter sports
	🌴 Dates		V Reindeer

Economic Profile

From the subsistence-agriculture economies of Afghanistan, Bhutan, and Nepal to the sophisticated, technology-driven societies of Japan and South Korea, Asian countries have attained disparate levels of development. These have been determined by a range of factors, including resource distribution, foreign investment, conflicts, and governing ideologies. Asia harbors two-thirds of the world's known reserves of oil and gas, concentrated in Siberia and the Arabian Peninsula, and 60 percent of the world's coal, found mainly in China, Siberia, and India. It also supplies 60 percent of the world's tin, most of it coming from Southeast Asia. Russia has immense stands of timber and Southeast Asia is endowed with valuable hardwoods such as teak and mahogany, though supplies are dwindling. More than half of the population, however, still depends on farming. Rice is the main staple crop, though wheat predominates in the north. Services and industries are becoming more significant, but heavy industry is confined mainly to Japan, China, and India. More widespread light industries are based on food processing, the manufacture of textiles and pharmaceuticals, and tourism.

Land Cover

The world's largest conifer forests still cloak much of Siberia, though huge swathes of forest have been cleared elsewhere. Arable land covers a large area, but has to support some of the highest population densities on Earth. Extensive barren areas, including the Plateau of Tibet, the deserts of Central Asia, and the arctic shoreline, make a large proportion of the continent unproductive.

PROPORTIONS OF TOTAL LAND AREA

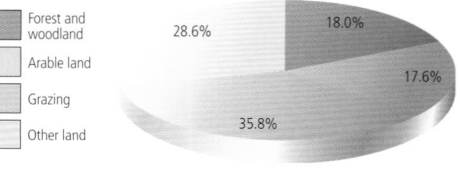

- Forest and woodland — 28.6%
- Arable land — 18.0%
- Grazing — 17.6%
- Other land — 35.8%

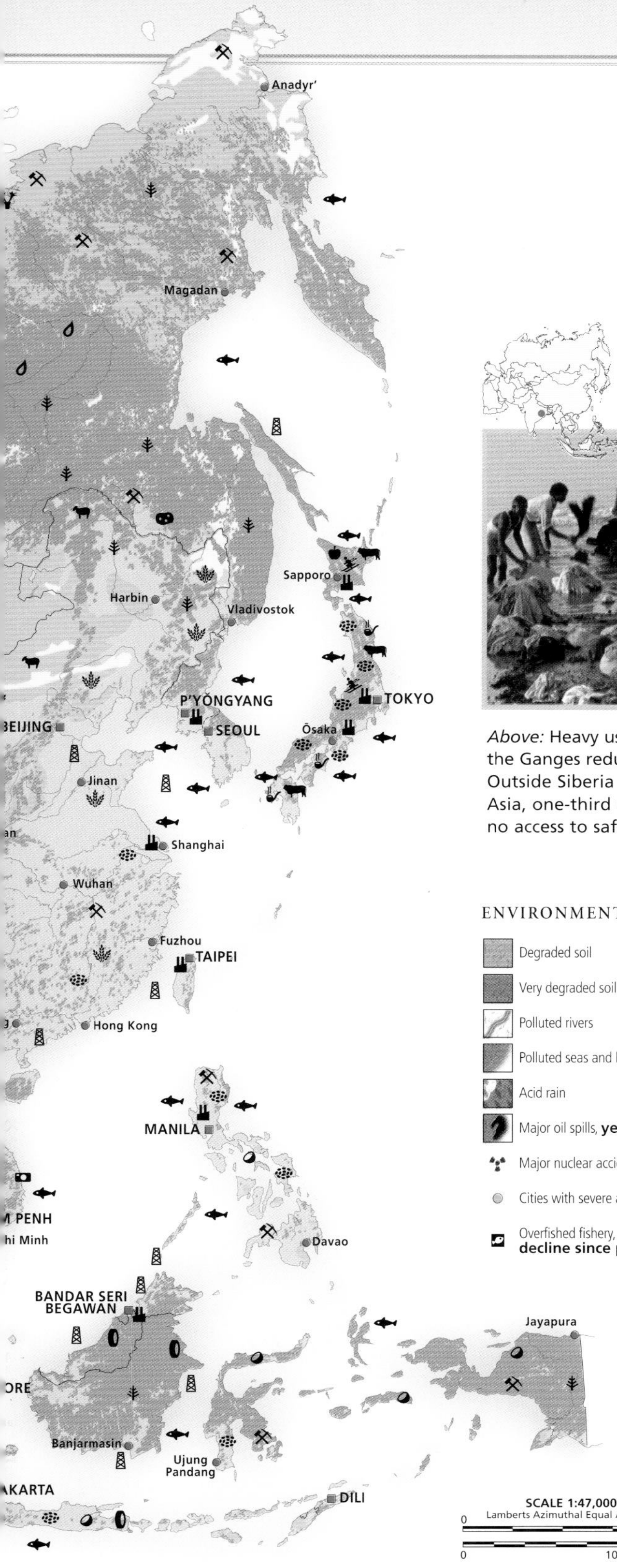

Right: Russia has decommissioned over 150 nuclear submarines. But few have been dismantled and most lie rusting in Arctic and eastern ports, posing a potential threat to the environment.

Above: The growth of aquaculture has led to habitat loss. About 60 percent of Asia's mangroves have been converted to shrimp ponds.

Above: Heavy use of rivers such as the Ganges reduces water quality. Outside Siberia and Southwest Asia, one-third of people have no access to safe drinking water.

ENVIRONMENTAL ISSUES

- Degraded soil
- Very degraded soil
- Polluted rivers
- Polluted seas and lakes
- Acid rain
- Major oil spills, **year**
- Major nuclear accidents, **year**
- Cities with severe air pollution
- Overfished fishery, **year of peak catch, decline since peak catch**

SCALE 1:47,000,000
Lamberts Azimuthal Equal Area Projection
0   1000 miles
0   1000 kilometers

Threats to the Environment

A desire to cater for impoverished, rapidly expanding populations is at the root of much recent environmental degradation in Asia, which has been compounded by neglect and failure to implement protective legislation. Intensive farming practices have increased agricultural output dramatically, but have also led to severe land degradation and water pollution. About 20 percent of vegetated land is degraded and more than half of drylands are affected by desertification. The continent also has some of the world's most polluted rivers. Demand for cultivable land has resulted in the virtual disappearance of Southeast Asia's species-rich lowland rain forests, while heavy logging has begun to threaten the integrity of Siberia's vast frontier forests (which could in turn contribute to global warming). Industrialization has invigorated local economies, especially in Japan, South Korea, Russia, China, Malaysia, Thailand, and India, but has also created some of the world's worst levels of air pollution and given rise to widespread acid rain.

Protecting the Environment

In western and Central Asia, a range of strategies has been implemented to combat the widespread problems of land degradation and desertification, including reforestation, sand-dune stabilization, and soil-fertility restoration programs. Japan has had notable success in reducing air pollution, and other governments are following its lead. In Nepal and Pakistan, for instance, users of gas- or battery-operated vehicles receive tax rebates, and the Indian city of Delhi has converted all its public transport to gas. Asian countries are at the forefront of reforestation: for example, China increased its forest coverage by more than 3.5 percent between 1993 and 2000. Large World Heritage areas have recently been designated in Siberia, and the number of protected areas is growing. However the overall proportion of land protected (3.7%) is low.

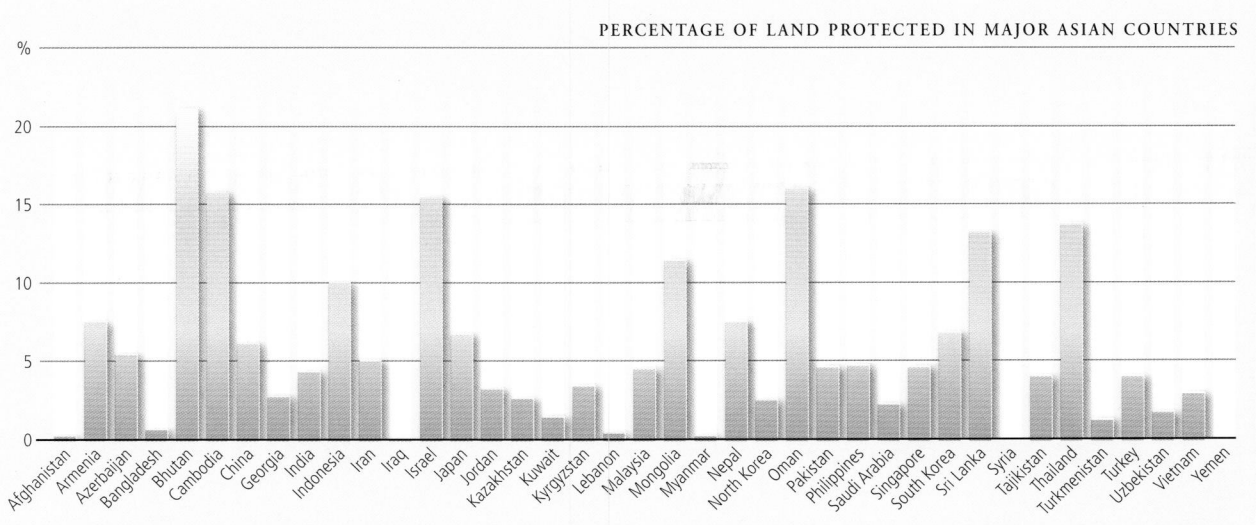

PERCENTAGE OF LAND PROTECTED IN MAJOR ASIAN COUNTRIES

TURKEY, CYPRUS, AND TRANSCAUCASIA
Armenia, Azerbaijan, Cyprus, Georgia, Turkey

Projecting westward from the Middle East, Turkey forms a land bridge between Europe and Asia. Divided by the Bosporus, it straddles the two continents, its small region of Eastern Thrace lying within Europe and the remainder of the country, Anatolia, forming Asia's westernmost edge. An arid plateau covers much of Anatolia's interior, giving way in the east to a series of ranges that extends into Transcaucasia. Here, the towering Caucasus form another natural boundary between Asia and Europe. Three nations occupy Transcaucasia: Armenia, Azerbaijan, and Georgia. All became Soviet republics in the 20th century before attaining independence in 1991. Turkey was the heart of the Ottoman Empire, which endured from the 12th century to the early 20th century, and from 1573 to 1878 included the mainly Greek island of Cyprus.

THE CAUCASUS

The Caucasus and the associated Lesser Caucasus mountains isolate and define the region known as Transcaucasia. The much higher Caucasus peaks form a great wall that runs from the Black Sea to the shores of the Caspian Sea and reaches Europe's highest point of 18,510 feet (5,642 m) at Elbrus in Russia. The Lesser Caucasus spread to the south across Armenia, merging with the ranges of eastern Turkey. In-between are lowlands and major river valleys, including the Kür–Aras lowlands of Azerbaijan, parts of which lie below sea level.

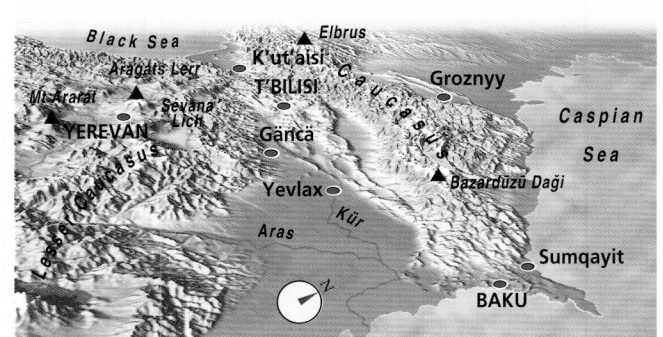

Near Cappadocia in Turkey, many traditional homes are carved out of eroded columns of soft volcanic rock.

Longitude east of Greenwich

POPULATION PATTERNS

In Turkey, the interior is less densely inhabited than the Black Sea and Aegean Sea coasts and European Turkey. Transcaucasia's inhabitants cluster on the Black Sea coast, along river valleys, and on foothills, shunning uplands and the Caspian lowlands. Cyprus is more densely populated in the south. Numerous peoples have fought over and settled in this region and ethnic diversity is high, with over 50 different groups in Transcaucasia alone. Turkey and Azerbaijan's populations are predominantly Muslim, whereas Christians are in the majority elsewhere.

Less than 2.6 persons per sq mile/1 per sq km
2.6–26 per sq mile/ 1–10 per sq km
26–65 per sq mile/ 10–25 per sq km
65–130 per sq mile/ 25–50 per sq km
130–260 per sq mile/ 50–100 per sq km
260–520 per sq mile/ 100–200 per sq km
520–1040 per sq mile/ 200–400 per sq km

ECONOMIC PROFILE

Metallic minerals, including chromium, manganese, mercury, and copper, are fairly widely distributed; the word Cyprus means "copper" in Greek and the island has long been renowned as a source of this metal. Oil reserves located in the Caspian Sea provide Azerbaijan with energy and valuable export revenue; the nation is also a major supplier of caviar. Traditional agriculture predominates in many areas, though industries and services have expanded rapidly in recent years, especially in Turkey. The production of textiles is important, along with metals, machinery, automobiles, food products, and some electronic goods in Transcaucasia.

Forest and woodland
Arable land
Grazing

Citrus fruits
Wine
Cotton
Tobacco
Sugar beet
Fishing
Industrial center
Oil production

Istanbul Turkey's largest urban, commercial, and industrial center occupies a strategic position on the Bosporus. This narrow waterway divides the city into European and Asian sectors, with the former being home to more than three-quarters of the population and most businesses. Founded as a Greek colony called Byzantium in the eighth century BC, the city became the capital of the Roman Empire in AD 330 and was renamed Constantinople. It remained the capital of the Byzantine (eastern Roman) Empire until it fell to the Ottoman Turks in 1453, under whom it became known as Istanbul. Constructed in AD 532–537 by the Emperor Justinian, the church of Hagia Sophia is the city's most remarkable Byzantine building and still its largest monument.

A Turkish invasion of Cyprus in 1974 led to the creation of Turkish and Greek sectors divided by a UN buffer zone.

Azerbaijan's oil is not as much in demand as it once was. Around 1900, Baku provided half the world's supplies.

ELEVATION

Feet	Meters
6562	2000
4921	1500
3281	1000
2461	750
1640	500
1312	400
984	300
656	200
328	100
0	0
Below sea level	
656	200
3281	1000
6562	2000
13,123	4000
19,685	6000
26,246	8000
32,808	10,000

SCALE 1:4,250,000
Lamberts Conformal Conic Projection
0 — 120 miles
0 — 120 kilometers

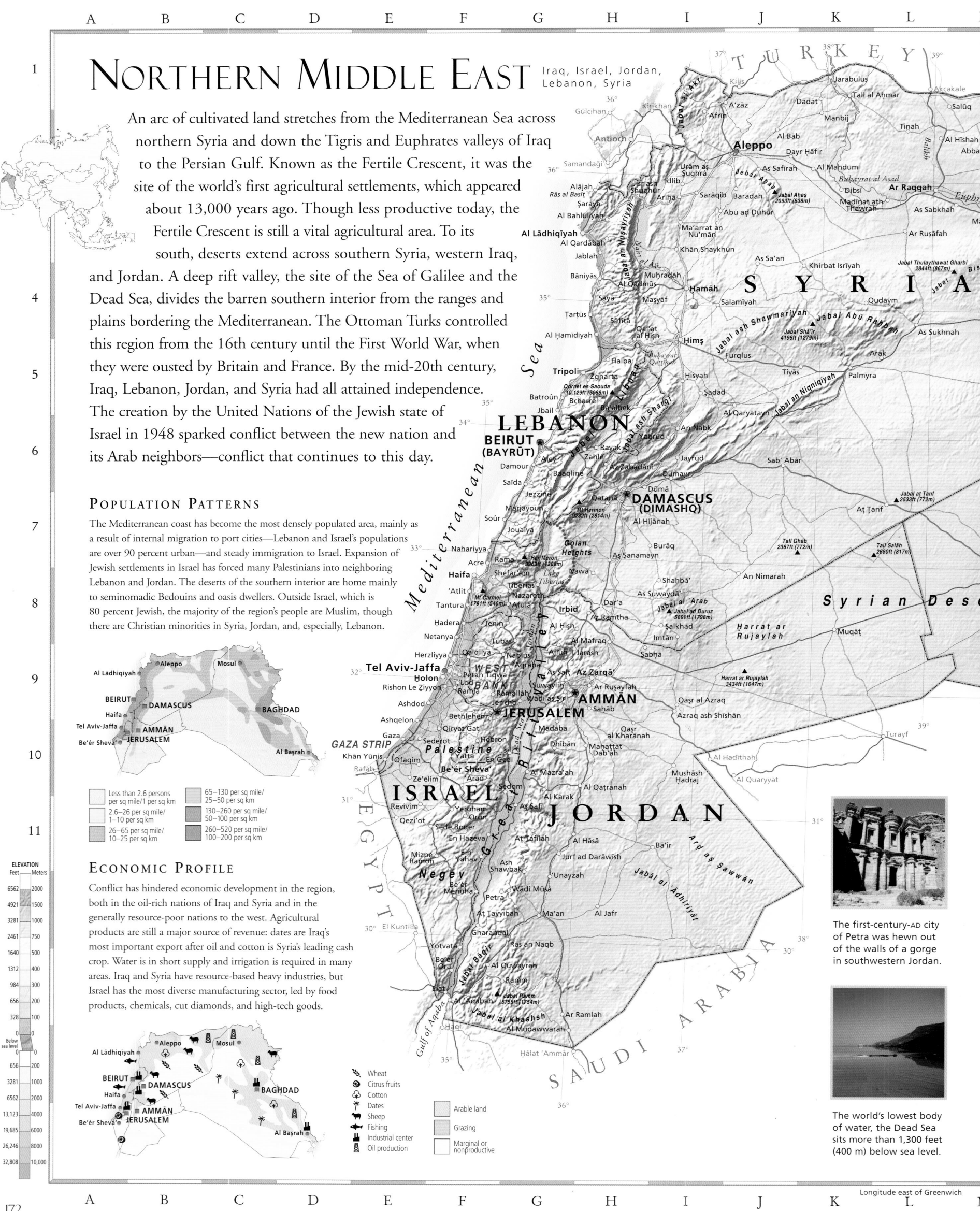

Northern Middle East

Iraq, Israel, Jordan,
Lebanon, Syria

An arc of cultivated land stretches from the Mediterranean Sea across northern Syria and down the Tigris and Euphrates valleys of Iraq to the Persian Gulf. Known as the Fertile Crescent, it was the site of the world's first agricultural settlements, which appeared about 13,000 years ago. Though less productive today, the Fertile Crescent is still a vital agricultural area. To its south, deserts extend across southern Syria, western Iraq, and Jordan. A deep rift valley, the site of the Sea of Galilee and the Dead Sea, divides the barren southern interior from the ranges and plains bordering the Mediterranean. The Ottoman Turks controlled this region from the 16th century until the First World War, when they were ousted by Britain and France. By the mid-20th century, Iraq, Lebanon, Jordan, and Syria had all attained independence. The creation by the United Nations of the Jewish state of Israel in 1948 sparked conflict between the new nation and its Arab neighbors—conflict that continues to this day.

POPULATION PATTERNS

The Mediterranean coast has become the most densely populated area, mainly as a result of internal migration to port cities—Lebanon and Israel's populations are over 90 percent urban—and steady immigration to Israel. Expansion of Jewish settlements in Israel has forced many Palestinians into neighboring Lebanon and Jordan. The deserts of the southern interior are home mainly to seminomadic Bedouins and oasis dwellers. Outside Israel, which is 80 percent Jewish, the majority of the region's people are Muslim, though there are Christian minorities in Syria, Jordan, and, especially, Lebanon.

Less than 2.6 persons per sq mile/1 per sq km
2.6–26 per sq mile/1–10 per sq km
26–65 per sq mile/10–25 per sq km
65–130 per sq mile/25–50 per sq km
130–260 per sq mile/50–100 per sq km
260–520 per sq mile/100–200 per sq km

ECONOMIC PROFILE

Conflict has hindered economic development in the region, both in the oil-rich nations of Iraq and Syria and in the generally resource-poor nations to the west. Agricultural products are still a major source of revenue: dates are Iraq's most important export after oil and cotton is Syria's leading cash crop. Water is in short supply and irrigation is required in many areas. Iraq and Syria have resource-based heavy industries, but Israel has the most diverse manufacturing sector, led by food products, chemicals, cut diamonds, and high-tech goods.

ELEVATION
Feet / Meters

Feet	Meters
6562	2000
4921	1500
3281	1000
2461	750
1640	500
1312	400
984	300
656	200
328	100
0	0
Below sea level	0
656	200
3281	1000
6562	2000
13,123	4000
19,685	6000
26,246	8000
32,808	10,000

Wheat
Citrus fruits
Cotton
Dates
Sheep
Fishing
Industrial center
Oil production

Arable land
Grazing
Marginal or nonproductive

The first-century-AD city of Petra was hewn out of the walls of a gorge in southwestern Jordan.

The world's lowest body of water, the Dead Sea sits more than 1,300 feet (400 m) below sea level.

Longitude east of Greenwich

O P 41° 42° Q 43° R 44° S T U V W X Y Z

TURKEY

Cizre
Nusaybin
Al Qāmishlī   Zākho
Jāghir   Qaratshuk   Summēl   Al 'Amādīyah   Al Amādīyah
Bāzār   Tall Kūjik   Dahūk   Zībār   Zēbār   Birkim   Sarī Kōrāwā
Tall Baydar   Tall 'Uwaynat   Agrah   10,951ft (3351m)   Rawānduz
's al 'Ayn   Tall Tamir   Tall Huqnah   Safahuddin   Küh-e Bari Ebrahim   45°
Şafih   Kubaybāt   Khān as Sür   Tall Kayt   Ranya   11,911ft (3650m)
Al Hasakah   Jabal Sinjār   Mosul   Qosh Tepe   Koi Sanjaq   Surdash   Panwin
Ash Shaddādah   Wardīyah   Hammām al 'Alīl   Arbīl   Taqtaq   As Sulaymānīyah
Abd al 'Azīz   Al Ba'āj   Tall 'Afar   Guwēr   Chamchamal
920m)   Ghūnā   Makhmūr   Altin Köprü   Qādir Karam   Arbat   Halabja
Al Bādī   Ash   Kirkūk   Tāza Khurmātū
ah   Al Hadr   Qoyyūrāh   Shārqāt   Dāqūq
Fedghāmī   35°
Aş Şuwār   Al Fathāh   Pārapāra
Dayr az Zawr   Tikrit   Tūz Khurmātū   Qasr-e
Al Busayrah   Bayjī   Jabal Hamrin   Sulaymān Beg   Shīrin
ayādīn   Umm al Tūz   Kifrī   Jalawlā
l 'Ashārah   Abū   Malhāt   Kalār   Khānaqin
Hardan   Ad Dawr   Qara Tepe

AL JAZĪRAH   Euphrates   Rāwah   Sāmarrā'   Tigris   Al Muqdādīyah   IRAN
As Sayyāl   Anka   'Ānah   Balad   Diltāwa   34°
Abū Kamāl   Al Qā'im   Fuhaymī   Ad Dujayl   Al Khālis   Mehrān
Al Hadīthah   Buhayrat   Ba'qūbah   Balad Rūz
Tharthar   ath Tharthār   Mandalī
Khān al Baghdādī   Khān al   Imām Hamid
Akāshat   Saniyah   Mashhādīyah   Tursāq
Muhaywir   Kubaysah   Hīt   Ar Ramādī   Kādhimain   Shandrūkh   33°
Wādi Hawrān   Al Habbānīyah   BAGHDAD   Badrah
Khān al Jīr   (BAGHDĀD)   Husayn al Ghafūs   Bagsaya   Mūlat al Mashkhūr
Ubaylah   Abū al Jīr   Al Fallūjah   Salmān Pāk   Jassān
Ar Rutbah   Al Mahmūdīyah   Sarābādī
Hawr al Habbānīyah   As Suwayrah   Al 'Azīzīyah   'Alī   32°
IRAQ   Ar Rahhālīyah   Buhayrat   Saddat al Hindīyah   An Nu'mānīyah   Hājī Muhsin   Shaykh Sa'd
ar Razāzah   Khān   'Alī al Gharbī   Shaykh Jūwī
An Nukhayb   al Mahāwīl   An Nu'mānīyah   Arab   Al Kūt   Hawr   Marhaj Kahlīl
Karbalā'   Al Hindīyah   Abdullah   Al Hayy   as Sa'dīyah   Al Kumayt
Bi'r Sābil   Al Hillah   Al Muwaffaqīyah   Tarād al Kahf   Musallam   Someydeh
Al Hāshimīyah   Ishaq   Ad Daghgharah   Fajir   Qal'at Sukkār   Al Halfāyah
Khān al Muşallā   Al Kifl   'Afak   Tahrīr   Ar Rifā'ī   Al Amārah   Sūsangerd
Aţ Taqtaqānah   Khān Jadwal   Ad Dīwānīyah   Telloh   31°
An Najaf   Al Kūfah   An Nasr   Qal'at Sālih   Tigris
Abū Shukhayr   Ad Dīwānīyah   Ash Shatrah
Al Ghammās   Imām al Hamzah   Ar Rumaythah   Al 'Uzayr
Khān ar   Ash Shanāfiyah   An Nasr
Rahbah   As Samāwah   Al Qurnah   Al Muzayri'ah
Judaidat   Ar Rihab   Al Khidr   An Nāsirīyah   Al Ma'qil   Al Basrah
al Hamir   Euphrates   Kharfīyah   Aradah   Ad Dayr   Khorramshahr
Şahrā' al Hijāra   Tall al Lahm   Sūq ash   Hawr al Hammār   Shu'aiba   Ābādān
Ma'ānīyah   Shuyūkh
Ash Shabakah   Al Qusayr   Jalibah   Az Zubayr   30°
As Salmān   Rumaila   Umm Qasr   Al Fāw
Zahrat al Batn   Qal'at Abū Ghar   Al Busayyah   Safwān   Bubiyān   Persian
Zahrat al Batn   Raudhatain   Island   Gulf
Al Haniyah   Wādī al Bātin
KUWAIT   KUWAIT
Nisāb   (AL KUWAYT)
SAUDI ARABIA   Ash Shu'bah   48°

Elat in Israel is a popular center for divers exploring the wonders of the Red Sea's extensive coral reefs.

The capital of Lebanon, Beirut was ravaged by civil war between 1975 and 1990, and is just starting to recover.

The Great Ziggurat of Ur is one of the best-preserved parts of the ancient city of Ur, near An Nāsirīyah in Iraq.

Jerusalem

Situated in a river valley linking the Mediterranean coast and the Dead Sea, the ancient city of Jerusalem is a place of pilgrimage for the adherents of three major faiths: Judaism, Christianity, and Islam. The Old City's many shrines reflect this diversity of beliefs, most notably around the Dome of the Rock. The oldest remaining Islamic temple and said to be the scene of Muhammad's ascension to heaven, it backs onto the Western Wall, the remains of a temple that constitute the most sacred site of Judaism. Nearby is the Church of the Holy Sepulchre, where Jesus is said to have been entombed before rising again.

Dome of the Rock

SCALE 1:3,250,000
Lamberts Conformal Conic Projection
0   100 miles
0   100 kilometers

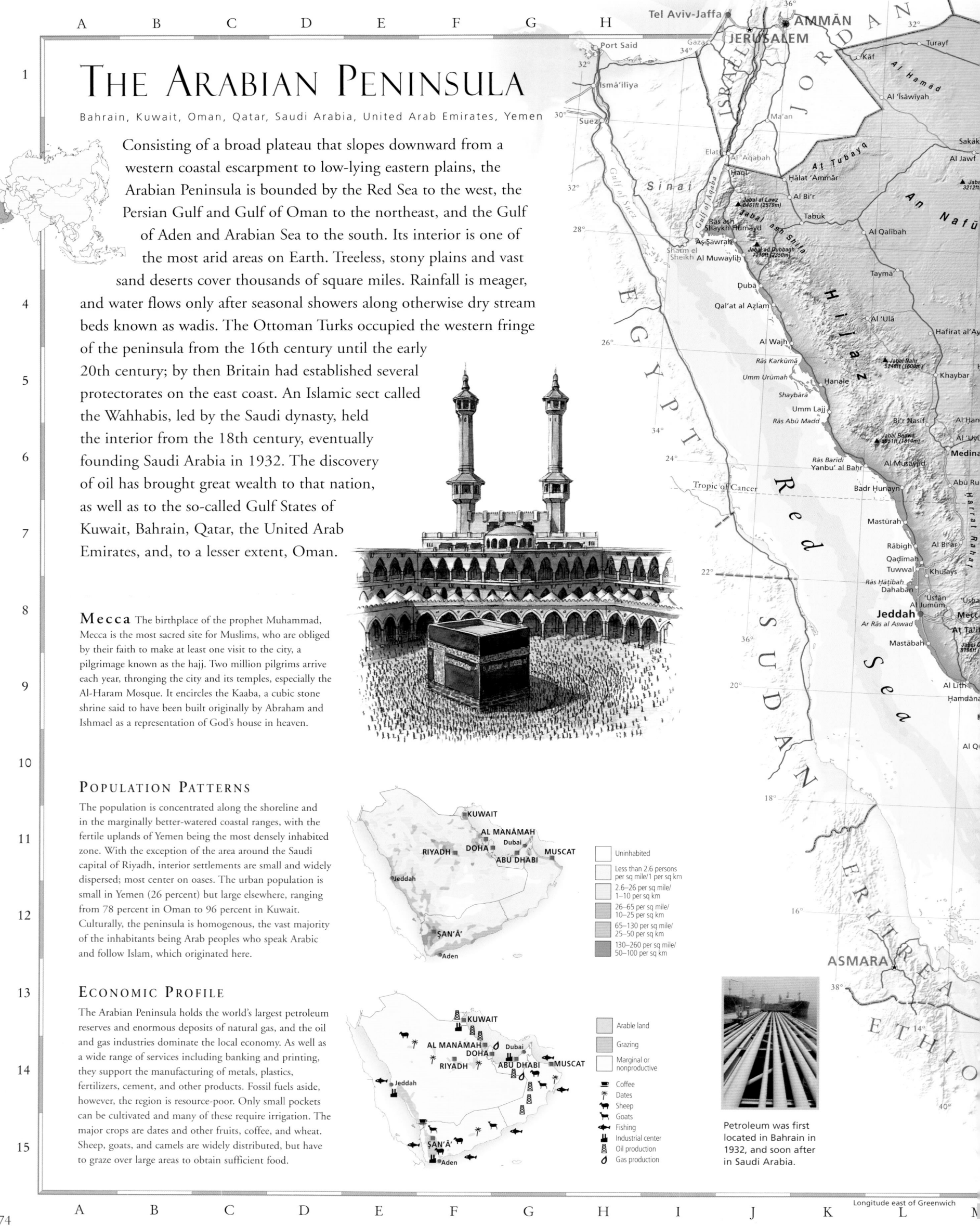

THE ARABIAN PENINSULA

Bahrain, Kuwait, Oman, Qatar, Saudi Arabia, United Arab Emirates, Yemen

Consisting of a broad plateau that slopes downward from a western coastal escarpment to low-lying eastern plains, the Arabian Peninsula is bounded by the Red Sea to the west, the Persian Gulf and Gulf of Oman to the northeast, and the Gulf of Aden and Arabian Sea to the south. Its interior is one of the most arid areas on Earth. Treeless, stony plains and vast sand deserts cover thousands of square miles. Rainfall is meager, and water flows only after seasonal showers along otherwise dry stream beds known as wadis. The Ottoman Turks occupied the western fringe of the peninsula from the 16th century until the early 20th century; by then Britain had established several protectorates on the east coast. An Islamic sect called the Wahhabis, led by the Saudi dynasty, held the interior from the 18th century, eventually founding Saudi Arabia in 1932. The discovery of oil has brought great wealth to that nation, as well as to the so-called Gulf States of Kuwait, Bahrain, Qatar, the United Arab Emirates, and, to a lesser extent, Oman.

Mecca The birthplace of the prophet Muhammad, Mecca is the most sacred site for Muslims, who are obliged by their faith to make at least one visit to the city, a pilgrimage known as the hajj. Two million pilgrims arrive each year, thronging the city and its temples, especially the Al-Haram Mosque. It encircles the Kaaba, a cubic stone shrine said to have been built originally by Abraham and Ishmael as a representation of God's house in heaven.

POPULATION PATTERNS

The population is concentrated along the shoreline and in the marginally better-watered coastal ranges, with the fertile uplands of Yemen being the most densely inhabited zone. With the exception of the area around the Saudi capital of Riyadh, interior settlements are small and widely dispersed; most center on oases. The urban population is small in Yemen (26 percent) but large elsewhere, ranging from 78 percent in Oman to 96 percent in Kuwait. Culturally, the peninsula is homogenous, the vast majority of the inhabitants being Arab peoples who speak Arabic and follow Islam, which originated here.

Uninhabited

Less than 2.6 persons per sq mile/1 per sq km

2.6–26 per sq mile/ 1–10 per sq km

26–65 per sq mile/ 10–25 per sq km

65–130 per sq mile/ 25–50 per sq km

130–260 per sq mile/ 50–100 per sq km

ECONOMIC PROFILE

The Arabian Peninsula holds the world's largest petroleum reserves and enormous deposits of natural gas, and the oil and gas industries dominate the local economy. As well as a wide range of services including banking and printing, they support the manufacturing of metals, plastics, fertilizers, cement, and other products. Fossil fuels aside, however, the region is resource-poor. Only small pockets can be cultivated and many of these require irrigation. The major crops are dates and other fruits, coffee, and wheat. Sheep, goats, and camels are widely distributed, but have to graze over large areas to obtain sufficient food.

Arable land

Grazing

Marginal or nonproductive

Coffee
Dates
Sheep
Goats
Fishing
Industrial center
Oil production
Gas production

Petroleum was first located in Bahrain in 1932, and soon after in Saudi Arabia.

Longitude east of Greenwich

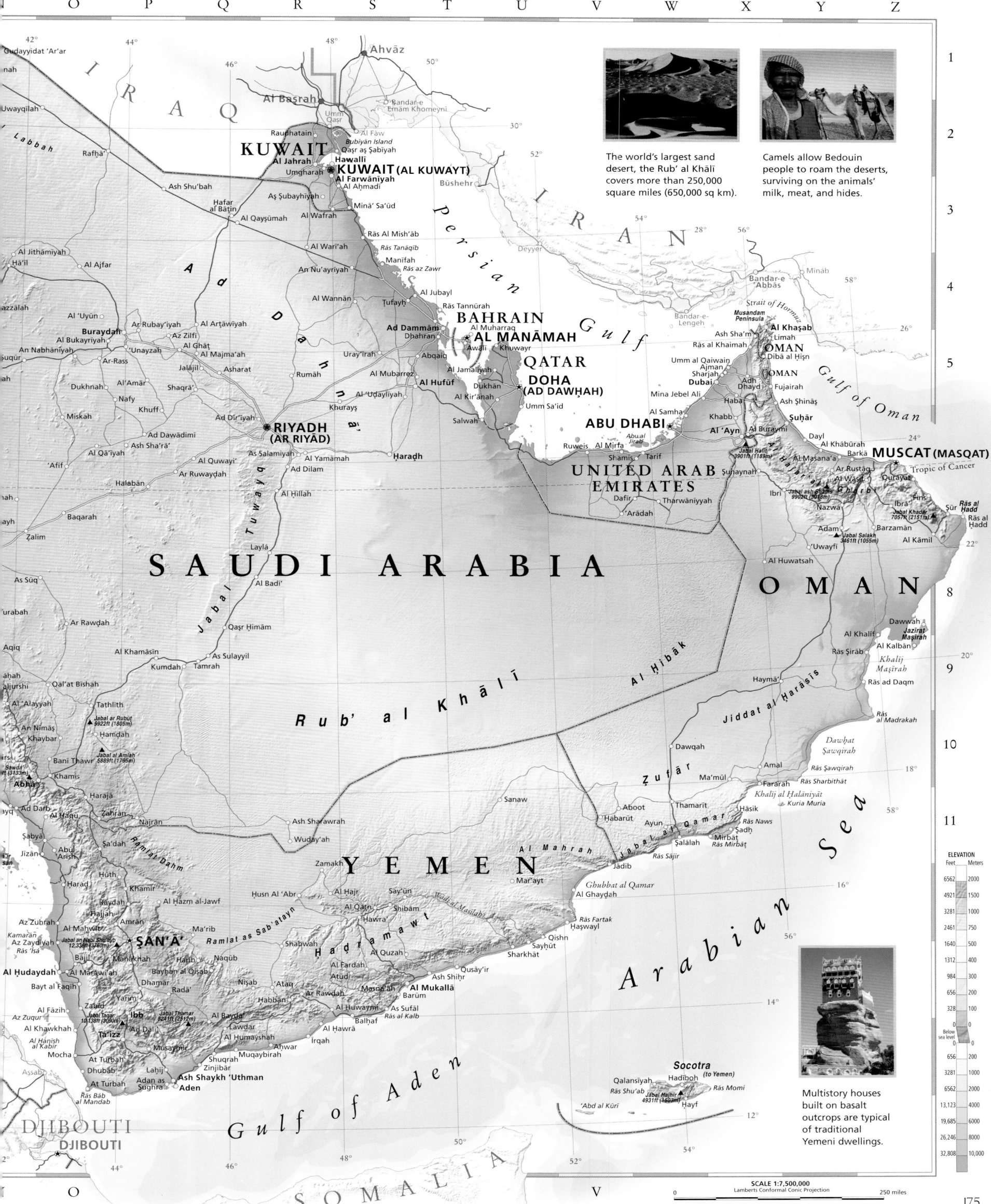

The world's largest sand desert, the Rub' al Khālī covers more than 250,000 square miles (650,000 sq km).

Camels allow Bedouin people to roam the deserts, surviving on the animals' milk, meat, and hides.

Multistory houses built on basalt outcrops are typical of traditional Yemeni dwellings.

SCALE 1:7,500,000
Lamberts Conformal Conic Projection

175

AFGHANISTAN, IRAN, AND PAKISTAN

A high, mainly barren plateau dominates the western half of this region, occupying most of Iran and extending into Afghanistan and Pakistan. It is bounded in the northwest by the forested Elburz Mountains and in the west by the Zagros Mountains. In northeastern Afghanistan, it rises to the lofty summits of the Hindu Kush and the Karakorams, offshoots of the Himalaya; in Pakistan, its crumpled eastern fringe abuts the broad, low valley of the Indus River. More than 97 percent of the inhabitants of this rugged and mostly arid land are Muslims, and their religion has profoundly influenced the region's history. Pakistan was founded in 1947 as a home for India's Muslims; Iran has been ruled by Islamic clerics since a revolution in 1979; and in the late 1990s Afghanistan was run by the Taliban, a fundamentalist Islamic regime that was toppled by a U.S.-led invasion in 2001.

At 28,251 feet (8,611m), K2, in the Karakoram range, is the world's second-highest peak.

Thriving around 2500 BC, Mohenjo Daro, near Sukkur, Pakistan, was one of Indus Valley's first cities.

THE KHYBER PASS

One of just a few passes permitting travel between Central Asia and the Indian Subcontinent, the Khyber Pass has long been of strategic importance to locals and foreign powers, from the Persians, who used it to reach the Indus in the fifth century BC, to the British, who made it the focus of local operations in the late 19th century. Consisting of a narrow opening in the Safed Koh Range, the pass reaches its highest point of 3,543 feet (1,080 m) at Landi Kotal. Its road and rail links facilitate travel between Kabul in Afghanistan and Peshawar in Pakistan.

Iran's Dasht-e Kavir is characterized by vast stony plains and low-lying salt pans (kavirs).

Iranian carpets, most of which are still woven by hand, are much in demand overseas.

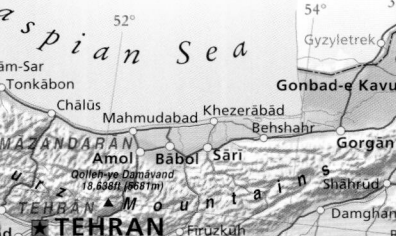

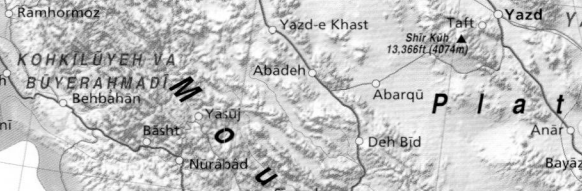

Longitude east of Greenwich

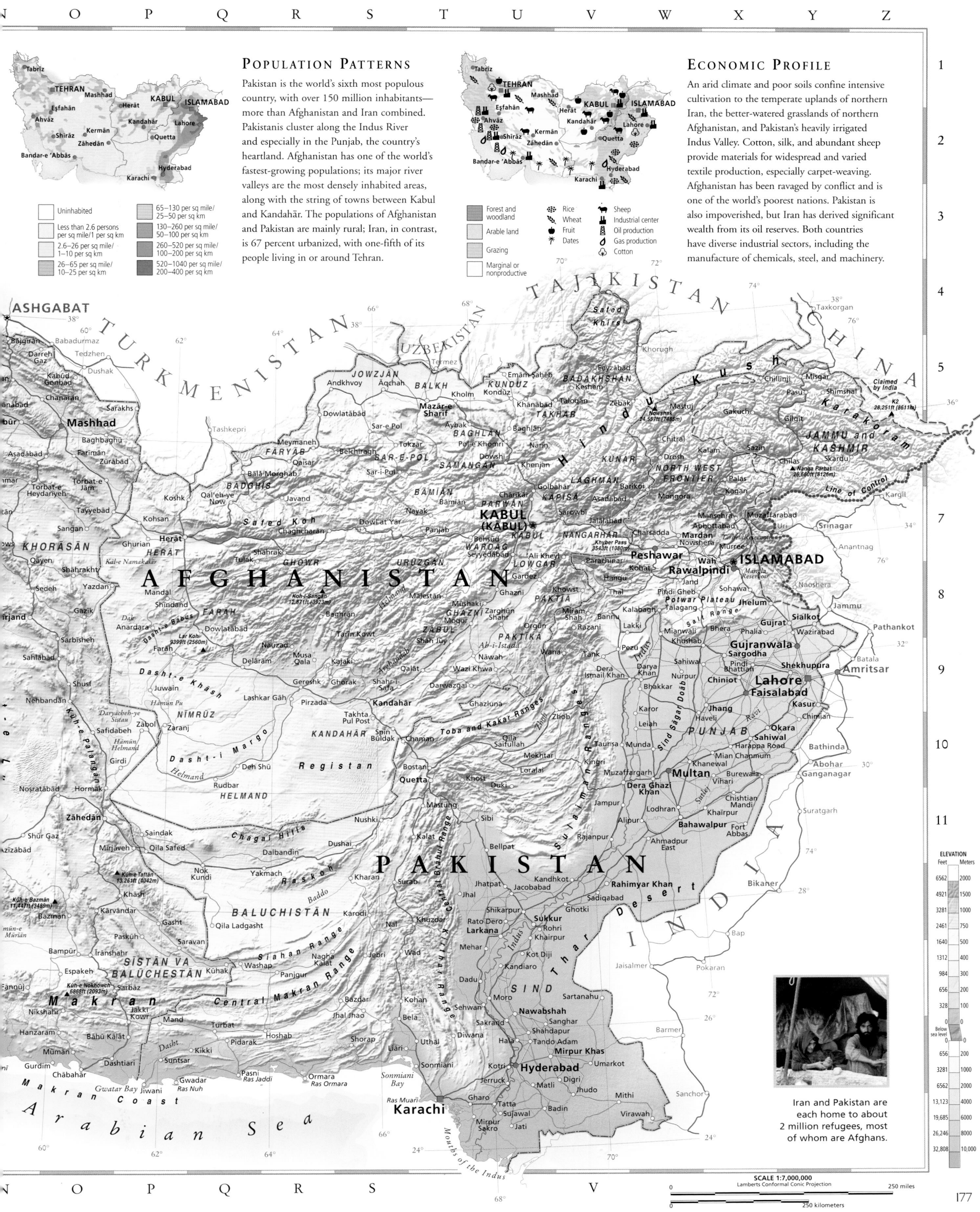

POPULATION PATTERNS

Pakistan is the world's sixth most populous country, with over 150 million inhabitants—more than Afghanistan and Iran combined. Pakistanis cluster along the Indus River and especially in the Punjab, the country's heartland. Afghanistan has one of the world's fastest-growing populations; its major river valleys are the most densely inhabited areas, along with the string of towns between Kabul and Kandahār. The populations of Afghanistan and Pakistan are mainly rural; Iran, in contrast, is 67 percent urbanized, with one-fifth of its people living in or around Tehran.

Uninhabited
Less than 2.6 persons per sq mile/1 per sq km
2.6–26 per sq mile/ 1–10 per sq km
26–65 per sq mile/ 10–25 per sq km
65–130 per sq mile/ 25–50 per sq km
130–260 per sq mile/ 50–100 per sq km
260–520 per sq mile/ 100–200 per sq km
520–1040 per sq mile/ 200–400 per sq km

Forest and woodland
Arable land
Grazing
Marginal or nonproductive

Rice
Wheat
Fruit
Dates
Sheep
Industrial center
Oil production
Gas production
Cotton

ECONOMIC PROFILE

An arid climate and poor soils confine intensive cultivation to the temperate uplands of northern Iran, the better-watered grasslands of northern Afghanistan, and Pakistan's heavily irrigated Indus Valley. Cotton, silk, and abundant sheep provide materials for widespread and varied textile production, especially carpet-weaving. Afghanistan has been ravaged by conflict and is one of the world's poorest nations. Pakistan is also impoverished, but Iran has derived significant wealth from its oil reserves. Both countries have diverse industrial sectors, including the manufacture of chemicals, steel, and machinery.

Iran and Pakistan are each home to about 2 million refugees, most of whom are Afghans.

SCALE 1:7,000,000
Lamberts Conformal Conic Projection
0 250 miles
0 250 kilometers

CENTRAL ASIA
Kazakhstan, Kyrgyzstan, Tajikistan, Turkmenistan, Uzbekistan

The peoples of Central Asia have long been linked by a shared Islamic religious and cultural heritage, traditionally pastoral and seminomadic lifestyles, and related, mainly Turkic languages. During the 19th century, they were brought even closer together when their lands were annexed by the Russian Empire. Subsequent Soviet control transformed an undeveloped region, rapidly industrializing farming, manufacturing, and mining, turning several villages into cities, and creating separate republics for each of the major ethnic groups—the Uzbeks, Kazaks, Tajiks, Turkmens, and Kyrgyz. After the fall of communism in 1991, all five republics became independent states. These nations occupy a wide, mainly arid and low-lying region. The grasslands of the Kazakh Steppe stretch across its northern third, spreading into Russia. South of the Aral Sea, deserts cover the Turan Lowland. In the east, a series of ranges climbs toward the Pamir and Tien Shan ranges, whose soaring peaks divide Central Asia from China.

Cotton is Turkmenistan's principal crop. Production centers on irrigated areas along the Amudar'ya River.

Russia's spacecraft-launching center is near Baykonur in Kazakhstan.

POPULATION PATTERNS

The scarcity of fresh water has restricted dense settlement to upland areas and the banks of major rivers, leaving the deserts and grasslands sparsely inhabited. During the Soviet era, Central Asia's population grew rapidly, due partly to an influx of Russians and Ukrainians and partly to improvements in medical services. Despite this, Central Asian society remains predominantly rural; indeed, with the departure of many Russians after the demise of the Soviet Union, the continuing focus on cotton production, and high birth rates in country areas, rural populations have grown recently, against the prevailing world trend.

Less than 2.6 persons per sq mile/1 per sq km	130–260 per sq mile/50–100 per sq km
2.6–26 per sq mile/1–10 per sq km	260–520 per sq mile/100–200 per sq km
26–65 per sq mile/10–25 per sq km	520–1040 per sq mile/200–400 per sq km
65–130 per sq mile/25–50 per sq km	

ECONOMIC PROFILE

Central Asia's mineral reserves include oil and gas deposits near the Caspian Sea and supplies of coal, iron ore, and chromium in Kazakhstan; these support a variety of heavy industries. Three-fifths of the land is desert, and large areas are used for grazing. Crops can be grown only in fertile upland pockets and irrigated areas. Soviet emphasis on the production of coal and oil in Kazakhstan and cotton elsewhere not only created severe environmental problems, but left these nations dependent on just a few commodities. Recent expansion of the gas industry (Turkmenistan has the world's fifth-largest reserves) is part of an attempt to diversify produce and alleviate widespread poverty.

Cereals
Cotton
Beef cattle
Sheep
Fishing
Industrial center
Mining
Oil production
Gas production
Fruit and vegetables

Forest and woodland
Arable land
Grazing
Marginal or nonproductive

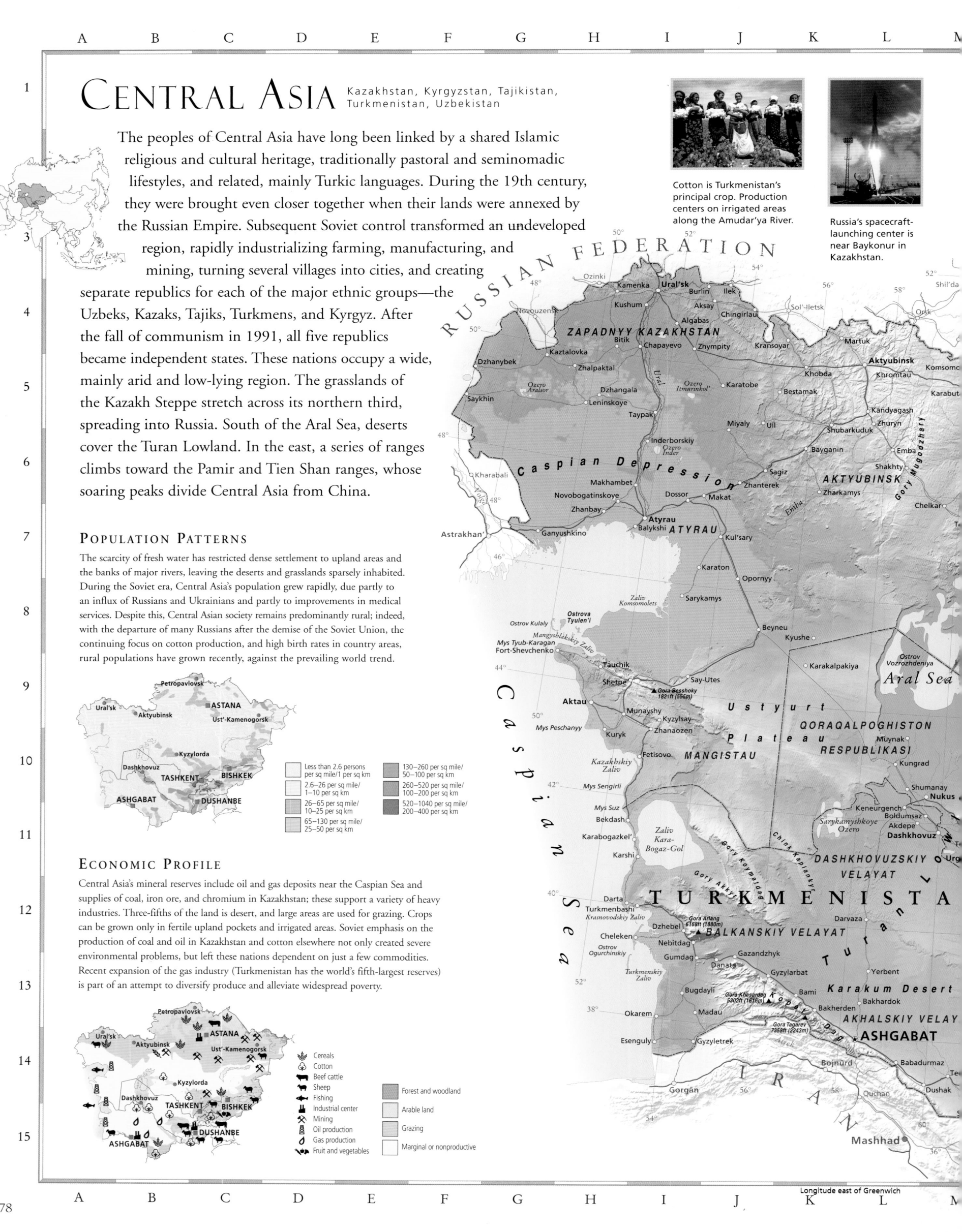

Longitude east of Greenwich

N O P Q R S T U V W X Y Z

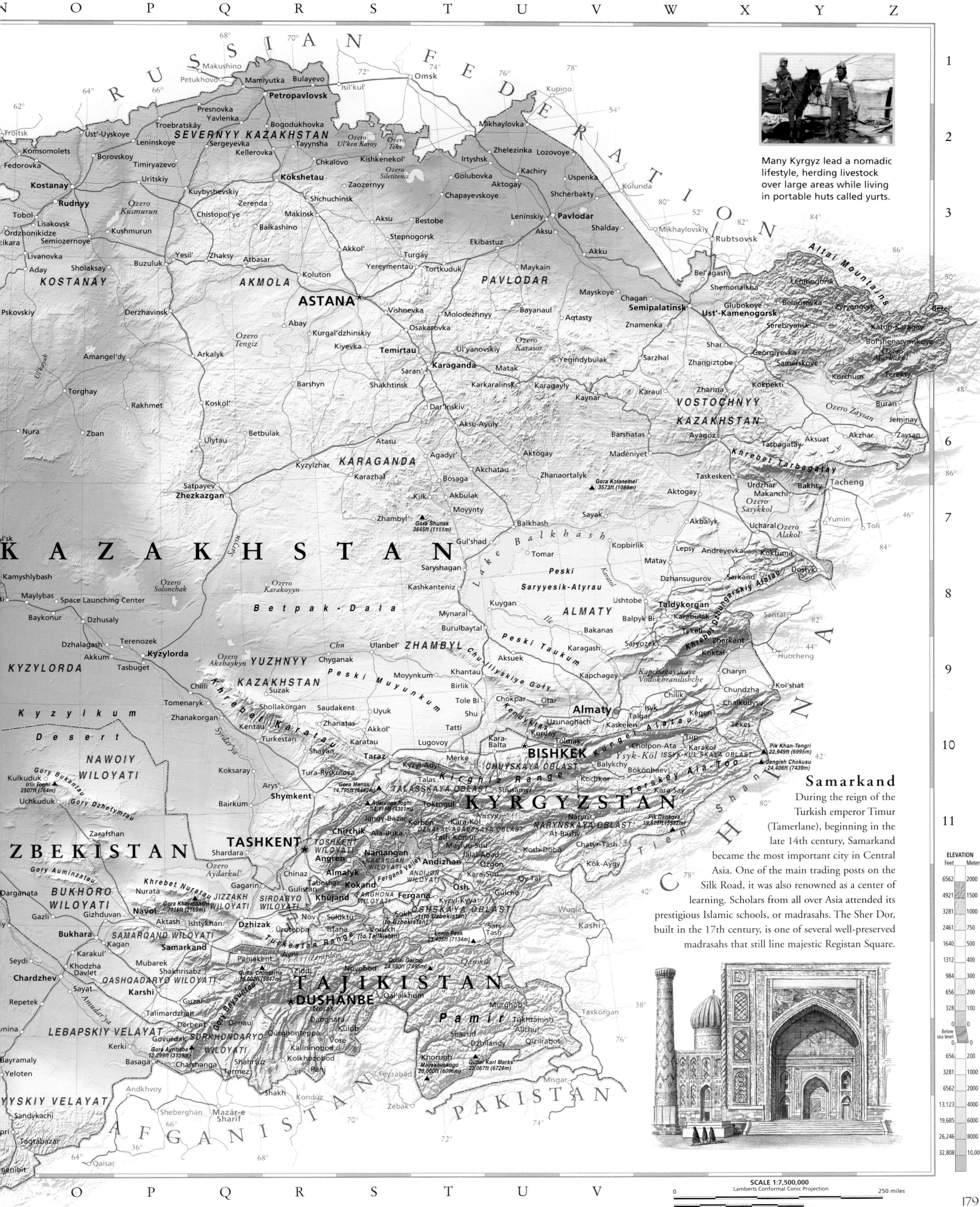

Many Kyrgyz lead a nomadic lifestyle, herding livestock over large areas while living in portable huts called yurts.

RUSSIAN FEDERATION

Makushino
Petukhovo
Mamlyutka
Bulayevo
Isil'kul'
Omsk
Kupino
Petropavlovsk
Presnovka
Yavlenka
Troebratskäy
Bogodukhovka
Mikhaylovka
Troitsk
Ust'-Uyskoye
Leninskoye
Sergeyevka
Kellerovka
Tayynsha
Irtyshsk
Zhelezinka
Lozovoye
Komsomolets
Borovskoy
Timiryazevo
Uritskiy
Kokshetau
Chkalovo
Kishkeneköl'
Zaozernyy
Golubovka
Aktogay
Uspenka
Shcherbakty
Kulunda
Fedorovka
Kostanay
Kuybyshevskiy
Zerenda
Ozero Ul'ken Karoy
Ozero Siletiteniz
Kachiry
Rudnyy
Makinsk
Shchuchinsk
Aksu
Bestobe
Stepnogorsk
Leninskiy
Pavlodar
Shalday
Mikhaylovskiy
Rubtsovsk
Ordzhonikidze
Semiozernoye
Kushmurun
Chistopol'ye
Balkashino
ASTANA
Kurgal'dzhinskiy
Turgay
Yereymentau
Tortkuduk
Maykain
Akku
Livanovka
Aday
Sholaksay
Buzuluk
Yesil'
Zhaksy
Atbasar
Temirtau
Ul'yanovskiy
Osakarovka
Bayanaul
Chagan
Semipalatinsk
Ust'-Kamenogorsk
tikara
Yesil'
Karaganda
Saran'
Shakhtinsk
Matak
Yegindybulak
Znamenka
Shar
Glubokoye
Belogorka
Zyryanovsk
Katon-Karagay
Betel'
Torghay
Rakhmet
Koskol'
Betbulak
Barshyn
Dar'inskiv
Aksu-Ayuly
Karkaralinsk
Karagayly
Kaynar
Zharma
Kokpekti
Samarskoye
Kurchum
Terekty
Zhezkazgan
KARAGANDA
Karazhal
Agadyr'
Akchatau
Zhanaortalyk
Gora Kotanemel' 3573ft (1089m)
Karaul
Zhangiztobe
Bakanas
Aktogay
Ayagoz
Barshatas
Madeniyet
Taskesken
Urdzhar
Makanchi
Ozero Sasykkol
Bakhty
Tacheng

KAZAKHSTAN

Satpayev
Ulytau
Gora Shumak 3645ft (1111m)
Kjik
Akbulak
Moyynty
Balkash
Sayak
Akbalyk
Uttaral
Ozero Alakol'
Yumin
Toli
Kyzylzhar
Bosaga
Kopbirlik
Lepsy
Andreyevka
Koktuma
Sarkand
Dostyk
Gul'shad
Tomar
Matay
Dzhansugurov

Lake Balkhash
Peski Saryyesik-Atyrau
Saryshagan
Kuygan
Ushtobe
Taldykorgan
Sarkand
Zharkent
Koktal
Santai
Huocheng
Kamyshlybash
Maylybas
Ozero Solonchak
Kashkanteniz
Mynaral
Balpyk Bi
Karabulak
Tekeli
Space Launching Center
Betpak-Dala
Burulbaytal
Saryozek
Kapchagay
Baykonur
Dzhusaly
Terenozek
Ile
Karagash
ALMATY
KYZYLORDA
Akkum
Kyzylorda
Tasbuget
Ozero Akzbaykyn
Ulanbel'
Moyynkum
Aksuek
Peski Taukum
Kyzylkum Desert
Chilli
Chyganak
Peski Muyunkum
Khantau
Kapchagayskoye Vodokhranilishche
Charyn
Chundzha
Kol'shat
Dzhalagash
YUZHNYY
Saudakent
Birlik
Tole Bi
Chokpar
Chilik
Chulliyskiye Gory
Zhanakorgan
Shollakorgan
KAZAKHSTAN
Suzak
Uyuk
Shu
Otar
Talgar
Isyk
Kegen
Tomenaryk
Zhanatas
Tatti
Kara-Balta
Almaty
Uzunagach
Kaskelen
Tekes
Tasbuget
Kentau
Karatau
Akköl'
Lugovoy
Merke
BISHKEK
Korday
Tüp
Karkara
Pik Khan-Tengri 22,949ft (6995m)
Khrebet Karatau
Turkestan
Shayan
Tura-Ryskulova
Taraz
Kyzyl-Adyr
CHUYSKAYA OBLAST
Balykchy
Bökönbaev
Karakol
Koksaray
Bairkum
Gora Menas 14,795ft (4464m)
Talas
Ysyk-Köl
Cholpon-Ata
ISSYK-KUL'SKAYA OBLAST
Shymkent
Adelunga Toghi 13,419ft (4301m)
TALASSKAYA OBLAST
Toktogul
Suusamyr
Kochkor
Kara-Say
Terskey Ala-Too
Dzhengish Chokusu 24,406ft (7439m)
Jangy-Bazar
Kirghiz Range
KYRGYZSTAN
Naryn
Pik Dankova 19,626ft (5982m)
Chirchik
Ala-Buka
Kerben
DZHALAL-ABADSKAYA OBLAST
Tash-Kömür
Mayluu-Suu
NARYNSKAYA OBLAST
At-Bashy
Kosh-Döbö
Chatyr-Tash
Kök-Aygy
UZBEKISTAN
TASHKENT
Shardara
TOSHKENT WILOYATI
Namangan
Andizhan
Jalal-Abad
Özgön
Kara-Suu
Oy-Tal
Angren
NAMANGAN WILOYATI
Kara-Su
Kashi
Almalyk
Taboshar
ANDIJON WILOYATI
Osh
Kyzyl-Kyya
Guicho
Wuqia
Chinaz
Chust
Fergana Valley
OSHSKAYA OBLAST
Gagarin
Nurata
JIZZAKH WILOYATI
SIRDARYO WILOYATI
Kokand
FERGHONA WILOYATI
Fergana
Gora Khayatbashi 7116ft (2169m)
Gulistan
Sokh (To Uzbekistan)
Yoruth (To Uzbekistan)
Kashi
Navoi
Khrebet Nuratau
Khujand
Nov
Sülüktü
Isfana
Lenin Peak 23,405ft (7134m)
Sary-Tash
Taxkorgan
BUKHORO WILOYATI
Aktash
Ishtykhan
Dzhizak
Uroteppa
Istana
Zöruth
Bukhara
Kagan
SAMARQAND WILOYATI
Samarkand
Ayni
Zeravshan
Panjakent
Qullai Chimtarga 18,003ft (5847m)
TAJIKISTAN
Novobod
Qullai Garmo 24,590ft (7495m)
Qayrakki
Gazli
Gory Auminzatau
Mubarek
Shakhrisabz
Qullai Karl Marks 23,067ft (6726m)
Karakul'
Gory Aydarkul'
Karshi
Guzar
DUSHANBE
Qal'aikhum
Murghob
Tükhtamish
Misgar
Seydi
QASHQADARYO WILOYATI
Nurak
Danghara
Chardzhev
Khodzha Davlet
Sayat
Derbent
Denau
Kulob
Vose
Shazud
Alichur
Qizilrabot
Pamir
LEBAPSKIY VELAYAT
Kerki
Govurdak
Gora Ayniaba 10,299ft (3139m)
SURKHONDARYO WILOYATI
Qurahonteppa
Kalininobod
Kolkhozobod
Khorugh
Dzhilandy
Repetek
Talimardzhan
Charshanga
Shahrtuz
Termez
Panj
Feyzabad
Bayramaly
Basaga
Khorugh 20,000ft (6096m)
Misgar
Yeloten
YYSKIY VELAYAT
Sandykachy
Andkhvoy
Sheberghan
Mazar-e Sharif
Konduz
Zébak
nina
Yaqeti
Togtabazar
AFGHANISTAN
Qaisar
PAKISTAN

CHINA

Altai Mountains
Leninogorsk
Zyryanovsk
Bol'shenarymskoye
Buran
Ozero Zaysan
Jeminay
Zaysan
VOSTOCHNYY KAZAKHSTAN
Khrebet Tarbagatay
Tarbagatay
Aksuat
Akzhar
Ucharal
Khrebet Dzhungarskiy Alatau
Khrebet Dzhungarskiy Alatau
Tien Shan
Kurgak Alatau

Samarkand

During the reign of the Turkish emperor Timur (Tamerlane), beginning in the late 14th century, Samarkand became the most important city in Central Asia. One of the main trading posts on the Silk Road, it was also renowned as a center of learning. Scholars from all over Asia attended its prestigious Islamic schools, or madrasahs. The Sher Dor, built in the 17th century, is one of several well-preserved madrasahs that still line majestic Registan Square.

ELEVATION

Feet	Meters
6562	2000
4921	1500
3281	1000
2461	750
1640	500
1312	400
984	300
656	200
328	100
Below sea level	
656	200
3281	1000
6562	2000
13,123	4000
19,685	6000
26,246	8000
32,808	10,000

SCALE 1:7,500,000
Lamberts Conformal Conic Projection

0 ————— 250 miles
0 ————— 250 kilometers

179

SOUTHERN ASIA

Bangladesh, Bhutan, India, Maldives, Nepal, Sri Lanka

Sometimes referred to as the Subcontinent, this region is dominated by India, the world's seventh-largest and second-most populous country. It also includes the Himalayan kingdoms of Nepal and Bhutan, low-lying Bangladesh, and the island nations of Sri Lanka and the Maldives. From their dizzy heights, the mountains of the Himalaya drop steeply to the wide, low plain of the Ganges River. West of the Gangetic Plain, the Thar Desert spreads into Pakistan; to the south, the triangular Deccan Plateau occupies most of central and southern India. In the early 16th century, much of Southern Asia was united by the Muslim Mughal dynasty, which ruled until it was undermined by the rise of the Hindu Marathas in the 18th century. Britain controlled most of the region from the early 19th century until 1948; before withdrawing, it created the states of West Pakistan and East Pakistan, which later became Pakistan and Bangladesh, and granted independence to Ceylon, now Sri Lanka.

POPULATION PATTERNS

More than one-sixth of the world's population lives in this region. India alone has more than 1 billion inhabitants and, given its growth rate—48,000 babies are born there every day—could surpass China as the world's most populous nation by 2050. High population densities occur on the Gangetic Plain and in the northeast—Bangladesh is one of the world's most densely populated countries—but only one-quarter of people live in cities. Most Indians and Nepalis are Hindu, whereas the majority of Bangladeshis are Muslim; Bhutan and Sri Lanka are predominantly Buddhist. Indigenous languages are many and varied, and English functions as a lingua franca.

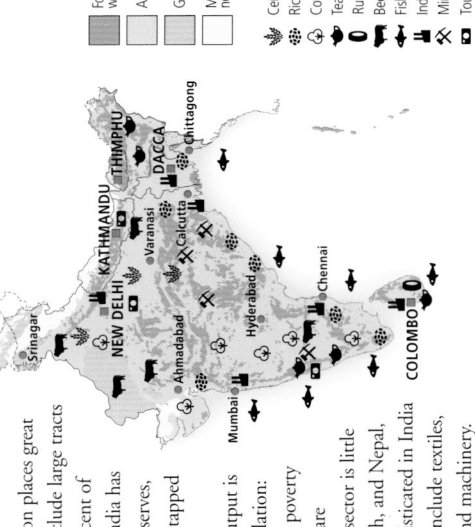

ECONOMIC PROFILE

The region's enormous population places great strain on its resources, which include large tracts of arable land (including 50 percent of India), forests, and minerals—India has the world's fourth-largest coal reserves, and oil and gas fields have been tapped in many areas. Most people are dependent on agriculture, yet output is insufficient to support the population: half of all Nepalis live below the poverty line and one-quarter of Indians are undernourished. The industrial sector is little developed in Bhutan, Bangladesh, and Nepal, but becoming increasingly sophisticated in India and Sri Lanka, where products include textiles, chemicals, computer software, and machinery.

Population density legend

- Uninhabited
- Less than 2.6 persons per sq mile/1 per sq km
- 2.6–26 per sq mile/ 1–10 per sq km
- 26–65 per sq mile/ 10–25 per sq km
- 65–130 per sq mile/ 25–50 per sq km
- 130–260 per sq mile/ 50–100 per sq km
- 260–520 per sq mile/ 100–200 per sq km
- 520–1040 per sq mile/ 200–400 per sq km
- 1040–2080 per sq mile/ 400–800 per sq km
- More than 2080 per sq mile/800 per sq km

Land use legend

- Forest and woodland
- Arable land
- Grazing
- Marginal or nonproductive
- Cereals
- Rice
- Cotton
- Tea
- Rubber
- Beef cattle
- Fishing
- Industrial center
- Mining
- Tourism

Tea is native to northeastern India. In the 19th century, the British greatly expanded its commercial cultivation.

In Sri Lanka, Tamil separatists have been waging war on the government since the 1980s.

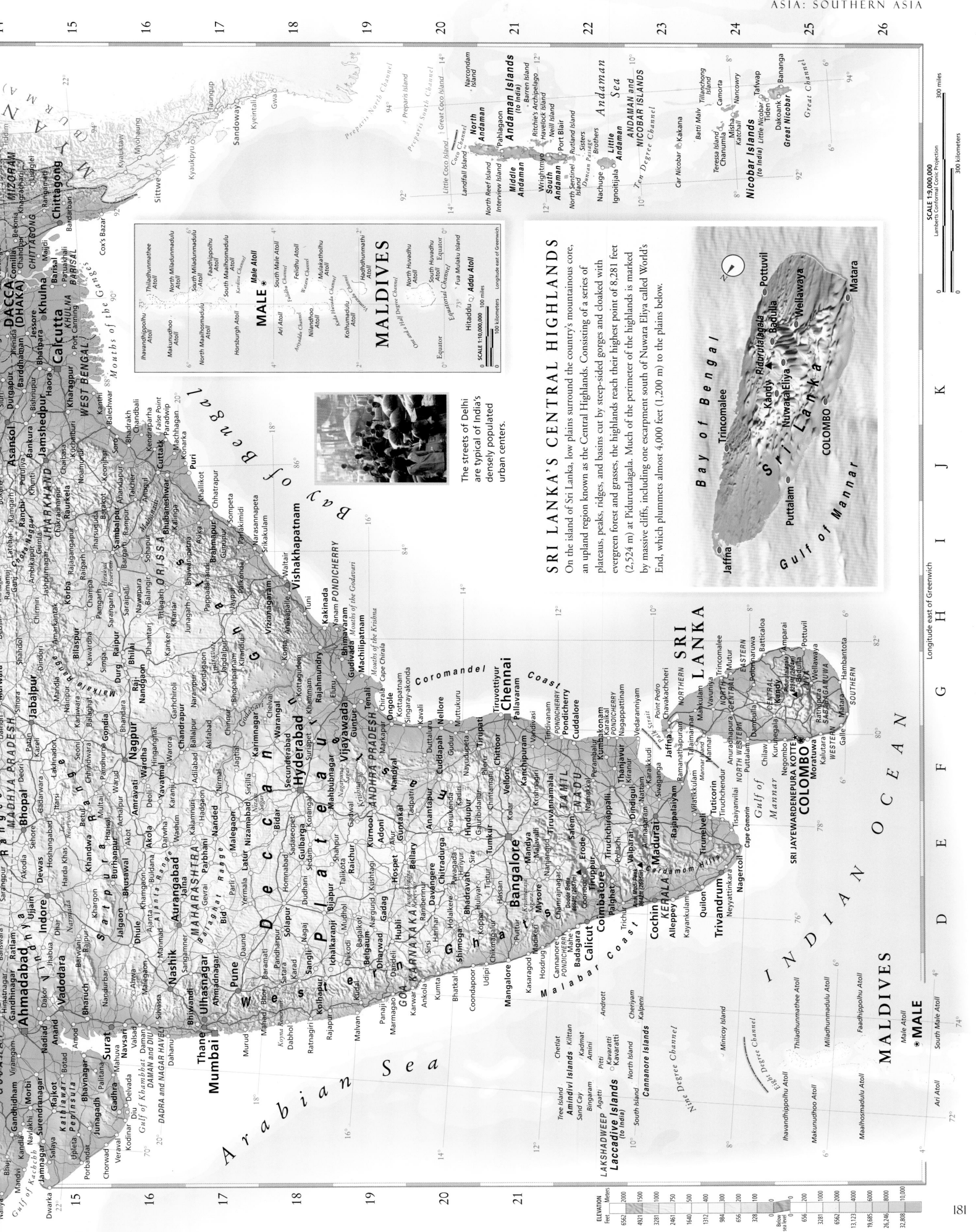

The streets of Delhi are typical of India's densely populated urban centers.

SRI LANKA'S CENTRAL HIGHLANDS

On the island of Sri Lanka, low plains surround the country's mountainous core, an upland region known as the Central Highlands. Consisting of a series of plateaus, peaks, ridges, and basins cut by steep-sided gorges and cloaked with evergreen forest and grasses, the highlands reach their highest point of 8,281 feet (2,524 m) at Pidurutalagala. Much of the perimeter of the highlands is marked by massive cliffs, including one escarpment south of Nuwara Eliya called World's End, which plummets almost 4,000 feet (1,200 m) to the plains below.

The Himalaya and the Gangetic Plain

Bangladesh, Bhutan, Nepal, Northern India

The world's tallest mountain range, the Himalaya forms a colossal barrier between the Subcontinent and Central Asia. Rising to the highest point on Earth, 29,035-foot (8,850-m) Mount Everest, it stretches for 1,550 miles (2,500 km) along the northern edge of India. Its southern flank yields abruptly to the densely populated and intensively farmed plain of the Ganges River. From its source in the western Himalaya, the Ganges flows south then east across northern India and into Bangladesh, branching repeatedly as it nears the Bay of Bengal to create one of the world's largest deltas. Cohesive states first took shape on the Gangetic Plain 3,000 years ago, and the valley was the heart of powerful Indian dynasties such as the Gupta (AD 300–550), the Mamluks (1206–1526), and the Mughals (1526–1761). Physical isolation helped preserve the autonomy of the kingdoms of Nepal, Sikkim, and Bhutan, though all were British protectorates during the 19th century, and in 1975 Sikkim acceded to India.

Up to 1,000 climbers a year now attempt an ascent of Mount Everest, which was first conquered in 1953.

Hindus view the Ganges as a holy river and visit places such as Varanasi to bathe in its waters.

The orchards of the fertile Kashmir Valley are one of India's most important sources of fruit and nuts.

POPULATION PATTERNS

This region includes the Subcontinent's least and most crowded areas. Above 16,000 feet (5,000 m), the Himalaya is virtually uninhabited. In contrast, population densities are among the world's highest in Bangladesh, which averages 2,000 people per square mile (770 per sq km); in Calcutta, where up to 100,000 people occupy each square mile of the city (40,000 per sq km); and in irrigated parts of the Gangetic Plain. The majority of people live in rural areas—Bhutan had no towns until the 1960s—and population growth rates are high. The region's peoples are a mix of Indo-European and Tibeto-Burman groups, with the latter, who include the Newar and Sherpa, generally occupying the higher land.

Uninhabited

Less than 2.6 persons per sq mile/1 per sq km

2.6–26 per sq mile/ 1–10 per sq km

26–65 per sq mile/ 10–25 per sq km

65–130 per sq mile/ 25–50 per sq km

130–260 per sq mile/ 50–100 per sq km

260–520 per sq mile/ 100–200 per sq km

520–1040 per sq mile/ 200–400 per sq km

1040–2080 per sq mile/ 400–800 per sq km

More than 2080 per sq mile/800 per sq km

ECONOMIC PROFILE

The region includes many large cities, but is little developed and its people mainly poor. On the Gangetic Plain, irrigation is used to grow wheat, cotton, and sugar. In the wetter Brahmaputra Valley and Bangladesh, tea is cultivated on the hillsides, rice on the plains. Despite its rugged terrain, the Himalaya has extensive arable land—mainly in foothills, basins, and river valleys—which produces wheat, corn, millet, and potatoes. On the upper slopes, sheep, goats, and yaks are herded between seasonal pastures. Minerals, including gold, sapphires, copper, and iron ore, are widespread, though difficult to access. The Himalaya and cities such as Agra, Delhi, and Varanasi are major tourist attractions.

Forest and woodland

Arable land

Grazing

Marginal or nonproductive

Cereals
Rice
Wheat
Fruit
Cotton
Tea
Dairy cattle
Fishing
Industrial center
Tourism

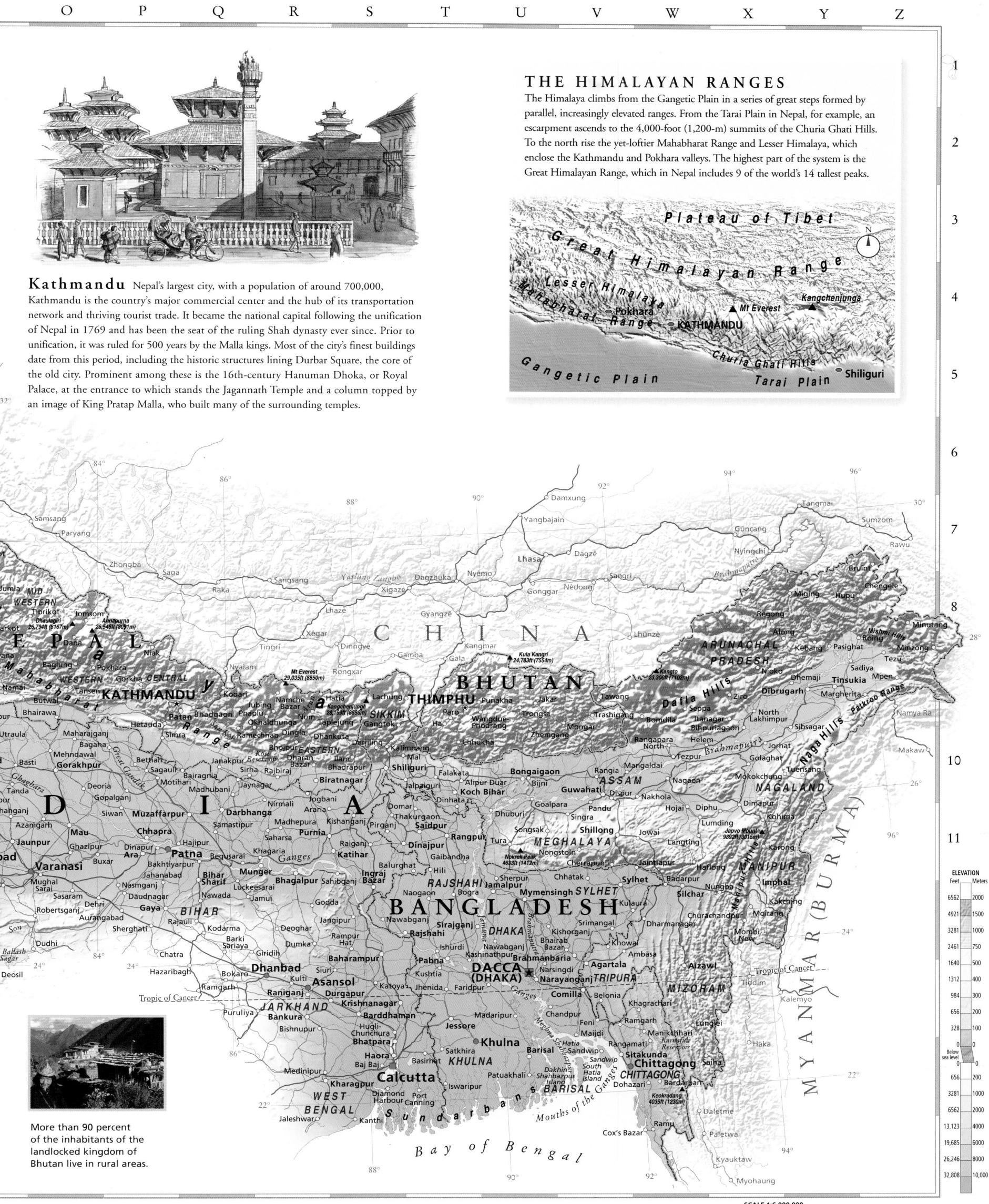

THE HIMALAYAN RANGES

The Himalaya climbs from the Gangetic Plain in a series of great steps formed by parallel, increasingly elevated ranges. From the Tarai Plain in Nepal, for example, an escarpment ascends to the 4,000-foot (1,200-m) summits of the Churia Ghati Hills. To the north rise the yet-loftier Mahabharat Range and Lesser Himalaya, which enclose the Kathmandu and Pokhara valleys. The highest part of the system is the Great Himalayan Range, which in Nepal includes 9 of the world's 14 tallest peaks.

Kathmandu Nepal's largest city, with a population of around 700,000, Kathmandu is the country's major commercial center and the hub of its transportation network and thriving tourist trade. It became the national capital following the unification of Nepal in 1769 and has been the seat of the ruling Shah dynasty ever since. Prior to unification, it was ruled for 500 years by the Malla kings. Most of the city's finest buildings date from this period, including the historic structures lining Durbar Square, the core of the old city. Prominent among these is the 16th-century Hanuman Dhoka, or Royal Palace, at the entrance to which stands the Jagannath Temple and a column topped by an image of King Pratap Malla, who built many of the surrounding temples.

More than 90 percent of the inhabitants of the landlocked kingdom of Bhutan live in rural areas.

EASTERN ASIA
China, Mongolia, North Korea, South Korea, Taiwan

In both size and population, China dwarfs not only its neighbors, but most other countries. The world's third-largest and most populous country, it occupies 3.7 million square miles (9.6 million sq km) and is home to 1.3 billion people. From the Plateau of Tibet, which covers one-quarter of the country, major rivers, including the Yellow and the Yangtze, run eastward through the central ranges to the intensely cultivated coastal plains. Northward-flowing rivers quickly peter out in the belt of arid land that spans northern China and Mongolia. In the northeast, the forested Changbai Mountains separate China from the Korean Peninsula. Early Chinese civilizations led the world in technology, becoming the first to develop products such as paper, cast iron, silk, and gunpowder. The 20th century saw a power struggle within China between the Nationalist Party and the Communist Party. The latter won out, proclaiming the People's Republic of China in 1949, while the Nationalists repaired to Taiwan. That island's subsequent declaration of independence has yet to be recognized by China.

Cities such as Seoul have absorbed most of the rapid population growth that has occurred in South Korea.

Near Guilin in southeastern China, rice fields form a patchwork between steep, jagged limestone outcrops.

POPULATION PATTERNS

China's population increases by 10 million every year, a situation that helps explain the government's controversial policy of permitting each family to have only one child. Most Chinese live in small villages and two-thirds occupy the eastern lowlands, which constitute less than one-third of the country. The population dwindles in northern and western China—just 2 million or so inhabit the vast Plateau of Tibet—and in Mongolia. The latter is one of the world's least densely populated countries: its 2.5 million people live in an area bigger than Alaska, with an average of just four people occupying each square mile (1.6 per sq km). Tiny Taiwan has almost ten times the population of Mongolia and, like the similarly crowded Korean Peninsula, is highly urbanized.

Uninhabited	130–260 per sq mile/ 50–100 per sq km
Less than 2.6 persons per sq mile/1 per sq km	260–520 per sq mile/ 100–200 per sq km
2.6–26 per sq mile/ 1–10 per sq km	520–1040 per sq mile/ 200–400 per sq km
26–65 per sq mile/ 10–25 per sq km	1040–2080 per sq mile/ 400–800 per sq km
65–130 per sq mile/ 25–50 per sq km	More than 2080 per sq mile/800 per sq km

ULAANBAATAR
Harbin
Changchun
Kashi
Ürümqi
BEIJING
P'YŎNGYANG
SEOUL
Lanzhou
Zhengzhou
Shanghai
Lhasa
Chongqing
TAIPEI
Hong Kong
Haikou

ECONOMIC PROFILE

With the world's largest workforce, abundant resources including coal, oil, iron ore, and hydroelectric power, and diverse, developed industries, China has huge economic potential. Until the late 1970s, this was held in check by strict government controls, but recent years have seen a degree of liberalization of production and trade, and consequent rises in productivity. A contrasting reluctance to relax state control has led to recession and food shortages in North Korea. South Korea and Taiwan have taken advantage of U.S. assistance to develop strong, technologically advanced industrial sectors, and both nations are now major producers of electronic goods. Though it has significant mineral reserves, including copper, coal, and oil, Mongolia is still dependent on its pastoral industry.

ULAANBAATAR
Harbin
Changchun
Kashi
Ürümqi
BEIJING
P'YONGYANG
SEOUL
Lanzhou
Zhengzhou
Shanghai
Lhasa
Chongqing
TAIPEI
Hong Kong
Haikou

	Forest and woodland
	Arable land
	Grazing
	Marginal or nonproductive

- Cereals
- Rice
- Beef cattle
- Sheep
- Fishing
- Industrial center
- Mining
- Oil production
- Timber

Immense dams are being built on the Three Gorges section of the Yangtze River.

About 70 percent of farming in Mongolia involves the rearing of domestic animals.

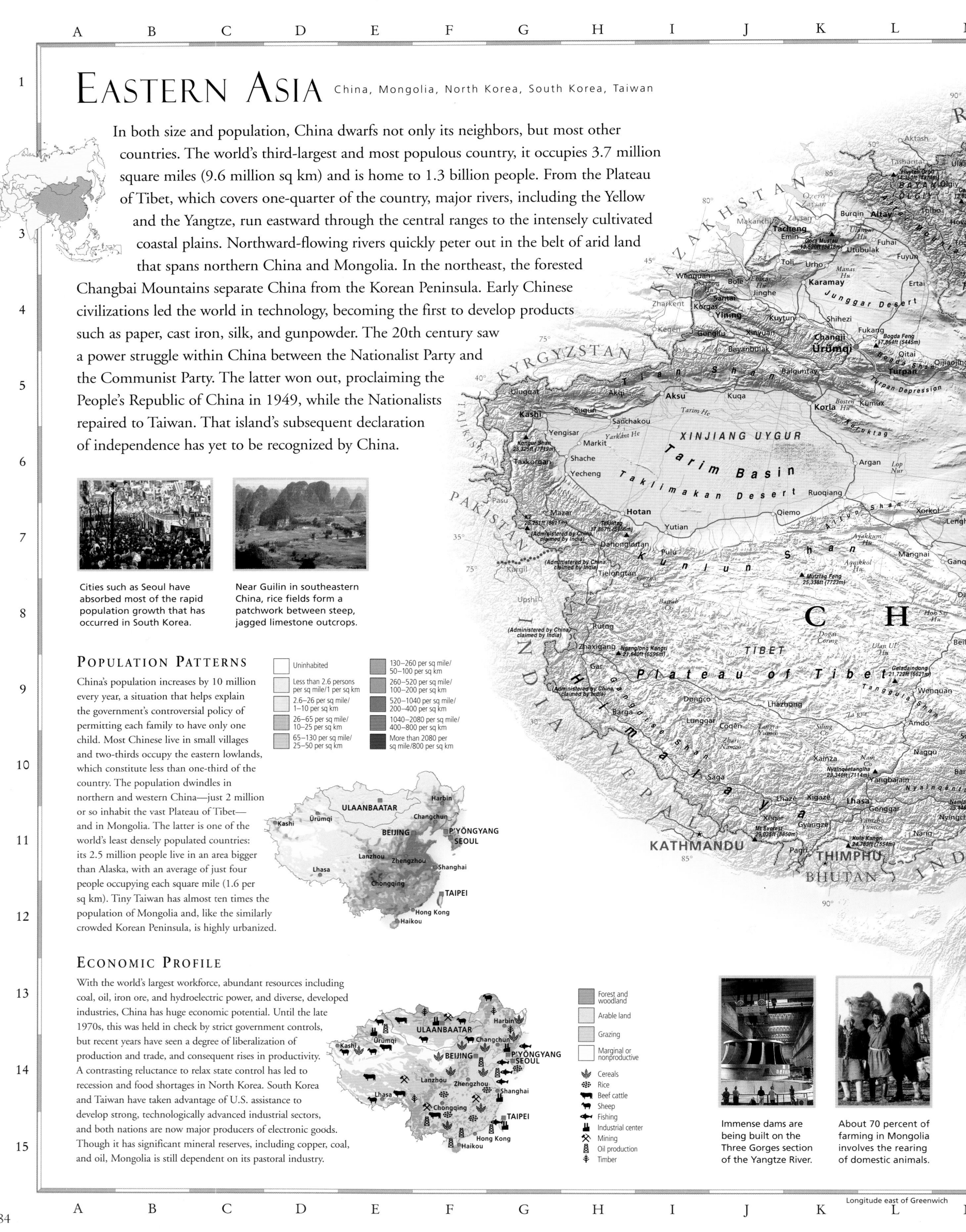

KAZAKHSTAN
Aktash
Tacheng
Emin
Karamay
Yining
Kashi
Aksu
Korla
XINJIANG UYGUR
Tarim Basin
Taklimakan Desert
Hotan
Junggar Desert
Ürümqi
Turpan
Turpan Depression
KYRGYZSTAN
TAJIKISTAN
PAKISTAN
C H
TIBET
Plateau of Tibet
I N D I A
NEPAL
KATHMANDU
THIMPHU
BHUTAN
Mt Everest
29,035ft (8850m)
Lhasa

Longitude east of Greenwich

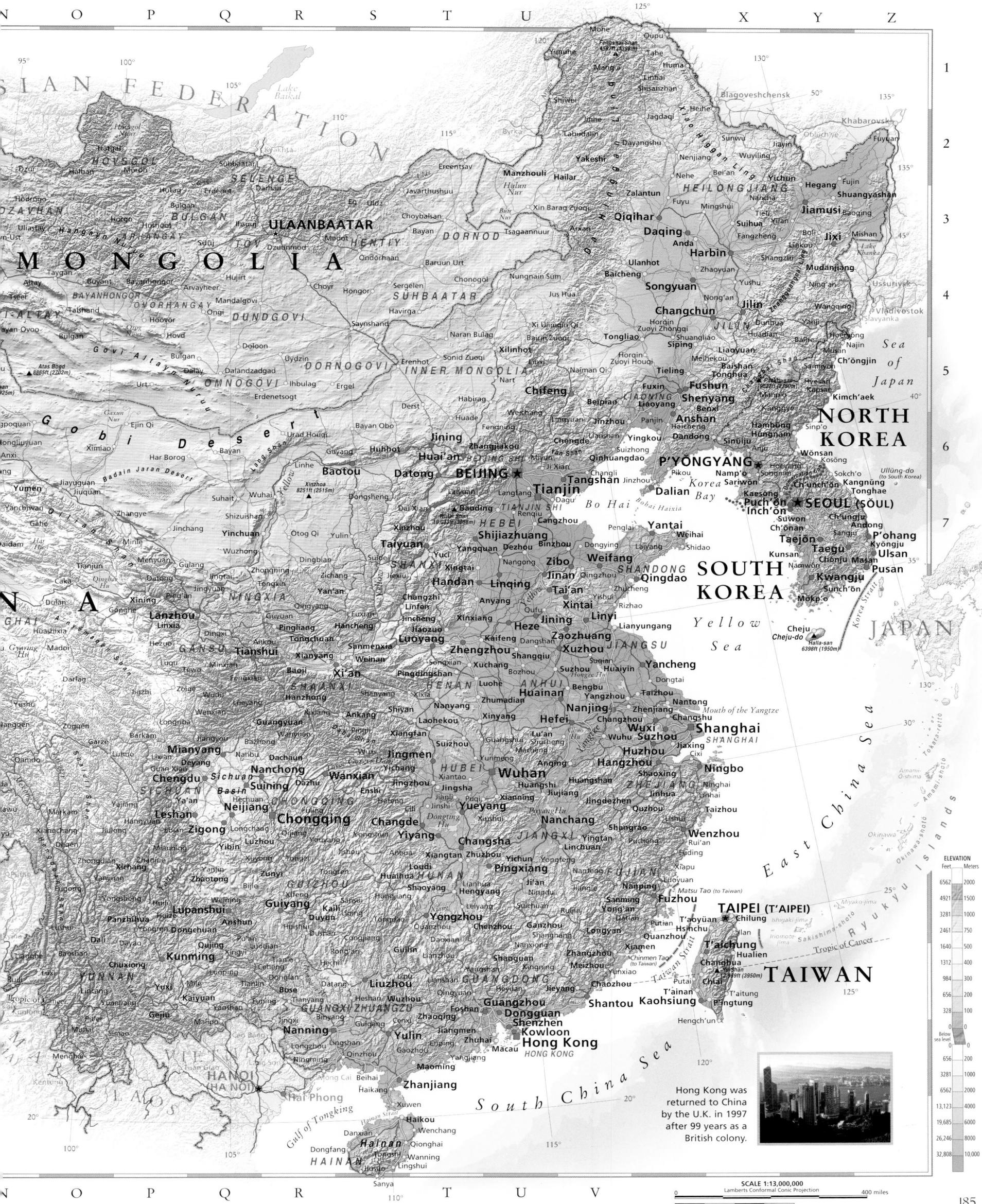

Hong Kong was
returned to China
by the U.K. in 1997
after 99 years as a
British colony.

ELEVATION

Feet	Meters
6562	2000
4921	1500
3281	1000
2461	750
1640	500
1312	400
984	300
656	200
328	100
0	Below sea level
656	200
3281	1000
6562	2000
13,123	4000
19,685	6000
26,246	8000
32,808	10,000

SCALE 1:13,000,000
Lamberts Conformal Conic Projection

0   400 miles

0   400 kilometers

NORTHEASTERN CHINA AND KOREA

Northeastern China, North Korea, South Korea

Northeastern China was formerly known as Manchuria and its major physical feature is the huge Manchurian Plain. This undulating lowland is bounded on three sides by mountains: the Da Hinggan Range in the west, which falls to the arid steppe of the interior; the Xiao Hinggan Range in the northeast, which lines the frontier with Russia; and a series of smaller ranges that extends into the Korean Peninsula. A narrow coastal strip links the southern end of the plain to China's populous eastern lowlands, site of the capital, Beijing. Manchuria was originally home to a distinctive people, the Manchus, and remained apart from early Chinese empires. Following the collapse of the Ming Dynasty in 1644, the Manchus took control of China, forming the Qing Dynasty. Its demise in the early 20th century allowed Japan to annex Korea and Manchuria before launching its offensive on the rest of Asia in 1941. The postwar division of Korea into Soviet- and U.S.-controlled sectors led to the Korean War of 1950–53 and the creation of communist North Korea and capitalist South Korea.

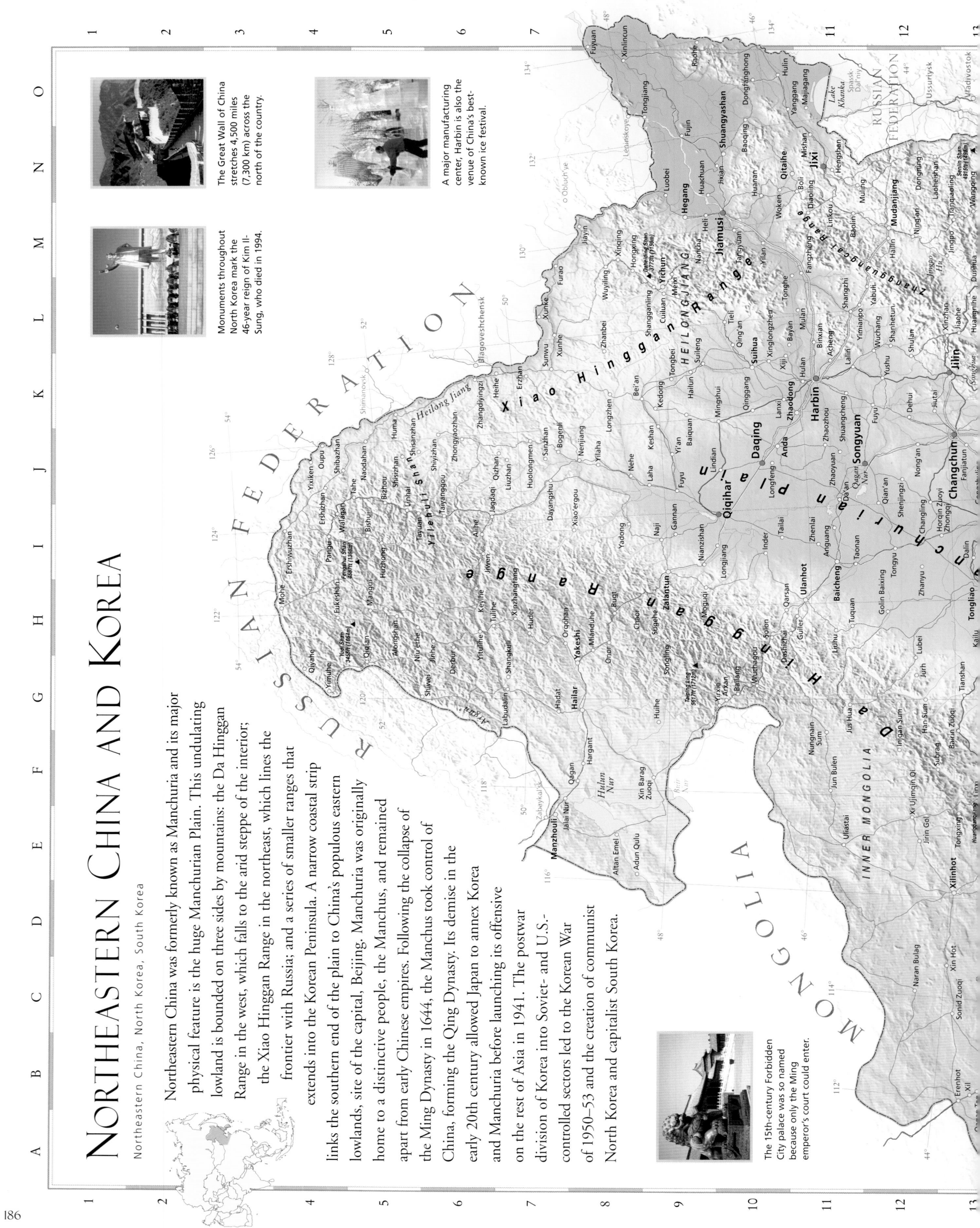

The Great Wall of China stretches 4,500 miles (7,300 km) across the north of the country.

Monuments throughout North Korea mark the 46-year reign of Kim Il-Sung, who died in 1994.

A major manufacturing center, Harbin is also the venue of China's best-known ice festival.

The 15th-century Forbidden City palace was so named because only the Ming emperor's court could enter.

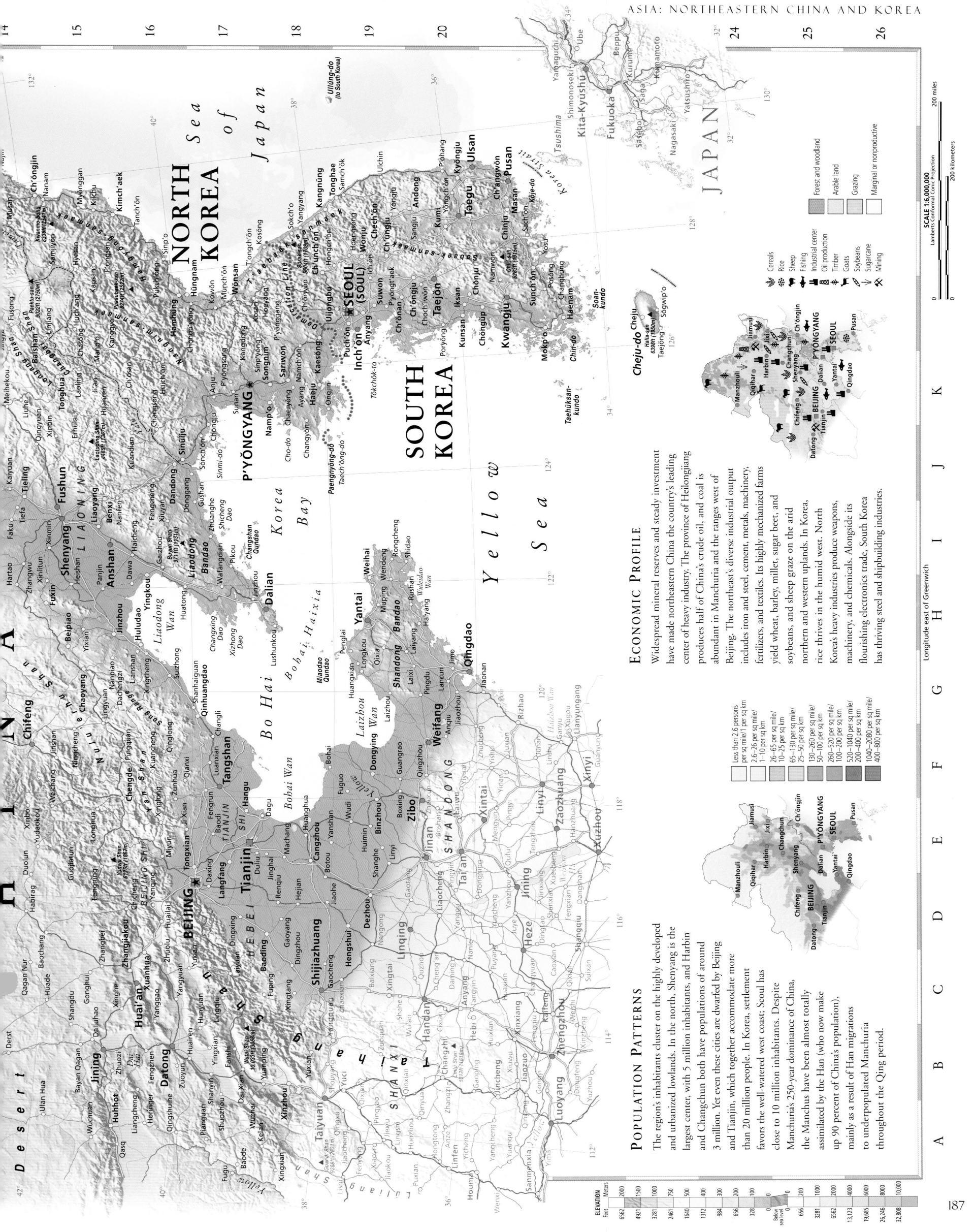

SOUTHEASTERN CHINA AND TAIWAN

The valleys of the Yellow and Yangtze rivers were the cradles of Chinese civilization, giving rise to China's first agricultural societies, around 9,000 years ago, and its first urban society, the Shang Dynasty, around 1800 BC. They remained the center of development under the Han, who united most of this region in 221 BC. The Han gradually expanded their territory westward beyond the broad Sichuan Basin to the plateaus of modern-day Gansu and the deep valleys and steep slopes of Yunnan, and southward through the eroded limestone hills of present-day Guangdong to the humid lowlands lining the South China Sea. The Yellow and Yangtze valleys, and the plains that divide them, are still the cultural and economic heart of modern China, and were developed intensively by the communist government during the second half of the 20th century. Taiwan also underwent dramatic economic growth in the 20th century, initially under Japanese rule (1895–1943) and then under the leadership of the Chinese Nationalist Party, which controlled the island until 2000.

An ancient system of waterways dating from the 7th century, China's Grand Canal links Beijing with Hangzhou.

About 6,000 life-size terra-cotta warriors guard the tomb of Emperor Qin Shi Huang (259–210 BC), at Xi'an in Shaanxi province.

POPULATION PATTERNS

The plains between the lower Yellow and Yangtze valleys now encompass 20 or so cities with more than 1 million inhabitants, including Shanghai, the nation's largest city, which has almost 13 million people. Other centers of population include the fertile Sichuan Basin, and the Pearl River Valley in the south. The Han are by far the largest ethnic group, but China's second-largest ethnic group, the Zhuang, cluster in the autonomous region of Guangxi Zhuangzu. Taiwan's mountainous terrain concentrates its large population on the northern and western coastal lowlands. Its indigenous Malayo-Polynesian inhabitants have, for the most part, been assimilated by Chinese immigrants, who began arriving in the 17th century.

Uninhabited

Less than 2.6 persons per sq mile/1 per sq km

2.6–26 per sq mile/ 1–10 per sq km

26–65 per sq mile/ 10–25 per sq km

65–130 per sq mile/ 25–50 per sq km

130–260 per sq mile/ 50–100 per sq km

260–520 per sq mile/ 100–200 per sq km

520–1040 per sq mile/ 200–400 per sq km

1040–2080 per sq mile/ 400–800 per sq km

More than 2080 per sq mile/800 per sq km

ECONOMIC PROFILE

The rich loess soils of the Yellow River have long provided wheat, millet, and cotton. Intensive farming of the fertile southeast and Sichuan Basin yields up to three crops a year, mainly of rice (of which China is the world's largest producer) and vegetables. Coal is abundant in Shanxi and Sichuan, which also has half of the nation's gas reserves; these resources underpin heavy industries in the interior. However, port cities such as Guangzhou and Shanghai have become the most prosperous centers, thanks to their long-established links with other Asian and Western trading partners and a recent influx of foreign investment. China is now the largest market for the exports—mainly electrical goods, metals, textiles, and plastics—that power Taiwan's thriving economy.

Forest and woodland

Arable land

Grazing

Marginal or nonproductive

Cereals
Rice
Beef cattle
Fishing
Industrial center
Mining
Oil production
Pigs
Gas production
Tea

Though resource-rich, the island of Hainan remains relatively undeveloped. Most of its people live by farming and fishing.

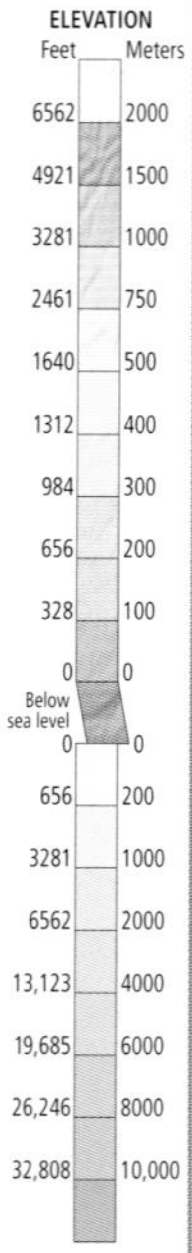

ELEVATION
Feet / Meters

6562 / 2000
4921 / 1500
3281 / 1000
2461 / 750
1640 / 500
1312 / 400
984 / 300
656 / 200
328 / 100
0 / 0
Below sea level
0 / 0
656 / 200
3281 / 1000
6562 / 2000
13,123 / 4000
19,685 / 6000
26,246 / 8000
32,808 / 10,000

Taiyuan
Lanzhou
Jinan
Xi'an
Zhengzhou
Huainan
Nanjing
Chengdu
Wuhan
Hangzhou
Shanghai
Chongqing
Changde
Nanchang
Changsha
Wenzhou
Guiyang
Kunming
Fuzhou
TAIPEI
Guangzhou
Nanning
Hong Kong
Kaohsiung
Haikou

Map labels

Linxi
Xiqing Shan
Lugu
Bayan Har Shan
Maqu
Chindu
Zhubgyugoin
Sangruma
Ru'nying
Zoigê
Bobso
Yushu
Chumda
Darlag
Xat'oi
Jigzhi
Tanggor
Hongyua
Song
Baitang
Zenda
Baima
Powo
Cairnyiggoin
Sanggam
Nanggên
Qagta
Loxur
Dege
Maniganggo
Sertar
Gana
Barkam
Shuafang
Zoggen
Rongbaca
Qiongla
SICHU
Tôba
Gamtog
Garzê
Qamdo
Qu'nyido
Baiyu
Luhuo
Jinchuan
Xiaojin
Guan X
Gyitang
Qêyr
Xinlong
Rinda
Danba
Day
Qiongla
Bamda
Yidun
Dawu
Kangding
Tianquan
Ya'an
Mei
Chuka
Batang
Litang
Gyawa
Gongga Shan 25,858ft (7514m)
Yingjing
Lesh
Markam
Chubalung
Mula
Lhabo
Jiulong
Jinkouhe
Qi
Yanjing
Sumdo
Zihag
Ganluo
Xiangcheng
Yuexi
Derong
Meigu
Soj
Degen
Dongmu
Warzhong
Yongshan
Renamo
Yanmen
Zhongdian
Xichang
Zhaoque
Da
Hexi
Butuo
Yi
Jodian
Yulongxue Shan 18,360ft (5596m)
Yanyuan
Puge
Zhaotong
Fugong
Weixi
Guangmao Shan 13,198ft (4023m)
Yimen
Ningnan
Dashuijing
Shigu
Jianchuan
Yongsheng
Huili
Huidong
Lushui
Eryuan
Jinjiang
Lixi
Luchang
Dongchuan
Diancang Shan 13,524ft (4122m)
Panzhihua
Yu
Caojian
Yangbi
Dali
Dayao
Yongren
Wuding
Zhany
Myitkyina
Yongping
Qiansuo
Yao'an
Tengchong
Baoshan
Weishan
Nanhua
Yipinglang
Songming
Liaoh
Lianghe
Chuxiong
Anning
Kunming
Luxi
Fengging
YUNNAN
Sanjiachang
Beicheng
Yiliang
Shiz
Yunxian
Yuxi
Mile
Bhamo
Yingjiang
Maotou Shan 10,848ft (3306m)
Longwu
Tonghai
Ruili
Wanding
Gengma
Uncang
Jiasa
Yangwu
Kaiyuan
Qi
Tropic of Cancer
Kutkare
Shuangjiang
Mojiang
Shiping
Hanshuh
Ya
Cangyuan
Jinggu
Yuanjiang
Gejiu
Mengzi
We
Shangyun
Pu'er
Simao
Na
Munai
Mengzhe
Jinghong
L
Menghai
Phonasali
La Chao
Mengla
Mengzhe
Jingzhou
Muang Khoua
Kengtung
Mengla
Muang
Namtha
Qi
Luang
MYANMAR (BURMA)
LAOS
VI

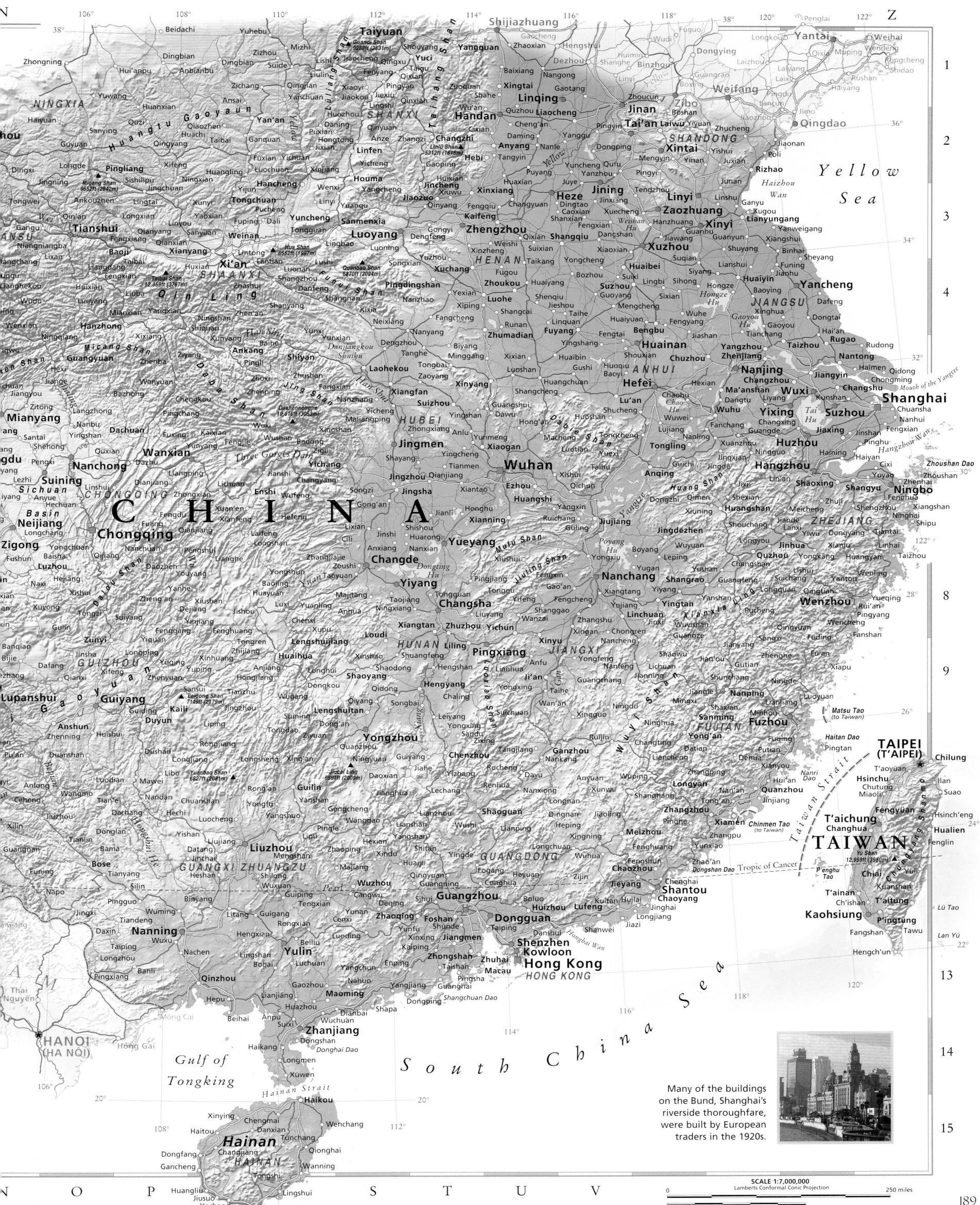

Many of the buildings
on the Bund, Shanghai's
riverside thoroughfare,
were built by European
traders in the 1920s.

SCALE 1:7,000,000
Lamberts Conformal Conic Projection

0   250 miles

0   250 kilometers

Mainland Southeast Asia

Cambodia, Laos, Myanmar (Burma), Thailand, Vietnam

The Southeast Asian mainland consists of a broad peninsula—sometimes referred to as the Indochina Peninsula—that extends southeastward from the borders of Bangladesh, India, and China, as well as part of its narrow offshoot, the Malay Peninsula. From the Chinese Himalaya, a series of mountain ranges divided by rivers fans out over the north. On the southern lowlands, these rivers, which include the Irrawaddy and the Mekong, have formed wide alluvial plains and deltas. In the 16th century, towns along the coast became bases for European traders. By the late 19th century, Britain controlled Burma (now Myanmar) and France ruled Indochina (present-day Laos, Cambodia, and Vietnam). Post-World War II decolonization led to civil wars in Indochina, including the Vietnam War of 1964–75. Only Thailand resisted colonization throughout its history; its independence and political stability have helped it become the region's leading economic power.

Population Patterns

Ethnically diverse, the inhabitants of Mainland Southeast Asia live mainly in rural villages. They are concentrated along the river valleys and especially the deltas of the Irrawaddy, Chao Phraya, Mekong, and Red rivers; they are sparsest in the heavily forested uplands of Cambodia, Laos, and the Myanmar–Thailand border. Though only about a quarter of the population is urban, the region has several large cities, most notably Bangkok (which is 20 times the size of Thailand's second city, Nonthaburi). Population growth is especially high in Laos and Cambodia; in contrast, Thailand has dramatically slowed its growth through social policies and education.

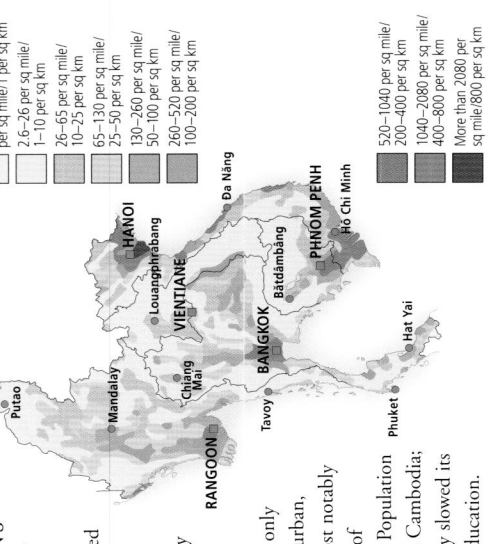

Eastern Myanmar is the world's second-biggest source of illegal opium.

Economic Profile

Agriculture is still the principal source of employment and many people, especially in the poorer countries of Cambodia, Laos, Vietnam, and Myanmar, depend on subsistence cultivation, mainly of rice, corn, and vegetables. Cash crops including rubber, palm oil, sugar, and tropical fruits make up the bulk of exports, whereas most manufactured goods are imported. Industrial development is most advanced in Thailand, which produces textiles, foodstuffs, and electrical goods, and has a thriving tourist trade. Cambodia, Laos, and Myanmar continue to exploit their extensive forests for timber, whereas Thailand now limits harvesting following overexploitation. The area where Myanmar, Thailand, and Laos meet, known as the "Golden Triangle," is a major source of opium, from which heroin is derived.

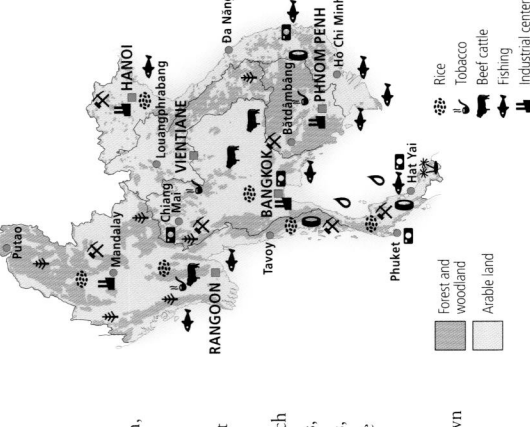

Most of the world's high-quality rubies come from mines in northern Myanmar.

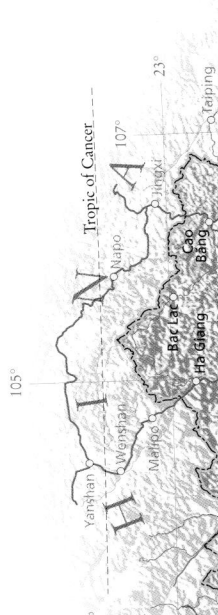
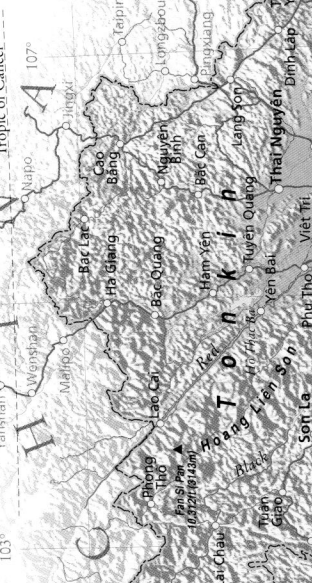

Rice is the most widespread crop in Vietnam, covering approximately 80 percent of the country's arable land.

Population density legend

- Less than 2.6 persons per sq mile/1 per sq km
- 2.6–26 per sq mile/1–10 per sq km
- 26–65 per sq mile/10–25 per sq km
- 65–130 per sq mile/25–50 per sq km
- 130–260 per sq mile/50–100 per sq km
- 260–520 per sq mile/100–200 per sq km
- 520–1040 per sq mile/200–400 per sq km
- 1040–2080 per sq mile/400–800 per sq km
- More than 2080 per sq mile/800 per sq km

Economic map legend

- Rice
- Tobacco
- Beef cattle
- Fishing
- Industrial center
- Mining
- Gas production
- Timber
- Rubber
- Tourism
- Palm oil

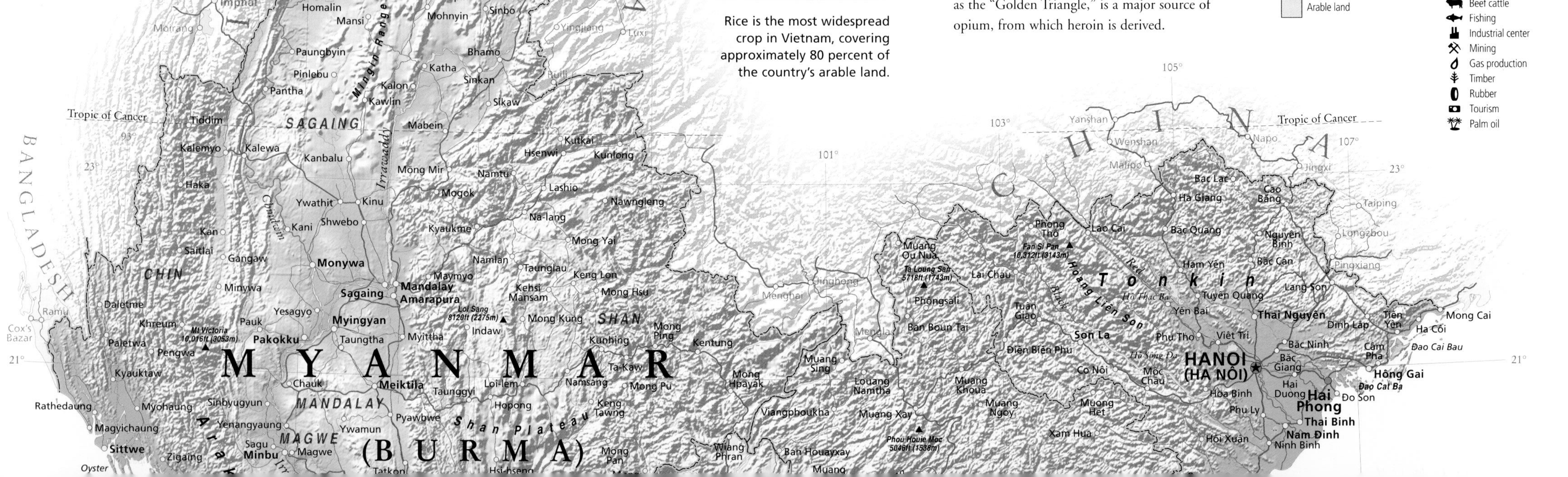

- Forest and woodland
- Arable land

Map labels (population patterns inset)

Putao, Mandalay, HANOI, Louangphrabang, VIENTIANE, Chiang Mai, BANGKOK, Da Nang, Batdâmbâng, PHNOM PENH, Hô Chi Minh, RANGOON, Tavoy, Hat Yai, Phuket

Map labels (economic profile inset)

Putao, Mandalay, HANOI, Louangphrabang, VIENTIANE, Chiang Mai, BANGKOK, Da Nang, Batdâmbâng, PHNOM PENH, Hô Chi Minh, RANGOON, Tavoy, Hat Yai, Phuket

Main map labels

CHINA, MYANMAR (BURMA), BANGLADESH, CAMBODIA (partial), TONKIN, HANOI (HA NOI), Hai Phong, Mong Cai, Haiphong, The Triangle, Hkakabo Razi (19,294ft [5881m]), Putao, Saramati (12,553ft [3826m]), KACHIN, SAGAING, MANDALAY, MAGWE, CHIN, SHAN, Shan Plateau, Arakan, Irrawaddy, Chindwin, Mandalay, Amarapura, Sittwe, Rathedaung, Cox's Bazar

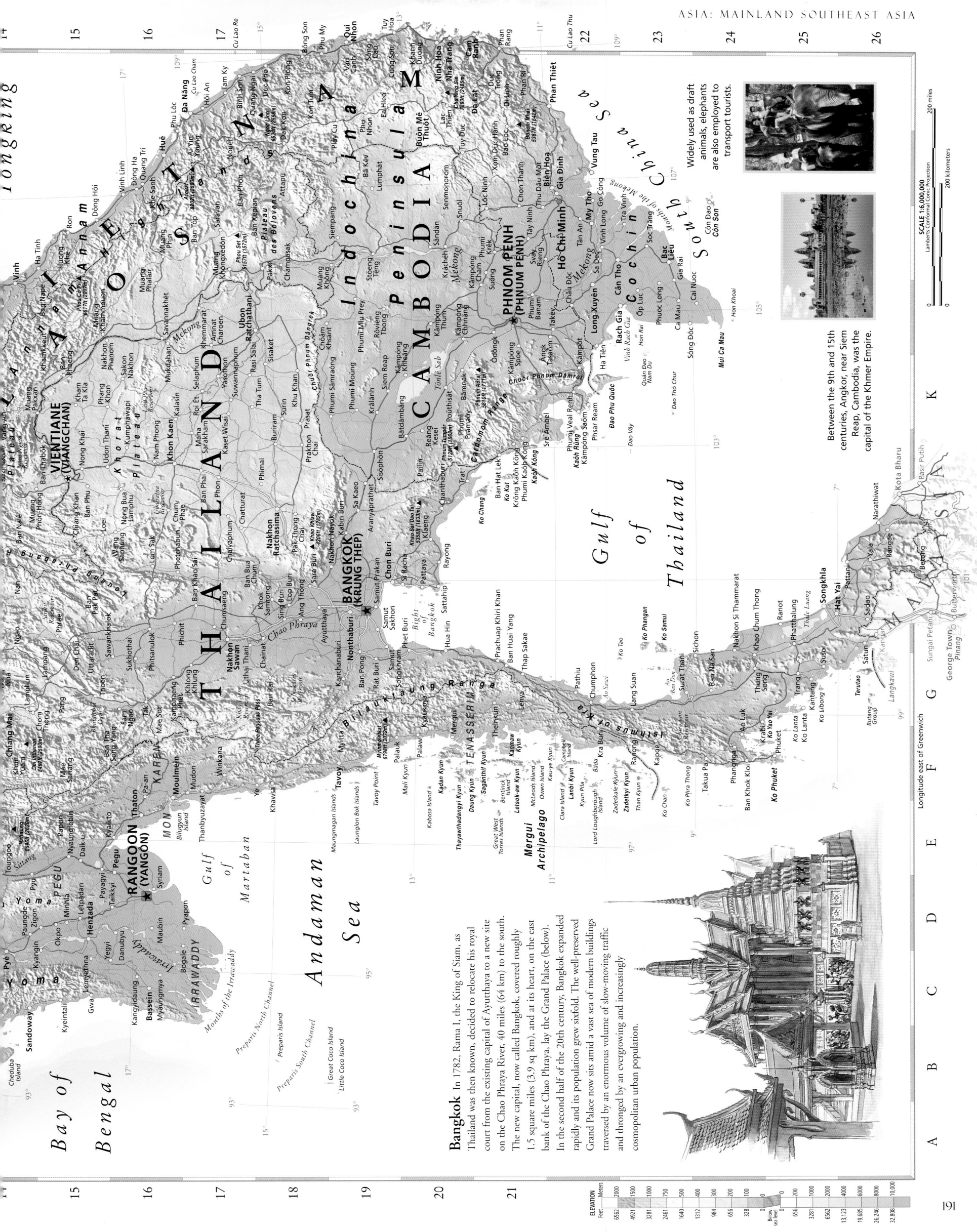

Bangkok In 1782, Rama I, the King of Siam, as Thailand was then known, decided to relocate his royal court from the existing capital of Ayutthaya to a new site on the Chao Phraya River, 40 miles (64 km) to the south. The new capital, now called Bangkok, covered roughly 1.5 square miles (3.9 sq km), and at its heart, on the east bank of the Chao Phraya, lay the Grand Palace (below). In the second half of the 20th century, Bangkok expanded rapidly and its population grew sixfold. The well-preserved Grand Palace now sits amid a vast sea of modern buildings traversed by an enormous volume of slow-moving traffic and thronged by an evergrowing and increasingly cosmopolitan urban population.

Widely used as draft animals, elephants are also employed to transport tourists.

Between the 9th and 15th centuries, Angkor, near Siem Reap, Cambodia, was the capital of the Khmer Empire.

SCALE 1:6,000,000
Lamberts Conformal Conic Projection

0   200 miles

0   200 kilometers

ELEVATION

Feet	Meters
6562	2000
4921	1500
3281	1000
2461	750
1640	500
1312	400
984	300
656	200
328	100
Below sea level	Below sea level
328	-200
656	-1000
3281	-2000
6562	-3000
13,123	-4000
19,685	-6000
26,246	-8000
32,808	-10,000

MARITIME SOUTHEAST ASIA

Brunei, East Timor, Indonesia, Malaysia, Philippines, Singapore

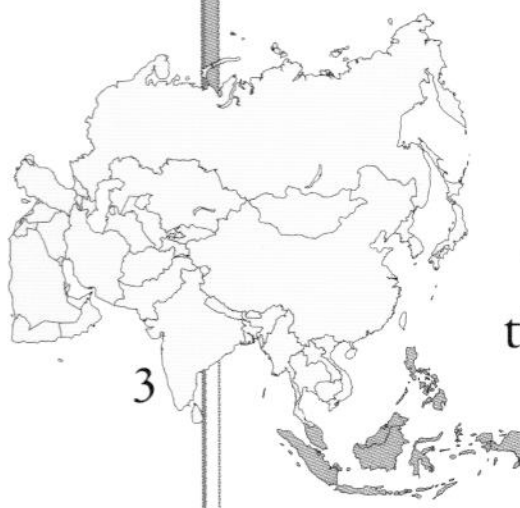

Scattered around the southeastern fringe of the Asian mainland are more than 20,000 islands. Ranging from the massive, rain-forest-cloaked landmass of Borneo—the world's third-largest island—to the tiny atolls of the Banda Sea, they form the largest island group on Earth, the Malay Archipelago. Divided mainly between the large countries of Malaysia (which includes the southern part of the Malay Peninsula), the Philippines, and Indonesia, it is also the site of the small states of Singapore, East Timor, and Brunei. Beginning in the 16th century, intense competition for control of the lucrative spice trade led various European powers to colonize large areas of the region. The Dutch seized most of present-day Indonesia, the British gradually gained control of Malaysia, the Portuguese established a foothold in Timor, and the Spanish occupied the Philippines (from where they were ousted by the U.S.A. in 1898). Since decolonization in the second half of the 20th century, Indonesia and Malaysia, in particular, have become major regional powers.

JAVA'S VOLCANOES

The islands of southern Indonesia formed as a result of subduction of the Indo-Australian Plate beneath the Eurasian Plate. This process continues to fuel the country's 76 volcanoes (more than any other nation), 22 of which are on Java. Sporadic and sometimes destructive volcanic activity takes place at Gunung Semeru in the east, Gunung Merapi near Yogyakarta, and Galunggung in the west. But the largest recorded eruption occurred on August 28, 1883, when Krakatau (Krakatoa) exploded, unleashing a tidal wave that killed 36,000 people.

Native to Borneo and Sumatra, the orangutan has become endangered due to habitat loss.

East Timor attained independence in 2002, following almost 25 years of Indonesian rule.

Controlled by the Dutch from 1619 to 1941, Jakarta became the capital of Indonesia in 1949.

Christmas Island (to Australia)

Longitude east of Greenwich

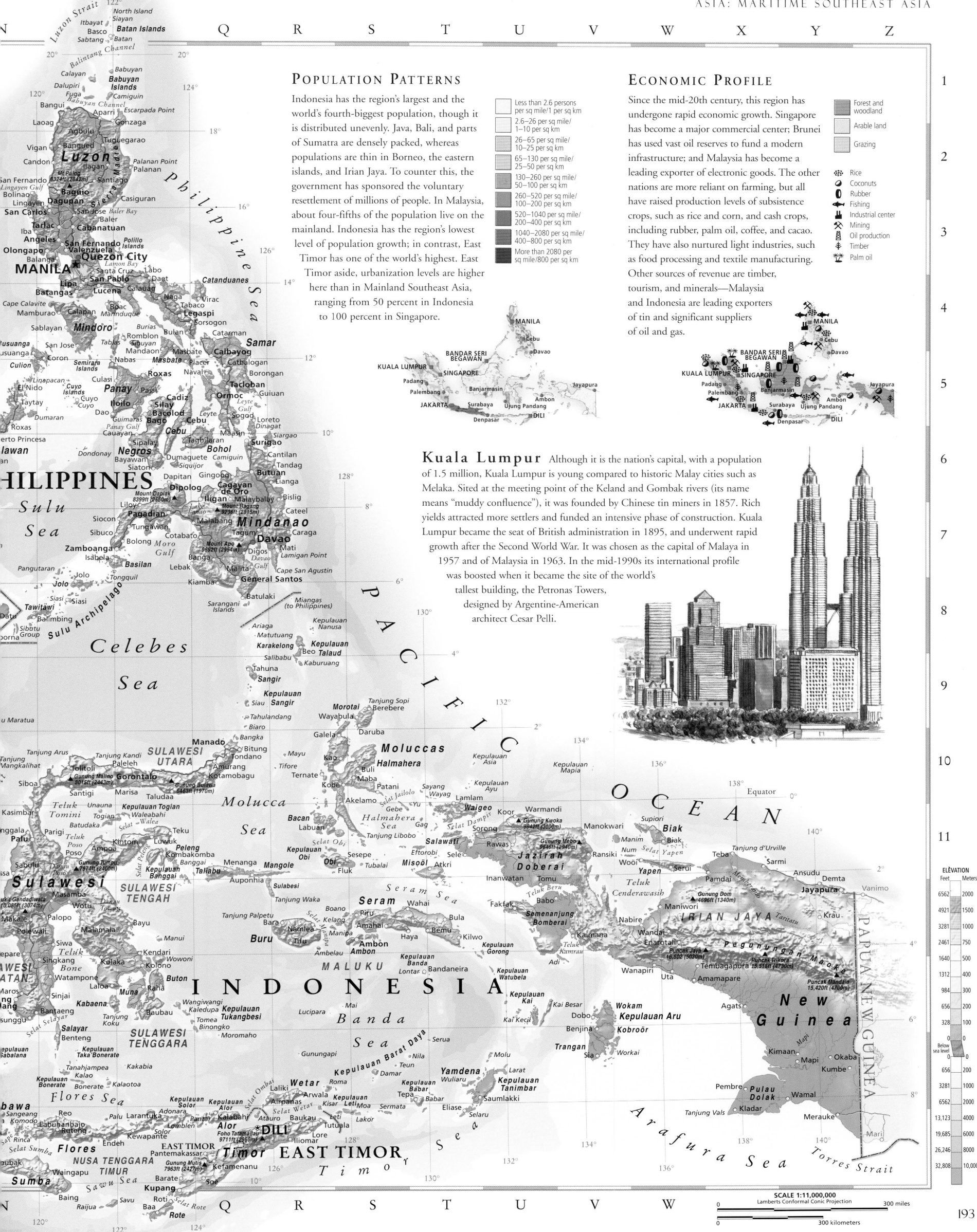

POPULATION PATTERNS

Indonesia has the region's largest and the world's fourth-biggest population, though it is distributed unevenly. Java, Bali, and parts of Sumatra are densely packed, whereas populations are thin in Borneo, the eastern islands, and Irian Jaya. To counter this, the government has sponsored the voluntary resettlement of millions of people. In Malaysia, about four-fifths of the population live on the mainland. Indonesia has the region's lowest level of population growth; in contrast, East Timor has one of the world's highest. East Timor aside, urbanization levels are higher here than in Mainland Southeast Asia, ranging from 50 percent in Indonesia to 100 percent in Singapore.

Less than 2.6 persons per sq mile/1 per sq km
2.6–26 per sq mile/ 1–10 per sq km
26–65 per sq mile/ 10–25 per sq km
65–130 per sq mile/ 25–50 per sq km
130–260 per sq mile/ 50–100 per sq km
260–520 per sq mile/ 100–200 per sq km
520–1040 per sq mile/ 200–400 per sq km
1040–2080 per sq mile/ 400–800 per sq km
More than 2080 per sq mile/800 per sq km

ECONOMIC PROFILE

Since the mid-20th century, this region has undergone rapid economic growth. Singapore has become a major commercial center; Brunei has used vast oil reserves to fund a modern infrastructure; and Malaysia has become a leading exporter of electronic goods. The other nations are more reliant on farming, but all have raised production levels of subsistence crops, such as rice and corn, and cash crops, including rubber, palm oil, coffee, and cacao. They have also nurtured light industries, such as food processing and textile manufacturing. Other sources of revenue are timber, tourism, and minerals—Malaysia and Indonesia are leading exporters of tin and significant suppliers of oil and gas.

Forest and woodland
Arable land
Grazing

Rice
Coconuts
Rubber
Fishing
Industrial center
Mining
Oil production
Timber
Palm oil

Kuala Lumpur

Although it is the nation's capital, with a population of 1.5 million, Kuala Lumpur is young compared to historic Malay cities such as Melaka. Sited at the meeting point of the Keland and Gombak rivers (its name means "muddy confluence"), it was founded by Chinese tin miners in 1857. Rich yields attracted more settlers and funded an intensive phase of construction. Kuala Lumpur became the seat of British administration in 1895, and underwent rapid growth after the Second World War. It was chosen as the capital of Malaya in 1957 and of Malaysia in 1963. In the mid-1990s its international profile was boosted when it became the site of the world's tallest building, the Petronas Towers, designed by Argentine-American architect Cesar Pelli.

ELEVATION
Feet	Meters
6562	2000
4921	1500
3281	1000
2461	750
1640	500
1312	400
984	300
656	200
328	100
Below sea level	
656	200
3281	1000
6562	2000
13,123	4000
19,685	6000
26,246	8000
32,808	10,000

SCALE 1:11,000,000
Lamberts Conformal Conic Projection
300 miles
300 kilometers

BRUNEI, MALAYSIA, AND SINGAPORE

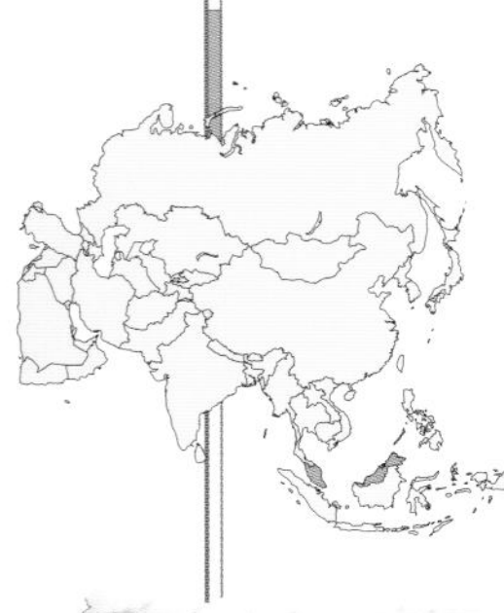

Malaysia comprises the southern third of the Malay Peninsula and the northern third of the island of Borneo. Divided by the South China Sea, these territories are known, respectively, as West (or Peninsular) Malaysia and East Malaysia (which is made up of the states of Sabah and Sarawak). Nestled on their fringes are two small independent states: Singapore, a tiny island republic on the southern tip of West Malaysia, and Brunei, a sultanate consisting of two enclaves on the north shore of East Malaysia. When the Portuguese arrived in the early 16th century, the Malay Peninsula and northern Borneo were divided into autonomous Islamic sultanates. In the 19th century, most of these states were brought under British control. Following Japanese occupation during the Second World War, the sultanates of the Malay Peninsula gained independence from Britain as Malaya in 1957; in 1963, they invited Singapore, Sabah, Sarawak, and Brunei to unite with them as Malaysia. All but Brunei accepted, though Singapore seceded peacefully in 1965. Today, these three states are among the most prosperous in Southeast Asia.

The jagged summit of Mount Kinabalu, Malaysia's highest peak, looms above a mosque near Kota Kinabalu.

Malaysia's largest port, George Town, occupies a sheltered position on the east side of the island of Pinang.

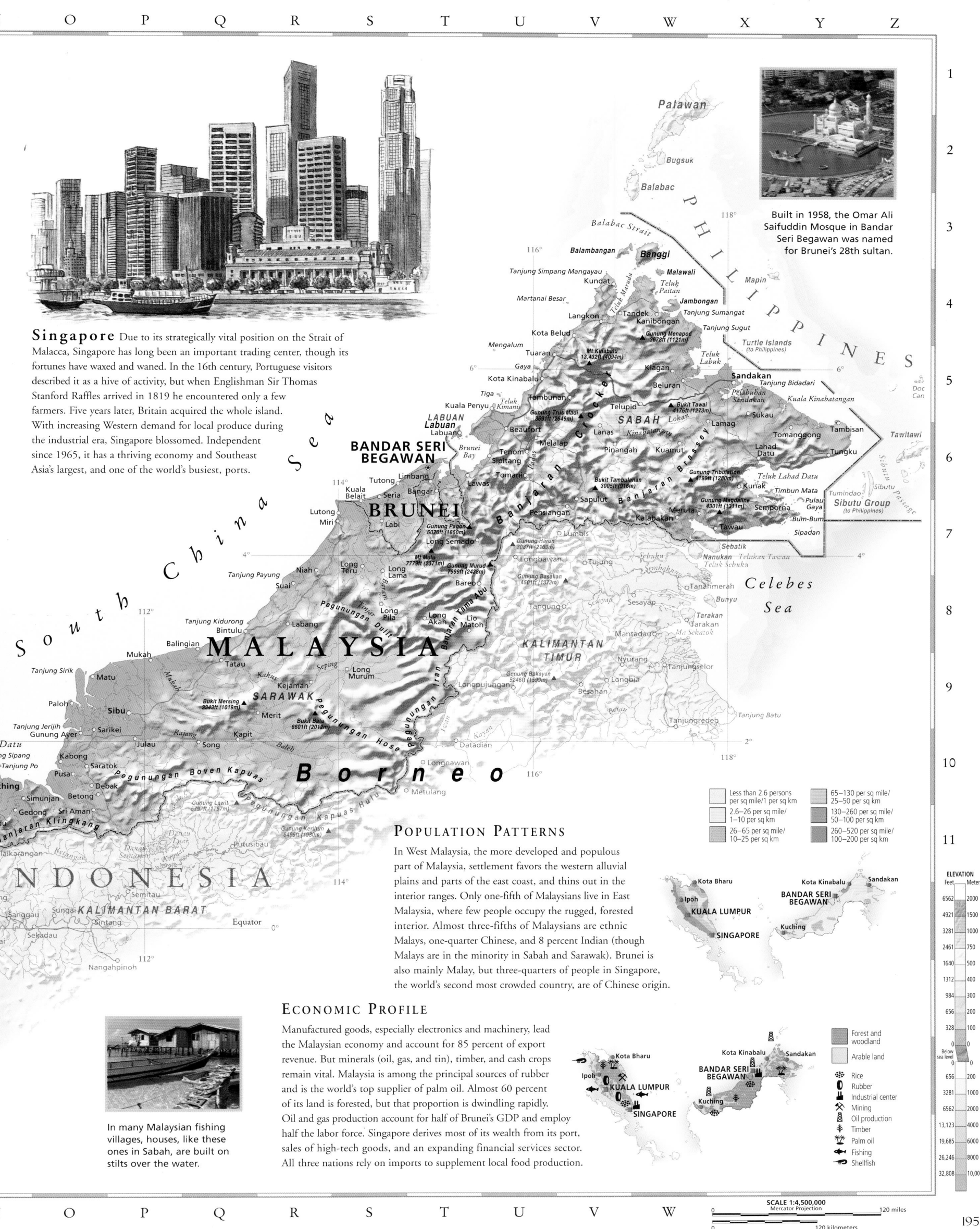

Singapore Due to its strategically vital position on the Strait of Malacca, Singapore has long been an important trading center, though its fortunes have waxed and waned. In the 16th century, Portuguese visitors described it as a hive of activity, but when Englishman Sir Thomas Stanford Raffles arrived in 1819 he encountered only a few farmers. Five years later, Britain acquired the whole island. With increasing Western demand for local produce during the industrial era, Singapore blossomed. Independent since 1965, it has a thriving economy and Southeast Asia's largest, and one of the world's busiest, ports.

Built in 1958, the Omar Ali Saifuddin Mosque in Bandar Seri Begawan was named for Brunei's 28th sultan.

In many Malaysian fishing villages, houses, like these ones in Sabah, are built on stilts over the water.

POPULATION PATTERNS

In West Malaysia, the more developed and populous part of Malaysia, settlement favors the western alluvial plains and parts of the east coast, and thins out in the interior ranges. Only one-fifth of Malaysians live in East Malaysia, where few people occupy the rugged, forested interior. Almost three-fifths of Malaysians are ethnic Malays, one-quarter Chinese, and 8 percent Indian (though Malays are in the minority in Sabah and Sarawak). Brunei is also mainly Malay, but three-quarters of people in Singapore, the world's second most crowded country, are of Chinese origin.

Less than 2.6 persons per sq mile/1 per sq km	65–130 per sq mile/ 25–50 per sq km
2.6–26 per sq mile/ 1–10 per sq km	130–260 per sq mile/ 50–100 per sq km
26–65 per sq mile/ 10–25 per sq km	260–520 per sq mile/ 100–200 per sq km

ECONOMIC PROFILE

Manufactured goods, especially electronics and machinery, lead the Malaysian economy and account for 85 percent of export revenue. But minerals (oil, gas, and tin), timber, and cash crops remain vital. Malaysia is among the principal sources of rubber and is the world's top supplier of palm oil. Almost 60 percent of its land is forested, but that proportion is dwindling rapidly. Oil and gas production account for half of Brunei's GDP and employ half the labor force. Singapore derives most of its wealth from its port, sales of high-tech goods, and an expanding financial services sector. All three nations rely on imports to supplement local food production.

Forest and woodland
Arable land

Rice
Rubber
Industrial center
Mining
Oil production
Timber
Palm oil
Fishing
Shellfish

ELEVATION

Feet	Meters
6562	2000
4921	1500
3281	1000
2461	750
1640	500
1312	400
984	300
656	200
328	100
0 Below sea level	0
656	200
3281	1000
6562	2000
13,123	4000
19,685	6000
26,246	8000
32,808	10,000

SCALE 1:4,500,000
Mercator Projection
0 — 120 miles
0 — 120 kilometers

195

THE PHILIPPINES

A physically fractured country made up of more than 7,000 mainly volcanic islands, the Philippines encompasses 116,000 square miles (300,000 sq km) of land between China and Indonesia. Its two largest islands, Luzon in the north and Mindanao in the south, account for two-thirds of the country's area. Most of the islands are mountainous with narrow coastal plains. The indigenous inhabitants, the Filipinos, are of Malay origin, but modern Philippine society displays conspicuous colonial influences. Following Ferdinand Magellan's visit in 1521, Spain controlled the archipelago (naming it after its king, Philip II) from 1565 until 1898, when it was ceded to the U.S.A. Under Spanish rule, most of the population converted to Catholicism; under the Americans, English became the colony's lingua franca. The Second World War, during which Japan occupied the islands, delayed independence, which was achieved in 1946. In 1986, the repressive, 21-year rule of Ferdinand Marcos was ended by a popular uprising. A fragile democracy has since been held, despite attempted coups, economic crises, and violence perpetrated by Muslim separatists, particularly on the islands of Mindanao and Basilan.

These rice terraces near Banaue, Luzon, were first built by the local Ifugao people 2,000 years ago.

Mayon in southeastern Luzon is a highly active volcano that poses a threat to nearby towns.

Manila

Spanish forces arrived in Manila, a trading post dating back to the 12th century, in 1571. Having ousted the local Muslim ruler, they constructed a fortress called Intramuros, whose 20-foot (6-m) walls eventually enclosed a town with 15 churches and 6 monasteries. Much of Intramuros was obliterated during the Second World War. Remnants of the Spanish colony include the church and monastery of San Augustin, built in 1599, and Fort Santiago, which dates from the mid-17th century.

San Augustin Church

Fort Santiago

POPULATION PATTERNS

The archipelago is densely though unevenly populated. The most developed area is central Luzon: Manila alone is home to 10 million people. Other areas, such as central Mindanao, Palawan, and northern Luzon, are sparsely inhabited. The population growth rate is high. Significant migration takes place, to the cities—urbanization has risen from 20 percent in 1900 to 63 percent in 2000—and overseas. More than 70 native languages are spoken; the official languages are Filipino (the Tagalog language of southern Luzon) and English.

ECONOMIC PROFILE

About 20 percent of the land is arable and agriculture is the biggest employer. Rice and corn are the staple crops, sugar and coconuts the main exports. Fishing is also important. Abundant minerals include some of the world's largest deposits of nickel, copper, and chromite. Electronic goods, mainly assembled in foreign-owned factories using imported parts, account for over half of exports. Other industrial products include textiles, metals, chemicals, and foodstuffs. Substantial income is also derived from tourism.

Less than 2.6 persons per sq mile/1 per sq km
2.6–26 per sq mile/1–10 per sq km
26–65 per sq mile/10–25 per sq km
65–130 per sq mile/25–50 per sq km
130–260 per sq mile/50–100 per sq km
260–520 per sq mile/100–200 per sq km
520–1040 per sq mile/200–400 per sq km
1040–2080 per sq mile/400–800 per sq km

Forest and woodland
Arable land
Grazing

Rice
Coconuts
Fishing
Industrial center
Mining
Oil production
Timber
Sugarcane

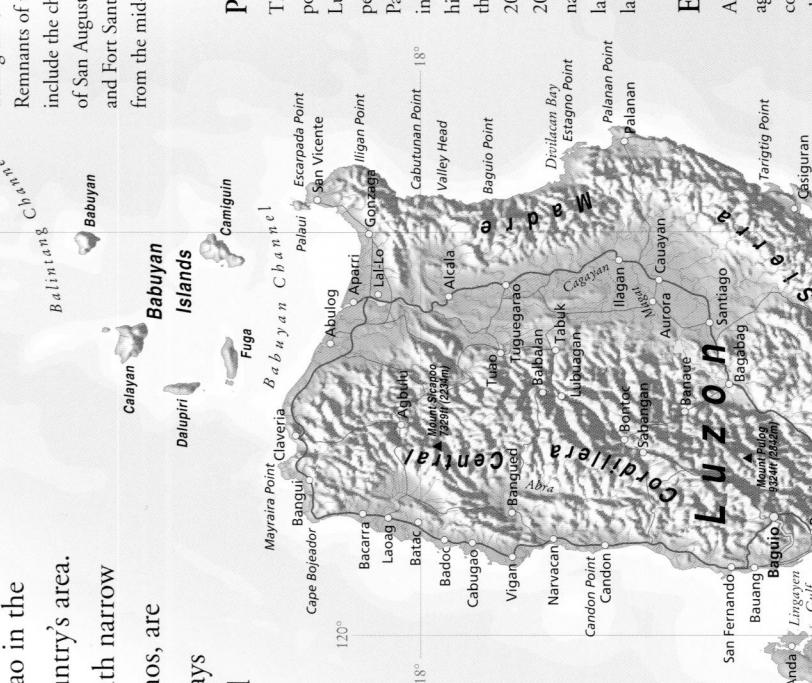
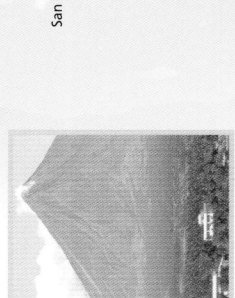

MANILA
Aparri
Dagupan
Roxas
Cebu
Legaspi
Davao
Zamboanga

PHILIPPINES

A distinctively Filipino mode of transport, jeepneys were originally modified U.S.-Army-surplus jeeps.

Up to 25 typhoons strike the Philippines each year. They are most common in the east around Samar and Leyte.

SCALE 1:4,000,000
Lamberts Conformal Conic Projection

0   120 miles

0   120 kilometers

ELEVATION

Feet	Meters
6562	2000
4921	1500
3281	1000
2461	750
1640	500
1312	400
984	300
656	200
328	100
0	0
Below sea level	Below sea level
656	200
1312	400
3281	1000
6562	2000
13,123	4000
19,685	6000
26,246	8000
32,808	10,000

Longitude east of Greenwich

Philippine Sea

South China Sea

Sulu Sea

Visayan Sea

Bohol Sea

Celebes Sea

Moro Gulf

Leyte Gulf

Davao Gulf

Panay Gulf

INDONESIA

Kepulauan Nanusa

Kepulauan Talaud

Miangas (to Philippines)

MALAYSIA

Luzon

Samar

Leyte

Biliran

Masbate

Ticao

Panay

Negros

Cebu

Bohol

Siquijor

Camiguin

Mindanao

Palawan

Mindoro

Tablas

Sibuyan

Romblon

Busuanga

Calamian Group

Culion

Dumaran

Cuyo Islands

Cagayan Islands

Semirata Islands

Dalanganem Islands

Calauit

Basilan

Jolo

Siasi

Tawitawi

Sibutu Group

Turtle Islands

Sarangani Islands

Sulu Archipelago

Tapul Group

Pangutaran Group

Samales Group

Cordillera Range

Diuata Mountains

Kalatungan Mountains

Zamboanga Peninsula

Davao

Cagayan de Oro

General Santos

Zamboanga

Pagadian

Dipolog

Cotabato

Iligan

Marawi

Butuan

Surigao

Tacloban

Ormoc

Calbayog

Catbalogan

Roxas

Iloilo

Bacolod

Bago

Silay

Cadiz

San Carlos

Toledo

Cebu

Mandaue

Lapu-Lapu

Dumaguete

Tagbilaran

Puerto Princesa

Mount Apo 9692ft (2954m)

Mount Dulang-dulang 9639ft (2938m)

Mount Kitanglad 9511ft (2899m)

Mount Hilong Hilong 6611ft (2012m)

Mount Malindang 7956ft (2425m)

Mount Matutum 7536ft (2295m)

Mount Ragang 9393ft (2815m)

Mount Dajak 8891ft (2710m)

Mount Canlaon 8087ft (2465m)

Mount Guiting-Guiting 6726ft (2050m)

Mount Mantalingajan 6739ft (2054m)

Cleopatra Needle 5226ft (1593m)

Victoria Peak 5607ft (1709m)

Mount Espetoah 2789ft (850m)

JAPAN

Although it occupies a strategically important position off the northeast coast of Asia, Japan remained isolated from outside influences for long periods of its history. It limited relations with its neighbors from the ninth century and adopted an official policy of isolation in 1639, soon after the arrival of the first Western missionaries and explorers. Only in the mid-19th century did it open up to foreign influences and trade.

Its subsequent attempts to expand its empire led to international conflicts and a devastating defeat in the Second World War. Yet the nation recovered spectacularly to become the world's second-strongest industrial power after the United States and wield an economic and political influence far out of proportion to its small size. Occupying a land area smaller than California, Japan consists of about 4,000 islands, dominated by the large islands of Hokkaidō, Honshū, Shikoku, and Kyūshū. In the interiors of these islands, mountain ranges are separated by river valleys and bounded by narrow coastal plains. Being situated on the Pacific Rim of Fire, the country experiences regular earthquakes and volcanic eruptions, which periodically wreak havoc on the land and its people.

POPULATION PATTERNS

About 80 percent of Japan is mountainous and has low-to-moderate levels of population density; the other 20 percent, however—mainly valleys and coastal plains—supports the bulk of the population and includes some of the world's most densely inhabited areas. Urban dwellers account for 80 percent of the inhabitants and the capital, Tokyo, is the world's largest urban center. The population is ethnically homogenous, with 99 percent being Japanese. About 84% follow both Buddhist and Shinto traditions. In recent years, a declining birth rate and rapidly aging population have heightened concerns about labor shortages and the cost of maintaining social services.

ECONOMIC PROFILE

Japan is an economic superpower despite having only a small area of cultivable land and modest mineral resources (small deposits of copper, coal, and iron ore and meager reserves of oil and gas). Its success is due mainly to government support and innovation: large subsidies and intensive farming practices have helped it become virtually self-sufficient in rice and produce large quantities of fruit and vegetables; heavy investment in education, research, and technology have created a sophisticated industrial sector renowned for machinery and electronic goods. Even the nation's impressive fish catches, accounting for 15 percent of world totals, are due in part to the use of technology-loaded, wide-ranging fishing boats. This industrial success has greatly increased export revenue; however, a recession in the late 1990s cast a shadow over the nation's economic future.

In winter, mountain-dwelling macaque monkeys stay warm by sitting in pools fed by hot springs.

Bullet trains began operating in 1964. They now have a top speed of 160 mph (260 km/h).

ELEVATION

Feet	Meters
6562	2000
4921	1500
3281	1000
2461	750
1640	500
1312	400
984	300
656	200
328	100
0	0
Below sea level	Below sea level
656	200
3281	1000
6562	2000
13,123	4000
19,685	6000
26,246	8000
32,808	10,000

Population density:

- Less than 2.6 persons per sq mile/1 per sq km
- 2.6–26 per sq mile/1–10 per sq km
- 26–65 per sq mile/10–25 per sq km
- 65–130 per sq mile/25–50 per sq km
- 130–260 per sq mile/50–100 per sq km
- 260–520 per sq mile/100–200 per sq km
- 520–1040 per sq mile/200–400 per sq km
- 1040–2080 per sq mile/400–800 per sq km
- More than 2080 per sq mile/800 per sq km

- Forest and woodland
- Arable land

- Rice
- Fruit
- Tobacco
- Beef cattle
- Fishing
- Industrial center
- Winter sports

Sapporo · Sendai · TOKYO · Nagoya · Osaka · Hiroshima · Kagoshima

PACIFIC OCEAN

Sea of Okhotsk

RUSSIAN FEDERATION

Kuril Islands

(Administered by Russian Federation claimed by Japan)

Sakhalin

La Pérouse Strait

HOKKAIDŌ

Sapporo · Asahikawa · Obihiro · Kushiro · Kitami · Tomakomai · Muroran · Hakodate · Otaru

JAPAN

Aomori · Hachinohe · Morioka · Akita · Yamagata · Sendai

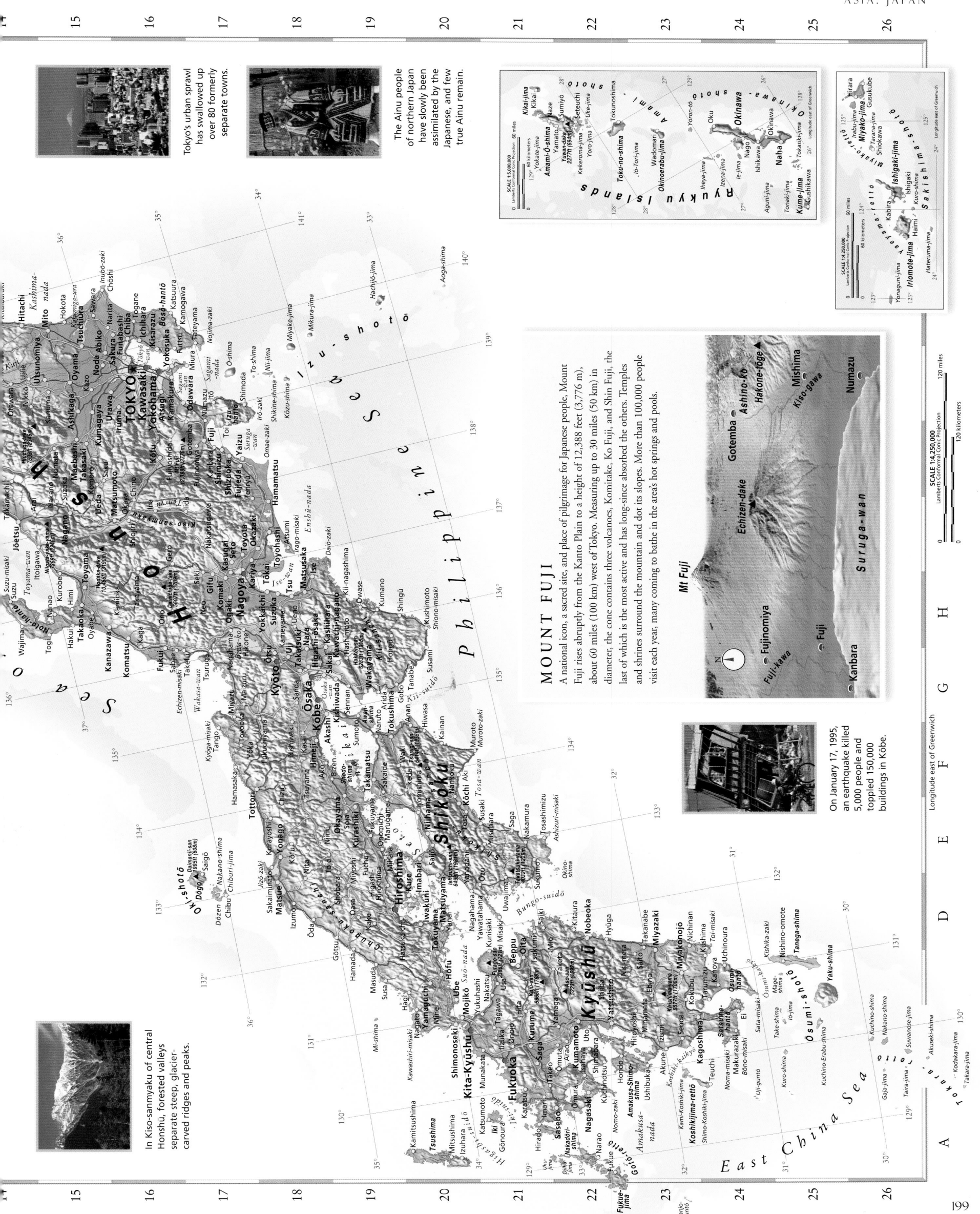

In Kiso-sanmyaku of central Honshū, forested valleys separate steep, glacier-carved ridges and peaks.

Tokyo's urban sprawl has swallowed up over 80 formerly separate towns.

The Ainu people of northern Japan have slowly been assimilated by the Japanese, and few true Ainu remain.

MOUNT FUJI

A national icon, a sacred site, and place of pilgrimage for Japanese people, Mount Fuji rises abruptly from the Kanto Plain to a height of 12,388 feet (3,776 m), about 60 miles (100 km) west of Tokyo. Measuring up to 30 miles (50 km) in diameter, the cone contains three volcanoes, Komitake, Ko Fuji, and Shin Fuji, the last of which is the most active and has long-since absorbed the others. Temples and shrines surround the mountain and dot its slopes. More than 100,000 people visit each year, many coming to bathe in the area's hot springs and pools.

On January 17, 1995, an earthquake killed 5,000 people and toppled 150,000 buildings in Kōbe.

SCALE 1:4,250,000
Lamberts Conformal Conic Projection

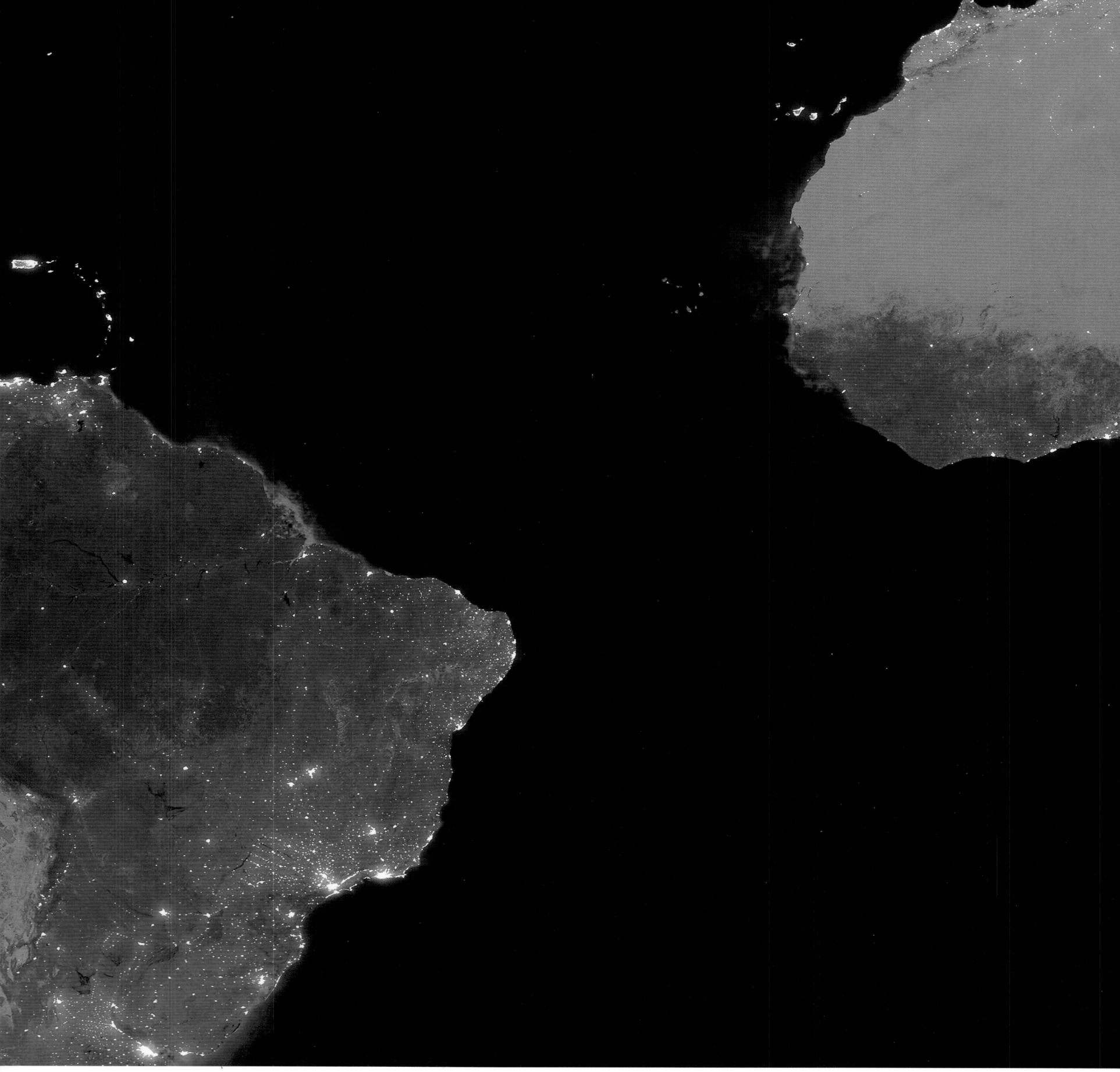

The Nile River, from the Aswan Dam to the Mediterranean, is illuminated at night.
This bright thread and the pockets of lights in the north and south indicate urbanized
areas. The Sahara and the tropical forests of the Congo Basin show little light.

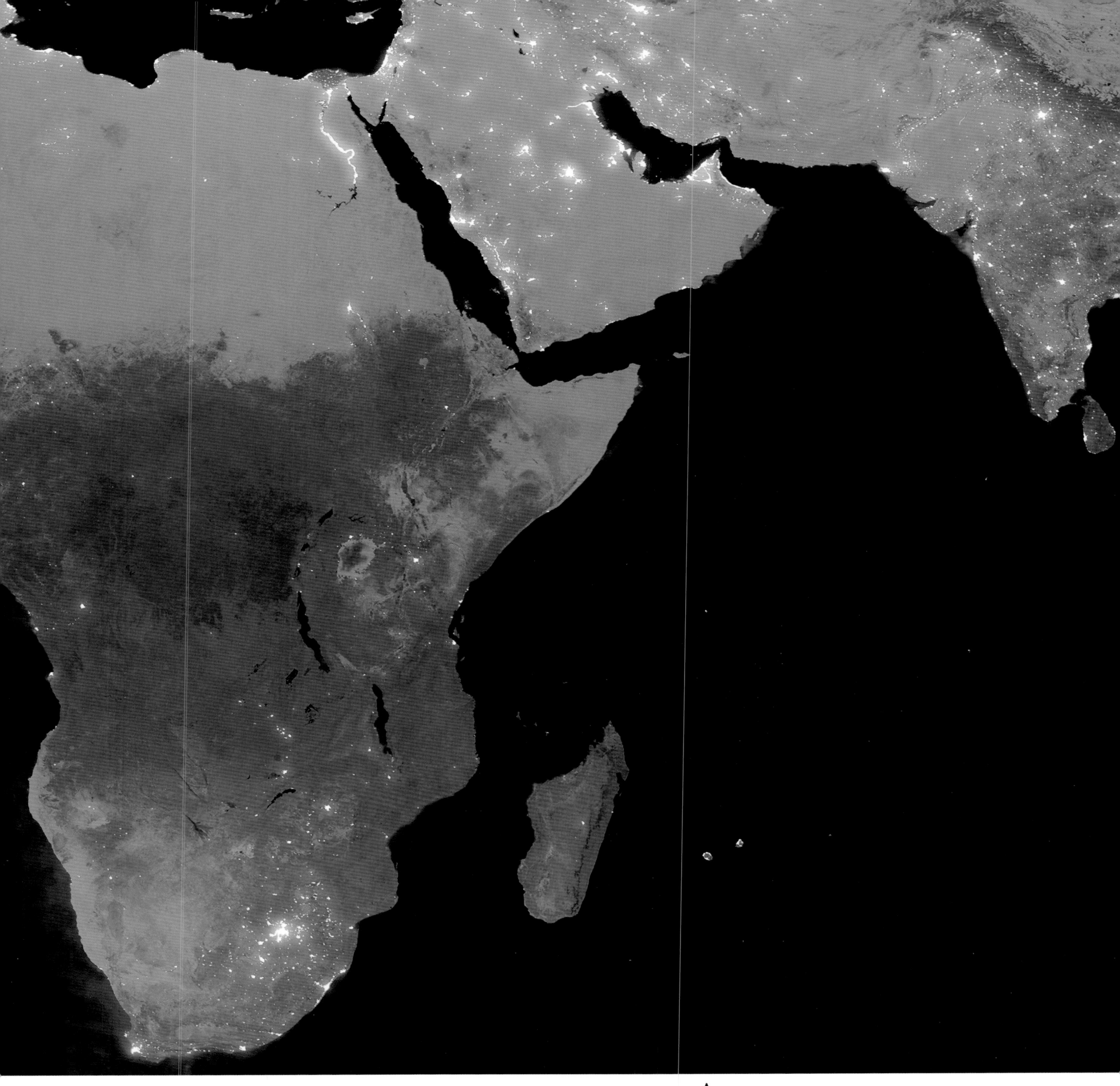

AFRICA

ABOVE AFRICA

Dominating the top third of the continent of Africa is the mighty Sahara, the largest region of dry land on the planet. Using radar imaging that can penetrate the Sahara's dry sands, satellites can "see" geological features that chronicle past climate changes and events that are not visible at ground level. Revealed are ancient drainage channels, scoured out in wetter times when forests and grasslands covered the region, and long valleys carved by wind-driven sand. Satellites also record ongoing change, such as the effects of the prolonged drought that sent huge clouds of dust billowing across the Atlantic. Africa's few volcanoes are concentrated in the Great Rift Valley, in the east of the continent, where two tectonic plates are slowly pulling apart. The Virunga volcanic chain lies near the southwestern end of the valley, straddling the borders of Rwanda, the Democratic Republic of Congo, and Uganda.

Namib Sand Sea, Namibia
Below: Land and ocean seem reversed in this false-color image of the vast Namib Sand Sea, on the west coast of southern Africa. The magenta areas are fields of high, steep sand dunes, while the orange area at the bottom is the South Atlantic Ocean. The bright green features in the upper right are rocky hills poking above the sand sea.

The Sahara Desert, northern Africa
Above right: A comet slamming into the Sahara Desert millions of years ago left the circular scars seen in this radar image. The concentric ring structure left of center is the main impact crater, with a diameter of 10.5 miles (17 km). Scientists believe the comet broke apart before impact, and to the right are two similar, but less distinct, scars.

Virunga Mountains, Central Africa
Below: The rugged Virunga volcanic chain in Central Africa is home to the endangered mountain gorilla. This false-color image, centered on Mount Karisimbi, graphically illustrates the threat to the gorilla's forest habitat, shown as green, by farmlands, shown as purple. The thin green lines are thought to be agricultural terracing.

Cape Verde and the Canary Islands
Right: A dust plume over 1,000 miles (1,600 km) long sweeps past the islands of Cape Verde (lower left), north to the Canary Islands (top center). The dust comes from the savanna lands just south of the Sahara, where long-term drought and overgrazing has stripped the dry soil bare, leading to erosion and catastrophic dust storms.

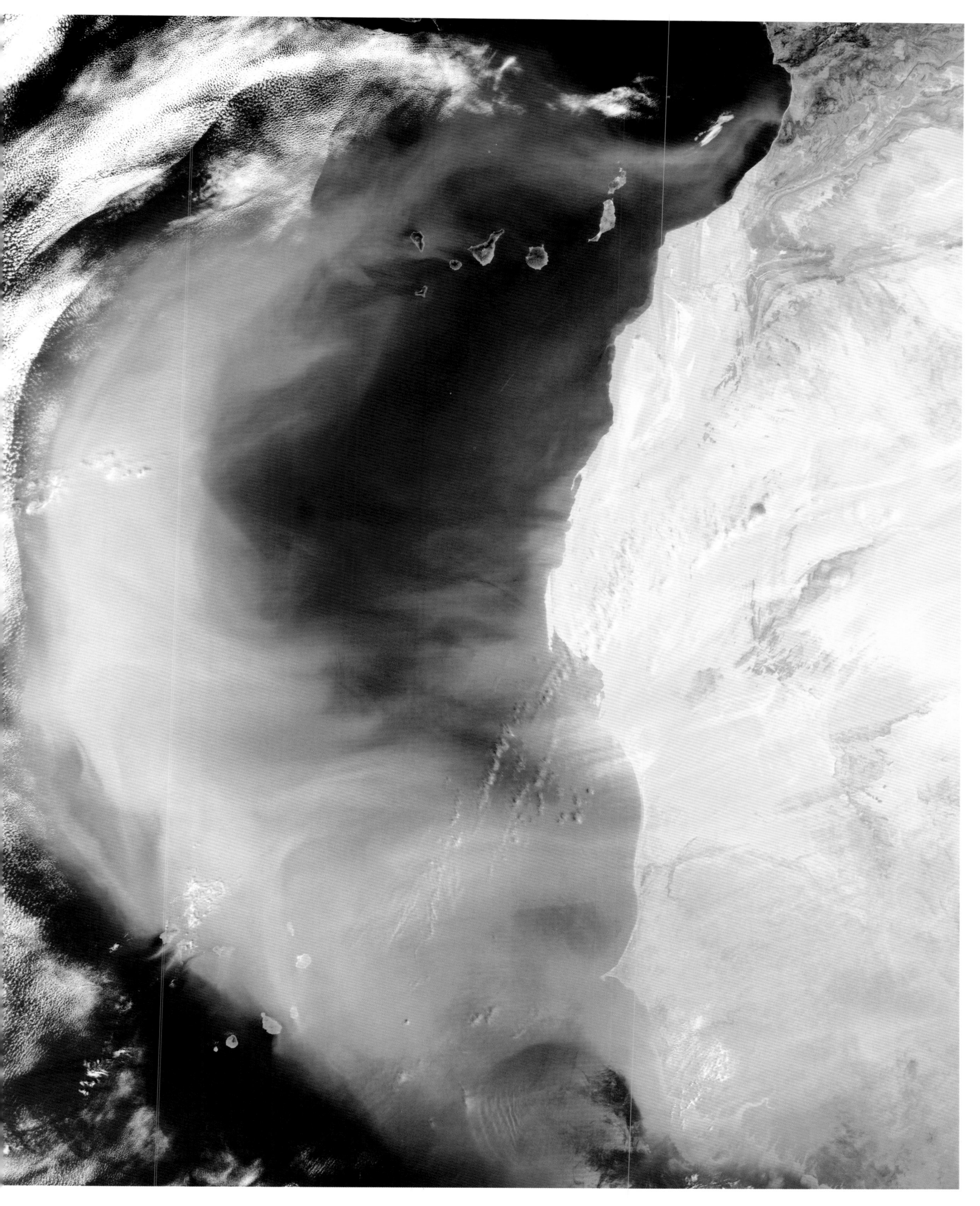

LAND AND ENVIRONMENT

The second-largest continent after Asia, Africa encompasses 11.7 million square miles (30 million sq km), almost one-fifth of Earth's land. It is separated from Europe by the Mediterranean Sea and from Asia by the Red Sea and Gulf of Aden. From Cap Blanc in the far north, it stretches about 5,000 miles (8,000 km) south to Cape Agulhas in South Africa. The northern half of the continent is far wider than the south, spanning 4,600 miles (7,360 km) between Cap Vert in Senegal and Rās Xaafuun in Somalia. Relative to the other continents, Africa has few extensive lowlands or high mountain ranges. It consists mainly of a huge plateau, rimmed by narrow coastal plains, which slopes gently from southeast to northwest. The highest areas are the Ethiopian Highlands and the East African Plateau, site of Africa's highest peak, Kilimanjaro. These uplands are riven by the Great Rift Valley, an extensive fault that runs for 4,000 miles (6,400 km) from the Red Sea to the Zambezi River.

SCALE 1:40,000,000
Lamberts Azimuthal Equal Area Projection
0   1000 miles
0   1000 kilometers

Left: The Atlas Mountains, which run from southwest to northeast across the center of this image, stretch for 1,200 miles (2,000 km), isolating the temperate northwest coast from the Sahara Desert.

Right: The dark green line at center here is the 4,160-mile (6,695-km) Nile, the world's longest river. Rising in the Ethiopian Highlands, it flows north through Sudan and Egypt to the Mediterranean Sea.

Below: The Suez Canal links the Mediterranean Sea to the Gulf of Suez and the Red Sea. Measuring approximately 100 miles (160 km) in length, it was completed in 1869 and is used by more than 50 ships a day.

NATURAL HAZARDS

Drought

Many parts of Africa receive rain only during an annual wet season. Fluctuations in this seasonal rainfall can result in drought—periods of rainfall well below the long-term average. With so many of the inhabitants of these regions dependent on subsistence agriculture, drought can, in turn, cause great hardship and loss of life. Sometimes, the losses are due to a misreading of natural long-term climatic patterns. In the Sahel region in the 1960s, for example, a succession of years of above-average rainfall (see graph, right) encouraged farmers to cultivate this normally arid region. When rainfall levels returned to the norm, the crops soon failed. By 1973, an estimated 100,000 people had starved to death.

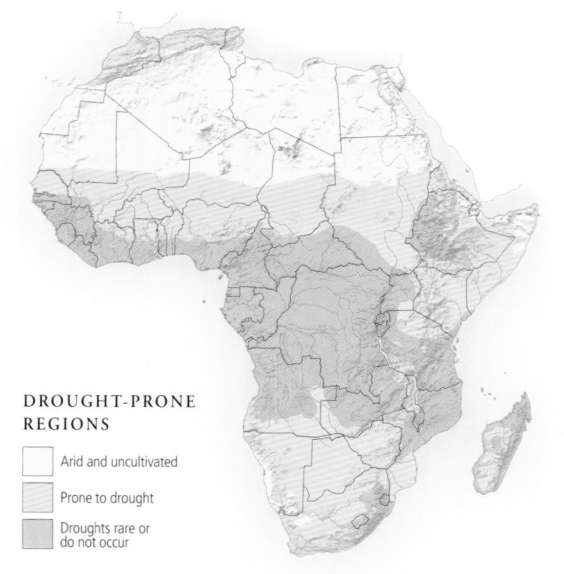

DROUGHT-PRONE REGIONS

- Arid and uncultivated
- Prone to drought
- Droughts rare or do not occur

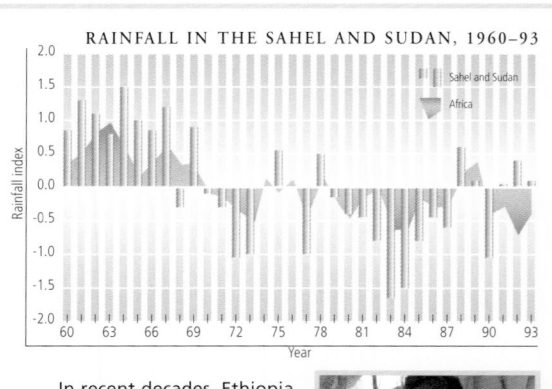

RAINFALL IN THE SAHEL AND SUDAN, 1960–93

Rainfall index / Year

Sahel and Sudan
Africa

In recent decades, Ethiopia has suffered a number of disastrous droughts, with the most severe one, in 1984, accounting for approximately 300,000 deaths. In 2003, an acute drought left about 11 million people facing severe food shortages.

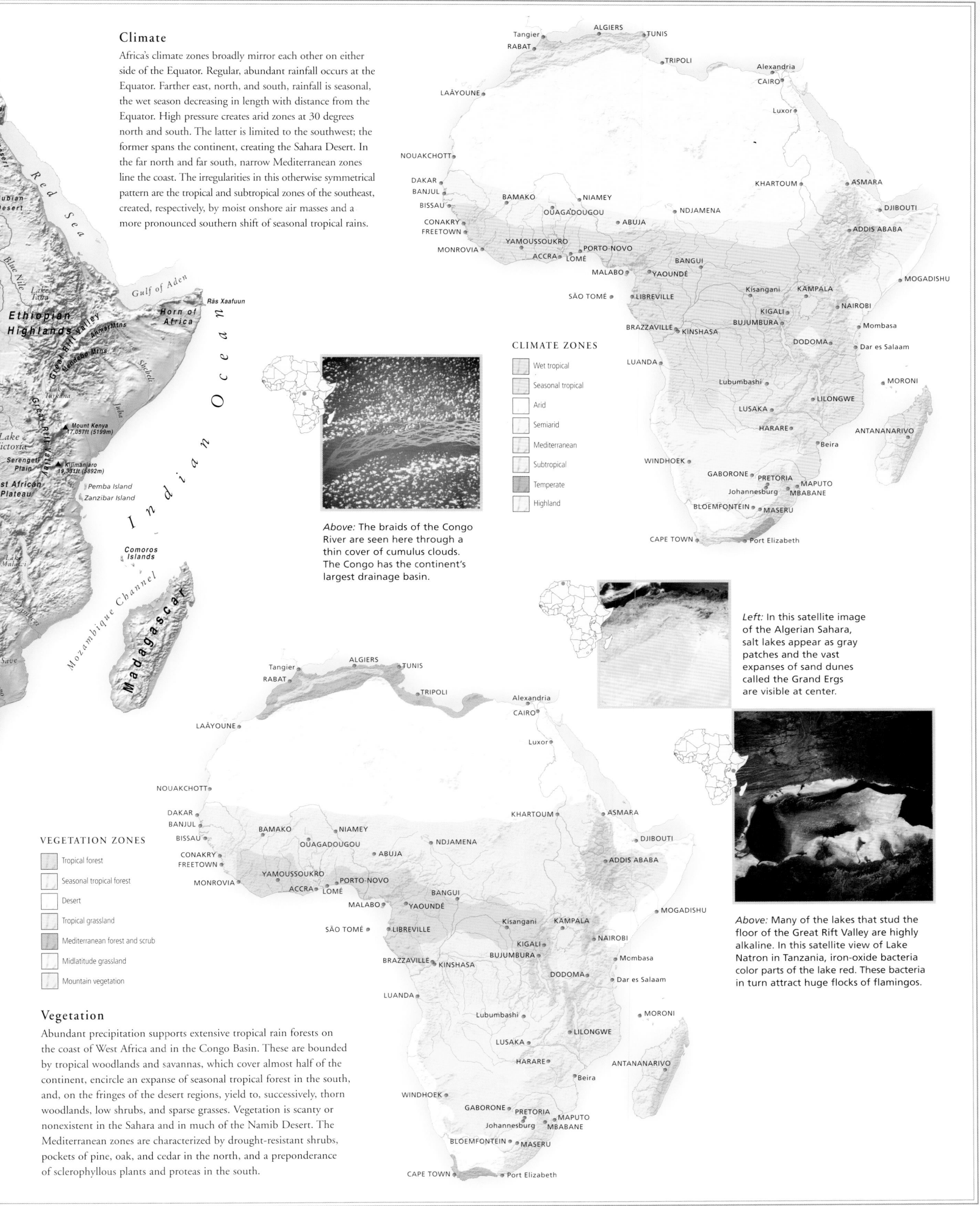

Climate

Africa's climate zones broadly mirror each other on either side of the Equator. Regular, abundant rainfall occurs at the Equator. Farther east, north, and south, rainfall is seasonal, the wet season decreasing in length with distance from the Equator. High pressure creates arid zones at 30 degrees north and south. The latter is limited to the southwest; the former spans the continent, creating the Sahara Desert. In the far north and far south, narrow Mediterranean zones line the coast. The irregularities in this otherwise symmetrical pattern are the tropical and subtropical zones of the southeast, created, respectively, by moist onshore air masses and a more pronounced southern shift of seasonal tropical rains.

CLIMATE ZONES

- Wet tropical
- Seasonal tropical
- Arid
- Semiarid
- Mediterranean
- Subtropical
- Temperate
- Highland

Above: The braids of the Congo River are seen here through a thin cover of cumulus clouds. The Congo has the continent's largest drainage basin.

Left: In this satellite image of the Algerian Sahara, salt lakes appear as gray patches and the vast expanses of sand dunes called the Grand Ergs are visible at center.

Above: Many of the lakes that stud the floor of the Great Rift Valley are highly alkaline. In this satellite view of Lake Natron in Tanzania, iron-oxide bacteria color parts of the lake red. These bacteria in turn attract huge flocks of flamingos.

VEGETATION ZONES

- Tropical forest
- Seasonal tropical forest
- Desert
- Tropical grassland
- Mediterranean forest and scrub
- Midlatitude grassland
- Mountain vegetation

Vegetation

Abundant precipitation supports extensive tropical rain forests on the coast of West Africa and in the Congo Basin. These are bounded by tropical woodlands and savannas, which cover almost half of the continent, encircle an expanse of seasonal tropical forest in the south, and, on the fringes of the desert regions, yield to, successively, thorn woodlands, low shrubs, and sparse grasses. Vegetation is scanty or nonexistent in the Sahara and in much of the Namib Desert. The Mediterranean zones are characterized by drought-resistant shrubs, pockets of pine, oak, and cedar in the north, and a preponderance of sclerophyllous plants and proteas in the south.

PEOPLES AND NATIONS

The continent-spanning Sahara Desert divides Africa's 800 million or so people into two major groups: the culturally homogenous, predominantly Arabic and Islamic peoples of the north; and the numerous, and culturally and linguistically diverse, indigenous peoples of the south. Other ethnic groups include the descendants of European colonists, found mainly in the far north and far south, and the Malagasy of Madagascar, whose ancestors migrated from Indonesia. The late-20th-century decolonization of Africa resulted in the creation of numerous states—now 53 countries in all—some of whose borders, especially in sub-Saharan Africa, cut across traditional ethnic territories. Resulting conflicts hinder attempts to alleviate poverty.

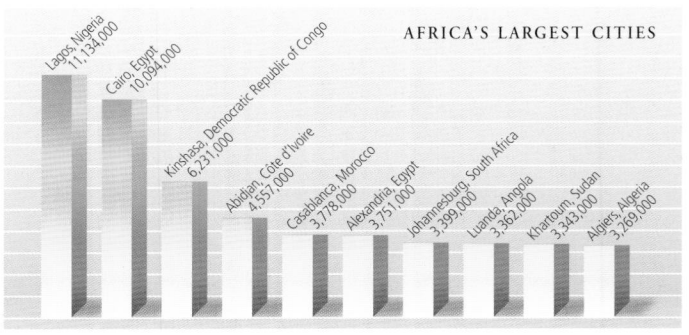

AFRICA'S LARGEST CITIES

Urbanization

Africa had few large towns or cities until the 20th century, and its proportion of urban dwellers remains low relative to other continents—approximately 40 percent. Yet recently urbanization has occurred more rapidly here than anywhere else: in 1950, just 15 percent of Africans lived in towns and cities. North Africa is considerably more urbanized than sub-Saharan Africa, though Lagos in Nigeria is the continent's biggest city. Africa's largest urban areas tend to be on the coast, and many are ports established by former colonial powers.

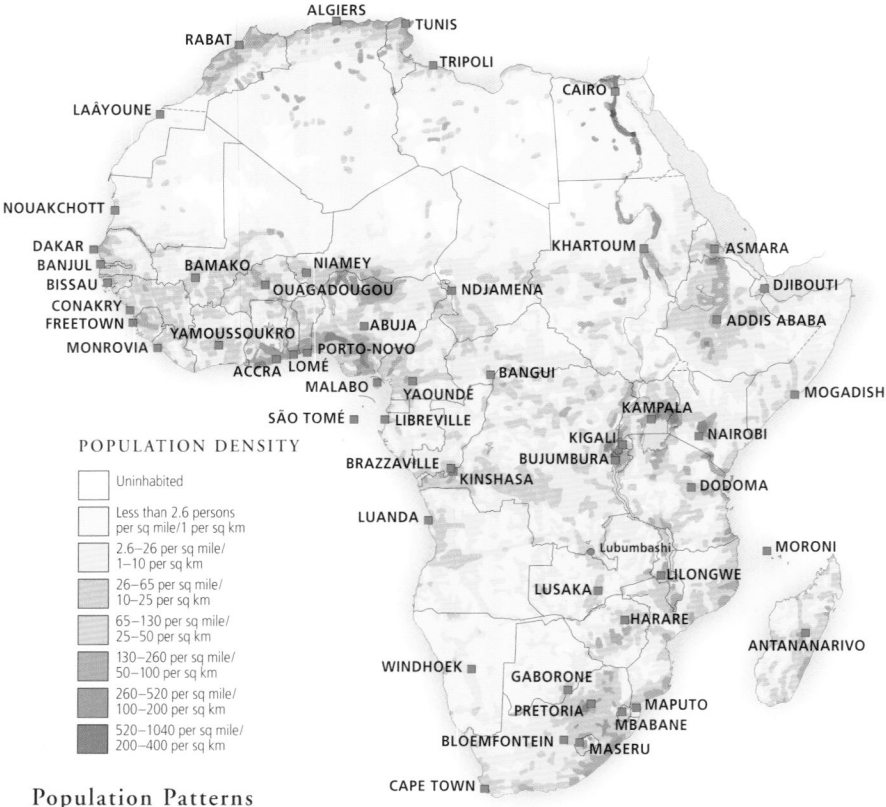

POPULATION DENSITY

Uninhabited

Less than 2.6 persons per sq mile/1 per sq km

2.6–26 per sq mile/ 1–10 per sq km

26–65 per sq mile/ 10–25 per sq km

65–130 per sq mile/ 25–50 per sq km

130–260 per sq mile/ 50–100 per sq km

260–520 per sq mile/ 100–200 per sq km

520–1040 per sq mile/ 200–400 per sq km

Right: Population growth in Lagos, Nigeria, is due mainly to rural–urban migration. In an effort to slow the city's expansion, the government recently moved the national capital from Lagos to Abuja.

Population Patterns

Relative to most other continents, Africa is underpopulated, having just 13 percent of the world's people but more than 20 percent of its land. This is due in part to the high proportion of arid land, which precludes widespread permanent settlement, but also to the effects of disease and conflict. The greatest population densities occur on the coasts of North and West Africa, along major rivers and around large lakes, and in well-watered upland areas such as the highlands of the Great Rift Valley. Despite its low density, Africa's population is growing rapidly and is likely to reach almost 1.5 billion by 2030 (during that time, its growth rate will probably stay high while rates on other continents decline steeply). About 40 percent of the current population is under 15.

FLASHPOINTS

Many of Africa's numerous and frequently violent regional disputes have centered on the control of lucrative natural resources and been stoked by interethnic rivalries.

Western Sahara

As soon as Spain left its colony of Western Sahara in 1976, Morocco annexed the territory, encouraging Moroccans to settle there and forcing native Saharawi people into Algeria. It then built a fortified wall, the so-called Berm, to keep out the Saharawi and their independence fighters, the Polisario Front. UN attempts to broker peace have so far failed.

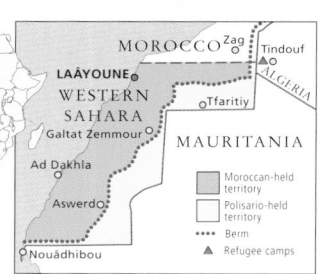

Trade Organizations

Intraregional trade has long been hampered by poor communications and a limited variety of commodities. However, the Abuja Treaty of 1991 established the African Economic Community, which aims to create an African common market by uniting the following regional organizations: the Economic Community of West African States (ECOWAS), the Economic Community of Central African States (ECCAS), the Southern African Development Community (SADC), the Common Market for Eastern and Southern Africa (COMESA), and the Arab Maghreb Union (AMU).

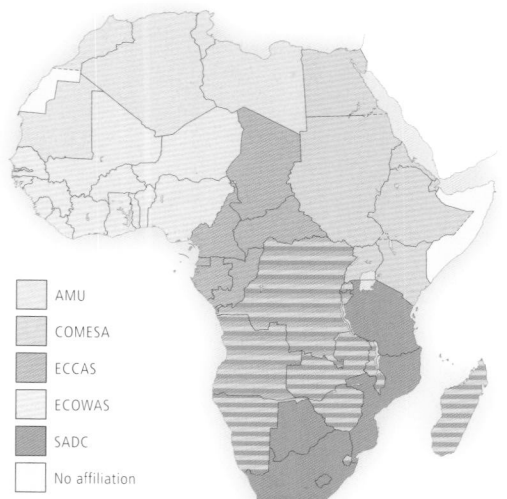

AMU

COMESA

ECCAS

ECOWAS

SADC

No affiliation

Democratic Republic of Congo

Ethnic disputes have fueled a civil war in the Democratic Republic of Congo that has claimed 3 million lives since 1998. Despite the formation in 2003 of a coalition government including the main rebel groups—the Movement for the Liberation of Congo (MLC) and the Rally for Congolese Democracy (RCD)—violence continues.

West Africa's Diamond Wars

In 1990, the rebel National Patriotic Front (NPF) took control of Liberia and began aiding Sierra Leone insurgents the Revolutionary United Front (RUF) in return for diamonds. This led to civil wars that have killed 300,000 people. The U.K. helped disarm the RUF in 2002, and the NPF was ousted in 2003, but the situation remains volatile.

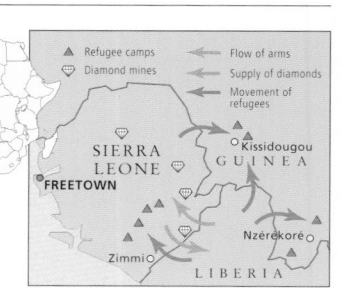

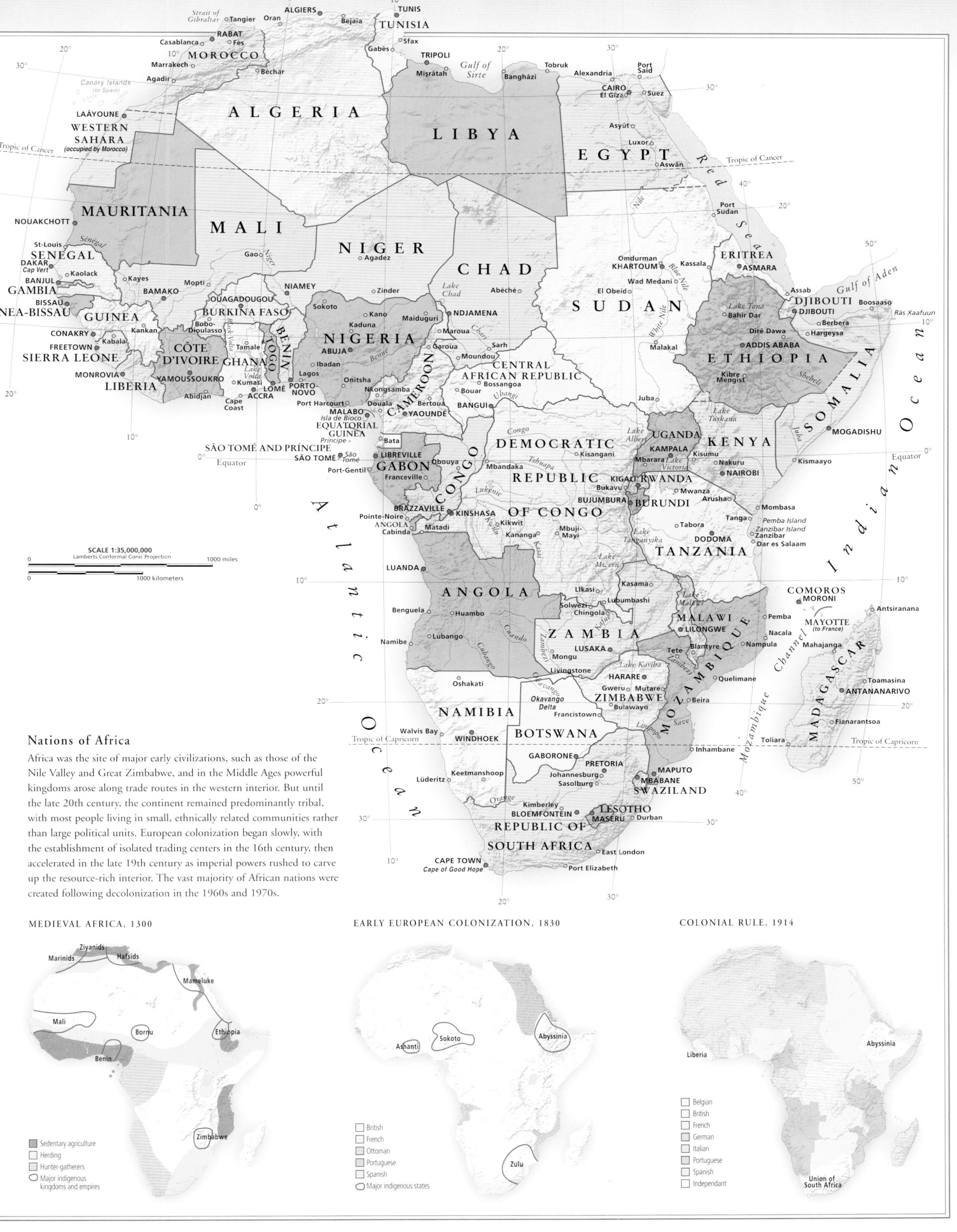

Strait of Gibraltar · Tangier · Oran · ALGIERS · Bejaia · TUNIS · TUNISIA · Sfax
Casablanca · RABAT · Fès · Gabès · TRIPOLI · Gulf of Sirte · Banghāzī · Tobruk · Port Said · Alexandria
Marrakech · Béchar · Mişrātah · CAIRO · El Gîza · Suez
Agadir

MOROCCO
Canary Islands (to Spain)
Tropic of Cancer
LAÀYOUNE
WESTERN SAHARA (occupied by Morocco)

ALGERIA
LIBYA
EGYPT
Asyūt · Luxor · Aswân · Tropic of Cancer

MAURITANIA
NOUAKCHOTT
MALI
NIGER
CHAD
Red Sea · Port Sudan
St-Louis · Senegal · Gao · Niger · Agadez · Omdurman · KHARTOUM · Kassala · ERITREA · ASMARA
SENEGAL · DAKAR · Cap Vert · Kaolack · Kayes · NIAMEY · Zinder · Lake Chad · Abéché · El Obeid · Wad Medani · Blue Nile · Assab · DJIBOUTI · DJIBOUTI · Boosaaso
GAMBIA · BANJUL · BAMAKO · Mopti · SUDAN · Bahīr Dar · Diré Dawa · Berbera · Hargeysa · Räs Xaafuun
BISSAU · GUINEA-BISSAU · OUAGADOUGOU · Sokoto · Kano · Kaduna · Maiduguri · NDJAMENA · Lake Tana · ADDIS ABABA
GUINEA · BURKINA FASO · Bobo-Dioulasso · NIGERIA · Marova · Sarh · Moundou · CENTRAL · ETHIOPIA · Shebeli
CONAKRY · Kankan · Kabala · Tamale · BENIN · ABUJA · Ibadan · Garoua · Benue · AFRICAN REPUBLIC · Kibre Mengist
FREETOWN · CÔTE · GHANA · Lake Volta · Lagos · Onitsha · Bouar · BANGUI · Juba · SOMALIA
SIERRA LEONE · D'IVOIRE · YAMOUSSOUKRO · LOMÉ · PORTO-NOVO · NKongsamba · Douala · Bertoua · Ubangi · Lake Turkana
MONROVIA · Kumasi · ACCRA · Port Harcourt · CAMEROON · YAOUNDÉ · Congo · UGANDA · KENYA
LIBERIA · Abidjan · Cape Coast · MALABO · Isla de Bioco · Bata · KAMPALA · Kisumu · Nakuru · MOGADISHU
SÃO TOMÉ AND PRÍNCIPE · EQUATORIAL GUINEA · LIBREVILLE · Obouya · DEMOCRATIC · Kisangani · Lake Albert · Mbarara · Lake Victoria · NAIROBI
SÃO TOMÉ · Príncipe · GABON · REPUBLIC · Mbandaka · KIGALI · RWANDA · Mwanza · Kismaayo · Equator
Equator · São Tomé · Port-Gentil · Franceville · OF CONGO · Bukavu · BUJUMBURA · BURUNDI · Arusha · Mombasa

ATLANTIC OCEAN
BRAZZAVILLE · KINSHASA · Kikwit · Kananga · Kasai · Lake Tanganyika · Tabora · Tanga · Pemba Island · Zanzibar Island · Zanzibar · Dar es Salaam
POINTE-NOIRE · ANGOLA · Matadi · Mbuji-Mayi · DODOMA · TANZANIA
Cabinda · LUANDA · Kasama · Lake Mweru · Lake Malawi · COMOROS · MORONI
ANGOLA · Likasi · Lubumbashi · Mwanza · MAYOTTE (to France)
Benguela · Huambo · Solwezi · Chingola · MALAWI · Pemba · Nacala · Antsiranana
Namibe · Lubango · ZAMBIA · LILONGWE · Nampula · Mahajanga
Mongu · LUSAKA · Tete · Blantyre · MOZAMBIQUE · Mozambique Channel · MADAGASCAR
Oshakati · Livingstone · Lake Kariba · Quelimane · Toamasina
Okavango Delta · HARARE · Gweru · Mutare · Beira · ANTANANARIVO
NAMIBIA · Francistown · Bulawayo · ZIMBABWE · Save · Fianarantsoa
Walvis Bay · BOTSWANA · Inhambane · Toliara · Tropic of Capricorn
WINDHOEK · GABORONE · Limpopo
Lüderitz · Keetmanshoop · PRETORIA · MAPUTO · MBABANE · SWAZILAND
Johannesburg · Sasolburg · Orange · Kimberley · LESOTHO · MASERU · Durban
BLOEMFONTEIN · REPUBLIC OF · East London
SOUTH AFRICA
CAPE TOWN · Cape of Good Hope · Port Elizabeth

SCALE 1:35,000,000
Lamberts Conformal Conic Projection
0 — 1000 miles
0 — 1000 kilometers

Nations of Africa

Africa was the site of major early civilizations, such as those of the Nile Valley and Great Zimbabwe, and in the Middle Ages powerful kingdoms arose along trade routes in the western interior. But until the late 20th century, the continent remained predominantly tribal, with most people living in small, ethnically related communities rather than large political units. European colonization began slowly, with the establishment of isolated trading centers in the 16th century, then accelerated in the late 19th century as imperial powers rushed to carve up the resource-rich interior. The vast majority of African nations were created following decolonization in the 1960s and 1970s.

MEDIEVAL AFRICA, 1300
Ziyanids · Marinids · Hafsids · Mameluke · Mali · Bornu · Ethiopia · Benin · Zimbabwe
☐ Sedentary agriculture
☐ Herding
☐ Hunter-gatherers
◯ Major indigenous kingdoms and empires

EARLY EUROPEAN COLONIZATION, 1830
Ashanti · Sokoto · Abyssinia · Zulu
☐ British
☐ French
☐ Ottoman
☐ Portuguese
☐ Spanish
◯ Major indigenous states

COLONIAL RULE, 1914
Liberia · Abyssinia
☐ Belgian
☐ British
☐ French
☐ German
☐ Italian
☐ Portuguese
☐ Spanish
☐ Independant
Union of South Africa

THE HUMAN IMPACT

Africa is where humans first evolved, and modification of the land to facilitate hunting and farming, as well as the excavation of minerals, have been happening there for thousands of years. As on most other continents, however, it was the arrival of European colonists that precipitated industrial-scale exploitation of natural resources—including people. An estimated 10 million Africans were deported as slaves between the 16th and 19th centuries. In addition, vast amounts of timber and huge quantities of minerals were shipped to foreign markets. Since decolonization, governments have faced the difficult balancing act of providing for impoverished populations while guarding against the exhaustion of resources. Environmental problems are exacerbated by population growth, inequitable land distribution, foreign penetration of local markets, corruption, weak institutions, and violent conflicts.

Land Cover

Two-thirds of Africa is arid or semiarid; much of this land is used, appropriately, for nomadic grazing. The proportion of arable land is low relative to other continents. Its quality varies, from fertile volcanic and alluvial soils to poor, leached soils in zones of high rainfall. Africa's forests represent 17 percent of global forest cover; one-fifth lies within the Democratic Republic of Congo.

PROPORTIONS OF TOTAL LAND AREA

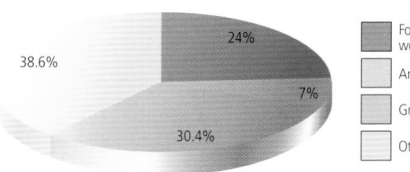

38.6%
24%
7%
30.4%

- Forest and woodland
- Arable land
- Grazing
- Other land

THE CHANGING FACE OF AFRICA

Desertification

Significant fluctuations in rainfall, including prolonged droughts, periodically reduce vegetation cover in semiarid areas of Africa. The impact of this natural cycle has been intensified by human modification of the land, especially the cultivation and grazing of marginal areas. These activities remove the natural vegetation that binds light soils together, making them vulnerable to erosion, and in turn inhibiting the regeneration of plants. Desertification, as this process is widely known, now threatens 46 percent of Africa, and more than half of this land is at high or very high risk. Around 485 million Africans are affected.

AREAS AT RISK OF DESERTIFICATION

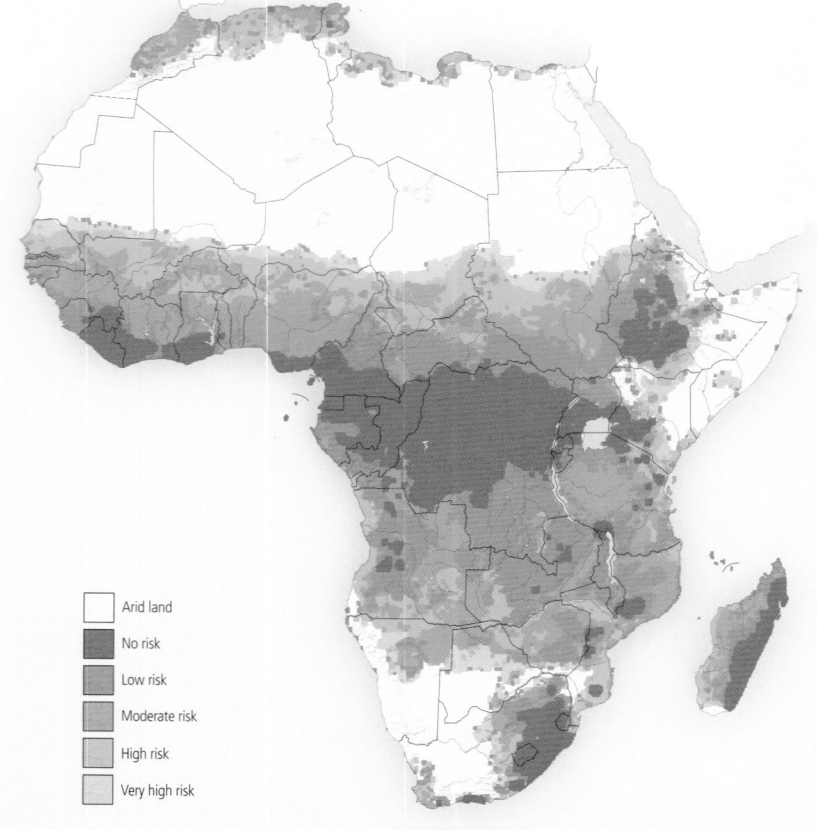

- Arid land
- No risk
- Low risk
- Moderate risk
- High risk
- Very high risk

Economic Profile

Africa is resource-wealthy, but due to its historical development and the uneven distribution of resources, Africans are not. About 44 percent live on the equivalent of less than US$1 a day, and almost 60 percent rely on subsistence farming. Yet minerals are abundant. Most North African nations, as well as Nigeria and Cameroon, have substantial oil and gas reserves. The Democratic Republic of Congo, Sierra Leone, and South Africa are important sources of diamonds. Uranium and gold are widespread in southern Africa, and the continent has a large part of the world's iron ore. Products from Africa's still-vast forests supply a higher proportion of GDP than on any other continent. The expansion of hydroelectric power has boosted energy output. Despite this, the industrial sector remains undeveloped. This is due in part to economic programs that have encouraged developing nations to focus on the export of only a few primary commodities. Such exporters are highly vulnerable in times of oversupply and falling prices. The current terms of world trade also prevent these countries from adding value to their raw products by processing them.

Protecting the Environment

Actions being taken to ameliorate land degradation include a return to the diverse farming systems used by many African farmers before industrial techniques were introduced. Some reforestation is taking place, but mainly in the form of monocultural plantations, which do not support the biological diversity of natural forests. More than 3,000 protected areas have, however, been created, covering 5.2 percent of the continent. Few more are likely to be established in the near future due to pressure on land, but increasing involvement of local people in the management of existing protected areas is helping to improve their effectiveness. Some 48 African countries have signed the Convention on International Trade in Endangered Species (CITES), which strictly controls trade in commodities such as ivory. However, some countries, notably in southern Africa where parks are well managed and elephants consequently abundant, contend that profits from a carefully controlled ivory trade could be used to fund the management of protected areas. Although air pollution is increasing in many cities, Africa emits just 3.5 percent of the world's carbon dioxide and a mere 7 percent of total greenhouse-gas emissions. Leaded petrol has been phased out in Egypt, Sudan, Libya, and Mauritius, and another 22 countries aim to follow suit by 2006.

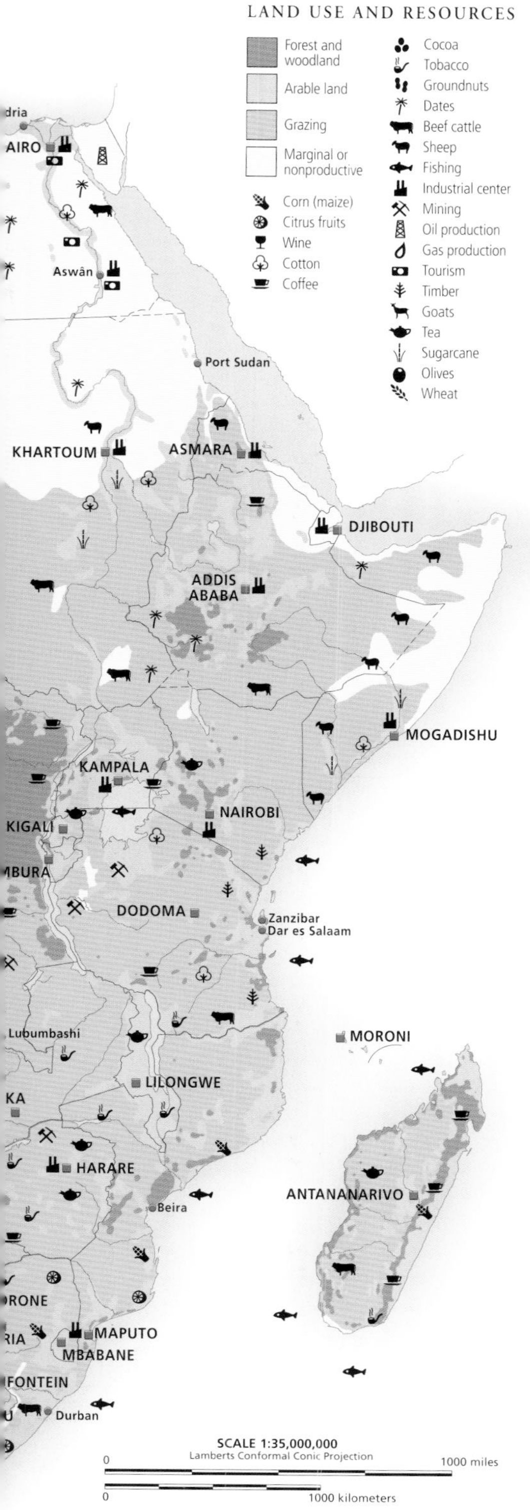

LAND USE AND RESOURCES
Forest and woodland
Arable land
Grazing
Marginal or nonproductive
Corn (maize)
Citrus fruits
Wine
Cotton
Coffee
Cocoa
Tobacco
Groundnuts
Dates
Beef cattle
Sheep
Fishing
Industrial center
Mining
Oil production
Gas production
Tourism
Timber
Goats
Tea
Sugarcane
Olives
Wheat
AIRO
Aswân
Port Sudan
KHARTOUM
ASMARA
DJIBOUTI
ADDIS ABABA
MOGADISHU
KAMPALA
NAIROBI
KIGALI
DODOMA
Zanzibar
Dar es Salaam
Lubumbashi
MORONI
LILONGWE
HARARE
Beira
ANTANANARIVO
MAPUTO
MBABANE
Durban
SCALE 1:35,000,000
Lamberts Conformal Conic Projection
1000 miles
1000 kilometers

Below: Almost 12.5 million acres (5 million ha) of Africa's forests (an area larger than Switzerland) are cleared each year—the highest rate of any continent. About 77 percent of Africa's frontier forests, most of which are in Central Africa, are thought to be at risk, with almost four-fifths of that number threatened by logging.

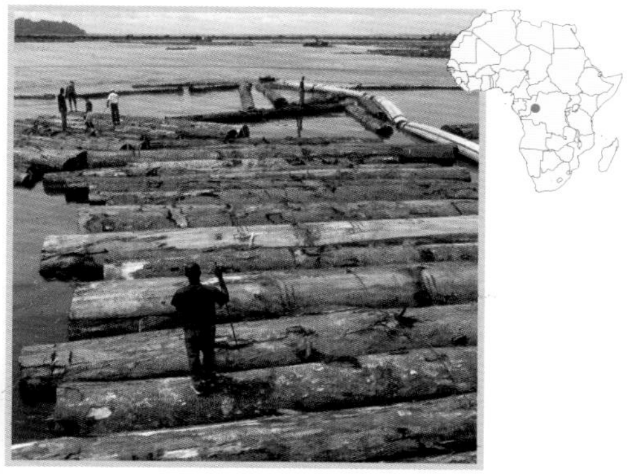

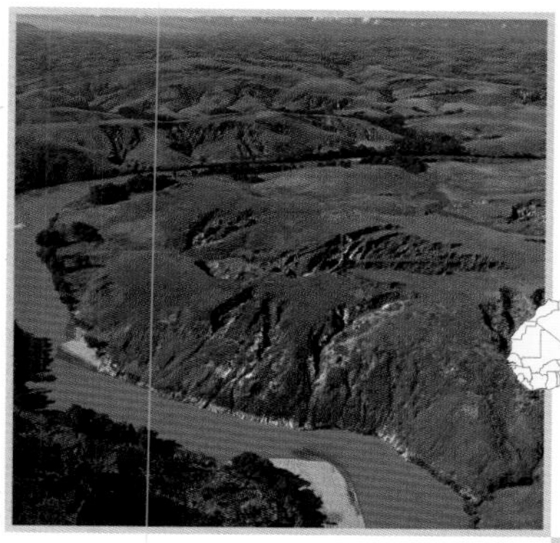

Left: Madagascar has lost about 80 percent of its original forest, which has left the island highly susceptible to erosion. Erosion is accelerated by the hilly terrain, resulting in bare slopes, deep gullies, and rivers choked with red sediments.

Right: Africa's diverse wildlife generates significant income from nature tourism and legal hunting. However, animal populations are threatened by habitat loss and poaching, which is fueled by the ready availability of arms. These pelts were seized from poachers in Kenya.

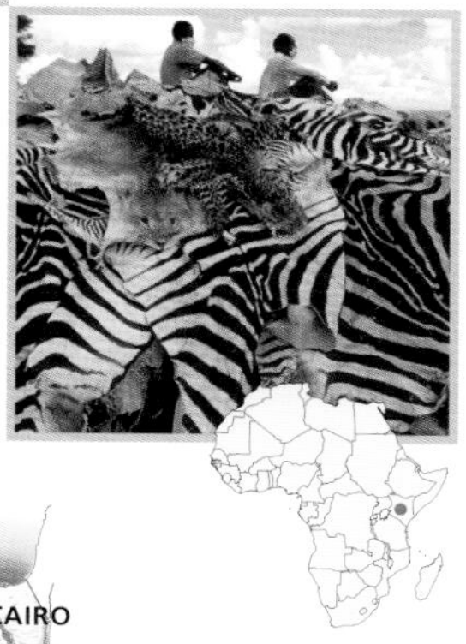

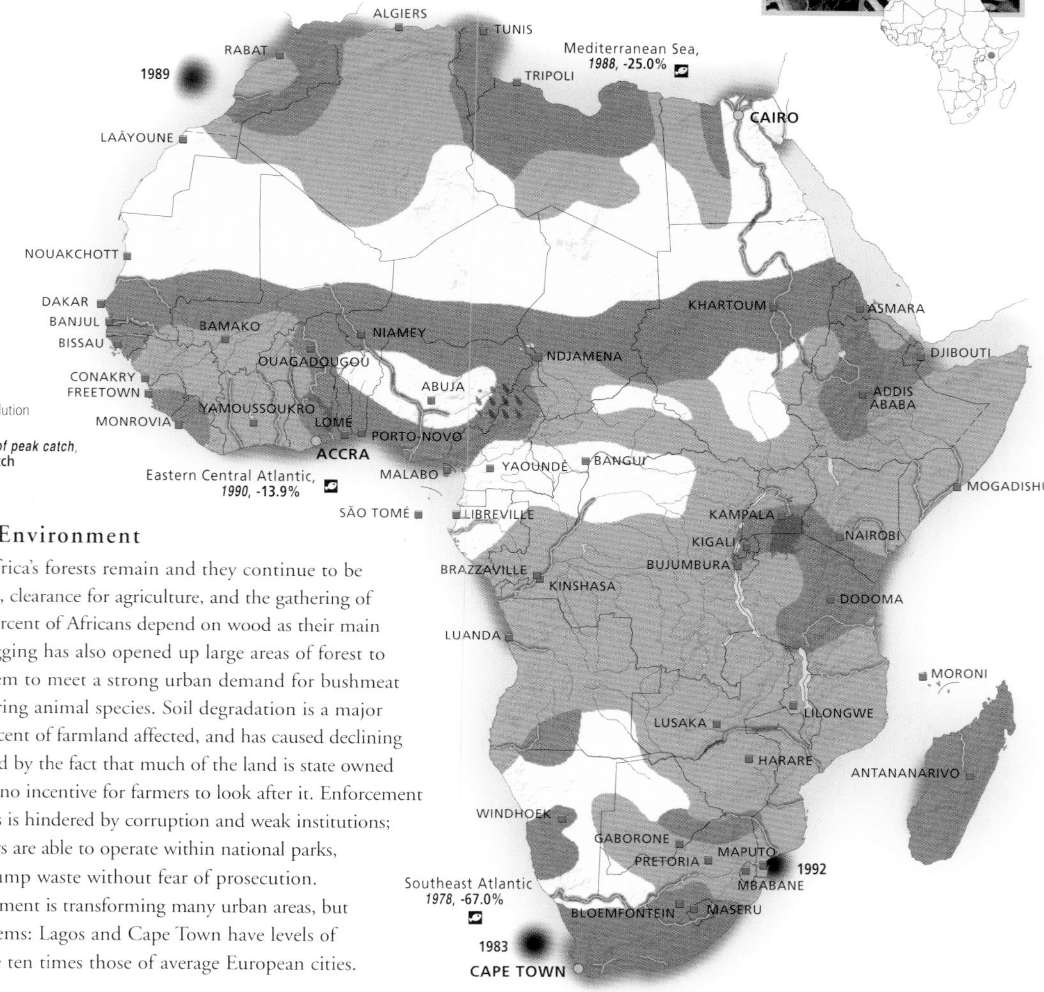

ENVIRONMENTAL ISSUES
Degraded soil
Very degraded soil
Polluted rivers
Polluted seas and lakes
Acid rain
Major oil spills, year
Cities with severe air pollution
Overfished fishery, year of peak catch, decline since peak catch
ALGIERS
TUNIS
RABAT
1989
Mediterranean Sea, 1988, -25.0%
TRIPOLI
CAIRO
LAÂYOUNE
NOUAKCHOTT
DAKAR
BANJUL
BISSAU
CONAKRY
FREETOWN
MONROVIA
BAMAKO
NIAMEY
OUAGADOUGOU
YAMOUSSOUKRO
ABUJA
LOMÉ
PORTO-NOVO
ACCRA
NDJAMENA
KHARTOUM
ASMARA
DJIBOUTI
ADDIS ABABA
Eastern Central Atlantic, 1990, -13.9%
MALABO
YAOUNDÉ
BANGUI
SÃO TOMÉ
LIBREVILLE
MOGADISHU
KAMPALA
NAIROBI
KIGALI
BUJUMBURA
BRAZZAVILLE
KINSHASA
DODOMA
LUANDA
MORONI
LUSAKA
LILONGWE
HARARE
ANTANANARIVO
WINDHOEK
GABORONE
PRETORIA
MAPUTO
1992
MBABANE
Southeast Atlantic 1978, -67.0%
BLOEMFONTEIN
MASERU
1983
CAPE TOWN

Threats to the Environment

Only one-third of Africa's forests remain and they continue to be threatened by logging, clearance for agriculture, and the gathering of wood for fuel—90 percent of Africans depend on wood as their main source of energy. Logging has also opened up large areas of forest to hunters, enabling them to meet a strong urban demand for bushmeat and in turn endangering animal species. Soil degradation is a major problem, with 65 percent of farmland affected, and has caused declining yields. It is exacerbated by the fact that much of the land is state owned and there is therefore no incentive for farmers to look after it. Enforcement of environmental laws is hindered by corruption and weak institutions; consequently, poachers are able to operate within national parks, and industries can dump waste without fear of prosecution. Western-style development is transforming many urban areas, but brings familiar problems: Lagos and Cape Town have levels of airborne lead that are ten times those of average European cities.

ENTAGE OF LAND PROTECTED IN MAJOR AFRICAN COUNTRIES

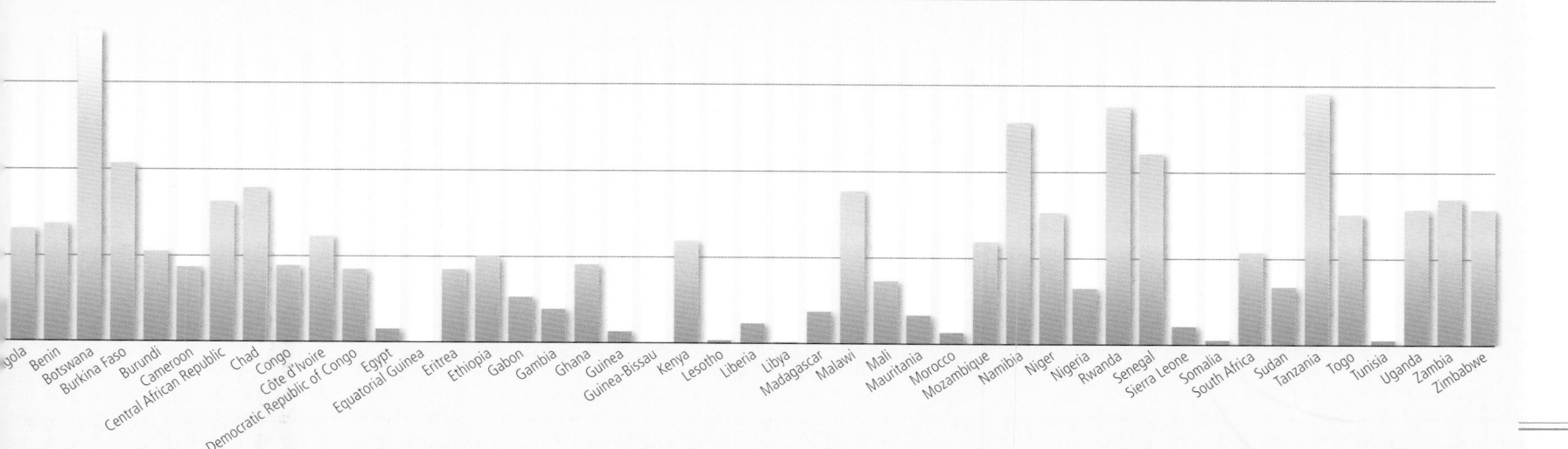

gola
Benin
Botswana
Burkina Faso
Burundi
Cameroon
Central African Republic
Chad
Congo
Côte d'Ivoire
Democratic Republic of Congo
Egypt
Equatorial Guinea
Eritrea
Ethiopia
Gabon
Gambia
Ghana
Guinea
Guinea-Bissau
Kenya
Lesotho
Liberia
Libya
Madagascar
Malawi
Mali
Mauritania
Morocco
Mozambique
Namibia
Niger
Nigeria
Rwanda
Senegal
Sierra Leone
Somalia
South Africa
Sudan
Tanzania
Togo
Tunisia
Uganda
Zambia
Zimbabwe

NORTHWESTERN AFRICA

Algeria, Libya, Morocco, Tunisia

Isolated from the rest of the continent by the Sahara Desert, Northwestern Africa is a transitional zone, between sea and remote interior, Europe and Africa, the West and the Middle East. Its distinctive and relatively homogenous culture was flavored by classical European civilizations and its original, nomadic Berber inhabitants, but derives mainly from the Arab peoples who invaded and settled here in the seventh century AD. This Arabic, Islamic heritage not only withstood subsequent occupation by the Ottoman Empire (between the 16th and 19th centuries), European colonial rule, and a torrid phase of decolonization, but also permeated almost every part of a vast, inhospitable region. Bounded by the Atlas Mountains in the northwest, the Sahara Desert occupies more than 80 percent of the land, confining major population centers and communications routes, sedentary farming, and industries to a narrow coastal strip.

POPULATION PATTERNS

The Sahara contains just a few isolated towns, scattered oases, and groups of nomadic pastoralists; the vast majority of the region's inhabitants dwell on the north coast. The population soared in the 20th century (Algeria's population doubled between 1960 and 1990), due to improving health services and persistent high fertility (even today, each woman has an average of four children). Migration to cities began under European rule and accelerated with industrialization, making this the most urbanized part of Africa. Libya is distinctly underpopulated and has to import skilled workers, whereas there is a steady outward flow of migrants from the other countries.

Uninhabited

Less than 2.6 persons per sq mile/1 per sq km

2.6–26 per sq mile/ 1–10 per sq km

26–65 per sq mile/ 10–25 per sq km

65–130 per sq mile/ 25–50 per sq km

130–260 per sq mile/ 50–100 per sq km

260–520 per sq mile/ 100–200 per sq km

The seminomadic Tuareg people roam the desert lands of Algeria, Libya, Mali, and Niger.

The Atlas Mountains are home to large numbers of Berbers, the region's original inhabitants.

Tangier Befitting a port that has at various times been ruled by the Phoenicians, Romans, Arabs, Spanish, Portuguese, and British, Tangier was for much of the 20th century designated an international zone. Since it became part of Morocco in 1956, many foreign residents have departed, but the city retains a cosmopolitan atmosphere. Encircled by 15th-century ramparts and surmounted by the Great Mosque, its whitewashed buildings climb a craggy limestone outcrop.

Great Mosque

ELEVATION

Feet	Meters
6562	2000
4921	1500
3281	1000
2461	750
1640	500
1312	400
984	300
656	200
328	100
	0
Below sea level	0
656	200
3281	1000
6562	2000
13,123	4000
19,685	6000
26,246	8000
32,808	10,000

Longitude west of Greenwich

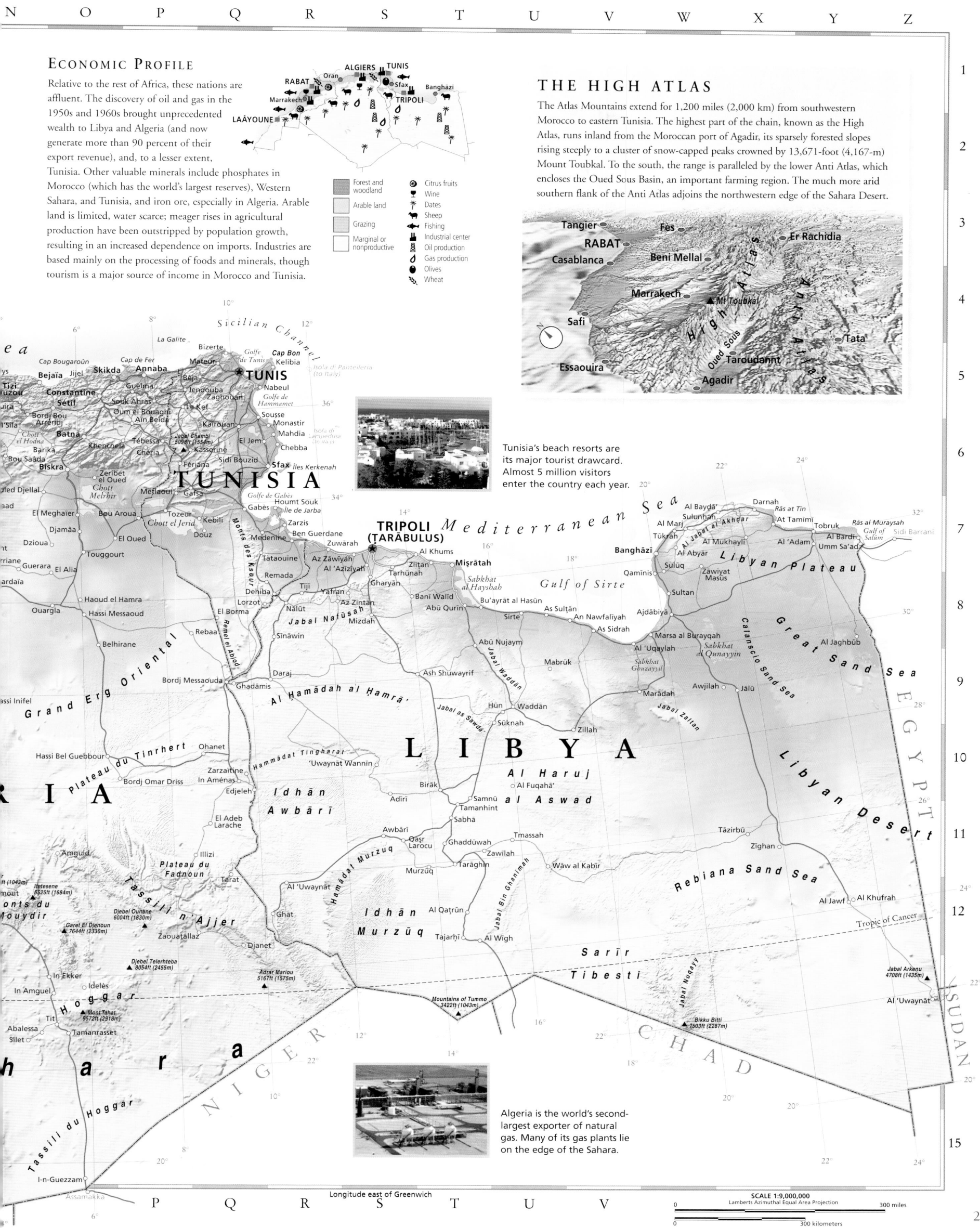

ECONOMIC PROFILE

Relative to the rest of Africa, these nations are affluent. The discovery of oil and gas in the 1950s and 1960s brought unprecedented wealth to Libya and Algeria (and now generate more than 90 percent of their export revenue), and, to a lesser extent, Tunisia. Other valuable minerals include phosphates in Morocco (which has the world's largest reserves), Western Sahara, and Tunisia, and iron ore, especially in Algeria. Arable land is limited, water scarce; meager rises in agricultural production have been outstripped by population growth, resulting in an increased dependence on imports. Industries are based mainly on the processing of foods and minerals, though tourism is a major source of income in Morocco and Tunisia.

Forest and woodland
Arable land
Grazing
Marginal or nonproductive

Citrus fruits
Wine
Dates
Sheep
Fishing
Industrial center
Oil production
Gas production
Olives
Wheat

THE HIGH ATLAS

The Atlas Mountains extend for 1,200 miles (2,000 km) from southwestern Morocco to eastern Tunisia. The highest part of the chain, known as the High Atlas, runs inland from the Moroccan port of Agadir, its sparsely forested slopes rising steeply to a cluster of snow-capped peaks crowned by 13,671-foot (4,167-m) Mount Toubkal. To the south, the range is paralleled by the lower Anti Atlas, which encloses the Oued Sous Basin, an important farming region. The much more arid southern flank of the Anti Atlas adjoins the northwestern edge of the Sahara Desert.

Tunisia's beach resorts are its major tourist drawcard. Almost 5 million visitors enter the country each year.

Algeria is the world's second-largest exporter of natural gas. Many of its gas plants lie on the edge of the Sahara.

SCALE 1:9,000,000
Lamberts Azimuthal Equal Area Projection
Longitude east of Greenwich

0   300 miles
0   300 kilometers

211

NORTHEASTERN AFRICA

Djibouti, Egypt, Eritrea, Ethiopia, Somalia, Sudan

At the northern end of the Great Rift Valley, the Ethiopian Highlands divides the Horn of Africa in the east from the barren expanses of the Sahara in the west. Rivers that descend from the highlands, and from the East African Plateau to the south, are the lifeblood of this predominantly arid and impoverished land.

The Shebeli and Juba are the only permanent rivers in Somalia and supply most of the nation's water. From Lake Tana, the Blue Nile flows east then west to join the White Nile at Khartoum; continuing north, the Nile forms a riverine oasis that constitutes Egypt's only fertile zone.

Since decolonization took place after the Second World War, the southern part of this region has been crippled by famines and political instability, including a long civil war that saw Eritrea secede from Ethiopia in 1993.

ECONOMIC PROFILE

The regional economy is undeveloped, and most people rely on subsistence farming of cereals, fruit and vegetables, sheep, cattle, goats, and camels—80 percent of Somalians are dependent on livestock. Cash crops include cotton and sugarcane, grown in the Nile Valley, and coffee from the Ethiopian Highlands (from whose Kaffa region the word "coffee" derives). Only Egypt has a developed industrial sector, based on engineering and the manufacture of metals and electronic goods. It also benefits from modest oil reserves, tourism, and revenue from the Suez Canal.

Forest and woodland
Arable land
Grazing
Marginal or nonproductive

Cotton
Coffee
Dates
Sugarcane
Beef cattle
Sheep
Oil production
Industrial center
Tourism

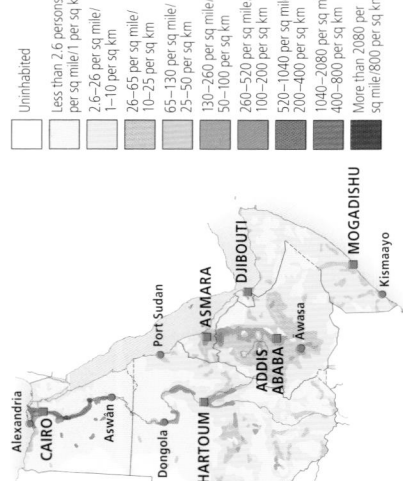

POPULATION PATTERNS

The highest population densities occur in the fertile Ethiopian Highlands and along the major rivers—99 percent of Egyptians live in the Nile Valley, an area that constitutes just 3 percent of the country. The deserts of the eastern Sahara, northern Ethiopia, and Somalia, and the swamps of southern Sudan deter settlement. In semiarid zones, many people, including 70 percent of Somalians, maintain a nomadic lifestyle. The Sahara separates the mainly Arabic peoples of the north from the diverse African groups of the south; however, the Middle East has influenced the entire region and most inhabitants are adherents of Islam.

Uninhabited
Less than 2.6 persons per sq mile/1 per sq km
2.6–26 per sq mile/1–10 per sq km
26–65 per sq mile/10–25 per sq km
65–130 per sq mile/25–50 per sq km
130–260 per sq mile/50–100 per sq km
260–520 per sq mile/100–200 per sq km
520–1040 per sq mile/200–400 per sq km
1040–2080 per sq mile/400–800 per sq km
More than 2080 per sq mile/800 per sq km

THE ETHIOPIAN HIGHLANDS

An enormous plateau, the Ethiopian Highlands cover most of Ethiopia and are bisected by the Great Rift Valley. The western highlands encompass the region's highest peak, 14,872-foot (4,533-m) Rás Dashen, Lake Tana, and Ethiopia's capital Addis Ababa, which sits about 8,000 feet (2,500 m) above sea level. The eastern highlands are narrower but almost as high, reaching 14,176 feet (4,321 m) at Batu. South of Addis Ababa, lakes and volcanic peaks stud the floor of the Great Rift Valley; northeast of the capital, the valley widens, the western wall forming a great escarpment that runs north to the Red Sea, the eastern side arcing toward the Gulf of Aden.

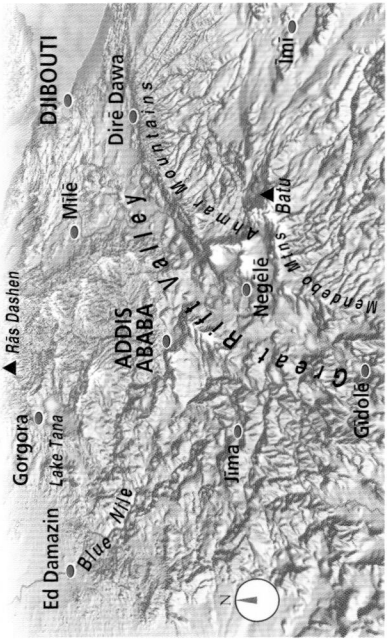

Completed in 1971, the Aswân Dam supplies half of Egypt's electricity.

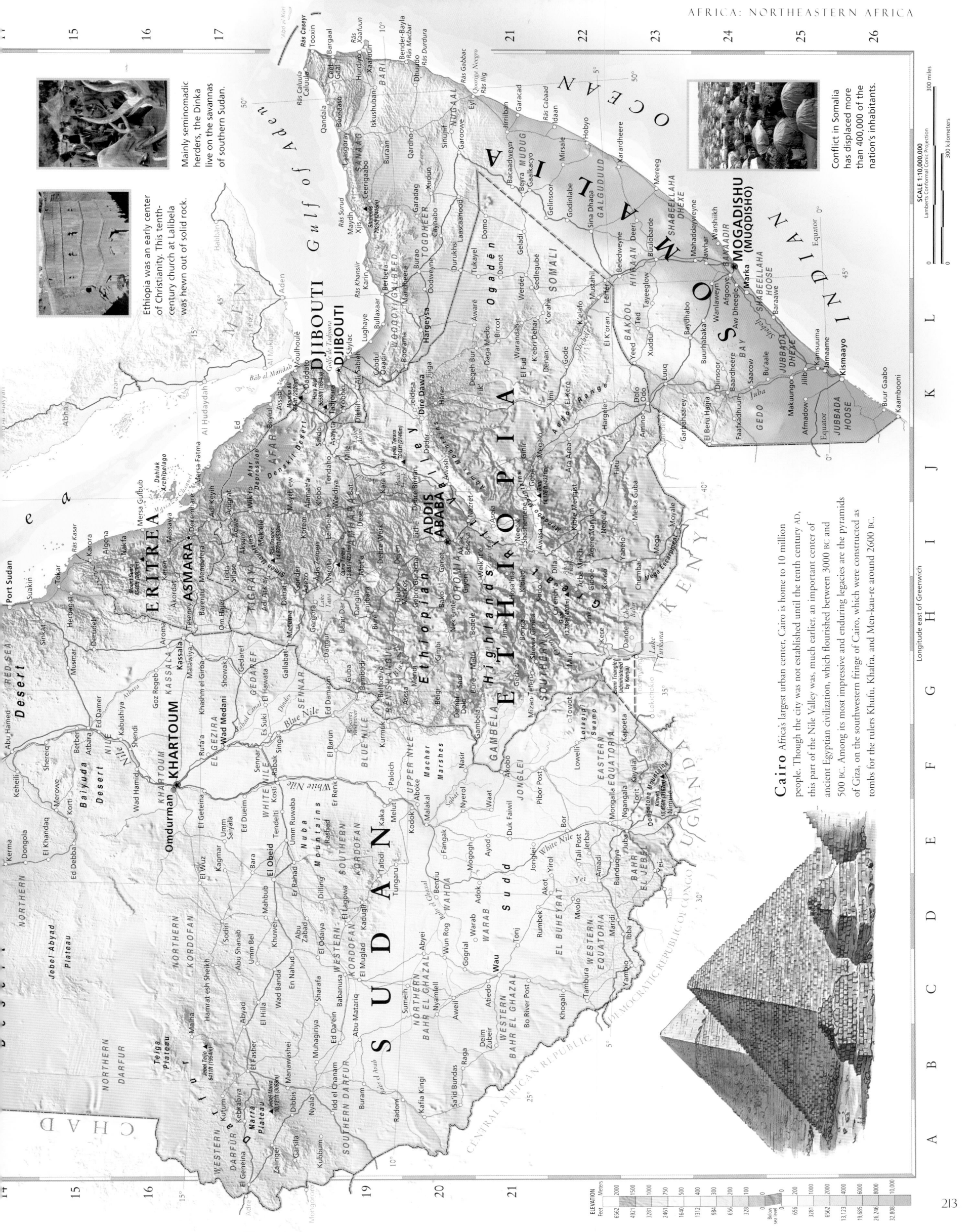

Mainly seminomadic herders, the Dinka live on the savannas of southern Sudan.

Ethiopia was an early center of Christianity. This tenth-century church at Lalibela was hewn out of solid rock.

Conflict in Somalia has displaced more than 400,000 of the nation's inhabitants.

Cairo Africa's largest urban center, Cairo is home to 10 million people. Though the city was not established until the tenth century AD, this part of the Nile Valley was, much earlier, an important center of ancient Egyptian civilization, which flourished between 3000 BC and 500 BC. Among its most impressive and enduring legacies are the pyramids of Giza, on the southwestern fringe of Cairo, which were constructed as tombs for the rulers Khufu, Khafra, and Men-kau-re around 2600 BC.

SCALE 1:10,000,000
Lamberts Conformal Conic Projection

Longitude east of Greenwich

213

WEST AFRICA

Benin, Burkina Faso, Cameroon, Chad, Côte d'Ivoire, Equatorial Guinea, Gambia, Ghana, Guinea, Guinea-Bissau, Liberia, Mali, Mauritania, Niger, Nigeria, Senegal, Sierra Leone, Togo

Isolated ranges and plateaus dot the West African landscape, but most of the terrain is low-lying. Distinctive environments and populations, however, divide the region into northern and southern sectors. Inhabited mainly by Muslim peoples, including Berbers and Arabs, the more arid northern two-thirds, sometimes called the Western Sudan, includes the western edge of the Sahara Desert, part of the scrubby Sahel, and wide savanna grasslands. The wetter southern third, the Guinea coast, is characterized by tropical rain forest and is home to diverse African peoples. In the Middle Ages, thriving trans-Saharan trade created prosperous kingdoms in the north. From the 16th century, the economic focus shifted to the coast with the arrival of European traders. European powers gradually took control of the region, relinquishing their hold only in the late 20th century.

Most inhabitants of the Sahel live near their livestock in traditional villages.

Djenné In the 14th century, Mali, located in the present-day country of the same name and centered on the cities of Djenné, Timbuktu, and Gao, was Africa's most powerful state. Larger than any contemporary state in Europe, it derived much of its wealth and power from its control of trans-Saharan trade in gold, salt, and slaves. Following its adoption of Islam, Mali became a center of Muslim scholarship and the site of several large mosques. The Great Mosque of Djenné was built in the 14th century, destroyed in 1896, and rebuilt in 1909. Made of sun-baked earth, it is the world's biggest mud-brick structure.

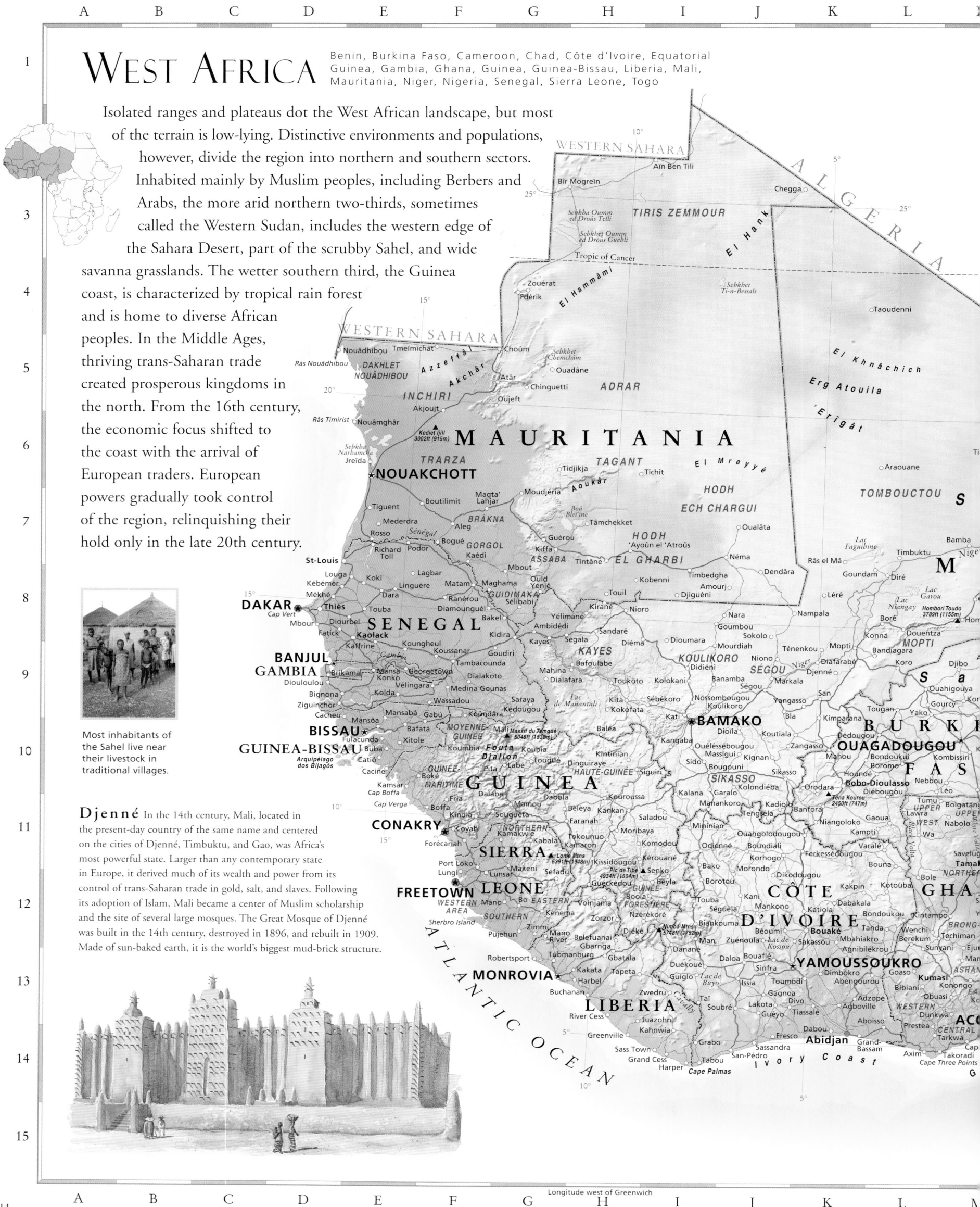

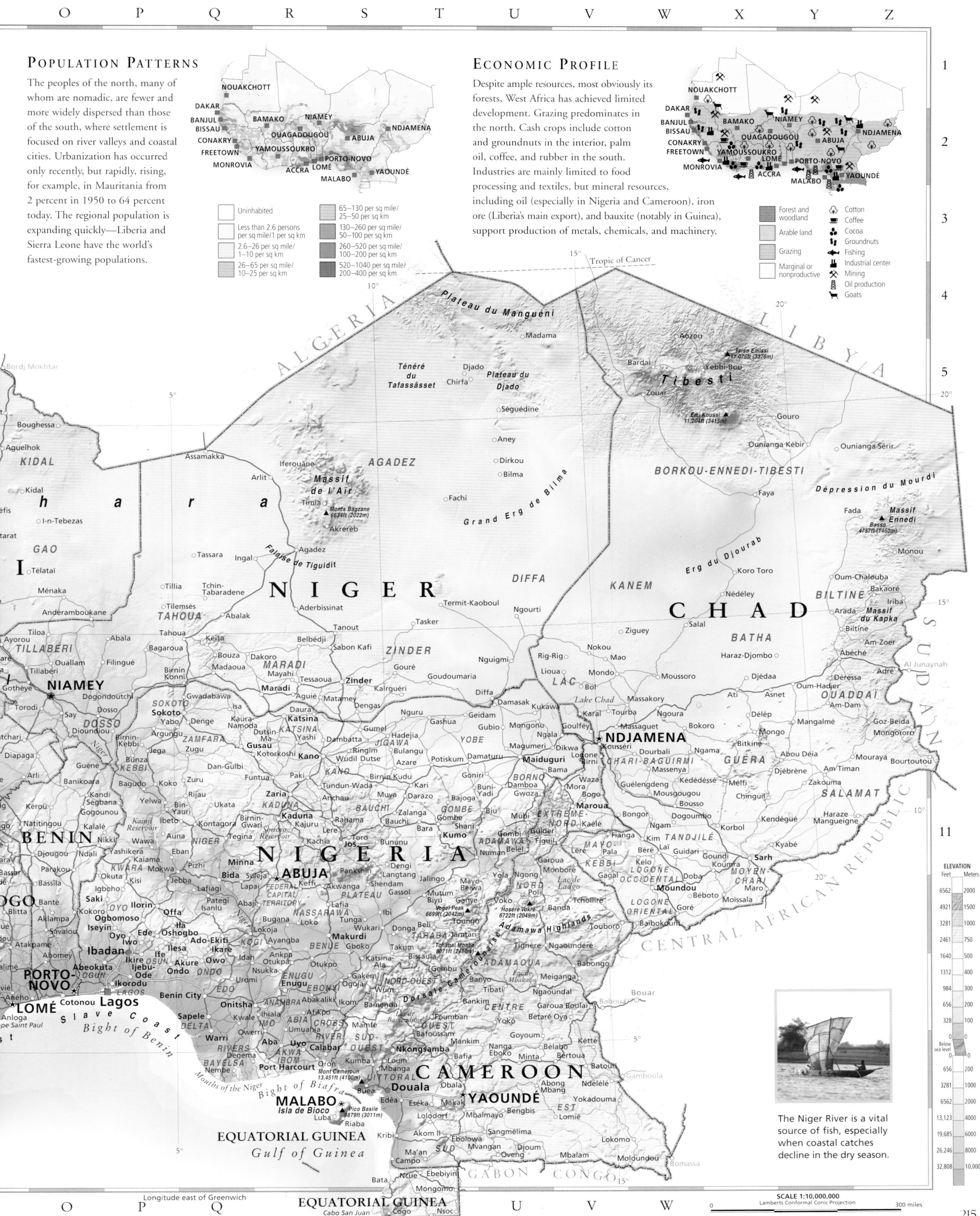

POPULATION PATTERNS

The peoples of the north, many of whom are nomadic, are fewer and more widely dispersed than those of the south, where settlement is focused on river valleys and coastal cities. Urbanization has occurred only recently, but rapidly, rising, for example, in Mauritania from 2 percent in 1950 to 64 percent today. The regional population is expanding quickly—Liberia and Sierra Leone have the world's fastest-growing populations.

- Uninhabited
- Less than 2.6 persons per sq mile/1 per sq km
- 2.6–26 per sq mile/ 1–10 per sq km
- 26–65 per sq mile/ 10–25 per sq km
- 65–130 per sq mile/ 25–50 per sq km
- 130–260 per sq mile/ 50–100 per sq km
- 260–520 per sq mile/ 100–200 per sq km
- 520–1040 per sq mile/ 200–400 per sq km

ECONOMIC PROFILE

Despite ample resources, most obviously its forests, West Africa has achieved limited development. Grazing predominates in the north. Cash crops include cotton and groundnuts in the interior, palm oil, coffee, and rubber in the south. Industries are mainly limited to food processing and textiles, but mineral resources, including oil (especially in Nigeria and Cameroon), iron ore (Liberia's main export), and bauxite (notably in Guinea), support production of metals, chemicals, and machinery.

- Forest and woodland
- Arable land
- Grazing
- Marginal or nonproductive
- Cotton
- Coffee
- Cocoa
- Groundnuts
- Fishing
- Industrial center
- Mining
- Oil production
- Goats

The Niger River is a vital source of fish, especially when coastal catches decline in the dry season.

ELEVATION

Feet	Meters
6562	2000
4921	1500
3281	1000
2461	750
1640	500
1312	400
984	300
656	200
328	100
0	0
Below sea level	
656	200
3281	1000
6562	2000
13,123	4000
19,685	6000
26,246	8000
32,808	10,000

SCALE 1:10,000,000
Lamberts Conformal Conic Projection
0 — 300 miles
0 — 300 kilometers

Longitude east of Greenwich

CENTRAL AND EAST AFRICA

Burundi, Central African Republic, Congo, Democratic Republic of Congo, Gabon, Kenya, Rwanda, São Tomé and Príncipe, Tanzania, Uganda

The Congo Basin covers most of Central Africa, extending from the west coast northeastward to the tablelands that cross the Central African Republic, east to the Mitumba and Ruwenzori mountains, and south into Angola and Zambia. A wet climate and dense cover of tropical rain forest make overland travel through the basin notoriously difficult, and the Congo and other rivers are still major communications routes. The dividing line between Central Africa and East Africa is the Great Rift Valley. On its eastern flank, the rain forests yield to savannas roamed by a great diversity of wild animals, as well as herds of cattle and sheep. Violence has plagued these countries in recent decades, including civil wars in Uganda and the Democratic Republic of Congo, and interethnic massacres in Rwanda and Burundi.

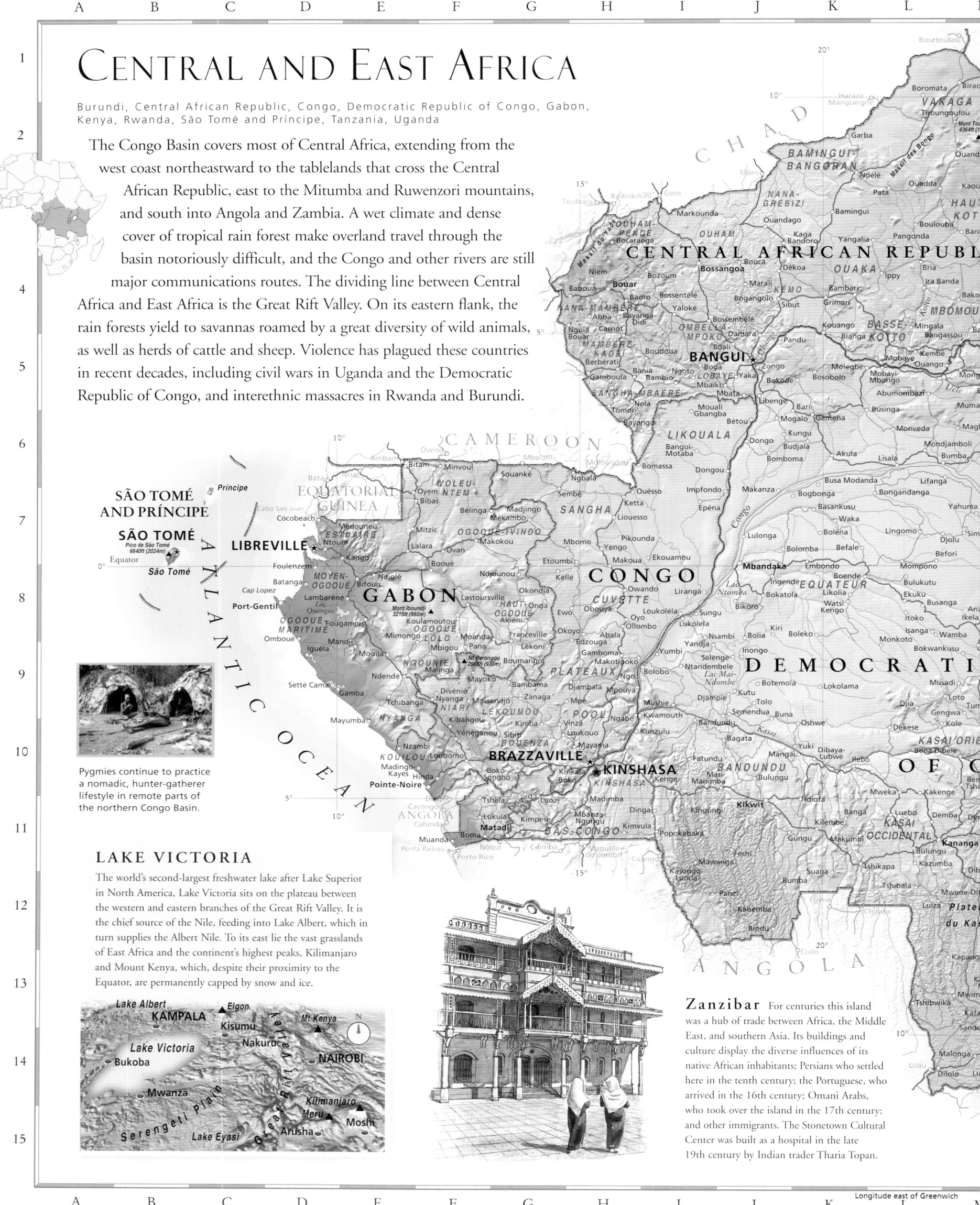

Pygmies continue to practice a nomadic, hunter-gatherer lifestyle in remote parts of the northern Congo Basin.

LAKE VICTORIA

The world's second-largest freshwater lake after Lake Superior in North America, Lake Victoria sits on the plateau between the western and eastern branches of the Great Rift Valley. It is the chief source of the Nile, feeding into Lake Albert, which in turn supplies the Albert Nile. To its east lie the vast grasslands of East Africa and the continent's highest peaks, Kilimanjaro and Mount Kenya, which, despite their proximity to the Equator, are permanently capped by snow and ice.

Zanzibar For centuries this island was a hub of trade between Africa, the Middle East, and southern Asia. Its buildings and culture display the diverse influences of its native African inhabitants; Persians who settled here in the tenth century; the Portuguese, who arrived in the 16th century; Omani Arabs, who took over the island in the 17th century; and other immigrants. The Stonetown Cultural Center was built as a hospital in the late 19th century by Indian trader Tharia Topan.

Longitude east of Greenwich

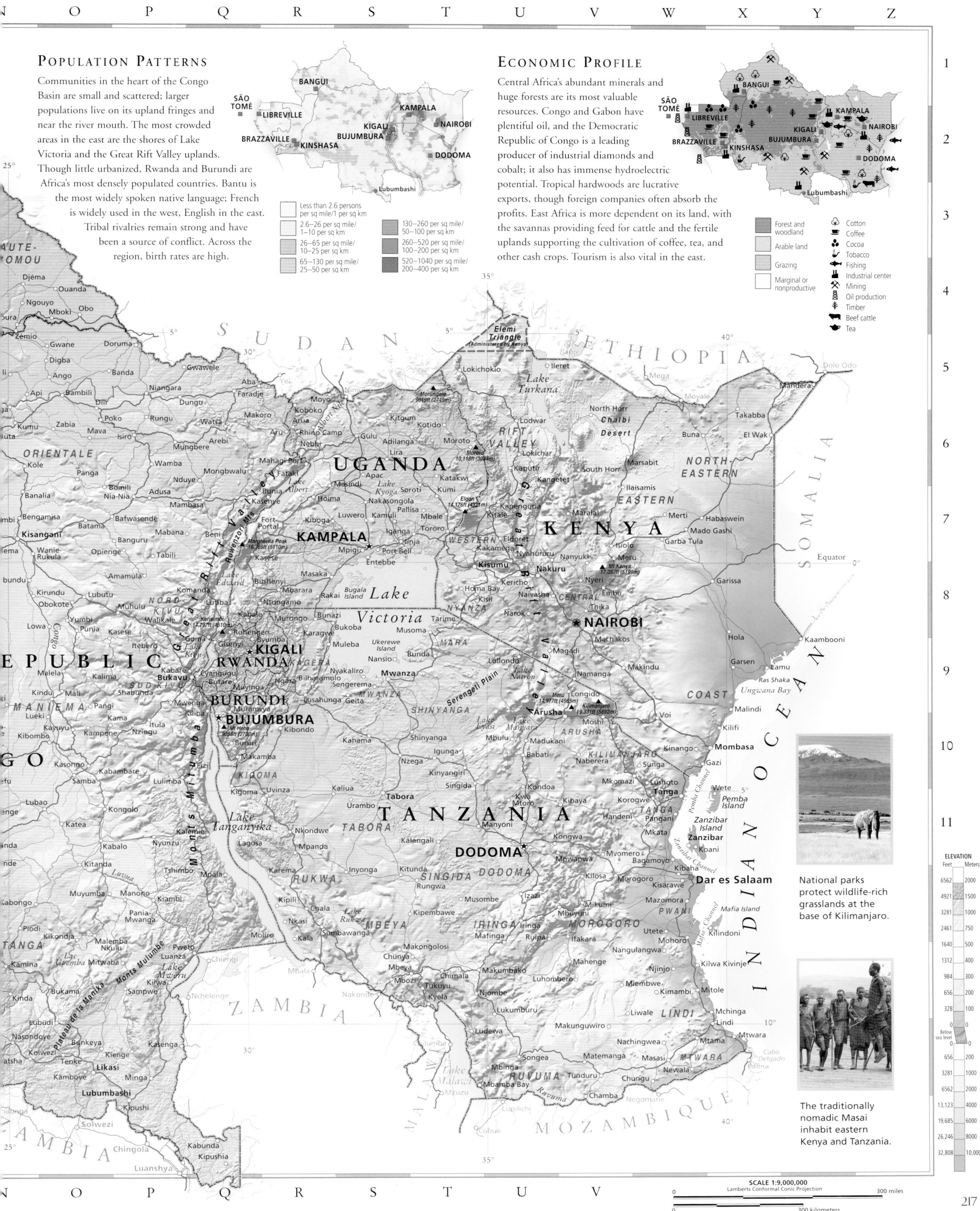

POPULATION PATTERNS

Communities in the heart of the Congo Basin are small and scattered; larger populations live on its upland fringes and near the river mouth. The most crowded areas in the east are the shores of Lake Victoria and the Great Rift Valley uplands. Though little urbanized, Rwanda and Burundi are Africa's most densely populated countries. Bantu is the most widely spoken native language; French is widely used in the west, English in the east. Tribal rivalries remain strong and have been a source of conflict. Across the region, birth rates are high.

Less than 2.6 persons per sq mile/1 per sq km
2.6–26 per sq mile/ 1–10 per sq km
26–65 per sq mile/ 10–25 per sq km
65–130 per sq mile/ 25–50 per sq km
130–260 per sq mile/ 50–100 per sq km
260–520 per sq mile/ 100–200 per sq km
520–1040 per sq mile/ 200–400 per sq km

ECONOMIC PROFILE

Central Africa's abundant minerals and huge forests are its most valuable resources. Congo and Gabon have plentiful oil, and the Democratic Republic of Congo is a leading producer of industrial diamonds and cobalt; it also has immense hydroelectric potential. Tropical hardwoods are lucrative exports, though foreign companies often absorb the profits. East Africa is more dependent on its land, with the savannas providing feed for cattle and the fertile uplands supporting the cultivation of coffee, tea, and other cash crops. Tourism is also vital in the east.

Forest and woodland
Arable land
Grazing
Marginal or nonproductive

Cotton
Coffee
Cocoa
Tobacco
Fishing
Industrial center
Mining
Oil production
Timber
Beef cattle
Tea

National parks protect wildlife-rich grasslands at the base of Kilimanjaro.

The traditionally nomadic Masai inhabit eastern Kenya and Tanzania.

ELEVATION
Feet	Meters
6562	2000
4921	1500
3281	1000
2461	750
1640	500
1312	400
984	300
656	200
328	100
0	0
Below sea level	
0	0
656	200
3281	1000
6562	2000
13,123	4000
19,685	6000
26,246	8000
32,808	10,000

SCALE 1:9,000,000
Lamberts Conformal Conic Projection
300 miles
300 kilometers

217

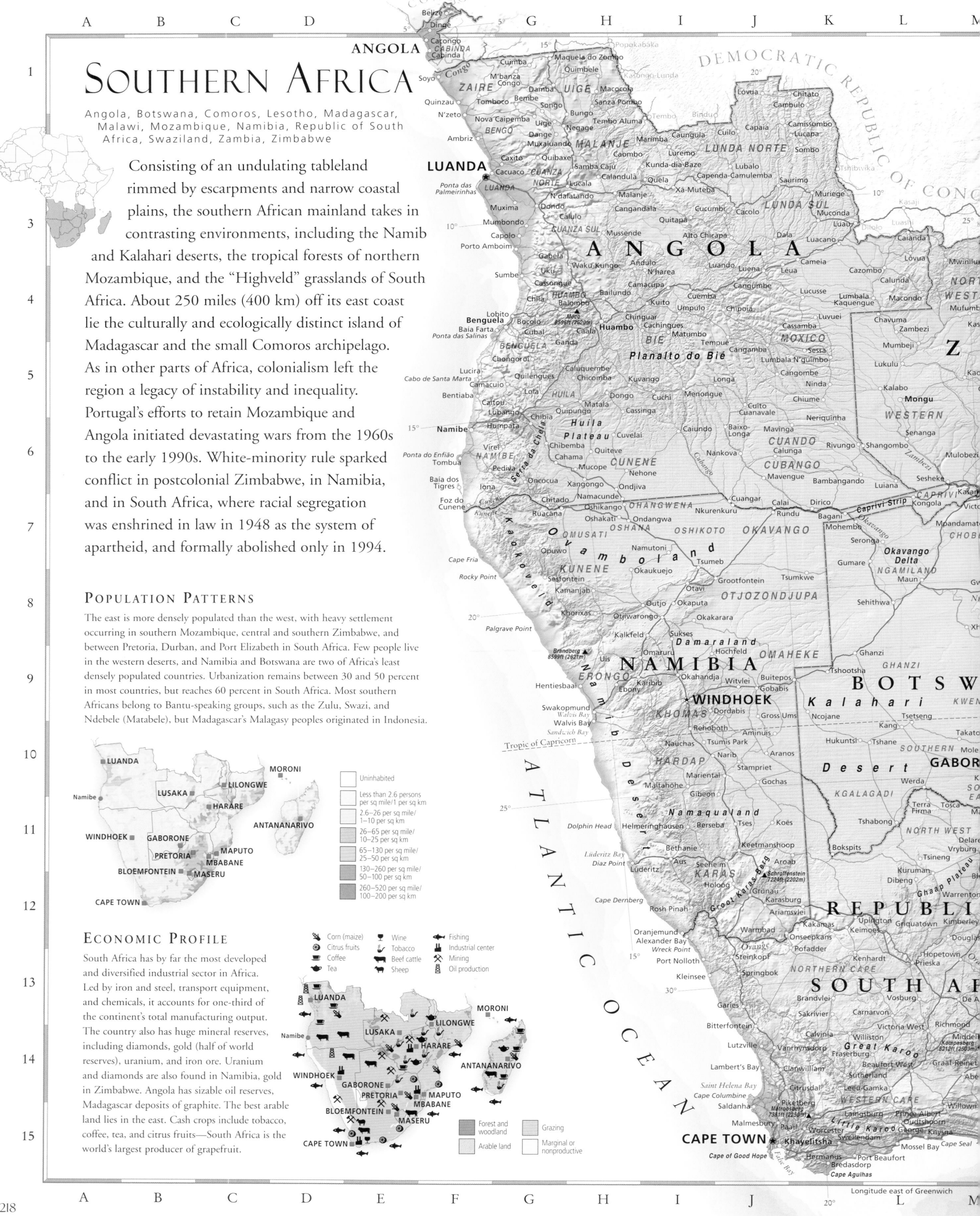

ANGOLA

SOUTHERN AFRICA

Angola, Botswana, Comoros, Lesotho, Madagascar,
Malawi, Mozambique, Namibia, Republic of South
Africa, Swaziland, Zambia, Zimbabwe

Consisting of an undulating tableland
rimmed by escarpments and narrow coastal
plains, the southern African mainland takes in
contrasting environments, including the Namib
and Kalahari deserts, the tropical forests of northern
Mozambique, and the "Highveld" grasslands of South
Africa. About 250 miles (400 km) off its east coast
lie the culturally and ecologically distinct island of
Madagascar and the small Comoros archipelago.
As in other parts of Africa, colonialism left the
region a legacy of instability and inequality.
Portugal's efforts to retain Mozambique and
Angola initiated devastating wars from the 1960s
to the early 1990s. White-minority rule sparked
conflict in postcolonial Zimbabwe, in Namibia,
and in South Africa, where racial segregation
was enshrined in law in 1948 as the system of
apartheid, and formally abolished only in 1994.

POPULATION PATTERNS

The east is more densely populated than the west, with heavy settlement
occurring in southern Mozambique, central and southern Zimbabwe, and
between Pretoria, Durban, and Port Elizabeth in South Africa. Few people live
in the western deserts, and Namibia and Botswana are two of Africa's least
densely populated countries. Urbanization remains between 30 and 50 percent
in most countries, but reaches 60 percent in South Africa. Most southern
Africans belong to Bantu-speaking groups, such as the Zulu, Swazi, and
Ndebele (Matabele), but Madagascar's Malagasy peoples originated in Indonesia.

| Uninhabited |
| Less than 2.6 persons per sq mile/1 per sq km |
| 2.6–26 per sq mile/1–10 per sq km |
| 26–65 per sq mile/10–25 per sq km |
| 65–130 per sq mile/25–50 per sq km |
| 130–260 per sq mile/50–100 per sq km |
| 260–520 per sq mile/100–200 per sq km |

ECONOMIC PROFILE

South Africa has by far the most developed
and diversified industrial sector in Africa.
Led by iron and steel, transport equipment,
and chemicals, it accounts for one-third of
the continent's total manufacturing output.
The country also has huge mineral reserves,
including diamonds, gold (half of world
reserves), uranium, and iron ore. Uranium
and diamonds are also found in Namibia, gold
in Zimbabwe. Angola has sizable oil reserves,
Madagascar deposits of graphite. The best arable
land lies in the east. Cash crops include tobacco,
coffee, tea, and citrus fruits—South Africa is the
world's largest producer of grapefruit.

Corn (maize) Wine Fishing
Citrus fruits Tobacco Industrial center
Coffee Beef cattle Mining
Tea Sheep Oil production

Forest and woodland
Arable land
Grazing
Marginal or nonproductive

Longitude east of Greenwich

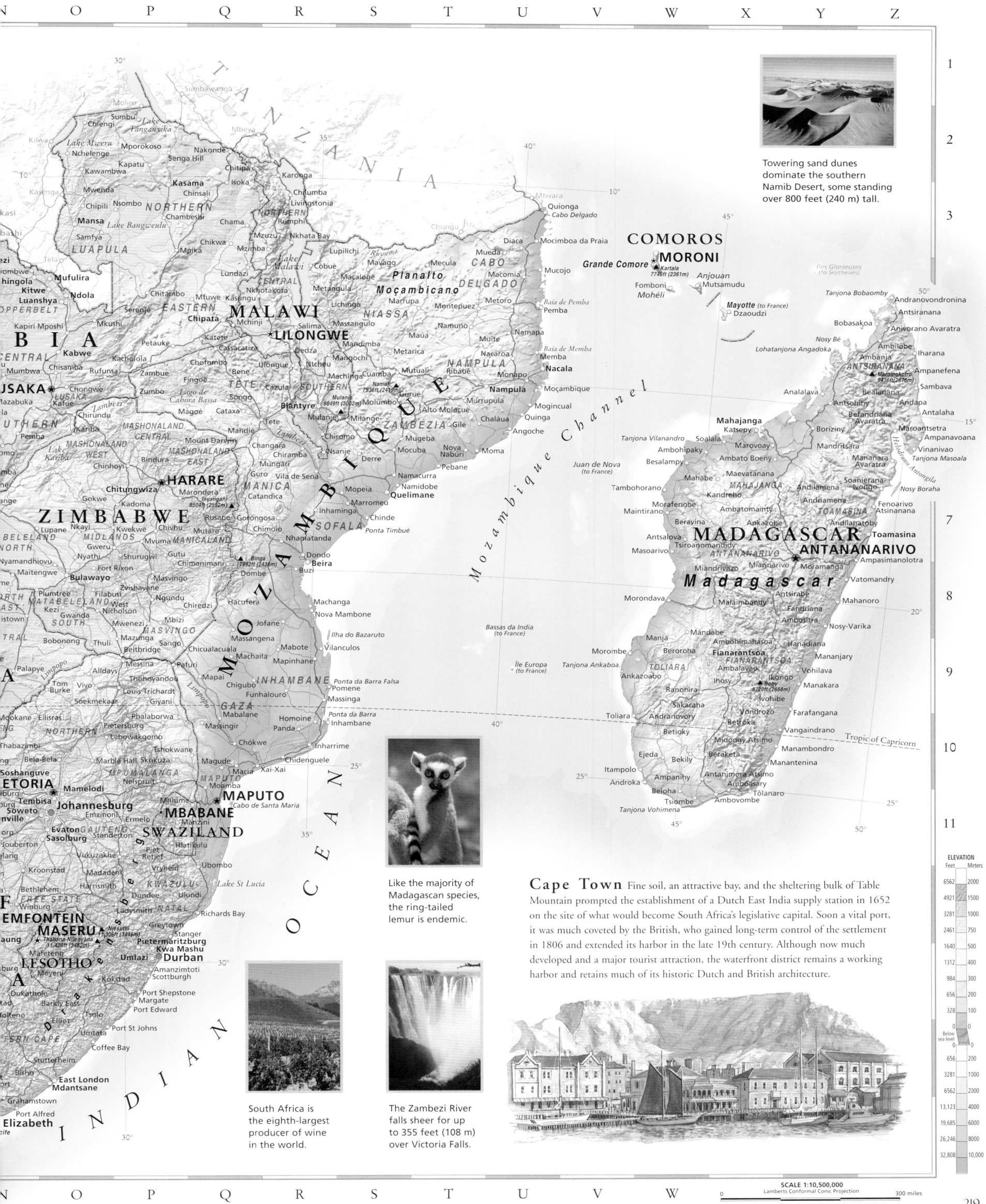

Towering sand dunes dominate the southern Namib Desert, some standing over 800 feet (240 m) tall.

Like the majority of Madagascan species, the ring-tailed lemur is endemic.

South Africa is the eighth-largest producer of wine in the world.

The Zambezi River falls sheer for up to 355 feet (108 m) over Victoria Falls.

Cape Town Fine soil, an attractive bay, and the sheltering bulk of Table Mountain prompted the establishment of a Dutch East India supply station in 1652 on the site of what would become South Africa's legislative capital. Soon a vital port, it was much coveted by the British, who gained long-term control of the settlement in 1806 and extended its harbor in the late 19th century. Although now much developed and a major tourist attraction, the waterfront district remains a working harbor and retains much of its historic Dutch and British architecture.

ELEVATION

Feet	Meters
6562	2000
4921	1500
3281	1000
2461	750
1640	500
1312	400
984	300
656	200
328	100
Below sea level	
656	200
3281	1000
6562	2000
13,123	4000
19,685	6000
26,246	8000
32,808	10,000

SCALE 1:10,500,000
Lamberts Conformal Conic Projection

0   300 miles

0   300 kilometers

Australia's eastern seaboard is illuminated at night while the sparsely populated interior remains dark. The north and south islands of New Zealand are clearly visible. The dots of light smattered throughout the Pacific are island nations such as Fiji.

OCEANIA

ABOVE OCEANIA

Satellites can record grand-scale natural happenings, from the calving of a huge iceberg on Antarctica's slowly diminishing Ross Ice Shelf, to devastating wildfires raging across the southeast of Australia. From space, the relative stability of the ancient landmass of Australia is in stark contrast to continuing geological activity in its near neighbors. New Zealand lies in the collision zone between the Indo-Australian and Pacific tectonic plates. Movement of these plates caused the volcanic activity that shaped much of the North Island, and the country's fertile pastures are a legacy of layers of volcanic ash. In the image of Mount Taranaki (Mt Egmont), above, simulated natural color emphasizes the contrast between the lush forests preserved within the circular boundary of Egmont National Park, which extends in a 6-mile (10-km) radius from the volcano's summit, and the bright-colored dairy pastures beyond.

Egmont National Park, New Zealand
Above: The snow-capped, symmetrical peak of Mount Taranaki (Mt Egmont), 8,261 feet (2,518 m), towers over the forests of Egmont National Park in the west of New Zealand's North Island. Taranaki began forming 70,000 years ago and last erupted in 1755. Nearby are two older volcanoes. The gray area, top right, is the city of New Plymouth.

Southeastern Australia and the Tasman Sea
Right: In January 2003 nearly 100 wildfires were burning in southeastern Australia. This satellite image, gathered on 10 January, shows smoke from fires near Sydney, center, and northeastern Victoria, lower left, streaking the skies above the Tasman Sea. Ten days after this image was taken, the smoke and haze reached beyond New Zealand.

Uluru and Kata Tjuta, Australia
Top: Shown in blue in this false-color image, Uluru, center right, and Kata Tjuta, 30 miles (50 km) to the west, poke through the dry plains of Central Australia. Both are part of an ancient bed of sedimentary rock that has been folded and pushed upward. Uluru is the weathered end of the bed, now standing vertically.

Ross Ice Shelf, Antarctica
Above: A huge iceberg, center, broke off the Ross Ice Shelf at the end of the Antarctic summer in March 2000, calving along pre-existing cracks in the ice shelf. At 180 miles (300 km) long and 25 miles (40 km) wide it is one of the largest known. It was locked in sea ice until the spring thaw, but began to drift soon after this image was taken.

LAND AND ENVIRONMENT

Extending from the Indian Ocean to the eastern Pacific, and from the Tropic of Cancer to the remote subantarctic territory of Macquarie Island, Oceania covers a vast area of ocean and about 3.4 million square miles (8.8 million sq km) of land. Of this, almost 3 million square miles (7.7 million sq km) is encompassed by the island continent of Australia; the remainder consists of the eastern half of New Guinea, the large island group of New Zealand, and about 10,000 smaller islands. Oceania is traditionally divided into four subregions named for the ethnic groups that first inhabited them: Australia, Melanesia, Micronesia, and Polynesia (which includes New Zealand). These subregions encompass diverse landscapes. Located in the middle of the Indo-Australian Plate, Australia is an ancient, stable land, with few high mountains and an arid interior. More recently formed, the islands of Melanesia and New Zealand lie on plate margins and have high, young peaks and active volcanoes. Elsewhere in Polynesia, and in Micronesia, most islands are the summits of undersea volcanoes, or tiny atolls.

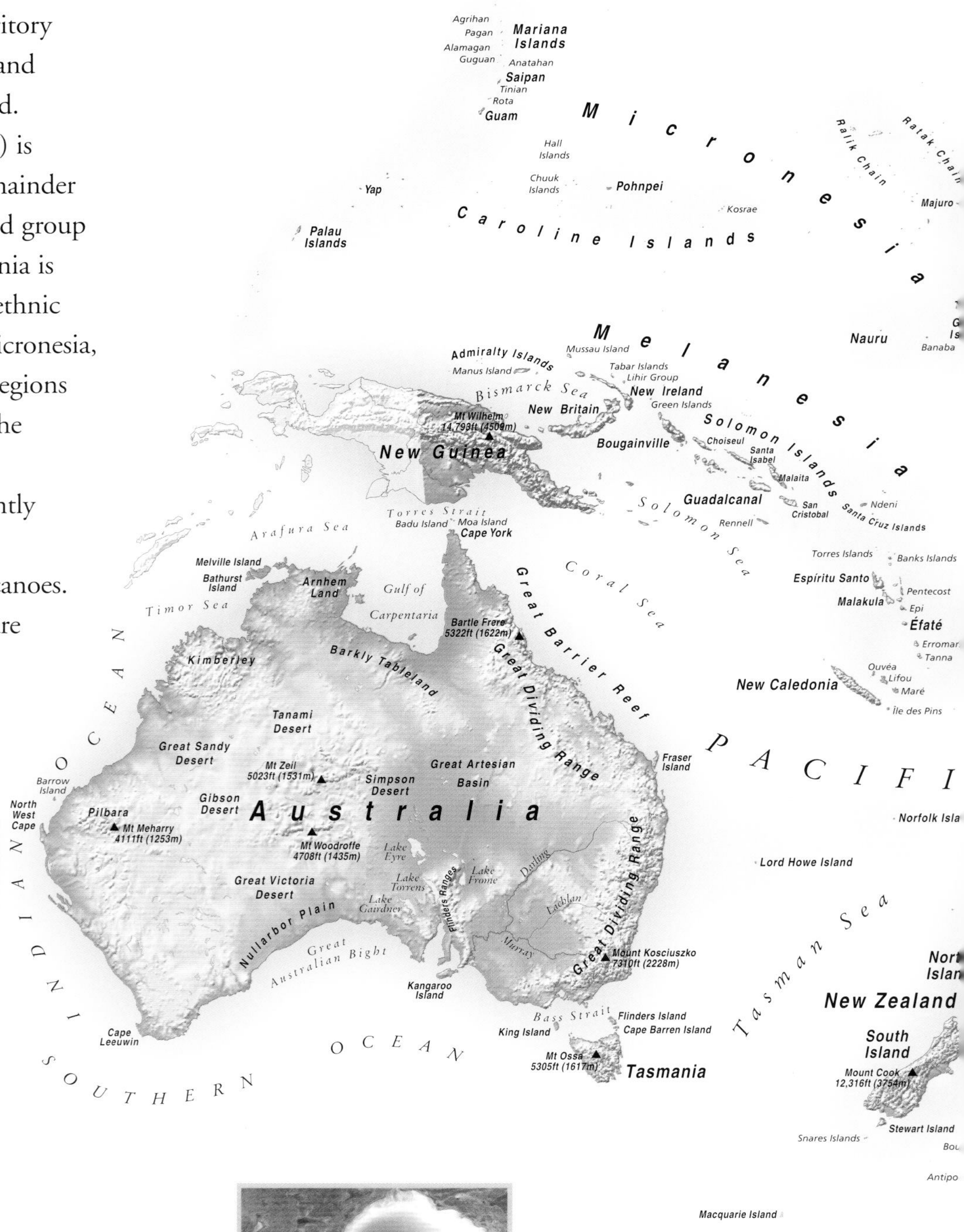

NATURAL HAZARDS

Wildfires

Long spells of dry weather combined with inflammable oils produced by widespread eucalypts and acacias make much of Australia highly susceptible to wildfires, or bushfires as they are known locally. Fire is part of the ecology of most Australian environments: many native plants are not only adapted to drought but can also withstand fire; indeed, some require fire to trigger germination. Wildfires are started naturally by lightning strikes. Increasingly, they are also caused by human carelessness or mischief, with the result that they occur regularly in urban areas. In dry, windy conditions, bushfires can move with astonishing speed, rapidly consuming vegetation, leaping roads and waterways, and, in severe cases, causing significant loss of life and property.

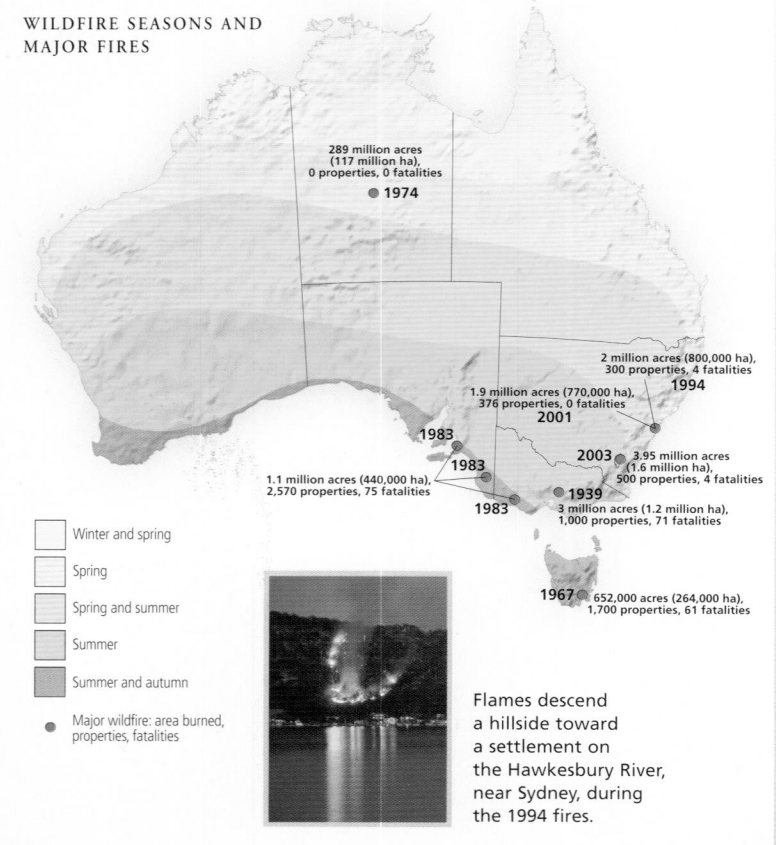

WILDFIRE SEASONS AND MAJOR FIRES

289 million acres (117 million ha), 0 properties, 0 fatalities
● 1974

2 million acres (800,000 ha), 300 properties, 4 fatalities
1994

1.9 million acres (770,000 ha), 376 properties, 0 fatalities
2001

1983

1983

2003 ● 3.95 million acres (1.6 million ha), 500 properties, 4 fatalities

1.1 million acres (440,000 ha), 2,570 properties, 75 fatalities

1983

● **1939** 3 million acres (1.2 million ha), 1,000 properties, 71 fatalities

1967 ● 652,000 acres (264,000 ha), 1,700 properties, 61 fatalities

☐ Winter and spring
☐ Spring
☐ Spring and summer
☐ Summer
☐ Summer and autumn
● Major wildfire: area burned, properties, fatalities

Flames descend a hillside toward a settlement on the Hawkesbury River, near Sydney, during the 1994 fires.

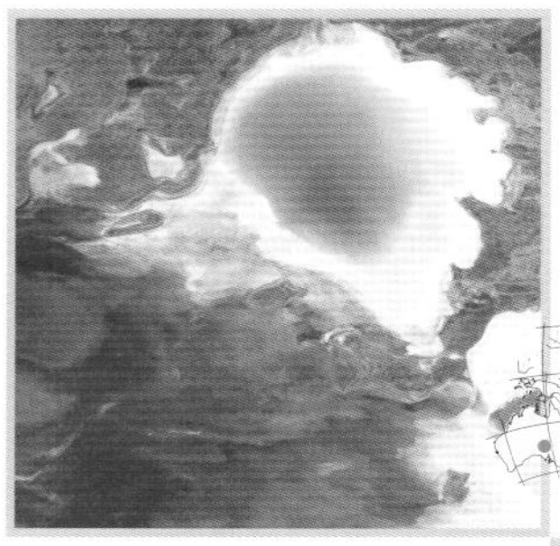

Right: The largest lake in Australia, Lake Eyre is part of a system that drains one-sixth of the continent. But only rarely does the lake fill with water; most of the time, it is dry and encrusted with salt.

Right: This chain of coral reefs is part of the northern end of Australia's Great Barrier Reef. The world's largest coral reef, it extends for over 1,200 miles (2,000 km) down the northeast coast of the continent.

(Map labels:)

Mariana Islands
Agrihan
Pagan
Alamagan
Guguan
Anatahan
Saipan
Tinian
Rota
Guam

Micronesia

Hall Islands
Yap
Chuuk Islands
Pohnpei
Kosrae
Majuro

Palau Islands

Caroline Islands

Ralik Chain
Ratak Chain

Nauru
Banaba

Melanesia

Admiralty Islands
Manus Island
Mussau Island
Tabar Islands
Lihir Group
New Ireland
New Britain
Green Islands
Mt Wilhelm 14,793ft (4504m)
Bougainville
Solomon Islands
Choiseul
Santa Isabel
Malaita
Guadalcanal
San Cristobal
Ndeni
Santa Cruz Islands
Rennell
Solomon Sea

New Guinea

Torres Strait
Badu Island
Moa Island
Cape York

Torres Islands
Banks Islands
Espíritu Santo
Pentecost
Epi
Makula
Malakula
Efaté
Errromar
Ouvéa
Lifou
Tanna
Maré
Île des Pins

Arafura Sea

Coral Sea

PACIFI

Timor Sea

Melville Island
Bathurst Island
Arnhem Land
Gulf of Carpentaria
Bartle Frere 5322ft (1622m)
Great Barrier Reef

New Caledonia

Kimberley
Barkly Tableland
Great Dividing Range

INDIAN OCEAN

Norfolk Island

Tanami Desert

Great Sandy Desert
Mt Zeil 5023ft (1531m)
Simpson Desert
Great Artesian Basin
Fraser Island

Barrow Island
North West Cape
Pilbara
Mt Meharry 4111ft (1253m)
Gibson Desert
Australia
Lake Eyre

Lord Howe Island

Great Victoria Desert
Mt Woodroffe 4708ft (1435m)
Lake Torrens
Lake Frome
Flinders Ranges
Lake Gairdner
Darling
Great Dividing Range

Nullarbor Plain
Murray
Lachlan
Mount Kosciuszko 7310ft (2228m)

Tasman Sea

North Island

New Zealand

Great Australian Bight
Kangaroo Island

Cape Leeuwin
King Island
Bass Strait
Flinders Island
Cape Barren Island

Cape Leeuwin

SOUTHERN OCEAN

Mt Ossa 5305ft (1617m)
Tasmania

South Island
Mount Cook 12,316ft (3754m)

Snares Islands
Stewart Island
Bou

Antipo

Macquarie Island

Climate

Most of the countries and territories of Oceania lie close to the Equator and therefore experience warm, humid conditions year-round. Rainfall varies little from month to month at the Equator, but farther north and south pronounced wet and dry seasons occur. During the Southern-Hemisphere summer, hurricanes (known locally as cyclones) occur above 5 degrees north and south. Seasonal tropical conditions—and cyclones—extend to the northern fringe of Australia. In middle latitudes, conditions are cooler, and moist onshore winds keep New Zealand and the east coast of Australia well-watered. The interior of Australia is, however, one of the most arid regions on Earth, and about half of the continent receives less than 12 inches (300 mm) of rain a year. Dry spells occasionally turn to droughts, especially in eastern Australia during El Niño episodes.

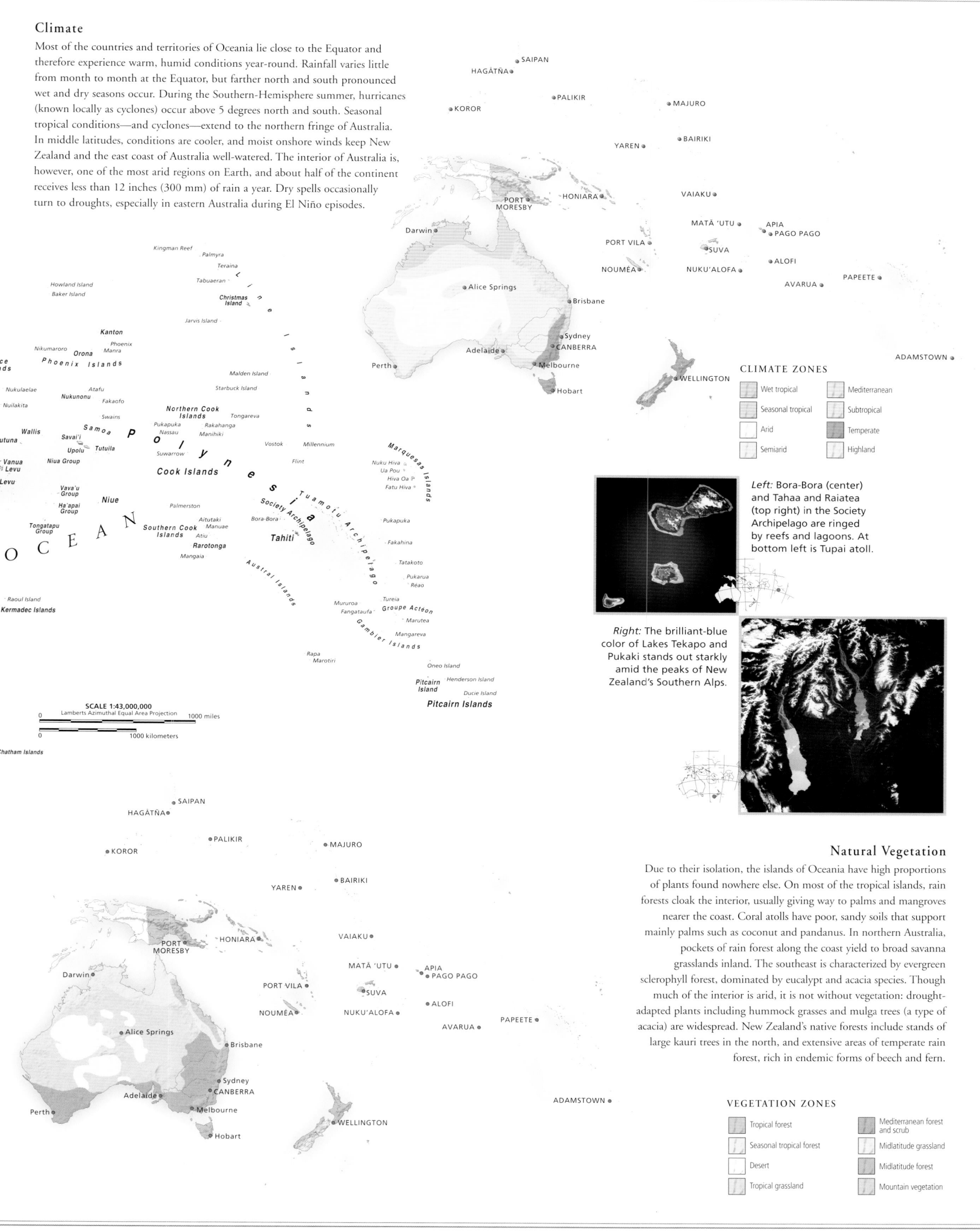

SCALE 1:43,000,000
Lamberts Azimuthal Equal Area Projection
0 —— 1000 miles
0 —— 1000 kilometers

CLIMATE ZONES

Wet tropical	Mediterranean
Seasonal tropical	Subtropical
Arid	Temperate
Semiarid	Highland

Left: Bora-Bora (center) and Tahaa and Raiatea (top right) in the Society Archipelago are ringed by reefs and lagoons. At bottom left is Tupai atoll.

Right: The brilliant-blue color of Lakes Tekapo and Pukaki stands out starkly amid the peaks of New Zealand's Southern Alps.

Natural Vegetation

Due to their isolation, the islands of Oceania have high proportions of plants found nowhere else. On most of the tropical islands, rain forests cloak the interior, usually giving way to palms and mangroves nearer the coast. Coral atolls have poor, sandy soils that support mainly palms such as coconut and pandanus. In northern Australia, pockets of rain forest along the coast yield to broad savanna grasslands inland. The southeast is characterized by evergreen sclerophyll forest, dominated by eucalypt and acacia species. Though much of the interior is arid, it is not without vegetation: drought-adapted plants including hummock grasses and mulga trees (a type of acacia) are widespread. New Zealand's native forests include stands of large kauri trees in the north, and extensive areas of temperate rain forest, rich in endemic forms of beech and fern.

VEGETATION ZONES

Tropical forest	Mediterranean forest and scrub
Seasonal tropical forest	Midlatitude grassland
Desert	Midlatitude forest
Tropical grassland	Mountain vegetation

Peoples and Nations

Home to about 32 million people, Oceania encompasses 14 nations and numerous dependencies. Its indigenous peoples form four major groups—Australian Aboriginal peoples, Melanesians, Micronesians, and Polynesians—who speak a huge variety of languages. Since the 18th century, large numbers of immigrants have settled in the region, particularly in Australia and New Zealand. Most came from Europe, especially the United Kingdom, making English the most widely spoken language in Australia and New Zealand.

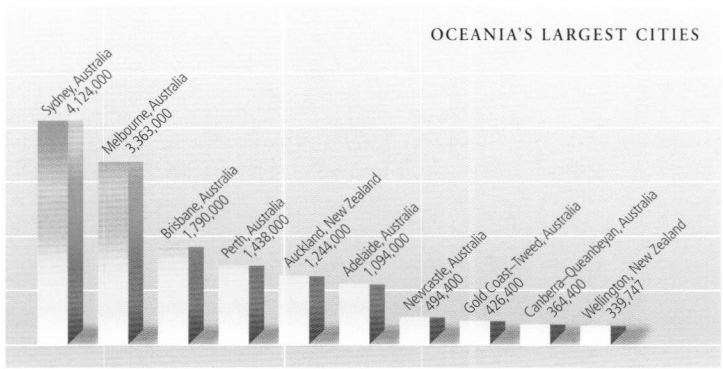

OCEANIA'S LARGEST CITIES

Sydney, Australia 4,124,000
Melbourne, Australia 3,363,000
Brisbane, Australia 1,790,000
Perth, Australia 1,438,000
Auckland, New Zealand 1,244,000
Adelaide, Australia 1,094,000
Newcastle, Australia 494,400
Gold Coast–Tweed, Australia 426,400
Canberra–Queanbeyan, Australia 364,400
Wellington, New Zealand 339,747

Urbanization

There is a stark contrast between Australia and New Zealand, where cities and towns accommodate around 90 percent of the inhabitants, and most of the rest of Oceania, where there are no major cities and the urban population is generally under 60 percent. An exception is the French territory of New Caledonia, where 82 percent of the inhabitants live in urban areas. In Papua New Guinea, just 19 percent of people live in towns and cities, but even here significant change has occurred in recent decades: in 1950, the urban population accounted for less than one percent of the total.

POPULATION DENSITY

Uninhabited

Less than 2.6 persons per sq mile/1 per sq km

2.6–26 per sq mile/ 1–10 per sq km

26–65 per sq mile/ 10–25 per sq km

Population Patterns

Australia accounts for most of Oceania's population, with about 20 million people. Another 5 million people inhabit New Guinea and about 4 million live in New Zealand. The remainder of Oceania's population is scattered across thousands of small islands. Population density is generally low but varies greatly. The highest concentrations of inhabitants occur on the southeast coast of Australia, in northern New Zealand and the Papua New Guinea highlands, and on the tiny islands of Nauru, the Cook Islands, and Tuvalu (where 11,000 people occupy just 10 square miles [26 sq km] of land). In contrast, the interior of Australia is one of the world's most sparsely populated regions, and many small Pacific islands are uninhabited. Growth rates are high in Micronesia and in Papua New Guinea, where the population is expected to double by 2030.

Flashpoints

Oceania has no major international boundary disputes, but ethnic rivalries have undermined political and economic stability in some countries and sparked a number of regional conflicts.

Fiji

Almost half of the people of Fiji are the descendants of Indian laborers brought to the islands by the British. The accession of a democratically elected, Indo-Fijian-dominated government prompted a military coup in 1987 led by indigenous Fijians, and the introduction of laws to ensure indigenous rule. Continuing Indo-Fijian participation in politics prompted another failed coup by indigenous Fijians in May 2000.

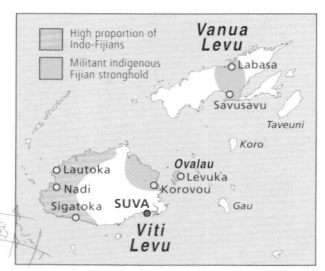

High proportion of Indo-Fijians
Militant indigenous Fijian stronghold

Solomon Islands

In 1998, inhabitants of Guadalcanal, resentful of the growing influence of immigrants from neighboring Malaita, founded the Isatabu Freedom Movement (IFM). It began a campaign to oust Malaitans, who responded by setting up the Malaita Eagle Force (MEF). Armed conflict between these groups claimed dozens of lives and wrecked the islands' economy. A degree of order was restored by the arrival of Australian security forces in 2003.

Bougainville

Politically, Bougainville is part of Papua New Guinea, but its inhabitants have strong cultural connections with the people of the Solomon Islands. Discontent among the islanders regarding the distribution of income from mineral reserves led to an armed secessionist revolt that lasted from 1988 to 2001. A peace accord reached in that year, providing an option of independence for Bougainville by 2011–16, has so far held.

Pacific Islands Forum

Pacific Islands Forum

The Pacific Islands Forum was founded as the South Pacific Forum in 1971 by Australia, the Cook Islands, Fiji, Nauru, New Zealand, Tonga, and the former Western Samoa (now Samoa) to facilitate trade and economic development in the Oceania region and provide a strong political voice for its member states in international affairs. The forum, which changed its name to the Pacific Islands Forum in October 1999, now includes a total of 16 independent and self-governing states. Its secretariat is based in Suva, Fiji, but annual meetings are hosted by each of the member countries and territories in turn.

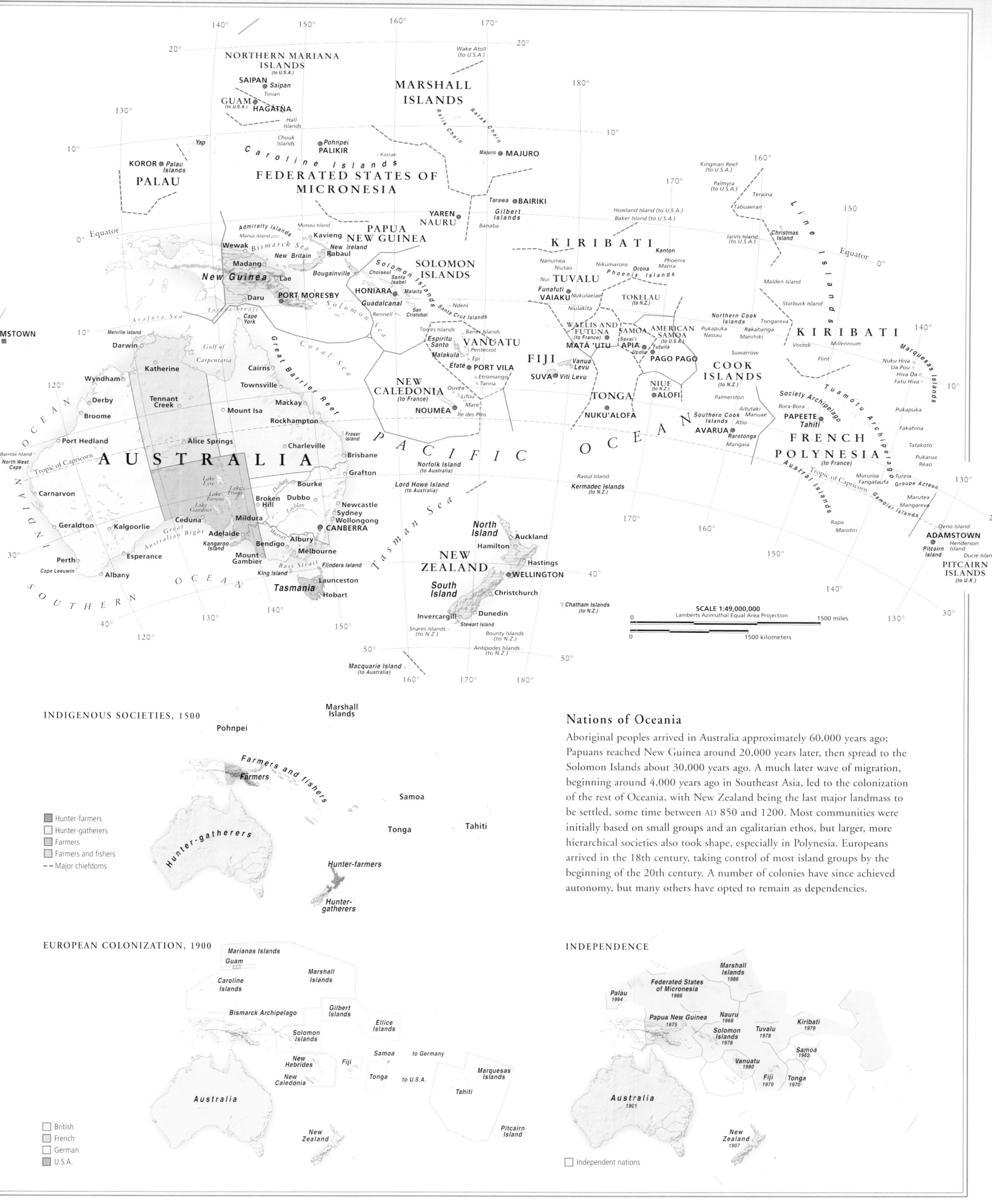

Nations of Oceania

Aboriginal peoples arrived in Australia approximately 60,000 years ago; Papuans reached New Guinea around 20,000 years later, then spread to the Solomon Islands about 30,000 years ago. A much later wave of migration, beginning around 4,000 years ago in Southeast Asia, led to the colonization of the rest of Oceania, with New Zealand being the last major landmass to be settled, some time between AD 850 and 1200. Most communities were initially based on small groups and an egalitarian ethos, but larger, more hierarchical societies also took shape, especially in Polynesia. Europeans arrived in the 18th century, taking control of most island groups by the beginning of the 20th century. A number of colonies have since achieved autonomy, but many others have opted to remain as dependencies.

INDIGENOUS SOCIETIES, 1500

- Hunter-farmers
- Hunter-gatherers
- Farmers
- Farmers and fishers
- -- Major chiefdoms

EUROPEAN COLONIZATION, 1900

- British
- French
- German
- U.S.A.

INDEPENDENCE

- Independent nations

THE HUMAN IMPACT

In well-watered New Guinea, agriculture began as early as 9,000 years ago; by 5,000 years ago, farmers there were clearing forest and digging extensive drainage systems. In Australia, by contrast, an arid climate and poor soils inhibited the development of sedentary agricultural societies. Mainly hunter-gatherers, early Aboriginal peoples did, however, divert waterways to trap fish, and burn woodlands to facilitate hunting, and may have contributed to the extinction of large mammal species, or megafauna. Some of the larger islands export cash crops such as sugar, palm oil, and cocoa, and many Melanesian islands have sizable mineral resources and forests. Europeans arriving in Oceania in the late 18th century imported the livestock, seeds, and technologies to permit rapid conversion of much larger tracts of land to agriculture. Their limited understanding of local conditions meant that they were often unaware of the havoc they were wreaking. In the industrial age, some problems have become acute. Dryland salinity threatens Australian water tables and soil; nuclear testing has contaminated land and ocean; and rising sea levels due to global warming threaten the livelihoods of entire island communities.

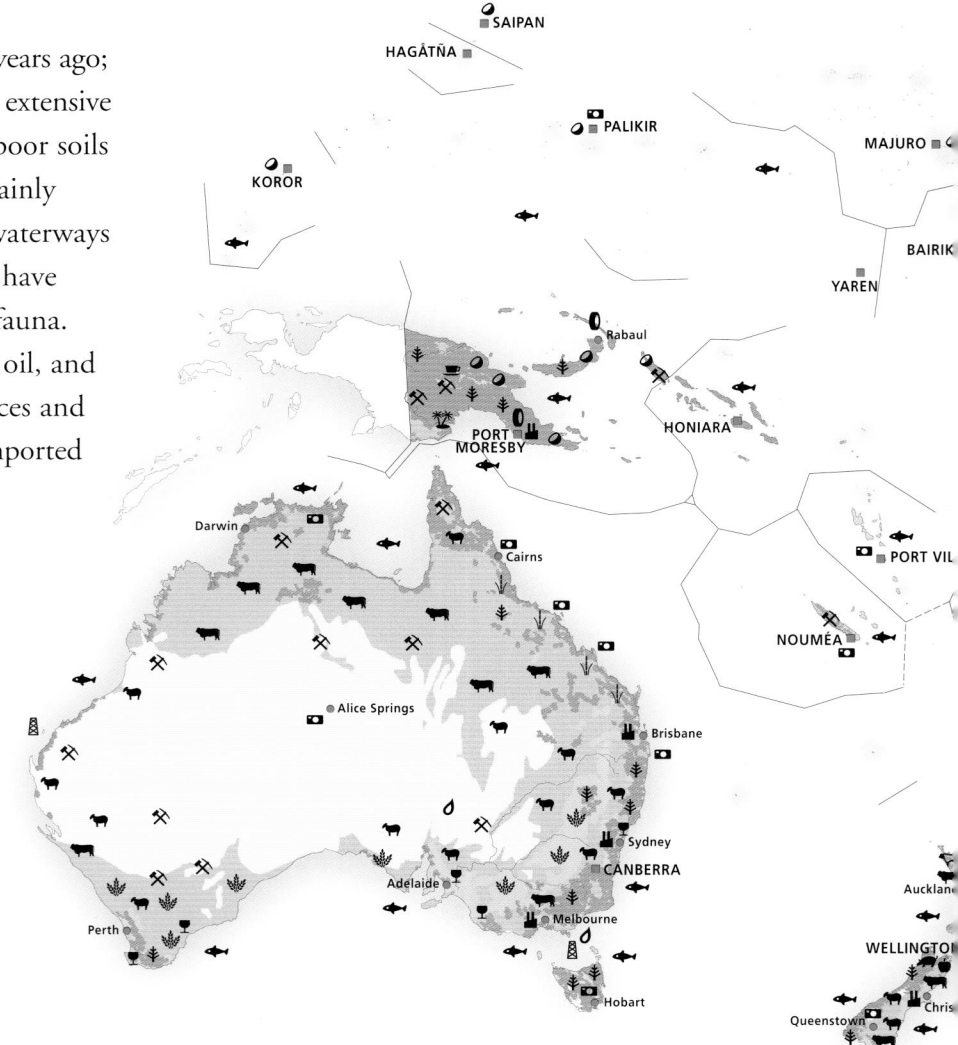

THE CHANGING FACE OF OCEANIA

Nuclear Testing

To foreign powers, the isolation and sparse populations of many parts of Oceania made them ideal for testing powerful weapons. In 1946, the U.S.A. relocated the inhabitants of Bikini and Enewetak to other other parts of the Marshall Islands, and for the next 12 years used the atolls for setting off nuclear explosions. The U.K. detonated 21 nuclear devices in Australia and the Pacific between 1952 and 1958, and France carried out 193 nuclear tests between 1966 and 1996 in French Polynesia. These tests contaminated the atmosphere and large tracts of land, and exposed service personnel and local people to fallout. Few residents of Bikini and Enewetak have been able to return home, and only in 2000 was the Maralinga site in Australia declared safe enough for its traditional owners to live there. In 1999, a French independent commission reported that radioactivity from French test sites continues to seep into fresh-water supplies, lagoons, and the sea.

NUCLEAR TEST SITES

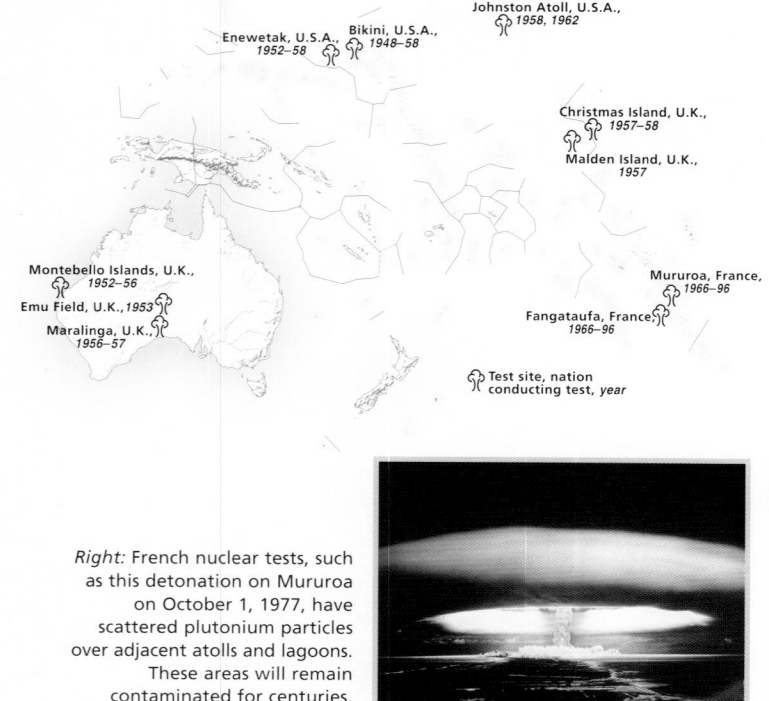

Johnston Atoll, U.S.A., 1958, 1962

Enewetak, U.S.A., 1952–58

Bikini, U.S.A., 1948–58

Christmas Island, U.K., 1957–58

Malden Island, U.K., 1957

Montebello Islands, U.K., 1952–56

Emu Field, U.K., 1953

Maralinga, U.K., 1956–57

Mururoa, France, 1966–96

Fangataufa, France, 1966–96

⚘ Test site, nation conducting test, *year*

Right: French nuclear tests, such as this detonation on Mururoa on October 1, 1977, have scattered plutonium particles over adjacent atolls and lagoons. These areas will remain contaminated for centuries.

Economic Profile

Australia and New Zealand have developed economies, with strong and diverse manufacturing sectors. However, most workers in these countries are employed in services such as the retail trade, banking, and tourism. Primary industries remain important: Australia's top exports are coal, crude oil, iron ore, gold, and wheat; New Zealand relies heavily on sales of dairy produce, meat, and timber. Elsewhere, the industrial sector is little developed, consisting mainly of the processing of raw materials. Many Melanesian islands have sizable mineral reserves and forests, and cash crops such as sugar, palm oil, and cocoa are exported by some of the larger islands. Tourism is a vital source of income for many Pacific communities, and some small islands have benefited from the sale of fishing rights to their disporportionately large maritime zones. However, most people outside Australia and New Zealand make a living from subsistence or small-scale commercial farming and fishing.

Land Cover

Abundant rainfall and volcanic soils make parts of Melanesia agriculturally productive, but arable land is scarce elsewhere. In Australia and New Zealand, in particular, most of the land is better suited to grazing, and in Australia livestock has to roam over large areas to find sufficient food. Though they are still being felled, forests cover almost one-quarter of Oceania. Australia's immense deserts account for much other land cover.

PROPORTIONS OF TOTAL LAND AREA

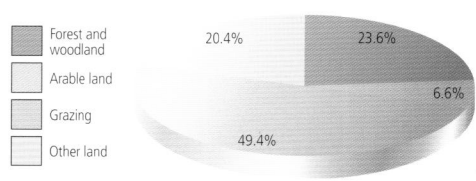

- Forest and woodland — 23.6%
- Arable land — 6.6%
- Grazing — 49.4%
- Other land — 20.4%

Australia has about 110 million sheep—down from a peak of 180 million in 1970—and their grazing contributes to land degradation. But wool remains an important export.

228

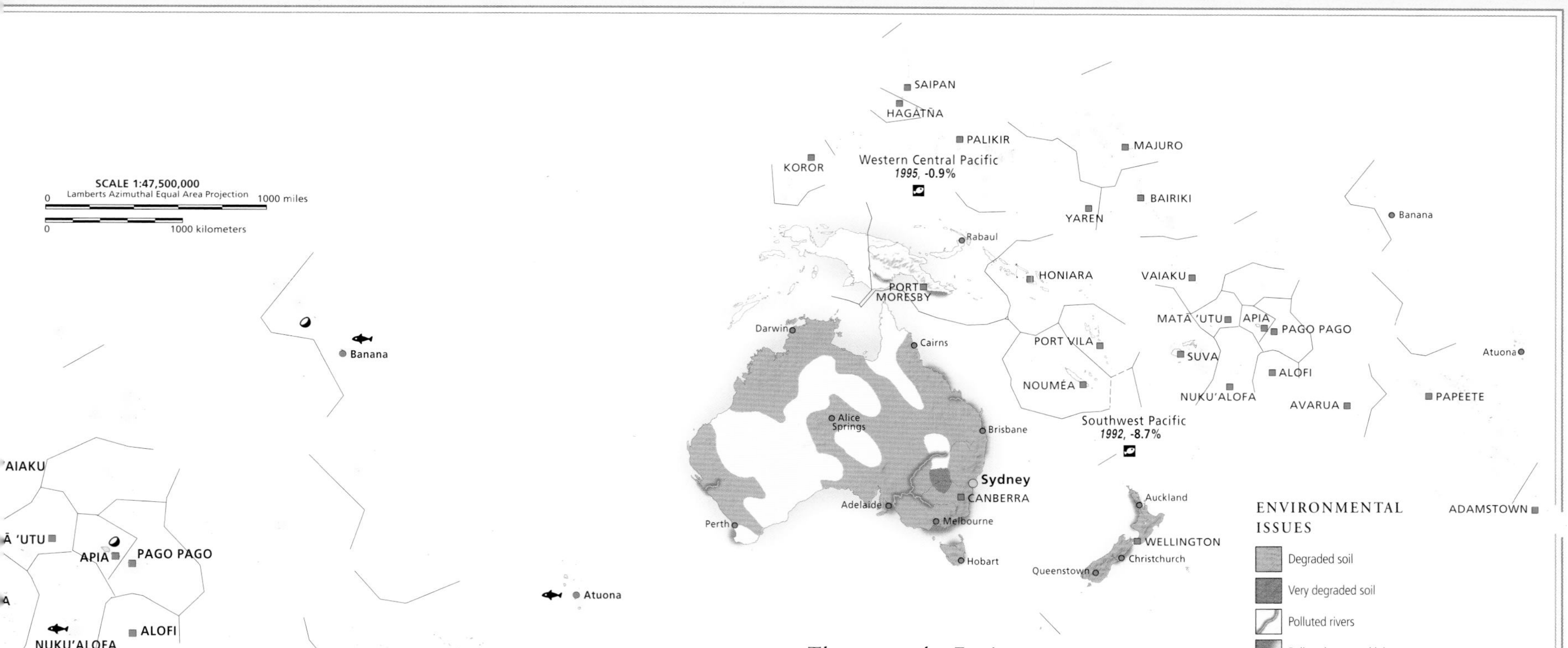

SCALE 1:47,500,000
Lamberts Azimuthal Equal Area Projection
0   1000 miles
0   1000 kilometers

SAIPAN
HAGÅTÑA
PALIKIR
KOROR
MAJURO
Western Central Pacific
1995, -0.9%
BAIRIKI
YAREN
Banana
Rabaul
HONIARA
VAIAKU
PORT
MORESBY
MATA'UTU
APIA
PAGO PAGO
Darwin
Cairns
PORT VILA
SUVA
Atuona
NOUMÉA
ALOFI
PAPEETE
NUKU'ALOFA
AVARUA
Alice
Springs
Brisbane
Southwest Pacific
1992, -8.7%
Sydney
CANBERRA
Adelaide
Perth
Melbourne
Auckland
ADAMSTOWN
Hobart
WELLINGTON
Queenstown
Christchurch

AIAKU
Å'UTU
APIA
PAGO PAGO
NUKU'ALOFA
ALOFI
Atuona
AVARUA
PAPEETE

ADAMSTOWN

Banana

ENVIRONMENTAL ISSUES

- Degraded soil
- Very degraded soil
- Polluted rivers
- Polluted seas and lakes
- Cities with severe air pollution
- Overfished fishery, *year of peak catch, decline since peak catch*

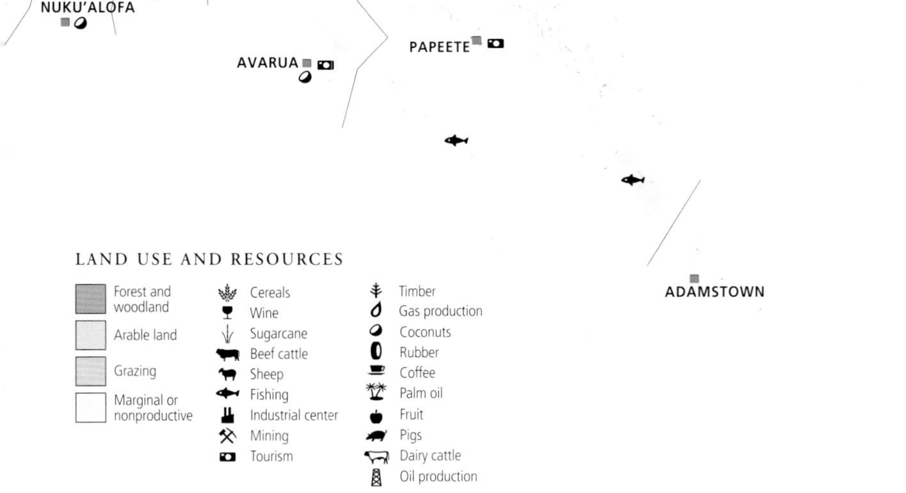

Threats to the Environment

Environmental damage increased greatly following the arrival of Europeans. Forest clearance and the hooves of livestock accelerated erosion; intensive farming of fragile soils resulted in plummeting fertility; and introduced species decimated native ecosystems. Australia now has the world's highest rate of mammalian extinctions; many New Zealand native species survive only on isolated islands; and introduced plant species predominate on many Pacific islands. Since Europeans arrived, more than 40 percent of Australia's original forests have been cleared, and forest cover in New Zealand has fallen from 70 to 16 percent. As a result of corruption, most notably in Papua New Guinea, foreign logging companies have been able to illegally harvest ancient rain forests. Waterways throughout Melanesia have been contaminated by waste from mining operations. Human waste disposal is problematic on remote, densely populated islands: water-borne diseases are the leading cause of death on Kiribati, and in Ebey Lagoon in the Marshall Islands pollution levels are 25,000 times higher than standard safety levels. Due to depletion of stratospheric ozone, ultraviolet levels in Australia and New Zealand are rising by about 10 percent each decade, significantly increasing the risk of skin cancer.

LAND USE AND RESOURCES

- Forest and woodland
- Arable land
- Grazing
- Marginal or nonproductive

- Cereals
- Wine
- Sugarcane
- Beef cattle
- Sheep
- Fishing
- Industrial center
- Mining
- Tourism
- Timber
- Gas production
- Coconuts
- Rubber
- Coffee
- Palm oil
- Fruit
- Pigs
- Dairy cattle
- Oil production

Left: Toxic waste from the Australian-operated Ok Tedi gold mine in Papua New Guinea has destroyed large areas of rain forest and poisoned fish and plants in the Fly, the country's longest river.

Left: Sea levels could rise by up to 3 feet (1 m) over the next century. This would spell disaster for densely inhabited, low-lying island groups such as Tuvalu, which rises just 12 feet (4 m) above sea level.

Right: Over 40 percent of Pacific coral reefs are threatened by pollution, urban development, tourism, and destructive exotic species such as the crown-of-thorns starfish.

Protecting the Environment

In the 1990s, Australian conservation and farming organizations established a coordinated farmland-management program called Landcare, designed to halt degradation. It has now been extended to cover other environments, including bushland, rivers, sand dunes, and coastline. Sustainable forestry practices are now the norm in Australia and New Zealand, and plantation forests are a major source of timber, providing, for example, 99 percent of annual roundwood output in New Zealand. The Pacific Islands Forum Fisheries Agency has had notable success in promoting sustainable fisheries throughout the region. Interest in alternative energy is growing: Vanuatu has declared it will switch to renewable sources by 2020. Overall, Oceania has the lowest proportion of human-dominated land after Antarctica, and the number of protected areas has grown sevenfold since 1960—the proportion of protected land, 7.1 percent, is just above the world average. The majority of states and territories in Oceania have also declared their waters to be whale sanctuaries.

PERCENTAGE OF LAND PROTECTED IN MAJOR COUNTRIES OF OCEANIA

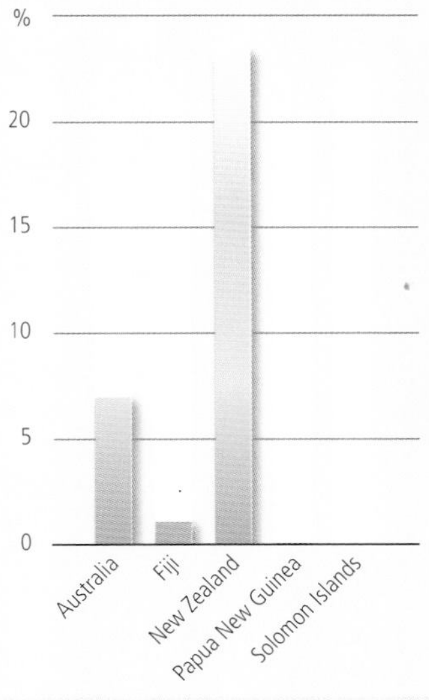

%
20
15
10
5
0
Australia
Fiji
New Zealand
Papua New Guinea
Solomon Islands

New Zealand's national parks help protect remnant populations of native flightless bird species, which have been easy prey for introduced predators. The ground-dwelling kakapo, the world's heaviest parrot, survives only on two small island reserves. As of 2003, just 86 kakapo remained.

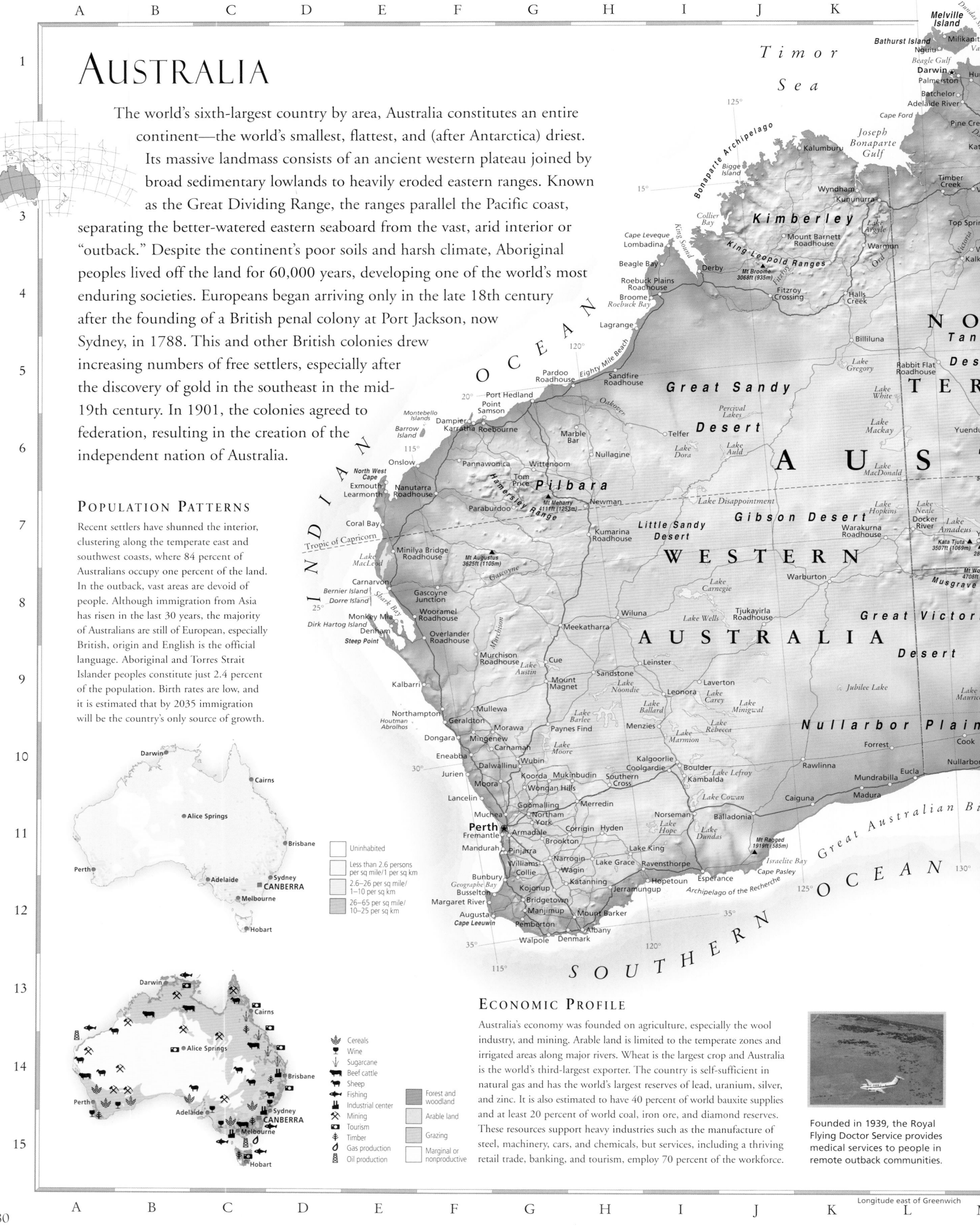

AUSTRALIA

The world's sixth-largest country by area, Australia constitutes an entire continent—the world's smallest, flattest, and (after Antarctica) driest. Its massive landmass consists of an ancient western plateau joined by broad sedimentary lowlands to heavily eroded eastern ranges. Known as the Great Dividing Range, the ranges parallel the Pacific coast, separating the better-watered eastern seaboard from the vast, arid interior or "outback." Despite the continent's poor soils and harsh climate, Aboriginal peoples lived off the land for 60,000 years, developing one of the world's most enduring societies. Europeans began arriving only in the late 18th century after the founding of a British penal colony at Port Jackson, now Sydney, in 1788. This and other British colonies drew increasing numbers of free settlers, especially after the discovery of gold in the southeast in the mid-19th century. In 1901, the colonies agreed to federation, resulting in the creation of the independent nation of Australia.

POPULATION PATTERNS

Recent settlers have shunned the interior, clustering along the temperate east and southwest coasts, where 84 percent of Australians occupy one percent of the land. In the outback, vast areas are devoid of people. Although immigration from Asia has risen in the last 30 years, the majority of Australians are still of European, especially British, origin and English is the official language. Aboriginal and Torres Strait Islander peoples constitute just 2.4 percent of the population. Birth rates are low, and it is estimated that by 2035 immigration will be the country's only source of growth.

Population density legend:
- Uninhabited
- Less than 2.6 persons per sq mile/1 per sq km
- 2.6–26 per sq mile/1–10 per sq km
- 26–65 per sq mile/10–25 per sq km

Economic activity legend:
- Cereals
- Wine
- Sugarcane
- Beef cattle
- Sheep
- Fishing
- Industrial center
- Mining
- Tourism
- Timber
- Gas production
- Oil production
- Forest and woodland
- Arable land
- Grazing
- Marginal or nonproductive

ECONOMIC PROFILE

Australia's economy was founded on agriculture, especially the wool industry, and mining. Arable land is limited to the temperate zones and irrigated areas along major rivers. Wheat is the largest crop and Australia is the world's third-largest exporter. The country is self-sufficient in natural gas and has the world's largest reserves of lead, uranium, silver, and zinc. It is also estimated to have 40 percent of world bauxite supplies and at least 20 percent of world coal, iron ore, and diamond reserves. These resources support heavy industries such as the manufacture of steel, machinery, cars, and chemicals, but services, including a thriving retail trade, banking, and tourism, employ 70 percent of the workforce.

Founded in 1939, the Royal Flying Doctor Service provides medical services to people in remote outback communities.

Longitude east of Greenwich

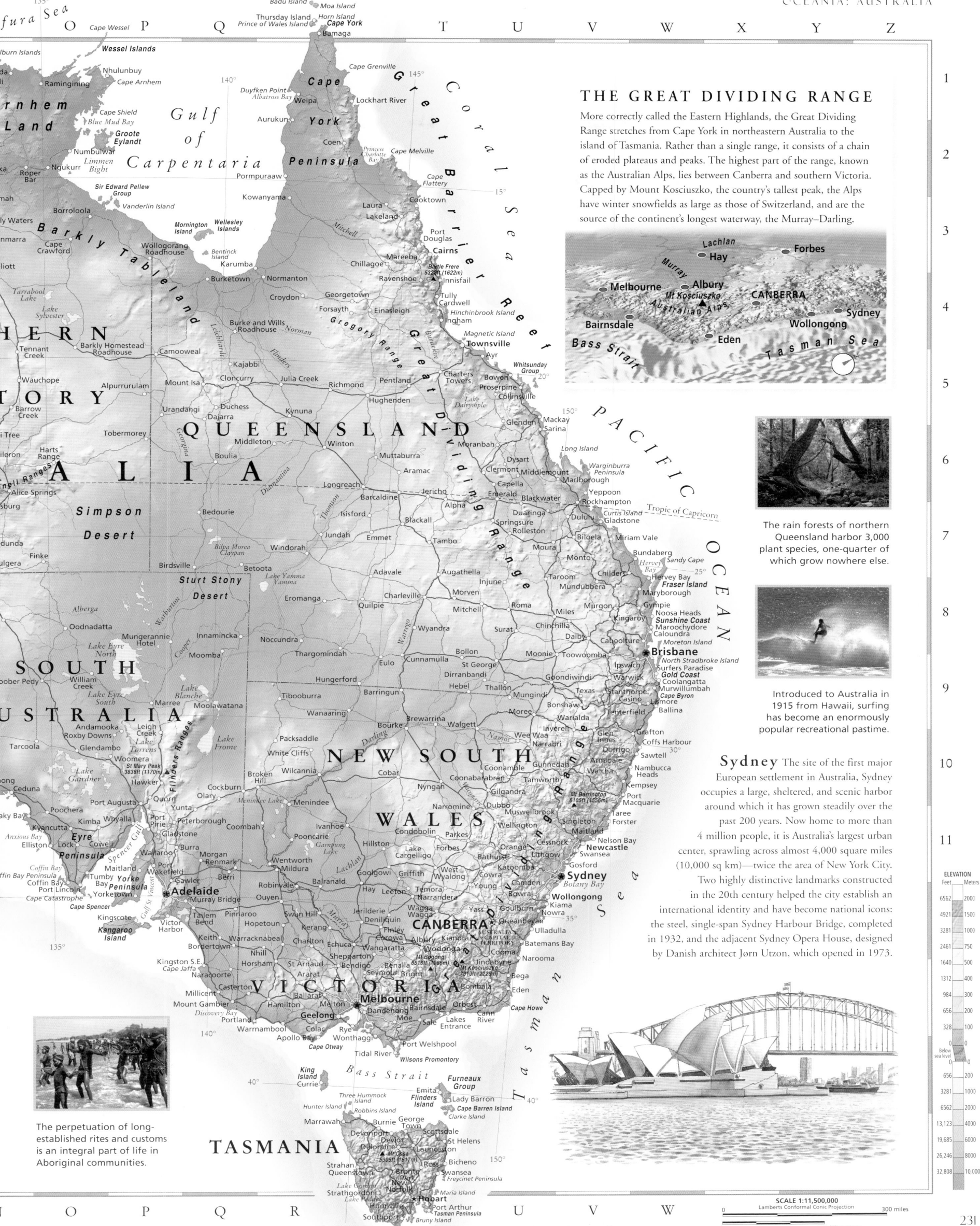

THE GREAT DIVIDING RANGE

More correctly called the Eastern Highlands, the Great Dividing Range stretches from Cape York in northeastern Australia to the island of Tasmania. Rather than a single range, it consists of a chain of eroded plateaus and peaks. The highest part of the range, known as the Australian Alps, lies between Canberra and southern Victoria. Capped by Mount Kosciuszko, the country's tallest peak, the Alps have winter snowfields as large as those of Switzerland, and are the source of the continent's longest waterway, the Murray–Darling.

The rain forests of northern Queensland harbor 3,000 plant species, one-quarter of which grow nowhere else.

Introduced to Australia in 1915 from Hawaii, surfing has become an enormously popular recreational pastime.

Sydney The site of the first major European settlement in Australia, Sydney occupies a large, sheltered, and scenic harbor around which it has grown steadily over the past 200 years. Now home to more than 4 million people, it is Australia's largest urban center, sprawling across almost 4,000 square miles (10,000 sq km)—twice the area of New York City. Two highly distinctive landmarks constructed in the 20th century helped the city establish an international identity and have become national icons: the steel, single-span Sydney Harbour Bridge, completed in 1932, and the adjacent Sydney Opera House, designed by Danish architect Jørn Utzon, which opened in 1973.

The perpetuation of long-established rites and customs is an integral part of life in Aboriginal communities.

ELEVATION	
Feet	Meters
6562	2000
4921	1500
3281	1000
2461	750
1640	500
1312	400
984	300
656	200
328	100
0	0
Below sea level	
656	200
3281	1000
6562	2000
13,123	4000
19,685	6000
26,240	8000
32,808	10,000

SCALE 1:11,500,000
Lamberts Conformal Conic Projection
0   300 miles
0   300 kilometers

231

NEW ZEALAND

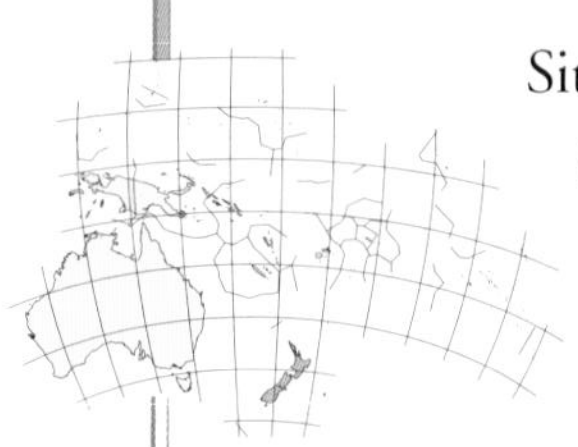

Situated 1,000 miles (1,600 km) southeast of Australia, its nearest neighbor, New Zealand consists of two large islands and several smaller ones. Both main islands straddle fault lines between the Indo-Australian and Pacific tectonic plates. Movement along these faults causes sporadic earthquakes and has formed active volcanoes and geysers in the North Island; over millions of years, it has also pushed up the steep-sided peaks of the Southern Alps, which form the backbone of the South Island. This rugged interior and the South Island's generally cold, wet climate concentrated the development of modern infrastructure in the North Island and along the drier, more fertile east coast of the South Island. Annexed by Britain in 1840, New Zealand became a self-governing colony in 1856 and a dominion in 1907, but did not achieve full independence until 1947. The descendants of British colonists now far outnumber the indigenous Maori, but Maori remains an official language and in recent years the government has made some reparations to Maori peoples for loss of traditional lands.

Wellington

Though Auckland is by far the largest city in New Zealand, Wellington is the country's national capital and major business center. The city occupies a large sheltered harbor—the flooded crater of an ancient volcano—at the southern end of the North Island. Europeans arrived in 1840 and moved their seat of government here in 1865. The foreshore, much of it reclaimed land, is the site of the commercial district and major government buildings including the parliament, with its distinctive executive office building, widely known as the Beehive. Designed by British architect Sir Basil Spence, it was begun in 1969 and completed in 1980.

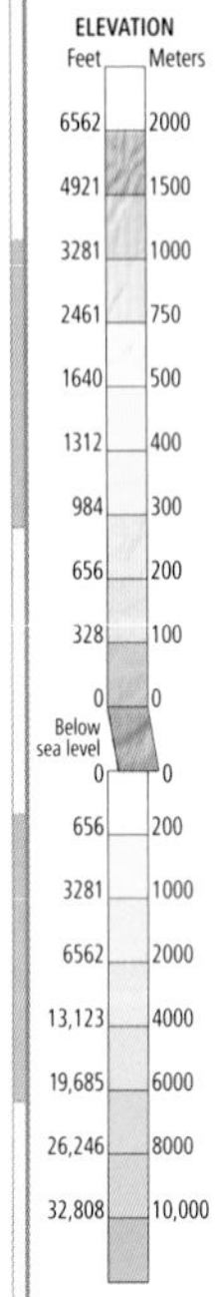

VOLCANO COUNTRY

Volcanic activity has fashioned the landscape of the North Island's central plateau and still has the potential to modify it further. Lake Taupo, the country's largest lake, occupies a crater formed by a massive volcanic explosion thought to have taken place in AD 186. To its south stretches a line of active volcanoes—Tongariro, Ngauruhoe, and Ruapehu—all of which erupted in the 20th century. In 1996, in the country's largest eruption in 400 years, Ruapehu spewed great clouds of steam and ash over the surrounding skifields; fortunately, there were no casualties. Farther west, the huge cone of Mount Taranaki (Mount Egmont) looms over the southwestern corner of the island. Now dormant, it last erupted in the 18th century.

Geothermal activity is concentrated around Rotorua in the North Island.

Home to approximately 1 million people, Auckland occupies an isthmus between two broad harbors.

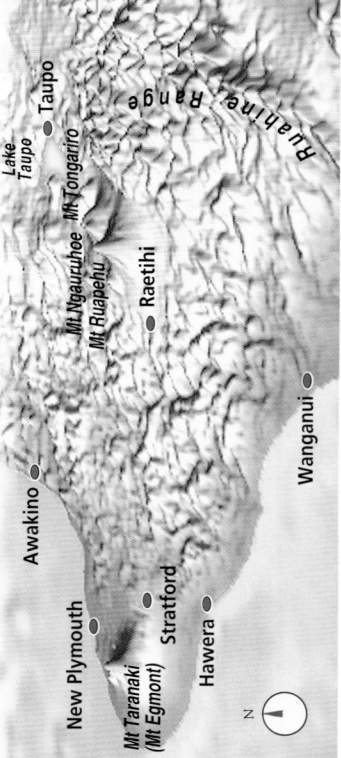

NEW ZEALAND

POPULATION PATTERNS

The North Island constitutes 42 percent of the country but is home to more than three-quarters of the population; indeed, more than 30 percent of New Zealanders live in the Auckland region. About 75 percent of inhabitants live in towns and cities. People of European extraction make up 80 percent of the population, and one in seven New Zealanders is Maori. Ethnic diversity is increasing, for example, climbed 140 percent between 1991 and 2001. Many Pacific Islander people have settled in New Zealand, and Auckland is recognized as the world's largest Polynesian city.

Uninhabited

	Less than 2.6 persons per sq mile/1 per sq km
	2.6–26 per sq mile/1–10 per sq km
	26–65 per sq mile/10–25 per sq km

Auckland
Hamilton
Napier
WELLINGTON
Christchurch
Dunedin
Queenstown
Invercargill

Cathedral Square is the heart of the South Island's largest city, Christchurch.

ECONOMIC PROFILE

New Zealand has a long association with wool, which was the country's leading agricultural product until the late 1970s. But the sheep population has declined, and dairy products and meat are now the nation's most valuable exports. Forests cover 30 percent of the country and forest products, overwhelmingly from plantations, constitute the third most lucrative export. New Zealand is self-sufficient in all energy sources except oil; two-thirds of its electricity comes from hydroelectric power and over 6 percent from geothermal power. Leading industries include foods and beverages (notably wine), machinery, metals, and textiles. However, services employ 65 percent of workers, with tourism alone generating 10 percent of GDP and supporting one in ten jobs.

Forest and woodland
Arable land
Grazing
Marginal or nonproductive

Fruit
Wine
Beef cattle
Sheep
Pigs
Fishing
Industrial center
Timber
Dairy cattle
Tourism

Auckland
Hamilton
Napier
WELLINGTON
Christchurch
Dunedin
Queenstown
Invercargill

SCALE 1:3,250,000
Lambert's Conformal Conic Projection

0   100 miles
0   100 kilometers

In the western South Island, Franz Josef Glacier (above) and Fox Glacier descend as far as the coastal lowlands.

The traditional welcome dance, or powhiri, is still performed for visitors to Maori meeting houses.

The southwest coast of the South Island is characterized by deep fjords, including spectacular Milford Sound.

Longitude east of Greenwich

PACIFIC OCEAN

233

MELANESIA

Fiji, Papua New Guinea, Solomon Islands, Vanuatu

The islands of Melanesia arc around the northeast coast of Australia, extend south toward the Tropic of Capricorn and spread east to the edge of the Western Hemisphere. They lie close to the boundary between the Indo-Australian and Pacific plates and have been shaped by relatively recent tectonic activity. Most are mountainous and many have active volcanoes and dark volcanic soil—the word Melanesia derives from the Greek terms *melas* (meaning "black") and *nesoi* ("islands"). Almost all are blanketed with a dense covering of tropical rain forest, though parts of this forest have been cleared. Independence has been achieved by all of the island groups except New Caledonia, which chose to remain part of France. However, many parts of Melanesia have been politically volatile in recent years. In New Caledonia in the 1980s, indigenous Kanak people began a campaign for independence that led to sporadic violence. Coups took place in Fiji in 1987 and 2000, and in Bougainville an armed independence movement fought a war against the Papua New Guinea government from 1988 to 2001.

In the Papua New Guinea highlands, men attending festivals called sing-sings wear paint and headdresses.

Bougainville's giant Panguna copper mine was closed down during the secessionist war and has not reopened.

Fiji's picturesque islands and highly developed tourist facilities attract up to 400,000 visitors a year.

Villagers on the island of Tanna in Vanuatu perform a traditional dance in sight of Yasur, a highly active volcano.

ELEVATION

Feet	Meters
6562	2000
4921	1500
3281	1000
2461	750
1640	500
1312	400
984	300
656	200
328	100
Below sea level 0	0
656	200
3281	1000
6562	2000
13,123	4000
19,685	6000
26,246	8000
32,808	10,000

Longitude east of Greenwich

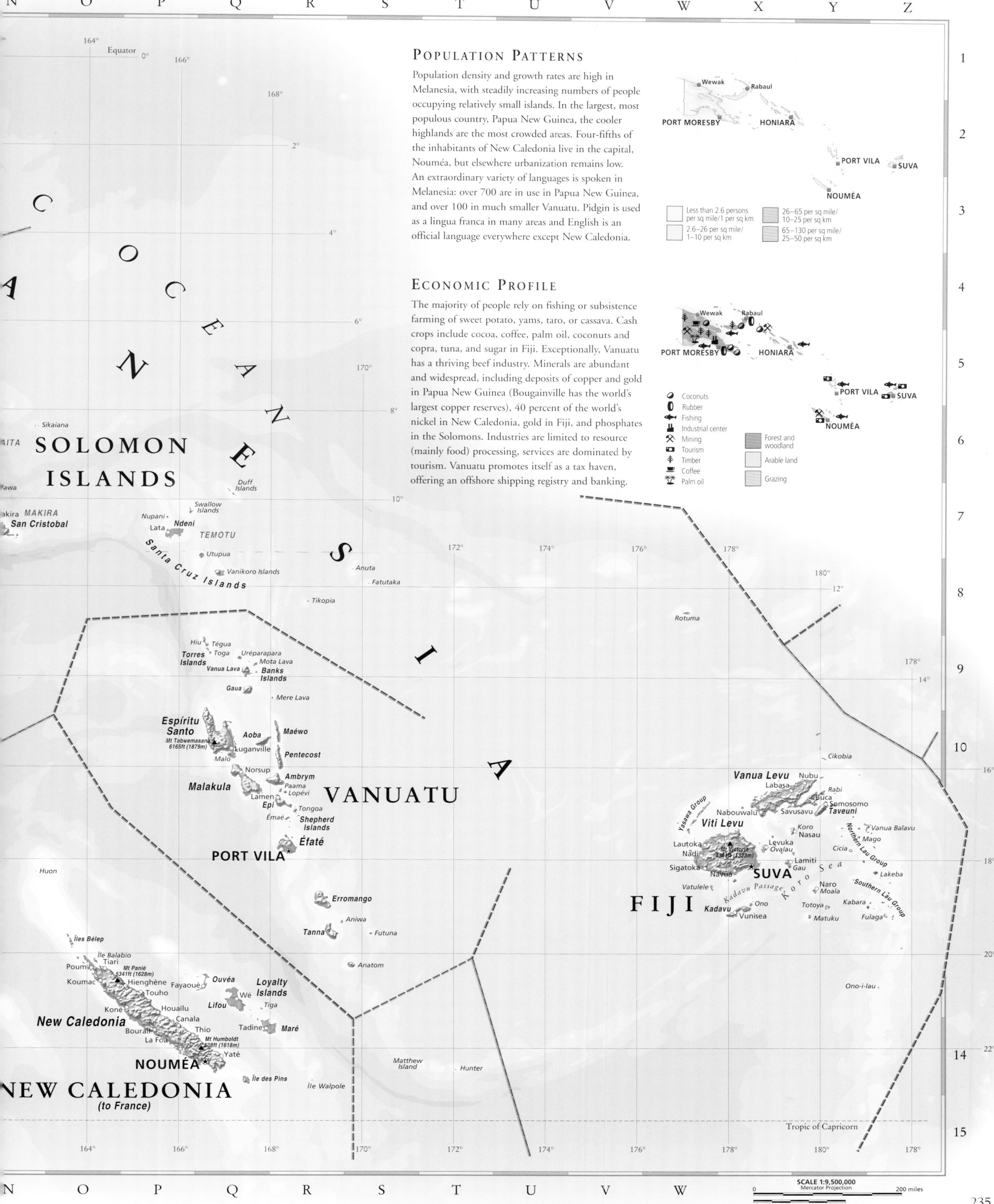

POPULATION PATTERNS

Population density and growth rates are high in Melanesia, with steadily increasing numbers of people occupying relatively small islands. In the largest, most populous country, Papua New Guinea, the cooler highlands are the most crowded areas. Four-fifths of the inhabitants of New Caledonia live in the capital, Nouméa, but elsewhere urbanization remains low. An extraordinary variety of languages is spoken in Melanesia: over 700 are in use in Papua New Guinea, and over 100 in much smaller Vanuatu. Pidgin is used as a lingua franca in many areas and English is an official language everywhere except New Caledonia.

Less than 2.6 persons per sq mile/1 per sq km
2.6–26 per sq mile/1–10 per sq km
26–65 per sq mile/10–25 per sq km
65–130 per sq mile/25–50 per sq km

ECONOMIC PROFILE

The majority of people rely on fishing or subsistence farming of sweet potato, yams, taro, or cassava. Cash crops include cocoa, coffee, palm oil, coconuts and copra, tuna, and sugar in Fiji. Exceptionally, Vanuatu has a thriving beef industry. Minerals are abundant and widespread, including deposits of copper and gold in Papua New Guinea (Bougainville has the world's largest copper reserves), 40 percent of the world's nickel in New Caledonia, gold in Fiji, and phosphates in the Solomons. Industries are limited to resource (mainly food) processing, services are dominated by tourism. Vanuatu promotes itself as a tax haven, offering an offshore shipping registry and banking.

Coconuts
Rubber
Fishing
Industrial center
Mining
Tourism
Timber
Coffee
Palm oil
Forest and woodland
Arable land
Grazing

SCALE 1:9,500,000
Mercator Projection
200 miles
200 kilometers

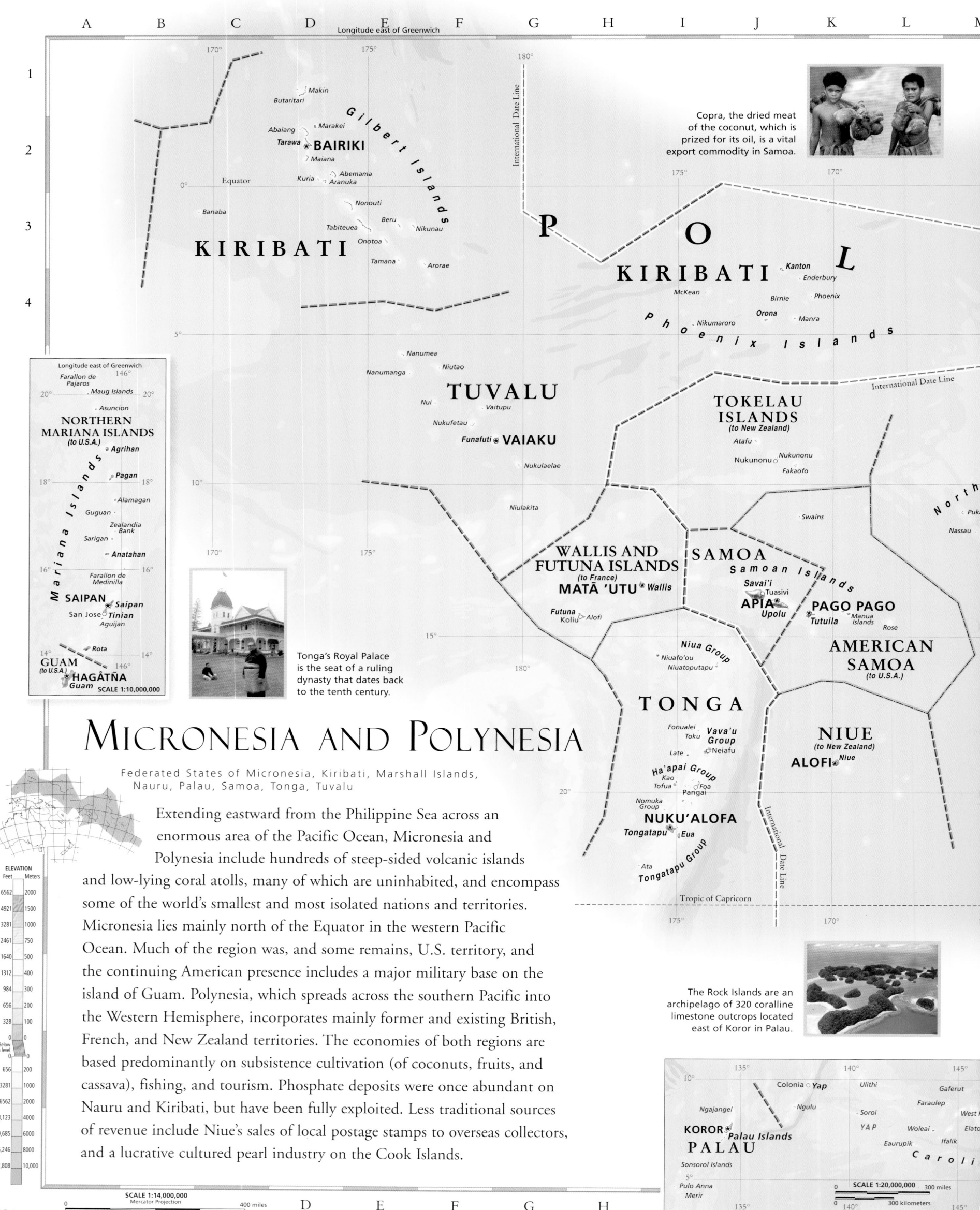

A B C D E F G H I J K L M

1

170° 175° 180°

Makin
Butaritari
Abaiang · Marakei
Tarawa · **BAIRIKI**
· Maiana
Equator 0°
Kuria Abemama
Aranuka
Banaba · Nonouti
Tabiteuea Beru
Onotoa Nikunau
Tamana
Arorae

Gilbert Islands

International Date Line

Copra, the dried meat of the coconut, which is prized for its oil, is a vital export commodity in Samoa.

175° 170°

P O L

KIRIBATI

Kanton
· Enderbury
McKean Birnie · Phoenix
· Orona · Manra
· Nikumaroro

Phoenix Islands

International Date Line

KIRIBATI

2

3

4

5°

Nanumea
Nanumanga Niutao
Nui Vaitupu
Nukufetau
Funafuti · **VAIAKU**
· Nukulaelae

TUVALU

Niulakita

TOKELAU ISLANDS
(to New Zealand)
Atafu
Nukunonu Nukunonu
Fakaofo

Swains

North...
Puka
Nassau

WALLIS AND FUTUNA ISLANDS
(to France)
MATĀ 'UTU · Wallis

Futuna
Koliu Alofi

SAMOA
Samoan Islands
Savai'i
· Tuasivi
APIA ·
Upolu
PAGO PAGO ·
Tutuila · Manua Islands
Rose

AMERICAN SAMOA
(to U.S.A.)

Niua Group
· Niuafo'ou
Niuatoputapu

15°

Tonga's Royal Palace is the seat of a ruling dynasty that dates back to the tenth century.

NIUE
(to New Zealand)
ALOFI · Niue

TONGA

Fonualei
Toku Vava'u Group
Late · Neiafu

Ha'apai Group
Kao
Tofua · Foa
· Pangai
Nomuka Group

NUKU'ALOFA
Tongatapu · Eua

· Ata
Tongatapu Group

International Date Line

20°

Tropic of Capricorn

175° 170°

146°

Farallon de Pajaros
· Maug Islands
20° · Asuncion 20°
NORTHERN MARIANA ISLANDS
(to U.S.A.)
· Agrihan
· Pagan
18° 18°
· Alamagan
· Guguan
Zealandia Bank
· Sarigan
· Anatahan
16° 16°
Farallon de Medinilla
SAIPAN · Saipan
San Jose · Tinian
· Aguijan
14° · Rota 14°
GUAM
(to U.S.A.) 146°
· **HAGÅTÑA**
Guam SCALE 1:10,000,000

Mariana Islands

MICRONESIA AND POLYNESIA

Federated States of Micronesia, Kiribati, Marshall Islands, Nauru, Palau, Samoa, Tonga, Tuvalu

Extending eastward from the Philippine Sea across an enormous area of the Pacific Ocean, Micronesia and Polynesia include hundreds of steep-sided volcanic islands and low-lying coral atolls, many of which are uninhabited, and encompass some of the world's smallest and most isolated nations and territories. Micronesia lies mainly north of the Equator in the western Pacific Ocean. Much of the region was, and some remains, U.S. territory, and the continuing American presence includes a major military base on the island of Guam. Polynesia, which spreads across the southern Pacific into the Western Hemisphere, incorporates mainly former and existing British, French, and New Zealand territories. The economies of both regions are based predominantly on subsistence cultivation (of coconuts, fruits, and cassava), fishing, and tourism. Phosphate deposits were once abundant on Nauru and Kiribati, but have been fully exploited. Less traditional sources of revenue include Niue's sales of local postage stamps to overseas collectors, and a lucrative cultured pearl industry on the Cook Islands.

ELEVATION
Feet Meters
6562 2000
4921 1500
3281 1000
2461 750
1640 500
1312 400
984 300
656 200
328 100
0 0
Below sea level
0 0
656 200
3281 1000
6562 2000
13,123 4000
19,685 6000
26,246 8000
32,808 10,000

The Rock Islands are an archipelago of 320 coralline limestone outcrops located east of Koror in Palau.

135° 140° 145°
10°
· Colonia · Yap Ulithi · Gaferut
Ngajangel · Ngulu · Sorol Faraulep
West
KOROR · YAP Woleai · Elato
· Palau Islands Eaurupik Ifalik
PALAU *Caroli...*
Sonsorol Islands
5°
Pulo Anna SCALE 1:20,000,000 300 miles
Merir 0 300 kilometers
135° 140° 145°

SCALE 1:14,000,000
Mercator Projection
0 400 miles
0 400 kilometers

D E F G H

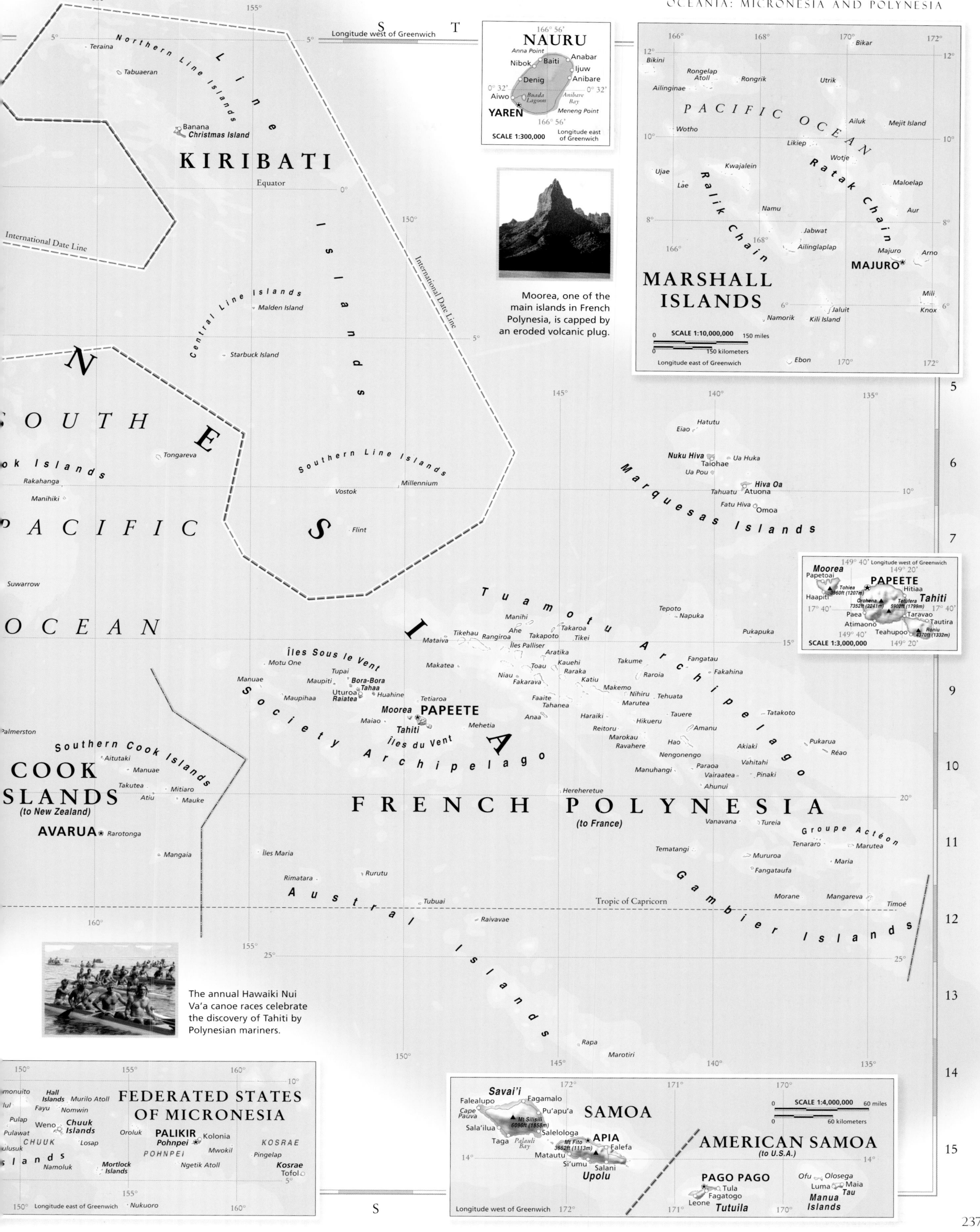

KIRIBATI

Northern Line Islands
Teraina
Tabuaeran
Banana
Christmas Island

Equator

International Date Line

Central Line Islands
Malden Island
Starbuck Island

Southern Line Islands
Vostok
Millennium
Flint

Line Islands

Longitude west of Greenwich

NAURU
Anna Point
Nibok · Baiti · Anabar
Denig · Ijuw
Aiwo · Anibare
Buada Lagoon · Anibare Bay
Meneng Point
YAREN
166° 56'
166° 56'
0° 32'
0° 32'
SCALE 1:300,000
Longitude east of Greenwich

Moorea, one of the main islands in French Polynesia, is capped by an eroded volcanic plug.

PACIFIC OCEAN

Bikar
Bikini
Rongelap Atoll · Rongrik
Utrik
Ailinginae
Ailuk
Wotho · Likiep · Wotje · Mejit Island
Ujae · Kwajalein
Lae · Namu · Maloelap
Jabwat · Aur
Ailinglaplap · Majuro · Arno
MAJURO
Mili
Jaluit · Knox
Namorik · Kili Island
Ebon

MARSHALL ISLANDS

Ralik Chain
Ratak Chain

SCALE 1:10,000,000
150 miles
150 kilometers
Longitude east of Greenwich

MICRONESIA

SOUTHE

Tongareva
Cook Islands
Rakahanga
Manihiki

PACIFIC

OCEAN

Suwarrow

Palmerston

COOK ISLANDS
(to New Zealand)
Southern Cook Islands
Aitutaki
Manuae
Takutea
Atiu · Mitiaro · Mauke
AVARUA · Rarotonga
Mangaia

Hatutu
Eiao
Nuku Hiva · Ua Huka
Taiohae
Ua Pou
Hiva Oa
Tahuatu · Atuona
Fatu Hiva · Omoa

Marquesas Islands

POLYNESIA

Tuamotu Archipelago

Îles Sous le Vent
Motu One
Manuae
Maupiti · Tupai
Uturoa · Bora-Bora
Raiatea · Tahaa
Maupihaa · Huahine
Tetiaroa
Moorea · **PAPEETE**
Maiao
Tahiti
Îles du Vent
Mehetia

Society Archipelago

Mataiva · Tikehau
Rangiroa · Ahe · Manihi
Takapoto · Takaroa
Îles Palliser · Tikei
Makatea · Aratika
Toau · Kauehi
Fakarava · Raraka · Katiu
Niau · Takume
Faaite · Makemo
Tahanea · Nihiru · Tehuata
Anaa · Marutea
Haraiki · Hikueru · Tauere · Amanu
Reitoru · Marokau · Akiaki
Ravahere · Hao · Pukarua · Réao
Nengonengo
Manuhangi · Paraoa · Vahitahi
Hereheretue · Vairaatea · Pinaki
Ahunui

Tepoto · Napuka
Pukapuka
Fangatau
Raroia · Fakahina
Tatakoto

Manihi

FRENCH POLYNESIA
(to France)

Vanavana · Tureia
Groupe Actéon
Tematangi · Tenararo · Marutea
Mururoa · Maria
Fangataufa
Morane · Mangareva · Timoé
Raivavae
Rimatara · Rururu
Îles Maria
Tubuai
Tropic of Capricorn

Austral Islands

Gambier Islands

Rapa
Marotiri

Moorea
Papetoai · **PAPEETE** · Hitiaa
Haapiti · Tohiea · Tahiti
3960ft (1207m) · Orohena · Tetufera
7352ft (2241m) · Tiarei
5902ft (1799m)
Paea · Taravao
Atimaono · Tautira
Teahupoo · Roniu
4370ft (1332m)
SCALE 1:3,000,000
149° 40' Longitude west of Greenwich
149° 20'
17° 40'

The annual Hawaiki Nui Va'a canoe races celebrate the discovery of Tahiti by Polynesian mariners.

FEDERATED STATES OF MICRONESIA
Hall Islands · Murilo Atoll
Namonuito
Fayu · Nomwin
Pulap
Pulusuk · Weno · **Chuuk Islands**
Pulawat · Losap
Oroluk · Kolonia
CHUUK · **PALIKIR**
Namoluk · Pohnpei
Mortlock Islands · Mwokil
Pingelap
Ngetik Atoll
Kosrae
KOSRAE
Tofol
Nukuoro
Longitude east of Greenwich

Savai'i
Falealupo · Fagamalo
Cape Pu'apu'a
Pauva · Mt Silisili
6096ft (1858m)
Sala'ilua · **SAMOA**
Taga · Salelologa
Palauli Bay · **APIA**
Mt Fito · Falefa
Matautu · 3652ft (1113m)
Si'umu
Salani · **Upolu**

AMERICAN SAMOA
(to U.S.A.)
PAGO PAGO · Ofu · Olosega
Leone · Tula · Luma · Maia
Fagatogo · Tau
Tutuila · **Manua Islands**
Longitude west of Greenwich
SCALE 1:4,000,000
60 miles
60 kilometers

Taken from NASA's Landsat 7 satellite, this image shows part of the Transantarctic Mountains. The glaciers visible at center and center right flow off the Antarctic plateau to the Ross Ice Shelf. The brown areas at left are the McMurdo Dry Valleys.

ANTARCTICA

Antarctica

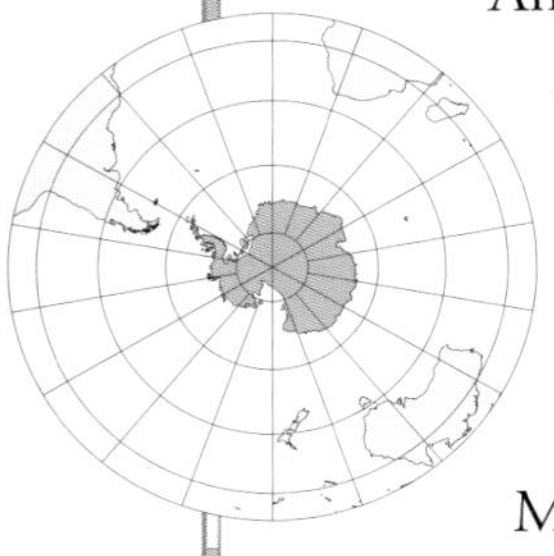

An almost circular landmass centered on the South Pole, Antarctica is the world's fifth-largest as well as its coldest, windiest, driest, and, on average, highest continent. A vast ice sheet covers 98 percent of the land. Among the few topographical features not totally obscured by the ice are the Transantarctic Mountains, which divide the continent into East and West Antarctica. In the east, the ice sheet hides a high plateau; to the west, it conceals a mountainous archipelago. Much of the surrounding ocean freezes in winter, effectively doubling the size of Antarctica, and for much of that season the sun does not rise. These severe conditions drastically restrict animal and plant distribution, and have prohibited permanent human occupation. Nevertheless, Antarctica is home to a fluctuating population of scientists and support staff based at a total of 42 research stations. Their numbers swell annually from around 1,000 in winter to approximately 4,000 in summer.

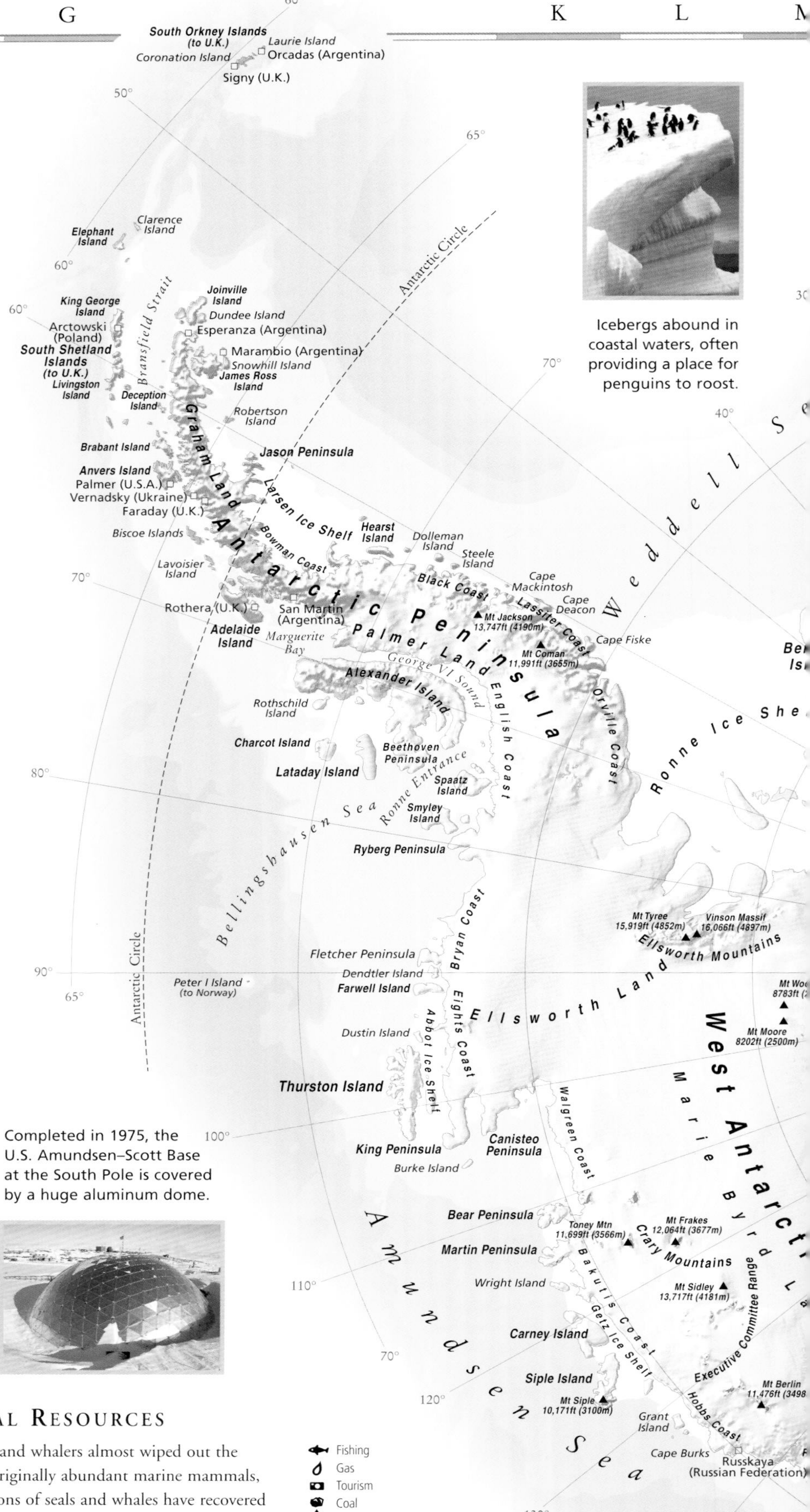

Icebergs abound in coastal waters, often providing a place for penguins to roost.

THE ANTARCTIC PENINSULA

The roughly circular outline of Antarctica is interrupted by the narrow Antarctic Peninsula, which extends 800 miles (1,300 km) toward the southern tip of South America. The peninsula is mountainous—rising to 13,747 feet (4,190 m) at Mount Jackson—capped by ice sheets and glaciers, and fringed by numerous islands, slender channels, and ice shelves. Nevertheless, it experiences the continent's mildest conditions and includes most of its few patches of ice-free land. From the end of the peninsula, an undersea ridge known as the Scotia Arc runs east then west, forming a great loop that eventually connects with Cape Horn in South America.

Completed in 1975, the U.S. Amundsen–Scott Base at the South Pole is covered by a huge aluminum dome.

THE ANTARCTIC TREATY

Seven countries—Argentina, Australia, Chile, France, New Zealand, Norway, and the United Kingdom—have at one time or other asserted sovereignty over parts of Antarctica. However, by becoming signatories to the Antarctic Treaty of 1959, they and 38 other nations have since agreed to suspend territorial claims and preserve the continent for nonmilitary scientific research. The Antarctic Treaty arose out of a worldwide scientific project called the International Geophysical Year, which began in 1957 and saw 12 nations establish numerous research stations across Antarctica.

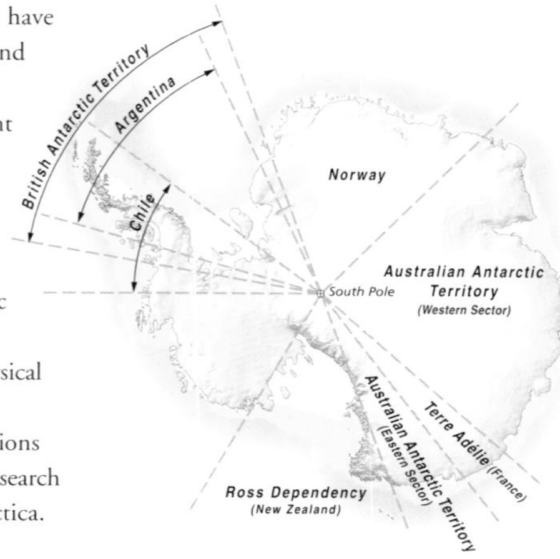

NATURAL RESOURCES

Early sealers and whalers almost wiped out the continent's originally abundant marine mammals, but populations of seals and whales have recovered in recent years, especially since the International Whaling Commission declared most of the Southern Ocean a whale sanctuary in 1994. Although 23 countries have agreed to manage Antarctic fisheries for sustainability, illegal fishing is steadily depleting stocks of Antarctic cod, finfish, and toothfish. Geologists concur that Antarctica may harbor great mineral wealth, including copper, gold, platinum, and oil. No economically exploitable reserves have been found, however, and, in any case, mining is banned under the Antarctic Treaty. Tourism is proving a more viable economic activity, with visitor numbers rising steadily.

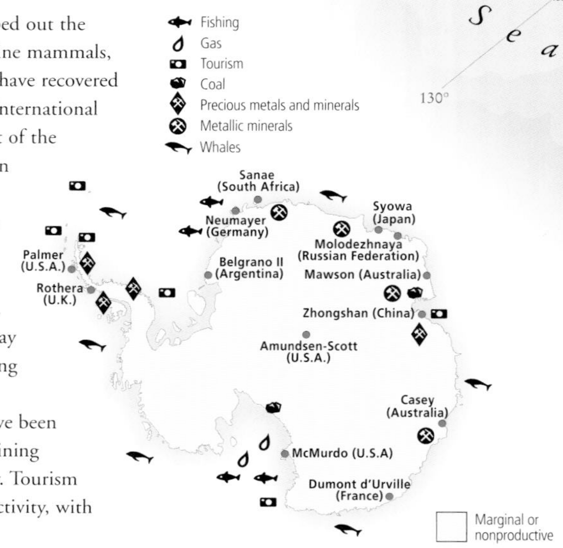

Fishing
Gas
Tourism
Coal
Precious metals and minerals
Metallic minerals
Whales

Marginal or nonproductive

Map labels

South Orkney Islands (to U.K.)
Coronation Island
Laurie Island
Orcadas (Argentina)
Signy (U.K.)
Elephant Island
Clarence Island
King George Island
Arctowski (Poland)
South Shetland Islands (to U.K.)
Livingston Island
Deception Island
Joinville Island
Dundee Island
Esperanza (Argentina)
Marambio (Argentina)
Snowhill Island
James Ross Island
Robertson Island
Bransfield Strait
Brabant Island
Anvers Island
Palmer (U.S.A.)
Vernadsky (Ukraine)
Faraday (U.K.)
Biscoe Islands
Lavoisier Island
Rothera (U.K.)
San Martin (Argentina)
Adelaide Island
Marguerite Bay
Rothschild Island
Charcot Island
Lataday Island
Alexander Island
Beethoven Peninsula
Smyley Island
Spaatz Island
Ryberg Peninsula
Graham Land
Antarctic Peninsula
Jason Peninsula
Larsen Ice Shelf
Bowman Coast
Hearst Island
Dolleman Island
Steele Island
Black Coast
Cape Mackintosh
Cape Deacon
Lassiter Coast
Mt Jackson 13,747ft (4190m)
Mt Coman 11,991ft (3685m)
Cape Fiske
Palmer Land
George VI Sound
English Coast
Orville Coast
Ronne Entrance
Weddell Sea
Ronne Ice Shelf
Bellingshausen Sea
Peter I Island (to Norway)
Fletcher Peninsula
Dendtler Island
Farwell Island
Dustin Island
Thurston Island
Eights Coast
Abbot Ice Shelf
Bryan Coast
Ellsworth Land
West Antarctica
Mt Tyree 15,919ft (4852m)
Vinson Massif 16,066ft (4897m)
Ellsworth Mountains
Mt Woe 8783ft
Mt Moore 8202ft (2500m)
King Peninsula
Burke Island
Canisteo Peninsula
Walgreen Coast
Marie Byrd Land
Bear Peninsula
Martin Peninsula
Wright Island
Toney Mtn 11,699ft (3566m)
Mt Frakes 12,064ft (3677m)
Crary Mountains
Mt Sidley 13,717ft (4181m)
Executive Committee Range
Bakutis Coast
Amundsen Sea
Carney Island
Siple Island
Mt Siple 10,171ft (3100m)
Grant Island
Getz Ice Shelf
Hobbs Coast
Mt Berlin 11,476ft (3498
Cape Burks
Russkaya (Russian Federation)
Weddell Sea
Be Is

Antarctic Peninsula detail map labels

Bellingshausen Sea
Adelaide Island
Drake Passage
South Shetland Islands
Alexander Island
Graham Land
Joinville Island
George VI Sound
Larsen Ice Shelf
James Ross Island
Palmer Land
Mt Jackson
Hearst Island
Mt Coman
Ronne Ice Shelf
Weddell Sea

Treaty map labels

British Antarctic Territory
Argentina
Chile
Norway
South Pole
Australian Antarctic Territory (Western Sector)
Terre Adélie (France)
Australian Antarctic Territory (Eastern Sector)
Ross Dependency (New Zealand)

Research stations (resources map)

Sanae (South Africa)
Neumayer (Germany)
Palmer (U.S.A.)
Rothera (U.K.)
Belgrano II (Argentina)
Syowa (Japan)
Molodezhnaya (Russian Federation)
Mawson (Australia)
Zhongshan (China)
Amundsen-Scott (U.S.A.)
Casey (Australia)
McMurdo (U.S.A.)
Dumont d'Urville (France)

The world's southernmost active volcano, Mount Erebus crowns Ross Island on the edge of the Ross Ice Shelf.

Evaporation of scant snowfall exposes bare sand in Victoria Land's Dry Valleys.

As summer nears, the pack ice begins to break up. Here, the silhouettes of seals stand out starkly against the ice.

ANTARCTICA IN FOCUS

Until the 20th century, Antarctica remained virtually unexplored. Although James Cook crossed the Antarctic Circle in 1773, he was blocked by ice, and it took another 65 years for the existence of a continent to be confirmed. The first human to set foot on this continent may have been the American John Davis in 1821, but it was 1899 before anyone spent a winter, and 1958 before a team crossed the icy expanse from one coast to the other.

The early 19th century saw sealers venture into the region, setting up bases on islands and almost destroying the fur seal populations. They were followed by 20th-century whalers, who killed 99 percent of blue whales, 97 percent of humpbacks, and 80 percent of fin whales before international agreements largely halted the practice.

The first permanent scientific bases were built in Antarctica in the 1950s. By studying the untouched ice layers, scientists have built up a picture of Earth's climate over the past 420,000 years. Fossil discoveries have shown that the continent was once lushly vegetated and had similar fauna to South America and Australia, providing evidence for the theory of continental drift, which states that Antarctica, Africa, India, South America, and Australia were once part of the supercontinent Gondwana. Current efforts are monitoring the ozone hole and the impact of global warming on Antarctic ice.

The lack of human impact that has made Antarctica a pristine laboratory for scientists has also made it a lure for adventurous tourists, whose numbers grew remarkably during the 1990s.

SCALE 1:48,000,000
Lambert Azimuthal Equal Area Projection

Tourism Boom

In 1956, the first plane carrying tourists flew over Antarctica without landing, a method of viewing the icy continent that remains popular today. It was not until the late 1960s, however, that tourist cruise ships began regular visits. In 1991–92, tourists outnumbered scientific personnel for the first time, and tourist numbers continued to grow dramatically throughout the decade that followed. The vast majority of tourists visit by cruise ship, but several dozen fly to Antarctica for a land-based adventure.

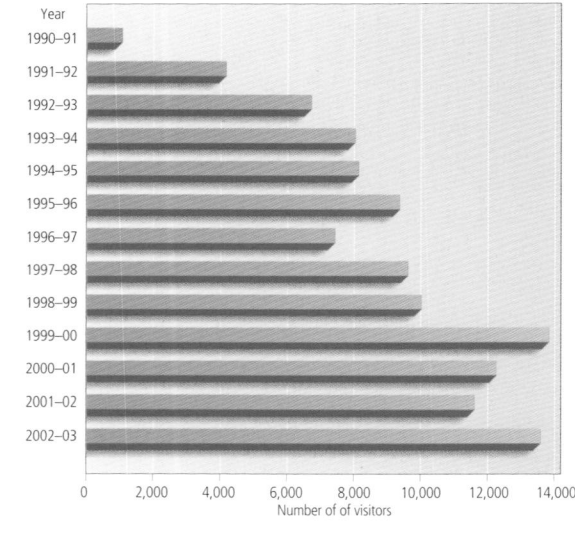

Number of of visitors

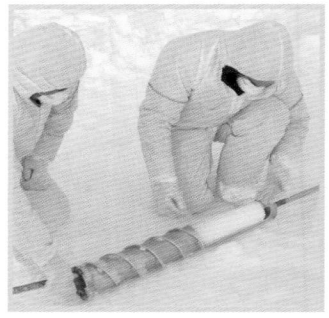

Most current tourism in Antarctica is ship-based, with visitors living aboard cruise liners and using inflatable craft to reach the shore. Land-based tourism would have a greater environmental impact.

The pristine layers of Antarctica's ice preserve a record of Earth's changing climate. Cores drilled out of the ice can reveal centuries of varying precipitation, temperature, and atmospheric composition.

ANNUAL MEAN TEMPERATURE

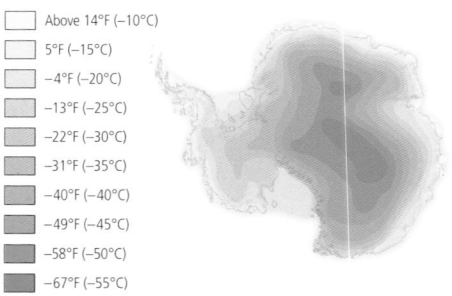

- Above 14°F (–10°C)
- 5°F (–15°C)
- –4°F (–20°C)
- –13°F (–25°C)
- –22°F (–30°C)
- –31°F (–35°C)
- –40°F (–40°C)
- –49°F (–45°C)
- –58°F (–50°C)
- –67°F (–55°C)

tons per square yard / kilogram per square meter   ANNUAL MEAN SNOWFALL

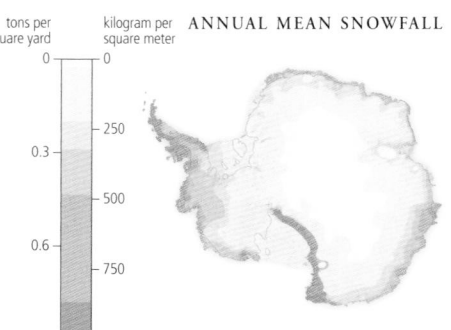

KATABATIC WINDS

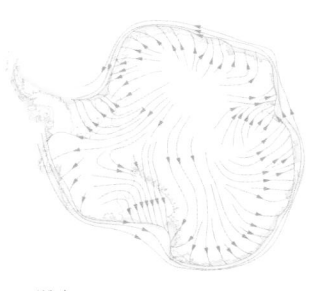

Wind

Cold, Dry, and Windy

Because of both its high elevation and its distance from the moderating effects of the ocean, Antarctica's eastern interior has by far the lowest temperatures. The continent receives little precipitation because the air is usually too cold to hold water vapor. Driven by gravity rather than pressure differences, katabatic winds blow constantly and become exceptionally strong near the coast.

Antarctic Exploration

In search of a great southern land, James Cook crossed the Antarctic Circle three times on his voyage of 1772–75. Although he did not see land, his descriptions of the rich marine life encouraged sealers and explorers to follow him. In 1820, Bellingshausen and Palmer both investigated the Antarctic Peninsula region, while later explorers revealed more southerly areas of the continent. Scott and Amundsen raced each other to the South Pole, with Amundsen reaching it first in 1911. More than 45 years later, a joint Commonwealth team made the first overland crossing of Antarctica.

Led by Robert Falcon Scott, a British team reached the South Pole on January 17, 1912, only to discover that Roald Amundsen's Norwegian team had arrived a month earlier, on December 14, 1911. All members of Scott's team perished on the return journey.

The plankton-rich Antarctic waters support vast swarms of small crustaceans known as krill, which are the main food of baleen whales, three seal species, penguins and other birds, and many fishes.

THE OZONE HOLE

High in the stratosphere, a layer containing a small amount of the gas known as ozone absorbs most of the Sun's harmful ultraviolet rays. Since the 1980s, scientists have been monitoring Antarctica's ozone hole, an area of depleted ozone that forms every September. Their work showed that the hole was growing dramatically, and industrial pollutants such as chlorofluorocarbons (CFCs) were identified as the culprit. As each southern spring begins, the atmospheric conditions trap these ozone-destroying chlorine compounds above Antarctica. Most countries agreed to phase out the use of CFCs under the 1987 Montreal Protocol, but the pollutants linger in the atmosphere. The 2000 ozone hole (shown in the image below) was the largest ever recorded, measuring about 11 million square miles (29 million sq km)—roughly three times the size of the United States.

Antarctica — Ozone hole September 2000

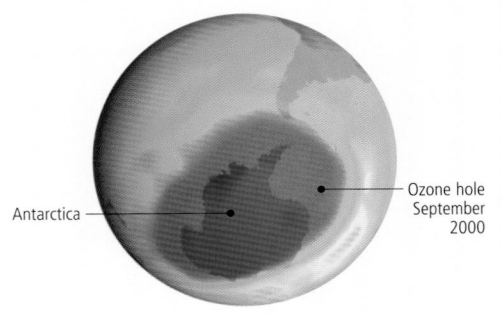

Insulated by thick layers of blubber, the Weddell seal spends the many months of winter darkness under the ice, using sonar to locate its food and breathing holes. It breeds on sea ice or land in summer.

POLAR OCEAN LIFE

- Antarctic Polar Frontal Zone
- Summer pack ice limit
- Winter pack ice limit
- Ice shelf
- High zooplankton concentration
- Medium zooplankton concentration
- Low zooplankton concentration
- Krill distribution
- Humpback whale migratory route
- Sei, blue, and fin whale distribution
- Penguin breeding colonies

Antarctic Animals

The only true land animals on Antarctica are tiny wingless midges and microscopic species that live in summer ponds. Some of the waters that surround the continent, however, are teeming, with blooms of phytoplankton and swarms of krill forming the center of a vast food web supporting fish, penguins, seabirds, seals, and whales. The Antarctic Polar Frontal Zone, where warm northern waters meet cold southern waters, acts as an oceanographic and biological barrier.

James Cook (U.K.) 1772–73

Thaddeus von Bellingshausen (Russia) 1819–1821

Charles Wilkes (U.S.A.) 1839–40

John Balleny (U.K.) 1839

to Australia

Atlantic Ocean

South Georgia

Southern Ocean

South Orkney Islands

Falkland Islands

South Shetland Islands

South America

Antarctic Peninsula

ANTARCTICA

Peter I Island

Indian Ocean

Pacific Ocean

Southern Ocean

Balleny Islands

Macquarie Island

SCALE 1:48,000,000
Lambert Azimuthal Equal Area Projection

REFERENCE

These tulip fields, picturesque and colorful in April bloom, are located in the Skagit River delta, south of Mount Vernon in western Washington, U.S.A. The area boasts some of the state's most productive land, much of which, including these agricultural flats, was reclaimed from swampland. The tractor gives perspective to the large scale of the tulip plantation.

GEOGRAPHICAL COMPARISONS

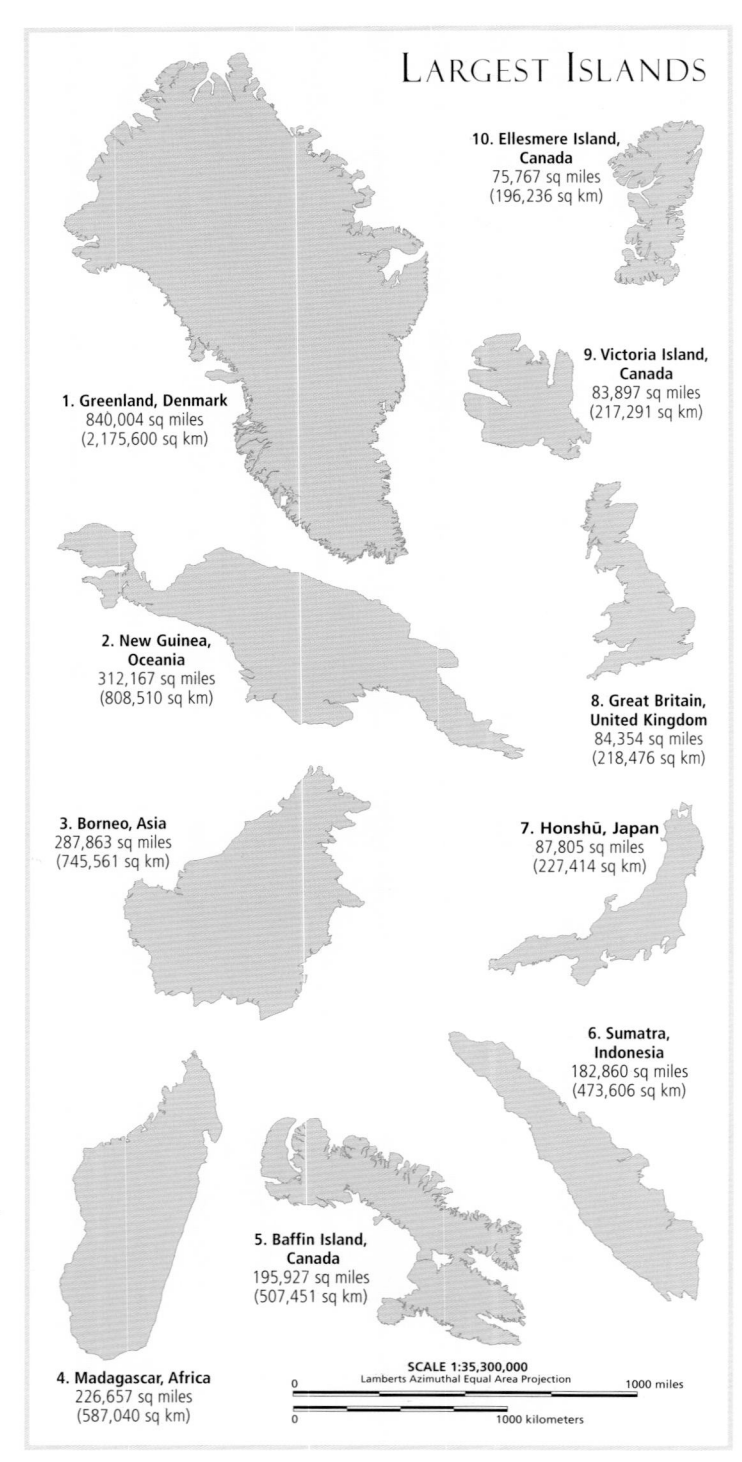

LARGEST ISLANDS

10. Ellesmere Island, Canada
75,767 sq miles
(196,236 sq km)

9. Victoria Island, Canada
83,897 sq miles
(217,291 sq km)

1. Greenland, Denmark
840,004 sq miles
(2,175,600 sq km)

2. New Guinea, Oceania
312,167 sq miles
(808,510 sq km)

8. Great Britain, United Kingdom
84,354 sq miles
(218,476 sq km)

3. Borneo, Asia
287,863 sq miles
(745,561 sq km)

7. Honshū, Japan
87,805 sq miles
(227,414 sq km)

6. Sumatra, Indonesia
182,860 sq miles
(473,606 sq km)

5. Baffin Island, Canada
195,927 sq miles
(507,451 sq km)

4. Madagascar, Africa
226,657 sq miles
(587,040 sq km)

SCALE 1:35,300,000
Lamberts Azimuthal Equal Area Projection
0 — 1000 miles
0 — 1000 kilometers

LARGEST COUNTRIES

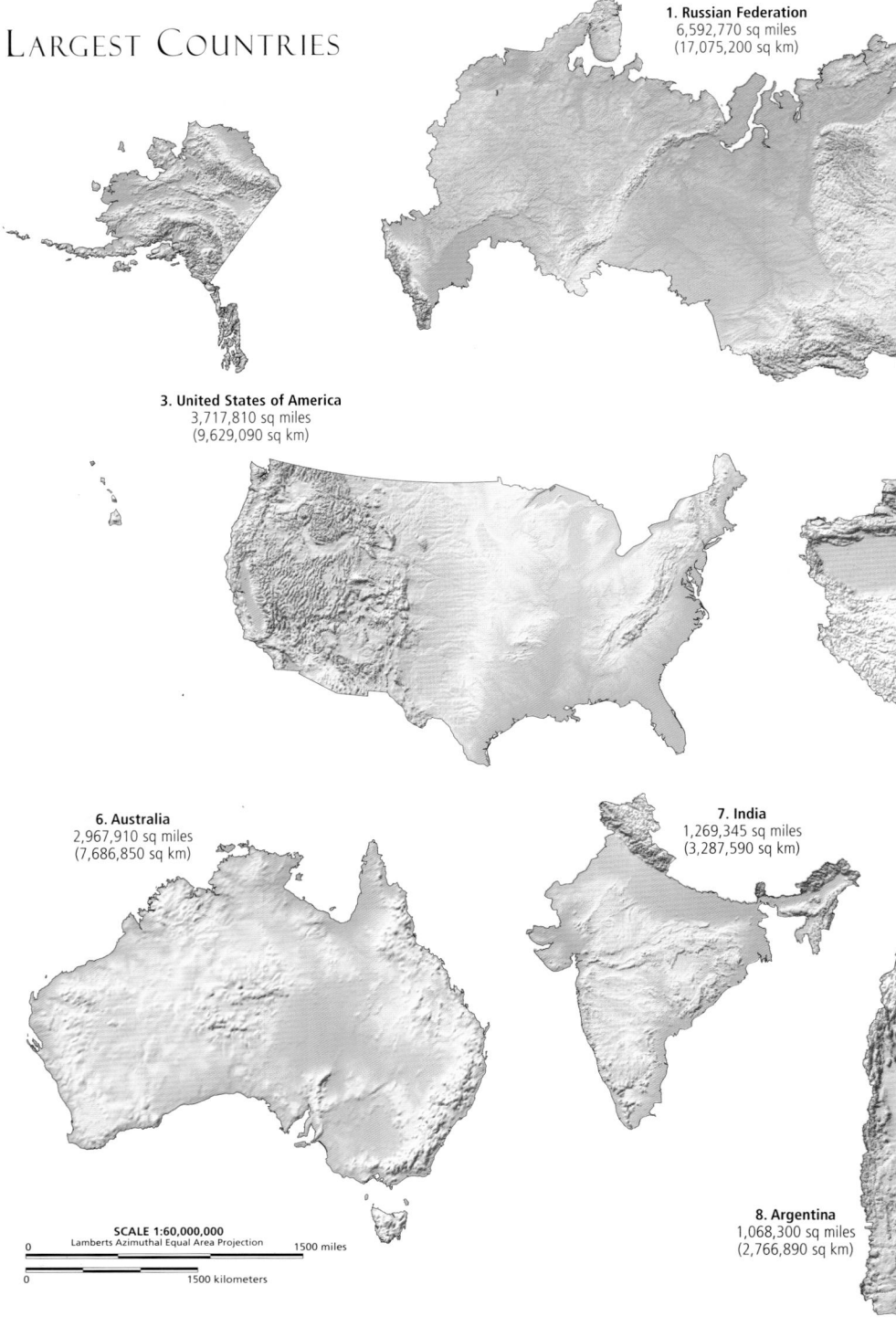

1. Russian Federation
6,592,770 sq miles
(17,075,200 sq km)

3. United States of America
3,717,810 sq miles
(9,629,090 sq km)

6. Australia
2,967,910 sq miles
(7,686,850 sq km)

7. India
1,269,345 sq miles
(3,287,590 sq km)

8. Argentina
1,068,300 sq miles
(2,766,890 sq km)

SCALE 1:60,000,000
Lamberts Azimuthal Equal Area Projection
0 — 1500 miles
0 — 1500 kilometers

LONGEST RIVERS

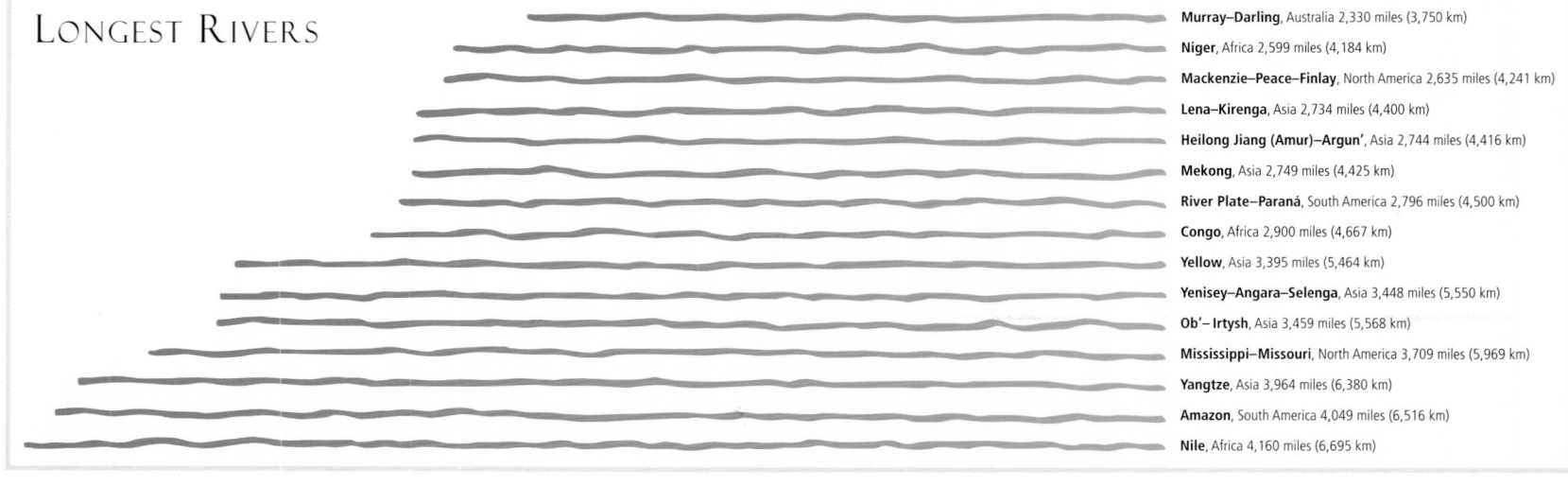

Murray–Darling, Australia 2,330 miles (3,750 km)

Niger, Africa 2,599 miles (4,184 km)

Mackenzie–Peace–Finlay, North America 2,635 miles (4,241 km)

Lena–Kirenga, Asia 2,734 miles (4,400 km)

Heilong Jiang (Amur)–Argun', Asia 2,744 miles (4,416 km)

Mekong, Asia 2,749 miles (4,425 km)

River Plate–Paraná, South America 2,796 miles (4,500 km)

Congo, Africa 2,900 miles (4,667 km)

Yellow, Asia 3,395 miles (5,464 km)

Yenisey–Angara–Selenga, Asia 3,448 miles (5,550 km)

Ob'–Irtysh, Asia 3,459 miles (5,568 km)

Mississippi–Missouri, North America 3,709 miles (5,969 km)

Yangtze, Asia 3,964 miles (6,380 km)

Amazon, South America 4,049 miles (6,516 km)

Nile, Africa 4,160 miles (6,695 km)

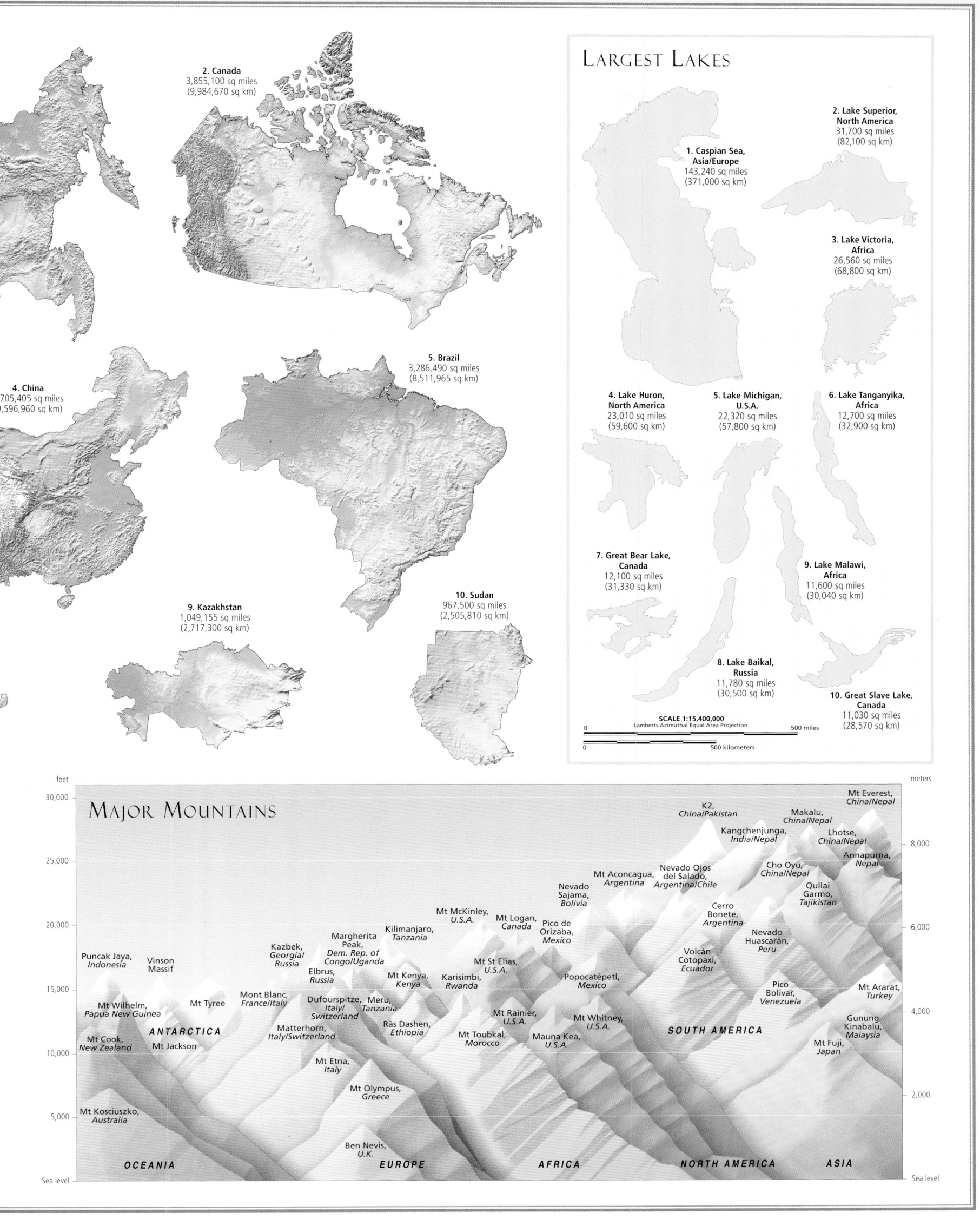

2. Canada
3,855,100 sq miles
(9,984,670 sq km)

4. China
705,405 sq miles
9,596,960 sq km)

5. Brazil
3,286,490 sq miles
(8,511,965 sq km)

9. Kazakhstan
1,049,155 sq miles
(2,717,300 sq km)

10. Sudan
967,500 sq miles
(2,505,810 sq km)

LARGEST LAKES

1. Caspian Sea, Asia/Europe
143,240 sq miles
(371,000 sq km)

2. Lake Superior, North America
31,700 sq miles
(82,100 sq km)

3. Lake Victoria, Africa
26,560 sq miles
(68,800 sq km)

4. Lake Huron, North America
23,010 sq miles
(59,600 sq km)

5. Lake Michigan, U.S.A.
22,320 sq miles
(57,800 sq km)

6. Lake Tanganyika, Africa
12,700 sq miles
(32,900 sq km)

7. Great Bear Lake, Canada
12,100 sq miles
(31,330 sq km)

9. Lake Malawi, Africa
11,600 sq miles
(30,040 sq km)

8. Lake Baikal, Russia
11,780 sq miles
(30,500 sq km)

10. Great Slave Lake, Canada
11,030 sq miles
(28,570 sq km)

SCALE 1:15,400,000
Lamberts Azimuthal Equal Area Projection
0   500 miles
0   500 kilometers

MAJOR MOUNTAINS

feet
30,000
25,000
20,000
15,000
10,000
5,000
Sea level

meters
8,000
6,000
4,000
2,000
Sea level

Mt Everest, *China/Nepal*
K2, *China/Pakistan*
Makalu, *China/Nepal*
Kangchenjunga, *India/Nepal*
Lhotse, *China/Nepal*
Cho Oyu, *China/Nepal*
Annapurna, *Nepal*
Nevado Ojos del Salado, *Argentina/Chile*
Mt Aconcagua, *Argentina*
Qullai Garmo, *Tajikistan*
Nevado Sajama, *Bolivia*
Cerro Bonete, *Argentina*
Mt McKinley, *U.S.A.*
Mt Logan, *Canada*
Pico de Orizaba, *Mexico*
Nevado Huascarán, *Peru*
Kilimanjaro, *Tanzania*
Volcán Cotopaxi, *Ecuador*
Margherita Peak, *Dem. Rep. of Congo/Uganda*
Mt St Elias, *U.S.A.*
Popocatépetl, *Mexico*
Kazbek, *Georgia/Russia*
Pico Bolívar, *Venezuela*
Puncak Jaya, *Indonesia*
Vinson Massif
Mt Kenya, *Kenya*
Karisimbi, *Rwanda*
Elbrus, *Russia*
Mt Ararat, *Turkey*
Nevado Huascarán, *Peru*
Mt Wilhelm, *Papua New Guinea*
Mt Tyree
Mont Blanc, *France/Italy*
Meru, *Tanzania*
Dufourspitze, *Italy/Switzerland*
Mt Rainier, *U.S.A.*
Mt Whitney, *U.S.A.*
Gunung Kinabalu, *Malaysia*
ANTARCTICA
Matterhorn, *Italy/Switzerland*
Rās Dashen, *Ethiopia*
SOUTH AMERICA
Mt Fuji, *Japan*
Mt Cook, *New Zealand*
Mt Jackson
Mt Toubkal, *Morocco*
Mauna Kea, *U.S.A.*
Mt Etna, *Italy*
Mt Olympus, *Greece*
Mt Kosciuszko, *Australia*
Ben Nevis, *U.K.*
OCEANIA
EUROPE
AFRICA
NORTH AMERICA
ASIA

TIME ZONES

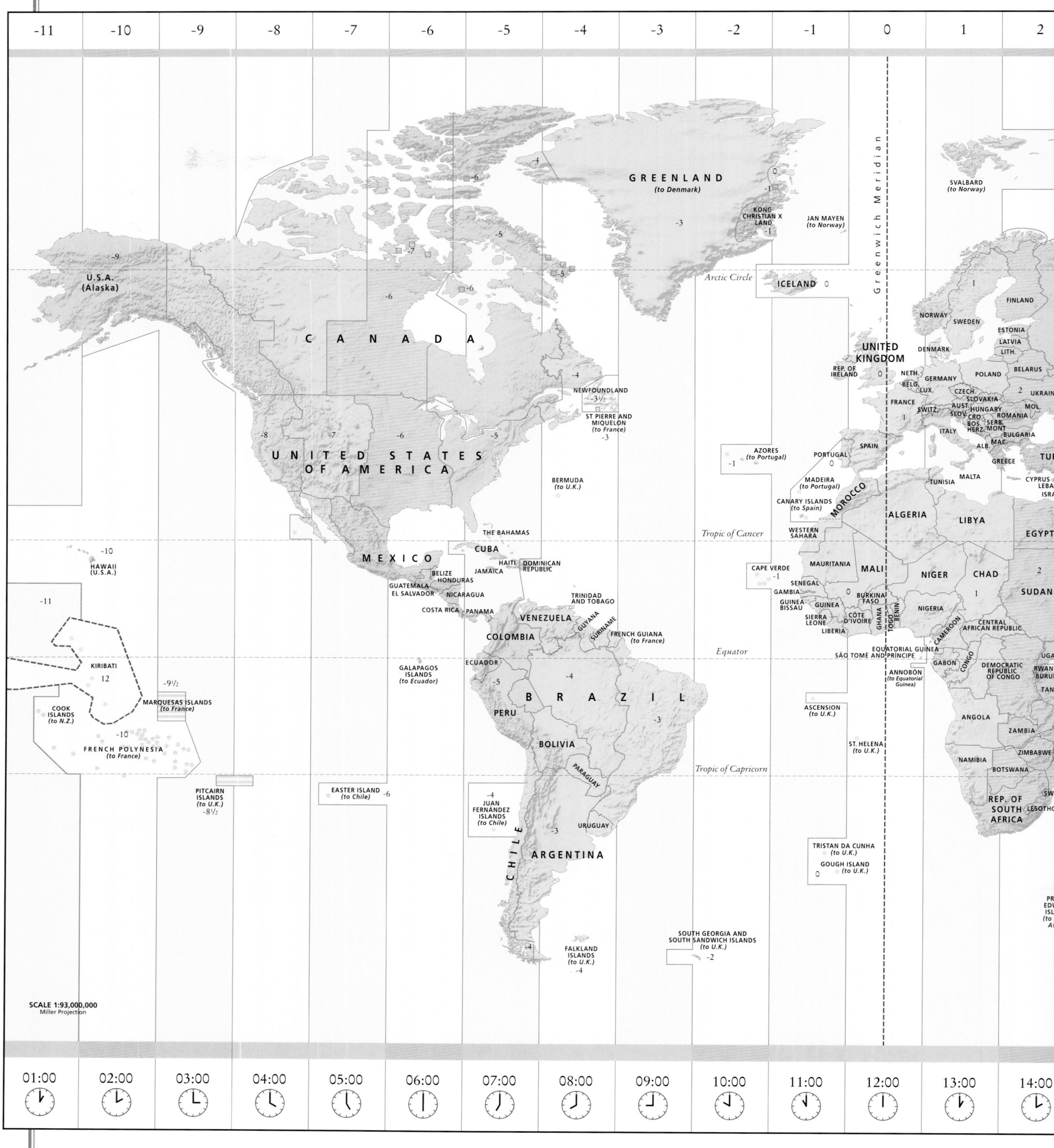

-11	-10	-9	-8	-7	-6	-5	-4	-3	-2	-1	0	1	2

Greenwich Meridian

GREENLAND
(to Denmark)

KONG
CHRISTIAN X
LAND
-1

JAN MAYEN
(to Norway)
-1

-4

-6

0

-1

-3

SVALBARD
(to Norway)

U.S.A.
(Alaska)
-9

-8

-7

-5

Arctic Circle

ICELAND   0

C A N A D A

NORWAY
SWEDEN
FINLAND

ESTONIA
LATVIA
LITH.

UNITED
KINGDOM

DENMARK
BELARUS

REP. OF
IRELAND   0
NETH.   GERMANY   POLAND
BELG.
LUX.   CZECH
SLOVAKIA   UKRAINE
FRANCE   SWITZ.   AUST. HUNGARY   MOL.
SLOV. CRO.   ROMANIA
ITALY   BOS. SERB.
HERZ. MONT.   BULGARIA
ALB.   MAC.
GREECE   TUR

NEWFOUNDLAND
-3½
ST PIERRE AND
MIQUELON
(to France)
-3

-6

-7

-8

UNITED STATES
OF AMERICA

-6

-5

BERMUDA
(to U.K.)

AZORES
(to Portugal)
-1

PORTUGAL
0

SPAIN

MADEIRA
(to Portugal)
CANARY ISLANDS
(to Spain)

MOROCCO

TUNISIA
MALTA

CYPRUS
LEBAN
ISR

Tropic of Cancer

THE BAHAMAS

WESTERN
SAHARA

ALGERIA

LIBYA

EGYPT

-10

HAWAII
(U.S.A.)

MEXICO

CUBA
HAITI
DOMINICAN
REPUBLIC

JAMAICA

CAPE VERDE
-1

MAURITANIA

MALI

NIGER

CHAD

2

SUDAN

-11

BELIZE
GUATEMALA HONDURAS
EL SALVADOR   NICARAGUA
COSTA RICA   PANAMA

SENEGAL
GAMBIA
GUINEA-
BISSAU   GUINEA

BURKINA
FASO

NIGERIA

KIRIBATI
12

TRINIDAD
AND TOBAGO

VENEZUELA
GUYANA
COLOMBIA   SURINAME
FRENCH GUIANA
(to France)

SIERRA
LEONE   CÔTE
D'IVOIRE

LIBERIA

GHANA
TOGO
BENIN

CENTRAL
AFRICAN REPUBLIC

CAMEROON

-9½

MARQUESAS ISLANDS
(to France)

Equator

EQUATORIAL GUINEA
SÃO TOMÉ AND PRINCIPE

GABON

UGA

COOK
ISLANDS
(to N.Z.)

-10

GALAPAGOS
ISLANDS
(to Ecuador)

ECUADOR
-5

-4

ANNOBÓN
(to Equatorial
Guinea)

CONGO

DEMOCRATIC
REPUBLIC
OF CONGO

RWANDA
BURUN

FRENCH POLYNESIA
(to France)

PERU

B R A Z I L

ASCENSION
(to U.K.)

ANGOLA

TANZ

PITCAIRN
ISLANDS
(to U.K.)
-8½

-9½

BOLIVIA

PARAGUAY

-3

Tropic of Capricorn

ST. HELENA
(to U.K.)

ZAMBIA

NAMIBIA

ZIMBABWE

BOTSWANA

EASTER ISLAND
(to Chile)   -6

-4
JUAN
FERNÁNDEZ
ISLANDS
(to Chile)

URUGUAY

TRISTAN DA CUNHA
(to U.K.)

GOUGH ISLAND
(to U.K.)
0

REP. OF
SOUTH
AFRICA

SWA

LESOTHO

-3

C
H
I
L
E

ARGENTINA

-4

FALKLAND
ISLANDS
(to U.K.)
-4

SOUTH GEORGIA AND
SOUTH SANDWICH ISLANDS
(to U.K.)
-2

PR
EDV
ISL
(to S
AF

SCALE 1:93,000,000
Miller Projection

01:00	02:00	03:00	04:00	05:00	06:00	07:00	08:00	09:00	10:00	11:00	12:00	13:00	14:00

| 4 | 5 | 6 | 7 | 8 | 9 | 10 | 11 | 12 | -11 |

FRANZ JOSEF LAND

SEVERNAYA ZEMLYA

NOVAYA ZEMLYA

NEW SIBERIA ISLANDS

R U S S I A N   F E D E R A T I O N

5

4

5

7

9

10

8

11

12

-9

KAZAKHSTAN

6

MONGOLIA

ALEUTIAN ISLANDS (U.S.A.) -10

UZBEKISTAN

KYRGYZSTAN

BAIJAN

TURKMENISTAN TAJIKISTAN

CHINA

KURIL ISLANDS (to Russian Federation)

IRAN

AFGHANISTAN 4½

NORTH KOREA

3½

PAKISTAN

NEPAL BHUTAN

5¼

JAPAN 9

SOUTH KOREA

JWAIT

5

BAN.

BAHRAIN QATAR U.A.E.

INDIA

MYANMAR (BURMA)

LAOS

8

RYUKYU ISLANDS (to Japan)

OMAN

5½

6½

4

SOCOTRA (to Yemen)

THAILAND

CAMB.

NORTHERN MARIANA ISLANDS (to U.S.A.)

10

GUAM (to U.S.A.)

JOHNSTON ATOLL (to U.S.A.)

-10

LACCADIVE ISLANDS (to India)

ANDAMAN AND NICOBAR ISLANDS (to India)

6

VIETNAM

7

PHILIPPINES

SRI LANKA

5½

PALAU

MICRONESIA

5

MALDIVES

BRUNEI

8

MALAYSIA

SINGAPORE

MARSHALL ISLANDS

12

BRITISH INDIAN OCEAN TERRITORY (to U.K.)

6

I N D O N E S I A

9

PAPUA NEW GUINEA

SOLOMON ISLANDS

NAURU

YCHELLES

6½

PAPUA NEW GUINEA

11

KIRIBATI 12

COCOS ISLANDS (to Australia)

CHRISTMAS ISLAND (to Australia)

EAST TIMOR

VANUATU

TUVALU

TOKELAU (to N.Z.) -10

MAURITIUS

CORAL SEA ISLANDS (to Australia)

NEW CALEDONIA (to France)

FIJI

SAMOA -10

SCAR

RÉUNION (to France)

9½

TONGA 13

FRENCH SOUTHERN AND ANTARCTIC TERRITORIES (to France)

5

A U S T R A L I A

8

10

NORFOLK ISLAND (to Australia) 11½

10½

LORD HOWE ISLAND (to Australia)

KERMADEC ISLANDS (to N.Z.)

12

-11

KERGUELEN ISLANDS (to France)

5

NEW ZEALAND

CHATHAM ISLANDS (to N.Z.) 12¼

HEARD AND MCDONALD ISLANDS (to Australia)

International Date Line

The standard time zone system is based on the theoretical division of the world into 24 zones of 15° of longitude. Each zone represents one hour of time. The middle meridian of each zone sets the time for that zone. The zero time zone is 7½° east and 7½° west of 0° longitude, the Greenwich (or prime) meridian. The time at this meridian is refered to as Greenwich mean time (GMT). Time zones to the west of the Greenwich meridian are earlier and zones to the east are later. The International Date Line has been designated at 180° longitude. The time is the same on both sides of this line but east of the International Date Line is one day earlier than it is to the west of the line.

Individual nations set their legal time based on this standard time zone system. For convenience certain islands or frontiers may be kept in a different time zone to the one in which they are physically located. For example, the South Island of New Zealand maintains the same time as the North Island despite its location in a different time zone. The time in certain nations or territories may differ from the rest of a zone by a fraction of an hour (for example India). This is indicated on the map by the striped areas. Some countries adjust the legal time for part of the year, particularly summer. They often advance their time by one hour to maximize the use of daylight hours.

On this map each zone is assigned a color. The numbers at the top of the map, and on each zone, signify the number of hours the zone is ahead or behind GMT. The 24-hour time and clocks at the bottom of the map indicate the time in each zone when it is 12:00 noon GMT.

| 16:00 | 17:00 | 18:00 | 19:00 | 20:00 | 21:00 | 22:00 | 23:00 | 24:00 | 01:00 |

The Greenwich meridian, located in London, England marks 0° longitude and the zero time zone.

	Area SQ MILES (SQ KM)	Population	Capital	Currency	Official Languages	Other Languages	Main Religions	Life Expectancy	Literacy Rate	Economy
NORTH AMERICA										
Antigua and Barbuda	171 (443)	68,720	Saint John's	East Caribbean dollar (XCD)	English	Local dialects	✝, ✢	71.02	89% (1960)	3.9%, 19.1%, 77%
The Bahamas	5,380 (13,940)	301,790	Nassau	Bahamian dollar (BSD)	English	Creole	✝ 70%, ✢ 19%, ∝ 6%, ✳ 5%	69.87	95.6%	3%, 7%, 90%
Barbados	166 (431)	279,250	Bridgetown	Barbadian dollar (BBD)	English		✝ 67%, ✢ 4%, ✳ 29%	73.49	97.4% (1995)	6%, 16%, 78%
Belize	8,870 (22,970)	279,460	Belmopan	Belizean dollar (BZD)	English	Spanish, Mayan, Garifuna (Carib), Creole	✢ 49.6%, ✝ 27%, ✳ 23.4%	71.46	94.1%	18%, 24%, 58%
Canada	3,474,920 (9,984,670)	32,805,040	Ottawa	Canadian dollar (CAD)	English, French		✢ 46%, ✝ 36%, ✳ 18%	79.69	97% (1986)	2%, 29%, 69%
Costa Rica	19,730 (51,100)	4,016,170	San José	Costa Rican colon (CRC)	Spanish	English	✢ 76.3%, ✝ 15.7%, ✳ 8%	76.22	96%	11%, 37%, 52%
Cuba	42,800 (110,860)	11,339,890	Havana	Cuban peso (CUP)	Spanish		✢, ✝, ✿, ✳	76.6	96.9%	7.6%, 34.5%, 57.9%
Dominica	291 (754)	69,030	Roseau	East Caribbean dollar (XCD)	English	French patois	✢ 77%, ✝ 15%, ✳ 8%	73.86	94%	NA
Dominican Republic	18,810 (48,730)	8,950,030	Santo Domingo	Dominican peso (DOP)	Spanish		✢ 95%	73.68	84.7%	11.1%, 34.1%, 54.8%
El Salvador	8,120 (21,040)	6,704,930	San Salvador	Salvadoran colon (SVC), U.S. dollar (USD)	Spanish	Nahua	✢ 83% ✝	70.32	80.2%	10%, 30%, 60%
Grenada	133 (344)	89,500	St George's	East Caribbean dollar (XCD)	English	French patois	✢ 53%, ✝ 47%	64.52	98% (1970)	7.7%, 23.9%, 68.4%
Guatemala	42,040 (108,890)	14,655,190	Guatemala	quetzal (GTQ), U.S. dollar (USD)	Spanish	Amerindian languages	✢, ✝, O	66.85	70.6%	23%, 20%, 57%
Haiti	10,710 (27,750)	7,790,340	Port-au-Prince	gourde (HTG)	French, Creole		✢ 80%, ✝ 16%, ✳ 4%	49.55	52.9%	30%, 20%, 50%
Honduras	43,280 (112,090)	6,975,200	Tegucigalpa	lempira (HNL)	Spanish	Amerindian dialects	✢ 97%, ✝	68.77	76.2%	18%, 32%, 50%
Jamaica	4,240 (10,990)	2,731,830	Kingston	Jamaican dollar (JMD)	English	Patois English	✝ 61.3%, ✢ 4%, ✳ 34.7%	75.64	87.9%	7%, 28%, 65%
Mexico	761,610 (1,972,550)	107,869,840	Mexico City	Mexican peso (MXN)	Spanish	Mayan, Nahuatl, other indigenous languages	✢ 89%, ✝ 6%, ✳ 5%	72.03	92.2%	5%, 26%, 69%
Nicaragua	50,000 (129,490)	5,334,680	Managua	gold cordoba (NIO)	Spanish	English, indigenous languages	✢ 85%, ✝	69.37	67.5%	33%, 23%, 44%
Panama	30,190 (78,200)	3,039,150	Panama City	balboa (PAB), U.S. dollar (USD)	Spanish	English	✢ 85%, ✝ 15%	75.89	92.6%	7%, 17%, 76%
St Kitts and Nevis	101 (261)	38,960	Basseterre	East Caribbean dollar (XCD)	English		✝, ✢	71.29	97% (1980)	3.5%, 25.8%, 70.7%
St Lucia	238 (616)	166,310	Castries	East Caribbean dollar (XCD)	English	French patois	✢ 90%, ✝ 10%	72.82	67% (1980)	7.9%, 19.6%, 72.5%
St Vincent and the Grenadines	150 (389)	117,530	Kingstown	East Caribbean dollar (XCD)	English	French patois	✝ 75%, ✢ 13%, ✳ 12%	72.82	96% (1970)	10%, 26%, 64%
Trinidad and Tobago	1,980 (5,130)	1,088,640	Port of Spain	Trinidad and Tobago dollar (TTD)	English	Hindi, French, Spanish, Chinese	✢ 29.4%, ✾ 23.8%, ✝ 14.3%, ☪ 5.8%, ✳ 26.7%	68.59	98.6%	1.6%, 43.2%, 55.2%
United States of America	3,717,810 (9,629,090)	295,734,130	Washington, D.C.	U.S. dollar (USD)	English	Spanish	✝ 56%, ✢ 28%, ✿ 2%, ✳ 14%	77.4	97% (1979)	2%, 18%, 80%
SOUTH AMERICA										
Argentina	1,068,300 (2,766,890)	39,537,940	Buenos Aires	Argentine peso (ARS)	Spanish	English, Italian, German, French	✢ 92%, ✝ 2%, ✿ 2%, ✳ 4%	75.48	97.1%	6%, 28%, 66%
Bolivia	424,160 (1,098,580)	8,857,870	La Paz, Sucre	boliviano (BOB)	Spanish, Quechua, Aymara		✢ 95%, ✝	64.42	87.2%	14%, 31%, 55%

Key to symbols: ∝ Christian ✢ Catholic ✿ Orthodox ✝ Protestant ◉ Buddhist ✾ Hindu ✡ Jewish ☪ Muslim ≡ Atheist O Indigenous ✳ Other ⚘ Agriculture ⚒ Industry ⚕ Services **NA** Not Available
Note: All literacy statistics are for 2003 unless otherwise stated.

AREA SQ MILES (SQ KM)	POPULATION	CAPITAL	CURRENCY	OFFICIAL LANGUAGES	OTHER LANGUAGES	MAIN RELIGIONS	LIFE EXPECTANCY	LITERACY RATE	ECONOMY		
3,286,490 (8,511,970)	186,112,790	Brasília	real (BRL)	Portuguese	Spanish, English, French	✚ 80%	63.55	86.4%	⛟ 9%, ⚒ 32%, ⚕ 59%		Brazil
292,260 (756,950)	15,984,780	Santiago	Chilean peso (CLP)	Spanish		✚ 89%, ✝ 11%, ✡ less than 1%	76.14	96.2%	⛟ 8%, ⚒ 38%, ⚕ 54%		Chile
439,740 (1,138,910)	42,954,280	Bogotá	Colombian peso (COP)	Spanish		✚ 90%, ✳ 10%	70.85	92.5%	⛟ 19%, ⚒ 26%, ⚕ 55%		Colombia
109,480 (283,560)	14,231,760	Quito	U.S. dollar (USD)	Spanish		✚ 95%, ✳ 5%	71.61	92.5%	⛟ 11%, ⚒ 25%, ⚕ 64%		Ecuador
83,000 (214,970)	710,660	Georgetown	Guyanese dollar (GYD)	English	Amerindian dialects, Creole, Hindi, Urdu	∝ 50%, ৯ 35%, ☾ 10%, ✳ 5%	62.59	98.8%	⛟ 36.1%, ⚒ 31.8%, ⚕ 32.1%		Guyana
157,050 (406,750)	6,347,880	Asunción	guarani (PYG)	Spanish, Guarani		✚ 90%, ✳ 10%	74.16	94%	⛟ 29%, ⚒ 26%, ⚕ 45%		Paraguay
496,230 (1,285,220)	29,309,290	Lima	nuevo sol (PEN)	Spanish, Quechua	Aymara	✚ 90%, ✳ 10%	70.59	90.9%	⛟ 10%, ⚒ 35%, ⚕ 55%		Peru
63,040 (163,270)	438,140	Paramaribo	Surinamese guilder (SRG)	Dutch	English, Sranang Tongo, Hindustani, Javanese	৯ 27.4%, ☾ 19.6%, ✚ 22.8%, ✝ 25.2%, ⊙ 5%	71.9	93% (1995)	⛟ 13%, ⚒ 22%, ⚕ 65%		Suriname
68,040 (176,220)	3,467,070	Montevideo	Uruguayan peso (UYU)	Spanish, Portunol, Brazilero		✚ 66%, ✝ 2%, ✡ 1%, ✳ 31%	75.66	98%	⛟ 6%, ⚒ 29%, ⚕ 65%		Uruguay
352,140 (912,050)	25,375,280	Caracas	bolivar (VEB)	Spanish	Indigenous dialects	✚ 96%, ✝ 2%, ✳ 2%	73.56	93.4%	⛟ 5%, ⚒ 40%, ⚕ 55%		Venezuela
11,100 (28,750)	3,654,960	Tirana	lek (ALL)	Albanian (Tosk is the official dialect)	Greek	☾ 70%, ✜ 20%, ✚ 10%	72.1	86.5%,	⛟ 52%, ⚒ 21%, ⚕ 27%		Albania
180 (470)	70,550	Andorra la Vella	euro (EUR)	Catalan	French, Castilian Spanish	✚	83.48	100%	NA		Andorra
32,380 (83,860)	8,221,260	Vienna	euro (EUR)	German		✚ 78%, ✝ 5%, ☾ and ✳ 17%	78	98%	⛟ 2%, ⚒ 29%, ⚕ 69%		Austria
80,150 (207,600)	10,300,480	Minsk	Belarusian ruble (BYB/BYR)	Belarusian	Russian	✜ 80%, ✳ 20%	68.28	99.6%	⛟ 13%, ⚒ 42%, ⚕ 45%		Belarus
11,780 (30,510)	10,313,490	Brussels	euro (EUR)	Dutch, French, German		✚ 75%, ✝ or ✳ 25%	78.13	98%	⛟ 1.4%, ⚒ 24%, ⚕ 74.6%		Belgium
19,740 (51,130)	4,025,480	Sarajevo	marka (BAM)	Croatian, Serbian, Bosnian		☾ 40%, ✜ 31%, ✚ 15%, ✝ 4%, ✳ 10%	72.02	NA	⛟ 16%, ⚒ 28%, ⚕ 56%		Bosnia and Herzegovina
42,820 (110,910)	7,377,370	Sofia	lev (BGL)	Bulgarian		✜ 83.8%, ☾ 12.1%, ✚ 1.7%, ✡ 0.8%, ✝ and ✳ 1.6%	71.5	98.6%	⛟ 14.5%, ⚒ 27.8%, ⚕ 57.7%		Bulgaria
21,830 (56,540)	4,449,290	Zagreb	kuna (HRK)	Croatian	Italian, Hungarian, Czech, Slovak, German	✚ 76.5%, ✜ 11.1%, ☾ 1.2%, ✝ 0.4%, ✳ 10.8%	74.13	98.5%	⛟ 10%, ⚒ 33%, ⚕ 57%		Croatia
30,450 (78,870)	10,230,740	Prague	Czech koruna (CZK)	Czech		≡ 39.8%, ✚ 39.2%, ✝ 4.6%, ✜ 3%, ✳ 13.4%	74.95	99.9% (1999)	⛟ 5%, ⚒ 41%, ⚕ 54%		Czech Republic
16,640 (43,090)	5,413,720	Copenhagen	Danish krone (DKK)	Danish	English, Faroese, Greenlandic, German	✝ 95%, ∝ 3%, ☾ 2%	76.91	100%	⛟ 3%, ⚒ 22%, ⚕ 75%		Denmark
17,460 (45,230)	1,395,850	Tallinn	Estonian kroon (EEK)	Estonian	Russian, Ukrainian, Finnish, other	✝, ✜, ✚, ✡, ∝	70.02	99.8%	⛟ 6%, ⚒ 28%, ⚕ 66%,		Estonia
130,130 (337,030)	5,203,940	Helsinki	euro (EUR)	Finnish	Swedish, Lapp, Russian	✝ 89%, ✜ 1%, ✳ 9%	77.75	100% (1980)	⛟ 3%, ⚒ 28%, ⚕ 69%		Finland
211,210 (547,030)	60,656,180	Paris	euro (EUR)	French	Provencal, Breton, Alsatian, Corsican, Basque, Flemish	✚ 83%-88%, ✝ 2%, ✡ 1%, ☾ 5%-10%, ✳ 4%	79.05	99% (1980)	⛟ 3.3%, ⚒ 25.7%, ⚕ 71%		France
137,850 (357,020)	82,431,390	Berlin	euro (EUR)	German		✝ 34%, ✚ 34%, ☾ 3.7%, ✳ 28.3%	77.78	99% (1977)	⛟ 1%, ⚒ 28%, ⚕ 71%		Germany
50,940 (131,940)	10,703,500	Athens	euro (EUR)	Greek	English, French	✜ 98%, ☾ 1.3%, ✳ 0.7%	78.74	97.5%	⛟ 8.3%, ⚒ 27.3%, ⚕ 64.4%		Greece

Key to symbols: ∝ Christian ✚ Catholic ✜ Orthodox ✝ Protestant ⊚ Buddhist ৯ Hindu ✡ Jewish ☾ Muslim ≡ Atheist ⊙ Indigenous ✳ Other ⛟ Agriculture ⚒ Industry ⚕ Services **NA** Not Available
Note: All literacy statistics are for 2003 unless otherwise stated.

EUROPE

	Area SQ MILES (SQ KM)	Population	Capital	Currency	Official Languages	Other Languages	Main Religions	Life Expectancy	Literacy Rate	Economy
Hungary	35,920 (93,030)	9,986,520	Budapest	forint (HUF)	Hungarian		✞ 67.5%, ✝ 25%, ≡ and ✳ 7.5%	71.9	99.4%	⚘ 6%, ⚒ 34%, ⛿ 60%
Iceland	39,770 (103,000)	283,440	Reykjavík	Icelandic krona (ISK)	Icelandic		✝ 93%, ∝ and ✳ 7%	79.66	99.9% (1997)	⚘ 15% (includes fishing 13%), ⚒ 21%, ⛿ 64%
Ireland, Republic of	27,140 (70,280)	4,001,530	Dublin	euro (EUR)	English, Irish (Gaelic)		✞ 91.6%, ✝ 2.5%, ✳ 5.9%	77.17	98% (1981)	⚘ 4%, ⚒ 38%, ⛿ 58%
Italy	116,310 (301,230)	58,103,030	Rome	euro (EUR)	Italian	German, French, Slovene, Albanian, Greek	✞, ✝, ✡, ☪	79.25	98.6%	⚘ 2.4%, ⚒ 30%, ⛿ 67.6%
Latvia	24,940 (64,590)	2,316,420	Rīga	Latvian lat (LVL)	Latvian	Lithuanian, Russian	✞, ✝, ✡	69	99.8%	⚘ 5%, ⚒ 24%, ⛿ 71%
Liechtenstein	62 (160)	33,720	Vaduz	Swiss franc (CHF)	German	Alemannic dialect	✞ 80%, ✝ 7.4%, ✳ 12.6%	79.1	100%	NA
Lithuania	25,170 (65,200)	3,577,950	Vilnius	litas (LTL)	Lithuanian	Polish, Russian	✞, ✝, ✡, ☪, ✡	69.42	99.6% (1981)	⚘ 9%, ⚒ 32%, ⛿ 59%
Luxembourg	1,000 (2,590)	465,250	Luxembourg	euro (EUR)	Luxembourgish	German, French	✞ (predominantly), ✝, ✡, ☪	77.48	100%	⚘ 1%, ⚒ 30%, ⛿ 69%
Macedonia (F.Y.R.O.M.)	9,780 (25,330)	2,079,060	Skopje	Macedonian denar (MKD)	Macedonian	Albanian, Turkish, Serbo-Croatian	✝ 67%, ☪ 30%, ✳ 3%	74.26	NA	⚘ 10%, ⚒ 32%, ⛿ 58%
Malta	122 (316)	406,260	Valletta	Maltese lira (MTL)	Maltese, English		✞ 91%	78.26	92.8%	⚘ 2.8%, ⚒ 25.5%, ⛿ 71.7%
Moldova	13,070 (33,840)	4,455,420	Chişinău	Moldovan leu (MDL)	Moldovan, Russian	Gagauz (a Turkish dialect)	✝ 98.5%, ✡ 1.5%	64.74	99.1%	⚘ 28%, ⚒ 21%, ⛿ 51%
Monaco	0.75 (1.95)	32,410	Monaco	euro (EUR)	French	English, Italian, Monegasque	✞ 90%	79.12	99%	NA
Netherlands	16,030 (41,530)	16,304,210	Amsterdam, The Hague	euro (EUR)	Dutch		✞ 31%, ✝ 21%, ☪ 4.4%, ✳ 43.6%	78.58	99% (2000)	⚘ 3.3%, ⚒ 26.3%, ⛿ 70.4%
Norway	125,180 (324,220)	4,586,160	Oslo	Norwegian krone (NOK)	Norwegian	Saami, Finnish	✝ 86%, ∝ 3%, ✳ 11%	78.94	100%	⚘ 2%, ⚒ 31%, ⛿ 67%
Poland	120,730 (312,690)	38,635,140	Warsaw	zloty (PLN)	Polish		✞ 95%, ✡, ✝ and ✳ 5%	73.66	99.8%	⚘ 4%, ⚒ 32%, ⛿ 64%
Portugal	35,670 (92,390)	10,135,380	Lisbon	euro (EUR)	Portuguese		✞ 94%, ✝	76.14	93.3%	⚘ 3.8%, ⚒ 30.5%, ⛿ 65.7%
Romania	91,700 (237,500)	22,178,400	Bucharest	leu (ROL)	Romanian	Hungarian, German	✝ 70%, ✞ 6%, ✝ 6%, ✳ 18%	70.39	98.4%	⚘ 15%, ⚒ 30%, ⛿ 55%
Russian Federation	6,592,770 (17,075,200)	143,736,790	Moscow	Russian ruble (RUR)	Russian		✝, ☪, ✳	67.5	99.6%	⚘ 7%, ⚒ 37%, ⛿ 56%
San Marino	24 (61)	28,880	San Marino	euro (EUR)	Italian		✞	81.33	96% (1976)	NA
Serbia and Montenegro	39,520 (102,350)	10,668,570	Belgrade	new Yugoslav dinar (YUM), euro (EUR)	Serbian, Albanian		✝ 65%, ☪ 19%, ✞ 4%, ✝ 1%, ✳ 11%	73.72	93% (1991)	⚘ 26%, ⚒ 36%, ⛿ 38%
Slovakia	18,860 (48,850)	5,444,900	Bratislava	Slovak koruna (SKK)	Slovak	Hungarian	✞ 60.3%, ≡ 9.7%, ✝ 8.4%, ✞ 4.1%, ✳ 17.5%	74.2	NA	⚘ 4%, ⚒ 32%, ⛿ 64%
Slovenia	7,830 (20,720)	1,940,630	Ljubljana	tolar (SIT)	Slovenian, Serbo-Croatian		✞ 70.8%, ✝ 1%, ☪ 1%, ≡ 4.3%, ✳ 22.9%	75.29	99.7%	⚘ 4%, ⚒ 35%, ⛿ 61%
Spain	194,900 (504,780)	40,341,460	Madrid	euro (EUR))	Castilian Spanish	Catalan, Galician, Basque	✞ 94%, ✳ 6%	79.08	97.9%	⚘ 4%, ⚒ 28%, ⛿ 68%
Sweden	173,730 (449,960)	8,879,790	Stockholm	Swedish krona (SEK)	Swedish	Saami, Finnish	✝ 87%, ✞, ✡, ☪, ✡, and ⚛ 13%	79.84	99% (1979)	⚘ 2%, ⚒ 28.7%, ⛿ 69.3%
Switzerland	15,940 (41,290)	7,346,070	Bern	Swiss franc (CHF)	German, French, Italian	Romansch, other	✞ 46.1%, ✝ 40%, ✳ 13.9%	79.86	99% (1980)	⚘ 2%, ⚒ 34%, ⛿ 64%

Key to symbols: ∝ Christian ✞ Catholic ✝ Orthodox ✝ Protestant ◎ Buddhist ⚛ Hindu ✡ Jewish ☪ Muslim ≡ Atheist ○ Indigenous ✳ Other ⚘ Agriculture ⚒ Industry ⛿ Services NA Not Available
Note: All literacy statistics are for 2003 unless otherwise stated.

ASIA

Area (sq miles / sq km)	Population	Capital	Currency	Official Languages	Other Languages	Main Religions	Life Expectancy	Literacy Rate	Economy		Country
33,090 (603,700)	47,425,340	Kiev	hryvnia (UAH)	Ukrainian	Russian, Romanian, Polish, Hungarian	✡, ♁, ✝, ✿	66.33	99.7%	NA		Ukraine
4,530 (244,820)	60,441,460	London	British pound (GBP)	English, Welsh, Scottish (Gaelic)		✡, ✝, ☪, ☬, ✿, ✳	77.99	99% (2000)	⚘ 1.7%, ⚒ 24.9%, ⚕ 73.4%		United Kingdom
.17 (0.44)	900	Vatican City	euro (EUR)	Italian, Latin, French		✡		NA	NA		Vatican City
50,000 (647,500)	30,241,190	Kabul	afghani (AFA)	Pashtu, Afghan Persian (Dari)	Turkic languages, other languages	☪ 99%, ✳ 1%	46.6	36% (1999)	⚘ 60%, ⚒ 20% (1990 est.)		Afghanistan
1,510 (29,800)	3,326,830	Yerevan	dram (AMD)	Armenian, Russian		∝ 98%, ✳ 2%	66.59	98.6%	⚘ 29%, ⚒ 32%, ⚕ 39%		Armenia
3,440 (86,600)	7,911,970	Baku	Azerbaijani manat (AZM)	Azerbaijani (Azeri), Russian	Armenian, other	☪ 93.4%, ♁ 4.8%, ✳ 1.8%	63.06	97% (1989)	⚘ 22%, ⚒ 33%, ⚕ 45%		Azerbaijan
57 (665)	688,350	Al Manāmah	Bahraini dinar (BHD)	Arabic, English, Farsi, Urdu		☪ 100%	73.47	89.1%	⚘ 1%, ⚒ 35%, ⚕ 64%		Bahrain
5,600 (144,000)	144,319,630	Dacca	taka (BDT)	Bangla (also known as Bengali)	English	☪ 83%, ☸ 16%, ✳ 1%	60.92	43.1%	⚘ 30%, ⚒ 18%, ⚕ 52%		Bangladesh
8,147 (47,000)	2,232,290	Thimphu	ngultrum (BTN), Indian rupee (INR)	Dzongkha	Tibetan dialects, Nepalese dialects	◉ 75%, ☸ 25%	53.19	42.2% (1995)	⚘ 45%, ⚒ 20%, ⚕ 35%		Bhutan
,230 (5,770)	372,360	Bandar Seri Begawan	Bruneian dollar (BND)	Malay	English, Chinese	☪ 67%, ◉ 13%, ∝ 10%, O and ✳ 10%	74.06	91.8%	⚘ 5%, ⚒ 45%, ⚕ 50%		Brunei
9,900 (181,040)	13,607,070	Phnom Penh	riel (KHR)	Khmer	French, English	◉ 95%, ✳ 5%	57.1	69.9%	⚘ 50%, ⚒ 15%, ⚕ 35%		Cambodia
,705,410 (9,569,960)	1,302,207,990	Beijing	yuan (CNY)	Mandarin, Cantonese, Shanghaiese	Fuzhou, Hokkien-Taiwanese, Xiang, Gan, Hakka, other	☪ 1%-2%, ∝ 3%-4%, ◉, ✳	71.86	86%	⚘ 17.7%, ⚒ 49.3%, ⚕ 33%		China
,570 (9,250)	780,130	Nicosia	Cypriot pound (CYP), Turkish lira (TRL)	Greek, Turkish, English		♁ 78%, ☪ 18%, ✳ 4%	77.08	97.6%	Gr: ⚘ 4.6%, ⚒ 19.9%, ⚕ 75.5%, Tk: ⚘ 8.3%, ⚒ 20.7%, ⚕ 71.0%		Cyprus
,800 (15,010)	1,040,880	Dili	U.S. dollar (USD)	Tetum, Portuguese	Indonesian, English, Tetum, Galole, Mambae, Kemak	✡ 90%, ☪ 4%, ✝ 3%, ☸ 0.5%, ◉, O	64.85	48% (2001)	⚘ 25.4%, ⚒ 17.2%, ⚕ 57.4%		East Timor
6,910 (69,700)	4,886,720	T'bilisi	lari (GEL)	Georgian	Russian, Armenian, Azeri	♁ 75%, ☪ 11%, ✳ 14%	64.67	99% (1999)	⚘ 25%, ⚒ 20%, ⚕ 55%		Georgia
,269,345 (3,287,590)	1,080,264,390	New Delhi	Indian rupee (INR)	Hindi	English, Bengali, Telugu, Marathi, Tamil, Urdu, other	☸ 81.3%, ☪ 12%, ∝ 2.3%, ✳ 4.4%	63.23	59.5%	⚘ 25%, ⚒ 26%, ⚕ 49%		India
741,100 (1,919,440)	241,973,880	Jakarta	Indonesian rupiah (IDR)	Bahasa Indonesia	English, Dutch, Javanese, local dialects	☪ 88%, ✝ 5%, ✡ 3%, ☸ 2%, ◉ 1%, ✳ 1%	68.63	88.5%	⚘ 17%, ⚒ 41%, ⚕ 42%		Indonesia
636,300 (1,648,000)	69,765,580	Tehran	Iranian rial (IRR)	Persian	Turkic, Kurdish, Luri, Balochi, Arabic, Turkish	☪ 99%, ✳ 1%	70.25	79.4%	⚘ 20%, ⚒ 24%, ⚕ 56%		Iran
68,750 (437,070)	26,074,910	Baghdad	Iraqi dinar (IQD)	Arabic, Kurdish	Assyrian, Armenian	☪ 97%, ∝ or ✳ 3%	67.38	40.4%	⚘ 6%, ⚒ 13%, ⚕ 81% (1993 est.)		Iraq
8,020 (20,070)	6,276,880	Jerusalem	new Israeli shekel (ILS)	Hebrew	Arabic, English	✿ 80.1%, ☪ 14.6%, ∝ 2.1%, ✳ 3.2%	78.86	95.4%	⚘ 4%, ⚒ 37%, ⚕ 59%		Israel
145,880 (377,840)	127,417,240	Tokyo	yen (JPY)	Japanese		◉ 84%, ✳ 16%	80.91	99% (1995)	⚘ 2%, ⚒ 36%, ⚕ 62%		Japan
35,640 (92,300)	5,759,730	Ammān	Jordanian dinar (JOD)	Arabic	English	☪ 92%, ∝ 6%, ✳ 2%	77.71	91.3%	⚘ 3.7%, ⚒ 26%, ⚕ 70.3%		Jordan
1,049,155 (2,717,300)	16,846,390	Astana	tenge (KZT)	Kazakh, Russian		☪ 47%, ♁ 44%, ✝ 2%, ✳ 7%	63.38	98.4% (1999)	⚘ 10%, ⚒ 30%, ⚕ 60%		Kazakhstan
6,880 (17,820)	2,335,650	Kuwait	Kuwaiti dinar (KD)	Arabic	English	☪ 85%, ∝, ☸, and ✳ 15%	76.46	83.5%	⚒ 60%, ⚕ 39.7%, ⚘ 0.3%		Kuwait
76,640 (198,500)	5,039,210	Bishkek	Kyrgyzstani som (KGS)	Kyrgyz, Russian		☪ 75%, ♁ 20%, ✳ 5%	63.56	97% (1989)	⚘ 38%, ⚒ 27%, ⚕ 35%		Kyrgyzstan

Key to symbols: ∝ Christian ✡ Catholic ♁ Orthodox ✝ Protestant ◉ Buddhist ☸ Hindu ✿ Jewish ☪ Muslim ≡ Atheist O Indigenous ✳ Other ⚘ Agriculture ⚒ Industry ⚕ Services NA Not Available
Note: All literacy statistics are for 2003 unless otherwise stated.

		AREA SQ MILES (SQ KM)	POPULATION	CAPITAL	CURRENCY	OFFICIAL LANGUAGES	OTHER LANGUAGES	MAIN RELIGIONS	LIFE EXPECTANCY	LITERACY RATE	ECONOMY
Laos		91,430 (236,800)	6,217,140	Vientiane	kip (LAK)	Lao	French, English, other	⊛ 60%, ✳ 40%	53.88	52.8%	⚘ 53%, ⚒ 22%, ⛏ 25%
Lebanon		4,020 (10,400)	3,826,020	Beirut	Lebanese pound (LBP)	Arabic	French, English, Armenian	☾ 70%, ⊶ 30%, ✧ less than 1%	71.79	87.4%	⚘ 12%, ⚒ 21%, ⛏ 67%
Malaysia		127,320 (329,750)	23,953,140	Kuala Lumpur	ringgit (MYR)	Bahasa Melayu	English, Chinese dialects, Iban, Kadazan	☾, ⊛, ⤫, ⊶, ✳	71.39	88.9%	⚘ 12%, ⚒ 40%, ⛏ 48%
Maldives		116 (300)	349,110	Male	rufiyaa (MVR)	Maldivian Dhivehi (dialect of Sinhala)	English	☾	62.93	97.2%	⚘ 20%, ⚒ 18%, ⛏ 62%
Mongolia		604,250 (1,565,000)	2,791,270	Ulaanbaatar	ogrog/tugrik (MNT)	Khalkha Mongol, Turkic, Russian		⊛ 96%, ☾ and ⊶ 4%	64.62	99.1%	⚘ 32%, ⚒ 30%, ⛏ 38%
Myanmar (Burma)		261,970 (678,500)	42,909,460	Rangoon	kyat (MMK)	Burmese	Minority ethnic groups have their own languages	⊛ 89%, ⤫ 4%, ☾ 4%, ✳ 3%	55.41	30% (1999)	⚘ 42%, ⚒ 17%, ⛏ 41%
Nepal		54,360 (140,800)	27,676,550	Kathmandu	Nepalese rupee (NPR)	Nepali	English, 12 other languages, about 30 major dialects	⊛ 86.2%, ⤨ 7.8%, ☾ 3.8%, ✳ 2.2%	58.61	45.2%	⚘ 41%, ⚒ 22%, ⛏ 37%
North Korea		46,540 (120,540)	22,912,180	P'yŏngyang	North Korean won (KPW)	Korean		⊛, ⤫, ✳	71.3	99%	⚘ 30%, ⚒ 42%, ⛏ 28%
Oman		82,030 (212,460)	3,001,580	Muscat	Omani rial (OMR)	Arabic	English, Baluchi, Urdu, Indian dialects	☾ 75%,	72.31	75.8%	⚘ 3%, ⚒ 40%, ⛏ 57%
Pakistan		310,400 (803,940)	156,689,150	Islamabad	Pakistani rupee (PKR)	Urdu, English	Punjabi, Sindhi, Siraiki, Pashtu, Balochi, other	☾ 97%, ⊶, ⤨, ✳ 3%	61.82	45.7%	⚘ 26%, ⚒ 24%, ⛏ 50%
Philippines		115,830 (300,000)	87,857,470	Manila	Philippine peso (PHP)	Filipino (based on Tagalog), English	Tagalog, Cebuano, Ilocan, Hiligaynon, Bicol, Waray, other	✟ 83%, ✢ 9%, ☾ 5%, ⊛ and ✳ 3%	68.12	95.9%	⚘ 17%, ⚒ 30%, ⛏ 53%
Qatar		4,420 (11,440)	863,050	Doha	Qatari rial (QAR)	Arabic	English	☾ 95%	72.88	82.5%	⚘ 1%, ⚒ 49%, ⛏ 50%
Saudi Arabia		756,980 (1,960,580)	25,934,590	Riyadh	Saudi riyal (SAR)	Arabic		☾ 100%	68.4	78.8%	⚘ 7%, ⚒ 48%, ⛏ 45%
Singapore		268 (693)	4,930,860	Singapore	Singapore dollar (SGD)	Chinese, Malay, Tamil, English		⊛, ☾, ⊶, ⤨, ✳	80.29	93.2%	⚒ 33%, ⛏ 67%
South Korea		38,020 (98,480)	48,893,070	Seoul	South Korean won (KRW)	Korean	English	⊶ 49%, ⊛ 47%, ✳ 4%	74.88	98.1%	⚘ 5%, ⚒ 44%, ⛏ 51%
Sri Lanka		25,330 (65,610)	20,064,780	Colombo, Sri Jayewardenepura Kotte	Sri Lankan rupee (LKR)	Sinhala	Tamil	⊛ 70%, ⤨ 15%, ⊶ 8%, ☾ 7%	72.35	92.3%	⚘ 21%, ⚒ 27%, ⛏ 52%
Syria		71,500 (185,180)	18,448,750	Damascus	Syrian pound (SYP)	Arabic	Kurdish, Armenian, Aramaic, Circassian, French, English	☾ 90%, ⊶ 10%, ✧ less than 1%	69.08	76.9%	⚘ 27%, ⚒ 23%, ⛏ 50%
Taiwan		13,980 (35,980)	22,894,380	Taipei	new Taiwan dollar (TWD)	Mandarin Chinese	Taiwanese (Min), Hakka dialects	⊛ 93%, ⊶ 4.5%, ✳ 2.5%	76.74	86% (1980)	⚘ 2%, ⚒ 32%, ⛏ 66%
Tajikistan		55,250 (143,100)	7,163,510	Dushanbe	somoni (TJS)	Tajik	Russian	☾ 90%	64.28	99.4%	⚘ 19%, ⚒ 25%, ⛏ 56%
Thailand		198,460 (514,000)	65,444,370	Bangkok	baht (THB)	Thai	English, ethnic and regional dialects	⊛ 95%, ☾ 3.8%, ⊶ 0.5%, ⤨ 0.1%, ✳ 0.6%	69.18	96%	⚘ 11%, ⚒ 40%, ⛏ 49%
Turkey		301,380 (780,580)	69,660,560	Ankara	Turkish lira (TRL)	Turkish	Kurdish, Arabic, Armenian, Greek	☾ 99.8%, ✳ 0.2%	71.52	86.5%	⚘ 14.5%, ⚒ 28.4%, ⛏ 57.1%
Turkmenistan		188,460 (488,100)	4,952,080	Ashgabat	Turkmen manat (TMM)	Turkmen, Russian, Uzbek		☾ 89%, ✟ 9%, ✳ 2%	61.1	98%	⚘ 27%, ⚒ 45%, ⛏ 28%
United Arab Emirates		32,000 (82,880)	2,563,210	Abu Dhabi	Emirati dirham (AED)	Arabic	Persian, English, Hindi, Urdu	☾ 96%, ⊶, ⤨, and ✳ 4%	74.52	77.9%	⚘ 3%, ⚒ 46%, ⛏ 51%
Uzbekistan		172,740 (447,400)	26,851,200	Tashkent	Uzbekistani sum (UZS)	Uzbek, Russian, Tajik		☾ 88%, ✟ 9%, ✳ 3%	63.9	99.3%	⚘ 33%, ⚒ 24%, ⛏ 43%
Vietnam		127,240 (329,560)	83,769,670	Hanoi	dong (VND)	Vietnamese	English, French, Chinese, Khmer	⊛, ⊶, ⬡, ☾	69.86	94%	⚘ 25%, ⚒ 35%, ⛏ 40%

Key to symbols: ⊶ Christian ✟ Catholic ⬡ Orthodox ✢ Protestant ⊛ Buddhist ⤨ Hindu ✧ Jewish ☾ Muslim ≡ Atheist O Indigenous ✳ Other ⚘ Agriculture ⚒ Industry ⛏ Services **NA** Not Available
Note: All literacy statistics are for 2003 unless otherwise stated.

254

AFRICA

Area sq miles (sq km)	Population	Capital	Currency	Official Languages	Other Languages	Main Religions	Life Expectancy	Literacy Rate	Economy		Country
203,850 (527,970)	20,727,060	Şan'ā'	Yemeni rial (YER)	Arabic		G, ☆, ∝, ⊛	60.59	50.2%	🌾 17%, ⚒ 40%, 🍴 43%		Yemen
919,590 (2,381,740)	33,892,390	Algiers	Algerian dinar (DZD)	Arabic	French, Berber dialects	G 99%, ∝ and ☆ 1%	70.24	70%	🌾 17%, ⚒ 33%, 🍴 50%		Algeria
481,350 (1,246,700)	11,190,790	Luanda	kwanza (AOA)	Portuguese	Bantu and African languages	O 47%, ♱ 38%, ✝ 15%	38.87	42% (1998)	🌾 6%, ⚒ 70%, 🍴 24%		Angola
43,480 (112,620)	7,460,030	Porto-Novo	Communaute Financiere Africaine franc (XOF)	French	Fon, Yoruba, tribal languages	O 50%, ∝ 30%, G 20%	49.69	40.9% (2000)	🌾 36%, ⚒ 14%, 🍴 50%		Benin
231,800 (600,370)	1,545,290	Gaborone	pula (BWP)	English	Setswana	O 85%, ∝ 15%	35.29	79.8%	🌾 4%, ⚒ 44% (including 36% mining), 🍴 52%		Botswana
105,870 (274,200)	13,925,310	Ouagadougou	Communaute Financiere Africaine franc (XOF)	French	African languages (belonging to Sudanic family)	O 40%, G 50%, ∝ 10%	46.11	26.6%	🌾 31%, ⚒ 28%, 🍴 41%		Burkina Faso
10,750 (27,830)	6,370,610	Bujumbura	Burundi franc (BIF)	Kirundi, French	Swahili	∝ 67%, O 23%, G 10%	45.94	51.6%	🌾 50%, ⚒ 18%, 🍴 32%		Burundi
183,570 (475,440)	16,380,010	Yaoundé	Communaute Financiere Africaine franc (XAF)	English, French	24 major African language groups	O 40%, ∝ 40%, G 20%	54.36	79%	🌾 44%, ⚒ 20%, 🍴 36%		Cameroon
1,560 (4,030)	418,220	Praia	Cape Verdean escudo (CVE)	Portuguese, Crioulo		♱, ✝	69.52	76.6%	🌾 11%, ⚒ 17%, 🍴 72%		Cape Verde
240,530 (622,980)	3,799,900	Bangui	Communaute Financiere Africaine franc (XAF)	French	Sangho, tribal languages	O 35%, ✝ 25%, ♱ 25%, G 15%	43.58	51%	🌾 55%, ⚒ 20%, 🍴 25%		Central African Republic
495,760 (1,284,000)	9,826,420	Ndjamena	Communaute Financiere Africaine franc (XAF)	French, Arabic	Sara, more than 120 languages and dialects	G 51%, ∝ 35%, ✳ 14%	51.27	47.5%	🌾 38%, ⚒ 13%, 🍴 49%		Chad
838 (2,170)	671,250	Moroni	Comoran franc (KMF)	Arabic, French	Shikomoro (a blend of Swahili and Arabic)	G 98%, ♱ 2%	60.79	56.5%	🌾 40%, ⚒ 4%, 🍴 56%		Comoros
132,050 (342,000)	3,039,130	Brazzaville	Communaute Financiere Africaine franc (XAF)	French	Monokutuba, Lingala, other language/dialects	∝ 50%, O 48%, G 2%	47.71	83.8%	🌾 10%, ⚒ 48%, 🍴 42%		Congo
124,500 (322,460)	17,693,380	Yamoussoukro	Communaute Financiere Africaine franc (XOF)	French	60 native dialects (Dioula the most widely spoken)	∝ 20-30%, G 35-40%, O 25-40%	44.72	50.9%	🌾 28%, ⚒ 29%, 🍴 43%		Côte d'Ivoire
909,040 (2,354,410)	60,085,000	Kinshasa	Congolese franc (CDF)	French	Lingala, Kingwana, Kikongo, Tshiluba	♱ 50%, ✝ 20%, ✳ 10%, G 10%, O 10%	49.13	65.5%	🌾 54%, ⚒ 9%, 🍴 37%		Democratic Republic of Congo
8,880 (23,000)	476,700	Djibouti	Djiboutian franc (DJF)	French, Arabic	Somali, Afar	G 94%, ∝ 6%	51.6	67.9%	🌾 3%, ⚒ 10%, 🍴 87%		Djibouti
386,660 (1,001,450)	77,505,760	Cairo	Egyptian pound (EGP)	Arabic	English, French	G 94%, ∝ and ✳ 6%	64.05	57.7%	🌾 14%, ⚒ 30%, 🍴 56%		Egypt
10,830 (28,050)	535,880	Malabo	Communaute Financiere Africaine franc (XAF)	Spanish, French	Pidgin English, Fang, Bubi, Ibo	∝, ✳	54.35	85.7%	🌾 20%, ⚒ 60%, 🍴 20%		Equatorial Guinea
46,840 (121,320)	4,561,600	Asmara	nakfa (ERN)	Afar, Arabic, Tigre, Kunama, Tigrinya, Cushitic languages		G, ∝, ♱, ✝	56.57	58.6%	🌾 17%, ⚒ 29%, 🍴 54%		Eritrea
435,190 (1,127,130)	69,113,730	Addis Ababa	birr (ETB)	Amharic, Tigrinya, Oromigna, Somali Guaragigna, Arabic	English, other local languages	G 45%-50%, ♱ 35%-40%, O 12%, ✳ 3%-8%	44.21	42.7%	🌾 52.3%, ⚒ 11.1%, 🍴 36.6%		Ethiopia
103,350 (267,670)	1,389,200	Libreville	Communaute Financiere Africaine franc (XAF)	French	Fang, Myene, Nzebi, Bapounou/Eschira, Bandjabi	∝ 55%-75%, O and G less than 1%	49.11	63.2% (1995)	🌾 10%, ⚒ 60%, 🍴 30%		Gabon
4,360 (11,300)	1,593,260	Banjul	dalasi (GMD)	English	Mandinka, Wolof, Fula, other indigenous languages	G 90%, ∝ 9%, O 1%	53.98	40.1%	🌾 21%, ⚒ 12%, 🍴 67%		Gambia
92,460 (239,460)	21,029,850	Accra	cedi (GHC)	English	African languages (e.g. Akan, Moshi-Dagomba, Ewe, Ga)	O 21%, G 16%, ∝ 63%	57.06	74.8%	🌾 36%, ⚒ 25%, 🍴 39%		Ghana
94,930 (245,860)	9,467,870	Conakry	Guinean franc (GNF)	French	Each ethnic group has its own language	G 85%, ∝ 8%, O 7%	46.28	35.9% (1995)	🌾 24%, ⚒ 38%, 🍴 38%		Guinea
13,950 (36,120)	1,416,030	Bissau	Communaute Financiere Africaine franc (XOF)	Portuguese	Crioulo, African languages	O 50%, G 45%, ∝ 5%	49.8	42.4%	🌾 54%, ⚒ 15%, 🍴 31%		Guinea-Bissau

Key to symbols: ∝ Christian ♱ Catholic O Orthodox ✝ Protestant ◉ Buddhist ⊛ Hindu ☆ Jewish G Muslim ≡ Atheist O Indigenous ✳ Other 🌾 Agriculture ⚒ Industry 🍴 Services NA Not Available
Note: All literacy statistics are for 2003 unless otherwise stated.

	Area SQ MILES (SQ KM)	Population	Capital	Currency	Official Languages	Other Languages	Main Religions	Life Expectancy	Literacy Rate	Economy
Kenya	224,960 (582,650)	32,368,100	Nairobi	Kenyan shilling (KES)	English, Kiswahili	Indigenous languages	✝ 45%, ∝ 33%, O 10%, G 10%, ✷ 2%	47.02	85.1%	⚘ 24%, ⛏ 13%, ⚕ 63%
Lesotho	11,720 (30,360)	1,867,040	Maseru	loti (LSL), South African rand (ZAR)	English	Sesotho (southern Sotho), Zulu, Xhosa	∝ 80%, O 20%	47	84.8%	⚘ 18%, ⛏ 38%, ⚕ 44%
Liberia	43,000 (111,370)	3,482,210	Monrovia	Liberian dollar (LRD)	English	20 ethnic group languages	O 40%, ∝ 40%, G 20%	51.8	57.5%	⚘ 60%, ⛏ 10%, ⚕ 30%
Libya	679,360 (1,759,540)	5,765,560	Tripoli	Libyan dinar (LYD)	Arabic, Italian, English		G 97%	75.86	82.6%	⚘ 7%, ⛏ 47%, ⚕ 46%
Madagascar	226,660 (587,040)	18,040,340	Antananarivo	Malagasy franc (MGF)	French, Malagasy		O 52%, ∝ 41%, G 7%	55.74	68.9%	⚘ 34%, ⛏ 11%, ⚕ 55%
Malawi	45,750 (118,480)	12,158,920	Lilongwe	Malawian kwacha (MWK)	English, Chichewa	Other regional languages	✝ 55%, ✛ 20%, G 20%, O 3%, ✷ 2%	36.59	62.7%	⚘ 40%, ⛏ 19%, ⚕ 41%
Mali	478,770 (1,240,000)	12,291,530	Bamako	Communaute Financiere Africaine franc (XOF)	French	Bambara, African languages	G 90%, O 9%, ∝ 1%	47.39	46.4%	⚘ 45%, ⛏ 17%, ⚕ 38%
Mauritania	397,960 (1,030,700)	3,086,860	Nouakchott	ouguiya (MRO)	Hassaniya Arabic, Wolof	Pulaar, Soninke, French	G 100%	51.53	41.7%	⚘ 25%, ⛏ 29%, ⚕ 46%
Mauritius	788 (2,040)	1,230,600	Port Louis	Mauritian rupee (MUR)	English, French	Creole, Hindi, Urdu, Hakka, Bhojpuri	✾ 52%, ∝ 28.3%, G 16.6%, ✷ 3.1%	71.53	85.6%	⚘ 6%, ⛏ 33%, ⚕ 61%
Morocco	172,410 (446,550)	32,725,850	Rabat	Moroccan dirham (MAD)	Arabic	Berber dialects, French	G 98.7%, ∝ 1.1%, ✢ 0.2%	69.73	51.7%	⚘ 15%, ⛏ 33%, ⚕ 52%
Mozambique	309,500 (801,590)	17,710,040	Maputo	metical (MZM)	Portuguese	Indigenous dialects	O 50%, ∝ 30%, G 20%	35.46	47.8%	⚘ 33%, ⛏ 25%, ⚕ 42%
Namibia	318,700 (825,420)	1,975,850	Windhoek	Namibian dollar (NAD), South African rand (ZAR)	English	Afrikaans, German, Oshivambo, Herero, Nama	∝ 80%-90%, O 10%-20%	38.97	84%	⚘ 11%, ⛏ 28%, ⚕ 61%
Niger	489,190 (1,267,000)	11,665,940	Niamey	Communaute Financiere Africaine franc (XOF)	French	Hausa, Djerma	G 80%, O and ∝ 20%	41.91	17.6%	⚘ 41%, ⛏ 17%, ⚕ 42%
Nigeria	356,670 (923,770)	140,601,620	Abuja	naira (NGN)	English	Hausa, Yoruba, Igbo (Ibo), Fulani	G 50%, ∝ 40%, O 10%	50.59	68%	⚘ 39%, ⛏ 33%, ⚕ 28%
Rwanda	10,170 (26,340)	8,098,620	Kigali	Rwandan franc (RWF)	Kinyarwanda, French, English	Bantu, Kiswahili (Swahili)	✛ 56.5%, ✝ 37.1%, G 4.6%, O 0.1%, ✷ 1.7%	38.66	70.4%	⚘ 46%, ⛏ 20%, ⚕ 34%
São Tomé and Príncipe	386 (1,000)	187,410	São Tomé	dobra (STD)	Portuguese		∝ 80%	65.93	79.3% (1991)	⚘ 25%, ⛏ 10%, ⚕ 65%
Senegal	75,750 (196,190)	11,126,830	Dakar	Communaute Financiere Africaine franc (XOF)	French	Wolof, Pulaar, Jola, Mandinka	G 94%, ∝ 5%, O 1%	62.93	40.2%	⚘ 18.5%, ⛏ 20.7%, ⚕ 60.8%
Seychelles	176 (455)	81,190	Victoria	Seychelles rupee (SCR)	English, French	Creole	✛ 86.6%, ✝ 6.8%, ∝ 2.5%, ✷ 4.1%	70.97	58% (1971)	⚘ 3.1%, ⛏ 26.3%, ⚕ 70.6%
Sierra Leone	27,700 (71,740)	6,017,640	Freetown	leone (SLL)	English	Mende, Temne, Krio	G 60%, O 30%, ∝ 10%	45.96	31.4% (1995)	⚘ 43%, ⛏ 27%, ⚕ 30%
Somalia	246,200 (637,660)	8,591,630	Mogadishu	Somali shilling (SOS)	Somali	Arabic, Italian, English	G	46.96	37.8% (2001)	⚘ 65%, ⛏ 10%, ⚕ 25%
South Africa, Republic of	471,010 (1,219,910)	42,552,330	Bloemfontein, Cape Town, Pretoria	rand (ZAR)	Afrikaans, English, Ndebele, Pedi, Sotho, Swazi, Tsonga, Tswana,	Official: Venda, Xhosa, Zulu	∝ 68%, G 2%, ✾ 1.5%, O 28.5%	45.43	86.4%	⚘ 3%, ⛏ 31%, ⚕ 66%
Sudan	967,500 (2,505,810)	40,187,490	Khartoum	Sudanese dinar (SDD)	Arabic	Nubian, Ta Bedawie, Nilotic, Nilo-Hamitic, Sudanic, English	G 70%, O 25%, ∝ 5%	57.33	61.1%	⚘ 43%, ⛏ 17%, ⚕ 40%
Swaziland	6,700 (17,360)	1,173,900	Mbabane	lilangeni (SZL)	English, siSwati		∝ and O 40%, ✛ 20%, G 10%, ✝, ✢, and ✷ 30%	37	81.6%	⚘ 10%, ⛏ 43%, ⚕ 47%
Tanzania	364,900 (945,090)	37,322,700	Dodoma	Tanzanian shilling (TZS)	Kiswahili, Swahili	Kiunguju, English, Arabic	mainland: ∝ 30%, G 35%, O 35%, Zanzibar: G 99%	51.7	78.2%	⚘ 48.4%, ⛏ 16.7%, ⚕ 34.9%
Togo	21,930 (56,790)	5,681,520	Lomé	Communaute Financiere Africaine franc (XOF)	French	Ewe, Mina, Kabye, Dagomba	O 51%, ∝ 29%, G 20%	54.02	60.9%	⚘ 42%, ⛏ 21%, ⚕ 37%

Key to symbols: ∝ Christian ✛ Catholic ✢ Orthodox ✝ Protestant ◉ Buddhist ✾ Hindu ✡ Jewish G Muslim ≡ Atheist O Indigenous ✷ Other ⚘ Agriculture ⛏ Industry ⚕ Services NA Not Available
Note: All literacy statistics are for 2003 unless otherwise stated.

AREA SQ MILES (SQ KM)	POPULATION	CAPITAL	CURRENCY	OFFICIAL LANGUAGES	OTHER LANGUAGES	MAIN RELIGIONS	LIFE EXPECTANCY	LITERACY RATE	ECONOMY		Country
63,170 (163,610)	10,137,250	Tunis	Tunisian dinar (TND)	Arabic	French	☾ 98%, ∝ 1%, ✡ and ✳ 1%	74.16	74.2%	⚘ 13%, ⚒ 33%, ⚙ 54%		Tunisia
91,140 (236,040)	27,202,150	Kampala	Ugandan shilling (UGX)	English	Niger-Congo/Nilo-Saharan languages Swahili, Arabic	✚ 33%, ✝ 33%, ☾ 16%, ○ 18%	43.81	69.9%	NA		Uganda
290,580 (752,610)	10,613,620	Lusaka	Zambian kwacha (ZMK)	English	Bemba, Kaonda, Lozi, Lunda, Luvale, Nyanja, Tonga, other	∝ 50%-75%, ☾ ✾ 24%-49%, ○ 1%	37.35	80.6%	⚘ 24%, ⚒ 25%, ⚙ 51%		Zambia
150,800 (390,580)	12,746,990	Harare	Zimbabwean dollar (ZWD)	English	Shona, Sindebele, minor tribal dialects	syncretic (blend of ∝ and ○) 50%, ∝ 25%, ○ 24%, ☾ and ✳ 1%	36.5	90.7%	⚘ 11%, ⚒ 14%, ⚙ 75%		Zimbabwe
2,967,910 (7,686,850)	20,090,440	Canberra	Australian dollar (AUD)	English	Indigenous languages	✝ 26.1%, ✚ 26%, ∝ 24.3%, ✳ 33.6%	80	100% (1980)	⚘ 3%, ⚒ 25%, ⚙ 72%		Australia
7,050 (18,270)	893,350	Suva	Fijian dollar (FJD)	English	Fijian, Hindustani	∝ 52%, ✾ 38%, ☾ 8%, ✳ 2%	68.56	93.7%	⚘ 17%, ⚒ 25%, ⚙ 58%		Fiji
313 (811)	103,090	Bairiki	Australian dollar (AUD)	English	I-Kiribati	✚ 52%, ✝ 40%, ☾ and ✳ 8%	60.54	NA	⚘ 30%, ⚒ 7%, ⚙ 63%		Kiribati
70 (181)	59,070	Majuro	U.S. dollar (USD)	Marshallese, English	Marshallese dialects (Malayo-Polynesian family), Japanese	∝	66.18	93.7% (1999)	⚘ 14%, ⚒ 16%, ⚙ 70%		Marshall Islands
271 (702)	138,740	Palikir	U.S. dollar (USD)	English	Trukese, Pohnpeian, Yapese, Kosrean, Ulithian, other	✚ 50%, ✝ 47%	NA	89% (1980)	⚘ 50%, ⚒ 4%, ⚙ 46%		Micronesia, Federated States of
8 (21)	13,050	Yaren	Australian dollar (AUD)	Nauruan	English	∝	61.57	NA	NA		Nauru
103,740 (268,680)	4,035,460	Wellington	New Zealand dollar (NZD)	English, Maori		✝ 52%, ✚ 15%, ✳ 33%	78.15	99% (1980)	⚘ 8%, ⚒ 23%, ⚙ 69%		New Zealand
177 (458)	20,300	Koror	U.S. dollar (USD)	English, Palauan, Tobi, Angaur, Japanese, Sonsoralese		∝ 49%, ○	69.19	92% (1980)	NA		Palau
178,700 (462,840)	5,545,270	Port Moresby	kina (PGK)	English, pidgin English, Motu	715 indigenous languages	✚ 22%, ✝ 44%, ○ 34%	63.83	66%	⚘ 30.4%, ⚒ 36.8%, ⚙ 32.8%		Papua New Guinea
1,140 (2,940)	177,290	Apia	tala (WST)	Samoan (Polynesian), English		∝ 99.7%, ✳ 0.3%	69.8	99.7%	⚘ 16%, ⚒ 18%, ⚙ 66%		Samoa
10,980 (28,450)	538,030	Honiara	Solomon Islands dollar (SBD)	Melanesian pidgin, English	120 indigenous languages	✝ 78%, ✚ 18%, ○ 4%	71.82	NA	⚘ 42%, ⚒ 11%, ⚙ 47%		Solomon Islands
289 (748)	112,420	Nuku'alofa	pa'anga (TOP)	Tongan, English		∝	68.56	98.5% (1996)	⚘ 30%, ⚒ 10%, ⚙ 60%		Tonga
10 (26)	11,640	Vaiaku	Australian dollar (AUD), Tuvaluan dollar	Tuvaluan, English, Samoan, I-Kiribati		✝ 98.4%, ✳ 1.6%	66.98	NA	NA		Tuvalu
4,710 (12,200)	205,750	Port Vila	vatu (VUV)	English, French, Pidgin	more than 100 local languages	✝ 61.7%, ✚ 15%, ○ 7.6%, ✳ 15.7%	61.33	53% (1979)	⚘ 26%, ⚒ 12%, ⚙ 62%		Vanuatu
77 (199)	73,320	Pago Pago	U.S. dollar (USD)	Samoan (Polynesian), English		∝ 50%, ✚ 20%, ✝ and ✳ 30%	75.53	97% (1980)	NA		American Samoa (U.S.A.)
39 (102)	13,250	The Valley	East Caribbean dollar (XCD)	English		✝ 85%, ✚ 3%, ✳ 12%	76.5	95%	⚘ 4%, ⚒ 18%, ⚙ 78%		Anguilla (U.K.)
75 (193)	71,570	Oranjestad	Aruban guilder/florin (AWG)	Dutch	Papiamento, English, Spanish	✚ 82%, ✝ 8%, ✳ 10%	78.67	97%	NA		Aruba (Netherlands)
2 (5)	no indigenous inhabitants										Ashmore Reef and Cartier Islands (Australia)
0.54 (1.4)	no indigenous inhabitants										Baker Island (U.S.A.)
21 (53)	65,370	Hamilton	Bermudian dollar (BMD)	English	Portuguese	✝ 66%, ✚ 15%, ✳ 19%	77.3	98% (1970)	⚘ 1%, ⚒ 10%, ⚙ 89%		Bermuda (U.K.)
23 (59)	uninhabited										Bouvetøya (Norway)

Key to symbols: ∝ Christian ✚ Catholic ✝ Orthodox ✝ Protestant ◉ Buddhist ✾ Hindu ✡ Jewish ☾ Muslim ≡ Atheist ○ Indigenous ✳ Other ⚘ Agriculture ⚒ Industry ⚙ Services NA Not Available
Note: All literacy statistics are for 2003 unless otherwise stated.

		AREA SQ MILES (SQ KM)	POPULATION	CAPITAL	CURRENCY	OFFICIAL LANGUAGES	OTHER LANGUAGES	MAIN RELIGIONS	LIFE EXPECTANCY	LITERACY RATE	ECONOMY
British Indian Ocean Territory (U.K.)		23 (60)	no indigenous inhabitants								
British Virgin Islands (U.K.)		59 (153)	22,640	Road Town	U.S. dollar (USD)	English		✝ 86%, ✤ 10%, ✱ 4%	75.85	97.8% (1991)	☙ 1.8%, ⚒ 6.2%, ⚕ 92%
Cayman Islands (U.K.)		101 (262)	44,270	George Town	Caymanian dollar (KYD)	English		✝, ✤	79.18	98% (1970)	☙ 1.4%, ⚒ 3.2%, ⚕ 95.4%
Christmas Island (Australia)		52 (135)	470	The Settlement	Australian dollar (AUD)	English	Chinese, Malay	◉ 36%, ☪ 25%, ∝ 18%, ✱ 21%	NA	NA	NA
Clipperton Island (France)		2 (6)	uninhabited								
Cocos Islands (Australia)		5 (14)	630		Australian dollar (AUD)	Malay (Cocos dialect), English		☪ 80%, ✱ 20%	NA	NA	NA
Cook Islands (N.Z.)		93 (240)	21,340	Avarua	New Zealand dollar (NZD)	English	Maori	∝	NA	95%	☙ 17%, ⚒ 7.8%, ⚕ 75.2%
Coral Sea Islands Territory (Australia)		1.1 (2.9)	no indigenous inhabitants								
Falkland Islands (U.K.)		4,700 (12,170)	2,970	Stanley	Falkland pound (FKP)	English		✝, ✤	NA	NA	NA
Faroe Islands (Denmark)		540 (1,400)	46,960	Torshavn	Danish krone (DKK)	Faroese, Danish		✝	78.74	NA	☙ 27%, ⚒ 11%, ⚕ 62%
French Guiana (France)		35,140 (91,000)	195,510	Cayenne	euro (EUR)	French		✤	76.69	83% (1982)	NA
French Polynesia (France)		1,610 (4,170)	270,490	Papeete	Comptoirs Francais du Pacifique franc (XPF)	French, Tahitian		✝ 54%, ✤ 30%, ✱ 16%	75.23	98% (1977)	☙ 6%, ⚒ 18%, ⚕ 76%
French Southern and Antarctic Lands (France)		3,020 (7,830)	no indigenous inhabitants								
Gibraltar (U.K.)		2.5 (6.5)	27,880	Gibraltar	Gibraltar pound (GIP)	English	Spanish, Italian, Portuguese, Russian	✤ 76.9%, ✝ 6.9%, ☪ 6.9%, ✿ 2.3%, ✱ 7%	79.23	above 80%	NA
Greenland (Denmark)		836,330 (2,166,090)	56,380	Nuuk	Danish krone (DKK)	Greenlandic (East Inuit), Danish, English		✝	68.69	NA	NA
Guadeloupe (France)		690 (1,780)	448,710	Basse-Terre	euro (EUR)	French	Creole patois	✤ 95%, ✵ and ○ 4%, ✝ 1%	77.35	90% (1982)	NA
Guam (U.S.A.)		212 (549)	169,970	Hagåtña	U.S. dollar (USD)	English, Chamorro, Japanese		✤ 85%, ✱ 15%	78.11	99% (1990)	☙ 7%, ⚒ 15%, ⚕ 78%
Guernsey (U.K.)		30 (78)	65,230	St Peter Port	British pound (GBP), Guernsey pound	English, French, Norman-French dialect		✝, ✤	79.9	NA	☙ 3%, ⚒ 10%, ⚕ 87%
Heard and McDonald Islands (Australia)		159 (412)	uninhabited								
Howland Island (U.S.A.)		0.6 (1.6)	uninhabited								
Isle of Man (U.K.)		221 (572)	75,050	Douglas	British pound (GBP), Manx pound	English, Manx Gaelic		✝, ✤, ∝	77.81	NA	☙ 1%, ⚒ 13%, ⚕ 86%
Jan Mayen (Norway)		144 (373)	no indigenous inhabitants								
Jarvis Island (U.S.A.)		1.7 (4.5)	uninhabited								
Jersey (U.K.)		45 (116)	90,810	St Helier	British pound (GBP), Jersey pound	English, French	Norman-French dialect	✝, ✤	78.78	NA	☙ 5%, ⚒ 2%, ⚕ 93%
Johnston Atoll (U.S.A.)		1.1 (2.8)	no indigenous inhabitants								

Key to symbols: ∝ Christian ✤ Catholic ✿ Orthodox ✝ Protestant ◉ Buddhist ✵ Hindu ✡ Jewish ☪ Muslim ≡ Atheist ○ Indigenous ✱ Other ☙ Agriculture ⚒ Industry ⚕ Services NA Not Available
Note: All literacy statistics are for 2003 unless otherwise stated.

AREA SQ MILES (SQ KM)	POPULATION	CAPITAL	CURRENCY	OFFICIAL LANGUAGES	OTHER LANGUAGES	MAIN RELIGIONS	LIFE EXPECTANCY	LITERACY RATE	ECONOMY		
0.4 (1.0)	uninhabited										Kingman Reef (U.S.A.)
420 (1,100)	432,900	Fort-de-France	euro (EUR)	French, Creole patois		✧ 95%, ℞ and O 5%	78.56	97.7%	⚘ 6%, ⚒ 11%, ⚕ 83%		Martinique (France)
140 (374)	193,630	Dzadaoudzi	euro (EUR)	French	Mahorian (a Swahili dialect)	☾ 97%, ∝ 3%	60.21	NA	NA		Mayotte (France)
2.4 (6.2)	no indigenous inhabitants										Midway Islands (U.S.A.)
39 (102)	9,340	Plymouth	East Caribbean dollar (XCD)	English		✚, ✧, ∝	78.2	97% (1970)	⚘ 5.4%, ⚒ 13.6%, ⚕ 81%		Montserrat (U.K.)
2.0 (5.2)	uninhabited										Navassa Island (U.S.A.)
371 (960)	219,960	Willemstad	Netherlands Antillean guilder (ANG)	Dutch	Papiamento, English, Spanish	✧, ✚, ✡	75.15	96.7%	⚘ 1%, ⚒ 15%, ⚕ 84%		Netherlands Antilles (Netherlands)
7,360 (19,060)	216,490	Nouméa	Comptoirs Francais du Pacifique franc (XPF)	French	33 Melanesian-Polynesian dialects	✧ 60%, ✚ 30%, ✱ 10%	73.27	91% (1976)	⚘ 5%, ⚒ 30%, ⚕ 65%		New Caledonia (France)
100 (260)	2,130	Alofi	New Zealand dollar (NZD)	Niuean, English		✚ 85%, ✱ 15%	NA	95%	⚘ NA, ⚒ NA, ⚕ 55%		Niue (N.Z.)
13 (34)	1,870	Kingston	Australian dollar (AUD)	English	Norfolk (mixture of 18th century English and ancient Tahitian)	✚ 55%, ✧ 11.5%, ✱ 33.5%	NA	NA	NA		Norfolk Island (Australia)
184 (477)	85,370	Saipan	U.S. dollar (USD)	English, Chamorro, Carolinian		∝	75.95	97% (1980)	NA		Northern Mariana Islands (U.S.A.)
5 (12)	no indigenous inhabitants										Palmyra Atoll (U.S.A.)
NA	no indigenous inhabitants										Paracel Islands (Occupied by China)
18 (47)	50	Adamstown	New Zealand dollar (NZD)	English	Pitcairnese	✚ 100%	NA	NA	NA		Pitcairn Islands (U.K.)
3,510 (9,100)	3,929,510	San Juan	U.S. dollar (USD)	Spanish, English		✧ 85%, ✚ and ✱ 15%	75.96	93.8% (2001)	⚘ 1%, ⚒ 45%, ⚕ 54%		Puerto Rico (U.S.A.)
970 (2,520)	776,950	Saint-Denis	euro (EUR), French franc (FRF)	French	Creole widely used	✧ 86%, ℞, ☾, ◉	73.18	88.9%	⚘ 8%, ⚒ 19%, ⚕ 73%		Réunion (France)
158 (410)	7,460	Jamestown	Saint Helenian pound (SHP)	English		✚, ✧	77.2	97% (1987)	NA		St Helena (U.K.)
93 (242)	7,010	St-Pierre	euro (EUR)	French		✧ 99%	77.93	99% (1982)	NA		St Pierre and Miquelon (France)
1,510 (3,900)	no indigenous inhabitants										South Georgia and Sandwich Islands (U.K.)
1,510 (62,050)	2,870	Longyearbyen	Norwegian krone (NOK)	Russian, Norwegian		NA	NA	NA	NA		Svalbard (Norway)
4 (10)	1,430	administrative center on each atoll	New Zealand dollar (NZD)	Tokelauan (a Polynesian language), English		✚ 70%, ✧ 28%, ✱ 2%	NA	NA	NA		Tokelau Islands (N.Z.)
166 (430)	20,560	Cockburn Town	U.S. dollar (USD)	English		✚ 86%, ✱ 14%	73.76	98% (1970)	NA		Turks and Caicos Islands (U.K.)
136 (352)	127,310	Charlotte Amalie	U.S. dollar (USD)	English	Spanish, Creole	✚ 59%, ✧ 34%, ✱ 7%	78.43	NA	NA		U.S. Virgin Islands (U.S.A.)
2.5 (6.5)	no indigenous inhabitants										Wake Atoll (U.S.A.)
106 (274)	16,030	Matā'Utu	Comptoirs Francais du Pacifique franc (XPF)	French, Wallisian (indigenous Polynesian language)		✧ 100%	NA	50% (1969)	NA		Wallis and Futuna Islands (France)

Key to symbols: ∝ Christian ✧ Catholic ✚ Orthodox ✚ Protestant ◉ Buddhist ℞ Hindu ✡ Jewish ☾ Muslim ≡ Atheist O Indigenous ✱ Other ⚘ Agriculture ⚒ Industry ⚕ Services NA Not Available
Note: All literacy statistics are for 2003 unless otherwise stated.

WORLD FACT FILE

Planet Earth Vital Statistics

DIAMETER: 7,926 miles (12,756 km)

AVERAGE DISTANCE FROM THE SUN: 93 million miles (150 million km)

ORBIT PERIOD: 365.25 days

ROTATION PERIOD: 23 hours 56 minutes

TOTAL SURFACE AREA: 196,940,000 sq miles (510,072,000 sq km)

TOTAL LAND AREA: 57,506,000 sq miles (148,940,000 sq km)

TOTAL WATER AREA: 139,434,000 sq miles (361,132,000 sq km)

†**TOTAL WORLD POPULATION:** 6,448,780,202

†**WORLD POPULATION GROWTH RATE:** 1.12% p.a.

AVERAGE LIFE EXPECTANCY: 63.95 years

AVERAGE LITERACY RATE: 77%

AVERAGE GDP PER CAPITA: US$7,900

† 2005 population figures

Largest Countries by Population

COUNTRY	POPULATION
1. China	1,302,207,990
2. India	1,080,264,390
3. United States	295,734,130
4. Indonesia	241,973,880
5. Brazil	186,112,790
6. Pakistan	156,689,150
7. Bangladesh	144,319,630
8. Russian Fed.	143,736,790
9. Nigeria	140,601,620
10. Japan	127,417,240

Smallest Countries by Population

COUNTRY	POPULATION
1. Vatican City	900
2. Tuvalu	11,640
3. Nauru	13,050
4. Palau	20,300
5. San Marino	28,880
6. Monaco	32,410
7. Liechtenstein	33,720
8. St Kitts and Nevis	38,960
9. Marshall Islands	59,070
10. Antigua and Barbuda	68,720

Largest Countries by Area

COUNTRY	TOTAL AREA
1. Russian Federation	6,592,770 sq miles (17,075,200 sq km)
2. Canada	3,474,920 sq miles (9,984,670 sq km)
3. United States of America	3,717,810 sq miles (9,629,090 sq km)
4. China	3,705,405 sq miles (9,596,960 sq km)
5. Brazil	3,286,490 sq miles (8,511,965 sq km)
6. Australia	2,967,910 sq miles (7,686,850 sq km)
7. India	1,269,345 sq miles (3,287,590 sq km)
8. Argentina	1,068,300 sq miles (2,766,890 sq km)
9. Kazakhstan	1,049,155 sq miles (2,717,300 sq km)
10. Sudan	967,500 sq miles (2,505,810 sq km)

Smallest Countries by Area

COUNTRY	TOTAL AREA
1. Vatican City	0.17 sq mile (0.44 sq km)
2. Monaco	0.75 sq mile (1.95 sq km)
3. Nauru	8 sq miles (21 sq km)
4. Tuvalu	10 sq miles (26 sq km)
5. San Marino	24 sq miles (61 sq km)
6. Liechtenstein	62 sq miles (160 sq km)
7. Marshall Islands	70 sq miles (181 sq km)
8. St Kitts and Nevis	101 sq miles (261 sq km)
9. Maldives	116 sq miles (300 sq km)
10. Malta	122 sq miles (316 sq km)

Largest Urban Agglomerations

AGGLOMERATION	COUNTRY	POPULATION
1. Tokyo	Japan	26,849,000
2. São Paulo	Brazil	19,591,000
3. Mexico City	Mexico	18,934,000
4. Mumbai	India	18,337,000
5. New York	United States	17,147,000
6. Dacca	Bangladesh	15,921,000
7. Delhi	India	15,335,000
8. Calcutta	India	14,299,000
9. Los Angeles	United States	13,766,000
10. Jakarta	Indonesia	13,156,000
11. Rhein-Ruhr*	Germany	12,944,000
12. Shanghai	China	12,665,000
13. Buenos Aires	Argentina	12,439,000
14. Karachi	Pakistan	11,830,000
15. Rio de Janeiro	Brazil	11,170,000
16. Lagos	Nigeria	11,134,000
17. Ōsaka	Japan	11,013,000
18. Manila	Philippines	10,864,000
19. Beijing	China	10,849,000
20. Cairo	Egypt	10,094,000

* Rhein-Ruhr includes Düsseldorf, Essen, Bonn, and Cologne.

Most Crowded Countries

COUNTRY	INHABITANTS
1. Monaco	26,784 per sq mile (16,620 per sq km)
2. Singapore	11,629 per sq mile (7,219 per sq km)
3. Vatican City	5,015 per sq mile (3,111 per sq km)
4. Malta	2,073 per sq mile (1,286 per sq km)
5. Maldives	1,877 per sq mile (1,164 per sq km)
6. Bangladesh	1,735 per sq mile (1,078 per sq km)
7. Bahrain	1,667 per sq mile (1,035 per sq km)
8. Taiwan	1,143 per sq mile (710 per sq km)
9. Barbados	1,042 per sq mile (648 per sq km)
10. Nauru	1,004 per sq mile (621 per sq km)

Least Crowded Countries

COUNTRY	INHABITANTS
1. Mongolia	2.9 per sq mile (1.8 per sq km)
2. Namibia	3.9 per sq mile (2.4 per sq km)
3. Australia	4.2 per sq mile (2.6 per sq km)
4. Botswana	4.3 per sq mile (2.6 per sq km)
5. Suriname	4.4 per sq mile (2.7 per sq km)
6. Iceland	4.6 per sq mile (2.8 per sq km)
7. Mauritania	4.8 per sq mile (3.0 per sq km)
8. Libya	5.3 per sq mile (3.3 per sq km)
9. Canada	5.8 per sq mile (3.6 per sq km)
10. Guyana	5.8 per sq mile (3.6 per sq km)

Most Widely Spoken Languages

LANGUAGE	NATIVE SPEAKERS
1. Mandarin Chinese	874 million
2. Hindi	366 million
3. English	341 million
4. Spanish	340 million
5. Bengali	207 million
6. Portuguese	176 million
7. Russian	167 million
8. Arabic	150 million
9. Japanese	125 million
10. German	100 million
11. Korean	78 million
12. French	77 million
13. Shanghainese (Wu)	77 million
14. Javanese	75 million
15. Cantonese (Yue)	71 million

Fastest Growing Populations*

COUNTRY	ANNUAL POPULATION GROWTH
1. Liberia	5.53%
2. Sierra Leone	4.54%
3. Eritrea	4.22%
4. Somalia	4.21%
5. Yemen	4.07%
6. Afghanistan	3.68%
7. Niger	3.63%
8. Democratic Republic of Congo	3.34%
9. Oman	3.27%
10. Uganda	3.11%

Fastest Shrinking Populations

COUNTRY	ANNUAL POPULATION GROWTH
1. Estonia	−1.14%
2. Bulgaria	−0.98%
3. Ukraine	−0.94%
4. Russian Federation	−0.64%
5. Latvia	−0.56%
6. Georgia	−0.53%
7. Hungary	−0.50%
8. Belarus	−0.40%
9. Kazakhstan	−0.37%
10. Romania	−0.26%

Major Classical Religions

RELIGION	ADHERENTS
1. Christianity	2 billion
2. Islam	1.3 billion
3. Hinduism	900 million
4. Buddhism	360 million
5. Confucianism	350 million
6. Taoism	187 million
7. Sikhism	23 million
8. Judaism	14 million
9. Baha'i	6 million
10. Jainism	4 million
11. Shinto	4 million
12. Zoroastrianism	500,000

* Countries with more than 1 million inhabitants

Richest Countries by GDP

COUNTRY	GDP PER CAPITA*
1. Luxembourg	US$44,000
2. United States	US$37,600
3. San Marino	US$34,600
4. Norway	US$31,800
5. Switzerland	US$31,700
6. Ireland	US$30,500
7. Canada	US$29,400
8. Belgium	US$29,000
9. Denmark	US$29,000
10. Japan	US$28,000

Poorest Countries by GDP

COUNTRY	GDP PER CAPITA*
1. East Timor	US$500
2. Somalia	US$550
3. Sierra Leone	US$580
4. Burundi	US$600
5. Democratic Republic of Congo	US$610
6. Tanzania	US$630
7. Malawi	US$670
8. Afghanistan	US$700
9. Comoros	US$720
10. Eritrea	US$740

Richest Countries by HDI

COUNTRY	HDI VALUE*
1. Norway	0.944
2. Iceland	0.942
3. Sweden	0.941
4. Australia	0.939
5. Netherlands	0.938
6. Belgium	0.937
7. United States	0.937
8. Canada	0.937
9. Japan	0.932
10. Switzerland	0.932

Poorest Countries by HDI

COUNTRY	HDI VALUE*
1. Sierra Leone	0.275
2. Niger	0.292
3. Burkina Faso	0.330
4. Mali	0.337
5. Burundi	0.337
6. Mozambique	0.356
7. Ethiopia	0.359
8. Central African Republic	0.363
9. Democratic Republic of Congo	0.363
10. Guinea-Bissau	0.373

* GDP (Gross Domestic Product) is the total value of all the goods and services produced each year. All GDP figures are in PPP (Purchasing Power Parity), which takes into account price differences between countries.

* HDI (Human Development Index) takes into account Gross Domestic Product (GDP), life expectancy, adult literacy rates, and education enrollments.

Most Educated Countries

COUNTRY	SCHOOL LIFE EXPECTANCY* (YEARS)
1. Norway	16.9
2. Finland	16.7
3. Australia	16.6
4. United Kingdom	16.4
5. New Zealand	16.2
6. Sweden	16.0
7. Netherlands	15.9
8. Belgium	15.8
9. Iceland	15.8
10. Denmark	15.6

Least Educated Countries

COUNTRY	SCHOOL LIFE EXPECTANCY* (YEARS)
1. Mali	2.1
2. Niger	2.3
3. Burkina Faso	2.8
4. Djibouti	3.4
5. Chad	3.9
6. Democratic Republic of Congo	4.3
7. Ethiopia	4.3
8. Eritrea	4.6
9. Burundi	4.9
10. Tanzania	5.0

* School life expectancy is the total number of years of schooling a child can expect to receive.

Hottest Places: Highest Temperatures by Continent

CONTINENT	LOCATION	DATE	TEMPERATURE
1. Africa	Al 'Azīzīyah, Libya	13 Sept. 1922	136°F (57.3°C)
2. North America	Death Valley, California	10 July 1913	134°F (56.7°C)
3. Asia	Tirat Tsvi, Israel	21 June 1942	129°F (53.9°C)
4. Oceania	Cloncurry, Australia	16 Jan. 1889	128°F (53.3°C)
5. Europe	Seville, Spain	4 Aug. 1881	122°F (50°C)
6. South America	Rivadavia, Argentina	11 Dec. 1905	120°F (48.9°C)
7. Antarctica	Vanda Station, Scott Coast	5 Jan. 1974	59°F (15°C)

Coldest Places: Lowest Temperatures by Continent

CONTINENT	LOCATION	DATE	TEMPERATURE
1. Antarctica	Vostok Station	21 July 1983	−129°F (−89°C)
2a. Asia	Oymyakon, Russian Federation	6 Feb. 1933	−90°F (−68°C)
2b. Asia	Verkhoyanskiy Khrebet, Russian Fed.	7 Feb. 1892	−90°F (−68°C)
3. North America	Northice, Greenland	9 Jan.1954	−87°F (−66°C)
4. Europe	Ust'-Shchuger, Russian Federation	Not known	−67°F (−55°C)
5. South America	Sarmiento, Argentina	1 June 1907	−27°F (−33°C)
6. Africa	Ifrane, Morocco	11 Feb. 1935	−11°F (−24°C)
7. Oceania	Charlotte Pass, Australia	29 June 1994	−9.4°F (−23°C)

Top Rail Networks

COUNTRY	LENGTH
1. United States	121,000 miles (194,700 km)
2. Russian Fed.	54,200 miles (87,200 km)
3. China	44,500 miles (71,600 km)
4. Canada	40,400 miles (65,000 km)
5. India	39,500 miles (63,500 km)
6. Germany	28,300 miles (45,500 km)
7. Australia	25,800 miles (41,600 km)
8. Argentina	21,400 miles (34,500 km)
9. France	20,300 miles (32,700 km)
10. Brazil	19,600 miles (31,500 km)

Top Road Networks

COUNTRY	LENGTH
1. United States	3,958,000 miles (6,370,000 km)
2. India	2,063,000 miles (3,320,000 km)
3. Brazil	1,230,000 miles (1,980,000 km)
4. China	870,000 miles (1,400,000 km)
5. Japan	716,000 miles (1,152,000 km)
6. Russian Fed.	592,000 miles (952,000 km)
7. Australia	567,000 miles (913,000 km)
8. Canada	561,000 miles (902,000 km)
9. France	555,000 miles (893,000 km)
10. Italy	416,000 miles (669,000 km)

Wettest Places: Highest Average Annual Precipitation by Continent

CONTINENT	LOCATION	PRECIPITATION
1. Asia	Mawsynram, India	467 in (11,862 mm)
2. Oceania	Mt Waialeale, Hawaii	460 in (11,684 mm)
3. Africa	Debundscha, Cameroon	405 in (10,287 mm)
4. South America	Quibdó, Colombia	354 in (8,992 mm)
5. North America	Henderson Lake, Canada	256 in (6,502 mm)
6. Europe	Crkvica, Bosnia-Herzegovina	183 in (4,648 mm)

Deadliest Earthquakes

LOCATION	DATE	DEATHS
1. Shanxi, China	1556	830,000
2. Tangshan, China	1976	255,000
3. Ḥalab (Aleppo), Syria	1138	230,000
4. near Xining, China	1927	200,000
5. Damghan, Iran	856	200,000
6. Gansu, China	1920	200,000
7. Ardabīl, Iran	893	150,000
8. Kwanto, Japan	1923	143,000
9. Ashgabat, Turkmenistan	1948	110,000
10. Messina, Italy	1908	100,000

Deadliest Volcanic Eruptions

LOCATION	DATE	DEATHS
1. Tambora, Indonesia	1815	92,000
2. Krakatau, Indonesia	1883	36,417
3. Mt Pelée, Martinique	1902	29,025
4. Ruiz, Colombia	1985	25,000
5. Unzen, Japan	1792	14,300
6. Laki, Iceland	1783	9,350
7. Kelut, Indonesia	1919	5,110
8. Galunggung, Indonesia	1882	4,011
9. Vesuvius, Italy	1631	3,500
10. Vesuvius, Italy	79	3,360

Driest Places: Lowest Average Annual Precipitation by Continent

CONTINENT	LOCATION	PRECIPITATION
1. South America	Quillagua, Chile	0.02 in (0.5 mm)
2. Africa	Wadi Halfa, Sudan	<0.1 in (<2.5 mm)
3. Antarctica	South Pole	0.8 in (20 mm)
4. North America	Batagues, Mexico	1.2 in (31 mm)
5. Asia	Aden, Yemen	1.8 in (46 mm)
6. Oceania	Mulka, Australia	4.1 in (104 mm)
7. Europe	Astrakhan, Russian Federation	6.4 in (163 mm)

GEOGRAPHIC TERMS

A

Abyssal plain
Flat area of the ocean floor generally extending from the base of the continental slope to the mid-ocean ridge.

Acid rain
Wet and dry deposition of oxides of nitrogen and sulfur derived from burning fossil fuels, smelting metals, and motor vehicle exhaust fumes. Results in damage to the natural and built environment.

Air mass
A large body of air of relatively constant temperature and humidity.

Alluvial fan
A deposit that radiates downslope from the point where a stream leaves a confined channel. Typically found along mountain fronts.

Alpine
High-altitude, high-relative-relief terrain that is actively affected by frost action, lies above the tree line, and has been subjected to glacial erosion.

Altitude
Height above sea level.

Antarctic Circle
Line of latitude at 66.5°S, poleward of which the Sun does not set at the summer solstice (21–22 December) and does not rise at the winter solstice (21–22 June).

Anticyclone
Area of high atmospheric pressure, generally stable and slow-moving, around which light winds spiral outward (clockwise in the Northern Hemisphere, anti clockwise in the Southern).

Arable
Strictly, a system of land use involving plowing. Usually refers to land that is tilled for crops.

Archipelago
Either a sea studded with islands or, nowadays, a group of islands.

Arctic Circle
Line of latitude at 66.5°N, poleward of which the Sun does not set at the summer solstice (21–22 June) and does not rise at the winter solstice (21–22 December).

Arid
Dry, either because of low precipitation or high evapotranspiration with respect to precipitation.

Asthenosphere
Part of Earth's mantle extending from the base of the lithosphere (at depths of 30–185 miles [50–300 km]) to depths of around 430 miles (700 km). It is in a partially molten state and is less resistant to deformation than the over- and underlying zones.

Atmosphere
Layer of air that envelops Earth. Dry air contains roughly 78% nitrogen, 21% oxygen, 1% argon, and 0.03% carbon dioxide.

Atmospheric pressure
The pressure exerted by the weight of the atmosphere above a point.

Atoll
Low, subcircular coral reef enclosing a lagoon. Found mainly in the Indian and Pacific oceans.

Avalanche
Sudden and rapid movement of ice, snow, and/or debris down a slope.

Axis
An imaginary line connecting the North and South poles, tilted at about 66.5° to the plane of Earth's orbit, around which Earth rotates.

B

Basin
1. The total area of land drained by a river and its tributaries. 2. Depression within which deposition occurs, ranging from a small hollow to a major structural feature. 3. Hollow in the ground, with a multitude of possible origins including subsidence, glacial erosion, and tectonics.

Bedrock
Consolidated, relatively unweathered rock either exposed at the ground surface or underlying the regolith.

Biodiversity
The range of flora and fauna present in an ecosystem.

Biomass
The total mass of organisms in an area.

Biome
A major ecological community of plants and animals that occupies a particular terrestrial or, less commonly, marine environment.

Biosphere
The zone in which life occurs on Earth, normally conceived as a zone of interaction with the lithosphere, atmosphere, and hydrosphere.

Border
An imaginary line that separates one administrative and/or political unit from another.

Boreal forest
The Northern Hemisphere coniferous forest, lying between approximately 55°N and 65°N.

C

Caldera
A large crater-like, steep-walled basin created by the collapse of a volcano. May contain a crater lake and subsidiary volcanoes.

Canal
An artificial waterway cut to carry irrigation water or to provide a route for shipping.

Carbon cycle
The carbon occurring as carbon dioxide in the atmosphere is absorbed and stored by plants. The plants, some animals, and bacteria obtain nourishment from the carbon and return some back to the atmosphere as carbon dioxide.

Cash crop
A crop grown for sale, by contrast with a subsistence crop grown for use by the grower.

Channel
1. A natural or artificial course for running water. 2. A narrow stretch of water between two landmasses. 3. A natural or dredged navigable waterway in an area of generally shallower water.

City
A very large permanent settlement lacking self-sufficiency in the production of food and usually dependent on manufacturing and commerce. The combined population of a city and its suburbs is known as an urban agglomeration. All city population statistics quoted in this atlas are of urban agglomerations.

Climate
The average pattern of weather that occurs in a place over an extended period of time. Several schemes divide Earth into distinct climatic zones.

Coniferous forest
A forest comprised mainly of cone-bearing, often evergreen trees that usually have needle-shaped or scaly leaves.

Continent
1. One of Earth's seven principal landmasses: Africa, Antarctica, Asia, Australia, Europe, North America, South America. 2. That part of Earth's crust composed of ancient, thick, low-density material.

Continental drift
The theory that the present distribution of the continents is a result of the fragmentation of one or more pre-existing supercontinents that have drifted apart. Subsequently subsumed within the plate tectonics model.

Continental shelf
The part of the continental crust below sea level. Usually very gently sloping. Terminated by the steeper continental slope, which forms the true edge of the continents.

Coral
A porous, calcareous rock consisting of the continuous skeleton secreted by coral polyps, bottom-dwelling marine invertebrates common at shallow depth in clear intertropical seas.

Coral reef
An extensive, solidified accumulation of coral; divided into atolls, fringing, and barrier.

Cordillera
A linear mountain chain.

Core
The central part of Earth, 2,200 miles (3,500 km) in diameter. Composed of nickel–iron alloys, solid in the inner core (800 miles [1,300 km] in diameter) and liquid in the outer.

Coriolis effect
Earth's rotation means that bodies moving over its surface such as air (winds) and water (ocean currents) are deflected to the right in the Northern Hemisphere and to the left in the Southern.

Crust
The outermost layer of Earth, 3.75–43 miles (6–70 km) thick and composed of low-density rocks.

Cyclone
An area of relatively low atmospheric pressure, typically 620–1,200 miles (1,000–2,000 km) across, into which low-level winds spiral anti clockwise in the Northern Hemisphere and clockwise in the Southern.

D

Deciduous forest
An area dominated by woody perennial plants that shed their leaves at a particular time, season, or growth stage, such as before the cold or dry season.

Deforestation
The removal of trees from an area. May occur naturally, but the main cause is clearance for timber, agriculture, and urbanization. The practice may cause significant environmental damage.

Delta
An accumulation of river-borne sediment deposited where a stream enters a body of standing water and its strength is reduced by the sudden decrease in flow velocity.

Dependency
A territory and its population governed or held in trust by another nation.

Desert
An area of moisture deficiency where precipitation is low relative to losses by evapotranspiration.

Desertification
Land degradation in arid areas resulting from factors including climatic variation and human activities such as deforestation, overgrazing, and cultivation of marginal land.

Distributary
A stream channel that splits from the main line of flow.

Drainage basin
An area drained by a river system.

Drought
May be defined meteorologically as a relatively long period of relatively low precipitation or, in human terms, taking account of impacts on agriculture, water supply, etc.

Dune
A mound or ridge of windblown sand found most commonly in deserts and coastal environments.

E

Earthquake
A shock or series of shocks in Earth's crust caused by a sudden release of pressure in the crust or upper mantle.

Ecosystem
An interacting system of organisms and the environment to which they are adapted.

El Niño
The replacement of cold upwelling waters along the west coast of South America by warm currents from the west and north. Occurs irregularly at intervals of 2–7 years. Associated with changes in global atmospheric and ocean circulation that cause major shifts in climate worldwide.

Endangered species
A plant or animal species in danger of extinction whose survival is unlikely if the factors causing its vulnerability continue operating.

Environment
Simply, the surroundings. These may be natural (e.g. biological or physical environments) or artificial (e.g. built or social environments).

Eon
1. The longest period of geological time, such as the Phanerozoic, the last 590 million years. 2. A thousand million years.

Epicenter
The point on Earth's surface that lies directly above the focus of an earthquake.

Equator
An imaginary line that is at right angles to Earth's axis of rotation lying midway between the two poles. It divides the world into the Northern and Southern hemispheres.

Era
A division of geological time. The Phanerozoic (see Eon) is divided into three eras: Paleozoic, Mesozoic, and Cenozoic.

Erosion
The process whereby material is loosened or dissolved and moved from at or near Earth's surface.

Estuary
That section of a river where it enters the sea and is influenced by marine processes, such as tides and marine water quality.

Evapotranspiration
Total water loss from the soil, including evaporation and transpiration from plant surfaces.

Evergreen
A woody perennial plant that retains its foliage throughout the year by continuously shedding and replacing a few leaves at a time.

F

Fault
A planar fracture surface in rock along which relative motion has occurred. The fracturing is an adjustment to stresses in the rock.

Fauna
A group of animals particular to a region or a period of time.

Floodplain
That part of a river valley that is inundated in times of flood.

Flora
A group of plants particular to a region or a period of time.

Forest
A large area of trees whose crowns touch to form a continuous canopy.

Fossil
The remains of an organism preserved within rock.

Fossil fuel
Combustible material derived from the fossilized remains of plants and animals. Includes coal, gas, and oil.

G

Geothermal energy
Anomalously hot zones in Earth's crust may give rise to hot springs, steam, and hot rocks at the surface. Such energy may be employed for human use.

Geyser
A spring or fountain of geothermally heated water that erupts intermittently.

Glaciation
1. An episode of marked extension of ice sheets and glaciers. 2. The occupation of an area by ice sheets or glaciers. 3. The action of ice on the landscape.

Glacier
A mass of ice sufficiently large to deform and flow under its own weight.

Global warming
The possibility that Earth is warming as a consequence of human activity over the past century or more.

Grassland
A region in which the vegetation is dominated by grasses and other herbs.

Grazing
1. An area where livestock feed on growing grass or other herbs. 2. The act of feeding livestock on such areas.

Greenhouse effect
A natural phenomenon that occurs when short-wave solar radiation passes through Earth's atmosphere, is absorbed at the surface, and is re-radiated as longer wavelength thermal radiation. This maintains Earth's average temperature at a point warm enough to sustain life. It is argued that an increase in the incidence of greenhouse gases such as carbon dioxide, as a result of fossil fuel combustion, is enhancing the greenhouse effect and causing global temperatures to rise.

Greenwich mean time (GMT)
The official time at the Greenwich meridian (0°) in Greenwich, U.K. from which all time is calculated.

Greenwich meridian
A theoretical line, extending from the North to the South Pole, that

runs through Greenwich, U.K. This is the prime meridian, the 0° of longitude, from which all other meridians are measured.

H

Habitat
The environment in which an organism lives.

Hemisphere
Earth's surface is bisected by the Equator, producing the Northern and Southern hemispheres. Less precisely, the continents of North and South America are referred to as the Western Hemisphere.

High latitude
Broadly, the areas poleward of the Arctic and Antarctic circles.

Humidity
The water vapor content of the atmosphere.

Hurricane
An intense cyclonic vortex that occurs mainly over tropical oceans. Around 400 miles (650 km) in diameter and 90–185 miles (150–300 km) high, with maximum wind speeds of 330 feet per second (100 m/s). Also known in various parts of the world as typhoon, tropical cyclone, and cyclone.

Hydroelectricity
Electricity generated using the power of running water to turn turbines.

Hydrosphere
The component of Earth's system pertaining to water in its fresh or saline, and its solid, liquid, or gaseous state.

I

Ice age
A period in Earth's history when ice is found relatively extensively on the surface. There have been at least six ice ages. The present one, the Cenozoic, began perhaps 42 million years ago. The latest advance in the present ice age ended around 13,000 years ago.

Ice cap
A large, dome-shaped body of ice displaying a generally outward and radial flow.

Indigenous
Indigenous plants and animals are those that occur naturally in a region. Indigenous people are descendants of the people who inhabited a territory before the formation of modern nation states.

International Date Line
A theoretical line at approximately 180° of longitude. Places just west of the line are 12 hours ahead of GMT; points just east are 12 hours behind. East of the line the date is one day earlier than to the west.

Irrigation
The supply of water by artificial means to assist plant growth.

Island
A landmass smaller than a continent that is enclosed by water.

L

Latitude
The distance north and south of the Equator. Latitude is given by the angle formed between a line from the center of Earth to the Equator and a line from the center of Earth to the relevant point on Earth's surface. The latitude of the Equator is thus 0° and that of the North Pole is 90°N.

Lava
Magma that is extruded from volcanic fissures and vents. The term is also applied to the cooled and solidified form of this material.

Lithosphere
Earth's crust and part of the upper mantle form a strong layer relative to the underlying and more easily deformable asthenosphere. Varies from a few miles thick over the mid-ocean ridge to over 180 miles (300 km) thick below some continents.

Longitude
The distance east and west of the Greenwich meridian. Longitude is given by the angle formed between a line from the axis of Earth to the Greenwich meridian and a line from the axis of Earth to the relevant point on Earth's surface. The angles are measured both east and west of the Greenwich meridian. 180°W thus coincides with 180°E.

M

Magma
Molten or partly molten rock generated by partial melting within Earth's crust or upper mantle. Magma may be intruded into the crust where it cools and solidifies to form intrusive rock or it may be extruded onto Earth's surface where it cools and solidifies to form volcanic rock.

Mantle
That part of Earth's interior between the core and the crust.

Map projection
A means of allowing the whole or part of the spherical surface of Earth to be represented on a flat map. Earth's lines of latitude and longitude are transformed into a net on a plane surface, the map projection. There are many ways in which this may be undertaken, but all introduce some form of distortion onto the resultant map.

Meridian
A line of longitude linking the North and South poles.

Mesa
An isolated, flat-topped hill bounded by steep slopes or cliffs.

Midlatitudes
Broadly, those areas of Earth lying between the tropics and the poles.

Mid-ocean ridge
A linear mountain chain rising 0.5–1.75 miles (1–3 km) from the ocean floor, developed where upwelling basaltic magma forms new ocean crust along a margin between divergent tectonic plates.

Mineral
1. A natural, inorganic substance of definite chemical composition, almost always in crystalline form, that cannot be physically separated into simpler compounds. 2. A loose term for inorganic material.

Monsoon
A markedly seasonal wind. The term has been extended to cover the rains that accompany these winds.

Mountain
A high-altitude, high-relative-relief topographic feature with a summit small in proportion to its base.

N

Northern Hemisphere
Refers to the half of Earth north of the Equator (0°).

North Pole
The northernmost geographical point on Earth. It marks the northern axis of Earth's rotation.

O

Oasis
An area in a hot desert where there is sufficient water to sustain plant life.

Ocean
1. The body of salt water that covers 71% of Earth's surface. 2. One of Earth's large bodies of salt water (the Arctic, Atlantic, Indian, Pacific, and Southern oceans).

Ozone layer
An ozone-enriched region of the stratosphere 9–21 miles (15–35 km) above Earth's surface. Absorbs much of the Sun's ultra-violet radiation, preventing the damaging radiation from reaching Earth's surface.

P

Pangaea
The name given to the supercontinent postulated by continental drift theory. This split to produce the northern and southern continents of Laurasia and Gondwana.

Pasture
1. A place with growing grass or other herbs on which livestock are grazed. 2. The growing grass or other herbs on which livestock are grazed.

Peninsula
A narrow neck of land projecting into a body of water.

Plain
An area of flat or rolling land devoid of prominent elevations or depressions.

Plate tectonics
The theory that the lithosphere is divided into seven major (and several minor) segments or plates that are being formed along the mid-ocean ridges and reworked down into the mantle along the deep-sea trenches. The plates carry the continents on them, explaining their movement over time. The zones of interaction between plates are often characterized by earthquakes, volcanoes, and tectonic activity.

Plateau
A broad, elevated area of flat or rolling land.

R

Rain forest
Largely evergreen forest characteristic of permanently wet regions of the tropics and midlatitudes.

Rain shadow
The leeward side of a topographic barrier where precipitation is low. Moist air is forced upward on the windward slopes. This causes rain, reducing the moisture content of the air, which is warmed and dried further as it descends the leeward slopes.

Reef
1. A narrow area of rock or sediment (including coral) usually covered at high tide, but often exposed at low tide. 2. A coral reef.

Regolith
The mantle or layer of rock fragments, alluvium, soil, blown sand, etc, that rests on bedrock. It forms almost all of the surface of Earth's land.

Renewable energy
Energy from (in practical terms) inexhaustible sources. Includes hydroelectricity, solar and geothermal energy, and wind power.

Resource
An element of the environment that may be used to meet human needs. Resources may be natural (such as water or minerals) or human (such as the entrepreneurial talents of a population).

Rift valley
A long, linear trough formed by faulting due to tension in the lithosphere.

Ring of Fire
A belt of volcanoes and associated tectonic activity found around the perimeter of the Pacific Ocean. Also known as the Rim of Fire.

S

Savanna
An area of open grassland with some trees and shrubs found in the tropics and subtropics. Characterized by seasonal wet and dry climates.

Sea
1. The body of salt water that covers 71% of Earth's surface. 2. A large body of salt water wholly or partly enclosed by the land.

Sea ice
Ice that forms on the sea surface at temperatures below around 30°F (-2°C). Covers large areas of the polar oceans. Known as fast ice when attached to land and pack ice when floating free.

Sea level
The elevation of the ocean surface. The term is often used synonymously with mean sea level, which varies slightly from place to place.

Seamount
An isolated submarine hill or mountain, usually of volcanic origin.

Solstice
Either of the two times of the year (21–22 June or 21–22 December) when the Sun is at its greatest distance from the Equator. At these times of year, there are the longest hours of either day or night.

Southern Hemisphere
Refers to the half of Earth south of the Equator (0°).

South Pole
The southernmost geographical point on Earth. It marks the southern axis of Earth's rotation.

State
1. A territorial unit with clearly defined and internationally accepted boundaries, having an independent existence and responsible for its own legal system. 2. A unit of regional government with some independence in relation to internal affairs.

Steppe
A midlatitude grassland biome stretching from Austria to China.

Strait
A narrow passage of water connecting two larger water bodies.

Subduction
Where tectonic plates collide, one of the plates may be drawn down into the mantle in a process known as subduction. The subducted plate is almost invariably that composed of denser, ocean crust. Friction along the surface of the subducting slab may give rise to earthquakes or melting, and thus volcanic activity.

Subsistence agriculture
Farming in which the products grown or raised are primarily for the support of the farmer and dependents.

T

Tectonic plate
One of the seven large and several smaller segments into which the lithosphere is divided.

Temperate
A climate without extremes of temperature.

Territory
1. The land, sea, and air ruled by a sovereign authority. 2. An area dependent upon a sovereign state, but having some authority. 3. A large tract of land with undefined boundaries. 4. In Australia, Canada, and the U.S.A., an area without full rights as a state or province.

Time zone
A division of Earth's surface selected so that standard time is the same across the whole area. Adjacent time zones usually differ by an hour. Each time zone should theoretically cover 15° of longitude.

Topography
The surface features of an area. Strictly refers not only to physical, but also to human features.

Tornado
A violent rotating storm with winds of high speed circulating round a funnel cloud around 330 feet (100 m) in diameter.

Trench (deep-sea)
A narrow, elongated, steep-sided depression 10,000 feet (3,000 m) or more deeper than the adjacent deep-sea floor. Thought to mark the zone along which one tectonic plate is subducted beneath another.

Tributary
A stream or river that flows into a larger river.

Tropic of Cancer
An imaginary line encircling Earth at 23.5°N that marks the most northerly point at which the noonday Sun is directly overhead at some stage of the year (21–22 June, the summer solstice). Denotes the northern limit of the tropics.

Tropic of Capricorn
An imaginary line encircling Earth at 23.5°S that marks the most southerly point at which the noonday Sun is directly overhead at some stage of the year (21–22 December, the summer solstice). Denotes the southern limit of the tropics.

Tundra
Vast, level, treeless, marshy regions, usually with permanently frozen subsoil, supporting mosses, lichens, herbs, and dwarf shrubs. Classically the northern part of Eurasia, but the term has been expanded to include similar terrains in the Arctic, Antarctica, and at high altitude.

V

Vegetation
The plant cover of an area.

Volcano
1. An opening or vent in Earth's crust through which lava, gas, pumice, and ash is emitted. 2. The landform produced by the accumulation of lava and other volcanic materials around a vent.

W

Weathering
The in-situ alteration of materials at or near Earth's surface by physical, chemical, and biological processes.

Wilderness
An extensive area of land that exists in a natural or nearly natural state.

Woodland
A vegetation community of widely spaced, mature trees.

100 Mile House – Akchâr

1

83 G 20 **100 Mile House**, British Columbia, Canada

A

130 H 1 **A Coruña**, Spain
130 J 1 **A Fonsagrada**, Spain
130 G 3 **A Guardia**, Spain
130 J 3 **A Gudiña**, Spain
137 B 17 **Aachen**, Germany
137 H 22 **Aalen**, Germany
133 J 16 **Aalst**, Netherlands
133 E 18 **Aalst**, Luxembourg
132 M 13 **Aalten**, Netherlands
133 D 17 **Aalter**, Belgium
138 F 6 **Aarau**, Switzerland
138 F 6 **Aare**, Switzerland
133 H 18 **Aarschot**, Belgium
133 F 17 **Aartselaar**, Belgium
177 T 9 **Ab-i-Istada**, Afghanistan
215 R 14 **Aba**, Nigeria
217 Q 5 **Aba**, Democratic Republic of Congo
188 L 4 **Aba**, China
176 G 9 **Ābādān**, Iran
176 J 9 **Ābādeh**, Iran
210 J 8 **Abadla**, Algeria
236 D 2 **Abaiang**, Kiribati
215 R 12 **Abaji**, Nigeria
74 M 6 **Abajo Peak**, Utah, U.S.A.
215 R 13 **Abakaliki**, Nigeria
153 N 13 **Abakan**, Russian Federation
215 P 8 **Abala**, Niger
216 H 8 **Abala**, Congo
215 Q 8 **Abalak**, Niger
211 N 14 **Abalessa**, Algeria
107 F 17 **Abancay**, Peru
176 J 9 **Abarqū**, Iran
198 L 3 **Abashiri**, Japan
198 L 4 **Abashiri-ko**, Japan
234 F 7 **Abau**, Papua New Guinea
179 R 4 **Abay**, Kazakhstan
213 I 22 **Ābaya Hāyk'**, Ethiopia
153 N 13 **Abaza**, Russian Federation
216 H 4 **Abba**, Central African Republic
172 M 2 **Abbah**, Syria
141 B 17 **Abbasanta**, Italy
129 P 2 **Abbeville**, France
60 M 12 **Abbeville**, South Carolina, U.S.A.
62 J 8 **Abbeville**, Louisiana, U.S.A.
63 R 6 **Abbeville**, Alabama, U.S.A.
63 U 5 **Abbeville**, Georgia, U.S.A.
125 B 20 **Abbeyfeale**, Republic of Ireland
240 J 8 **Abbot Ice Shelf**, Antarctica
127 P 14 **Abbotsbury**, United Kingdom
64 E 11 **Abbotsford**, Wisconsin, U.S.A.
83 G 22 **Abbotsford**, British Columbia, Canada
177 X 7 **Abbottabad**, Pakistan
175 V 15 **'Abd al Kūrī**, Yemen
215 Y 9 **Abéché**, Chad
133 A 19 **Abele**, Belgium
236 D 2 **Abemama**, Kiribati
214 L 13 **Abengourou**, Côte d'Ivoire
135 B 26 **Åbenrå**, Denmark
215 P 13 **Abeokuta**, Nigeria
126 M 8 **Aberaeron**, United Kingdom
127 O 10 **Aberdare**, United Kingdom
126 L 6 **Aberdaron**, United Kingdom
218 M 14 **Aberdeen**, Republic of South Africa
124 J 10 **Aberdeen**, United Kingdom
61 V 2 **Aberdeen**, Maryland, U.S.A.
61 Q 10 **Aberdeen**, North Carolina, U.S.A.
63 N 3 **Aberdeen**, Mississippi, U.S.A.
66 M 7 **Aberdeen**, South Dakota, U.S.A.
76 F 7 **Aberdeen**, Washington, U.S.A.
84 K 2 **Aberdeen Lake**, Nunavut, Canada
126 M 7 **Aberdyfi**, United Kingdom
127 P 9 **Abergavenny**, United Kingdom
126 L 8 **Aberporth**, United Kingdom
126 L 6 **Abersoch**, United Kingdom
127 O 10 **Abertillery**, United Kingdom
126 M 7 **Aberystwyth**, United Kingdom
140 E 9 **Abetone**, Italy
155 T 3 **Abez'**, Russian Federation
175 N 11 **Abhā**, Saudi Arabia
176 H 5 **Abhar**, Iran
215 R 13 **Abia**, Nigeria
214 K 14 **Abidjan**, Côte d'Ivoire
199 K 15 **Abiko**, Japan
70 M 6 **Abilene**, Texas, U.S.A.
127 T 10 **Abingdon**, United Kingdom
60 M 7 **Abingdon**, Virginia, U.S.A.
58 I 13 **Abington**, Pennsylvania, U.S.A.
75 P 8 **Abiquia Reservoir**, New Mexico, U.S.A.
212 E 10 **Abnûb**, Egypt
182 G 7 **Abohar**, India
214 L 13 **Aboisso**, Côte d'Ivoire
213 E 20 **Aboke**, Sudan
215 O 13 **Abomey**, Benin
215 U 14 **Abong Mbang**, Cameroon
175 V 11 **Aboot**, Oman
197 C 19 **Aborlan**, Philippines
215 Y 10 **Abou Déia**, Chad
175 T 5 **Abqaiq**, Saudi Arabia
196 F 7 **Abra**, Philippines
110 I 5 **Abra Pampa**, Argentina
93 O 4 **Abraham's Bay**, The Bahamas
212 D 13 **'Abri**, Sudan
43 H 16 **Abrolhos Bank**, Atlantic Ocean
150 H 10 **Abrud**, Romania
148 D 8 **Abruka**, Estonia
140 I 13 **Abruzzo**, Italy
56 K 6 **Absaroka Range**, Montana/Wyoming, U.S.A.
139 R 6 **Abtenau**, Austria
172 I 3 **Abū aḍ Ḍuhūr**, Syria
173 R 7 **Abū al Jīr**, Iraq
175 W 6 **Abu al Jirab**, United Arab Emirates
175 O 11 **Abū 'Arīsh**, Saudi Arabia
175 W 6 **Abu Dhabi**, United Arab Emirates
212 D 8 **Abu Haggag**, Egypt
213 F 14 **Abu Hamed**, Sudan
173 O 5 **Abū Ḥardān**, Syria
173 O 5 **Abū Kamāl**, Syria
213 B 19 **Abu Matariq**, Sudan
176 K 13 **Abu Musa**, Iran
211 T 8 **Abū Nujaym**, Libya
211 T 8 **Abū Qurin**, Libya
174 M 6 **Abū Rubayq**, Saudi Arabia
213 C 17 **Abu Shanab**, Sudan
212 E 12 **Abu Simbel**, Egypt
173 T 9 **Abū Şukhayr**, Iraq
213 D 18 **Abu Zabad**, Sudan
212 F 9 **Abu Zenîma**, Egypt
215 R 12 **Abuja**, Nigeria
196 G 5 **Abulog**, Philippines
216 L 5 **Abumombazi**, Democratic Republic of Congo
108 D 13 **Abunā**, Brazil
198 J 6 **Abuta**, Japan
213 C 17 **Abyad**, Sudan
213 C 20 **Abyei**, Sudan
108 K 11 **Açailândia**, Brazil
90 I 7 **Acajutla**, El Salvador
131 P 6 **Acalá de Henares**, Spain
89 Q 11 **Acambaro**, Mexico
88 M 10 **Acaponeta**, Mexico
89 Q 14 **Acapulco**, Mexico
108 K 10 **Acará**, Brazil
108 N 11 **Acaraú**, Brazil
108 F 9 **Acari Mountains**, Brazil
104 M 3 **Acarigua**, Venezuela
150 H 8 **Acâș**, Romania
89 S 13 **Acatlan**, Mexico
89 S 12 **Acatzingo**, Mexico
61 W 5 **Accomac**, Virginia, U.S.A.
192 B 8 **Aceh**, Indonesia
141 K 16 **Acerno**, Italy
105 N 4 **Achaguas**, Venezuela
181 E 16 **Achalpur**, India
171 U 6 **Achaseli**, Georgia
186 K 11 **Acheng**, China
139 N 6 **Achenkirch**, Austria
157 P 13 **Achikulak**, Russian Federation
125 A 16 **Achill Island**, Republic of Ireland
153 N 12 **Achinsk**, Russian Federation
156 J 11 **Achuyevo**, Russian Federation
170 D 12 **Acipayam**, Turkey
141 K 22 **Acireale**, Italy
70 K 6 **Ackerly**, Texas, U.S.A.
93 N 4 **Acklins Island**, The Bahamas
127 Z 6 **Acle**, United Kingdom
64 J 11 **Acme**, Michigan, U.S.A.
91 P 9 **Acoyapa**, Nicaragua
140 C 8 **Acqui Terme**, Italy
108 B 13 **Acre**, Brazil
172 F 7 **Acre**, Israel
141 M 18 **Acri**, Italy
89 R 11 **Actopan**, Mexico
108 O 12 **Açu**, Brazil
215 T 15 **Acurenam**, Equatorial Guinea
175 N 7 **Ad Dafīnah**, Saudi Arabia
173 U 9 **Ad Daghgharah**, Iraq
175 P 4 **Ad Dahnā'**, Saudi Arabia
210 B 12 **Ad Dakhla**, Western Sahara
175 P 14 **Aḍ Ḍāli'**, Yemen
175 T 5 **Ad Dammām**, Saudi Arabia
175 N 11 **Ad Darb**, Saudi Arabia
175 P 6 **Ad Dawādimī**, Saudi Arabia
173 S 5 **Ad Dawr**, Iraq
173 Y 11 **Ad Dayr**, Iraq
175 R 6 **Ad Dilam**, Saudi Arabia
175 Q 6 **Ad Dir'īyah**, Saudi Arabia
173 U 9 **Ad Dīwānīyah**, Iraq
173 T 6 **Ad Dujayl**, Iraq
144 K 8 **Ada**, Serbia and Montenegro
69 O 11 **Ada**, Oklahoma, U.S.A.
78 F 14 **Adak**, Alaska, U.S.A.
78 F 14 **Adak Island**, Alaska, U.S.A.
175 Y 7 **Adam**, Oman
215 U 13 **Adamaoua**, Cameroon
147 H 23 **Adamas**, Greece
215 U 11 **Adamawa**, Nigeria
215 U 12 **Adamawa Highlands**, Cameroon
58 H 7 **Adams**, New York, U.S.A.
41 Y 15 **Adam's Rock**, Pitcairn Island
41 Y 14 **Adamstown**, Pitcairn Island
175 P 14 **Adan as Sughra**, Yemen
170 K 13 **Adana**, Turkey
159 W 9 **Adana Trough**, Mediterranean Sea
198 K 13 **Adatara-san**, Japan
231 S 7 **Adavale**, Queensland, Australia
77 M 19 **Adaven**, Nevada, U.S.A.
179 N 4 **Aday**, Kazakhstan
213 I 20 **Addis Ababa**, Ethiopia
181 L 20 **Addu Atoll**, Maldives
63 U 6 **Adel**, Georgia, U.S.A.
231 P 12 **Adelaide**, South Australia, Australia
240 H 5 **Adelaide Island**, Antarctica
230 M 2 **Adelaide River**, Northern Territory, Australia
241 U 14 **Adélie Coast**, Antarctica
241 U 14 **Adélie Land**, Antarctica
179 S 11 **Adelunga Toghi**, Uzbekistan
131 S 7 **Ademuz**, Spain
175 P 14 **Aden**, Yemen
215 R 8 **Aderbissinat**, Niger
175 X 5 **Adh Dhayd**, United Arab Emirates
193 U 13 **Adi**, Indonesia
213 I 18 **Ādī Ārk'ay**, Ethiopia
213 I 17 **Adi Keyih**, Eritrea
213 I 17 **Ādīgrat**, Ethiopia
170 D 11 **Adigüzel Baraji**, Turkey
181 F 17 **Adilabad**, India
217 T 6 **Adilanga**, Uganda
171 S 10 **Adilcevaz**, Turkey
77 H 15 **Adin**, California, U.S.A.
133 A 18 **Adinkerke**, Belgium
211 S 11 **Adīrī**, Libya
58 J 8 **Adirondack Mountains**, New York, U.S.A.
213 H 18 **Ādīs Zemen**, Ethiopia
171 N 12 **Adıyaman**, Turkey
150 L 10 **Adjud**, Romania
156 L 14 **Adler**, Russian Federation
138 G 7 **Adliswil**, Switzerland
76 G 6 **Admiralty Inlet**, Washington, U.S.A.
79 X 11 **Admiralty Island**, Alaska, U.S.A.
234 D 2 **Admiralty Islands**, Papua New Guinea
215 Q 12 **Ado-Ekiti**, Nigeria
213 D 21 **Adok**, Sudan
193 P 15 **Adonara**, Indonesia
181 E 19 **Adoni**, India
131 P 13 **Adra**, Spain
210 K 11 **Adrar**, Algeria
214 H 5 **Adrar**, Mauritania
211 R 13 **Adrar Mariou**, Algeria
210 B 14 **Adrar Souttouf**, Western Sahara
215 Z 9 **Adré**, Chad
65 L 16 **Adrian**, Michigan, U.S.A.
70 I 2 **Adrian**, Texas, U.S.A.
140 I 9 **Adriatic Sea**, Europe
186 E 8 **Adun Qulu**, China
217 P 7 **Adusa**, Democratic Republic of Congo
149 H 14 **Adutiškis**, Lithuania
158 K 9 **Adventure Bank**, Mediterranean Sea
213 I 17 **Ādwa**, Ethiopia
214 K 13 **Adzopé**, Côte d'Ivoire
155 S 4 **Adz'va**, Russian Federation
155 S 4 **Adz'vavom**, Russian Federation
147 I 17 **Aegean Sea**, Greece
148 G 6 **Aegviidu**, Estonia
173 V 9 **'Afak**, Iraq
147 O 24 **Afantou**, Greece
213 J 18 **Afar**, Ethiopia
213 J 17 **Afar Depression**, Ethiopia
177 R 8 **Afghanistan**, Asia
213 M 24 **Afgooye**, Somalia
175 O 6 **'Afif**, Saudi Arabia
215 R 13 **Afikpo**, Nigeria
210 M 7 **Aflou**, Algeria
213 K 25 **Afmadow**, Somalia
79 Q 11 **Afognak Island**, Alaska, U.S.A.
108 M 13 **Afrânio**, Brazil
38 G 10 **Africana Seamount**, Indian Ocean
172 J 2 **'Afrīn**, Syria
170 L 11 **Afşin**, Turkey
132 I 8 **Afsluitdijk**, Netherlands
108 I 9 **Afuá**, Brazil
172 G 8 **'Afula**, Israel
170 F 10 **Afyon**, Turkey
215 R 7 **Agadez**, Niger
215 S 6 **Agadez**, Niger
210 F 9 **Agadir**, Morocco
42 K 9 **Agadir Canyon**, Atlantic Ocean
179 T 6 **Agadyr'**, Kazakhstan
183 V 13 **Agartala**, India
41 T 12 **Agassiz Fracture Zone**, Pacific Ocean
147 M 21 **Agathonisi**, Greece
193 X 13 **Agats**, Indonesia
181 B 22 **Agatti**, India
78 B 12 **Agattu Island**, Alaska, U.S.A.
78 B 12 **Agattu Strait**, Alaska, U.S.A.
214 K 13 **Agboville**, Côte d'Ivoire
196 G 6 **Agbulu**, Philippines
171 W 9 **Ağcabädi**, Azerbaijan
171 W 9 **Ağdam**, Azerbaijan
171 W 8 **Ağdaş**, Azerbaijan
129 R 14 **Agde**, France
129 N 13 **Agen**, France
213 I 22 **Āgere Maryam**, Ethiopia
171 W 10 **Aghband**, Azerbaijan
147 M 22 **Agia Marina**, Greece
147 K 17 **Agia Paraskevi**, Greece
153 R 14 **Aginskoye**, Russian Federation
147 F 16 **Agiokampos**, Greece
147 H 14 **Ágion Óros**, Greece
147 I 16 **Agios Efstratios**, Greece
147 H 21 **Agios Georgios**, Greece
147 E 22 **Ágios Ilías**, Greece
147 L 21 **Agios Kirykos**, Greece
147 D 16 **Agnantero**, Greece
76 E 13 **Agness**, Oregon, U.S.A.
214 K 13 **Agnibilékrou**, Côte d'Ivoire
196 E 9 **Agno**, Philippines
182 J 10 **Agra**, India
131 R 4 **Ágreda**, Spain
171 S 9 **Ağri**, Turkey
141 I 23 **Agrigento**, Italy
236 B 6 **Agrihan**, Northern Mariana Islands
147 C 18 **Agrinio**, Greece
141 K 17 **Agropoli**, Italy
155 R 14 **Agryz**, Russian Federation
171 X 8 **Ağsu**, Azerbaijan
196 H 11 **Agta Point**, Philippines
88 J 3 **Agua Prieta**, Mexico
111 I 16 **Aguada Cecilio**, Argentina
93 T 8 **Aguadilla**, Puerto Rico
91 V 14 **Aguadulce**, Panama
91 N 4 **Agúan**, Honduras
89 O 10 **Aguascalientes**, Mexico
89 O 10 **Aguascalientes**, Mexico
112 J 6 **Agudos**, Brazil
215 R 9 **Aguié**, Niger
236 B 8 **Aguijan**, Northern Mariana Islands
74 I 12 **Aguila**, Arizona, U.S.A.
131 N 2 **Aguilar de Campóo**, Spain
90 I 7 **Aguilares**, El Salvador
131 R 12 **Águilas**, Spain
89 O 12 **Aguililla**, Mexico
43 N 18 **Agulhas Bank**, Atlantic Ocean/Indian Ocean
43 O 19 **Agulhas Basin**, Atlantic Ocean
38 G 10 **Agulhas Basin Plateau**, Indian Ocean
112 M 6 **Agulhas Negras**, Brazil
38 H 10 **Agulhas Plateau**, Indian Ocean
43 M 19 **Agulhas Ridge**, Atlantic Ocean
199 N 24 **Aguni-jima**, Japan
197 M 20 **Agusan**, Philippines
197 G 16 **Agutaya**, Philippines
176 G 3 **Ahar**, Iran
233 G 18 **Ahaura**, New Zealand
137 C 14 **Ahaus**, Germany
232 I 5 **Ahipara**, New Zealand
232 I 5 **Ahipara Bay**, New Zealand
232 J 12 **Ahititi**, New Zealand
79 O 13 **Ahklun Mountains**, Alaska, U.S.A.
171 R 11 **Ahlat**, Turkey
137 E 15 **Ahlen**, Germany
181 C 14 **Ahmadabad**, India
181 C 17 **Ahmadnagar**, India
177 W 11 **Ahmadpur East**, Pakistan
213 J 21 **Ahmar Mountains**, Ethiopia
88 J 7 **Ahome**, Mexico
176 G 9 **Āhū**, Iran
90 I 7 **Ahuachapán**, El Salvad
176 G 9 **Ahvāz**, Iran
181 C 16 **Ahwa**, India
175 R 14 **Aḥwar**, Yemen
191 N 17 **Ai Yin Young**, Vietnam
234 A 5 **Aiambak**, Papua New Guinea
137 J 23 **Aichach**, Germany
139 S 2 **Aigen**, Austria
170 I 15 **Aigialousa**, Cyprus
147 G 21 **Aigina**, Greece
147 G 20 **Aigina**, Greece
147 E 14 **Aiginio**, Greece
147 D 19 **Aigio**, Greece
138 C 10 **Aigle**, Switzerland
113 F 15 **Aiguá**, Uruguay
198 I 13 **Aikawa**, Japan
188 K 11 **Ailao Shan**, China
231 N 6 **Aileron**, Northern Territory, Australia
91 Z 13 **Ailigandi**, Panama
237 W 1 **Ailinginae**, Marshall Islands
237 Y 3 **Ailinglaplap**, Marshall Islands
237 Y 2 **Ailuk**, Marshall Islands
110 H 8 **Aimogasta**, Argentina
211 P 6 **Aïn Beïda**, Algeria
214 I 2 **Aïn Ben Tili**, Mauritani
210 J 7 **Aïn Beni Mathar**, Moro
210 M 5 **Aïn Defla**, Algeria
210 M 6 **Aïn Deheb**, Algeria
211 N 6 **Aïn el Hadjel**, Algeria
210 K 8 **Aïn Sefra**, Algeria
210 K 6 **Aïn Temouchent**, Alger
148 F 9 **Ainaži**, Latvia
147 B 19 **Ainos**, Greece
131 U 3 **Ainsa**, Spain
66 K 12 **Ainsworth**, Nebraska, U.S.A.
107 K 20 **Aiquile**, Bolivia
192 G 9 **Air**, Indonesia
85 Q 1 **Air Force Island**, Nunav Canada
192 D 10 **Airbangis**, Indonesia
128 M 14 **Aire-sur-l'Adour**, France
138 G 9 **Airolo**, Switzerland
193 R 14 **Airpanas**, Indonesia
111 F 20 **Aisén**, Chile
131 T 9 **Aitana**, Spain
234 B 3 **Aitape**, Papua New Guinea
67 R 5 **Aitkin**, Minnesota, U.S.
237 P 10 **Aitutaki**, Cook Islands
150 I 10 **Aiud**, Romania
148 H 11 **Aiviekste**, Latvia
237 U 1 **Aiwo**, Nauru
129 U 14 **Aix-en-Provence**, Franc
129 V 10 **Aix-les-Bains**, France
183 W 13 **Aizawl**, India
148 G 11 **Aizkraukle**, Latvia
148 C 11 **Aizpute**, Latvia
198 K 13 **Aizu-Wakamatsu**, Japa
129 X 15 **Ajaccio**, France
182 L 12 **Ajaigarh**, India
181 D 16 **Ajanta**, India
181 D 16 **Ajanta Range**, India
211 W 8 **Ajdābiyā**, Libya
144 A 7 **Ajdovščina**, Slovenia
172 G 9 **'Ajlūn**, Jordan
175 X 5 **Ajman**, United Arab Emirates
180 D 12 **Ajmer**, India
182 H 5 **Ajnala**, India
74 I 14 **Ajo**, Arizona, U.S.A.
198 K 5 **Akabira**, Japan
210 L 11 **Akabli**, Algeria
213 I 20 **Āk'ak'ī**, Ethiopia
233 H 21 **Akaroa**, New Zealand
233 I 21 **Akaroa Harbour**, New Zealand
173 N 6 **Akāshat**, Iraq
199 G 18 **Akashi**, Japan
179 W 7 **Akbalyk**, Kazakhstan
157 W 5 **Akbulak**, Russian Federation
179 T 7 **Akbulak**, Kazakhstan
171 N 11 **Akşşadağ**, Turkey
171 O 13 **Akşşakale**, Turkey
170 G 7 **Akşşakoca**, Turkey
214 F 5 **Akchâr**, Mauritania

Country · Internal administrative region: State/Province/Territory/Dependent territory · Capital city · Mountain range/Undersea ridge · Mountain peak/Volcano/Seamount · Geographic feature · Headland/Point/Cape/Peninsula · Desert · Island/Island group · Antarctic base · Ocean · Sea · Bay/Gulf/Channel/Strait · Lake · Salt pan/Dry/Intermittent lake

T 6	Akchatau, Kazakhstan	
D 13	Akdağlar, Turkey	
K 10	Akdağmadeni, Turkey	
L 11	Akdepe, Turkmenistan	
S 10	Akelamo, Indonesia	
M 6	Aketi, Democratic Republic of Congo	
S 7	Akhalk'alak'i, Georgia	
L 13	Akhalskiy Velayat, Turkmenistan ▣	
S 7	Akhalts'ikhe, Georgia	
C 10	Akhisar, Turkey	
E 10	Akhmīm, Egypt	
H 4	Akhnoor, India	
Q 9	Akhtubinsk, Russian Federation	
F 20	Aki, Japan	
G 8	Akiéni, Gabon	
O 9	Akimiski Island, Québec, Canada ✣	
K 14	Akinci Burnu, Turkey ▶	
J 10	Akita, Japan	
F 5	Akjoujt, Mauritania	
G 9	Akka, Morocco	
M 5	Akkeshi, Japan	
M 5	Akkeshi-wan, Japan ≈	
S 10	Akkol', Kazakhstan	
S 3	Akkol', Kazakhstan	
B 12	Akköy, Turkey	
V 3	Akku, Kazakhstan	
O 9	Akkum, Kazakhstan	
M 8	Akkuş, Turkey	
O 12	Aklampa, Benin	
B 9	Aklavik, Northwest Territories, Canada	
R 4	Akmola, Kazakhstan ▣	
H 12	Akniste, Latvia	
F 18	Akō, Japan	
F 21	Akobo, Sudan	
E 14	Akodia, India	
E 16	Akola, India	
T 15	Akom II, Cameroon	
H 16	Akordat, Eritrea	
D 22	Akot, Sudan	
E 16	Akot, India	
S 5	Akpatok Island, Nunavut, Canada ✣	
H 5	Akqi, China	
K 26	Akra Agios Ioannis, Greece ▶	
H 15	Akra Akrathos, Greece ▶	
H 14	Akra Arapis, Greece ▶	
C 19	Akra Araxos, Greece ✣	
H 15	Akra Drepano, Greece ▶	
I 19	Akra Kafireas, Greece ▶	
G 15	Akra Kassandras, Greece ▶	
R 10	Akra Krios, Mediterranean Sea ▶	
I 26	Akra Lithino, Greece ▶	
F 23	Akra Maleas, Greece ▶	
K 19	Akra Meston, Greece ▶	
F 25	Akra Paliouri, Greece ▶	
M 25	Akra Paraspori, Greece ▶	
L 26	Akra Sideros, Greece ▶	
K 17	Akra Sigri, Greece	
G 25	Akra Spatha, Greece ▶	
E 24	Akra Tainaro, Greece ▶	
S 7	Akrérèb, Niger	
N 17	Akron, Ohio, U.S.A.	
L 3	Aksai Chin, India ▣	
N 7	Aksakovo, Bulgaria	
I 11	Aksaray, Turkey	
O 9	Aksay, Russian Federation	
J 4	Aksay, Kazakhstan	
G 11	Akşehir, Turkey	
F 11	Akşehir Gölü, Turkey ❧	
G 13	Akseki, Turkey	
S 3	Aksu, Kazakhstan	
U 3	Aksu, Kazakhstan	
I 5	Aksu, China	
T 6	Aksu-Ayuly, Kazakhstan	
Y 6	Aksuat, Kazakhstan	
U 9	Aksuek, Kazakhstan	
I 17	Āksum, Ethiopia	
P 12	Aktash, Uzbekistan	
H 9	Aktau, Kazakhstan	
U 3	Aktau, Kazakhstan	
U 6	Aktogay, Kazakhstan	
W 7	Aktogay, Kazakhstan	
K 20	Aktsyabrski, Belarus	

178	L 6	Aktyubinsk, Kazakhstan ▣
178	L 5	Aktyubinsk, Kazakhstan
216	K 6	Akula, Democratic Republic of Congo
85	P 5	Akulivik, Québec, Canada
199	B 23	Akune, Japan
215	Q 13	Akure, Nigeria
134	C 10	Akureyri, Iceland
199	B 26	Akuseki-shima, Japan ✣
78	K 13	Akutan Island, Alaska, U.S.A. ✣
215	R 14	Akwa Ibom, Nigeria ▣
215	R 12	Akwanga, Nigeria
179	Y 6	Akzhar, Kazakhstan
171	O 12	Akziyaret, Turkey
211	W 7	Al Abyār, Libya
211	Y 7	Al 'Adam, Libya
175	S 3	Al Aḥmadī, Kuwait
175	O 4	Al Ajfar, Saudi Arabia
175	N 9	Al 'Alayyah, Saudi Arabia
173	S 1	Al Amādīyah, Iraq
173	Y 9	Al 'Amārah, Iraq
172	F 13	Al 'Aqabah, Jordan
175	N 9	Al 'Aqīq, Saudi Arabia
210	B 12	Al Argoub, Western Sahara
175	Q 4	Al Arṭāwīyah, Saudi Arabia
173	O 4	Al 'Ashārah, Syria
175	X 6	Al 'Ayn, United Arab Emirates
211	S 8	Al 'Azīzīyah, Libya
173	U 8	Al 'Azīzīyah, Iraq
173	P 2	Al Ba'āj, Iraq
172	J 2	Al Bāb, Syria
173	P 3	Al Bādī, Iraq
175	Q 8	Al Badī', Saudi Arabia
175	N 9	Al Bāḥah, Saudi Arabia
172	H 3	Al Bahlūlīyah, Syria
211	Y 7	Al Bardī, Libya
173	Z 11	Al Baṣrah, Iraq
211	W 7	Al Baydā', Libya
175	Q 13	Al Baydā', Yemen
174	M 7	Al Bi'ār, Saudi Arabia
174	K 3	Al Bi'r, Saudi Arabia
175	N 11	Al Birk, Saudi Arabia
175	O 5	Al Bukayrīyah, Saudi Arabia
175	X 6	Al Buraymī, Oman
173	N 4	Al Buşayrah, Syria
173	W 12	Al Buşayyah, Iraq
173	S 7	Al Fallūjah, Iraq
175	S 13	Al Fardah, Yemen
175	S 3	Al Farwānīyah, Kuwait
173	S 4	Al Fatḥah, Iraq
173	Z 12	Al Fāw, Iraq
175	O 13	Al Fāzih, Yemen
211	U 10	Al Fuqahā', Libya
173	U 10	Al Ghammās, Iraq
175	P 5	Al Ghāt, Saudi Arabia
175	V 12	Al Ghaydah, Yemen
173	S 7	Al Ḥabbānīyah, Iraq
173	Q 6	Al Ḥadīthah, Iraq
173	R 3	Al Ḥaḍr, Iraq
210	E 10	Al Haggounia, Western Sahara
175	X 6	Al Hajar'al Gharbī, Oman ▲▲
175	R 12	Al Ḥajr, Yemen
173	Y 9	Al Ḥalfāyah, Iraq
174	L 1	Al Ḥamād, Saudi Arabia ◇
211	Q 9	Al Ḥamādah al Ḥamrā', Libya ◇
172	H 4	Al Ḥamīdīyah, Syria
174	M 6	Al Ḥanākīyah, Saudi Arabia
175	O 14	Al Ḥanīsh al Kabīr, Yemen ✣
173	W 14	Al Haniyah, Iraq ◇
175	O 11	Al Haqū, Saudi Arabia
211	U 10	Al Haruj al Aswad, Libya ◇
172	G 11	Al Ḥāsā, Jordan
173	O 2	Al Ḥasakah, Syria
173	U 9	Al Hāshimīyah, Iraq
173	O 2	Al Hawl, Syria
175	R 14	Al Ḥawrā, Yemen
175	W 9	Al Ḥayy, Iraq
175	P 12	Al Ḥazm al-Jawf, Yemen
175	V 9	Al Ḥibāk, Saudi Arabia ◇

172	H 7	Al Hījānah, Syria
173	T 8	Al Ḥillah, Iraq
175	R 7	Al Ḥillah, Saudi Arabia
173	T 8	Al Hindīyah, Iraq
172	L 2	Al Hīshah, Syria
172	G 8	Al Ḥiṣn, Jordan
210	J 6	Al Hoceima, Morocco
175	O 13	Al Ḥudaydah, Yemen
175	P 6	Al Hufūf, Saudi Arabia
175	Q 14	Al Ḥumayshah, Yemen
175	X 8	Al Ḥuwatsah, Oman
175	S 13	Al Ḥuwaymi, Yemen
174	L 1	Al 'Īsāwīyah, Saudi Arabia
211	W 7	Al Jabal al Akhḍar, Libya ◇
172	H 12	Al Jafr, Jordan
211	Y 8	Al Jaghbūb, Libya
175	R 2	Al Jahrah, Kuwait
175	U 5	Al Jamālīyah, Qatar
211	Y 12	Al Jawf, Libya
174	M 2	Al Jawf, Saudi Arabia
173	N 2	Al Jazīrah, Syria ◇
175	N 4	Al Jithāmīyah, Saudi Arabia
175	T 4	Al Jubayl, Saudi Arabia
174	M 8	Al Jumūm, Saudi Arabia
175	Z 9	Al Kalbān, Oman
172	G 11	Al Karak, Jordan
212	F 11	Al Karnak, Egypt
175	Y 6	Al Khābūrah, Oman
175	Z 9	Al Khalīf, Oman
173	U 6	Al Khāliş, Iraq
175	P 9	Al Khamāsīn, Saudi Arabia
175	Y 5	Al Khaşab, Oman
175	O 14	Al Khawkhah, Yemen
173	V 10	Al Khiḍr, Iraq
211	Y 7	Al Khufrah, Libya
211	T 7	Al Khums, Libya
173	T 9	Al Kifl, Iraq
175	U 5	Al Kir'ānah, Qatar
173	T 9	Al Kūfah, Iraq
173	X 9	Al Kumayt, Iraq
173	W 8	Al Kūt, Iraq
175	N 2	Al Labbah, Saudi Arabia ◇
172	H 3	Al Lādhiqīyah, Syria
174	M 9	Al Lith, Saudi Arabia
173	R 11	Al Ma'ānīyah, Iraq
172	H 8	Al Mafraq, Jordan
210	F 10	Al Mahbas, Western Sahara
172	K 2	Al Mahdum, Syria
173	T 7	Al Maḥmūdīyah, Iraq
175	U 11	Al Mahrah, Yemen ◇
175	O 12	Al Maḥwīt, Yemen
175	Q 5	Al Majma'ah, Saudi Arabia
173	Q 1	Al Mālikīyah, Syria
175	T 5	Al Manāmah, Bahrain ♞
173	Z 11	Al Ma'qil, Iraq
175	O 13	Al Marāwi'ah, Yemen
211	W 7	Al Marj, Libya
175	Y 6	Al Masana'a, Oman
173	N 4	Al Mayādīn, Syria
172	G 10	Al Mazra'ah, Jordan
175	V 6	Al Mirfa, United Arab Emirates
175	T 5	Al Mubarrez, Saudi Arabia
172	G 14	Al Mudawwarah, Jordan
175	T 5	Al Muharraq, Bahrain
175	T 13	Al Mukallā, Yemen
211	X 7	Al Mukhaylī, Libya
173	U 6	Al Muqdādīyah, Iraq
174	L 6	Al Musayjid, Saudi Arabia
173	W 9	Al Muwaffaqīyah, Iraq
175	N 7	Al Muwayh, Saudi Arabia
174	J 3	Al Muwayliḥ, Saudi Arabia
173	Y 11	Al Muzayri'ah, Iraq
172	H 4	Al Qadmūs, Syria
173	P 5	Al Qā'im, Iraq
175	O 6	Al Qā'īyah, Saudi Arabia
174	L 3	Al Qalibah, Saudi Arabia
173	O 1	Al Qāmishlī, Syria
172	H 3	Al Qardābah, Syria
172	I 5	Al Qaryatayn, Syria
175	S 12	Al Qaṭn, Yemen
172	H 10	Al Qaṭrānah, Jordan
211	T 12	Al Qaṭrūn, Libya

175	Q 3	Al Qayşūmah, Saudi Arabia
174	M 10	Al Qunfidhah, Saudi Arabia
173	Y 11	Al Qurnah, Iraq
173	W 11	Al Qusayr, Iraq
175	Q 6	Al Quwayi', Saudi Arabia
172	F 13	Al Quwayrah, Jordan
175	S 13	Al Quzah, Yemen
175	W 6	Al Samha, United Arab Emirates
175	S 5	Al 'Uḍaylīyah, Saudi Arabia
174	L 4	Al 'Ulā, Saudi Arabia
211	V 9	Al 'Uqaylah, Libya
211	R 12	Al 'Uwaynāt, Libya
211	Z 13	Al 'Uwaynāt, Libya
175	O 2	Al 'Uwayqīlah, Saudi Arabia
174	M 6	Al 'Uyūn, Saudi Arabia
175	O 4	Al 'Uyūn, Saudi Arabia
173	Y 10	Al 'Uzayr, Iraq
175	S 3	Al Wafrah, Kuwait
174	J 4	Al Wajh, Saudi Arabia
175	S 4	Al Wannān, Saudi Arabia
175	R 3	Al Wari'ah, Saudi Arabia
175	Y 6	Al Wāsiţ, Oman
211	T 12	Al Wīgh, Libya
175	R 6	Al Yamāmah, Saudi Arabia
179	S 11	Ala-Buka, Kyrgyzstan
170	G 11	Ala Dağı, Turkey ▲
63	O 4	Alabama, U.S.A. ▣
63	O 5	Alabama, Alabama, U.S.A. ❧
196	H 12	Alabat, Philippines ✣
170	J 9	Alaca, Turkey
170	K 7	Alaşşam, Turkey
63	V 8	Alachua, Florida, U.S.A.
157	O 14	Alagir, Russian Federation
108	O 13	Alagoas, Brazil ▣
109	N 14	Alagoinhas, Brazil
131	S 4	Alagón, Spain
197	L 22	Alah, Philippines ❧
172	H 3	Alājah, Syria
91	P 12	Alajuela, Costa Rica
236	B 7	Alamagan, Northern Mariana Islands ✣
175	P 5	Al'Amār, Saudi Arabia
213	I 18	Ālamat'ā, Ethiopia
91	Q 7	Alamicamba, Nicaragua
196	E 9	Alaminos, Philippines
77	M 20	Alamo, Nevada, U.S.A.
74	H 11	Alamo Lake, Arizona, U.S.A. ❧
75	Q 13	Alamogordo, New Mexico, U.S.A.
75	Q 7	Alamosa, Colorado, U.S.A.
135	I 19	Åland, Finland ✣
135	I 19	Ålands Hav, Finland ≈
170	G 13	Alanya, Turkey
170	C 11	Alaşehir, Turkey
79	P 6	Alaska, U.S.A. ▣
79	P 9	Alaska Range, Alaska, U.S.A. ▲
78	L 13	Alaskan Peninsula, Alaska, U.S.A. ▶
171	Z 8	Ālāt, Azerbaijan
157	Q 2	Alatyr', Russian Federation
106	B 10	Alausí, Ecuador
171	T 8	Alaverdi, Armenia
135	K 16	Alavus, Finland
153	V 7	Alazeya, Russian Federation ❧
131	R 9	Albacete, Spain
145	K 17	Albania, Europe ▣
230	H 12	Albany, Western Australia, Australia
232	K 8	Albany, New Zealand
58	K 9	Albany, New York, U.S.A.
60	H 7	Albany, Kentucky, U.S.A.
63	S 6	Albany, Georgia, U.S.A.
71	N 6	Albany, Texas, U.S.A.
76	G 10	Albany, Oregon, U.S.A.
84	L 10	Albany, Ontario, Canada ❧
132	G 13	Albasserdam, Netherlands
231	R 1	Albatross Bay, Queensland, Australia ≈
232	K 10	Albatross Point, New Zealand ▶
196	K 13	Albay Gulf, Philippines ≈

61	P 10	Albemarle, North Carolina, U.S.A.
61	V 8	Albemarle Sound, North Carolina, U.S.A. ≈
140	B 9	Albenga, Italy
109	G 20	Alberdi, Paraguay
231	O 8	Alberga, South Australia, Australia ❧
130	H 5	Albergaria-a-Velha, Portugal
129	Q 2	Albert, France
67	S 10	Albert Lea, Minnesota, U.S.A.
217	R 6	Albert Nile, Uganda ❧
61	T 7	Alberta, Virginia, U.S.A.
83	I 16	Alberta, Canada ▣
143	J 23	Albertirsa, Hungary
129	V 10	Albertville, France
63	R 2	Albertville, Alabama, U.S.A.
129	Q 13	Albi, France
58	A 10	Albion, Pennsylvania, U.S.A.
65	K 15	Albion, Michigan, U.S.A.
67	N 13	Albion, Nebraska, U.S.A.
158	B 9	Alboran Ridge, Mediterranean Sea ◇
131	O 14	Alboran Sea, Africa/Spain ◇
135	C 23	Ålborg, Denmark
130	H 12	Albufeira, Portugal
138	I 9	Albula Alpen, Switzerland ▲
75	Q 10	Albuquerque, New Mexico, U.S.A.
130	J 8	Alburquerque, Spain
231	T 12	Albury, New South Wales, Australia
130	H 10	Alcácer do Sal, Portugal
196	H 6	Alcala, Philippines
130	L 13	Alcalá de los Gazules, Spain
131	O 12	Alcalá la Real, Spain
141	H 22	Alcamo, Italy
131	T 5	Alcañiz, Spain
130	J 8	Alcántara, Spain
131	Q 10	Alcaraz, Spain
131	N 12	Alcaudete, Spain
131	P 8	Alcázar de San Juan, Spain
127	S 8	Alcester, United Kingdom
151	Y 6	Alchevs'k, Ukraine
131	T 6	Alcorisa, Spain
113	B 15	Alcorta, Argentina
131	U 7	Alcossebre, Spain
73	W 12	Alcova, Wyoming, U.S.A.
131	T 9	Alcoy, Spain
131	Y 7	Alcúdia, Spain
38	K 5	Aldabra Islands, Seychelles ✣
89	S 9	Aldama, Mexico
153	U 11	Aldan, Russian Federation ❧
153	T 12	Aldan, Russian Federation
127	Z 8	Aldeburgh, United Kingdom
58	I 7	Alder Creek, New York, U.S.A.
125	J 25	Alderney, United Kingdom ✣
127	U 11	Aldershot, United Kingdom
65	D 17	Aledo, Illinois, U.S.A.
214	F 7	Aleg, Mauritania
42	O 11	Alegranza, Canary Islands ✣
112	O 5	Alegre, Brazil
112	E 12	Alegrete, Brazil
154	H 10	Alekhovshchina, Russian Federation
154	J 14	Aleksandrov, Russian Federation
157	R 7	Aleksandrov Gay, Russian Federation
146	I 7	Aleksandrovo, Bulgaria
155	T 11	Aleksandrovsk, Russian Federation
153	X 13	Aleksandrovsk-Sakhalinskiy, Russian Federation
156	L 6	Alekseyevka, Russian Federation
157	N 7	Alekseyevskaya, Russian Federation

157	S 1	Alekseyevskoye, Russian Federation
156	K 2	Aleksin, Russian Federation
144	N 13	Aleksinac, Serbia and Montenegro
112	N 6	Além Paraíba, Brazil
129	N 5	Alençon, France
108	H 10	Alenquer, Brazil
78	D 8	Alenuihaha Channel, Hawaii, U.S.A. ≈
172	J 2	Aleppo, Syria
129	Z 15	Aléria, France
81	P 1	Alert, Nunavut, Canada
107	G 15	Alerta, Peru
129	S 13	Alès, France
150	G 8	Aleşd, Romania
140	C 8	Alessandria, Italy
135	B 16	Ålesund, Norway
41	P 2	Aleutian Basin, Pacific Ocean ◇
78	E 13	Aleutian Islands, Alaska, U.S.A. ✣
79	N 12	Aleutian Range, Alaska, U.S.A. ▲
41	O 2	Aleutian Trench, Pacific Ocean ◇
79	W 11	Alexander Archipelago, Alaska, U.S.A. ✣
218	I 12	Alexander Bay, Republic of South Africa
63	Q 4	Alexander City, Alabama, U.S.A.
240	I 6	Alexander Island, Antarctica ✣
233	D 23	Alexandra, New Zealand
212	D 7	Alexandria, Egypt
150	J 13	Alexandria, Romania
61	U 3	Alexandria, Virginia, U.S.A.
62	I 6	Alexandria, Louisiana, U.S.A.
67	P 6	Alexandria, Minnesota, U.S.A.
86	J 10	Alexandria, Ontario, Canada
58	H 6	Alexandria Bay, New York, U.S.A.
146	K 13	Alexandroupoli, Greece
172	G 6	'Aley, Lebanon
152	L 13	Aleysk, Russian Federation
146	M 6	Alfatar, Bulgaria
112	L 5	Alfenas, Brazil
140	G 9	Alfonsine, Italy
127	W 4	Alford, United Kingdom
127	S 5	Alfreton, United Kingdom
178	I 4	Algabas, Kazakhstan
130	G 12	Algarve, Portugal ◇
130	L 14	Algeciras, Spain
213	I 15	Algena, Eritrea
210	K 11	Algeria, Africa ▣
158	D 8	Algerian Basin, Mediterranean Sea ◇
158	I 8	Algerian–Tyrrhenian Trough, Mediterranean Sea ◇
141	A 16	Alghero, Italy
210	M 5	Algiers, Algeria ♞
131	T 9	Alginet, Spain
130	L 13	Algodonales, Spain
64	H 11	Algoma, Wisconsin, U.S.A.
67	R 11	Algona, Iowa, U.S.A.
173	V 8	'Alī, Iraq
173	X 8	'Alī al Gharbī, Iraq
171	Y 9	Ālī Bayramli, Azerbaijan
177	V 7	'Alī Kheyl, Afghanistan
213	K 19	Ali Sabieh, Djibouti
170	B 10	Aliağa, Turkey
147	F 19	Aliartos, Greece
144	L 10	Alibunar, Serbia and Montenegro
131	T 10	Alicante, Spain
71	P 13	Alice, Texas, U.S.A.
92	J 10	Alice Shoal, Jamaica ≈
231	O 6	Alice Springs, Northern Territory, Australia
92	J 2	Alice Town, The Bahamas
63	O 4	Aliceville, Alabama, U.S.A.
179	U 14	Alichur, Tajikistan
183	I 8	Aligarh, India
186	I 6	Alihe, China
147	N 24	Alimia, Greece ✣

105	W 8	**Alimimuni Peak**, Suriname ▲
197	H 22	**Alimpaya Point**, Philippines ▶
177	W 11	**Alipur**, Pakistan
183	T 10	**Alipur Duar**, India
130	J 8	**Aliseda**, Spain
147	H 19	**Aliveri**, Greece
130	K 9	**Aljucén**, Spain
77	M 19	**Alkali Flat**, Nevada, U.S.A. ■
132	H 9	**Alkmaar**, Netherlands
183	N 11	**Allahabad**, India
79	Q 5	**Allakaket**, Alaska, U.S.A.
153	V 10	**Allakh-Yun'**, Russian Federation
219	O 9	**Alldays**, Republic of South Africa
58	E 10	**Allegeny Plateau**, New York, U.S.A. ◇
58	C 14	**Allegheny Mountains**, Pennsylvania/West Virginia, U.S.A. ▲
197	K 14	**Allen**, Philippines
61	O 14	**Allendale**, South Carolina, U.S.A.
89	P 5	**Allende**, Mexico
89	Q 7	**Allende**, Mexico
58	H 13	**Allentown**, Pennsylvania, U.S.A.
181	D 23	**Alleppey**, India
138	K 7	**Allgäuer Alpen**, Austria/Germany ▲
66	H 12	**Alliance**, Nebraska, U.S.A.
181	E 23	**Allinagaram**, India
63	V 6	**Alma**, Georgia, U.S.A.
64	K 13	**Alma**, Michigan, U.S.A.
66	L 15	**Alma**, Nebraska, U.S.A.
86	M 6	**Alma**, Québec, Canada
131	U 4	**Almacelles**, Spain
130	M 9	**Almadén**, Spain
131	O 9	**Almagro**, Spain
179	S 12	**Almalyk**, Uzbekistan
131	S 9	**Almansa**, Spain
130	M 7	**Almanzor**, Spain ▲
109	K 14	**Almas**, Brazil
179	V 8	**Almaty**, Kazakhstan ■
179	V 10	**Almaty**, Kazakhstan
131	Q 4	**Almazán**, Spain
108	I 10	**Almeirim**, Brazil
130	H 8	**Almeirim**, Portugal
132	N 11	**Almelo**, Netherlands
131	Q 4	**Almenar de Soria**, Spain
130	K 9	**Almendralejo**, Spain
132	I 11	**Almere**, Netherlands
131	Q 13	**Almería**, Spain
157	T 2	**Al'met'yevsk**, Russian Federation
135	F 24	**Älmhult**, Sweden
91	S 13	**Almirante**, Panama
130	H 11	**Almodôvar**, Portugal
130	J 12	**Almonte**, Spain
182	L 7	**Almora**, India
131	O 13	**Almuñécar**, Spain
125	J 14	**Alnwick**, United Kingdom
236	J 10	**Alofi**, Niue ■
236	H 8	**Alofi**, Wallis and Futuna Islands ■
148	G 9	**Aloja**, Latvia
183	X 8	**Along**, India
186	G 5	**Alongshan**, China
147	G 17	**Alonnisos**, Greece ■
193	Q 15	**Alor**, Indonesia ■
194	A 5	**Alor Setar**, Malaysia
234	G 7	**Alotau**, Papua New Guinea
130	I 8	**Alpalhao**, Portugal
64	L 11	**Alpena**, Michigan, U.S.A.
231	T 7	**Alpha**, Queensland, Australia
45	R 7	**Alpha Ridge**, Arctic Ocean ▲
65	E 17	**Alphe**, Illinois, U.S.A.
132	G 12	**Alphen**, Netherlands
70	H 9	**Alpine**, Texas, U.S.A.
74	M 12	**Alpine**, Arizona, U.S.A.
140	A 6	**Alps**, Europe ▲
231	P 5	**Alpurrurulam**, Northern Territory, Australia
129	W 5	**Alsace**, France ■
131	Q 2	**Alsasua**, Spain
137	G 17	**Alsfeld**, Germany
148	C 11	**Alsunga**, Latvia

134	K 7	**Alta**, Norway
110	J 10	**Alta Gracia**, Argentina
91	O 10	**Alta Gracia**, Nicaragua
134	K 7	**Altaelva**, Norway ↘
105	O 3	**Altagracia de Orituco**, Venezuela
184	L 2	**Altai Mountains**, Asia ▲
63	V 5	**Altamaha**, Georgia, U.S.A. ↘
108	I 10	**Altamira**, Brazil
110	G 7	**Altamira**, Chile
91	P 11	**Altamira**, Costa Rica
141	M 16	**Altamura**, Italy
186	E 8	**Altan Emel**, China
61	Q 7	**Altavista**, Virginia, U.S.A.
184	L 3	**Altay**, China
185	N 4	**Altay**, Mongolia
138	G 8	**Altdorf**, Switzerland
131	U 10	**Altea**, Spain
137	N 17	**Altenberg**, Germany
137	L 17	**Altenburg**, Germany
130	I 8	**Alter do Chão**, Portugal
134	I 8	**Altevatnet**, Norway ↘
139	Q 4	**Altheim**, Austria
173	T 3	**Altin Köprü**, Iraq
107	H 20	**Altiplano**, Bolivia ◇
71	T 7	**Alto**, Texas, U.S.A.
109	H 16	**Alto Araguaia**, Brazil
218	J 3	**Alto Chicapa**, Angola
90	F 4	**Alto Cuchumatanes**, Guatemala ▲
130	I 6	**Alto da Torre**, Portugal ▲
104	I 4	**Alto de Tamar**, Colombia ▲
109	H 16	**Alto Garças**, Brazil
219	T 6	**Alto Molócuè**, Mozambique
104	G 5	**Alto Musinga**, Colombia ▲
108	K 13	**Alto Parnaíba**, Brazil
107	G 15	**Alto Purús**, Peru ↘
111	G 19	**Alto Río Senguerr**, Argentina
137	K 21	**Amberg**, Germany
127	U 12	**Alton**, United Kingdom
69	W 8	**Alton**, Missouri, U.S.A.
58	D 13	**Altoona**, Pennsylvania, U.S.A.
137	L 24	**Altötting**, Germany
127	Q 4	**Altrincham**, United Kingdom
184	K 7	**Altun Shan**, China ▲
77	I 15	**Alturas**, California, U.S.A.
68	K 11	**Altus**, Oklahoma, U.S.A.
151	S 2	**Altynivka**, Ukraine
148	I 10	**Alūksne**, Latvia
151	U 13	**Alupka**, Ukraine
181	E 19	**Alur**, India
151	U 12	**Alushta**, Ukraine
68	L 8	**Alva**, Oklahoma, U.S.A.
71	Q 6	**Alvarado**, Texas, U.S.A.
89	T 12	**Alvarado**, Mexico
108	D 11	**Alvarães**, Brazil
135	D 17	**Alvdal**, Norway
135	E 18	**Alvdalen**, Sweden ↘
135	F 18	**Älvdalen**, Sweden
135	A 18	**Alvik**, Norway
71	T 11	**Alvin**, Texas, U.S.A.
135	H 19	**Alvkarleby**, Sweden
134	J 12	**Älvsbyn**, Sweden
182	I 9	**Alwar**, India
149	F 16	**Alytus**, Lithuania
73	Z 8	**Alzada**, Montana, U.S.A.
137	E 20	**Alzey**, Germany
215	Y 9	**Am-Dam**, Chad
215	Y 10	**Am Timan**, Chad
215	Z 8	**Am-Zoer**, Chad
213	D 22	**Amadi**, Sudan
173	S 1	**Amādīyah**, Iraq
85	Q 3	**Amadjuak Lake**, Nunavut, Canada ↘
193	S 12	**Amahai**, Indonesia
199	A 23	**Amakusa-nada**, Japan ≈
199	B 23	**Amakusa-Shimo-shima**, Japan ■
175	X 10	**Amal**, Oman
135	F 20	**Åmål**, Sweden
141	K 16	**Amalfi**, Italy
147	C 20	**Amaliada**, Greece
193	X 13	**Amamapare**, Indonesia
109	H 19	**Amambaí**, Brazil
199	N 21	**Amami-Ō-shima**, Japan ■
199	N 23	**Amami shotō**, Japan ■

217	P 8	**Amamula**, Democratic Republic of Congo
234	A 3	**Amanab**, Papua New Guinea
140	I 12	**Amandola**, Italy
179	P 5	**Amangel'dy**, Kazakhstan
141	M 19	**Amantea**, Italy
219	P 13	**Amanzimtoti**, Republic of South Africa
108	I 8	**Amapá**, Brazil
108	I 9	**Amapá**, Brazil ■
190	D 11	**Amarapura**, Myanmar
77	L 21	**Amargosa Valley**, Nevada, U.S.A.
70	J 2	**Amarillo**, Texas, U.S.A.
181	H 15	**Amarkantak**, India
170	H 7	**Amasra**, Turkey
170	K 8	**Amasya**, Turkey
108	C 11	**Amataurá**, Brazil
133	I 20	**Amay**, Belgium
108	F 11	**Amazon**, Brazil/Peru ↘
108	C 11	**Amazon Basin**, Brazil ◇
42	F 13	**Amazon Cone**, Atlantic Ocean ◇
104	L 11	**Amazonas**, Colombia ■
105	O 8	**Amazonas**, Venezuela ■
106	C 11	**Amazonas**, Peru ■
108	D 11	**Amazonas**, Brazil ■
182	I 7	**Ambala**, India
219	X 9	**Ambalavao**, Madagascar
219	Z 5	**Ambanja**, Madagascar
153	W 7	**Ambarchik**, Russian Federation
154	H 5	**Ambarnyy**, Russian Federation
183	V 12	**Ambāsa**, India
106	B 9	**Ambato**, Ecuador
219	X 6	**Ambato Boeny**, Madagascar
219	X 7	**Ambatomainty**, Madagascar
193	R 12	**Ambelau**, Indonesia ■
137	K 21	**Amberg**, Germany
64	G 10	**Amberg**, Wisconsin, U.S.A.
90	L 1	**Ambergris Cay**, Belize ■
129	U 9	**Ambérieu-en-Bugey**, France
233	H 19	**Amberley**, New Zealand
86	C 12	**Amberley**, Ontario, Canada
181	H 14	**Ambikapur**, India
196	F 12	**Ambil**, Philippines ■
219	Z 5	**Ambilobe**, Madagascar
79	O 5	**Ambler**, Alaska, U.S.A.
107	D 15	**Ambo**, Peru
219	X 10	**Amboasary**, Madagascar
219	X 9	**Ambohimahasoa**, Madagascar
219	W 6	**Ambohipaky**, Madagascar
193	S 12	**Ambon**, Indonesia
193	S 12	**Ambon**, Indonesia ■
219	X 8	**Ambositra**, Madagascar
219	X 11	**Ambovombe**, Madagascar
77	M 24	**Amboy**, California, U.S.A.
218	F 2	**Ambriz**, Angola
235	R 10	**Ambrym**, Vanuatu ■
78	D 13	**Amchitka Island**, Alaska, U.S.A. ■
78	E 14	**Amchitka Islands**, Alaska, U.S.A. ■
78	D 14	**Amchitka Pass**, Alaska, U.S.A. ≈
155	S 1	**Amderma**, Russian Federation
184	L 9	**Amdo**, China
89	N 11	**Ameca**, Mexico
132	K 5	**Ameland**, Netherlands ■
61	S 6	**Amelia Court House**, Virginia, U.S.A.
73	O 12	**American Falls**, Idaho, U.S.A.
73	O 12	**American Falls Reservoir**, Idaho, U.S.A. ↘
236	L 9	**American Samoa**, U.S.A. ■
43	J 22	**American–Antarctic Ridge**, Atlantic Ocean ▲
63	S 5	**Americus**, Georgia, U.S.A.
132	J 12	**Amersfoort**, Netherlands
127	V 10	**Amersham**, United Kingdom
241	W 6	**Amery Ice Shelf**, Antarctica ◇
57	Q 8	**Ames**, Iowa, U.S.A.

127	S 12	**Amesbury**, United Kingdom
147	C 18	**Amfilochia**, Greece
147	E 19	**Amfissa**, Greece
153	T 11	**Amga**, Russian Federation ↘
153	U 11	**Amga**, Russian Federation
153	W 15	**Amgu**, Russian Federation
153	Z 6	**Amguema**, Russian Federation
211	O 11	**Amguid**, Algeria
153	V 13	**Amgun**, Russian Federation ↘
213	I 19	**Amhara**, Ethiopia ■
58	M 9	**Amherst**, Massachusetts, U.S.A.
87	U 9	**Amherst**, Nova Scotia, Canada
129	Q 2	**Amiens**, France
181	A 22	**Amindivi Islands**, India ■
181	B 22	**Amini**, India ■
213	K 23	**Amino**, Ethiopia
218	J 10	**Aminuis**, Namibia
38	K 5	**Amirante Islands**, Seychelles ■
38	K 5	**Amirante Trench**, Indian Ocean ◇
83	N 16	**Amisk Lake**, Saskatchewan, Canada ↘
62	L 7	**Amite**, Louisiana, U.S.A.
78	G 14	**Amlia Island**, Alaska, U.S.A. ■
126	L 4	**Amlwch**, United Kingdom
172	H 9	**Ammān**, Jordan ♣
126	M 9	**Ammanford**, United Kingdom
134	H 12	**Ammarnäs**, Sweden
45	N 13	**Ammassalik**, Greenland
137	J 25	**Ammersee**, Germany ↘
170	I 15	**Ammóchostos**, Cyprus
191	L 17	**Amnat Charoen**, Thailand
181	C 15	**Amod**, India
176	J 5	**Amol**, Iran
131	Q 1	**Amorebieta**, Spain
147	K 23	**Amorgos**, Greece ■
63	N 2	**Amory**, Mississippi, U.S.A.
86	G 6	**Amos**, Québec, Canada
135	B 20	**Åmot**, Norway
214	J 8	**Amourj**, Mauritania
90	L 8	**Ampala**, Honduras
219	Z 6	**Ampanavoana**, Madagascar
219	Z 5	**Ampanefena**, Madagascar
219	W 10	**Ampanihy**, Madagascar
181	H 25	**Amparai**, Sri Lanka
219	Z 8	**Ampasimanolotra**, Madagascar
42	K 9	**Ampere Seamount**, Atlantic Ocean ▲
193	O 11	**Ampoa**, Indonesia
131	U 6	**Amposta**, Spain
127	V 8	**Ampthill**, United Kingdom
87	R 6	**Amqui**, Québec, Canada
175	P 12	**Amrān**, Yemen
181	E 16	**Amravati**, India
182	H 5	**Amritsar**, India
136	E 7	**Amrum**, Germany ■
132	H 11	**Amstelveen**, Netherlands
132	H 11	**Amsterdam**, Netherlands ♣
39	N 10	**Amsterdam Fracture Zone**, Indian Ocean ◇
39	O 10	**Amsterdam Island**, Indian Ocean ■
139	U 4	**Amstetten**, Austria
179	O 13	**Amudar'ya**, Turkmenistan ↘
78	H 15	**Amukta Pass**, Alaska, U.S.A. ≈
45	P 8	**Amund Ringnes Island**, Canada ■
81	O 3	**Amund Ringnes Island**, Nunavut, Canada ■
41	S 15	**Amundsen Abyssal Plain**, Pacific Ocean ◇
241	P 9	**Amundsen Coast**, Antarctica
45	N 6	**Amundsen Gulf**, Arctic Ocean ≈
82	D 7	**Amundsen Gulf**, Northwest Territories, Canada ≈
231	P 9	**Amundsen-Scott**, Antarctica ⬡

240	I 9	**Amundsen Sea**, Antarctica ≈
192	L 12	**Amuntai**, Indonesia
153	U 14	**Amur**, Russian Federation ↘
193	Q 10	**Amurang**, Indonesia
131	P 2	**Amurrio**, Spain
153	V 13	**Amursk**, Russian Federation
147	B 17	**Amvrakikos Kolpos**, Greece ≈
151	Y 7	**Amvrosiyivka**, Ukraine
175	O 5	**An Nabhānīyah**, Saudi Arabia
172	I 6	**An Nabk**, Syria
174	L 2	**An Nafūd**, Saudi Arabia ■
173	T 9	**An Najaf**, Iraq
173	W 11	**An Nāşirīyah**, Iraq
173	W 10	**An Naşr**, Iraq
211	V 8	**An Nawfalīyah**, Libya
172	J 8	**An Nimarah**, Syria
175	N 10	**An Nimāş**, Saudi Arabia
175	S 4	**An Nu'ayrīyah**, Saudi Arabia
173	U 8	**An Nukhayb**, Iraq
173	U 8	**An Nu'mānīyah**, Iraq
173	V 8	**An Nu'mānīyah**, Iraq
237	V 1	**Anabar**, Nauru
105	Q 3	**Anaco**, Venezuela
73	O 6	**Anaconda**, Montana, U.S.A.
153	Z 7	**Anadyr'**, Russian Federation
147	K 24	**Anafi**, Greece ■
109	M 15	**Anagé**, Brazil
141	I 14	**Anagni**, Italy
173	P 5	**'Ānah**, Iraq
77	K 25	**Anaheim**, California, U.S.A.
89	Q 6	**Anáhuac**, Mexico
181	D 23	**Anai Mudi Peak**, India ▲
181	H 18	**Anakapalle**, India
219	Y 5	**Analalava**, Madagascar
108	E 11	**Anamã**, Brazil
215	R 13	**Anambra**, Nigeria ■
170	H 14	**Anamur**, Turkey
170	H 14	**Anamur Burnu**, Turkey ▶
199	G 20	**Anan**, Japan
181	C 15	**Anand**, India
181	J 16	**Anandapur**, India
181	E 20	**Anantapur**, India
182	H 4	**Anantnag**, India
156	J 12	**Anapa**, Russian Federation
109	J 16	**Anápolis**, Brazil
176	K 10	**Anār**, Iran
176	K 8	**Anārak**, Iran
177	P 8	**Anardara**, Afghanistan
236	A 7	**Anatahan**, Northern Mariana Islands ■
170	D 10	**Anatolia**, Turkey ◇
146	I 12	**Anatolikí Makedonía Kai Thráki**, Greece ■
235	S 13	**Anatom**, Vanuatu ■
110	K 8	**Añatuya**, Argentina
159	U 9	**Anaximander Mountains**, Mediterranean Sea ◇
189	P 1	**Anbianbu**, China
107	C 14	**Ancash**, Peru ■
128	L 7	**Ancenis**, France
215	R 11	**Anchau**, Nigeria
79	R 9	**Anchorage**, Alaska, U.S.A.
107	C 16	**Ancón**, Peru
140	I 11	**Ancona**, Italy
111	E 17	**Ancud**, Chile
186	J 10	**Anda**, China
196	E 8	**Anda**, Philippines
107	E 17	**Andahuaylas**, Peru
110	K 8	**Andalgalá**, Argentina
130	L 12	**Andalucía**, Spain ■
63	Q 6	**Andalusia**, Alabama, U.S.A.
181	O 23	**Andaman and Nicobar Islands**, India ■
39	R 3	**Andaman Basin**, Indian Ocean ◇
181	O 21	**Andaman Islands**, India ■
191	D 18	**Andaman Sea**, Asia ≈
231	P 9	**Andamooka**, South Australia, Australia
219	Z 5	**Andapa**, Madagascar

138	I 9	**Andeer**, Switzerland
133	I 21	**Andenne**, Belgium
133	F 21	**Anderlues**, Belgium
138	G 9	**Andermatt**, Switzerland
128	L 12	**Andernos-les-Bains**, France
60	L 11	**Anderson**, South Carolina, U.S.A.
65	J 18	**Anderson**, Indiana, U.S.A.
69	S 8	**Anderson**, Missouri, U.S.A.
79	R 7	**Anderson**, Alaska, U.S.A. ↘
82	C 9	**Anderson**, Northwest Territories, Canada ↘
110	G 13	**Andes**, South America ▲
134	G 8	**Andfjorden**, Norway ≈
181	F 19	**Andhra Pradesh**, India ■
179	T 12	**Andijon Wiloyati**, Uzbekistan ■
219	Y 7	**Andilamena**, Madagascar
219	Y 7	**Andilanatoby**, Madagascar
176	G 8	**Andīmeshk**, Iran
179	T 12	**Andizhan**, Uzbekistan
177	R 5	**Andkhvoy**, Afghanistan
106	D 10	**Andoas**, Peru
187	M 20	**Andong**, South Korea
131	W 2	**Andorra**, Europe ■
131	W 2	**Andorra La Vella**, Andorra ♣
127	S 11	**Andover**, United Kingdom
134	G 8	**Andoya**, Norway ■
112	H 5	**Andradina**, Brazil
219	Z 4	**Andranovondronina**, Madagascar
219	W 10	**Andranovory**, Madagascar
131	X 8	**Andratx**, Spain
78	E 14	**Andreanof Islands**, Alaska, U.S.A. ■
154	F 14	**Andreapol'**, Russian Federation
112	M 6	**Andrelândia**, Brazil
38	K 3	**Andrew Tablemount**, Indian Ocean ▲
70	J 6	**Andrews**, Texas, U.S.A.
179	X 7	**Andreyevka**, Kazakhstan
141	M 15	**Andria**, Italy
219	Y 7	**Andriamena**, Madagascar
151	X 8	**Andriyivka**, Ukraine
219	W 10	**Androka**, Madagascar
147	I 20	**Andros**, Greece ■
92	K 3	**Andros Island**, The Bahamas ■
92	K 2	**Andros Town**, The Bahamas
157	S 4	**Androsovka**, Russian Federation
181	C 22	**Andrott**, India ■
134	I 8	**Andselv**, Norway
131	N 11	**Andújar**, Spain
218	H 4	**Andulo**, Angola
93	W 7	**Anegada**, Virgin Islands, United Kingdom ■
215	N 13	**Aného**, Togo
197	C 18	**Anepahan**, Philippines
131	U 2	**Aneto**, Spain ▲
215	U 6	**Aney**, Niger
189	U 9	**Anfu**, China
191	H 18	**Ang Thong**, Thailand
153	O 11	**Angara**, Russian Federation ↘
153	P 13	**Angarsk**, Russian Federation
135	G 16	**Ånge**, Sweden
105	R 6	**Angel Falls**, Venezuela ◇
196	F 10	**Angeles**, Philippines
135	E 24	**Ängelholm**, Sweden
136	N 12	**Angermünde**, Germany
128	M 7	**Angers**, France
135	J 15	**Ångesön**, Sweden ■
191	L 21	**Ångk Tasaôm**, Cambodia
126	L 4	**Anglesey**, United Kingdom ■
71	S 11	**Angleton**, Texas, U.S.A.
217	O 5	**Ango**, Democratic Republic of Congo
219	U 6	**Angoche**, Mozambique
176	M 13	**Angohrān**, Iran
111	F 15	**Angol**, Chile
218	H 3	**Angola**, Africa ■
43	M 16	**Angola Basin**, Atlantic Ocean ◇
234	C 3	**Angoram**, Papua New Guinea
129	N 10	**Angoulême**, France

■ Country ■ Internal administrative region: State/Province/Territory/Dependent territory ♣ Capital city ◇ Mountain range/ Undersea ridge ▲ Mountain peak/ Volcano/Seamount ◇ Geographic feature ▶ Headland/Point/ Cape/Peninsula ■ Desert ■ Island/Island group ⬡ Antarctic base ≈ Ocean ≈ Sea ≈ Bay/Gulf/Channel/Strait ■ Lake ↘ Salt pan/Dry/ Intermittent lake

N 1 **Angra do Heroísmo**, Azores
M 7 **Angra dos Reis**, Brazil
S 11 **Angren**, Uzbekistan
N 5 **Angu**, Democratic Republic of Congo
I 11 **Anguang**, China
T 3 **Angüés**, Spain
X 7 **Anguilla**, United Kingdom, United Kingdom ▣
J 3 **Anguilla Cay**, The Bahamas 🏝
D 24 **Anholt**, Denmark 🏝
S 8 **Anhua**, China
W 5 **Anhui**, China ▣
H 16 **Anhumas**, Brazil
J 10 **Ani**, Japan
N 9 **Aniak**, Alaska, U.S.A.
V 1 **Anibare**, Nauru
V 1 **Anibare Bay**, Nauru ≈
N 15 **Animas Peak**, New Mexico, U.S.A. ▲
M 15 **Anitaguipan Point**, Philippines ▶
Z 4 **Anivorano Avaratra**, Madgascar
S 12 **Aniwa**, Vanuatu 🏝
R 9 **Anjiang**, China
W 4 **Anjouan**, Comoros 🏝
K 17 **Anju**, North Korea
O 5 **Anka**, Iraq
Q 5 **Ankang**, China
H 9 **Ankara**, Turkey
V 9 **Ankazoabo**, Madgascar
Y 7 **Ankazobe**, Madgascar
S 13 **Ankeny**, Iowa, U.S.A.
M 9 **Anklam**, Germany
C 20 **Ankola**, India
R 9 **Ankou**, China
P 3 **Ankouzhen**, China
R 13 **Ankpa**, Nigeria
N 10 **Anlong**, China
T 6 **Anlu**, China
L 15 **Ann Arbor**, Michigan, U.S.A.
M 5 **Anna**, Russian Federation
F 22 **Anna**, Illinois, U.S.A.
U 1 **Anna Point**, Nauru ▶
P 5 **Annaba**, Algeria
M 15 **Annam**, Vietnam ◇
K 14 **Annam Highlands**, Laos ⛰
V 3 **Annapolis**, Maryland, U.S.A.
T 11 **Annapolis Royal**, Nova Scotia, Canada
P 8 **Annapurna**, Nepal ▲
V 9 **Annecy**, France
L 11 **Anning**, China
R 3 **Anniston**, Alabama, U.S.A.
T 11 **Annonay**, France
J 26 **Ano Viannos**, Greece
R 14 **Anpu**, China
W 6 **Anqing**, China
F 20 **Anqiu**, China
J 20 **Ans**, Belgium
Q 1 **Ansai**, China
I 21 **Ansbach**, Germany
A 10 **Anse à la Mouche**, Seychelles
B 10 **Anse Royal**, Seychelles
H 16 **Anshan**, China
O 10 **Anshun**, China
F 13 **Ansina**, Uruguay
L 14 **Ansley**, Nebraska, U.S.A.
M 6 **Anson**, Texas, U.S.A.
Y 11 **Ansudu**, Indonesia
F 18 **Antabamba**, Peru
Z 6 **Antalaha**, Madgascar
F 13 **Antalya**, Turkey
V 9 **Antalya Basin**, Mediterranean Sea ◇
F 13 **Antalya Körfezi**, Turkey ≈
Y 7 **Antananarivo**, Madgascar 🏛
X 7 **Antananarivo**, Madgascar ▣
W 10 **Antanimora Atsimo**, Madgascar
H 4 **Antarctic Peninsula**, Antarctica ▶
241 Q 7 **Antarctica**
131 N 13 **Antequera**, Spain
75 Q 14 **Anthony**, New Mexico, U.S.A.
210 F 9 **Anti Atlas**, Morocco ⛰
129 X 14 **Antibes**, France
64 F 11 **Antigo**, Wisconsin, U.S.A.
87 W 9 **Antigonish**, Nova Scotia, Canada
90 H 6 **Antigua**, Guatemala
93 Y 9 **Antigua**, Antigua and Barbuda 🏝
93 Z 8 **Antigua and Barbuda**, North America □
147 F 25 **Antikythira**, Greece 🏝
147 H 23 **Antimilos**, Greece 🏝
170 L 14 **Antioch**, Turkey
104 H 5 **Antioquia**, Colombia ▣
147 I 22 **Antiparos**, Greece 🏝
147 A 17 **Antipaxoi**, Greece 🏝
152 M 8 **Antipayuta**, Russian Federation
41 P 13 **Antipodes Islands**, New Zealand 🏝
110 F 5 **Antofagasta**, Chile
110 F 5 **Antofagasta**, Chile ▣
110 H 7 **Antofagasta de la Sierra**, Argentina
111 I 21 **Antonio de Biedma**, Argentina
125 F 15 **Antrim**, United Kingdom
140 H 13 **Antrodoco**, Italy
219 W 7 **Antsalova**, Madgascar
219 X 8 **Antsirabe**, Madgascar
219 Z 4 **Antsiranana**, Madgascar
219 Z 5 **Antsiranana**, Madgascar ▣
148 H 9 **Antsla**, Estonia
219 Y 5 **Antsohihy**, Madgascar
187 M 14 **Antu**, China
111 F 14 **Antuco**, Chile
133 G 17 **Antwerp**, Belgium
133 G 17 **Antwerpen**, Belgium ▣
181 I 16 **Anugul**, India
180 C 11 **Anupgarh**, India
181 G 24 **Anuradhapura**, Sri Lanka
235 S 8 **Anuta**, Solomon Islands 🏝
240 H 4 **Anvers Island**, Antarctica 🏝
185 N 6 **Anxi**, China
189 S 7 **Anxiang**, China
231 O 11 **Anxious Bay**, South Australia, Australia ≈
187 L 19 **Anyang**, South Korea
189 U 2 **Anyang**, China
147 K 23 **Anydro**, Greece 🏝
185 O 8 **A'nyêmaqên Shan**, China ⛰
149 G 14 **Anykščiai**, Lithuania
189 V 10 **Anyuan**, China
189 N 7 **Anyue**, China
189 S 2 **Anze**, China
133 D 19 **Anzegem**, Belgium
216 M 8 **Anzi**, Democratic Republic of Congo
141 H 15 **Anzio**, Italy
105 Q 4 **Anzoátegui**, Venezuela ▣
191 G 23 **Ao Ban Don**, Thailand ≈
191 F 24 **Ao Luk**, Thailand
191 G 22 **Ao Sawi**, Thailand ≈
235 Q 10 **Aoba**, Vanuatu 🏝
199 L 20 **Aoga-shima**, Japan 🏝
234 M 7 **Aola**, Solomon Islands
198 J 9 **Aomori**, Japan
182 K 9 **Aonla**, India
140 A 6 **Aosta**, Italy
210 C 11 **Aoufist**, Western Sahara
214 G 7 **Aoukâr**, Mauritania ⛰
210 L 11 **Aoulef**, Algeria
215 W 5 **Aozou**, Chad
217 S 6 **Apac**, Uganda
68 M 11 **Apache**, Oklahoma, U.S.A.
74 L 15 **Apache Peak**, Arizona, U.S.A. ▲
63 T 8 **Apalachee Bay**, Florida, U.S.A. ≈
63 S 8 **Apalachicola**, Florida, U.S.A.
112 H 4 **Aparecida do Taboado**, Brazil
196 H 5 **Aparri**, Philippines
144 I 8 **Apatin**, Serbia and Montenegro
154 H 3 **Apatity**, Russian Federation
89 O 12 **Apatzingán**, Mexico
148 I 9 **Ape**, Latvia
132 L 12 **Apeldoorn**, Netherlands
140 D 9 **Apennines**, Italy ⛰
217 N 5 **Api**, Democratic Republic of Congo
182 M 7 **Api**, Nepal ▲
236 J 8 **Apia**, Samoa 🏛
107 F 19 **Aplao**, Peru
108 N 12 **Apodi**, Brazil
105 V 6 **Apoera**, Suriname
231 R 14 **Apollo Bay**, Victoria, Australia
107 I 18 **Apolo**, Bolivia
112 H 3 **Aporé**, Brazil
112 H 4 **Aporé**, Brazil ∿
64 E 7 **Apostle Islands**, Wisconsin, U.S.A. 🏝
44 M 14 **Apostolens Tommefinger**, Greenland ▲
112 E 10 **Apóstoles**, Argentina
151 T 8 **Apostolove**, Ukraine
57 U 11 **Appalachian Mountains**, Georgia, U.S.A. ⛰
140 I 13 **Appennino Abruzzese**, Italy ⛰
140 B 9 **Appennino Ligure**, Italy ⛰
141 L 16 **Appennino Lucano**, Italy ⛰
141 K 15 **Appennino Napoletano**, Italy ⛰
140 E 9 **Appennino Tosco-Emiliano**, Italy ⛰
140 H 11 **Appennino Umbro-Marchigiano**, Italy ⛰
138 I 7 **Appenzell**, Switzerland
132 N 6 **Appingedam**, Netherlands
64 G 12 **Appleton**, Wisconsin, U.S.A.
61 S 6 **Appomattox**, Virginia, U.S.A.
156 L 13 **Apsheronsk**, Russian Federation
129 U 13 **Apt**, France
112 H 7 **Apucarana**, Brazil
159 O 7 **Apulian Plateau**, Mediterranean Sea ◇
105 N 5 **Apure**, Venezuela ▣
105 N 4 **Apure**, Venezuela ∿
107 F 18 **Apurímac**, Peru ▣
107 E 16 **Apurímac**, Peru ∿
177 S 5 **Āqchah**, Afghanistan
176 K 8 **Áqdā**, Iran
184 K 7 **Aqqikkol Hu**, China 💧
172 G 9 **'Aqraba**, Israel
173 S 1 **'Aqrah**, Iraq
179 V 4 **Aqtasty**, Kazakhstan
109 G 18 **Aquidauana**, Brazil
128 L 12 **Aquitaine**, France ▣
173 S 8 **Ar Raḩḩālīyah**, Iraq
173 S 7 **Ar Ramādī**, Iraq
172 G 13 **Ar Ramlah**, Jordan
172 H 8 **Ar Ramtha**, Jordan
172 L 3 **Ar Raqqah**, Syria
174 L 8 **Ar Rās al Aswad**, Saudi Arabia ▶
175 O 5 **Ar-Rass**, Saudi Arabia
175 O 8 **Ar Rawḑah**, Saudi Arabia
175 R 13 **Ar Rawḑah**, Yemen
173 W 10 **Ar Rifā'ī**, Iraq
173 V 10 **Ar Rihab**, Iraq ◇
175 P 5 **Ar Rubay'iyah**, Saudi Arabia
173 V 10 **Ar Rumaythah**, Iraq
172 L 3 **Ar Ruşāfah**, Syria
172 H 9 **Ar Ruşayfah**, Jordan
175 Z 6 **Ar Rustāq**, Oman
173 N 8 **Ar Ruţbah**, Iraq
175 P 6 **Ar Ruwayḑah**, Saudi Arabia
183 P 11 **Ara**, India
213 J 22 **Āra Ārba**, Ethiopia
63 Q 2 **Arab**, Alabama, U.S.A.
173 V 8 **Arab Abdullah**, Iraq
38 M 2 **Arabian Basin**, Indian Ocean ◇
175 V 13 **Arabian Sea**,Asia 🌊
170 I 7 **Araş**, Turkey
109 O 14 **Aracaju**, Brazil
108 O 11 **Aracati**, Brazil
112 I 5 **Araçatuba**, Brazil
172 F 10 **'Arad**, Israel
150 F 10 **Arad**, Romania
215 Y 8 **Arada**, Chad
175 V 7 **'Arādah**, United Arab Emirates
173 Y 11 **Aradah**, Iraq
193 V 14 **Arafura Sea**, Asia/Oceania 🌊
40 K 9 **Arafura Shelf**, Pacific Ocean ◇
171 T 8 **Aragats Lerr**, Armenia ▲
131 S 5 **Aragón**, Spain ▣
105 O 3 **Aragua**, Venezuela ▣
109 J 14 **Araguaçu**, Brazil
108 J 13 **Araguaia**, Brazil ∿
108 J 12 **Araguaína**, Brazil
109 J 17 **Araguari**, Brazil
199 I 14 **Arai**, Japan
176 H 7 **Arāk**, Iran
211 N 12 **Arak**, Algeria
172 L 5 **Arak**, Syria
190 B 13 **Arakan**, Myanmar ▣
190 B 12 **Arakan Yoma**, Myanmar ⛰
178 L 9 **Aral Sea**, Kazakhstan/Uzbekistan 💧
179 N 7 **Aral'sk**, Kazakhstan
231 S 6 **Aramac**, Queensland, Australia
234 B 6 **Aramia**, Papua New Guinea ∿
127 N 6 **Aran Fawddwy**, United Kingdom ▲
125 A 18 **Aran Islands**, Republic of Ireland 🏝
131 O 4 **Aranda de Duero**, Spain
144 L 11 **Aranđelovac**, Serbia and Montenegro
131 O 7 **Aranjuez**, Spain
218 J 10 **Aranos**, Namibia
236 D 2 **Aranuka**, Kiribati 🏝
191 J 19 **Aranyaprathet**, Thailand
199 B 22 **Arao**, Japan
66 K 15 **Arapahoe**, Nebraska, U.S.A.
233 J 16 **Arapawa Island**, New Zealand 🏝
108 O 13 **Arapiraca**, Brazil
171 N 10 **Arapkir**, Turkey
112 H 7 **Arapongas**, Brazil
175 N 1 **'Ar'ar**, Saudi Arabia
104 K 10 **Araracuara**, Colombia
112 I 11 **Araranguá**, Brazil
112 J 6 **Araraquara**, Brazil
108 H 12 **Araras**, Brazil
231 R 13 **Ararat**, Victoria, Australia
183 R 11 **Araria**, India
171 R 9 **Aras**, Turkey
171 S 9 **Aras**, Azerbaijan/Turkey ∿
171 R 10 **Aras Güneyi Dağlari**, Turkey ⛰
171 N 12 **Aratürk Baraji**, Turkey 💧
104 K 5 **Arauca**, Colombia ▣
104 L 5 **Arauca**, Colombia
104 M 5 **Arauca**, Venezuela ∿
111 F 15 **Araucania**, Chile ▣
111 E 14 **Arauco**, Chile
180 C 13 **Aravalli Range**, India ⛰
109 K 17 **Araxá**, Brazil
171 W 10 **Araz**, Azerbaijan ∿
213 H 22 **Ārba Minch**, Ethiopia
173 V 4 **Arbat**, Iraq
141 D 18 **Arbatax**, Italy
139 U 3 **Arbesbach**, Austria
173 T 2 **Arbīl**, Iraq
135 G 20 **Arboga**, Sweden
104 G 4 **Arboletes**, Colombia
138 I 6 **Arbon**, Switzerland
124 I 12 **Arbroath**, United Kingdom
128 L 12 **Arcachon**, France
58 D 9 **Arcade**, New York, U.S.A.
62 I 4 **Arcadia**, Louisiana, U.S.A.
63 W 11 **Arcadia**, Florida, U.S.A.
105 T 8 **Arcarai Mountains**, Guyana ⛰
77 E 15 **Arcata**, California, U.S.A.
89 Q 13 **Arcelia**, Mexico
230 I 12 **Archipelago of the Recherche**, Western Australia, Australia 🏝
91 S 12 **Archipiélago de Bocas del Toro**, Panama 🏝
92 J 4 **Archipiélago de Camagüey**, Cuba 🏝
111 E 23 **Archipiélago de la Reina Adelaida**, Chile 🏝
91 X 15 **Archipiélago de las Perlas**, Panama 🏝
92 G 4 **Archipiélago de los Canarreros**, Cuba 🏝
111 E 20 **Archipiélago de los Chonos**, Chile 🏝
92 J 5 **Archipiélago de los Jardines de la Reina**, Cuba 🏝
92 H 3 **Archipiélago de Sabana**, Cuba 🏝
91 Y 12 **Archipiélago de San Blas**, Panama 🏝
91 P 10 **Archipiélago de Solentiname**, Nicaragua 🏝
41 W 2 **Archipiélago Juan Fernández**, Juan Fernández Islands 🏝
140 F 12 **Arcidosso**, Italy
73 N 11 **Arco**, Idaho, U.S.A.
130 L 13 **Arcos de la Frontera**, Spain
81 Q 4 **Arctic Bay**, Nunavut, Canada
45 Q 8 **Arctic Ocean** ◎
240 G 3 **Arctowski**, Antarctica ⁙
171 U 8 **Arcvašen**, Armenia
172 I 11 **Arḑ aş Şawwān**, Jordan ⛰
146 J 11 **Arda**, Bulgaria ∿
176 H 3 **Ardabīl**, Iran
176 H 3 **Ardabīl**, Iran ▣
171 S 8 **Ardahan**, Turkey
176 K 8 **Ardakān**, Iran
157 Q 2 **Ardatov**, Russian Federation
86 E 10 **Ardbeg**, Ontario, Canada
125 E 17 **Ardee**, Republic of Ireland
133 H 23 **Ardennes**, Belgium ◇
176 J 7 **Ardestān**, Iran
69 N 12 **Ardmore**, Oklahoma, U.S.A.
150 H 7 **Ardusat**, Romania
135 F 15 **Åre**, Sweden
217 Q 6 **Arebi**, Democratic Republic of Congo
93 U 7 **Arecibo**, Puerto Rico
197 F 19 **Arena**, Philippines 🏝
91 P 11 **Arenal**, Costa Rica ∿
109 G 15 **Arenápolis**, Brazil
130 M 7 **Arenas de San Pedro**, Spain
135 B 21 **Arendal**, Norway
133 H 16 **Arendonk**, Belgium
147 E 23 **Areopoli**, Greece
107 G 19 **Arequipa**, Peru
107 F 20 **Arequipa**, Peru ▣
140 G 11 **Arezzo**, Italy
147 F 17 **Argalasti**, Greece
184 L 6 **Argan**, China
131 O 7 **Arganda**, Spain
129 N 4 **Argentan**, France
110 J 11 **Argentina**, South America □
110 J 9 **Argentina**, Argentina
43 F 19 **Argentine Abyssal Plain**, Atlantic Ocean ◇
43 G 18 **Argentine Basin**, Atlantic Ocean ◇
177 S 9 **Arghandab**, Afghanistan ∿
159 Q 9 **Argolikos Basin**, Mediterranean Sea ◇
147 E 21 **Argolikos Kolpos**, Greece ≈
147 E 21 **Argos**, Greece
147 C 14 **Argos Orestiko**, Greece
147 B 19 **Argostoli**, Greece
186 G 6 **Argun'**, China ∿
215 P 10 **Argungu**, Nigeria
87 T 12 **Argyle**, Nova Scotia, Canada
185 P 3 **Arhangay**, Mongolia ▣
135 C 24 **Århus**, Denmark
181 L 18 **Ari Atoll**, Maldives 🏝
193 Q 8 **Ariaga**, Indonesia 🏝
218 J 12 **Ariamsvlei**, Namibia
113 B 15 **Arias**, Argentina
104 K 11 **Arica**, Colombia
106 D 9 **Arica**, Peru
110 F 2 **Arica**, Chile
199 G 19 **Arida**, Japan
172 I 3 **Arīḩā**, Syria
144 K 13 **Arilje**, Serbia and Montenegro
109 G 14 **Arinos**, Brazil ∿
108 F 12 **Aripuanã**, Brazil ∿
108 E 13 **Ariquemes**, Brazil
105 N 4 **Arismendi**, Venezuela
181 K 18 **Ariyaddu Channel**, Maldives ≈
131 Q 5 **Ariza**, Spain
74 H 11 **Arizona**, U.S.A. ▣
135 E 20 **Årjäng**, Sweden
134 H 12 **Arjeplog**, Sweden
157 O 5 **Arkadak**, Russian Federation
69 U 12 **Arkadelphia**, Arkansas, U.S.A.
179 Q 5 **Arkalyk**, Kazakhstan
69 T 11 **Arkansas**, U.S.A. ▣
69 O 8 **Arkansas**, U.S.A., U.S.A. ∿
69 N 7 **Arkansas City**, Kansas, U.S.A.
154 K 6 **Arkhangel'sk**, Russian Federation
154 L 7 **Arkhangel'skaya Oblast'**, Russian Federation ▣
153 P 6 **Arkhipelag Nordenshel'da**, Russian Federation 🏝
147 F 18 **Arkitsa**, Greece
125 F 19 **Arklow**, Republic of Ireland
129 T 14 **Arles**, France
61 U 3 **Arlington**, District of Columbia, U.S.A.
67 O 9 **Arlington**, South Dakota, U.S.A.
71 Q 6 **Arlington**, Texas, U.S.A.
215 Q 6 **Arlit**, Niger
133 K 25 **Arlon**, Belgium
230 G 11 **Armadale**, Western Australia, Australia
125 E 16 **Armagh**, United Kingdom
212 F 11 **Armant**, Egypt
147 M 26 **Armathia**, Greece 🏝
156 M 12 **Armavir**, Russian Federation
104 H 7 **Armenia**, Colombia
171 T 8 **Armenia**, Asia □
231 V 10 **Armidale**, New South Wales, Australia
73 Q 4 **Armington**, Montana, U.S.A.
84 L 10 **Armstrong**, Ontario, Canada
147 G 14 **Arnaia**, Greece
85 R 5 **Arnaud**, Québec, Canada ∿
133 D 15 **Arnemuiden**, Netherlands
68 J 9 **Arnett**, Oklahoma, U.S.A.
132 K 13 **Arnhem**, Netherlands
231 N 1 **Arnhem Land**, Northern Territory, Australia ◇
146 D 13 **Arnissa**, Greece
237 Z 3 **Arno**, Marshall Islands 🏝
140 E 10 **Arno**, Italy ∿
134 I 6 **Arnøya**, Norway 🏝
137 I 17 **Arnstadt**, Germany
218 K 11 **Aroab**, Namibia
84 M 11 **Aroland**, Ontario, Canada
213 H 16 **Aroma**, Sudan
42 M 12 **Arona**, Canary Islands
140 C 6 **Arona**, Italy
236 F 3 **Arorae**, Kiribati 🏝
197 J 14 **Aroroy**, Philippines
138 I 8 **Arosa**, Switzerland
214 D 10 **Arquipélago dos Bijagós**, Guinea-Bissau 🏝
124 G 13 **Arran**, United Kingdom 🏝
129 Q 2 **Arras**, France
129 N 15 **Arreau**, France
42 O 11 **Arrecife**, Canary Islands
113 C 15 **Arrecifes**, Argentina
89 P 10 **Arriaga**, Mexico
89 V 14 **Arriaga**, Mexico

Country ▣ Internal administrative region: State/Province/Territory/Dependent territory 🏛 Capital city ⛰ Mountain range/Undersea ridge ▲ Mountain peak/Volcano/Seamount ◇ Geographic feature ▶ Headland/Point/Cape/Peninsula 🏜 Desert 🏝 Island/Island group ⁙ Antarctic base ◎ Ocean 🌊 Sea ≈ Bay/Gulf/Channel/Strait 💧 Lake ⚑ Salt pan/Dry/Intermittent lake ∿ River

130	M 1	**Arriondas**, Spain
113	G 14	**Arroio Grande**, Brazil
77	H 23	**Arroyo Grande**, California, U.S.A.
135	C 23	**Års**, Denmark
157	S 1	**Arsk**, Russian Federation
147	C 17	**Arta**, Greece
131	Z 8	**Artà**, Spain
171	U 9	**Artashat**, Armenia
89	O 13	**Arteaga**, Mexico
92	G 4	**Artemisa**, Cuba
151	X 6	**Artemivs'k**, Ukraine
141	H 14	**Artena**, Italy
137	J 16	**Artern**, Germany
131	V 4	**Artesa de Segre**, Spain
75	S 13	**Artesia**, New Mexico, U.S.A.
66	I 13	**Arthur**, Nebraska, U.S.A.
233	G 19	**Arthur's Pass**, New Zealand
82	C 10	**Artic Red**, Northwest Territories, Canada ∿
112	E 12	**Artigas**, Uruguay
112	E 12	**Artigas**, Uruguay ▣
171	T 8	**Art'ik**, Armenia
151	O 10	**Artsyz**, Ukraine
171	Q 7	**Artvin**, Turkey
217	R 6	**Aru**, Democratic Republic of Congo
217	R 6	**Arua**, Uganda
109	I 15	**Aruanã**, Brazil
93	R 12	**Aruba**, The Netherlands, The Netherlands ▣
108	E 11	**Arumã**, Brazil
183	R 9	**Arun**, Nepal ∿
183	X 8	**Arunachal Pradesh**, India ▣
127	V 13	**Arundel**, United Kingdom
217	V 10	**Arusha**, Tanzania ▣
217	V 10	**Arusha**, Tanzania
75	R 4	**Arvada**, Colorado, U.S.A.
185	P 4	**Arvayheer**, Mongolia
82	N 11	**Arviat**, Nunavut, Canada
84	L 4	**Arviat**, Nunavut, Canada
134	I 12	**Arvidsjaur**, Sweden
135	E 20	**Arvika**, Sweden
193	R 14	**Arwala**, Indonesia
186	G 10	**Arxan**, China
179	R 11	**Arys'**, Kazakhstan
141	C 15	**Arzachena**, Italy
157	O 1	**Arzamas**, Russian Federation
210	L 6	**Arzew**, Algeria
157	O 12	**Arzgir**, Russian Federation
172	J 3	**As Sa'an**, Syria
172	M 3	**As Sabkhah**, Syria
172	G 11	**Aş Şafi**, Jordan
173	N 1	**Aş Şafiḩ**, Syria
172	J 2	**As Safīrah**, Syria
175	R 6	**As Salamiyah**, Saudi Arabia
173	U 12	**As Salmān**, Iraq
172	G 9	**As Salţ**, Jordan
173	V 10	**As Samāwah**, Iraq
172	H 7	**Aş Şanamayn**, Syria
174	J 3	**Aş Şawrah**, Saudi Arabia
173	O 5	**As Sayyāl**, Syria
211	V 8	**As Sidrah**, Libya
175	R 3	**Aş Şubayhīyah**, Kuwait
175	S 13	**As Sufāl**, Yemen
172	L 4	**As Sukhnah**, Syria
173	U 3	**As Sulaymānīyah**, Iraq
175	Q 9	**As Sulayyil**, Saudi Arabia
211	U 8	**As Sulţān**, Libya
175	O 8	**As Sūq**, Saudi Arabia
173	O 3	**Aş Şuwār**, Syria
172	H 8	**As Suwaydā'**, Syria
173	T 8	**As Suwayrah**, Iraq
176	G 6	**Asadābād**, Iran
177	O 6	**Asadābād**, Iran
177	V 7	**Asadābād**, Afghanistan
171	V 8	**Asaği**, Azerbaijan
198	K 4	**Asahi-dake**, Japan ▲
198	K 4	**Asahikawa**, Japan
176	H 4	**Asālem**, Iran
183	R 13	**Asansol**, India
213	J 19	**Āsayita**, Ethiopia
58	J 13	**Asbury Park**, New Jersey, U.S.A.
43	K 25	**Ascension**, U.K. ▣
88	L 3	**Ascensión**, Mexico
137	F 19	**Aschaffenburg**, Germany
140	I 12	**Ascoli Piceno**, Italy
141	L 15	**Ascoli Satriano**, Italy
213	I 21	**Āsela**, Ethiopia
135	H 14	**Åsele**, Sweden
146	I 10	**Asenovgrad**, Bulgaria
134	B 10	**Ásgarður**, Iceland
69	W 9	**Ash Flat**, Arkansas, U.S.A.
74	J 10	**Ash Fork**, Arizona, U.S.A.
173	S 11	**Ash Shabakah**, Iraq
173	O 2	**Ash Shaddādah**, Syria
175	X 5	**Ash Sha'm**, United Arab Emirates
173	V 12	**Ash Shāmīyah**, Iraq ◇
173	U 10	**Ash Shanāfīyah**, Iraq
175	P 6	**Ash Sha'rā'**, Saudi Arabia
175	R 11	**Ash Sharawrah**, Saudi Arabia
173	S 3	**Ash Sharqāţ**, Iraq
173	W 10	**Ash Shaṭrah**, Iraq
172	G 11	**Ash Shawbak**, Jordan
175	P 14	**Ash Shaykh 'Uthman**, Yemen
175	T 13	**Ash Shiḩr**, Yemen
175	X 5	**Ash Şhināş**, Oman
175	P 3	**Ash Shu'bah**, Saudi Arabia
175	N 11	**Ash Shuqayq**, Saudi Arabia
211	T 9	**Ash Shuwayrif**, Libya
175	Q 5	**Asharat**, Saudi Arabia
127	S 5	**Ashbourne**, United Kingdom
233	G 21	**Ashburton**, New Zealand
127	S 6	**Ashby de la Zouch**, United Kingdom
172	E 9	**Ashdod**, Israel
69	S 13	**Ashdown**, Arkansas, U.S.A.
61	Q 9	**Asheboro**, North Carolina, U.S.A.
69	O 11	**Asher**, Oklahoma, U.S.A.
60	M 9	**Asheville**, North Carolina, U.S.A.
127	Y 12	**Ashford**, United Kingdom
178	L 14	**Ashgabat**, Turkmenistan 🏛
198	K 5	**Ashibetsu**, Japan
199	J 15	**Ashikaga**, Japan
198	K 10	**Ashiro**, Japan
199	E 22	**Ashizuri-misaki**, Japan ▶
59	R 1	**Ashland**, Maine, U.S.A.
60	L 4	**Ashland**, Kentucky, U.S.A.
64	E 8	**Ashland**, Wisconsin, U.S.A.
65	N 17	**Ashland**, Ohio, U.S.A.
68	J 7	**Ashland**, Kansas, U.S.A.
77	G 14	**Ashland**, Oregon, U.S.A.
66	L 6	**Ashley**, North Dakota, U.S.A.
149	H 16	**Ashmyany**, Belarus
198	L 5	**Ashoro**, Japan
172	E 10	**Ashqelon**, Israel
65	O 15	**Ashtabula**, Ohio, U.S.A.
171	T 8	**Ashtarak**, Armenia
73	Q 10	**Ashton**, Idaho, U.S.A.
197	J 15	**Asid Gulf**, Philippines ≈
181	F 17	**Asifabad**, India
181	I 17	**Asika**, India
210	I 6	**Asilah**, Morocco
152	M 12	**Asino**, Russian Federation
149	K 18	**Asipovichy**, Belarus
171	P 9	**Aşkale**, Turkey
127	T 3	**Askern**, United Kingdom
135	D 20	**Askim**, Norway
155	T 14	**Askino**, Russian Federation
135	A 18	**Askøy**, Norway 🏝
176	G 2	**Aşlāndūz**, Iran
213	I 17	**Asmara**, Eritrea 🏛
135	F 24	**Åsnen**, Sweden 💧
215	X 9	**Asnet**, Chad
199	C 22	**Aso-san**, Japan ▲
147	F 23	**Asopos**, Greece
213	G 20	**Āsosa**, Ethiopia
139	X 5	**Aspang-Markt**, Austria
75	P 5	**Aspen**, Colorado, U.S.A.
70	M 5	**Aspermont**, Texas, U.S.A.
213	K 18	**Assab**, Eritrea
214	G 7	**Assaba**, Mauritania ▣
183	V 10	**Assam**, India ▣
215	Q 6	**Assamakka**, Niger
61	X 5	**Assateague Island**, Virginia, U.S.A. 🏝
133	F 18	**Asse**, Belgium
132	M 7	**Assen**, Netherlands
133	I 21	**Assesse**, Belgium
84	H 10	**Assiniboine**, Manitoba, Canada ∿
112	I 6	**Assis**, Brazil
109	B 14	**Assis Brasil**, Brazil
140	H 12	**Assisi**, Italy
135	D 18	**Åsta**, Norway ∿
147	M 25	**Astakida**, Greece 🏝
147	C 18	**Astakos**, Greece
179	R 4	**Astana**, Kazakhstan 🏛
176	H 3	**Āstārā**, Iran
133	K 16	**Asten**, Netherlands
140	B 8	**Asti**, Italy
107	H 17	**Astillero**, Peru
127	T 4	**Aston**, United Kingdom
130	L 3	**Astorga**, Spain
76	F 8	**Astoria**, Oregon, U.S.A.
157	R 11	**Astrakhan'**, Russian Federation
151	V 9	**Astrakhanka**, Ukraine
157	R 10	**Astrakhanskaya Oblast'**, Russian Federation ▣
43	N 23	**Astrid Ridge**, Atlantic Ocean ⛰
234	D 4	**Astrolabe Bay**, Papua New Guinea ≈
147	E 21	**Astros**, Greece
149	F 18	**Astryna**, Belarus
130	L 1	**Asturias**, Spain ▣
147	L 23	**Astypalaia**, Greece 🏝
241	S 2	**Asuka**, Antarctica ⁙
236	A 5	**Asuncion**, Northern Mariana Islands 🏝
107	I 16	**Asunción**, Bolivia
109	G 20	**Asunción**, Paraguay 🏛
90	I 6	**Asunción Mita**, Guatemala
148	J 13	**Asvyeya**, Belarus
212	F 12	**Aswân**, Egypt
212	E 10	**Asyût**, Egypt
179	U 11	**At-Bashy**, Kyrgyzstan
172	G 11	**Aţ Ţafīlah**, Jordan
174	M 8	**Aţ Ţā'if**, Saudi Arabia
211	X 7	**At Tamīmī**, Libya
172	L 7	**Aţ Ţanf**, Syria
173	T 9	**Aţ Ţaqţaqānah**, Iraq
172	G 12	**Aţ Ţayyibah**, Jordan
173	N 3	**At Tibnī**, Syria
174	K 2	**Aţ Ţubayq**, Saudi Arabia ◇
175	O 14	**At Turbah**, Yemen
175	P 14	**At Turbah**, Yemen
236	H 11	**Ata**, Tonga 🏝
110	F 8	**Atacama**, Chile ▣
110	F 2	**Atacama Desert**, Chile ◇
236	J 6	**Atafu**, Tokelau Islands 🏝
215	N 12	**Atakpamé**, Togo
107	E 15	**Atalaya**, Peru
175	R 13	**'Ataq**, Yemen
214	G 5	**Atâr**, Mauritania
185	O 5	**Atas Bogd**, Mongolia ▲
179	S 6	**Atasu**, Kazakhstan
193	Q 15	**Atauro**, Indonesia 🏝
213	F 15	**Atbara**, Sudan
213	G 16	**Atbara**, Sudan ∿
179	Q 4	**Atbasar**, Kazakhstan
62	J 9	**Atchafalaya Bay**, Louisiana, U.S.A. ≈
69	Q 3	**Atchison**, Kansas, U.S.A.
133	E 20	**Ath**, Belgium
83	I 18	**Athabasca**, Alberta, Canada ∿
147	G 20	**Athens**, Greece 🏛
60	I 10	**Athens**, Tennessee, U.S.A.
63	U 2	**Athens**, Georgia, U.S.A.
65	N 19	**Athens**, Ohio, U.S.A.
71	R 6	**Athens**, Texas, U.S.A.
170	H 15	**Athiénou**, Cyprus
125	D 18	**Athlone**, Republic of Ireland
58	M 9	**Athol**, Massachusetts, U.S.A.
147	H 15	**Athos**, Greece ▲
215	X 9	**Ati**, Chad
107	E 19	**Atico**, Peru
213	C 21	**Atiedo**, Sudan
131	P 5	**Atienza**, Spain
84	K 11	**Atikokan**, Ontario, Canada
90	I 7	**Atiquizaya**, El Salvador
90	G 6	**Atitlán**, Guatemala
237	P 10	**Atiu**, Cook Islands 🏝
153	X 10	**Atka**, Russian Federation
78	G 14	**Atka**, Alaska, U.S.A.
78	G 14	**Atka Island**, Alaska, U.S.A. 🏝
157	P 5	**Atkarsk**, Russian Federation
193	T 11	**Atkri**, Indonesia
63	S 3	**Atlanta**, Georgia, U.S.A.
64	K 11	**Atlanta**, Michigan, U.S.A.
72	L 10	**Atlanta**, Idaho, U.S.A.
61	V 10	**Atlantic**, North Carolina, U.S.A.
67	R 13	**Atlantic**, Iowa, U.S.A.
58	J 15	**Atlantic City**, New Jersey, U.S.A.
38	J 14	**Atlantic–Indian–Antarctic Basin**, Southern Ocean ◇
43	K 20	**Atlantic–Indian Ridge**, Atlantic Ocean/Indian Ocean ⛰
42	G 10	**Atlantic Ocean** 🌊
104	H 2	**Atlantico**, Colombia ▣
42	F 9	**Atlantis Fracture Zone**, Atlantic Ocean ◇
210	H 9	**Atlas Mountains**, Morocco ⛰
210	L 7	**Atlas Saharien**, Algeria ⛰
83	B 15	**Atlin Lake**, British Columbia, Canada 💧
172	F 8	**'Atlit**, Israel
63	P 6	**Atmore**, Alabama, U.S.A.
107	J 22	**Atocha**, Bolivia
69	P 12	**Atoka**, Oklahoma, U.S.A.
191	N 17	**Atouat**, Laos ▲
176	M 4	**Atrak**, Iran ∿
199	K 16	**Atsugi**, Japan
198	J 12	**Atsumi**, Japan
199	I 18	**Atsumi**, Japan
198	J 5	**Atsuta**, Japan
191	N 18	**Attapu**, Laos
147	O 24	**Attavyros**, Greece ▲
84	M 10	**Attawapiskat**, Ontario, Canada ∿
85	O 9	**Attawapiskat**, Ontario, Canada
84	L 9	**Attawapiskat Lake**, Ontario, Canada 💧
139	R 5	**Attersee**, Austria 💧
133	K 25	**Attert**, Belgium
58	D 8	**Attica**, New York, U.S.A.
65	H 18	**Attica**, Indiana, U.S.A.
147	G 22	**Attiki**, Greece ▣
127	Y 7	**Attleborough**, United Kingdom
78	B 11	**Attu Island**, Alaska, U.S.A. 🏝
175	S 13	**Atūd**, Yemen
111	H 14	**Atuel**, Argentina ∿
178	I 7	**Atyrau**, Kazakhstan ▣
178	I 7	**Atyrau**, Kazakhstan
64	L 12	**Au Sable Point**, Michigan, U.S.A. ▶
234	B 2	**Aua Island**, Papua New Guinea 🏝
133	K 26	**Aubange**, Belgium
129	S 12	**Aubenas**, France
129	Q 7	**Aubigny-sur-Nère**, France
129	Q 12	**Aubin**, France
58	G 8	**Auburn**, New York, U.S.A.
59	N 10	**Auburn**, Massachusetts, U.S.A.
63	R 4	**Auburn**, Alabama, U.S.A.
65	E 19	**Auburn**, Illinois, U.S.A.
67	Q 15	**Auburn**, Nebraska, U.S.A.
76	G 7	**Auburn**, Washington, U.S.A.
77	H 18	**Auburn**, California, U.S.A.
129	Q 9	**Aubusson**, France
148	D 12	**Auce**, Latvia
129	N 14	**Auch**, France
232	K 8	**Auckland**, New Zealand
232	J 8	**Auckland**, New Zealand ▣
41	O 13	**Auckland Islands**, New Zealand 🏝
128	H 5	**Audierne**, France
213	J 22	**Audo Range**, Ethiopia ⛰
137	L 18	**Aue**, Germany
137	L 18	**Auerbach**, Germany
231	T 7	**Augathella**, Queensland, Australia
137	I 24	**Augsburg**, Germany
148	H 13	**Augšzemes Augstiene**, Latvia ⛰
230	F 12	**Augusta**, Western Australia, Australia
141	L 23	**Augusta**, Italy
59	P 6	**Augusta**, Maine, U.S.A.
63	V 3	**Augusta**, Georgia, U.S.A.
64	D 11	**Augusta**, Wisconsin, U.S.A.
65	D 18	**Augusta**, Illinois, U.S.A.
73	P 4	**Augusta**, Montana, U.S.A.
110	G 6	**Augusta Victoria**, Chile
142	N 9	**Augustów**, Poland
234	M 6	**Auki**, Solomon Islands
75	R 2	**Ault**, Colorado, U.S.A.
215	P 11	**Auna**, Nigeria
85	S 6	**Aupaluk**, Québec, Canada
193	R 12	**Auponhia**, Indonesia
237	Z 3	**Aur**, Marshall Islands 🏝
192	F 9	**Aur**, Malaysia 🏝
64	G 8	**Aura**, Michigan, U.S.A.
182	L 10	**Auraiya**, India
183	P 12	**Aurangabad**, India
128	J 6	**Auray**, France
136	D 10	**Aurich**, Germany
129	Q 11	**Aurillac**, France
135	B 18	**Aurlandsvangen**, Norway
196	H 8	**Aurora**, Philippines
65	G 16	**Aurora**, Illinois, U.S.A.
75	R 4	**Aurora**, Colorado, U.S.A.
108	K 10	**Aurora do Pará**, Brazil
231	R 2	**Aurukun**, Queensland, Australia
218	I 11	**Aus**, Namibia
67	T 10	**Austin**, Minnesota, U.S.A.
71	P 9	**Austin**, Texas, U.S.A.
77	L 17	**Austin**, Nevada, U.S.A.
41	T 10	**Austral Fracture Zone**, Pacific Ocean ◇
41	S 10	**Austral Islands**, French Polynesia 🏝
231	N 6	**Australia**, Oceania □
231	U 12	**Australian Capital Territory**, Australia ▣
139	P 7	**Austria**, Europe □
134	G 9	**Austvågøy**, Norway 🏝
108	F 11	**Autazes**, Brazil
89	N 11	**Autlán**, Mexico
129	S 8	**Autun**, France
129	Q 10	**Auvergne**, France ▣
129	R 6	**Auxerre**, France
105	R 6	**Auyan Tepuí**, Venezuela ▲
69	U 7	**Ava**, Missouri, U.S.A.
129	S 7	**Avallon**, France
58	I 15	**Avalon**, New Jersey, U.S.A.
85	Z 10	**Avalon Peninsula**, Newfoundland and Labrador, Canada ▶
112	J 7	**Avaré**, Brazil
237	N 11	**Avarua**, Cook Islands 🏛
127	R 11	**Avebury**, United Kingdom
108	H 11	**Aveiro**, Brazil
130	H 5	**Aveiro**, Portugal ▣
130	H 6	**Aveiro**, Portugal
141	K 16	**Avellino**, Italy
141	J 16	**Aversa**, Italy
72	K 4	**Avery**, Idaho, U.S.A.
42	E 12	**Aves Ridge**, Atlantic Ocean ⛰
129	S 2	**Avesnes-sur-Helpe**, France
135	G 19	**Avesta**, Sweden
110	L 7	**Aviá Terai**, Argentina
112	C 10	**Avia Teray**, Argentina
124	H 10	**Aviemore**, United Kingdom
129	T 13	**Avignon**, France
131	N 6	**Ávila**, Spain
130	L 1	**Avilés**, Spain
148	I 6	**Avinurme**, Estonia
147	G 19	**Avlida**, Greece
141	K 23	**Avola**, Italy
127	R 9	**Avon**, United Kingdom ∿
58	E 8	**Avon**, New York, U.S.A.
63	W 11	**Avon Park**, Florida, U.S.A.
74	I 12	**Avondale**, Arizona, U.S.A.
128	L 4	**Avranches**, France
150	I 11	**Avrig**, Romania
213	L 24	**Aw Dheegle**, Somalia
198	J 12	**Awa-shima**, Japan 🏝
199	G 19	**Awaji-shima**, Japan 🏝
232	K 11	**Awakino**, New Zealand
175	T 5	**Awālī**, Bahrain
232	I 5	**Awanui**, New Zealand
213	L 21	**Āwarē**, Ethiopia
232	J 6	**Awarua**, New Zealand
233	B 21	**Awarua Point**, New Zealand ▶
213	I 21	**Āwasa**, Ethiopia
213	J 20	**Āwash**, Ethiopia
213	J 19	**Āwash**, Ethiopia ∿
233	I 17	**Awatere**, New Zealand
211	S 11	**Awbārī**, Libya
213	C 20	**Aweil**, Sudan
63	P 5	**Awin**, Alabama, U.S.A.
211	X 9	**Awjilah**, Libya
210	C 13	**Awserd**, Western Sahara
81	O 2	**Axel Heiberg Island**, Nunavut, Canada 🏝
146	E 13	**Axios**, Greece ∿
127	O 13	**Axminster**, United Kingdom
107	E 17	**Ayacucho**, Peru
107	E 18	**Ayacucho**, Peru ▣
113	D 18	**Ayacucho**, Argentina
179	X 6	**Ayagoz**, Kazakhstan
184	L 7	**Ayakkum Hu**, China 💧
130	I 12	**Ayamonte**, Spain
153	V 12	**Ayan**, Russian Federation
170	J 7	**Ayancik**, Turkey
187	K 18	**Ayang**, North Korea
105	T 6	**Ayanganna Mountain**, Guyana ▲
215	R 12	**Ayangba**, Nigeria
107	G 18	**Ayaviri**, Peru
177	T 6	**Āybak**, Afghanistan
151	Y 5	**Aydar**, Ukraine ∿
170	C 11	**Aydin**, Turkey
170	B 11	**Aydin Dağlari**, Turkey
213	J 19	**Āyelu Terara**, Ethiopia
194	E 10	**Ayer Hitam**, Malaysia
131	S 3	**Ayerbe**, Spain
153	R 10	**Aykhal**, Russian Federation
233	H 20	**Aylesbury**, New Zealand
127	U 9	**Aylesbury**, United Kingdom
131	P 5	**Ayllón**, Spain
82	J 10	**Aylmer Lake**, Northwest Territories, Canada 💧
127	Z 6	**Aylsham**, United Kingdom
179	R 13	**Ayní**, Tajikistan
213	E 21	**Ayod**, Sudan
131	S 9	**Ayora**, Spain
215	N 8	**Ayorou**, Niger
214	H 7	**'Ayoûn el 'Atroûs**, Mauritania
231	U 5	**Ayr**, Queensland, Australia
125	G 14	**Ayr**, United Kingdom
170	I 12	**Ayranci**, Turkey
179	N 8	**Ayteke Bi**, Kazakhstan
146	M 9	**Aytos**, Bulgaria
175	W 11	**Ayun**, Oman
191	H 18	**Ayutthaya**, Thailand
170	A 9	**Ayvacik**, Turkey
170	B 9	**Ayvalik**, Turkey
172	H 6	**Az Zabadānī**, Syria
172	H 9	**Az Zarqā'**, Jordan
211	S 7	**Az Zāwīyah**, Libya
175	O 13	**Az Zaydīyah**, Yemen
175	P 5	**Az Zilfī**, Saudi Arabia
211	R 8	**Az Zintān**, Libya
173	Z 12	**Az Zubayr**, Iraq
175	O 12	**Az Zuhrah**, Yemen
175	O 14	**Az Zuqur**, Yemen 🏝
91	N 6	**Azacualpa**, Honduras
76	F 13	**Azalea**, Oregon, U.S.A.
183	O 11	**Azamgarh**, India
176	F 4	**Āzarbāyjān-e Gharbī**, Iran ▣
176	G 3	**Āzarbāyjān-e Sharqī**, Iran ▣
215	S 10	**Azare**, Nigeria
149	L 20	**Azarychy**, Belarus
172	J 1	**A'zāz**, Syria
210	G 7	**Azemmour**, Morocco
171	V 10	**Azerbaijan**, Asia □
213	H 18	**Āzezo**, Ethiopia
210	H 8	**Azilal**, Morocco
177	N 11	**'Azīzābād**, Iran

□ Country ▣ Internal administrative region: State/Province/Territory/Dependent territory 🏛 Capital city ⛰ Mountain range/Undersea ridge ▲ Mountain peak/Volcano/Seamount ◇ Geographic feature ▶ Headland/Point/Cape/Peninsula ◭ Desert 🏝 Island/Island group ⁙ Antarctic base 🌊 Ocean ◗ Sea ≈ Bay/Gulf/Channel/Strait 💧 Lake ⊟ Salt pan/Dry/Intermittent lake ∿ R

O 1	Azores, Portugal [■]
J 8	Azores-Biscay Rise, Atlantic Ocean [ridge]
L 10	Azov, Russian Federation
I 9	Azraq ash Shīshān, Jordan
I 7	Azrou, Morocco
H 13	Aztec, Arizona, U.S.A.
O 8	Aztec, New Mexico, U.S.A.
Q 8	Azua, Dominican Republic
L 10	Azuaga, Spain
B 10	Azuay, Ecuador [■]
C 17	Azul, Argentina
E 5	Azzeffâl, Mauritania [mtn range]

R 9	B. Everett Jordan Reservoir, North Carolina, U.S.A. [lake]
N 19	Bâ Kêv, Cambodia
P 15	Baa, Indonesia
H 5	Ba'albek, Lebanon
G 6	Baaqline, Lebanon
L 24	Baardheere, Somalia
K 17	Bāb al Mandab, Africa/Asia [sea]
G 7	Baba Burnu, Turkey [headland]
A 9	Baba Burun, Turkey [headland]
N 12	Babadag, Romania
X 7	Babadağ Dağl, Azerbaijan [peak]
L 14	Babadurmaz, Turkmenistan
B 7	Babaeski, Turkey
C 19	Babanusa, Sudan
T 14	Babar, Indonesia
U 10	Babati, Tanzania
I 11	Babayevo, Russian Federation
O 2	Babb, Montana, U.S.A.
N 14	Babbacombe Bay, United Kingdom
F 9	Babi Besar, Malaysia [island]
E 18	Babine Lake, British Columbia, Canada [lake]
U 12	Babo, Indonesia
J 5	Bābol, Iran
V 13	Babongo, Cameroon
K 15	Baboquivari Peak, Arizona, U.S.A. [peak]
G 4	Baboua, Central African Republic
L 19	Babruysk, Belarus
H 4	Babuyan, Philippines [island]
D 18	Babuyan, Philippines
G 5	Babuyan Channel, Philippines [channel]
H 4	Babuyan Islands, Philippines [island]
M 11	Băc Can, Vietnam
M 12	Băc Giang, Vietnam
L 10	Bac Lac, Vietnam
M 23	Bac Liêu, Vietnam
M 12	Băc Ninh, Vietnam
L 11	Băc Quang, Vietnam
N 21	Bacaadweyn, Somalia
L 11	Bacabal, Brazil
I 11	Bacajá, Brazil [river]
Z 12	Bacalar, Mexico
R 11	Bacan, Indonesia
F 6	Bacarra, Philippines
L 9	Bacău, Romania
V 5	Baccarat, France
K 7	Bach, Austria
D 19	Bacharach, Germany
K 1	Back, Nunavut, Canada [river]
J 9	Bačka Palanka, Serbia and Montenegro
J 8	Bačka Topola, Serbia and Montenegro
G 22	Backnang, Germany
J 17	Bacolod, Philippines
J 6	Bácum, Mexico
S 6	Bad Aussee, Austria
D 22	Bad Bergzabern, Germany
H 9	Bad Bramstedt, Germany
N 12	Bad Freienwalde, Germany
R 6	Bad Goisern, Austria
Q 7	Bad Hofgastein, Austria
E 14	Bad Iburg, Germany
R 5	Bad Ischl, Austria
S 8	Bad Kleinkirchheim, Austria

137	D 20	Bad Kreuznach, Germany
137	I 17	Bad Langensalza, Germany
139	T 3	Bad Leonfelden, Austria
137	H 21	Bad Mergentheim, Germany
137	H 19	Bad Neustadt an der Saale, Germany
136	H 10	Bad Oldesloe, Germany
139	X 8	Bad Radkersburg, Austria
137	L 25	Bad Reichenhall, Germany
137	H 17	Bad Salzungen, Germany
136	H 9	Bad Segeberg, Germany
139	U 7	Bad St Leonhard, Austria
137	J 25	Bad Tölz, Germany
137	G 25	Bad Waldsee, Germany
191	F 22	Bada, Myanmar [island]
181	D 22	Badagara, India
189	N 11	Badahe, China
185	O 7	Badain Jaran Desert, China [feature]
130	J 9	Badajoz, Spain
177	V 5	Badakhshān, Afghanistan [■]
175	N 1	Badanah, Saudi Arabia
180	F 9	Badarinath Peaks, India [peak]
183	W 11	Badarpur, India
87	X 8	Baddeck, Nova Scotia, Canada
177	R 12	Baddo, Pakistan [river]
139	X 4	Baden, Austria
137	E 22	Baden Baden, Germany
137	E 23	Baden-wurttemberg, Germany [■]
139	Q 7	Badgastein, Austria
177	Q 7	Bādghīs, Afghanistan [■]
132	H 11	Badhoevedorp, Netherlands
131	Z 7	Badia d'Alcúdia, Spain [bay]
131	X 8	Badia de Palma, Spain [bay]
177	U 15	Badin, Pakistan
66	G 6	Badlands, North Dakota, U.S.A. [feature]
196	F 6	Badoc, Philippines
189	R 6	Badong, China
215	N 12	Badou, Togo
174	L 6	Badr Ḩunayn, Saudi Arabia
173	W 7	Badrah, Iraq
182	L 6	Badrinath Peaks, India [peak]
231	R 1	Badu Island, Queensland, Australia [island]
181	G 25	Badulla, Sri Lanka
131	N 12	Baena, Spain
131	O 11	Baeza, Spain
214	E 10	Bafatá, Guinea-Bissau
45	O 9	Baffin Basin, Arctic Ocean [feature]
45	N 10	Baffin Bay, Arctic Ocean [feature]
85	Q 1	Baffin Island, Nunavut, Canada [island]
215	T 14	Bafia, Cameroon
215	T 14	Bafoussam, Cameroon
176	L 9	Bāfq, Iran
170	K 7	Bafra, Turkey
170	L 7	Bafra Burnu, Turkey [headland]
217	P 7	Bafwasende, Democratic Republic of Congo
196	G 8	Bagabag, Philippines
196	F 11	Bagac, Philippines
196	F 11	Bagac Bay, Philippines [bay]
91	O 11	Bagaces, Costa Rica
183	O 10	Bagaha, India
181	D 19	Bagalkot, India
217	W 11	Bagamoyo, Tanzania
197	N 21	Baganga, Philippines
218	K 7	Bagani, Namibia
197	J 22	Baganian Peninsula, Philippines [cape]
192	D 9	Bagansiapiapi, Indonesia
215	P 9	Bagaroua, Niger
216	J 10	Bagata, Democratic Republic of Congo
112	F 13	Bagé, Brazil
182	L 7	Bageshwar, India
73	V 15	Baggs, Wyoming, U.S.A.
126	M 12	Baggy Point, United Kingdom [headland]
177	O 6	Baghbaghū, Iran
173	T 7	Baghdad, Iraq [capital]
141	I 21	Bagheria, Italy

176	L 10	Bāghīn, Iran
177	T 6	Baghlān, Afghanistan [■]
177	U 6	Baghlān, Afghanistan
177	R 8	Baghrān, Afghanistan
183	O 9	Baglung, Nepal
197	I 17	Bago, Philippines
140	E 6	Bagolino, Italy
149	B 16	Bagrationovsk, Russian Federation
108	J 10	Bagre, Brazil
173	W 8	Bagsaya, Iraq
127	L 11	Bagshot, United Kingdom
106	B 12	Bagua, Peru
215	P 10	Bagudo, Nigeria
196	F 8	Baguio, Philippines
196	H 6	Baguio Point, Philippines [headland]
92	K 1	Bahamas, The, North America
183	R 13	Baharampur, India
212	D 9	Bahariya Oasis, Egypt [feature]
151	W 7	Bahatyr, Ukraine
194	D 9	Bahau, Malaysia
177	W 11	Bahawalnagar, Pakistan
170	L 13	Bahşşe, Turkey
109	M 14	Bahia, Brazil [■]
111	K 16	Bahía Anegada, Argentina [bay]
88	G 6	Bahía Asunción, Mexico [bay]
113	B 19	Bahía Blanca, Argentina [bay]
113	B 19	Bahía Blanca, Argentina
111	I 19	Bahía Bustamante, Argentina
111	I 19	Bahía Camarones, Argentina [bay]
89	Z 12	Bahía Chetumal, Mexico [bay]
90	J 4	Bahía de Amatique, Guatemala [bay]
106	B 7	Bahía de Ancón de Sardinas, Ecuador [bay]
88	G 6	Bahía de Ballenas, Mexico [bay]
88	M 11	Bahía de Banderas, Mexico [bay]
91	R 10	Bahía de Bluefields, Nicaragua [bay]
89	V 11	Bahía de Campeche, Mexico [bay]
106	A 9	Bahía de Caráquez, Ecuador [bay]
90	L 1	Bahía de Chetumal, Belize [bay]
111	E 26	Bahía de Cook, Chile [bay]
91	Q 14	Bahía de Coronado, Costa Rica [bay]
89	Z 11	Bahía de Espíritu Santo, Mexico [bay]
90	K 8	Bahía de Jiquilisco, El Salvador [bay]
89	Z 11	Bahía de la Ascensión, Mexico [bay]
88	I 8	Bahía de La Paz, Mexico [bay]
88	G 4	Bahía de los Ángeles, Mexico
106	A 9	Bahía de Mania, Ecuador [bay]
91	X 14	Bahía de Panamá, Panama [bay]
91	W 15	Bahía de Parita, Panama [bay]
89	P 13	Bahía de Petacalco, Mexico [bay]
93	R 7	Bahía de Samaná, Dominican Republic [bay]
91	R 10	Bahía de San Juan del Norte, Nicaragua [bay]
111	H 24	Bahía de San Sebastián, Argentina [bay]
106	A 9	Bahía de Santa Elena, Ecuador [bay]
88	K 7	Bahía de Santa María, Mexico [bay]
106	A 12	Bahía de Sechura, Peru [bay]
91	N 4	Bahía de Trujillo, Honduras [bay]
93	R 7	Bahía Escocesa, Dominican Republic [bay]
111	H 23	Bahía Grande, Argentina [bay]
88	I 4	Bahía Kino, Mexico
111	I 21	Bahía Laura, Argentina [bay]
104	G 7	Bahía Magdalena, Colombia [bay]

88	H 8	Bahía Magdalena, Mexico [bay]
111	I 26	Bahía Nassau, Chile [bay]
109	G 18	Bahía Negra, Paraguay
111	F 25	Bahía Otway, Chile [bay]
110	F 8	Bahía Salada, Chile [bay]
111	E 23	Bahía Salvación, Chile [bay]
113	E 16	Bahía Samborombón, Argentina [bay]
107	E 18	Bahía San Nicolás, Peru [bay]
88	G 5	Bahía Sebastián Vizcaíno, Mexico [bay]
88	F 5	Bahía Tortugas, Mexico
113	B 20	Bahía Unión, Argentina [bay]
213	H 19	Bahir Dar, Ethiopia
213	A 19	Bahr el Arab, Sudan [river]
213	D 20	Bahr el Ghazal, Sudan [river]
213	E 23	Bahr el Jebel, Sudan [■]
182	M 9	Bahraich, India
175	U 4	Bahrain, Asia [■]
177	P 14	Bahū Kālāt, Iran
149	M 15	Bahushewsk, Belarus
190	L 13	Bai Thuong, Vietnam
151	N 12	Baia, Romania
108	J 10	Baía de Marajó, Brazil [bay]
219	U 5	Baia de Memba, Mozambique [bay]
219	U 4	Baia de Pemba, Mozambique [bay]
108	L 10	Baía de São Marcos, Brazil [bay]
218	F 6	Baía dos Tigres, Angola
218	F 4	Baía Farta, Angola
150	I 8	Baia Mare, Romania
108	J 10	Baião, Brazil
176	L 8	Baiazeh, Iran
215	W 12	Baïbokoum, Chad
186	H 11	Baicheng, China
150	K 12	Băicoi, Romania
87	Q 5	Baie-Comeau, Québec, Canada
128	H 6	Baie de Audierne, France [bay]
128	K 7	Baie de Bourgneuf, France [bay]
128	H 5	Baie de Douarnenez, France [bay]
128	M 3	Baie de Seine, France [bay]
128	J 4	Baie de St-Brieuc, France [bay]
87	N 7	Baie-St-Paul, Québec, Canada
87	R 5	Baie-Trinité, Québec, Canada
85	X 9	Baie Verte, Newfoundland and Labrador, Canada
187	M 14	Baihe, China
189	R 5	Baihe, China
186	G 10	Bailang, China
150	K 10	Băile Tuşnad, Romania
131	O 11	Bailén, Spain
108	J 9	Bailique, Brazil
133	J 22	Baillonville, Belgium
218	H 4	Bailundo, Angola
188	K 4	Baima, China
234	C 5	Baimuru, Papua New Guinea
63	S 6	Bainbridge, Georgia, U.S.A.
193	O 15	Baing, Indonesia
186	K 9	Baiquan, China
172	I 11	Bā'ir, Jordan
184	I 8	Bairab Co, China [lake]
183	Q 10	Bairagnia, India
79	O 5	Baird Mountains, Alaska, U.S.A. [mtn range]
236	D 2	Bairiki, Kiribati [capital]
186	F 13	Bairin Qiao, China
186	F 13	Bairin Zuoqi, China
179	Q 11	Bairkum, Kazakhstan
231	T 13	Bairnsdale, Victoria, Australia
189	O 7	Baisha, China
187	K 14	Baishan, China
187	L 14	Baishan, China
182	M 8	Baitadi, Nepal
188	I 4	Baitang, China
237	U 1	Baiti, Nauru
189	U 1	Baixiang, China

218	J 6	Baixo-Longa, Angola
188	J 5	Baiyü, China
213	F 15	Baiyuda Desert, Sudan [feature]
183	S 14	Baj Baj, India
143	I 25	Baja, Hungary
88	F 2	Baja California, Mexico [headland]
88	F 4	Baja California Norte, Mexico
88	G 7	Baja California Sur, Mexico [■]
182	M 8	Bajang, Nepal
192	G 9	Bajau, Indonesia [island]
177	N 7	Bajestān, Iran
177	O 5	Bājgīrān, Iran
175	O 13	Bājil, Yemen
91	S 14	Bajo Boquete, Panama
111	G 21	Bajo Caracoles, Argentina
215	T 11	Bajoga, Nigeria
157	U 1	Bakaly, Russian Federation
179	V 8	Bakanas, Kazakhstan
215	Z 8	Bakaoré, Chad
214	G 8	Bakel, Senegal
73	Z 4	Baker, Montana, U.S.A.
76	K 11	Baker, Oregon, U.S.A.
77	L 23	Baker, California, U.S.A.
41	P 7	Baker Island, U.S.A. [■]
84	K 3	Baker Lake, Nunavut, Canada [lake]
77	J 23	Bakersfield, California, U.S.A.
127	S 4	Bakewell, United Kingdom
178	L 13	Bakhardok, Turkmenistan
151	T 12	Bakhcyisaray, Ukraine
178	K 13	Bakherden, Turkmenistan
151	S 2	Bakhmach, Ukraine
153	N 10	Bakhta, Russian Federation
183	Q 11	Bakhtiyarpur, India
179	Y 7	Bakhty, Kazakhstan
170	D 7	Bakirköy, Turkey
146	O 13	Bakiröy, Turkey
134	D 10	Bakkaflói, Iceland [bay]
182	H 5	Bakloh, India
213	H 20	Bako, Ethiopia
214	I 11	Bako, Côte d'Ivoire
143	G 24	Bakony, Hungary [mtn range]
213	L 23	Bakool, Somalia [■]
234	H 4	Bakop, Papua New Guinea
216	M 4	Bakouma, Central African Republic
157	O 13	Baksan, Russian Federation
171	Z 8	Baku, Azerbaijan [■]
171	S 7	Bakuriani, Georgia
240	K 10	Bakutis Coast, Antarctica [feature]
127	N 5	Bala, United Kingdom
170	H 10	Balâ, Turkey
177	Q 6	Bālā Morghāb, Afghanistan
197	B 21	Balabac, Philippines
197	A 21	Balabac, Philippines [island]
197	A 21	Balabac Strait, Philippines [channel]
151	U 7	Balabyne, Ukraine
173	T 6	Balad, Iraq
173	U 6	Balad Rūz, Iraq
181	G 15	Balaghat, India
181	D 17	Balaghat Range, India [mtn range]
131	V 4	Balaguer, Spain
171	V 6	Balakän, Azerbaijan
151	T 13	Balaklava, Ukraine
151	W 5	Balakliya, Ukraine
157	R 5	Balakovo, Russian Federation
195	V 3	Balambangan, Malaysia [island]
196	F 11	Balanga, Philippines
181	H 16	Balangir, India
157	O 5	Balashov, Russian Federation
143	J 21	Balassagyarmat, Hungary
143	G 24	Balaton, Hungary [lake]
196	G 7	Balatong, Philippines
108	F 10	Balbina, Brazil
91	W 13	Balboa, Panama
125	F 17	Balbriggan, Republic of Ireland
113	D 18	Balcarce, Argentina
146	N 7	Balchik, Bulgaria

233	E 25	Balclutha, New Zealand
70	N 10	Balcones Escarpment, Texas, U.S.A. [mtn range]
61	T 12	Bald Head Island, North Carolina, U.S.A. [island]
69	W 10	Bald Knob, Arkansas, U.S.A.
63	W 7	Baldwin, Florida, U.S.A.
64	C 11	Baldwin, Wisconsin, U.S.A.
64	J 13	Baldwin, Michigan, U.S.A.
58	G 8	Baldwinsville, New York, U.S.A.
73	S 3	Baldy Mountain, Montana, U.S.A. [peak]
84	H 9	Baldy Mountain, Manitoba, Canada [peak]
74	M 12	Baldy Peak, Arizona, U.S.A. [peak]
158	E 8	Balearic Channel, Mediterranean Sea [sea]
131	V 9	Balearic Islands, Spain [island]
195	R 10	Baleh, Malaysia [river]
196	H 9	Baler, Philippines
196	H 9	Baler Bay, Philippines [bay]
181	K 16	Baleshwar, India
155	Q 13	Balezino, Russian Federation
184	K 5	Balguntay, China
175	S 14	Balḩaf, Yemen
180	C 13	Bali, India
192	L 14	Bali, Indonesia [island]
192	L 15	Bali, Indonesia [■]
192	K 14	Bali Sea, Indonesia [sea]
192	D 9	Balige, Indonesia
170	C 9	Balikesir, Turkey
172	L 2	Balīkh, Syria [river]
192	M 11	Balikpapan, Indonesia
197	E 25	Balimbing, Philippines
197	L 20	Balingasag, Philippines
137	F 24	Balingen, Germany
195	P 8	Balingian, Malaysia
197	L 19	Balingoan, Philippines
196	G 3	Balintang Channel, Philippines [channel]
216	M 5	Balitondo, Central African Republic
175	N 9	Baljurshī, Saudi Arabia
132	J 8	Balk, Netherlands
146	F 8	Balkan Mountains, Bulgaria [mtn range]
178	J 12	Balkanskiy Velayat, Turkmenistan
179	Q 3	Balkashino, Kazakhstan
177	T 5	Balkh, Afghanistan [■]
179	U 7	Balkhash, Kazakhstan
124	G 11	Ballachulish, United Kingdom
230	J 11	Balladonia, Western Australia, Australia
125	C 17	Ballaghaderreen, Republic of Ireland
181	F 17	Ballalpur, India
125	G 14	Ballantrae, United Kingdom
231	R 13	Ballarat, Victoria, Australia
241	S 15	Balleny Islands, Antarctica [island]
231	W 9	Ballina, New South Wales, Australia
125	B 16	Ballina, Republic of Ireland
125	C 18	Ballinasloe, Republic of Ireland
70	M 7	Ballinger, Texas, U.S.A.
125	F 15	Ballymena, United Kingdom
125	C 16	Ballysadare, Republic of Ireland
111	G 20	Balmaceda, Chile
70	H 8	Balmorhea, Texas, U.S.A.
218	G 4	Balombo, Angola
180	H 13	Balotra, India
179	W 8	Balpyk Bi, Kazakhstan
183	N 9	Balrampur, India
231	R 11	Balranald, New South Wales, Australia
150	I 13	Balş, Romania
91	P 12	Balsa, Costa Rica [river]
106	C 13	Balsas, Peru
108	K 12	Balsas, Brazil
89	R 13	Balsas, Mexico [river]
138	E 7	Balsthal, Switzerland
151	O 7	Balta, Ukraine

Country [■] Internal administrative region: State/Province/Territory/Dependent territory   [⚓] Capital city   [▲▲] Mountain range   [▲] Mountain peak/Volcano/Seamount   [◇] Geographic feature   [►] Headland/Point/Cape/Peninsula   [▲] Desert   [⛬] Island/Island group   [⊞] Antarctic base   [◆] Ocean   [≈] Sea   [≈] Bay/Gulf/Channel/Strait   [↘] Lake   [↙] Salt pan/Dry/Intermittent lake   [↘] River

Balta Berilovac – Battle Creek

144 O 13 **Balta Berilovac**, Serbia and Montenegro
150 M 8 **Bălți**, Moldova
135 G 26 **Baltic Sea**, Europe
61 U 2 **Baltimore**, Maryland, U.S.A.
149 A 15 **Baltiysk**, Russian Federation
177 R 12 **Baluchistān**, Pakistan
197 J 15 **Balud**, Philippines
183 S 11 **Balurghat**, India
197 M 25 **Balut**, Philippines
148 I 10 **Balvi**, Latvia
179 V 10 **Balykchy**, Kyrgyzstan
178 I 7 **Balykshi**, Kazakhstan
177 N 11 **Bam**, Iran
215 U 10 **Bama**, Nigeria
189 P 11 **Bama**, China
231 R 1 **Bamaga**, Queensland, Australia
216 G 9 **Bambama**, Congo
218 K 6 **Bambangando**, Angola
216 K 4 **Bambari**, Central African Republic
137 I 20 **Bamberg**, Germany
61 O 14 **Bamberg**, South Carolina, U.S.A.
217 O 5 **Bambili**, Democratic Republic of Congo
216 I 5 **Bambio**, Central African Republic
213 G 19 **Bambudi**, Ethiopia
109 K 17 **Bambui**, Brazil
188 I 6 **Bamda**, China
215 S 13 **Bamenda**, Cameroon
83 F 22 **Bamfield**, British Columbia, Canada
178 K 13 **Bami**, Turkmenistan
177 T 7 **Bāmīān**, Afghanistan
177 T 7 **Bāmīān**, Afghanistan
186 J 13 **Bamiancheng**, China
216 K 3 **Bamingui**, Central African Republic
216 K 2 **Bamingui-Bangoran**, Central African Republic
191 K 20 **Bâmnak**, Cambodia
127 N 12 **Bampton**, United Kingdom
177 O 13 **Bampūr**, Iran
190 K 13 **Ban Ban**, Laos
190 I 12 **Ban Boun Tai**, Laos
191 I 17 **Ban Bua Chum**, Thailand
191 J 21 **Ban Hat Lek**, Thailand
190 H 13 **Ban Houayxay**, Laos
191 G 21 **Ban Huai Yang**, Thailand
191 H 17 **Ban Khao Sai**, Thailand
191 E 24 **Ban Khok Kloi**, Thailand
191 G 24 **Ban Na San**, Thailand
191 I 14 **Ban Nalè**, Laos
191 L 15 **Ban Napè**, Laos
191 H 15 **Ban Pak Pat**, Thailand
191 K 15 **Ban Phaeng**, Laos
191 J 17 **Ban Phai**, Thailand
191 M 17 **Ban Phon**, Laos
191 J 15 **Ban Phu**, Thailand
191 G 19 **Ban Pong**, Thailand
191 G 18 **Ban Rai**, Thailand
191 F 15 **Ban Tha Song Yang**, Thailand
191 J 15 **Ban Thabôk**, Laos
191 M 17 **Ban Tôp**, Laos
191 K 14 **Ban Vang-An**, Laos
191 M 18 **Ban Xepian**, Laos
213 M 24 **Banaadir**, Somalia
236 C 3 **Banaba**, Kiribati
217 N 7 **Banalia**, Democratic Republic of Congo
237 P 2 **Banana**, Kiribati
181 O 25 **Bananga**, India
146 M 13 **Banarli**, Turkey
180 D 13 **Banas**, India
196 G 8 **Banaue**, Philippines
170 E 10 **Banaz**, Turkey
184 M 10 **Banbar**, China
125 F 16 **Banbridge**, United Kingdom
127 S 8 **Banbury**, United Kingdom
89 Z 12 **Banco Chinchorro**, Mexico
92 G 10 **Banco Gorda**, Jamaica
197 D 21 **Bancoran**, Philippines
86 G 11 **Bancroft**, Ontario, Canada
215 U 12 **Banda**, Cameroon
217 P 5 **Banda**, Democratic Republic of Congo
182 L 11 **Banda**, India
192 B 8 **Banda Aceh**, Indonesia
39 V 5 **Banda Sea**, Indian Ocean
193 S 13 **Banda Sea**, Indonesia
193 T 13 **Bandaneira**, Indonesia
176 L 12 **Bandar-e 'Abbās**, Iran
176 H 4 **Bandar-e Anzalī**, Iran
176 G 9 **Bandar-e Emām Khomeynī**, Iran
176 K 13 **Bandar-e Lengeh**, Iran
176 J 13 **Bandar-e Moghūyeh**, Iran
192 G 13 **Bandar Lampung**, Indonesia
195 S 6 **Bandar Seri Begawan**, Brunei
130 I 3 **Bande**, Spain
110 K 9 **Bandera**, Argentina
71 N 10 **Bandera**, Texas, U.S.A.
182 H 3 **Bandipur**, India
170 C 8 **Bandirma**, Turkey
76 E 12 **Bandon**, Oregon, U.S.A.
216 J 10 **Bandundu**, Democratic Republic of Congo
216 I 10 **Bandundu**, Democratic Republic of Congo
192 H 14 **Bandung**, Indonesia
150 M 13 **Băneasa**, Romania
92 M 6 **Banes**, Cuba
124 I 9 **Banff**, United Kingdom
83 I 20 **Banff**, Alberta, Canada
216 K 11 **Banga**, Democratic Republic of Congo
197 L 23 **Banga**, Philippines
197 N 21 **Bangai Point**, Philippines
181 D 21 **Bangalore**, India
195 T 6 **Bangar**, Malaysia
216 M 5 **Bangassou**, Central African Republic
193 P 11 **Banggai**, Indonesia
195 W 3 **Banggi**, Malaysia
211 W 7 **Banghāzī**, Libya
192 G 11 **Bangka**, Indonesia
193 Q 10 **Bangka**, Indonesia
192 K 14 **Bangkalan**, Indonesia
192 D 10 **Bangkinang**, Indonesia
192 F 11 **Bangko**, Indonesia
191 I 19 **Bangkok**, Thailand
183 U 12 **Bangladesh**, Asia
126 M 4 **Bangor**, United Kingdom
59 R 5 **Bangor**, Maine, U.S.A.
196 F 7 **Bangued**, Philippines
216 J 5 **Bangui**, Central African Republic
196 F 5 **Bangui**, Philippines
216 I 6 **Bangui-Motaba**, Congo
217 P 7 **Banguru**, Democratic Republic of Congo
216 M 3 **Bani**, Central African Republic
196 E 10 **Bani Point**, Philippines
175 O 10 **Banī Thawr**, Saudi Arabia
211 S 8 **Banī Walīd**, Libya
216 H 5 **Bania**, Central African Republic
234 G 7 **Baniara**, Papua New Guinea
215 O 10 **Banikoara**, Benin
172 H 4 **Bāniyās**, Syria
144 G 10 **Banja Luka**, Bosnia and Herzegovina
195 V 7 **Banjaran Brassey**, Malaysia
195 U 7 **Banjaran Crocker**, Malaysia
195 N 11 **Banjaran Klingkang**, Malaysia
195 T 9 **Banjaran Tama Abu**, Malaysia
192 L 12 **Banjarmasin**, Indonesia
214 D 9 **Banjul**, Gambia
215 N 9 **Bankilaré**, Niger
215 T 13 **Bankim**, Cameroon
72 K 9 **Banks**, Idaho, U.S.A.
82 E 5 **Banks Island**, Northwest Territories, Canada
235 R 9 **Banks Islands**, Vanuatu
76 J 6 **Banks Lake**, Washington, U.S.A.
233 I 20 **Banks Peninsula**, New Zealand
183 R 13 **Bankura**, India
189 P 13 **Banli**, China
177 V 8 **Bannu**, Pakistan
189 N 9 **Banqiao**, China
143 J 20 **Banská Bystrica**, Slovakia
146 G 13 **Bansko**, Bulgaria
181 C 14 **Banswara**, India
193 O 13 **Bantaeng**, Indonesia
197 K 16 **Bantayan**, Philippines
197 J 16 **Bantayan**, Philippines
215 O 12 **Bantè**, Benin
125 A 21 **Bantry Bay**, Republic of Ireland
215 U 13 **Banyo**, Cameroon
192 K 14 **Banyuwangi**, Indonesia
241 W 13 **Banzare Coast**, Antarctica
39 O 13 **Banzare Seamount**, Indian Ocean
191 N 21 **Bao Lôc**, Vietnam
187 C 15 **Baochang**, China
187 A 17 **Baode**, China
187 E 17 **Baodi**, China
187 D 18 **Baoding**, China
189 P 3 **Baoji**, China
189 R 8 **Baojing**, China
186 M 11 **Baolin**, China
186 O 10 **Baoqing**, China
216 H 4 **Baoro**, Central African Republic
188 J 10 **Baoshan**, China
185 S 6 **Baotou**, China
189 V 5 **Baoyi**, China
189 X 4 **Baoying**, China
180 C 12 **Bap**, India
175 O 7 **Baqarah**, Saudi Arabia
173 U 6 **Ba'qūbah**, Iraq
145 I 17 **Bar**, Serbia and Montenegro
150 M 6 **Bar**, Ukraine
59 S 6 **Bar Harbor**, Maine, U.S.A.
129 T 4 **Bar-le-Duc**, France
213 E 17 **Bara**, Sudan
215 T 11 **Bara**, Nigeria
193 R 12 **Bara**, Indonesia
182 M 10 **Bara Banki**, India
213 L 25 **Baraawe**, Somalia
172 J 3 **Baradah**, Syria
113 C 15 **Baradero**, Argentina
93 Q 8 **Barahona**, Dominican Republic
181 I 15 **Barakot**, India
195 S 7 **Baram**, Malaysia
181 C 18 **Baramati**, India
182 H 3 **Baramula**, India
149 H 19 **Baranavichy**, Belarus
79 W 11 **Baranof Island**, Alaska, U.S.A.
133 J 22 **Baraque de Fraiture**, Belgium
193 P 15 **Barate**, Indonesia
109 L 18 **Barbacena**, Brazil
112 M 5 **Barbacena**, Brazil
93 Z 11 **Barbados**, North America
131 U 3 **Barbastro**, Spain
130 K 14 **Barbate**, Spain
81 P 1 **Barbeau Peak**, Nunavut, Canada
128 M 10 **Barbezieux-St-Hilaire**, France
104 J 6 **Barbosa**, Colombia
93 Y 8 **Barbuda**, Antigua and Barbuda
231 S 6 **Barcaldine**, Queensland, Australia
130 J 10 **Barcarrota**, Spain
105 P 3 **Barcelona**, Venezuela
131 X 5 **Barcelona**, Spain
108 E 10 **Barcelos**, Brazil
143 G 26 **Barcs**, Hungary
155 T 13 **Barda**, Russian Federation
215 W 5 **Bardai**, Chad
183 W 14 **Bardarban**, Bangladesh
134 C 11 **Bárðarbunga**, Iceland
110 G 13 **Bardas Blancas**, Argentina
183 S 13 **Barddhaman**, India
143 L 19 **Bardejov**, Slovakia
140 A 7 **Bardonecchia**, Italy
126 K 6 **Bardsey Island**, United Kingdom
126 K 6 **Bardsey Sound**, United Kingdom
125 G 19 **Bardsley Island**, United Kingdom
60 H 5 **Bardstown**, Kentucky, U.S.A.
182 L 9 **Bareilly**, India
45 T 10 **Barents Plain**, Arctic Ocean
134 N 5 **Barents Sea**, Europe
45 U 13 **Barents Trough**, Arctic Ocean
213 H 17 **Barentu**, Eritrea
195 T 8 **Bareo**, Malaysia
184 H 9 **Barga**, China
213 O 19 **Bargaal**, Somalia
181 I 16 **Bargarh**, India
127 Z 11 **Barham**, United Kingdom
213 O 19 **Bari**, Somalia
216 K 6 **Bari**, Democratic Republic of Congo
141 N 15 **Bari**, Italy
211 O 6 **Barika**, Algeria
177 W 7 **Barikoi**, Afghanistan
104 L 4 **Barinas**, Venezuela
104 L 4 **Barinas**, Venezuela
212 E 11 **Bârîs**, Egypt
183 U 14 **Barisal**, Bangladesh
183 V 14 **Barisal**, Bangladesh
192 L 11 **Barito**, Indonesia
175 Y 6 **Barkā**, Oman
188 L 5 **Barkam**, China
148 I 11 **Barkava**, Latvia
183 Q 12 **Barki Sariaya**, India
60 D 7 **Barkley Lake**, Kentucky, U.S.A.
219 O 13 **Barkly East**, Republic of South Africa
231 P 5 **Barkly Homestead Roadhouse**, Northern Territory, Australia
231 O 3 **Barkly Tableland**, Northern Territory, Australia
184 M 5 **Barkol**, China
150 M 10 **Bârlad**, Romania
141 M 15 **Barletta**, Italy
142 E 11 **Barlinek**, Poland
180 B 13 **Barmer**, India
126 M 6 **Barmouth**, United Kingdom
126 M 6 **Barmouth Bay**, United Kingdom
43 N 25 **Barn Long Point**, St Helena
152 M 13 **Barnaul**, Russian Federation
127 V 10 **Barnet**, United Kingdom
132 J 12 **Barneveld**, Netherlands
70 K 8 **Barnhart**, Texas, U.S.A.
127 S 3 **Barnsley**, United Kingdom
59 P 11 **Barnstable**, Massachusetts, U.S.A.
126 M 12 **Barnstaple**, United Kingdom
61 N 14 **Barnwell**, South Carolina, U.S.A.
104 L 3 **Barquisimeto**, Venezuela
109 L 14 **Barra**, Brazil
124 D 11 **Barra**, United Kingdom
108 G 12 **Barra de São Manuel**, Brazil
109 G 15 **Barra do Bugres**, Brazil
108 L 12 **Barra do Corda**, Brazil
109 I 16 **Barra do Garças**, Brazil
112 H 12 **Barra do Ribeiro**, Brazil
89 S 8 **Barra Jesús María**, Mexico
91 S 5 **Barra Kruta**, Honduras
42 F 11 **Barracuda Fracture Zone**, Atlantic Ocean
42 F 11 **Barracuda Ridge**, Atlantic Ocean
108 L 13 **Barragem de Sobradinho**, Brazil
109 J 17 **Barragen de São Simão**, Brazil
104 J 3 **Barranca**, Venezuela
107 C 15 **Barranca**, Peru
105 R 4 **Barrancas**, Venezuela
104 I 2 **Barranquilla**, Colombia
58 M 9 **Barre**, Massachusetts, U.S.A.
110 G 11 **Barreal**, Argentina
109 L 14 **Barreiras**, Brazil
108 E 12 **Barreirinha do Baeta**, Brazil
130 G 9 **Barreiro**, Portugal
181 O 21 **Barren Island**, India
112 K 5 **Barretos**, Brazil
86 E 12 **Barrie**, Ontario, Canada
87 T 12 **Barrington**, Nova Scotia, Canada
231 S 9 **Barringun**, New South Wales, Australia
125 E 19 **Barrow**, Republic of Ireland
79 O 2 **Barrow**, Alaska, U.S.A.
231 N 5 **Barrow Creek**, Northern Territory, Australia
127 O 1 **Barrow-in-Furness**, United Kingdom
230 E 6 **Barrow Island**, Western Australia, Australia
127 O 11 **Barry**, United Kingdom
86 H 10 **Barrys Bay**, Ontario, Canada
179 W 6 **Barshatas**, Kazakhstan
179 R 5 **Barshyn**, Kazakhstan
77 L 23 **Barstow**, California, U.S.A.
148 C 12 **Bārta**, Latvia
136 L 8 **Barth**, Germany
105 U 5 **Bartica**, Guyana
170 H 7 **Bartin**, Turkey
231 T 3 **Bartle Frere**, Queensland, Australia
69 P 8 **Bartlesville**, Oklahoma, U.S.A.
60 A 10 **Bartlett**, Tennessee, U.S.A.
66 M 13 **Bartlett**, Nebraska, U.S.A.
58 M 5 **Barton**, Vermont, U.S.A.
127 U 3 **Barton-upon-Humber**, United Kingdom
142 K 8 **Bartoszyce**, Poland
63 W 11 **Bartow**, Florida, U.S.A.
175 S 13 **Barūm**, Yemen
192 M 10 **Barung**, Indonesia
192 K 15 **Barung**, Indonesia
192 C 9 **Barus**, Indonesia
185 T 4 **Baruun Urt**, Mongolia
181 C 15 **Barwani**, India
143 F 14 **Barycz**, Poland
149 K 16 **Barysaw**, Belarus
157 Q 3 **Barysh**, Russian Federation
175 Z 7 **Barzamān**, Oman
216 H 11 **Bas-Congo**, Democratic Republic of Congo
179 P 14 **Basaga**, Turkmenistan
110 L 8 **Basail**, Argentina
77 J 19 **Basalt**, Nevada, U.S.A.
216 K 7 **Basankusu**, Democratic Republic of Congo
196 H 2 **Basco**, Philippines
137 D 26 **Basel**, Germany
138 D 6 **Basel**, Switzerland
157 O 4 **Bashmakovo**, Russian Federation
176 H 10 **Bāsht**, Iran
151 S 8 **Bashtanka**, Ukraine
197 H 23 **Basilan**, Philippines
197 H 23 **Basilan Strait**, Philippines
127 X 10 **Basildon**, United Kingdom
141 M 17 **Basilicata**, Italy
73 U 9 **Basin**, Wyoming, U.S.A.
127 T 11 **Basingstoke**, United Kingdom
183 T 14 **Basirhat**, India
171 T 11 **Başkale**, Turkey
216 M 7 **Basoko**, Democratic Republic of Congo
77 K 14 **Basque**, Oregon, U.S.A.
231 S 14 **Bass Strait**, Tasmania, Australia
140 G 6 **Bassano del Grappa**, Italy
215 N 11 **Bassar**, Togo
219 U 8 **Bassas da India**, France
216 L 4 **Basse-Kotto**, Central African Republic
128 L 4 **Basse-Normandie**, France
93 Y 9 **Basse-Terre**, Guadeloupe
191 C 16 **Bassein**, Myanmar
131 V 3 **Bassella**, Spain
93 X 8 **Basseterre**, St Kitts and Nevis
66 L 12 **Bassett**, Nebraska, U.S.A.
215 O 12 **Bassila**, Benin
215 Z 7 **Basso**, Chad
67 U 3 **Basswood Lake**, Minnesota, U.S.A.
176 K 12 **Bastak**, Iran
176 G 3 **Bastānābād**, Iran
183 N 10 **Basti**, India
129 Z 14 **Bastia**, France
133 K 23 **Bastogne**, Belgium
62 J 4 **Bastrop**, Louisiana, U.S.
71 Q 10 **Bastrop**, Texas, U.S.A.
215 S 15 **Bata**, Equatorial Guine
196 F 11 **Bataan Peninsula**, Philippines
196 F 6 **Batac**, Philippines
153 T 9 **Batagay**, Russian Federation
112 H 5 **Bataguassu**, Brazil
146 H 11 **Batak**, Bulgaria
192 L 13 **Batakan**, Indonesia
182 H 5 **Batala**, India
192 F 10 **Batam**, Indonesia
217 O 7 **Batama**, Democratic Republic of Congo
153 T 10 **Batamay**, Russian Federation
196 H 2 **Batan**, Philippines
196 K 13 **Batan**, Philippines
196 H 3 **Batan Islands**, Philippines
188 J 7 **Batang**, China
216 D 8 **Batanga**, Gabon
196 G 12 **Batangas**, Philippines
197 E 16 **Batas**, Philippines
58 D 8 **Batavia**, New York, U.S
39 S 8 **Batavia Seamount**, Indi Ocean
156 L 10 **Bataysk**, Russian Federation
197 H 16 **Batbatan**, Philippines
230 M 1 **Batchelor**, Northern Territory, Australia
191 J 20 **Bătdâmbâng**, Cambodi
231 U 12 **Batemans Bay**, New So Wales, Australia
61 N 12 **Batesburg**, South Carolina, U.S.A.
62 M 2 **Batesville**, Mississippi, U.S.A.
69 W 9 **Batesville**, Arkansas, U.S.A.
71 N 12 **Batesville**, Texas, U.S.A.
127 Q 11 **Bath**, United Kingdom
58 F 9 **Bath**, New York, U.S.A.
59 P 6 **Bath**, Maine, U.S.A.
87 R 9 **Bath**, New Brunswick, Canada
215 X 8 **Batha**, Chad
182 H 7 **Bathinda**, India
132 L 11 **Bathmen**, Netherlands
231 U 11 **Bathurst**, New South Wales, Australia
87 S 7 **Bathurst**, New Brunswic Canada
45 O 7 **Bathurst Island**, Canada
82 H 9 **Bathurst Inlet**, Nunavut, Canada
82 I 8 **Bathurst Inlet**, Nunavut, Canada
230 L 1 **Bathurst Island**, Northe Territory, Australia
81 O 3 **Bathurst Island**, Nunavu Canada
213 J 19 **Batī**, Ethiopia
170 E 13 **Bati Toroslar**, Turkey
171 Q 12 **Batman**, Turkey
211 O 6 **Batna**, Algeria
144 L 12 **Batočina**, Serbia and Montenegro
62 K 7 **Baton Rouge**, Louisiana, U.S.A.
182 H 4 **Batote**, India
215 V 14 **Batouri**, Cameroon
172 G 5 **Batroûn**, Lebanon
134 M 5 **Båtsfjord**, Norway
181 N 24 **Batti Malv**, India
181 G 24 **Batticaloa**, Sri Lanka
127 X 12 **Battle**, United Kingdom
65 J 15 **Battle Creek**, Michigan, U.S.A.

Country · Internal administrative region: State/Province/Territory/Dependent territory · Capital city · Mountain range/Undersea ridge · Mountain peak/Volcano/Seamount · Geographic feature · Headland/Point/Cape/Peninsula · Desert · Island/Island group · Antarctic base · Ocean · Sea · Bay/Gulf/Channel/Strait · Lake · Salt pan/Dry/Intermittent lake · F

Blakeney Point – Bounty Trough

Y 5 **Blakeney Point**, United Kingdom ▶
D 10 **Blake–Bahama Ridge**, Atlantic Ocean ⛰
Y 9 **Blanc-Sablon**, Newfoundland and Labrador, Canada
L 17 **Blanco**, Bolivia ∿
O 10 **Blanco**, Texas, U.S.A.
Q 13 **Blandford Forum**, United Kingdom
Y 4 **Blanes**, Spain
B 8 **Blangkejeren**, Indonesia
C 16 **Blankenberge**, Belgium
C 18 **Blankenheim**, Germany
R 5 **Blantyre**, Malawi
M 11 **Blaye**, France
B 6 **Bled**, Slovenia
C 20 **Bléharies**, Belgium
J 17 **Blenheim**, New Zealand
C 14 **Blenheim**, Ontario, Canada
R 11 **Blessing**, Texas, U.S.A.
E 18 **Blessington**, Republic of Ireland
U 9 **Bletchley**, United Kingdom
M 5 **Blida**, Algeria
A 22 **Bligh Sound**, New Zealand ≈
B 9 **Blind River**, Ontario, Canada
L 12 **Bliss**, Idaho, U.S.A.
J 15 **Blitar**, Indonesia
N 12 **Blitta**, Togo
N 12 **Block Island**, Rhode Island, U.S.A. ※
N 11 **Block Island Sound**, Rhode Island, U.S.A. ≈
N 12 **Bloemfontein**, Republic of South Africa ⚑
M 12 **Bloemhof**, Republic of South Africa
O 7 **Blois**, France
B 10 **Blönduós**, Iceland
C 14 **Bloody Foreland**, Republic of Ireland ▶
I 20 **Bloomfield**, Indiana, U.S.A.
U 14 **Bloomfield**, Iowa, U.S.A.
F 18 **Bloomington**, Illinois, U.S.A.
I 20 **Bloomington**, Indiana, U.S.A.
T 8 **Bloomington**, Minnesota, U.S.A.
R 7 **Blountstown**, Florida, U.S.A.
J 7 **Bludenz**, Austria
R 5 **Blue Hill**, Maine, U.S.A.
P 6 **Blue Mesa Reservoir**, Colorado, U.S.A. ∽
J 7 **Blue Mountain**, New York, U.S.A. ▲
S 11 **Blue Mountain**, Arkansas, U.S.A. ▲
J 11 **Blue Mountains**, Oregon, U.S.A. ⛰
O 2 **Blue Mud Bay**, Northern Territory, Australia ≈
G 19 **Blue Nile**, Ethiopia/Sudan ∿
F 19 **Blue Nile**, Sudan ▣
O 2 **Blue Rapids**, Kansas, U.S.A.
H 19 **Blue River**, British Columbia, Canada
Q 9 **Bluefields**, Nicaragua
O 6 **Bluestone Lake**, West Virginia, U.S.A. ∽
C 26 **Bluff**, New Zealand
M 7 **Bluff**, Utah, U.S.A.
J 9 **Blumenau**, Brazil
K 9 **Blunt**, South Dakota, U.S.A.
T 4 **Blyth**, United Kingdom
N 25 **Blythe**, California, U.S.A.
Z 9 **Blytheville**, Arkansas, U.S.A.
U 3 **Blyton**, United Kingdom
G 12 **Bo**, Sierra Leone
F 18 **Bo Hai**, China ≈
C 21 **Bo River Post**, Sudan
B 16 **Boa Vista**, Cape Verde ※
E 8 **Boa Vista**, Brazil

196 H 13 **Boac**, Philippines
91 O 9 **Boaco**, Nicaragua
216 J 5 **Boali**, Central African Republic
193 R 12 **Boano**, Indonesia ※
197 D 17 **Boayan**, Philippines ※
189 R 13 **Bobai**, China
219 Z 4 **Bobasakoa**, Madgascar
140 D 8 **Bobbio**, Italy
137 I 24 **Bobingen**, Germany
142 F 9 **Bobolice**, Poland
219 O 9 **Bobonong**, Botswana
149 L 16 **Bobr**, Belarus
143 E 15 **Bóbr**, Poland ∿
156 M 6 **Bobrov**, Russian Federation
151 Q 3 **Bobrovytsya**, Ukraine
142 O 10 **Bobrowniki**, Poland
151 R 7 **Bobrynets'**, Ukraine
188 M 4 **Bobso**, China
219 X 9 **Boby**, Madgascar ▲
90 L 1 **Boca Bacalar Chico**, Belize ※
91 T 14 **Boca Chica**, Panama
108 C 13 **Boca do Acre**, Brazil
216 H 3 **Bocaranga**, Central African Republic
91 T 13 **Bocas del Toro**, Panama
85 R 11 **Bochart**, Québec, Canada
137 C 14 **Bocholt**, Germany
137 C 16 **Bochum**, Germany
218 G 4 **Bocoio**, Angola
150 F 11 **Bocşa**, Romania
216 I 5 **Boda**, Central African Republic
135 H 23 **Böda**, Sweden
153 R 12 **Bodaybo**, Russian Federation
43 J 15 **Bode Verde Fracture Zone**, Atlantic Ocean ◇
134 J 12 **Boden**, Sweden
127 P 8 **Bodenham**, United Kingdom
137 G 26 **Bodensee**, Germany ∽
126 L 14 **Bodmin**, United Kingdom
126 L 14 **Bodmin Moor**, United Kingdom ◇
134 G 10 **Bodø**, Norway
170 B 12 **Bodrum**, Turkey
216 K 8 **Boende**, Democratic Republic of Congo
71 O 10 **Boerne**, Texas, U.S.A.
214 F 11 **Boffa**, Guinea
191 D 17 **Bogale**, Myanmar
62 M 7 **Bogalusa**, Louisiana, U.S.A.
216 J 4 **Bogangolo**, Central African Republic
170 K 10 **Boğazliyan**, Turkey
216 K 7 **Bogbonga**, Democratic Republic of Congo
184 L 4 **Bogda Feng**, China ▲
184 L 4 **Bogda Shan**, China ⛰
146 E 12 **Bogdanci**, Macedonia (F.Y.R.O.M.)
186 J 7 **Bogenli**, China
234 C 3 **Bogia**, Papua New Guinea
127 U 13 **Bognor Regis**, United Kingdom
215 V 10 **Bogo**, Cameroon
197 K 16 **Bogo**, Philippines
179 R 2 **Bogodukhovka**, Kazakhstan
192 H 14 **Bogor**, Indonesia
157 O 1 **Bogorodsk**, Russian Federation
104 I 7 **Bogotá**, Colombia ⚑
153 N 12 **Bogotol**, Russian Federation
183 T 12 **Bogra**, Bangladesh
153 O 12 **Boguchany**, Russian Federation
156 M 7 **Boguchar**, Russian Federation
214 F 7 **Bogué**, Mauritania
187 F 18 **Bohai**, China
187 G 18 **Bohai Haixia**, China ≈
187 E 18 **Bohai Wan**, China ≈
143 B 18 **Bohemia**, Czech Republic ◇
143 A 18 **Bohemian Forest**, Czech Republic/Germany ◇
143 D 19 **Bohemian Massif**, Czech Republic ⛰

136 E 13 **Bohmte**, Germany
151 V 4 **Bohodukhiv**, Ukraine
197 K 18 **Bohol**, Philippines ※
197 K 19 **Bohol Sea**, Philippines ◠
197 J 18 **Bohol Strait**, Philippines ≈
64 L 10 **Bois Blanc Island**, Michigan, U.S.A. ※
72 K 10 **Boise**, Idaho, U.S.A.
68 F 7 **Boise City**, Oklahoma, U.S.A.
136 H 11 **Boizenburg**, Germany
141 J 15 **Bojano**, Italy
176 M 5 **Bojnūrd**, Iran
183 Q 13 **Bokaro**, India
216 J 8 **Bokatola**, Democratic Republic of Congo
214 F 10 **Boké**, Guinea
135 A 20 **Boknafjorden**, Norway ≈
216 G 10 **Boko**, Congo
216 G 10 **Boko-Songho**, Congo
216 J 5 **Bokode**, Democratic Republic of Congo
179 V 10 **Bökönbaev**, Kyrgyzstan
215 W 10 **Bokoro**, Chad
157 N 8 **Bokovskaya**, Russian Federation
218 K 11 **Bokspits**, Botswana
234 J 5 **Boku**, Papua New Guinea
216 M 9 **Bokwankusu**, Democratic Republic of Congo
215 V 9 **Bol**, Chad
217 N 9 **Bolaiti**, Democratic Republic of Congo
129 N 3 **Bolbec**, France
150 L 11 **Boldu**, Romania
178 M 11 **Boldumsaz**, Turkmenistan
184 J 4 **Bole**, China
216 K 8 **Boleko**, Democratic Republic of Congo
216 K 7 **Bolena**, Democratic Republic of Congo
143 E 15 **Bolesławiec**, Poland
157 R 2 **Bolgar**, Russian Federation
151 N 11 **Bolhrad**, Ukraine
186 N 11 **Boli**, China
216 J 8 **Bolia**, Democratic Republic of Congo
193 N 3 **Bolinao**, Philippines
60 B 10 **Bolivar**, Tennessee, U.S.A.
69 T 6 **Bolivar**, Missouri, U.S.A.
104 I 4 **Bolívar**, Colombia ▣
105 Q 5 **Bolívar**, Venezuela ▣
106 B 9 **Bolívar**, Ecuador ▣
107 J 19 **Bolivia**, South America ▣
144 N 12 **Boljevac**, Serbia and Montenegro
156 J 3 **Bolkhov**, Russian Federation
129 T 13 **Bollene**, France
135 G 18 **Bollnäs**, Sweden
231 T 8 **Bollon**, Queensland, Australia
41 Q 13 **Bollons Tablemount**, Pacific Ocean ▲
135 H 16 **Bollstabruk**, Sweden
135 E 24 **Bolmen**, Sweden ∽
216 I 9 **Bolobo**, Democratic Republic of Congo
140 F 9 **Bologna**, Italy
107 E 15 **Bolognesi**, Peru
106 F 13 **Bolognesi**, Peru
154 G 13 **Bologoye**, Russian Federation
216 J 7 **Bolomba**, Democratic Republic of Congo
197 I 22 **Bolong**, Philippines
149 C 15 **Bol'shakovo**, Russian Federation
157 T 5 **Bol'shaya Chernigovka**, Russian Federation
157 T 4 **Bol'shaya Glushitsa**, Russian Federation
179 Z 5 **Bol'shenarymskoye**, Kazakhstan
155 P 4 **Bol'shezemel'skaya Tundra**, Russian Federation ◇
157 X 1 **Bol'shoy Iremel'**, Russian Federation ▲
153 O 9 **Bol'shoy Porog**, Russian Federation
157 P 1 **Bol'shoye Murashkino**, Russian Federation

127 T 4 **Bolsover**, United Kingdom
132 J 7 **Bolsward**, Netherlands
131 T 3 **Boltaña**, Spain
127 Q 3 **Bolton**, United Kingdom
170 G 8 **Bolu**, Turkey
234 G 6 **Bolubolu**, Papua New Guinea
134 A 9 **Bolungarvík**, Iceland
189 U 12 **Boluo**, China
140 F 5 **Bolzano**, Italy
112 I 11 **Bom Jesus**, Brazil
109 L 15 **Bom Jesus da Lapa**, Brazil
112 I 10 **Bom Retiro**, Brazil
216 F 11 **Boma**, Democratic Republic of Congo
216 H 6 **Bomassa**, Congo
231 U 13 **Bombala**, New South Wales, Australia
130 G 8 **Bombarral**, Portugal
216 J 6 **Bomboma**, Democratic Republic of Congo
183 W 9 **Bomdila**, India
217 O 7 **Bomili**, Democratic Republic of Congo
135 A 19 **Bømlo**, Norway ※
176 F 4 **Bonāb**, Iran
93 S 13 **Bonaire**, Netherlands Antilles ※
91 P 6 **Bonanza**, Nicaragua
93 Q 7 **Bonao**, Dominican Republic
230 I 3 **Bonaparte Archipelago**, Western Australia, Australia ※
85 Z 10 **Bonavista**, Newfoundland and Labrador, Canada
85 Y 10 **Bonavista Bay**, Newfoundland and Labrador, Canada ≈
216 M 5 **Bondo**, Democratic Republic of Congo
196 H 12 **Bondoc Peninsula**, Philippines ▶
214 L 12 **Bondoukou**, Côte d'Ivoire
73 R 11 **Bondurant**, Wyoming, U.S.A.
193 O 14 **Bonerate**, Indonesia ※
191 O 18 **Bông Son**, Vietnam
213 H 21 **Bonga**, Ethiopia
197 H 14 **Bongabong**, Philippines
183 U 10 **Bongaigaon**, India
216 L 7 **Bongandanga**, Democratic Republic of Congo
197 E 25 **Bongao**, Philippines
197 K 22 **Bongo**, Philippines ※
215 V 11 **Bongor**, Chad
71 R 4 **Bonham**, Texas, U.S.A.
129 Y 15 **Bonifacio**, France
63 Q 7 **Bonifay**, Florida, U.S.A.
40 L 5 **Bonin Trench**, Pacific Ocean ◇
109 G 18 **Bonito**, Brazil
137 C 17 **Bonn**, Germany
129 P 9 **Bonnat**, France
72 K 2 **Bonners Ferry**, Idaho, U.S.A.
129 V 9 **Bonneville**, France
74 I 3 **Bonneville Salt Flats**, Utah, U.S.A. ◇
83 K 17 **Bonnyville**, Alberta, Canada
199 B 24 **Bōno-misaki**, Japan ▶
191 O 21 **Bonom Mhai**, Vietnam ▲
231 V 9 **Bonshaw**, New South Wales, Australia
192 M 11 **Bontang**, Indonesia
196 G 7 **Bontoc**, Philippines
193 N 13 **Bontosunggu**, Indonesia
143 I 25 **Bonyhád**, Hungary
38 B 8 **Booby Island**, Seychelles ※
214 I 12 **Boola**, Guinea
61 N 8 **Boone**, North Carolina, U.S.A.
67 S 12 **Boone**, Iowa, U.S.A.
63 N 1 **Booneville**, Mississippi, U.S.A.
213 K 20 **Boorama**, Somalia
133 G 18 **Boortmeerbeek**, Belgium
213 O 19 **Boosaaso**, Somalia
82 K 5 **Boothia Peninsula**, Nunavut, Canada ▶
127 O 3 **Bootle**, United Kingdom
216 F 8 **Booué**, Gabon

137 D 19 **Boppard**, Germany
112 H 13 **Boqueirão**, Brazil
89 O 5 **Boquillas del Carmen**, Mexico
213 E 22 **Bor**, Sudan
143 A 18 **Bor**, Czech Republic
144 N 12 **Bor**, Serbia and Montenegro
170 J 12 **Bor**, Turkey
184 M 4 **Bor- Üdzüür**, Mongolia
73 N 10 **Borah Peak**, Idaho, U.S.A. ▲
135 E 22 **Borås**, Sweden
176 H 10 **Borāzjān**, Iran
108 F 11 **Borba**, Brazil
241 Q 14 **Borchgrevink Coast**, Antarctica ◇
171 Q 7 **Borşşka**, Turkey
128 M 11 **Bordeaux**, France
87 V 9 **Borden**, Prince Edward Island, Canada
81 N 3 **Borden Island**, Northwest Territories, Canada ※
81 Q 4 **Borden Peninsula**, Nunavut, Canada ▶
231 Q 12 **Bordertown**, South Australia, Australia
211 O 6 **Bordj Bou Arréridj**, Algeria
211 Q 9 **Bordj Messaouda**, Algeria
210 L 14 **Bordj Mokhtar**, Algeria
211 P 10 **Bordj Omar Driss**, Algeria
241 P 2 **Borg Massif**, Antarctica ⛰
134 D 10 **Borgarfjörður**, Iceland
134 A 11 **Borgarnes**, Iceland
132 N 8 **Borger**, Netherlands
70 K 2 **Borger**, Texas, U.S.A.
135 H 24 **Borgholm**, Sweden
141 M 20 **Borgia**, Italy
140 F 6 **Borgo Valsugana**, Italy
140 B 6 **Borgomanero**, Italy
157 N 6 **Borisoglebsk**, Russian Federation
219 Y 6 **Boriziny**, Madgascar
106 C 11 **Borja**, Peru
131 R 4 **Borja**, Spain
148 J 13 **Borkavichy**, Belarus
137 C 15 **Borken**, Germany
215 X 6 **Borkou-Ennedi-Tibesti**, Chad ▣
136 C 10 **Borkum**, Germany ※
135 G 19 **Borlänge**, Sweden
140 E 5 **Bormio**, Italy
137 L 16 **Borna**, Germany
132 J 5 **Borndiep**, Netherlands ≈
132 N 11 **Borne**, Netherlands
192 J 10 **Borneo**, Indonesia ※
135 F 26 **Bornholm**, Denmark ※
215 U 10 **Borno**, Nigeria ▣
170 B 10 **Bornova**, Turkey
151 O 10 **Borodino**, Ukraine
151 O 3 **Borodyanka**, Ukraine
216 L 1 **Boromata**, Central African Republic
197 M 16 **Borongan**, Philippines
214 I 12 **Borotou**, Côte d'Ivoire
127 S 1 **Boroughbridge**, United Kingdom
151 X 5 **Borova**, Ukraine
154 G 12 **Borovichi**, Russian Federation
179 O 2 **Borovskoy**, Kazakhstan
231 O 3 **Borroloola**, Northern Territory, Australia
150 J 8 **Borşa**, Romania
134 K 6 **Børselv**, Norway
126 M 7 **Borth**, United Kingdom
176 G 7 **Borūjerd**, Iran
151 Q 3 **Boryspil'**, Ukraine
151 R 2 **Borzna**, Ukraine
153 S 14 **Borzya**, Russian Federation
141 B 17 **Bosa**, Italy
179 T 6 **Bosaga**, Kazakhstan
144 F 9 **Bosanska Dubica**, Bosnia and Herzegovina
144 F 9 **Bosanska Gradiška**, Bosnia and Herzegovina
144 E 11 **Bosanski Petrovac**, Bosnia and Herzegovina
126 K 13 **Boscastle**, United Kingdom

189 O 12 **Bose**, China
189 W 2 **Boshan**, China
144 H 10 **Bosna**, Bosnia and Herzegovina ∿
144 G 11 **Bosnia and Herzegovina**, Europe ▣
199 L 16 **Bōsō-hantō**, Japan ▶
216 K 5 **Bosobolo**, Democratic Republic of Congo
170 D 7 **Bosporus**, Turkey ≈
216 I 4 **Bossangoa**, Central African Republic
216 I 4 **Bossembélé**, Central African Republic
216 I 4 **Bossentélé**, Central African Republic
62 H 4 **Bossier City**, Louisiana, U.S.A.
177 T 10 **Bostan**, Pakistan
184 K 5 **Bosten Hu**, China ∽
127 W 5 **Boston**, United Kingdom
59 O 9 **Boston**, Massachusetts, U.S.A.
69 S 9 **Boston Mountains**, Arkansas, U.S.A. ⛰
58 C 13 **Boswell**, Pennsylvania, U.S.A.
181 B 15 **Botad**, India
231 V 12 **Botany Bay**, New South Wales, Australia ≈
216 J 9 **Botemola**, Democratic Republic of Congo
146 I 9 **Botev**, Bulgaria ▲
146 G 8 **Botevgrad**, Bulgaria
130 I 4 **Boticas**, Portugal
157 Q 15 **Botlikh**, Russian Federation
196 E 10 **Botolan**, Philippines
150 L 8 **Botoşani**, Romania
187 E 18 **Botou**, China
135 I 14 **Botsmark**, Sweden
218 K 9 **Botswana**, Africa ▣
134 K 13 **Bottenviken**, Sweden ≈
137 C 15 **Bottrop**, Germany
112 J 6 **Botucatu**, Brazil
146 B 12 **Botun**, Macedonia (F.Y.R.O.M.)
211 P 7 **Bou Aroua**, Algeria
214 H 7 **Boû Bleï'îne**, Mauritania ∽
210 F 9 **Bou Izakarn**, Morocco
211 N 6 **Bou Saâda**, Algeria
214 J 13 **Bouaflé**, Côte d'Ivoire
214 K 12 **Bouaké**, Côte d'Ivoire
216 H 4 **Bouar**, Central African Republic
210 K 8 **Bouârfa**, Morocco
216 J 4 **Bouca**, Central African Republic
87 U 8 **Bouctouche**, New Brunswick, Canada
216 I 5 **Boudoua**, Central African Republic
216 G 10 **Bouenza**, Congo ▣
234 I 5 **Bougainville**, Papua New Guinea ※
210 L 7 **Bougtob**, Algeria
133 I 24 **Bouillon**, Belgium
211 N 5 **Bouira**, Algeria
210 C 11 **Boujdour**, Western Sahara
210 D 11 **Boukra**, Western Sahara
230 I 10 **Boulder**, Western Australia, Australia
75 R 3 **Boulder**, Colorado, U.S.A.
77 N 22 **Boulder City**, Nevada, U.S.A.
210 I 7 **Boulemane**, Morocco
231 Q 6 **Boulia**, Queensland, Australia
129 O 1 **Boulogne-sur-Mer**, France
216 L 3 **Boulouba**, Central African Republic
210 H 8 **Boumalne Dadès**, Morocco
216 G 9 **Boumango**, Gabon
214 L 11 **Bouna**, Côte d'Ivoire
77 J 19 **Boundary Peak**, Nevada, U.S.A. ▲
214 J 11 **Boundiali**, Côte d'Ivoire
41 Y 14 **Bounty Bay**, Pitcairn Island ≈
41 P 13 **Bounty Islands**, New Zealand ※
41 P 12 **Bounty Trough**, Pacific Ocean ◇

ountry ▣ Internal administrative region: State/Province/Territory/Dependent territory ⚑ Capital city ⛰ Mountain range/Undersea ridge ▲ Mountain peak/Volcano/Seamount ◇ Geographic feature ▶ Headland/Point/Cape/Peninsula ◢ Desert ※ Island/Island group ∷ Antarctic base ◎ Ocean ◠ Sea ≈ Bay/Gulf/Channel/Strait ∽ Lake ◫ Salt pan/Dry/Intermittent lake ∿ River

▫ Country ▫ Internal administrative region: State/Province/Territory/Dependent territory ▪ Capital city ▲ Mountain range/Undersea ridge ▲ Mountain peak/Volcano/Seamount ◇ Geographic feature ▶ Headland/Point/Cape/Peninsula ▨ Desert ⊞ Island/Island group ⊞ Antarctic base ◌ Ocean ◌ Sea ≈ Bay/Gulf/Channel/Strait ᔕ Lake ᔕ Salt pan/Dry/Intermittent lake River

274

▣ Country   ▣ Internal administrative region: State/Province/Territory/Dependent territory   ▪️ Capital city   ▲▲ Mountain range   ▲ Mountain peak/Volcano/Seamount   ◇ Geographic feature   ▶ Headland/Point/Cape/Peninsula   ▲ Desert   ≈ Island/Island group   ▦ Antarctic base   Ⓞ Ocean   Ⓢ Sea   ≈ Bay/Gulf/Channel/Strait   ↳ Lake   ↳ Salt pan/Dry/Intermittent lake   ↳ River

275

196 J 11 **Calagua Islands**, Philippines 🏝
131 R 3 **Calahorra**, Spain
218 J 7 **Calai**, Angola
129 P 1 **Calais**, France
59 T 4 **Calais**, Maine, U.S.A.
108 E 13 **Calama**, Brazil
110 G 5 **Calama**, Chile
104 I 3 **Calamar**, Colombia
104 J 8 **Calamar**, Colombia
196 G 12 **Calamba**, Philippines
197 E 15 **Calamian Group**, Philippines 🏝
150 H 10 **Călan**, Romania
197 F 17 **Calandagan**, Philippines 🏝
218 H 2 **Calandula**, Angola
192 B 8 **Calang**, Indonesia
211 X 8 **Calanscio Sand Sea**, Libya ◇
196 G 13 **Calapan**, Philippines
151 N 8 **Călărași**, Moldova
150 M 13 **Călărași**, Romania
131 R 5 **Calatayud**, Spain
196 I 12 **Calauag**, Philippines
197 E 14 **Calawit**, Philippines 🏝
196 G 4 **Calayan**, Philippines 🏝
197 K 15 **Calbayog**, Philippines
137 J 14 **Calbe**, Germany
62 H 8 **Calcasieu Lake**, Louisiana, U.S.A. ◡
108 I 8 **Calçoene**, Brazil
108 I 9 **Calçoene**, Brazil ∫
183 S 14 **Calcutta**, India
130 G 8 **Caldas da Rainha**, Portugal
110 F 8 **Caldera**, Chile
126 L 10 **Caldey Island**, United Kingdom 🏝
127 P 10 **Caldicot**, United Kingdom
171 T 10 **Caldiran**, Turkey
69 N 7 **Caldwell**, Kansas, U.S.A.
71 R 9 **Caldwell**, Texas, U.S.A.
72 J 10 **Caldwell**, Idaho, U.S.A.
87 U 11 **Caledonia**, Nova Scotia, Canada
63 P 4 **Calera**, Alabama, U.S.A.
110 F 3 **Caleta Buena**, Chile
110 F 4 **Caleta Lobos**, Chile
111 I 20 **Caleta Olivia**, Argentina
77 M 26 **Calexico**, California, U.S.A.
83 J 20 **Calgary**, Alberta, Canada
63 S 2 **Calhoun**, Georgia, U.S.A.
104 G 7 **Cali**, Colombia
197 M 16 **Calicoan**, Philippines 🏝
181 D 22 **Calicut**, India
77 N 20 **Caliente**, Nevada, U.S.A.
77 H 22 **California**, U.S.A., U.S.A. ▣
77 H 21 **California Aqueduct**, California, U.S.A. ∫
171 Y 9 **Cälilabad**, Azerbaijan
197 G 14 **Calintaan**, Philippines
77 M 26 **Calipatria**, California, U.S.A.
77 F 18 **Calistoga**, California, U.S.A.
141 L 16 **Calitri**, Italy
89 Y 11 **Calkiní**, Mexico
86 F 9 **Callander**, Ontario, Canada
107 C 16 **Callao**, Peru
61 V 5 **Callao**, Virginia, U.S.A.
126 L 14 **Callington**, United Kingdom
91 V 14 **Calobre**, Panama
231 W 8 **Caloundra**, Queensland, Australia
141 K 23 **Caltagirone**, Italy
141 J 22 **Caltanissetta**, Italy
218 G 3 **Calulo**, Angola
218 L 4 **Calunda**, Angola
218 J 6 **Calunga**, Angola
218 G 5 **Caluquembe**, Angola
197 G 18 **Calusa**, Philippines 🏝
213 O 18 **Caluula**, Somalia
197 H 15 **Caluya**, Philippines 🏝
129 Y 14 **Calvi**, France
218 K 14 **Calvinia**, Republic of South Africa
190 N 12 **Câm Pha**, Vietnam
191 O 20 **Cam Ranh**, Vietnam
109 N 15 **Camaçari**, Brazil
89 O 8 **Camacho**, Mexico
218 F 5 **Camacuio**, Angola
218 I 4 **Camacupa**, Angola
92 K 5 **Camagüey**, Cuba
109 N 15 **Camamu**, Brazil
107 F 19 **Camaná**, Peru
109 H 17 **Camapuã**, Brazil
112 H 13 **Camaquã**, Brazil
42 N 5 **Câmara de Lobos**, Madeira
111 I 19 **Camarones**, Argentina
85 U 12 **Cambellton**, New Brunswick, Canada
127 U 11 **Camberley**, United Kingdom
191 K 20 **Cambodia**, Asia □
126 J 15 **Camborne**, United Kingdom
129 R 2 **Cambrai**, France
126 M 9 **Cambrian Mountains**, United Kingdom ⛰
232 L 10 **Cambridge**, New Zealand
127 W 8 **Cambridge**, United Kingdom
59 N 9 **Cambridge**, Massachusetts, U.S.A.
61 V 4 **Cambridge**, Maryland, U.S.A.
65 O 18 **Cambridge**, Ohio, U.S.A.
67 S 7 **Cambridge**, Minnesota, U.S.A.
72 J 9 **Cambridge**, Idaho, U.S.A.
82 I 7 **Cambridge Bay**, Nunavut, Canada
218 K 1 **Cambulo**, Angola
231 U 12 **Camden**, New South Wales, Australia
58 H 8 **Camden**, New York, U.S.A.
59 Q 6 **Camden**, Maine, U.S.A.
60 D 8 **Camden**, Tennessee, U.S.A.
61 P 12 **Camden**, South Carolina, U.S.A.
63 P 5 **Camden**, Alabama, U.S.A.
69 U 13 **Camden**, Arkansas, U.S.A.
69 U 5 **Camdenton**, Missouri, U.S.A.
218 K 3 **Cameia**, Angola
62 H 8 **Cameron**, Louisiana, U.S.A.
64 C 10 **Cameron**, Wisconsin, U.S.A.
69 S 2 **Cameron**, Missouri, U.S.A.
71 Q 9 **Cameron**, Texas, U.S.A.
74 K 9 **Cameron**, Arizona, U.S.A.
194 B 7 **Cameron Highlands**, Malaysia
194 B 7 **Cameron Highlands**, Malaysia ⛰
233 A 25 **Cameron Mountains**, New Zealand ⛰
215 T 14 **Cameroon**, Africa □
108 J 10 **Cametá**, Brazil
170 B 12 **Camişşi Gölü**, Turkey ◡
196 H 5 **Camiguin**, Philippines 🏝
197 L 19 **Camiguin**, Philippines 🏝
196 F 9 **Camiling**, Philippines
63 T 6 **Camilla**, Georgia, U.S.A.
110 F 2 **Camiña**, Chile
130 H 3 **Caminha**, Portugal
107 L 22 **Camiri**, Bolivia
218 K 2 **Camissombo**, Angola
108 M 10 **Camocim**, Brazil
231 P 5 **Camooweal**, Queensland, Australia
181 O 24 **Camorta**, India 🏝
197 L 17 **Camotes Islands**, Philippines 🏝
74 J 11 **Camp Verde**, Arizona, U.S.A.
90 M 6 **Campamento**, Honduras
141 K 15 **Campania**, Italy ▣
65 M 18 **Campbell Hill**, Ohio, U.S.A. ▲
41 O 13 **Campbell Island**, New Zealand 🏝
191 F 22 **Campbell Island**, Myanmar 🏝
41 O 12 **Campbell Plateau**, Pacific Ocean ◇
83 E 21 **Campbell River**, British Columbia, Canada
86 G 12 **Campbellford**, Ontario, Canada
60 H 6 **Campbellsville**, Kentucky, U.S.A.
87 R 7 **Campbellton**, New Brunswick, Canada
125 F 14 **Campbeltown**, United Kingdom
89 X 11 **Campeche**, Mexico
89 Y 12 **Campeche**, Mexico ▣
130 L 10 **Campillo de Llerena**, Spain
108 O 12 **Campina Grande**, Brazil
112 I 4 **Campina Verde**, Brazil
109 K 19 **Campinas**, Brazil
112 K 7 **Campinas**, Brazil
215 T 15 **Campo**, Cameroon
112 L 5 **Campo Belo**, Brazil
112 I 10 **Campo Belo do Sul**, Brazil
112 J 4 **Campo Florido**, Brazil
109 M 14 **Campo Formoso**, Brazil
110 K 7 **Campo Gallo**, Argentina
109 H 18 **Campo Grande**, Brazil
112 H 7 **Campo Mourão**, Brazil
112 G 10 **Campo Novo**, Brazil
109 G 15 **Campo Novo de Parecis**, Brazil
105 N 6 **Campo Troco**, Colombia
104 H 8 **Campoalegre**, Colombia
141 J 14 **Campobasso**, Italy
141 H 22 **Campobello di Mazara**, Italy
112 O 6 **Campos**, Brazil
109 K 15 **Campos Belos**, Brazil
112 H 10 **Campos Novos**, Brazil
150 J 11 **Câmpulung**, Romania
83 K 18 **Camrose**, Alberta, Canada
170 B 8 **Can**, Turkey
191 M 23 **Cân Tho**, Vietnam
81 O 11 **Canada**, North America □
45 O 4 **Canada Basin**, Arctic Ocean ◇
70 L 1 **Canadian**, Texas, U.S.A.
70 K 2 **Canadian**, Texas, U.S.A. ∫
45 P 4 **Canadian Abyssal Plain**, Arctic Ocean ◇
170 A 8 **Canakkale**, Turkey
147 K 14 **Çanakkale**, Turkey ▣
111 G 26 **Canal Ballenero**, Chile ≈
108 I 9 **Canal do Norte**, Brazil ∫
83 I 21 **Canal Flats**, British Columbia, Canada
107 A 18 **Canal Isabela**, Ecuador ≈
111 E 22 **Canal Ladrillero**, Chile ≈
111 F 19 **Canal Moraleda**, Chile ≈
235 P 14 **Canala**, New Caledonia
110 I 13 **Canalejas**, Argentina
88 J 3 **Cananea**, Mexico
112 K 8 **Cananéia**, Brazil
106 B 10 **Cañar**, Ecuador
106 B 10 **Cañar**, Ecuador ▣
42 L 11 **Canary Islands**, Spain ▣
91 P 12 **Cañas**, Costa Rica
89 N 8 **Canatlán**, Mexico
130 K 7 **Cañaveral**, Spain
109 N 16 **Canavieiras**, Brazil
91 U 14 **Cañazas**, Panama
140 G 5 **Canazei**, Italy
231 U 12 **Canberra**, Australian Capital Territory, Australia ⌂
67 P 8 **Canby**, Minnesota, U.S.A.
77 H 15 **Canby**, California, U.S.A.
89 Z 10 **Cancún**, Mexico
112 E 10 **Candelaria**, Argentina
90 J 6 **Candelaria**, Honduras
170 I 9 **Candir**, Turkey
79 N 6 **Candle**, Alaska, U.S.A.
66 L 2 **Cando**, North Dakota, U.S.A.
196 F 7 **Candon**, Philippines
196 F 7 **Candon Point**, Philippines ▶
113 E 15 **Canelones**, Uruguay
113 F 16 **Canelones**, Uruguay ▣
111 E 15 **Cañete**, Chile
131 R 7 **Cañete**, Spain
107 E 17 **Cangallo**, Peru
218 J 5 **Cangamba**, Angola
218 H 3 **Cangandala**, Angola
130 K 1 **Cangas del Narcea**, Spain
218 J 5 **Cangombe**, Angola
112 G 13 **Canguçu**, Brazil
218 J 4 **Cangumbe**, Angola
189 S 12 **Cangwu**, China
188 J 12 **Cangyuan**, China
187 E 18 **Cangzhou**, China
85 S 8 **Caniapiscau**, Québec, Canada ∫
141 J 23 **Canicatti**, Italy
170 K 7 **Canik Dağlari**, Turkey ⛰
108 N 11 **Canindé**, Brazil
197 G 16 **Canipo**, Philippines 🏝
240 K 9 **Canisteo Peninsula**, Antarctica ▶
170 I 8 **Cankiri**, Turkey
231 U 13 **Cann River**, Victoria, Australia
124 E 11 **Canna**, United Kingdom 🏝
181 D 22 **Cannanore**, India
181 B 23 **Cannanore Islands**, India 🏝
129 W 14 **Cannes**, France
127 R 6 **Cannock**, United Kingdom
76 F 9 **Cannon Beach**, Oregon, U.S.A.
66 I 6 **Cannonball**, North Dakota, U.S.A. ∫
105 N 8 **Caño Colorado**, Colombia
112 H 12 **Canoas**, Brazil
112 I 10 **Canoas**, Brazil ∫
112 I 9 **Canoinhas**, Brazil
75 R 5 **Canon City**, Colorado, U.S.A.
93 Y 12 **Canouan**, St Vincent and the Grenadines 🏝
87 Y 9 **Canso**, Nova Scotia, Canada
107 D 16 **Canta**, Peru
131 O 1 **Cantabria**, Spain ▣
108 F 11 **Cantagalo**, Brazil
233 G 20 **Canterbury**, New Zealand ▣
127 Y 11 **Canterbury**, United Kingdom
87 R 9 **Canterbury**, New Brunswick, Canada
233 H 21 **Canterbury Bight**, New Zealand ≈
233 G 20 **Canterbury Plains**, New Zealand ◇
197 N 19 **Cantilan**, Philippines
130 L 12 **Cantillana**, Spain
108 M 13 **Canto do Buriti**, Brazil
58 F 11 **Canton**, Pennsylvania, U.S.A.
58 H 5 **Canton**, New York, U.S.A.
62 L 4 **Canton**, Mississippi, U.S.A.
63 S 2 **Canton**, Georgia, U.S.A.
65 E 18 **Canton**, Illinois, U.S.A.
65 O 17 **Canton**, Ohio, U.S.A.
79 R 8 **Cantwell**, Alaska, U.S.A.
113 D 16 **Cañuelas**, Argentina
108 F 11 **Canumã**, Brazil
108 D 12 **Canutama**, Brazil
127 X 10 **Canvey Island**, United Kingdom
70 J 3 **Canyon**, Texas, U.S.A.
73 R 9 **Canyon**, Wyoming, U.S.A.
73 Q 6 **Canyon Ferry Lake**, Montana, U.S.A. ◡
76 F 13 **Canyonville**, Oregon, U.S.A.
190 M 10 **Cao Băng**, Vietnam
188 J 10 **Caojian**, China
218 H 2 **Caombo**, Angola
189 V 3 **Caoxian**, China
197 F 24 **Cap**, Philippines 🏝
210 B 13 **Cap Barbas**, Western Sahara ▶
158 J 9 **Cap Blanc**, Mediterranean Sea ▶
214 E 11 **Cap Boffa**, Guinea ▶
211 R 5 **Cap Bon**, Tunisia ▶
211 O 5 **Cap Bougaroûn**, Algeria ▶
158 G 5 **Cap de Creus**, Mediterranean Sea ▶
211 O 5 **Cap de Fer**, Algeria ▶
131 Y 7 **Cap de Formentor**, Spain ▶
128 K 2 **Cap de la Hague**, France ▶
86 M 9 **Cap-de-la-Madeleine**, Québec, Canada
131 Y 8 **Cap de ses Salines**, Spain ▶
131 Z 7 **Cap des Freu**, Spain ▶
158 C 9 **Cap des Trois Fourches**, Mediterranean Sea ▶
210 E 10 **Cap Draâ**, Morocco ▶
158 D 9 **Cap Ferrat**, Mediterranean Sea ▶
128 K 4 **Cap Fréhel**, France ▶
87 U 5 **Cap Gaspé**, Québec, Canada ▶
93 P 6 **Cap-Haïtien**, Haiti
85 R 5 **Cap Hopes Advance**, Québec, Canada ▶
210 D 10 **Cap Juby**, Morocco ▶
216 D 8 **Cap Lopez**, Gabon ▶
210 F 8 **Cap Rhir**, Morocco ▶
70 J 6 **Cap Rock Escarpment**, Texas, U.S.A. ⛰
214 E 11 **Cap Verga**, Guinea ▶
214 D 8 **Cap Vert**, Senegal ▶
85 P 4 **Cap Wolstenholme**, Québec, Canada ▶
218 J 2 **Capaia**, Angola
112 G 9 **Capanema**, Brazil
112 J 7 **Capão Bonito**, Brazil
196 F 10 **Capas**, Philippines
241 Q 14 **Cape Adare**, Antarctica ▶
218 K 15 **Cape Agulhas**, Republic of South Africa ▶
59 O 9 **Cape Ann**, Massachusetts, U.S.A. ▶
170 J 15 **Cape Apostolos Andreas**, Cyprus ▶
170 G 15 **Cape Arnaoutis**, Cyprus ▶
231 P 1 **Cape Arnhem**, Northern Territory, Australia ▶
82 F 7 **Cape Baring**, Northwest Territories, Canada ▶
231 T 14 **Cape Barren Island**, Tasmania, Australia 🏝
232 L 7 **Cape Barrier**, New Zealand ▶
43 M 18 **Cape Basin**, Atlantic Ocean ◇
82 D 7 **Cape Bathurst**, Northwest Territories, Canada ▶
85 X 8 **Cape Bauld**, Newfoundland and Labrador, Canada ▶
76 E 13 **Cape Blanco**, Oregon, U.S.A. ▶
196 F 5 **Cape Bojeador**, Philippines ▶
38 L 15 **Cape Boothby**, Indian Ocean ▶
87 Y 8 **Cape Breton Island**, Nova Scotia, Canada 🏝
232 J 5 **Cape Brett**, New Zealand ▶
197 B 20 **Cape Buliluyan**, Philippines ▶
240 L 12 **Cape Burks**, Antarctica ▶
231 W 9 **Cape Byron**, New South Wales, Australia ▶
196 F 13 **Cape Calavite**, Philippines ▶
233 J 17 **Cape Campbell**, New Zealand ▶
63 X 10 **Cape Canaveral**, Florida, U.S.A.
63 Y 10 **Cape Canaveral**, Florida, U.S.A. ▶
87 Y 9 **Cape Canso**, Nova Scotia, Canada ▶
86 A 7 **Cape Cargantua**, Ontario, Canada ▶
231 O 12 **Cape Catastrophe**, South Australia, Australia ▶
61 W 6 **Cape Charles**, Virginia, U.S.A.
61 W 6 **Cape Charles**, Virginia, U.S.A. ▶
241 R 14 **Cape Cheetham**, Antarctica ▶
44 L 12 **Cape Chidley**, Arctic Ocean ▶
181 G 19 **Cape Chirala**, India ▶
84 L 6 **Cape Churchill**, Manitoba, Canada ▶
125 B 21 **Cape Clear**, Republic of Ireland ▶
59 P 10 **Cape Cod**, Massachusetts, U.S.A. ▶
59 P 10 **Cape Cod Bay**, Massachusetts, U.S.A. ≈
45 Q 9 **Cape Columbia**, Arctic Ocean ▶
218 J 14 **Cape Columbine**, Repu of South Africa ▶
232 L 7 **Cape Colville**, New Zealand ▶
181 E 24 **Cape Comorin**, India ▶
83 D 21 **Cape Cook**, British Columbia, Canada ▶
63 W 12 **Cape Coral**, Florida, U.S
126 I 15 **Cape Cornwall**, United Kingdom ▶
231 O 3 **Cape Crawford**, Northe Territory, Australia
234 E 5 **Cape Cretin**, Papua Nev Guinea ▶
82 D 7 **Cape Dalhousie**, Northwest Territories, Canada ▶
241 X 5 **Cape Darnley**, Antarctica ▶
240 K 5 **Cape Deacon**, Antarctica ▶
218 I 12 **Cape Dernberg**, Namibia ▶
76 F 8 **Cape Disappointment**, Washington, U.S.A. ▶
111 L 23 **Cape Dolphin**, Falkland Islands ▶
81 R 7 **Cape Dorchester**, Nunavut, Canada ▶
85 P 3 **Cape Dorset**, Nunavut, Canada
85 T 1 **Cape Dyer**, Nunavut, Canada ▶
59 P 7 **Cape Elizabeth**, Maine, U.S.A. ▶
196 H 9 **Cape Encanto**, Philippines ▶
233 H 15 **Cape Farewell**, New Zealand ▶
61 T 12 **Cape Fear**, North Caroli U.S.A. ▶
240 K 5 **Cape Fiske**, Antarctica
231 T 2 **Cape Flattery**, Queensland, Australia
76 F 5 **Cape Flattery**, Washington, U.S.A. ▶
230 L 2 **Cape Ford**, Northern Territory, Australia ▶
233 F 17 **Cape Foulwind**, New Zealand ▶
241 T 14 **Cape Freshfield**, Antarctica ▶
218 F 7 **Cape Fria**, Namibia ▶
170 H 15 **Cape Gata**, Cyprus ▶
87 X 9 **Cape George**, Nova Sco Canada
69 Z 6 **Cape Girardeau**, Missou U.S.A.
234 C 3 **Cape Girgir**, Papua New Guinea ▶
241 X 13 **Cape Goodenough**, Antarctica ▶
241 U 14 **Cape Gray**, Antarctica
170 I 15 **Cape Greko**, Cyprus ▶
231 S 1 **Cape Grenville**, Queensland, Australia
234 I 4 **Cape Hanpan**, Papua Ne Guinea ▶
61 X 10 **Cape Hatteras**, North Carolina, U.S.A. ▶
85 O 8 **Cape Henrietta Maria**, Ontario, Canada ▶
61 W 7 **Cape Henry**, Virginia, U.S.A. ▶
111 I 26 **Cape Horn**, Chile ▶
231 U 13 **Cape Howe**, New South Wales, Australia ▶
241 T 15 **Cape Hudson**, Antarctica ▶
86 C 10 **Cape Hurd**, Ontario, Canada ▶
231 Q 13 **Cape Jaffa**, South Australia, Australia ▶
232 I 4 **Cape Karikari**, New Zealand ▶
241 W 14 **Cape Keltie**, Antarctica
232 N 13 **Cape Kidnappers**, New Zealand ▶
83 B 18 **Cape Knox**, British Columbia, Canada ▶
170 H 15 **Cape Kormakitis**, Cyprus ▶
85 T 5 **Cape Labrador**, Newfoundland and Labrador, Canada ▶
230 G 12 **Cape Leeuwin**, Western Australia, Australia ▶

□ Country ▣ Internal administrative region: State/Province/Territory/Dependent territory ⌂ Capital city ⛰ Mountain range/Undersea ridge ▲ Mountain peak/Volcano/Seamount ◇ Geographic feature ▶ Headland/Point/Cape/Peninsula ⌓ Desert 🏝 Island/Island group ⁙ Antarctic base ◎ Ocean ◠ Sea ≈ Bay/Gulf/Channel/Strait ◡ Lake ⚑ Salt pan/Dry/Intermittent lake ∫

Cape Leveque – Cayo Romano

I 3 **Cape Leveque**, Western Australia, Australia
V 6 **Cape Leveque**, Indian Ocean
V 11 **Cape Lookout**, North Carolina, U.S.A.
K 5 **Cape Mackintosh**, Antarctica
B 11 **Cape Malheureux**, Mauritius
H 4 **Cape Maria van Diemen**, New Zealand
I 15 **Cape May**, New Jersey, U.S.A.
I 15 **Cape May**, New Jersey, U.S.A.
S 2 **Cape Melville**, Queensland, Australia
A 21 **Cape Melville**, Philippines
E 16 **Cape Mendocino**, California, U.S.A.
T 2 **Cape Mercy**, Nunavut, Canada
K 24 **Cape Meredith**, Falkland Islands
K 9 **Cape Mohican**, Alaska, U.S.A.
W 15 **Cape Morse**, Indian Ocean
F 6 **Cape Nelson**, Papua New Guinea
M 11 **Cape Newenham**, Alaska, U.S.A.
M 7 **Cape Nome**, Alaska, U.S.A.
Y 7 **Cape North**, Nova Scotia, Canada
O 2 **Cape Norvegia**, Antarctica
J 15 **Cape of Good Hope**, Republic of South Africa
N 18 **Cape of Good Hope**, Atlantic Ocean
R 14 **Cape Otway**, Victoria, Australia
L 17 **Cape Palliser**, New Zealand
I 14 **Cape Palmas**, Côte d'Ivoire
E 7 **Cape Parry**, Northwest Territories, Canada
J 11 **Cape Pasley**, Western Australia, Australia
Q 15 **Cape Penck**, Indian Ocean
Y 11 **Cape Poinsett**, Antarctica
L 4 **Cape Prince Alfred**, Northwest Territories, Canada
A 25 **Cape Providence**, New Zealand
N 15 **Cape Recife**, Republic of South Africa
H 4 **Cape Reinga**, New Zealand
R 14 **Cape Romain**, South Carolina, U.S.A.
W 13 **Cape Romano**, Florida, U.S.A.
O 10 **Cape Runaway**, New Zealand
E 8 **Cape Sable**, Atlantic Ocean
X 14 **Cape Sable**, Florida, U.S.A.
T 13 **Cape Sable Island**, Nova Scotia, Canada
N 23 **Cape San Agustin**, Philippines
D 21 **Cape Scott**, British Columbia, Canada
M 15 **Cape Seal**, Republic of South Africa
O 1 **Cape Shield**, Northern Territory, Australia
F 2 **Cape Siemens**, Papua New Guinea
I 8 **Cape Siri**, Papua New Guinea
N 4 **Cape Southampton**, Nunavut, Canada
P 12 **Cape Spencer**, South Australia, Australia
H 4 **Cape St George**, Papua New Guinea
233 J 15 **Cape Stephens**, New Zealand
84 L 7 **Cape Tatnam**, Manitoba, Canada
233 J 16 **Cape Terawhiti**, New Zealand
218 J 15 **Cape Town**, Republic of South Africa
233 M 15 **Cape Turnagain**, New Zealand
85 U 6 **Cape Uivak**, Newfoundland and Labrador, Canada
43 A 16 **Cape Verde**, Atlantic Ocean
42 I 12 **Cape Verde Basin**, Atlantic Ocean
42 J 11 **Cape Verde Plateau**, Atlantic Ocean
241 X 12 **Cape Waldron**, Antarctica
234 E 6 **Cape Ward Hunt**, Papua New Guinea
231 O 1 **Cape Wessel**, Northern Territory, Australia
85 O 2 **Cape Wilson**, Nunavut, Canada
124 G 8 **Cape Wrath**, United Kingdom
231 R 1 **Cape York**, Queensland, Australia
231 R 1 **Cape York Peninsula**, Queensland, Australia
109 M 16 **Capelinha**, Brazil
231 U 6 **Capella**, Queensland, Australia
132 G 13 **Capelle aan den IJssel**, Netherlands
133 L 25 **Capellen**, Luxembourg
218 I 2 **Capenda-Camulemba**, Angola
140 I 13 **Capestrano**, Italy
75 R 12 **Capitan Peak**, New Mexico, U.S.A.
197 G 17 **Capnoyan**, Philippines
141 A 16 **Capo Caccia**, Italy
141 C 19 **Capo Carbonara**, Italy
141 N 19 **Capo Colonna**, Italy
141 D 16 **Capo Comino**, Italy
141 B 15 **Capo del Falcone**, Italy
141 B 18 **Capo della Frasca**, Italy
141 K 24 **Capo delle Correnti**, Italy
141 K 21 **Capo di Milazzo**, Italy
141 D 17 **Capo di Monte Santu**, Italy
141 K 21 **Capo d'Orlando**, Italy
141 I 21 **Capo Gallo**, Italy
158 L 9 **Capo Granitola**, Mediterranean Sea
141 L 23 **Capo Murro di Porco**, Italy
141 L 17 **Capo Palinuro**, Italy
141 N 20 **Capo Rizzuto**, Italy
141 H 21 **Capo San Vito**, Italy
141 O 18 **Capo Santa Maria di Leuca**, Italy
141 J 24 **Capo Scaramia**, Italy
141 B 20 **Capo Spartivento**, Italy
141 N 17 **Capo Spulico**, Italy
141 N 18 **Capo Trionto**, Italy
141 L 20 **Capo Vaticano**, Italy
218 G 3 **Capolo**, Angola
170 J 11 **Cappadocia**, Turkey
141 J 16 **Capri**, Italy
218 L 7 **Caprivi**, Namibia
218 K 7 **Caprivi Strip**, Namibia
78 D 9 **Captain Cook**, Hawaii, U.S.A.
104 I 9 **Caquetá**, Colombia
104 J 10 **Caquetá**, Colombia
181 N 23 **Car Nicobar**, India
197 H 15 **Carabao**, Philippines
105 N 3 **Carabobo**, Venezuela
105 S 5 **Carabobo**, Venezuela
150 I 13 **Caracal**, Romania
108 E 8 **Caracaraí**, Brazil
105 O 2 **Caracas**, Venezuela
108 L 13 **Caracol**, Brazil
107 I 20 **Caracollo**, Bolivia
197 N 22 **Caraga**, Philippines
111 F 15 **Carahue**, Chile
196 J 12 **Caramoan Peninsula**, Philippines
112 M 5 **Carandaí**, Brazil
150 G 11 **Caransebeș**, Romania
87 T 7 **Caraquet**, New Brunswick, Canada
106 A 9 **Caráquez**, Ecuador
91 Q 5 **Caratasca**, Honduras
91 R 14 **Carate**, Costa Rica
108 C 11 **Carauari**, Brazil
131 R 11 **Caravaca de la Cruz**, Spain
109 N 17 **Caravelas**, Brazil
112 G 11 **Carazinho**, Brazil
130 H 1 **Carballo**, Spain
58 H 11 **Carbondale**, Pennsylvania, U.S.A.
65 F 22 **Carbondale**, Illinois, U.S.A.
75 P 4 **Carbondale**, Colorado, U.S.A.
131 R 13 **Carboneras**, Spain
131 R 7 **Carboneras de Guadazaón**, Spain
113 B 15 **Carcaraña**, Argentina
129 Q 14 **Carcassonne**, France
106 B 8 **Carchi**, Ecuador
181 E 22 **Cardamom Hills**, India
89 T 12 **Cardel**, Mexico
131 N 10 **Cárdena**, Spain
89 V 13 **Cárdenas**, Mexico
92 H 4 **Cárdenas**, Cuba
127 O 11 **Cardiff**, United Kingdom
126 K 8 **Cardigan**, United Kingdom
126 L 7 **Cardigan Bay**, United Kingdom
191 J 21 **Cardomom Range**, Cambodia
113 E 15 **Cardona**, Uruguay
233 D 23 **Cardrona**, New Zealand
83 K 21 **Cardston**, Alberta, Canada
231 T 4 **Cardwell**, Queensland, Australia
150 G 7 **Carei**, Romania
128 L 3 **Carentan**, France
72 M 11 **Carey**, Idaho, U.S.A.
38 L 6 **Cargados Carajos Bank**, Indian Ocean
38 M 6 **Cargados Carajos Islands**, Mauritius
128 I 5 **Carhaix-Plouguer**, France
112 O 5 **Cariacica**, Brazil
105 Q 2 **Cariaco**, Venezuela
106 B 11 **Cariamanga**, Ecuador
141 N 18 **Cariati**, Italy
92 I 13 **Caribbean Sea**, North America
59 R 1 **Caribou**, Maine, U.S.A.
83 H 15 **Caribou Mountains**, Alberta, Canada
197 L 16 **Carigara**, Philippines
131 S 5 **Cariñena**, Spain
109 L 15 **Carinhanha**, Brazil
105 R 3 **Caripito**, Venezuela
86 I 11 **Carleton Place**, Ontario, Canada
219 N 11 **Carletonville**, Republic of South Africa
77 M 16 **Carlin**, Nevada, U.S.A.
65 E 20 **Carlinville**, Illinois, U.S.A.
125 I 15 **Carlisle**, United Kingdom
58 F 13 **Carlisle**, Pennsylvania, U.S.A.
141 B 19 **Carloforte**, Italy
113 B 16 **Carlos Casares**, Argentina
125 E 19 **Carlow**, Republic of Ireland
75 T 14 **Carlsbad**, New Mexico, U.S.A.
38 K 2 **Carlsberg Ridge**, Indian Ocean
83 O 19 **Carlyle**, Saskatchewan, Canada
65 F 21 **Carlyle Lake**, Illinois, U.S.A.
82 B 13 **Carmacks**, Yukon Territory, Canada
126 L 9 **Carmarthen**, United Kingdom
126 L 10 **Carmarthen Bay**, United Kingdom
129 P 13 **Carmaux**, France
126 L 3 **Carmel Head**, United Kingdom
90 I 2 **Carmelita**, Guatemala
113 D 15 **Carmelo**, Uruguay
104 I 3 **Carmen**, Colombia
110 G 7 **Carmen**, Chile
74 K 15 **Carmen**, Arizona, U.S.A.
110 G 5 **Carmen Alto**, Chile
113 B 20 **Carmen de Patagones**, Argentina
110 H 13 **Carmensa**, Argentina
65 G 22 **Carmi**, Illinois, U.S.A.
130 L 12 **Carmona**, Spain
91 O 12 **Carmona**, Costa Rica
124 G 10 **Carn Eighe**, United Kingdom
230 G 10 **Carnamah**, Western Australia, Australia
218 L 13 **Carnarvon**, Republic of South Africa
230 E 8 **Carnarvon**, Western Australia, Australia
240 K 11 **Carney Island**, Antarctica
127 P 1 **Carnforth**, United Kingdom
216 H 4 **Carnot**, Central African Republic
124 I 12 **Carnoustie**, United Kingdom
125 F 20 **Carnsore Point**, Republic of Ireland
63 Y 13 **Carol City**, Florida, U.S.A.
108 K 12 **Carolina**, Brazil
236 L 15 **Caroline Islands**, Federated States of Micronesia
141 J 21 **Caronia**, Italy
143 J 18 **Carpathian Mountains**, Europe
129 T 13 **Carpentras**, France
140 F 8 **Carpi**, Italy
77 I 24 **Carpinteria**, California, U.S.A.
63 S 8 **Carrabelle**, Florida, U.S.A.
140 D 9 **Carrara**, Italy
131 P 7 **Carrascosa del Campo**, Spain
125 A 20 **Carrauntuohil**, Republic of Ireland
93 Y 12 **Carriacou**, Grenada
89 N 6 **Carrillo**, Mexico
66 L 4 **Carrington**, North Dakota, U.S.A.
110 F 8 **Carrizal Bajo**, Chile
70 M 12 **Carrizo Springs**, Texas, U.S.A.
75 R 12 **Carrizozo**, New Mexico, U.S.A.
67 R 12 **Carroll**, Iowa, U.S.A.
63 S 3 **Carrollton**, Georgia, U.S.A.
170 L 8 **Carșamba**, Turkey
140 I 13 **Carsoli**, Italy
77 I 18 **Carson City**, Nevada, U.S.A.
104 H 2 **Cartagena**, Colombia
131 S 12 **Cartagena**, Spain
104 H 6 **Cartago**, Colombia
91 Q 12 **Cartago**, Costa Rica
60 G 8 **Carthage**, Tennessee, U.S.A.
62 M 4 **Carthage**, Mississippi, U.S.A.
71 T 6 **Carthage**, Texas, U.S.A.
91 X 13 **Carti Suitupo**, Panama
84 H 10 **Cartwright**, Manitoba, Canada
85 W 8 **Cartwright**, Newfoundland and Labrador, Canada
108 O 13 **Caruarú**, Brazil
105 Q 2 **Carúpano**, Venezuela
197 D 17 **Caruray**, Philippines
108 K 10 **Carutapera**, Brazil
77 K 18 **Carvers**, Nevada, U.S.A.
112 K 6 **Casa Branca**, Brazil
74 J 13 **Casa Grande**, Arizona, U.S.A.
210 H 7 **Casablanca**, Morocco
141 K 14 **Casacalenda**, Italy
140 B 7 **Casale**, Italy
104 K 6 **Casanare**, Colombia
91 N 10 **Casares**, Nicaragua
88 L 3 **Casas Grandes**, Mexico
131 R 9 **Casas Ibáñez**, Spain
112 H 11 **Casca**, Brazil
38 A 9 **Cascade**, Seychelles
72 K 9 **Cascade**, Idaho, U.S.A.
233 C 21 **Cascade Point**, New Zealand
76 G 13 **Cascade Range**, Canada/U.S.A.
72 K 9 **Cascade Reservoir**, Idaho, U.S.A.
41 U 3 **Cascadia Basin**, Pacific Ocean
108 N 11 **Cascavel**, Brazil
112 G 8 **Cascavel**, Brazil
59 P 7 **Casco Bay**, Maine, U.S.A.
141 J 15 **Caserta**, Italy
64 L 13 **Caseville**, Michigan, U.S.A.
241 Y 11 **Casey**, Antarctica
65 G 20 **Casey**, Illinois, U.S.A.
196 I 9 **Casiguran**, Philippines
196 H 9 **Casiguran Sound**, Philippines
113 B 15 **Casilda**, Argentina
231 W 9 **Casino**, New South Wales, Australia
107 B 15 **Casma**, Peru
131 T 5 **Caspe**, Spain
73 W 12 **Casper**, Wyoming, U.S.A.
178 G 6 **Caspian Depression**, Kazakhstan/Russian Federation
157 S 14 **Caspian Sea**, Asia/Europe
64 M 13 **Cass City**, Michigan, U.S.A.
219 Q 5 **Cassacatiza**, Mozambique
218 J 4 **Cassamba**, Angola
83 D 15 **Cassiar**, British Columbia, Canada
83 C 14 **Cassiar Mountains**, Yukon Territory, Canada
109 I 17 **Cassilândia**, Brazil
218 H 5 **Cassinga**, Angola
141 I 15 **Cassino**, Italy
218 H 4 **Cassongue**, Angola
184 M 2 **Cast Uul**, Mongolia
140 D 11 **Castagneto Carducci**, Italy
108 F 12 **Castanha**, Brazil
108 K 10 **Castanhal**, Brazil
110 G 10 **Castaño**, Argentina
138 I 10 **Castasegna**, Switzerland
140 C 8 **Casteggio**, Italy
130 J 7 **Castel Branco**, Portugal
141 J 14 **Castél di Sangro**, Italy
129 V 13 **Castellane**, France
110 L 7 **Castelli**, Argentina
113 D 17 **Castelli**, Argentina
131 U 7 **Castelló de la Plana**, Spain
129 P 14 **Castelnaudary**, France
140 E 9 **Castelnovo ne' Monti**, Italy
130 I 7 **Castelo Branco**, Portugal
141 B 16 **Castelsardo**, Italy
141 I 22 **Casteltermini**, Italy
141 H 22 **Castelvetrano**, Italy
231 Q 13 **Casterton**, Victoria, Australia
140 E 12 **Castiglione della Pescaia**, Italy
110 F 8 **Castilla**, Chile
131 Q 8 **Castilla-La Mancha**, Spain
130 K 4 **Castilla Y Leõn**, Spain
113 G 15 **Castillos**, Uruguay
127 P 12 **Castle Cary**, United Kingdom
74 L 5 **Castle Dale**, Utah, U.S.A.
74 H 13 **Castle Dome Peak**, Arizona, U.S.A.
127 S 6 **Castle Donnington**, United Kingdom
125 H 15 **Castle Douglas**, United Kingdom
42 B 7 **Castle Harbour**, Bermuda
72 M 10 **Castle Peak**, Idaho, U.S.A.
75 R 4 **Castle Rock**, Colorado, U.S.A.
43 N 26 **Castle Rock Point**, St Helena
125 B 17 **Castlebar**, Republic of Ireland
127 T 2 **Castleford**, United Kingdom
83 I 21 **Castlegar**, British Columbia, Canada
129 Q 14 **Castres**, France
93 Z 11 **Castries**, St Lucia
111 F 18 **Castro**, Chile
112 I 8 **Castro**, Brazil
130 I 5 **Castro Daire**, Portugal
130 H 11 **Castro Verde**, Portugal
130 J 1 **Castropol**, Spain
141 M 18 **Castrovillari**, Italy
130 L 9 **Castuera**, Spain
233 A 23 **Caswell Sound**, New Zealand
171 Q 9 **Cat**, Turkey
92 L 3 **Cat Island**, The Bahamas
84 K 10 **Cat Lake**, Ontario, Canada
91 N 5 **Catacamas**, Honduras
62 J 6 **Catahoula Lake**, Louisiana, U.S.A.
171 S 12 **Çatak**, Turkey
109 J 17 **Catalão**, Brazil
146 O 12 **Çatalca**, Turkey
131 W 4 **Cataluña**, Spain
170 J 6 **Catalzeytin**, Turkey
110 I 8 **Catamarca**, Argentina
110 H 7 **Catamarca**, Argentina
111 G 16 **Catán Lil**, Argentina
219 Q 7 **Catandica**, Mozambique
196 L 12 **Catanduanes**, Philippines
141 K 22 **Catania**, Italy
141 M 20 **Catanzaro**, Italy
71 N 12 **Catarina**, Texas, U.S.A.
197 L 14 **Catarman**, Philippines
219 Q 6 **Cataxa**, Mozambique
197 L 15 **Catbalogan**, Philippines
197 N 21 **Cateel**, Philippines
214 E 10 **Catió**, Guinea-Bissau
233 D 25 **Catlins**, New Zealand
89 Q 8 **Catorce**, Mexico
111 H 15 **Catriel**, Argentina
110 J 13 **Catriló**, Argentina
58 K 10 **Catskill**, New York, U.S.A.
58 I 10 **Catskill Mountains**, New York, U.S.A.
196 H 8 **Cauayan**, Philippines
197 I 18 **Cauayan**, Philippines
104 G 8 **Cauca**, Colombia
104 I 4 **Cauca**, Colombia
104 H 4 **Caucasia**, Colombia
156 L 13 **Caucasus**, Russian Federation
171 Q 5 **Caucasus**, Georgia
110 H 10 **Caucete**, Argentina
197 N 19 **Cauit Point**, Philippines
218 I 2 **Caungula**, Angola
110 F 13 **Cauquenes**, Chile
105 Q 6 **Caura**, Venezuela
87 R 6 **Causapscal**, Québec, Canada
67 N 2 **Cavalier**, North Dakota, U.S.A.
232 J 5 **Cavalli Islands**, New Zealand
214 I 13 **Cavally**, Liberia
125 D 16 **Cavan**, Republic of Ireland
170 E 13 **Cavdir**, Turkey
233 F 21 **Cave**, New Zealand
60 K 5 **Cave Run Lake**, Kentucky, U.S.A.
197 G 19 **Cavili**, Philippines
196 G 11 **Cavite**, Philippines
108 L 11 **Caxias**, Brazil
112 H 11 **Caxias do Sul**, Brazil
218 G 2 **Caxito**, Angola
170 F 11 **Cay**, Turkey
92 I 3 **Cay Sal**, The Bahamas
106 C 8 **Cayambe**, Ecuador
171 P 8 **Cayeli**, Turkey
105 Z 6 **Cayenne**, French Guiana
170 G 9 **Cayirhan**, Turkey
92 I 7 **Cayman Brac**, Cayman Islands
92 I 7 **Cayman Islands**, United Kingdom, United Kingdom
42 B 11 **Cayman Trench**, Atlantic Ocean
92 H 8 **Cayman Trench**, Cayman Islands
213 M 20 **Caynabo**, Somalia
92 G 5 **Cayo del Rosario**, Cuba
92 H 5 **Cayo Largo**, Cuba
92 K 4 **Cayo Romano**, Cuba

Country · Internal administrative region: State/Province/Territory/Dependent territory · Capital city · Mountain range/Undersea ridge · Mountain peak/Volcano/Seamount · Geographic feature · Headland/Point/Cape/Peninsula · Desert · Island/Island group · Antarctic base · Ocean · Sea · Bay/Gulf/Channel/Strait · Lake · Salt pan/Dry/Intermittent lake · River

Cayo Sabinal – Chelforó

92 K 5 **Cayo Sabinal**, Cuba
91 S 6 **Cayos Miskitos**, Nicaragua
150 L 12 **Căzănești**, Romania
129 O 14 **Cazères**, France
218 L 4 **Cazombo**, Angola
219 R 5 **Cazula**, Mozambique
108 N 12 **Ceará**, Brazil
43 H 14 **Ceara Abyssal Plain**, Atlantic Ocean
42 G 13 **Ceara Ridge**, Atlantic Ocean
89 N 6 **Ceballos**, Mexico
131 P 4 **Cebollera**, Spain
197 K 18 **Cebu**, Philippines
197 K 17 **Cebu**, Philippines
143 I 24 **Cece**, Hungary
67 T 11 **Cedar**, Iowa, U.S.A.
74 I 7 **Cedar City**, Utah, U.S.A.
67 T 11 **Cedar Falls**, Iowa, U.S.A.
69 X 4 **Cedar Hill**, Missouri, U.S.A.
61 W 5 **Cedar Island**, Virginia, U.S.A.
63 U 9 **Cedar Key**, Florida, U.S.A.
84 H 8 **Cedar Lake**, Manitoba, Canada
67 U 12 **Cedar Rapids**, Iowa, U.S.A.
63 S 2 **Cedartown**, Georgia, U.S.A.
90 L 8 **Cedeño**, Honduras
41 V 4 **Cedros Trench**, Pacific Ocean
231 N 10 **Ceduna**, South Australia, Australia
142 D 11 **Cedynia**, Poland
130 G 1 **Cée**, Spain
213 O 19 **Ceel Gaal**, Somalia
213 N 19 **Ceerigaabo**, Somalia
141 J 21 **Cefalù**, Italy
158 L 8 **Cefalu Basin**, Mediterranean Sea
143 J 23 **Cegléd**, Hungary
189 O 11 **Ceheng**, China
170 K 9 **Cekerek**, Turkey
89 Q 11 **Celaya**, Mexico
40 J 7 **Celebes Sea**, Pacific Ocean
193 P 8 **Celebes Sea**, Asia
89 X 10 **Celestún**, Mexico
60 H 8 **Celina**, Tennessee, U.S.A.
65 K 18 **Celina**, Ohio, U.S.A.
144 D 7 **Celje**, Slovenia
136 H 13 **Celle**, Germany
133 D 20 **Celles**, Belgium
171 T 11 **Çelo Daglari**, Turkey
125 D 21 **Celtic Sea**, Republic of Ireland
42 K 7 **Celtic Shelf**, Atlantic Ocean
60 G 9 **Center Hill Lake**, Tennessee, U.S.A.
63 P 4 **Centerville**, Alabama, U.S.A.
67 T 14 **Centerville**, Iowa, U.S.A.
69 X 6 **Centerville**, Missouri, U.S.A.
71 R 8 **Centerville**, Texas, U.S.A.
140 F 8 **Cento**, Italy
217 V 8 **Central**, Kenya
219 N 5 **Central**, Zambia
219 N 9 **Central**, Botswana
219 Q 4 **Central**, Malawi
234 E 7 **Central**, Papua New Guinea
234 L 6 **Central**, Solomon Islands
234 M 8 **Central**, Solomon Islands
181 G 24 **Central**, Sri Lanka
183 P 9 **Central**, Nepal
216 H 4 **Central African Republic**, Africa
138 E 9 **Central Alps**, Switzerland
40 K 5 **Central Basin**, Pacific Ocean
177 T 12 **Central Brāhui Range**, Pakistan
60 F 6 **Central City**, Kentucky, U.S.A.
148 H 11 **Central Highlands of Vidzemes**, Latvia
237 Q 5 **Central Line Islands**, Kiribati
177 Q 13 **Central Makran Range**, Pakistan
41 P 6 **Central Pacific Basin**, Pacific Ocean
138 D 7 **Central Plateau**, Switzerland
234 A 4 **Central Range**, Papua New Guinea
153 Q 9 **Central Siberian Plateau**, Russian Federation
111 F 14 **Central Valley**, Chile
77 H 16 **Central Valley**, California, U.S.A.
65 F 21 **Centralia**, Illinois, U.S.A.
76 G 8 **Centralia**, Washington, U.S.A.
215 U 13 **Centre**, Cameroon
129 P 7 **Centre**, France
38 B 12 **Centre de Flacq**, Mauritius
233 B 25 **Centre Island**, New Zealand
189 R 12 **Cenxi**, China
141 I 14 **Ceprano**, Italy
110 K 9 **Ceres**, Argentina
141 L 15 **Cerignola**, Italy
170 I 9 **Cerikli**, Turkey
170 H 8 **Cerkeş**, Turkey
146 N 12 **Cerkezköy**, Turkey
144 B 8 **Cerknica**, Slovenia
171 O 12 **Cermik**, Turkey
151 N 12 **Cerna**, Romania
150 M 13 **Cernavodă**, Romania
89 Q 7 **Cerralvo**, Mexico
145 K 19 **Cërrik**, Albania
89 Q 10 **Cerritos**, Mexico
110 G 11 **Cerro Amarillo**, Argentina
111 F 21 **Cerro Arenales**, Chile
107 A 19 **Cerro Azol**, Ecuador
112 J 8 **Cerro Azul**, Brazil
89 S 10 **Cerro Azul**, Mexico
107 J 23 **Cerro Bonete**, Bolivia
110 G 8 **Cerro Bonete**, Argentina
113 F 15 **Cerro Catedral**, Uruguay
111 F 23 **Cerro Cervantes**, Argentina
110 J 11 **Cerro Champaqui**, Argentina
91 R 13 **Cerro Chirripó Grande**, Costa Rica
111 H 20 **Cerro Cojudo Blanco**, Argentina
88 F 2 **Cerro de La Encantada**, Mexico
110 G 10 **Cerro de Olivares**, Chile
107 D 15 **Cerro de Pasco**, Peru
110 G 8 **Cerro de Petro**, Chile
93 U 8 **Cerro de Punta**, Puerto Rico
110 H 6 **Cerro del Rincón**, Argentina
89 R 9 **Cerro del Tigre**, Mexico
105 P 7 **Cerro Duida**, Venezuela
104 I 7 **Cerro El Nevado**, Colombia
88 H 6 **Cerro Encantado**, Mexico
111 F 22 **Cerro Fitz Roy**, Argentina
110 H 7 **Cerro Galán**, Argentina
105 Q 6 **Cerro Guaiquinima**, Venezuela
111 F 20 **Cerro Hudson**, Chile
88 L 8 **Cerro Huehueto**, Mexico
112 F 13 **Cerro Largo**, Uruguay
90 K 6 **Cerro Las Minas**, Honduras
110 F 9 **Cerro Las Tórtolas**, Chile
111 F 22 **Cerro Lautaron**, Chile
105 O 7 **Cerro Marahuaca**, Venezuela
111 F 21 **Cerro Mellizo Sur**, Chile
107 I 22 **Cerro Milliri**, Bolivia/Chile
111 F 22 **Cerro Murallón**, Chile
110 H 13 **Cerro Nevado**, Argentina
105 O 7 **Cerro Ovana**, Venezuela
111 F 23 **Cerro Paine**, Chile
105 O 6 **Cerro Paraque**, Venezuela
111 H 14 **Cerro Payún**, Argentina
89 R 8 **Cerro Peña Nevada**, Mexico
110 H 6 **Cerro Pular**, Chile
91 S 13 **Cerro Punta**, Panama
111 F 21 **Cerro San Lorenzo**, Argentina
109 G 20 **Cerro San Rafael**, Paraguay
111 F 20 **Cerro San Valentín**, Chile
91 O 7 **Cerro Saslaya**, Nicaragua
88 J 5 **Cerro Seberi**, Mexico
89 U 12 **Cerro Sta Martha**, Mexico
89 O 12 **Cerro Tancitaro**, Mexico
113 B 19 **Cerro Tres Picos**, Argentina
110 G 12 **Cerro Tupungato**, Argentina
88 H 3 **Cerro Viejo**, Mexico
107 C 15 **Cerro Yerupaja**, Peru
140 F 11 **Certaldo**, Italy
131 V 4 **Cervera**, Spain
140 H 9 **Cervia**, Italy
130 J 1 **Cervo**, Spain
104 J 3 **Cesar**, Colombia
140 G 9 **Cesena**, Italy
148 G 10 **Cēsis**, Latvia
143 D 16 **Česká Lípa**, Czech Republic
143 F 17 **Česká Třebová**, Czech Republic
143 C 19 **České Budějovice**, Czech Republic
143 C 20 **Český Krumlov**, Czech Republic
170 A 11 **Çeşme**, Turkey
231 V 11 **Cessnock**, New South Wales, Australia
148 H 11 **Cesvaine**, Latvia
130 L 14 **Ceuta**, Spain
138 G 10 **Cevio**, Switzerland
170 K 13 **Ceyhan**, Turkey
171 P 13 **Ceylanpinar**, Turkey
39 P 4 **Ceylon Plain**, Indian Ocean
177 O 14 **Chābahār**, Iran
106 C 12 **Chachapoyas**, Peru
149 N 19 **Chachersk**, Belarus
110 K 7 **Chaco**, Argentina
215 W 8 **Chad**, Africa
61 R 12 **Chadbourn**, North Carolina, U.S.A.
111 I 14 **Chadileo**, Argentina
66 H 11 **Chadron**, Nebraska, U.S.A.
187 K 18 **Chaeryŏng**, North Korea
177 P 11 **Chagai Hills**, Pakistan
179 W 4 **Chagan**, Kazakhstan
177 R 7 **Chaghcharān**, Afghanistan
39 N 5 **Chagos Archipelago**, British Indian Ocean Territory
39 N 5 **Chagos Trench**, Indian Ocean
39 N 4 **Chagos–Laccadive Ridge**, Indian Ocean
176 I 8 **Chahār Mahall Va Bakhtīārī**, Iran
181 J 15 **Chaibasa**, India
38 K 4 **Chain Ridge**, Indian Ocean
191 H 18 **Chainat**, Thailand
111 F 18 **Chaitén**, Chile
191 I 17 **Chaiyaphum**, Thailand
112 D 13 **Chajarí**, Argentina
181 J 15 **Chakradharpur**, India
182 J 6 **Chakrata**, India
217 R 12 **Chala**, Tanzania
107 E 19 **Chala**, Peru
129 N 11 **Chalais**, France
90 J 6 **Chalatenango**, El Salvador
219 T 6 **Chaláua**, Mozambique
217 V 6 **Chalbi Desert**, Kenya
127 T 14 **Chale**, United Kingdom
87 S 7 **Chaleur Bay**, New Brunswick, Canada
189 T 9 **Chaling**, China
147 N 24 **Chalki**, Greece
147 G 19 **Chalkida**, Greece
179 X 9 **Chalkudysu**, Kazakhstan
128 K 8 **Challans**, France
107 J 21 **Challapata**, Bolivia
40 L 6 **Challenger Deep**, Pacific Ocean
41 V 11 **Challenger Fracture Zone**, Pacific Ocean
41 O 12 **Challenger Plateau**, Pacific Ocean
72 M 9 **Challis**, Idaho, U.S.A.
129 T 8 **Chalon-sur-Saône**, France
129 S 4 **Châlons-en-Champagne**, France
176 I 5 **Chālūs**, Iran
137 L 21 **Cham**, Germany
219 Q 3 **Chama**, Zambia
177 S 10 **Chaman**, Pakistan
217 V 15 **Chamba**, Tanzania
182 I 5 **Chamba**, India
66 L 10 **Chamberlain**, South Dakota, U.S.A.
59 Q 2 **Chamberlain Lake**, Maine, U.S.A.
74 M 10 **Chambers**, Arizona, U.S.A.
58 E 14 **Chambersburg**, Pennsylvania, U.S.A.
129 V 10 **Chambéry**, France
219 P 3 **Chambeshi**, Zambia
173 U 3 **Chamchamāl**, Iraq
91 W 14 **Chame**, Panama
90 J 5 **Chamelec**, Honduras
110 I 10 **Chamical**, Argentina
182 L 7 **Chamoli**, India
129 W 9 **Chamonix-Mont-Blanc**, France
181 H 15 **Champa**, India
129 T 4 **Champagne-Ardenne**, France
65 G 18 **Champaign**, Illinois, U.S.A.
191 L 18 **Champasak**, Laos
58 K 5 **Champlain**, New York, U.S.A.
89 X 12 **Champotón**, Mexico
181 D 22 **Chamrajnagar**, India
157 P 2 **Chamzinka**, Russian Federation
110 F 7 **Chañaral**, Chile
177 O 5 **Chanārān**, Iran
110 F 13 **Chanco**, Chile
182 K 8 **Chandausi**, India
181 J 16 **Chandbali**, India
63 N 8 **Chandeleur Islands**, Mississippi, U.S.A.
63 N 8 **Chandeleur Sound**, Mississippi, U.S.A.
180 E 13 **Chanderi**, India
182 J 6 **Chandigarh**, India
74 J 13 **Chandler**, Arizona, U.S.A.
87 T 6 **Chandler**, Québec, Canada
183 U 13 **Chandpur**, Bangladesh
181 F 17 **Chandrapur**, India
219 Q 6 **Changara**, Mozambique
187 K 15 **Changbai Shan**, China
186 J 13 **Changchun**, China
189 S 8 **Changde**, China
189 Z 11 **Changhua**, Taiwan
187 L 22 **Changhŭng**, South Korea
194 C 14 **Changi**, Singapore
184 K 4 **Changji**, China
189 Q 15 **Changjiang**, China
187 F 17 **Changli**, China
186 I 12 **Changling**, China
189 T 8 **Changsha**, China
189 X 8 **Changshan**, China
187 I 17 **Changshan Qundao**, China
189 Y 5 **Changshu**, China
187 J 16 **Changsong**, North Korea
189 W 10 **Changting**, China
187 J 14 **Changtu**, China
91 S 13 **Changuinola**, Panama
187 N 21 **Ch'angwŏn**, South Korea
189 Y 6 **Changxing**, China
187 H 17 **Changxing Dao**, China
189 S 6 **Changyang**, China
187 J 18 **Changyŏn**, North Korea
189 U 3 **Changyuan**, China
189 T 2 **Changzhi**, China
189 Y 5 **Changzhou**, China
147 H 26 **Chania**, Greece
125 J 26 **Channel Islands**, United Kingdom
77 I 24 **Channel Islands**, California, U.S.A.
85 X 11 **Channel-Port-aux-Basques**, Newfoundland and Labrador, Canada
127 Z 12 **Channel Tunnel**, France/United Kingdom
70 J 2 **Channing**, Texas, U.S.A.
153 Z 6 **Chantal'skiy**, Russian Federation
191 I 20 **Chanthaburi**, Thailand
128 L 8 **Chantonnay**, France
181 N 24 **Chanumla**, India
69 Q 6 **Chanute**, Kansas, U.S.A.
107 B 14 **Chao**, Peru
189 W 5 **Chao Hu**, China
191 G 17 **Chao Phraya**, Thailand
189 W 5 **Chaohu**, China
186 H 8 **Chaor**, China
210 I 6 **Chaouèn**, Morocco
187 G 15 **Chaoyang**, China
189 W 12 **Chaoyang**, China
189 W 12 **Chaozhou**, China
104 H 7 **Chaparral**, Colombia
178 I 4 **Chapayevo**, Kazakhstan
157 S 4 **Chapayevsk**, Russian Federation
179 T 3 **Chapayevskoye**, Kazakhstan
112 G 10 **Chapecó**, Brazil
127 R 4 **Chapel-en-le-Frith**, United Kingdom
86 B 7 **Chapleau**, Ontario, Canada
83 M 19 **Chaplin**, Saskatchewan, Canada
156 M 4 **Chaplygin**, Russian Federation
151 T 10 **Chaplynka**, Ukraine
60 M 5 **Chapmanville**, West Virginia, U.S.A.
107 L 22 **Charagua**, Bolivia
107 H 20 **Charana**, Bolivia
110 K 8 **Charata**, Argentina
89 P 9 **Charcas**, Mexico
240 I 6 **Charcot Island**, Antarctica
127 P 13 **Chard**, United Kingdom
179 O 13 **Chardzhev**, Turkmenistan
215 W 10 **Chari-Baguirmi**, Chad
177 U 7 **Chārīkār**, Afghanistan
67 T 14 **Chariton**, Iowa, U.S.A.
105 U 5 **Charity**, Guyana
64 L 12 **Charity Island**, Michigan, U.S.A.
182 I 8 **Charkhi Dadri**, India
133 G 21 **Charleroi**, Belgium
67 T 11 **Charles City**, Iowa, U.S.A.
65 E 15 **Charles Mound**, Illinois, U.S.A.
87 N 8 **Charlesbourg**, Québec, Canada
233 F 17 **Charleston**, New Zealand
61 Q 15 **Charleston**, South Carolina, U.S.A.
61 N 4 **Charleston**, West Virginia, U.S.A.
77 M 21 **Charleston Peak**, Nevada, U.S.A.
231 T 8 **Charleville**, Queensland, Australia
129 S 3 **Charleville-Mézières**, France
64 J 10 **Charlevoix**, Michigan, U.S.A.
42 G 6 **Charlie–Gibbs Fracture Zone**, Atlantic Ocean
61 O 10 **Charlotte**, North Carolina, U.S.A.
65 K 14 **Charlotte**, Michigan, U.S.A.
93 V 8 **Charlotte Amalie**, Virgin Islands, U.S.A.
63 W 12 **Charlotte Harbor**, Florida, U.S.A.
61 S 5 **Charlottesville**, Virginia, U.S.A.
87 V 8 **Charlottetown**, Prince Edward Island, Canada
93 Z 13 **Charlotteville**, Trinidad and Tobago
231 R 12 **Charlton**, Victoria, Australia
81 T 11 **Charlton Island**, Nunav Canada
129 V 5 **Charmes**, France
127 P 13 **Charmouth**, United Kingdom
177 W 7 **Charsadda**, Pakistan
179 P 14 **Charshanga**, Turkmenistan
231 T 5 **Charters Towers**, Queensland, Australia
129 P 5 **Chartres**, France
179 X 9 **Charyn**, Kazakhstan
113 D 16 **Chascomús**, Argentina
149 K 15 **Chashniki**, Belarus
67 S 8 **Chaska**, Minnesota, U.S
187 K 15 **Chasŏng**, North Korea
155 P 9 **Chasovo**, Russian Federation
79 S 6 **Chatanika**, Alaska, U.S.
129 S 7 **Château-Chinon**, Franc
129 N 6 **Château-du-Loir**, Franc
129 R 4 **Château-Thierry**, Franc
128 L 6 **Châteaubriant**, France
129 O 6 **Châteaudun**, France
86 L 11 **Châteauguay**, Québec, Canada
128 H 5 **Châteaulin**, France
129 P 8 **Châteauroux**, France
129 N 8 **Châtellerault**, France
127 X 11 **Chatham**, United Kingdom
86 B 14 **Chatham**, Ontario, Canada
87 T 8 **Chatham**, New Brunsw Canada
41 P 12 **Chatham Islands**, Pacifi Ocean
79 X 11 **Chatham Strait**, Alaska, U.S.A.
129 O 8 **Châtillon-sur-Indre**, Fra
129 T 6 **Châtillon-sur-Seine**, France
183 P 12 **Chatra**, India
60 H 10 **Chattanooga**, Tennesse U.S.A.
63 S 7 **Chattaoochee**, Florida, U.S.A.
127 W 7 **Chatteris**, United Kingdom
191 I 17 **Chatturat**, Thailand
179 V 11 **Chatyr-Tash**, Kyrgyzstan
191 L 22 **Châu Đôc**, Vietnam
190 C 12 **Chauk**, Myanmar
182 L 9 **Chauka**, India
129 T 5 **Chaumont**, France
181 G 23 **Chavakachcheri**, Sri Lan
154 J 5 **Chavan'ga**, Russian Federation
108 J 9 **Chaves**, Brazil
130 J 4 **Chaves**, Portugal
218 L 4 **Chavuma**, Zambia
149 N 17 **Chavusy**, Belarus
155 S 14 **Chaykovskiy**, Russian Federation
110 J 11 **Chazón**, Argentina
63 Q 3 **Cheaha Mountain**, Alabama, U.S.A.
143 A 17 **Cheb**, Czech Republic
211 R 6 **Chebba**, Tunisia
157 R 1 **Cheboksary**, Russian Federation
64 K 10 **Cheboygan**, Michigan, U.S.A.
157 P 13 **Chechenskaya Respubli** Russian Federation
187 M 19 **Chech'ŏn**, South Korea
143 K 16 **Chęciny**, Poland
69 Q 10 **Checotah**, Oklahoma, U.S.A.
127 P 11 **Cheddar**, United Kingdo
191 B 14 **Cheduba Island**, Myanmar
78 L 9 **Chefornak**, Alaska, U.S.A.
214 K 3 **Chegga**, Mauritania
76 G 8 **Chehalis**, Washington, U.S.A.
187 L 23 **Cheju**, South Korea
187 L 23 **Cheju-do**, South Korea
154 K 11 **Chekshino**, Russian Federation
178 I 12 **Cheleken**, Turkmenistan
111 I 15 **Chelforó**, Argentina

Country · Internal administrative region: State/Province/Territory/Dependent territory · Capital city · Mountain range/Undersea ridge · Mountain peak/Volcano/Seamount · Geographic feature · Headland/Point/Cape/Peninsula · Desert · Island/Island group · Antarctic base · Ocean · Sea · Bay/Gulf/Channel/Strait · Lake · Salt pan/Dry/Intermittent lake

M 7 **Chelkar**, Kazakhstan
O 15 **Chełm**, Poland
I 10 **Chełmno**, Poland
X 10 **Chelmsford**, United Kingdom
I 11 **Chełmża**, Poland
L 14 **Cheltenham**, New Zealand
Q 9 **Cheltenham**, United Kingdom
S 8 **Chelva**, Spain
G 18 **Chelvai**, India
I 11 **Chelyabinsk**, Russian Federation
Q 6 **Chelyuskin**, Russian Federation
G 8 **Chemaïa**, Morocco
N 15 **Chemenibit**, Turkmenistan
L 17 **Chemnitz**, Germany
H 12 **Chemult**, Oregon, U.S.A.
S 6 **Chena Hot Springs**, Alaska, U.S.A.
I 11 **Chenachane**, Algeria
H 22 **Ch'ench'a**, Ethiopia
M 6 **Cheney Reservoir**, Kansas, U.S.A. 💧
U 2 **Cheng'an**, China
E 16 **Chengde**, China
N 6 **Chengdu**, China
Z 8 **Chengele**, India
W 12 **Chenghai**, China
Q 5 **Chengkou**, China
R 15 **Chengmai**, China
G 21 **Chennai**, India
G 18 **Chenoa**, Illinois, U.S.A.
R 8 **Chenxi**, China
T 10 **Chenzhou**, China
I 11 **Chepelare**, Bulgaria
B 13 **Chepén**, Peru
I 10 **Chepes**, Argentina
X 13 **Chepo**, Panama
P 10 **Chepstow**, United Kingdom
Q 11 **Cheraw**, South Carolina, U.S.A.
L 3 **Cherbourg**, France
S 10 **Cherdyn'**, Russian Federation
M 12 **Cherepanovo**, Russian Federation
I 12 **Cherepovets**, Russian Federation
M 9 **Cherevkovo**, Russian Federation
P 6 **Chéria**, Algeria
C 23 **Cheriyam**, India 🏝
R 5 **Cherkasy**, Ukraine
N 13 **Cherkessk**, Russian Federation
K 12 **Cherlak**, Russian Federation
S 12 **Chermoz**, Russian Federation
Q 2 **Chernaya**, Russian Federation
F 9 **Cherni Vrŭkh**, Bulgaria ▲
Q 2 **Chernihiv**, Ukraine
W 8 **Cherninivka**, Ukraine
K 7 **Chernivtsi**, Ukraine
P 2 **Chernobyl**, Ukraine
N 10 **Chernoostrovskoye**, Russian Federation
T 14 **Chernushka**, Russian Federation
N 3 **Chernyakhiv**, Ukraine
C 16 **Chernyakhovsk**, Russian Federation
S 13 **Chernyshevsk**, Russian Federation
R 10 **Chernyshevskiy**, Russian Federation
W 4 **Chernyy Otrog**, Russian Federation
Q 11 **Cherokee**, Iowa, U.S.A.
L 8 **Cherokee**, Oklahoma, U.S.A.
K 8 **Cherokee Lake**, Tennessee, U.S.A. 💧
V 11 **Cherrapunji**, India
I 14 **Cherry Hill**, New Jersey, U.S.A.
W 7 **Cherskiy**, Russian Federation
J 3 **Chervonohrad**, Ukraine
151 Y 5 **Chervonooskil's'ke Vodoskhovyshche**, Ukraine 💧
151 P 9 **Chervonoznam''yanka**, Ukraine
149 K 18 **Chervyen'**, Belarus
149 N 18 **Cherykaw**, Belarus
65 L 14 **Chesaning**, Michigan, U.S.A.
61 V 7 **Chesapeake**, Virginia, U.S.A.
61 V 4 **Chesapeake Bay**, Maryland, U.S.A. ≈
61 V 3 **Chesapeake Beach**, Maryland, U.S.A.
155 N 4 **Cheshskaya Guba**, Russian Federation ≈
127 P 4 **Chester**, United Kingdom
61 O 11 **Chester**, South Carolina, U.S.A.
61 T 6 **Chester**, Virginia, U.S.A.
65 E 22 **Chester**, Illinois, U.S.A.
73 Q 2 **Chester**, Montana, U.S.A.
77 H 16 **Chester**, California, U.S.A.
87 U 11 **Chester**, Nova Scotia, Canada
127 S 4 **Chesterfield**, United Kingdom
84 M 3 **Chesterfield Inlet**, Nunavut, Canada ≈
59 Q 3 **Chesuncook Lake**, Maine, U.S.A. 💧
87 X 8 **Chéticamp**, Nova Scotia, Canada
181 B 22 **Chetlat**, India 🏝
89 Z 12 **Chetumal**, Mexico
233 J 15 **Chetwode Islands**, New Zealand 🏝
83 G 17 **Chetwynd**, British Columbia, Canada
78 L 9 **Chevak**, Alaska, U.S.A.
233 I 19 **Cheviot**, New Zealand
213 H 23 **Che'w Bahir**, Ethiopia 💧
76 K 6 **Chewelah**, Washington, U.S.A.
68 J 10 **Cheyenne**, Oklahoma, U.S.A.
73 Z 14 **Cheyenne**, Wyoming, U.S.A.
73 Y 11 **Cheyenne**, Wyoming/Utah, U.S.A. ∿
75 U 5 **Cheyenne Wells**, Colorado, U.S.A.
183 P 11 **Chhapra**, India
183 V 11 **Chhatak**, Bangladesh
182 L 12 **Chhatarpur**, India
181 I 17 **Chhatrapur**, India
181 F 15 **Chhindwara**, India
183 T 10 **Chhukha**, Bhutan
189 Z 12 **Chiai**, Taiwan
191 I 15 **Chiang Khan**, Thailand
191 G 14 **Chiang Mai**, Thailand
190 H 13 **Chiang Rai**, Thailand
89 X 14 **Chiapas**, Mexico ▣
171 S 6 **Chiat'ura**, Georgia
140 D 5 **Chiavenno**, Italy
199 L 16 **Chiba**, Japan
218 G 6 **Chibemba**, Angola
218 G 6 **Chibia**, Angola
85 R 11 **Chibougamau**, Québec, Canada
199 D 17 **Chibu**, Japan
199 D 17 **Chiburi-jima**, Japan 🏝
65 H 16 **Chicago**, Illinois, U.S.A.
79 W 11 **Chichagof Island**, Alaska, U.S.A. 🏝
210 G 8 **Chichaoua**, Morocco
90 G 5 **Chiché**, Guatemala
187 D 16 **Chicheng**, China
127 U 13 **Chichester**, United Kingdom
105 N 2 **Chichiriviche**, Venezuela
60 I 10 **Chickamauga Lake**, Tennessee, U.S.A. 💧
68 L 11 **Chickasha**, Oklahoma, U.S.A.
79 T 7 **Chicken**, Alaska, U.S.A.
106 B 13 **Chiclayo**, Peru
111 H 19 **Chico**, Argentina ∿
77 G 17 **Chico**, California, U.S.A.
218 H 5 **Chicomba**, Angola
219 Q 9 **Chicualacuala**, Mozambique
219 R 10 **Chidenguele**, Mozambique
137 L 25 **Chiemsee**, Germany 💧
219 O 2 **Chiengi**, Zambia
191 F 23 **Chieo Lan Reservoir**, Thailand 💧
140 B 8 **Chieri**, Italy
140 J 13 **Chieti**, Italy
187 F 14 **Chifeng**, China
87 T 10 **Chigneco Bay**, New Brunswick, Canada ≈
107 I 22 **Chiguana**, Bolivia
219 Q 9 **Chigubo**, Mozambique
88 M 5 **Chihuahua**, Mexico
88 M 5 **Chihuahua**, Mexico ▣
179 Q 9 **Chiili**, Kazakhstan
154 E 13 **Chikhachevo**, Russian Federation
181 C 21 **Chikmagalur**, India
181 C 19 **Chikodi**, India
219 Q 3 **Chikwa**, Zambia
198 J 7 **Chikyū-misaki**, Japan ▶
218 G 4 **Chila**, Angola
177 Y 6 **Chilas**, Pakistan
182 H 2 **Chilas**, India
181 F 24 **Chilaw**, Sri Lanka
231 V 7 **Childers**, Queensland, Australia
70 M 3 **Childress**, Texas, U.S.A.
111 F 15 **Chile**, South America □
111 G 20 **Chile Chico**, Chile
110 H 9 **Chilecito**, Argentina
127 Y 11 **Chilham**, United Kingdom
179 W 9 **Chilik**, Kazakhstan
219 N 4 **Chililabombwe**, Zambia
231 S 3 **Chillagoe**, Queensland, Australia
111 F 14 **Chillán**, Chile
113 C 18 **Chillar**, Argentina
65 F 17 **Chillicothe**, Illinois, U.S.A.
65 M 19 **Chillicothe**, Ohio, U.S.A.
69 T 2 **Chillicothe**, Missouri, U.S.A.
107 H 20 **Chilliculco**, Peru
177 Y 5 **Chillinji**, Pakistan
76 G 13 **Chiloquin**, Oregon, U.S.A.
89 R 13 **Chilpancingo**, Mexico
127 T 10 **Chiltern Hills**, United Kingdom ⛰
64 G 12 **Chilton**, Wisconsin, U.S.A.
219 R 3 **Chilumba**, Malawi
189 Z 10 **Chilung**, Taiwan
217 T 13 **Chimala**, Tanzania
90 G 6 **Chimaltenango**, Guatemala
91 X 14 **Chimán**, Panama
219 Q 8 **Chimanimani**, Zimbabwe
133 F 23 **Chimay**, Belgium
106 B 9 **Chimborazo**, Ecuador ▲
106 B 9 **Chimborazo**, Ecuador ▣
107 B 14 **Chimbote**, Peru
234 C 5 **Chimbu**, Papua New Guinea ▣
177 Y 10 **Chimian**, Pakistan
219 Q 7 **Chimoio**, Mozambique
190 B 11 **Chin**, Myanmar ▣
187 L 22 **Chin-do**, South Korea 🏝
187 E 14 **China**, Asia □
89 R 7 **China**, Mexico
90 H 4 **Chinajá**, Guatemala
90 M 8 **Chinandega**, Nicaragua
70 G 10 **Chinati Peak**, Texas, U.S.A. ▲
179 R 12 **Chinaz**, Uzbekistan
107 D 17 **Chincha Alta**, Peru
83 G 16 **Chinchaga**, Alberta, Canada ∿
231 V 8 **Chinchilla**, Queensland, Australia
219 S 7 **Chinde**, Mozambique
188 H 4 **Chindu**, China
190 C 8 **Chindwin**, Myanmar ∿
178 J 4 **Chingirlau**, Kazakhstan
219 N 4 **Chingola**, Zambia
218 H 4 **Chinguar**, Angola
214 G 5 **Chinguetti**, Mauritania
215 X 11 **Chinguil**, Chad
219 P 6 **Chinhoyi**, Zimbabwe
177 X 9 **Chiniot**, Pakistan
187 M 21 **Chinju**, South Korea
178 J 11 **Chink Kaplankyr**, Uzbekistan ⛰
74 M 9 **Chinle**, Arizona, U.S.A.
189 X 11 **Chinmen Tao**, Taiwan 🏝
181 F 17 **Chinnur**, India
199 I 16 **Chino**, Japan
129 N 7 **Chinon**, France
73 S 2 **Chinook**, Montana, U.S.A.
41 P 3 **Chinook Trough**, Pacific Ocean ◇
219 Q 3 **Chinsali**, Zambia
181 E 21 **Chintamani**, India
140 G 7 **Chioggia**, Italy
147 K 19 **Chios**, Greece
147 K 19 **Chios**, Greece 🏝
219 Q 4 **Chipata**, Zambia
219 O 3 **Chipili**, Zambia
87 S 9 **Chipman**, New Brunswick, Canada
218 J 4 **Chipoia**, Angola
127 R 11 **Chippenham**, United Kingdom
64 D 11 **Chippewa Falls**, Wisconsin, U.S.A.
127 S 8 **Chipping Campden**, United Kingdom
127 S 9 **Chipping Norton**, United Kingdom
127 W 9 **Chipping Ongar**, United Kingdom
127 Q 10 **Chipping Sodbury**, United Kingdom
59 R 3 **Chiputneticook Lakes**, Maine, U.S.A. 💧
107 D 15 **Chiquian**, Peru
89 Z 10 **Chiquilá**, Mexico
90 I 5 **Chiquimula**, Guatemala
104 I 6 **Chiquinquira**, Colombia
157 N 8 **Chir**, Russian Federation ∿
181 G 19 **Chirala**, India
219 R 6 **Chiramba**, Mozambique
182 I 8 **Chirawa**, India
179 R 11 **Chirchik**, Uzbekistan
219 P 8 **Chiredzi**, Zimbabwe
215 T 5 **Chirfa**, Niger
187 M 21 **Chiri-san**, South Korea ▲
74 M 15 **Chiricahua Peak**, Arizona, U.S.A. ▲
104 J 3 **Chiriguana**, Colombia
79 O 13 **Chirikof Island**, Alaska, U.S.A. 🏝
91 T 14 **Chiriquí Grande**, Panama
181 H 15 **Chirmiri**, India
219 R 6 **Chiromo**, Mozambique
146 J 10 **Chirpan**, Bulgaria
91 Q 11 **Chirripo**, Costa Rica ∿
219 O 6 **Chirundu**, Zambia
176 J 13 **Chīrūyeh**, Iran
219 O 5 **Chisamba**, Zambia
85 P 9 **Chisasibi**, Québec, Canada
90 H 4 **Chisec**, Guatemala
189 Z 12 **Ch'ishan**, Taiwan
157 V 2 **Chishmy**, Russian Federation
177 X 11 **Chishtian Mandi**, Pakistan
151 O 9 **Chişinău**, Moldova ⌂
150 F 9 **Chişineu-Criş**, Romania
157 S 1 **Chistopol'**, Russian Federation
179 Q 3 **Chistopol'ye**, Kazakhstan
153 R 14 **Chita**, Russian Federation
218 G 7 **Chitado**, Angola
219 P 4 **Chitambo**, Zambia
218 K 1 **Chitato**, Angola
79 S 9 **Chitina**, Alaska, U.S.A.
219 Q 2 **Chitipa**, Malawi
198 K 6 **Chitose**, Japan
181 D 20 **Chitradurga**, India
177 W 6 **Chitral**, Pakistan
91 V 15 **Chitré**, Panama
183 W 14 **Chittagong**, Bangladesh
183 W 14 **Chittagong**, Bangladesh ▣
180 D 13 **Chittaurgarh**, India
181 F 21 **Chittoor**, India
219 O 7 **Chitungwiza**, Zimbabwe
218 K 5 **Chiume**, Angola
140 B 7 **Chivasso**, Italy
219 P 7 **Chivhu**, Zimbabwe
90 G 4 **Chixoy**, Guatemala ∿
154 M 4 **Chizha**, Russian Federation
199 F 18 **Chizu**, Japan
179 R 2 **Chkalovo**, Kazakhstan
154 L 14 **Chkalovsk**, Russian Federation
143 L 16 **Chmielnik**, Poland
187 J 18 **Cho-do**, North Korea 🏝
191 L 18 **Chŏâm Khsant**, Cambodia
218 M 7 **Chobe**, Botswana ▣
187 L 20 **Choch'iwŏn**, South Korea
104 G 6 **Chocó**, Colombia ▣
197 K 18 **Chocolate Hills**, Philippines ⛰
104 J 6 **Chocontá**, Colombia
142 G 11 **Chodzież**, Poland
111 I 15 **Choele Choel**, Argentina
219 Q 5 **Chofombo**, Mozambique
234 K 5 **Choiseul**, Solomon Islands 🏝
111 L 24 **Choiseul Sound**, Falkland Islands ≈
88 K 6 **Choix**, Mexico
142 H 10 **Chojnice**, Poland
198 K 11 **Chōkai-san**, Japan ▲
71 O 12 **Choke Canyon Lake**, Texas, U.S.A. 💧
179 U 9 **Chokpar**, Kazakhstan
153 V 7 **Chokurdakh**, Russian Federation
219 Q 10 **Chókwe**, Mozambique
128 M 7 **Cholet**, France
111 G 18 **Cholila**, Argentina
179 V 10 **Cholpon-Ata**, Kyrgyzstan
90 M 8 **Choluteca**, Honduras
191 G 15 **Chom Thong**, Thailand
219 N 6 **Choma**, Zambia
143 B 16 **Chomutov**, Czech Republic
191 H 19 **Chon Buri**, Thailand
191 N 21 **Chon Thanh**, Vietnam
187 L 19 **Ch'ŏnan**, South Korea
106 A 9 **Chone**, Ecuador
187 N 14 **Ch'ŏngjin**, North Korea
187 L 20 **Ch'ŏngju**, South Korea
187 J 17 **Chŏngju**, North Korea
189 Z 5 **Chongming**, China
218 F 5 **Chongoroi**, Angola
187 K 17 **Chŏngp'yŏng**, North Korea
189 O 7 **Chongqing**, China
189 P 7 **Chongqing**, China ▣
189 V 8 **Chongren**, China
187 L 21 **Chŏngŭp**, South Korea
219 O 5 **Chongwe**, Zambia
187 L 21 **Chŏnju**, South Korea
185 T 4 **Chonogol**, Mongolia
150 G 6 **Chop**, Ukraine
127 P 3 **Chorley**, United Kingdom
150 K 6 **Chortkiv**, Ukraine
181 A 15 **Chorwad**, India
187 L 18 **Ch'ŏrwŏn**, South Korea
142 L 10 **Chorzele**, Poland
111 G 14 **Chos Malal**, Argentina
187 K 16 **Ch'osan**, North Korea
199 L 16 **Chōshi**, Japan
142 E 11 **Choszczno**, Poland
106 B 13 **Chota**, Peru
181 I 14 **Chota Nagpur**, India ⛰
73 P 4 **Choteau**, Montana, U.S.A.
210 L 6 **Chott ech Chergui**, Algeria 💧
211 N 6 **Chott el Hodna**, Algeria 💧
211 P 7 **Chott el Jerid**, Tunisia 💧
211 O 7 **Chott Melrhir**, Algeria 💧
214 G 5 **Choûm**, Mauritania
69 Q 9 **Chouteau**, Oklahoma, U.S.A.
185 S 3 **Choybalsan**, Mongolia
185 R 4 **Choyr**, Mongolia
233 H 20 **Christchurch**, New Zealand
127 S 13 **Christchurch**, United Kingdom
237 P 2 **Christmas Island**, Kiribati 🏝
192 G 15 **Christmas Island**, Australia 🏝
79 S 8 **Christochina**, Alaska, U.S.A.
147 K 21 **Christos**, Greece
143 E 17 **Chrudim**, Czech Republic
146 I 13 **Chrysoupoli**, Greece
143 J 17 **Chrzanów**, Poland
179 R 9 **Chu**, Kazakhstan ∿
179 T 9 **Chu-Iliyskiye Gory**, Kazakhstan ⛰
191 O 20 **Chu Yang Sin**, Vietnam ▲
189 Z 6 **Chuansha**, China
189 P 11 **Chuanshan**, China
188 J 7 **Chubalung**, China
111 H 18 **Chubut**, Argentina ▣
111 H 18 **Chubut**, Argentina ∿
153 Z 5 **Chuckchi Sea**, Russian Federation/U.S.A. 🌊
91 Z 14 **Chucunaque**, Panama ∿
151 N 4 **Chudniv**, Ukraine
154 F 11 **Chudovo**, Russian Federation
149 I 20 **Chudzin**, Belarus
79 S 9 **Chugach Mountains**, Alaska, U.S.A. ⛰
199 D 19 **Chūgoku-sanchi**, Japan ⛰
73 Z 13 **Chugwater**, Wyoming, U.S.A.
151 W 4 **Chuhuyiv**, Ukraine
188 I 7 **Chuka**, China
45 S 4 **Chukchi Abyssal Plain**, Arctic Ocean ◇
45 R 5 **Chukchi Plateau**, Arctic Ocean ◇
78 J 3 **Chukchi Sea**, Russian Federation/U.S.A. 🌊
154 L 12 **Chukhloma**, Russian Federation
153 Z 6 **Chukotskiy Poluostrov**, Russian Federation ▶
77 K 26 **Chula Vista**, California, U.S.A.
153 T 12 **Chul'man**, Russian Federation
126 M 13 **Chulmleigh**, United Kingdom
152 L 12 **Chulym**, Russian Federation
155 T 3 **Chum**, Russian Federation
191 I 16 **Chum Phae**, Thailand
182 K 4 **Chumatang**, India
213 I 23 **Chumba**, Ethiopia
110 I 9 **Chumbicha**, Argentina
188 I 4 **Chumda**, China
153 V 12 **Chumikan**, Russian Federation
191 G 22 **Chumphon**, Thailand
191 H 17 **Chumsaeng**, Thailand
187 M 18 **Ch'unch'ŏn**, South Korea
179 X 9 **Chundzha**, Kazakhstan
218 M 5 **Chunga**, Zambia
187 M 19 **Ch'ungju**, South Korea
217 W 14 **Chungu**, Tanzania
189 Z 12 **Chungyang Shanmo**, Taiwan ⛰
217 S 13 **Chunya**, Tanzania
191 K 21 **Chuŏr Phnum Dâmrei**, Cambodia ⛰
191 K 18 **Chuŏr Phnum Dângrek**, Thailand ⛰
110 G 4 **Chuquicamata**, Chile
107 K 22 **Chuquisaca**, Bolivia ▣
138 I 8 **Chur**, Switzerland
183 X 12 **Churachandpur**, India
153 U 10 **Churapcha**, Russian Federation
61 U 5 **Church**, Virginia, U.S.A.
127 P 7 **Church Stretton**, United Kingdom
81 P 10 **Churchill**, Canada ∿
84 K 6 **Churchill**, Manitoba, Canada
85 U 8 **Churchill Falls**, Newfoundland and Labrador, Canada
182 H 8 **Churu**, India
104 M 2 **Churuguara**, Venezuela
198 L 6 **Chūrui**, Japan
182 K 4 **Chushul**, India
155 T 12 **Chusovoy**, Russian Federation
85 S 11 **Chute-des-Passes**, Québec, Canada
151 U 4 **Chutove**, Ukraine
189 Z 11 **Chutung**, Taiwan
237 O 15 **Chuuk**, Federated States of Micronesia ▣
237 O 15 **Chuuk Islands**, Federated States of Micronesia 🏝
157 Q 1 **Chuvashskaya Respublika**, Russian Federation ▣
188 K 10 **Chuxiong**, China
179 U 10 **Chuyskaya Oblast'**, Kyrgyzstan ▣
189 W 5 **Chuzhou**, China
179 R 9 **Chyganak**, Kazakhstan

ountry ▣ Internal administrative region: State/Province/Territory/Dependent territory ⌂ Capital city ⛰ Mountain range/Undersea ridge ▲ Mountain peak/Volcano/Seamount ◇ Geographic feature ▶ Headland/Point/Cape/Peninsula ◓ Desert 🏝 Island/Island group ⁙ Antarctic base ◎ Ocean 🌊 Sea ≈ Bay/Gulf/Channel/Strait 💧 Lake ⚑ Salt pan/Dry/Intermittent lake ∿ River

Country · Internal administrative region: State/Province/Territory/Dependent territory · Capital city · Mountain range/Undersea ridge · Mountain peak/Volcano/Seamount · Geographic feature · Headland/Point/Cape/Peninsula · Desert · Island/Island group · Antarctic base · Ocean · Sea · Bay/Gulf/Channel/Strait · Lake · Salt pan/Dry/Intermittent lake · R

Country ▫ Internal administrative region: State/Province/Territory/Dependent territory ♣ Capital city ▲ Mountain range/Undersea ridge ▲ Mountain peak/Volcano/Seamount ◇ Geographic feature ▶ Headland/Point/Cape/Peninsula ▲ Desert ⚓ Island/Island group ⚓ Antarctic base ◇ Ocean ≈ Sea ≈ Bay/Gulf/Channel/Strait ⚓ Lake ⚓ Salt pan/Dry/Intermittent lake ⚓ River

□ Country ■ Internal administrative region: State/Province/Territory/Dependent territory ⚓ Capital city ⛰ Mountain range/Undersea ridge ▲ Mountain peak/Volcano/Seamount ◇ Geographic feature ► Headland/Point/Cape/Peninsula Desert ⇄ Island/Island group ⊞ Antarctic base ○ Ocean Sea ≈ Bay/Gulf/Channel/Strait Lake Salt pan/Dry/Intermittent lake Ri

73 N 4 **Dayr az Zawr**, Syria
72 J 2 **Dayr Ḥāfir**, Syria
0 H 10 **Dayton**, Tennessee, U.S.A.
5 L 19 **Dayton**, Ohio, U.S.A.
4 T 10 **Dayton**, Texas, U.S.A.
6 K 9 **Dayton**, Washington, U.S.A.
7 X 9 **Daytona Beach**, Florida, U.S.A.
89 U 10 **Dayu**, China
1 J 11 **Dayville**, Oregon, U.S.A.
89 P 6 **Dazhu**, China
18 M 13 **De Aar**, Republic of South Africa
32 H 7 **De Cocksdorp**, Netherlands
3 Q 7 **De Funiak Springs**, Florida, U.S.A.
33 B 16 **De Haan**, Belgium
6 G 16 **De Kalb**, Illinois, U.S.A.
4 T 4 **De Kalb**, Texas, U.S.A.
63 W 13 **De-Kastri-Nysh**, Russian Federation
32 H 7 **De Koog**, Netherlands
9 N 4 **De Long Mountains**, Alaska, U.S.A. ▲
32 O 11 **De Lutte**, Netherlands
33 A 17 **De Panne**, Belgium
1 G 12 **De Pere**, Wisconsin, U.S.A.
9 S 13 **De Queen**, Arkansas, U.S.A.
2 H 7 **De Ridder**, Louisiana, U.S.A.
4 S 13 **De Soto**, Iowa, U.S.A.
1 L 9 **De Tour Village**, Michigan, U.S.A.
9 W 12 **De Witt**, Iowa, U.S.A.
9 X 12 **De Witt**, Arkansas, U.S.A.
72 G 10 **Dead Sea**, Israel
8 M 4 **Deadman's Cay**, The Bahamas
27 Z 11 **Deal**, United Kingdom
6 M 15 **Dearborn**, Michigan, U.S.A.
8 D 16 **Dease Lake**, British Columbia, Canada
I 8 **Dease Strait**, Nunavut, Canada
L 21 **Death Valley**, California, U.S.A.
K 21 **Death Valley**, California, U.S.A. ◇
95 O 10 **Debak**, Malaysia
51 Y 6 **Debal'tseve**, Ukraine
46 B 12 **Debar**, Macedonia (F.Y.R.O.M.)
43 L 17 **Dębica**, Poland
63 X 9 **Debin**, Russian Federation
43 M 14 **Dęblin**, Poland
42 D 11 **Dębno**, Poland
3 J 20 **Debre Birhan**, Ethiopia
13 H 19 **Debre Markos**, Ethiopia
13 J 19 **Debre Werk'**, Ethiopia
43 M 22 **Debrecen**, Hungary
45 K 15 **Dečani**, Serbia and Montenegro
P 2 **Decatur**, Alabama, U.S.A.
S 3 **Decatur**, Georgia, U.S.A.
F 19 **Decatur**, Illinois, U.S.A.
K 17 **Decatur**, Indiana, U.S.A.
P 12 **Decatur**, Nebraska, U.S.A.
P 5 **Decatur**, Texas, U.S.A.
1 E 18 **Deccan Plateau**, India ◇
40 H 3 **Deception Island**, Antarctica ⚓
1 C 19 **Decimomannu**, Italy
19 R 8 **Decize**, France
U 10 **Decorah**, Iowa, U.S.A.
32 M 9 **Dedemsvaart**, Netherlands
3 J 20 **Deder**, Ethiopia
2 K 8 **Dedo de Deus**, Brazil ▲
1 V 7 **Dedop'listsqaro**, Georgia
9 R 5 **Dedza**, Malawi
4 I 11 **Dee**, United Kingdom 🝠
H 10 **Deep River**, Ontario, Canada
S 11 **Deer Island**, New Brunswick, Canada ⚓
R 6 **Deer Isle**, Maine, U.S.A. ⚓
X 10 **Deer Lake**, Newfoundland and Labrador, Canada

76 K 6 **Deer Park**, Washington, U.S.A.
63 Y 12 **Deerfield Beach**, Florida, U.S.A.
213 M 23 **Deeri**, Somalia
79 N 6 **Deering**, Alaska, U.S.A.
65 K 17 **Defiance**, Ohio, U.S.A.
188 I 5 **Dêgê**, China
213 L 21 **Degeh Bur**, Ethiopia
87 P 7 **Dégelis**, Québec, Canada
215 N 14 **Degema**, Nigeria
137 L 22 **Deggendorf**, Germany
156 M 8 **Degtevo**, Russian Federation
176 J 10 **Deh Bīd**, Iran
177 Q 10 **Deh Shū**, Afghanistan
211 Q 8 **Dehiba**, Tunisia
176 F 7 **Dehlorān**, Iran
182 J 7 **Dehra Dun**, India
183 O 12 **Dehri**, India
189 X 10 **Dehua**, China
186 K 12 **Dehui**, China
213 B 21 **Deim Zubeir**, Sudan
133 D 18 **Deinze**, Belgium
150 I 8 **Dej**, Romania
213 I 19 **Dejen**, Ethiopia
189 P 8 **Dejiang**, China
213 I 17 **Dekemhare**, Eritrea
216 L 10 **Dekese**, Democratic Republic of Congo
216 J 4 **Dékoa**, Central African Republic
38 I 11 **Del Cano Rise**, Indian Ocean ▲
70 L 11 **Del Rio**, Texas, U.S.A.
158 L 9 **Dela Basin**, Mediterranean Sea ◇
77 I 22 **Delano**, California, U.S.A.
177 Q 9 **Delārām**, Afghanistan
218 M 11 **Delareyville**, Republic of South Africa
58 I 10 **Delaware**, New York, U.S.A.
61 W 3 **Delaware**, U.S.A. ▣
65 M 18 **Delaware**, Ohio, U.S.A.
61 X 2 **Delaware Bay**, Delaware, U.S.A. ≈
70 G 7 **Delaware Mountains**, Texas, U.S.A.
146 E 11 **Delčevo**, Macedonia (F.Y.R.O.M.)
61 S 12 **Delco**, North Carolina, U.S.A.
138 D 6 **Delémont**, Switzerland
215 X 9 **Délép**, Chad
132 F 13 **Delft**, Netherlands
132 N 6 **Delfzijl**, Netherlands
213 E 14 **Delgo**, Sudan
182 J 8 **Delhi**, India
182 J 8 **Delhi**, India ▣
176 I 7 **Delijān**, Iran
82 E 11 **Déline**, Northwest Territories, Canada
137 K 15 **Delitzsch**, Germany
211 N 5 **Dellys**, Algeria
136 E 12 **Delmenhorst**, Germany
231 S 15 **Deloraine**, Tasmania, Australia
147 J 21 **Delos**, Greece ⚓
63 Y 12 **Delray Beach**, Florida, U.S.A.
215 Q 13 **Delta**, Nigeria ▣
74 J 4 **Delta**, Utah, U.S.A.
75 O 5 **Delta**, Colorado, U.S.A.
105 S 3 **Delta Amacuro**, Venezuela ▣
79 S 7 **Delta Junction**, Alaska, U.S.A.
63 X 9 **Deltona**, Florida, U.S.A.
181 B 16 **Delvada**, India
216 L 11 **Demba**, Democratic Republic of Congo
213 G 20 **Dembī Dolo**, Ethiopia
217 N 5 **Dembia**, Central African Republic
42 G 12 **Demerara Abyssal Plain**, Atlantic Ocean ◇
42 F 12 **Demerara Plateau**, Atlantic Ocean ◇
156 H 1 **Demidov**, Russian Federation
75 O 14 **Deming**, New Mexico, U.S.A.
170 D 10 **Demirci**, Turkey

170 C 10 **Demirköprü Baraji**, Turkey 🝠
146 N 11 **Demirköy**, Turkey
136 L 9 **Demmin**, Germany
216 M 9 **Democratic Republic Of Congo**, Africa ▣
63 O 4 **Demopolis**, Alabama, U.S.A.
193 Y 12 **Demta**, Indonesia
154 F 13 **Demyansk**, Russian Federation
132 H 7 **Den Burg**, Netherlands
191 H 15 **Den Chai**, Thailand
132 H 8 **Den Helder**, Netherlands
132 I 8 **Den Oever**, Netherlands
213 J 18 **Denakil Desert**, Ethiopia
79 R 8 **Denali**, Alaska, U.S.A.
213 L 22 **Denan**, Ethiopia
179 Q 14 **Denau**, Uzbekistan
127 O 4 **Denbigh**, United Kingdom
86 H 11 **Denbigh**, Ontario, Canada
192 H 12 **Dendang**, Indonesia
214 J 8 **Dendâra**, Mauritania
133 E 19 **Denderleeuw**, Belgium
133 F 18 **Dendermonde**, Belgium
240 J 8 **Dendtler Island**, Antarctica ⚓
132 N 11 **Denekamp**, Netherlands
215 S 9 **Dengas**, Niger
215 Q 10 **Denge**, Nigeria
189 T 3 **Dengfeng**, China
215 S 11 **Dengi**, Nigeria
189 S 5 **Dengzhou**, China
230 E 8 **Denham**, Western Australia, Australia
131 U 9 **Denia**, Spain
237 U 1 **Denig**, Nauru
231 S 12 **Deniliquin**, New South Wales, Australia
77 J 14 **Denio**, Nevada, U.S.A.
67 Q 12 **Denison**, Iowa, U.S.A.
71 Q 4 **Denison**, Texas, U.S.A.
170 D 12 **Denizli**, Turkey
230 G 12 **Denmark**, Western Australia, Australia
135 C 25 **Denmark**, Europe ▣
61 N 13 **Denmark**, South Carolina, U.S.A.
45 O 14 **Denmark Strait**, Arctic Ocean ≈
127 Z 8 **Dennington**, United Kingdom
192 L 15 **Denpasar**, Indonesia
61 V 3 **Denton**, Maryland, U.S.A.
71 Q 5 **Denton**, Texas, U.S.A.
234 G 6 **D'Entrecasteaux Islands**, Papua New Guinea ⚓
75 R 4 **Denver**, Colorado, U.S.A.
180 C 13 **Deogarh**, India
183 R 12 **Deoghar**, India
181 F 16 **Deoli**, India
181 F 14 **Deori**, India
183 P 10 **Deoria**, India
183 N 13 **Deosil**, India
86 H 8 **Depot-Forbes**, Québec, Canada
241 W 5 **Depot Peak**, Antarctica ▲
215 Y 6 **Dépression Du Mourdi**, Chad ◇
153 U 8 **Deputatskiy**, Russian Federation
188 J 8 **Dêqên**, China
189 S 12 **Deqing**, China
177 W 11 **Dera Ghazi Khan**, Pakistan
177 V 9 **Dera Ismail Khan**, Pakistan
150 M 5 **Derazhnya**, Ukraine
157 S 15 **Derbent**, Russian Federation
179 Q 14 **Derbent**, Uzbekistan
87 V 10 **Derbert**, Nova Scotia, Canada
186 H 6 **Derbur**, China
230 I 4 **Derby**, Western Australia, Australia
127 S 5 **Derby**, United Kingdom
69 N 6 **Derby**, Kansas, U.S.A.
215 Y 9 **Déréssa**, Chad
151 T 6 **Deriyivka**, Ukraine
151 Z 6 **Derkul**, Ukraine 🝠
188 J 8 **Dêrong**, China
219 S 6 **Derre**, Mozambique

59 N 8 **Derry**, New Hampshire, U.S.A.
127 X 6 **Dersingham**, United Kingdom
187 B 14 **Derst**, China
213 H 15 **Derudeb**, Sudan
144 H 10 **Derventa**, Bosnia and Herzegovina
75 T 8 **Des Moines**, New Mexico, U.S.A.
65 H 16 **Des Plaines**, Illinois, U.S.A.
67 S 13 **Des Moines**, Iowa, U.S.A.
67 S 12 **Des Moines**, Iowa/Missouri, U.S.A. 🝠
110 H 11 **Desaguadero**, Argentina
88 E 2 **Descanso**, Mexico
213 I 19 **Desē**, Ethiopia
111 I 21 **Deseado**, Argentina
111 H 20 **Deseado**, Argentina 🝠
88 H 3 **Desemboque**, Mexico
74 I 3 **Deseret Peak**, Utah, U.S.A. ▲
77 M 25 **Desert Center**, California, U.S.A.
74 I 2 **Desert Peak**, Utah, U.S.A. ▲
74 K 9 **Desert View**, Arizona, U.S.A.
42 O 5 **Deserta Grande**, Madeira ⚓
110 I 10 **Desiderio Tello**, Argentina
147 D 15 **Deskati**, Greece
151 Q 3 **Desna**, Ukraine 🝠
197 M 17 **Desolation Point**, Philippines ▶
144 M 12 **Despotovac**, Serbia and Montenegro
137 K 15 **Dessau**, Germany
133 E 18 **Destelbergen**, Belgium
150 E 11 **Deta**, Romania
219 N 7 **Dete**, Zimbabwe
137 F 14 **Detmold**, Germany
65 M 15 **Detroit**, Michigan, U.S.A.
87 S 4 **Détroit de Jacques-Cartier**, Québec, Canada ≈
87 T 4 **Détroit d'Honguedo**, Québec, Canada ≈
67 P 5 **Detroit Lakes**, Minnesota, U.S.A.
133 K 16 **Deurne**, Netherlands
139 Y 5 **Deutschkreutz**, Austria
139 V 8 **Deutschlandsberg**, Austria
150 H 10 **Deva**, Romania
170 K 9 **Deveci Dağlari**, Turkey
170 K 11 **Develi**, Turkey
132 L 11 **Deventer**, Netherlands
180 B 12 **Devikot**, India
233 H 15 **Devil River Peak**, New Zealand ▲
64 D 8 **Devil's Island**, Wisconsin, U.S.A. ⚓
66 L 3 **Devil's Lake**, North Dakota, U.S.A.
66 L 3 **Devil's Lake**, North Dakota, U.S.A. 🝠
73 Y 8 **Devil's Tower**, Wyoming, U.S.A. ▲
146 H 11 **Devin**, Bulgaria
71 O 11 **Devine**, Texas, U.S.A.
146 M 8 **Devnya**, Bulgaria
81 P 4 **Devon Island**, Nunavut, Canada ⚓
231 S 15 **Devonport**, Tasmania, Australia
170 G 7 **Devrek**, Turkey
181 E 15 **Dewas**, India
127 S 3 **Dewsbury**, United Kingdom
189 N 6 **Deyang**, China
176 M 8 **Deyhuk**, Iran
181 I 12 **Deyyer**, Iran
176 G 8 **Dezful**, Iran
187 D 19 **Dezhou**, China
175 T 5 **Dhahran**, Saudi Arabia
183 U 12 **Dhaka**, Bangladesh ▣
181 P 13 **Dhamār**, Yemen
181 G 16 **Dhamtari**, India
183 R 13 **Dhanbad**, India

182 M 8 **Dhangadhi**, Nepal
183 R 10 **Dhankuta**, Nepal
181 D 15 **Dhar**, India
183 R 10 **Dharan Bazar**, Nepal
183 W 12 **Dharmanagar**, India
181 C 19 **Dharwad**, India
183 O 8 **Dhaulagiri**, Nepal ▲
183 Y 9 **Dhemaji**, India
172 G 10 **Dhībān**, Jordan
175 O 14 **Dhubāb**, Yemen
183 U 11 **Dhuburi**, India
181 D 16 **Dhule**, India
213 O 20 **Dhuudo**, Somalia
191 O 21 **Di Linh**, Vietnam
147 J 26 **Dia**, Greece ⚓
77 G 21 **Diablo Range**, California, U.S.A. ▲
219 U 3 **Diaca**, Mozambique
214 F 9 **Dialakoto**, Senegal
113 C 14 **Diamante**, Argentina
231 Q 7 **Diamantina**, Queensland, Australia 🝠
39 S 9 **Diamantina Deep**, Indian Ocean ◇
39 R 9 **Diamantina Fracture Zone**, Indian Ocean ◇
183 S 14 **Diamond Harbour**, India
75 N 2 **Diamond Peak**, Colorado, U.S.A. ▲
73 R 14 **Diamondville**, Wyoming, U.S.A.
214 F 8 **Diamounguél**, Senegal
43 N 25 **Diana's Peak**, St Helena ▲
189 S 13 **Dianbai**, China
188 K 10 **Diancang Shan**, China ▲
189 P 6 **Dianjiang**, China
186 M 11 **Diaoling**, China
218 H 11 **Diaz Point**, Namibia ▶ ◇
175 X 5 **Dibā al Ḥiṣn**, Oman
216 P 11 **Dibaya**, Democratic Republic of Congo
216 K 10 **Dibaya-Lubwe**, Democratic Republic of Congo
213 A 18 **Dibbis**, Sudan
218 L 12 **Dibeng**, Republic of South Africa
183 X 9 **Dibrugarh**, India
172 K 3 **Dibsī**, Syria
70 L 5 **Dickens**, Texas, U.S.A.
66 H 5 **Dickinson**, North Dakota, U.S.A.
60 E 8 **Dickson**, Tennessee, U.S.A.
171 P 11 **Dicle Baraji**, Turkey 🝠
132 L 13 **Didam**, Netherlands
127 T 10 **Didcot**, United Kingdom
180 D 12 **Didwana**, India
146 L 12 **Didymoteicho**, Greece
129 U 12 **Die**, France
137 F 20 **Dieburg**, Germany
39 N 5 **Diego Garcia**, British Indian Ocean Territory ⚓
214 H 12 **Diéké**, Guinea
133 K 23 **Diekirch**, Luxembourg ▣
133 L 24 **Diekirch**, Luxembourg
132 H 11 **Diemen**, Netherlands
190 J 12 **Điện Biên Phu**, Vietnam
191 L 14 **Điện Châu**, Vietnam
148 G 12 **Dienvidsusēja**, Latvia 🝠
136 E 13 **Diepholz**, Germany
129 O 2 **Dieppe**, France
132 L 12 **Dieren**, Netherlands
69 S 12 **Dierks**, Arkansas, U.S.A.
133 I 18 **Diest**, Belgium
215 U 9 **Diffa**, Niger
215 U 8 **Diffa**, Niger ▣
217 O 5 **Digba**, Democratic Republic of Congo
87 T 11 **Digby**, Nova Scotia, Canada
68 I 4 **Dighton**, Kansas, U.S.A.
129 V 13 **Digne-les-Bains**, France
129 S 9 **Digoin**, France
197 M 23 **Digos**, Philippines
177 V 14 **Digri**, Pakistan
213 K 24 **Diinsoor**, Somalia
129 T 7 **Dijon**, France
134 G 13 **Dikanäs**, Sweden
213 K 19 **Dikhil**, Djibouti
170 B 10 **Dikili**, Turkey
153 S 11 **Dikimdya**, Russian Federation

214 J 12 **Dikodougou**, Côte d'Ivoire
133 B 18 **Diksmuide**, Belgium
153 N 6 **Dikson**, Russian Federation
215 V 10 **Dikwa**, Nigeria
213 I 22 **Dīla**, Ethiopia
217 O 5 **Dili**, Democratic Republic of Congo
193 Q 15 **Dili**, East Timor ▣
171 U 8 **Dilijan**, Armenia
71 N 12 **Dilley**, Texas, U.S.A.
137 C 21 **Dilligen**, Germany
213 D 18 **Dilling**, Sudan
137 I 23 **Dillingen**, Germany
79 N 11 **Dillingham**, Alaska, U.S.A.
61 R 11 **Dillon**, South Carolina, U.S.A.
73 O 8 **Dillon**, Montana, U.S.A.
216 L 14 **Dilolo**, Democratic Republic of Congo
133 K 18 **Dilsen**, Belgium
173 T 6 **Diltāwa**, Iraq
183 X 11 **Dimapur**, India
216 M 11 **Dimbelenge**, Democratic Republic of Congo
214 K 13 **Dimbokro**, Côte d'Ivoire
146 J 10 **Dimitrovgrad**, Bulgaria
157 S 2 **Dimitrovgrad**, Russian Federation
145 O 14 **Dimitrovgrad**, Serbia and Montenegro
70 J 3 **Dimmit**, Texas, U.S.A.
197 M 18 **Dinagat**, Philippines
197 M 18 **Dinagat**, Philippines ⚓
183 T 11 **Dinajpur**, Bangladesh
128 K 5 **Dinan**, France
133 H 22 **Dinant**, Belgium
183 P 11 **Dinapur**, India
170 E 11 **Dinar**, Turkey
144 E 11 **Dinaric Alps**, Bosnia and Herzegovina ▲
213 G 18 **Dinder**, Sudan 🝠
181 E 15 **Dindigul**, India
181 G 15 **Dindori**, India
216 I 11 **Dinga**, Democratic Republic of Congo
196 G 10 **Dingalan Bay**, Philippines ≈
189 P 1 **Dingbian**, China
189 Q 1 **Dingbian**, China
218 F 1 **Dinge**, Angola
183 R 10 **Dingla**, Nepal
125 A 20 **Dingle**, Republic of Ireland
125 A 20 **Dingle Bay**, Republic of Ireland ≈
58 I 11 **Dingmans Ferry**, Pennsylvania, U.S.A.
189 U 11 **Dingnan**, China
137 L 23 **Dingolfing**, Germany
189 V 3 **Dingtao**, China
214 G 10 **Dinguiraye**, Guinea
87 Y 7 **Dingwall**, Nova Scotia, Canada
189 N 2 **Dingxi**, China
187 D 17 **Dingxing**, China
187 C 18 **Dingzhou**, China
190 N 13 **Dinh Lâp**, Vietnam
183 T 10 **Dinhata**, India
137 H 22 **Dinkelsbühl**, Germany
75 N 3 **Dinosaur**, Colorado, U.S.A.
133 F 15 **Dinteloord**, Netherlands
132 M 13 **Dinxperlo**, Netherlands
112 G 9 **Dionísio Cerqueira**, Brazil
109 I 20 **Dioniso Cerqueira**, Brazil
214 D 9 **Diouloulou**, Senegal
215 P 10 **Dioundiou**, Niger
214 E 8 **Diourbel**, Senegal
182 M 8 **Dipayal**, Nepal
183 W 11 **Diphu**, India
197 J 20 **Dipolog**, Philippines
133 L 25 **Dippach**, Luxembourg
213 K 20 **Dirē Dawa**, Ethiopia
39 Z 1 **Direction Island**, Cocos Islands ⚓
91 N 9 **Diriamba**, Nicaragua
218 K 7 **Dirico**, Angola
230 E 8 **Dirk Hartog Island**, Western Australia, Australia ⚓
215 U 6 **Dirkou**, Niger

Country ▣ Internal administrative region: State/Province/Territory/Dependent territory   ⚓ Capital city   ▲ Mountain range/Undersea ridge   ▲ Mountain peak/Volcano/Seamount   ◇ Geographic feature   ▶ Headland/Point/Cape/Peninsula   ▲ Desert   ⚓ Island/Island group   ▲ Antarctic base   Ocean   Sea   ≈ Bay/Gulf/Channel/Strait   Lake   🝠 Salt pan/Dry/Intermittent lake   🝠 River

◻ Country ◼ Internal administrative region: State/Province/Territory/Dependent territory ♟ Capital city ▲ Mountain range/Undersea ridge ▲ Mountain peak/Volcano/Seamount ◇ Geographic feature ▶ Headland/Point/Cape/Peninsula ▲ Desert ☷ Island/Island group ☷ Antarctic base Ocean Sea ≈ Bay/Gulf/Channel/Strait Lake Salt pan/Dry/Intermittent lake

R 10 **Dunn**, North Carolina, U.S.A.
V 9 **Dunnellon**, Florida, U.S.A.
K 13 **Dunning**, Nebraska, U.S.A.
D 24 **Dunrobin**, New Zealand
K 2 **Dunseith**, North Dakota, U.S.A.
G 15 **Dunsmuir**, California, U.S.A.
U 9 **Dunstable**, United Kingdom
D 23 **Dunstan Mountains**, New Zealand ⛰
F 10 **Dunte**, Latvia
K 13 **Dunvegan Lake**, Northwest Territories, Canada 💧
E 14 **Duolun**, China
F 10 **Dupnista**, Bulgaria
I 8 **Dupree**, South Dakota, U.S.A.
O 3 **Dupuyer**, Montana, U.S.A.
C 11 **Durand**, Wisconsin, U.S.A.
L 14 **Durand**, Michigan, U.S.A.
P 1 **Durango**, Spain
O 7 **Durango**, Colorado, U.S.A.
M 7 **Durango**, Mexico ▣
N 8 **Durango**, Mexico
O 4 **Durango**, Honduras
O 6 **Durankulak**, Bulgaria
O 13 **Durant**, Oklahoma, U.S.A.
E 15 **Durazno**, Uruguay
E 15 **Durazno**, Uruguay ▣
P 13 **Durban**, Republic of South Africa
O 13 **Dúrcal**, Spain
B 17 **Düren**, Germany
G 16 **Durg**, India
R 13 **Durgapur**, India
J 15 **Durham**, United Kingdom
R 9 **Durham**, North Carolina, U.S.A.
E 10 **Duri**, Indonesia
N 9 **Durlești**, Moldova
J 14 **Durmitor**, Serbia and Montenegro ▲
G 8 **Durness**, United Kingdom
Y 3 **Dürnkrut**, Austria
J 18 **Durrës**, Albania
Q 10 **Dursley**, United Kingdom
D 9 **Dursunbey**, Turkey
A 6 **Duru**, Papua New Guinea
M 20 **Durukhsi**, Somalia
O 12 **Durusu Gölü**, Turkey 💧
I 15 **D'Urville Island**, New Zealand 🏝
S 11 **Dushai**, Pakistan
M 14 **Dushak**, Turkmenistan
P 10 **Dushan**, China
R 13 **Dushanbe**, Tajikistan 🏛
G 11 **Dushore**, Pennsylvania, U.S.A.
A 24 **Dusky Sound**, New Zealand ≈
C 16 **Düsseldorf**, Germany
J 8 **Dustin Island**, Antarctica 🏝
F 11 **Dusunmudo**, Indonesia
K 14 **Dutch Harbor**, Alaska, U.S.A.
S 7 **Dutovo**, Russian Federation
S 10 **Dutse**, Nigeria
R 10 **Dutsin-Ma**, Nigeria
F 20 **Duttaluru**, India
U 14 **Duvan**, Russian Federation
R 1 **Duyfken Point**, Queensland, Australia ▶
P 10 **Duyun**, China
M 15 **Duża**, Poland
G 8 **Düzce**, Turkey
K 7 **Dve Mogili**, Bulgaria
K 6 **Dvinskaya Guba**, Russian Federation ≈
X 4 **Dvorichna**, Ukraine
A 15 **Dwarka**, India
G 17 **Dwight**, Illinois, U.S.A.
K 5 **Dworshak Reservoir**, Idaho, U.S.A. 💧
Z 7 **Dyakove**, Ukraine
B 8 **Dyersburg**, Tennessee, U.S.A.
153 T 10 **Dyeundyu**, Russian Federation
151 U 4 **Dykan'ka**, Ukraine
127 Y 12 **Dymchurch**, United Kingdom
151 P 3 **Dymer**, Ukraine
151 X 6 **Dymytrov**, Ukraine
143 M 18 **Dynów**, Poland
231 U 6 **Dysart**, Queensland, Australia
147 D 20 **Dytiki Ellas**, Greece ▣
147 D 14 **Dytiki Makedonia**, Greece ▣
157 V 1 **Dyurtyuli**, Russian Federation
219 X 4 **Dzaoudzi**, France
171 Z 10 **Džarskij**, Azerbaijan
185 N 3 **Dzavhan**, Mongolia ▣
157 O 1 **Dzerzhinsk**, Russian Federation
151 X 6 **Dzerzhyns'k**, Ukraine
179 O 9 **Dzhalagash**, Kazakhstan
179 T 11 **Dzhalal-Abadskaya Oblast'**, Kyrgyzstan ▣
178 H 5 **Dzhangala**, Kazakhstan
151 U 11 **Dzhankoy**, Ukraine
179 X 8 **Dzhansugurov**, Kazakhstan
178 F 5 **Dzhanybek**, Kazakhstan
151 S 10 **Dzharylhats'ka Zatoka**, Ukraine ≈
178 I 12 **Dzhebel**, Turkmenistan
179 T 14 **Dzhilandy**, Tajikistan
179 Q 12 **Dzhizak**, Uzbekistan
156 K 13 **Dzhubga**, Russian Federation
151 N 6 **Dzhuryn**, Ukraine
179 O 8 **Dzhusaly**, Kazakhstan
142 K 10 **Działdowo**, Poland
89 Y 10 **Dzilam de Bravo**, Mexico
211 O 7 **Dzioua**, Algeria
149 J 14 **Dzisna**, Belarus 〰
149 F 21 **Dzivin**, Belarus
185 N 2 **Dzur**, Mongolia
185 R 3 **Dzuunmod**, Mongolia
149 I 18 **Dzyarzhynsk**, Belarus
149 J 22 **Dzyarzhynsk**, Belarus
149 I 17 **Dzyarzhynskaya Hara**, Belarus ▲

E

191 O 19 **Ea Hleo**, Vietnam
75 U 5 **Eads**, Colorado, U.S.A.
74 M 11 **Eagar**, Arizona, U.S.A.
79 T 6 **Eagle**, Alaska, U.S.A.
85 W 8 **Eagle**, Newfoundland and Labrador, Canada 〰
59 Q 2 **Eagle Lake**, Maine, U.S.A.
59 R 1 **Eagle Lake**, Maine, U.S.A. 💧
77 H 16 **Eagle Lake**, California, U.S.A. 💧
70 M 12 **Eagle Pass**, Texas, U.S.A.
64 F 9 **Eagle River**, Wisconsin, U.S.A.
127 W 3 **Easington**, United Kingdom
127 T 1 **Easingwold**, United Kingdom
60 L 11 **Easley**, South Carolina, U.S.A.
158 C 9 **East Alboran Basin**, Mediterranean Sea ◇
127 X 6 **East Anglia**, United Kingdom ◇
241 R 4 **East Antarctica**, Antarctica ◇
58 D 9 **East Aurora**, New York, U.S.A.
234 E 5 **East Bay**, Papua New Guinea ≈
62 M 9 **East Bay**, Louisiana, U.S.A. ≈
93 Q 5 **East Caicos**, Turks and Caicos Islands 🏝
232 O 10 **East Cape**, New Zealand ▶
40 L 7 **East Caroline Basin**, Pacific Ocean ◇
185 X 12 **East China Sea**, China/Japan 🌊
127 Y 6 **East Dereham**, United Kingdom
111 L 24 **East Falkland**, Falkland Islands 🏝
127 W 12 **East Grinstead**, United Kingdom
58 M 12 **East Hampton**, New York, U.S.A.
39 R 8 **East Indiaman Ridge**, Indian Ocean ⛰
124 H 13 **East Kilbride**, United Kingdom
65 O 17 **East Liverpool**, Ohio, U.S.A.
219 O 14 **East London**, Republic of South Africa
126 L 14 **East Looe**, United Kingdom
40 M 6 **East Mariana Basin**, Pacific Ocean ◇
159 P 9 **East Mediterranean Ridge**, Mediterranean Sea ◇
234 H 4 **East New Britain**, Papua New Guinea ▣
43 N 16 **East Point**, Tristan da Cunha ▶
63 S 3 **East Point**, Georgia, U.S.A.
43 I 21 **East Scotia Basin**, Atlantic Ocean ◇
234 C 4 **East Sepik**, Papua New Guinea ▣
38 K 2 **East Sheba Ridge**, Indian Ocean ⛰
153 V 5 **East Siberian Sea**, Russian Federation 🌊
65 E 21 **East St Louis**, Illinois, U.S.A.
193 R 15 **East Timor**, Asia □
127 X 13 **Eastbourne**, United Kingdom
41 X 3 **Easter Island**, Chile ▣
214 G 12 **Eastern**, Sierra Leone ▣
217 W 7 **Eastern**, Kenya ▣
219 P 4 **Eastern**, Zambia ▣
181 G 24 **Eastern**, Sri Lanka ▣
183 R 10 **Eastern**, Nepal ▣
219 N 14 **Eastern Cape**, Republic of South Africa ▣
212 F 9 **Eastern Desert**, Egypt ◇
213 F 22 **Eastern Equatoria**, Sudan ▣
181 F 20 **Eastern Ghats**, India ⛰
234 D 5 **Eastern Highlands**, Papua New Guinea ▣
127 T 12 **Eastleigh**, United Kingdom
85 Q 10 **Eastmain**, Québec, Canada 〰
85 P 10 **Eastmain**, Québec, Canada
63 U 5 **Eastman**, Georgia, U.S.A.
127 Q 14 **Easton**, United Kingdom
58 I 12 **Easton**, Pennsylvania, U.S.A.
61 V 3 **Easton**, Maryland, U.S.A.
127 T 5 **Eastwood**, United Kingdom
63 T 3 **Eatonton**, Georgia, U.S.A.
64 D 11 **Eau Claire**, Wisconsin, U.S.A.
236 L 15 **Eaurupik**, Federated States of Micronesia 🏝
215 P 11 **Eban**, Nigeria
89 R 10 **Ebano**, Mexico
127 O 9 **Ebbw Vale**, United Kingdom
215 T 15 **Ebebiyin**, Equatorial Guinea
139 S 5 **Ebensee**, Austria
170 G 11 **Eber Gölü**, Turkey 💧
136 M 12 **Eberswalde-Finow**, Germany
198 J 5 **Ebetsu**, Japan
188 M 7 **Ebian**, China
199 C 23 **Ebino**, Japan
184 J 4 **Ebinur Hu**, China 💧
141 K 16 **Eboli**, Italy
215 T 5 **Ebolowa**, Cameroon
237 Y 5 **Ebon**, Marshall Islands 🏝
218 H 9 **Ebony**, Namibia
215 R 13 **Ebonyi**, Nigeria ▣
131 T 5 **Ebro**, Spain 〰
170 A 8 **Eceabat**, Turkey
210 L 6 **Ech Chélif**, Algeria
138 B 9 **Echallens**, Switzerland
146 I 12 **Echinos**, Greece
199 G 16 **Echizen-misaki**, Japan ▶
76 J 9 **Echo**, Oregon, U.S.A.
82 G 10 **Echo Bay**, Northwest Territories, Canada
86 A 8 **Echo Bay**, Ontario, Canada
133 K 17 **Echt**, Netherlands
133 M 24 **Echternach**, Luxembourg
231 S 12 **Echuca**, Victoria, Australia
130 M 12 **Écija**, Spain
64 K 9 **Eckermann**, Michigan, U.S.A.
136 H 8 **Eckernförde**, Germany
106 A 9 **Ecuador**, South America □
213 J 17 **Ed**, Eritrea
213 B 19 **Ed Da'ein**, Sudan
213 G 19 **Ed Damazin**, Sudan
213 F 15 **Ed Damer**, Sudan
213 E 15 **Ed Debba**, Sudan
213 E 17 **Ed Dueim**, Sudan
132 I 10 **Edam**, Netherlands
124 I 7 **Eday**, United Kingdom 🏝
60 D 7 **Eddyville**, Kentucky, U.S.A.
215 P 12 **Ede**, Nigeria
132 K 13 **Ede**, Netherlands
215 S 14 **Edéa**, Cameroon
231 U 13 **Eden**, New South Wales, Australia
125 I 15 **Eden**, United Kingdom 〰
70 M 8 **Eden**, Texas, U.S.A.
233 C 25 **Edendale**, New Zealand
61 V 8 **Edenton**, North Carolina, U.S.A.
146 D 13 **Edessa**, Greece
232 M 10 **Edgecumbe**, New Zealand
66 M 6 **Edgeley**, North Dakota, U.S.A.
66 G 11 **Edgemont**, South Dakota, U.S.A.
45 U 11 **Edgeoya**, Svalbard 🏝
124 I 13 **Edinburgh**, United Kingdom
71 P 15 **Edinburgh**, Texas, U.S.A.
150 M 7 **Edineț**, Moldova
146 M 11 **Edirne**, Turkey ▣
170 B 6 **Edirne**, Turkey
211 Q 10 **Edjeleh**, Algeria
60 H 7 **Edmonton**, Kentucky, U.S.A.
83 J 18 **Edmonton**, Alberta, Canada
87 Q 7 **Edmundston**, New Brunswick, Canada
71 R 11 **Edna**, Texas, U.S.A.
215 Q 13 **Edo**, Nigeria ▣
140 E 5 **Edolo**, Italy
170 B 9 **Edremit**, Turkey
170 A 9 **Edremit Körfezi**, Turkey ≈
83 I 18 **Edson**, Alberta, Canada
110 J 13 **Eduardo Castex**, Argentina
241 N 11 **Edward VII Peninsula**, Antarctica ▶
241 X 4 **Edward VIII Gulf**, Antarctica ≈
70 K 8 **Edwards Plateau**, Texas, U.S.A. ◇
65 F 20 **Edwardsville**, Illinois, U.S.A.
216 H 9 **Edzouga**, Congo
78 M 10 **Eek**, Alaska, U.S.A.
133 D 17 **Eeklo**, Belgium
132 N 5 **Eemshaven**, Netherlands
235 R 11 **Éfaté**, Vanuatu 🏝
139 S 3 **Eferding**, Austria
65 G 20 **Effingham**, Illinois, U.S.A.
193 T 11 **Eftorobi**, Indonesia 🏝
185 S 3 **Eg**, Mongolia
158 K 8 **Egadi Valley**, Mediterranean Sea ◇
79 N 11 **Egegik**, Alaska, U.S.A.
143 K 22 **Eger**, Hungary
43 M 26 **Egg Island**, St Helena 🏝
139 W 2 **Eggenburg**, Austria
137 L 24 **Eggenfelden**, Germany
133 H 20 **Eghezée**, Belgium
134 D 10 **Egilsstaðir**, Iceland
170 F 12 **Eğirdir**, Turkey
170 F 11 **Eğirdir Gölü**, Turkey 💧
129 P 10 **Égletons**, France
80 M 3 **Eglinton Island**, Northwest Territories, Canada 🏝
153 Z 6 **Egvekinot**, Russian Federation
212 C 10 **Egypt**, Africa □
137 G 24 **Ehingen**, Germany
199 C 24 **Ei**, Japan
132 M 12 **Eibergen**, Netherlands
139 V 8 **Eibiswald**, Austria
135 B 19 **Eidfjord**, Norway
137 B 19 **Eifel**, Germany ⛰
138 F 9 **Eiger**, Switzerland ▲
124 F 11 **Eigg**, United Kingdom 🏝
181 B 25 **Eight Degree Channel**, Maldives ≈
240 J 8 **Eights Coast**, Antarctica ◇
230 H 5 **Eighty Mile Beach**, Western Australia, Australia ◇
137 L 16 **Eilenburg**, Germany
172 F 11 **Ein Yahav**, Israel
231 S 4 **Einasleigh**, Queensland, Australia
137 H 15 **Einbeck**, Germany
133 J 16 **Eindhoven**, Netherlands
42 G 6 **Eirik Ridge**, Atlantic Ocean ⛰
134 B 11 **Eiríksjökull**, Iceland ▲
108 B 12 **Eirunepé**, Brazil
137 H 17 **Eisenach**, Germany
139 U 6 **Eisenerz**, Austria
139 U 9 **Eisenkappel**, Austria
139 Y 5 **Eisenstadt**, Austria
137 I 18 **Eisfeld**, Germany
149 F 17 **Eišiškės**, Lithuania
137 J 15 **Eisleben Lutherstadt**, Germany
131 W 9 **Eivissa**, Spain
131 S 3 **Ejea de los Caballeros**, Spain
219 W 10 **Ejeda**, Madgascar
185 P 6 **Ejin Qi**, China
171 T 9 **Ejmiatsin**, Armenia
89 T 14 **Ejutla**, Mexico
73 Y 6 **Ekalaka**, Montana, U.S.A.
233 K 15 **Eketahuna**, New Zealand
179 U 3 **Ekibastuz**, Kazakhstan
153 Q 9 **Ekonda**, Russian Federation
216 I 7 **Ekouamou**, Congo
135 F 23 **Eksjö**, Sweden
79 O 11 **Ekuk**, Alaska, U.S.A.
216 L 8 **Ekuku**, Democratic Republic of Congo
85 N 9 **Ekwan**, Ontario, Canada 〰
211 Q 11 **El Adeb Larache**, Algeria
212 D 8 **El 'Alamein**, Egypt
211 O 8 **El Alia**, Algeria
130 L 12 **El Arahal**, Spain
88 H 5 **El Arco**, Mexico
210 K 7 **El Aricha**, Algeria
212 G 7 **El 'Arîsh**, Egypt
212 F 10 **El Balyana**, Egypt
88 L 3 **El Barreal**, Mexico 💧
213 F 19 **El Barun**, Sudan
105 N 4 **El Baúl**, Venezuela
210 L 7 **El Bayadh**, Algeria
213 J 24 **El Beru Hagia**, Somalia
91 R 9 **El Bluff**, Nicaragua
111 G 17 **El Bolsón**, Argentina
211 Q 8 **El Borma**, Tunisia
213 D 22 **El Buheyrat**, Sudan ▣
111 H 17 **El Caín**, Argentina
77 K 26 **El Cajon**, California, U.S.A.
104 K 6 **El Campin**, Colombia
71 R 11 **El Campo**, Texas, U.S.A.
107 L 18 **El Carmen**, Bolivia
106 B 8 **El Carmen**, Ecuador
89 N 7 **El Casco**, Mexico
77 M 26 **El Centro**, California, U.S.A.
107 M 20 **El Cerro**, Bolivia
89 W 13 **El Chichónal**, Mexico ▲
88 G 2 **El Chinero**, Mexico
89 Z 10 **El Cuyo**, Mexico
104 F 9 **El Diviso**, Colombia
104 K 9 **El Dorado**, Colombia
69 O 6 **El Dorado**, Kansas, U.S.A.
69 V 14 **El Dorado**, Arkansas, U.S.A.
88 L 8 **El Dorado**, Mexico
104 J 11 **El Encanto**, Colombia
90 J 4 **El Estor**, Guatemala
212 E 9 **El Faiyûm**, Egypt
213 B 17 **El Fasher**, Sudan
212 E 9 **El Fashn**, Egypt
213 K 21 **El Fud**, Ethiopia
88 K 6 **El Fuerte**, Mexico
213 A 17 **El Geneina**, Sudan
213 F 17 **El Geteina**, Sudan
213 F 17 **El Gezira**, Sudan ▣
212 E 8 **El Gîza**, Egypt
210 M 9 **El Goléa**, Algeria
90 J 4 **El Golfete**, Guatemala 💧
88 G 2 **El Golfo de Santa Clara**, Mexico
214 G 4 **El Hammâmi**, Mauritania ⛰
214 J 4 **El Hank**, Mauritania ⛰
91 S 14 **El Hato del Volcán**, Panama
213 G 18 **El Hawata**, Sudan
42 L 12 **El Hierro**, Canary Islands 🏝
213 C 18 **El Hilla**, Sudan
210 M 9 **El Homr**, Algeria
210 G 7 **El Jadida**, Morocco
211 Q 6 **El Jem**, Tunisia
210 G 8 **El Kelaâ des Srarhna**, Morocco
213 K 22 **Ēl Kerē**, Ethiopia
213 E 15 **El Khandaq**, Sudan
212 E 11 **El Khârga**, Egypt
213 L 22 **Ēl K'oran**, Ethiopia
213 D 19 **El Lagowa**, Sudan
91 X 13 **El Llano**, Panama
93 S 7 **El Macao**, Dominican Republic
212 E 8 **El Mansûra**, Egypt
105 R 5 **El Manteco**, Venezuela
211 O 7 **El Meghaïer**, Algeria
212 E 9 **El Minya**, Egypt
131 O 6 **El Molar**, Spain
214 I 6 **El Mreyyé**, Mauritania ⛰
213 C 19 **El Muglad**, Sudan
90 L 5 **El Negrito**, Honduras
197 E 16 **El Nido**, Philippines
213 D 18 **El Obeid**, Sudan
213 C 18 **El Odaiya**, Sudan
106 A 11 **El Oro**, Ecuador ▣
89 O 6 **El Oro**, Mexico
211 O 7 **El Oued**, Algeria
65 F 17 **El Paso**, Illinois, U.S.A.
70 E 7 **El Paso**, Texas, U.S.A.
131 U 6 **El Perelló**, Spain
91 X 13 **El Porvenir**, Panama
90 I 5 **El Progreso**, Guatemala
90 I 6 **El Progreso**, Guatemala
107 L 19 **El Puente**, Bolivia
90 M 8 **El Puente**, Nicaragua
130 K 13 **El Puerto de Santa María**, Spain
212 D 11 **El Qasr**, Egypt
91 Z 15 **El Real**, Panama
68 M 10 **El Reno**, Oklahoma, U.S.A.
212 F 11 **El Ridisîya Bahari**, Egypt
130 K 11 **El Ronquillo**, Spain
212 E 8 **El Saff**, Egypt
88 H 3 **El Sahuaro**, Mexico
111 H 21 **El Salado**, Argentina
88 M 8 **El Salto**, Mexico
110 G 7 **El Salvador**, Chile
197 L 20 **El Salvador**, Philippines
90 J 7 **El Salvador**, North America □
93 S 7 **El Seibo**, Dominican Republic
110 G 13 **El Sosneado**, Argentina
88 M 4 **El Sueco**, Mexico
130 K 3 **El Teleno**, Spain ▲
105 Q 4 **El Tigre**, Venezuela
110 F 9 **El Toro**, Chile
113 B 14 **El Trebol**, Argentina
212 F 9 **El Tûr**, Egypt
111 G 24 **El Turbio**, Argentina
91 W 14 **El Valle**, Panama
131 W 5 **El Vendrell**, Spain
90 M 8 **El Viejo**, Nicaragua
104 K 4 **El Vigía**, Venezuela
217 X 6 **El Wak**, Kenya
213 D 17 **El Wuz**, Sudan
147 F 23 **Elafonisos**, Greece 🏝
147 L 26 **Elasa**, Greece 🏝

□ ountry ▣ Internal administrative region: State/Province/Territory/Dependent territory 🏛 Capital city ⛰ Mountain range/Undersea ridge ▲ Mountain peak/Volcano/Seamount ◇ Geographic feature ▶ Headland/Point/Cape/Peninsula ◣ Desert 🏝 Island/Island group ⁙ Antarctic base ◎ Ocean 🌊 Sea ≈ Bay/Gulf/Channel/Strait 💧 Lake ⛶ Salt pan/Dry/Intermittent lake 〰 River

147 E 15	Elassona, Greece	
172 F 13	Elat, Israel	
236 M 15	Elato, Federated States of Micronesia	
171 O 11	Elazığ, Turkey	
63 Q 6	Elba, Alabama, U.S.A.	
145 K 19	Elbasan, Albania	
136 I 11	Elbe, Czech Republic/Germany	
76 H 8	Elbe, Washington, U.S.A.	
63 U 2	Elberton, Georgia, U.S.A.	
170 M 11	Elbistan, Turkey	
142 J 8	Elbląg, Poland	
83 M 19	Elbow, Saskatchewan, Canada	
157 N 14	Elbrus, Russian Federation ▲	
132 K 10	Elburg, Netherlands	
176 I 5	Elburz Mountains, Iran ⋀	
131 S 10	Elche, Spain	
131 R 10	Elche de la Sierra, Spain	
131 S 10	Elda, Spain	
153 U 11	El'dikan, Russian Federation	
69 U 5	Eldon, Missouri, U.S.A.	
112 F 9	Eldorado, Argentina	
65 G 22	Eldorado, Illinois, U.S.A.	
70 L 9	Eldorado, Texas, U.S.A.	
108 J 12	Eldorado dos Carajás, Brazil	
217 U 7	Eldoret, Kenya	
147 G 20	Elefsina, Greece	
148 E 12	Eleja, Latvia	
217 U 4	Elemi Triangle, Kenya ◇	
146 K 8	Elena, Bulgaria	
75 P 13	Elephant Butte Reservoir, New Mexico, U.S.A. ⬡	
240 G 2	Elephant Island, Antarctica	
92 L 2	Eleuthera, The Bahamas	
124 I 9	Elgin, United Kingdom	
65 G 16	Elgin, Illinois, U.S.A.	
66 I 6	Elgin, North Dakota, U.S.A.	
71 Q 9	Elgin, Texas, U.S.A.	
76 K 10	Elgin, Oregon, U.S.A.	
217 T 7	Elgon, Kenya ▲	
193 T 15	Eliase, Indonesia	
75 T 12	Elida, New Mexico, U.S.A.	
146 G 9	Elin Pelin, Bulgaria	
217 N 8	Elipa, Democratic Republic of Congo	
108 L 13	Eliseu Martins, Brazil	
157 O 11	Elista, Russian Federation	
58 J 13	Elizabeth, New Jersey, U.S.A.	
61 W 8	Elizabeth City, North Carolina, U.S.A.	
60 L 8	Elizabethton, Tennessee, U.S.A.	
60 G 6	Elizabethtown, Kentucky, U.S.A.	
61 S 11	Elizabethtown, North Carolina, U.S.A.	
142 M 9	Ełk, Poland	
68 J 10	Elk City, Oklahoma, U.S.A.	
72 L 7	Elk City, Idaho, U.S.A.	
83 K 18	Elk Point, Alberta, Canada	
67 S 7	Elk River, Minnesota, U.S.A.	
65 J 16	Elkhart, Indiana, U.S.A.	
68 G 7	Elkhart, Kansas, U.S.A.	
65 G 14	Elkhorn, Wisconsin, U.S.A.	
146 L 10	Elkhovo, Bulgaria	
61 O 8	Elkin, North Carolina, U.S.A.	
61 P 3	Elkins, West Virginia, U.S.A.	
77 M 16	Elko, Nevada, U.S.A.	
83 J 21	Elko, British Columbia, Canada	
60 F 10	Elkton, Tennessee, U.S.A.	
61 R 4	Elkton, Virginia, U.S.A.	
63 N 2	Ellaville, Georgia, U.S.A.	
81 N 2	Ellef Ringnes Island, Nunavut, Canada ⇌	
66 M 6	Ellendale, North Dakota, U.S.A.	
76 I 8	Ellensburg, Washington, U.S.A.	
127 P 6	Ellesmere, United Kingdom	
81 P 1	Ellesmere Island, Nunavut, Canada ⇌	
127 P 4	Ellesmere Port, United Kingdom	
63 S 1	Ellijay, Georgia, U.S.A.	
219 O 14	Elliot, Republic of South Africa	
86 C 9	Elliot Lake, Ontario, Canada	
231 N 3	Elliott, Northern Territory, Australia	
61 Q 5	Elliott Knob, Virginia, U.S.A. ▲	
219 N 10	Ellisras, Republic of South Africa	
231 O 11	Elliston, South Australia, Australia	
124 J 10	Ellon, United Kingdom	
59 R 5	Ellsworth, Maine, U.S.A.	
64 C 11	Ellsworth, Wisconsin, U.S.A.	
240 J 8	Ellsworth Land, Antarctica ◇	
240 L 8	Ellsworth Mountains, Antarctica ⋀	
137 H 22	Ellwangen, Germany	
76 G 7	Elma, Washington, U.S.A.	
170 E 13	Elmalı, Turkey	
138 K 7	Elmen, Austria	
58 F 10	Elmira, New York, U.S.A.	
87 W 8	Elmira, Prince Edward Island, Canada	
136 G 10	Elmshorn, Germany	
68 I 8	Elmwood, Oklahoma, U.S.A.	
74 K 13	Eloy, Arizona, U.S.A.	
132 K 13	Elst, Netherlands	
137 M 16	Elsterwerda, Germany	
232 J 13	Eltham, New Zealand	
157 Q 8	El'ton, Russian Federation	
181 Q 19	Eluru, India	
148 H 8	Elva, Estonia	
130 J 9	Elvas, Portugal	
135 E 18	Elverum, Norway	
108 A 12	Elvira, Brazil	
65 J 18	Elwood, Indiana, U.S.A.	
65 N 16	Elyria, Ohio, U.S.A.	
137 G 14	Elze, Germany	
235 R 11	Émaé, Vanuatu ⇌	
177 U 5	Emām Şāḩeb, Afghanistan	
178 K 7	Emba, Kazakhstan	
178 L 6	Emba, Kazakhstan ⇌	
90 J 7	Embalse Cerrón Grande, El Salvador	
111 H 15	Embalse Cerros Colorados, Argentina ⬡	
90 H 5	Embalse Chixoy, Guatemala	
131 Q 8	Embalse de Alarcón, Spain ⬡	
130 L 5	Embalse de Almendra, Spain ⬡	
131 Q 6	Embalse de Buendía, Spain ⬡	
130 M 8	Embalse de Cijara, Spain ⬡	
130 M 8	Embalse de Garcia Sola, Spain ⬡	
105 R 4	Embalse de Guri, Venezuela	
131 N 12	Embalse de Iznajar, Spain ⬡	
130 L 9	Embalse de Orellana, Spain ⬡	
130 K 8	Embalse de Valdecañas, Spain ⬡	
130 M 9	Embalse del Zújar, Spain ⬡	
111 H 15	Embalse Ezequiel Ramos Mexia, Argentina ⬡	
111 H 18	Embalse Florentino Ameghino, Argentina ⬡	
110 J 5	Embarcación, Argentina	
216 K 8	Embondo, Democratic Republic of Congo	
128 K 7	Embouchure de la Loire, France ≈	
217 V 8	Embu, Kenya	
136 D 10	Emden, Germany	
188 M 7	Emei, China	
231 U 6	Emerald, Queensland, Australia	
74 K 5	Emery, Utah, U.S.A.	
170 D 10	Emet, Turkey	
234 B 6	Emeti, Papua New Guinea	
215 X 6	Emi Koussi, Chad ▲	
158 F 8	Emile Baudot Escarpment, Mediterranean Sea ◇	
140 F 9	Emilia-Romagna, Italy ☐	
89 X 13	Emiliano Zapata, Mexico	
184 J 3	Emin, China	
234 F 2	Emirau Island, Papua New Guinea ⇌	
170 F 10	Emirdağ, Turkey	
231 T 14	Emita, Tasmania, Australia	
136 C 13	Emlichheim, Germany	
148 D 7	Emmaste, Estonia	
132 K 9	Emmeloord, Netherlands	
132 N 9	Emmen, Netherlands	
137 B 14	Emmerich, Germany	
231 S 7	Emmet, Queensland, Australia	
67 R 11	Emmetsburg, Iowa, U.S.A.	
78 L 8	Emmonak, Alaska, U.S.A.	
70 I 11	Emory Peak, Texas, U.S.A. ▲	
88 I 5	Empalme, Mexico	
112 C 10	Empedrado, Argentina	
41 O 3	Emperor Trough, Pacific Ocean ◇	
140 E 10	Empoli, Italy	
61 T 7	Emporia, Virginia, U.S.A.	
69 P 5	Emporia, Kansas, U.S.A.	
58 D 11	Emporium, Pennsylvania, U.S.A.	
136 D 12	Ems, Germany ≈	
86 F 10	Emsdale, Ontario, Canada	
219 P 11	Emzinoni, Republic of South Africa	
172 F 10	En Gedi, Israel	
172 F 11	'En Hazeva, Israel	
213 C 18	En Nahud, Sudan	
193 W 12	Enarotali, Indonesia	
109 G 20	Encarnación, Paraguay	
71 N 13	Encinal, Texas, U.S.A.	
77 K 26	Encinitas, California, U.S.A.	
75 R 11	Encino, New Mexico, U.S.A.	
110 H 11	Encón, Argentina	
112 H 12	Encruzilhada do Sul, Brazil	
143 L 21	Encs, Hungary	
194 E 9	Endau, Malaysia	
41 T 3	Endeavour Seamount, Pacific Ocean ▲	
193 O 15	Endeh, Indonesia	
236 K 4	Enderbury, Kiribati ⇌	
38 H 14	Enderby Abyssal Plain, Indian Ocean ◇	
241 U 3	Enderby Land, Antarctica ◇	
58 H 10	Endicott, New York, U.S.A.	
79 P 4	Endicott Mountains, Alaska, U.S.A. ⋀	
230 F 10	Eneabba, Western Australia, Australia	
113 D 19	Energía, Argentina	
146 K 13	Enez, Turkey	
170 A 7	Enez, Turkey	
127 W 10	Enfield, United Kingdom	
58 L 10	Enfield, Connecticut, U.S.A.	
61 T 8	Enfield, North Carolina, U.S.A.	
87 V 10	Enfield, Nova Scotia, Canada	
234 B 4	Enga, Papua New Guinea ☐	
64 J 9	Engadine, Michigan, U.S.A.	
135 C 15	Engan, Norway	
198 L 4	Engaru, Japan	
138 G 8	Engelberg, Switzerland	
139 R 3	Engelhartszell, Austria	
157 Q 5	Engel's, Russian Federation	
132 H 6	Engelschmangat, Netherlands ≈	
132 L 5	Engelsmanplaat, Netherlands ≈	
192 E 13	Enggano, Indonesia ⇌	
133 E 20	Enghien, Belgium	
125 I 19	England, United Kingdom	
69 W 12	England, Arkansas, U.S.A.	
85 X 9	Englee, Newfoundland and Labrador, Canada	
86 E 7	Englehart, Ontario, Canada	
43 K 25	English Bay, Ascension ≈	
127 Q 14	English Channel, France/United Kingdom ≈	
240 J 6	English Coast, Antarctica ◇	
148 E 10	Engure, Latvia	
148 E 10	Engures ezers, Latvia ⬡	
68 M 8	Enid, Oklahoma, U.S.A.	
198 J 6	Eniwa, Japan	
132 I 9	Enkhuizen, Netherlands	
141 J 22	Enna, Italy	
82 L 12	Ennadai Lake, Nunavut, Canada ⬡	
125 B 19	Ennis, Republic of Ireland	
73 P 8	Ennis, Montana, U.S.A.	
125 E 19	Enniscorthy, Republic of Ireland	
125 D 16	Enniskillen, United Kingdom	
139 T 4	Enns, Austria	
189 S 13	Enping, China	
128 L 5	Enree, France	
132 N 11	Enschede, Netherlands	
88 F 2	Ensenada, Mexico	
189 Q 7	Enshi, China	
199 I 18	Enshū-nada, Japan ≈	
217 S 8	Entebbe, Uganda	
63 R 6	Enterprise, Alabama, U.S.A.	
74 H 7	Enterprise, Utah, U.S.A.	
76 L 10	Enterprise, Oregon, U.S.A.	
83 H 14	Enterprise, Northwest Territories, Canada	
197 D 17	Enterprise Point, Philippines ▶	
83 H 19	Entrance, Alberta, Canada	
113 C 14	Entre Ríos, Argentina ☐	
130 H 8	Entroncamento, Portugal	
108 B 13	Envira, Brazil	
132 K 11	Epe, Netherlands	
216 I 7	Epéna, Congo	
129 S 4	Épernay, France	
58 G 13	Ephrata, Pennsylvania, U.S.A.	
76 J 7	Ephrata, Washington, U.S.A.	
235 R 11	Epi, Vanuatu ⇌	
129 V 5	Épinal, France	
170 H 15	Episkopi, Cyprus	
127 W 10	Epping, United Kingdom	
127 V 11	Epsom, United Kingdom	
111 J 14	Epu-pel, Argentina	
127 U 3	Epworth, United Kingdom	
216 K 8	Equateur, Democratic Republic of Congo ☐	
181 L 20	Equatorial Channel, Maldives ≈	
215 R 15	Equatorial Guinea, Africa ☐	
210 I 8	Er Rachidia, Morocco	
213 E 18	Er Rahad, Sudan	
210 J 9	Er Raoui, Algeria ◇	
213 F 19	Er Renk, Sudan	
159 W 10	Eratosthenes Seamount, Mediterranean Sea ▲	
170 L 8	Erbaa, Turkey	
171 T 11	Erşşek, Turkey	
171 S 10	Erciş, Turkey	
170 K 11	Erciyes Dağı, Turkey ▲	
143 I 23	Érd, Hungary	
170 C 8	Erdek, Turkey	
170 J 13	Erdemli, Turkey	
185 Q 3	Erdenet, Mongolia	
185 Q 5	Erdenetsogt, Mongolia	
137 K 24	Erding, Germany	
112 H 10	Erechim, Brazil	
185 T 2	Ereentsav, Mongolia	
170 I 12	Ereğli, Turkey	
170 G 7	Ereğli, Turkey	
186 B 13	Erenhot, China	
210 I 8	Erfoud, Morocco	
137 I 17	Erfurt, Germany	
210 H 13	'Erg Chech, Algeria	
215 W 8	Erg du Djourab, Chad ◇	
210 I 10	Erg Iabès, Algeria ◇	
210 G 11	Erg Iguidi, Algeria ◇	
171 O 11	Ergani, Turkey	
185 S 5	Ergel, Mongolia	
146 L 13	Ergene, Turkey ↳	
148 G 11	Ērgļi, Latvia	
187 J 15	Erhulai, China	
43 N 18	Erica Seamount, Atlantic Ocean ▲	
130 F 9	Ericeira, Portugal	
58 B 10	Erie, Pennsylvania, U.S.A.	
147 A 15	Eriekoussa, Greece ⇌	
84 I 10	Eriksdale, Manitoba, Canada	
198 L 6	Erimo, Japan	
198 L 7	Erimo-misaki, Japan ▶	
124 E 11	Eriskay, United Kingdom ⇌	
213 H 16	Eritrea, Africa ☐	
136 M 13	Erkner, Germany	
137 I 20	Erlangen, Germany	
231 N 7	Erldunda, Northern Territory, Australia	
219 P 11	Ermelo, Republic of South Africa	
132 J 11	Ermelo, Netherlands	
170 H 13	Ermenek, Turkey	
147 F 21	Ermioni, Greece	
147 I 21	Ermoupoli, Greece	
137 E 17	Erndtebrück, Germany	
139 X 3	Ernstbrunn, Austria	
181 E 22	Erode, India	
231 R 8	Eromanga, Queensland, Australia	
218 H 9	Erongo, Namibia ☐	
133 F 22	Erquelinnes, Belgium	
125 B 16	Erris Head, Republic of Ireland ▶	
59 N 5	Errol, New Hampshire, U.S.A.	
235 R 12	Erromango, Vanuatu ⇌	
145 L 20	Ersekë, Albania	
186 I 4	Ershiwuzhan, China	
186 J 4	Ershizhan, China	
67 P 4	Erskine, Minnesota, U.S.A.	
184 L 4	Ertai, China	
171 R 12	Eruh, Turkey	
112 G 13	Erval, Brazil	
137 F 15	Erwitte, Germany	
147 F 19	Erythres, Greece	
188 J 10	Eryuan, China	
186 K 7	Erzhan, China	
153 O 14	Erzin, Russian Federation	
170 L 13	Erzin, Turkey	
171 O 9	Erzincan, Turkey	
171 Q 9	Erzurum, Turkey	
149 D 14	Eržvilkas, Lithuania	
210 E 11	Es Semara, Western Sahara	
213 F 18	Es Suki, Sudan	
234 G 7	Esa-ala, Papua New Guinea	
198 J 7	Esan-misaki, Japan ▶	
198 I 8	Esashi, Japan	
198 K 3	Esashi, Japan	
135 B 25	Esbjerg, Denmark	
197 J 17	Escalante, Philippines	
74 K 7	Escalante, Utah, U.S.A.	
89 N 6	Escalón, Mexico	
64 H 10	Escanaba, Michigan, U.S.A.	
89 X 12	Escárcega, Mexico	
196 I 5	Escarpada Point, Philippines ▶	
133 F 16	Escaut, Belgium ↳	
133 K 26	Esch-sur-Alzette, Luxembourg	
137 H 16	Eschwege, Germany	
107 H 19	Escoma, Bolivia	
77 K 26	Escondido, California, U.S.A.	
91 Q 9	Escondido, Nicaragua ↳	
88 M 9	Escuinapa, Mexico	
90 I 7	Escuintla, Guatemala	
215 T 14	Eséka, Cameroon	
170 D 13	Esen, Turkey	
178 I 14	Esenguly, Turkmenistan	
176 J 7	Eşfahān, Iran	
176 I 8	Eşfahān, Iran	
176 M 5	Esfarāyen, Iran	
85 T 8	Esker, Newfoundland and Labrador, Canada	
135 G 21	Eskilstuna, Sweden	
170 F 9	Eskişehir, Turkey	
176 F 6	Eslāmābād-e Gharb, Iran	
92 K 5	Esmeralda, Cuba	
106 B 7	Esmeraldas, Ecuador	
106 A 8	Esmeraldas, Ecuador ☐	
177 O 13	Espakeh, Iran	
129 Q 12	Espalion, France	
75 Q 9	Espanola, New Mexico, U.S.A.	
86 C 9	Espanola, Ontario, Canada	
136 F 13	Espelkamp, Germany	
230 I 12	Esperance, Western Australia, Australia	
240 H 3	Esperanza, Antarctica	
107 G 15	Esperanza, Peru	
111 G 23	Esperanza, Argentina	
88 J 5	Esperanza, Mexico	
130 M 10	Espiel, Spain	
104 I 7	Espinal, Colombia	
130 G 5	Espinho, Portugal	
109 M 17	Espírito Santo, Brazil ☐	
235 P 10	Espíritu Santo, Vanuatu ⇌	
109 I 14	Esplanada, Brazil	
135 L 19	Espoo, Finland	
130 H 4	Esposende, Portugal	
111 G 18	Esquel, Argentina	
112 C 12	Esquina, Argentina	
210 F 8	Essaouira, Morocco	
137 C 15	Essen, Germany	
105 U 6	Essequibo, Guyana ↳	
86 B 14	Essex, Ontario, Canada	
153 Y 10	Esso, Russian Federation	
215 V 15	Est, Cameroon ☐	
196 I 7	Estagno Point, Philippines ▶	
109 N 14	Estância, Brazil	
140 G 7	Este, Italy	
110 K 9	Esteban Rams, Argentina	
91 N 3	Estelí, Nicaragua	
131 Q 2	Estella, Spain	
70 L 3	Estelline, Texas, U.S.A.	
130 M 14	Estepona, Spain	
79 R 7	Ester, Alaska, U.S.A.	
67 Q 10	Estherville, Iowa, U.S.A.	
61 N 15	Estill, South Carolina, U.S.A.	
148 F 7	Estonia, Europe ☐	
111 I 26	Estrecho de Le Maire, Argentina ≈	
111 I 24	Estrecho Nelson, Chile ≈	
130 I 9	Estremoz, Portugal	
216 D 7	Estuaire, Gabon ☐	
182 K 9	Etah, India	
129 U 3	Étain, France	
81 Y 9	Étamamiou, Québec, Canada	
85 W 10	Etamamiou, Québec, Canada	
129 P 5	Étampes, France	
182 K 10	Etawah, India	
213 G 21	Ethiopia, Africa ☐	
213 G 20	Ethiopian Highlands, Ethiopia ⋀	
170 H 9	Etimesğut, Turkey	
78 K 9	Etolin Strait, Alaska, U.S.A. ≈	
216 H 7	Etoumbi, Congo	
129 N 3	Étretat, France	
146 H 9	Etropole, Bulgaria	
128 M 15	Etsaut, France	
133 L 24	Ettelbruck, Luxembourg	
236 I 11	Eua, Tonga	
230 L 10	Eucla, Western Australia, Australia	
65 N 16	Euclid, Ohio, U.S.A.	
63 R 5	Eufaula, Alabama, U.S.A.	
68 Q 11	Eufaula, Oklahoma, U.S.A.	
69 P 10	Eufaula Lake, Oklahoma, U.S.A. ⬡	
76 F 11	Eugene, Oregon, U.S.A.	
231 S 9	Eulo, Queensland, Australia	
62 J 7	Eunice, Louisiana, U.S.A.	
75 U 14	Eunice, New Mexico, U.S.A.	
133 L 20	Eupen, Belgium	
172 L 3	Euphrates, Syria/Iraq ↳	
62 M 3	Eupora, Mississippi, U.S.A.	

☐ Country   ☐ Internal administrative region: State/Province/Territory/Dependent territory   ☀ Capital city   ⋀ Mountain range/Undersea ridge   ▲ Mountain peak/Volcano/Seamount   ◇ Geographic feature   ▶ Headland/Point/Cape/Peninsula   ▲ Desert   ⇌ Island/Island group   ⚑ Antarctic base   Ocean   Sea   ≈ Bay/Gulf/Channel/Strait   Lake   Salt pan/Dry/Intermittent lake

M 2 **Eureka**, Montana, U.S.A.
J 4 **Eureka**, Utah, U.S.A.
E 15 **Eureka**, California, U.S.A.
M 17 **Eureka**, Nevada, U.S.A.
F 13 **Europoort**, Netherlands ◇
C 18 **Euskirchen**, Germany
W 9 **Eustis**, Florida, U.S.A.
O 4 **Eutaw**, Alabama, U.S.A.
E 19 **Eutsuk Lake**, British Columbia, Canada 💧
O 4 **Evans Strait**, Nunavut, Canada ≈
H 15 **Evanston**, Illinois, U.S.A.
Q 15 **Evanston**, Wyoming, U.S.A.
H 22 **Evansville**, Indiana, U.S.A.
O 8 **Evant**, Texas, U.S.A.
O 11 **Evaton**, Republic of South Africa
J 12 **Evaz**, Iran
Y 9 **Evensk**, Russian Federation
D 13 **Everett**, Pennsylvania, U.S.A.
H 6 **Everett**, Washington, U.S.A.
X 14 **Everglades**, Florida, U.S.A. ◇
P 6 **Evergreen**, Alabama, U.S.A.
R 8 **Evesham**, United Kingdom
K 15 **Evijärvi**, Finland 💧
B 21 **Evje**, Norway
I 10 **Evora**, Portugal ▣
I 9 **Évora**, Portugal
O 4 **Évreux**, France
K 13 **Evros**, Greece 〰
H 19 **Evvoia**, Greece 🏝
B 7 **Ewa Beach**, Hawaii, U.S.A.
M 16 **Ewing Seamount**, Atlantic Ocean ▲
G 8 **Ewo**, Congo
S 3 **Excelsior Springs**, Missouri, U.S.A.
N 13 **Exe**, United Kingdom 〰
L 11 **Executive Committee Range**, Antarctica ⛰
N 13 **Exeter**, United Kingdom
J 21 **Exeter**, California, U.S.A.
R 13 **Exira**, Iowa, U.S.A.
O 14 **Exminster**, United Kingdom
N 12 **Exmoor**, United Kingdom ◇
W 5 **Exmore**, Virginia, U.S.A.
E 6 **Exmouth**, Western Australia, Australia
O 14 **Exmouth**, United Kingdom
T 7 **Exmouth Plateau**, Indian Ocean ◇
H 14 **Exton**, Pennsylvania, U.S.A.
K 8 **Extremadura**, Spain ▣
V 11 **Extrême-Nord**, Cameroon ▣
L 3 **Exuma Cays**, The Bahamas 🏝
Y 7 **Eye**, United Kingdom
O 21 **Eyl**, Somalia
P 10 **Eymoutiers**, France
O 11 **Eyre Peninsula**, South Australia, Australia ▶
H 20 **Eyreton**, New Zealand
J 12 **Ezernieki**, Latvia
U 7 **Ezhou**, China
A 9 **Ezine**, Turkey

L 17 **Faadhippolhu Atoll**, Maldives 🏝
J 24 **Faafxadhuun**, Somalia
E 7 **Fabens**, Texas, U.S.A.
T 7 **Fachi**, Niger
G 19 **Facundo**, Argentina
Y 7 **Fada**, Chad
G 9 **Faenza**, Italy
J 10 **Făgăraș**, Romania
G 20 **Fagersta**, Sweden
G 10 **Făget**, Romania
C 11 **Fagurhólsmýri**, Iceland
N 1 **Faial**, Azores 🏝
138 G 9 **Faido**, Switzerland
124 J 6 **Fair Isle**, United Kingdom 🏝
79 R 7 **Fairbanks**, Alaska, U.S.A.
65 G 21 **Fairfield**, Illinois, U.S.A.
71 R 7 **Fairfield**, Texas, U.S.A.
72 L 11 **Fairfield**, Idaho, U.S.A.
77 G 19 **Fairfield**, California, U.S.A.
233 F 21 **Fairlie**, New Zealand
61 P 2 **Fairmont**, West Virginia, U.S.A.
67 N 15 **Fairmont**, Nebraska, U.S.A.
67 R 10 **Fairmont**, Minnesota, U.S.A.
75 Q 5 **Fairplay**, Colorado, U.S.A.
64 I 10 **Fairport**, Michigan, U.S.A.
68 L 9 **Fairview**, Oklahoma, U.S.A.
177 X 9 **Faisalabad**, Pakistan
66 I 8 **Faith**, South Dakota, U.S.A.
183 N 10 **Faizabad**, India
93 U 8 **Fajardo**, Puerto Rico
173 W 9 **Fajir**, Iraq
236 J 6 **Fakaofo**, Tokelau Islands 🏝
127 Y 6 **Fakenham**, United Kingdom
193 U 12 **Fakfak**, Indonesia
146 M 10 **Fakiya**, Bulgaria
135 D 26 **Fakse Bugt**, Denmark ≈
187 I 14 **Faku**, China
128 M 4 **Falaise**, France
215 R 7 **Falaise de Tiguidit**, Niger ⛰
183 T 10 **Falakata**, India
104 M 2 **Falcón**, Venezuela ▣
140 I 10 **Falconara Marittima**, Italy
150 M 8 **Fălești**, Moldova
71 P 14 **Falfurrias**, Texas, U.S.A.
136 L 13 **Falkensee**, Germany
124 H 13 **Falkirk**, United Kingdom
43 F 20 **Falkland Escarpment**, Atlantic Ocean ◇
111 J 24 **Falkland Islands**, U.K. ▣
43 F 20 **Falkland Plateau**, Atlantic Ocean ◇
111 K 24 **Falkland Sound**, Falkland Islands ≈
147 G 23 **Falkonera**, Greece 🏝
135 E 22 **Falköping**, Sweden
59 O 11 **Fall River**, Massachusetts, U.S.A.
77 J 17 **Fallon**, Nevada, U.S.A.
67 Q 15 **Falls City**, Nebraska, U.S.A.
61 S 8 **Falls Lake Reserve**, North Carolina, U.S.A. 💧
126 J 15 **Falmouth**, United Kingdom
60 J 4 **Falmouth**, Kentucky, U.S.A.
61 T 4 **Falmouth**, Virginia, U.S.A.
92 K 8 **Falmouth**, Jamaica
126 J 15 **Falmouth Bay**, United Kingdom ≈
218 J 15 **False Bay**, Republic of South Africa ≈
78 L 13 **False Pass**, Alaska, U.S.A.
181 J 16 **False Point**, India ▶
135 D 26 **Falster**, Denmark 🏝
150 L 8 **Fălticeni**, Romania
135 G 19 **Falun**, Sweden
110 H 9 **Famatina**, Argentina
176 H 6 **Famenin**, Iran
190 J 11 **Fan Si Pan**, Vietnam ▲
189 X 6 **Fanchang**, China
219 Y 8 **Fandriana**, Madgascar
190 G 13 **Fang**, Thailand
213 E 20 **Fangak**, Sudan
189 T 4 **Fangcheng**, China
189 Z 12 **Fangshan**, Taiwan
189 R 5 **Fangxian**, China
186 M 11 **Fangzheng**, China
186 J 13 **Fanjiatun**, China
177 N 13 **Fannūj**, Iran
140 H 10 **Fano**, Italy
135 B 25 **Fanø**, Denmark 🏝
189 Y 8 **Fanshan**, China
187 B 17 **Fanshi**, China
182 M 8 **Far Western**, Nepal ▣
240 H 4 **Faraday**, Antarctica ⁙
217 Q 5 **Faradje**, Democratic Republic of Congo
219 Y 10 **Farafangana**, Madgascar
177 Q 8 **Farāh**, Afghanistan ▣
177 P 9 **Farāh**, Afghanistan
236 A 8 **Farallon de Medinilla**, Northern Mariana Islands 🏝
236 A 5 **Farallon de Pajaros**, Northern Mariana Islands 🏝
214 H 11 **Faranah**, Guinea
175 X 10 **Fararah**, Oman
236 M 14 **Faraulep**, Federated States of Micronesia 🏝
127 T 13 **Fareham**, United Kingdom
79 P 8 **Farewell**, Alaska, U.S.A.
233 H 15 **Farewell Spit**, New Zealand ▶
179 S 12 **Farghona Wiloyati**, Uzbekistan ▣
63 V 7 **Fargo**, Georgia, U.S.A.
67 O 5 **Fargo**, North Dakota, U.S.A.
67 S 9 **Faribault**, Minnesota, U.S.A.
182 J 9 **Faridabad**, India
182 H 6 **Faridkot**, India
183 T 13 **Faridpur**, Bangladesh
177 O 6 **Farīmān**, Iran
127 S 10 **Faringdon**, United Kingdom
135 G 24 **Färjestaden**, Sweden
59 P 5 **Farmington**, Maine, U.S.A.
75 O 8 **Farmington**, New Mexico, U.S.A.
61 R 6 **Farmville**, Virginia, U.S.A.
127 U 11 **Farnborough**, United Kingdom
127 T 11 **Farnham**, United Kingdom
130 H 12 **Faro**, Portugal ▣
130 H 12 **Faro**, Portugal
82 C 13 **Faro**, Yukon Territory, Canada
45 R 15 **Faroe Islands**, Denmark 🏝
45 Q 15 **Faroe–Iceland Ridge**, Arctic Ocean ⛰
42 K 5 **Faroe–Shetland Trough**, Atlantic Ocean ◇
135 I 22 **Fårösund**, Sweden 🏝
135 I 22 **Fårösund**, Sweden
38 K 6 **Farquhar Islands**, Seychelles 🏝
69 X 5 **Farrington**, Missouri, U.S.A.
176 J 10 **Fārs**, Iran ▣
147 E 17 **Farsala**, Greece
73 S 13 **Farson**, Wyoming, U.S.A.
70 I 3 **Farwell**, Texas, U.S.A.
240 J 8 **Farwell Island**, Antarctica 🏝
177 R 6 **Fāryāb**, Afghanistan ▣
176 J 11 **Fasā**, Iran
141 N 16 **Fasano**, Italy
151 P 4 **Fastiv**, Ukraine
217 R 6 **Fataki**, Democratic Republic of Congo
182 I 7 **Fatehabad**, India
182 L 9 **Fatehgarh**, India
182 M 11 **Fatehpur**, India
156 J 4 **Fatezh**, Russian Federation
214 D 8 **Fatick**, Senegal
216 I 10 **Fatundu**, Democratic Republic of Congo
235 S 8 **Fatutaka**, Solomon Islands 🏝
134 G 10 **Fauske**, Norway
127 Y 11 **Faversham**, United Kingdom
134 A 11 **Faxaflói**, Iceland ≈
215 X 7 **Faya**, Chad
235 Q 13 **Fayaoué**, New Caledonia
62 K 5 **Fayette**, Mississippi, U.S.A.
63 O 3 **Fayette**, Alabama, U.S.A.
60 F 10 **Fayetteville**, Tennessee, U.S.A.
61 R 10 **Fayetteville**, North Carolina, U.S.A.
65 L 20 **Fayetteville**, Ohio, U.S.A.
69 S 9 **Fayetteville**, Arkansas, U.S.A.
214 G 4 **Fdérik**, Mauritania
129 N 3 **Fécamp**, France
144 H 13 **Federacija Bosna Hercegovina**, Bosnia and Herzegovina ▣
112 D 13 **Federación**, Argentina
112 D 13 **Federal**, Argentina
215 R 12 **Federal Capital Territory**, Nigeria ▣
237 Q 14 **Federated States of Micronesia**, Oceania □
173 O 3 **Fedghāmī**, Syria
179 O 2 **Fedorovka**, Kazakhstan
136 I 8 **Fehmarn**, Germany 🏝
136 I 7 **Fehmarnbelt**, Germany ≈
139 X 8 **Fehring**, Austria
108 B 13 **Feijó**, Brazil
109 N 14 **Feira de Santana**, Brazil
170 K 12 **Feke**, Turkey
131 Y 8 **Felanitx**, Spain
139 X 8 **Feldbach**, Austria
138 I 7 **Feldkirch**, Austria
139 S 8 **Feldkirchen in Kärnten**, Austria
38 C 8 **Félicité**, Seychelles 🏝
181 L 18 **Felidhu Atoll**, Maldives 🏝
89 Z 11 **Felipe Carrillo Puerto**, Mexico
127 Z 9 **Felixstowe**, United Kingdom
140 G 6 **Feltre**, Italy
135 E 17 **Femunden**, Norway 💧
171 O 8 **Fener Burnu**, Turkey ▶
147 J 14 **Fengari**, Greece ▲
187 I 16 **Fengcheng**, China
189 U 8 **Fengcheng**, China
189 P 7 **Fengdu**, China
189 P 8 **Fenggang**, China
189 Z 7 **Fenghua**, China
189 Q 8 **Fenghuang**, China
189 W 11 **Fenghuang**, China
189 Q 6 **Fengjie**, China
189 Z 11 **Fenglin**, Taiwan
187 E 15 **Fengning**, China
188 J 11 **Fengqing**, China
189 U 3 **Fengqiu**, China
187 F 17 **Fengrun**, China
186 I 4 **Fengshui Shan**, China ▲
189 V 11 **Fengshun**, China
189 V 5 **Fengtai**, China
189 O 4 **Fengxian**, China
189 V 3 **Fengxian**, China
189 Z 6 **Fengxian**, China
189 P 3 **Fengxiang**, China
189 V 8 **Fengxin**, China
189 W 4 **Fengyang**, China
189 Z 11 **Fengyüan**, Taiwan
187 B 16 **Fengzhen**, China
183 V 13 **Feni**, Bangladesh
234 I 3 **Feni Islands**, Papua New Guinea 🏝
65 E 14 **Fennimore**, Wisconsin, U.S.A.
219 Z 7 **Fenoarivo Atsinanana**, Madgascar
237 N 14 **Fayu**, Federated States of Micronesia 🏝
189 S 1 **Fenyang**, China
151 V 12 **Feodosiya**, Ukraine
65 I 21 **Ferdinand**, Indiana, U.S.A.
177 N 7 **Ferdows**, Iran
146 K 13 **Feres**, Greece
213 L 22 **Fērfēr**, Ethiopia
179 T 12 **Fergana**, Uzbekistan
179 S 12 **Fergana Valley**, Uzbekistan ◇
67 P 6 **Fergus Falls**, Minnesota, U.S.A.
234 G 6 **Fergusson Island**, Papua New Guinea 🏝
211 P 6 **Fériana**, Tunisia
214 K 11 **Ferkessédougou**, Côte d'Ivoire
140 I 11 **Fermo**, Italy
130 K 5 **Fermoselle**, Spain
125 C 20 **Fermoy**, Republic of Ireland
110 J 8 **Fernández**, Argentina
63 W 7 **Fernandina Beach**, Florida, U.S.A.
43 I 14 **Fernando de Noronha**, Brazil 🏝
112 I 4 **Fernandópolis**, Brazil
77 I 17 **Fernley**, Nevada, U.S.A.
141 M 16 **Ferrandina**, Italy
140 G 8 **Ferrara**, Italy
130 H 10 **Ferreira do Alentejo**, Portugal
62 K 6 **Ferriday**, Louisiana, U.S.A.
130 I 1 **Ferrol**, Spain
210 I 7 **Fès**, Morocco
216 J 11 **Feshi**, Democratic Republic of Congo
66 K 4 **Fessenden**, North Dakota, U.S.A.
69 Y 5 **Festus**, Missouri, U.S.A.
150 M 13 **Fetești-Gara**, Romania
170 D 13 **Fethiye**, Turkey
178 I 10 **Fetisovo**, Kazakhstan
124 K 4 **Fetlar**, United Kingdom 🏝
137 H 22 **Feuchtwangen**, Germany
129 S 10 **Feurs**, France
177 V 5 **Feyzābād**, Afghanistan
127 N 5 **Ffestiniog**, United Kingdom
110 H 8 **Fiambalá**, Argentina
219 X 9 **Fianarantsoa**, Madgascar
219 X 9 **Fianarantsoa**, Madgascar ▣
215 V 11 **Fianga**, Chad
213 I 20 **Fichē**, Ethiopia
137 J 20 **Fichtelgebirge**, Germany ⛰
140 G 12 **Ficulle**, Italy
140 E 8 **Fidenza**, Italy
145 J 20 **Fier**, Albania
138 F 10 **Fiesch**, Switzerland
64 J 12 **Fife Lake**, Michigan, U.S.A.
124 I 12 **Fife Ness**, United Kingdom ▶
129 P 12 **Figeac**, France
130 G 7 **Figueira da Foz**, Portugal
131 Y 3 **Figueres**, Spain
210 K 8 **Figuig**, Morocco
215 V 11 **Figuil**, Cameroon
235 W 12 **Fiji**, Oceania □
213 K 21 **Fīk'**, Ethiopia
219 O 8 **Filabusi**, Zimbabwe
91 O 10 **Filadelfia**, Costa Rica
109 F 18 **Filadélfia**, Paraguay
143 K 21 **Filakovo**, Slovakia
241 N 5 **Filchner Ice Shelf**, Antarctica ◇
127 V 1 **Filey**, United Kingdom
127 V 1 **Filey Head**, United Kingdom ▶
150 H 12 **Filiași**, Romania
147 C 22 **Filiatra**, Greece
215 P 9 **Filingué**, Niger
147 B 17 **Filippiada**, Greece
74 I 5 **Fillmore**, Utah, U.S.A.
77 J 24 **Fillmore**, California, U.S.A.
213 J 23 **Fīltu**, Ethiopia
241 P 1 **Fimbul Ice Shelf**, Antarctica ◇
241 P 2 **Fimbulheimen**, Antarctica ⛰
131 P 12 **Fiñana**, Spain
65 L 17 **Findlay**, Ohio, U.S.A.
58 F 9 **Finger Lakes**, New York, U.S.A. 💧
219 P 5 **Fingoè**, Mozambique
170 E 14 **Finike**, Turkey
234 D 4 **Finisterre Range**, Papua New Guinea ⛰
231 O 7 **Finke**, Northern Territory, Australia
135 L 18 **Finland**, Europe □
83 E 16 **Finlay**, British Columbia, Canada 〰
231 S 12 **Finley**, New South Wales, Australia
67 N 4 **Finley**, North Dakota, U.S.A.
175 Z 7 **Fins**, Oman
234 E 5 **Finschhafen**, Papua New Guinea
138 F 9 **Finsteraarhorn**, Switzerland ▲
233 A 25 **Fiordland**, New Zealand ◇
83 J 15 **Firebag**, Alberta, Canada 〰
140 F 9 **Firenzuola**, Italy
113 B 15 **Firmat**, Argentina
129 S 11 **Firminy**, France
154 G 13 **Firovo**, Russian Federation
182 K 10 **Firozabad**, India
182 H 6 **Firozpur**, India
125 G 14 **Firth of Clyde**, United Kingdom ≈
124 I 12 **Firth of Forth**, United Kingdom ≈
124 F 12 **Firth of Lorn**, United Kingdom ≈
232 L 8 **Firth of Thames**, New Zealand ≈
176 J 11 **Fīrūzābād**, Iran
176 J 6 **Fīrūzkūh**, Iran
39 Y 15 **Fisher Bay**, Indian Ocean ≈
85 N 4 **Fisher Strait**, Nunavut, Canada ≈
126 K 9 **Fishguard**, United Kingdom
126 J 8 **Fishguard Bay**, United Kingdom ≈
129 R 3 **Fismes**, France
124 J 5 **Fitful Head**, United Kingdom ▶
111 H 20 **Fitz Roy**, Argentina
107 F 16 **Fitzcarrald**, Peru
230 J 4 **Fitzroy**, Western Australia, Australia 〰
230 J 4 **Fitzroy Crossing**, Western Australia, Australia
86 C 10 **Fitzwilliam Island**, Ontario, Canada 🏝
141 G 14 **Fiumicino**, Italy
140 D 9 **Fivizzano**, Italy
217 Q 10 **Fizi**, Democratic Republic of Congo
135 C 19 **Flå**, Norway
134 C 12 **Flaga**, Iceland
74 K 10 **Flagstaff**, Arizona, U.S.A.
43 N 25 **Flagstaff Bay**, St Helena ≈
59 O 4 **Flagstaff Lake**, Maine, U.S.A. 💧
85 P 8 **Flaherty Island**, Ontario, Canada 🏝
127 V 1 **Flamborough**, United Kingdom
127 V 1 **Flamborough Head**, United Kingdom ▶
137 K 14 **Fläming**, Germany ⛰
74 M 2 **Flaming Gorge Reservoir**, Utah/Wyoming, U.S.A. 💧
63 X 14 **Flamingo**, Florida, U.S.A.
133 C 19 **Flanders**, Belgium ◇
135 G 14 **Flåsjön**, Sweden 💧
38 B 11 **Flat Island**, Mauritius 🏝
73 N 3 **Flathead Lake**, Montana, U.S.A. 💧
139 S 8 **Flattnitz**, Austria
42 B 7 **Flatts Village**, Bermuda
127 O 2 **Fleetwood**, United Kingdom
135 A 21 **Flekkefjord**, Norway
42 G 7 **Flemish Cap**, Atlantic Ocean ⛰
135 B 26 **Flensburg**, Denmark
136 G 7 **Flensburg**, Germany
128 M 4 **Flers**, France
240 I 8 **Fletcher Peninsula**, Antarctica ▶
138 B 8 **Fleurier**, Switzerland
132 I 10 **Flevoland**, Netherlands ▣
84 H 7 **Flin Flon**, Manitoba, Canada
231 R 5 **Flinders**, Queensland, Australia 〰
231 T 14 **Flinders Island**, Tasmania, Australia 🏝
231 P 10 **Flinders Ranges**, South Australia, Australia ⛰
237 S 7 **Flint**, Kiribati 🏝
127 O 4 **Flint**, United Kingdom
65 L 14 **Flint**, Michigan, U.S.A.
69 O 7 **Flint Hills**, Kansas, U.S.A. ◇
135 E 18 **Flisa**, Norway 〰
135 E 19 **Flisa**, Norway
65 G 21 **Flora**, Illinois, U.S.A.
129 S 12 **Florac**, France
63 Q 6 **Florala**, Alabama, U.S.A.
140 F 10 **Florence**, Italy
58 A 13 **Florence**, Pennsylvania, U.S.A.
61 P 12 **Florence**, South Carolina, U.S.A.

ountry ▣ Internal administrative region: State/Province/Territory/Dependent territory 🏛 Capital city ⛰ Mountain range/Undersea ridge ▲ Mountain peak/Volcano/Seamount ◇ Geographic feature ▶ Headland/Point/Cape/Peninsula 🏜 Desert 🏝 Island/Island group ⁙ Antarctic base 🌊 Ocean ⛵ Sea ≈ Bay/Gulf/Channel/Strait 💧 Lake ◩ Salt pan/Dry/Intermittent lake 〰 River

B 11 **Gabriel Island**, Mauritius 🏝
J 9 **Gabrovo**, Bulgaria ▣
J 8 **Gabrovo**, Bulgaria
F 9 **Gabú**, Guinea-Bissau
H 14 **Gacko**, Bosnia and Herzegovina
V 8 **Gädäbäy**, Azerbaijan
D 19 **Gadag**, India
F 15 **Gadarwara**, India
A 16 **Gadhra**, India
R 2 **Gadsden**, Alabama, U.S.A.
E 19 **Gadwal**, India
J 12 **Găeşti**, Romania
I 15 **Gaeta**, Italy
M 14 **Gaferut**, Federated States of Micronesia 🏝
N 10 **Gaffney**, South Carolina, U.S.A.
P 7 **Gafsa**, Tunisia
T 11 **Gag**, Indonesia 🏝
V 12 **Gagal**, Chad
J 1 **Gagarin**, Russian Federation
Q 12 **Gagarin**, Uzbekistan
O 17 **Gagliano del Capo**, Italy
J 13 **Gagnoa**, Côte d'Ivoire
T 9 **Gagnon**, Québec, Canada
O 7 **Gahe**, China
T 11 **Gaibandha**, Bangladesh
P 13 **Gaillac**, France
T 2 **Gainesville**, Georgia, U.S.A.
V 8 **Gainesville**, Florida, U.S.A.
V 8 **Gainesville**, Missouri, U.S.A.
Q 4 **Gainesville**, Texas, U.S.A.
U 4 **Gainsborough**, United Kingdom
I 16 **Gaizhou**, China
G 11 **Gaiziņkalns**, Latvia ▲
B 26 **Gaja-jima**, Japan 🏝
S 13 **Gakem**, Nigeria
S 8 **Gakona**, Alaska, U.S.A.
X 6 **Gakuch**, Pakistan
T 8 **Galapagos Fracture Zone**, Pacific Ocean ◇
A 17 **Galapagos Islands**, Ecuador 🏝
I 13 **Galashiels**, United Kingdom
N 8 **Galata**, Bulgaria
M 11 **Galaţi**, Romania
F 14 **Galatista**, Greece
M 12 **Gáldar**, Canary Islands
C 17 **Galdhøpiggen**, Norway ▲
L 4 **Galeana**, Mexico
S 10 **Galela**, Indonesia
E 15 **Galena**, Illinois, U.S.A.
O 7 **Galena**, Alaska, U.S.A.
Z 14 **Galeota Point**, Trinidad and Tobago ▶
Z 14 **Galera Point**, Trinidad and Tobago ▶
E 17 **Galesburg**, Illinois, U.S.A.
D 12 **Galesville**, Wisconsin, U.S.A.
E 10 **Galeton**, Pennsylvania, U.S.A.
N 22 **Galguduud**, Somalia ▣
H 13 **Galicea Mare**, Romania
L 13 **Galich**, Russian Federation
I 2 **Galicia**, Spain ▣
K 8 **Galicia Bank**, Atlantic Ocean ◇
H 18 **Gallabat**, Sudan
C 6 **Gallarate**, Italy
F 8 **Gallatin**, Tennessee, U.S.A.
F 25 **Galle**, Sri Lanka
G 24 **Gallegos**, Argentina ∿
O 17 **Gallipoli**, Italy
B 8 **Gallipoli**, Turkey
A 8 **Gallipoli Peninsula**, Turkey ▶
N 20 **Gallipolis**, Ohio, U.S.A.
J 10 **Gällivare**, Sweden
N 9 **Gallup**, New Mexico, U.S.A.
D 12 **Galtat Zemmour**, Western Sahara
T 11 **Galveston**, Texas, U.S.A.
T 10 **Galveston Bay**, Texas, U.S.A. ≈

110 K 11 **Gálvez**, Argentina
183 N 7 **Galwa**, Nepal
125 B 18 **Galway**, Republic of Ireland
125 B 18 **Galway Bay**, Republic of Ireland ≈
216 D 9 **Gamba**, Gabon
194 D 8 **Gambang**, Malaysia
213 G 21 **Gambēla**, Ethiopia
213 F 21 **Gambēla**, Ethiopia ▣
214 D 9 **Gambia**, Africa □
214 E 9 **Gambia**, Gambia ∿
42 J 12 **Gambia Abyssal Plain**, Atlantic Ocean ◇
216 H 9 **Gamboma**, Congo
216 H 5 **Gamboula**, Central African Republic
171 W 8 **Gamiş Dağl**, Azerbaijan ▲
188 J 5 **Gamtog**, China
189 V 9 **Gan**, China ∿
188 K 5 **Gana**, China
74 M 9 **Ganado**, Arizona, U.S.A.
86 I 12 **Gananoque**, Ontario, Canada
176 H 10 **Ganāveh**, Iran
171 V 8 **Gäncä**, Azerbaijan
189 Q 15 **Gancheng**, China
218 G 5 **Ganda**, Angola
85 Y 10 **Gander**, Newfoundland and Labrador, Canada
131 U 5 **Gandesa**, Spain
181 A 14 **Gandhidham**, India
181 C 14 **Gandhinagar**, India
131 T 9 **Gandía**, Spain
111 H 17 **Gangán**, Argentina
182 G 7 **Ganganagar**, India
180 E 12 **Gangapur**, India
190 C 11 **Gangaw**, Myanmar
184 H 9 **Gangdise Shan**, China ⛰
137 B 17 **Gangelt**, Germany
129 S 13 **Ganges**, France
182 K 9 **Ganges**, India/Bangladesh ∿
39 P 1 **Ganges Cone**, Indian Ocean ◇
180 G 12 **Gangetic Plain**, India ◇
183 S 10 **Gangtok**, India
189 O 3 **Gangu**, China
188 L 7 **Ganluo**, China
186 I 9 **Gannan**, China
129 R 9 **Gannat**, France
73 S 11 **Gannett Peak**, Wyoming, U.S.A. ▲
184 M 7 **Ganq**, China
189 Q 2 **Ganquan**, China
139 Y 3 **Gänserndorf**, Austria
189 N 3 **Gansu**, China
189 N 3 **Gansu**, China ▣
171 P 5 **Gant'iadi**, Georgia
215 T 12 **Ganye**, Nigeria
189 X 3 **Ganyu**, China
178 G 7 **Ganyushkino**, Kazakhstan
189 U 10 **Ganzhou**, China
189 V 8 **Gao'an**, China
187 C 18 **Gaocheng**, China
189 T 2 **Gaoping**, China
189 V 1 **Gaotang**, China
189 N 8 **Gaoxian**, China
187 D 18 **Gaoyang**, China
189 X 4 **Gaoyou**, China
189 X 4 **Gaoyou Hu**, China ◣
189 R 13 **Gaozhou**, China
129 V 12 **Gap**, France
196 G 10 **Gapan**, Philippines
184 H 9 **Gar**, China
213 O 21 **Garacad**, Somalia
91 Y 15 **Garachiné**, Panama
213 M 20 **Garadag**, Somalia
108 O 13 **Garanhuns**, Brazil
216 K 2 **Garba**, Central African Republic
217 W 7 **Garba Tula**, Kenya
213 K 23 **Garbahaarey**, Somalia
77 E 16 **Garberville**, California, U.S.A.
136 G 13 **Garbsen**, Germany
112 I 6 **Garça**, Brazil
136 J 13 **Gardelegen**, Germany
68 I 5 **Garden City**, Kansas, U.S.A.

64 J 9 **Garden Island**, Michigan, U.S.A. 🏝
177 U 8 **Gardez**, Afghanistan
73 R 8 **Gardiner**, Montana, U.S.A.
63 W 11 **Gardner**, Florida, U.S.A.
41 Q 5 **Gardner Pinnacles**, Hawaii 🏝
78 E 13 **Gareloi Island**, Alaska, U.S.A. 🏝
140 B 9 **Garessio**, Italy
211 O 12 **Garet El Djenoun**, Algeria ▲
75 Q 5 **Garfield**, Colorado, U.S.A.
127 S 2 **Garforth**, United Kingdom
148 B 13 **Gargždai**, Lithuania
181 G 16 **Garhchiroli**, India
112 H 11 **Garibaldi**, Brazil
218 J 13 **Garies**, Republic of South Africa
217 X 8 **Garissa**, Kenya
61 S 11 **Garland**, North Carolina, U.S.A.
71 Q 5 **Garland**, Texas, U.S.A.
149 E 15 **Garliava**, Lithuania
176 H 3 **Garmī**, Iran
137 I 26 **Garmisch-Partenkirchen**, Germany
176 J 6 **Garmsār**, Iran
69 Q 5 **Garnett**, Kansas, U.S.A.
231 R 11 **Garnpung Lake**, New South Wales, Australia ◣
128 M 11 **Garonne**, France ∿
213 N 20 **Garoowe**, Somalia
215 U 11 **Garoua**, Cameroon
215 V 13 **Garoua Boulai**, Cameroon
234 F 4 **Garove Island**, Papua New Guinea 🏝
73 O 6 **Garrison**, Montana, U.S.A.
84 K 1 **Garry Lake**, Nunavut, Canada ◣
217 X 9 **Garsen**, Kenya
213 A 18 **Garsila**, Sudan
127 P 2 **Garstang**, United Kingdom
127 O 8 **Garth**, United Kingdom
192 H 14 **Garut**, Indonesia
233 C 24 **Garvie Mountains**, New Zealand ⛰
181 I 14 **Garwa**, India
142 M 13 **Garwolin**, Poland
65 H 16 **Gary**, Indiana, U.S.A.
188 K 5 **Garzê**, China
104 H 8 **Garzón**, Colombia
128 M 13 **Gascony**, France ◇
230 F 8 **Gascoyne**, Western Australia, Australia ∿
230 F 8 **Gascoyne Junction**, Western Australia, Australia
39 S 7 **Gascoyne Plain**, Indian Ocean ◇
177 P 12 **Gasht**, Iran
215 T 10 **Gashua**, Nigeria
234 G 5 **Gasmata**, Papua New Guinea
87 T 5 **Gaspé**, Québec, Canada
198 K 12 **Gassan**, Japan ▲
215 T 12 **Gassol**, Nigeria
61 O 10 **Gastonia**, North Carolina, U.S.A.
147 C 20 **Gastouni**, Greece
111 G 17 **Gastre**, Argentina
150 F 11 **Gătaia**, Romania
154 E 11 **Gatchina**, Russian Federation
82 J 6 **Gateshead Island**, Nunavut, Canada 🏝
71 P 8 **Gatesville**, Texas, U.S.A.
86 I 10 **Gatineau**, Québec, Canada
60 K 9 **Gatlinburg**, Tennessee, U.S.A.
91 W 13 **Gatún**, Panama
235 Y 12 **Gau**, Fiji 🏝
235 Q 9 **Gaua**, Vanuatu 🏝
148 G 9 **Gauja**, Latvia ∿
181 E 21 **Gauribidanur**, India
135 C 19 **Gausta**, Norway ▲
219 O 11 **Gauteng**, Republic of South Africa ▣
176 I 12 **Gāvbandī**, Iran
147 H 26 **Gavdopoula**, Greece 🏝
147 H 26 **Gavdos**, Greece 🏝
108 C 12 **Gaviãozinho**, Brazil

135 H 19 **Gävle**, Sweden
154 J 13 **Gavrilov-Yam**, Russian Federation
231 P 11 **Gawler**, South Australia, Australia
185 P 6 **Gaxun Nur**, China ◣
183 P 12 **Gaya**, India
195 U 5 **Gaya**, Malaysia 🏝
64 K 11 **Gaylord**, Michigan, U.S.A.
155 R 10 **Gayny**, Russian Federation
219 Q 9 **Gaza**, Mozambique ▣
172 E 10 **Gaza**, Israel
172 E 10 **Gaza Strip**, Israel ◇
178 J 13 **Gazandzhyk**, Turkmenistan
217 X 10 **Gazi**, Kenya
170 M 13 **Gaziantep**, Turkey
177 O 8 **Gazīk**, Iran
170 G 14 **Gazipaşa**, Turkey
179 O 12 **Gazli**, Uzbekistan
214 H 12 **Gbarnga**, Liberia
214 H 13 **Gbatala**, Liberia
215 S 12 **Gboko**, Nigeria
142 I 8 **Gdańsk**, Poland
154 D 11 **Gdov**, Russian Federation
142 I 8 **Gdynia**, Poland
193 S 11 **Gebe**, Indonesia 🏝
212 G 11 **Gebel Hamâta**, Egypt ▲
212 F 9 **Gebel Katherîna**, Egypt ▲
213 I 20 **Gebre Guracha**, Ethiopia
170 E 8 **Gebze**, Turkey
213 G 21 **Gech'a**, Ethiopia
213 G 17 **Gedaref**, Sudan
213 G 18 **Gedaref**, Sudan ▣
213 L 21 **Gedlegubē**, Ethiopia
213 K 24 **Gedo**, Somalia ▣
195 N 11 **Gedong**, Malaysia
135 D 26 **Gedser**, Denmark
133 H 17 **Geel**, Belgium
231 S 13 **Geelong**, Victoria, Australia
215 T 9 **Geidam**, Nigeria
83 L 15 **Geikie**, Saskatchewan, Canada ∿
135 C 18 **Geilo**, Norway
217 S 9 **Geita**, Tanzania
188 L 12 **Gejiu**, China
141 J 23 **Gela**, Italy
184 L 9 **Geladaindong**, China ▲
213 M 21 **Geladī**, Ethiopia
132 K 12 **Gelderland**, Netherlands ▣
137 B 15 **Geldern**, Germany
133 J 16 **Geldrop**, Netherlands
133 K 18 **Geleen**, Netherlands
156 K 12 **Gelendzhik**, Russian Federation
213 M 22 **Gelinsoor**, Somalia
194 C 9 **Gemas**, Malaysia
133 G 20 **Gembloux**, Belgium
215 T 13 **Gembu**, Nigeria
216 K 6 **Gemena**, Democratic Republic of Congo
170 L 10 **Gemerek**, Turkey
170 D 8 **Gemlik**, Turkey
134 A 10 **Gemlufall**, Iceland
140 I 5 **Gemona del Friuli**, Italy
212 F 10 **Gemsa**, Egypt
111 J 14 **General Acha**, Argentina
110 H 13 **General Alvear**, Argentina
113 D 16 **General Belgrano**, Argentina
110 J 11 **General Cabrera**, Argentina
89 P 7 **General Cepreda**, Mexico
113 A 20 **General Conesa**, Argentina
112 C 9 **General José de San Martín**, Argentina
113 E 17 **General Juan Madariaga**, Argentina
113 C 18 **General La Madrid**, Argentina
110 G 1 **General Lagos**, Chile
113 E 17 **General Lavalle**, Argentina
197 M 16 **General MacArthur**, Philippines
110 I 6 **General Martín Miguel de Güemes**, Argentina
113 A 17 **General Pico**, Argentina
113 B 16 **General Pinto**, Argentina
111 H 15 **General Roca**, Argentina

197 M 23 **General Santos**, Philippines
146 N 6 **General-Toshevo**, Bulgaria
113 A 16 **General Villegas**, Argentina
65 E 16 **Geneseo**, Illinois, U.S.A.
213 I 20 **Genet**, Ethiopia
138 A 10 **Geneva**, Switzerland
58 F 8 **Geneva**, New York, U.S.A.
188 J 11 **Gengma**, China
216 M 9 **Gengwa**, Democratic Republic of Congo
133 J 18 **Genk**, Belgium
140 C 9 **Genoa**, Italy
192 G 14 **Genteng**, Indonesia
136 K 13 **Genthin**, Germany
194 C 8 **Genting Highlands**, Malaysia
230 G 12 **Geographe Bay**, Western Australia, Australia ≈
218 L 15 **George**, Republic of South Africa
85 T 6 **George**, Québec, Canada ∿
43 N 26 **George Island**, St Helena 🏝
233 A 23 **George Sound**, New Zealand ≈
231 T 15 **George Town**, Tasmania, Australia
194 A 6 **George Town**, Malaysia
92 H 7 **George Town**, Cayman Islands ⌂
92 M 3 **George Town**, The Bahamas
241 T 14 **George V Coast**, Antarctica ◇
241 S 14 **George V Land**, Antarctica ◇
240 I 5 **George VI Sound**, Antarctica ≈
71 P 12 **George West**, Texas, U.S.A.
214 E 9 **Georgetown**, Gambia
231 S 4 **Georgetown**, Queensland, Australia
43 K 25 **Georgetown**, Ascension ⌂
105 U 5 **Georgetown**, Guyana ⌂
60 I 5 **Georgetown**, Kentucky, U.S.A.
61 W 3 **Georgetown**, Delaware, U.S.A.
61 R 13 **Georgetown**, South Carolina, U.S.A.
93 Z 12 **Georgetown**, St Vincent and the Grenadines
171 T 6 **Georgia**, Asia □
63 S 4 **Georgia**, U.S.A. ▣
86 D 10 **Georgian Bay**, Ontario, Canada ≈
231 P 5 **Georgina**, Queensland, Australia ∿
179 X 5 **Georgiyevka**, Kazakhstan
157 O 13 **Georgiyevsk**, Russian Federation
136 D 10 **Georgsheil**, Germany
137 K 17 **Gera**, Germany
133 E 19 **Geraardsbergen**, Belgium
147 E 22 **Geraki**, Greece
69 X 5 **Gerald**, Missouri, U.S.A.
230 F 10 **Geraldton**, Western Australia, Australia
171 Q 12 **Gercüş**, Turkey
170 H 8 **Gerede**, Turkey
177 R 9 **Gereshk**, Afghanistan
131 Q 12 **Gérgal**, Spain
77 J 16 **Gerlach**, Nevada, U.S.A.
143 K 19 **Gerlachovský štit**, Slovakia ▲
137 H 17 **Germany**, Europe □
199 I 16 **Gero**, Japan
170 K 7 **Gerze**, Turkey
135 I 19 **Geta**, Finland
131 O 7 **Getafe**, Spain
58 F 14 **Gettysburg**, Pennsylvania, U.S.A.
66 K 8 **Gettysburg**, South Dakota, U.S.A.
240 K 10 **Getz Ice Shelf Range**, Antarctica ◇
171 S 11 **Gevaş**, Turkey
146 E 12 **Gevgelija**, Macedonia (F.Y.R.O.M.)
181 D 17 **Gevrai**, India

194 B 14 **Geylang**, Singapore
139 V 3 **Gföhl**, Austria
218 L 12 **Ghaap Plateau**, Republic of South Africa ◇
211 Q 9 **Ghadāmis**, Libya
211 T 11 **Ghaddūwah**, Libya
183 N 10 **Ghaghara**, India ∿
214 M12 **Ghana**, Africa □
218 K 9 **Ghanzi**, Botswana
218 L 9 **Ghanzi**, Botswana ▣
172 F 12 **Gharandal**, Jordan
211 N 8 **Ghardaïa**, Algeria
177 T 15 **Gharo**, Pakistan
211 S 8 **Gharyān**, Libya
211 R 12 **Ghāt**, Libya
210 K 6 **Ghazaouet**, Algeria
182 J 8 **Ghaziabad**, India
183 O 11 **Ghazipur**, India
177 T 9 **Ghazluna**, Pakistan
177 U 8 **Ghaznī**, Afghanistan
177 T 8 **Ghaznī**, Afghanistan ▣
175 N 4 **Ghazzālah**, Saudi Arabia
133 D 18 **Ghent**, Belgium
150 K 9 **Gheorgheni**, Romania
150 I 8 **Gherla**, Romania
177 R 9 **Ghorak**, Afghanistan
177 V 12 **Ghotki**, Pakistan
177 R 8 **Ghowr**, Afghanistan ▣
175 V 12 **Ghubbat al Qamar**, Yemen ≈
173 O 2 **Ghūnā**, Syria
177 P 7 **Ghurian**, Afghanistan
191 N 22 **Gia Đinh**, Vietnam
191 L 23 **Gia Rai**, Vietnam
146 E 13 **Giannitsa**, Greece
141 L 22 **Giarre**, Italy
73 N 7 **Gibbonsville**, Idaho, U.S.A.
42 A 8 **Gibb's Hill**, Bermuda ▲
218 I 10 **Gibeon**, Namibia
130 J 12 **Gibraleón**, Spain
130 L 14 **Gibraltar**, Gibraltar ⌂
130 L 14 **Gibraltar**, U.K. ▣
230 J 7 **Gibson Desert**, Western Australia, Australia ◇
71 Q 10 **Giddings**, Texas, U.S.A.
135 H 14 **Gideälven**, Sweden ∿
213 H 22 **Gīdolē**, Ethiopia
129 Q 6 **Gien**, France
137 F 18 **Giessen**, Germany
132 N 7 **Gieten**, Netherlands
76 K 6 **Gifford**, Washington, U.S.A.
136 H 13 **Gifhorn**, Germany
199 H 17 **Gifu**, Japan
130 L 1 **Gijón**, Spain
74 K 13 **Gila**, Arizona, U.S.A. ∿
74 I 13 **Gila Bend**, Arizona, U.S.A.
74 L 12 **Gila Mountains**, Arizona, U.S.A. ⛰
176 H 4 **Gīlān**, Iran ▣
150 H 9 **Gilău**, Romania
171 Y 7 **Giläzi**, Azerbaijan
236 D 1 **Gilbert Islands**, Kiribati 🏝
108 K 13 **Gilbués**, Brazil
73 R 2 **Gildford**, Montana, U.S.A.
219 T 6 **Gilé**, Mozambique
212 B 12 **Gilf Kebir Plateau**, Egypt ◇
231 U 10 **Gilgandra**, New South Wales, Australia
177 Y 6 **Gilgit**, Pakistan
182 H 2 **Gilgit**, India
43 O 26 **Gill Point**, St Helena ▶
84 K 7 **Gillam**, Manitoba, Canada
73 X 9 **Gillette**, Wyoming, U.S.A.
127 Q 12 **Gillingham**, United Kingdom
127 X 11 **Gillingham**, United Kingdom
241 W 6 **Gillock Island**, Antarctica 🏝
65 G 17 **Gilman**, Illinois, U.S.A.
77 G 20 **Gilroy**, California, U.S.A.
213 G 20 **Gīmbī**, Ethiopia
197 L 20 **Gingoog**, Philippines
213 J 21 **Gīnīr**, Ethiopia
147 H 17 **Gioura**, Greece 🏝
177 P 10 **Girdi**, Iran
124 J 11 **Girdle Ness**, United Kingdom ▶
171 N 8 **Giresun**, Turkey

□ Country ▣ Internal administrative region: State/Province/Territory/Dependent territory ⌂ Capital city ⛰ Mountain range/Undersea ridge ▲ Mountain peak/Volcano/Seamount ◇ Geographic feature ▶ Headland/Point/Cape/Peninsula ◗ Desert 🏝 Island/Island group ⁙ Antarctic base 🌊 Ocean ◓ Sea ≈ Bay/Gulf/Channel/Strait ◣ Lake ⚑ Salt pan/Dry/Intermittent lake ∿ River

170	M 8	Giresun Dağlari, Turkey ▲▲
212	F 10	Girga, Egypt
183	R 12	Giridih, India
131	Y 3	Girona, Spain
128	L 10	Gironde, France ↳
125	G 14	Girvan, United Kingdom
232	O 12	Gisborne, New Zealand
232	O 11	Gisborne, New Zealand ▣
217	Q 9	Gisenyi, Rwanda
135	E 23	Gislaved, Sweden
129	P 3	Gisors, France
133	B 17	Gistel, Belgium
140	J 12	Giulianova, Italy
150	K 14	Giurgiu, Romania
133	E 21	Givry, Belgium
219	P 9	Giyani, Republic of South Africa
213	I 20	Giyon, Ethiopia
179	P 12	Gizhduvan, Uzbekistan
153	Y 9	Gizhiga, Russian Federation
234	K 6	Gizo, Solomon Islands
142	M 9	Giżycko, Poland
145	I 17	Gjiri i Drinit, Albania ≈
145	K 21	Gjirokastër, Albania
84	L 1	Gjoa Haven, Nunavut, Canada
134	B 10	Gjögur, Iceland
135	D 18	Gjøvik, Norway
87	Y 8	Glace Bay, Nova Scotia, Canada
79	V 10	Glacier Bay, Alaska, U.S.A. ≈
71	T 6	Gladewater, Texas, U.S.A.
231	V 7	Gladstone, Queensland, Australia
231	P 11	Gladstone, South Australia, Australia
64	H 9	Gladstone, Michigan, U.S.A.
135	D 18	Glåma, Norway ↳
197	M 24	Glan, Philippines
132	O 12	Glanerbrug, Netherlands
138	H 7	Glarus, Switzerland
127	P 9	Glasbury, United Kingdom
68	M 3	Glasco, Kansas, U.S.A.
124	H 13	Glasgow, United Kingdom
60	G 7	Glasgow, Kentucky, U.S.A.
73	W 3	Glasgow, Montana, U.S.A.
70	H 10	Glass Mountains, Texas, U.S.A. ▲▲
127	P 12	Glastonbury, United Kingdom
155	R 12	Glazov, Russian Federation
156	J 4	Glazunovka, Russian Federation
139	W 7	Gleisdorf, Austria
74	K 7	Glen Canyon, Utah, U.S.A. ◇
231	V 10	Glen Innes, New South Wales, Australia
79	S 8	Glenallen, Alaska, U.S.A.
233	F 23	Glenavy, New Zealand
86	C 14	Glencoe, Ontario, Canada
74	I 12	Glendale, Arizona, U.S.A.
231	O 10	Glendambo, South Australia, Australia
231	U 5	Glenden, Queensland, Australia
73	Y 4	Glendive, Montana, U.S.A.
73	Y 12	Glendo, Wyoming, U.S.A.
73	Z 12	Glendo Reservoir, Wyoming, U.S.A. ↳
105	T 6	Glendor Mountains, Guyana ▲▲
61	U 5	Glenns, Virginia, U.S.A.
72	K 12	Glenns Ferry, Idaho, U.S.A.
63	V 5	Glennville, Georgia, U.S.A.
233	C 22	Glenorchy, New Zealand
58	K 8	Glens Falls, New York, U.S.A.
125	C 15	Glenties, Republic of Ireland
67	G 14	Glenwood, Iowa, U.S.A.
69	T 12	Glenwood, Arkansas, U.S.A.
75	N 13	Glenwood, New Mexico, U.S.A.

75	P 4	Glenwood Springs, Colorado, U.S.A.
138	F 9	Gletsch, Switzerland
142	K 11	Glinojeck, Poland
143	I 17	Gliwice, Poland
74	L 12	Globe, Arizona, U.S.A.
139	X 5	Gloggnitz, Austria
143	F 14	Głogów, Poland
134	F 7	Glomfjord, Norway
134	I 13	Glommersträsk, Sweden
127	R 4	Glossop, United Kingdom
234	F 4	Gloucester, Papua New Guinea
127	Q 9	Gloucester, United Kingdom
59	O 9	Gloucester, Massachusetts, U.S.A.
61	V 6	Gloucester, Virginia, U.S.A.
156	M 8	Glubokiy, Russian Federation
179	X 4	Glubokoye, Kazakhstan
157	Q 6	Gmelinka, Russian Federation
139	R 8	Gmünd, Austria
139	U 2	Gmünd, Austria
139	S 5	Gmunden, Austria
142	H 11	Gniewkowo, Poland
142	H 12	Gniezno, Poland
145	M 15	Gnjilane, Serbia and Montenegro
191	N 22	Go Công, Vietnam
181	C 20	Goa, India ▣
183	U 11	Goalpara, India
213	J 21	Goba, Ethiopia
218	J 9	Gobabis, Namibia
42	K 7	Goban Spur, Atlantic Ocean ⌁
111	I 15	Gobernador Duval, Argentina
111	H 21	Gobernador Gregores, Argentina
111	G 23	Gobernador Mayer, Argentina
187	A 14	Gobi Desert, China ◇
199	G 19	Gobo, Japan
137	B 15	Goch, Germany
218	J 10	Gochas, Namibia
127	U 12	Godalming, United Kingdom
181	F 17	Godavari, India ↳
87	Q 5	Godbout, Québec, Canada
183	R 12	Godda, India
213	K 22	Godē, Ethiopia
86	C 12	Goderich, Ontario, Canada
213	M 22	Godinlabe, Somalia
143	J 22	Gödöllő, Hungary
84	K 7	Gods, Manitoba, Canada ↳
84	J 8	Gods Lake, Manitoba, Canada ↳
234	A 6	Goe, Papua New Guinea
133	E 15	Goes, Netherlands
139	V 2	Göfritz, Austria
86	C 7	Gogama, Ontario, Canada
215	O 11	Gogounou, Benin
213	C 20	Gogrial, Sudan
182	K 10	Gohad, India
109	J 16	Goiânia, Brazil
109	J 16	Goiás, Brazil
109	J 16	Goiás, Brazil ▣
112	G 7	Goio-Erê, Brazil
133	I 15	Goirle, Netherlands
170	A 8	Gökçeada, Turkey ⌁
170	B 12	Gökova Körfezi, Turkey ≈
170	L 12	Göksun, Turkey
219	O 7	Gokwe, Zimbabwe
135	C 18	Gol, Norway
182	L 9	Gola, India
183	X 10	Golaghat, India
71	Q 12	Golaid, Texas, U.S.A.
172	G 7	Golan Heights, Israel ◇
177	U 7	Golbahār, Afghanistan
170	M 12	Gölbasi, Turkey
65	G 23	Golconda, Illinois, U.S.A.
77	K 15	Golconda, Nevada, U.S.A.
170	E 8	Gölcük, Turkey
76	E 13	Gold Beach, Oregon, U.S.A.
231	W 9	Gold Coast, Queensland, Australia ◇

79	R 8	Gold Creek, Alaska, U.S.A.
142	M 8	Gołdap, Poland
83	I 20	Golden, British Columbia, Canada
233	H 15	Golden Bay, New Zealand ≈
39	R 8	Golden Dragon Seamount, Indian Ocean ▲
62	L 9	Golden Meadow, Louisiana, U.S.A.
76	I 9	Goldendale, Washington, U.S.A.
77	K 20	Goldfield, Nevada, U.S.A.
61	T 10	Goldsboro, North Carolina, U.S.A.
71	O 8	Goldthwaite, Texas, U.S.A.
171	R 8	Göle, Turkey
142	D 10	Goleniów, Poland
176	L 4	Golestān, Iran ▣
77	I 24	Goleta, California, U.S.A.
131	W 5	Golf de Sant Jordi, Spain ≈
211	Q 7	Golfe de Gabès, Tunisia ≈
211	R 5	Golfe de Hammamet, Tunisia ≈
93	O 7	Golfe de la Gonâve, Haiti ≈
128	J 4	Golfe de St-Malo, France ≈
213	L 19	Golfe de Tadjoura, Djibouti ≈
211	Q 5	Golfe de Tunis, Tunisia ≈
158	G 5	Golfe du Lion, Mediterranean Sea ≈
91	R 14	Golfito, Costa Rica
158	E 7	Golfo de Valencia, Mediterranean Sea ≈
131	Q 13	Golfo de Almería, Spain ≈
111	F 17	Golfo de Ancud, Chile ≈
111	E 14	Golfo de Arauco, Chile ≈
92	G 4	Golfo de Batabanó, Cuba ≈
130	J 12	Golfo de Cádiz, Portugal/Spain ≈
91	T 15	Golfo de Chiriquí, Panama ≈
111	E 18	Golfo de Corcovado, Chile ≈
90	L 8	Golfo de Fonseca, Honduras ≈
92	K 6	Golfo de Guacanayabo, Cuba ≈
91	U 13	Golfo de los Mosquitos, Panama ≈
131	S 12	Golfo de Mazarrón, Spain ≈
91	U 15	Golfo de Montijo, Panama ≈
91	P 13	Golfo de Nicoya, Costa Rica ≈
111	E 21	Golfo de Penas, Chile ≈
111	I 20	Golfo de San Jorge, Argentina ≈
91	Y 14	Golfo de San Miguel, Panama ≈
89	U 14	Golfo de Tehuantepec, Mexico ≈
104	G 4	Golfo de Urabá, Colombia ≈
131	U 8	Golfo de Valencia, Spain ≈
141	C 19	Golfo di Cagliari, Italy ≈
141	H 21	Golfo di Castellammare, Italy ≈
141	B 15	Golfo di Catania, Italy ≈
141	B 15	Golfo di dell'Asinara, Italy ≈
141	I 15	Golfo di Gaeta, Italy ≈
141	L 20	Golfo di Gioia, Italy ≈
141	M 14	Golfo di Manfredonia, Italy ≈
141	I 16	Golfo di Napoli, Italy ≈
141	L 24	Golfo di Noto, Italy ≈
141	B 18	Golfo di Oristano, Italy ≈
141	D 17	Golfo di Orosei, Italy ≈
141	B 19	Golfo di Palmas, Italy ≈
141	L 18	Golfo di Policastro, Italy ≈
141	K 17	Golfo di Salerno, Italy ≈
141	M 20	Golfo di Santa Eufemia, Italy ≈
141	N 20	Golfo di Squillace, Italy ≈
141	N 18	Golfo di Taranto, Italy ≈

140	I 7	Golfo di Trieste, Italy ≈
91	R 14	Golfo Dulce, Costa Rica ≈
111	J 17	Golfo Nuevo, Argentina ≈
111	J 17	Golfo San José, Argentina ≈
111	J 17	Golfo San Matías, Argentina ≈
111	E 23	Golfo Trinidad, Chile ≈
186	H 12	Golin Baixing, China
185	N 8	Golmud, China
196	F 12	Golo, Philippines ⌁
176	H 7	Golpāyegān, Iran
124	H 9	Golspie, United Kingdom
179	T 3	Golubovka, Kazakhstan
146	H 11	Golyam Perelik, Bulgaria ▲
146	I 11	Golyam Persenk, Bulgaria ▲
217	Q 9	Goma, Democratic Republic of Congo
180	G 12	Gomati, India ↳
215	T 11	Gombe, Nigeria
215	T 11	Gombe, Nigeria ▣
215	U 11	Gombi, Nigeria
38	E 8	Gombrani Island, Rodrigues Island ⌁
88	L 4	Gómez Farías, Mexico
89	N 7	Gómez Palacio, Mexico
93	O 7	Gonaïves, Haiti
176	L 5	Gonbad-e Kavus, Iran
183	N 10	Gonda, India
213	H 18	Gonder, Ethiopia
181	F 15	Gondia, India
170	C 8	Gönen, Turkey
189	S 7	Gong'an, China
189	R 11	Gongcheng, China
188	L 7	Gongga Shan, China ▲
184	L 11	Gonggar, China
185	P 8	Gonghe, China
187	C 15	Gonghui, China
184	J 4	Gongliu, China
185	N 6	Gongpoquan, China
189	T 3	Gongyi, China
186	J 13	Gongzhuling, China
215	T 10	Goniri, Nigeria
199	A 21	Gōnoura, Japan
196	H 6	Gonzaga, Philippines
71	Q 10	Gonzales, Texas, U.S.A.
77	G 21	Gonzales, California, U.S.A.
91	Y 14	Gonzalo Vásquez, Panama
61	T 5	Goochland, Virginia, U.S.A.
234	G 6	Goodenough Island, Papua New Guinea ⌁
72	L 12	Gooding, Idaho, U.S.A.
68	G 3	Goodland, Kansas, U.S.A.
38	B 11	Goodlands, Mauritius
78	M 10	Goodnews, Alaska, U.S.A.
231	S 11	Goolgowi, New South Wales, Australia
230	G 11	Goomalling, Western Australia, Australia
231	U 9	Goondiwindi, Queensland, Australia
132	M 11	Goor, Netherlands
111	L 24	Goose Green, Falkland Islands
77	I 14	Goose Lake, California, U.S.A. ↳
183	P 10	Gopalganj, India
182	K 7	Gopeshwar, India
143	F 14	Góra, Poland
178	J 12	Gora Arlang, Turkmenistan ▲
179	P 14	Gora Ayribaba, Turkmenistan ▲
152	M 14	Gora Belukha, Russian Federation ▲
178	I 9	Gora Besshoky, Kazakhstan ▲
155	U 10	Gora Denezhkin Kamen', Russian Federation ▲
155	U 9	Gora Isherim, Russian Federation ▲
178	J 13	Gora Khasardag, Turkmenistan ▲
179	P 12	Gora Khayatbashi, Uzbekistan ▲
155	U 11	Gora Konzhakovskiy Kamen', Russian Federation ▲

179	V 7	Gora Kotanemel', Kazakhstan ▲
155	S 7	Gora Kozhim-Iz, Russian Federation ▲
153	Z 8	Gora Ledyanaya, Russian Federation ▲
153	X 13	Gora Lopatina, Russian Federation ▲
179	S 10	Gora Manas, Kyrgyzstan ▲
153	O 13	Gora Munku Sardyk, Russian Federation ▲
184	K 3	Gora Mustau, China ▲
155	T 5	Gora Narodnaya, Russian Federation ▲
153	X 10	Gora Nukh Yablonevyy, Russian Federation ▲
155	U 3	Gora Payyer, Russian Federation ▲
153	W 9	Gora Pobeda, Russian Federation ▲
179	T 7	Gora Shunak, Kazakhstan ▲
178	K 13	Gora Tagarev, Turkmenistan ▲
153	V 14	Gora Tardoki-Yani, Russian Federation ▲
155	T 6	Gora Tel'pos-Iz, Russian Federation ▲
152	J 8	Gora Telposiz, Russian Federation ▲
183	O 10	Gorakhpur, India
144	I 13	Goražde, Bosnia and Herzegovina
61	S 5	Gordonsville, Virginia, U.S.A.
233	D 25	Gore, New Zealand
215	W 12	Goré, Chad
86	B 9	Gore Bay, Ontario, Canada
58	M 5	Gore Mountain, Vermont, U.S.A. ▲
170	J 11	Göreme, Turkey
125	E 19	Gorey, Republic of Ireland
176	K 5	Gorgān, Iran
233	D 23	Gorge Creek, New Zealand
214	F 7	Gorgol, Mauritania ▣
213	H 18	Gorgora, Ethiopia
171	T 6	Gori, Georgia
133	H 14	Gorinchem, Netherlands
171	V 9	Goris, Armenia
154	I 14	Goritsy, Russian Federation
140	I 6	Gorizia, Italy
183	P 9	Gorkha, Nepal
154	M 14	Gor'kovskoye Vodokhranilishche, Russian Federation ↳
143	L 18	Gorlice, Poland
137	O 16	Görlitz, Germany
146	H 7	Gorni Dŭbnik, Bulgaria
144	L 12	Gornji Milanovac, Serbia and Montenegro
152	M 13	Gorno Altaysk, Russian Federation
152	L 13	Gornyak, Russian Federation
157	R 5	Gornyy, Russian Federation
157	P 7	Gornyy Balykley, Russian Federation
154	L 14	Gorodets, Russian Federation
157	P 3	Gorodishche, Russian Federation
157	N 11	Gorodovikovsk, Russian Federation
234	D 4	Goroka, Papua New Guinea
219	R 7	Gorongosa, Mozambique
193	P 10	Gorontalo, Indonesia
132	L 12	Gorssel, Netherlands
178	I 11	Gory Akkyr, Turkmenistan ▲▲
179	N 12	Gory Auminzatau, Uzbekistan ▲▲
179	Q 14	Gory Baysuntau, Uzbekistan ▲▲
179	N 10	Gory Bukantau, Uzbekistan ▲▲
153	P 7	Gory Byrranga, Russian Federation ▲▲
179	O 11	Gory Dzhetymtau, Uzbekistan ▲▲
153	P 8	Gory Kamen', Russian Federation ▲▲

178	J 11	Gory Koymatdag, Turkmenistan ▲▲
178	L 7	Gory Mugodzhary, Kazakhstan ▲▲
153	O 9	Gory Putorana, Russian Federation ▲▲
143	K 15	Góry Świętokrzyskie, Poland ▲▲
142	E 11	Gorzów Wielkopolski, Poland
231	V 11	Gosford, New South Wales, Australia
198	J 9	Goshogawara, Japan
137	N 14	Goslar, Germany
127	T 13	Gosport, United Kingdom
133	G 21	Gosselies, Belgium
135	B 15	Gossen, Norway
146	C 11	Gostivar, Macedonia (F.Y.R.O.M.)
142	G 13	Gostyń, Poland
142	J 12	Gostynin, Poland
199	J 7	Gotemba, Japan
137	I 17	Gotha, Germany
135	D 22	Gothenburg, Sweden
66	K 14	Gothenburg, Nebraska, U.S.A.
215	O 9	Gothèye, Niger
135	I 23	Gotland, Sweden ⌁
199	A 23	Gotō-rettō, Japan ⌁
146	G 12	Gotse Delchev, Bulgaria
135	I 22	Gotska Sandön, Sweden ⌁
199	D 19	Gōtsu, Japan
137	H 15	Göttingen, Germany
132	G 13	Gouda, Netherlands
214	F 9	Goudiri, Senegal
215	T 9	Goudoumaria, Niger
43	I 19	Gough Fracture Zone, Atlantic Ocean ⌁
43	K 19	Gough Island, U.K. ⌁
231	U 12	Goulburn, New South Wales, Australia
231	N 1	Goulburn Islands, Northern Territory, Australia ⌁
241	O 9	Gould Coast, Antarctica ◇
215	V 10	Goulféy, Cameroon
215	X 11	Goundi, Chad
215	S 9	Gouré, Niger
129	P 3	Gournay-en-Bray, France
215	Y 6	Gouro, Chad
58	H 6	Gouverneur, New York, U.S.A.
109	M 17	Governador Valadares, Brazil
185	N 4	Govi-Altay, Mongolia ▣
185	O 5	Govi Altayn Nuruu, Mongolia ▲▲
183	N 12	Govind Ballash Pant Sagar, India ↳
179	P 14	Govurdak, Turkmenistan
58	C 9	Gowanda, New York, U.S.A.
86	D 7	Gowganda, Ontario, Canada
112	C 11	Goya, Argentina
171	X 8	Göyşşay, Azerbaijan
170	F 8	Göynük, Turkey
171	Q 10	Göynük, Turkey
215	U 14	Goyoum, Cameroon
171	Y 10	Göytäpä, Azerbaijan
215	Z 10	Goz-Beïda, Chad
213	G 16	Goz Regeb, Sudan
184	I 8	Gozha Co, China ↳
141	J 25	Gozo, Malta ⌁
218	M 14	Graaf-Reinet, Republic of South Africa
214	I 14	Grabo, Côte d'Ivoire
86	I 9	Gracefield, Québec, Canada
67	O 7	Graceville, Minnesota, U.S.A.
90	K 6	Gracias, Honduras
42	N 1	Graciosa, Azores ⌁
42	O 11	Graciosa, Canary Islands ⌁
144	H 10	Gradačac, Bosnia and Herzegovina
146	L 9	Gradets, Bulgaria
130	L 1	Grado, Spain
140	I 6	Grado, Italy
75	T 10	Grady, New Mexico, U.S.A.

▣ Country   ▣ Internal administrative region: State/Province/Territory/Dependent territory   ⚓ Capital city   ▲▲ Mountain range/Undersea ridge   ▲ Mountain peak/Volcano/Seamount   ◇ Geographic feature   ▶ Headland/Point/Cape/Peninsula   ▤ Desert   ⌁ Island/Island group   ▦ Antarctic base   ⊚ Ocean   ⌇ Sea   ≈ Bay/Gulf/Channel/Strait   ↳ Lake   ↳ Salt pan/Dry/Intermittent lake   R

- W 10 **Grafton**, New South Wales, Australia
- P 2 **Grafton**, West Virginia, U.S.A.
- N 2 **Grafton**, North Dakota, U.S.A.
- O 3 **Graham Island**, Nunavut, Canada 🏝
- C 19 **Graham Island**, British Columbia, Canada 🏝
- H 3 **Graham Land**, Antarctica ◇
- N 15 **Grahamstown**, Republic of South Africa
- K 12 **Grajaú**, Brazil
- M 9 **Grajewo**, Poland
- N 10 **Gramatikovo**, Bulgaria
- H 11 **Grampian Mtns**, United Kingdom ⛰
- N 11 **Gramzow**, Germany
- G 21 **Gran Altiplanicie Central**, Argentina ⛰
- M 12 **Gran Canaria**, Canary Islands 🏝
- K 6 **Gran Chaco**, Argentina/Paraguay ◇
- E 15 **Gran Pajonal**, Peru ◇
- O 12 **Gran Tarajal**, Canary Islands
- J 7 **Granada**, Colombia
- O 12 **Granada**, Spain
- U 6 **Granada**, Colorado, U.S.A.
- N 9 **Granada**, Nicaragua
- M 10 **Granby**, Québec, Canada
- H 7 **Grand**, South Dakota, U.S.A. ∿
- K 1 **Grand Bahama**, The Bahamas 🏝
- F 7 **Grand Banks of Newfoundland**, Atlantic Ocean ◇
- K 14 **Grand-Bassam**, Côte d'Ivoire
- S 10 **Grand Bay**, New Brunswick, Canada
- C 13 **Grand Bend**, Ontario, Canada
- P 5 **Grand Caicos**, Turks and Caicos Islands 🏝
- J 9 **Grand Canyon**, Arizona, U.S.A.
- H 9 **Grand Canyon**, Arizona, U.S.A. ◇
- H 7 **Grand Cayman**, Cayman Islands 🏝
- I 14 **Grand Cess**, Liberia
- J 6 **Grand Coulee**, Washington, U.S.A.
- T 7 **Grand Erg de Bilma**, Niger ◇
- J 9 **Grand Erg Occidental**, Algeria ◇
- N 10 **Grand Erg Oriental**, Algeria ◇
- Q 8 **Grand Falls**, New Brunswick, Canada
- N 3 **Grand Forks**, North Dakota, U.S.A.
- I 14 **Grand Haven**, Michigan, U.S.A.
- I 8 **Grand Island**, Michigan, U.S.A. 🏝
- M 14 **Grand Island**, Nebraska, U.S.A.
- B 10 **Grand Junction**, Tennessee, U.S.A.
- N 5 **Grand Junction**, Colorado, U.S.A.
- I 8 **Grand Lake**, Louisiana, U.S.A. 💧
- K 18 **Grand Lake**, Ohio, U.S.A. 💧
- X 10 **Grand Lake**, Newfoundland and Labrador, Canada 💧
- S 9 **Grand Lake**, New Brunswick, Canada 💧
- R 8 **Grand Lake o' the Cherokees**, Oklahoma, U.S.A. 💧
- T 5 **Grand Manan Channel**, Maine, U.S.A. ≈
- S 11 **Grand Manan Island**, New Brunswick, Canada 🏝
- J 8 **Grand Marais**, Michigan, U.S.A.
- V 3 **Grand Marais**, Minnesota, U.S.A.
- 86 L 9 **Grand-Mère**, Québec, Canada
- 67 V 2 **Grand Portage**, Minnesota, U.S.A.
- 65 J 14 **Grand Rapids**, Michigan, U.S.A.
- 67 R 4 **Grand Rapids**, Minnesota, U.S.A.
- 84 I 8 **Grand Rapids**, Manitoba, Canada
- 86 I 9 **Grand-Remous**, Québec, Canada
- 73 R 10 **Grand Teton**, Wyoming, U.S.A. ▲
- 64 J 11 **Grand Traverse Bay**, Michigan, U.S.A. ≈
- 93 Q 5 **Grand Turk**, Turks and Caicos Islands 🏝
- 72 J 11 **Grand View**, Idaho, U.S.A.
- 107 L 21 **Grande**, Bolivia/Brazil ∿
- 91 Q 8 **Grande**, Nicaragua ∿
- 38 B 11 **Grande Baie**, Mauritius
- 83 H 18 **Grande Cache**, Alberta, Canada
- 219 W 4 **Grande Comore**, Comoros 🏝
- 87 W 6 **Grande-Entrée**, Québec, Canada
- 83 H 18 **Grande Prairie**, Alberta, Canada
- 38 A 12 **Grande Rivière Noire**, Mauritius
- 38 C 12 **Grande Rivière Sud-Est**, Mauritius
- 87 T 5 **Grande-Vallée**, Québec, Canada
- 70 J 8 **Grandfalls**, Texas, U.S.A.
- 68 L 12 **Grandfield**, Oklahoma, U.S.A.
- 130 G 10 **Grândola**, Portugal
- 76 I 9 **Grandview**, Washington, U.S.A.
- 73 S 14 **Granger**, Wyoming, U.S.A.
- 72 K 6 **Grangeville**, Idaho, U.S.A.
- 65 E 21 **Granite City**, Illinois, U.S.A.
- 67 P 8 **Granite Falls**, Minnesota, U.S.A.
- 73 S 7 **Granite Peak**, Montana, U.S.A. ▲
- 74 I 3 **Granite Peak**, Utah, U.S.A. ▲
- 66 I 14 **Grant**, Nebraska, U.S.A.
- 240 L 11 **Grant Island**, Antarctica 🏝
- 127 U 5 **Grantham**, United Kingdom
- 75 O 10 **Grants**, New Mexico, U.S.A.
- 76 F 13 **Grants Pass**, Oregon, U.S.A.
- 74 J 3 **Grantsville**, Utah, U.S.A.
- 128 L 4 **Granville**, France
- 72 J 12 **Grasmere**, Idaho, U.S.A.
- 135 I 19 **Gräsö**, Sweden 🏝
- 77 H 17 **Grass Valley**, California, U.S.A.
- 141 M 16 **Grassano**, Italy
- 129 W 13 **Grasse**, France
- 73 S 5 **Grassrange**, Montana, U.S.A.
- 66 G 4 **Grassy Butte**, North Dakota, U.S.A.
- 138 H 9 **Graubünden**, Switzerland ▣
- 131 U 3 **Graus**, Spain
- 112 H 12 **Gravatai**, Brazil
- 133 K 14 **Grave**, Netherlands
- 72 L 6 **Grave Peak**, Idaho, U.S.A. ▲
- 140 D 5 **Gravedona**, Italy
- 86 F 11 **Gravenhurst**, Ontario, Canada
- 127 X 11 **Gravesend**, United Kingdom
- 129 U 7 **Gray**, France
- 63 T 4 **Gray**, Georgia, U.S.A.
- 64 K 11 **Grayling**, Michigan, U.S.A.
- 65 G 21 **Grayville**, Illinois, U.S.A.
- 156 I 6 **Grayvoron**, Russian Federation
- 139 W 7 **Graz**, Austria
- 92 L 1 **Great Abaco**, The Bahamas 🏝
- 230 K 11 **Great Australian Bight**, Western Australia, Australia ≈
- 92 J 2 **Great Bahama Bank**, The Bahamas ≈
- 232 L 7 **Great Barrier Island**, New Zealand 🏝
- 231 S 1 **Great Barrier Reef**, Queensland, Australia ◇
- 58 L 10 **Great Barrington**, Massachusetts, U.S.A.
- 77 M 17 **Great Basin**, Nevada/Utah, U.S.A. ◇
- 82 F 10 **Great Bear Lake**, Northwest Territories, Canada 💧
- 68 L 5 **Great Bend**, Kansas, U.S.A.
- 125 J 14 **Great Britain**, United Kingdom 🏝
- 181 N 25 **Great Channel**, India ≈
- 191 B 19 **Great Coco Island**, Myanmar 🏝
- 73 U 13 **Great Divide Basin**, Wyoming, U.S.A. ◇
- 231 T 13 **Great Dividing Range**, Victoria, Australia ⛰
- 127 X 9 **Great Dunmow**, United Kingdom
- 232 I 4 **Great Exhibition Bay**, New Zealand ≈
- 92 L 3 **Great Exuma Island**, The Bahamas 🏝
- 73 Q 4 **Great Falls**, Montana, U.S.A.
- 183 P 10 **Great Gandak**, India ∿
- 127 Q 2 **Great Harwood**, United Kingdom
- 143 L 24 **Great Hungarian Plain**, Hungary ◇
- 93 N 5 **Great Inagua Island**, The Bahamas 🏝
- 218 K 14 **Great Karoo**, Republic of South Africa ⛰
- 127 Q 8 **Great Malvern**, United Kingdom
- 232 L 8 **Great Mercury Island**, New Zealand 🏝
- 42 I 10 **Great Meteor Tablemount**, Atlantic Ocean ▲
- 181 O 25 **Great Nicobar**, India 🏝
- 127 X 7 **Great Ouse**, United Kingdom ∿
- 85 Q 2 **Great Plain of the Koukdjuak**, Nunavut, Canada ◇
- 56 M 5 **Great Plains**, U.S.A., U.S.A. ◇
- 213 H 22 **Great Rift Valley**, Africa ◇
- 172 F 12 **Great Rift Valley**, Jordan ◇
- 58 J 8 **Great Sacandaga Lake**, New York, U.S.A. 💧
- 74 J 2 **Great Salt Lake**, Utah, U.S.A. 💧
- 74 I 3 **Great Salt Lake Desert**, Utah, U.S.A. ◇
- 68 M 7 **Great Salt Plains Lake**, Oklahoma, U.S.A. 💧
- 212 B 9 **Great Sand Sea**, Egypt/Libya ◇
- 230 J 5 **Great Sandy Desert**, Western Australia, Australia ◇
- 82 H 13 **Great Slave Lake**, Northwest Territories, Canada 💧
- 60 J 10 **Great Smoky Mountains**, North Carolina, U.S.A. ⛰
- 83 F 16 **Great Snow Mountain**, British Columbia, Canada ▲
- 42 A 7 **Great Sound**, Bermuda ≈
- 126 M 12 **Great Torrington**, United Kingdom
- 230 L 8 **Great Victoria Desert**, Western Australia, Australia ◇
- 59 S 5 **Great Wass Island**, Maine, U.S.A. 🏝
- 191 E 21 **Great West Torres Islands**, Myanmar 🏝
- 127 Z 6 **Great Yarmouth**, United Kingdom
- 173 S 2 **Great Zab**, Iraq ∿
- 92 I 5 **Greater Antilles**, Cuba 🏝
- 39 S 4 **Greater Sunda Islands**, Indonesia 🏝
- 111 H 24 **Greec**, Chile
- 147 C 17 **Greece**, Europe ▣
- 58 E 8 **Greece**, New York, U.S.A.
- 75 S 3 **Greeley**, Colorado, U.S.A.
- 61 P 13 **Greeleyville**, South Carolina, U.S.A.
- 74 L 4 **Green**, Utah, U.S.A. ∿
- 64 H 11 **Green Bay**, Wisconsin, U.S.A. ≈
- 64 H 12 **Green Bay**, Wisconsin, U.S.A.
- 63 W 8 **Green Cove Springs**, Florida, U.S.A.
- 234 I 4 **Green Islands**, Papua New Guinea 🏝
- 83 L 17 **Green Lake**, Saskatchewan, Canada
- 58 L 8 **Green Mountains**, Vermont, U.S.A. ⛰
- 234 A 3 **Green River**, Papua New Guinea
- 74 L 5 **Green River**, Utah/Wyoming, U.S.A.
- 60 H 6 **Green River Lake**, Kentucky, U.S.A. 💧
- 65 I 19 **Greencastle**, Indiana, U.S.A.
- 60 L 8 **Greeneville**, Tennessee, U.S.A.
- 58 L 9 **Greenfield**, Massachusetts, U.S.A.
- 69 S 6 **Greenfield**, Missouri, U.S.A.
- 75 R 6 **Greenhorn Mountain**, Colorado, U.S.A. ▲
- 45 P 11 **Greenland**, Denmark ▣
- 45 S 12 **Greenland Plain**, Arctic Ocean ◇
- 45 R 13 **Greenland Sea**, Arctic Ocean ◗
- 58 M 12 **Greenport**, New York, U.S.A.
- 61 P 8 **Greensboro**, North Carolina, U.S.A.
- 58 B 13 **Greensburg**, Pennsylvania, U.S.A.
- 62 L 7 **Greensburg**, Louisiana, U.S.A.
- 65 J 20 **Greensburg**, Indiana, U.S.A.
- 68 K 6 **Greensburg**, Kansas, U.S.A.
- 214 H 14 **Greenville**, Liberia
- 59 Q 4 **Greenville**, Maine, U.S.A.
- 60 M 11 **Greenville**, South Carolina, U.S.A.
- 61 T 9 **Greenville**, North Carolina, U.S.A.
- 62 K 3 **Greenville**, Mississippi, U.S.A.
- 63 Q 5 **Greenville**, Alabama, U.S.A.
- 63 T 7 **Greenville**, Florida, U.S.A.
- 65 K 18 **Greenville**, Ohio, U.S.A.
- 69 Y 7 **Greenville**, Missouri, U.S.A.
- 71 R 5 **Greenville**, Texas, U.S.A.
- 77 H 16 **Greenville**, California, U.S.A.
- 127 W 10 **Greenwich**, United Kingdom
- 65 N 17 **Greenwich**, Ohio, U.S.A.
- 60 M 12 **Greenwood**, South Carolina, U.S.A.
- 62 H 4 **Greenwood**, Louisiana, U.S.A.
- 62 M 3 **Greenwood**, Mississippi, U.S.A.
- 69 V 10 **Greers Ferry Lake**, Arkansas, U.S.A. 💧
- 66 L 11 **Gregory**, South Dakota, U.S.A.
- 231 R 4 **Gregory Range**, Queensland, Australia ⛰
- 136 M 9 **Greifswald**, Germany
- 136 M 8 **Greifswalder Bodden**, Germany ≈
- 139 U 4 **Grein**, Austria
- 137 K 18 **Greiz**, Germany
- 154 K 3 **Gremikha**, Russian Federation
- 135 D 24 **Grenå**, Denmark
- 62 M 3 **Grenada**, Mississippi, U.S.A.
- 93 Y 13 **Grenada**, North America ▣
- 62 M 2 **Grenada Lake**, Mississippi, U.S.A. 💧
- 58 A 11 **Greenville**, Pennsylvania, U.S.A.
- 138 D 7 **Grenchen**, Switzerland
- 129 U 11 **Grenoble**, France
- 93 Y 13 **Grenville**, Grenada
- 133 E 14 **Grevelingen**, Netherlands ≈
- 137 D 14 **Greven**, Germany
- 147 C 15 **Grevena**, Greece
- 137 B 16 **Grevenbroich**, Germany
- 133 L 24 **Grevenmacher**, Luxembourg ▣
- 133 M 25 **Grevenmacher**, Luxembourg
- 136 I 9 **Grevesmühlen**, Germany
- 233 F 18 **Grey**, New Zealand ∿
- 85 X 9 **Grey Islands**, Newfoundland and Labrador, Canada 🏝
- 73 V 9 **Greybull**, Wyoming, U.S.A.
- 233 F 18 **Greymouth**, New Zealand
- 219 P 12 **Greytown**, Republic of South Africa
- 233 L 16 **Greytown**, New Zealand
- 157 N 5 **Gribanovskiy**, Russian Federation
- 139 S 4 **Grieskirchen**, Austria
- 63 S 3 **Griffin**, Georgia, U.S.A.
- 231 S 11 **Griffith**, New South Wales, Australia
- 171 Q 6 **Grigoleti**, Georgia
- 151 O 9 **Grigoriopol**, Moldova
- 216 K 4 **Grimari**, Central African Republic
- 137 L 16 **Grimma**, Germany
- 136 L 9 **Grimmen**, Germany
- 127 V 3 **Grimsby**, United Kingdom
- 134 C 9 **Grímsey**, Iceland 🏝
- 134 C 10 **Grímsstaðir**, Iceland
- 134 A 12 **Grindavík**, Iceland
- 138 F 9 **Grindelwald**, Switzerland
- 144 C 6 **Grintovec**, Slovenia ▲
- 218 L 12 **Griquatown**, Republic of South Africa
- 81 P 3 **Grise Fiord**, Nunavut, Canada
- 144 E 10 **Grmeč**, Bosnia and Herzegovina ⛰
- 133 H 17 **Grobbendonk**, Belgium
- 148 B 11 **Grobiņa**, Latvia
- 139 S 6 **Gröbming**, Austria
- 143 G 16 **Grodków**, Poland
- 132 M 12 **Groenlo**, Netherlands
- 142 L 13 **Grójec**, Poland
- 43 I 15 **Groll Seamount**, Atlantic Ocean ▲
- 135 E 14 **Grong**, Norway
- 132 M 6 **Groningen**, Netherlands ▣
- 132 M 6 **Groningen**, Netherlands
- 70 L 2 **Groom**, Texas, U.S.A.
- 218 I 12 **Groot Karas Berg**, Namibia ⛰
- 231 P 2 **Groote Eylandt**, Northern Territory, Australia 🏝
- 218 J 8 **Grootfontein**, Namibia
- 218 J 9 **Gross Ums**, Namibia
- 140 F 12 **Grosseto**, Italy
- 139 P 7 **Grossglockner**, Austria ▲
- 85 W 7 **Groswater Bay**, Newfoundland and Labrador, Canada ≈
- 58 B 11 **Grove City**, Pennsylvania, U.S.A.
- 63 O 6 **Grove Hill**, Alabama, U.S.A.
- 59 N 5 **Groveton**, New Hampshire, U.S.A.
- 157 Q 14 **Groznyy**, Russian Federation
- 146 M 10 **Grudovo**, Bulgaria
- 142 I 10 **Grudziądz**, Poland
- 218 J 12 **Grünau**, Namibia
- 148 E 12 **Gruzdžiai**, Lithuania
- 156 M 4 **Gryazi**, Russian Federation
- 154 K 12 **Gryazovets**, Russian Federation
- 138 D 9 **Gstaad**, Switzerland
- 194 C 6 **Gua Musang**, Malaysia
- 91 S 13 **Guabito**, Panama
- 110 I 7 **Guachipas**, Argentina
- 131 P 6 **Guadalajara**, Spain
- 89 O 11 **Guadalajara**, Mexico
- 234 K 7 **Guadalcanal**, Solomon Islands 🏝
- 234 M 7 **Guadalcanal**, Solomon Islands ▣
- 110 H 12 **Guadales**, Argentina
- 130 L 12 **Guadalquivir**, Spain ∿
- 41 V 4 **Guadalupe**, Mexico 🏝
- 130 M 8 **Guadalupe**, Spain
- 89 Q 7 **Guadalupe**, Mexico
- 89 N 8 **Guadalupe**, Mexico
- 70 F 7 **Guadalupe Mountains**, Texas, U.S.A. ⛰
- 70 G 7 **Guadalupe Peak**, Texas, U.S.A. ▲
- 93 Y 9 **Guadeloupe**, France ▣
- 93 X 9 **Guadeloupe Passage**, Montserrat ≈
- 131 N 9 **Guadiana**, Spain ∿
- 131 P 12 **Guadix**, Spain
- 41 X 12 **Guafo Fracture Zone**, Pacific Ocean ◇
- 112 H 12 **Guaíba**, Brazil
- 104 M 8 **Guainía**, Colombia ▣
- 104 M 8 **Guainía**, Colombia ∿
- 112 F 7 **Guaíra**, Brazil
- 109 D 14 **Guajará-Mirim**, Brazil
- 113 C 15 **Gualeguay**, Argentina
- 112 C 13 **Gualeguay**, Argentina ∿
- 113 D 14 **Gualeguaychu**, Argentina
- 110 L 11 **Gualeguaychú**, Argentina
- 111 G 18 **Gualjaina**, Argentina
- 236 A 9 **Guam**, Guam 🏝
- 236 A 9 **Guam**, U.S.A. ▣
- 113 B 18 **Guamini**, Argentina
- 88 K 7 **Guamúchil**, Mexico
- 188 M 6 **Guan Xian**, China
- 92 H 4 **Guanabacoa**, Cuba
- 91 N 3 **Guanaja**, Honduras
- 89 P 11 **Guanajuato**, Mexico
- 89 P 10 **Guanajuato**, Mexico ▣
- 109 L 15 **Guanambi**, Brazil
- 104 M 4 **Guanare**, Venezuela
- 110 G 9 **Guandacol**, Argentina
- 189 S 1 **Guandi Shan**, China ▲
- 92 F 4 **Guane**, Cuba
- 189 V 9 **Guangchang**, China
- 189 X 6 **Guangde**, China
- 189 U 11 **Guangdong**, China ▣
- 189 X 8 **Guangfeng**, China
- 189 T 13 **Guanghai**, China
- 188 K 9 **Guangmao Shan**, China ▲
- 189 N 11 **Guangnan**, China
- 189 T 12 **Guangning**, China
- 187 F 19 **Guangrao**, China
- 189 U 5 **Guangshui**, China
- 189 Q 12 **Guangxi Zhuangzu**, China ▣
- 189 O 5 **Guangyuan**, China
- 189 W 9 **Guangze**, China
- 189 T 12 **Guangzhou**, China
- 189 W 3 **Guanhu**, China
- 92 M 6 **Guantánamo**, Cuba
- 92 M 6 **Guantánamo Bay Naval Base**, U.S.A., U.S.A.
- 189 X 3 **Guanyun**, China
- 91 R 12 **Guápiles**, Costa Rica
- 109 E 15 **Guaporé**, Brazil ∿
- 107 H 19 **Guaqui**, Bolivia
- 112 O 5 **Guarapari**, Brazil
- 112 H 8 **Guarapuava**, Brazil
- 112 J 8 **Guaraqueçaba**, Brazil
- 112 J 9 **Guaratuba**, Brazil
- 107 I 17 **Guarayos**, Bolivia
- 130 J 5 **Guarda**, Portugal ▣
- 130 J 6 **Guarda**, Portugal
- 105 O 4 **Guárico**, Venezuela ▣
- 112 L 7 **Guarujá**, Brazil
- 88 K 7 **Guasave**, Mexico
- 90 H 6 **Guatemala**, Guatemala 🏛
- 90 I 4 **Guatemala**, North America ▣
- 41 X 7 **Guatemala Basin**, Pacific Ocean ◇
- 105 O 2 **Guatire**, Venezuela
- 104 K 9 **Guaviare**, Colombia ▣
- 104 M 7 **Guaviare**, Colombia ∿
- 93 U 8 **Guayama**, Puerto Rico
- 106 A 10 **Guayaquil**, Ecuador
- 107 K 15 **Guayaramerin**, Bolivia
- 106 A 10 **Guayas**, Ecuador ▣
- 88 I 5 **Guaymas**, Mexico
- 90 H 6 **Guazacapán**, Guatemala
- 213 G 19 **Guba**, Ethiopia

Country ▣ Internal administrative region: State/Province/Territory/Dependent territory 🏛 Capital city ⛰ Mountain range/Undersea ridge ▲ Mountain peak/Volcano/Seamount ◇ Geographic feature ▶ Headland/Point/Cape/Peninsula ◓ Desert 🏝 Island/Island group ⁂ Antarctic base 🌊 Ocean ◗ Sea ≈ Bay/Gulf/Channel/Strait 💧 Lake ⚑ Salt pan/Dry/Intermittent lake ∿ River

Guba – Hamilton

152 M 8 **Guba**, Russian Federation
155 R 1 **Guba Dolgaya**, Russian Federation
155 T 11 **Gubakha**, Russian Federation
142 D 13 **Gubin**, Poland
215 U 10 **Gubio**, Nigeria
171 P 5 **Gudaut'a**, Georgia
175 O 1 **Gudayyidat 'Ar'ar**, Saudi Arabia
157 Q 14 **Gudermes**, Russian Federation
41 X 15 **Gudgeon Harbour**, Pitcairn Island
181 G 19 **Gudivada**, India
181 F 20 **Gudur**, India
214 H 12 **Guéckédou**, Guinea
215 V 10 **Guélengdeng**, Chad
211 P 5 **Guelma**, Algeria
210 F 9 **Guelmine**, Morocco
86 E 13 **Guelph**, Ontario, Canada
89 R 8 **Güémez**, Mexico
215 O 10 **Guéné**, Benin
215 X 10 **Guéra**, Chad
211 N 8 **Guerara**, Algeria
210 J 7 **Guercif**, Morocco
129 P 9 **Guéret**, France
125 J 25 **Guernsey**, United Kingdom
73 Z 12 **Guernsey**, Wyoming, U.S.A.
214 G 7 **Guérou**, Mauritania
89 Q 6 **Guerrero**, Mexico
89 Q 13 **Guerrero**, Mexico
88 G 5 **Guerrero Negro**, Mexico
214 J 13 **Guéyo**, Côte d'Ivoire
213 H 22 **Gugē**, Ethiopia
236 A 7 **Guguan**, Northern Mariana Islands
42 G 13 **Guiana Basin**, Atlantic Ocean
105 O 6 **Guiana Highlands**, South America
189 W 6 **Guichi**, China
113 E 14 **Guichón**, Uruguay
215 W 11 **Guidari**, Chad
215 V 11 **Guider**, Cameroon
214 G 8 **Guidimaka**, Mauritania
189 P 10 **Guiding**, China
189 Q 12 **Guigang**, China
214 I 13 **Guiglo**, Côte d'Ivoire
130 L 6 **Guijuelo**, Spain
127 U 11 **Guildford**, United Kingdom
186 H 11 **Guiler**, China
59 Q 4 **Guilford**, Maine, U.S.A.
189 R 11 **Guilin**, China
129 W 12 **Guillestre**, France
42 M 12 **Güimar**, Canary Islands
197 I 17 **Guimaras**, Philippines
63 O 2 **Guin**, Alabama, U.S.A.
197 L 18 **Guindulman**, Philippines
214 F 10 **Guinea**, Africa
43 L 14 **Guinea Basin**, Atlantic Ocean
214 E 10 **Guinea-Bissau**, Africa
214 I 12 **Guinée-Forestière**, Guinea
214 F 10 **Guinée-Maritime**, Guinea
92 H 4 **Güines**, Cuba
128 J 5 **Guingamp**, France
189 R 12 **Guiping**, China
127 Y 6 **Guist**, United Kingdom
130 I 1 **Guitiriz**, Spain
197 M 16 **Guiuan**, Philippines
189 O 9 **Guiyang**, China
189 T 10 **Guiyang**, China
189 O 9 **Guizhou**, China
181 B 14 **Gujarat**, India
177 Y 9 **Gujranwala**, Pakistan
177 Y 8 **Gujrat**, Pakistan
185 P 8 **Gulang**, China
181 E 18 **Gulbarga**, India
148 I 10 **Gulbene**, Latvia
179 U 12 **Gülchö**, Kyrgyzstan
234 C 6 **Gulf**, Papua New Guinea
191 I 22 **Gulf of Thailand**, Thailand
213 M 18 **Gulf of Aden**, Africa/Asia
79 Q 11 **Gulf of Alaska**, Alaska, U.S.A.
153 Z 6 **Gulf of Anadyr**, Russian Federation
174 I 3 **Gulf of Aqaba**, Asia
82 L 4 **Gulf of Boothia**, Nunavut, Canada
135 I 19 **Gulf of Bothnia**, Sweden
88 G 3 **Gulf of California**, Mexico
231 Q 2 **Gulf of Carpentaria**, Queensland, Australia
147 E 19 **Gulf of Corinth**, Greece
104 G 3 **Gulf of Darién**, Colombia
135 L 20 **Gulf of Finland**, Europe
142 J 7 **Gulf of Gdańsk**, Europe
140 C 10 **Gulf of Genoa**, Italy
106 A 10 **Gulf of Guayaquil**, Ecuador
215 R 15 **Gulf of Guinea**, Africa
90 M 3 **Gulf of Honduras**, Honduras
181 A 14 **Gulf of Kachchh**, India
181 B 16 **Gulf of Khambhat**, India
59 P 9 **Gulf of Maine**, Maine, U.S.A.
181 F 24 **Gulf of Mannar**, Sri Lanka
191 E 17 **Gulf of Martaban**, Myanmar
57 R 15 **Gulf of Mexico**, North America
175 Y 5 **Gulf of Oman**, Asia
91 X 15 **Gulf of Panama**, Panama
234 C 6 **Gulf of Papua**, Papua New Guinea
105 R 3 **Gulf of Paria**, Venezuela
148 E 9 **Gulf of Riga**, Estonia/Latvia
212 C 7 **Gulf of Salûm**, Egypt/Libya
211 V 8 **Gulf of Sirte**, Libya
159 O 13 **Gulf of Sirte**, Mediterranean Sea
87 W 5 **Gulf of St Lawrence**, Québec, Canada
212 F 8 **Gulf of Suez**, Egypt
151 Y 9 **Gulf of Taganrog**, Russian Federation/Ukraine
39 S 3 **Gulf of Thailand**, Indian Ocean
189 Q 14 **Gulf of Tongking**, China
144 A 8 **Gulf of Trieste**, Slovenia
104 K 2 **Gulf of Venezuela**, Venezuela
140 H 7 **Gulf of Venice**, Italy
63 O 8 **Gulf Shores**, Alabama, U.S.A.
231 P 12 **Gulf St Vincent**, South Australia, Australia
57 T 13 **Gulfport**, Mississippi, U.S.A.
189 O 8 **Gulin**, China/Vietnam
189 V 7 **Guling**, China
179 R 12 **Gulistan**, Uzbekistan
170 B 12 **Güllük Körfezi**, Turkey
170 A 9 **Gülpinar**, Turkey
171 Q 5 **Gulrip'shi**, Georgia
179 U 7 **Gul'shad**, Kazakhstan
217 S 6 **Gulu**, Uganda
146 K 10 **Gülübovo**, Bulgaria
146 I 7 **Gulyantsi**, Bulgaria
218 L 7 **Gumare**, Botswana
178 I 13 **Gumdag**, Turkmenistan
215 S 10 **Gumel**, Nigeria
181 I 15 **Gumla**, India
180 E 13 **Guna**, India
213 I 19 **Guna Terara**, Ethiopia
139 Q 4 **Gundertshausen**, Austria
170 L 12 **Güney Doğu Toroslar**, Turkey
216 J 11 **Gungu**, Democratic Republic of Congo
157 R 15 **Gunib**, Russian Federation
45 P 13 **Gunnbjørn Fjeld**, Greenland
231 U 10 **Gunnedah**, New South Wales, Australia
38 B 11 **Gunners Quoin**, Mauritius
74 K 5 **Gunnison**, Utah, U.S.A.
75 P 5 **Gunnison**, Colorado, U.S.A.
181 E 19 **Guntakal**, India
63 Q 2 **Guntersville Lake**, Alabama, U.S.A.
181 G 19 **Guntur**, India
192 B 8 **Gunung Abongabong**, Indonesia
195 O 10 **Gunung Ayer**, Malaysia
194 C 7 **Gunung Batu Puteh**, Malaysia
194 E 10 **Gunung Belumut**, Malaysia
194 C 7 **Gunung Benum**, Malaysia
194 A 6 **Gunung Bintang**, Malaysia
193 Q 10 **Gunung Bulawa**, Indonesia
194 C 6 **Gunung Camah**, Malaysia
193 W 12 **Gunung Dom**, Indonesia
192 D 11 **Gunung Kerinci**, Indonesia
193 U 11 **Gunung Kwoka**, Indonesia
194 D 5 **Gunung Lawit**, Malaysia
194 D 9 **Gunung Ledang**, Malaysia
194 C 7 **Gunung Liang Timur**, Malaysia
195 X 7 **Gunung Magdaline**, Malaysia
193 O 10 **Gunung Malino**, Indonesia
194 D 6 **Gunung Mandi Angin**, Malaysia
193 V 11 **Gunung Mebo**, Indonesia
195 W 4 **Gunung Menapod**, Malaysia
195 T 7 **Gunung Murud**, Malaysia
193 Q 15 **Gunung Mutis**, Indonesia
194 C 5 **Gunung Noring**, Malaysia
195 T 7 **Gunung Pagon**, Malaysia
192 K 15 **Gunung Semeru**, Indonesia
192 I 14 **Gunung Slamet**, Indonesia
194 D 6 **Gunung Tahan**, Malaysia
194 D 7 **Gunung Tapis**, Malaysia
195 X 6 **Gunung Tribulation**, Malaysia
195 U 5 **Gunung Trus Madi**, Malaysia
193 P 11 **Gunung Tumpu**, Indonesia
193 R 14 **Gunungapi**, Indonesia
192 C 10 **Gunungsitoli**, Indonesia
181 I 17 **Gunupur**, India
137 H 23 **Günzburg**, Germany
187 E 15 **Guojiatun**, China
189 V 4 **Guoyang**, China
150 K 8 **Gura Humorului**, Romania
182 H 3 **Gurais**, India
186 A 13 **Gurban Obo**, China
177 O 14 **Gurdim**, Iran
180 B 13 **Gurha**, India
112 I 4 **Gurinhatã**, Brazil
139 T 8 **Gurk**, Austria
219 Q 6 **Guro**, Mozambique
219 S 5 **Guruè**, Mozambique
170 M 11 **Gürün**, Turkey
108 I 10 **Gurupá**, Brazil
109 J 14 **Gurupi**, Brazil
156 M 1 **Gus'-Khrustal'nyy**, Russian Federation
215 Q 10 **Gusau**, Nigeria
149 C 16 **Gusev**, Russian Federation
187 I 17 **Gushan**, China
189 V 5 **Gushi**, China
199 M 25 **Gushikawa**, Japan
141 B 18 **Guspini**, Italy
139 X 7 **Güssing**, Austria
139 V 5 **Gusswerk**, Austria
241 W 5 **Gustav Bull Mountains**, Antarctica
79 W 10 **Gustavus**, Alaska, U.S.A.
199 O 26 **Gusukube**, Japan
137 E 14 **Gütersloh**, Germany
69 N 9 **Guthrie**, Oklahoma, U.S.A.
70 M 4 **Guthrie**, Texas, U.S.A.
74 M 13 **Guthrie**, Arizona, U.S.A.
189 X 9 **Gutian**, China
67 V 11 **Guttenberg**, Iowa, U.S.A.
219 P 7 **Gutu**, Zimbabwe
183 V 10 **Guwahati**, India
173 S 2 **Guwēr**, Iraq
105 S 6 **Guyana**, South America
185 R 6 **Guyang**, China
68 G 8 **Guymon**, Oklahoma, U.S.A.
189 O 2 **Guyuan**, China
179 P 13 **Guzar**, Uzbekistan
149 B 16 **Gvardeysk**, Russian Federation
191 C 15 **Gwa**, Myanmar
215 Q 9 **Gwadabawa**, Nigeria
177 P 14 **Gwadar**, Pakistan
182 J 11 **Gwalior**, India
219 O 8 **Gwanda**, Zimbabwe
217 O 5 **Gwane**, Democratic Republic of Congo
177 P 14 **Gwatar Bay**, Iran
217 Q 5 **Gwawele**, Democratic Republic of Congo
142 G 10 **Gwda**, Poland
219 O 7 **Gweru**, Zimbabwe
218 M 8 **Gweta**, Botswana
64 H 9 **Gwinn**, Michigan, U.S.A.
215 U 10 **Gwoza**, Nigeria
147 M 23 **Gyali**, Greece
184 K 11 **Gyangzê**, China
185 N 9 **Gyaring Hu**, China
147 I 21 **Gyaros**, Greece
188 K 7 **Gyawa**, China
153 N 7 **Gyda**, Russian Federation
153 N 7 **Gydanskiy Poluostrov**, Russian Federation
188 I 6 **Gyitang**, China
231 W 8 **Gympie**, Queensland, Australia
143 L 24 **Gyomaendrőd**, Hungary
143 K 22 **Gyöngyös**, Hungary
143 H 22 **Győr**, Hungary
84 I 9 **Gypsumville**, Manitoba, Canada
147 E 23 **Gytheio**, Greece
143 L 24 **Gyula**, Hungary
171 T 8 **Gyumri**, Armenia
178 J 13 **Gyzylarbat**, Turkmenistan
178 I 14 **Gyzyletrek**, Turkmenistan

H

183 T 9 **Ha**, Bhutan
190 N 12 **Ha Côi**, Vietnam
190 L 10 **Ha Giang**, Vietnam
191 L 22 **Ha Tiên**, Vietnam
191 M 15 **Ha Tinh**, Vietnam
148 F 8 **Häädemeeste**, Estonia
137 K 24 **Haag in Oberbayern**, Germany
132 N 12 **Haaksbergen**, Netherlands
236 I 10 **Ha'apai Group**, Tonga
135 L 15 **Haapajärvi**, Finland
148 E 7 **Haapsalu**, Estonia
132 G 11 **Haarlem**, Netherlands
233 D 21 **Haast**, New Zealand
175 X 5 **Haba**, United Arab Emirates
175 V 11 **Ḩabarūt**, Oman
217 X 7 **Habaswein**, Kenya
133 J 25 **Habay-la-Neuve**, Belgium
175 R 13 **Ḩabbān**, Yemen
158 C 9 **Habibas Escarpment**, Mediterranean Sea
187 D 14 **Habirag**, China
104 H 10 **Hacha**, Colombia
199 L 19 **Hachijō-jima**, Japan
198 K 9 **Hachinohe**, Japan
171 R 9 **Haciömer**, Turkey
58 J 12 **Hackensack**, New Jersey, U.S.A.
219 Q 8 **Hacufera**, Mozambique
186 G 7 **Hadat**, China
215 S 10 **Hadejia**, Nigeria
172 F 8 **Ḩadera**, Israel
135 B 25 **Haderslev**, Denmark
181 E 17 **Hadgaon**, India
181 L 19 **Hadhdhunmathi Atoll**, Maldives
175 W 14 **Hadīboh**, Yemen
170 H 13 **Hadim**, Turkey
127 Y 8 **Hadleigh**, United Kingdom
82 H 5 **Hadley Bay**, Nunavut, Canada
175 R 13 **Ḩaḑramawt**, Yemen
134 G 8 **Hadseløy**, Norway
135 C 24 **Hadsund**, Denmark
151 T 3 **Hadyach**, Ukraine
187 K 18 **Haeju**, North Korea
187 L 22 **Haenam**, South Korea
175 Q 3 **Ḩafar al Bāţin**, Saudi Arabia
170 M 9 **Hafik**, Turkey
174 L 4 **Hafirat al'Aydā**, Saudi Arabia
183 W 11 **Haflong**, India
134 A 11 **Hafnarfjörður**, Iceland
236 A 9 **Hagåtña**, Guam
137 D 16 **Hagen**, Germany
72 L 12 **Hagerman**, Idaho, U.S.A.
61 T 2 **Hagerstown**, Maryland, U.S.A.
135 F 20 **Hagfors**, Sweden
199 C 20 **Hagi**, Japan
125 B 18 **Hag's Head**, Republic of Ireland
129 X 4 **Haguenau**, France
190 M 12 **Hai Duong**, Vietnam
190 M 12 **Hai Phong**, Vietnam
189 Y 4 **Hai'an**, China
187 I 16 **Haicheng**, China
172 F 8 **Haifa**, Israel
189 R 14 **Haikang**, China
189 R 15 **Haikou**, China
175 N 4 **Ḩā'il**, Saudi Arabia
186 G 8 **Hailar**, China
186 M 12 **Hailin**, China
127 W 13 **Hailsham**, United Kingdom
186 K 9 **Hailun**, China
134 L 13 **Hailuoto**, Finland
189 Z 5 **Haimen**, China
199 M 26 **Haimi**, Japan
189 Q 15 **Hainan**, China
189 Q 15 **Hainan**, China
189 Q 15 **Hainan Strait**, China
133 E 21 **Hainaut**, Belgium
139 Z 4 **Hainburg an der Donau**, Austria
79 W 10 **Haines**, Alaska, U.S.A.
63 W 10 **Haines City**, Florida, U.S.A.
83 A 14 **Haines Junction**, Yukon Territory, Canada
139 W 4 **Hainfeld**, Austria
189 Y 6 **Haining**, China
189 Y 10 **Haitan Dao**, China
93 O 8 **Haiti**, North America
189 Q 15 **Haitou**, China
189 Z 6 **Haiyan**, China
187 H 20 **Haiyang**, China
189 O 2 **Haiyuan**, China
189 X 3 **Haizhou Wan**, China
143 M 22 **Hajdúböszörmény**, Hungary
143 M 23 **Hajdúszoboszló**, Hungary
173 V 8 **Hājī Muḩsin**, Iraq
198 I 13 **Hajiki-zaki**, Japan
183 Q 11 **Hajipur**, India
175 O 12 **Ḩajjah**, Yemen
176 L 12 **Ḩājjīābād**, Iran
142 O 11 **Hajnówka**, Poland
190 B 10 **Haka**, Myanmar
171 T 12 **Hakkâri**, Turkey
199 G 19 **Hakken-san**, Japan
198 K 9 **Hakkōda-san**, Japan
198 K 3 **Hako-dake**, Japan
198 J 8 **Hakodate**, Japan
199 H 15 **Hakui**, Japan
177 U 14 **Hala**, Pakistan
175 P 7 **Halabān**, Saudi Arabia
173 V 4 **Halabja**, Iraq
212 H 13 **Halaib**, Sudan
212 G 12 **Halaib Triangle**, Sudan
174 J 2 **Ḩālat 'Ammār**, Saudi Arabia
172 H 5 **Halba**, Lebanon
185 O 2 **Halban**, Mongolia
137 I 14 **Halberstadt**, Germany
135 D 20 **Halden**, Norway
182 L 8 **Haldwani**, India
127 Q 4 **Hale**, United Kingdom
78 D 8 **Haleakala**, Hawaii, U.S.A.
127 R 7 **Halesowen**, United Kingdom
127 Z 7 **Halesworth**, United Kingdom
77 I 19 **Half Dome**, California, U.S.A.
171 N 13 **Halfeti**, Turkey
233 C 26 **Halfmoon Bay**, New Zealand
132 H 11 **Halfweg**, Netherlands
86 G 10 **Haliburton Highlands**, Ontario, Canada
127 R 2 **Halifax**, United Kingdo
87 V 11 **Halifax**, Nova Scotia, Canada
85 O 1 **Hall Beach**, Nunavut, Canada
139 N 7 **Hall in Tirol**, Austria
237 O 14 **Hall Islands**, Federated States of Micronesia
85 S 3 **Hall Peninsula**, Nunavu Canada
187 L 23 **Halla-san**, South Korea
133 F 19 **Halle**, Belgium
137 K 16 **Halle**, Germany
139 Q 6 **Hallein**, Austria
71 Q 11 **Hallettsville**, Texas, U.S.
241 N 3 **Halley**, Antarctica
66 H4 **Halliday**, North Dakota, U.S.A.
230 K 4 **Halls Creek**, Western Australia, Australia
139 R 6 **Hallstatt**, Austria
138 F 7 **Hallwiler See**, Switzerland
126 L 13 **Hallworthy**, United Kingdom
193 S 10 **Halmahera**, Indonesia
193 S 11 **Halmahera Sea**, Indonesia
135 E 24 **Halmstad**, Sweden
127 X 9 **Halstead**, United Kingdom
133 F 15 **Halsteren**, Netherlands
127 N 15 **Halwell**, United Kingdo
190 L 11 **Ham Yên**, Vietnam
199 C 19 **Hamada**, Japan
176 G 6 **Hamadān**, Iran
176 G 6 **Hamadān**, Iran
211 R 12 **Hamādat Murzuq**, Libya
210 J 9 **Hamaguir**, Algeria
172 I 4 **Ḩamāh**, Syria
199 I 18 **Hamamatsu**, Japan
135 D 18 **Hamar**, Norway
199 F 17 **Hamasaka**, Japan
198 J 3 **Hamatonbetsu**, Japan
181 G 26 **Hambantota**, Sri Lanka
136 H 10 **Hamburg**, Germany
58 C 9 **Hamburg**, New York, U.S.A.
67 Q 15 **Hamburg**, Iowa, U.S.A.
175 O 10 **Ḩamḑah**, Saudi Arabia
174 M 9 **Ḩamdānah**, Saudi Arabi
135 L 18 **Hämeenlinna**, Finland
137 G 14 **Hameln**, Germany
230 F 6 **Hamersley Range**, Western Australia, Australia
187 L 16 **Hamgyŏng-sanmaek**, North Korea
187 L 16 **Hamhŭng**, North Korea
184 M 5 **Hami**, China
170 F 9 **Hamidye**, Turkey
231 R 13 **Hamilton**, Victoria, Australia
232 K 10 **Hamilton**, New Zealand
42 A 7 **Hamilton**, Bermuda
124 H 13 **Hamilton**, United Kingdom
63 O 2 **Hamilton**, Alabama, U.S.A.
65 D 18 **Hamilton**, Illinois, U.S.A.

Country · Internal administrative region: State/Province/Territory/Dependent territory · Capital city · Mountain range/Undersea ridge · Mountain peak/Volcano/Seamount · Geographic feature · Headland/Point/Cape/Peninsula · Desert · Island/Island group · Antarctic base · Ocean · Sea · Bay/Gulf/Channel/Strait · Lake · Salt pan/Dry/Intermittent lake · R

K 19 **Hamilton**, Ohio, U.S.A.
P 7 **Hamilton**, Texas, U.S.A.
M 6 **Hamilton**, Montana, U.S.A.
E 13 **Hamilton**, Ontario, Canada
F 6 **Hamilton Bank**, Atlantic Ocean ◇
W 8 **Hamilton Inlet**, Newfoundland and Labrador, Canada ◣
N 19 **Hamina**, Finland
I 5 **Hamirpur**, India
Q 11 **Hamlet**, North Carolina, U.S.A.
M 6 **Hamlin**, Texas, U.S.A.
D 15 **Hamm**, Germany
G 10 **Hammada du Drâa**, Algeria ◇
Q 10 **Hammādat Tingharat**, Libya ◇
R 2 **Ḩammān al ʻAlīl**, Iraq
G 16 **Hammarstrand**, Sweden
H 19 **Hamme-Mille**, Belgium
G 15 **Hammerdal**, Sweden
L 7 **Hammond**, Louisiana, U.S.A.
H 16 **Hammond**, Indiana, U.S.A.
I 14 **Hammonton**, New Jersey, U.S.A.
I 22 **Hamois**, Belgium
F 23 **Hampden**, New Zealand
O 8 **Hampton**, New Hampshire, U.S.A.
O 14 **Hampton**, South Carolina, U.S.A.
V 6 **Hampton**, Virginia, U.S.A.
V 14 **Hampton**, Arkansas, U.S.A.
I 12 **Hampton**, Oregon, U.S.A.
T 10 **Hampton**, New Brunswick, Canada
C 17 **Hamrat esh Sheikh**, Sudan
N 12 **Hāmūn-e Jaz Mūrīān**, Iran ◣
P 10 **Hāmūn Helmand**, Iran ◣
P 9 **Hāmūn Pu**, Afghanistan ◣
S 9 **Hamur**, Turkey
Q 5 **Han Shui**, China ∿
G 12 **Han Sum**, China
D 8 **Hana**, Hawaii, U.S.A.
K 5 **Ḩanale**, Saudi Arabia
K 10 **Hanamaki**, Japan
F 19 **Hanau**, Germany
R 3 **Hancheng**, China
I 10 **Hancock**, New York, U.S.A.
S 2 **Hancock**, Maryland, U.S.A.
U 2 **Handan**, China
W 11 **Handeni**, Tanzania
I 20 **Handlová**, Slovakia
D 17 **Hanestad**, Norway
Y 5 **Hanga Roa**, Easter Island
O 3 **Hangayn Nuruu**, Mongolia ⛰
V 8 **Hangu**, Pakistan
E 17 **Hangu**, China
P 11 **Hangyuan**, China
Y 6 **Hangzhou**, China
Z 6 **Hangzhou Wan**, China ≈
P 11 **Hani**, Turkey
K 20 **Hanko**, Finland
L 6 **Hanksville**, Utah, U.S.A.
K 5 **Hanle**, India
L 10 **Hanli**, Turkey
H 18 **Hanmer Springs**, New Zealand
G 16 **Hann-Münden**, Germany
K 19 **Hanna**, Alberta, Canada
O 10 **Hannah Bay**, Ontario, Canada ≈
W 2 **Hannibal**, Missouri, U.S.A.
G 13 **Hannover**, Germany
I 20 **Hannut**, Belgium
F 25 **Hanöbukten**, Sweden ≈
L 12 **Hanoi**, Vietnam ⌂
D 12 **Hanover**, Ontario, Canada
W 4 **Hansen Mountains**, Antarctica ⛰
H 8 **Hansi**, India
H 20 **Hantsavichy**, Belarus
B 23 **Hantsholm**, Denmark
G 7 **Hanumangarh**, India
177 O 14 **Hanzaram**, Iran
189 O 4 **Hanzhong**, China
189 W 3 **Hanzhuang**, China
183 S 14 **Haora**, India
211 O 8 **Haoud el Hamra**, Algeria
210 E 10 **Haouza**, Western Sahara
70 K 3 **Happy**, Texas, U.S.A.
77 F 14 **Happy Camp**, California, U.S.A.
85 V 8 **Happy Valley Goose Bay**, Newfoundland and Labrador, Canada
174 J 2 **Ḩaql**, Saudi Arabia
185 P 6 **Har Borog**, China
185 N 7 **Har Hu**, China ◣
172 G 7 **Har Meron**, Israel ▲
185 N 3 **Har Nuur**, Mongolia ◣
184 M 3 **Har Us Nuur**, Mongolia ◣
213 K 18 **Hara Alol**, Djibouti ▲
175 O 12 **Ḩaraḑ**, Yemen
175 S 6 **Ḩaraḑh**, Saudi Arabia
149 L 14 **Haradok**, Belarus
149 H 18 **Haradzyeya**, Belarus
175 O 11 **Ḩarajā**, Saudi Arabia
198 L 13 **Haramachi**, Japan
177 X 10 **Harappa Road**, Pakistan
219 P 6 **Harare**, Zimbabwe ⌂
215 X 9 **Haraz-Djombo**, Chad
215 Y 11 **Haraze Mangueigne**, Chad
214 H 13 **Harbel**, Liberia
186 K 11 **Harbin**, China
64 K 10 **Harbor Springs**, Michigan, U.S.A.
85 Y 11 **Harbour Breton**, Newfoundland and Labrador, Canada
181 E 15 **Harda Khas**, India
135 A 19 **Hardangerfjorden**, Norway ≈
218 I 10 **Hardap**, Namibia ◘
61 O 15 **Hardeeville**, South Carolina, U.S.A.
132 J 11 **Harderwijk**, Netherlands
73 V 7 **Hardin**, Montana, U.S.A.
182 L 9 **Hardoi**, India
69 W 8 **Hardy**, Arkansas, U.S.A.
133 C 19 **Harelbeke**, Belgium
132 M 6 **Haren**, Netherlands
213 K 20 **Hārer**, Ethiopia
186 F 8 **Hargant**, China
213 K 22 **Hargele**, Ethiopia
213 L 20 **Hargeysa**, Somalia
148 H 9 **Hargla**, Estonia
175 Q 13 **Harīb**, Yemen
182 K 7 **Haridwar**, India
181 D 20 **Harihar**, India
233 E 19 **Harihari**, New Zealand
133 F 14 **Haringvliet**, Netherlands ≈
181 E 15 **Harisal**, India
61 V 11 **Harkers Island**, North Carolina, U.S.A.
60 K 7 **Harlan**, Kentucky, U.S.A.
126 M 6 **Harlech**, United Kingdom
73 T 2 **Harlem**, Montana, U.S.A.
132 J 7 **Harlingen**, Netherlands
71 Q 15 **Harlingen**, Texas, U.S.A.
127 W 9 **Harlow**, United Kingdom
73 S 6 **Harlowton**, Montana, U.S.A.
170 D 9 **Harmancik**, Turkey
76 I 12 **Harney Basin**, Oregon, U.S.A. ◇
76 J 12 **Harney Lake**, Oregon, U.S.A. ◣
135 H 16 **Härnösand**, Sweden
131 P 2 **Haro**, Spain
214 I 14 **Harper**, Liberia
68 M 7 **Harper**, Kansas, U.S.A.
76 K 12 **Harper**, Oregon, U.S.A.
172 J 8 **Ḩarrat ar Rujaylah**, Jordan ⛰
172 J 9 **Harrat ar Rujaylah**, Jordan ▲
174 M 6 **Ḩarrat Rahaţ**, Saudi Arabia ⛰
85 P 10 **Harricanaw**, Québec, Canada ∿
60 J 9 **Harriman**, Tennessee, U.S.A.
42 B 7 **Harrington Sound**, Bermuda ≈
124 E 9 **Harris**, United Kingdom ⁂
41 R 3 **Harris Seamount**, Pacific Ocean ▲
58 F 13 **Harrisburg**, Pennsylvania, U.S.A.
65 G 22 **Harrisburg**, Illinois, U.S.A.
69 X 10 **Harrisburg**, Arkansas, U.S.A.
219 O 12 **Harrismith**, Republic of South Africa
64 K 12 **Harrison**, Michigan, U.S.A.
66 F 12 **Harrison**, Nebraska, U.S.A.
69 U 9 **Harrison**, Arkansas, U.S.A.
61 R 4 **Harrisonburg**, Virginia, U.S.A.
69 S 4 **Harrisonville**, Missouri, U.S.A.
64 F 13 **Harrisville**, Wisconsin, U.S.A.
64 L 11 **Harrisville**, Michigan, U.S.A.
127 S 2 **Harrogate**, United Kingdom
176 G 6 **Harsīn**, Iran
134 H 8 **Harstad**, Norway
64 I 13 **Hart**, Michigan, U.S.A.
187 H 14 **Hartao**, China
139 X 6 **Hartberg**, Austria
135 B 19 **Hårteigen**, Norway ▲
58 L 10 **Hartford**, Connecticut, U.S.A.
60 E 6 **Hartford**, Kentucky, U.S.A.
65 J 15 **Hartford**, Michigan, U.S.A.
87 R 9 **Hartland**, New Brunswick, Canada
126 L 12 **Hartland Point**, United Kingdom ▶
125 K 15 **Hartlepool**, United Kingdom
70 J 1 **Hartley**, Texas, U.S.A.
39 S 9 **Hartog Ridge**, Indian Ocean ⛰
231 O 6 **Harts Range**, Northern Territory, Australia
69 U 7 **Hartville**, Missouri, U.S.A.
63 U 2 **Hartwell Reservoir**, Georgia/South Carolina, U.S.A. ◣
87 U 3 **Harve-St-Pierre**, Québec, Canada
66 K 4 **Harvey**, North Dakota, U.S.A.
87 R 10 **Harvey**, New Brunswick, Canada
127 Z 9 **Harwich**, United Kingdom
182 H 7 **Haryana**, India ◘
137 H 15 **Harz**, Germany ⛰
170 J 11 **Hasan Dağl**, Turkey ▲
176 L 12 **Ḩasan Langī**, Iran
136 D 12 **Haselünne**, Germany
199 G 19 **Hashimoto**, Japan
176 I 5 **Hashtgerd**, Iran
175 X 11 **Ḩāsik**, Oman
70 M 5 **Haskell**, Texas, U.S.A.
127 U 12 **Haslemere**, United Kingdom
181 D 21 **Hassan**, India
133 J 18 **Hasselt**, Belgium
137 I 19 **Hassfurt**, Germany
211 O 10 **Hassi Bel Guebbour**, Algeria
211 N 9 **Hassi Inifel**, Algeria
211 O 8 **Hassi Messaoud**, Algeria
135 E 25 **Hässleholm**, Sweden
232 N 13 **Hastings**, New Zealand
127 X 13 **Hastings**, United Kingdom
65 J 15 **Hastings**, Michigan, U.S.A.
66 M 15 **Hastings**, Nebraska, U.S.A.
67 T 8 **Hastings**, Minnesota, U.S.A.
175 V 12 **Ḩaşwayl**, Yemen
191 H 26 **Hat Yai**, Thailand
75 P 13 **Hatch**, New Mexico, U.S.A.
150 H 11 **Haţeg**, Romania
199 M 26 **Hateruma-jima**, Japan ⁂
127 T 3 **Hatfield**, United Kingdom
185 P 2 **Hatgal**, Mongolia
126 M 13 **Hatherleigh**, United Kingdom
182 J 9 **Hathras**, India
183 R 9 **Hatia**, Nepal
183 V 14 **Hatia**, Bangladesh ⁂
199 D 19 **Hatsukaichi**, Japan
181 F 14 **Hatta**, India
61 W 10 **Hatteras**, North Carolina, U.S.A.
42 D 10 **Hatteras Abyssal Plain**, Atlantic Ocean ◇
61 X 9 **Hatteras Island**, North Carolina, U.S.A. ⁂
62 M 6 **Hattiesburg**, Mississippi, U.S.A.
42 J 6 **Hatton Ridge**, Atlantic Ocean ⛰
233 M 14 **Hatuma**, New Zealand
143 J 22 **Hatvan**, Hungary
135 A 20 **Haugesund**, Norway
139 X 2 **Haugsdorf**, Austria
135 B 19 **Haukeligrend**, Norway
135 N 16 **Haukivesi**, Finland ◣
112 C 10 **Haumonía**, Argentina
232 K 8 **Hauraki Gulf**, New Zealand ≈
137 D 24 **Hausach**, Germany
216 G 8 **Haut-Ogooué**, Gabon ◘
214 H 10 **Haute-Guinée**, Guinea ◘
216 M 3 **Haute-Kotto**, Central African Republic ◘
217 N 3 **Haute-Mbomou**, Central African Republic ◘
129 O 3 **Haute-Normandie**, France ◘
210 J 7 **Hauts Plateaux**, Morocco ◇
65 E 18 **Havana**, Illinois, U.S.A.
92 G 3 **Havana**, Cuba ⌂
127 U 13 **Havant**, United Kingdom
136 L 13 **Havel**, Germany ∿
133 I 21 **Havelange**, Belgium
177 W 10 **Haveli**, Pakistan
233 I 16 **Havelock**, New Zealand
61 U 10 **Havelock**, North Carolina, U.S.A.
181 N 21 **Havelock Island**, India ⁂
132 L 9 **Havelte**, Netherlands
126 K 9 **Haverfordwest**, United Kingdom
127 X 8 **Haverhill**, United Kingdom
133 I 22 **Haversin**, Belgium
185 T 4 **Havirga**, Mongolia
143 E 18 **Havlíčkův Brod**, Czech Republic
73 S 2 **Havre**, Montana, U.S.A.
85 W 12 **Havre Aubert**, Québec, Canada
85 U 10 **Havre-St-Pierre**, Québec, Canada
151 W 7 **Havrylivka**, Ukraine
170 B 6 **Havsa**, Turkey
170 K 8 **Havza**, Turkey
78 D 9 **Hawaii**, Hawaii, U.S.A. ⁂
78 A 9 **Hawaii**, U.S.A. ◘
78 A 6 **Hawaiian Islands**, Hawaii, U.S.A. ⁂
175 S 2 **Hawallī**, Kuwait
232 J 13 **Hawera**, New Zealand
127 R 1 **Hawes**, United Kingdom
78 E 8 **Hawi**, Hawaii, U.S.A.
125 I 14 **Hawick**, United Kingdom
73 Z 13 **Hawk Springs**, Wyoming, U.S.A.
232 N 13 **Hawke Bay**, New Zealand ≈
231 P 10 **Hawker**, South Australia, Australia
232 M 13 **Hawke's Bay**, New Zealand ◘
85 X 9 **Hawkes Bay**, Newfoundland and Labrador, Canada
86 K 10 **Hawkesbury**, Ontario, Canada
63 T 5 **Hawkinsville**, Georgia, U.S.A.
233 I 19 **Hawkswood**, New Zealand
173 S 7 **Hawr al Ḩabbānīyah**, Iraq ◣
173 Y 11 **Hawr al Hammār**, Iraq ◣
173 W 9 **Hawr as Sa'dīyah**, Iraq ◣
175 S 12 **Ḩawra'**, Yemen
77 J 19 **Hawthorne**, Nevada, U.S.A.
127 T 1 **Haxby**, United Kingdom
231 S 12 **Hay**, New South Wales, Australia
127 O 8 **Hay-on-Wye**, United Kingdom
82 H 13 **Hay River**, Northwest Territories, Canada
66 H 12 **Hay Springs**, Nebraska, U.S.A.
193 S 12 **Haya**, Indonesia
198 L 10 **Hayachine-san**, Japan ▲
79 N 6 **Haycock**, Alaska, U.S.A.
176 F 4 **Haydarābād**, Iran
74 L 13 **Hayden**, Arizona, U.S.A.
66 J 9 **Hayes**, South Dakota, U.S.A.
175 W 15 **Ḩayf**, Yemen
77 M 21 **Hayfod Peak**, Nevada, U.S.A. ▲
126 J 15 **Hayle**, United Kingdom
127 T 13 **Hayling Island**, United Kingdom ⁂
175 X 9 **Haymā'**, Oman
170 H 10 **Haymana**, Turkey
61 T 3 **Haymarket**, Virginia, U.S.A.
62 I 4 **Haynesville**, Louisiana, U.S.A.
63 Q 5 **Hayneville**, Alabama, U.S.A.
170 C 7 **Hayrabolu**, Turkey
68 K 4 **Hays**, Kansas, U.S.A.
73 T 3 **Hays**, Montana, U.S.A.
151 O 6 **Haysyn**, Ukraine
64 D 9 **Hayward**, Wisconsin, U.S.A.
77 G 19 **Hayward**, California, U.S.A.
127 W 12 **Haywards Heath**, United Kingdom
60 K 6 **Hazard**, Kentucky, U.S.A.
181 I 14 **Hazaribag**, India
183 P 13 **Hazaribagh**, India
41 O 9 **Hazel Holme Bank**, Pacific Ocean ▲
63 V 5 **Hazelhurst**, Georgia, U.S.A.
81 N 3 **Hazen Strait**, Nunavut, Canada ≈
62 L 5 **Hazlelhurst**, Mississippi, U.S.A.
72 K 5 **Headquarters**, Idaho, U.S.A.
64 F 10 **Heafford Junction**, Wisconsin, U.S.A.
77 F 18 **Healdsburg**, California, U.S.A.
79 R 7 **Healy**, Alaska, U.S.A.
39 O 12 **Heard Island**, Australia ⁂
71 R 8 **Hearne**, Texas, U.S.A.
86 B 4 **Hearst**, Ontario, Canada
240 J 4 **Hearst Island**, Antarctica ⁂
71 N 14 **Hebbronville**, Texas, U.S.A.
187 C 17 **Hebei**, China ◘
231 T 9 **Hebel**, Queensland, Australia
74 L 11 **Heber**, Arizona, U.S.A.
73 Q 9 **Hebgen Lake**, Montana, U.S.A. ◣
189 T 2 **Hebi**, China
172 F 10 **Hebron**, Israel
66 I 5 **Hebron**, North Dakota, U.S.A.
67 N 15 **Hebron**, Nebraska, U.S.A.
85 U 6 **Hebron**, Newfoundland and Labrador, Canada
83 C 19 **Hecate Strait**, British Columbia, Canada ≈
89 Y 11 **Hecelchakán**, Mexico
189 P 11 **Hechi**, China
133 J 17 **Hechtel**, Belgium
189 O 7 **Hechuan**, China
135 F 16 **Hede**, Sweden
133 I 14 **Hedel**, Netherlands
132 G 10 **Heemskerk**, Netherlands
132 K 8 **Heerenveen**, Netherlands
132 H 9 **Heerhugowaard**, Netherlands
133 L 19 **Heerlen**, Netherlands
133 I 19 **Heers**, Belgium
133 J 14 **Heesh**, Netherlands
189 V 5 **Hefei**, China
189 R 7 **Hefeng**, China
186 M 9 **Hegang**, China
136 F 8 **Heide**, Germany
137 F 21 **Heidelberg**, Germany
139 U 2 **Heidenreichstein**, Austria
186 K 7 **Heihe**, China
137 G 22 **Heilbronn**, Germany
139 Q 7 **Heiligenblut**, Austria
139 X 7 **Heiligenkreuz**, Austria
186 K 5 **Heilong Jiang**, China ∿
186 K 9 **Heilongjiang**, China ◘
134 B 12 **Heimaey**, Iceland ⁂
135 M 18 **Heinola**, Finland
137 B 16 **Heinsberg**, Germany
187 H 15 **Heishan**, China
133 H 18 **Heist-op-den-Berg**, Belgium
187 D 18 **Hejian**, China
189 O 8 **Hejiang**, China
171 N 11 **Hekimhan**, Turkey
134 B 11 **Hekla**, Iceland ▲
142 I 8 **Hel**, Poland
183 X 10 **Helem**, India
73 P 5 **Helena**, Montana, U.S.A.
124 G 13 **Helensburgh**, United Kingdom
232 J 8 **Helensville**, New Zealand
136 E 9 **Helgoländer Bucht**, Germany ≈
186 M 9 **Heli**, China
38 B 15 **Hell-Bourg**, Réunion
134 B 11 **Hella**, Iceland
135 A 21 **Helleland**, Norway
159 Q 10 **Hellenic Trench**, Mediterranean Sea ◇
133 F 14 **Hellevoetsluis**, Netherlands
131 R 10 **Hellín**, Spain
56 H 6 **Hells Canyon**, Idaho/Oregon, U.S.A. ◇
177 Q 11 **Helmand**, Afghanistan ◘
177 P 10 **Helmand**, Afghanistan ∿
218 H 11 **Helmeringhausen**, Namibia
133 J 15 **Helmond**, Netherlands
124 H 9 **Helmsdale**, United Kingdom
127 T 1 **Helmsley**, United Kingdom
219 Z 6 **Helodrano Antongila**, Madgascar ≈
187 M 14 **Helong**, China
135 E 25 **Helsingborg**, Sweden
135 M 19 **Helsinki**, Finland ⌂
126 J 15 **Helston**, United Kingdom
212 E 8 **Helwân**, Egypt
127 V 9 **Hemel Hempstead**, United Kingdom
66 H 12 **Hemingford**, Nebraska, U.S.A.
136 G 10 **Hemmoor**, Germany
71 R 9 **Hempstead**, Texas, U.S.A.
135 H 18 **Hemränge**, Sweden
127 Z 6 **Hemsby**, United Kingdom
232 K 7 **Hen and Chickens Islands**, New Zealand ⁂
189 T 4 **Henan**, China ◘
198 J 9 **Henashi-zaki**, Japan ▶
60 E 5 **Henderson**, Kentucky, U.S.A.
60 C 9 **Henderson**, Tennessee, U.S.A.
61 S 8 **Henderson**, North Carolina, U.S.A.
71 T 6 **Henderson**, Texas, U.S.A.
60 L 10 **Hendersonville**, North Carolina, U.S.A.
60 F 8 **Hendersonville**, Tennessee, U.S.A.
127 W 10 **Hendon**, United Kingdom
176 J 13 **Hendorābī**, Iran ⁂
105 W 7 **Hendrik Top**, Suriname ▲
234 C 5 **Henganofi**, Papua New Guinea
189 Z 13 **Hengch'un**, Taiwan
188 I 7 **Hengduan Shan**, China ⛰
132 N 11 **Hengelo**, Netherlands
186 N 11 **Hengshan**, China
189 T 9 **Hengshan**, China
187 C 19 **Hengshui**, China
189 Q 12 **Hengxian**, China
189 T 9 **Hengyang**, China
151 U 10 **Heniches'k**, Ukraine
68 M 9 **Hennessey**, Oklahoma, U.S.A.
136 L 12 **Hennigsdorf**, Germany
71 O 4 **Henrietta**, Texas, U.S.A.

Country ◘ Internal administrative region: State/Province/Territory/Dependent territory ⌂ Capital city ⛰ Mountain range/Undersea ridge ▲ Mountain peak/Volcano/Seamount ◇ Geographic feature ▶ Headland/Point/Cape/Peninsula ◓ Desert ⁂ Island/Island group ⊞ Antarctic base ◎ Ocean ◒ Sea ≈ Bay/Gulf/Channel/Strait ◣ Lake ⚑ Salt pan/Dry/Intermittent lake ∿ River

65 F 17 **Henry**, Illinois, U.S.A.
69 P 10 **Henryetta**, Oklahoma, U.S.A.
218 H 9 **Hentiesbaai**, Namibia
185 S 3 **Hentiy**, Mongolia ▣
191 D 15 **Henzada**, Myanmar
189 U 11 **Heping**, China
76 J 10 **Heppner**, Oregon, U.S.A.
189 Q 13 **Hepu**, China
177 P 7 **Herāt**, Afghanistan ▣
177 P 7 **Herāt**, Afghanistan
213 H 15 **Herbagat**, Sudan
137 H 23 **Herbrechtingen**, Germany
145 I 16 **Herceg-Novi**, Serbia and Montenegro
134 C 10 **Herðubreið**, Iceland ▲
91 Q 12 **Heredia**, Costa Rica
127 P 9 **Hereford**, United Kingdom
70 J 3 **Hereford**, Texas, U.S.A.
232 I 5 **Herekino**, New Zealand
131 O 8 **Herencia**, Spain
133 H 17 **Herentals**, Belgium
137 F 14 **Herford**, Germany
69 O 4 **Herington**, Kansas, U.S.A.
138 H 6 **Herisau**, Switzerland
124 K 3 **Herma Ness**, United Kingdom ▶
139 R 9 **Hermagor**, Austria
89 P 6 **Hermanas**, Mexico
69 W 4 **Hermann**, Missouri, U.S.A.
231 N 7 **Hermannsburg**, Northern Territory, Australia
218 K 15 **Hermanus**, Republic of South Africa
76 J 9 **Hermiston**, Oregon, U.S.A.
234 C 2 **Hermit Islands**, Papua New Guinea 🏝
88 I 4 **Hermosillo**, Mexico
62 M 1 **Hernando**, Mississippi, U.S.A.
137 D 15 **Herne**, Germany
127 Z 11 **Herne Bay**, United Kingdom
135 B 24 **Herning**, Denmark
159 S 11 **Herodotus Abyssal Plain**, Mediterranean Sea ◇
159 V 10 **Herodotus Basin**, Mediterranean Sea ◇
159 R 11 **Herodotus Rise**, Mediterranean Sea ◇
159 P 12 **Herodotus Trough**, Mediterranean Sea ◇
112 C 9 **Herradura**, Argentina
137 F 23 **Herrenberg**, Germany
131 N 2 **Herrera de Pisuerga**, Spain
130 M 9 **Herrera del Duque**, Spain
82 A 8 **Herschel Island**, Yukon Territory, Canada 🏝
127 V 9 **Hertford**, United Kingdom
133 K 20 **Herve**, Belgium
231 W 7 **Hervey Bay**, Queensland, Australia ≈
231 W 8 **Hervey Bay**, Queensland, Australia
137 H 15 **Herzberg**, Germany
137 M 15 **Herzberg**, Germany
172 F 9 **Herzliya**, Israel
129 P 2 **Hesdin**, France
136 D 11 **Hesel**, Germany
189 Q 12 **Heshan**, China
41 P 6 **Hess Tablemount**, Pacific Ocean ▲
137 G 18 **Hessen**, Germany ▣
127 O 4 **Heswall**, United Kingdom
183 P 10 **Hetauda**, Nepal
66 H 6 **Hettinger**, North Dakota, U.S.A.
143 K 22 **Heves**, Hungary
188 L 8 **Hexi**, China
189 O 5 **Hexi**, China
189 S 11 **Hexian**, China
189 X 5 **Hexian**, China
127 P 1 **Heysham**, United Kingdom
189 U 12 **Heyuan**, China
189 U 3 **Heze**, China
189 N 9 **Hezhang**, China
185 P 9 **Hezuo**, China
63 Y 13 **Hialeah**, Florida, U.S.A.
69 Q 2 **Hiawatha**, Kansas, U.S.A.
67 T 4 **Hibbing**, Minnesota, U.S.A.
60 B 7 **Hickman**, Kentucky, U.S.A.
61 N 9 **Hickory**, North Carolina, U.S.A.
90 K 1 **Hicks Cay**, Belize 🏝
61 O 5 **Hico**, West Virginia, U.S.A.
71 P 7 **Hico**, Texas, U.S.A.
198 K 6 **Hidaka**, Japan
198 K 6 **Hidaka-sanmyaku**, Japan ⛰
89 Q 11 **Hidalgo**, Mexico ▣
88 M 6 **Hidalgo del Parral**, Mexico
136 L 7 **Hiddensee**, Germany 🏝
139 U 6 **Hieflau**, Austria
235 P 13 **Hienghène**, New Caledonia
199 D 19 **Higashi-Hiroshima**, Japan
199 G 18 **Higashi-ōsaka**, Japan
199 A 21 **Higashi-suidō**, Japan ≈
64 K 12 **Higgins Lake**, Michigan, U.S.A. ≀
210 H 8 **High Atlas**, Morocco ⛰
64 J 10 **High Island**, Michigan, U.S.A. 🏝
71 U 10 **High Island**, Texas, U.S.A.
83 H 15 **High Level**, Alberta, Canada
196 F 10 **High Peak**, Philippines ▲
70 K 1 **High Plains**, Texas, U.S.A. ◇
58 J 11 **High Point**, New Jersey, U.S.A. ▲
61 P 9 **High Point**, North Carolina, U.S.A.
63 V 8 **High Springs**, Florida, U.S.A.
126 M 13 **High Willhays**, United Kingdom ▲
127 U 10 **High Wycombe**, United Kingdom
127 T 11 **Highclere**, United Kingdom
65 H 15 **Highland Park**, Illinois, U.S.A.
60 K 10 **Highlands**, North Carolina, U.S.A.
66 L 9 **Highmore**, South Dakota, U.S.A.
213 M 23 **Hiiraan**, Somalia ▣
148 D 6 **Hiiumaa**, Estonia 🏝
174 K 3 **Hijaz**, Saudi Arabia ⛰
199 H 17 **Hikone**, Japan
232 J 6 **Hikurangi**, New Zealand
232 O 10 **Hikurangi**, New Zealand ▲
137 I 18 **Hildburghausen**, Germany
137 H 14 **Hildesheim**, Germany
183 T 11 **Hili**, Bangladesh
90 K 2 **Hill Bank**, Belize
67 R 5 **Hill City**, Minnesota, U.S.A.
68 J 3 **Hill City**, Kansas, U.S.A.
72 L 11 **Hill City**, Idaho, U.S.A.
241 Q 12 **Hillary Coast**, Antarctica ◇
132 G 11 **Hillegom**, Netherlands
135 D 25 **Hillerød**, Denmark
58 M 8 **Hillsboro**, New Hampshire, U.S.A.
64 E 13 **Hillsboro**, Wisconsin, U.S.A.
65 F 20 **Hillsboro**, Illinois, U.S.A.
65 L 20 **Hillsboro**, Ohio, U.S.A.
71 Q 7 **Hillsboro**, Texas, U.S.A.
93 Y 12 **Hillsborough**, Grenada
231 S 11 **Hillston**, New South Wales, Australia
61 P 7 **Hillsville**, Virginia, U.S.A.
78 E 8 **Hilo**, Hawaii, U.S.A.
197 L 17 **Hilongos**, Philippines
61 O 15 **Hilton Head Island**, South Carolina, U.S.A.
171 O 12 **Hilvan**, Turkey
132 I 11 **Hilversum**, Netherlands
182 J 5 **Himachal Pradesh**, India ▣
182 I 4 **Himalaya**, India ⛰
145 K 21 **Himarë**, Albania
233 K 14 **Himatangi**, New Zealand
181 C 14 **Himatnagar**, India
199 F 18 **Himeji**, Japan
199 H 15 **Himi**, Japan
172 I 5 **Ḥimṣ**, Syria
197 N 20 **Hinatuan**, Philippines
151 N 9 **Hînceşti**, Moldova
93 P 7 **Hinche**, Haiti
231 T 4 **Hinchinbrook Island**, Queensland, Australia 🏝
79 S 10 **Hinchinbrook Island**, Alaska, U.S.A. 🏝
127 S 7 **Hinckley**, United Kingdom
67 S 6 **Hinckley**, Minnesota, U.S.A.
216 F 10 **Hinda**, Congo
180 E 12 **Hindaun**, India
127 U 12 **Hindhead**, United Kingdom
233 G 21 **Hinds**, New Zealand
177 U 6 **Hindu Kush**, Afghanistan ⛰
181 E 20 **Hindupur**, India
181 F 16 **Hinganghat**, India
171 R 10 **Hinis**, Turkey
197 I 18 **Hinobaan**, Philippines
139 N 7 **Hintertux**, Austria
199 A 21 **Hirado**, Japan
181 H 15 **Hirakud Reservoir**, India ≀
199 O 26 **Hirara**, Japan
181 E 20 **Hiriyur**, India
198 L 6 **Hiroo**, Japan
198 J 9 **Hirosaki**, Japan
199 D 19 **Hiroshima**, Japan
129 S 2 **Hirson**, France
182 H 8 **Hisar**, India
170 G 7 **Hisarönü**, Turkey
93 O 6 **Hispaniola**, Dominican Republic 🏝
172 I 5 **Ḥisyah**, Syria
173 R 6 **Hīt**, Iraq
199 C 21 **Hita**, Japan
199 L 14 **Hitachi**, Japan
181 L 20 **Hitaddu**, Maldives
127 V 9 **Hitchin**, United Kingdom
199 C 23 **Hitoyoshi**, Japan
135 C 15 **Hitra**, Norway 🏝
235 P 9 **Hiu**, Vanuatu 🏝
199 J 14 **Hiuchiga-take**, Japan ▲
199 F 20 **Hiwasa**, Japan
82 I 13 **Hjalmar Lake**, Northwest Territories, Canada ≀
135 G 21 **Hjälmaren**, Sweden ≀
135 C 23 **Hjørring**, Denmark
190 F 5 **Hkakabo Razi**, Myanmar ▲
219 P 11 **Hlatikulu**, Swaziland
151 S 5 **Hlobyne**, Ukraine
143 H 21 **Hlohovec**, Slovakia
151 T 1 **Hlukhiv**, Ukraine
149 K 19 **Hlusk**, Belarus
149 J 15 **Hlybokaye**, Belarus
191 M 22 **Hô Chi Minh**, Vietnam
190 K 12 **Hô Sông Đa**, Vietnam ≀
190 K 11 **Hô Thac Ba**, Vietnam ≀
190 L 12 **Hoa Binh**, Vietnam
190 K 11 **Hoang Liên Son**, Vietnam ⛰
231 T 15 **Hobart**, Tasmania, Australia
68 K 11 **Hobart**, Oklahoma, U.S.A.
75 U 13 **Hobbs**, New Mexico, U.S.A.
240 L 11 **Hobbs Coast**, Antarctica ◇
63 Y 11 **Hobe Sound**, Florida, U.S.A.
135 C 24 **Hobro**, Denmark
213 N 22 **Hobyo**, Somalia
139 R 8 **Hochalmspitze**, Austria ▲
138 F 7 **Hochdorf**, Switzerland
218 I 9 **Hochfeld**, Namibia
139 T 6 **Hochreichart**, Austria ▲
139 U 5 **Hochschwab**, Austria ⛰
140 F 4 **Hochwilde**, Austria/Italy ▲
199 H 15 **Hodaka-dake**, Japan ▲
60 G 6 **Hodgenville**, Kentucky, U.S.A.
214 I 7 **Hodh Ech Chargui**, Mauritania ▣
214 I 7 **Hodh El Gharbi**, Mauritania ▣
143 K 25 **Hódmezővásárhely**, Hungary
143 G 20 **Hodonín**, Czech Republic
185 O 3 **Hödrögö**, Mongolia
132 F 13 **Hoek van Holland**, Netherlands
187 M 19 **Hoengsŏng**, South Korea
133 K 18 **Hoensbroek**, Netherlands
187 N 14 **Hoeryŏng**, North Korea
187 L 18 **Hoeyang**, North Korea
137 K 18 **Hof**, Germany
134 D 11 **Höfn**, Iceland
134 C 11 **Hofsjökull**, Iceland ◇
134 B 10 **Hofsós**, Iceland
199 C 20 **Hōfu**, Japan
61 W 6 **Hog Island**, Virginia, U.S.A. 🏝
66 G 13 **Hogback Mountain**, Nebraska, U.S.A. ▲
211 O 14 **Hoggar**, Algeria ⛰
135 G 23 **Högsby**, Sweden
184 M 8 **Hoh Sai Hu**, China ≀
139 O 7 **Hohe Tauern**, Austria ⛰
139 Y 2 **Hohenau an der March**, Austria
139 S 6 **Hoher Dachstein**, Austria ▲
151 Q 3 **Hoholiv**, Ukraine
191 O 17 **Hôi An**, Vietnam
190 L 13 **Hôi Xuân**, Vietnam
217 R 7 **Hoima**, Uganda
68 L 5 **Hoisington**, Kansas, U.S.A.
183 W 11 **Hojai**, India
232 H 6 **Hokianga Harbour**, New Zealand ≈
233 F 19 **Hokitika**, New Zealand
198 K 5 **Hokkaidō**, Japan 🏝
199 L 15 **Hokota**, Japan
171 T 9 **Hoktemberyan**, Armenia
217 X 9 **Hola**, Kenya
151 S 10 **Hola Prystan**, Ukraine
181 D 20 **Holalkere**, India
107 K 18 **Holanda**, Bolivia
127 W 6 **Holbeach**, United Kingdom
73 O 13 **Holbrook**, Idaho, U.S.A.
74 L 10 **Holbrook**, Arizona, U.S.A.
74 J 5 **Holden**, Utah, U.S.A.
127 V 2 **Holderness**, United Kingdom ◇
66 L 15 **Holdrege**, Nebraska, U.S.A.
92 L 6 **Holguín**, Cuba
143 G 20 **Holíč**, Slovakia
135 E 18 **Höljes**, Sweden
139 X 2 **Hollabrunn**, Austria
65 I 14 **Holland**, Michigan, U.S.A.
133 G 14 **Hollands Diep**, Netherlands ≈
133 K 24 **Hollange**, Belgium
58 D 13 **Hollidaysburg**, Pennsylvania, U.S.A.
68 J 11 **Hollis**, Oklahoma, U.S.A.
77 G 21 **Hollister**, California, U.S.A.
132 J 5 **Hollum**, Netherlands
61 T 11 **Holly Ridge**, North Carolina, U.S.A.
62 L 1 **Holly Springs**, Mississippi, U.S.A.
63 Y 13 **Hollywood**, Florida, U.S.A.
134 B 10 **Hólmavík**, Iceland
127 T 2 **Holme-upon-Spalding-Moor**, United Kingdom
127 R 3 **Holmfirth**, United Kingdom
234 E 6 **Holnicote Bay**, Papua New Guinea ≈
150 J 2 **Holoby**, Ukraine
172 F 9 **Ḥolon**, Israel
218 J 12 **Holoog**, Namibia
63 X 10 **Holopaw**, Florida, U.S.A.
135 B 24 **Holstebro**, Denmark
67 Q 12 **Holstein**, Iowa, U.S.A.
126 L 13 **Holsworthy**, United Kingdom
127 Y 5 **Holt**, United Kingdom
132 L 11 **Holten**, Netherlands
151 V 6 **Holubivka**, Ukraine
132 K 6 **Holwerd**, Netherlands
79 N 8 **Holy Cross**, Alaska, U.S.A.
126 L 4 **Holy Island**, United Kingdom 🏝
126 L 4 **Holyhead**, United Kingdom
126 L 4 **Holyhead Bay**, United Kingdom ≈
58 L 10 **Holyoke**, Massachusetts, U.S.A.
75 U 3 **Holyoke**, Colorado, U.S.A.
127 O 4 **Holywell**, United Kingdom
137 J 25 **Holzkirchen**, Germany
137 G 15 **Holzminden**, Germany
217 T 8 **Homa Bay**, Kenya
190 C 8 **Homalin**, Myanmar
137 D 21 **Homburg**, Germany
85 R 1 **Home Bay**, Nunavut, Canada ≈
39 Z 2 **Home Island**, Cocos Islands 🏝
39 Z 2 **Home Island Settlement**, Cocos Islands
149 L 20 **Homel'skaya Voblasts'**, Belarus ▣
62 I 4 **Homer**, Louisiana, U.S.A.
79 Q 10 **Homer**, Alaska, U.S.A.
63 U 6 **Homerville**, Georgia, U.S.A.
63 Y 14 **Homestead**, Florida, U.S.A.
134 F 12 **Hommelstø**, Norway
181 E 18 **Homnabad**, India
219 R 10 **Homoine**, Mozambique
197 M 17 **Homonhon**, Philippines 🏝
149 N 20 **Homyel'**, Belarus
191 L 24 **Hon Khoai**, Vietnam 🏝
191 L 23 **Hon Rai**, Vietnam 🏝
104 I 6 **Honda**, Colombia
197 D 18 **Honda Bay**, Philippines ≈
199 B 22 **Hondo**, Japan
71 N 11 **Hondo**, Texas, U.S.A.
75 R 12 **Hondo**, New Mexico, U.S.A.
90 J 1 **Hondo**, Belize ∽
90 L 5 **Honduras**, North America □
60 L 12 **Honea Path**, South Carolina, U.S.A.
135 D 19 **Hønefoss**, Norway
77 I 16 **Honey Lake**, California, U.S.A. ≀
190 N 12 **Hông Gai**, Vietnam
189 U 13 **Hong Kong**, China
189 U 13 **Hong Kong**, China ▣
189 U 6 **Hong'an**, China
187 M 18 **Hongch'ŏn**, South Korea
189 V 12 **Honghai Wan**, China ≈
189 T 7 **Honghu**, China
189 R 9 **Hongjiang**, China
185 N 6 **Hongliuyuan**, China
185 S 4 **Hongor**, Mongolia
189 P 11 **Hongshui He**, China ∽
185 S 2 **Hongtong**, China
199 H 19 **Hongū**, Japan
186 M 8 **Hongxing**, China
188 M 7 **Hongya**, China
188 M 5 **Hongyuan**, China
189 X 4 **Hongze**, China
189 X 4 **Hongze Hu**, China ≀
234 L 6 **Honiara**, Solomon Islands ⌂
127 O 13 **Honiton**, United Kingdom
198 J 11 **Honjō**, Japan
134 K 5 **Honningsvåg**, Norway
78 E 8 **Honokaa**, Hawaii, U.S.A.
78 D 9 **Honokohau**, Hawaii, U.S.A.
78 C 7 **Honolulu**, Hawaii, U.S.A.
199 H 17 **Honshū**, Japan 🏝
132 G 11 **Hoofddorp**, Netherlands
136 F 7 **Hooge**, Germany 🏝
132 M 8 **Hoogersmilde**, Netherlands
132 M 9 **Hoogeveen**, Netherlands
132 I 9 **Hoogkarspel**, Netherlands
127 T 11 **Hook**, United Kingdom
125 E 20 **Hook Head**, Republic of Ireland ▶
68 H 7 **Hooker**, Oklahoma, U.S.A.
79 W 10 **Hoonah**, Alaska, U.S.A.
78 L 8 **Hooper Bay**, Alaska, U.S.A.
132 I 9 **Hoorn**, Netherlands
65 K 19 **Hoosier Hill**, Indiana, U.S.A. ▲
185 P 4 **Höövör**, Mongolia
171 Q 7 **Hopa**, Turkey
127 P 5 **Hope**, United Kingdom
69 T 13 **Hope**, Arkansas, U.S.A.
79 R 9 **Hope**, Alaska, U.S.A.
83 G 22 **Hope**, British Columbia, Canada
62 M 8 **Hopedale**, Louisiana, U.S.A.
85 V 7 **Hopedale**, Newfoundla and Labrador, Canada
89 Y 11 **Hopelchén**, Mexico
230 I 12 **Hopetoun**, Western Australia, Australia
231 R 12 **Hopetoun**, Victoria, Australia
218 M 13 **Hopetown**, Republic of South Africa
190 E 8 **Hopin**, Myanmar
60 E 7 **Hopkinsville**, Kentucky, U.S.A.
190 E 12 **Hopong**, Myanmar
76 F 7 **Hoquiam**, Washington, U.S.A.
150 J 7 **Hora Hoverla**, Ukraine
171 R 9 **Horasan**, Turkey
131 N 8 **Horcajo de los Montes**, Spain
185 O 3 **Horgo**, Mongolia
151 N 12 **Horia**, Romania
187 A 16 **Horinger**, China
41 P 10 **Horizon Deep**, Pacific Ocean ▲
149 N 16 **Horki**, Belarus
241 N 8 **Horlick Mountains**, Antarctica ⛰
151 X 6 **Horlivka**, Ukraine
177 O 11 **Hormak**, Iran
176 L 13 **Hormoz**, Iran 🏝
176 L 12 **Hormozgān**, Iran ▣
139 W 2 **Horn**, Austria
231 R 1 **Horn Island**, Queenslan Australia 🏝
63 N 8 **Horn Island**, Mississippi, U.S.A. 🏝
82 F 13 **Horn Mountains**, Northwest Territories, Canada ⛰
134 H 12 **Hornavan**, Sweden ≀
77 G 14 **Hornbrook**, California, U.S.A.
127 V 4 **Horncastle**, United Kingdom
91 T 14 **Hornconcitos**, Panama
58 E 9 **Hornell**, New York, U.S.
85 N 11 **Hornepayne**, Ontario, Canada
127 V 2 **Hornsea**, United Kingd
150 K 6 **Horodenka**, Ukraine
151 Q 1 **Horodnya**, Ukraine
151 Q 5 **Horodyshche**, Ukraine
198 J 3 **Horonobe**, Japan
198 K 6 **Horoshiri-dake**, Japan ▲
232 K 10 **Horotiu**, New Zealand
185 W 4 **Horqin Zouyi Zhongqi**, China
187 H 14 **Horqin Zuoyi Houqi**, China
186 I 13 **Horqin Zuoyi Zhongqi**, China
181 L 17 **Horsburgh Atoll**, Maldives 🏝
39 Y 1 **Horsburgh Island**, Cocos Islands 🏝
135 C 25 **Horsens**, Denmark
72 K 10 **Horseshoe Bend**, Idaho, U.S.A.
42 J 9 **Horseshoe Seamounts**, Atlantic Ocean ▲
231 R 13 **Horsham**, Victoria, Australia
127 V 12 **Horsham**, United Kingdom
133 L 16 **Horst**, Netherlands
42 N 1 **Horta**, Azores
69 Q 2 **Horton**, Kansas, U.S.A.
82 E 8 **Horton**, Northwest Territories, Canada ∽
138 F 8 **Horw**, Switzerland
127 Q 3 **Horwich**, United Kingdo
150 L 4 **Horyn**, Ukraine ∽
213 I 21 **Hosa'ina**, Ethiopia
181 D 21 **Hosdrug**, India
215 U 12 **Hoséré Vokre**, Cameroon ▲
177 R 14 **Hoshab**, Pakistan
181 E 15 **Hoshangabad**, India
182 I 6 **Hoshiarpur**, India

□ Country ▣ Internal administrative region: State/Province/Territory/Dependent territory ⌂ Capital city ⛰ Mountain range/Undersea ridge ▲ Mountain peak/Volcano/Seamount ◇ Geographic feature ▶ Headland/Point/Cape/Peninsula ☗ Desert 🏝 Island/Island group ⁙ Antarctic base 🌀 Ocean ∿ Sea ≈ Bay/Gulf/Channel/Strait ≀ Lake ⚑ Salt pan/Dry/Intermittent lake ∽ R

Country ▣ Internal administrative region: State/Province/Territory/Dependent territory · ⚓ Capital city · ▲ Mountain range/Undersea ridge · ▲ Mountain peak/Volcano/Seamount · ✦ Geographic feature · ▶ Headland/Point/Cape/Peninsula · ▲ Desert · ✖ Island/Island group · ⠿ Antarctic base · ⦿ Ocean · ● Sea · ≈ Bay/Gulf/Channel/Strait · ↳ Lake · ↳ Salt pan/Dry/Intermittent lake · ↳ River

295

38 K 6 **Île Tromelin**, Indian Ocean 🏝
235 R 14 **Île Walpole**, New Caledonia 🏝
216 K 10 **Ilebo**, Democratic Republic of Congo
157 V 5 **Ilek**, Russian Federation
178 J 4 **Ilek**, Kazakhstan
217 U 5 **Ileret**, Kenya
235 O 13 **Îles Bélep**, New Caledonia 🏝
128 K 4 **Îles Chausey**, France 🏝
234 L 12 **Îles Chesterfield**, New Caledonia 🏝
128 H 6 **Îles de Glénan**, France 🏝
129 W 15 **Îles de Hyères**, France 🏝
87 X 7 **Îles de la Madeleine**, Québec, Canada 🏝
87 U 3 **Îles de Mingan**, Québec, Canada 🏝
219 Y 4 **Îles Glorieuses**, Seychelles 🏝
211 R 6 **Îles Kerkenah**, Tunisia 🏝
215 P 12 **Ilesa**, Nigeria
127 W 10 **Ilford**, United Kingdom
126 M 11 **Ilfracombe**, United Kingdom
170 I 8 **Ilgaz**, Turkey
170 I 8 **Ilgaz Dağlari**, Turkey
170 G 11 **Ilgin**, Turkey
108 J 9 **Ilha Caviana**, Brazil 🏝
112 K 8 **Ilha Comprida**, Brazil 🏝
108 J 9 **Ilha Curuá**, Brazil 🏝
42 O 5 **Ilha da Madeira**, Madeira 🏝
43 I 16 **Ilha da Trindade**, Brazil 🏝
112 J 8 **Ilha das Peças**, Brazil 🏝
108 J 8 **Ilha de Maracá**, Brazil 🏝
108 J 9 **Ilha de Marajó**, Brazil 🏝
42 O 4 **Ilha de Porto Santo**, Madeira 🏝
112 J 10 **Ilha de Santa Catarina**, Brazil 🏝
112 J 9 **Ilha de São Francisco**, Brazil 🏝
112 L 7 **Ilha de São Sebastião**, Brazil 🏝
219 R 8 **Ilha do Bazaruto**, Mozambique 🏝
112 O 7 **Ilha do Cabo Frio**, Brazil 🏝
112 K 8 **Ilha do Cardoso**, Brazil 🏝
112 M 7 **Ilha Grande**, Brazil 🏝
108 J 9 **Ilha Janaucu**, Brazil 🏝
108 J 9 **Ilha Mexiana**, Brazil 🏝
42 O 5 **Ilhas Desertas**, Madeira 🏝
43 I 16 **Ilhas Martin Vas**, Atlantic Ocean 🏝
109 N 15 **Ilhéus**, Brazil
150 G 10 **Ilia**, Romania
79 O 10 **Iliamna Lake**, Alaska, U.S.A. 💧
171 N 10 **Ilic**, Turkey
197 K 21 **Iligan**, Philippines
197 K 20 **Iligan Bay**, Philippines ≈
196 I 5 **Iligan Point**, Philippines ▶
197 G 15 **Ilin**, Philippines 🏝
155 S 12 **Il'inskiy**, Russian Federation
193 R 15 **Iliomar**, East Timor
171 R 12 **Ilisu Baraji**, Turkey 💧
127 R 2 **Ilkley**, United Kingdom
197 K 21 **Illana Bay**, Philippines ≈
110 F 10 **Illapel**, Chile
137 H 24 **Illertissen**, Germany
151 Q 10 **Illichivs'k**, Ukraine
65 D 17 **Illinois**, U.S.A. ▣
65 E 18 **Illinois**, Illinois, U.S.A. 〰
151 O 6 **Illintsi**, Ukraine
211 Q 11 **Illizi**, Algeria
137 I 18 **Ilmenau**, Germany
127 P 13 **Ilminster**, United Kingdom
107 G 20 **Ilo**, Peru
197 E 16 **Iloc**, Philippines 🏝
197 I 17 **Iloilo**, Philippines
215 P 12 **Ilorin**, Nigeria
157 O 8 **Ilovlya**, Russian Federation
143 E 14 **Iłowa**, Poland
153 Y 9 **Il'pyrskiy**, Russian Federation
128 I 6 **Îls de Groix**, France 🏝
148 H 13 **Ilūkste**, Latvia
45 N 12 **Ilulissat**, Greenland
149 I 16 **Il'ya**, Belarus
199 D 20 **Imabari**, Japan
198 J 8 **Imabetsu**, Japan
173 U 9 **Imām al Hamzah**, Iraq
173 U 7 **Imām Ḩamid**, Iraq
170 K 13 **Imamoğlu**, Turkey
199 B 21 **Imari**, Japan
42 F 6 **Imarssuak Seachannel**, Atlantic Ocean ≈
107 G 19 **Imata**, Peru
135 O 18 **Imatra**, Finland
106 B 8 **Imbabura**, Ecuador ▣
213 K 22 **Īmī**, Ethiopia
210 G 8 **Imi-n-Tanoute**, Morocco
171 X 9 **Imişli**, Azerbaijan
77 K 16 **Imlay**, Nevada, U.S.A.
210 B 12 **Imlili**, Western Sahara
137 H 26 **Immenstadt**, Germany
127 V 3 **Immingham**, United Kingdom
63 X 12 **Immokalee**, Florida, U.S.A.
215 R 13 **Imo**, Nigeria ▣
140 G 9 **Imola**, Italy
234 A 3 **Imonda**, Papua New Guinea
108 K 11 **Imperatriz**, Brazil
140 B 10 **Imperia**, Italy
107 D 17 **Imperial**, Peru
66 I 15 **Imperial**, Nebraska, U.S.A.
216 J 7 **Impfondo**, Congo
183 X 12 **Imphal**, India
170 D 8 **Imrali**, Turkey 🏝
170 A 8 **Imroz**, Turkey
138 L 7 **Imst**, Austria
172 I 8 **Imtān**, Syria
88 I 3 **Imuris**, Mexico
197 D 17 **Imuruan Bay**, Philippines ≈
211 Q 10 **In Aménas**, Algeria
211 O 13 **In Amguel**, Algeria
211 O 13 **In Ekker**, Algeria
210 M 11 **In Salah**, Algeria
199 I 16 **Ina**, Japan
43 N 16 **Inaccessible Island**, Tristan da Cunha 🏝
233 G 17 **Inangahua Junction**, New Zealand
193 U 12 **Inanwatan**, Indonesia
107 H 16 **Iñapari**, Peru
134 L 8 **Inari**, Finland
153 Q 10 **Inarigda**, Russian Federation
134 M 8 **Inarijärvi**, Finland 💧
198 J 13 **Inawashiro-ko**, Japan 💧
110 G 7 **Inca de Oro**, Chile
170 J 6 **Ince Burun**, Turkey ▶
170 I 14 **Incekum Burnu**, Turkey ▶
214 F 5 **Inchiri**, Mauritania ▣
187 L 19 **Inch'ŏn**, South Korea
133 H 20 **Incourt**, Belgium
148 F 11 **Inčukalns**, Latvia
213 I 17 **Inda Silasē**, Ethiopia
135 F 15 **Indalsälven**, Sweden 〰
190 E 12 **Indaw**, Myanmar
69 S 3 **Independence**, Missouri, U.S.A.
45 R 10 **Independence Fjord**, Greenland ≈
69 P 7 **Indepenence**, Kansas, U.S.A.
186 I 10 **Inder**, China
178 I 6 **Inderborskiy**, Kazakhstan
183 O 11 **India**, Asia □
85 W 7 **Indian Harbour**, Newfoundland and Labrador, Canada
61 U 4 **Indian Head**, Maryland, U.S.A.
65 L 18 **Indian Lake**, Ohio, U.S.A. 💧
39 P 7 **Indian Ocean** 🌊
77 M 21 **Indian Springs**, Nevada, U.S.A.
74 M 10 **Indian Wells**, Arizona, U.S.A.
58 C 12 **Indiana**, Pennsylvania, U.S.A.
65 H 18 **Indiana**, U.S.A. ▣
65 I 19 **Indianapolis**, Indiana, U.S.A.
62 L 3 **Indianola**, Mississippi, U.S.A.
67 S 13 **Indianola**, Iowa, U.S.A.
39 U 14 **Indian–Antarctic Basin**, Indian Ocean ◇
39 U 12 **Indian–Antarctic Ridge**, Indian Ocean ⛰
155 O 3 **Indiga**, Russian Federation
153 U 7 **Indigirka**, Russian Federation 〰
77 L 25 **Indio**, California, U.S.A.
234 M 6 **Indispensable Strait**, Solomon Islands ≈
191 M 19 **Indochina Peninsula**, Cambodia ◇
192 H 13 **Indonesia**, Asia □
181 D 15 **Indore**, India
181 G 17 **Indravati**, India 〰
149 E 18 **Indura**, Belarus
177 W 9 **Indus**, India/Pakistan 〰
170 I 6 **Inebolu**, Turkey
170 E 9 **Inegöl**, Turkey
196 H 11 **Infanta**, Philippines
130 M 1 **Infiesto**, Spain
215 Q 7 **Ingal**, Niger
216 J 8 **Ingende**, Democratic Republic of Congo
110 K 5 **Ingeniero Guillermo Neuva Juárez**, Argentina
111 G 17 **Ingeniero Jacobacci**, Argentina
231 T 4 **Ingham**, Queensland, Australia
127 Q 1 **Ingleborough**, United Kingdom ▲
127 Q 1 **Ingleton**, United Kingdom
232 J 12 **Inglewood**, New Zealand
127 W 4 **Ingoldmells**, United Kingdom
137 J 22 **Ingolstadt**, Germany
73 V 5 **Ingomar**, Montana, U.S.A.
87 Y 7 **Ingonish**, Nova Scotia, Canada
183 S 11 **Ingraj Bazar**, India
241 W 6 **Ingrid Christensen Coast**, Antarctica ◇
219 R 10 **Inhambane**, Mozambique
219 Q 9 **Inhambane**, Mozambique ▣
219 R 7 **Inhaminga**, Mozambique
219 R 10 **Inharrime**, Mozambique
151 R 8 **Inhul**, Ukraine 〰
151 S 8 **Inhulets**, Ukraine 〰
125 A 17 **Inishbofin**, Republic of Ireland 🏝
125 B 18 **Inisheer**, Republic of Ireland 🏝
125 B 18 **Inishmore**, Republic of Ireland 🏝
125 A 17 **Inishturk**, Republic of Ireland 🏝
186 F 12 **Injgan Sum**, China
213 H 19 **Injibara**, Ethiopia
231 U 8 **Injune**, Queensland, Australia
233 I 18 **Inland Kaikoura Range**, New Zealand ⛰
60 M 10 **Inman**, South Carolina, U.S.A.
137 K 24 **Inn**, Germany 〰
231 Q 8 **Innamincka**, South Australia, Australia
124 E 13 **Inner Hebrides**, United Kingdom 🏝
38 B 9 **Inner Islands**, Seychelles 🏝
186 E 12 **Inner Mongolia**, China ▣
138 F 9 **Innertkirchen**, Switzerland
231 T 4 **Innisfail**, Queensland, Australia
138 M 7 **Innsbruck**, Austria
216 J 9 **Inongo**, Democratic Republic of Congo
142 H 11 **Inowrocław**, Poland
107 J 20 **Inquisivi**, Bolivia
138 C 7 **Ins**, Switzerland
150 M 12 **Insurăţei**, Romania
155 T 4 **Inta**, Russian Federation
138 E 9 **Interlaken**, Switzerland
67 S 2 **International Falls**, Minnesota, U.S.A.
181 N 21 **Interview Island**, India 🏝
112 C 11 **Intiyaco**, Argentina
150 K 11 **Întorsura Buzăului**, Romania
154 K 5 **Intsy**, Russian Federation
106 E 10 **Intutu**, Peru
199 L 15 **Inubō-zaki**, Japan ▶
85 P 6 **Inukjuak**, Québec, Canada
82 C 9 **Inuvik**, Northwest Territories, Canada
124 G 12 **Inveraray**, United Kingdom
233 C 25 **Invercargill**, New Zealand
231 V 10 **Inverell**, New South Wales, Australia
124 H 10 **Inverness**, United Kingdom
63 V 9 **Inverness**, Florida, U.S.A.
87 X 8 **Inverness**, Nova Scotia, Canada
39 R 4 **Investigator Ridge**, Indian Ocean ⛰
152 M 13 **Inya**, Russian Federation
219 Q 7 **Inyangani**, Zimbabwe ▲
77 K 22 **Inyocern**, California, U.S.A.
217 S 12 **Inyonga**, Tanzania
157 Q 3 **Inza**, Russian Federation
157 X 2 **Inzer**, Russian Federation
199 C 25 **Iō-jima**, Japan 🏝
199 N 23 **Iō-Tori-jima**, Japan 🏝
147 B 16 **Ioannina**, Greece
69 Q 6 **Iola**, Kansas, U.S.A.
218 G 6 **Iona**, Angola
124 E 12 **Iona**, United Kingdom 🏝
87 Y 8 **Iona**, Nova Scotia, Canada
150 I 12 **Ioneşti**, Romania
65 K 14 **Ionia**, Michigan, U.S.A.
159 O 9 **Ionian Basin**, Mediterranean Sea ◇
147 A 17 **Ionian Islands**, Greece 🏝
159 P 9 **Ionian Sea**, Mediterannean ◒
147 B 17 **Ionioi Nisoi**, Greece ▣
147 J 23 **Ios**, Greece 🏝
62 I 7 **Iowa**, Louisiana, U.S.A.
67 R 12 **Iowa**, U.S.A. ▣
67 V 13 **Iowa City**, Iowa, U.S.A.
67 T 11 **Iowa Falls**, Iowa, U.S.A.
90 I 6 **Ipala**, Guatemala
109 L 17 **Ipatinga**, Brazil
157 N 11 **Ipatovo**, Russian Federation
147 B 16 **Ipeiros**, Greece ▣
143 I 21 **Ipel**, Slovakia 〰
104 G 9 **Ipiales**, Colombia
197 I 21 **Ipil**, Philippines
112 I 8 **Ipiranga**, Brazil
108 A 13 **Ipixuna**, Brazil
194 B 7 **Ipoh**, Malaysia
216 L 4 **Ippy**, Central African Republic
170 B 7 **Ipsala**, Turkey
231 W 9 **Ipswich**, Queensland, Australia
127 Z 8 **Ipswich**, United Kingdom
108 M 11 **Ipu**, Brazil
85 R 3 **Iqaluit**, Nunavut, Canada
185 N 7 **Iqe**, China
107 F 19 **Iquipi**, Peru
110 F 3 **Iquique**, Chile
106 F 11 **Iquitos**, Peru
216 L 4 **Ira Banda**, Central African Republic
199 N 26 **Irabu-jima**, Japan 🏝
199 I 18 **Irago-misaki**, Japan ▶
112 G 10 **Iraí**, Brazil
147 J 23 **Irakleia**, Greece 🏝
146 F 13 **Irakleia**, Greece
0 J 26 **Irakleiou**, Greece
109 M 15 **Iramaia**, Brazil
176 K 7 **Iran**, Asia □
176 K 9 **Iranian Plateau**, Iran ◇
177 O 13 **Īrānshahr**, Iran
89 P 11 **Irapuato**, Mexico
173 R 8 **Iraq**, Asia □
112 I 9 **Irati**, Brazil
155 R 6 **Irayel'**, Russian Federation
148 C 9 **Irbe Strait**, Estonia/Latvia ≈
172 H 8 **Irbid**, Jordan
109 M 14 **Irecê**, Brazil
125 D 17 **Ireland, Republic of**, Europe □
42 A 7 **Ireland Island**, Bermuda 🏝
179 N 6 **Irgiz**, Kazakhstan
210 H 8 **Irhil M'Goun**, Morocco ▲
176 F 4 **Īrī Dāgh**, Iran ▲
193 W 12 **Irian Jaya**, Indonesia ▣
215 Z 8 **Iriba**, Chad
196 J 13 **Iriga**, Philippines
217 U 12 **Iringa**, Tanzania ▣
217 U 12 **Iringa**, Tanzania
199 M 26 **Iriomote-jima**, Japan 🏝
91 O 4 **Iriona**, Honduras
108 H 11 **Iriri**, Brazil 〰
125 G 17 **Irish Sea**, Republic of Ireland/United Kingdom ◒
108 K 10 **Irituia**, Brazil
153 P 14 **Irkutsk**, Russian Federation
179 N 10 **Irlir Toghi**, Uzbekistan ▲
170 I 9 **Irmak**, Turkey
42 H 5 **Irminger Basin**, Atlantic Ocean ◇
199 J 18 **Irō-zaki**, Japan ▶
64 H 9 **Iron Mountain**, Michigan, U.S.A.
64 G 9 **Iron River**, Michigan, U.S.A.
65 M 21 **Ironton**, Ohio, U.S.A.
64 E 8 **Ironwood**, Michigan, U.S.A.
86 E 6 **Iroquois Falls**, Ontario, Canada
151 P 3 **Irpin'**, Ukraine
175 R 14 **Īrqah**, Yemen
190 C 13 **Irrawaddy**, Myanmar 〰
191 C 17 **Irrawaddy**, Myanmar ▣
151 N 3 **Irsha**, Ukraine 〰
152 K 10 **Irtysh**, Russian Federation 〰
179 U 2 **Irtyshsk**, Kazakhstan
199 K 16 **Iruma**, Japan
107 I 19 **Irupana**, Bolivia
71 Q 5 **Irving**, Texas, U.S.A.
60 F 5 **Irvington**, Kentucky, U.S.A.
233 G 20 **Irwell**, New Zealand
215 Q 9 **Isa**, Nigeria
234 L 5 **Isabel**, Solomon Islands ▣
66 I 7 **Isabel**, South Dakota, U.S.A.
197 H 23 **Isabela**, Philippines
151 N 11 **Isaccea**, Romania
134 A 10 **Ísafjörður**, Iceland
199 B 22 **Isahaya**, Japan
216 L 8 **Isanga**, Democratic Republic of Congo
215 Q 12 **Isanlu**, Nigeria
138 K 8 **Ischgl**, Austria
141 J 16 **Ischia**, Italy
199 H 18 **Ise**, Japan
199 H 18 **Ise-wan**, Japan ≈
41 Q 15 **Iselin Seamount**, Pacific Ocean ▲
217 N 7 **Isengi**, Democratic Republic of Congo
141 J 14 **Isernia**, Italy
215 P 12 **Iseyin**, Nigeria
179 R 12 **Isfana**, Kyrgyzstan
173 U 9 **Ishaq**, Iraq
199 N 26 **Ishigaki**, Japan
199 N 26 **Ishigaki-jima**, Japan 🏝
198 J 5 **Ishikari-wan**, Japan ≈
199 N 24 **Ishikawa**, Japan
152 K 11 **Ishim**, Russian Federation
198 L 12 **Ishinomaki**, Japan
199 E 20 **Ishizuchi-san**, Japan ▲
179 Q 12 **Ishtykhan**, Uzbekistan
183 T 12 **Ishurdi**, Bangladesh
152 K 11 **Isil'kul'**, Russian Federation
217 V 7 **Isiolo**, Kenya
217 P 6 **Isiro**, Democratic Republic of Congo
231 S 7 **Isisford**, Queensland, Australia
170 L 13 **Iskenderun**, Turkey
170 K 13 **Iskenderun Körfezi**, Turkey ≈
170 J 8 **Iskilip**, Turkey
146 H 7 **Iskŭr**, Bulgaria 〰
213 O 19 **Iskushuban**, Somalia
41 W 2 **Isla Alejandro Selkirk**, Juan Fernández Islands 🏝
88 H 4 **Isla Ángel de la Guarda**, Mexico 🏝
111 G 25 **Isla Aracena**, Chile 🏝
107 B 18 **Isla Baltra**, Ecuador 🏝
93 P 8 **Isla Beata**, Dominican Republic 🏝
105 P 1 **Isla Blanquilla**, Venezuela 🏝
111 E 21 **Isla Campana**, Chile 🏝
88 I 7 **Isla Carmen**, Mexico 🏝
88 F 5 **Isla Cedros**, Mexico 🏝
88 J 8 **Isla Cerralvo**, Mexico 🏝
111 F 23 **Isla Chatham**, Chile 🏝
111 G 25 **Isla Clarence**, Chile 🏝
105 Q 2 **Isla Coche**, Venezuela 🏝
91 T 15 **Isla Coiba**, Panama 🏝
111 F 24 **Isla Contreras**, Chile 🏝
89 W 12 **Isla de Aguada**, Mexico
131 P 15 **Isla de Alborán**, Spain 🏝
88 K 8 **Isla de Altamura**, Mexico 🏝
215 R 15 **Isla de Bioco**, Equatorial Guinea 🏝
91 Q 14 **Isla de Caño**, Costa Rica 🏝
111 E 18 **Isla de Chiloé**, Chile 🏝
91 T 13 **Isla de Colón**, Panama 🏝
89 Z 11 **Isla de Cozumel**, Mexico 🏝
91 N 3 **Isla de Guanaja**, Honduras 🏝
92 G 5 **Isla de la Juventud**, Cuba 🏝
111 J 26 **Isla de los Estados**, Argentina 🏝
105 Q 2 **Isla de Margarita**, Venezuela 🏝
91 O 10 **Isla de Ometepe**, Nicaragua 🏝
91 N 3 **Isla de Roatán**, Honduras 🏝
90 M 4 **Isla de Utila**, Honduras 🏝
91 Y 14 **Isla del Rey**, Panama 🏝
91 R 9 **Isla del Venado**, Nicaragua 🏝
111 F 25 **Isla Desolación**, Chile 🏝
111 E 23 **Isla Duque de York**, Chile 🏝
111 E 22 **Isla Esmeralda**, Chile 🏝
107 C 19 **Isla Española**, Ecuador 🏝
88 J 8 **Isla Espíritu Santo**, Mexico 🏝
107 A 19 **Isla Fernandina**, Ecuador 🏝
113 B 20 **Isla Flamenco**, Argentina 🏝
113 B 20 **Isla Gama**, Argentina 🏝
107 C 18 **Isla Genovesa**, Ecuador
111 H 26 **Isla Gordon**, Chile 🏝
111 H 25 **Isla Grande de Tierra del Fuego**, Chile 🏝
88 E 4 **Isla Guadalupe**, Mexico
111 E 18 **Isla Guafo**, Chile 🏝
111 E 19 **Isla Guamblin**, Chile 🏝
111 F 23 **Isla Hanover**, Chile 🏝
111 H 26 **Isla Hoste**, Chile 🏝
107 A 19 **Isla Isabela**, Ecuador 🏝
111 F 19 **Isla James**, Chile 🏝
111 F 21 **Isla Javier**, Chile 🏝
91 T 15 **Isla Jicarón**, Panama 🏝
111 F 23 **Isla Jorge Montt**, Chile 🏝
105 P 2 **Isla La Tortuga**, Venezuela 🏝
111 I 26 **Isla Lennox**, Chile 🏝
111 G 26 **Isla Londonderry**, Chile
111 E 23 **Isla Madre de Dios**, Chile 🏝
111 F 19 **Isla Magdalena**, Chile 🏝
107 A 18 **Isla Marchena**, Ecuador
88 L 10 **Isla Maria Cleofas**, Mexico 🏝
88 L 10 **Isla María Madre**, Mexico 🏝
88 L 10 **Isla María Magdelena**, Mexico 🏝
111 F 19 **Isla Melchor**, Chile 🏝
111 E 15 **Isla Mocha**, Chile 🏝
93 T 8 **Isla Mona**, Puerto Rico 🏝
91 T 15 **Isla Montuosa**, Panama 🏝
111 E 22 **Isla Mornington**, Chile 🏝
111 H 26 **Isla Navarino**, Chile 🏝
111 I 26 **Isla Nueva**, Chile 🏝
105 O 2 **Isla Orchila**, Venezuela 🏝
91 T 15 **Isla Parida**, Panama 🏝

□ Country ▣ Internal administrative region: State/Province/Territory/Dependent territory 🏛 Capital city ⛰ Mountain range/Undersea ridge ▲ Mountain peak/Volcano/Seamount ◇ Geographic feature ▶ Headland/Point/Cape/Peninsula ⏶ Desert 🏝 Island/Island group ⁜ Antarctic base 🌊 Ocean ◒ Sea ≈ Bay/Gulf/Channel/Strait 💧 Lake ⚑ Salt pan/Dry/Intermittent lake 〰 Ri

Country ▣ Internal administrative region: State/Province/Territory/Dependent territory ⚓ Capital city ▲▲ Mountain range/ Undersea ridge ▲ Mountain peak/ Volcano/Seamount ◇ Geographic feature ▶ Headland/Point/ Cape/Peninsula ▲ Desert ⚓ Island/Island group 🏕 Antarctic base Ocean Sea ≈ Bay/Gulf/Channel/Strait 🝖 Lake Salt pan/Dry/ Intermittent lake 🝖 River

297

□ Country   **▣** Internal administrative region: State/Province/Territory/Dependent territory   **♣** Capital city   **▲▲** Mountain range/Undersea ridge   **▲** Mountain peak/Volcano/Seamount   **◇** Geographic feature   **▶** Headland/Point/Cape/Peninsula   **▲** Desert   **⇄** Island/Island group   **✹** Antarctic base   **☊** Ocean   **🌊** Sea   **≈** Bay/Gulf/Channel/Strait   Lake   Salt pan/Dry/Intermittent lake

F 7 **Kaédi**, Mauritania
V 11 **Kaélé**, Cameroon
J 5 **Kaeo**, New Zealand
K 18 **Kaesŏng**, North Korea
K 1 **Kāf**, Saudi Arabia
M 13 **Kafakumba**, Democratic Republic of Congo
E 9 **Kaffrine**, Senegal
A 20 **Kafia Kingi**, Sudan
O 5 **Kafue**, Zambia
H 16 **Kaga**, Japan
K 3 **Kaga Bandoro**, Central African Republic
X 7 **Kagan**, Pakistan
O 13 **Kagan**, Uzbekistan
R 9 **Kagera**, Tanzania ◘
S 9 **Kağizman**, Turkey
E 17 **Kagmar**, Sudan
C 24 **Kagoshima**, Japan
M 5 **Kāhak**, Iran
S 10 **Kahama**, Tanzania
Q 4 **Kaharlyk**, Ukraine
J 12 **Kahemba**, Democratic Republic of Congo
M 12 **Kahnūj**, Iran
I 14 **Kahnwia**, Liberia
I 5 **Kahoe**, New Zealand
V 1 **Kahoka**, Missouri, U.S.A.
C 8 **Kahoolawe**, Hawaii, U.S.A. 🏝
L 12 **Kahramanmaraş**, Turkey
N 12 **Kahta**, Turkey
U 13 **Kai Besar**, Indonesia 🏝
U 13 **Kai Kecil**, Indonesia 🏝
P 11 **Kaiama**, Nigeria
H 20 **Kaiapoi**, New Zealand
K 8 **Kaibito**, Arizona, U.S.A.
T 3 **Kaifeng**, China
J 6 **Kaikohe**, New Zealand
I 18 **Kaikoura**, New Zealand
I 18 **Kaikoura Peninsula**, New Zealand ▶
P 9 **Kaili**, China
H 13 **Kailu**, China
D 7 **Kailua**, Hawaii, U.S.A.
V 12 **Kaimana**, Indonesia
D 7 **Käina**, Estonia
F 20 **Kainan**, Japan
D 5 **Kainantu**, Papua New Guinea
X 7 **Kaindorf**, Austria
P 11 **Kainji Reservoir**, Nigeria 💧
K 10 **Kainulasjärvi**, Sweden
I 7 **Kaipara Harbour**, New Zealand ≈
S 13 **Kaiping**, China
N 14 **Kairakau Beach**, New Zealand
B 3 **Kairiru**, Papua New Guinea 🏝
Q 6 **Kairouan**, Tunisia
D 6 **Kairuku**, Papua New Guinea
W 7 **Kaiser Wilhelm II Land**, Antarctica ◇
D 21 **Kaiserslautern**, Germany
F 15 **Kaišiadorys**, Lithuania
E 25 **Kaitangata**, New Zealand
I 10 **Kaitumälven**, Sweden ∿
C 7 **Kaiwi Channel**, Hawaii, U.S.A. ≈
Q 6 **Kaixian**, China
J 14 **Kaiyuan**, China
M 11 **Kaiyuan**, China
M 14 **Kajaani**, Finland
Q 5 **Kajabbi**, Queensland, Australia
R 9 **Kajaki**, Afghanistan
C 8 **Kajang**, Malaysia
R 11 **Kajuru**, Nigeria
E 19 **Kaka**, Sudan
E 25 **Kaka Point**, New Zealand
P 14 **Kakabia**, Indonesia 🏝
K 23 **Kakal**, Philippines ∿
K 12 **Kakamas**, Republic of South Africa
T 7 **Kakamega**, Kenya
N 23 **Kakana**, India
K 13 **Kakaramea**, New Zealand
H 13 **Kakata**, Liberia
K 13 **Kakatahi**, New Zealand
183 X 12 **Kakching**, India
199 D 19 **Kake**, Japan
216 L 10 **Kakenge**, Democratic Republic of Congo
151 T 9 **Kakhovka Tavriys'k**, Ukraine
151 T 8 **Kakhovs'ke Vodoskhovyshche**, Ukraine 💧
176 I 11 **Kākī**, Iran
181 H 18 **Kakinada**, India
214 K 12 **Kakpin**, Côte d'Ivoire
79 S 3 **Kaktovik**, Alaska, U.S.A.
198 K 12 **Kakuda**, Japan
195 Q 9 **Kakus**, Malaysia ∿
177 O 8 **Kāl-e Namakasār**, Afghanistan 💧
217 R 12 **Kala**, Tanzania
177 V 8 **Kalabagh**, Pakistan
193 Q 15 **Kalabahi**, Indonesia
195 W 7 **Kalabakan**, Malaysia
218 L 5 **Kalabo**, Zambia
156 M 7 **Kalach**, Russian Federation
157 O 8 **Kalach-na-Donu**, Russian Federation
86 H 12 **Kaladar**, Ontario, Canada
218 K 9 **Kalahari Desert**, Botswana ◇
135 L 14 **Kalajoki**, Finland ∿
135 K 14 **Kalajoki**, Finland
215 P 11 **Kalalé**, Benin
177 W 6 **Kalam**, Pakistan
147 F 14 **Kalamaria**, Greece
147 D 22 **Kalamata**, Greece
65 J 15 **Kalamazoo**, Michigan, U.S.A.
181 E 17 **Kalamnuri**, India
147 B 18 **Kalamos**, Greece 🏝
147 D 16 **Kalampaka**, Greece
151 T 12 **Kalamyts'ka Zatoka**, Ukraine ≈
151 S 10 **Kalanchak**, Ukraine
217 T 11 **Kalangali**, Tanzania
193 O 14 **Kalao**, Indonesia 🏝
193 O 14 **Kalaotoa**, Indonesia 🏝
173 V 5 **Kalār**, Iraq
191 K 16 **Kalasin**, Thailand
177 T 11 **Kalat**, Pakistan
197 K 21 **Kalatungan Mountains**, Philippines ⛰
147 D 20 **Kalavryta**, Greece
230 F 9 **Kalbarri**, Western Australia, Australia
170 I 9 **Kalecik**, Turkey
193 Q 13 **Kaledupa**, Indonesia 🏝
217 N 10 **Kalema**, Democratic Republic of Congo
217 Q 11 **Kalémié**, Democratic Republic of Congo
190 C 10 **Kalemyo**, Myanmar
154 G 5 **Kalevala**, Russian Federation
190 C 10 **Kalewa**, Myanmar
157 X 2 **Kalga**, Russian Federation
230 I 10 **Kalgoorlie**, Western Australia, Australia
197 H 15 **Kalibo**, Philippines
217 O 9 **Kalima**, Democratic Republic of Congo
192 I 11 **Kalimantan Barat**, Indonesia ◘
192 M 12 **Kalimantan Selatan**, Indonesia ◘
192 J 12 **Kalimantan Tengah**, Indonesia ◘
192 L 10 **Kalimantan Timur**, Indonesia ◘
183 S 10 **Kalimpang**, India
181 I 16 **Kalinga**, India
149 B 15 **Kaliningrad**, Russian Federation
149 B 15 **Kaliningradskaya Oblast'**, Russian Federation ◘
179 R 14 **Kalininobod**, Tajikistan
157 O 5 **Kalininsk**, Russian Federation
149 L 21 **Kalinkavichy**, Belarus
72 M 3 **Kalispell**, Montana, U.S.A.
143 H 14 **Kalisz**, Poland
142 F 10 **Kalisz Pomorski**, Poland
217 R 11 **Kaliua**, Tanzania
170 D 13 **Kalkan**, Turkey
230 M 4 **Kalkarindji**, Northern Territory, Australia
64 J 11 **Kalkaska**, Michigan, U.S.A.
218 I 8 **Kalkfeld**, Namibia
135 F 15 **Kallsjön**, Sweden 💧
135 G 24 **Kalmar**, Sweden
148 F 11 **Kalnciems**, Latvia
143 I 25 **Kalocsa**, Hungary
219 N 6 **Kalomo**, Zambia
190 D 9 **Kalon**, Myanmar
182 K 6 **Kalpa**, India
181 C 23 **Kalpeni**, India 🏝
182 L 11 **Kalpi**, India
215 S 9 **Kalrguéri**, Niger
149 H 14 **Kaltanėnai**, Lithuania
156 J 2 **Kaluga**, Russian Federation
230 K 2 **Kalumburu**, Western Australia, Australia
135 D 25 **Kalundborg**, Denmark
150 I 5 **Kalush**, Ukraine
181 F 25 **Kalutara**, Sri Lanka
156 I 2 **Kaluzhskaya Oblast'**, Russian Federation ◘
149 E 16 **Kalvarija**, Lithuania
154 I 14 **Kalyazin**, Russian Federation
147 M 22 **Kalymnos**, Greece 🏝
147 M 22 **Kalymnos**, Greece
151 N 5 **Kalynivka**, Ukraine
217 O 10 **Kama**, Democratic Republic of Congo
155 S 10 **Kama**, Russian Federation ∿
191 C 14 **Kama**, Myanmar
198 L 10 **Kamaishi**, Japan
199 J 16 **Kamakura**, Japan
214 G 11 **Kamakwie**, Sierra Leone
170 I 10 **Kaman**, Turkey
218 G 8 **Kamanjab**, Namibia
175 O 12 **Kamarān**, Yemen 🏝
214 G 11 **Kamaron**, Sierra Leone
230 I 10 **Kambalda**, Western Australia, Australia
217 O 14 **Kambove**, Democratic Republic of Congo
153 Y 9 **Kamchatka Peninsula**, Russian Federation ▶
146 K 7 **Kamen**, Bulgaria
152 M 12 **Kamen'-na-Obi**, Russian Federation
217 N 11 **Kamende**, Democratic Republic of Congo
154 M 5 **Kamenka**, Russian Federation
157 O 4 **Kamenka**, Russian Federation
178 H 4 **Kamenka**, Kazakhstan
156 L 13 **Kamennomostskiy**, Russian Federation
156 L 9 **Kamenolomni**, Russian Federation
156 M 8 **Kamensk-Shakhtinskiy**, Russian Federation
152 J 10 **Kamensk-Ural'skiy**, Russian Federation
199 H 18 **Kameyama**, Japan
199 B 23 **Kami-Koshiki-jima**, Japan 🏝
142 D 9 **Kamień Pomorski**, Poland
143 J 15 **Kamieńsk**, Poland
198 K 4 **Kamikawa**, Japan
82 L 11 **Kamilukuak Lake**, Nunavut, Canada 💧
150 K 1 **Kamin'-Kashyrs'kyy**, Ukraine
217 N 13 **Kamina**, Democratic Republic of Congo
199 H 16 **Kamioka**, Japan
199 A 20 **Kamitsushima**, Japan
83 H 21 **Kamloops**, British Columbia, Canada
41 O 4 **Kammu Seamount**, Pacific Ocean ▲
171 U 8 **Kamo**, Armenia
199 L 16 **Kamogawa**, Japan
217 S 7 **Kampala**, Uganda 🏛
192 E 8 **Kampar**, Malaysia
132 K 10 **Kampen**, Netherlands
217 O 10 **Kampene**, Democratic Republic of Congo
191 G 16 **Kamphaeng Phet**, Thailand
191 M 20 **Kâmpóng Cham**, Cambodia
191 L 20 **Kâmpóng Chhnăng**, Cambodia
191 K 19 **Kâmpóng Khleăng**, Cambodia
191 K 22 **Kâmpóng Saôm**, Cambodia
194 F 10 **Kampong Sedili Kechil**, Malaysia
191 K 21 **Kâmpóng Spoe**, Cambodia
191 L 20 **Kâmpóng Thum**, Cambodia
191 K 22 **Kâmpôt**, Cambodia
194 A 7 **Kampung Koh**, Malaysia
214 E 10 **Kamsar**, Guinea
157 R 1 **Kamskoye Ust'ye**, Russian Federation
155 S 11 **Kamskoye Vodokhanilishche**, Russian Federation 💧
213 K 25 **Kamsuuma**, Somalia
198 L 6 **Kamui-dake**, Japan ▲
198 I 6 **Kamui-misaki**, Japan ▶
217 S 7 **Kamuli**, Uganda
150 M 2 **Kam"yane**, Ukraine
150 L 6 **Kam"yanets'-Podil's'kyy**, Ukraine
151 U 8 **Kam"yanka**, Ukraine
149 E 20 **Kamyanyets**, Belarus
176 F 6 **Kāmyārān**, Iran
149 K 15 **Kamyen'**, Belarus
157 P 7 **Kamyshin**, Russian Federation
179 N 8 **Kamyshlybash**, Kazakhstan
157 R 11 **Kamyzyak**, Russian Federation
190 C 11 **Kan**, Myanmar
74 J 7 **Kanab**, Utah, U.S.A.
78 E 14 **Kanaga Island**, Alaska, U.S.A. 🏝
85 U 8 **Kanairiktoktok**, Newfoundland and Labrador, Canada ∿
147 B 17 **Kanallaki**, Greece
216 L 11 **Kananga**, Democratic Republic of Congo
157 Q 1 **Kanash**, Russian Federation
199 H 15 **Kanazawa**, Japan
190 D 10 **Kanbalu**, Myanmar
199 J 17 **Kanbara**, Japan
191 G 19 **Kanchanaburi**, Thailand
181 F 21 **Kanchipuram**, India
177 S 10 **Kandahār**, Afghanistan ◘
177 S 9 **Kandahār**, Afghanistan
154 H 3 **Kandalaksha**, Russian Federation
154 H 4 **Kandalakshskiy Zaliv**, Russian Federation ≈
215 N 11 **Kandé**, Togo
177 V 12 **Kandhkot**, Pakistan
215 O 10 **Kandi**, Benin
177 U 13 **Kandiaro**, Pakistan
147 B 18 **Kandila**, Greece
170 F 7 **Kandira**, Turkey
181 A 14 **Kandla**, India
219 W 7 **Kandreho**, Madgascar
234 F 5 **Kandrian**, Papua New Guinea
181 G 25 **Kandy**, Sri Lanka
178 L 5 **Kandyagash**, Kazakhstan
58 C 11 **Kane**, Pennsylvania, U.S.A.
42 G 10 **Kane Fracture Zone**, Atlantic Ocean ◇
215 W 8 **Kanem**, Chad ◘
78 C 7 **Kaneohe**, Hawaii, U.S.A.
148 I 9 **Kanepi**, Estonia
218 L 10 **Kang**, Botswana
197 F 24 **Kang Tipayan Dakula**, Philippines 🏝
44 M 12 **Kangaamiut**, Greenland
170 M 10 **Kangal**, Turkey
176 M 14 **Kangān**, Iran
194 A 4 **Kangar**, Malaysia
231 P 12 **Kangaroo Island**, South Australia, Australia 🏝
135 M 17 **Kangasniemi**, Finland
183 S 9 **Kangchenjunga**, India/Nepal ▲
188 L 6 **Kangding**, China
187 K 17 **Kangdong**, North Korea
85 S 1 **Kangeeak Point**, Nunavut, Canada ▶
45 N 12 **Kangerlussaq**, Greenland
45 O 11 **Kangersuatsiaq**, Greenland
217 U 6 **Kangetet**, Kenya
187 L 16 **Kanggye**, North Korea
85 T 6 **Kangiqsualujjuaq**, Québec, Canada
85 R 4 **Kangiqsujuaq**, Québec, Canada
85 R 5 **Kangirsuk**, Québec, Canada
187 M 18 **Kangnŭng**, South Korea
216 E 7 **Kango**, Gabon
187 I 14 **Kangping**, China
182 I 5 **Kangra**, India
183 W 9 **Kangto**, India ▲
191 C 16 **Kangyidaung**, Myanmar
214 J 12 **Kani**, Côte d'Ivoire
190 C 11 **Kani**, Myanmar
195 W 4 **Kanibongan**, Malaysia
154 M 2 **Kanin Kamen'**, Russian Federation ◇
154 L 2 **Kanin Nos**, Russian Federation
151 Q 4 **Kaniv**, Ukraine
181 F 15 **Kaniwara**, India
144 K 7 **Kanjiža**, Serbia and Montenegro
65 H 17 **Kankakee**, Illinois, U.S.A.
214 H 11 **Kankan**, Guinea
181 G 16 **Kanker**, India
191 F 21 **Kanmaw Kyun**, Myanmar 🏝
61 O 10 **Kannapolis**, North Carolina, U.S.A.
182 K 10 **Kannauj**, India
215 R 10 **Kano**, Nigeria
215 S 10 **Kano**, Nigeria ◘
199 C 24 **Kanoya**, Japan
182 M 10 **Kanpur**, India
68 L 5 **Kansas**, U.S.A. ◘
69 O 3 **Kansas**, Kansas, U.S.A. ∿
69 R 3 **Kansas City**, Missouri, U.S.A.
153 O 12 **Kansk**, Russian Federation
191 G 25 **Kantang**, Thailand
156 L 7 **Kantemirovka**, Russian Federation
183 S 15 **Kanthi**, India
236 J 4 **Kanton**, Kiribati 🏝
199 K 15 **Kanuma**, Japan
182 H 9 **Kanwat**, India
218 M 10 **Kanye**, Botswana
236 I 10 **Kao**, Tonga 🏝
193 S 10 **Kao**, Indonesia
191 J 21 **Kaôh Kŏng**, Cambodia 🏝
191 J 22 **Kaôh Rŭng**, Cambodia 🏝
189 Z 12 **Kaohsiung**, Taiwan
218 G 7 **Kaokoveld**, Namibia ◇
214 E 8 **Kaolack**, Senegal
218 M 5 **Kaoma**, Zambia
216 M 3 **Kaouadja**, Central African Republic
136 M 7 **Kap Arkona**, Germany ▶
45 Q 13 **Kap Brewster**, Greenland ▶
44 M 14 **Kap Farvel**, Greenland ▶
45 R 9 **Kap Morris Jesup**, Greenland ▶
171 V 10 **Kapan**, Armenia
216 M 13 **Kapanga**, Democratic Republic of Congo
219 P 2 **Kapatu**, Zambia
179 V 9 **Kapchagay**, Kazakhstan
179 W 9 **Kapchagayskoye Vodokhranilishche**, Kazakhstan 💧
133 E 16 **Kapelle**, Netherlands
133 G 16 **Kapellen**, Belgium
135 I 20 **Kapellskär**, Sweden
217 U 7 **Kapenguria**, Kenya
139 V 6 **Kapfenberg**, Austria
170 C 8 **Kapidaği Peninsula**, Turkey ▶
219 O 4 **Kapiri Mposhi**, Zambia
177 V 7 **Kāpīsā**, Afghanistan ◘
195 Q 10 **Kapit**, Malaysia
233 K 15 **Kapiti Island**, New Zealand 🏝
191 F 23 **Kapoe**, Thailand
213 F 23 **Kapoeta**, Sudan
143 H 25 **Kaposvár**, Hungary
137 D 19 **Kappel**, Germany
136 H 7 **Kappeln**, Germany
187 M 15 **Kapsan**, North Korea
192 I 11 **Kapuas**, Indonesia ∿
86 C 5 **Kapuskasing**, Ontario, Canada
157 Q 8 **Kapustin Yar**, Russian Federation
217 U 6 **Kaputir**, Kenya
143 G 23 **Kapuvár**, Hungary
149 I 19 **Kapyl'**, Belarus
215 N 11 **Kara**, Togo
179 U 10 **Kara-Balta**, Kyrgyzstan
170 H 12 **Kara Dağ**, Turkey ▲
171 O 8 **Kara Dağ**, Turkey ▲
179 T 11 **Kara-Köl**, Kyrgyzstan
213 J 19 **Kara K'orē**, Ethiopia
179 W 11 **Kara-Say**, Kyrgyzstan
152 M 6 **Kara Sea**, Russian Federation 🌊
179 T 12 **Kara-Suu**, Kyrgyzstan
178 I 11 **Karabogazkel'**, Turkmenistan
170 H 7 **Karabük**, Turkey
179 W 8 **Karabulak**, Kazakhstan
170 A 10 **Karaburun**, Turkey
178 M 5 **Karabutak**, Kazakhstan
170 E 13 **Karaca Yarimadasi**, Turkey ▶
170 D 8 **Karacabey**, Turkey
170 D 7 **Karacaköy**, Turkey
170 H 14 **Karaçal Tepe**, Turkey ▲
156 M 13 **Karachayevo Cherkesskaya Respublika**, Russian Federation ◘
156 M 13 **Karachayevsk**, Russian Federation
156 I 3 **Karachev**, Russian Federation
177 T 15 **Karachi**, Pakistan
181 C 18 **Karad**, India
179 S 6 **Karaganda**, Kazakhstan ◘
179 T 5 **Karaganda**, Kazakhstan
179 V 9 **Karagash**, Kazakhstan
179 U 5 **Karagayly**, Kazakhstan
153 Z 9 **Karaginskiy Zaliv**, Russian Federation ≈
171 O 10 **Karagöl Dağlari**, Turkey ⛰
217 R 8 **Karagwe**, Tanzania
181 F 22 **Karaikal**, India
181 F 23 **Karaikkudi**, India
176 I 6 **Karaj**, Iran
194 C 8 **Karak**, Malaysia
178 K 9 **Karakalpakiya**, Uzbekistan
171 O 12 **Karakeşşi**, Turkey
170 I 9 **Karakeşşili**, Turkey
193 R 8 **Karakelong**, Indonesia 🏝
171 P 10 **Karakoşşan**, Turkey
179 W 10 **Karakol**, Kyrgyzstan
177 Y 5 **Karakoram**, Pakistan ⛰
180 D 6 **Karakoram Range**, India ⛰
179 O 13 **Karakul'**, Uzbekistan
178 L 13 **Karakum Desert**, Turkmenistan ◇
171 R 9 **Karakurt**, Turkey
215 V 9 **Karal**, Chad
148 C 8 **Karala**, Estonia
170 H 13 **Karaman**, Turkey
184 K 4 **Karamay**, China
233 G 16 **Karamea**, New Zealand
233 G 17 **Karamea Bight**, New Zealand ≈
192 L 13 **Karamian**, Indonesia 🏝
232 K 10 **Karamu**, New Zealand
181 E 16 **Karanji**, India
146 M 7 **Karapelit**, Bulgaria
170 I 12 **Karapinar**, Turkey
218 I 12 **Karas**, Namibia ◘
218 J 12 **Karasburg**, Namibia
134 L 7 **Kárásjohka**, Norway
170 F 7 **Karasu**, Turkey
152 L 12 **Karasuk**, Russian Federation
170 K 13 **Karataş**, Turkey
179 S 10 **Karatau**, Kazakhstan
178 J 5 **Karatobe**, Kazakhstan
179 V 8 **Karatol**, Kazakhstan ∿
178 I 7 **Karaton**, Kazakhstan
134 I 11 **Karats**, Sweden 💧

Country ◘ Internal administrative region: State/Province/Territory/Dependent territory 🏛 Capital city ⛰ Mountain range/Undersea ridge ▲ Mountain peak/Volcano/Seamount ◇ Geographic feature ▶ Headland/Point/Cape/Peninsula 🏜 Desert 🏝 Island/Island group ⁘ Antarctic base Ⓞ Ocean 🌊 Sea ≈ Bay/Gulf/Channel/Strait 💧 Lake ⚑ Salt pan/Dry/Intermittent lake ∿ River

199 B 21 **Karatsu**, Japan
179 W 5 **Karaul**, Kazakhstan
139 S 9 **Karawanken**, Austria ⛰
179 S 6 **Karazhal**, Kazakhstan
173 T 8 **Karbalā'**, Iraq
135 G 17 **Kårböle**, Sweden
143 L 23 **Karcag**, Hungary
147 D 17 **Karditsa**, Greece
181 L 17 **Kardiva Channel**, Maldives ≈
148 D 6 **Kärdla**, Estonia
181 F 15 **Kareli**, India
149 H 18 **Karelichy**, Belarus
217 R 12 **Karema**, Tanzania
191 F 16 **Karen**, Myanmar ▣
180 E 13 **Karera**, India
134 J 8 **Karesuando**, Finland
152 M 11 **Kargasok**, Russian Federation
170 J 7 **Kargi**, Turkey
182 I 3 **Kargil**, India
154 J 9 **Kargopol'**, Russian Federation
142 E 13 **Kargowa**, Poland
215 T 10 **Kari**, Nigeria
219 O 6 **Kariba**, Zimbabwe
218 H 9 **Karibib**, Namibia
134 L 7 **Karigasniemi**, Finland
192 I 11 **Karimata**, Indonesia ⛬
181 F 18 **Karimnagar**, India
213 M 19 **Karin**, Somalia
217 Q 8 **Karisimbi**, Democratic Republic of Congo/Rwanda ▲
199 I 17 **Kariya**, Japan
234 D 4 **Karkar Island**, Papua New Guinea ⛬
179 U 5 **Karkaralinsk**, Kazakhstan
171 U 9 **Karki**, Azerbaijan
151 R 11 **Karkinits'ka Zatoka**, Ukraine ≈
148 G 8 **Karksi-Nuia**, Estonia
185 N 5 **Karlik Shan**, China ▲
142 E 9 **Karlino**, Poland
171 Q 10 **Karliova**, Turkey
151 U 5 **Karlivka**, Ukraine
146 I 9 **Karlovo**, Bulgaria
143 B 17 **Karlovy Vary**, Czech Republic
135 F 25 **Karlshamn**, Sweden
135 F 20 **Karlskoga**, Sweden
135 G 25 **Karlskrona**, Sweden
137 E 22 **Karlsruhe**, Germany
135 F 20 **Karlstad**, Sweden
67 O 2 **Karlstad**, Minnesota, U.S.A.
139 U 2 **Karlstift**, Austria
149 N 19 **Karma**, Belarus
183 W 14 **Karnafuli Reservoir**, Bangladesh ➘
182 J 7 **Karnal**, India
182 M 8 **Karnali**, Nepal ʃ
181 D 20 **Karnataka**, India ▣
71 P 11 **Karnes City**, Texas, U.S.A.
139 P 9 **Karnische Alpen**, Austria ⛰
140 G 5 **Karnische Alps**, Austria/Italy ⛰
146 M 9 **Karnobat**, Bulgaria
139 S 9 **Kärnten**, Austria ▣
177 S 12 **Karodi**, Pakistan
183 X 11 **Karong**, India
219 R 2 **Karonga**, Malawi
177 W 9 **Karor**, Pakistan
213 I 15 **Karora**, Eritrea
193 N 11 **Karossa**, Indonesia
147 L 22 **Karpáthio Pélagos**, Greece ◒
147 M 26 **Karpathos**, Greece
147 M 25 **Karpathos**, Greece ⛬
147 D 18 **Karpenisi**, Greece
154 M 7 **Karpogory**, Russian Federation
230 F 6 **Karratha**, Western Australia, Australia
171 S 8 **Kars**, Turkey
135 L 14 **Kärsämäki**, Finland
148 J 11 **Kārsava**, Latvia
178 I 11 **Karshi**, Turkmenistan
179 P 13 **Karshi**, Uzbekistan
170 E 8 **Kartal**, Turkey
219 W 4 **Kartala**, Comoros ▲
152 I 11 **Kartaly**, Russian Federation
142 H 8 **Kartuzy**, Poland
231 Q 3 **Karumba**, Queensland, Australia
177 O 12 **Kārvāndar**, Iran
181 C 20 **Karwar**, India
138 M 7 **Karwendelgebirge**, Austria ⛰
147 B 18 **Karya**, Greece
153 R 14 **Karymskoye**, Russian Federation
147 H 20 **Karystos**, Greece
170 D 13 **Kaş**, Turkey
84 L 9 **Kasabonika**, Ontario, Canada
216 J 10 **Kasai**, Democratic Republic of Congo ʃ
199 F 18 **Kasai**, Japan
216 L 11 **Kasai Occidental**, Democratic Republic of Congo ▣
216 M 10 **Kasai Oriental**, Democratic Republic of Congo ▣
216 M 14 **Kasaji**, Democratic Republic of Congo
219 P 3 **Kasama**, Zambia
218 M 7 **Kasane**, Botswana
181 C 21 **Kasaragod**, India
81 O 9 **Kasba Lake**, Nunavut, Canada ➘
210 H 7 **Kasba Tadla**, Morocco
218 M 4 **Kasempa**, Zambia
217 P 14 **Kasenga**, Democratic Republic of Congo
217 Q 7 **Kasenye**, Democratic Republic of Congo
217 O 8 **Kasese**, Democratic Republic of Congo
217 Q 7 **Kasese**, Uganda
191 K 17 **Kaset Wisai**, Thailand
182 K 9 **Kasganj**, India
84 L 11 **Kashabowie**, Ontario, Canada
176 I 7 **Kāshān**, Iran
156 M 8 **Kashary**, Russian Federation
81 T 11 **Kashechewan**, Ontario, Canada
85 P 10 **Kashechewen**, Ontario, Canada
79 O 9 **Kashegelok**, Alaska, U.S.A.
184 G 5 **Kashi**, China
199 H 18 **Kashihara**, Japan
199 L 14 **Kashima-nada**, Japan ≈
154 I 13 **Kashin**, Russian Federation
183 T 12 **Kashinathpur**, Bangladesh
182 K 8 **Kashipur**, India
156 L 2 **Kashira**, Russian Federation
199 I 14 **Kashiwazaki**, Japan
179 T 8 **Kashkanteniz**, Kazakhstan
177 N 6 **Kāshmar**, Iran
182 H 3 **Kashmir Valley**, India ◇
193 N 11 **Kasimbar**, Indonesia
157 N 2 **Kasimov**, Russian Federation
179 V 10 **Kaskelen**, Kazakhstan
152 I 10 **Kasli**, Russian Federation
83 I 21 **Kaslo**, British Columbia, Canada
217 O 10 **Kasongo**, Democratic Republic of Congo
216 I 12 **Kasongo-Lunda**, Democratic Republic of Congo
147 M 26 **Kasos**, Greece ⛬
171 T 6 **Kaspi**, Georgia
157 R 14 **Kaspiysk**, Russian Federation
213 H 16 **Kassala**, Sudan
213 G 16 **Kassala**, Sudan ▣
147 G 15 **Kassandreia**, Greece
137 G 16 **Kassel**, Germany
211 P 6 **Kasserine**, Tunisia
147 A 16 **Kassiopi**, Greece
170 I 7 **Kastamonu**, Turkey
147 G 26 **Kastelli**, Greece
147 J 26 **Kastelli**, Greece
133 H 17 **Kasterlee**, Belgium
147 C 14 **Kastoria**, Greece
156 K 5 **Kastornoye**, Russian Federation
147 B 18 **Kastos**, Greece ⛬
149 O 18 **Kastsyukovichy**, Belarus
199 I 17 **Kasugai**, Japan
199 L 15 **Kasumiga-ura**, Japan ➘
157 S 15 **Kasumkent**, Russian Federation
219 Q 4 **Kasungu**, Malawi
177 Y 9 **Kasur**, Pakistan
230 M 7 **Kata Tjuta**, Northern Territory, Australia ▲
182 K 2 **Kataklik**, India
217 N 10 **Katako-Kombe**, Democratic Republic of Congo
217 T 6 **Katakwi**, Uganda
79 T 10 **Katalla**, Alaska, U.S.A.
217 N 13 **Katanga**, Democratic Republic of Congo ▣
230 H 12 **Katanning**, Western Australia, Australia
147 B 20 **Katastari**, Greece
181 O 24 **Katchall**, India ⛬
217 O 11 **Katea**, Democratic Republic of Congo
147 E 15 **Katerini**, Greece
219 Q 5 **Katete**, Zambia
190 E 9 **Katha**, Myanmar
230 M 2 **Katherine**, Northern Territory, Australia
181 A 15 **Kathiawar Peninsula**, India ▶
183 Q 9 **Kathmandu**, Nepal ⌂
183 S 11 **Katihar**, India
232 L 9 **Katikati**, New Zealand
214 K 12 **Katiola**, Côte d'Ivoire
146 D 11 **Katlanovo**, Macedonia (F.Y.R.O.M.)
147 D 20 **Kato Achaïa**, Greece
146 H 12 **Kato Nevrokopi**, Greece
147 E 18 **Kato Tithorea**, Greece
179 Z 4 **Katon-Karagay**, Kazakhstan
194 B 14 **Katong**, Singapore
231 U 11 **Katoomba**, New South Wales, Australia
143 I 17 **Katowice**, Poland
183 S 13 **Katoya**, India
135 G 21 **Katrineholm**, Sweden
219 X 6 **Katsepy**, Madgascar
215 R 9 **Katsina**, Nigeria
215 R 10 **Katsina**, Nigeria ▣
215 S 13 **Katsina-Ala**, Nigeria
199 A 21 **Katsumoto**, Japan
199 L 16 **Katsuura**, Japan
147 N 24 **Kattavia**, Greece
135 D 23 **Kattegat**, Denmark ≈
134 H 13 **Kattisavan**, Sweden
232 I 6 **Katui**, New Zealand
191 F 22 **Kau-ye Kyun**, Myanmar ⛬
78 A 6 **Kauai**, Hawaii, U.S.A. ⛬
78 A 7 **Kauai Channel**, Hawaii, U.S.A. ≈
137 I 25 **Kaufbeuren**, Germany
135 K 17 **Kauhajoki**, Finland
134 L 10 **Kaukonen**, Finland
148 I 6 **Kauksi**, Estonia
78 D 9 **Kauna Point**, Hawaii, U.S.A. ▶
78 C 7 **Kaunakakai**, Hawaii, U.S.A.
149 E 15 **Kaunas**, Lithuania
234 C 3 **Kaup**, Papua New Guinea
135 B 17 **Kaupanger**, Norway
215 Q 9 **Kaura-Namoda**, Nigeria
135 K 15 **Kaustinen**, Finland
134 K 8 **Kautokeino**, Norway
233 L 14 **Kauwhata**, New Zealand
146 D 12 **Kavadarci**, Macedonia (F.Y.R.O.M.)
145 J 19 **Kavajë**, Albania
170 B 8 **Kavak**, Turkey
146 H 13 **Kavala**, Greece
181 G 20 **Kavali**, India
176 I 11 **Kavār**, Iran
181 B 22 **Kavaratti**, India ⛬
181 B 22 **Kavaratti**, India
146 O 7 **Kavarna**, Bulgaria
234 G 2 **Kavieng**, Papua New Guinea
69 O 7 **Kaw Lake**, Oklahoma, U.S.A. ➘
199 G 19 **Kawachi-nagano**, Japan
232 J 6 **Kawakawa**, New Zealand
219 O 2 **Kawambwa**, Zambia
181 G 15 **Kawardha**, India
86 G 11 **Kawartha Lakes**, Ontario, Canada ➘
199 K 16 **Kawasaki**, Japan
199 B 20 **Kawashiri-misaki**, Japan ▶
232 K 7 **Kawau Island**, New Zealand ⛬
232 M 12 **Kaweka**, New Zealand ▲
232 J 10 **Kawhia**, New Zealand
232 J 10 **Kawhia Harbour**, New Zealand ≈
77 L 19 **Kawich Peak**, Nevada, U.S.A. ▲
190 D 9 **Kawlin**, Myanmar
192 E 13 **Kayaapu**, Indonesia
191 E 14 **Kayah**, Myanmar ▣
79 T 10 **Kayak Island**, Alaska, U.S.A. ⛬
181 D 23 **Kayankulam**, India
73 W 10 **Kaycee**, Wyoming, U.S.A.
216 M 13 **Kayembe-Mukulu**, Democratic Republic of Congo
74 L 8 **Kayenta**, Arizona, U.S.A.
179 V 5 **Kaynar**, Kazakhstan
170 K 11 **Kayseri**, Turkey
192 G 12 **Kayuagung**, Indonesia
217 O 10 **Kayuyu**, Democratic Republic of Congo
153 O 8 **Kayyerkan**, Russian Federation
170 A 9 **Kaz Daği**, Turkey
153 T 7 **Kazach'ye**, Russian Federation
178 H 10 **Kazakhskiy Zaliv**, Kazakhstan ≈
179 Q 8 **Kazakhstan**, Asia ■
84 J 4 **Kazan**, Nunavut, Canada ʃ
157 R 1 **Kazan'**, Russian Federation
151 S 7 **Kazanka**, Ukraine
146 J 9 **Kazanlŭk**, Bulgaria
171 T 5 **Kazbek**, Georgia ▲
176 I 10 **Kāzerūn**, Iran
143 K 21 **Kazincbarcika**, Hungary
149 E 15 **Kazlu Rūda**, Lithuania
199 K 15 **Kazo**, Japan
82 L 11 **Kazon**, Nunavut, Canada ʃ
178 G 5 **Kaztalovka**, Kazakhstan
216 L 11 **Kazumba**, Democratic Republic of Congo
142 G 11 **Kcynia**, Poland
147 H 21 **Kea**, Greece ⛬
78 E 9 **Keaau**, Hawaii, U.S.A.
78 D 8 **Keahole Point**, Hawaii, U.S.A. ▶
74 L 9 **Keams**, Arizona, U.S.A.
66 L 15 **Kearney**, Nebraska, U.S.A.
171 N 11 **Keban**, Turkey
171 O 10 **Keban Baraji**, Turkey ➘
183 Y 9 **Kebang**, India
215 P 10 **Kebbi**, Nigeria ▣
214 D 8 **Kébémèr**, Senegal
211 Q 7 **Kebili**, Tunisia
213 A 17 **Kebkabiya**, Sudan
134 I 9 **Kebnekaise**, Sweden ▲
213 L 21 **K'ebrī Dehar**, Ethiopia
143 J 24 **Kecskemét**, Hungary
194 A 5 **Kedah**, Malaysia ▣
149 E 14 **Kėdainiai**, Lithuania
215 W 10 **Kédédéssé**, Chad
87 R 7 **Kedgwick**, New Brunswick, Canada
214 F 6 **Kediet Ijill**, Mauritania ▲
192 J 14 **Kediri**, Indonesia
186 K 9 **Kedong**, China
214 G 9 **Kédougou**, Senegal
143 H 17 **Kędzierzyn-Koźle**, Poland
82 C 12 **Keele Peak**, Yukon Territory, Canada ▲
197 C 22 **Keenapusan**, Philippines ⛬
58 M 8 **Keene**, New Hampshire, U.S.A.
218 J 11 **Keetmanshoop**, Namibia
159 O 8 **Kefallinia Valley**, Mediterranean Sea ◇
147 A 19 **Kefallonia**, Greece ⛬
159 P 8 **Kefallonia**, Mediterranean Sea ⛬
147 M 23 **Kefalos**, Greece
193 Q 15 **Kefamenanu**, Indonesia
215 R 12 **Keffi**, Nigeria
134 A 11 **Keflavik**, Iceland
83 H 16 **Keg River**, Alberta, Canada
179 X 10 **Kegen**, Kazakhstan
213 F 14 **Keheili**, Sudan
137 D 23 **Kehl**, Germany
148 G 6 **Kehra**, Estonia
190 F 11 **Kehsi Mansam**, Myanmar
127 R 2 **Keighley**, United Kingdom
148 F 6 **Keila**, Estonia
218 K 12 **Keimoes**, Republic of South Africa
215 Q 8 **Keïta**, Niger
135 M 16 **Keitele**, Finland ➘
231 Q 12 **Keith**, South Australia, Australia
195 R 9 **Kejaman**, Malaysia
233 J 17 **Kekerengu**, New Zealand
199 N 22 **Kekeroma-jima**, Japan ⛬
143 K 22 **Kékes**, Hungary ▲
153 V 11 **Kekra**, Russian Federation
213 L 22 **K'elafo**, Ethiopia
187 A 18 **Kelan**, China
193 R 12 **Kelang**, Indonesia ⛬
194 B 8 **Kelang**, Malaysia
194 C 5 **Kelantan**, Malaysia ʃ
194 C 6 **Kelantan**, Malaysia ▣
211 R 5 **Kelibia**, Tunisia
170 M 8 **Kelkit**, Turkey ʃ
171 O 9 **Kelkit**, Turkey
216 G 8 **Kéllé**, Congo
179 R 2 **Kellerovka**, Kazakhstan
65 M 16 **Kelley's Island**, Ohio, U.S.A. ⛬
72 K 4 **Kellogg**, Idaho, U.S.A.
134 N 10 **Kelloselkä**, Finland
125 E 17 **Kells**, Republic of Ireland
148 D 13 **Kelmė**, Lithuania
133 L 20 **Kelmis**, Belgium
215 W 11 **Kelo**, Chad
83 H 21 **Kelowna**, British Columbia, Canada
76 G 9 **Kelso**, Washington, U.S.A.
194 E 10 **Keluang**, Malaysia
192 F 11 **Kelume**, Indonesia
154 I 6 **Kem'**, Russian Federation
171 O 10 **Kemah**, Turkey
171 N 10 **Kemaliye**, Turkey
216 L 5 **Kembé**, Central African Republic
170 D 13 **Kemer**, Turkey
152 M 12 **Kemerovo**, Russian Federation
134 L 12 **Kemi**, Finland
134 M 11 **Kemijärvi**, Finland ➘
134 M 11 **Kemijärvi**, Finland
134 M 10 **Kemijoki**, Finland ʃ
157 P 2 **Kemlya**, Russian Federation
73 R 14 **Kemmerer**, Wyoming, U.S.A.
137 K 20 **Kemnath**, Germany
216 J 4 **Kémo**, Central African Republic ▣
71 R 6 **Kemp**, Texas, U.S.A.
241 U 4 **Kemp Land**, Antarctica ◇
92 L 3 **Kemp's Bay**, The Bahamas
231 V 10 **Kempsey**, New South Wales, Australia
137 H 25 **Kempten**, Germany
79 Q 9 **Kenai**, Alaska, U.S.A.
79 Q 10 **Kenai Peninsula**, Alaska, U.S.A. ▶
63 X 10 **Kenansville**, Florida, U.S.A.
127 P 1 **Kendal**, United Kingdom
63 Y 13 **Kendall**, Florida, U.S.A.
65 K 16 **Kendallville**, Indiana, U.S.A.
193 P 12 **Kendari**, Indonesia
192 I 12 **Kendawangan**, Indonesia
215 X 11 **Kendégué**, Chad
181 J 16 **Kendraparha**, India
179 U 9 **Kendyktas**, Kazakhstan ⛰
158 G 7 **Kene Plateau**, Mediterranean Sea ◇
214 H 12 **Kenema**, Sierra Leone
178 L 11 **Keneurgench**, Turkmenistan
190 F 11 **Keng Lon**, Myanmar
190 F 12 **Keng Tawng**, Myanmar
216 I 10 **Kenge**, Democratic Republic of Congo
218 K 13 **Kenhardt**, Republic of South Africa
127 S 7 **Kenilworth**, United Kingdom
210 H 6 **Kénitra**, Morocco
125 B 20 **Kenmare**, Republic of Ireland
66 I 2 **Kenmare**, North Dakota, U.S.A.
59 O 7 **Kennebunkport**, Maine, U.S.A.
79 Q 10 **Kennedy Entrance**, Alaska, U.S.A. ≈
62 L 8 **Kenner**, Louisiana, U.S.A
69 Y 8 **Kennett**, Missouri, U.S.A
76 J 9 **Kennewick**, Washington, U.S.A.
84 J 10 **Kenora**, Ontario, Canad
65 H 15 **Kenosha**, Wisconsin, U.S.A.
87 V 8 **Kensington**, Prince Edward Island, Canada
70 G 8 **Kent**, Texas, U.S.A.
82 I 8 **Kent Peninsula**, Nunavut, Canada ▶
179 R 10 **Kentau**, Kazakhstan
65 H 17 **Kentland**, Indiana, U.S.A
146 F 13 **Kentriki Makedonia**, Greece ▣
60 I 6 **Kentucky**, U.S.A. ▣
60 K 6 **Kentucky**, Kentucky, U.S.A. ʃ
60 D 7 **Kentucky Lake**, Kentuck U.S.A. ➘
190 G 12 **Kentung**, Myanmar
217 U 7 **Kenya**, Africa ■
183 W 14 **Keokradang**, Bangladesh ▲
181 J 15 **Keonjhar**, India
192 F 12 **Kepahiang**, Indonesia
145 J 20 **Kepi i Gjuhëzës**, Albania ▶
145 J 18 **Kepi i Rodonit**, Albania ▶
143 H 15 **Kępno**, Poland
193 Q 14 **Kepulauan Alor**, Indonesia ⛬
192 G 9 **Kepulauan Anambas**, Indonesia ⛬
193 V 13 **Kepulauan Aru**, Indonesia ⛬
193 U 10 **Kepulauan Asia**, Indonesia ⛬
193 U 10 **Kepulauan Ayu**, Indonesia ⛬
193 T 14 **Kepulauan Babar**, Indonesia ⛬
193 T 13 **Kepulauan Banda**, Indonesia ⛬
193 P 11 **Kepulauan Banggai**, Indonesia ⛬
192 C 9 **Kepulauan Banyak**, Indonesia ⛬
193 R 14 **Kepulauan Barat Daya**, Indonesia ⛬
192 C 11 **Kepulauan Batu**, Indonesia ⛬
193 O 14 **Kepulauan Bonerate**, Indonesia ⛬
193 U 12 **Kepulauan Gorong**, Indonesia ⛬
193 U 13 **Kepulauan Kai**, Indonesia ⛬
192 L 14 **Kepulauan Kangean**, Indonesia ⛬
192 J 13 **Kepulauan Karimunjawa**, Indonesia ⛬
192 L 13 **Kepulauan Laut Kecil**, Indonesia ⛬
193 S 14 **Kepulauan Leti**, Indonesia ⛬
192 G 11 **Kepulauan Lingga**, Indonesia ⛬
193 V 10 **Kepulauan Mapia**, Indonesia ⛬

■ Country ▣ Internal administrative region: State/Province/Territory/Dependent territory ⌂ Capital city ⛰ Mountain range/Undersea ridge ▲ Mountain peak/Volcano/Seamount ◇ Geographic feature ▶ Headland/Point/Cape/Peninsula ◓ Desert ⛬ Island/Island group ∷ Antarctic base ◎ Ocean ◒ Sea ≈ Bay/Gulf/Channel/Strait ➘ Lake ▦ Salt pan/Dry/Intermittent lake ʃ Ri

Kepulauan Nanusa – Kingston

R 8 Kepulauan Nanusa, Indonesia
H 8 Kepulauan Natuna, Indonesia
R 11 Kepulauan Obi, Indonesia
N 14 Kepulauan Sabalana, Indonesia
R 9 Kepulauan Sangir, Indonesia
P 14 Kepulauan Solor, Indonesia
O 14 Kepulauan Taka'Bonerate, Indonesia
R 8 Kepulauan Talaud, Indonesia
H 10 Kepulauan Tambelan, Indonesia
U 14 Kepulauan Tanimbar, Indonesia
M 14 Kepulauan Tengah, Indonesia
P 11 Kepulauan Togian, Indonesia
Q 13 Kepulauan Tukangbesi, Indonesia
U 13 Kepulauan Watubela, Indonesia
D 23 Kerala, India
R 12 Kerang, Victoria, Australia
H 20 Keratea, Greece
S 11 Kerben, Kyrgyzstan
W 11 Kerch, Ukraine
W 12 Kerch Strait, Ukraine
H 22 Kere, Ethiopia
C 6 Kerema, Papua New Guinea
I 6 Kerempe Burun, Turkey
I 16 Keren, Eritrea
N 11 Kerguelen Islands, France
M 11 Kerguelen Plateau, Indian Ocean
U 8 Kericho, Kenya
J 5 Kerikeri, New Zealand
P 14 Kerki, Turkmenistan
A 16 Kerkyra, Greece
E 14 Kerma, Sudan
P 11 Kermadec Islands, New Zealand
P 11 Kermadec Ridge, Pacific Ocean
P 11 Kermadec Trench, Pacific Ocean
M 11 Kermān, Iran
M 10 Kermān, Iran
F 6 Kermānshāh, Iran
F 6 Kermānshāh, Iran
I 7 Kermit, Texas, U.S.A.
K 22 Keros, Greece
O 11 Kérou, Benin
H 11 Kérouané, Guinea
L 19 Kerrobert, Saskatchewan, Canada
N 10 Kerrville, Texas, U.S.A.
A 19 Kerry Head, Republic of Ireland
P 11 Kershaw, South Carolina, U.S.A.
I 11 Kertamulia, Indonesia
H 15 Keryneia, Cyprus
K 9 Kerzaz, Algeria
D 8 Kerzers, Switzerland
B 7 Keşan, Turkey
K 9 Keshan, China
V 5 Keshem, Afghanistan
L 16 Kessel, Netherlands
G 5 Kesten'ga, Russian Federation
I 15 Keswick, United Kingdom
G 24 Keszthely, Hungary
M 11 Ket', Russian Federation
I 11 Ketapang, Indonesia
O 10 Ketchenery, Russian Federation
Y 12 Ketchikan, Alaska, U.S.A.
M 10 Ketchum, Idaho, U.S.A.
J 10 Ketelmeer, Netherlands
L 9 Kętrzyn, Poland
H 7 Ketta, Congo
V 14 Kétté, Cameroon
127 U 7 Kettering, United Kingdom
65 L 19 Kettering, Ohio, U.S.A.
76 K 5 Kettle Falls, Washington, U.S.A.
135 L 16 Keuruu, Finland
65 E 17 Kewanee, Illinois, U.S.A.
193 P 15 Kewapante, Indonesia
64 G 8 Keweenaw Bay, Michigan, U.S.A.
64 H 7 Keweenaw Peninsula, Michigan, U.S.A.
64 H 7 Keweenaw Point, Michigan, U.S.A.
63 Y 13 Key Biscayne, Florida, U.S.A.
86 D 10 Key Harbour, Ontario, Canada
63 Y 14 Key Largo, Florida, U.S.A.
63 Y 14 Key Largo, Florida, U.S.A.
63 W 15 Key West, Florida, U.S.A.
213 F 23 Keyala, Sudan
68 G 7 Keyes, Oklahoma, U.S.A.
186 H 6 Keyihe, China
61 R 2 Keyser, West Virginia, U.S.A.
69 P 8 Keystone Lake, Oklahoma, U.S.A.
61 S 6 Keysville, Virginia, U.S.A.
69 U 3 Keytesville, Missouri, U.S.A.
219 O 8 Kezi, Zimbabwe
143 K 19 Kežmarok, Slovakia
218 K 10 Kgalagadi, Botswana
219 N 10 Kgatleng, Botswana
153 V 14 Khabarovsk, Russian Federation
175 X 6 Khabb, United Arab Emirates
156 L 12 Khadyzhensk, Russian Federation
151 P 9 Khadzhybeys'kyy Lyman, Ukraine
183 Q 11 Khagaria, India
183 V 13 Khagrachari, Bangladesh
177 U 12 Khairpur, Pakistan
177 X 11 Khaïrpur, Pakistan
212 D 7 Khalig el 'Arab, Egypt
175 Y 11 Khalīj al Ḩalāniyāt, Oman
159 R 12 Khalīj Bumbah, Mediterranean Sea
175 Z 9 Khalīj Maşīrah, Oman
181 I 17 Khallikot, India
155 U 2 Khal'mer-Yu, Russian Federation
149 K 16 Khalopyenichy, Belarus
191 K 15 Kham Ta Kla, Thailand
181 D 16 Khamgaon, India
176 K 13 Khamīr, Iran
175 P 12 Khamir, Yemen
175 O 10 Khamis, Saudi Arabia
191 K 15 Khamkkeut, Laos
181 G 18 Khammam, India
153 S 10 Khampa, Russian Federation
153 R 11 Khamra, Russian Federation
173 Q 6 Khān al Baghdādī, Iraq
173 T 8 Khan al Maḩāwīl, Iraq
173 T 7 Khān al Mashāhīdah, Iraq
173 T 9 Khān al Muşallá, Iraq
173 T 10 Khān ar Rahbah, Iraq
173 P 2 Khān as Sūr, Iraq
173 U 9 Khān Jadwal, Iraq
172 I 3 Khān Shaykhūn, Syria
172 E 10 Khān Yūnis, Israel
177 U 5 Khānābād, Afghanistan
173 V 5 Khānaqīn, Iraq
181 E 15 Khandwa, India
153 U 10 Khandyga, Russian Federation
177 W 10 Khanewal, Pakistan
191 O 20 Khanh Duong, Vietnam
153 S 12 Khani, Russian Federation
182 I 6 Khanna, India
179 T 9 Khantau, Kazakhstan
152 K 10 Khanty-Mansiysk, Russian Federation
191 H 24 Khao Chum Thong, Thailand
191 I 18 Khao Khiaw, Thailand
191 G 17 Khao Laem Reservoir, Thailand
191 I 20 Khao Sai Dao Tai, Thailand
182 I 2 Khapalu, India
157 R 9 Kharabali, Russian Federation
183 S 14 Kharagpur, India
177 S 12 Kharan, Pakistan
182 G 8 Kharbara, India
173 X 11 Kharfiyah, Iraq
176 H 10 Khārg Islands, Iran
181 D 15 Khargon, India
181 H 16 Khariar, India
151 V 4 Kharkiv, Ukraine
154 J 2 Kharlovka, Russian Federation
146 K 11 Kharmanli, Bulgaria
154 K 11 Kharovsk, Russian Federation
213 F 16 Khartoum, Sudan
213 F 16 Khartoum, Sudan
157 Q 14 Khasav'yurt, Russian Federation
177 P 12 Khāsh, Iran
152 L 8 Khashgort, Russian Federation
213 G 17 Khashm el Girba, Sudan
171 S 6 Khashuri, Georgia
146 K 11 Khaskovo, Bulgaria
146 J 11 Khaskovo, Bulgaria
153 P 8 Khatanga, Russian Federation
153 Q 8 Khatanga, Russian Federation
153 Q 7 Khatangskiy Zaliv, Russian Federation
153 Z 7 Khatyrka, Russian Federation
181 A 14 Khavda, India
191 F 18 Khawsa, Myanmar
175 N 10 Khawsh, Saudi Arabia
174 L 5 Khaybar, Saudi Arabia
175 O 10 Khaybar, Saudi Arabia
218 K 15 Khayelitsha, Republic of South Africa
155 S 2 Khaypudyrskaya Guba, Russian Federation
191 K 14 Khê Bo, Vietnam
191 N 16 Khe Sanh, Vietnam
182 M 7 Khela, India
210 I 7 Khemisset, Morocco
191 L 17 Khemmarat, Thailand
211 P 6 Khenchela, Algeria
210 I 7 Khenifra, Morocco
177 U 6 Khenjan, Afghanistan
151 S 9 Kherson, Ukraine
176 J 5 Khezerābād, Iran
153 R 14 Khilok, Russian Federation
172 K 4 Khirbat Isrīyah, Syria
191 G 17 Khlong Khlung, Thailand
150 M 5 Khmel'nyts'kyy, Ukraine
151 Q 6 Khmel'ove, Ukraine
151 N 5 Khmil'nyk, Ukraine
178 K 5 Khobda, Kazakhstan
171 R 6 Khobi, Georgia
151 O 4 Khodorkiv, Ukraine
179 O 13 Khodzha Davlet, Uzbekistan
213 C 22 Khogali, Sudan
191 H 18 Khok Samrong, Thailand
154 E 13 Kholm, Russian Federation
177 T 5 Kholm, Afghanistan
153 X 14 Kholmsk, Russian Federation
149 M 21 Kholmyech, Belarus
218 I 9 Khomas, Namibia
176 H 7 Khomeyn, Iran
176 I 8 Khomeynīshahr, Iran
191 J 16 Khon Kaen, Thailand
176 J 12 Khonj, Iran
153 V 9 Khonuu, Russian Federation
153 V 14 Khor, Russian Federation
177 O 7 Khorāsān, Iran
191 J 16 Khorat Plateau, Thailand
155 S 3 Khorey-Ver, Russian Federation
153 Q 13 Khorinsk, Russian Federation
218 H 8 Khorixas, Namibia
151 T 10 Khorly, Ukraine
151 T 3 Khorol, Ukraine
151 S 4 Khorol, Ukraine
176 G 7 Khorramābād, Iran
176 F 9 Khorramshahr, Iran
179 T 14 Khorugh, Tajikistan
157 R 10 Khosheutovo, Russian Federation
177 T 10 Khost, Pakistan
150 L 6 Khotyn, Ukraine
210 H 7 Khouribga, Morocco
183 V 12 Khowai, India
176 H 11 Khowr-e Soltānī, Iran
177 V 8 Khowst, Afghanistan
149 M 21 Khoyniki, Belarus
153 U 9 Khrebet Cherskogo, Russian Federation
153 U 12 Khrebet Dzhugdzhur, Russian Federation
179 W 9 Khrebet Dzhungarskiy Alatau, Kazakhstan
179 Q 9 Khrebet Karatau, Kazakhstan
153 P 14 Khrebet Khamar-Daban, Russian Federation
153 X 10 Khrebet Kolymskiy, Russian Federation
179 P 12 Khrebet Nuratau, Uzbekistan
153 T 8 Khrebet Orulgan, Russian Federation
155 S 1 Khrebet Pay-Khoy, Russian Federation
153 T 12 Khrebet Synnagyn, Russian Federation
179 X 6 Khrebet Tarbagatay, Kazakhstan
190 B 12 Khreum, Myanmar
178 L 5 Khromtau, Kazakhstan
191 K 18 Khu Khan, Thailand
175 P 6 Khuff, Saudi Arabia
179 R 12 Khŭjand, Tajikistan
174 L 7 Khulays, Saudi Arabia
183 T 14 Khulna, Bangladesh
183 T 14 Khulna, Bangladesh
191 F 14 Khun Yuam, Thailand
181 J 14 Khunti, India
175 R 6 Khurayş, Saudi Arabia
182 J 9 Khurja, India
177 W 9 Khushab, Pakistan
150 H 7 Khust, Ukraine
175 U 5 Khuwayr, Qatar
213 D 18 Khuwei, Sudan
177 T 12 Khuzdar, Pakistan
176 G 9 Khūzestān, Iran
157 R 4 Khvalynsk, Russian Federation
176 L 7 Khvor, Iran
176 I 11 Khvormūj, Iran
176 F 3 Khvoy, Iran
154 H 12 Khvoynaya, Russian Federation
177 V 7 Khyber Pass, Afghanistan
234 L 5 Kia, Solomon Islands
231 U 12 Kiama, New South Wales, Australia
197 L 24 Kiamba, Philippines
217 P 12 Kiambi, Democratic Republic of Congo
79 N 5 Kiana, Alaska, U.S.A.
231 T 12 Kiandra, New South Wales, Australia
217 W 12 Kibaha, Tanzania
216 F 10 Kibangou, Congo
197 L 21 Kibawe, Philippines
217 V 11 Kibaya, Tanzania
217 R 7 Kiboga, Uganda
217 O 10 Kibombo, Democratic Republic of Congo
217 R 10 Kibondo, Tanzania
213 I 22 Kibre Mengist, Ethiopia
146 C 12 Kičevo, Macedonia (F.Y.R.O.M.)
155 N 11 Kichmengskiy Gorodok, Russian Federation
197 L 22 Kidapawan, Philippines
127 Q 7 Kidderminster, United Kingdom
214 G 8 Kidira, Senegal
127 T 9 Kidlington, United Kingdom
127 R 5 Kidsgrove, United Kingdom
126 M 10 Kidwelly, United Kingdom
136 H 8 Kiel, Germany
64 G 12 Kiel, Wisconsin, U.S.A.
143 K 15 Kielce, Poland
136 H 8 Kieler Bucht, Germany
217 P 14 Kienge, Democratic Republic of Congo
234 J 5 Kieta, Papua New Guinea
151 P 3 Kiev, Ukraine
151 P 3 Kiev Reservoir, Ukraine
214 G 7 Kiffa, Mauritania
145 H 14 Kifino Selo, Bosnia and Herzegovina
147 G 20 Kifisia, Greece
147 E 18 Kifisos, Greece
173 U 5 Kifrī, Iraq
217 Q 9 Kigali, Rwanda
217 Q 10 Kigoma, Tanzania
217 Q 11 Kigoma, Tanzania
78 D 8 Kihei, Hawaii, U.S.A.
232 L 10 Kihikihi, New Zealand
148 F 8 Kihnu, Estonia
199 H 19 Kii-nagashima, Japan
199 G 19 Kii-sanchi, Japan
199 G 19 Kii-suidō, Japan
179 T 7 Kiik, Kazakhstan
199 O 21 Kikai, Japan
199 O 21 Kikai-jima, Japan
144 L 8 Kikinda, Serbia and Montenegro
177 Q 14 Kikki, Pakistan
159 S 9 Kikladhes Plateau, Mediterranean Sea
155 O 14 Kiknur, Russian Federation
217 O 12 Kikondja, Democratic Republic of Congo
234 C 5 Kikori, Papua New Guinea
234 C 5 Kikori, Papua New Guinea
216 J 11 Kikwit, Democratic Republic of Congo
78 A 6 Kilauea, Hawaii, U.S.A.
78 E 9 Kilauea, Hawaii, U.S.A.
187 M 15 Kilchu, North Korea
125 E 18 Kilcock, Republic of Ireland
125 E 18 Kildare, Republic of Ireland
216 K 11 Kilembe, Democratic Republic of Congo
71 T 6 Kilgore, Texas, U.S.A.
237 Y 4 Kili Island, Marshall Islands
217 Q 10 Kiliba, Democratic Republic of Congo
217 X 10 Kilifi, Kenya
217 V 9 Kilimanjaro, Tanzania
217 V 10 Kilimanjaro, Tanzania
217 X 12 Kilindoni, Tanzania
148 F 8 Kilingi-Nõmme, Estonia
170 M 13 Kilis, Turkey
172 J 1 Kilis, Syria
125 B 19 Kilkee, Republic of Ireland
125 D 19 Kilkenny, Republic of Ireland
126 K 13 Kilkhampton, United Kingdom
146 F 13 Kilkis, Greece
125 B 20 Killarney, Republic of Ireland
86 D 9 Killarney, Ontario, Canada
66 H 4 Killdeer, North Dakota, U.S.A.
71 P 8 Killeen, Texas, U.S.A.
85 T 5 Killiniq, Québec, Canada
124 G 13 Kilmarnock, United Kingdom
155 Q 14 Kil'mez', Russian Federation
217 V 12 Kilosa, Tanzania
125 B 19 Kilrush, Republic of Ireland
181 B 22 Kilttan, India
217 P 13 Kilwa, Democratic Republic of Congo
217 W 13 Kilwa Kivinje, Tanzania
193 T 12 Kilwo, Indonesia
215 W 11 Kim, Chad
75 T 7 Kim, Colorado, U.S.A.
193 X 14 Kimaan, Indonesia
217 W 13 Kimambi, Tanzania
216 G 10 Kimba, Congo
231 O 11 Kimba, South Australia, Australia
66 G 14 Kimball, Nebraska, U.S.A.
234 G 4 Kimbe, Papua New Guinea
218 M 12 Kimberley, Republic of South Africa
230 K 3 Kimberley, Western Australia, Australia
187 M 16 Kimch'aek, North Korea
85 R 4 Kimmirut, Nunavut, Canada
147 I 23 Kimolos, Greece
216 G 11 Kimpese, Democratic Republic of Congo
198 I 13 Kimpoku-san, Japan
216 H 11 Kimvula, Democratic Republic of Congo
195 V 6 Kinabatangan, Malaysia
217 W 10 Kinango, Kenya
147 L 22 Kinaros, Greece
86 C 12 Kincardine, Ontario, Canada
217 N 13 Kinda, Democratic Republic of Congo
62 I 7 Kinder, Louisiana, U.S.A.
83 L 19 Kindersley, Saskatchewan, Canada
214 F 11 Kindia, Guinea
217 O 9 Kindu, Democratic Republic of Congo
157 T 3 Kinel'-Cherkasy, Russian Federation
154 L 13 Kineshma, Russian Federation
77 H 21 King City, California, U.S.A.
111 K 23 King George Bay, Falkland Islands
240 G 3 King George Island, Antarctica
81 S 9 King George Islands, Nunavut, Canada
231 R 14 King Island, Tasmania, Australia
241 X 7 King Leopold and Queen Astrid Coast, Antarctica
230 I 3 King Leopold Ranges, Western Australia, Australia
83 D 16 King Mountain, British Columbia, Canada
240 J 9 King Peninsula, Antarctica
230 I 3 King Sound, Western Australia, Australia
84 L 1 King William Island, Nunavut, Canada
231 W 8 Kingaroy, Queensland, Australia
68 M 9 Kingfisher, Oklahoma, U.S.A.
154 D 11 Kingisepp, Russian Federation
68 M 6 Kingman, Kansas, U.S.A.
74 G 10 Kingman, Arizona, U.S.A.
41 Q 7 Kingman Reef, U.S.A.
177 V 10 Kingri, Pakistan
125 M 19 King's, United Kingdom
127 X 6 King's Lynn, United Kingdom
58 L 12 Kings Park, New York, U.S.A.
74 L 2 Kings Peak, Utah, U.S.A.
127 T 12 King's Worthy, United Kingdom
127 N 15 Kingsbridge, United Kingdom
127 T 11 Kingsclere, United Kingdom
231 P 12 Kingscote, South Australia, Australia
63 W 6 Kingsland, Georgia, U.S.A.
60 L 8 Kingsport, Tennessee, U.S.A.
233 C 23 Kingston, New Zealand
58 J 10 Kingston, New York, U.S.A.
59 N 11 Kingston, Rhode Island, U.S.A.
65 D 19 Kingston, Illinois, U.S.A.

Country | Internal administrative region: State/Province/Territory/Dependent territory | Capital city | Mountain range/Undersea ridge | Mountain peak/Volcano/Seamount | Geographic feature | Headland/Point/Cape/Peninsula | Desert | Island/Island group | Antarctic base | Ocean | Sea | Bay/Gulf/Channel/Strait | Lake | Salt pan/Dry/Intermittent lake | River

▣ Country ▣ Internal administrative region: State/Province/Territory/Dependent territory ★ Capital city ▲ Mountain range/Undersea ridge ▲ Mountain peak/Volcano/Seamount ◇ Geographic feature ► Headland/Point/Cape/Peninsula ▲ Desert ▱ Island/Island group ⊞ Antarctic base ⊘ Ocean ⟆ Sea ≈ Bay/Gulf/Channel/Strait ⟍ Lake ↳ Salt pan/Dry/Intermittent lake ↷ Ri[ver]

302

0	F 8	**Köroğlu Dağlari,** Turkey ▲
0	G 8	**Köroğlu Tepesi,** Turkey ▲
7	W 11	**Korogwe,** Tanzania
7	L 23	**Koronadal,** Philippines
7	D 23	**Koroni,** Greece
6	I 15	**Koror,** Palau
3	K 24	**Körös,** Hungary ↘
	N 3	**Korosten',** Ukraine
1	O 4	**Korostyshiv,** Ukraine
5	M 17	**Korpilahti,** Finland
1	Q 5	**Korsun'-Shevchenkivs'kyy,** Ukraine
3	B 18	**Kortemark,** Belgium
8	E 15	**Korti,** Sudan
3	C 19	**Kortrijk,** Belgium
3	Y 9	**Koryakskiy Khrebet,** Russian Federation ▲▲
5	N 10	**Koryazhma,** Russian Federation
2	N 10	**Korycin,** Poland
9	R 1	**Koryukivka,** Ukraine
7	M 22	**Kos,** Greece
7	M 23	**Kos,** Greece ⚓
1	U 10	**Kosa Arabats'ka Strilka,** Ukraine ≈
1	V 10	**Kosa Biryuchyy Ostriv,** Ukraine ▶
7	L 17	**Kosan,** North Korea
	F 13	**Kościan,** Poland
2	H 9	**Kościerzyna,** Poland
	M 4	**Kosciusko,** Mississippi, U.S.A.
8	G 6	**Kose,** Estonia
2	M 14	**Kosh-Agach,** Russian Federation
	U 11	**Kosh-Döbö,** Kyrgyzstan
	B 23	**Koshiki-kaikyō,** Japan ≈
9	A 23	**Koshikijima-rettō,** Japan ⚓
7	P 7	**Koshk,** Afghanistan
3	R 10	**Kosi Reservoir,** Nepal ↘
3	L 20	**Košice,** Slovakia
0	J 7	**Kosiv,** Ukraine
4	K 12	**Kosjerić,** Serbia and Montenegro
9	Q 5	**Koskol',** Kazakhstan
7	M 18	**Kosŏng,** North Korea
5	L 15	**Kosovo,** Serbia and Montenegro ▣
5	L 15	**Kosovska Mitrovica,** Serbia and Montenegro
7	R 15	**Kosrae,** Federated States of Micronesia ⚓
7	R 15	**Kosrae,** Federated States of Micronesia ▣
9	P 6	**Kössen,** Austria
9	O 4	**Kostanay,** Kazakhstan ▣
9	O 3	**Kostanay,** Kazakhstan
6	H 10	**Kostenets,** Bulgaria
3	F 18	**Kosti,** Sudan
6	F 9	**Kostinbrod,** Bulgaria
0	L 3	**Kostopil',** Ukraine
4	K 13	**Kostroma,** Russian Federation
4	L 12	**Kostromskaya Oblast',** Russian Federation
2	D 12	**Kostrzyn,** Poland
1	X 6	**Kostyantynivka,** Ukraine
5	S 4	**Kos'yu,** Russian Federation
2	F 8	**Koszalin,** Poland
3	K 17	**Koszyce,** Poland
7	U 13	**Kot Diji,** Pakistan
2	I 9	**Kot Putli,** India
0	D 13	**Kota,** India
5	V 4	**Kota Belud,** Malaysia
4	C 5	**Kota Bharu,** Malaysia
5	V 4	**Kota Kinabalu,** Malaysia
4	F 10	**Kota Tinggi,** Malaysia
2	F 13	**Kotaagung,** Indonesia
2	M 12	**Kotabaru,** Indonesia
2	F 13	**Kotabumi,** Indonesia
2	Q 10	**Kotamobagu,** Indonesia
2	D 10	**Kotapinang,** Indonesia
2	K 12	**Kotare,** New Zealand
6	L 8	**Kotel,** Bulgaria
5	O 13	**Kotel'nich,** Russian Federation
7	O 9	**Kotel'nikovo,** Russian Federation
1	U 4	**Kotel'va,** Ukraine
217	T 6	**Kotido,** Uganda
135	N 18	**Kotka,** Finland
155	N 10	**Kotlas,** Russian Federation
182	G 4	**Kotli,** India
145	I 16	**Kotor,** Serbia and Montenegro
144	G 10	**Kotor Varoš,** Bosnia and Herzegovina
215	R 10	**Kotorkoshi,** Nigeria
214	L 12	**Kotouba,** Côte d'Ivoire
151	O 8	**Kotovs'k,** Ukraine
149	F 18	**Kotra,** Belarus ↘
177	U 14	**Kotri,** Pakistan
139	Q 9	**Kötschach,** Austria
181	G 18	**Kottagudem,** India
181	G 19	**Kottapatnam,** India
216	L 4	**Kotto,** Central African Republic ↘
153	R 8	**Kotuy,** Russian Federation ↘
79	N 5	**Kotzebue,** Alaska, U.S.A.
78	M 5	**Kotzebue Sound,** Alaska, U.S.A. ≈
216	K 4	**Kouango,** Central African Republic
214	G 10	**Koubia,** Guinea
216	E 10	**Kouilou,** Congo ▣
170	G 15	**Koúklia,** Cyprus
216	E 8	**Koulamoutou,** Gabon
235	O 13	**Koumac,** New Caledonia
214	F 10	**Koumbia,** Guinea
215	X 11	**Koumra,** Chad
214	F 9	**Koúndara,** Guinea
214	E 9	**Koungheul,** Senegal
105	Y 6	**Kourou,** French Guiana
214	H 11	**Kouroussa,** Guinea
214	F 9	**Koussanar,** Senegal
215	V 10	**Kousséri,** Chad
147	D 16	**Koutsochero,** Greece
135	N 18	**Kouvola,** Finland
154	G 3	**Kovdor,** Russian Federation
150	J 2	**Kovel',** Ukraine
157	N 1	**Kovrov,** Russian Federation
157	O 3	**Kovylkino,** Russian Federation
231	R 3	**Kowanyama,** Queensland, Australia
189	U 13	**Kowloon,** China
187	L 17	**Kowŏn,** North Korea
170	C 12	**Köycegiz,** Turkey
154	L 5	**Koyda,** Russian Federation
79	O 6	**Koykuyuk,** Alaska, U.S.A.
181	C 18	**Koyna Reservoir,** India ↘
146	G 7	**Koynare,** Bulgaria
79	N 6	**Koyuk,** Alaska, U.S.A.
170	M 9	**Koyulhisar,** Turkey
170	K 12	**Kozan,** Turkey
147	D 15	**Kozani,** Greece
144	F 9	**Kozara,** Bosnia and Herzegovina ▲▲
151	Q 3	**Kozelets',** Ukraine
156	J 3	**Kozel'sk,** Russian Federation
153	R 7	**Kozhevnikovo,** Russian Federation
143	L 14	**Kozienice,** Poland
146	G 6	**Kozloduy,** Bulgaria
157	Q 1	**Koz'modem'yansk,** Russian Federation
199	K 18	**Kōzu-shima,** Japan ⚓
151	O 5	**Kozyatyn,** Ukraine
215	N 13	**Kpalimé,** Togo
191	F 22	**Kra Buri,** Thailand
191	G 25	**Krabi,** Thailand
191	M 20	**Krâchéh,** Cambodia
144	L 12	**Kragujevac,** Serbia and Montenegro
192	G 14	**Krakatau,** Indonesia ▲
143	K 13	**Kraków,** Poland
191	K 19	**Krâlänh,** Cambodia
93	S 13	**Kralendijk,** Netherlands Antilles
144	L 12	**Kraljevo,** Serbia and Montenegro
143	B 17	**Kralovice,** Czech Republic
151	X 6	**Kramators'k,** Ukraine
133	F 7	**Krammer,** Netherlands ≈
147	F 21	**Kranidi,** Greece
144	B 7	**Kranj,** Slovenia
194	A 13	**Kranji Reservoir,** Singapore ↘
178	K 4	**Kransoyar,** Kazakhstan
143	H 16	**Krapkowice,** Poland
152	K 6	**Krasino,** Russian Federation
148	I 13	**Kräslava,** Latvia
149	N 18	**Krasnapollye,** Belarus
157	N 1	**Krasnaya,** Russian Federation
156	L 13	**Krasnaya Polyana,** Russian Federation
149	I 19	**Krasnaya Slabada,** Belarus
151	O 8	**Krasni Okny,** Ukraine
143	M 15	**Kraśnik,** Poland
157	Q 6	**Krasnoarmeysk,** Russian Federation
151	X 7	**Krasnoarmiys'k,** Ukraine
155	N 9	**Krasnoborsk,** Russian Federation
156	K 12	**Krasnodar,** Russian Federation
156	L 11	**Krasnodarskiy Kray,** Russian Federation ▣
156	M 11	**Krasnogvardeyskoye,** Russian Federation
151	V 5	**Krasnohrad,** Ukraine
155	S 12	**Krasnokamsk,** Russian Federation
157	U 5	**Krasnokholm,** Russian Federation
151	W 5	**Krasnopavlivka,** Ukraine
151	T 10	**Krasnoperekops'k,** Ukraine
151	U 3	**Krasnopillya,** Ukraine
153	N 9	**Krasnosel'kup,** Russian Federation
154	J 4	**Krasnoshchel'ye,** Russian Federation
151	S 6	**Krasnosillya,** Ukraine
151	O 2	**Krasnoslobodsk,** Russian Federation
155	U 13	**Krasnoufimsk,** Russian Federation
157	W 2	**Krasnousol'skiy,** Russian Federation
155	T 10	**Krasnovishersk,** Russian Federation
178	H 12	**Krasnovodskiy Zaliv,** Turkmenistan ≈
153	N 12	**Krasnoyarsk,** Russian Federation
156	H 2	**Krasnoye,** Russian Federation
143	O 15	**Krasnystaw,** Poland
156	G 2	**Krasnyy,** Russian Federation
154	I 13	**Krasnyy Kholm,** Russian Federation
157	Q 6	**Krasnyy Kut,** Russian Federation
151	Z 6	**Krasnyy Luch,** Ukraine
151	X 5	**Krasnyy Lyman,** Ukraine
157	P 6	**Krasnyy Yar,** Russian Federation
157	S 10	**Krasnyy Yar,** Russian Federation
157	R 11	**Krasnyye Barrikady,** Russian Federation
146	E 10	**Kratovo,** Macedonia (F.Y.R.O.M.)
193	Y 12	**Krau,** Indonesia
157	R 13	**Kraynovka,** Russian Federation
137	B 16	**Krefeld,** Germany
151	T 6	**Kremenchuk,** Ukraine
151	S 5	**Kremenchuts'ka Vodoskhovyshche,** Ukraine ↘
150	K 4	**Kremenets',** Ukraine
151	Y 5	**Kreminna,** Ukraine
150	J 4	**Kremintsi,** Ukraine
75	Q 3	**Kremmling,** Colorado, U.S.A.
139	V 3	**Krems an der Donau,** Austria
146	F 11	**Kresna,** Bulgaria
147	D 21	**Krestena,** Greece
155	Q 4	**Krestovka,** Russian Federation
153	R 11	**Krestyakh,** Russian Federation
148	B 13	**Kretinga,** Lithuania
139	Q 8	**Kreuzeck,** Austria ▲
138	H 6	**Kreuzlingen,** Switzerland
215	S 15	**Kribi,** Cameroon
139	W 6	**Krieglach,** Austria
147	C 18	**Krikellos,** Greece
139	O 7	**Krimml,** Austria
181	E 19	**Krishna,** India ↘
181	E 21	**Krishnagiri,** India
183	S 13	**Krishnanagar,** India
181	D 21	**Krishnaraja Sagara,** India ↘
135	B 22	**Kristiansand,** Norway
135	F 25	**Kristianstad,** Sweden
135	C 15	**Kristiansund,** Norway
135	J 17	**Kristinestad,** Finland
147	J 26	**Kriti,** Greece ▣
146	E 10	**Kriva Palanka,** Macedonia (F.Y.R.O.M.)
158	M 4	**Krk,** Mediterranean Sea ▣
151	U 11	**Krms'ky Pivostriv,** Ukraine ▶
142	H 7	**Krokowa,** Poland
134	B 10	**Króksfjarðarnes,** Iceland
151	S 2	**Krolevets',** Ukraine
156	J 4	**Kromy,** Russian Federation
137	J 19	**Kronach,** Germany
191	J 21	**Krŏng Kaôh Kŏng,** Cambodia
153	Z 10	**Kronotskiy Poluostrov,** Russian Federation ▶
153	Z 11	**Kronotskiy Zaliv,** Russian Federation ≈
219	N 12	**Kroonstad,** Republic of South Africa
156	L 11	**Kropotkin,** Russian Federation
143	M 18	**Krosno,** Poland
143	G 14	**Krotoszyn,** Poland
62	J 7	**Krotz Springs,** Louisiana, U.S.A.
144	D 7	**Krško,** Slovenia
146	J 12	**Krumovgrad,** Bulgaria
144	J 11	**Krupanj,** Serbia and Montenegro
143	I 21	**Krupina,** Slovakia
144	M 13	**Kruševac,** Serbia and Montenegro
149	N 17	**Kryichaw,** Belarus
156	J 12	**Krymsk,** Russian Federation
151	T 13	**Krymski Hori,** Ukraine ▲▲
143	L 18	**Krynica,** Poland
151	P 7	**Kryve Ozero,** Ukraine
151	T 7	**Kryvyy Rih,** Ukraine
151	N 7	**Kryzhopil',** Ukraine
143	I 15	**Krzepice,** Poland
210	K 10	**Ksabi,** Algeria
210	M 6	**Ksar Chellala,** Algeria
210	M 6	**Ksar el Boukhari,** Algeria
210	I 6	**Ksar el Kebir,** Morocco
157	O 1	**Kstovo,** Russian Federation
195	S 6	**Kuala Belait,** Brunei
194	B 6	**Kuala Kangsar,** Malaysia
194	C 5	**Kuala Kerai,** Malaysia
195	Y 5	**Kuala Kinabatangan,** Malaysia ↘
194	C 7	**Kuala Lipis,** Malaysia
194	C 8	**Kuala Lumpur,** Malaysia ▣
194	C 8	**Kuala Lumpur,** Malaysia ▣
195	U 5	**Kuala Penyu,** Malaysia
194	B 8	**Kuala Selangor,** Malaysia
194	E 6	**Kuala Terengganu,** Malaysia
192	K 11	**Kualakurun,** Indonesia
195	W 6	**Kuamut,** Malaysia
187	F 16	**Kuancheng,** China
187	J 16	**Kuandian,** China
189	Z 12	**Kuanshan,** Taiwan
194	E 8	**Kuantan,** Malaysia
173	O 1	**Kubaybāt,** Syria
173	R 7	**Kubaysah,** Iraq
213	A 18	**Kubbum,** Sudan
234	B 5	**Kubeai,** Papua New Guinea
146	L 6	**Kubrat,** Bulgaria
144	M 11	**Kučevo,** Serbia and Montenegro
181	J 15	**Kuchaiburi,** India
195	N 10	**Kuching,** Malaysia
199	B 25	**Kuchino-Erabu-shima,** Japan ⚓
199	B 26	**Kuchino-shima,** Japan ⚓
199	B 22	**Kuchinotsu,** Japan
181	L 19	**Kuda Huvadu Channel,** Maldives ↘
181	C 19	**Kudal,** India
175	N 10	**Kudayd,** Saudi Arabia
143	F 16	**Kudowa-Zdrój,** Poland
192	J 14	**Kudus,** Indonesia
155	S 11	**Kudymkar,** Russian Federation
139	O 6	**Kufstein,** Austria
82	G 9	**Kugluktuk,** Nunavut, Canada
82	C 8	**Kugmallit Bay,** Northwest Territories, Canada ≈
177	N 12	**Kūh-e Bazmān,** Iran ▲
176	F 5	**Kūh-e Chehel Chashmeh,** Iran ▲
176	L 12	**Kūh-e Fūrgun,** Iran ▲
176	H 8	**Kūh-e Garbosh,** Iran ▲
173	T 2	**Kūh-e Ḥājī Ebrāhīm,** Iraq ▲
176	F 5	**Kūh-e-Haji Ebrahim,** Iran ▲
176	K 12	**Kūh-e Hormoz,** Iran ▲
176	L 11	**Kūh-e Ilazārān,** Iran ▲
176	M 8	**Kūh-e Nāy Band,** Iran ▲
177	O 13	**Kūh-e Nokhowch,** Iran ▲
177	O 9	**Kūh-e Palangān,** Iran ▲
176	I 11	**Kūh-e Shīb,** Iran ▲▲
177	P 12	**Kūh-e Taftān,** Iran ▲
177	Q 13	**Kūhak,** Iran
176	H 3	**Kuhha-ye Sabalan,** Iran ▲
135	N 14	**Kuhmo,** Finland
189	V 12	**Kuitan,** China
218	I 4	**Kuito,** Angola
198	L 9	**Kuji,** Japan
199	K 14	**Kuji,** Japan ↘
199	C 21	**Kujū-san,** Japan ▲
215	U 9	**Kukawa,** Nigeria
145	L 16	**Kukës,** Albania
194	E 10	**Kukup,** Malaysia
144	J 8	**Kula,** Serbia and Montenegro
146	E 6	**Kula,** Bulgaria
170	C 10	**Kula,** Turkey
184	K 11	**Kula Kangri,** China ▲
197	F 23	**Kulassein,** Philippines ⚓
183	V 12	**Kulaura,** Bangladesh
148	C 11	**Kuldīga,** Latvia
157	N 1	**Kulebaki,** Russian Federation
231	N 7	**Kulgera,** Northern Territory, Australia
179	O 10	**Kulkuduk,** Uzbekistan
182	J 5	**Kullu,** India
137	J 19	**Kulmbach,** Germany
179	S 14	**Külob,** Tajikistan
171	Q 11	**Kulp,** Turkey
178	J 7	**Kul'sary,** Kazakhstan
183	R 13	**Kulti,** India
170	H 10	**Kulu,** Turkey
152	L 12	**Kulunda,** Russian Federation
157	O 12	**Kuma,** Russian Federation ↘
199	K 15	**Kumagaya,** Japan
198	I 7	**Kumaishi,** Japan
199	C 22	**Kumamoto,** Japan
199	H 19	**Kumano,** Japan
146	D 10	**Kumanovo,** Macedonia (F.Y.R.O.M.)
233	E 18	**Kumara Junction,** New Zealand
230	H 7	**Kumarina Roadhouse,** Western Australia, Australia
215	S 14	**Kumba,** Cameroon
181	F 22	**Kumbakonam,** India
193	Y 14	**Kumbe,** Indonesia
170	F 10	**Kümbet,** Turkey
175	P 9	**Kumdah,** Saudi Arabia
199	M 25	**Kume-jima,** Japan ⚓
199	W 3	**Kumertau,** Russian Federation
217	T 7	**Kumi,** Uganda
187	M 20	**Kumi,** South Korea
135	G 21	**Kumla,** Sweden
136	L 9	**Kummerower See,** Germany ↘
215	T 11	**Kumo,** Nigeria
191	J 16	**Kumphawapi,** Thailand
181	C 20	**Kumta,** India
217	N 6	**Kumu,** Democratic Republic of Congo
184	L 5	**Kümüx,** China
195	X 6	**Kunak,** Malaysia
177	V 6	**Kunar,** Afghanistan ▣
148	H 5	**Kunda,** Estonia
182	M 11	**Kunda,** India
218	I 2	**Kunda-dia-Baze,** Angola
195	V 4	**Kundat,** Malaysia
234	C 4	**Kundiawa,** Papua New Guinea
192	F 10	**Kundur,** Indonesia ⚓
177	U 5	**Kunduz,** Afghanistan ▣
218	G 8	**Kunene,** Namibia ▣
218	F 7	**Kunene,** Namibia ↘
179	V 10	**Kungei Alatau,** Kyrgyzstan ▲▲
83	C 20	**Kunghit Island,** British Columbia, Canada ⚓
178	L 10	**Kungrad,** Uzbekistan
135	D 23	**Kungsbacka,** Sweden
216	J 6	**Kungu,** Democratic Republic of Congo
155	T 13	**Kungur,** Russian Federation
190	F 12	**Kunhing,** Myanmar
199	D 21	**Kunisaki,** Japan
190	F 10	**Kunlong,** Myanmar
184	H 7	**Kunlun Shan,** China ▲▲
188	L 11	**Kunming,** China
187	L 20	**Kunsan,** South Korea
189	Y 5	**Kunshan,** China
143	K 24	**Kunszentmárton,** Hungary
234	I 4	**Kunua,** Papua New Guinea
230	K 3	**Kununurra,** Western Australia, Australia
216	H 10	**Kunzulu,** Democratic Republic of Congo
154	G 3	**Kuolayarvi,** Russian Federation
135	N 15	**Kuopio,** Finland
193	P 15	**Kupang,** Indonesia
234	E 7	**Kupiano,** Papua New Guinea
148	G 13	**Kupiškis,** Lithuania
79	X 11	**Kupreanof Island,** Alaska, U.S.A. ⚓
151	X 4	**Kup"yans'k,** Ukraine
184	J 5	**Kuqa,** China
171	V 7	**Kür,** Azerbaijan/Turkey ↘
153	N 13	**Kuragino,** Russian Federation
199	E 19	**Kurashiki,** Japan
199	E 18	**Kurayoshi,** Japan
179	Y 5	**Kurchum,** Kazakhstan
176	E 2	**Kurdistan,** Iran ◇
146	J 12	**Kürdzhali,** Bulgaria ▣
146	J 11	**Kürdzhali,** Bulgaria
199	D 20	**Kure,** Japan
170	I 7	**Küre,** Turkey
170	H 7	**Küre Dağlari,** Turkey ▲▲
148	D 8	**Kuressaare,** Estonia
179	R 5	**Kurgal'dzhinskiy,** Kazakhstan
152	J 11	**Kurgan,** Russian Federation
156	M 12	**Kurganinsk,** Russian Federation
236	D 2	**Kuria,** Kiribati ⚓
175	Y 11	**Kuria Muria,** Oman ⚓
135	K 16	**Kurikka,** Finland
40	M 2	**Kuril Basin,** Pacific Ocean ◇
153	Y 14	**Kuril Islands,** Russian Federation ⚓
40	M 3	**Kuril Trench,** Pacific Ocean ◇
157	R 6	**Kurilovka,** Russian Federation
153	Y 14	**Kuril'sk,** Russian Federation
91	Q 8	**Kurinwás,** Nicaragua ↘
156	M 1	**Kurlovskiy,** Russian Federation
213	G 19	**Kurmuk,** Sudan
181	E 19	**Kurnool,** India
199	N 26	**Kuro-shima,** Japan ⚓
199	H 15	**Kurobe,** Japan
199	K 14	**Kuroiso,** Japan
233	E 22	**Kurow,** New Zealand
143	M 14	**Kurów,** Poland

Laguna de Bay – Langdon

G 11 **Laguna de Bay**, Philippines
Q 5 **Laguna de Caratasca**, Honduras
O 11 **Laguna de Chapala**, Mexico
T 13 **Laguna de Chiriqui**, Panama
Q 7 **Laguna de Huaunta**, Nicaragua
R 9 **Laguna de Perlas**, Nicaragua
R 9 **Laguna de Perlas**, Nicaragua
K 17 **Laguna de San Luis**, Bolivia
X 12 **Laguna de Términos**, Mexico
J 19 **Laguna e Karavastasë**, Albania
P 4 **Laguna Ibans**, Honduras
R 7 **Laguna Karatá**, Nicaragua
Q 14 **Laguna Madre**, Texas, U.S.A.
S 8 **Laguna Madre**, Mexico
J 17 **Laguna Rogaguado**, Bolivia
U 14 **Laguna Superior**, Mexico
R 6 **Laguna Taberis**, Nicaragua
G 7 **Laguna Veneta**, Italy
G 4 **Lagunas**, Chile
J 9 **Laha**, China
X 6 **Lahad Datu**, Malaysia
D 7 **Lahaina**, Hawaii, U.S.A.
F 12 **Lahat**, Indonesia
D 7 **Lahe**, Myanmar
B 10 **Lahewa**, Indonesia
P 14 **Laḥij**, Yemen
E 18 **Lahn**, Germany
E 24 **Laholmsbukten**, Sweden
Y 9 **Lahore**, Pakistan
M 18 **Lahti**, Finland
W 11 **Laï**, Chad
J 11 **Lai Chau**, Vietnam
Q 7 **Laifeng**, China
O 4 **L'Aigle**, France
L 15 **Laingsburg**, Republic of South Africa
J 8 **Lainioälven**, Sweden
E 12 **Lais**, Indonesia
S 1 **Laishevo**, Russian Federation
W 2 **Laiwu**, China
G 20 **Laixi**, China
G 20 **Laiyang**, China
C 17 **Laiyuan**, China
G 19 **Laizhou**, China
G 19 **Laizhou Wan**, China
S 6 **Lajanurpekhi**, Georgia
H 12 **Lajeado**, Brazil
O 1 **Lajes**, Azores
I 10 **Lajes**, Brazil
N 1 **Lajes do Pico**, Azores
K 11 **Lajkovac**, Serbia and Montenegro
J 19 **Lake Abbe**, Ethiopia
I 13 **Lake Abert**, Oregon, U.S.A.
F 6 **Lake Abitibi**, Ontario, Canada
R 6 **Lake Albert**, Uganda/Democratic Republic of Congo
M 7 **Lake Amadeus**, Northern Territory, Australia
L 3 **Lake Argyle**, Western Australia, Australia
I 8 **Lake Arthur**, Louisiana, U.S.A.
M 9 **Lake Athabasca**, Alberta/Saskatchewan, Canada
J 6 **Lake Auld**, Western Australia, Australia
G 9 **Lake Austin**, Western Australia, Australia
Q 13 **Lake Baikal**, Russian Federation
T 8 **Lake Balkhash**, Kazakhstan
230 I 9 **Lake Ballard**, Western Australia, Australia
219 O 3 **Lake Bangweulu**, Zambia
230 H 9 **Lake Barlee**, Western Australia, Australia
233 E 22 **Lake Benmore**, New Zealand
67 P 9 **Lake Benton**, Minnesota, U.S.A.
63 T 5 **Lake Blackshear**, Georgia, U.S.A.
231 Q 9 **Lake Blanche**, South Australia, Australia
144 B 6 **Lake Bled**, Slovenia
197 L 23 **Lake Buluan**, Philippines
230 I 9 **Lake Carey**, Western Australia, Australia
231 T 11 **Lake Cargelligo**, New South Wales, Australia
230 I 8 **Lake Carnegie**, Western Australia, Australia
215 V 9 **Lake Chad**, Chad
58 L 5 **Lake Champlain**, Vermont, U.S.A.
62 H 7 **Lake Charles**, Louisiana, U.S.A.
76 I 6 **Lake Chelan**, Washington, U.S.A.
64 E 9 **Lake Chippewa**, Wisconsin, U.S.A.
60 J 8 **Lake City**, Tennessee, U.S.A.
61 Q 12 **Lake City**, South Carolina, U.S.A.
63 V 7 **Lake City**, Florida, U.S.A.
64 K 12 **Lake City**, Michigan, U.S.A.
83 I 15 **Lake Claire**, Alberta, Canada
233 G 19 **Lake Coleridge**, New Zealand
71 S 9 **Lake Conroe**, Texas, U.S.A.
138 H 5 **Lake Constance**, Switzerland
230 I 10 **Lake Cowan**, Western Australia, Australia
60 I 7 **Lake Cumberland**, Kentucky, U.S.A.
231 T 5 **Lake Dalrymple**, Queensland, Australia
230 I 7 **Lake Disappointment**, Western Australia, Australia
127 P 1 **Lake District**, United Kingdom
230 I 6 **Lake Dora**, Western Australia, Australia
230 I 11 **Lake Dundas**, Western Australia, Australia
217 Q 8 **Lake Edward**, Democratic Republic of Congo/Uganda
233 H 21 **Lake Ellesmere**, New Zealand
58 A 9 **Lake Erie**, Pennsylvania, U.S.A.
65 M 16 **Lake Erie**, Ohio, U.S.A.
86 C 15 **Lake Erie**, Ontario, Canada
217 U 10 **Lake Eyasi**, Tanzania
231 O 8 **Lake Eyre North**, South Australia, Australia
231 O 9 **Lake Eyre South**, South Australia, Australia
71 S 5 **Lake Fork Reservoir**, Texas, U.S.A.
231 Q 10 **Lake Frome**, South Australia, Australia
231 O 10 **Lake Gairdner**, South Australia, Australia
129 V 9 **Lake Geneva**, France/Switzerland
58 K 7 **Lake George**, New York, U.S.A.
63 W 9 **Lake George**, Florida, U.S.A.
64 F 8 **Lake Gogebic**, Michigan, U.S.A.
231 S 15 **Lake Gordon**, Tasmania, Australia
230 H 11 **Lake Grace**, Western Australia, Australia
230 K 5 **Lake Gregory**, Western Australia, Australia
233 B 25 **Lake Hauroko**, New Zealand
74 H 11 **Lake Havasu City**, Arizona, U.S.A.
233 D 22 **Lake Hawea**, New Zealand
230 I 11 **Lake Hope**, Western Australia, Australia
230 L 7 **Lake Hopkins**, Western Australia, Australia
64 L 10 **Lake Huron**, Michigan, U.S.A.
86 A 10 **Lake Huron**, Ontario, Canada
71 T 11 **Lake Jackson**, Texas, U.S.A.
219 O 6 **Lake Kariba**, Zimbabwe
71 N 4 **Lake Kemp**, Texas, U.S.A.
60 L 11 **Lake Keowee**, South Carolina, U.S.A.
186 O 11 **Lake Khanka**, China
230 H 11 **Lake King**, Western Australia, Australia
217 Q 9 **Lake Kivu**, Rwanda/Democratic Republic of Congo
72 L 2 **Lake Koocanusa**, Montana, U.S.A.
217 S 7 **Lake Kyoga**, Uganda
154 F 9 **Lake Ladoga**, Russian Federation
197 K 21 **Lake Lanao**, Philippines
230 I 10 **Lake Lefroy**, Western Australia, Australia
71 Q 5 **Lake Lewisville**, Texas, U.S.A.
71 R 7 **Lake Limestone**, Texas, U.S.A.
64 G 7 **Lake Linden**, Michigan, U.S.A.
71 S 9 **Lake Livingston**, Texas, U.S.A.
83 I 20 **Lake Louise**, Alberta, Canada
230 L 6 **Lake MacDonald**, Western Australia, Australia
230 L 6 **Lake Mackay**, Western Australia, Australia
230 E 7 **Lake MacLeod**, Western Australia, Australia
197 M 19 **Lake Mainit**, Philippines
219 R 4 **Lake Malawi**, Malawi
233 B 24 **Lake Manapouri**, New Zealand
84 I 10 **Lake Manitoba**, Manitoba, Canada
217 U 10 **Lake Manyara**, Tanzania
104 K 3 **Lake Maracaibo**, Venezuela
61 P 13 **Lake Marion**, South Carolina, U.S.A.
230 I 10 **Lake Marmion**, Western Australia, Australia
63 Q 4 **Lake Martin**, Alabama, U.S.A.
61 W 9 **Lake Mattamuskeet**, North Carolina, U.S.A.
230 M 9 **Lake Maurice**, South Australia, Australia
66 I 14 **Lake McConaughy**, Nebraska, U.S.A.
74 G 9 **Lake Mead**, Arizona/Nevada, U.S.A.
85 V 8 **Lake Melville**, Newfoundland and Labrador, Canada
58 L 4 **Lake Memphremagog**, Vermont, U.S.A.
70 K 2 **Lake Meredith**, Texas, U.S.A.
65 I 15 **Lake Michigan**, Michigan, U.S.A.
230 J 9 **Lake Minigwal**, Western Australia, Australia
230 G 10 **Lake Moore**, Western Australia, Australia
61 P 13 **Lake Moultrie**, South Carolina, U.S.A.
234 A 5 **Lake Murray**, Papua New Guinea
61 N 12 **Lake Murray**, South Carolina, U.S.A.
86 E 11 **Lake Muskoka**, Ontario, Canada
217 P 13 **Lake Mweru**, Democratic Republic of Congo/Zambia
212 F 12 **Lake Nasser**, Egypt
217 U 9 **Lake Natron**, Tanzania
196 G 13 **Lake Naujan**, Philippines
230 L 7 **Lake Neale**, Northern Territory, Australia
91 O 10 **Lake Nicaragua**, Nicaragua
84 L 11 **Lake Nipigon**, Ontario, Canada
86 E 9 **Lake Nipissing**, Ontario, Canada
230 H 9 **Lake Noondie**, Western Australia, Australia
61 O 9 **Lake Norman**, North Carolina, U.S.A.
212 E 13 **Lake Nuba**, Sudan
71 T 5 **Lake o' the Pines**, Texas, U.S.A.
66 J 9 **Lake Oahe**, South Dakota, U.S.A.
63 U 3 **Lake Oconee**, Georgia, U.S.A.
69 U 5 **Lake of the Ozarks**, Missouri, U.S.A.
84 J 11 **Lake of the Woods**, Canada/U.S.A.
233 D 21 **Lake Ohau**, New Zealand
146 B 13 **Lake Ohrid**, Macedonia (F.Y.R.O.M.)
63 X 12 **Lake Okeechobee**, Florida, U.S.A.
154 H 9 **Lake Onega**, Russian Federation
81 U 14 **Lake Ontario**, Ontario, Canada
77 H 17 **Lake Oroville**, California, U.S.A.
69 T 11 **Lake Ouachita**, Arkansas, U.S.A.
76 K 12 **Lake Owyhee**, Oregon, U.S.A.
71 S 6 **Lake Palestine**, Texas, U.S.A.
231 S 15 **Lake Pedder**, Tasmania, Australia
148 I 7 **Lake Peipus**, Estonia
58 K 6 **Lake Placid**, New York, U.S.A.
58 J 7 **Lake Pleasant**, New York, U.S.A.
62 L 8 **Lake Pontchartrain**, Louisiana, U.S.A.
233 B 25 **Lake Poteriteri**, New Zealand
74 K 7 **Lake Powell**, Utah, U.S.A.
64 F 12 **Lake Poygan**, Wisconsin, U.S.A.
146 C 13 **Lake Prespa**, Macedonia (F.Y.R.O.M.)
154 D 12 **Lake Pskov**, Russian Federation
233 E 21 **Lake Pukaki**, New Zealand
230 I 10 **Lake Rebecca**, Western Australia, Australia
86 E 10 **Lake Rosseau**, Ontario, Canada
232 M 10 **Lake Rotorua**, New Zealand
217 S 12 **Lake Rukwa**, Tanzania
66 I 3 **Lake Sakakawea**, North Dakota, U.S.A.
145 J 16 **Lake Scutari**, Serbia and Montenegro
63 S 7 **Lake Seminole**, Georgia, U.S.A.
65 F 19 **Lake Shelbyville**, Illinois, U.S.A.
63 S 2 **Lake Sidney Lanier**, Georgia, U.S.A.
86 F 12 **Lake Simcoe**, Ontario, Canada
63 U 3 **Lake Sinclair**, Georgia, U.S.A.
65 M 15 **Lake St Clair**, Canada/U.S.A.
84 K 10 **Lake St Joseph**, Ontario, Canada
219 Q 12 **Lake St Lucia**, Republic of South Africa
233 H 18 **Lake Sumner**, New Zealand
75 S 11 **Lake Sumner**, New Mexico, U.S.A.
57 S 5 **Lake Superior**, U.S.A./Canada, U.S.A./Canada
231 O 4 **Lake Sylvester**, Northern Territory, Australia
196 G 12 **Lake Taal**, Philippines
77 H 18 **Lake Tahoe**, California, U.S.A.
213 H 18 **Lake Tana**, Ethiopia
217 Q 11 **Lake Tanganyika**, Africa
232 M 11 **Lake Tarawera**, New Zealand
232 L 12 **Lake Taupo**, New Zealand
71 R 5 **Lake Tawakoni**, Texas, U.S.A.
233 B 23 **Lake Te Anau**, New Zealand
233 E 21 **Lake Tekapo**, New Zealand
233 F 21 **Lake Tekapo**, New Zealand
69 O 13 **Lake Texoma**, Oklahoma, U.S.A.
172 G 8 **Lake Tiberias**, Israel
107 H 19 **Lake Titicaca**, Peru
231 P 10 **Lake Torrens**, South Australia, Australia
217 U 5 **Lake Turkana**, Ethiopia/Kenya
176 F 3 **Lake Urmia**, Iran
217 S 8 **Lake Victoria**, Africa
233 K 16 **Lake Wairarapa**, New Zealand
233 C 23 **Lake Wakatipu**, New Zealand
63 W 10 **Lake Wales**, Florida, U.S.A.
67 R 4 **Lake Walker**, Minnesota, U.S.A.
233 D 22 **Lake Wanaka**, New Zealand
230 I 8 **Lake Wells**, Western Australia, Australia
230 L 5 **Lake White**, Western Australia, Australia
71 P 7 **Lake Whitney**, Texas, U.S.A.
64 G 12 **Lake Winnebago**, Wisconsin, U.S.A.
67 R 4 **Lake Winnibigoshish**, Minnesota, U.S.A.
84 I 9 **Lake Winnipeg**, Manitoba, Canada
84 H 8 **Lake Winnipegosis**, Manitoba, Canada
59 O 7 **Lake Winnipesaukee**, New Hampshire, U.S.A.
63 Y 12 **Lake Worth**, Florida, U.S.A.
231 R 8 **Lake Yamma Yamma**, Queensland, Australia
235 Z 12 **Lakeba**, Fiji
231 S 3 **Lakeland**, Queensland, Australia
63 U 6 **Lakeland**, Georgia, U.S.A.
63 W 10 **Lakeland**, Florida, U.S.A.
231 T 13 **Lakes Entrance**, Victoria, Australia
76 E 12 **Lakeside**, Oregon, U.S.A.
77 I 14 **Lakeview**, Oregon, U.S.A.
58 C 10 **Lakewood**, New York, U.S.A.
58 J 14 **Lakewood**, New Jersey, U.S.A.
75 R 4 **Lakewood**, Colorado, U.S.A.
154 F 9 **Lakhdenpokh'ya**, Russian Federation
182 M 9 **Lakhimpur**, India
181 F 15 **Lakhnadon**, India
181 A 14 **Lakhpat**, India
177 V 8 **Lakki**, Pakistan
147 E 23 **Lakonikos Kolpos**, Greece
193 S 15 **Lakor**, Indonesia
214 J 13 **Lakota**, Côte d'Ivoire
66 M 3 **Lakota**, North Dakota, U.S.A.
134 L 5 **Laksefjorden**, Norway
134 K 6 **Lakselv**, Norway
181 A 22 **Lakshadweep**, India
144 G 10 **Laktaši**, Bosnia and Herzegovina
196 H 6 **Lal-Lo**, Philippines
170 B 6 **Lalapaşa**, Turkey
146 L 11 **Lalapaşa**, Turkey
216 E 7 **Lalara**, Gabon
176 G 8 **Lālī**, Iran
213 I 19 **Lalībela**, Ethiopia
193 R 14 **Laliki**, Indonesia
186 K 11 **Lalin**, China
130 I 2 **Lalín**, Spain
193 O 13 **Laloa**, Indonesia
191 K 16 **Lam Pao Reservoir**, Thailand
195 X 6 **Lamag**, Malaysia
69 S 6 **Lamar**, Missouri, U.S.A.
139 S 4 **Lambach**, Austria
128 J 5 **Lamballe**, France
216 E 8 **Lambaréné**, Gabon
106 A 13 **Lambayeque**, Peru
218 J 14 **Lambert's Bay**, Republic of South Africa
127 S 10 **Lambourn**, United Kingdom
73 W 7 **Lame Deer**, Montana, U.S.A.
130 H 5 **Lamego**, Portugal
235 R 11 **Lamen**, Vanuatu
70 J 6 **Lamesa**, Texas, U.S.A.
141 M 20 **Lamezia**, Italy
147 E 18 **Lamia**, Greece
197 N 23 **Lamigan Point**, Philippines
197 H 23 **Lamitan**, Philippines
235 Y 11 **Lamiti**, Fiji
193 T 10 **Lamlam**, Indonesia
196 H 11 **Lamon Bay**, Philippines
191 G 15 **Lampang**, Thailand
71 P 8 **Lampasas**, Texas, U.S.A.
89 Q 6 **Lampazos**, Mexico
126 M 8 **Lampeter**, United Kingdom
191 G 14 **Lamphun**, Thailand
192 G 13 **Lampung**, Indonesia
217 X 9 **Lamu**, Kenya
189 Z 12 **Lan Yü**, Taiwan
78 C 7 **Lanai**, Hawaii, U.S.A.
78 D 8 **Lanai City**, Hawaii, U.S.A.
195 V 6 **Lanas**, Malaysia
191 F 22 **Lanbi Kyun**, Myanmar
197 I 20 **Lanboyan Point**, Philippines
127 P 1 **Lancaster**, United Kingdom
58 G 14 **Lancaster**, Pennsylvania, U.S.A.
59 N 6 **Lancaster**, New Hampshire, U.S.A.
61 O 11 **Lancaster**, South Carolina, U.S.A.
65 E 14 **Lancaster**, Wisconsin, U.S.A.
65 M 19 **Lancaster**, Ohio, U.S.A.
69 U 1 **Lancaster**, Missouri, U.S.A.
77 J 24 **Lancaster**, California, U.S.A.
45 N 8 **Lancaster Sound**, Arctic Ocean
81 P 4 **Lancaster Sound**, Nunavut, Canada
230 F 11 **Lancelin**, Western Australia, Australia
171 R 6 **Lanch'khut'i**, Georgia
140 J 13 **Lanciano**, Italy
111 F 16 **Lanco**, Chile
187 G 20 **Lancun**, China
137 L 23 **Landau an der Isar**, Germany
137 E 21 **Landau in der Pfalz**, Germany
138 K 7 **Landeck**, Austria
73 T 12 **Lander**, Wyoming, U.S.A.
132 I 5 **Landerum**, Netherlands
181 N 20 **Landfall Island**, India
138 I 8 **Landquart**, Switzerland
126 I 15 **Land's End**, United Kingdom
80 L 3 **Lands End**, Northwest Territories, Canada
137 I 24 **Landsberg**, Germany
137 K 23 **Landshut**, Germany
185 Q 6 **Lang Shan**, China
190 M 11 **Lang Son**, Vietnam
191 G 23 **Lang Suan**, Thailand
66 M 2 **Langdon**, North Dakota, U.S.A.

ountry · Internal administrative region: State/Province/Territory/Dependent territory · Capital city · Mountain range/Undersea ridge · Mountain peak/Volcano/Seamount · Geographic feature · Headland/Point/Cape/Peninsula · Desert · Island/Island group · Antarctic base · Ocean · Sea · Bay/Gulf/Channel/Strait · Lake · Salt pan/Dry/Intermittent lake · River

⊡ Country | ⊡ Internal administrative region: State/Province/Territory/Dependent territory | ◆ Capital city | ▲ Mountain range/Undersea ridge | ▲ Mountain peak/Volcano/Seamount | ◇ Geographic feature | ▶ Headland/Point/Cape/Peninsula | ▲ Desert | ⊠ Island/Island group | Antarctic base | Ocean | Sea | Bay/Gulf/Channel/Strait | Lake | Salt pan/Dry/Intermittent lake

- P 6 Lewiston, Maine, U.S.A.
- J 6 Lewiston, Idaho, U.S.A.
- E 13 Lewistown, Pennsylvania, U.S.A.
- S 5 Lewistown, Montana, U.S.A.
- I 5 Lexington, Kentucky, U.S.A.
- C 9 Lexington, Tennessee, U.S.A.
- P 9 Lexington, North Carolina, U.S.A.
- Q 5 Lexington, Virginia, U.S.A.
- L 14 Lexington, Nebraska, U.S.A.
- I 10 Lexington, Oregon, U.S.A.
- V 4 Lexington Park, Maryland, U.S.A.
- P 3 Leyland, United Kingdom
- L 16 Leyte, Philippines
- M 16 Leyte Gulf, Philippines ≈
- N 17 Leżajsk, Poland
- J 17 Lezhë, Albania
- N 6 Lezhi, China
- I 5 L'gov, Russian Federation
- K 7 Lhabo, China
- K 10 Lhasa, China
- J 10 Lhazê, China
- J 9 Lhazhong, China
- C 8 Lhokseumawe, Indonesia
- C 8 Lhoksukon, Indonesia
- X 5 L'Hospitalet de Llobregat, Spain
- W 10 Liancheng, China
- N 20 Lianga, Philippines
- B 16 Liangcheng, China
- O 4 Liangdang, China
- I 10 Lianghe, China
- Q 7 Lianghe, China
- N 4 Lianghekou, China
- P 6 Liangping, China
- U 9 Lianhua, China
- Q 13 Lianjiang, China
- X 9 Lianjiang, China
- U 11 Lianping, China
- G 16 Lianshan, China
- S 11 Lianshan, China
- X 4 Lianshui, China
- X 3 Lianyungang, China
- T 11 Lianzhou, China
- U 2 Liaocheng, China
- I 17 Liaodong Bandao, China ▶
- H 16 Liaodong Wan, China ≈
- M 10 Liaohu, China
- I 15 Liaoning, China ▪
- I 15 Liaoyang, China
- J 14 Liaoyuan, China
- C 14 Liard, Yukon Territory, Canada ↳
- D 15 Liard Plateau, British Columbia, Canada ◇
- S 14 Liari, Pakistan
- I 6 Libano, Colombia
- L 2 Libby, Montana, U.S.A.
- J 5 Libenge, Democratic Republic of Congo
- H 7 Liberal, Kansas, U.S.A.
- D 16 Liberec, Czech Republic
- H 13 Liberia, Africa ▪
- O 11 Liberia, Costa Rica
- M 4 Libertad, Venezuela
- K 19 Liberty, Indiana, U.S.A.
- J 24 Libin, Belgium
- J 12 Libmanan, Philippines
- P 10 Libo, China
- M 11 Libourne, France
- J 24 Libramont, Belgium
- K 18 Librazhd, Albania
- D 7 Libreville, Gabon ♣
- S 10 Libya, Africa ▪
- X 10 Libyan Desert, Libya ◇
- B 13 Libyan Desert, Sudan ◇
- W 7 Libyan Plateau, Libya ◇
- C 8 Libyan Plateau, Egypt ◇
- F 13 Licantén, Chile
- J 23 Licata, Italy
- Q 11 Lice, Turkey
- S 6 Lichfield, United Kingdom
- R 4 Lichinga, Mozambique
- N 11 Lichtenburg, Republic of South Africa

- 137 I 19 Lichtenfels, Germany
- 132 M 13 Lichtenvoorde, Netherlands
- 133 C 18 Lichtervelde, Belgium
- 189 Q 7 Lichuan, China
- 189 W 9 Lichuan, China
- 69 V 6 Licking, Missouri, U.S.A.
- 149 G 17 Lida, Belarus
- 77 K 20 Lida, Nevada, U.S.A.
- 135 E 21 Lidköping, Sweden
- 141 G 14 Lido di Ostia, Italy
- 142 J 10 Lidzbark, Poland
- 142 K 9 Lidzbark Warmiński, Poland
- 138 I 7 Liechtenstein, Europe ▪
- 133 K 21 Liège, Belgium
- 133 J 20 Liège, Belgium
- 135 O 15 Lieksa, Finland
- 139 P 8 Lienz, Austria
- 148 B 11 Liepāja, Latvia
- 133 G 17 Lier, Belgium
- 138 E 6 Liestal, Switzerland
- 135 M 16 Lievestuore, Finland
- 139 T 6 Liezen, Austria
- 216 M 6 Lifanga, Democratic Republic of Congo
- 125 E 18 Liffey, Republic of Ireland ↳
- 235 Q 12 Lifou, New Caledonia ≈
- 196 J 13 Ligao, Philippines
- 88 I 7 Ligui, Mexico
- 140 C 8 Liguria, Italy ▪
- 140 A 12 Ligurian Sea, Europe ≊
- 234 H 3 Lihir Group, Papua New Guinea
- 234 H 3 Lihir Island, Papua New Guinea
- 78 A 6 Lihue, Hawaii, U.S.A.
- 148 F 7 Lihula, Estonia
- 188 J 9 Lijiang, China
- 217 O 14 Likasi, Democratic Republic of Congo
- 216 M 6 Likati, Democratic Republic of Congo
- 154 H 13 Likhoslavl', Russian Federation
- 237 Y 2 Likiep, Marshall Islands ≈
- 216 K 8 Likolia, Democratic Republic of Congo
- 216 I 6 Likouala, Congo
- 192 I 10 Liku, Indonesia
- 189 T 9 Liling, China
- 129 R 1 Lille, France
- 133 H 17 Lille, Belgium
- 135 D 18 Lillehammer, Norway
- 83 G 21 Lillooet, British Columbia, Canada
- 219 R 5 Lilongwe, Malawi ♣
- 38 C 9 L'Îlot Frégate, Seychelles
- 197 I 21 Liloy, Philippines
- 107 C 16 Lima, Peru ♣
- 107 C 16 Lima, Peru ▪
- 109 G 19 Lima, Paraguay
- 65 L 17 Lima, Ohio, U.S.A.
- 73 O 9 Lima, Montana, U.S.A.
- 175 X 5 Limah, Oman
- 111 G 16 Limay, Argentina ↳
- 111 I 14 Limay Mahuida, Argentina
- 195 T 6 Limbang, Malaysia
- 148 F 7 Limbaži, Latvia
- 133 K 16 Limburg, Netherlands ▪
- 137 I 18 Limburg, Germany
- 133 I 18 Limburg, Belgium ▪
- 135 F 18 Limedsforsen, Sweden
- 112 K 6 Limeira, Brazil
- 125 C 19 Limerick, Republic of Ireland
- 59 S 14 Limestone, Maine, U.S.A.
- 135 B 23 Limfjorden, Denmark ≈
- 134 L 13 Liminka, Finland
- 135 F 23 Limmared, Sweden
- 231 O 2 Limmen Bight, Northern Territory, Australia ≈
- 147 G 18 Limni, Greece
- 147 D 14 Limni Aliakmonas, Greece ↳
- 146 F 12 Limni Kerkinitis, Greece ↳
- 147 D 18 Limni Trichonida, Greece ↳
- 146 D 13 Limni Vegoritis, Greece ↳

- 147 I 15 Limnos, Greece ≈
- 129 O 10 Limoges, France
- 75 T 4 Limon, Colorado, U.S.A.
- 91 S 12 Limón, Costa Rica
- 140 A 9 Limone Piemonte, Italy
- 129 O 10 Limousin, France ▪
- 129 Q 15 Limoux, France
- 219 P 9 Limpopo, Mozambique/Botswana ↳
- 154 H 1 Linakhamari, Russian Federation
- 189 Y 6 Lin'an, China
- 197 K 23 Linao Bay, Philippines ≈
- 197 K 23 Linao Point, Philippines ▶
- 197 E 16 Linapacan, Philippines ≈
- 197 E 15 Linapacan Strait, Philippines ≈
- 110 F 13 Linares, Chile
- 131 O 11 Linares, Spain
- 89 Q 8 Linares, Mexico
- 147 I 18 Linaria, Greece
- 188 J 11 Lincang, China
- 189 V 8 Linchuan, China
- 233 H 20 Lincoln, New Zealand
- 113 B 16 Lincoln, Argentina
- 127 U 4 Lincoln, United Kingdom
- 59 R 4 Lincoln, Maine, U.S.A.
- 65 F 18 Lincoln, Illinois, U.S.A.
- 67 P 14 Lincoln, Nebraska, U.S.A.
- 76 F 10 Lincoln City, Oregon, U.S.A.
- 127 V 3 Lincolnshire Wolds, United Kingdom ◇
- 137 G 26 Lindau, Germany
- 105 U 5 Linden, Guyana
- 60 D 9 Linden, Tennessee, U.S.A.
- 63 O 5 Linden, Alabama, U.S.A.
- 71 U 5 Linden, Texas, U.S.A.
- 217 W 13 Lindi, Tanzania ▪
- 217 X 14 Lindi, Tanzania
- 186 J 9 Lindian, China
- 147 O 24 Lindos, Greece
- 86 G 12 Lindsay, Ontario, Canada
- 237 Q 1 Line Islands, Kiribati ≈
- 189 S 2 Linfen, China
- 196 F 9 Lingayen, Philippines
- 196 F 9 Lingayen Gulf, Philippines ≈
- 189 R 3 Lingbao, China
- 189 W 4 Lingbi, China
- 136 D 13 Lingen, Germany
- 127 W 12 Lingfield, United Kingdom
- 192 F 11 Lingga, Indonesia ≈
- 192 M 7 Lingkabau, Malaysia
- 216 L 7 Lingomo, Democratic Republic of Congo
- 187 C 17 Lingqiu, China
- 189 Q 10 Lingshan, China
- 189 S 2 Lingshi, China
- 189 R 15 Lingshui, China
- 189 P 3 Lingtai, China
- 214 E 8 Linguère, Senegal
- 187 G 15 Lingyuan, China
- 186 I 5 Linhai, China
- 189 Z 7 Linhai, China
- 109 M 17 Linhares, Brazil
- 185 R 6 Linhe, China
- 187 L 15 Linjiang, China
- 135 G 22 Linköping, Sweden
- 186 M 11 Linkou, China
- 148 F 12 Linkuva, Lithuania
- 189 T 2 Linlü Shan, China ▲
- 71 P 15 Linn, Texas, U.S.A.
- 137 B 17 Linnich, Germany
- 189 V 1 Linqing, China
- 189 U 4 Linquan, China
- 112 I 6 Lins, Brazil
- 189 X 3 Linshu, China
- 189 O 7 Linshui, China
- 138 H 8 Linthal, Switzerland
- 65 H 20 Linton, Indiana, U.S.A.
- 66 K 6 Linton, North Dakota, U.S.A.
- 189 Q 3 Lintong, China
- 186 F 13 Linxi, China
- 188 M 2 Linxia, China
- 187 E 19 Linyi, China
- 189 W 3 Linyi, China
- 189 R 3 Linyi, China

- 189 P 3 Linyou, China
- 139 T 3 Linz, Austria
- 195 T 8 Lio Matoh, Malaysia
- 150 J 2 Lioboml', Ukraine
- 141 L 16 Lioni, Italy
- 215 U 9 Lioua, Chad
- 216 H 7 Liouesso, Congo
- 196 G 12 Lipa, Philippines
- 150 L 7 Lipcani, Moldova
- 156 L 4 Lipetsk, Russian Federation
- 156 L 4 Lipetskaya Oblast', Russian Federation ▪
- 142 D 11 Lipiany, Poland
- 189 Q 10 Liping, China
- 142 I 11 Lipno, Poland
- 150 F 10 Lipova, Romania
- 137 C 15 Lippe, Germany ↳
- 137 E 15 Lippstadt, Germany
- 142 N 9 Lipsk, Poland
- 143 J 19 Liptovský Mikuláš, Slovakia
- 189 R 11 Lipu, China
- 217 S 6 Lira, Uganda
- 216 I 8 Liranga, Congo
- 179 N 3 Lisakovsk, Kazakhstan
- 216 L 6 Lisala, Democratic Republic of Congo
- 130 F 9 Lisboa, Portugal ▪
- 130 G 9 Lisbon, Portugal ♣
- 67 N 6 Lisbon, North Dakota, U.S.A.
- 59 P 6 Lisbon Falls, Maine, U.S.A.
- 146 E 11 Lisec, Macedonia (F.Y.R.O.M.) ▲
- 189 R 1 Lishi, China
- 186 J 13 Lishu, China
- 189 Y 8 Lishui, China
- 129 N 4 Lisieux, France
- 126 L 14 Liskeard, United Kingdom
- 156 L 6 Liski, Russian Federation
- 231 W 9 Lismore, New South Wales, Australia
- 127 T 12 Liss, United Kingdom
- 125 B 19 Listowel, Republic of Ireland
- 188 K 7 Litang, China
- 189 Q 12 Litang, China
- 65 F 20 Litchfield, Illinois, U.S.A.
- 147 B 21 Lithakia, Greece
- 231 U 11 Lithgow, New South Wales, Australia
- 149 C 14 Lithuania, Europe ▪
- 139 U 1 Litschau, Austria
- 181 N 22 Little Andaman, India ≈
- 73 U 8 Little Bighorn, Montana, U.S.A. ↳
- 92 I 7 Little Cayman, Cayman Islands ≈
- 191 B 19 Little Coco Island, Myanmar ≈
- 74 K 9 Little Colorado, Arizona, U.S.A. ↳
- 86 C 9 Little Current, Ontario, Canada
- 58 I 8 Little Falls, New York, U.S.A.
- 67 P 6 Little Falls, Minnesota, U.S.A.
- 67 Q 6 Little Falls, Minnesota, U.S.A.
- 84 J 9 Little Grand Rapids, Manitoba, Canada
- 93 O 5 Little Inagua Island, The Bahamas ≈
- 218 K 15 Little Karoo, Republic of South Africa
- 66 G 4 Little Missouri, North Dakota, U.S.A. ↳
- 181 O 24 Little Nicobar, India ≈
- 69 V 11 Little Rock, Arkansas, U.S.A.
- 64 I 13 Little Sable Point, Michigan, U.S.A. ▶
- 230 I 7 Little Sandy Desert, Western Australia, Australia ◇
- 78 D 13 Little Sitkin Island, Alaska, U.S.A. ≈
- 173 S 3 Little Zab, Iraq ↳
- 127 R 3 Littleborough, United Kingdom
- 70 I 4 Littlefield, Texas, U.S.A.
- 127 V 13 Littlehampton, United Kingdom

- 127 X 7 Littleport, United Kingdom
- 215 S 14 Littoral, Cameroon ▪
- 151 N 5 Lityn, Ukraine
- 189 P 4 Liuba, China
- 187 K 14 Liuhe, China
- 186 H 11 Liuhu, China
- 189 Q 11 Liujiang, China
- 189 R 1 Liulin, China
- 189 T 8 Liuyang, China
- 186 J 7 Liuzhan, China
- 189 Q 11 Liuzhou, China
- 150 H 7 Livada, Romania
- 148 H 12 Livāni, Latvia
- 179 N 4 Livanovka, Kazakhstan
- 63 U 7 Live Oak, Florida, U.S.A.
- 60 E 6 Livermore, Kentucky, U.S.A.
- 127 O 4 Liverpool, United Kingdom
- 87 U 12 Liverpool, Nova Scotia, Canada
- 127 O 3 Liverpool Bay, United Kingdom ≈
- 71 T 9 Livingston, Texas, U.S.A.
- 73 R 7 Livingston, Montana, U.S.A.
- 90 J 4 Livingston, Guatemala
- 62 L 7 Livingstone, Louisiana, U.S.A.
- 219 N 7 Livingstone, Zambia
- 219 R 3 Livingstonia, Malawi
- 144 F 12 Livno, Bosnia and Herzegovina
- 156 K 4 Livny, Russian Federation
- 140 E 11 Livorno, Italy
- 217 V 13 Liwale, Tanzania
- 142 M 12 Liwiec, Poland ↳
- 189 O 4 Lixan, China
- 188 L 9 Lixi, China
- 189 S 7 Lixian, China
- 147 A 19 Lixouri, Greece
- 189 X 5 Liyang, China
- 126 J 15 Lizard, United Kingdom
- 126 J 15 Lizard Point, United Kingdom ▶
- 144 K 12 Ljig, Serbia and Montenegro
- 144 B 7 Ljubljana, Slovenia ♣
- 144 J 11 Ljubovija, Serbia and Montenegro
- 135 I 23 Ljugarn, Sweden
- 135 G 16 Ljungan, Sweden ↳
- 135 F 24 Ljungby, Sweden
- 135 G 17 Ljusdal, Sweden
- 135 G 17 Ljusnan, Sweden ↳
- 126 L 5 Llanaelhaearn, United Kingdom
- 126 M 5 Llanberis, United Kingdom
- 127 O 5 Llandderfel, United Kingdom
- 126 M 9 Llandeilo, United Kingdom
- 126 L 9 Llandissilio, United Kingdom
- 127 N 9 Llandovery, United Kingdom
- 127 O 8 Llandrindod Wells, United Kingdom
- 126 N 4 Llandudno, United Kingdom
- 126 M 5 Llandwrog, United Kingdom
- 126 M 10 Llanelli, United Kingdom
- 126 M 4 Llanerchymedd, United Kingdom
- 131 N 1 Llanes, Spain
- 126 M 4 Llanfairpwllgwyngyll, United Kingdom
- 127 O 6 Llangadfan, United Kingdom
- 126 M 6 Llangelynin, United Kingdom
- 127 O 8 Llangollen, United Kingdom
- 127 N 7 Llangurig, United Kingdom
- 126 L 5 Llanllyfni, United Kingdom

- 70 I 5 Llano Estacado, Texas, U.S.A. ▲
- 104 K 9 Llanos, Colombia ◇
- 126 M 8 Llanrhystud, United Kingdom
- 127 N 5 Llanrwst, United Kingdom
- 127 O 10 Llantrisant, United Kingdom
- 127 N 11 Llantwit Major, United Kingdom
- 131 U 4 Lleida, Spain
- 130 K 10 Llerena, Spain
- 126 L 5 Lleyn Peninsula, United Kingdom ◇
- 107 I 22 Llica, Bolivia
- 131 T 8 Lliria, Spain
- 131 W 3 Llivia, Spain
- 197 M 16 Llorente, Philippines
- 83 K 18 Lloydminster, Saskatchewan, Canada
- 131 Y 8 Llucmajor, Spain
- 74 K 6 Loa, Utah, U.S.A.
- 140 B 9 Loano, Italy
- 137 O 16 Löbau, Germany
- 216 I 5 Lobaye, Central African Republic
- 111 L 15 Loberia, Argentina
- 113 D 18 Loberia, Argentina
- 142 E 10 Łobez, Poland
- 218 G 4 Lobito, Angola
- 196 G 12 Lobo, Philippines
- 130 K 9 Lobón, Spain
- 101 O 11 Lobos, Canary Islands ≈
- 113 D 16 Lobos, Argentina
- 191 M 21 Lôc Ninh, Vietnam
- 138 G 10 Locarno, Switzerland
- 124 G 12 Loch Lomond, United Kingdom ↳
- 124 H 10 Loch Ness, United Kingdom ↳
- 124 H 11 Loch Rannoch, United Kingdom ↳
- 124 G 9 Loch Shin, United Kingdom ↳
- 132 M 12 Lochem, Netherlands
- 129 O 7 Loches, France
- 124 F 13 Lochgilphead, United Kingdom
- 124 G 9 Lochinver, United Kingdom
- 142 M 12 Łochów, Poland
- 231 O 11 Lock, South Australia, Australia
- 58 E 12 Lock Haven, Pennsylvania, U.S.A.
- 125 I 14 Lockerbie, United Kingdom
- 231 S 1 Lockhart River, Queensland, Australia
- 141 M 21 Locri, Italy
- 172 F 9 Lod, Israel
- 127 Z 7 Loddon, United Kingdom
- 129 R 13 Lodève, France
- 154 G 10 Lodeynoye Pole, Russian Federation
- 73 V 8 Lodge Grass, Montana, U.S.A.
- 177 W 11 Lodhran, Pakistan
- 140 D 7 Lodi, Italy
- 77 F 9 Lodi, California, U.S.A.
- 134 G 9 Lødingen, Norway
- 216 M 10 Lodja, Democratic Republic of Congo
- 217 U 6 Lodwar, Kenya
- 143 J 14 Łódź, Poland
- 191 I 15 Loei, Thailand
- 139 P 6 Lofer, Austria
- 134 F 9 Lofoten, Norway
- 157 O 7 Log, Russian Federation
- 60 M 5 Logan, West Virginia, U.S.A.
- 74 K 1 Logan, Utah, U.S.A.
- 75 T 10 Logan, New Mexico, U.S.A.
- 65 I 18 Logansport, Indiana, U.S.A.
- 215 V 10 Logone Birni, Cameroon
- 215 W 11 Logone Occidental, Chad
- 215 W 12 Logone Oriental, Chad ▪
- 131 Q 3 Logroño, Spain
- 182 H 8 Loharu, India
- 219 Y 5 Lohatanjona Angadoka, Madagascar ▶

- Z 12 **Lusk**, Wyoming, U.S.A.
- 9 O 9 **Lussac-les-Châteaux**, France
- 8 I 6 **Lustenau**, Austria
- 7 L 14 **Lutherstadt Wittenberg**, Germany
- 7 Q 8 **Lutiba**, Democratic Republic of Congo
- 6 H 8 **Lütjenburg**, Germany
- 7 V 9 **Luton**, United Kingdom
- 5 R 7 **Lutong**, Malaysia
- I 12 **Lutselk'e**, Northwest Territories, Canada
- 0 K 3 **Luts'k**, Ukraine
- 7 T 7 **Lutterworth**, United Kingdom
- 1 Z 6 **Lutuhyne**, Ukraine
- 6 I 10 **Lützow**, Germany
- 1 U 2 **Lützow-Holm Bay**, Antarctica ≈
- 8 J 14 **Lutzville**, Republic of South Africa
- 3 K 23 **Luuq**, Somalia
- P 10 **Luverne**, Minnesota, U.S.A.
- 7 O 12 **Luvua**, Democratic Republic of Congo ∿
- 8 K 4 **Luvuei**, Angola
- 7 S 7 **Luwero**, Uganda
- 3 P 11 **Luwuk**, Indonesia
- 3 L 25 **Luxembourg**, Luxembourg 🏛
- 3 K 25 **Luxembourg**, Europe □
- 3 L 26 **Luxembourg**, Luxembourg ▣
- 3 I 23 **Luxembourg**, Belgium ▣
- 9 V 6 **Luxeuil-les-Bains**, France
- 8 I 11 **Luxi**, China
- 8 M 11 **Luxi**, China
- 9 R 8 **Luxi**, China
- 2 F 11 **Luxor**, Egypt
- 5 O 10 **Luza**, Russian Federation
- 8 F 7 **Luzern**, Switzerland
- 9 N 8 **Luzhou**, China
- 9 J 16 **Luziânia**, Brazil
- 6 G 8 **Luzon**, Philippines 🏝
- 6 G 3 **Luzon Strait**, Philippines ≈
- 0 I 4 **L'viv**, Ukraine
- V 5 **Lyakhovskiye Ostrova**, Russian Federation 🏝
- 46 J 8 **Lyaskovets**, Bulgaria
- 35 I 14 **Lycksele**, Sweden
- 27 Y 12 **Lydd**, United Kingdom
- 49 K 22 **Lyel'chytsy**, Belarus
- 49 K 15 **Lyepyel'**, Belarus
- 47 F 21 **Lygourio**, Greece
- 27 O 14 **Lyme Bay**, United Kingdom ≈
- 27 P 13 **Lyme Regis**, United Kingdom
- 27 S 13 **Lymington**, United Kingdom
- 42 K 8 **Łyna**, Poland ∿
- R 6 **Lynchburg**, Virginia, U.S.A.
- 27 S 13 **Lyndhurst**, United Kingdom
- 9 P 4 **Lyndon**, Kansas, U.S.A.
- 35 A 21 **Lyngdal**, Norway
- 4 I 6 **Lynn Lake**, Manitoba, Canada
- 51 R 3 **Lynovytsya**, Ukraine
- 27 N 11 **Lynton**, United Kingdom
- 49 H 15 **Lyntupy**, Belarus
- 29 T 10 **Lyon**, France
- 3 V 5 **Lyons**, Georgia, U.S.A.
- 3 M 5 **Lyons**, Kansas, U.S.A.
- 49 M 15 **Lyozna**, Belarus
- 51 T 3 **Lypova Dolyna**, Ukraine
- 33 B 19 **Lys**, Belgium ∿
- 57 P 1 **Lyskovo**, Russian Federation
- 55 U 12 **Lys'va**, Russian Federation
- 51 Y 5 **Lysychans'k**, Ukraine
- 27 O 2 **Lytham St Anne's**, United Kingdom
- 33 H 20 **Lyttelton**, New Zealand
- 3 G 21 **Lytton**, British Columbia, Canada
- 49 J 20 **Lyuban'**, Belarus
- 50 M 4 **Lyubar**, Ukraine
- 51 P 1 **Lyubech**, Ukraine
- 156 L 1 **Lyubertsy**, Russian Federation
- 150 K 1 **Lyubeshiv**, Ukraine
- 154 G 12 **Lyubytine**, Russian Federation
- 156 J 2 **Lyudinovo**, Russian Federation

M

- 181 B 26 **Maalhosmadulu Atoll**, Maldives 🏝
- 219 N 6 **Maamba**, Zambia
- 215 T 15 **Ma'an**, Cameroon
- 172 G 12 **Ma'an**, Jordan
- 134 M 11 **Maaninkavaara**, Finland
- 189 X 5 **Ma'anshan**, China
- 133 J 16 **Maarheeze**, Netherlands
- 135 J 19 **Maarianhamina**, Finland
- 172 I 3 **Ma'arrat an Nu'mān**, Syria
- 132 I 12 **Maarssen**, Netherlands
- 133 H 14 **Maas**, Netherlands ∿
- 133 K 18 **Maaseik**, Belgium
- 197 L 18 **Maasin**, Philippines
- 132 F 13 **Maasland**, Netherlands
- 133 K 18 **Maasmechelen**, Belgium
- 133 K 19 **Maastricht**, Netherlands
- 193 S 10 **Maba**, Indonesia
- 196 F 10 **Mabalacat**, Philippines
- 219 Q 10 **Mabalane**, Mozambique
- 217 P 7 **Mabana**, Democratic Republic of Congo
- 190 E 10 **Mabein**, Myanmar
- 197 N 22 **Mabini**, Philippines
- 127 W 4 **Mablethorpe**, United Kingdom
- 219 R 9 **Mabote**, Mozambique
- 87 X 8 **Mabou**, Nova Scotia, Canada
- 211 U 9 **Mabrūk**, Libya
- 196 H 1 **Mabudis**, Philippines 🏝
- 241 V 5 **Mac Robertson Land**, Antarctica ◇
- 113 A 18 **Macachín**, Argentina
- 112 O 6 **Macaé**, Brazil
- 219 S 4 **Macaloge**, Mozambique
- 194 C 5 **Macang**, Malaysia
- 108 I 9 **Macapá**, Brazil
- 106 A 11 **Macará**, Ecuador
- 91 V 15 **Macaracas**, Panama
- 106 C 10 **Macas**, Ecuador
- 189 U 13 **Macau**, China
- 109 L 15 **Macaúbas**, Brazil
- 111 L 23 **Macbride Head**, Falkland Islands ▶
- 63 V 7 **Macclenny**, Florida, U.S.A.
- 127 Q 4 **Macclesfield**, United Kingdom
- 39 N 12 **MacDonald Islands**, Australia ▣
- 230 N 6 **MacDonnell Ranges**, Northern Territory, Australia ⛰
- 130 J 4 **Macedo de Cavaleiros**, Portugal
- 146 C 11 **Macedonia (F.Y.R.O.M.)**, Europe □
- 108 O 13 **Maceió**, Brazil
- 140 I 11 **Macerata**, Italy
- 153 S 11 **Macha**, Russian Federation
- 106 B 8 **Machachi**, Ecuador
- 219 Q 9 **Machaila**, Mozambique
- 217 V 9 **Machakos**, Kenya
- 106 A 10 **Machala**, Ecuador
- 187 E 18 **Machang**, China
- 219 R 8 **Machanga**, Mozambique
- 90 I 3 **Machaquilá**, Guatemala ∿
- 213 F 20 **Machar Marshes**, Sudan ◇
- 107 L 22 **Machareti**, Bolivia
- 189 U 6 **Macheng**, China
- 181 J 16 **Machhagan**, India
- 59 S 5 **Machias**, Maine, U.S.A.
- 42 O 5 **Machico**, Madeira
- 181 G 19 **Machilipatnam**, India
- 219 R 5 **Machinga**, Malawi
- 104 K 3 **Machiques**, Venezuela
- 127 N 7 **Machynlleth**, United Kingdom
- 219 Q 10 **Macia**, Mozambique
- 151 N 12 **Măcin**, Romania
- 231 U 5 **Mackay**, Queensland, Australia
- 73 N 10 **Mackay**, Idaho, U.S.A.
- 82 D 10 **Mackenzie**, Northwest Territories, Canada ∿
- 241 X 6 **Mackenzie Bay**, Antarctica ≈
- 82 B 8 **Mackenzie Bay**, Yukon Territory, Canada ≈
- 81 N 3 **Mackenzie King Island**, Northwest Territories, Canada 🏝
- 82 C 11 **Mackenzie Mountains**, Yukon Territory, Canada ⛰
- 64 K 10 **Mackinaw City**, Michigan, U.S.A.
- 83 K 18 **Macklin**, Saskatchewan, Canada
- 233 D 26 **Maclennan**, New Zealand
- 218 H 1 **Macocola**, Angola
- 65 D 18 **Macomb**, Illinois, U.S.A.
- 141 B 17 **Macomer**, Italy
- 219 U 4 **Macomia**, Mozambique
- 63 T 4 **Macon**, Georgia, U.S.A.
- 63 N 4 **Macon**, Mississippi, U.S.A.
- 65 L 20 **Macon**, Ohio, U.S.A.
- 69 U 2 **Macon**, Missouri, U.S.A.
- 129 T 9 **Mâcon**, France
- 218 L 4 **Macondo**, Angola
- 231 T 10 **Macquarie**, New South Wales, Australia ∿
- 41 N 13 **Macquarie Island**, Australia 🏝
- 125 B 20 **Macroom**, Republic of Ireland
- 90 J 5 **Macuelizo**, Honduras
- 104 J 10 **Macuje**, Colombia
- 172 G 10 **Mādabā**, Jordan
- 219 P 12 **Madadeni**, Republic of South Africa
- 219 W 7 **Madagascar**, Africa □
- 219 W 8 **Madagascar**, Madgascar 🏝
- 38 K 8 **Madagascar Basin**, Indian Ocean ◇
- 38 J 8 **Madagascar Plateau**, Indian Ocean ◇
- 38 J 9 **Madagascar Ridge**, Indian Ocean ⛰
- 215 U 5 **Madama**, Niger
- 146 I 12 **Madan**, Bulgaria
- 234 D 4 **Madang**, Papua New Guinea
- 234 D 4 **Madang**, Papua New Guinea ▣
- 215 Q 9 **Madaoua**, Niger
- 183 U 13 **Madaripur**, Bangladesh
- 178 I 13 **Madau**, Turkmenistan
- 59 R 1 **Madawaska**, Maine, U.S.A.
- 42 N 4 **Madeira**, Portugal ▣
- 108 D 13 **Madeira**, Brazil ∿
- 42 J 10 **Madeira Ridge**, Atlantic Ocean ⛰
- 77 H 15 **Madeline**, California, U.S.A.
- 64 E 8 **Madeline Island**, Wisconsin, U.S.A. 🏝
- 171 O 11 **Maden**, Turkey
- 179 W 6 **Madeniyet**, Kazakhstan
- 77 I 20 **Madera**, California, U.S.A.
- 88 K 4 **Madera**, Mexico
- 183 R 11 **Madhepura**, India
- 183 Q 10 **Madhubani**, India
- 182 M 12 **Madhya Pradesh**, India ▣
- 181 C 21 **Madikeri**, India
- 69 O 13 **Madill**, Oklahoma, U.S.A.
- 216 H 11 **Madimba**, Democratic Republic of Congo
- 172 M 3 **Ma'din**, Syria
- 172 K 3 **Madīnat ath Thawrah**, Syria
- 216 E 10 **Madingo-Kayes**, Congo
- 107 I 17 **Madini**, Bolivia ∿
- 63 U 3 **Madison**, Georgia, U.S.A.
- 63 U 7 **Madison**, Florida, U.S.A.
- 65 F 14 **Madison**, Wisconsin, U.S.A.
- 65 J 20 **Madison**, Indiana, U.S.A.
- 67 O 9 **Madison**, South Dakota, U.S.A.
- 61 R 6 **Madison Heights**, Virginia, U.S.A.
- 60 E 6 **Madisonville**, Kentucky, U.S.A.
- 60 J 10 **Madisonville**, Tennessee, U.S.A.
- 71 R 8 **Madisonville**, Texas, U.S.A.
- 192 J 14 **Madiun**, Indonesia
- 216 G 7 **Madjingo**, Gabon
- 148 G 11 **Madliena**, Latvia
- 217 W 7 **Mado Gashi**, Kenya
- 86 H 12 **Madoc**, Ontario, Canada
- 185 O 9 **Madoi**, China
- 148 H 11 **Madona**, Latvia
- 76 H 11 **Madras**, Oregon, U.S.A.
- 107 H 16 **Madre de Dios**, Peru ▣
- 107 G 17 **Madre de Dios**, Bolivia/Peru ∿
- 131 O 6 **Madrid**, Spain 🏛
- 131 O 7 **Madrid**, Spain ▣
- 217 U 10 **Madukani**, Tanzania
- 230 K 10 **Madura**, Western Australia, Australia
- 192 K 14 **Madura**, Indonesia 🏝
- 181 E 23 **Madurai**, India
- 191 F 14 **Mae Hong Son**, Thailand
- 191 F 15 **Mae Sariang**, Thailand
- 191 F 16 **Mae Sot**, Thailand
- 199 J 15 **Maebashi**, Japan
- 219 X 6 **Maevatanana**, Madgascar
- 235 R 10 **Maéwo**, Vanuatu 🏝
- 84 H 8 **Mafeking**, Manitoba, Canada
- 219 N 13 **Mafeteng**, Lesotho
- 217 W 13 **Mafia Channel**, Tanzania ≈
- 217 X 12 **Mafia Island**, Tanzania 🏝
- 218 M 11 **Mafikeng**, Republic of South Africa
- 217 U 12 **Mafinga**, Tanzania
- 112 I 9 **Mafra**, Brazil
- 153 X 10 **Magadan**, Russian Federation
- 217 V 9 **Magadi**, Kenya
- 111 F 24 **Magallanes**, Chile ▣
- 131 X 8 **Magalluf**, Spain
- 196 H 8 **Magat**, Philippines ∿
- 69 T 10 **Magazine Mountain**, Arkansas, U.S.A. ▲
- 216 M 6 **Magbakele**, Democratic Republic of Congo
- 153 T 13 **Magdagachi**, Russian Federation
- 104 I 2 **Magdalena**, Colombia ▣
- 104 I 4 **Magdalena**, Colombia ∿
- 107 L 17 **Magdalena**, Bolivia
- 113 D 16 **Magdalena**, Argentina
- 75 P 11 **Magdalena**, New Mexico, U.S.A.
- 88 I 3 **Magdalena**, Mexico
- 88 I 3 **Magdalena**, Mexico ∿
- 137 J 14 **Magdeburg**, Germany
- 199 C 25 **Mage-shima**, Japan 🏝
- 140 C 7 **Magenta**, Italy
- 134 K 5 **Magerøya**, Norway 🏝
- 212 E 9 **Maghâgha**, Egypt
- 214 F 8 **Maghama**, Mauritania
- 210 K 6 **Maghnia**, Algeria
- 131 O 11 **Magina**, Spain ▲
- 141 O 17 **Maglie**, Italy
- 234 F 4 **Magma Point**, Papua New Guinea ▶
- 231 T 4 **Magnetic Island**, Queensland, Australia 🏝
- 152 I 11 **Magnitogorsk**, Russian Federation
- 69 T 14 **Magnolia**, Arkansas, U.S.A.
- 235 Y 11 **Mago**, Fiji 🏝
- 219 P 6 **Màgoé**, Mozambique
- 86 M 11 **Magog**, Québec, Canada
- 214 F 7 **Magta' Lahjar**, Mauritania
- 219 Q 10 **Magude**, Mozambique
- 215 U 10 **Magumeri**, Nigeria
- 84 K 4 **Maguse Lake**, Nunavut, Canada ≋
- 190 C 13 **Magwe**, Myanmar ▣
- 190 C 13 **Magwe**, Myanmar
- 190 A 13 **Magyichaung**, Myanmar
- 191 J 17 **Maha Sarakham**, Thailand
- 176 F 4 **Mahābād**, Iran
- 219 W 6 **Mahabe**, Madgascar
- 183 N 9 **Mahabharat Range**, Nepal ⛰
- 181 B 18 **Mahad**, India
- 213 M 24 **Mahaddayweyne**, Somalia
- 217 R 6 **Mahagi Port**, Democratic Republic of Congo
- 182 G 8 **Mahajan**, India
- 219 X 6 **Mahajanga**, Madgascar
- 219 X 7 **Mahajanga**, Madgascar ▣
- 192 L 10 **Mahakam**, Indonesia ∿
- 176 H 7 **Mahallāt**, Iran
- 176 M 10 **Māhān**, Iran
- 181 I 16 **Mahanadi**, India ∿
- 219 Y 8 **Mahanoro**, Madgascar
- 183 P 10 **Maharajganj**, India
- 181 D 17 **Maharashtra**, India ▣
- 172 H 10 **Mahaṭṭat Dab'ah**, Jordan
- 213 D 18 **Mahbub**, Sudan
- 181 F 19 **Mahbubnagar**, India
- 211 R 6 **Mahdia**, Tunisia
- 181 D 22 **Mahe**, India
- 38 B 10 **Mahé**, Seychelles 🏝
- 38 B 12 **Mahébourg**, Mauritius
- 217 V 13 **Mahenge**, Tanzania
- 233 F 23 **Maheno**, New Zealand
- 232 O 12 **Mahia**, New Zealand
- 232 O 12 **Mahia Peninsula**, New Zealand ▶
- 149 M 17 **Mahilyow**, Belarus
- 149 M 18 **Mahilyowskaya Voblasts'**, Belarus ▣
- 136 M 13 **Mahlow**, Germany
- 176 J 5 **Mahmudabad**, Iran
- 182 M 10 **Mahmudabad**, India
- 67 P 4 **Mahnomen**, Minnesota, U.S.A.
- 182 K 11 **Mahoba**, India
- 232 K 11 **Mahoenui**, New Zealand
- 131 Z 7 **Mahon**, Spain
- 131 R 9 **Mahora**, Spain
- 181 B 16 **Mahuva**, India
- 182 I 10 **Mahwa**, India
- 193 S 13 **Mai**, Indonesia 🏝
- 236 D 2 **Maiana**, Kiribati 🏝
- 104 K 2 **Maicao**, Colombia
- 108 H 9 **Maicuru**, Brazil ∿
- 127 U 10 **Maidenhead**, United Kingdom
- 127 X 11 **Maidstone**, United Kingdom
- 215 U 10 **Maiduguri**, Nigeria
- 182 M 12 **Maihar**, India
- 183 V 13 **Maijdi**, Bangladesh
- 181 G 16 **Maikala Range**, India ⛰
- 192 D 12 **Maileppe**, Indonesia
- 129 S 5 **Mailly-le-Camp**, France
- 137 F 20 **Main**, Germany ∿
- 43 K 26 **Main Base**, Ascension
- 86 C 10 **Main Channel**, Ontario, Canada ≈
- 137 K 23 **Mainburg**, Germany
- 59 P 4 **Maine**, U.S.A. ▣
- 124 H 7 **Mainland**, United Kingdom 🏝
- 124 J 4 **Mainland**, United Kingdom 🏝
- 182 K 10 **Mainpuri**, India
- 219 W 7 **Maintirano**, Madgascar
- 137 E 19 **Mainz**, Germany
- 43 B 17 **Maio**, Cape Verde 🏝
- 113 D 17 **Maipú**, Argentina
- 105 O 2 **Maiquetía**, Venezuela
- 139 W 2 **Maissau**, Austria
- 110 F 10 **Maitencillo**, Chile
- 219 N 8 **Maitengwe**, Botswana
- 231 V 11 **Maitland**, New South Wales, Australia
- 231 P 11 **Maitland**, South Australia, Australia
- 241 Q 1 **Maitri**, Antarctica ⁘
- 199 G 17 **Maizuru**, Japan
- 145 J 20 **Maja e Çikes**, Albania ▲
- 145 K 15 **Maja Jezercë**, Albania ▲
- 89 Z 12 **Majahual**, Mexico
- 144 N 11 **Majdanpek**, Serbia and Montenegro
- 193 N 12 **Majene**, Indonesia
- 144 H 10 **Majevica**, Bosnia and Herzegovina ⛰
- 186 O 11 **Majiagang**, China
- 189 S 12 **Majiang**, China
- 189 S 8 **Majitang**, China
- 131 X 8 **Majorca**, Spain 🏝
- 237 Z 3 **Majuro**, Marshall Islands 🏛
- 237 Z 3 **Majuro**, Marshall Islands 🏝
- 215 T 14 **Makak**, Cameroon
- 193 N 12 **Makale**, Indonesia
- 217 Q 10 **Makamba**, Burundi
- 179 Y 7 **Makanchi**, Kazakhstan
- 216 J 7 **Makanza**, Democratic Republic of Congo
- 232 O 12 **Makaraka**, New Zealand
- 151 O 3 **Makariv**, Ukraine
- 153 X 14 **Makarov**, Russian Federation
- 45 R 8 **Makarov Basin**, Arctic Ocean ◇
- 40 M 5 **Makarov Seamount**, Pacific Ocean ▲
- 157 O 5 **Makarovo**, Russian Federation
- 154 M 13 **Makar'yev**, Russian Federation
- 193 N 11 **Makassar Strait**, Indonesia ≈
- 178 J 6 **Makat**, Kazakhstan
- 190 E 7 **Makaw**, Myanmar
- 214 G 11 **Makeni**, Sierra Leone
- 157 R 14 **Makhachkala**, Russian Federation
- 178 I 6 **Makhambet**, Kazakhstan
- 173 S 3 **Makhmūr**, Iraq
- 233 F 22 **Makikihi**, New Zealand
- 236 D 1 **Makin**, Kiribati 🏝
- 217 V 9 **Makindu**, Kenya
- 179 R 3 **Makinsk**, Kazakhstan
- 235 N 7 **Makira**, Solomon Islands ▣
- 85 V 7 **Makkovik**, Newfoundland and Labrador, Canada
- 143 L 25 **Makó**, Hungary
- 216 F 7 **Makokou**, Gabon
- 217 S 13 **Makongolosi**, Tanzania
- 217 Q 6 **Makoro**, Democratic Republic of Congo
- 216 H 9 **Makotipoko**, Congo
- 216 H 7 **Makoua**, Congo
- 147 K 24 **Makra**, Greece 🏝
- 147 D 18 **Makrakomi**, Greece
- 177 O 13 **Makran**, Iran ◇
- 177 N 14 **Makran Coast**, Iran ◇
- 147 H 20 **Makronisi**, Greece 🏝
- 154 H 13 **Maksatikha**, Russian Federation
- 176 E 2 **Mākū**, Iran
- 217 T 13 **Makumbako**, Tanzania
- 216 K 11 **Makumbi**, Democratic Republic of Congo
- 217 V 14 **Makunguwiro**, Tanzania
- 181 L 16 **Makunudhoo Atoll**, Maldives 🏝
- 199 B 24 **Makurazaki**, Japan
- 215 S 12 **Makurdi**, Nigeria
- 78 J 13 **Makushin Volcano**, Alaska, U.S.A. ▲
- 213 K 25 **Makuungo**, Somalia
- 183 T 10 **Mal**, India
- 107 C 17 **Mala**, Peru
- 197 K 21 **Malabang**, Philippines
- 181 C 21 **Malabar Coast**, India ◇
- 215 S 14 **Malabo**, Equatorial Guinea 🏛
- 143 G 21 **Malacky**, Slovakia
- 73 P 13 **Malad City**, Idaho, U.S.A.
- 149 I 16 **Maladzyechna**, Belarus
- 131 N 13 **Málaga**, Spain
- 131 O 9 **Malagón**, Spain
- 219 X 8 **Malaimbandy**, Madgascar
- 234 M 6 **Malaita**, Solomon Islands 🏝
- 235 N 6 **Malaita**, Solomon Islands ▣
- 213 E 20 **Malakal**, Sudan
- 182 I 9 **Malakhera**, India
- 182 L 8 **Malakheti**, Nepal
- 235 P 11 **Malakula**, Vanuatu 🏝
- 234 D 4 **Malalamai**, Papua New Guinea
- 234 B 6 **Malam**, Papua New Guinea
- 193 O 12 **Malamala**, Indonesia
- 197 D 19 **Malanao**, Philippines 🏝
- 192 J 14 **Malang**, Indonesia
- 218 H 3 **Malanje**, Angola
- 218 H 2 **Malanje**, Angola ▣

□ Country ▣ Internal administrative region: State/Province/Territory/Dependent territory 🏛 Capital city ⛰ Mountain range/Undersea ridge ▲ Mountain peak/Volcano/Seamount ◇ Geographic feature ▶ Headland/Point/Cape/Peninsula ☗ Desert 🏝 Island/Island group ⁘ Antarctic base 🌊 Ocean ◒ Sea ≈ Bay/Gulf/Channel/Strait ≋ Lake ⚑ Salt pan/Dry/Intermittent lake ∿ River

Malanzán – Marion

110 H 10 Malanzán, Argentina
135 H 20 Mälaren, Sweden
110 G 13 Malargüe, Argentina
86 G 7 Malartic, Québec, Canada
149 E 22 Malaryta, Belarus
171 N 11 Malatya, Turkey
182 G 7 Malaut, India
181 E 21 Malavalli, India
195 W 4 Malawali, Malaysia
219 Q 4 Malawi, Africa
213 H 17 Malawiya, Sudan
194 D 7 Malay Peninsula, Malaysia
154 G 11 Malaya Vishera, Russian Federation
197 L 21 Malaybalay, Philippines
176 G 6 Malāyer, Iran
194 D 7 Malaysia, Asia
171 R 10 Malazgirt, Turkey
142 I 9 Malbork, Poland
136 L 10 Malchin, Germany
136 K 10 Malchow, Germany
133 D 17 Maldegem, Belgium
133 K 14 Malden, Netherlands
69 Y 8 Malden, Missouri, U.S.A.
237 Q 4 Malden Island, Kiribati
181 K 19 Maldives, Asia
127 X 9 Maldon, United Kingdom
113 F 16 Maldonado, Uruguay
113 G 16 Maldonado, Uruguay
181 L 18 Male, Maldives
181 L 17 Male Atoll, Maldives
143 G 21 Malé Karpaty, Slovakia
181 E 17 Malegaon, India
181 C 16 Malegaon, India
217 O 9 Malela, Democratic Republic of Congo
217 O 13 Malemba Nkulu, Democratic Republic of Congo
177 T 8 Mālestān, Afghanistan
213 B 17 Malha, Sudan
173 R 5 Malḩāt, Iraq
76 J 13 Malheur Lake, Oregon, U.S.A.
214 F 10 Mali, Africa
217 O 9 Mali, Democratic Republic of Congo
191 F 20 Mali Kyun, Myanmar
189 S 6 Maliangping, China
197 J 22 Maligay Bay, Philippines
125 E 14 Malin, Republic of Ireland
125 D 14 Malin Head, Republic of Ireland
217 X 9 Malindi, Kenya
216 F 9 Malinga, Gabon
185 Q 14 Malipo, China
145 L 20 Maliq, Albania
197 M 23 Malita, Philippines
146 L 13 Malkara, Turkey
124 F 11 Mallaig, United Kingdom
212 E 9 Mallawi, Egypt
84 K 3 Mallery Lake, Nunavut, Canada
125 C 20 Mallow, Republic of Ireland
234 G 4 Malmal, Papua New Guinea
133 L 21 Malmédy, Belgium
218 J 15 Malmesbury, Republic of South Africa
127 R 10 Malmesbury, United Kingdom
135 E 25 Malmö, Sweden
155 Q 14 Malmyzh, Russian Federation
150 K 10 Malnaș, Romania
235 Q 10 Malo, Vanuatu
108 G 9 Maloca, Brazil
237 Z 2 Maloelap, Marshall Islands
196 G 11 Malolos, Philippines
58 J 5 Malone, New York, U.S.A.
216 M 14 Malonga, Democratic Republic of Congo
154 J 7 Maloshuyka, Russian Federation
135 A 16 Måløy, Norway
155 O 4 Malozemel'skaya Tundra, Russian Federation
180 D 12 Malpura, India
141 I 25 Malta, Europe
141 K 25 Malta, Malta
148 I 12 Malta, Latvia
73 U 3 Malta, Montana, U.S.A.
141 I 24 Malta Channel, Italy
158 M 10 Malta Plateau, Mediterranean Sea
159 N 11 Malta Ridge, Mediterranean Sea
158 K 9 Malta Trough, Mediterranean Sea
218 I 10 Maltahöhe, Namibia
127 T 3 Maltby, United Kingdom
127 W 4 Maltby le Marsh, United Kingdom
127 U 1 Malton, United Kingdom
193 R 13 Maluku, Indonesia
135 F 19 Malung, Sweden
197 H 23 Maluso, Philippines
234 M 6 Malu'u, Solomon Islands
181 B 19 Malvan, India
69 U 12 Malvern, Arkansas, U.S.A.
151 O 3 Malyn, Ukraine
157 T 1 Mamadysh, Russian Federation
197 L 19 Mambajao, Philippines
217 Q 7 Mambasa, Democratic Republic of Congo
216 H 5 Mambéré-Kadéï, Central African Republic
196 F 13 Mamburao, Philippines
38 B 9 Mamelles, Seychelles
219 O 11 Mamelodi, Republic of South Africa
215 S 13 Mamfé, Cameroon
110 G 3 Mamiña, Chile
179 Q 1 Mamlyutka, Kazakhstan
171 W 10 Mammadbajli, Azerbaijan
74 L 13 Mammoth, Arizona, U.S.A.
73 R 8 Mammoth Hot Springs, Wyoming, U.S.A.
149 A 16 Mamonovo, Russian Federation
107 K 17 Mamoré, Bolivia
108 C 10 Mamori, Brazil
108 C 12 Mamoriá, Brazil
214 G 11 Mamou, Guinea
193 N 12 Mamuju, Indonesia
175 X 10 Ma'mūl, Oman
214 I 12 Man, Côte d'Ivoire
106 A 9 Manabí, Ecuador
108 F 11 Manacapuru, Brazil
131 Y 8 Manacor, Spain
193 Q 10 Manado, Indonesia
91 N 9 Managua, Nicaragua
219 Y 9 Manakara, Madgascar
175 P 13 Manākhah, Yemen
234 C 3 Manam, Papua New Guinea
219 X 10 Manambondro, Madgascar
197 F 16 Manamoc, Philippines
219 Z 6 Mananara Avaratra, Madgascar
219 Y 9 Mananjary, Madgascar
219 X 10 Manantenina, Madgascar
233 C 24 Manapouri, New Zealand
184 K 3 Manas Hu, China
61 T 3 Manassas, Virginia, U.S.A.
43 N 26 Manati Bay, St Helena
108 F 10 Manaus, Brazil
170 F 13 Manavgat, Turkey
213 B 18 Manawashei, Sudan
232 L 13 Manawatu-Wanganui, New Zealand
172 K 2 Manbij, Syria
64 J 11 Mancelona, Michigan, U.S.A.
127 R 3 Manchester, United Kingdom
58 L 8 Manchester, Vermont, U.S.A.
59 N 8 Manchester, New Hampshire, U.S.A.
60 J 6 Manchester, Kentucky, U.S.A.
60 G 10 Manchester, Tennessee, U.S.A.
187 H 14 Manchurian Plain, China
170 M 10 Mancilik, Turkey
177 P 14 Mand, Pakistan
219 W 8 Mandabe, Madgascar
194 A 13 Mandai, Singapore
177 P 8 Mandal, Afghanistan
190 C 12 Mandalay, Myanmar
190 D 11 Mandalay, Myanmar
185 Q 2 Mandalgovi, Mongolia
173 V 6 Mandalī, Iraq
66 J 5 Mandan, North Dakota, U.S.A.
197 J 15 Mandaon, Philippines
141 C 18 Mandas, Italy
197 K 17 Mandaue, Philippines
217 Y 5 Mandera, Kenya
92 K 8 Mandeville, Jamaica
180 B 12 Mandha, India
213 L 20 Mandheera, Somalia
182 J 6 Mandi, India
219 Q 6 Mandié, Mozambique
219 S 5 Mandimba, Mozambique
216 E 9 Mandji, Gabon
181 G 15 Mandla, India
135 B 25 Mandø, Denmark
219 Z 6 Mandritsara, Madgascar
181 D 14 Mandsaur, India
230 G 11 Mandurah, Western Australia, Australia
141 O 17 Manduria, Italy
181 A 14 Mandvi, India
181 E 21 Mandya, India
212 E 10 Manfalût, Egypt
141 L 14 Manfredonia, Italy
234 H 3 Manga, Papua New Guinea
216 K 10 Mangai, Democratic Republic of Congo
234 G 3 Mangai, Papua New Guinea
237 P 11 Mangaia, Cook Islands
232 L 11 Mangakino, New Zealand
183 V 10 Mangaldai, India
151 N 14 Mangalia, Romania
215 Y 10 Mangalmé, Chad
181 C 21 Mangalore, India
232 I 5 Mangamuka, New Zealand
219 N 12 Mangaung, Republic of South Africa
232 M 13 Mangaweka, New Zealand
232 K 7 Mangawhai, New Zealand
137 J 26 Mangfallgebirge, Germany
192 H 12 Manggar, Indonesia
234 M 8 Manggautu, Solomon Islands
178 J 10 Mangistau, Kazakhstan
182 G 4 Mangla Reservoir, India/Pakistan
184 L 7 Mangnai, China
215 N 11 Mango, Togo
219 R 5 Mangochi, Malawi
193 R 11 Mangole, Indonesia
232 I 5 Mangonui, New Zealand
92 K 3 Mangrove Cay, The Bahamas
130 J 6 Mangualde, Portugal
112 H 9 Mangueirinha, Brazil
186 H 5 Mangui, China
68 J 11 Mangum, Oklahoma, U.S.A.
178 G 8 Mangyshlakskiy Zaliv, Kazakhstan
69 O 3 Manhattan, Kansas, U.S.A.
133 K 22 Manhay, Belgium
140 H 6 Maniago, Italy
219 Q 7 Manica, Mozambique
219 P 7 Manicaland, Zimbabwe
108 E 12 Manicoré, Brazil
87 P 3 Manicouagan, Québec, Canada
217 O 9 Maniema, Democratic Republic of Congo
175 S 4 Manifah, Saudi Arabia
188 J 5 Maniganggo, China
84 J 10 Manigotagan, Manitoba, Canada
237 O 7 Manihiki, Cook Islands
41 Q 9 Manihiki Plateau, Pacific Ocean
44 M 12 Maniitsoq, Greenland
183 W 13 Manikchhari, Bangladesh
182 M 12 Manikpur, India
196 G 11 Manila, Philippines
74 M 2 Manila, Utah, U.S.A.
196 G 11 Manila Bay, Philippines
193 V 11 Manim, Indonesia
231 N 1 Maningrida, Northern Territory, Australia
193 R 12 Manipa, Indonesia
183 X 11 Manipur, India
183 X 12 Manipur Hills, India
170 B 10 Manisa, Turkey
109 H 14 Manissauá-Miçu, Brazil
64 I 12 Manistee, Michigan, U.S.A.
64 J 12 Manistee, Michigan, U.S.A.
64 I 9 Manistique, Michigan, U.S.A.
64 J 9 Manistique Lake, Michigan, U.S.A.
84 I 7 Manitoba, Canada
64 I 11 Manitou Islands, Michigan, U.S.A.
86 C 10 Manitoulin Island, Ontario, Canada
84 M 11 Manitouwadge, Ontario, Canada
86 I 9 Maniwaki, Québec, Canada
193 W 12 Maniwori, Indonesia
104 H 6 Manizales, Colombia
219 W 9 Manja, Madgascar
176 H 5 Manjil, Iran
230 G 12 Manjimup, Western Australia, Australia
67 R 9 Mankato, Minnesota, U.S.A.
215 U 14 Mankim, Cameroon
214 J 12 Mankono, Côte d'Ivoire
181 G 24 Mankulam, Sri Lanka
181 C 16 Manmad, India
192 E 13 Manna, Indonesia
181 F 24 Mannar, Sri Lanka
181 F 24 Mannar Island, Sri Lanka
137 F 21 Mannheim, Germany
61 P 13 Manning, South Carolina, U.S.A.
66 H 5 Manning, North Dakota, U.S.A.
214 G 12 Mano, Sierra Leone
214 G 12 Mano River, Liberia
193 V 11 Manokwari, Indonesia
150 L 7 Manoleasa, Romania
217 P 12 Manono, Democratic Republic of Congo
129 V 13 Manosque, France
187 K 15 Manp'o, North Korea
236 K 4 Manra, Kiribati
131 W 4 Manresa, Spain
219 O 3 Mansa, Zambia
182 H 7 Mansa, India
214 E 9 Mansa Konko, Gambia
214 E 9 Mansabá, Guinea-Bissau
177 X 7 Mansehra, Pakistan
85 P 4 Mansel Island, Nunavut, Canada
127 T 5 Mansfield, United Kingdom
58 F 10 Mansfield, Pennsylvania, U.S.A.
62 G 5 Mansfield, Louisiana, U.S.A.
65 N 17 Mansfield, Ohio, U.S.A.
69 S 11 Mansfield, Arkansas, U.S.A.
190 D 9 Mansi, Myanmar
214 E 10 Mansôa, Guinea-Bissau
170 K 12 Mansurlu, Turkey
106 A 9 Manta, Ecuador
77 H 19 Manteca, California, U.S.A.
104 M 5 Mantecal, Venezuela
61 W 8 Manteo, North Carolina, U.S.A.
129 P 4 Mantes-la-Jolie, France
74 K 4 Manti, Utah, U.S.A.
91 N 5 Manto, Honduras
147 G 18 Mantoudi, Greece
140 E 7 Mantova, Italy
154 M 12 Manturovo, Russian Federation
236 K 8 Manua Islands, American Samoa
237 P 10 Manuae, Cook Islands
108 H 12 Manuelzinho, Brazil
193 P 12 Manui, Indonesia
176 M 12 Manūjān, Iran
197 E 25 Manuk Manka, Philippines
232 K 8 Manukau, New Zealand
232 J 9 Manukau Harbour, New Zealand
234 D 2 Manus, Papua New Guinea
234 D 2 Manus Island, Papua New Guinea
62 H 6 Many, Louisiana, U.S.A.
217 T 11 Manyoni, Tanzania
131 P 9 Manzanares, Spain
89 N 12 Manzanillo, Mexico
176 I 6 Manzariyeh, Iran
186 E 7 Manzhouli, China
140 G 13 Manziana, Italy
219 P 11 Manzini, Swaziland
215 V 9 Mao, Chad
189 R 13 Maoming, China
188 J 11 Maotou Shan, China
219 Q 9 Mapai, Mozambique
89 W 15 Mapastepec, Mexico
193 Y 14 Mapi, Indonesia
193 Y 14 Mapi, Indonesia
197 D 22 Mapin, Philippines
219 R 9 Mapinhane, Mozambique
83 L 20 Maple Creek, Saskatchewan, Canada
63 P 4 Maplesville, Alabama, U.S.A.
234 B 3 Maprik, Papua New Guinea
233 H 16 Mapua, New Zealand
108 G 9 Mapuera, Brazil
219 Q 11 Maputo, Mozambique
219 Q 10 Maputo, Mozambique
188 L 3 Maqu, China
131 N 7 Maqueda, Spain
196 K 12 Maqueda Channel, Philippines
218 G 1 Maquela do Zombo, Angola
111 H 17 Maquinchao, Argentina
67 W 12 Maquoketa, Iowa, U.S.A.
113 E 18 Mar del Plata, Argentina
217 T 9 Mara, Tanzania
108 D 10 Maraã, Brazil
108 J 11 Marabá, Brazil
104 J 2 Maracaibo, Venezuela
109 H 18 Maracaju, Brazil
105 N 3 Maracay, Venezuela
211 W 9 Marādah, Libya
215 R 9 Maradi, Niger
215 R 9 Maradi, Niger
176 F 4 Marāgheh, Iran
236 D 2 Marakei, Kiribati
217 V 7 Maralal, Kenya
216 J 4 Marali, Central African Republic
240 H 3 Marambio, Antarctica
194 D 8 Maran, Malaysia
74 K 14 Marana, Arizona, U.S.A.
131 Q 5 Maranchón, Spain
176 F 3 Marand, Iran
108 K 12 Maranhão, Brazil
106 C 11 Marañón, Peru
150 L 10 Mărășești, Romania
141 L 17 Maratea, Italy
63 X 15 Marathon, Florida, U.S.A.
70 I 10 Marathon, Texas, U.S.A.
84 M 12 Marathon, Ontario, Canada
232 O 11 Marau Point, New Zealand
197 L 21 Marawi, Philippines
175 U 12 Mar'ayt, Yemen
171 Y 8 Märäzä, Azerbaijan
130 M 14 Marbella, Spain
230 H 6 Marble Bar, Western Australia, Australia
74 K 9 Marble Canyon, Arizona, U.S.A.
219 O 10 Marble Hall, Republic of South Africa
65 N 16 Marble Head, Ohio, U.S.A.
69 Y 6 Marble Hill, Missouri, U.S.A.
73 R 12 Marbleton, Wyoming, U.S.A.
137 F 17 Marburg, Germany
109 H 14 Marcelândia, Brazil
139 Z 3 March, Austria
127 W 7 March, United Kingdom
140 I 11 Marche, Italy
133 J 22 Marche-en-Famenne, Belgium
139 Z 3 Marchegg, Austria
130 L 12 Marchena, Spain
107 E 18 Marcona, Peru
113 B 14 Marcos Juárez, Argentin
177 W 7 Mardan, Pakistan
171 P 12 Mardin, Turkey
171 P 12 Mardin Dağlari, Turkey
235 R 14 Maré, New Caledonia
89 V 14 Mare Muerto, Mexico
65 D 19 Maredosia, Illinois, U.S.A.
231 T 3 Mareeba, Queensland, Australia
110 H 10 Mareyes, Argentina
70 H 9 Marfa, Texas, U.S.A.
230 F 12 Margaret River, Western Australia, Australia
219 P 13 Margate, Republic of South Africa
127 Z 11 Margate, United Kingdo
63 Y 13 Margate, Florida, U.S.A.
183 Y 9 Margherita, India
217 R 7 Margherita Peak, Uganda
150 G 8 Marghita, Romania
197 J 21 Margosatubig, Philippin
240 I 5 Marguerite Bay, Antarctica
173 X 9 Marhaj Kahlīl, Iraq
151 U 8 Marhanets', Ukraine
210 L 6 Marhoum, Algeria
234 A 6 Mari, Papua New Guinea
110 G 5 María Elena, Chile
231 T 15 Maria Island, Tasmania, Australia
139 P 8 Maria Luggau, Austria
236 A 8 Mariana Islands, Northe Mariana Islands
40 L 6 Mariana Trench, Pacific Ocean
92 G 4 Marianao, Cuba
63 S 7 Marianna, Florida, U.S.A.
38 C 8 Marianne, Seychelles
135 G 23 Mariannelund, Sweden
112 D 12 Mariano Loza, Argentina
143 A 17 Mariánské Lázně, Czech Republic
139 V 5 Mariazell, Austria
175 Q 12 Ma'rib, Yemen
144 D 6 Maribor, Slovenia
74 J 13 Maricopa, Arizona, U.S.A.
77 I 23 Maricopa, California, U.S.A.
213 D 22 Maridi, Sudan
240 L 9 Marie Byrd Land, Antarctica
41 T 15 Marie Byrd Seamount, Pacific Ocean
93 Y 9 Marie-Galante, Guadeloupe, France
92 G 4 Mariel, Cuba
133 G 23 Mariembourg, Belgium
137 M 18 Marienberg, Germany
218 J 10 Mariental, Namibia
135 F 21 Mariestad, Sweden
63 S 2 Marietta, Georgia, U.S.A.
65 O 19 Marietta, Ohio, U.S.A.
149 E 16 Marijampolė, Lithuania
112 I 6 Marília, Brazil
218 H 2 Marimba, Angola
77 G 21 Marina, California, U.S.A.
140 D 10 Marina di Carrara, Italy
149 J 18 Mar"ina Horka, Belarus
196 H 13 Marinduque, Philippines
64 H 11 Marinette, Wisconsin, U.S.A.
112 G 7 Maringá, Brazil
130 G 7 Marinha Grande, Portuga
60 D 6 Marion, Kentucky, U.S.A.
60 M 9 Marion, North Carolina, U.S.A.
61 Q 12 Marion, South Carolina, U.S.A.
61 N 7 Marion, Virginia, U.S.A.
65 F 22 Marion, Illinois, U.S.A.
65 J 18 Marion, Indiana, U.S.A.
65 M 18 Marion, Ohio, U.S.A.
67 V 12 Marion, Iowa, U.S.A.

Country · Internal administrative region: State/Province/Territory/Dependent territory · Capital city · Mountain range/Undersea ridge · Mountain peak/Volcano/Seamount · Geographic feature · Headland/Point/Cape/Peninsula · Desert · Island/Island group · Antarctic base · Ocean · Sea · Bay/Gulf/Channel/Strait · Lake · Salt pan/Dry/Intermittent lake · Riv

X 7 **Maripasoula**, French Guiana
I 20 **Mariposa**, California, U.S.A.
P 10 **Marisa**, Indonesia
K 12 **Marismas del Guadalquivir**, Spain ◇
K 11 **Maritsa**, Bulgaria ∿
X 8 **Mariupol'**, Ukraine
F 11 **Mariveles**, Philippines
F 7 **Märjamaa**, Estonia
G 7 **Marjayoun**, Lebanon
W 3 **Mark Twain Lake**, Missouri, U.S.A. 💧
L 24 **Marka**, Somalia
J 7 **Markam**, China
F 19 **Markapur**, India
H 7 **Markazī**, Iran ▣
M 12 **Markelo**, Netherlands
I 10 **Markermeer**, Netherlands ≈
Q 6 **Market Drayton**, United Kingdom
T 7 **Market Harborough**, United Kingdom
V 4 **Market Rasen**, United Kingdom
U 2 **Market Weighton**, United Kingdom
F 12 **Markham**, Ontario, Canada
H 6 **Markit**, China
Z 4 **Markivka**, Ukraine
K 9 **Marknesse**, Netherlands
I 3 **Markounda**, Central African Republic
Y 7 **Markovo**, Russian Federation
Q 5 **Marks**, Russian Federation
J 6 **Marksville**, Louisiana, U.S.A.
K 19 **Marktredwitz**, Germany
N 8 **Marla**, South Australia, Australia
V 6 **Marlborough**, Queensland, Australia
I 17 **Marlborough**, New Zealand ▣
S 11 **Marlborough**, United Kingdom
S 10 **Marlborough Downs**, United Kingdom ◇
Q 8 **Marlin**, Texas, U.S.A.
P 4 **Marlinton**, West Virginia, U.S.A.
U 10 **Marlow**, United Kingdom
C 19 **Marmagao**, India
N 12 **Marmande**, France
C 8 **Marmara**, Turkey
C 8 **Marmara**, Turkey 🏝
T 6 **Marmara Trough**, Mediterranean Sea ◇
N 13 **Marmaraereğlisi**, Turkey
C 13 **Marmaris**, Turkey
G 5 **Marmolada**, Italy ▲
F 9 **Marne**, Germany
U 7 **Marneuli**, Georgia
X 12 **Maro**, Chad
N 8 **Maroa**, Venezuela
Z 6 **Maroantsetra**, Madgascar
Z 5 **Maromokotro**, Madgascar ▲
P 7 **Marondera**, Zimbabwe
X 8 **Maroni**, French Guiana ∿
W 8 **Maroochydore**, Queensland, Australia
O 5 **Maroon Peak**, Colorado, U.S.A. ▲
I 6 **Maropiu**, New Zealand
N 13 **Maros**, Indonesia
V 11 **Maroua**, Cameroon
X 6 **Marovoay**, Madgascar
S 9 **Marquesas Fracture Zone**, Pacific Ocean ◇
T 8 **Marquesas Islands**, French Polynesia 🏝
W 15 **Marquesas Keys**, Florida, U.S.A. 🏝
H 8 **Marquette**, Michigan, U.S.A.
R 8 **Marquez**, Texas, U.S.A.
A 17 **Marra Plateau**, Sudan ◇
G 10 **Marradi**, Italy
G 8 **Marrakech**, Morocco
231 S 15 **Marrawah**, Tasmania, Australia
231 P 9 **Marree**, South Australia, Australia
219 S 7 **Marromeu**, Mozambique
219 S 4 **Marrupa**, Mozambique
211 W 8 **Marsa al Burayqah**, Libya
212 G 11 **Marsa Alam**, Egypt
212 C 7 **Marsa Matrûh**, Egypt
217 V 6 **Marsabit**, Kenya
141 G 22 **Marsala**, Italy
132 H 8 **Marsdiep**, Netherlands ≈
129 U 14 **Marseille**, France
92 L 1 **Marsh Harbour**, The Bahamas
62 J 8 **Marsh Island**, Louisiana, U.S.A. 🏝
67 P 9 **Marshall**, Minnesota, U.S.A.
69 T 3 **Marshall**, Missouri, U.S.A.
69 U 9 **Marshall**, Arkansas, U.S.A.
71 T 6 **Marshall**, Texas, U.S.A.
237 W 4 **Marshall Islands**, Oceania □
67 T 12 **Marshalltown**, Iowa, U.S.A.
64 E 11 **Marshfield**, Wisconsin, U.S.A.
195 V 4 **Martanai Besar**, Malaysia 🏝
192 L 12 **Martapura**, Indonesia
192 F 13 **Martapura**, Indonesia
133 K 24 **Martelange**, Belgium
86 F 8 **Marten River**, Ontario, Canada
59 O 11 **Martha's Vineyard**, Massachusetts, U.S.A. 🏝
138 C 10 **Martigny**, Switzerland
143 I 19 **Martin**, Slovakia
60 C 8 **Martin**, Tennessee, U.S.A.
66 I 11 **Martin**, South Dakota, U.S.A.
240 K 10 **Martin Peninsula**, Antarctica ▶
141 N 16 **Martina Franca**, Italy
233 L 16 **Martinborough**, New Zealand
89 S 11 **Martínez**, Mexico
93 Y 11 **Martinique**, France, France ▣
93 Y 10 **Martinique Passage**, Dominica ≈
147 F 19 **Martino**, Greece
65 O 18 **Martins Ferry**, Ohio, U.S.A.
61 S 2 **Martinsburg**, West Virginia, U.S.A.
61 Q 7 **Martinsville**, Virginia, U.S.A.
65 I 20 **Martinsville**, Indiana, U.S.A.
233 L 14 **Marton**, New Zealand
178 K 4 **Martuk**, Kazakhstan
171 U 9 **Martuni**, Armenia
199 E 19 **Marugame**, Japan
109 O 14 **Maruim**, Brazil
179 N 14 **Mary**, Turkmenistan
231 W 8 **Maryborough**, Queensland, Australia
61 T 3 **Maryland**, U.S.A. ▣
74 J 6 **Marysvale**, Utah, U.S.A.
65 L 18 **Marysville**, Ohio, U.S.A.
69 O 2 **Marysville**, Kansas, U.S.A.
76 H 6 **Marysville**, Washington, U.S.A.
77 G 18 **Marysville**, California, U.S.A.
60 J 9 **Maryville**, Tennessee, U.S.A.
69 R 1 **Maryville**, Missouri, U.S.A.
179 N 15 **Maryyskiy Velayat**, Turkmenistan ▣
90 G 6 **Masagua**, Guatemala
217 R 8 **Masaka**, Uganda
192 L 13 **Masalembu Besar**, Indonesia 🏝
192 L 13 **Masalembu Kecil**, Indonesia 🏝
171 Y 10 **Masalli**, Azerbaijan
193 O 12 **Masamba**, Indonesia
187 M 21 **Masan**, South Korea
217 W 14 **Masasi**, Tanzania
107 L 21 **Masavi**, Bolivia
91 N 9 **Masaya**, Nicaragua
197 J 14 **Masbate**, Philippines
197 J 15 **Masbate**, Philippines 🏝
38 L 6 **Mascarene Basin**, Indian Ocean ◇
38 K 7 **Mascarene Plain**, Indian Ocean ◇
38 L 5 **Mascarene Ridge**, Indian Ocean ⛰
219 N 12 **Maseru**, Lesotho 🏛
127 S 1 **Masham**, United Kingdom
177 O 6 **Mashhad**, Iran
176 L 10 **Mashīz**, Iran
219 P 6 **Mashonaland Central**, Zimbabwe ▣
219 Q 6 **Mashonaland East**, Zimbabwe ▣
219 O 6 **Mashonaland West**, Zimbabwe ▣
134 K 7 **Masi**, Norway
216 J 10 **Masi-Manimba**, Democratic Republic of Congo
88 J 6 **Masiáca**, Mexico
217 R 7 **Masindi**, Uganda
171 T 9 **Masis**, Armenia
107 E 14 **Masisea**, Peru
176 G 8 **Masjed Soleymān**, Iran
175 S 13 **Masna'ah**, Yemen
219 W 7 **Masoarivo**, Madgascar
60 M 3 **Mason**, West Virginia, U.S.A.
71 N 9 **Mason**, Texas, U.S.A.
233 B 26 **Mason Bay**, New Zealand ≈
65 F 18 **Mason City**, Illinois, U.S.A.
67 T 10 **Mason City**, Iowa, U.S.A.
42 N 12 **Maspalomas**, Canary Islands
140 E 10 **Massa**, Italy
140 F 12 **Massa Marittimo**, Italy
59 N 9 **Massachusetts**, U.S.A. ▣
59 O 9 **Massachusetts Bay**, Massachusetts, U.S.A. ≈
215 V 10 **Massaguet**, Chad
215 W 9 **Massakory**, Chad
219 Q 9 **Massangena**, Mozambique
219 R 4 **Massangulo**, Mozambique
213 I 16 **Massawa**, Eritrea
213 I 16 **Massawa Channel**, Eritrea ≈
58 I 5 **Massena**, New York, U.S.A.
215 W 10 **Massenya**, Chad
83 C 19 **Masset**, British Columbia, Canada
86 C 9 **Massey**, Ontario, Canada
129 R 11 **Massif Central**, France ⛰
93 N 8 **Massif de la Hotte**, Haiti ⛰
215 S 6 **Massif de L'aïr**, Niger ⛰
216 L 3 **Massif des Bongo**, Central African Republic ⛰
215 Z 8 **Massif du Kapka**, Chad ⛰
214 G 10 **Massif du Tamgué**, Guinea ▲
216 H 4 **Massif du Yadé**, Central African Republic ⛰
215 Z 7 **Massif Ennedi**, Chad ⛰
219 R 9 **Massinga**, Mozambique
219 Q 10 **Massingir**, Mozambique
241 Y 9 **Masson Island**, Antarctica 🏝
174 L 8 **Mastābah**, Saudi Arabia
171 Z 8 **Mastağa**, Azerbaijan
233 L 15 **Masterton**, New Zealand
92 K 2 **Mastic Point**, The Bahamas
177 W 5 **Mastuj**, Pakistan
177 T 11 **Mastung**, Pakistan
174 L 7 **Mastūrah**, Saudi Arabia
199 C 19 **Masuda**, Japan
219 P 8 **Masvingo**, Zimbabwe
219 P 8 **Masvingo**, Zimbabwe ▣
172 H 4 **Maşyāf**, Syria
149 E 21 **Masyevichy**, Belarus
236 H 8 **Matā 'Utu**, Wallis and Futuna Islands 🏛
219 N 7 **Matabeleland North**, Zimbabwe ▣
219 O 8 **Matabeleland South**, Zimbabwe ▣
86 E 7 **Matachewan**, Ontario, Canada
216 G 11 **Matadi**, Democratic Republic of Congo
70 L 4 **Matador**, Texas, U.S.A.
91 N 8 **Matagalpa**, Nicaragua
85 P 11 **Matagami**, Québec, Canada
71 R 12 **Matagorda Bay**, Texas, U.S.A. ≈
71 R 12 **Matagorda Island**, Texas, U.S.A. 🏝
71 R 12 **Matagorda Peninsula**, Texas, U.S.A. ▶
179 U 5 **Matak**, Kazakhstan
192 G 9 **Matak**, Indonesia 🏝
232 M 9 **Matakana Island**, New Zealand 🏝
232 O 10 **Matakaoa Point**, New Zealand ▶
218 H 5 **Matala**, Angola
214 F 8 **Matam**, Senegal
232 L 10 **Matamata**, New Zealand
215 R 9 **Matamey**, Niger
89 S 7 **Matamoros**, Mexico
197 I 23 **Matanal Point**, Philippines ▶
87 Q 5 **Matane**, Québec, Canada
92 H 4 **Matanzas**, Cuba
181 G 25 **Matara**, Sri Lanka
147 C 19 **Mataragka**, Greece
192 L 15 **Mataram**, Indonesia
231 N 2 **Mataranka**, Northern Territory, Australia
131 X 4 **Mataró**, Spain
232 M 10 **Matata**, New Zealand
233 D 25 **Mataura**, New Zealand
233 C 24 **Mataura**, New Zealand ∿
41 Y 5 **Mataveri**, Easter Island
232 N 11 **Matawai**, New Zealand
179 W 8 **Matay**, Kazakhstan
107 L 17 **Mategua**, Bolivia
89 Q 9 **Matehuala**, Mexico
217 V 14 **Matemanga**, Tanzania
141 M 16 **Matera**, Italy
143 N 21 **Mátészalka**, Hungary
211 Q 5 **Mateur**, Tunisia
86 E 6 **Matheson**, Ontario, Canada
61 V 6 **Mathews**, Virginia, U.S.A.
71 P 13 **Mathis**, Texas, U.S.A.
182 I 9 **Mathura**, India
197 N 22 **Mati**, Philippines
109 L 15 **Matias Cardoso**, Brazil
85 T 8 **Matimekosh**, Québec, Canada
91 R 12 **Matina**, Costa Rica
148 G 9 **Matīši**, Latvia
177 U 14 **Matli**, Pakistan
127 S 5 **Matlock**, United Kingdom
197 K 14 **Matnog**, Philippines
109 H 14 **Mato Grosso**, Brazil ▣
112 F 6 **Mato Grosso do Sul**, Brazil ▣
130 H 5 **Matosinhos**, Portugal
139 P 8 **Matrei in Osttirol**, Austria
218 J 15 **Matroosberg**, Republic of South Africa ▲
189 Y 10 **Matsu Tao**, Taiwan 🏝
199 D 18 **Matsue**, Japan
198 I 8 **Matsumae**, Japan
199 I 16 **Matsumoto**, Japan
199 H 18 **Matsusaka**, Japan
199 D 20 **Matsuyama**, Japan
86 F 9 **Mattawa**, Ontario, Canada
59 R 4 **Mattawamkeag**, Maine, U.S.A.
138 D 11 **Matterhorn**, Switzerland ▲
77 M 15 **Matterhorn**, Nevada, U.S.A. ▲
139 Y 5 **Mattersburg**, Austria
235 S 14 **Matthew Island**, Vanuatu 🏝
93 N 6 **Matthew Town**, The Bahamas
139 Q 4 **Mattighofen**, Austria
65 G 19 **Mattoon**, Illinois, U.S.A.
195 O 9 **Matu**, Malaysia
107 D 16 **Matucana**, Peru
235 Y 12 **Matuku**, Fiji 🏝
218 I 4 **Matumbo**, Angola
105 R 3 **Maturín**, Venezuela
193 Q 8 **Matutuang**, Indonesia 🏝
183 O 11 **Mau**, India
180 F 13 **Mau Rampur**, India
219 S 5 **Maúa**, Mozambique
129 S 2 **Maubeuge**, France
191 D 16 **Maubin**, Myanmar
43 L 23 **Maud Rise**, Atlantic Ocean ⛰
182 L 11 **Maudaha**, India
108 G 11 **Maués**, Brazil
236 A 5 **Maug Islands**, Northern Mariana Islands 🏝
183 N 12 **Mauganj**, India
78 D 7 **Maui**, Hawaii, U.S.A. 🏝
237 P 10 **Mauke**, Cook Islands 🏝
110 F 13 **Maule**, Chile ▣
111 F 17 **Maullín**, Chile
65 L 16 **Maumee**, Ohio, U.S.A.
218 L 8 **Maun**, Botswana
78 E 8 **Mauna Kea**, Hawaii, U.S.A. ▲
78 E 9 **Mauna Loa**, Hawaii, U.S.A. ▲
232 J 6 **Maungatapere**, New Zealand
191 F 19 **Maungmagan Islands**, Myanmar 🏝
76 H 10 **Maupin**, Oregon, U.S.A.
129 Q 11 **Mauriac**, France
214 F 6 **Mauritania**, Africa □
38 A 11 **Mauritius**, Indian Ocean □
38 K 8 **Mauritius Trench**, Indian Ocean ◇
42 I 6 **Maury Seachannel**, Atlantic Ocean ≈
64 E 13 **Mauston**, Wisconsin, U.S.A.
139 R 7 **Mauterndorf**, Austria
217 O 6 **Mava**, Democratic Republic of Congo
219 S 4 **Mavago**, Mozambique
218 J 6 **Mavengue**, Angola
218 K 6 **Mavinga**, Angola
216 I 11 **Mawanga**, Democratic Republic of Congo
189 P 10 **Mawei**, China
241 X 4 **Mawson**, Antarctica ⁙
241 W 4 **Mawson Coast**, Antarctica ◇
241 T 15 **Mawson Peninsula**, Antarctica ▶
66 J 4 **Max**, North Dakota, U.S.A.
110 I 8 **Maxán**, Argentina
89 Y 10 **Maxcanú**, Mexico
135 K 15 **Maxmo**, Finland
153 U 11 **Maya**, Russian Federation ∿
188 M 4 **Maya**, China
192 I 11 **Maya**, Indonesia 🏝
90 I 4 **Maya Mountains**, Guatemala ⛰
93 O 4 **Mayaguana Island**, The Bahamas 🏝
93 T 8 **Mayagüez**, Puerto Rico
215 R 9 **Mayahi**, Niger
179 T 14 **Mayakovskogo**, Tajikistan ▲
216 H 10 **Mayama**, Congo
176 L 5 **Mayamey**, Iran
213 I 18 **Maych'ew**, Ethiopia
213 M 19 **Maydh**, Somalia
128 M 5 **Mayenne**, France
233 F 21 **Mayfield**, New Zealand
60 C 7 **Mayfield**, Kentucky, U.S.A.
146 M 11 **Mayha Dağl**, Turkey ▲
75 R 13 **Mayhill**, New Mexico, U.S.A.
179 U 4 **Maykain**, Kazakhstan
156 L 12 **Maykop**, Russian Federation
179 T 11 **Mayluu-Suu**, Kyrgyzstan
179 N 8 **Maylybas**, Kazakhstan
190 E 11 **Maymyo**, Myanmar
157 R 3 **Mayna**, Russian Federation
63 U 8 **Mayo**, Florida, U.S.A.
82 B 12 **Mayo**, Yukon Territory, Canada
215 T 12 **Mayo-Belwa**, Nigeria
215 V 11 **Mayo-Kébbi**, Chad ▣
216 F 9 **Mayoko**, Congo
113 B 19 **Mayor Buratovich**, Argentina
232 M 9 **Mayor Island**, New Zealand 🏝
109 F 17 **Mayor Pablo Lagerenza**, Paraguay
219 X 4 **Mayotte**, France 🏝
196 G 5 **Mayraira Point**, Philippines ▶
139 N 7 **Mayrhofen**, Austria
153 U 13 **Mayskiy**, Russian Federation
179 V 4 **Mayskoye**, Kazakhstan
60 J 4 **Maysville**, Kentucky, U.S.A.
197 E 16 **Maytiguid**, Philippines 🏝
193 R 10 **Mayu**, Indonesia 🏝
216 E 10 **Mayumba**, Gabon
66 K 15 **Maywood**, Nebraska, U.S.A.
113 A 18 **Maza**, Argentina
219 N 5 **Mazabuka**, Zambia
76 I 5 **Mazama**, Washington, U.S.A.
129 Q 14 **Mazamet**, France
106 F 10 **Mazán**, Peru
176 J 5 **Māzandarān**, Iran ▣
184 G 7 **Mazar**, China
177 T 5 **Mazār-e Sharīf**, Afghanistan
141 G 22 **Mazara del Vallo**, Italy
131 R 12 **Mazarrón**, Spain
158 C 9 **Mazarron Escarpment**, Mediterranean Sea ◇
88 J 4 **Mazatán**, Mexico
90 F 6 **Mazatenango**, Guatemala
88 L 9 **Mazatlán**, Mexico
74 J 11 **Mazatzal Peak**, Arizona, U.S.A. ▲
148 D 12 **Mažeikiai**, Lithuania
148 D 9 **Mazirbe**, Latvia
88 J 4 **Mazocahui**, Mexico
217 W 12 **Mazomora**, Tanzania
219 P 9 **Mazunga**, Zimbabwe
149 L 21 **Mazyr**, Belarus
219 P 11 **Mbabane**, Swaziland 🏛
214 K 12 **Mbahiakro**, Côte d'Ivoire
216 J 5 **Mbaïki**, Central African Republic
215 V 15 **Mbalam**, Cameroon
217 T 7 **Mbale**, Uganda
215 T 15 **Mbalmayo**, Cameroon
234 M 7 **Mbalo**, Solomon Islands
217 T 14 **Mbamba Bay**, Tanzania
216 J 8 **Mbandaka**, Democratic Republic of Congo
215 S 14 **Mbanga**, Cameroon
218 G 1 **M'banza Congo**, Angola
216 H 11 **Mbanza-Ngungu**, Democratic Republic of Congo
217 R 8 **Mbarara**, Uganda
216 J 5 **Mbata**, Central African Republic
217 S 12 **Mbeya**, Tanzania ▣
217 T 13 **Mbeya**, Tanzania
216 F 9 **Mbigou**, Gabon
217 U 14 **Mbinga**, Tanzania
219 P 8 **Mbizi**, Zimbabwe
217 O 4 **Mboki**, Central African Republic
216 G 7 **Mbomo**, Congo
216 M 4 **Mbomou**, Central African Republic ▣
214 D 8 **Mbour**, Senegal
214 G 8 **Mbout**, Mauritania
217 S 13 **Mbozi**, Tanzania
216 M 11 **Mbuji-Mayi**, Democratic Republic of Congo
217 U 10 **Mbulu**, Tanzania
217 U 12 **Mbuyuni**, Tanzania
87 R 10 **McAdam**, New Brunswick, Canada
69 P 11 **McAlester**, Oklahoma, U.S.A.
71 P 15 **McAllen**, Texas, U.S.A.
61 P 11 **McBee**, South Carolina, U.S.A.
83 G 19 **McBride**, British Columbia, Canada
72 K 8 **McCall**, Idaho, U.S.A.
70 J 8 **McCamey**, Texas, U.S.A.
73 P 12 **McCammon**, Idaho, U.S.A.
82 I 5 **McClintock Channel**, Nunavut, Canada ≈
58 F 12 **McClure**, Pennsylvania, U.S.A.

Country □ Internal administrative region: State/Province/Territory/Dependent territory ▣ Capital city 🏛 Mountain range/Undersea ridge ⛰ Mountain peak/Volcano/Seamount ▲ Geographic feature ◇ Headland/Point/Cape/Peninsula ▶ Desert ◭ Island/Island group 🏝 Antarctic base ⁙ Ocean ◎ Sea 🌊 Bay/Gulf/Channel/Strait ≈ Lake 💧 Salt pan/Dry/Intermittent lake ⚑ River ∿

■ Country ▪ Internal administrative region: State/Province/Territory/Dependent territory ⌖ Capital city ▲ Mountain range/ Undersea ridge ▲ Mountain peak/ Volcano/Seamount ◇ Geographic feature ▶ Headland/Point/ Cape/Peninsula ⊇ Desert ⊞ Island/Island group ⊞ Antarctic base ⊇ Ocean ⊇ Sea ≈ Bay/Gulf/Channel/Strait ⤴ Lake ⤴ Salt pan/Dry/Intermittent lake ⤴ River

312

Mikhaylovka – Mongu

9 U 2 Mikhaylovka, Kazakhstan
2 L 13 Mikhaylovskiy, Russian Federation
Y 7 Mikhaytov Island, Antarctica
5 N 17 Mikkeli, Finland
7 V 12 Mikumi, Tanzania
5 P 8 Mikun', Russian Federation
9 L 18 Mikura-jima, Japan
S 6 Milaca, Minnesota, U.S.A.
1 B 25 Miladhunmadulu Atoll, Maldives
0 C 7 Milan, Italy
B 8 Milan, Tennessee, U.S.A.
T 1 Milan, Missouri, U.S.A.
9 S 6 Milange, Mozambique
4 N 11 Milanovac, Serbia and Montenegro
0 B 12 Milas, Turkey
9 H 19 Milavidy, Belarus
O 8 Milbank, South Dakota, U.S.A.
R 5 Milbridge, Maine, U.S.A.
7 W 7 Mildenhall, United Kingdom
1 R 11 Mildura, Victoria, Australia
3 J 19 Mīlē, Ethiopia
8 M 11 Mile, China
1 V 8 Miles, Queensland, Australia
X 6 Miles City, Montana, U.S.A.
I 11 Milford, Pennsylvania, U.S.A.
L 12 Milford, Connecticut, U.S.A.
N 10 Milford, Massachusetts, U.S.A.
N 8 Milford, New Hampshire, U.S.A.
W 3 Milford, Delaware, U.S.A.
I 6 Milford, Utah, U.S.A.
6 K 9 Milford Haven, United Kingdom
N 3 Milford Lake, Kansas, U.S.A.
3 A 22 Milford Sound, New Zealand
3 B 22 Milford Sound, New Zealand
7 Z 4 Mili, Marshall Islands
3 G 14 Milicz, Poland
) M 1 Milikapiti, Northern Territory, Australia
3 Z 11 Mil'kovo, Russian Federation
1 Y 10 Mill Island, Antarctica
P 3 Mill Island, Nunavut, Canada
9 R 13 Millau, France
R 6 Mille Lacs, Minnesota, U.S.A.
U 4 Milledgeville, Georgia, U.S.A.
7 S 6 Millennium, Kiribati
5 M 8 Millerovo, Russian Federation
F 13 Millersburg, Pennsylvania, U.S.A.
N 17 Millersburg, Ohio, U.S.A.
) B 9 Millesimo, Italy
1 Q 13 Millicent, South Australia, Australia
R 3 Millinocket, Maine, U.S.A.
O 3 Millport, Alabama, U.S.A.
G 13 Mills Lake, Northwest Territories, Canada
R 10 Milltown, New Brunswick, Canada
5 B 19 Milltown Malbay, Republic of Ireland
I 15 Millville, New Jersey, U.S.A.
M 18 Millwood, Ohio, U.S.A.
T 13 Millwood Lake, Arkansas, U.S.A.
4 G 7 Milne Bay, Papua New Guinea
4 H 7 Milne Bay, Papua New Guinea
7 P 1 Milnthorpe, United Kingdom
Q 4 Milo, Maine, U.S.A.
7 H 23 Milos, Greece

151 Z 4 Milove, Ukraine
233 E 25 Milton, New Zealand
58 F 12 Milton, Pennsylvania, U.S.A.
63 P 7 Milton, Florida, U.S.A.
76 K 9 Milton-Freewater, Oregon, U.S.A.
127 U 9 Milton Keynes, United Kingdom
69 N 3 Miltonvale, Kansas, U.S.A.
65 H 14 Milwaukee, Wisconsin, U.S.A.
42 E 11 Milwaukee Deep, Atlantic Ocean
128 L 13 Mimizan, France
216 F 8 Mimongo, Gabon
188 M 7 Min, China
77 K 19 Mina, Nevada, U.S.A.
175 W 5 Mina Jebel Ali, United Arab Emirates
175 S 3 Minā' Sa'ūd, Kuwait
176 M 13 Mīnāb, Iran
199 B 23 Minamata, Japan
113 F 15 Minas, Uruguay
92 K 5 Minas, Cuba
87 U 10 Minas Basin, Nova Scotia, Canada
87 T 10 Minas Channel, Nova Scotia, Canada
112 F 13 Minas de Corrales, Uruguay
92 F 4 Minas de Matahambre, Cuba
109 L 16 Minas Gerais, Brazil
89 V 13 Minatitlán, Mexico
190 C 13 Minbu, Myanmar
214 I 11 Mininian, Côte d'Ivoire
111 F 18 Minchinmávida, Chile
197 M 21 Mindanao, Philippines
197 K 22 Mindanao, Philippines
137 H 24 Mindelheim, Germany
43 A 15 Mindelo, Cape Verde
136 F 13 Minden, Germany
62 H 4 Minden, Louisiana, U.S.A.
86 F 11 Minden, Ontario, Canada
196 G 13 Mindoro, Philippines
197 F 14 Mindoro Strait, Philippines
199 C 20 Mine, Japan
125 D 20 Mine Head, Republic of Ireland
127 N 11 Minehead, United Kingdom
71 S 6 Mineola, Texas, U.S.A.
71 O 6 Mineral Wells, Texas, U.S.A.
157 O 13 Mineral'nyye Vody, Russian Federation
74 I 6 Minersville, Utah, U.S.A.
141 M 15 Minervino Murge, Italy
217 P 14 Minga, Democratic Republic of Congo
171 W 8 Mingäşşevir, Azerbaijan
171 W 7 Mingäçevir Su Anbari, Azerbaijan
216 L 4 Mingala, Central African Republic
230 G 10 Mingenew, Western Australia, Australia
189 T 5 Minggang, China
190 D 9 Mingin Range, Myanmar
186 K 10 Mingshui, China
124 D 11 Mingulay, United Kingdom
189 W 9 Mingxi, China
191 D 15 Minhla, Myanmar
189 X 10 Minhou, China
181 B 24 Minicoy Island, India
73 N 12 Minidoka, Idaho, U.S.A.
230 F 7 Minilya Bridge Roadhouse, Western Australia, Australia
182 H 2 Minimarg, India
185 P 7 Minle, China
215 Q 11 Minna, Nigeria
67 R 8 Minneapolis, Minnesota, U.S.A.
68 J 6 Minneola, Kansas, U.S.A.
67 O 6 Minnesota, U.S.A.
67 R 8 Minnesota, Minnesota, U.S.A.
131 Z 7 Minorca, Spain

66 J 3 Minot, North Dakota, U.S.A.
149 J 17 Minsk, Belarus
142 L 13 Mińsk Mazowiecki, Poland
149 J 18 Minskaya Voblasts', Belarus
215 U 14 Minta, Cameroon
79 Q 7 Minto, Alaska, U.S.A.
87 S 9 Minto, New Brunswick, Canada
82 F 7 Minto Inlet, Northwest Territories, Canada
83 N 20 Minton, Saskatchewan, Canada
141 J 15 Minturno, Italy
183 Z 8 Minutang, India
216 F 6 Minvoul, Gabon
185 Q 9 Minxian, China
157 X 1 Minyar, Russian Federation
183 Z 9 Minzong, India
64 L 11 Mio, Michigan, U.S.A.
149 H 18 Mir, Belarus
130 H 6 Mira, Portugal
108 J 13 Miracema do Tocantins, Brazil
177 V 8 Miram Shah, Pakistan
113 D 18 Miramar, Argentina
87 T 7 Miramichi Bay, New Brunswick, Canada
129 N 12 Miramont-de-Guyenne, France
105 O 3 Miranda, Venezuela
109 G 17 Miranda, Brazil
131 P 2 Miranda de Ebro, Spain
130 J 4 Mirandela, Portugal
112 H 5 Mirandópolis, Brazil
145 M 20 Miras, Albania
175 X 11 Mirbāţ, Oman
195 R 7 Miri, Malaysia
231 V 7 Miriam Vale, Queensland, Australia
177 P 11 Mīrjāveh, Iran
241 Y 8 Mirny, Antarctica
153 R 11 Mirnyy, Russian Federation
142 F 10 Mirosławiec, Poland
177 U 14 Mirpur Khas, Pakistan
177 U 15 Mirpur Sakro, Pakistan
213 N 22 Mirsale, Somalia
147 F 22 Mirtoö Pelagos, Greece
159 R 9 Mirtoon Basin, Mediterranean Sea
183 N 12 Mirzapur, India
199 D 21 Misaki, Japan
198 K 9 Misawa, Japan
87 U 6 Miscou Island, New Brunswick, Canada
177 Y 5 Misgar, Pakistan
182 H 1 Misgar, India
181 O 24 Misha, India
186 N 11 Mishan, China
183 Z 8 Mishmi Hills, India
234 C 5 Misiki, Papua New Guinea
112 F 10 Misiones, Argentina
175 O 6 Miskah, Saudi Arabia
143 L 21 Miskolc, Hungary
193 T 11 Misoöl, Indonesia
211 T 7 Mişrātah, Libya
66 J 11 Mission, South Dakota, U.S.A.
85 N 9 Missisa Lake, Ontario, Canada
86 E 13 Mississauga, Ontario, Canada
57 S 11 Mississippi, U.S.A., U.S.A.
62 K 3 Mississippi, U.S.A.
62 M 9 Mississippi Delta, Louisiana, U.S.A.
62 M 7 Mississippi Sound, Mississippi, U.S.A.
73 N 5 Missoula, Montana, U.S.A.
210 J 7 Missour, Morocco
56 M 5 Missouri, U.S.A., U.S.A.
69 S 5 Missouri, U.S.A.
71 S 10 Missouri City, Texas, U.S.A.
67 P 12 Missouri Valley, Iowa, U.S.A.
85 R 11 Mistassini, Québec, Canada

139 Y 2 Mistelbach, Austria
92 F 7 Misteriosa Bank, Cayman Islands
151 Y 5 Mistky, Ukraine
158 L 11 Misurata Valley, Mediterranean Sea
108 H 8 Mitaraka, Brazil
231 R 3 Mitchell, Queensland, Australia
231 T 8 Mitchell, Queensland, Australia
67 N 10 Mitchell, South Dakota, U.S.A.
76 I 11 Mitchell, Oregon, U.S.A.
125 C 20 Mitchelstown, Republic of Ireland
177 V 15 Mithi, Pakistan
237 P 10 Mitiaro, Cook Islands
199 L 15 Mito, Japan
217 W 13 Mitole, Tanzania
198 K 6 Mitsuishi, Japan
199 A 20 Mitsushima, Japan
138 J 7 Mittelberg, Austria
138 L 8 Mittelberg, Austria
139 P 7 Mittersill, Austria
137 M 26 Mittlespitze, Germany
104 L 9 Mitú, Colombia
217 P 13 Mitwaba, Democratic Republic of Congo
216 E 7 Mitzic, Gabon
199 K 17 Miura, Japan
199 L 18 Miyake-jima, Japan
198 L 10 Miyako, Japan
199 O 26 Miyako-jima, Japan
199 N 26 Miyako-rettō, Japan
199 C 23 Miyakonojō, Japan
178 J 5 Miyaly, Kazakhstan
199 D 23 Miyazaki, Japan
199 G 17 Miyazu, Japan
199 D 19 Miyoshi, Japan
187 E 16 Miyun, China
213 G 21 Mīzan Teferī, Ethiopia
211 S 8 Mizdah, Libya
125 A 21 Mizen Head, Republic of Ireland
150 I 6 Mizhhir''ya, Ukraine
189 R 1 Mizhi, China
150 L 12 Mizil, Romania
146 G 7 Miziya, Bulgaria
183 W 13 Mizoram, India
172 E 11 Mizpe Ramon, Israel
241 T 3 Mizuho, Antarctica
135 F 22 Mjölby, Sweden
217 W 11 Mkata, Tanzania
217 W 10 Mkomazi, Tanzania
219 O 4 Mkushi, Zambia
143 D 16 Mladá Boleslav, Czech Republic
144 L 11 Mladenovac, Serbia and Montenegro
142 K 11 Mława, Poland
159 N 5 Mljet, Mediterranean Sea
134 F 11 Mo i Rana, Norway
193 S 14 Moa, Indonesia
93 N 6 Moa, Cuba
231 R 1 Moa Island, Queensland, Australia
74 M 5 Moab, Utah, U.S.A.
235 Y 12 Moala, Fiji
219 Q 10 Moamba, Mozambique
233 G 18 Moana, New Zealand
216 F 8 Moanda, Gabon
176 I 8 Mobārakeh, Iran
216 L 5 Mobaye, Central African Republic
216 L 5 Mobayi-Mbongo, Democratic Republic of Congo
69 U 3 Moberly, Missouri, U.S.A.
63 O 7 Mobile, Alabama, U.S.A.
63 O 7 Mobile Bay, Alabama, U.S.A.
66 K 7 Mobridge, South Dakota, U.S.A.
190 L 12 Môc Châu, Vietnam
93 Q 7 Moca, Dominican Republic
219 U 5 Moçambique, Mozambique
175 O 14 Mocha, Yemen
41 X 12 Mocha Fracture Zone, Pacific Ocean

219 U 3 Mocimboa da Praia, Mozambique
218 H 4 Môco, Angola
104 G 9 Mocoa, Colombia
112 K 5 Mococa, Brazil
88 M 4 Moctezuma, Mexico
219 S 6 Mocuba, Mozambique
129 W 11 Modane, France
140 F 8 Modena, Italy
74 H 6 Modena, Utah, U.S.A.
77 H 20 Modesto, California, U.S.A.
90 J 4 Modesto Méndez, Guatemala
141 K 24 Modica, Italy
139 X 4 Mödling, Austria
185 R 3 Modot, Mongolia
144 H 10 Modriča, Bosnia and Herzegovina
231 S 13 Moe, Victoria, Australia
232 K 7 Moehau, New Zealand
105 X 6 Moengo, Suriname
137 C 15 Moers, Germany
182 H 6 Moga, India
213 M 24 Mogadishu, Somalia
216 J 6 Mogalo, Democratic Republic of Congo
198 J 12 Mogami, Japan
190 E 8 Mogaung, Myanmar
112 J 5 Mogi-Guaçu, Brazil
146 C 12 Mogila, Macedonia (F.Y.R.O.M.)
142 H 12 Mogilno, Poland
219 U 5 Mogincual, Mozambique
153 S 13 Mogocha, Russian Federation
213 E 20 Mogogh, Sudan
190 E 10 Mogok, Myanmar
91 N 7 Mogotón, Nicaragua
186 H 9 Moguqi, China
143 I 26 Mohács, Hungary
210 H 7 Mohammedia, Morocco
58 J 8 Mohawk, New York, U.S.A.
186 H 4 Mohe, China
219 W 4 Mohéli, Comoros
218 K 7 Mohembo, Botswana
45 R 13 Mohns Ridge, Arctic Ocean
190 E 9 Mohnyin, Myanmar
107 H 18 Moho, Peru
217 W 13 Mohoro, Tanzania
150 M 6 Mohyliv-Podil's'kyy, Ukraine
183 X 12 Moirang, India
147 I 26 Moires, Greece
112 B 13 Moisés Ville, Argentina
87 S 3 Moisie, Québec, Canada
215 X 12 Moïssala, Chad
77 J 23 Mojave, California, U.S.A.
77 K 23 Mojave Desert, California, U.S.A.
188 K 12 Mojiang, China
199 C 20 Mojikō, Japan
145 J 14 Mojkovac, Serbia and Montenegro
183 X 10 Mokokchung, India
233 D 25 Mokoreta, New Zealand
187 L 21 Mokp'o, South Korea
215 P 11 Mokwa, Nigeria
133 I 17 Mol, Belgium
141 N 15 Mola di Bari, Italy
89 R 11 Molango, Mexico
147 F 23 Molaoi, Greece
135 B 15 Molde, Norway
151 N 9 Moldova, Europe
87 T 11 Molega Lake, Nova Scotia, Canada
216 K 5 Molegbe, Democratic Republic of Congo
218 M 10 Molepolole, Botswana
149 G 14 Molėtai, Lithuania
141 M 15 Molfetta, Italy
131 R 6 Molina de Aragón, Spain
65 E 16 Moline, Illinois, U.S.A.
69 P 7 Moline, Kansas, U.S.A.
217 R 12 Moliro, Democratic Republic of Congo
141 K 14 Molise, Italy
141 L 17 Moliterno, Italy
139 Q 8 Möll, Austria
107 F 20 Mollendo, Peru

131 V 4 Mollerussa, Spain
136 I 10 Mölln, Germany
151 V 8 Molochans'k, Ukraine
151 V 9 Molochnyy Lyman, Ukraine
241 V 2 Molodezhnaya, Antarctica
179 T 4 Molodezhnyy, Kazakhstan
78 D 7 Molokai, Hawaii, U.S.A.
41 R 5 Molokai Fracture Zone, Pacific Ocean
147 E 18 Molos, Greece
215 V 15 Moloundou, Cameroon
219 N 13 Molteno, Republic of South Africa
193 U 14 Molu, Indonesia
193 Q 11 Molucca Sea, Indonesia
193 T 10 Moluccas, Indonesia
219 S 5 Molumbo, Mozambique
219 T 6 Moma, Mozambique
217 X 10 Mombasa, Kenya
183 X 12 Mombi New, India
146 J 12 Momchilgrad, Bulgaria
196 H 12 Mompog Passage, Philippines
216 L 8 Mompono, Democratic Republic of Congo
104 I 3 Mompós, Colombia
153 U 8 Momskiy Khrebet, Russian Federation
191 E 16 Mon, Myanmar
135 E 26 Møn, Denmark
129 X 13 Monaco, Monaco
129 W 13 Monaco, Europe
42 J 9 Monaco Basin, Atlantic Ocean
105 R 3 Monagas, Venezuela
70 I 8 Monahans, Texas, U.S.A.
219 U 5 Monapo, Mozambique
211 R 6 Monastir, Tunisia
141 B 19 Monastir, Italy
198 K 6 Monbetsu, Japan
215 U 11 Monboré, Cameroon
154 H 3 Monchegorsk, Russian Federation
137 B 16 Mönchengladbach, Germany
139 Y 4 Mönchhof, Austria
61 Q 14 Moncks Corner, South Carolina, U.S.A.
89 P 6 Monclova, Mexico
87 U 9 Moncton, New Brunswick, Canada
141 I 21 Mondello, Italy
216 L 6 Mondjamboli, Democratic Republic of Congo
215 V 9 Mondo, Chad
130 J 1 Mondoñedo, Spain
140 A 9 Mondovì, Italy
141 I 15 Mondragone, Italy
139 R 5 Mondsee, Austria
147 F 23 Monemvasia, Greece
58 B 13 Monessen, Pennsylvania, U.S.A.
130 J 2 Monforte, Spain
130 I 9 Monforte, Portugal
190 N 11 Mong Cai, Vietnam
190 F 13 Mong Hang, Myanmar
190 H 12 Mong Hpayak, Myanmar
190 F 11 Mong Hsu, Myanmar
190 F 11 Mong Kung, Myanmar
190 E 10 Möng Mir, Myanmar
190 F 13 Mong Pan, Myanmar
190 G 12 Mong Ping, Myanmar
190 G 12 Mong Pu, Myanmar
190 F 11 Mong Yai, Myanmar
216 M 5 Monga, Democratic Republic of Congo
213 E 22 Mongalla, Sudan
183 V 10 Mongar, Bhutan
217 Q 6 Mongbwalu, Democratic Republic of Congo
140 A 9 Mongioie, Italy
215 X 10 Mongo, Chad
185 N 4 Mongolia, Asia
215 T 15 Mongomo, Equatorial Guinea
215 U 10 Mongonu, Nigeria
177 W 7 Mongora, Pakistan
215 Z 10 Mongororo, Chad
218 L 5 Mongu, Zambia

Country ■ Internal administrative region: State/Province/Territory/Dependent territory ■ Capital city ▲ Mountain range/Undersea ridge ▲ Mountain peak/Volcano/Seamount ◆ Geographic feature ▶ Headland/Point/Cape/Peninsula ▲ Desert Island/Island group Antarctic base Ocean Sea Bay/Gulf/Channel/Strait Lake Salt pan/Dry/Intermittent lake River

64	F 10	**Monico**, Wisconsin, U.S.A.
90	I 6	**Monjas**, Guatemala
230	E 8	**Monkey Mia**, Western Australia, Australia
197	N 21	**Monkeyo**, Philippines
142	N 10	**Mońki**, Poland
216	L 9	**Monkoto**, Democratic Republic of Congo
127	P 9	**Monmouth**, United Kingdom
65	E 17	**Monmouth**, Illinois, U.S.A.
77	J 19	**Mono Lake**, California, U.S.A.
59	Q 11	**Monomoy Island**, Massachusetts, U.S.A.
141	N 15	**Monopoli**, Italy
143	J 23	**Monor**, Hungary
215	Z 7	**Monou**, Chad
129	O 12	**Monpazier**, France
131	S 6	**Monreal del Campo**, Spain
58	J 11	**Monroe**, New York, U.S.A.
61	P 10	**Monroe**, North Carolina, U.S.A.
62	J 4	**Monroe**, Louisiana, U.S.A.
65	L 15	**Monroe**, Michigan, U.S.A.
65	F 15	**Monroe**, Wisconsin, U.S.A.
69	V 2	**Monroe City**, Missouri, U.S.A.
65	I 20	**Monroe Lake**, Indiana, U.S.A.
58	B 13	**Monroeville**, Pennsylvania, U.S.A.
63	P 6	**Monroeville**, Alabama, U.S.A.
214	G 13	**Monrovia**, Liberia
133	E 21	**Mons**, Belgium
137	B 18	**Monschau**, Germany
132	F 13	**Monster**, Netherlands
129	W 9	**Mont Blanc**, France/Switzerland ▲
215	S 14	**Mont Cameroun**, Cameroon ▲
38	B 12	**Mont Cocotte**, Mauritius ▲
85	S 10	**Mont de Babel**, Québec, Canada ▲
128	M 13	**Mont-de-Marsan**, France
45	O 13	**Mont Forel**, Greenland ▲
216	E 8	**Mont Iboundji**, Gabon ▲
87	S 5	**Mont Jacques Cartier**, Québec, Canada ▲
87	Q 6	**Mont-Joli**, Québec, Canada
86	J 9	**Mont-Laurier**, Québec, Canada
87	S 5	**Mont Louis**, Québec, Canada
129	W 12	**Mont Pelat**, France ▲
105	Y 8	**Mont St-Marcel**, French Guiana ▲
211	O 13	**Mont Tahat**, Algeria ▲
129	W 11	**Mont Thabor**, France ▲
216	M 2	**Mont Toussoro**, Central African Republic ▲
129	U 13	**Mont Ventoux**, France ▲
85	T 9	**Mont Wright**, Québec, Canada ▲
85	R 9	**Mont Yapeitso**, Québec, Canada ▲
79	S 10	**Montague Island**, Alaska, U.S.A.
128	L 8	**Montaigu**, France
131	S 6	**Montalbán**, Spain
140	F 13	**Montalto di Castro**, Italy
106	C 10	**Montalvo**, Ecuador
146	G 7	**Montana**, Bulgaria ▣
146	F 7	**Montana**, Bulgaria
73	Q 5	**Montana**, U.S.A. ▣
91	P 5	**Montañas de Colón**, Honduras ▲
129	Q 6	**Montargis**, France
129	O 13	**Montauban**, France
58	M 12	**Montauk**, New York, U.S.A.
59	N 12	**Montauk Point**, New York, U.S.A.
129	S 6	**Montbard**, France
129	V 6	**Montbéliard**, France
131	V 5	**Montblanc**, Spain
129	S 5	**Montceau-les-Mines**, France
108	H 10	**Monte Alegre**, Brazil
140	J 13	**Monte Amaro**, Italy ▲
109	M 16	**Monte Azul**, Brazil
106	E 12	**Monte Bello**, Peru
111	F 24	**Monte Burney**, Chile ▲
129	X 13	**Monte Carlo**, Monaco
140	I 13	**Monte Carno**, Italy ▲
112	D 12	**Monte Caseros**, Argentina
129	Y 14	**Monte Cinto**, France ▲
93	P 6	**Monte Cristi**, Dominican Republic
111	H 25	**Monte Darwin**, Chile ▲
111	H 24	**Monte Dinero**, Argentina
129	Y 15	**Monte Incudine**, France ▲
111	F 19	**Monte Macá**, Chile ▲
111	F 18	**Monte Melimoyu**, Chile ▲
141	J 15	**Monte Miletto**, Italy ▲
109	N 16	**Monte Pascoal**, Brazil ▲
110	K 7	**Monte Quemado**, Argentina
129	Y 15	**Monte Rotondo**, France ▲
141	L 14	**Monte Sant'Angelo**, Italy
109	N 14	**Monte Santo**, Brazil
140	A 8	**Monte Viso**, Italy ▲
75	Q 7	**Monte Vista**, Colorado, U.S.A.
86	J 10	**Montebello**, Québec, Canada
230	F 6	**Montebello Islands**, Western Australia, Australia
112	F 9	**Montecarlo**, Argentina
140	F 13	**Montefiascone**, Italy
92	K 8	**Montego Bay**, Jamaica
129	T 12	**Montélimar**, France
64	F 13	**Montello**, Wisconsin, U.S.A.
130	H 9	**Montemor-o-nova**, Portugal
89	Q 7	**Montemorelos**, Mexico
112	G 12	**Montenegro**, Brazil
145	I 15	**Montenegro**, Serbia and Montenegro
219	T 4	**Montepuez**, Mozambique
61	Q 4	**Monterey**, Virginia, U.S.A.
77	G 21	**Monterey**, California, U.S.A.
77	G 21	**Monterey Bay**, California, U.S.A. ≈
104	H 4	**Montería**, Colombia
107	L 20	**Montero**, Bolivia
89	Q 7	**Monterrey**, Mexico
109	L 16	**Montes Claros**, Brazil
113	E 16	**Montevideo**, Uruguay
67	P 8	**Montevideo**, Minnesota, U.S.A.
68	I 6	**Montezuma**, Kansas, U.S.A.
127	O 7	**Montgomery**, United Kingdom
63	R 5	**Montgomery**, Alabama, U.S.A.
138	C 10	**Monthey**, Switzerland
58	I 11	**Monticello**, New York, U.S.A.
60	I 7	**Monticello**, Kentucky, U.S.A.
62	L 6	**Monticello**, Mississippi, U.S.A.
67	V 11	**Monticello**, Iowa, U.S.A.
69	V 2	**Monticello**, Missouri, U.S.A.
69	W 13	**Monticello**, Arkansas, U.S.A.
74	M 6	**Monticello**, Utah, U.S.A.
130	G 9	**Montijo**, Portugal
129	P 9	**Montluçon**, France
129	R 4	**Montmirail**, France
231	V 7	**Monto**, Queensland, Australia
131	N 11	**Montoro**, Spain
58	L 6	**Montpelier**, Vermont, U.S.A.
73	Q 13	**Montpelier**, Idaho, U.S.A.
129	S 14	**Montpellier**, France
86	L 10	**Montréal**, Québec, Canada
83	M 17	**Montreal Lake**, Saskatchewan, Canada
83	M 17	**Montreal Lake**, Saskatchewan, Canada
86	A 8	**Montreal River**, Ontario, Canada
138	C 9	**Montreux**, Switzerland
124	J 11	**Montrose**, United Kingdom
58	H 10	**Montrose**, Pennsylvania, U.S.A.
69	W 14	**Montrose**, Arkansas, U.S.A.
75	O 6	**Montrose**, Colorado, U.S.A.
215	S 7	**Monts Bagzane**, Niger ▲
211	Q 7	**Monts des Ksour**, Tunisia ▲
211	N 12	**Monts du Mouydir**, Algeria ▲
217	Q 12	**Monts Mitumba**, Democratic Republic of Congo ▲
217	O 13	**Monts Mulumbe**, Democratic Republic of Congo ▲
87	P 8	**Monts Notre Dame**, Québec, Canada ▲
93	X 9	**Montserrat**, United Kingdom, United Kingdom ▣
131	N 5	**Montuenga**, Spain
74	M 7	**Monument Valley**, Utah, U.S.A. ◇
216	L 6	**Monveda**, Democratic Republic of Congo
190	D 11	**Monywa**, Myanmar
140	C 6	**Monza**, Italy
107	D 14	**Monzón**, Peru
131	U 4	**Monzón**, Spain
219	N 10	**Mookane**, Botswana
231	Q 9	**Moolawatana**, South Australia, Australia
231	Q 9	**Moomba**, South Australia, Australia
231	U 9	**Moonie**, Queensland, Australia
230	G 10	**Moora**, Western Australia, Australia
71	N 11	**Moore**, Texas, U.S.A.
73	N 10	**Moore**, Idaho, U.S.A.
73	S 5	**Moore**, Montana, U.S.A.
61	R 3	**Moorefield**, West Virginia, U.S.A.
67	O 5	**Moorhead**, Minnesota, U.S.A.
73	R 11	**Moose**, Wyoming, U.S.A.
85	O 10	**Moose**, Ontario, Canada ⌁
79	R 10	**Moose Pass**, Alaska, U.S.A.
59	Q 3	**Moosehead Lake**, Maine, U.S.A. ⌁
85	O 10	**Moosonee**, Ontario, Canada
219	S 7	**Mopeia**, Mozambique
177	T 8	**Moqor**, Afghanistan
107	G 20	**Moquegua**, Peru
107	H 19	**Moquegua**, Peru ▣
143	H 23	**Mór**, Hungary
215	V 10	**Mora**, Cameroon
130	H 9	**Mora**, Portugal
135	F 18	**Mora**, Sweden
131	O 8	**Mora**, Spain
75	N 9	**Mora**, New Mexico, U.S.A.
182	K 8	**Moradabad**, India
219	W 7	**Morafenobe**, Madagascar
142	J 9	**Morąg**, Poland
90	J 5	**Morales**, Guatemala
219	Y 8	**Moramanga**, Madagascar
73	R 10	**Moran**, Wyoming, U.S.A.
231	U 6	**Moranbah**, Queensland, Australia
181	F 25	**Moratuwa**, Sri Lanka
143	G 17	**Morava**, Czech Republic ⌁
143	E 19	**Morava**, Czech Republic ◇
143	E 19	**Moravské Budějovice**, Czech Republic
230	F 10	**Morawa**, Western Australia, Australia
124	H 9	**Moray Firth**, United Kingdom ≈
90	L 5	**Morazán**, Honduras
137	C 20	**Morbach**, Germany
181	B 14	**Morbi**, India
139	Y 5	**Mörbisch**, Austria
141	J 15	**Morcone**, Italy
156	M 5	**Mordovo**, Russian Federation
66	I 8	**Moreau**, South Dakota, U.S.A. ⌁
127	P 1	**Morecambe**, United Kingdom
127	P 1	**Morecambe Bay**, United Kingdom ≈
231	U 9	**Moree**, New South Wales, Australia
234	A 6	**Morehead**, Papua New Guinea
60	K 5	**Morehead**, Kentucky, U.S.A.
61	U 11	**Morehead City**, North Carolina, U.S.A.
89	P 11	**Morelia**, Mexico
131	T 6	**Morella**, Spain
89	R 12	**Morelos**, Mexico ▣
182	J 10	**Morena**, India
83	C 20	**Moresby Island**, British Columbia, Canada ⌁
127	S 9	**Moreton-in-Marsh**, United Kingdom
231	W 8	**Moreton Island**, Queensland, Australia ⌁
129	V 8	**Morez**, France
170	H 15	**Morfou**, Cyprus
170	G 15	**Morfou Bay**, Cyprus ≈
231	Q 11	**Morgan**, South Australia, Australia
62	K 8	**Morgan City**, Louisiana, U.S.A.
77	G 20	**Morgan Hill**, California, U.S.A.
61	V 8	**Morgans Corner**, North Carolina, U.S.A.
61	N 9	**Morganton**, North Carolina, U.S.A.
61	P 2	**Morgantown**, West Virginia, U.S.A.
138	B 9	**Morges**, Switzerland
198	J 7	**Mori**, Japan
75	Q 10	**Moriarty**, New Mexico, U.S.A.
194	B 9	**Morib**, Malaysia
214	H 11	**Moribaya**, Guinea
104	L 8	**Morichal**, Colombia
198	K 10	**Morioka**, Japan
128	I 4	**Morlaix**, France
141	M 18	**Mormanno**, Italy
38	A 9	**Morne Seychellois**, Seychelles ▲
41	X 13	**Mornington Abyssal Plain**, Pacific Ocean ◇
231	P 3	**Mornington Island**, Queensland, Australia ⌁
177	U 13	**Moro**, Pakistan
197	J 22	**Moro Gulf**, Philippines ≈
234	E 5	**Morobe**, Papua New Guinea
234	E 5	**Morobe**, Papua New Guinea ▣
210	F 8	**Morocco**, Africa ▣
65	H 17	**Morocco**, Indiana, U.S.A.
150	K 1	**Morochne**, Ukraine
217	V 12	**Morogoro**, Tanzania ▣
217	V 12	**Morogoro**, Tanzania
89	P 11	**Moroleón**, Mexico
193	Q 14	**Moromaho**, Indonesia ⌁
219	V 9	**Morombe**, Madagascar
92	J 5	**Morón**, Cuba
185	P 2	**Mörön**, Mongolia
106	C 10	**Morona**, Ecuador
106	C 10	**Morona-Santiago**, Ecuador ▣
219	W 8	**Morondava**, Madagascar
214	J 11	**Morondo**, Côte d'Ivoire
219	W 4	**Moroni**, Comoros
193	S 9	**Morotai**, Indonesia ⌁
217	T 6	**Moroto**, Uganda ▲
217	T 6	**Moroto**, Uganda
157	N 9	**Morozovsk**, Russian Federation
109	L 14	**Morpara**, Brazil
232	L 10	**Morrinsville**, New Zealand
67	P 7	**Morris**, Minnesota, U.S.A.
84	I 11	**Morris**, Manitoba, Canada
58	J 12	**Morristown**, New Jersey, U.S.A.
60	K 8	**Morristown**, Tennessee, U.S.A.
77	H 22	**Morro Bay**, California, U.S.A.
109	M 14	**Morro do Chapéu**, Brazil
157	N 3	**Morshanka**, Russian Federation
134	G 10	**Morsvikboth**, Norway
126	M 12	**Morte Bay**, United Kingdom ≈
112	B 13	**Morteros**, Argentina
93	N 4	**Mortimer's**, The Bahamas
237	P 15	**Mortlock Islands**, Federated States of Micronesia ⌁
70	I 4	**Morton**, Texas, U.S.A.
76	G 8	**Morton**, Washington, U.S.A.
217	T 5	**Morungole**, Uganda ▲
231	T 8	**Morven**, Queensland, Australia
156	J 2	**Mosal'sk**, Russian Federation
156	K 1	**Moscow**, Russian Federation ▣
60	B 10	**Moscow**, Tennessee, U.S.A.
72	J 5	**Moscow**, Idaho, U.S.A.
241	X 12	**Moscow University Ice Shelf**, Antarctica ◇
137	C 19	**Mosel**, Germany ⌁
76	J 8	**Moses Lake**, Washington, U.S.A.
217	V 10	**Moshi**, Tanzania
151	R 5	**Moshny**, Ukraine
142	G 13	**Mosina**, Poland
134	F 12	**Mosjøen**, Norway
134	F 9	**Moskenesøy**, Norway ⌁
156	K 1	**Moskovskaya Oblast'**, Russian Federation ▣
143	G 22	**Moson-magyaróvár**, Hungary
85	P 5	**Mosquito Bay**, Québec, Canada ≈
91	R 8	**Mosquito Coast**, Nicaragua ◇
63	X 9	**Mosquito Lagoon**, Florida, U.S.A. ⌁
135	D 20	**Moss**, Norway
233	C 24	**Mossburn**, New Zealand
218	L 15	**Mossel Bay**, Republic of South Africa
216	F 9	**Mossendjo**, Congo
108	O 12	**Mossoró**, Brazil
210	L 6	**Mostaganem**, Algeria
145	G 14	**Mostar**, Bosnia and Herzegovina
112	I 13	**Mostardas**, Brazil
151	Q 8	**Mostove**, Ukraine
156	M 13	**Mostovskoy**, Russian Federation
150	H 4	**Mostys'ka**, Ukraine
173	R 2	**Mosul**, Iraq
213	I 19	**Mot'a**, Ethiopia
131	P 8	**Mota del Cuervo**, Spain
235	Q 9	**Mota Lava**, Vanuatu ⌁
90	I 5	**Motagua**, Guatemala ⌁
149	G 21	**Motal'**, Belarus
135	F 21	**Motala**, Sweden
182	K 11	**Moth**, India
183	P 10	**Motihari**, India
131	R 8	**Motilla del Palancar**, Spain
232	M 10	**Motiti Island**, New Zealand ⌁
131	Q 1	**Motrico**, Spain
150	G 12	**Motru**, Romania
198	I 7	**Motsuta-misaki**, Japan ▶
66	H 6	**Mott**, North Dakota, U.S.A.
232	N 11	**Motu**, New Zealand ⌁
41	X 5	**Motu Nui**, Easter Island ⌁
233	H 16	**Motueka**, New Zealand
232	J 12	**Motueka**, New Zealand ⌁
234	I 5	**Motupena Point**, Papua New Guinea ▶
216	I 6	**Mouali Gbangba**, Congo
214	G 7	**Moudjéria**, Mauritania
135	K 17	**Mouhijärvi**, Finland
216	E 9	**Mouila**, Gabon
213	K 18	**Moulhoulê**, Djibouti
129	R 8	**Moulins**, France
191	F 16	**Moulmein**, Myanmar
63	O 2	**Moulton**, Alabama, U.S.A.
63	T 6	**Moultrie**, Georgia, U.S.A.
65	F 23	**Mound City**, Illinois, U.S.A.
69	Q 1	**Mound City**, Missouri, U.S.A.
129	N 5	**Mortagne-au-Perche**, France
215	W 12	**Moundou**, Chad
61	O 2	**Moundsville**, West Virginia, U.S.A.
110	G 11	**Mount Aconcagua**, Argentina ▲
111	K 23	**Mt Adam**, Falkland Islands ▲
76	H 8	**Mt Adams**, Washington, U.S.A. ▲
61	O 8	**Mount Airy**, North Carolina, U.S.A.
234	E 6	**Mt Albert Edward**, Papua New Guinea ▲
241	Y 10	**Mt Amundsen**, Antarctica ▲
233	C 26	**Mt Anglem**, New Zealand ▲
197	M 22	**Mount Apo**, Philippines ▲
171	T 9	**Mt Ararat**, Turkey ▲
233	F 20	**Mt Arrowsmith**, New Zealand ▲
64	G 8	**Mt Arvon**, Michigan, U.S.A. ▲
233	C 22	**Mt Aspiring**, New Zealand ▲
83	J 20	**Mt Assiniboine**, British Columbia, Canada ▲
230	F 7	**Mt Augustus**, Western Australia, Australia ▲
197	G 14	**Mount Baco**, Philippines ▲
76	H 5	**Mt Baker**, Washington, U.S.A. ▲
234	I 4	**Mt Balbi**, Papua New Guinea ▲
196	H 12	**Mount Banahao**, Philippines ▲
234	E 5	**Mt Bangeta**, Papua New Guinea ▲
74	H 8	**Mt Bangs**, Arizona, U.S.A. ▲
230	H 12	**Mount Barker**, Western Australia, Australia
230	K 3	**Mount Barnett Roadhouse**, Western Australia, Australia
231	V 10	**Mt Barrington**, New South Wales, Australia ▲
85	V 7	**Mt Benedict**, Newfoundland and Labrador, Canada ▲
240	M 11	**Mt Berlin**, Antarctica ▲
216	F 9	**Mt Berongou**, Congo ▲
79	T 8	**Mt Blackburn**, Alaska, U.S.A. ▲
231	T 12	**Mt Bogong**, Victoria, Australia ▲
79	T 9	**Mt Bona**, Alaska, U.S.A. ▲
234	B 5	**Mt Bosavi**, Papua New Guinea ▲
230	J 4	**Mt Broome**, Western Australia, Australia ▲
197	I 17	**Mount Canlaon**, Philippines ▲
197	L 14	**Mount Capotoah**, Philippines ▲
233	C 22	**Mt Cardrona**, New Zealand ▲
81	X 11	**Mt Carleton**, New Brunswick, Canada ▲
65	I 21	**Mount Carmel**, Indiana, U.S.A.
172	F 8	**Mt Carmel**, Israel ▲
85	U 5	**Mt Caubvick**, Newfoundland and Labrador, Canada ▲
241	N 9	**Mt Chapman**, Antarctica ▲
73	N 2	**Mount Cleveland**, Montana, U.S.A. ▲
241	W 3	**Mt Codrington**, Antarctica ▲
83	H 19	**Mt Columbia**, British Columbia/Alberta, Canada ▲
240	K 5	**Mt Coman**, Antarctica ▲
233	E 20	**Mount Cook**, New Zealand
233	E 20	**Mt Cook**, New Zealand ▲
241	W 4	**Mt Cook**, Antarctica ▲
197	J 20	**Mount Dapiak**, Philippines ▲
219	P 6	**Mount Darwin**, Zimbabwe
58	C 14	**Mt Davis**, Pennsylvania, U.S.A. ▲
59	R 6	**Mount Desert Island**, Maine, U.S.A. ⌁

▣ Country ▣ Internal administrative region: State/Province/Territory/Dependent territory ⚓ Capital city ▲ Mountain range/ Undersea ridge ▲ Mountain peak/ Volcano/Seamount ◇ Geographic feature ▶ Headland/Point/ Cape/Peninsula ▲ Desert ⌁ Island/Island group Antarctic base Ocean Sea ≈ Bay/Gulf/Channel/Strait ⌁ Lake Salt pan/Dry/ Intermittent lake

Mt Doonerak – Mungerannie Hotel

9 Q 5 **Mt Doonerak**, Alaska, U.S.A. ▲
9 P 11 **Mt Douglas**, Alaska, U.S.A. ▲
34 E 2 **Mt Dremsel**, Papua New Guinea ▲
33 C 22 **Mt Earnslaw**, New Zealand ▲
5 Q 4 **Mount Elbert**, Colorado, U.S.A. ▲
41 W 3 **Mt Elkins**, Antarctica ▲
4 L 6 **Mt Ellen**, Utah, U.S.A. ▲
41 Q 12 **Mt Erebus**, Antarctica ▲
34 D 5 **Mt Eruki**, Papua New Guinea ▲
41 K 22 **Mount Etna**, Italy ▲
3 N 6 **Mount Evans**, Montana, U.S.A. ▲
33 R 9 **Mt Everest**, China/Nepal ▲
0 H 8 **Mt Fairweather**, Canada/U.S.A. ▲
3 A 17 **Mt Fogo**, Cape Verde ▲
5 D 12 **Mount Forest**, Ontario, Canada
40 L 10 **Mt Frakes**, Antarctica ▲
99 J 16 **Mt Fuji**, Japan ▲
31 Q 13 **Mount Gambier**, South Australia, Australia
34 C 5 **Mt Giluwe**, Papua New Guinea ▲
4 M 14 **Mt Graham**, Arizona, U.S.A. ▲
3 L 9 **Mount Greylock**, Massachusetts, U.S.A. ▲
97 I 14 **Mount Guitinguitin**, Philippines ▲
0 L 9 **Mt Guyot**, Tennessee, U.S.A. ▲
34 C 4 **Mount Hagen**, Papua New Guinea
96 G 13 **Mount Halcon**, Philippines ▲
9 S 7 **Mt Harper**, Alaska, U.S.A. ▲
5 P 5 **Mt Harvard**, Colorado, U.S.A. ▲
3 A 15 **Mt Hay**, British Columbia, Canada ▲
9 S 7 **Mt Hayes**, Alaska, U.S.A. ▲
33 K 15 **Mt Hector**, New Zealand ▲
17 Q 10 **Mt Hehan**, Burundi ▲
33 H 20 **Mt Herbert**, New Zealand ▲
72 H 7 **Mt Hermon**, Syria ▲
97 M 19 **Mount Hilonghilong**, Philippines ▲
6 H 10 **Mt Hood**, Oregon, U.S.A. ▲
5 F 14 **Mount Horeb**, Wisconsin, U.S.A.
35 Q 14 **Mt Humboldt**, New Caledonia ▲
41 U 14 **Mt Hunt**, Antarctica ▲
33 G 20 **Mount Hutt**, New Zealand
33 F 20 **Mt Hutt**, New Zealand ▲
31 Q 5 **Mount Isa**, Queensland, Australia
96 J 12 **Mount Isarog**, Philippines ▲
40 K 5 **Mt Jackson**, Antarctica ▲
5 H 10 **Mt Jefferson**, Oregon, U.S.A. ▲
7 L 18 **Mt Jefferson**, Nevada, U.S.A. ▲
9 Q 3 **Mt Katahdin**, Maine, U.S.A. ▲
9 P 11 **Mt Katmai**, Alaska, U.S.A. ▲
17 V 8 **Mt Kenya**, Kenya ▲
95 V 5 **Mt Kinabalu**, Malaysia ▲
41 Q 10 **Mt Kirkpatrick**, Antarctica ▲
31 T 13 **Mt Kosciuszko**, New South Wales, Australia ▲
96 I 12 **Mount Labo**, Philippines ▲
41 Q 12 **Mt Lister**, Antarctica ▲
0 H 9 **Mt Livermore**, Texas, U.S.A. ▲
3 A 14 **Mt Logan**, Yukon Territory, Canada ▲
33 B 23 **Mt Lyall**, New Zealand ▲
41 R 13 **Mt Mackintosh**, Antarctica ▲
230 G 9 **Mount Magnet**, Western Australia, Australia
197 J 20 **Mount Malindang**, Philippines ▲
58 L 5 **Mt Mansfield**, Vermont, U.S.A. ▲
197 B 19 **Mount Mantalingajan**, Philippines ▲
79 R 9 **Mt Marcus Baker**, Alaska, U.S.A. ▲
58 J 6 **Mt Marcy**, New York, U.S.A. ▲
74 K 5 **Mt Marvine**, Utah, U.S.A. ▲
197 L 23 **Mount Matutum**, Philippines ▲
232 M 10 **Mount Maunganui**, New Zealand
196 K 13 **Mount Mayon**, Philippines ▲
241 R 11 **Mt McClintock**, Antarctica ▲
72 M 8 **Mount McGuire**, Idaho, U.S.A. ▲
79 Q 8 **Mt McKinley**, Alaska, U.S.A. ▲
230 G 7 **Mt Meharry**, Western Australia, Australia ▲
241 U 5 **Mt Menzies**, Antarctica ▲
79 S 3 **Mt Michelson**, Alaska, U.S.A. ▲
241 Q 10 **Mt Miller**, Antarctica ▲
241 R 14 **Mt Minto**, Antarctica ▲
60 M 9 **Mt Mitchell**, North Carolina, U.S.A. ▲
240 M 8 **Mt Moore**, Antarctica ▲
58 A 14 **Mount Morris**, Pennsylvania, U.S.A.
58 E 9 **Mount Morris**, New York, U.S.A.
195 T 7 **Mt Mulu**, Malaysia ▲
241 U 14 **Mt Murchison**, Antarctica ▲
83 D 14 **Mt Murray**, Yukon Territory, Canada ▲
232 L 12 **Mt Ngauruhoe**, New Zealand ▲
61 T 10 **Mount Olive**, North Carolina, U.S.A.
147 E 15 **Mt Olympus**, Greece ▲
76 F 6 **Mt Olympus**, Washington, U.S.A. ▲
233 F 22 **Mt Orr**, New Zealand ▲
231 S 15 **Mt Ossa**, Tasmania, Australia ▲
235 P 13 **Mt Panié**, New Caledonia ▲
196 F 10 **Mount Pinatubo**, Philippines ▲
77 I 23 **Mt Pinos**, California, U.S.A. ▲
58 B 13 **Mount Pleasant**, Pennsylvania, U.S.A.
61 Q 14 **Mount Pleasant**, South Carolina, U.S.A.
64 K 13 **Mount Pleasant**, Michigan, U.S.A.
67 V 13 **Mount Pleasant**, Iowa, U.S.A.
71 S 5 **Mount Pleasant**, Texas, U.S.A.
74 K 4 **Mount Pleasant**, Utah, U.S.A.
234 M 7 **Mt Popomanaseu**, Solomon Islands ▲
196 G 8 **Mount Pulog**, Philippines ▲
83 F 20 **Mt Queen Bess**, British Columbia, Canada ▲
197 L 21 **Mount Ragang**, Philippines ▲
230 J 11 **Mt Ragged**, Western Australia, Australia ▲
76 H 7 **Mt Rainier**, Washington, U.S.A. ▲
83 C 16 **Mt Ratz**, British Columbia, Canada ▲
83 H 19 **Mt Robson**, British Columbia, Canada ▲
61 N 7 **Mt Rogers**, Virginia, U.S.A. ▲
233 F 19 **Mt Rolleston**, New Zealand ▲
105 S 6 **Mt Roraima**, Brazil/Guyana ▲
233 L 16 **Mt Ross**, New Zealand ▲
232 K 12 **Mt Ruapehu**, New Zealand ▲
66 G 10 **Mt Rushmore**, South Dakota, U.S.A. ▲
241 X 9 **Mt Sandow**, Antarctica ▲
83 E 20 **Mt Saugstad**, British Columbia, Canada ▲
68 L 11 **Mt Scott**, Oklahoma, U.S.A. ▲
76 G 13 **Mt Scott**, Oregon, U.S.A. ▲
241 N 8 **Mt Seelig**, Antarctica ▲
77 G 15 **Mount Shasta**, California, U.S.A.
77 G 15 **Mt Shasta**, California, U.S.A. ▲
196 G 6 **Mount Sicapoo**, Philippines ▲
240 L 10 **Mt Sidley**, Antarctica ▲
234 G 7 **Mt Simpson**, Papua New Guinea ▲
234 H 4 **Mt Sinewit**, Papua New Guinea ▲
240 K 11 **Mt Siple**, Antarctica ▲
82 D 13 **Mt Sir James MacBrian**, Northwest Territories, Canada ▲
234 B 5 **Mt Sisa**, Papua New Guinea ▲
233 B 24 **Mt Solitary**, New Zealand ▲
241 S 14 **Mt Southard**, Antarctica ▲
79 T 9 **Mt St Elias**, Alaska, U.S.A. ▲
76 G 8 **Mt St Helens**, Washington, U.S.A. ▲
233 D 22 **Mt St Mary**, New Zealand ▲
60 K 5 **Mount Sterling**, Kentucky, U.S.A.
233 J 16 **Mt Stokes**, New Zealand ▲
241 X 9 **Mt Strathcona**, Antarctica ▲
234 E 5 **Mt Strong**, Papua New Guinea ▲
213 H 16 **Mount Suara**, Eritrea ▲
68 G 3 **Mount Sunflower**, Kansas, U.S.A. ▲
83 E 16 **Mt Sylvia**, British Columbia, Canada ▲
234 D 5 **Mt Tabletop**, Papua New Guinea ▲
235 P 10 **Mt Tabwemasana**, Vanuatu ▲
234 J 5 **Mt Takuan**, Papua New Guinea ▲
232 J 12 **Mt Taranaki (Mt Egmont)**, New Zealand ▲
75 O 10 **Mt Taylor**, New Mexico, U.S.A. ▲
74 H 9 **Mt Tipton**, Arizona, U.S.A. ▲
232 L 12 **Mt Tongariro**, New Zealand ▲
79 Q 9 **Mt Torbert**, Alaska, U.S.A. ▲
210 G 8 **Mt Toubkal**, Morocco ▲
170 G 15 **Mount Troödos**, Cyprus ▲
74 I 8 **Mt Trumbull**, Arizona, U.S.A. ▲
240 L 7 **Mt Tyree**, Antarctica ▲
234 G 4 **Mt Ulawun**, Papua New Guinea ▲
233 H 18 **Mt Una**, New Zealand ▲
58 E 13 **Mt Union**, Pennsylvania, U.S.A.
111 L 23 **Mt Usborne**, Falkland Islands ▲
79 N 12 **Mt Veniaminof**, Alaska, U.S.A. ▲
63 O 6 **Mount Vernon**, Alabama, U.S.A.
65 F 21 **Mount Vernon**, Illinois, U.S.A.
65 G 22 **Mount Vernon**, Indiana, U.S.A.
69 S 7 **Mount Vernon**, Missouri, U.S.A.
76 H 6 **Mount Vernon**, Washington, U.S.A.
65 M 18 **Mt Vernon**, Ohio, U.S.A.
241 T 3 **Mt Victor**, Antarctica ▲
234 E 6 **Mt Victoria**, Papua New Guinea ▲
235 X 11 **Mt Victoria**, Fiji ▲
190 C 12 **Mt Victoria**, Myanmar ▲
234 F 6 **Mt Victory**, Papua New Guinea ▲
80 I 12 **Mt Waddington**, British Columbia, Canada ▲
59 N 6 **Mt Washington**, New Hampshire, U.S.A. ▲
77 K 21 **Mt Whitney**, California, U.S.A. ▲
64 E 9 **Mt Whittlesey**, Wisconsin, U.S.A. ▲
234 C 4 **Mt Wilhelm**, Papua New Guinea ▲
83 D 16 **Mt Will**, British Columbia, Canada ▲
75 O 7 **Mt Wilson**, Colorado, U.S.A. ▲
230 M 8 **Mt Woodroffe**, South Australia, Australia ▲
240 M 8 **Mt Woollard**, Antarctica ▲
79 T 8 **Mt Wrangell**, Alaska, U.S.A. ▲
230 M 6 **Mt Zeil**, Northern Territory, Australia ▲
75 P 2 **Mt Zirkel**, Colorado, U.S.A. ▲
72 K 11 **Mountain Home**, Idaho, U.S.A.
69 V 9 **Mountain View**, Arkansas, U.S.A.
211 T 13 **Mountains of Tummo**, Libya ▲
126 J 15 **Mount's Bay**, United Kingdom ≈
231 V 7 **Moura**, Queensland, Australia
108 E 10 **Moura**, Brazil
130 I 10 **Moura**, Portugal
215 Z 10 **Mouraya**, Chad
232 M 10 **Mourea**, New Zealand
133 C 19 **Mouscron**, Belgium
215 W 10 **Mousgougou**, Chad
213 K 18 **Moussa Ali**, Djibouti ▲
215 W 9 **Moussoro**, Chad
131 V 6 **Mouth of the Ebro**, Spain ◇
125 A 19 **Mouth of the Shannon**, Republic of Ireland ◇
189 Z 5 **Mouth of the Yangtze**, China ◇
108 J 9 **Mouths of the Amazon**, Brazil ◇
183 U 15 **Mouths of the Ganges**, Bangladesh ◇
181 H 19 **Mouths of the Godavari**, India ◇
177 T 15 **Mouths of the Indus**, Pakistan ◇
191 B 17 **Mouths of the Irrawaddy**, Myanmar ◇
181 G 19 **Mouths of the Krishna**, India ◇
191 M 23 **Mouths of the Mekong**, Vietnam ◇
215 Q 14 **Mouths of the Niger**, Nigeria ◇
138 D 7 **Moutier**, Switzerland
129 V 10 **Moûtiers**, France
147 D 17 **Mouzaki**, Greece
218 J 5 **Moxico**, Angola ■
213 I 23 **Moyale**, Ethiopia
210 H 8 **Moyen Atlas**, Morocco ⛰
215 X 11 **Moyen-Chari**, Chad ■
216 D 8 **Moyen-Ogooué**, Gabon ■
219 N 13 **Moyeni**, Lesotho
214 F 10 **Moyenne-Guinée**, Guinea ■
217 R 5 **Moyo**, Uganda
192 M 15 **Moyo**, Indonesia ✦
106 C 12 **Moyobamba**, Peru
134 G 9 **Moysalen**, Norway ▲
179 T 9 **Moyynkum**, Kazakhstan
179 T 7 **Moyynty**, Kazakhstan
219 Q 9 **Mozambique**, Africa ■
219 T 8 **Mozambique Channel**, Mozambique ≈
38 I 10 **Mozambique Escarpment**, Indian Ocean ⛰
38 I 9 **Mozambique Ridge**, Indian Ocean ⛰
157 P 13 **Mozdok**, Russian Federation
156 J 1 **Mozhaysk**, Russian Federation
155 R 14 **Mozhga**, Russian Federation
217 Q 12 **Mpala**, Democratic Republic of Congo
217 R 11 **Mpanda**, Tanzania
218 M 7 **Mpandamatenga**, Botswana
216 H 9 **Mpé**, Congo
183 Z 9 **Mpen**, India
217 S 7 **Mpigi**, Uganda
219 P 3 **Mpika**, Zambia
219 P 2 **Mporokoso**, Zambia
216 H 9 **Mpouya**, Congo
219 O 10 **Mpumalanga**, Republic of South Africa ■
217 U 11 **Mpwapwa**, Tanzania
142 L 9 **Mrągowo**, Poland
157 W 3 **Mrakovo**, Russian Federation
146 D 12 **Mrešičko**, Macedonia (F.Y.R.O.M.)
144 F 11 **Mrkonjić-Grad**, Bosnia and Herzegovina
151 Q 2 **Mryn**, Ukraine
211 N 6 **M'sila**, Algeria
149 N 17 **Mstsislaw**, Belarus
217 W 14 **Mtama**, Tanzania
156 J 3 **Mtsensk**, Russian Federation
171 T 6 **Mts'khet'a**, Georgia
217 W 14 **Mtwara**, Tanzania ■
217 X 14 **Mtwara**, Tanzania
216 F 11 **Muanda**, Democratic Republic of Congo
191 L 15 **Muang Khammouan**, Laos
191 M 18 **Muang Không**, Laos
191 L 17 **Muang Khôngxédôn**, Laos
190 J 12 **Muang Khoua**, Laos
190 J 12 **Muang Ngoy**, Laos
190 I 11 **Muang Ou Nua**, Laos
190 H 13 **Muang Pakbeng**, Laos
191 K 14 **Muang Pakxan**, Laos
191 L 16 **Muang Phalan**, Laos
191 M 16 **Muang Phin**, Laos
191 I 14 **Muang Phôn-Hông**, Laos
190 H 12 **Muang Sing**, Laos
190 J 13 **Muang Souy**, Laos
191 I 14 **Muang Xaignabouri**, Laos
190 I 12 **Muang Xay**, Laos
194 C 10 **Muar**, Malaysia
194 D 9 **Muar**, Malaysia ∿
192 E 12 **Muaraaman**, Indonesia
192 F 12 **Muarabeliti**, Indonesia
192 E 11 **Muarabungo**, Indonesia
192 F 13 **Muaradua**, Indonesia
192 F 12 **Muaraenim**, Indonesia
192 C 11 **Muarasiberut**, Indonesia
179 P 13 **Mubarek**, Uzbekistan
215 U 11 **Mubi**, Nigeria
127 P 7 **Much Wenlock**, United Kingdom
230 G 11 **Muchea**, Western Australia, Australia
188 M 8 **Muchuan**, China
124 F 11 **Muck**, United Kingdom ✦
219 U 4 **Mucojo**, Mozambique
218 K 3 **Muconda**, Angola
218 H 6 **Mucope**, Angola
170 J 10 **Mucur**, Turkey
109 N 17 **Mucuri**, Brazil
66 H 8 **Mud Butte**, South Dakota, U.S.A.
194 A 5 **Muda**, Malaysia ∿
186 M 12 **Mudanjiang**, China
170 D 8 **Mudanya**, Turkey
73 V 13 **Muddy Gap**, Wyoming, U.S.A.
181 D 19 **Mudhol**, India
191 F 17 **Mudon**, Myanmar
213 N 21 **Mudug**, Somalia ■
219 U 3 **Mueda**, Mozambique
189 U 7 **Mufu Shan**, China ⛰
219 O 4 **Mufulira**, Zambia
218 M 4 **Mufumbwe**, Zambia
171 Y 9 **Muğan Düzü**, Azerbaijan ◇
219 S 6 **Mugeba**, Mozambique
183 O 12 **Mughal Sarai**, India
176 J 7 **Mūghār**, Iran
170 C 12 **Muğla**, Turkey
213 B 18 **Muhagiriya**, Sudan
212 G 13 **Muhammad Qol**, Sudan
173 O 7 **Muḩaywīr**, Iraq
241 Q 2 **Mühlig-Hofmann Mountains**, Antarctica ⛰
139 S 3 **Mühlviertel**, Austria ⛰
172 H 4 **Muḩradah**, Syria
148 E 7 **Muhu**, Estonia ✦
217 P 8 **Muhulu**, Democratic Republic of Congo
213 G 22 **Mui**, Ethiopia
191 L 24 **Mui Ca Mau**, Vietnam ▶
219 T 5 **Muite**, Mozambique
150 H 6 **Mukacheve**, Ukraine
195 P 9 **Mukah**, Malaysia
195 P 9 **Mukah**, Malaysia ∿
191 L 16 **Mukdahan**, Thailand
230 G 10 **Mukinbudin**, Western Australia, Australia
192 E 12 **Mukomuko**, Indonesia
182 G 6 **Muktsar**, India
188 K 7 **Mula**, China
91 Z 13 **Mula-tupo**, Panama
181 L 18 **Mulakatholhu Atoll**, Maldives ✦
186 L 11 **Mulan**, China
196 I 13 **Mulanay**, Philippines
219 R 6 **Mulanje**, Malawi
219 S 5 **Mulanje**, Malawi ▲
173 W 8 **Mūlat al Mashkhūr**, Iraq
182 I 3 **Mulbekh**, India
79 O 10 **Mulchatna**, Alaska, U.S.A. ∿
111 F 14 **Mulchén**, Chile
73 Z 10 **Mule Creek**, Wyoming, U.S.A.
217 S 9 **Muleba**, Tanzania
88 I 6 **Mulegé**, Mexico
70 I 4 **Muleshoe**, Texas, U.S.A.
131 P 12 **Mulhacén**, Spain ▲
129 W 6 **Mulhouse**, France
186 M 11 **Muling**, China
124 F 12 **Mull**, United Kingdom ✦
125 G 15 **Mull of Galloway**, United Kingdom ▶
125 F 14 **Mull of Kintyre**, United Kingdom ▶
124 F 13 **Mull of Oa**, United Kingdom ▶
230 F 9 **Mullewa**, Western Australia, Australia
137 D 25 **Müllheim**, Germany
125 D 17 **Mullingar**, Republic of Ireland
126 J 15 **Mullion**, United Kingdom
218 M 6 **Mulobezi**, Zambia
181 F 15 **Multai**, India
177 W 10 **Multan**, Pakistan
216 M 5 **Muma**, Democratic Republic of Congo
177 O 14 **Mūmān**, Iran
181 B 17 **Mumbai**, India
218 L 5 **Mumbeji**, Zambia
218 G 3 **Mumbondo**, Angola
219 N 5 **Mumbwa**, Zambia
234 E 5 **Mumeng**, Papua New Guinea
157 R 11 **Mumra**, Russian Federation
193 P 13 **Muna**, Indonesia ✦
89 Y 11 **Muna**, Mexico
180 A 12 **Munabao**, India
188 J 12 **Munai**, China
199 B 21 **Munakata**, Japan
178 H 9 **Munayshy**, Kazakhstan
83 E 15 **Muncho Lake**, British Columbia, Canada
187 L 17 **Munch'ŏn**, North Korea
65 J 18 **Muncie**, Indiana, U.S.A.
58 F 11 **Muncy**, Pennsylvania, U.S.A.
177 W 10 **Munda**, Pakistan
70 M 5 **Munday**, Texas, U.S.A.
127 X 7 **Mundford**, United Kingdom
112 F 7 **Mundo Novo**, Brazil
230 K 10 **Mundrabilla**, Western Australia, Australia
231 V 8 **Mundubbera**, Queensland, Australia
131 Q 9 **Munera**, Spain
60 G 6 **Munfordville**, Kentucky, U.S.A.
219 Q 6 **Mungári**, Mozambique
217 P 6 **Mungbere**, Democratic Republic of Congo
183 R 11 **Munger**, India
231 P 8 **Mungerannie Hotel**, South Australia, Australia

Country ■ Internal administrative region: State/Province/Territory/Dependent territory · Capital city · ⛰ Mountain range/Undersea ridge · ▲ Mountain peak/Volcano/Seamount · ◇ Geographic feature · ▶ Headland/Point/Cape/Peninsula · Desert · ✦ Island/Island group · Antarctic base · Ocean · Sea · ≈ Bay/Gulf/Channel/Strait · Lake · Salt pan/Dry/Intermittent lake · ∿ River

◻ Country ◻ Internal administrative region: State/Province/Territory/Dependent territory ⚓ Capital city ▲ Mountain range/ Undersea ridge ▲ Mountain peak/ Volcano/Seamount ◇ Geographic feature ▶ Headland/Point/ Cape/Peninsula ⁂ Desert ⥮ Island/Island group ⊞ Antarctic base ⏘ Ocean ⏗ Sea ≈ Bay/Gulf/Channel/Strait ⌁ Lake ⊡ Salt pan/Dry/ Intermittent lake ⌁ River

Page	Grid	Name
39	N 4	Nanping, China
89	Y 10	Nanri Dao, China ⌷
5	T 9	Nansen Basin, Arctic Ocean ◇
5	S 10	Nansen Cordillera, Arctic Ocean ▲
5	O 1	Nansen Sound, Nunavut, Canada ⌷
7	S 9	Nansio, Tanzania
28	L 7	Nantes, France
5	E 14	Nanticoke, Ontario, Canada
	J 20	Nanton, Alberta, Canada
89	Y 5	Nantong, China
9	P 11	Nantucket, Massachusetts, U.S.A.
9	P 11	Nantucket Island, Massachusetts, U.S.A. ⌷
9	P 11	Nantucket Sound, Massachusetts, U.S.A. ≈
27	Q 5	Nantwich, United Kingdom
86	E 5	Nanumanga, Tuvalu ⌷
86	E 5	Nanumea, Tuvalu ⌷
80	E 6	Nanutarra Roadhouse, Western Australia, Australia
89	S 7	Nanxian, China
89	U 11	Nanxiong, China
89	T 5	Nanyang, China
8	K 13	Nanyo, Japan
7	V 7	Nanyuki, Kenya
89	S 5	Nanzhang, China
89	S 4	Nanzhao, China
6	J 5	Naodahan, China
3	T 12	Naogaon, Bangladesh
82	H 4	Naoshera, India
	G 19	Napa, California, U.S.A.
	H 9	Napaktulik Lake, Nunavut, Canada ↘
	N 13	Napier, New Zealand
	W 3	Napier Mountains, Antarctica ▲
	J 16	Naples, Italy
	W 13	Naples, Florida, U.S.A.
	K 2	Naples, Idaho, U.S.A.
06	B 8	Napo, Ecuador ▣
06	D 9	Napo, Ecuador/Peru ↘
06	O 12	Napo, Peru ↘
	L 16	Napoleon, Ohio, U.S.A.
	K 6	Napoleon, North Dakota, U.S.A.
75	Q 13	Naqūb, Yemen
99	H 18	Nara, Japan
	U 9	Nara Visa, New Mexico, U.S.A.
49	I 15	Narach, Belarus
81	Q 13	Naracoorte, South Australia, Australia
	G 17	Narainpur, India
	C 12	Naran Bulag, China
6	B 10	Naranjal, Ecuador
06	D 11	Naranjal, Peru
	S 10	Naranjos, Mexico
99	A 22	Narao, Japan
81	I 18	Narasannapeta, India
1	I 26	Narathiwat, Thailand
3	U 13	Narayanganj, Bangladesh
29	R 15	Narbonne, France
81	O 20	Narcondam Island, India ⌷
2	C 13	Naré, Argentina
2	D 10	Nares Abyssal Plain, Atlantic Ocean ◇
	F 10	Nares Deep, Atlantic Ocean ◇
	Q 1	Nares Strait, Nunavut, Canada ⌷
2	L 11	Narew, Poland ↘
81	D 19	Nargund, India
8	J 10	Narib, Namibia
7	F 9	Narin, Afghanistan
04	F 9	Nariño, Colombia ▣
99	L 16	Narita, Japan
82	J 6	Narkanda, India
81	D 15	Narmada, India ↘
35	Y 12	Naro, Fiji
56	K 1	Naro-Fominsk, Russian Federation
7	U 8	Narok, Kenya
81	U 13	Narooma, New South Wales, Australia
81	U 10	Narrabri, New South Wales, Australia
231	T 12	Narrandera, New South Wales, Australia
230	G 11	Narrogin, Western Australia, Australia
231	T 11	Narromine, New South Wales, Australia
61	O 6	Narrows, Virginia, U.S.A.
44	M 13	Narsarsuaq, Greenland
183	U 13	Narsingdi, Bangladesh
187	D 14	Nart, China
199	F 19	Naruto, Japan
148	J 5	Narva, Estonia
148	J 5	Narva Bay, Estonia ≈
196	F 7	Narvacan, Philippines
134	H 9	Narvik, Norway
155	P 3	Nar'yan-Mar, Russian Federation
179	T 11	Naryn, Kyrgyzstan
179	V 11	Naryn, Kyrgyzstan
179	V 11	Naryn, Kyrgyzstan ↘
179	V 11	Narynskaya Oblast', Kyrgyzstan ▣
156	J 4	Naryshkino, Russian Federation
235	Y 11	Nasau, Fiji
76	G 8	Naselle, Washington, U.S.A.
181	C 16	Nashik, India
59	N 9	Nashua, New Hampshire, U.S.A.
73	W 3	Nashua, Montana, U.S.A.
60	F 8	Nashville, Tennessee, U.S.A.
65	F 21	Nashville, Illinois, U.S.A.
69	T 13	Nashville, Arkansas, U.S.A.
42	F 10	Nashville Seamount, Atlantic Ocean ▲
213	F 20	Nasir, Sudan
85	U 8	Naskaupi, Newfoundland and Labrador, Canada ↘
183	P 12	Nasmganj, India
141	K 11	Naso, Italy
217	N 14	Nasondoye, Democratic Republic of Congo
215	R 12	Nassarawa, Nigeria ▣
236	M 7	Nassau, Cook Islands ⌷
92	L 2	Nassau, The Bahamas ⬛
135	F 23	Nässjö, Sweden
85	Q 7	Nastapoca, Québec, Canada ↘
85	P 7	Nastapoka Islands, Ontario, Canada ⌷
199	K 14	Nasu-dake, Japan ▲
196	F 12	Nasugbu, Philippines
219	N 8	Nata, Botswana
104	H 7	Natagaima, Colombia
108	O 12	Natal, Brazil
192	C 10	Natal, Indonesia
38	I 9	Natal Basin, Indian Ocean ◇
38	H 9	Natal Valley, Indian Ocean ◇
176	I 7	Naṭanz, Iran
87	V 3	Natashquan, Québec, Canada
62	K 6	Natchez, Mississippi, U.S.A.
62	I 5	Natchitoches, Louisiana, U.S.A.
234	D 7	National Capital District, Papua New Guinea ▣
215	N 11	Natitingou, Benin
198	K 12	Natori, Japan
58	B 12	Natrona Heights, Pennsylvania, U.S.A.
181	E 23	Nattam, India
191	E 14	Nattaung, Myanmar ▲
192	H 9	Natuna Besar, Indonesia
39	S 9	Naturaliste Fracture Zone, Indian Ocean ◇
39	T 9	Naturaliste Plateau, Indian Ocean ◇
218	I 10	Nauchas, Namibia
138	K 8	Nauders, Austria
136	L 13	Nauen, Germany
180	C 11	Naukh, India
237	U 1	Nauru, Oceania ▣
106	E 11	Nauta, Peru
89	T 11	Nautla, Mexico
177	R 9	Nauzad, Afghanistan
131	N 8	Navahermosa, Spain
149	H 18	Navahrudak, Belarus
75	O 8	Navajo Lake, New Mexico, U.S.A. ↘
74	L 7	Navajo Mount, Utah, U.S.A. ▲
197	K 16	Naval, Philippines
130	L 7	Navalmoral de la Mata, Spain
149	K 14	Navapolatsk, Belarus
131	R 2	Navarra, Spain ▣
93	N 7	Navassa Island, U.S.A., U.S.A.
149	G 18	Navavel'nya, Belarus
110	F 12	Navidad, Chile
181	A 14	Navlakhi, India
156	I 4	Navlya, Russian Federation
179	P 12	Navoi, Uzbekistan
88	J 6	Navojoa, Mexico
181	C 16	Navsari, India
235	W 12	Navua, Fiji
172	H 8	Nawá, Syria
183	S 12	Nawabganj, Bangladesh
183	U 12	Nawabganj, Bangladesh
177	U 13	Nawabshah, Pakistan
183	Q 12	Nawada, India
177	T 9	Nāwah, Afghanistan
182	H 9	Nawalgarh, India
181	H 16	Nawapara, India
190	F 10	Nawngleng, Myanmar
179	O 10	Nawoiy Wiloyati, Uzbekistan ▣
171	V 10	Naxşivan, Azerbaijan
189	N 8	Naxi, China
147	J 22	Naxos, Greece
147	J 22	Naxos, Greece ⌷
104	G 7	Naya, Colombia
177	T 7	Nayak, Afghanistan
89	N 10	Nayar, Mexico
88	M 10	Nayarit, Mexico ▣
198	K 4	Nayoro, Japan
181	F 20	Nayudupeta, India
172	G 8	Nazareth, Israel
38	L 6	Nazareth Bank, Indian Ocean ◇
107	E 18	Nazca, Peru
199	O 22	Naze, Japan
170	C 11	Nazilli, Turkey
157	P 14	Nazran', Russian Federation
213	I 20	Nazrēt, Ethiopia
175	Y 2	Nazwá, Oman
219	O 2	Nchelenge, Zambia
218	K 9	Ncojane, Botswana
215	T 15	Ncue, Equatorial Guinea
218	G 3	N'dalatando, Angola
215	O 11	Ndali, Benin
216	K 3	Ndélé, Central African Republic
215	V 14	Ndélélé, Cameroon
216	E 9	Ndendé, Gabon
235	P 7	Ndeni, Solomon Islands ⌷
215	V 10	Ndjamena, Chad ⬛
216	E 8	Ndjolé, Gabon
216	G 8	Ndjounou, Gabon
219	O 4	Ndola, Zambia
217	Q 6	Nduye, Democratic Republic of Congo
147	F 17	Nea Anchialos, Greece
147	F 15	Nea Moudania, Greece
146	G 13	Nea Zichni, Greece
76	F 6	Neah Bay, Washington, U.S.A.
147	F 23	Neapoli, Greece
147	K 26	Neapoli, Greece
78	B 11	Near Islands, Alaska, U.S.A. ⌷
127	N 10	Neath, United Kingdom
217	R 6	Nebbi, Uganda
178	I 12	Nebitdag, Turkmenistan
66	H 13	Nebraska, U.S.A. ▣
67	P 15	Nebraska City, Nebraska, U.S.A.
64	E 12	Necedah, Wisconsin, U.S.A.
71	T 7	Neches, Texas, U.S.A. ↘
137	F 21	Neckar, Germany ↘
113	D 19	Necochea, Argentina
215	X 8	Nédéley, Chad
133	K 17	Nederweert, Netherlands
151	T 3	Nedryhayliv, Ukraine
73	T 10	Needle Mountain, Wyoming, U.S.A. ▲
77	N 24	Needles, California, U.S.A. ↘
84	H 10	Neepawa, Manitoba, Canada
171	Z 9	Neftşala, Azerbaijan
155	S 14	Neftekamsk, Russian Federation
157	P 12	Neftekumsk, Russian Federation
152	L 10	Nefteyugansk, Russian Federation
126	L 5	Nefyn, United Kingdom
218	G 2	Negage, Angola
192	L 15	Negara, Indonesia
213	I 21	Negēlē, Ethiopia
213	I 22	Negēlē, Ethiopia
194	C 9	Negeri Sembilan, Malaysia ▣
172	E 12	Negev, Israel ◇
217	W 15	Negomane, Tanzania
181	F 25	Negombo, Sri Lanka
144	O 11	Negotin, Serbia and Montenegro
150	I 12	Negreni, Romania
106	A 11	Negritos, Peru
111	H 15	Negro, South America ↘
197	I 18	Negros, Philippines ⌷
151	N 14	Negru Vodă, Romania
177	O 9	Nehbandān, Iran
186	J 8	Nehe, China
150	K 11	Nehoiu, Romania
218	H 6	Nehone, Angola
236	J 10	Neiafu, Tonga
93	P 8	Neiba, Dominican Republic
189	N 7	Neijiang, China
181	N 22	Neill Island, India ⌷
104	H 8	Neiva, Colombia
189	S 4	Neixiang, China
89	T 14	Nejapa Tequisistlán, Mexico
213	H 20	Nek'emtē, Ethiopia
154	F 14	Nelidovo, Russian Federation
67	N 12	Neligh, Nebraska, U.S.A.
181	G 20	Nellore, India
233	I 16	Nelson, New Zealand
233	I 16	Nelson, New Zealand ▣
83	I 21	Nelson, British Columbia, Canada
231	V 11	Nelson Bay, New South Wales, Australia
219	P 10	Nelspruit, Republic of South Africa
197	E 16	Nelyan Point, Philippines ▶
214	J 7	Néma, Mauritania
149	D 15	Neman, Lithuania ↘
149	C 15	Neman, Russian Federation
215	Q 14	Nembe, Nigeria
147	E 20	Nemea, Greece
149	G 15	Nemenčinė, Lithuania
198	N 4	Nemuro, Japan
198	N 4	Nemuro-hantō, Japan ▶
198	M 3	Nemuro-kaikyō, Japan ≈
198	N 4	Nemuro-wan, Japan ≈
151	N 6	Nemyriv, Ukraine
79	R 7	Nenana, Alaska, U.S.A. ↘
194	E 8	Nenasi, Malaysia
155	R 2	Nenetskiy Avtonomnyy Okrug, Russian Federation ▣
186	J 8	Nenjiang, China
199	H 17	Neo, Japan
147	L 20	Neo Karlovasi, Greece
67	Q 13	Neola, Iowa, U.S.A.
183	O 8	Nepal, Asia ▣
182	M 9	Nepalganj, Nepal
86	I 11	Nepean, Ontario, Canada
143	B 18	Nepomuk, Czech Republic
153	S 14	Nerchinsk, Russian Federation
148	G 12	Nereta, Latvia
145	G 14	Neretva, Bosnia and Herzegovina ↘
218	K 6	Neriquinha, Angola
149	F 15	Neris, Lithuania ↘
131	N 13	Nerja, Spain
153	T 12	Neryungri, Russian Federation
132	K 5	Nes, Netherlands
146	N 9	Nesebür, Bulgaria
68	J 5	Ness City, Kansas, U.S.A.
149	D 15	Nesterov, Russian Federation
84	J 11	Nestor Falls, Ontario, Canada
146	H 12	Nestos, Greece ↘
172	F 8	Netanya, Israel
132	H 10	Netherlands, Europe ▣
93	S 12	Netherlands Antilles, The Netherlands, The Netherlands ▣
85	Q 2	Nettilling Lake, Nunavut, Canada ↘
137	J 23	Neuberg, Germany
136	M 10	Neubrandenburg, Germany
136	J 9	Neubukow, Germany
138	C 7	Neuchâtel, Switzerland
136	M 13	Neuenhagen, Germany
129	L 5	Neufchâteau, France
133	J 24	Neufchâteau, Belgium
129	O 2	Neufchâtel-en-Bray, France
139	S 3	Neufelden, Austria
139	W 4	Neulengbach, Austria
137	J 21	Neumarkt, Germany
241	O 1	Neumayer, Antarctica ▦
136	H 9	Neumünster, Germany
129	P 6	Neung-sur-Beuvron, France
137	C 21	Neunkirchen, Germany
139	W 5	Neunkirchen, Austria
111	H 15	Neuquén, Argentina
111	G 15	Neuquén, Argentina ▣
111	G 14	Neuquén, Argentina ↘
136	L 12	Neuruppin, Germany
139	Y 5	Neusiedler See, Austria ↘
137	C 16	Neuss, Germany
137	J 17	Neustadt, Germany
137	K 22	Neustadt, Germany
136	G 13	Neustadt, Germany
136	I 9	Neustadt, Germany
137	E 21	Neustadt, Germany
137	I 20	Neustadt an der Aisch, Germany
136	L 11	Neustrelitz, Germany
136	F 9	Neuwerk, Germany ⌷
137	D 18	Neuwied, Germany
69	S 6	Nevada, Missouri, U.S.A.
77	J 18	Nevada, U.S.A. ▣
77	H 17	Nevada City, California, U.S.A.
89	N 12	Nevada de Colima, Mexico ▲
107	F 19	Nevado Ampato, Peru ▲
110	G 13	Nevado Campanario, Argentina ▲
107	F 18	Nevado Coropuna, Peru ▲
110	H 5	Nevado de Chañi, Argentina ▲
110	H 5	Nevado de Poquis, Chile ▲
89	Q 12	Nevado de Tolúca, Mexico ▲
104	H 8	Nevado del Huila, Colombia ▲
104	I 6	Nevado del Ruiz, Colombia ▲
107	C 14	Nevado Huascarán, Peru ▲
107	I 19	Nevado Illampu, Bolivia ▲
110	H 8	Nevado Ojos del Salado, Argentina ▲
107	I 20	Nevado Sajama, Bolivia ▲
110	H 6	Nevados de Cachi, Argentina ▲
154	E 14	Nevel', Russian Federation
129	R 8	Nevers, France
157	N 12	Nevinnomyssk, Russian Federation
93	X 8	Nevis, St Kitts and Nevis ⌷
170	J 11	Nevşehir, Turkey
63	N 2	New Albany, Mississippi, U.S.A.
65	J 21	New Albany, Indiana, U.S.A.
127	T 12	New Alresford, United Kingdom
105	V 5	New Amsterdam, Guyana
59	O 11	New Bedford, Massachusetts, U.S.A.
61	U 10	New Bern, North Carolina, U.S.A.
71	T 4	New Boston, Texas, U.S.A.
71	P 10	New Braunfels, Texas, U.S.A.
234	F 4	New Britain, Papua New Guinea
87	S 8	New Brunswick, Canada ▣
235	N 14	New Caledonia, New Caledonia
235	O 15	New Caledonia, France ▣
41	N 10	New Caledonia Trough, Pacific Ocean ◇
58	A 11	New Castle, Pennsylvania, U.S.A.
60	H 4	New Castle, Kentucky, U.S.A.
58	J 12	New City, New York, U.S.A.
182	J 8	New Delhi, India ⬛
61	N 13	New Ellenton, South Carolina, U.S.A.
59	N 9	New England, New Hampshire, U.S.A. ◇
42	E 8	New England Seamounts, Atlantic Ocean ▲
127	S 12	New Forest, United Kingdom ◇
234	K 6	New Georgia, Solomon Islands ⌷
234	J 6	New Georgia Islands, Solomon Islands ⌷
234	K 5	New Georgia Sound, Solomon Islands ≈
87	W 9	New Glasgow, Nova Scotia, Canada
234	A 4	New Guinea, Indonesia/Papua New Guinea ⌷
59	N 7	New Hampshire, U.S.A. ▣
234	G 2	New Hanover, Papua New Guinea ⌷
58	L 11	New Haven, Connecticut, U.S.A.
83	D 18	New Hazelton, British Columbia, Canada
41	O 10	New Hebrides Trench, Pacific Ocean ◇
62	J 8	New Iberia, Louisiana, U.S.A.
234	G 3	New Ireland, Papua New Guinea ⌷
234	H 2	New Ireland, Papua New Guinea ▣
58	I 14	New Jersey, U.S.A. ▣
65	N 19	New Lexington, Ohio, U.S.A.
86	F 7	New Liskeard, Ontario, Canada
58	M 11	New London, Connecticut, U.S.A.
64	G 12	New London, Wisconsin, U.S.A.
61	R 4	New Market, Virginia, U.S.A.
72	J 8	New Meadows, Idaho, U.S.A.
75	O 11	New Mexico, U.S.A. ▣
231	S 15	New Norfolk, Tasmania, Australia
62	L 8	New Orleans, Louisiana, U.S.A.
65	N 18	New Philadelphia, Ohio, U.S.A.
77	I 14	New Pine Creek, California, U.S.A.
232	J 12	New Plymouth, New Zealand
92	K 2	New Providence, The Bahamas ⌷
126	L 8	New Quay, United Kingdom
87	S 6	New Richmond, Québec, Canada
62	K 7	New Roads, Louisiana, U.S.A.
58	K 12	New Rochelle, New York, U.S.A.
66	L 4	New Rockford, North Dakota, U.S.A.
127	Y 12	New Romney, United Kingdom
125	E 20	New Ross, Republic of Ireland
87	U 11	New Ross, Nova Scotia, Canada

Country ▣ Internal administrative region: State/Province/Territory/Dependent territory　⬛ Capital city　▲ Mountain range/Undersea ridge　▲ Mountain peak/Volcano/Seamount　◇ Geographic feature　▶ Headland/Point/Cape/Peninsula　▲ Desert　⌷ Island/Island group　▦ Antarctic base　≋ Ocean　⤳ Sea　≈ Bay/Gulf/Channel/Strait　↘ Lake　⬏ Salt pan/Dry/Intermittent lake　↝ River

Page	Ref	Name
153	T 6	New Siberia Islands, Russian Federation ⇄
63	X 9	New Smyrna Beach, Florida, U.S.A.
231	T 10	New South Wales, Australia ◫
66	H 3	New Town, North Dakota, U.S.A.
67	R 9	New Ulm, Minnesota, U.S.A.
58	F 9	New York, U.S.A. ◫
58	K 12	New York, New York, U.S.A.
233	I 14	New Zealand, Oceania ◫
217	W 14	Newala, Tanzania
58	J 12	Newark, New Jersey, U.S.A.
58	F 8	Newark, New York, U.S.A.
61	W 2	Newark, Delaware, U.S.A.
65	N 18	Newark, Ohio, U.S.A.
77	M 17	Newark Lake, Nevada, U.S.A. ↘
127	U 5	Newark-on-Trent, United Kingdom
76	G 10	Newberg, Oregon, U.S.A.
61	N 12	Newberry, South Carolina, U.S.A.
86	I 11	Newboro, Ontario, Canada
58	J 11	Newburgh, New York, U.S.A.
127	T 11	Newbury, United Kingdom
59	O 9	Newburyport, Massachusetts, U.S.A.
127	P 1	Newby Bridge, United Kingdom
231	V 11	Newcastle, New South Wales, Australia
125	F 16	Newcastle, United Kingdom
73	Z 10	Newcastle, Wyoming, U.S.A.
86	F 12	Newcastle, Ontario, Canada
87	S 8	Newcastle, New Brunswick, Canada
126	L 9	Newcastle Emlyn, United Kingdom
127	Q 5	Newcastle-under-Lyme, United Kingdom
125	J 15	Newcastle upon Tyne, United Kingdom
58	D 8	Newfane, New York, U.S.A.
85	X 10	Newfoundland, Newfoundland and Labrador, Canada
85	V 9	Newfoundland and Labrador, Canada ◫
42	F 8	Newfoundland Ridge, Atlantic Ocean ⛰
42	G 8	Newfoundland Seamounts, Atlantic Ocean ⛰
127	W 13	Newhaven, United Kingdom
230	H 7	Newman, Western Australia, Australia
65	G 19	Newman, Illinois, U.S.A.
127	W 8	Newmarket, United Kingdom
59	O 8	Newmarket, New Hampshire, U.S.A.
86	E 12	Newmarket, Ontario, Canada
63	S 3	Newnan, Georgia, U.S.A.
127	T 13	Newport, United Kingdom
126	K 8	Newport, United Kingdom
127	Q 6	Newport, United Kingdom
58	F 13	Newport, Pennsylvania, U.S.A.
58	M 5	Newport, Vermont, U.S.A.
58	M 8	Newport, New Hampshire, U.S.A.
59	N 11	Newport, Rhode Island, U.S.A.
60	K 9	Newport, Tennessee, U.S.A.
69	W 10	Newport, Arkansas, U.S.A.
76	F 10	Newport, Oregon, U.S.A.
76	L 6	Newport, Washington, U.S.A.
126	K 8	Newport Bay, United Kingdom ≈
61	V 7	Newport News, Virginia, U.S.A.
127	U 8	Newport Pagnell, United Kingdom
126	J 14	Newquay, United Kingdom
125	F 16	Newry, United Kingdom
127	Q 2	Newton, United Kingdom
59	O 10	Newton, Massachusetts, U.S.A.
67	T 13	Newton, Iowa, U.S.A.
69	N 5	Newton, Kansas, U.S.A.
127	N 14	Newton Abbot, United Kingdom
125	G 15	Newton Stewart, United Kingdom
127	O 7	Newtown, United Kingdom
154	M 13	Neya, Russian Federation
176	J 8	Neyestānak, Iran
177	N 6	Neyshābūr, Iran
181	E 24	Neyyattinkara, India
192	I 10	Ngabang, Indonesia
216	H 10	Ngabé, Congo
190	E 7	Ngagahtawng, Myanmar
236	J 14	Ngajangel, Palau ⇄
215	V 10	Ngala, Nigeria
215	W 11	Ngam, Chad
215	W 10	Ngama, Chad
218	L 8	Ngamiland, Botswana ◫
213	E 23	Ngangala, Sudan
184	I 8	Nganglong Kangri, China ▲
191	H 14	Ngao, Thailand
215	U 13	Ngaoundal, Cameroon
215	U 12	Ngaoundéré, Cameroon
217	R 9	Ngara, Tanzania
216	H 6	Ngbala, Congo
237	P 15	Ngetik Atoll, Federated States of Micronesia ⇄
234	L 6	Nggatokae, Solomon Islands ⇄
216	H 9	Ngo, Congo
191	O 18	Ngoc Linh, Vietnam ▲
215	U 12	Ngong, Cameroon
216	I 5	Ngoto, Central African Republic
216	E 9	Ngounié, Gabon ◫
215	W 9	Ngoura, Chad
215	U 8	Ngourti, Niger
217	N 4	Ngouyo, Central African Republic
216	H 5	Nguia Bouar, Central African Republic
215	U 9	Nguigmi, Niger
230	L 1	Nguiu, Northern Territory, Australia
231	O 2	Ngukurr, Northern Territory, Australia
236	J 14	Ngulu, Federated States of Micronesia ⇄
219	P 8	Ngundu, Zimbabwe
215	S 9	Nguru, Nigeria
190	M 11	Nguyên, Vietnam
191	O 20	Nha Trang, Vietnam
219	R 7	Nhamatanda, Mozambique
108	G 10	Nhamundá, Brazil
218	I 4	N'harea, Angola
231	R 12	Nhill, Victoria, Australia
231	O 1	Nhulunbuy, Northern Territory, Australia
217	P 7	Nia-Nia, Democratic Republic of Congo
58	C 8	Niagara Falls, New York, U.S.A.
86	F 13	Niagara Falls, Ontario, Canada
195	R 7	Niah, Malaysia
183	P 9	Niak, Nepal
215	P 9	Niamey, Niger ★
217	P 5	Niangara, Democratic Republic of Congo
189	O 3	Niangniangba, China
186	I 9	Nianzishan, China
216	F 9	Niari, Congo
192	B 10	Nias, Indonesia ⇄
219	S 4	Niassa, Mozambique ◫
237	U 1	Nibok, Nauru
91	P 8	Nicaragua, North America ◫
42	C 11	Nicaraguan Rise, Atlantic Ocean ⛰
141	M 19	Nicastro, Italy
129	X 13	Nice, France
63	Q 7	Niceville, Florida, U.S.A.
199	D 23	Nichinan, Japan
61	R 12	Nichols, South Carolina, U.S.A.
181	N 24	Nicobar Islands, India ⇄
141	J 22	Nicosia, Italy
170	H 15	Nicosia, Cyprus ★
91	O 12	Nicoya, Costa Rica
143	K 16	Nida, Poland ↘
149	B 14	Nida, Lithuania
146	D 13	Nidže Kožuf, Macedonia (F.Y.R.O.M.) ▲
142	K 10	Nidzica, Poland
136	F 7	Niebüll, Germany
133	M 25	Niederanven, Luxembourg
139	U 3	Niederösterreich, Austria ◫
136	F 12	Niedersachsen, Germany ◫
143	M 15	Niedrzwica, Poland
216	H 4	Niem, Central African Republic
136	G 13	Nienburg, Germany
137	O 16	Niesky, Germany
132	K 11	Nieuw-Milligen, Netherlands
105	V 6	Nieuw Nickerie, Suriname
132	I 13	Nieuwegein, Netherlands
133	E 15	Nieuwerkerk, Netherlands
132	G 13	Nieuwerkerk aan den IJssel, Netherlands
132	N 6	Nieuwolda, Netherlands
133	A 17	Nieuwpoort, Belgium
170	J 12	Niğde, Turkey
215	R 8	Niger, Africa ◫
215	Q 11	Niger, Nigeria ◫
215	Q 12	Niger, Nigeria/Niger ↘
42	M 13	Niger Cone, Atlantic Ocean ◇
215	R 11	Nigeria, Africa ◫
43	O 17	Nightingale Island, Tristan da Cunha ⇄
198	K 13	Nihonmatsu, Japan
199	K 18	Nii-jima, Japan ⇄
198	J 13	Niigata, Japan
199	I 15	Niigata-yake-yama, Japan ▲
199	E 20	Niihama, Japan
78	A 7	Niihau, Hawaii, U.S.A. ⇄
199	E 18	Niimi, Japan
198	J 13	Niitsu, Japan
131	Q 13	Nijar, Spain
132	J 12	Nijkerk, Netherlands
133	K 14	Nijmegen, Netherlands
132	M 11	Nijverdal, Netherlands
147	E 16	Nikaia, Greece
154	N 1	Nikel', Russian Federation
134	I 9	Nikkaluokta, Sweden
215	O 11	Nikki, Benin
199	K 14	Nikkō, Japan
153	W 12	Nikolayevsk-na-Amure, Russian Federation
157	Q 3	Nikol'sk, Russian Federation
146	I 7	Nikopol, Bulgaria
151	U 8	Nikopol', Ukraine
170	M 8	Niksar, Turkey
177	O 13	Nīkshahr, Iran
145	I 15	Nikšić, Serbia and Montenegro
236	I 4	Nikumaroro, Kiribati ⇄
236	E 3	Nikunau, Kiribati ⇄
193	T 14	Nila, Indonesia ⇄
181	L 18	Nilandhoo Atoll, Maldives ⇄
212	E 10	Nile, Egypt/Sudan ↘
213	F 16	Nile, Sudan ↘
212	E 7	Nile Delta, Egypt ◇
159	V 12	Nile Fan, Mediterranean Sea ◇
65	I 16	Niles, Michigan, U.S.A.
89	U 14	Niltepec, Mexico
214	I 12	Nimba Mountains, Côte d'Ivoire/Guinea ▲
129	S 13	Nîmes, France
177	Q 10	Nīmrūz, Afghanistan ◫
213	E 23	Nimule, Sudan
218	K 5	Ninda, Angola
181	A 23	Nine Degree Channel, India ≈
39	Q 8	Ninetyeast Ridge, Indian Ocean ⛰
186	M 12	Ning'an, China
189	Z 7	Ningbo, China
187	F 15	Ningcheng, China
189	Y 9	Ningde, China
189	V 9	Ningdu, China
189	X 6	Ningguo, China
189	Z 7	Ninghai, China
189	W 10	Ninghua, China
185	R 14	Ningming, China
188	L 9	Ningnan, China
189	O 5	Ningqiang, China
189	Q 4	Ningshan, China
189	O 2	Ningxia, China ◫
189	P 3	Ningxian, China
189	S 8	Ningxiang, China
189	S 10	Ningyuan, China
190	M 13	Ninh Binh, Vietnam
191	O 20	Ninh Hoa, Vietnam
234	C 2	Ninigo Group, Papua New Guinea ⇄
198	K 9	Ninohe, Japan
66	I 11	Niobrara, Nebraska, U.S.A. ↘
67	N 12	Niobrara, Nebraska, U.S.A.
183	X 9	Nioko, India
128	M 9	Niort, France
83	M 17	Nipawin, Saskatchewan, Canada
84	L 11	Nipigon, Ontario, Canada
77	M 23	Nipton, California, U.S.A.
181	F 17	Nirmal, India
183	R 11	Nirmali, India
144	N 13	Niš, Serbia and Montenegro
173	U 14	Nişāb, Iraq
175	Q 13	Nişab, Yemen
199	C 25	Nishino-omote, Japan
199	F 18	Nishiwaki, Japan
199	C 22	Nisi-mera, Japan
143	M 16	Nisko, Poland
135	E 24	Nissan, Sweden ↘
234	I 4	Nissan Island, Papua New Guinea ⇄
135	B 20	Nisser, Norway ↘
147	M 23	Nisyros, Greece ⇄
199	E 18	Nita, Japan
112	N 7	Niterói, Brazil
143	H 21	Nitra, Slovakia
236	I 9	Niua Group, Tonga ⇄
236	I 9	Niuafo'ou, Tonga ⇄
236	I 9	Niuatoputapu, Tonga ⇄
236	K 10	Niue, Niue ⇄
236	K 10	Niue, New Zealand ◫
186	H 5	Niu'erhe, China
236	G 7	Niulakita, Tuvalu ⇄
236	F 5	Niutao, Tuvalu ⇄
133	F 20	Nivelles, Belgium
69	T 7	Nixa, Missouri, U.S.A.
71	P 11	Nixon, Texas, U.S.A.
181	E 17	Nizam Sagar, India ↘
181	F 17	Nizamabad, India
154	M 13	Nizhegorodskaya Oblast', Russian Federation ◫
157	S 1	Nizhnekamsk, Russian Federation
153	O 13	Nizhneudinsk, Russian Federation
152	L 10	Nizhnevartovsk, Russian Federation
153	T 7	Nizhneyyansk, Russian Federation
157	N 8	Nizhniy Chir, Russian Federation
157	O 3	Nizhniy Lomov, Russian Federation
157	P 1	Nizhniy Novgorod, Russian Federation
152	J 10	Nizhniy Tagil, Russian Federation
155	N 4	Nizhnyaya Pesha, Russian Federation
153	N 9	Nizhnyaya Tunguska, Russian Federation ↘
151	R 2	Nizhyn, Ukraine
170	M 13	Nizip, Turkey
145	I 14	Njegoš, Serbia and Montenegro ▲
219	P 12	Njesuthi, Lesotho ▲
217	W 13	Njinjo, Tanzania
217	T 13	Njombe, Tanzania
217	R 12	Nkasi, Tanzania
219	O 7	Nkayi, Zimbabwe
219	R 3	Nkhata Bay, Malawi
219	R 4	Nkhotakota, Malawi
217	R 11	Nkondwe, Tanzania
215	S 14	Nkongsamba, Cameroon
218	J 7	Nkurenkuru, Namibia
190	F 8	Nmai Hka, Myanmar ↘
181	J 15	Noamundi, India
199	D 22	Nobeoka, Japan
198	J 7	Noboribetsu, Japan
109	G 15	Nobres, Brazil
231	R 8	Noccundra, Queensland, Australia
89	S 13	Nochixtlán, Mexico
141	N 16	Noci, Italy
199	K 15	Noda, Japan
86	E 9	Noelville, Ontario, Canada
74	K 15	Nogales, Arizona, U.S.A.
88	I 3	Nogales, Mexico
129	O 5	Nogent-le-Rotrou, France
153	O 10	Noginsk, Russian Federation
156	L 1	Noginsk, Russian Federation
113	C 14	Nogoyá, Argentina
182	H 8	Nohar, India
137	C 20	Nohfelden, Germany
130	H 2	Noia, Spain
128	K 7	Noirmoutier-en-l'Île, France
199	L 17	Nojima-zaki, Japan ▶
177	Q 12	Nok Kundi, Pakistan
180	C 11	Nokha, India
135	L 18	Nokia, Finland
215	V 9	Nokou, Chad
183	U 11	Nokrek Peak, India ▲
216	H 5	Nola, Central African Republic
141	J 16	Nola, Italy
155	P 13	Nolinsk, Russian Federation
199	B 24	Noma-misaki, Japan ▶
78	M 7	Nome, Alaska, U.S.A.
199	B 22	Nomo-zaki, Japan ▶
236	I 10	Nomuka Group, Tonga ⇄
237	O 14	Nomwin, Federated States of Micronesia ⇄
191	I 16	Nong Bua Lamphu, Thailand
191	J 15	Nong Khai, Thailand
186	J 12	Nong'an, China
183	V 11	Nongstoin, India
236	E 3	Nonouti, Kiribati ⇄
191	H 19	Nonthaburi, Thailand
129	N 10	Nontron, France
132	G 8	Nooderhaaks, Netherlands ⇄
133	I 15	Noord-Brabant, Netherlands ◫
132	H 9	Noord-Holland, Netherlands ◫
79	N 5	Noorvik, Alaska, U.S.A.
231	W 8	Noosa Heads, Queensland, Australia
179	R 13	Norak, Tajikistan
197	L 23	Norala, Philippines
86	F 6	Noranda, Québec, Canada
215	U 12	Nord, Cameroon ◫
134	I 6	Nord-Kvaløy, Norway ⇄
215	T 13	Nord-Ouest, Cameroon ◫
129	Q 1	Nord-pas-de-Calais, France ◫
45	U 11	Nordaustlandet, Svalbard ⇄
136	D 10	Norden, Germany
136	C 10	Norderney, Germany ⇄
136	F 8	Norderoogsand, Germany ⇄
135	B 17	Nordfjordeid, Norway
134	G 10	Nordfold, Norway
136	E 8	Nordfriesische Inseln, Germany ◇
137	I 15	Nordhausen, Germany
136	C 13	Nordhorn, Germany
134	K 5	Nordkapp, Norway ▶
135	F 14	Nordli, Norway
137	I 22	Nördlingen, Germany
135	I 15	Nordmaling, Sweden
135	B 15	Nordmøre, Norway ↘
135	B 16	Nordøyane, Norway ⇄
137	E 15	Nordrhein-Westfalen, Germany ◫
136	F 8	Nordstrand, Germany ⇄
153	R 7	Nordvik, Russian Federation
135	C 19	Noresund, Norway
61	V 7	Norfolk, Virginia, U.S.A.
67	N 12	Norfolk, Nebraska, U.S.A.
41	O 10	Norfolk Island, Australia ⇄
69	V 8	Norfork Lake, Arkansas, U.S.A. ↘
71	P 14	Norias, Texas, U.S.A.
153	O 8	Noril'sk, Russian Federation
86	F 11	Norland, Ontario, Canada
61	P 8	Norlina, North Carolina, U.S.A.
65	G 18	Normal, Illinois, U.S.A.
231	R 4	Norman, Queensland, Australia ↘
69	N 10	Norman, Oklahoma, U.S.A.
82	D 11	Norman Wells, Northwest Territories, Canada
234	G 7	Normanby Island, Papua New Guinea ⇄
128	L 4	Normandy, France ◫
231	R 4	Normanton, Queensland, Australia
111	G 17	Ñorquinco, Argentina
135	F 19	Norra Ny, Sweden
134	G 12	Norra Storfjället, Sweden ▲
135	G 14	Norråker, Sweden
135	C 23	Nørresundby, Denmark
60	J 8	Norris Lake, Tennessee, U.S.A. ↘
135	G 21	Norrköping, Sweden
135	I 20	Norrtälje, Sweden
230	I 11	Norseman, Western Australia, Australia
135	C 20	Norsjö, Norway ↘
235	Q 10	Norsup, Vanuatu
104	J 4	Norte de Santander, Colombia ◫
58	L 9	North Adams, Massachusetts, U.S.A.
159	R 7	North Aegean Trough, Mediterranean Sea ◇
42	E 10	North American Basin, Atlantic Ocean ◇
181	N 20	North Andaman, India ⇄
60	M 13	North Augusta, South Carolina, U.S.A.
39	U 6	North Australian Basin, Indian Ocean ◇
197	A 21	North Balabac Strait, Philippines ≈
83	L 18	North Battleford, Saskatchewan, Canada
86	F 9	North Bay, Ontario, Canada
81	S 10	North Belcher Islands, Nunavut, Canada ⇄
76	E 12	North Bend, Oregon, U.S.A.
67	T 7	North Branch, Minnesota, U.S.A.
93	P 5	North Caicos, Turks and Caicos Islands ⇄
232	I 4	North Cape, New Zealand ▶
61	N 9	North Carolina, U.S.A. ◫
181	G 24	North Central, Sri Lanka ◫
125	E 14	North Channel, Republic of Ireland/United Kingdom ≈
86	B 9	North Channel, Ontario, Canada ≈
61	P 14	North Charleston, South Carolina, U.S.A.
66	I 4	North Dakota, U.S.A. ◫
127	U 12	North Downs, United Kingdom ◇
219	N 8	North East, Botswana ◫
58	B 9	North East, Pennsylvania, U.S.A.
217	X 6	North-Eastern, Kenya ◫
41	O 9	North Fiji Basin, Pacific Ocean ◇
127	Z 11	North Foreland, United Kingdom ▶
77	M 15	North Fork, Nevada, U.S.A.

◫ Country   ◫ Internal administrative region: State/Province/Territory/Dependent territory   ★ Capital city   ⛰ Mountain range/Undersea ridge   ▲ Mountain peak/Volcano/Seamount   ◇ Geographic feature   ▶ Headland/Point/Cape/Peninsula   ▲ Desert   ⇄ Island/Island group   ⬚ Antarctic base   ⊚ Ocean   ⌇ Sea   ≈ Bay/Gulf/Channel/Strait   ↘ Lake   ⬚ Salt pan/Dry/Intermittent lake   ≋ Ri... / Intermittent lake

J 7 **North Head**, New Zealand ▶
V 6 **North Horr**, Kenya
L 20 **North Huvadhu Atoll**, Maldives ⛬
S 8 **North Ikaria Basin**, Mediterranean Sea ◇
M 11 **North Island**, New Zealand ⛬
A 9 **North Island**, Seychelles ⛬
B 23 **North Island**, India ⛬
H 1 **North Island**, Philippines ⛬
E 20 **North Islet**, Philippines ⛬
Q 5 **North Keeling Island**, Cocos Islands ⛬
M 17 **North Korea**, Asia ◘
X 9 **North Lakhimpur**, India
L 17 **North Maalhosmadulu Atoll**, Maldives ⛬
N 2 **North Magnetic Pole**, Nunavut, Canada ◇
L 16 **North Miladunmadulu Atoll**, Maldives ⛬
G 13 **North Platte**, Nebraska, U.S.A. ∫
A 9 **North Point**, Seychelles ▶
K 25 **North Point**, Ascension ▶
N 16 **North Point**, Tristan da Cunha ▶
L 11 **North Point**, Michigan, U.S.A. ▶
S 8 **North Pole**, Arctic Ocean ◇
R 7 **North Pole**, Alaska, U.S.A.
K 10 **North Powder**, Oregon, U.S.A.
N 21 **North Reef Island**, India ⛬
J 9 **North Rim**, Arizona, U.S.A.
I 6 **North Ronaldsay**, United Kingdom ⛬
K 18 **North Saskatchewan**, Saskatchewan, Canada ∫
M 6 **North Sea**, Atlantic Ocean ◢
N 22 **North Sentinel Island**, India ⛬
J 4 **North Solomons**, Papua New Guinea ◘
W 3 **North Somercotes**, United Kingdom
W 9 **North Stradbroke Island**, Queensland, Australia ⛬
J 12 **North Taranaki Bight**, New Zealand ≈
O 9 **North Twin Island**, Québec, Canada ⛬
F 23 **North Ubian**, Philippines ⛬
E 10 **North Uist**, United Kingdom ⛬
D 18 **North Verde**, Philippines ⛬
J 20 **North Vernon**, Indiana, U.S.A.
Z 5 **North Walsham**, United Kingdom
L 11 **North West**, Republic of South Africa ◘
E 6 **North West Cape**, Western Australia, Australia ▶
W 6 **North West Frontier**, Pakistan ◘
G 11 **North West Highlands**, United Kingdom ⛰
F 24 **North Western**, Sri Lanka ◘
M 4 **North-Western**, Zambia ◘
F 13 **North York**, Ontario, Canada
S 1 **Northallerton**, United Kingdom
G 11 **Northam**, Western Australia, Australia
E 9 **Northampton**, Western Australia, Australia
U 8 **Northampton**, United Kingdom
L 9 **Northampton**, Massachusetts, U.S.A.
K 7 **Northeast Cape**, Alaska, U.S.A. ▶
R 3 **Northeast Pacific Basin**, Pacific Ocean ◇
137 H 15 **Northeim**, Germany
213 D 14 **Northern**, Sudan ◘
214 G 11 **Northern**, Sierra Leone ◘
219 O 10 **Northern**, Republic of South Africa ◘
219 P 3 **Northern**, Zambia ◘
219 Q 3 **Northern**, Malawi ◘
234 F 6 **Northern**, Papua New Guinea ◘
181 G 23 **Northern**, Sri Lanka ◘
213 C 20 **Northern Bahr el Ghazal**, Sudan ◘
218 K 13 **Northern Cape**, Republic of South Africa ◘
90 L 2 **Northern Cay**, Belize ⛬
236 L 7 **Northern Cook Islands**, Cook Islands ⛬
213 B 15 **Northern Darfur**, Sudan ◘
154 L 8 **Northern Dvina**, Russian Federation ∫
125 E 15 **Northern Ireland**, United Kingdom ◘
213 D 16 **Northern Kordofan**, Sudan ◘
90 K 2 **Northern Lagoon**, Belize ◣
235 Y 11 **Northern Lau Group**, Fiji ⛬
236 A 6 **Northern Mariana Islands**, U.S.A. ◘
140 D 8 **Northern Plain**, Italy ◇
231 N 4 **Northern Territory**, Australia ◘
67 S 8 **Northfield**, Minnesota, U.S.A.
232 J 6 **Northland**, New Zealand ◘
87 U 8 **Northumberland Strait**, Prince Edward Island, Canada ≈
58 J 8 **Northville**, New York, U.S.A.
42 E 5 **Northwest Atlantic Mid-Ocean Channel**, Atlantic Ocean ◇
78 K 7 **Northwest Cape**, Alaska, U.S.A. ▶
41 N 3 **Northwest Pacific Basin**, Pacific Ocean ◇
82 H 11 **Northwest Territories**, Canada ◘
127 Q 4 **Northwich**, United Kingdom
45 R 4 **Northwind Plain**, Arctic Ocean ◇
68 J 2 **Norton**, Kansas, U.S.A.
78 M 7 **Norton Sound**, Alaska, U.S.A. ≈
60 E 6 **Nortonville**, Kentucky, U.S.A.
58 K 12 **Norwalk**, Connecticut, U.S.A.
65 M 17 **Norwalk**, Ohio, U.S.A.
135 B 19 **Norway**, Europe ◘
84 J 8 **Norway House**, Manitoba, Canada
45 S 15 **Norwegian Basin**, Arctic Ocean ◇
135 A 16 **Norwegian Sea**, Norway ◢
127 Z 6 **Norwich**, United Kingdom
58 M 11 **Norwich**, Connecticut, U.S.A.
146 N 9 **Nos Emine**, Bulgaria ▶
146 O 7 **Nos Kaliakra**, Bulgaria ▶
146 O 7 **Nos Shabla**, Bulgaria ▶
198 N 4 **Nosapu-misaki**, Japan ▶
198 I 2 **Noshappu-misaki**, Japan ▶
198 J 10 **Noshiro**, Japan
155 Q 2 **Nosovaya**, Russian Federation
177 O 11 **Noṣratābād**, Iran
124 I 8 **Noss Head**, United Kingdom ▶
219 Y 5 **Nosy Bé**, Madgascar ⛬
219 Z 7 **Nosy Boraha**, Madgascar ⛬
219 Y 8 **Nosy-Varika**, Madgascar
74 I 4 **Notch Peak**, Utah, U.S.A. ▲
142 E 11 **Noteć**, Poland ∫
147 J 23 **Notio Aigaio**, Greece ◘
147 A 16 **Notio Steno Kerkyras**, Greece ≈
147 G 19 **Notios Evvoïkos Kolpos**, Greece ≈
141 K 24 **Noto**, Italy
199 H 15 **Noto-hantō**, Japan ▶
198 M 3 **Notoro-ko**, Japan ◣
85 Y 9 **Notre Dame Bay**, Newfoundland and Labrador, Canada ≈
86 E 11 **Nottawasaga Bay**, Ontario, Canada ≈
85 P 10 **Nottaway**, Québec, Canada ∫
127 T 5 **Nottingham**, United Kingdom
85 P 4 **Nottingham Island**, Nunavut, Canada ⛬
210 A 14 **Nouâdhibou**, Western Sahara
214 D 5 **Nouâdhibou**, Mauritania
214 E 6 **Nouakchott**, Mauritania ♜
214 E 6 **Nouâmghâr**, Mauritania
191 N 17 **Nouei**, Vietnam
235 Q 14 **Nouméa**, New Caledonia ♜
179 R 12 **Nov**, Tajikistan
109 J 15 **Nova**, Brazil
112 G 5 **Nova Alvorada**, Brazil
218 F 2 **Nova Caipemba**, Angola
112 N 6 **Nova Friburgo**, Brazil
112 M 6 **Nova Iguaçu**, Brazil
219 R 8 **Nova Mambone**, Mozambique
219 T 6 **Nova Nabúri**, Mozambique
151 R 8 **Nova Odesa**, Ukraine
87 W 10 **Nova Scotia**, Canada ◘
41 P 8 **Nova Trough**, Pacific Ocean ◇
144 K 13 **Nova Varoš**, Serbia and Montenegro
146 K 9 **Nova Zagora**, Bulgaria
140 B 7 **Novara**, Italy
77 F 19 **Novato**, California, U.S.A.
152 L 6 **Novaya Zemlya**, Russian Federation ⛬
143 H 22 **Nové Zámky**, Slovakia
154 G 12 **Novgorodskaya Oblast'**, Russian Federation ◘
151 S 1 **Novhorod-Sivers'kyy**, Ukraine
151 S 7 **Novhorodka**, Ukraine
144 K 8 **Novi Bečej**, Serbia and Montenegro
146 G 9 **Novi-Iskŭr**, Bulgaria
140 C 8 **Novi Ligure**, Italy
145 L 14 **Novi Pazar**, Serbia and Montenegro
146 M 7 **Novi Pazar**, Bulgaria
144 K 9 **Novi Sad**, Serbia and Montenegro
108 E 10 **Novo Airão**, Brazil
108 F 11 **Novo Aripuanã**, Brazil
112 H 12 **Novo Hamburgo**, Brazil
144 C 8 **Novo Mesto**, Slovenia
146 F 12 **Novo Selo**, Macedonia (F.Y.R.O.M.)
157 N 6 **Novoanninskiy**, Russian Federation
151 Q 6 **Novoarkhanhel's'k**, Ukraine
151 Y 8 **Novoazovs'k**, Ukraine
179 S 13 **Novobod**, Tajikistan
178 H 6 **Novobogatinskoye**, Kazakhstan
151 V 8 **Novobohdanivka**, Ukraine
157 Q 1 **Novocheboksarsk**, Russian Federation
156 L 9 **Novocherkassk**, Russian Federation
154 K 6 **Novodvinsk**, Russian Federation
150 M 3 **Novohrad-Volyns'kyy**, Ukraine
156 M 6 **Novokhopersk**, Russian Federation
157 S 4 **Novokuybyshevsk**, Russian Federation
152 M 13 **Novokuznetsk**, Russian Federation
241 R 1 **Novolazarevskaya**, Antarctica ⁙
151 V 6 **Novomoskovs'k**, Ukraine
156 L 3 **Novomoskovsk**, Russian Federation
157 N 6 **Novonikolayevskiy**, Russian Federation
157 P 8 **Novonikol'skoye**, Russian Federation
151 U 10 **Novoolekisiyivka**, Ukraine
151 U 7 **Novopokrovka**, Ukraine
151 Z 4 **Novopskov**, Ukraine
156 K 12 **Novorossiysk**, Russian Federation
153 Q 7 **Novorybnaya**, Russian Federation
151 T 11 **Novoselivs'ke**, Ukraine
157 V 4 **Novosergiyevka**, Russian Federation
156 L 9 **Novoshakhtinsk**, Russian Federation
152 M 12 **Novosibirsk**, Russian Federation
157 R 4 **Novospasskoye**, Russian Federation
151 U 10 **Novotroyits'ke**, Ukraine
151 Q 7 **Novoukrayinka**, Ukraine
157 R 6 **Novouzensk**, Russian Federation
156 G 4 **Novozybkov**, Russian Federation
149 M 18 **Novy Bykhaw**, Belarus
143 H 18 **Nový Jičín**, Czech Republic
155 P 4 **Novyy Bor**, Russian Federation
151 S 8 **Novyy Buh**, Ukraine
151 R 3 **Novyy Bykiv**, Ukraine
156 K 6 **Novyy Oskol**, Russian Federation
152 M 8 **Novyy Port**, Russian Federation
152 M 9 **Novyy Urengoy**, Russian Federation
153 V 13 **Novyy Urgal**, Russian Federation
143 I 15 **Nowa**, Poland
143 M 16 **Nowa Dęba**, Poland
143 F 16 **Nowa Ruda**, Poland
142 E 10 **Nowogard**, Poland
231 U 12 **Nowra**, New South Wales, Australia
177 W 6 **Nowshak**, Pakistan ▲
177 W 7 **Nowshera**, Pakistan
142 K 12 **Nowy Dwór Mazowiecki**, Poland
143 L 18 **Nowy Sącz**, Poland
143 K 18 **Nowy Targ**, Poland
152 M 9 **Noyabr'sk**, Russian Federation
129 R 3 **Noyon**, France
128 K 6 **Nozay**, France
216 I 8 **Nsambi**, Democratic Republic of Congo
219 R 6 **Nsanje**, Malawi
215 T 15 **Nsoc**, Equatorial Guinea
219 P 3 **Nsombo**, Zambia
215 Q 13 **Nsukka**, Nigeria
216 I 9 **Ntandembele**, Democratic Republic of Congo
219 R 5 **Ntcheu**, Malawi
216 D 7 **Ntoum**, Gabon
217 R 8 **Ntungamo**, Uganda
218 M 8 **Ntwetwe Pan**, Botswana ◣
188 J 9 **Nu Shan**, China ⛰
213 E 18 **Nuba Mountains**, Sudan ⛰
213 G 14 **Nubian Desert**, Sudan ◇
235 Y 10 **Nubu**, Fiji
89 U 13 **Nudo de Zempoaltépetl**, Mexico ▲
84 J 4 **Nueltin Lake**, Nunavut, Canada ◣
90 K 5 **Nueva Arcadia**, Honduras
104 L 3 **Nueva Bolivia**, Venezuela
89 X 12 **Nueva Coahuila**, Mexico
105 P 2 **Nueva Esparta**, Venezuela ◘
110 I 13 **Nueva Galia**, Argentina
92 G 5 **Nueva Gerona**, Cuba
91 Q 10 **Nueva Guinea**, Nicaragua
106 C 8 **Nueva Loja**, Ecuador
111 G 19 **Nueva Lubecka**, Argentina
90 J 6 **Nueva Ocotepeque**, Honduras
110 L 6 **Nueva Pompeya**, Argentina
89 P 5 **Nueva Rosita**, Mexico
90 I 7 **Nueva San Salvador**, El Salvador
89 R 8 **Nueva Villa de Padilla**, Mexico
113 C 16 **Nueve de Julio**, Argentina
92 L 5 **Nuevitas**, Cuba
89 Q 6 **Nuevo Laredo**, Mexico
89 R 7 **Nuevo León**, Mexico ◘
213 O 20 **Nugaal**, Somalia ◘
234 J 3 **Nuguria Islands**, Papua New Guinea ⛬
182 I 9 **Nuh**, India
232 O 12 **Nuhaka**, New Zealand
236 F 5 **Nui**, Tuvalu ⛬
79 Q 3 **Nuiqsut**, Alaska, U.S.A.
234 J 5 **Nukiki**, Solomon Islands
234 B 3 **Nuku**, Papua New Guinea
236 I 11 **Nuku'alofa**, Tonga ♜
236 F 6 **Nukufetau**, Tuvalu ⛬
236 G 6 **Nukulaelae**, Tuvalu ⛬
234 L 4 **Nukumanu Islands**, Papua New Guinea ⛬
236 K 6 **Nukunonu**, Tokelau Islands ⛬
236 J 6 **Nukunonu**, Tokelau Islands
237 P 15 **Nukuoro**, Federated States of Micronesia ⛬
178 M 10 **Nukus**, Uzbekistan
230 H 6 **Nullagine**, Western Australia, Australia
230 M 10 **Nullarbor**, South Australia, Australia
230 L 10 **Nullarbor Plain**, Western Australia, Australia ◇
187 F 15 **Nulu'erhu Shan**, China ⛰
183 R 9 **Num**, Nepal
193 V 11 **Num**, Indonesia ⛬
215 U 11 **Numan**, Nigeria
133 G 14 **Numansdorp**, Netherlands
199 J 15 **Numata**, Japan
199 K 17 **Numazu**, Japan
231 O 2 **Numbulwar**, Northern Territory, Australia
84 J 2 **Nunavut**, Canada ◘
127 S 7 **Nuneaton**, United Kingdom
183 X 12 **Nungba**, India
186 F 11 **Nungnain Sum**, China
78 L 9 **Nunivak Island**, Alaska, U.S.A. ⛬
153 Z 6 **Nunligran**, Russian Federation
132 K 11 **Nunspeet**, Netherlands
141 C 17 **Nuoro**, Italy
235 P 7 **Nupani**, Solomon Islands ⛬
175 N 5 **Nuqrah**, Saudi Arabia
104 G 6 **Nuquí**, Colombia
179 N 6 **Nura**, Kazakhstan
176 I 10 **Nūrābād**, Iran
179 P 12 **Nurata**, Uzbekistan
137 I 21 **Nuremberg**, Germany
88 J 5 **Nuri**, Mexico
157 S 2 **Nurlat**, Russian Federation
135 N 14 **Nurmes**, Finland
177 W 9 **Nurpur**, Pakistan
182 I 5 **Nurpur**, India
192 M 14 **Nusa Tenggara Barat**, Indonesia ◘
193 O 15 **Nusa Tenggara Timur**, Indonesia ◘
171 Q 13 **Nusaybin**, Turkey
177 S 11 **Nushki**, Pakistan
45 O 11 **Nuugaatsiaq**, Greenland
44 M 12 **Nuuk**, Greenland ♜
45 N 11 **Nuussuaq**, Greenland ▶
45 O 10 **Nuussuaq**, Greenland
152 K 9 **Nyagan'**, Russian Federation
217 U 7 **Nyahururu**, Kenya
184 K 10 **Nyainqêntanglha**, China ▲
184 L 10 **Nyainqêntanglha Shan**, China ⛰
217 S 9 **Nyakaliro**, Tanzania
213 A 18 **Nyala**, Sudan
219 O 8 **Nyamandhiovu**, Zimbabwe
213 C 20 **Nyamlell**, Sudan
154 K 9 **Nyandoma**, Russian Federation
216 E 10 **Nyanga**, Gabon ◘
216 F 9 **Nyanga**, Congo
217 T 8 **Nyanza**, Kenya ◘
149 I 19 **Nyasvizh**, Belarus
219 O 7 **Nyathi**, Zimbabwe
191 E 15 **Nyaunglebin**, Myanmar
135 E 18 **Nybergsund**, Norway
135 C 25 **Nyborg**, Denmark
135 G 24 **Nybro**, Sweden
217 V 8 **Nyeri**, Kenya
213 E 20 **Nyerol**, Sudan
184 M 11 **Nyingchi**, China
143 N 22 **Nyírbátor**, Hungary
143 M 22 **Nyíregyháza**, Hungary
135 D 26 **Nykøbing**, Denmark
135 H 21 **Nyköping**, Sweden
135 H 21 **Nynäshamn**, Sweden
231 T 10 **Nyngan**, New South Wales, Australia
149 G 18 **Nyoman**, Belarus ∫
138 A 9 **Nyon**, Switzerland
129 U 12 **Nyons**, France
155 S 10 **Nyrob**, Russian Federation
143 G 16 **Nysa**, Poland
198 J 10 **Nyūdō-zaki**, Japan ▶
217 P 11 **Nyunzu**, Democratic Republic of Congo
192 M 9 **Nyurang**, Indonesia
153 S 10 **Nyurba**, Russian Federation
153 S 11 **Nyuya**, Russian Federation
151 U 9 **Nyzhni Sirohozy**, Ukraine
151 U 9 **Nyzhni Torhayi**, Ukraine
151 U 11 **Nyzhn'ohirs'kyy**, Ukraine
216 E 10 **Nzambi**, Congo
217 S 10 **Nzega**, Tanzania
214 H 12 **Nzérékoré**, Guinea
218 F 2 **N'zeto**, Angola
217 P 10 **Nzingu**, Democratic Republic of Congo

O

198 H 8 **Ō-shima**, Japan ⛬
199 K 17 **Ō-shima**, Japan ⛬
78 C 7 **Oahu**, Hawaii, U.S.A. ⛬
59 O 11 **Oak Bluffs**, Massachusetts, U.S.A.
74 J 4 **Oak City**, Utah, U.S.A.
65 H 14 **Oak Creek**, Wisconsin, U.S.A.
75 P 3 **Oak Creek**, Colorado, U.S.A.
76 G 6 **Oak Harbor**, Washington, U.S.A.
65 H 16 **Oak Lawn**, Illinois, U.S.A.
60 J 8 **Oak Ridge**, Tennessee, U.S.A.
62 I 7 **Oakdale**, Louisiana, U.S.A.
127 U 6 **Oakham**, United Kingdom
77 I 20 **Oakhurst**, California, U.S.A.
61 Q 2 **Oakland**, Maryland, U.S.A.
67 P 13 **Oakland**, Nebraska, U.S.A.
76 F 12 **Oakland**, Oregon, U.S.A.
77 G 19 **Oakland**, California, U.S.A.
68 I 3 **Oakley**, Kansas, U.S.A.
73 N 13 **Oakley**, Idaho, U.S.A.
230 H 5 **Oakover**, Western Australia, Australia ∫
76 G 12 **Oakridge**, Oregon, U.S.A.
232 J 12 **Oakura**, New Zealand
232 J 6 **Oakura**, New Zealand
233 F 23 **Oamaru**, New Zealand
199 D 19 **Ōasa**, Japan
77 Q 5 **Oasis**, Nevada, U.S.A.
241 R 14 **Oates Land**, Antarctica ◇
89 T 14 **Oaxaca**, Mexico
89 S 14 **Oaxaca**, Mexico ◘
152 L 10 **Ob'**, Russian Federation ∫
86 B 5 **Oba**, Ontario, Canada
215 T 14 **Obala**, Cameroon
124 F 12 **Oban**, United Kingdom
233 D 23 **Obelisk**, New Zealand ▲
112 F 10 **Oberá**, Argentina
139 Q 8 **Oberdrauburg**, Austria
68 I 2 **Oberlin**, Kansas, U.S.A.
139 Q 5 **Oberndorf**, Austria
139 Q 4 **Oberösterreich**, Austria ◘
137 K 20 **Oberpfälzer Wald**, Germany ◇
139 Y 6 **Oberpullendorf**, Austria
137 H 26 **Oberstdorf**, Germany

Country ◘ Internal administrative region: State/Province/Territory/Dependent territory ♜ Capital city ⛰ Mountain range/Undersea ridge ▲ Mountain peak/Volcano/Seamount ◇ Geographic feature ▶ Headland/Point/Cape/Peninsula ☗ Desert ⛬ Island/Island group ⁙ Antarctic base ◎ Ocean ◢ Sea ≈ Bay/Gulf/Channel/Strait ◣ Lake ⚑ Salt pan/Dry/Intermittent lake ∫ River

Obervellach – Orleans

139	R 8	**Obervellach**, Austria
139	X 6	**Oberwart**, Austria
193	S 11	**Obi**, Indonesia
108	G 10	**Óbidos**, Brazil
198	L 5	**Obihiro**, Japan
65	G 20	**Oblong**, Illinois, U.S.A.
153	U 14	**Obluch'ye**, Russian Federation
156	K 1	**Obninsk**, Russian Federation
217	O 4	**Obo**, Central African Republic
217	O 8	**Obokote**, Democratic Republic of Congo
149	K 14	**Obol'**, Belarus
151	S 5	**Obolon'**, Ukraine
142	G 12	**Oborniki**, Poland
216	H 8	**Obouya**, Congo
156	J 5	**Oboyan'**, Russian Federation
154	K 7	**Obozerskiy**, Russian Federation
142	E 12	**Obra**, Poland
144	K 11	**Obrenovac**, Serbia and Montenegro
77	F 14	**O'Brien**, Oregon, U.S.A.
146	N 7	**Obrochishte**, Bulgaria
170	H 11	**Obruk**, Turkey
152	L 8	**Obskaya**, Russian Federation
45	X 10	**Obskaya Guba**, Arctic Ocean
151	P 4	**Obukhiv**, Ukraine
155	P 10	**Ob''yachevo**, Russian Federation
151	W 9	**Obytichna Kosa**, Ukraine
151	V 10	**Obytichna Zatoka**, Ukraine
63	W 9	**Ocala**, Florida, U.S.A.
75	R 9	**Ocate**, New Mexico, U.S.A.
232	K 6	**Ocean Beach**, New Zealand
58	J 15	**Ocean City**, New Jersey, U.S.A.
61	X 4	**Ocean City**, Maryland, U.S.A.
76	F 8	**Ocean Park**, Washington, U.S.A.
63	N 7	**Ocean Springs**, Mississippi, U.S.A.
42	G 9	**Oceanographer Fracture Zone**, Atlantic Ocean
77	K 26	**Oceanside**, California, U.S.A.
151	Q 9	**Ochakiv**, Ukraine
171	Q 6	**Och'amch'ire**, Georgia
155	S 13	**Ocher**, Russian Federation
198	N 4	**Ochiishi-misaki**, Japan
92	L 8	**Ocho Rios**, Jamaica
63	X 13	**Ochopee**, Florida, U.S.A.
137	H 20	**Ochsenfurt**, Germany
63	U 5	**Ocilla**, Georgia, U.S.A.
63	U 5	**Ocmulgeee**, Georgia, U.S.A.
90	F 6	**Ocos**, Guatemala
89	W 13	**Ocosingo**, Mexico
91	N 7	**Ocotal**, Nicaragua
61	W 10	**Ocracoke Island**, North Carolina, U.S.A.
107	J 21	**Ocurí**, Bolivia
199	D 18	**Ōda**, Japan
198	J 9	**Ōdate**, Japan
199	K 17	**Odawara**, Japan
71	Q 13	**Odem**, Texas, U.S.A.
130	G 11	**Odemira**, Portugal
170	C 11	**Ödemiş**, Turkey
135	C 25	**Odense**, Denmark
136	N 12	**Oder**, Germany/Poland
136	M 9	**Oderhaff**, Germany
140	H 6	**Oderzo**, Italy
151	Q 10	**Odesa**, Ukraine
70	J 7	**Odessa**, Texas, U.S.A.
76	J 7	**Odessa**, Washington, U.S.A.
214	I 11	**Odienné**, Côte d'Ivoire
191	L 21	**Ŏdŏngk**, Cambodia
132	N 8	**Odoorn**, Netherlands
150	K 10	**Odorheiu Secuiesc**, Romania
143	K 14	**Odrzywół**, Poland
144	J 9	**Odžaci**, Serbia and Montenegro
108	M 12	**Oeiras**, Brazil
66	G 11	**Oelrichs**, South Dakota, U.S.A.
137	K 18	**Oelsnitz**, Germany
231	N 1	**Oenpelli**, Northern Territory, Australia
171	P 8	**Of**, Turkey
172	E 10	**Ofaqim**, Israel
215	P 12	**Offa**, Nigeria
137	F 19	**Offenbach**, Germany
137	D 23	**Offenburg**, Germany
147	K 23	**Ofidoussa**, Greece
198	L 11	**Ōfunato**, Japan
198	J 10	**Oga**, Japan
198	K 11	**Ogachi**, Japan
213	M 21	**Ogadēn**, Ethiopia
199	H 17	**Ogaki**, Japan
66	I 14	**Ogallala**, Nebraska, U.S.A.
198	K 9	**Ogawara-ko**, Japan
215	P 12	**Ogbomoso**, Nigeria
74	J 2	**Ogden**, Utah, U.S.A.
63	W 4	**Ogeechee**, Georgia, U.S.A.
198	I 13	**Ogi**, Japan
82	A 10	**Ogilvie Mountains**, Yukon Territory, Canada
215	S 13	**Ogoja**, Nigeria
84	M 10	**Ogoki**, Ontario, Canada
216	G 7	**Ogooué-Ivindo**, Gabon
216	F 8	**Ogooué-Lolo**, Gabon
216	D 8	**Ogooué-Maritime**, Gabon
146	F 11	**Ograzden**, Macedonia (F.Y.R.O.M.)
148	F 11	**Ogre**, Latvia
215	O 13	**Ogun**, Nigeria
171	W 7	**Oğuz**, Azerbaijan
41	X 15	**Oh Dear**, Pitcairn Island
232	L 13	**Ohakune**, New Zealand
211	Q 10	**Ohanet**, Algeria
218	I 7	**Ohangwena**, Namibia
233	K 15	**Ohau**, New Zealand
232	K 10	**Ohaupo**, New Zealand
110	F 12	**O'Higgins**, Chile
57	U 9	**Ohio**, U.S.A., U.S.A.
143	B 16	**Ohře**, Czech Republic
146	B 12	**Ohrid**, Macedonia (F.Y.R.O.M.)
232	K 12	**Ohura**, New Zealand
108	I 8	**Oiapoque**, Brazil
108	I 8	**Oiapoque**, Brazil
85	S 1	**Oikiqtarjuaq**, Nunavut, Canada
133	I 15	**Oirschot**, Netherlands
199	C 21	**Ōita**, Japan
147	E 18	**Oiti**, Greece
64	D 10	**Ojibwa**, Wisconsin, U.S.A.
199	A 22	**Ojika-jima**, Japan
89	N 4	**Ojinaga**, Mexico
199	J 14	**Ojiya**, Japan
88	M 4	**Ojo de Laguna**, Mexico
234	A 4	**Ok Tedi**, Papua New Guinea
156	K 2	**Oka**, Russian Federation
193	Y 14	**Okaba**, Indonesia
218	I 9	**Okahandja**, Namibia
232	I 5	**Okaihau**, New Zealand
85	U 6	**Okak Islands**, Newfoundland and Labrador, Canada
218	I 8	**Okakarara**, Namibia
218	I 8	**Okaputa**, Namibia
177	X 10	**Okara**, Pakistan
178	I 13	**Okarem**, Turkmenistan
233	E 19	**Okarito Lagoon**, New Zealand
218	H 8	**Okaukuejo**, Namibia
218	J 7	**Okavango**, Namibia
218	K 7	**Okavango**, Botswana
218	L 7	**Okavango Delta**, Botswana
199	I 16	**Okaya**, Japan
199	F 19	**Okayama**, Japan
199	I 17	**Okazaki**, Japan
63	Y 11	**Okeechobee**, Florida, U.S.A.
126	M 13	**Okehampton**, United Kingdom
153	W 12	**Okha**, Russian Federation
183	Q 9	**Okhaldhunga**, Nepal
155	S 13	**Okhansk**, Russian Federation
153	W 11	**Okhotsk**, Russian Federation
151	V 9	**Okhrimivka**, Ukraine
151	U 4	**Okhtyrka**, Ukraine
199	D 17	**Oki-shotō**, Japan
199	O 24	**Okinawa**, Japan
199	O 25	**Okinawa-shotō**, Japan
199	E 22	**Okino-shima**, Japan
199	N 23	**Okinoerabu-jima**, Japan
68	L 10	**Oklahoma**, U.S.A.
69	N 10	**Oklahoma City**, Oklahoma, U.S.A.
69	Q 10	**Okmulgee**, Oklahoma, U.S.A.
216	G 8	**Okondja**, Gabon
216	H 8	**Okoyo**, Congo
191	D 15	**Okpo**, Myanmar
134	J 6	**Øksfjord**, Norway
155	P 3	**Oksino**, Russian Federation
157	U 2	**Oktyabr'skiy**, Russian Federation
157	O 9	**Oktyabr'skiy**, Russian Federation
153	Z 11	**Oktyabr'skiy**, Russian Federation
154	L 10	**Oktyabr'skiy**, Russian Federation
157	W 4	**Oktyabr'skoye**, Russian Federation
199	N 24	**Oku**, Japan
154	G 12	**Okulovka**, Russian Federation
198	H 7	**Okushiri-tō**, Japan
215	O 12	**Okuta**, Nigeria
69	T 11	**Ola**, Arkansas, U.S.A.
91	V 14	**Olá**, Panama
148	F 11	**Olaine**, Latvia
77	K 22	**Olancha**, California, U.S.A.
135	H 24	**Öland**, Sweden
231	Q 10	**Olary**, South Australia, Australia
69	R 4	**Olathe**, Kansas, U.S.A.
113	C 17	**Olavarría**, Argentina
143	G 15	**Oława**, Poland
141	C 16	**Olbia**, Italy
82	A 9	**Old Crow**, Yukon Territory, Canada
73	R 9	**Old Faithful**, Wyoming, U.S.A.
58	I 7	**Old Forge**, New York, U.S.A.
79	P 12	**Old Harbor**, Alaska, U.S.A.
125	C 21	**Old Head of Kinsale**, Republic of Ireland
59	R 4	**Old Town**, Maine, U.S.A.
83	N 19	**Old Wives Lake**, Saskatchewan, Canada
132	K 10	**Oldebroek**, Netherlands
136	E 11	**Oldenburg**, Germany
136	I 8	**Oldenburg in Holstein**, Germany
132	N 11	**Oldenzaal**, Netherlands
134	K 6	**Olderfjord**, Norway
127	R 3	**Oldham**, United Kingdom
58	D 10	**Olean**, New York, U.S.A.
142	M 9	**Olecko**, Poland
153	S 11	**Olekminsk**, Russian Federation
151	R 6	**Oleksandrivka**, Ukraine
151	W 7	**Oleksandrivka**, Ukraine
151	S 6	**Oleksandriya**, Ukraine
154	I 2	**Olenegorsk**, Russian Federation
153	R 8	**Olenëk**, Russian Federation
153	S 7	**Olenekskiy Zaliv**, Russian Federation
151	S 11	**Olenevka**, Ukraine
154	I 4	**Olenitsa**, Russian Federation
143	G 15	**Oleśnica**, Poland
143	I 16	**Olesno**, Poland
150	M 2	**Olevs'k**, Ukraine
134	G 11	**Ølfjellet**, Norway
184	M 2	**Ölgiy**, Mongolia
130	I 12	**Olhão**, Portugal
112	J 5	**Olímpia**, Brazil
60	K 5	**Olive Hill**, Kentucky, U.S.A.
130	J 9	**Olivenza**, Spain
83	L 14	**Oliver Lake**, Saskatchewan, Canada
67	Q 8	**Olivia**, Minnesota, U.S.A.
157	P 7	**Ol'khovka**, Russian Federation
143	J 17	**Olkusz**, Poland
110	H 4	**Ollagüe**, Chile
127	T 4	**Ollerton**, United Kingdom
216	H 8	**Ollombo**, Congo
131	N 5	**Olmedo**, Spain
106	B 12	**Olmos**, Peru
65	G 21	**Olney**, Illinois, U.S.A.
71	O 5	**Olney**, Texas, U.S.A.
143	G 18	**Olomouc**, Czech Republic
154	G 9	**Olonets**, Russian Federation
196	F 11	**Olongapo**, Philippines
128	M 14	**Oloron-Ste-Marie**, France
131	X 3	**Olot**, Spain
153	R 14	**Olovyannaya**, Russian Federation
149	K 18	**Ol'sa**, Belarus
142	K 9	**Olsztyn**, Poland
142	K 10	**Olsztynek**, Poland
150	I 10	**Olt**, Romania
138	E 6	**Olten**, Switzerland
150	L 13	**Oltenița**, Romania
171	R 8	**Oltu**, Turkey
197	I 22	**Olutanga**, Philippines
76	G 7	**Olympia**, Washington, U.S.A.
153	Z 8	**Olyutorskiy**, Russian Federation
153	Z 9	**Olyutorskiy Zaliv**, Russian Federation
213	H 17	**Om Hajēr**, Eritrea
198	J 8	**Ōma**, Japan
198	J 8	**Ōma-zaki**, Japan
199	J 18	**Omae-zaki**, Japan
198	K 11	**Ōmagari**, Japan
125	E 15	**Omagh**, United Kingdom
106	F 11	**Omaguas**, Peru
67	P 14	**Omaha**, Nebraska, U.S.A.
218	J 9	**Omaheke**, Namibia
76	J 6	**Omak**, Washington, U.S.A.
233	D 23	**Omakau**, New Zealand
233	M 14	**Omakere**, New Zealand
171	U 6	**Omalo**, Georgia
175	Y 8	**Oman**, Asia
233	E 22	**Omarama**, New Zealand
218	I 9	**Omaruru**, Namibia
216	I 4	**Ombella-Mpoko**, Central African Republic
216	D 9	**Omboué**, Gabon
213	F 16	**Omdurman**, Sudan
151	T 5	**Omel'nyk**, Ukraine
64	L 12	**Omer**, Michigan, U.S.A.
89	R 14	**Ometepec**, Mexico
176	G 9	**Omīdīyeh**, Iran
132	M 10	**Ommen**, Netherlands
185	Q 5	**Ömnögovi**, Mongolia
213	G 22	**Omo Wenz**, Ethiopia
153	X 8	**Omolon**, Russian Federation
153	X 8	**Omolon**, Russian Federation
152	K 11	**Omsk**, Russian Federation
153	X 9	**Omsukchan**, Russian Federation
198	K 3	**Ōmū**, Japan
199	B 22	**Ōmura**, Japan
146	L 8	**Omurtag**, Bulgaria
218	G 7	**Omusati**, Namibia
199	B 22	**Ōmuta**, Japan
155	Q 12	**Omutninsk**, Russian Federation
64	D 12	**Onalaska**, Wisconsin, U.S.A.
67	R 6	**Onamia**, Minnesota, U.S.A.
64	K 10	**Onaway**, Michigan, U.S.A.
198	M 5	**Onbetsu**, Japan
218	G 6	**Oncócua**, Angola
218	H 7	**Ondangwa**, Namibia
143	M 19	**Ondava**, Slovakia
181	F 14	**Onder**, India
218	H 6	**Ondjiva**, Angola
215	P 13	**Ondo**, Nigeria
215	Q 13	**Ondo**, Nigeria
185	S 4	**Öndörhaan**, Mongolia
181	K 20	**One and a Half Degree Channel**, Maldives
154	J 7	**Onega**, Russian Federation
58	H 8	**Oneida**, New York, U.S.A.
58	H 8	**Oneida Lake**, New York, U.S.A.
66	M 12	**O'Neill**, Nebraska, U.S.A.
58	I 9	**Oneonta**, New York, U.S.A.
63	Q 2	**Oneonta**, Alabama, U.S.A.
150	L 10	**Onești**, Romania
154	I 6	**Onezhskaya Guba**, Russian Federation
216	G 8	**Onga**, Gabon
232	K 12	**Ongarue**, New Zealand
185	Q 4	**Ongi**, Mongolia
187	K 18	**Ongjin**, North Korea
181	G 19	**Ongole**, India
171	S 6	**Oni**, Georgia
215	Q 13	**Onitsha**, Nigeria
153	U 11	**Onnes**, Russian Federation
235	X 12	**Ono**, Fiji
199	H 16	**Ono**, Japan
235	Z 13	**Ono-i-lau**, Fiji
199	B 21	**Ōnojō**, Japan
199	E 19	**Onomichi**, Japan
186	H 8	**Onor**, China
236	E 3	**Onotoa**, Kiribati
218	J 12	**Onseepkans**, Republic of South Africa
230	E 6	**Onslow**, Western Australia, Australia
61	T 12	**Onslow Bay**, North Carolina, U.S.A.
76	L 11	**Ontario**, Oregon, U.S.A.
86	C 7	**Ontario**, Canada
131	T 9	**Ontinyent**, Spain
64	F 8	**Ontonagon**, Michigan, U.S.A.
234	L 4	**Ontong Java Atoll**, Solomon Islands
231	O 8	**Oodnadatta**, South Australia, Australia
213	L 20	**Oodweyne**, Somalia
230	M 10	**Ooldea**, South Australia, Australia
69	Q 8	**Oologah Lake**, Oklahoma, U.S.A.
133	D 18	**Oost-Vlaanderen**, Belgium
132	I 6	**Oost-Vlieland**, Netherlands
133	B 17	**Oostende**, Belgium
132	J 5	**Oosterend**, Netherlands
133	H 15	**Oosterhout**, Netherlands
133	E 15	**Oosterschelde**, Netherlands
133	C 15	**Oostersscheldekering**, Netherlands
132	L 7	**Oosterwolde**, Netherlands
133	C 17	**Oostkamp**, Belgium
133	A 18	**Oostvleteren**, Belgium
191	L 23	**Ŏp Luc**, Vietnam
217	N 8	**Opala**, Democratic Republic of Congo
155	O 11	**Oparino**, Russian Federation
143	L 16	**Opatów**, Poland
143	H 17	**Opava**, Czech Republic
63	S 4	**Opelika**, Alabama, U.S.A.
62	I 7	**Opelousas**, Louisiana, U.S.A.
234	G 4	**Open Bay**, Papua New Guinea
73	W 2	**Opheim**, Montana, U.S.A.
132	J 13	**Opheusden**, Netherlands
217	P 7	**Opienge**, Democratic Republic of Congo
151	U 4	**Opishnya**, Ukraine
154	D 13	**Opochka**, Russian Federation
143	K 14	**Opoczno**, Poland
143	H 16	**Opole**, Poland
178	J 8	**Opornyy**, Kazakhstan
232	N 10	**Opotiki**, New Zealand
63	Q 6	**Opp**, Alabama, U.S.A.
135	D 16	**Oppdal**, Norway
141	M 21	**Oppido Mamertina**, Italy
232	J 13	**Opunake**, New Zealand
218	G 7	**Opuwo**, Namibia
74	L 14	**Oracle**, Arizona, U.S.A.
150	G 8	**Oradea**, Romania
182	K 11	**Orai**, India
74	L 9	**Oraibi**, Arizona, U.S.A.
210	K 6	**Oran**, Algeria
110	J 5	**Orán**, Argentina
151	P 2	**Orane**, Ukraine
218	M 13	**Orange**, Republic of Sout Africa
231	U 11	**Orange**, New South Wales, Australia
129	T 13	**Orange**, France
71	V 9	**Orange**, Texas, U.S.A.
43	N 16	**Orange Cone**, Atlantic Ocean
90	K 1	**Orange Walk**, Belize
61	O 13	**Orangeburg**, South Carolina, U.S.A.
234	F 7	**Orangerie Bay**, Papua New Guinea
86	E 12	**Orangeville**, Ontario, Canada
196	F 11	**Orani**, Philippines
136	L 12	**Oranienburg**, Germany
218	I 12	**Oranjemund**, Namibia
93	R 13	**Oranjestad**, Aruba
218	M 8	**Orapa**, Botswana
197	M 15	**Oras**, Philippines
150	H 10	**Orăștie**, Romania
143	J 19	**Orava**, Slovakia
150	F 11	**Oravița**, Romania
233	B 25	**Orawia**, New Zealand
140	F 13	**Orbetello**, Italy
231	T 13	**Orbost**, Victoria, Australi
240	I 1	**Orcadas**, Antarctica
131	Q 10	**Orcera**, Spain
230	L 4	**Ord**, Western Australia, Australia
130	H 1	**Ordes**, Spain
170	M 8	**Ordu**, Turkey
75	T 6	**Ordway**, Colorado, U.S.A
179	N 3	**Ordzhonikidze**, Kazakhstan
171	X 9	**Ordzonikidze**, Azerbaijan
143	A 17	**Ore Mountains**, Czech Republic
135	G 20	**Örebro**, Sweden
65	F 14	**Oregon**, Wisconsin, U.S.A
76	H 12	**Oregon**, U.S.A., U.S.A.
76	G 10	**Oregon City**, Oregon, U.S.A.
151	T 6	**Orel**, Ukraine
156	J 3	**Orel**, Russian Federation
106	D 13	**Orellana**, Peru
170	C 12	**Ören**, Turkey
157	W 5	**Orenburg**, Russian Federation
157	V 4	**Orenburgskaya Oblast'**, Russian Federation
113	C 19	**Orense**, Argentina
146	L 12	**Orestiada**, Greece
233	C 25	**Oreti**, New Zealand
232	K 8	**Orewa**, New Zealand
75	Q 14	**Organ Peak**, New Mexico, U.S.A.
105	Y 6	**Organabo**, French Guian
177	U 8	**Orgūn**, Afghanistan
151	N 8	**Orhei**, Moldova
131	S 2	**Orhi**, Spain
90	M 6	**Orica**, Honduras
77	E 15	**Orick**, California, U.S.A.
217	O 6	**Orientale**, Democratic Republic of Congo
113	C 19	**Oriente**, Argentina
131	S 11	**Orihuela**, Spain
151	V 8	**Orikhiv**, Ukraine
151	V 5	**Oril'**, Ukraine
151	V 5	**Oril'ka**, Ukraine
86	F 12	**Orillia**, Ontario, Canada
73	Y 12	**Orin**, Wyoming, U.S.A.
105	O 4	**Orinoco**, Venezuela
234	B 6	**Oriomo**, Papua New Guinea
181	I 16	**Orissa**, India
148	E 7	**Orissaare**, Estonia
141	B 18	**Oristano**, Italy
135	O 16	**Orivesi**, Finland
108	G 10	**Oriximiná**, Brazil
89	S 12	**Orizaba**, Mexico
135	E 24	**Örkelljunga**, Sweden
124	H 7	**Orkney Islands**, United Kingdom
70	H 7	**Orla**, Texas, U.S.A.
112	K 5	**Orlândia**, Brazil
63	W 10	**Orlando**, Florida, U.S.A.
59	P 10	**Orleans**, Massachusetts, U.S.A.
77	F 15	**Orleans**, California, U.S.A

Country · Internal administrative region: State/Province/Territory/Dependent territory · Capital city · Mountain range/Undersea ridge · Mountain peak/Volcano/Seamount · Geographic feature · Headland/Point/Cape/Peninsula · Desert · Island/Island group · Antarctic base · Ocean · Sea · Bay/Gulf/Channel/Strait · Lake · Salt pan/Dry/Intermittent lake · Riv

P 6 **Orléans**, France
K 4 **Orlovskaya Oblast'**, Russian Federation ▣
N 10 **Orlovskiy**, Russian Federation
Q 4 **Orly**, France
R 14 **Ormara**, Pakistan
L 16 **Ormoc**, Philippines
X 9 **Ormond Beach**, Florida, U.S.A.
P 3 **Ormskirk**, United Kingdom
G 14 **Ormylia**, Greece
K 9 **Orneta**, Poland
I 21 **Ornö**, Sweden 🏝
P 3 **Orno Peak**, Colorado, U.S.A. ▲
I 15 **Örnsköldsvik**, Sweden
K 5 **Orofino**, Idaho, U.S.A.
P 4 **Orog Nuur**, Mongolia 💧
Q 14 **Orogrande**, New Mexico, U.S.A.
P 15 **Oroluk**, Federated States of Micronesia 🏝
H 20 **Oromia**, Ethiopia ▣
S 9 **Oromocto**, New Brunswick, Canada
S 14 **Oron**, Nigeria
F 11 **Oron**, Israel
J 4 **Orona**, Kiribati 🏝
K 20 **Oroquieta**, Philippines
J 26 **Oros Kofinas**, Greece ▲
D 17 **Orosei**, Italy
L 25 **Orosháza**, Hungary
K 15 **Orovada**, Nevada, U.S.A.
G 17 **Oroville**, California, U.S.A.
G 7 **Orphan Knoll**, Atlantic Ocean ▲
H 7 **Orqohan**, China
M 16 **Orsha**, Belarus
D 11 **Orsières**, Switzerland
H 11 **Orsk**, Russian Federation
G 12 **Orşova**, Romania
H 13 **Orta Toroslar**, Turkey ⛰
I 12 **Ortaköy**, Turkey
Y 3 **Orth an der Donau**, Austria
L 14 **Orthez**, France
I 16 **Orthon**, Bolivia ∿
I 1 **Ortigueira**, Spain
J 5 **Ortiz**, Mexico
J 13 **Ortona**, Italy
O 7 **Ortonville**, Minnesota, U.S.A.
F 3 **Orūmīyeh**, Iran
J 20 **Oruro**, Bolivia
I 21 **Oruro**, Bolivia ▣
D 22 **Orust**, Sweden 🏝
G 12 **Orvieto**, Italy
K 6 **Orville Coast**, Antarctica ◇
O 16 **Orwell**, Ohio, U.S.A.
H 6 **Oryakhovo**, Bulgaria
D 7 **Orzinuovi**, Italy
O 11 **Orzola**, Canary Islands
M 9 **Orzysz**, Poland
S 13 **Osa**, Russian Federation
T 10 **Osage**, Iowa, U.S.A.
G 18 **Ōsaka**, Japan
G 18 **Ōsaka-wan**, Japan ≈
S 4 **Osakarovka**, Kazakhstan
P 6 **Osborn Plateau**, Indian Ocean ◇
L 3 **Osborne**, Kansas, U.S.A.
C 16 **Oschiri**, Italy
L 12 **Oscoda**, Michigan, U.S.A.
J 11 **Osečina**, Serbia and Montenegro
I 11 **Osgoode**, Ontario, Canada
T 12 **Osh**, Kyrgyzstan
H 7 **Oshakati**, Namibia
I 7 **Oshamambe**, Japan
H 7 **Oshana**, Namibia ▣
F 12 **Oshawa**, Ontario, Canada
L 12 **Oshika-hantō**, Japan ▶
H 7 **Oshikango**, Namibia
I 7 **Oshikoto**, Namibia ▣
I 7 **Oshima-hantō**, Japan ▶
G 12 **Oshkosh**, Wisconsin, U.S.A.
H 14 **Oshkosh**, Nebraska, U.S.A.
P 12 **Oshogbo**, Nigeria

179 T 12 **Oshskaya Oblast'**, Kyrgyzstan ▣
216 K 10 **Oshwe**, Democratic Republic of Congo
67 T 13 **Oskaloosa**, Iowa, U.S.A.
135 G 23 **Oskarshamn**, Sweden
151 X 4 **Oskol**, Ukraine ∿
135 D 20 **Oslo**, Norway 🏛
135 C 21 **Oslofjorden**, Norway ≈
170 J 8 **Osmancik**, Turkey
170 E 8 **Osmaneli**, Turkey
170 L 13 **Osmaniye**, Turkey
148 E 6 **Osmussaar**, Estonia 🏝
136 E 13 **Osnabrück**, Germany
146 D 10 **Osogovske Planine**, Macedonia (F.Y.R.O.M.) ⛰
112 I 12 **Osório**, Brazil
111 E 16 **Osorno**, Chile
131 N 3 **Osorno**, Spain
83 H 22 **Osoyoos**, British Columbia, Canada
135 A 19 **Osøyra**, Norway
133 J 14 **Oss**, Netherlands
64 D 11 **Osseo**, Wisconsin, U.S.A.
153 Y 9 **Ossora**, Russian Federation
154 F 13 **Ostashkov**, Russian Federation
151 P 3 **Oster**, Ukraine
136 J 12 **Osterburg**, Germany
135 F 16 **Östersund**, Sweden
136 C 10 **Ostfriesische Inseln**, Germany 🏝
135 I 19 **Östhammar**, Sweden
140 F 8 **Ostiglia**, Italy
143 H 18 **Ostrava**, Czech Republic
142 J 9 **Ostróda**, Poland
150 L 4 **Ostroh**, Ukraine
142 L 11 **Ostrołęka**, Poland
154 D 13 **Ostrov**, Russian Federation
153 Q 5 **Ostrov**, Russian Federation 🏝
153 N 6 **Ostrov Arkticheskogo Instituta**, Russian Federation 🏝
153 X 6 **Ostrov Ayon**, Russian Federation 🏝
153 T 6 **Ostrov Bel'kovskiy**, Russian Federation 🏝
152 M 6 **Ostrov Belyy**, Russian Federation 🏝
153 U 5 **Ostrov Bennetta**, Russian Federation 🏝
153 Z 10 **Ostrov Beringa**, Russian Federation 🏝
153 U 6 **Ostrov Bol'shaya Lyakhovskiy**, Russian Federation 🏝
153 R 7 **Ostrov Bol'shoy Begichev**, Russian Federation 🏝
171 Z 8 **Ostrov Bulla**, Azerbaijan 🏝
155 R 1 **Ostrov Dolgiy**, Russian Federation 🏝
153 N 4 **Ostrov Dzheksona**, Russian Federation 🏝
154 D 10 **Ostrov Gogland**, Russian Federation 🏝
153 O 3 **Ostrov Greem-Bell**, Russian Federation 🏝
153 O 5 **Ostrov Isachenko**, Russian Federation 🏝
153 Y 14 **Ostrov Iturup**, Russian Federation 🏝
153 Z 9 **Ostrov Karaginskiy**, Russian Federation 🏝
154 I 1 **Ostrov Kil'din**, Russian Federation 🏝
155 O 2 **Ostrov Kolguyev**, Russian Federation 🏝
153 P 4 **Ostrov Komsomolets**, Russian Federation 🏝
153 T 6 **Ostrov Kotel'nyy**, Russian Federation 🏝
178 G 8 **Ostrov Kulaly**, Kazakhstan 🏝
153 Y 14 **Ostrov Kunashir**, Russian Federation 🏝
153 U 6 **Ostrov Malyy Lyakhovskiy**, Russian Federation 🏝
153 R 5 **Ostrov Malyy Taymyr**, Russian Federation 🏝
153 Z 10 **Ostrov Mednyy**, Russian Federation 🏝

152 K 6 **Ostrov Mezhdusharskiy**, Russian Federation 🏝
154 L 4 **Ostrov Morzhovets**, Russian Federation 🏝
153 U 6 **Ostrov Novaya Sibir'**, Russian Federation 🏝
178 H 12 **Ostrov Ogurchinskiy**, Turkmenistan 🏝
153 P 5 **Ostrov Oktyabr'skoy Revolyutsii**, Russian Federation 🏝
153 N 7 **Ostrov Oleniy**, Russian Federation 🏝
153 Z 12 **Ostrov Onekotan**, Russian Federation 🏝
153 Z 12 **Ostrov Paramushir**, Russian Federation 🏝
153 P 4 **Ostrov Pioner**, Russian Federation 🏝
153 N 3 **Ostrov Rudol'fa**, Russian Federation 🏝
153 Z 13 **Ostrov Shiashkotan**, Russian Federation 🏝
153 P 4 **Ostrov Shmidta**, Russian Federation 🏝
153 N 7 **Ostrov Sibiryakova**, Russian Federation 🏝
153 Z 13 **Ostrov Simushir**, Russian Federation 🏝
153 T 6 **Ostrov Stolbovoy**, Russian Federation 🏝
153 Y 14 **Ostrov Urup**, Russian Federation 🏝
153 O 4 **Ostrov Ushakova**, Russian Federation 🏝
153 O 5 **Ostrov Uyedineniya**, Russian Federation 🏝
155 R 1 **Ostrov Vaygach**, Russian Federation 🏝
153 N 6 **Ostrov Vil'kitskogo**, Russian Federation 🏝
153 O 4 **Ostrov Vise**, Russian Federation 🏝
178 L 9 **Ostrov Vozrozhdeniya**, Uzbekistan 🏝
153 V 5 **Ostrov Zhokhova**, Russian Federation 🏝
153 U 5 **Ostrova De-Longa**, Russian Federation 🏝
153 O 6 **Ostrova Izvestiy Ts. I. K.**, Russian Federation 🏝
153 W 6 **Ostrova Medvezh'i**, Russian Federation 🏝
178 H 8 **Ostrova Tyulen'i**, Kazakhstan 🏝
154 L 13 **Ostrovskoye**, Russian Federation
142 M 11 **Ostrów Mazowiecki**, Poland
143 H 14 **Ostrów Wielkopolski**, Poland
143 L 15 **Ostrowiec Świętokrzyski**, Poland
143 H 14 **Ostrzeszów**, Poland
136 M 8 **Ostseebad Göhren**, Germany
139 O 8 **Osttirol**, Austria ▣
141 O 16 **Ostuni**, Italy
146 I 8 **Osŭm**, Bulgaria ∿
199 C 24 **Ōsumi-hantō**, Japan ▶
199 C 24 **Ōsumi-kaikyō**, Japan ≈
199 B 25 **Ōsumi-shotō**, Japan 🏝
215 P 13 **Osun**, Nigeria ▣
130 M 12 **Osuna**, Spain
58 G 7 **Oswego**, New York, U.S.A.
127 P 6 **Oswestry**, United Kingdom
151 W 9 **Osypenko**, Ukraine
233 E 22 **Otago**, New Zealand ▣
233 F 24 **Otago Peninsula**, New Zealand ▶
232 J 6 **Otaika**, New Zealand
233 K 15 **Otaki**, New Zealand
179 U 9 **Otar**, Kazakhstan
198 J 5 **Otaru**, Japan
106 B 8 **Otavalo**, Ecuador
218 I 8 **Otavi**, Namibia
199 K 14 **Ōtawara**, Japan
233 E 22 **Otematata**, New Zealand
148 H 8 **Otepää**, Estonia
76 J 8 **Othello**, Washington, U.S.A.
147 A 15 **Othonoi**, Greece 🏝
233 G 19 **Otira**, New Zealand
218 I 8 **Otjiwarongo**, Namibia
218 J 8 **Otjozondjupa**, Namibia ▣

127 S 2 **Otley**, United Kingdom
185 R 7 **Otog Qi**, China
198 J 3 **Otoineppu**, Japan
232 K 11 **Otorohanga**, New Zealand
233 E 20 **Otorokua Point**, New Zealand ▶
135 B 20 **Otra**, Norway ∿
141 O 17 **Otranto**, Italy
159 O 6 **Otranto Valley**, Mediterranean Sea ◇
153 Y 7 **Otrozhnyy**, Russian Federation
65 J 15 **Otsego**, Michigan, U.S.A.
199 G 18 **Ōtsu**, Japan
135 D 17 **Otta**, Norway
65 F 17 **Ottawa**, Illinois, U.S.A.
69 Q 4 **Ottawa**, Kansas, U.S.A.
86 I 10 **Ottawa**, Ontario, Canada 🏛
86 H 9 **Ottawa**, Québec, Canada ∿
81 S 9 **Ottawa Islands**, Nunavut, Canada 🏝
135 G 25 **Ottenby**, Sweden
139 V 3 **Ottenschlag**, Austria
136 F 10 **Otterndorf**, Germany
140 D 8 **Ottone**, Italy
67 U 14 **Ottumwa**, Iowa, U.S.A.
215 R 13 **Otukpa**, Nigeria
215 R 13 **Otukpo**, Nigeria
110 K 8 **Otumpa**, Argentina
142 L 13 **Otwock**, Poland
138 K 8 **Ötztaler Alpen**, Austria ⛰
198 K 10 **Ōu-sanmyaku**, Japan ⛰
69 U 13 **Ouachita**, Arkansas, U.S.A. ∿
69 S 11 **Ouachita Mountains**, Arkansas, U.S.A. ⛰
214 G 5 **Ouadâne**, Mauritania
216 L 3 **Ouadda**, Central African Republic
215 Y 9 **Ouaddaï**, Chad ▣
216 K 4 **Ouaka**, Central African Republic ▣
214 J 7 **Oualâta**, Mauritania
215 O 9 **Ouallam**, Niger
105 Z 7 **Ouanary**, French Guiana
217 O 4 **Ouanda**, Central African Republic
216 J 3 **Ouandago**, Central African Republic
216 M 2 **Ouandja**, Central African Republic
216 L 5 **Ouango**, Central African Republic
214 K 11 **Ouangolodougou**, Côte d'Ivoire
211 O 8 **Ouargla**, Algeria
133 F 14 **Oude-Tonge**, Netherlands
133 D 19 **Oudenaarde**, Belgium
218 L 15 **Oudtshoorn**, Republic of South Africa
210 H 7 **Oued Zem**, Morocco
216 H 7 **Ouésso**, Congo
215 T 13 **Ouest**, Cameroon ▣
216 I 3 **Ouham**, Central African Republic ▣
216 H 3 **Ouham-Pendé**, Central African Republic ▣
210 K 6 **Oujda**, Morocco
214 G 5 **Oujeft**, Mauritania
210 G 9 **Oulad Teïma**, Morocco
214 G 8 **Ould Yenjé**, Mauritania
211 N 7 **Ouled Djellal**, Algeria
134 L 13 **Oulu**, Finland
135 M 14 **Oulujärvi**, Finland 💧
134 L 13 **Oulujoki**, Finland ∿
215 Y 8 **Oum-Chalouba**, Chad
211 O 6 **Oum el Bouaghi**, Algeria
215 Y 9 **Oum-Hadjer**, Chad
210 F 8 **Ounara**, Morocco
134 K 10 **Ounasjoki**, Finland ∿
127 U 7 **Oundle**, United Kingdom
215 X 6 **Ounianga Kébir**, Chad
215 Y 6 **Ounianga Sérir**, Chad
186 J 4 **Oupu**, China
135 C 18 **Øure Ardel**, Norway
130 I 3 **Ourense**, Spain
108 N 13 **Ouricuri**, Brazil
109 J 19 **Ourinhos**, Brazil
133 J 22 **Ourthe**, Belgium ∿
127 T 2 **Ouse**, United Kingdom ∿

125 D 10 **Outer Hebrides**, United Kingdom 🏝
64 E 8 **Outer Island**, Wisconsin, U.S.A. 🏝
64 I 10 **Outer Island**, Michigan, U.S.A. 🏝
218 I 8 **Outjo**, Namibia
233 E 24 **Outram**, New Zealand
235 Q 13 **Ouvéa**, New Caledonia 🏝
231 R 12 **Ouyen**, Victoria, Australia
170 I 14 **Ovacik**, Turkey
235 X 11 **Ovalau**, Fiji 🏝
110 F 10 **Ovalle**, Chile
218 G 7 **Ovamboland**, Namibia ◇
216 F 7 **Ovan**, Gabon
130 H 5 **Ovar**, Portugal
215 U 15 **Oveng**, Cameroon
133 G 19 **Overijse**, Belgium
132 M 11 **Overijssel**, Netherlands ▣
134 K 11 **Överkalix**, Sweden
69 R 4 **Overland Park**, Kansas, U.S.A.
230 F 8 **Overlander Roadhouse**, Western Australia, Australia
133 J 17 **Overpelt**, Belgium
77 N 21 **Overton**, Nevada, U.S.A.
151 N 13 **Ovidiu**, Romania
130 L 1 **Oviedo**, Spain
93 Q 8 **Oviedo**, Dominican Republic
148 C 9 **Ovišrags**, Latvia ▶
185 P 4 **Övörhangay**, Mongolia ▣
134 J 9 **Övre Soppero**, Sweden
151 O 2 **Ovruch**, Ukraine
233 E 25 **Owaka**, New Zealand
216 H 8 **Owando**, Congo
199 H 19 **Owase**, Japan
67 S 9 **Owatonna**, Minnesota, U.S.A.
233 C 26 **Owen Head**, New Zealand ▶
191 F 21 **Owen Island**, Myanmar 🏝
233 H 17 **Owen River**, New Zealand
86 D 11 **Owen Sound**, Ontario, Canada
234 E 6 **Owen Stanley Range**, Papua New Guinea ⛰
77 K 21 **Owens Lake**, California, U.S.A. 💧
60 E 5 **Owensboro**, Kentucky, U.S.A.
215 R 14 **Owerri**, Nigeria
215 Q 13 **Owo**, Nigeria
65 L 14 **Owosso**, Michigan, U.S.A.
76 K 13 **Owyhee**, Oregon, U.S.A. ∿
77 M 14 **Owyhee**, Nevada, U.S.A.
83 O 19 **Oxbow**, Saskatchewan, Canada
135 H 21 **Oxelösund**, Sweden
233 G 20 **Oxford**, New Zealand
127 S 10 **Oxford**, United Kingdom
58 H 9 **Oxford**, New York, U.S.A.
61 S 8 **Oxford**, North Carolina, U.S.A.
62 M 2 **Oxford**, Mississippi, U.S.A.
65 L 14 **Oxford**, Michigan, U.S.A.
77 I 24 **Oxnard**, California, U.S.A.
127 W 11 **Oxted**, United Kingdom
179 U 12 **Oy Tal**, Kyrgyzstan
199 H 15 **Oyabe**, Japan
199 K 15 **Oyama**, Japan
216 E 7 **Oyem**, Gabon
83 K 19 **Oyen**, Alberta, Canada
135 D 20 **Øyeren**, Norway 💧
215 P 12 **Oyo**, Nigeria ▣
216 H 8 **Oyo**, Congo
215 P 12 **Oyo**, Nigeria
107 C 15 **Oyón**, Peru
190 A 13 **Oyster Island**, Myanmar 🏝
171 T 11 **Özalp**, Turkey
197 K 21 **Ozamiz**, Philippines
69 T 10 **Ozark**, Arkansas, U.S.A.
69 T 7 **Ozark**, Missouri, U.S.A.
69 S 8 **Ozark Plateau**, Missouri, U.S.A. ◇
41 Q 10 **Ozbourn Seamount**, Pacific Ocean ▲
143 K 21 **Ózd**, Hungary

153 Z 12 **Ozernovskiy**, Russian Federation
156 H 1 **Ozernyy**, Russian Federation
179 Q 9 **Ozero Akzhaykyn**, Kazakhstan 💧
179 X 7 **Ozero Alakol'**, Kazakhstan 💧
178 G 5 **Ozero Aralsor**, Kazakhstan 💧
179 Q 12 **Ozero Aydarkul'**, Uzbekistan 💧
154 I 10 **Ozero Beloye**, Russian Federation 💧
154 F 12 **Ozero Il'men'**, Russian Federation 💧
154 H 3 **Ozero Imandra**, Russian Federation 💧
178 I 6 **Ozero Inder**, Kazakhstan 💧
178 I 5 **Ozero Itmurinkol'**, Kazakhstan 💧
179 R 8 **Ozero Karakoyyn**, Kazakhstan 💧
179 U 5 **Ozero Karasor**, Kazakhstan 💧
154 H 4 **Ozero Kovdozero**, Russian Federation 💧
154 J 8 **Ozero Kozhozero**, Russian Federation 💧
154 K 11 **Ozero Kubenskoye**, Russian Federation 💧
179 P 3 **Ozero Kusmurun**, Kazakhstan 💧
154 J 9 **Ozero Lacha**, Russian Federation 💧
154 G 7 **Ozero Leksozero**, Russian Federation 💧
154 I 3 **Ozero Lovozero**, Russian Federation 💧
157 O 10 **Ozero Manych-Gudilo**, Russian Federation 💧
179 Z 5 **Ozero Markakol'**, Kazakhstan 💧
154 G 4 **Ozero Pyaozero**, Russian Federation 💧
179 X 7 **Ozero Sasykkol**, Kazakhstan 💧
154 H 7 **Ozero Segozerskoye**, Russian Federation 💧
153 Y 14 **Ozero Shikotan**, Russian Federation 🏝
179 S 2 **Ozero Siletiteniz**, Kazakhstan 💧
179 P 8 **Ozero Solonchak**, Kazakhstan 💧
153 Q 6 **Ozero Taymyr**, Russian Federation 💧
179 S 2 **Ozero Teke**, Kazakhstan 💧
179 Q 5 **Ozero Tengiz**, Kazakhstan 💧
154 G 5 **Ozero Topozero**, Russian Federation 💧
179 S 2 **Ozero Ul'ken Karoy**, Kazakhstan 💧
154 I 3 **Ozero Umbozero**, Russian Federation 💧
154 J 8 **Ozero Vodlozero**, Russian Federation 💧
154 J 10 **Ozero Vozhe**, Russian Federation 💧
154 I 7 **Ozero Vygozero**, Russian Federation 💧
151 N 11 **Ozero Yalpuh**, Ukraine 💧
179 Y 6 **Ozero Zaysan**, Kazakhstan 💧
149 C 16 **Ozersk**, Russian Federation
156 L 2 **Ozery**, Russian Federation
179 T 12 **Özgön**, Kyrgyzstan
141 C 16 **Ozieri**, Italy
143 H 16 **Ozimek**, Poland
157 S 5 **Ozinki**, Russian Federation
70 K 9 **Ozona**, Texas, U.S.A.
142 J 13 **Ozorków**, Poland
199 D 21 **Ōzu**, Japan
89 S 10 **Ozuluama**, Mexico
171 R 7 **Ozurget'i**, Georgia

P

191 F 16 **Pa-an**, Myanmar
235 R 11 **Paama**, Vanuatu 🏝
44 M 13 **Paamiut**, Greenland
218 J 15 **Paarl**, Republic of South Africa
143 J 14 **Pabianice**, Poland

Country ▣ Internal administrative region: State/Province/Territory/Dependent territory 🏛 Capital city ⛰ Mountain range/Undersea ridge ▲ Mountain peak/Volcano/Seamount ◇ Geographic feature ▶ Headland/Point/Cape/Peninsula ◠ Desert 🏝 Island/Island group ⁙ Antarctic base 🌊 Ocean ≋ Sea ≈ Bay/Gulf/Channel/Strait 💧 Lake ⊡ Salt pan/Dry/Intermittent lake ∿ River

Pabna – Patten

183 T 13 **Pabna**, Bangladesh
149 G 15 **Pabradė**, Lithuania
106 B 13 **Pacasmayo**, Peru
147 K 24 **Pachia**, Greece
141 K 24 **Pachino**, Italy
107 E 14 **Pachitea**, Peru
147 H 26 **Páchnes**, Greece
89 R 11 **Pachuca**, Mexico
41 R 7 **Pacific Ocean**
197 K 17 **Pacijan**, Philippines
231 R 10 **Packsaddle**, New South Wales, Australia
76 H 8 **Packwood**, Washington, U.S.A.
91 X 13 **Pacora**, Panama
192 D 11 **Padang**, Indonesia
192 D 10 **Padangsidimpuan**, Indonesia
192 I 11 **Padangtikar**, Indonesia
154 H 7 **Padany**, Russian Federation
195 U 6 **Padas**, Malaysia
107 K 23 **Padcaya**, Bolivia
137 F 15 **Paderborn**, Germany
107 K 21 **Padilla**, Bolivia
150 L 12 **Padina**, Romania
140 G 7 **Padova**, Italy
71 Q 14 **Padre Island**, Texas, U.S.A.
141 D 16 **Padru**, Italy
126 K 14 **Padstow**, United Kingdom
60 C 6 **Paducah**, Kentucky, U.S.A.
70 M 4 **Paducah**, Texas, U.S.A.
182 J 4 **Padum**, India
187 L 14 **Paektu-san**, China/North Korea
187 J 19 **Paengnyŏng-do**, South Korea
232 L 9 **Paeroa**, New Zealand
170 G 15 **Pafos**, Cyprus
219 P 9 **Pafuri**, Mozambique
158 M 4 **Pag**, Mediterranean Sea
108 H 11 **Paga-Conta**, Brazil
197 J 21 **Pagadian**, Philippines
192 D 12 **Pagai Selatan**, Indonesia
192 D 12 **Pagai Utara**, Indonesia
236 B 6 **Pagan**, Northern Mariana Islands
147 F 17 **Pagasitikos Kolpos**, Greece
192 L 12 **Pagatan**, Indonesia
146 L 13 **Pağayiğit**, Turkey
74 K 8 **Page**, Arizona, U.S.A.
149 C 14 **Pagėgiai**, Lithuania
61 P 11 **Pageland**, South Carolina, U.S.A.
236 K 8 **Pago Pago**, American Samoa
75 P 7 **Pagosa Springs**, Colorado, U.S.A.
184 K 11 **Pagri**, China
194 D 8 **Pahang**, Malaysia
194 D 8 **Pahang**, Malaysia
233 L 15 **Pahiatua**, New Zealand
181 N 21 **Pahlagaon**, India
191 F 14 **Pai**, Thailand
148 G 7 **Paide**, Estonia
127 N 14 **Paignton**, United Kingdom
232 J 5 **Paihia**, New Zealand
135 M 17 **Päijänne**, Finland
191 J 20 **Pailin**, Cambodia
111 F 16 **Paillaco**, Chile
128 J 4 **Paimpol**, France
192 D 11 **Painan**, Indonesia
65 O 16 **Painesville**, Ohio, U.S.A.
74 K 9 **Painted Desert**, Arizona, U.S.A.
60 L 5 **Paintsville**, Kentucky, U.S.A.
131 Q 2 **País Vasco**, Spain
76 I 13 **Paisley**, Oregon, U.S.A.
106 A 12 **Paita**, Peru
134 K 10 **Pajala**, Sweden
191 I 18 **Pak Thong Chai**, Thailand
105 Q 7 **Pakaraima Mountains**, Brazil/Venezuela
86 E 10 **Pakesley**, Ontario, Canada
215 R 10 **Paki**, Nigeria
177 U 12 **Pakistan**, Asia
190 C 12 **Pakokku**, Myanmar
143 I 25 **Paks**, Hungary
177 U 8 **Paktīā**, Afghanistan
177 U 9 **Paktīkā**, Afghanistan
191 L 18 **Pakxé**, Laos
215 V 11 **Pala**, Chad
107 K 17 **Palacios**, Bolivia
71 S 12 **Palacios**, Texas, U.S.A.
131 Y 4 **Palafrugell**, Spain
170 H 15 **Palaichóri**, Cyprus
147 G 26 **Palaiochora**, Greece
147 B 18 **Palairos**, Greece
182 I 5 **Palam Pur**, India
147 D 16 **Palamas**, Greece
131 Y 4 **Palamós**, Spain
153 Y 9 **Palana**, Russian Federation
196 I 7 **Palanan**, Philippines
196 I 7 **Palanan Point**, Philippines
148 B 13 **Palanga**, Lithuania
192 K 12 **Palangkaraya**, Indonesia
181 B 14 **Palanpur**, India
219 N 9 **Palapye**, Botswana
177 X 6 **Palas**, Pakistan
153 X 10 **Palatka**, Russian Federation
63 W 8 **Palatka**, Florida, U.S.A.
236 I 15 **Palau**, Oceania
141 C 15 **Palau**, Italy
236 I 15 **Palau Islands**, Palau
40 K 7 **Palau Trench**, Pacific Ocean
196 H 5 **Palaui**, Philippines
191 F 19 **Palauk**, Myanmar
191 F 20 **Palaw**, Myanmar
197 D 19 **Palawan**, Philippines
197 B 19 **Palawan Passage**, Philippines
40 I 7 **Palawan Trough**, Pacific Ocean
148 F 6 **Paldiski**, Estonia
193 O 10 **Paleleh**, Indonesia
192 G 12 **Palembang**, Indonesia
77 M 25 **Palen Dry Lake**, California, U.S.A.
111 F 18 **Palena**, Chile
131 N 3 **Palencia**, Spain
141 I 21 **Palermo**, Italy
172 F 10 **Palestine**, Israel
71 S 7 **Palestine**, Texas, U.S.A.
190 B 12 **Paletwa**, Myanmar
181 D 22 **Palghat**, India
218 G 8 **Palgrave Point**, Namibia
180 C 13 **Pali**, India
237 P 15 **Palikir**, Federated States of Micronesia
197 K 23 **Palimbang**, Philippines
133 I 24 **Paliseul**, Belgium
181 B 15 **Palitana**, India
181 F 23 **Palk Strait**, Sri Lanka
181 I 17 **Palkonda**, India
157 Q 7 **Pallasovka**, Russian Federation
181 G 21 **Pallavaram**, India
217 T 7 **Pallisa**, Uganda
73 Q 11 **Pallisades Reservoir**, Idaho, U.S.A.
233 K 16 **Palliser Bay**, New Zealand
182 G 8 **Pallu**, India
77 L 25 **Palm Springs**, California, U.S.A.
131 Y 8 **Palma**, Spain
130 M 11 **Palma del Río**, Spain
92 M 6 **Palma Soriano**, Cuba
91 R 13 **Palmar**, Costa Rica
112 I 12 **Palmares do Sul**, Brazil
108 K 13 **Palmas**, Brazil
112 H 9 **Palmas**, Brazil
77 J 24 **Palmdale**, California, U.S.A.
112 G 10 **Palmeira das Missões**, Brazil
108 L 12 **Palmeiras**, Brazil
112 I 8 **Palmeiras**, Brazil
240 H 4 **Palmer**, Antarctica
79 Q 9 **Palmer**, Alaska, U.S.A.
240 I 5 **Palmer Land**, Antarctica
230 L 1 **Palmerston**, Northern Territory, Australia
233 F 24 **Palmerston**, New Zealand
237 N 10 **Palmerston**, Cook Islands
233 L 15 **Palmerston North**, New Zealand
141 L 21 **Palmi**, Italy
104 H 7 **Palmira**, Colombia
172 K 5 **Palmyra**, Syria
41 Q 7 **Palmyra Atoll**, U.S.A.
77 F 20 **Palo Alto**, California, U.S.A.
104 G 4 **Palo de las Letras**, Colombia
91 Z 15 **Palo de las Letras**, Panama
110 M 7 **Palo Santo**, Argentina
195 O 9 **Paloh**, Malaysia
213 F 19 **Paloich**, Sudan
134 K 9 **Palojoensuu**, Finland
107 H 18 **Palomani**, Peru
89 U 13 **Palomares**, Mexico
193 O 12 **Palopo**, Indonesia
107 E 18 **Palpa**, Peru
171 P 11 **Palu**, Turkey
193 N 11 **Palu**, Indonesia
193 O 15 **Palu**, Indonesia
196 F 13 **Paluan**, Philippines
192 H 14 **Pamanukan**, Indonesia
193 X 12 **Pamdai**, Indonesia
181 H 15 **Pamgarh**, India
139 Z 5 **Pamhagen**, Austria
129 P 15 **Pamiers**, France
179 U 14 **Pamir**, Tajikistan
61 V 10 **Pamlico Sound**, North Carolina, U.S.A.
70 L 2 **Pampa**, Texas, U.S.A.
110 K 7 **Pampa de los Guanacos**, Argentina
107 K 20 **Pampa Grande**, Bolivia
110 I 13 **Pampas**, Argentina
104 J 5 **Pamplona**, Colombia
131 R 2 **Pamplona**, Spain
182 I 3 **Pampur**, India
170 E 8 **Pamukova**, Turkey
216 F 9 **Pana**, Gabon
65 F 20 **Pana**, Illinois, U.S.A.
89 Z 10 **Panabá**, Mexico
197 H 21 **Panabutan Bay**, Philippines
77 N 20 **Panaca**, Nevada, U.S.A.
197 D 18 **Panagtaran Point**, Philippines
146 H 9 **Panagyurishte**, Bulgaria
192 G 14 **Panaitan**, Indonesia
181 C 19 **Panaji**, India
91 V 14 **Panama**, North America
41 Y 7 **Panama Basin**, Pacific Ocean
91 W 13 **Panama Canal**, Panama
63 R 8 **Panama City**, Florida, U.S.A.
91 X 14 **Panama City**, Panama
197 L 18 **Panaon**, Philippines
197 I 16 **Panay**, Philippines
197 I 18 **Panay Gulf**, Philippines
144 L 10 **Pančevo**, Serbia and Montenegro
150 F 9 **Pâncota**, Romania
219 R 10 **Panda**, Mozambique
196 K 12 **Pandan**, Philippines
197 I 15 **Pandan**, Philippines
197 B 20 **Pandanan**, Philippines
192 L 11 **Pandang**, Indonesia
192 G 14 **Pandeglang**, Indonesia
148 G 13 **Pandėlys**, Lithuania
181 D 18 **Pandharpur**, India
230 F 6 **Pannawonica**, Western Australia, Australia
181 F 15 **Pandhurna**, India
107 I 16 **Pando**, Bolivia
91 S 12 **Pandora**, Costa Rica
216 J 5 **Pandu**, Democratic Republic of Congo
183 V 11 **Pandu**, India
148 F 13 **Panevėžys**, Lithuania
191 G 15 **Pang**, Thailand
217 O 6 **Panga**, Democratic Republic of Congo
236 I 10 **Pangai**, Tonga
217 W 11 **Pangani**, Tanzania
197 I 21 **Panganuran**, Philippines
217 O 9 **Pangi**, Democratic Republic of Congo
192 C 9 **Pangkalanbrandan**, Indonesia
192 J 12 **Pangkalanbuun**, Indonesia
192 G 12 **Pangkalpinang**, Indonesia
194 A 7 **Pangkor**, Malaysia
197 K 19 **Panglao**, Philippines
85 S 2 **Pangnirtung**, Nunavut, Canada
216 L 3 **Pangonda**, Central African Republic
186 I 4 **Pangu**, China
111 F 16 **Panguipulli**, Chile
74 J 6 **Panguitch**, Utah, U.S.A.
234 J 5 **Panguna**, Papua New Guinea
197 F 23 **Pangutaran**, Philippines
197 F 23 **Pangutaran Group**, Philippines
70 K 2 **Panhandle**, Texas, U.S.A.
217 P 12 **Pania-Mwanga**, Democratic Republic of Congo
182 I 7 **Panipat**, India
179 R 14 **Panj**, Tajikistan
177 T 7 **Panjāb**, Afghanistan
179 Q 13 **Panjakent**, Tajikistan
177 R 13 **Panjgur**, Pakistan
187 H 15 **Panjin**, China
215 S 11 **Pankshin**, Nigeria
182 L 12 **Panna**, India
112 H 5 **Panorama**, Brazil
187 K 14 **Panshi**, China
194 A 7 **Pantai Remis**, Malaysia
109 G 17 **Pantanal**, Brazil
193 Q 15 **Pantar**, Indonesia
141 G 24 **Pantelleria**, Italy
193 Q 15 **Pantemakassar**, East Timor
190 C 9 **Pantha**, Myanmar
192 D 10 **Panti**, Indonesia
89 S 10 **Pánuco**, Mexico
89 R 10 **Pánuco**, Mexico
189 N 10 **Panxian**, China
188 L 9 **Panzhihua**, China
216 J 12 **Panzi**, Democratic Republic of Congo
90 I 5 **Panzos**, Guatemala
141 M 19 **Paola**, Italy
65 I 21 **Paoli**, Indiana, U.S.A.
143 G 23 **Pápa**, Hungary
124 I 6 **Papa Westray**, United Kingdom
109 F 14 **Papagaio**, Brazil
232 L 12 **Papakai**, New Zealand
232 J 7 **Paparoa**, New Zealand
136 D 11 **Papenburg**, Germany
67 P 14 **Papillion**, Nebraska, U.S.A.
148 G 13 **Papilys**, Lithuania
110 F 6 **Paposo**, Chile
181 H 17 **Pappadahandi**, India
234 H 5 **Papua New Guinea**, Oceania
191 E 15 **Papun**, Myanmar
91 P 12 **Paquera**, Costa Rica
108 I 11 **Pará**, Brazil
230 G 7 **Paraburdoo**, Western Australia, Australia
177 V 8 **Parachinar**, Pakistan
144 M 12 **Paraćin**, Serbia and Montenegro
108 N 11 **Paracuru**, Brazil
86 I 7 **Paradis**, Québec, Canada
181 J 16 **Paradwip**, India
108 K 10 **Paragominas**, Brazil
69 Y 9 **Paragould**, Arkansas, U.S.A.
107 M 18 **Paragua**, Bolivia
109 F 19 **Paraguay**, South America
109 G 19 **Paraguay**, Paraguay
108 O 13 **Paraíba**, Brazil
112 N 6 **Paraíba do Sul**, Brazil
135 K 19 **Parainen**, Finland
89 V 12 **Paraíso**, Mexico
89 W 12 **Paraíso**, Mexico
215 O 11 **Parakou**, Benin
105 X 6 **Paramaribo**, Suriname
147 B 16 **Paramythia**, Greece
110 L 10 **Paraná**, Argentina/Brazil
112 C 13 **Paraná**, Argentina
112 H 8 **Paraná**, Brazil
109 K 14 **Paranã**, Brazil
112 J 9 **Paranaguá**, Brazil
112 H 4 **Paranaíba**, Brazil
112 I 4 **Paranaíba**, Brazil
109 I 18 **Paranapanema**, Brazil
112 G 7 **Paranavaí**, Brazil
197 K 22 **Parang**, Philippines
109 L 17 **Paraopeba**, Brazil
173 T 4 **Pārāpāra**, Iraq
112 M 7 **Parati**, Brazil
108 I 12 **Parauapebas**, Brazil
181 E 17 **Parbhani**, India
136 J 10 **Parchim**, Germany
143 N 14 **Parczew**, Poland
230 G 5 **Pardoo Roadhouse**, Western Australia, Australia
143 E 17 **Pardubice**, Czech Republic
176 F 2 **Pareh**, Iran
232 H 4 **Parengarenga Harbour**, New Zealand
86 K 7 **Parent**, Québec, Canada
233 F 22 **Pareora**, New Zealand
193 N 12 **Parepare**, Indonesia
147 B 17 **Parga**, Greece
193 O 11 **Parigi**, Indonesia
108 G 10 **Parintins**, Brazil
129 Q 4 **Paris**, France
60 J 5 **Paris**, Kentucky, U.S.A.
60 D 8 **Paris**, Tennessee, U.S.A.
65 H 19 **Paris**, Illinois, U.S.A.
71 S 4 **Paris**, Texas, U.S.A.
73 Q 13 **Paris**, Idaho, U.S.A.
176 L 10 **Pārīz**, Iran
64 E 9 **Park Falls**, Wisconsin, U.S.A.
67 Q 5 **Park Rapids**, Minnesota, U.S.A.
135 K 17 **Parkano**, Finland
74 G 11 **Parker**, Arizona, U.S.A.
61 N 3 **Parkersburg**, West Virginia, U.S.A.
231 T 11 **Parkes**, New South Wales, Australia
67 N 11 **Parkston**, South Dakota, U.S.A.
181 I 17 **Parlakimidi**, India
181 D 17 **Parli**, India
140 D 8 **Parma**, Italy
65 N 16 **Parma**, Ohio, U.S.A.
108 M 11 **Parnaíba**, Brazil
108 K 13 **Parnaíba**, Brazil
147 E 18 **Parnassos**, Greece
139 Z 4 **Parndorf**, Austria
147 E 22 **Parnon**, Greece
148 F 8 **Pärnu**, Estonia
148 F 7 **Pärnu-Jaagupi**, Estonia
148 F 8 **Pärnu laht**, Estonia
183 T 9 **Paro**, Bhutan
147 J 22 **Paros**, Greece
147 J 22 **Paros**, Greece
74 I 6 **Parowan**, Utah, U.S.A.
61 W 5 **Parramore Island**, Virginia, U.S.A.
89 P 7 **Parras**, Mexico
91 Q 13 **Parrita**, Costa Rica
87 U 10 **Parrsboro**, Nova Scotia, Canada
85 O 1 **Parry Bay**, Nunavut, Canada
81 N 4 **Parry Channel**, Nunavut, Canada
80 M 3 **Parry Islands**, Nunavut, Canada
86 E 10 **Parry Sound**, Ontario, Canada
142 F 9 **Parsęta**, Poland
60 D 9 **Parsons**, Tennessee, U.S.A.
69 Q 7 **Parsons**, Kansas, U.S.A.
138 J 8 **Partenen**, Austria
128 M 8 **Parthenay**, France
143 I 20 **Partizánske**, Slovakia
127 W 4 **Partney**, United Kingdom
108 H 9 **Paru**, Brazil
108 G 10 **Paru de Oeste**, Brazil
180 D 12 **Parvatsar**, India
177 U 7 **Parwān**, Afghanistan
149 L 19 **Parychy**, Belarus
71 T 10 **Pasadena**, Texas, U.S.A.
77 J 24 **Pasadena**, California, U.S.A.
170 B 8 **Paşalimani**, Turkey
192 D 12 **Pasapuat**, Indonesia
90 K 7 **Pasaquina**, El Salvador
63 N 7 **Pascagoula**, Mississippi, U.S.A.
150 L 8 **Paşcani**, Romania
107 D 15 **Pasco**, Peru
76 J 9 **Pasco**, Washington, U.S.A.
196 J 13 **Pascual**, Philippines
136 N 10 **Pasewalk**, Germany
83 L 14 **Pasfield Lake**, Saskatchewan, Canada
196 G 11 **Pasig**, Philippines
183 Y 8 **Pasighat**, India
171 Q 9 **Pasinler**, Turkey
90 I 3 **Pasión**, Guatemala
194 C 5 **Pasir Mas**, Malaysia
194 D 5 **Pasir Putih**, Malaysia
177 P 12 **Paskūh**, Iran
142 J 9 **Pasłęk**, Poland
142 J 8 **Pasłęka**, Poland
177 Q 14 **Pasni**, Pakistan
90 H 2 **Paso Caballos**, Guatemala
111 H 18 **Paso de Indios**, Argentina
112 E 12 **Paso de los Libres**, Argentina
113 E 14 **Paso de los Toros**, Uruguay
91 R 13 **Paso Real**, Costa Rica
111 H 19 **Paso Río Mayo**, Argentina
77 H 22 **Paso Robles**, California, U.S.A.
82 F 5 **Passage Point**, Northwest Territories, Canada
139 W 6 **Passail**, Austria
137 M 23 **Passau**, Germany
139 R 3 **Passau**, Austria
197 I 16 **Passi**, Philippines
112 H 10 **Passo Fundo**, Brazil
112 K 5 **Passos**, Brazil
149 I 15 **Pastavy**, Belarus
106 C 9 **Pastaza**, Ecuador
104 G 9 **Pasto**, Colombia
177 Y 5 **Pasu**, Pakistan
192 K 14 **Pasuruan**, Indonesia
148 F 13 **Pasvalys**, Lithuania
216 L 3 **Pata**, Central African Republic
197 G 24 **Pata**, Philippines
111 G 22 **Patagonia**, Argentina
181 B 14 **Patan**, India
181 F 14 **Patan**, India
183 Q 9 **Patan**, Nepal
193 S 10 **Patani**, Indonesia
127 Q 10 **Patchway**, United Kingdom
232 J 13 **Patea**, New Zealand
215 Q 12 **Pategi**, Nigeria
127 S 1 **Pateley Bridge**, United Kingdom
139 R 8 **Paternion**, Austria
141 K 22 **Paterno**, Italy
58 J 12 **Paterson**, New Jersey, U.S.A.
182 I 5 **Pathankot**, India
73 W 12 **Pathfinder Reservoir**, Wyoming, U.S.A.
191 G 22 **Pathiu**, Thailand
182 I 7 **Patiala**, India
197 G 24 **Patikul**, Philippines
183 Y 9 **Patkroo Range**, India
147 L 21 **Patmos**, Greece
183 P 11 **Patna**, India
196 I 11 **Patnanongan**, Philippines
171 S 10 **Patnos**, Turkey
65 I 21 **Patoka Lake**, Indiana, U.S.A.
108 O 12 **Patos**, Brazil
109 K 17 **Patos de Minas**, Brazil
110 H 9 **Patquía**, Argentina
0 D 19 **Patra**, Greece
147 C 19 **Patraïkos Kolpos**, Greece
134 A 10 **Patreksfjörður**, Iceland
127 W 3 **Patrington**, United Kingdom
191 I 26 **Pattani**, Thailand
191 H 20 **Pattaya**, Thailand
59 R 3 **Patten**, Maine, U.S.A.

Country · Internal administrative region: State/Province/Territory/Dependent territory · Capital city · Mountain range/Undersea ridge · Mountain peak/Volcano/Seamount · Geographic feature · Headland/Point/Cape/Peninsula · Desert · Island/Island group · Antarctic base · Ocean · Sea · Bay/Gulf/Channel/Strait · Lake · Salt pan/Dry/Intermittent lake · Riv

Page	Grid	Entry
	R 2	**Patton Seamount**, Pacific Ocean ▲
3	U 14	**Patuakhali**, Bangladesh
	P 5	**Patuca**, Honduras ⌇
	P 12	**Pátzcuaro**, Mexico
8	M 14	**Pau**, France
8	C 13	**Pauini**, Brazil
0	C 12	**Pauk**, Myanmar
	E 8	**Paulatuk**, Northwest Territories, Canada
8	O 13	**Paulista**, Brazil
8	N 13	**Paulo Afonso**, Brazil
	N 11	**Pauls Valley**, Oklahoma, U.S.A.
0	C 9	**Paungbyin**, Myanmar
1	D 14	**Paungde**, Myanmar
2	K 7	**Pauri**, India
1	E 20	**Pavagada**, India
6	L 3	**Pavelets**, Russian Federation
0	C 7	**Pavia**, Italy
8	C 11	**Pãvilosta**, Latvia
6	J 8	**Pavlikeni**, Bulgaria
0	J 3	**Pavlivka**, Ukraine
9	U 4	**Pavlodar**, Kazakhstan ◻
9	U 3	**Pavlodar**, Kazakhstan
1	V 6	**Pavlohrad**, Ukraine
7	O 1	**Pavlovo**, Russian Federation
6	M 6	**Pavlovsk**, Russian Federation
6	L 11	**Pavlovskaya**, Russian Federation
0	F 9	**Pavullo nel Frignano**, Italy
4	A 15	**Pawai**, Singapore
	P 8	**Pawhuska**, Oklahoma, U.S.A.
	O 8	**Pawnee**, Oklahoma, U.S.A.
7	H 26	**Paximadia**, Greece ☷
7	A 17	**Paxoi**, Greece ☷
	S 8	**Paxson**, Alaska, U.S.A.
1	E 15	**Payagyi**, Myanmar
2	D 11	**Payakumbuh**, Indonesia
8	C 8	**Payerne**, Switzerland
	J 10	**Payette**, Idaho, U.S.A.
0	G 10	**Paynes Find**, Western Australia, Australia
	Q 7	**Paynesville**, Minnesota, U.S.A.
8	L 6	**Pays de la Loire**, France ◻
2	E 13	**Paysandu**, Uruguay ◻
3	D 14	**Paysandú**, Uruguay
	K 11	**Payson**, Arizona, U.S.A.
	K 3	**Payson**, Utah, U.S.A.
2	G 12	**Payung**, Indonesia
4	K 6	**Paz de Ariporo**, Colombia
	Q 7	**Pazar**, Turkey
0	F 7	**Pazarbaşi Burnu**, Turkey ▶
0	M 12	**Pazarcik**, Turkey
6	H 10	**Pazardzhik**, Bulgaria ◻
6	H 10	**Pazardzhik**, Bulgaria
	H 16	**Peace**, Alberta, Canada ⌇
	H 17	**Peace River**, Alberta, Canada
	H 9	**Peach Springs**, Arizona, U.S.A.
	F 16	**Peanut**, California, U.S.A.
	M 14	**Pearce**, Arizona, U.S.A.
9	R 12	**Pearl**, China ⌇
	L 5	**Pearl**, Mississippi, U.S.A. ⌇
	B 7	**Pearl City**, Hawaii, U.S.A.
	B 7	**Pearl Harbor**, Hawaii, U.S.A. ≈
	U 6	**Pearson**, Georgia, U.S.A.
	N 2	**Peary Channel**, Nunavut, Canada ≈
	R 10	**Peary Land**, Greenland ◇
	N 8	**Peawanuck**, Ontario, Canada
9	T 6	**Pebane**, Mozambique
06	12	**Pebas**, Peru
1	L 23	**Pebble Island**, Falkland Islands ☷
15	K 15	**Peć**, Serbia and Montenegro
	I 8	**Pecan Island**, Louisiana, U.S.A.
35	P 3	**Pechora**, Russian Federation ⌇
155	S 5	**Pechora**, Russian Federation
155	Q 2	**Pechorskaya Guba**, Russian Federation ≈
152	K 6	**Pechorskoye More**, Russian Federation ≋
70	H 8	**Pecos**, Texas, U.S.A.
75	S 12	**Pecos**, New Mexico/Texas, U.S.A. ⌇
133	C 20	**Pecq**, Belgium
143	H 26	**Pécs**, Hungary
91	W 15	**Pedasí**, Panama
93	P 8	**Pedernales**, Dominican Republic
218	F 6	**Pediva**, Angola
109	M 16	**Pedra Azul**, Brazil
43	B 17	**Pedra Badejo**, Cape Verde
109	E 14	**Pedras Negras**, Brazil
91	S 14	**Pedregal**, Panama
112	K 4	**Pedregulho**, Brazil
89	N 7	**Pedriceña**, Mexico
108	K 13	**Pedro Afonso**, Brazil
92	K 9	**Pedro Bank**, Jamaica ≈
110	G 5	**Pedro de Valdivia**, Chile
109	G 18	**Pedro Juan Caballero**, Paraguay
112	G 13	**Pedro Osório**, Brazil
65	M 20	**Peebles**, Ohio, U.S.A.
58	K 11	**Peekskill**, New York, U.S.A.
125	G 16	**Peel**, United Kingdom
82	B 10	**Peel**, Yukon Territory/Northwest Territories, Canada ⌇
136	M 9	**Peene**, Germany ⌇
136	M 8	**Peenemünde**, Germany
233	I 20	**Pegasus Bay**, New Zealand ≈
137	J 20	**Pegnitz**, Germany
191	D 15	**Pegu**, Myanmar ◻
191	E 16	**Pegu**, Myanmar
191	D 14	**Pegu Yoma**, Myanmar ▲▲
192	B 8	**Pegunungan Barisan**, Indonesia ▲▲
195	P 10	**Pegunungan Boven Kapuas**, Malaysia ▲▲
195	R 8	**Pegunungan Dulit**, Malaysia ▲▲
195	R 9	**Pegunungan Hose**, Malaysia ▲▲
195	T 10	**Pegunungan Iran**, Indonesia/Malaysia ▲▲
193	X 12	**Pegunungan Maoke**, Indonesia ▲▲
192	K 11	**Pegunungan Muller**, Indonesia ▲▲
192	J 11	**Pegunungan Schwaner**, Indonesia ▲▲
127	Z 11	**Pegwell Bay**, United Kingdom ▶
113	B 17	**Pehuajó**, Argentina
0	G 20	**Peiraias**, Greece
194	B 14	**Peirce Reservoir**, Singapore ⌇
109	J 14	**Peixe**, Brazil
192	H 10	**Pejantan**, Indonesia ☷
194	E 8	**Pekan**, Malaysia
192	E 10	**Pekanbaru**, Indonesia
194	B 8	**Pelabuhan Kelang**, Malaysia
195	X 5	**Pelabuhan Sandakan**, Malaysia ▶
192	M 10	**Pelawanbesar**, Indonesia
86	B 15	**Pelee Island**, Ontario, Canada ☷
86	B 15	**Pelee Point**, Ontario, Canada ▶
193	P 11	**Peleng**, Indonesia ☷
143	D 18	**Pelhřimov**, Czech Republic
92	K 1	**Pelican Point**, The Bahamas
146	C 13	**Pelister**, Macedonia (F.Y.R.O.M.) ▲
63	Q 3	**Pell City**, Alabama, U.S.A.
134	K 11	**Pello**, Finland
136	F 8	**Pellworm**, Germany ☷
82	B 13	**Pelly**, Yukon Territory, Canada ⌇
84	M 1	**Pelly Bay**, Nunavut, Canada
82	B 12	**Pelly Crossing**, Yukon Territory, Canada
75	O 12	**Pelona Mountain**, New Mexico, U.S.A. ▲
147	D 21	**Peloponnese**, Greece ▲
147	E 22	**Peloponnisos**, Greece ◻
159	Q 9	**Peloponnisos–Cretan Ridge**, Mediterranean Sea ◇
112	H 13	**Pelotas**, Brazil
112	H 10	**Pelotas**, Brazil
194	F 9	**Pemanggil**, Malaysia ☷
192	I 10	**Pemangkat**, Indonesia
192	C 9	**Pematangsiantar**, Indonesia
219	N 6	**Pemba**, Zambia
219	U 4	**Pemba**, Mozambique
217	W 11	**Pemba Channel**, Tanzania ≈
217	X 11	**Pemba Island**, Tanzania ☷
230	G 12	**Pemberton**, Western Australia, Australia
83	G 21	**Pemberton**, British Columbia, Canada
67	N 2	**Pembina**, North Dakota, U.S.A.
64	G 10	**Pembine**, Wisconsin, U.S.A.
193	X 14	**Pembre**, Indonesia
126	K 10	**Pembroke**, United Kingdom
86	H 10	**Pembroke**, Ontario, Canada
127	O 9	**Pen y Fan**, United Kingdom ▲
127	R 1	**Pen-y-ghent**, United Kingdom ▲
131	N 1	**Pena Prieta**, Spain ▲
130	I 5	**Penafiel**, Portugal
131	N 4	**Peñafiel**, Spain
131	O 5	**Peñalara**, Spain ▲
108	L 11	**Penalva**, Brazil
112	I 5	**Penápolis**, Brazil
130	M 6	**Peñaranda de Bracamonte**, Spain
130	L 10	**Peñarroya-Pueblonuevo**, Spain
127	O 11	**Penarth**, United Kingdom ▶
72	K 3	**Pend Oreille Lake**, Idaho, U.S.A. ⌇
76	J 9	**Pendleton**, Oregon, U.S.A.
217	N 11	**Penge**, Democratic Republic of Congo
189	Y 12	**P'enghu Tao**, Taiwan ☷
187	G 19	**Penglai**, China
189	P 7	**Pengshui**, China
190	B 12	**Pengwa**, Myanmar
189	O 6	**Pengxi**, China
192	L 15	**Penida**, Indonesia ☷
111	G 25	**Península Brecknock**, Chile ▶
91	V 15	**Península de Azuero**, Panama ▶
111	G 20	**Península de Brunswick**, Chile ▶
91	O 12	**Península de Nicoya**, Costa Rica ▶
91	R 14	**Península de Osa**, Costa Rica ▶
111	E 20	**Península de Taitao**, Chile ▶
111	H 26	**Península Hardy**, Chile ▶
111	I 25	**Península Mitre**, Argentina ▶
107	D 18	**Península Paracas**, Peru ▶
104	L 1	**Península Paraguaná**, Venezuela ▶
111	E 21	**Península Tres Montes**, Chile ▶
111	J 17	**Península Valdés**, Argentina ▶
113	B 19	**Península Verde**, Argentina ▶
111	E 22	**Península Wharton**, Chile ▶
87	S 6	**Péninsule de Gaspé**, Québec, Canada ▶
85	P 5	**Pèninsule d'Ungava**, Québec, Canada ▶
131	U 7	**Peñíscola**, Spain
173	V 3	**Penjwin**, Iraq
127	R 6	**Penkridge**, United Kingdom
128	H 6	**Penmarch**, France
140	J 13	**Penne**, Italy
241	Q 14	**Pennell Coast**, Antarctica ◇
125	I 14	**Pennines**, United Kingdom ▲
127	R 1	**Pennines Dales**, United Kingdom ◇
60	L 7	**Pennington Gap**, Virginia, U.S.A.
58	H 14	**Pennsville**, New Jersey, U.S.A.
58	E 12	**Pennsylvania**, U.S.A. ◻
231	N 10	**Penong**, South Australia, Australia
91	V 14	**Penonomé**, Panama
41	R 8	**Penrhyn Basin**, Pacific Ocean ◇
125	I 15	**Penrith**, United Kingdom ◇
126	J 15	**Penryn**, United Kingdom
63	P 7	**Pensacola**, Florida, U.S.A.
241	N 6	**Pensacola Mountains**, Antarctica ▲
107	M 18	**Pensamiento**, Bolivia
195	U 7	**Pensiangan**, Malaysia
235	R 10	**Pentecost**, Vanuatu ☷
83	H 21	**Penticton**, British Columbia, Canada
126	K 14	**Pentire Point**, United Kingdom ▶
231	T 5	**Pentland**, Queensland, Australia
124	H 7	**Pentland Firth**, United Kingdom ≈
181	E 20	**Penukonda**, India
127	O 8	**Penybont**, United Kingdom
127	N 10	**Penywaun**, United Kingdom
131	S 6	**Penza**, Russian Federation
126	I 15	**Penzance**, United Kingdom
137	J 25	**Penzberg**, Germany
157	P 4	**Penzenskaya Oblast'**, Russian Federation ◻
153	Y 9	**Penzhinskaya Guba**, Russian Federation ≈
65	F 17	**Peoria**, Illinois, U.S.A.
232	K 9	**Pepepe**, New Zealand
194	B 7	**Perak**, Malaysia ◻
194	B 7	**Perak**, Malaysia ⌇
131	S 6	**Perales del Alfambra**, Spain
147	I 26	**Perama**, Greece
181	F 22	**Perambalur**, India
134	N 12	**Peranka**, Finland
87	U 6	**Percé**, Québec, Canada
139	X 4	**Perchtoldsdorf**, Austria
230	J 5	**Percival Lakes**, Western Australia, Australia ◇
150	H 6	**Perechyn**, Ukraine
104	H 6	**Pereira**, Colombia
112	H 5	**Pereira Barreto**, Brazil
157	N 8	**Perelazovskiy**, Russian Federation
154	H 12	**Pereslavl-Zalesskiy**, Russian Federation
157	V 5	**Perevolotskiy**, Russian Federation
151	Q 4	**Pereyaslav-Khmel'nyts'kyy**, Ukraine
77	H 14	**Perez**, California, U.S.A.
139	T 4	**Perg**, Austria
113	C 15	**Pergamino**, Argentina
194	D 5	**Perhentian Besar**, Malaysia ☷
135	K 15	**Perhonjoki**, Finland ⌇
85	S 10	**Péribonca**, Québec, Canada ⌇
110	I 6	**Perico**, Argentina
88	L 7	**Pericos**, Mexico
129	O 11	**Périgueux**, France
111	G 20	**Perito Moreno**, Argentina
136	K 11	**Perleberg**, Germany
194	A 4	**Perlis**, Malaysia ◻
155	T 12	**Perm'**, Russian Federation
145	L 21	**Përmet**, Albania
155	T 12	**Permskaya Oblast'**, Russian Federation ◻
108	O 13	**Pernambuco**, Brazil
43	J 14	**Pernambuco Abyssal Plain**, Atlantic Ocean ◇
43	I 14	**Pernambuco Seamounts**, Atlantic Ocean ▲▲
146	F 9	**Pernik**, Bulgaria ◻
146	F 9	**Pernik**, Bulgaria
139	W 5	**Pernitz**, Austria
89	S 12	**Perote**, Mexico
129	R 15	**Perpignan**, France
126	J 14	**Perranporth**, United Kingdom
71	O 5	**Perrin**, Texas, U.S.A.
63	T 4	**Perry**, Georgia, U.S.A.
63	T 8	**Perry**, Florida, U.S.A.
69	N 9	**Perry**, Oklahoma, U.S.A.
69	Q 3	**Perry Lake**, Kansas, U.S.A. ⌇
70	L 1	**Perryton**, Texas, U.S.A.
107	L 18	**Perseverancia**, Bolivia
175	T 3	**Persian Gulf**, Asia ≈
230	G 11	**Perth**, Western Australia, Australia
124	I 12	**Perth**, United Kingdom
86	I 11	**Perth**, Ontario, Canada
39	T 8	**Perth Basin**, Indian Ocean ◇
128	L 9	**Pertuis Breton**, France ≈
128	L 9	**Pertuis d'Antioche**, France ≈
107	E 15	**Peru**, South America ◻
65	J 18	**Peru**, Indiana, U.S.A.
107	J 16	**Perú**, Bolivia
41	Y 9	**Peru Basin**, Pacific Ocean ◇
140	G 11	**Perugia**, Italy
112	G 12	**Perugorria**, Argentina
112	K 8	**Peruíbe**, Brazil
41	Z 7	**Peru–Chile Trench**, Pacific Ocean ◇
133	D 21	**Peruwelz**, Belgium
151	Q 7	**Pervomays'k**, Ukraine
151	T 11	**Pervomays'ke**, Ukraine
156	M 3	**Pervomayskiy**, Russian Federation
157	W 5	**Pervomayskiy**, Russian Federation
151	V 5	**Pervomays'kyy**, Ukraine
153	Y 8	**Pervorechenskiy**, Russian Federation
152	I 10	**Pervoural'sk**, Russian Federation
140	H 10	**Pesaro**, Italy
140	J 13	**Pescara**, Italy
177	W 7	**Peshawar**, Pakistan
145	L 21	**Peshkopi**, Albania
146	H 10	**Peshtera**, Bulgaria
179	R 9	**Peski Muyunkum**, Kazakhstan ◇
179	V 8	**Peski Saryyesik-Atyrau**, Kazakhstan ◇
179	U 9	**Peski Taukum**, Kazakhstan ◇
90	L 7	**Pespire**, Honduras
154	H 12	**Pestovo**, Russian Federation
157	S 5	**Perelyub**, Russian Federation
150	J 4	**Peremyshlyany**, Ukraine
151	V 5	**Pereshchepyne**, Ukraine
154	J 14	**Pereslavl'-Zalesskiy**, Russian Federation
157	V 5	**Perevolotskiy**, Russian Federation
151	Q 4	**Pereyaslav-Khmel'nyts'kyy**, Ukraine
77	H 14	**Perez**, California, U.S.A.
139	T 4	**Perg**, Austria
83	K 16	**Peter Pond Lake**, Saskatchewan, Canada ⌇
86	B 6	**Peterbell**, Ontario, Canada
231	P 11	**Peterborough**, South Australia, Australia
127	V 7	**Peterborough**, United Kingdom
86	F 12	**Peterborough**, Ontario, Canada
124	J 10	**Peterhead**, United Kingdom
45	P 12	**Petermann Bjerg**, Greenland ▲
61	T 6	**Petersburg**, Virginia, U.S.A.
79	X 11	**Petersburg**, Alaska, U.S.A.
127	T 12	**Petersfield**, United Kingdom
87	T 9	**Petitcodiac**, New Brunswick, Canada
83	F 15	**Petitot**, British Columbia, Canada ⌇
89	Z 11	**Peto**, Mexico
64	K 10	**Petoskey**, Michigan, U.S.A.
172	F 9	**Petah Tiqwa**, Israel
147	D 22	**Petalidi**, Greece
77	F 19	**Petaluma**, California, U.S.A.
133	K 26	**Pètange**, Luxembourg
89	P 13	**Petatlán**, Mexico
219	P 5	**Petauke**, Zambia
64	E 12	**Petenwell Lake**, Wisconsin, U.S.A. ⌇
240	H 8	**Peter I Island**, Norway ☷
172	G 12	**Petra**, Jordan
146	F 12	**Petrich**, Bulgaria
151	P 9	**Petrivka**, Ukraine
151	U 9	**Petrivka**, Ukraine
104	J 4	**Petrólea**, Colombia
108	N 13	**Petrolina**, Brazil
179	R 1	**Petropavlovsk**, Kazakhstan
153	Z 11	**Petropavlovsk-Kamchatskiy**, Russian Federation
112	N 6	**Petrópolis**, Brazil
150	H 11	**Petroşani**, Romania
157	P 4	**Petrovsk**, Russian Federation
153	Q 14	**Petrovsk-Zabaykal'skiy**, Russian Federation
154	G 9	**Petrozavodsk**, Russian Federation
150	M 7	**Petruşeni**, Moldova
151	U 6	**Petrykivka**, Ukraine
132	G 9	**Petten**, Netherlands
71	P 12	**Pettus**, Texas, U.S.A.
152	J 11	**Petukhovo**, Russian Federation
156	L 1	**Petushki**, Russian Federation
127	U 12	**Petworth**, United Kingdom
139	S 3	**Peuerbach**, Austria
192	C 8	**Peureula**, Indonesia
153	X 6	**Pevek**, Russian Federation
143	G 21	**Pezinok**, Slovakia
177	V 9	**Pezu**, Pakistan
137	J 23	**Pfaffenhofen an der Ilm**, Germany
137	F 22	**Pforzheim**, Germany
137	G 25	**Pfullendorf**, Germany
138	K 8	**Pfunds**, Austria
219	P 10	**Phalaborwa**, Republic of South Africa
177	X 8	**Phalia**, Pakistan
180	C 12	**Phalodi**, India
191	O 21	**Phan Rang**, Vietnam
191	O 21	**Phan Ri**, Vietnam
191	O 22	**Phan Thiêt**, Vietnam
191	K 15	**Phang Khon**, Thailand
191	F 24	**Phangnga**, Thailand
183	R 9	**Phaplu**, Nepal
191	H 25	**Phatthalung**, Thailand
191	H 14	**Phayao**, Thailand
63	R 4	**Phenix City**, Alabama, U.S.A.
191	H 20	**Phet Buri**, Thailand
191	I 16	**Phetchabun**, Thailand
191	H 17	**Phichit**, Thailand
58	I 14	**Philadelphia**, Pennsylvania, U.S.A.
79	R 4	**Philip Smith Mountains**, Alaska, U.S.A. ▲
133	G 22	**Philippeville**, Belgium
61	P 3	**Philippi**, West Virginia, U.S.A.
40	K 6	**Philippine Basin**, Pacific Ocean ◇
196	L 11	**Philippine Sea**, Asia ≋
40	J 5	**Philippine Trench**, Pacific Ocean ◇
197	F 20	**Philippines**, Asia ◻
73	O 6	**Philipsburg**, Montana, U.S.A.
68	L 2	**Phillipsburg**, Kansas, U.S.A.
191	J 18	**Phimai**, Thailand
191	H 16	**Phitsanulok**, Thailand
191	L 21	**Phnom Penh**, Cambodia ⚑
191	K 21	**Phnum Aôral**, Cambodia ▲
191	J 20	**Phnum Tumpôr**, Cambodia ▲
236	K 4	**Phoenix**, Kiribati ☷
74	I 12	**Phoenix**, Arizona, U.S.A.
236	H 4	**Phoenix Islands**, Kiribati ☷
191	J 17	**Phon**, Thailand
190	K 11	**Phong Thô**, Vietnam
190	I 11	**Phôngsali**, Laos
191	J 14	**Phou Bia**, Laos ▲
191	L 15	**Phou Cô Pi**, Laos ▲
190	I 13	**Phou Houie Moc**, Laos ▲
190	J 13	**Phou San**, Laos ▲
191	M 17	**Phou Set**, Laos ▲

■ Country   ◻ Internal administrative region: State/Province/Territory/Dependent territory   ⚑ Capital city   ▲▲ Mountain range/ Undersea ridge   ▲ Mountain peak/ Volcano/Seamount   ◇ Geographic feature   ▶ Headland/Point/ Cape/Peninsula   ▲ Desert   ☷ Island/Island group   Antarctic base   ⊘ Ocean   ≋ Sea   ≈ Bay/Gulf/Channel/Strait   Lake   Salt pan/Dry/ Intermittent lake   ⌇ River

323

80 B 12 **Pokaran**, India

32 K 9 **Pokeno**, New Zealand

83 O 9 **Pokhara**, Nepal

57 T 3 **Pokhvistnevo**, Russian Federation

34 L 9 **Pokka**, Finland

17 O 6 **Poko**, Democratic Republic of Congo

53 T 11 **Pokrovsk**, Russian Federation

56 K 9 **Pokrovskoye**, Russian Federation

76 J 10 **Pol-e Fāsā**, Iran

77 U 6 **Pol-e Khomrī**, Afghanistan

43 J 20 **Polana**, Slovakia ▲

42 F 11 **Poland**, Europe ▣

42 G 9 **Polanów**, Poland

70 G 9 **Polatli**, Turkey

49 K 14 **Polatsk**, Belarus

5 R 9 **Pole Plain**, Arctic Ocean ◇

93 N 12 **Polewali**, Indonesia

15 U 12 **Poli**, Cameroon

89 X 2 **Poli**, China

42 D 10 **Police**, Poland

47 K 17 **Polichnitos**, Greece

29 U 8 **Poligny**, France

96 H 11 **Polillo**, Philippines 🏝

96 H 10 **Polillo Islands**, Philippines 🏝

96 H 10 **Polillo Strait**, Philippines ≈

70 G 15 **Polis**, Cyprus

51 O 2 **Polis'ke**, Ukraine

81 E 22 **Pollachi**, India

31 Y 7 **Pollença**, Spain

32 J 9 **Pollok**, New Zealand

51 W 8 **Polohy**, Ukraine

97 L 23 **Polomoloc**, Philippines

81 G 24 **Polonnaruwa**, Sri Lanka

50 M 4 **Polonne**, Ukraine

50 H 12 **Polovragi**, Romania

26 L 15 **Polperro**, United Kingdom

46 J 7 **Polski Trŭmbesh**, Bulgaria

2 M 4 **Polson**, Montana, U.S.A.

51 U 5 **Poltava**, Ukraine

48 H 7 **Põltsamaa**, Estonia

54 M 4 **Poluostrov Kanin**, Russian Federation ▶

54 I 1 **Poluostrov Rybachiy**, Russian Federation ▶

53 O 7 **Poluostrov Taymyr**, Russian Federation ▶

52 M 7 **Poluostrov Yamal**, Russian Federation ▶

48 I 8 **Põlva**, Estonia

47 I 23 **Polyaigos**, Greece 🏝

54 I 1 **Polyarnyy**, Russian Federation

55 T 5 **Polyarnyy Ural**, Russian Federation ⛰

47 G 14 **Polygyros**, Greece

46 E 13 **Polykastro**, Greece

36 F 3 **Polynesia**, Oceania ◇

30 H 7 **Pombal**, Portugal

19 R 9 **Pomene**, Mozambique

42 F 9 **Pomerania**, Poland ⛰

5 N 20 **Pomeroy**, Ohio, U.S.A.

34 G 4 **Pomio**, Papua New Guinea

36 N 9 **Pommersche Bucht**, Germany ≈

7 K 24 **Pomona**, California, U.S.A.

0 K 3 **Pomona**, Belize

46 N 9 **Pomorie**, Bulgaria

54 I 6 **Pomorskiy Bereg**, Russian Federation ◇

55 O 3 **Pomorskiy Proliv**, Russian Federation ≈

3 Y 13 **Pompano Beach**, Florida, U.S.A.

41 J 16 **Pompei**, Italy

9 N 8 **Ponca City**, Oklahoma, U.S.A.

3 U 8 **Ponce**, Puerto Rico

3 M 8 **Pond Creek**, Oklahoma, U.S.A.

81 H 19 **Pondicherry**, India ▣

0 M 9 **Poneloya**, Nicaragua

30 K 2 **Ponferrada**, Spain

43 M 15 **Poniatowa**, Poland

57 V 3 **Ponomarevka**, Russian Federation

154 L 4 **Ponoy**, Russian Federation

197 L 17 **Ponson**, Philippines 🏝

133 F 21 **Pont-à-Celles**, Belgium

129 U 4 **Pont-à-Mousson**, France

140 A 7 **Pont-Canavese**, Italy

109 N 17 **Ponta da Baleia**, Brazil ▶

219 R 10 **Ponta da Barra**, Mozambique ▶

219 R 9 **Ponta da Barra Falsa**, Mozambique ▶

218 F 2 **Ponta das Palmeirinhas**, Angola ▶

218 F 4 **Ponta das Salinas**, Angola ▶

42 O 2 **Ponta Delgada**, Azores 🏛

218 F 6 **Ponta do Enfião**, Angola ▶

43 A 15 **Ponta do Sol**, Cape Verde

42 N 5 **Ponta do Sol**, Madeira

112 I 8 **Ponta Grossa**, Brazil

112 J 11 **Ponta Imbituba**, Brazil ▶

109 H 18 **Ponta Porã**, Brazil

219 S 7 **Ponta Timbué**, Mozambique ▶

129 V 8 **Pontarlier**, France

128 K 7 **Pontchâteau**, France

109 K 14 **Ponte Alta do Tocantins**, Brazil

130 H 4 **Ponte da Barca**, Portugal

130 H 4 **Ponte de Lima**, Portugal

130 H 8 **Ponte de Sor**, Portugal

130 H 3 **Ponteareas**, Spain

140 I 5 **Pontebba**, Italy

127 T 3 **Pontefract**, United Kingdom

109 F 15 **Pontes e Lacerda**, Brazil

130 H 2 **Pontevedra**, Spain

65 G 17 **Pontiac**, Illinois, U.S.A.

65 M 14 **Pontiac**, Michigan, U.S.A.

194 E 10 **Pontian Kechil**, Malaysia

192 I 11 **Pontianak**, Indonesia

128 J 5 **Pontivy**, France

129 P 4 **Pontoise**, France

84 I 8 **Ponton**, Manitoba, Canada

63 N 2 **Pontotoc**, Mississippi, U.S.A.

140 D 9 **Pontremoli**, Italy

131 V 4 **Ponts**, Spain

127 O 10 **Pontypool**, United Kingdom

127 O 10 **Pontypridd**, United Kingdom

91 V 15 **Ponuga**, Panama

149 J 15 **Ponya**, Belarus 〰

231 O 11 **Poochera**, South Australia, Australia

216 H 9 **Pool**, Congo ▣

127 R 13 **Poole**, United Kingdom

127 R 14 **Poole Bay**, United Kingdom ≈

231 R 11 **Pooncarie**, New South Wales, Australia

232 K 6 **Poor Knights Islands**, New Zealand 🏝

151 V 6 **Popasne**, Ukraine

104 G 8 **Popayán**, Colombia

148 C 10 **Pope**, Latvia

133 A 19 **Poperinge**, Belgium

73 X 3 **Poplar**, Montana, U.S.A.

69 Y 7 **Poplar Bluff**, Missouri, U.S.A.

62 M 7 **Poplarville**, Mississippi, U.S.A.

89 R 12 **Popocatépetl**, Mexico ▲

216 I 11 **Popokabaka**, Democratic Republic of Congo

140 I 13 **Popoli**, Italy

234 E 6 **Popondetta**, Papua New Guinea

146 L 7 **Popovo**, Bulgaria

143 K 19 **Poprad**, Slovakia

90 I 3 **Poptún**, Guatemala

233 M 14 **Porangahau**, New Zealand

109 J 15 **Porangatu**, Brazil

181 A 15 **Porbandar**, India

42 J 6 **Porcupine Abyssal Plain**, Atlantic Ocean ◇

140 H 6 **Pordenone**, Italy

157 Q 2 **Poretskoye**, Russian Federation

234 B 4 **Porgera**, Papua New Guinea

135 J 18 **Pori**, Finland

233 K 16 **Porirua**, New Zealand

134 I 11 **Porjus**, Sweden

154 E 12 **Porkhov**, Russian Federation

127 N 12 **Porlock**, United Kingdom

231 R 2 **Pormpuraaw**, Queensland, Australia

128 K 7 **Pornic**, France

197 L 17 **Poro**, Philippines 🏝

153 X 13 **Poronaysk**, Russian Federation

147 G 21 **Poros**, Greece

149 F 19 **Porozava**, Belarus

241 W 13 **Porpoise Bay**, Antarctica ≈

43 L 25 **Porpoise Point**, Ascension ▶

138 C 6 **Porrentruy**, Switzerland

140 E 9 **Porreta Terme**, Italy

134 K 6 **Porsangen**, Norway ≈

135 C 20 **Porsgrunn**, Norway

93 N 8 **Port-à-Piment**, Haiti

83 F 22 **Port Alberni**, British Columbia, Canada

219 N 15 **Port Alfred**, Republic of South Africa

76 G 6 **Port Angeles**, Washington, U.S.A.

92 L 8 **Port Antonio**, Jamaica

231 T 15 **Port Arthur**, Tasmania, Australia

71 U 10 **Port Arthur**, Texas, U.S.A.

93 O 7 **Port-au-Prince**, Haiti 🏛

231 P 10 **Port Augusta**, South Australia, Australia

218 K 15 **Port Beaufort**, Republic of South Africa

217 S 7 **Port Bell**, Uganda

181 N 22 **Port Blair**, India

71 T 10 **Port Bolivar**, Texas, U.S.A.

86 D 14 **Port Burwell**, Ontario, Canada

183 T 14 **Port Canning**, India

87 R 4 **Port-Cartier**, Québec, Canada

233 F 24 **Port Chalmers**, New Zealand

63 W 12 **Port Charlotte**, Florida, U.S.A.

65 M 16 **Port Clinton**, Ohio, U.S.A.

86 F 14 **Port Colborne**, Ontario, Canada

93 O 6 **Port-de-Paix**, Haiti

194 C 9 **Port Dickson**, Malaysia

231 T 3 **Port Douglas**, Queensland, Australia

219 P 13 **Port Edward**, Republic of South Africa

86 C 11 **Port Elgin**, Ontario, Canada

87 U 9 **Port Elgin**, New Brunswick, Canada

219 N 15 **Port Elizabeth**, Republic of South Africa

126 M 10 **Port Eynon**, United Kingdom

232 L 7 **Port Fitzroy**, New Zealand

216 D 8 **Port-Gentil**, Gabon

62 L 5 **Port Gibson**, Mississippi, U.S.A.

124 G 13 **Port Glasgow**, United Kingdom

79 P 10 **Port Graham**, Alaska, U.S.A.

215 R 14 **Port Harcourt**, Nigeria

83 E 21 **Port Hardy**, British Columbia, Canada

87 X 9 **Port Hawkesbury**, Nova Scotia, Canada

230 G 5 **Port Hedland**, Western Australia, Australia

79 N 12 **Port Heiden**, Alaska, U.S.A.

90 K 4 **Port Honduras**, Belize ≈

64 M 12 **Port Hope**, Michigan, U.S.A.

85 X 8 **Port Hope Simpson**, Newfoundland and Labrador, Canada

92 M 3 **Port Howe**, The Bahamas

65 M 14 **Port Huron**, Michigan, U.S.A.

126 K 14 **Port Isaac Bay**, United Kingdom ≈

71 Q 15 **Port Isabel**, Texas, U.S.A.

156 K 10 **Port Katon**, Russian Federation

71 R 12 **Port Lavaca**, Texas, U.S.A.

231 O 12 **Port Lincoln**, South Australia, Australia

214 F 11 **Port Loko**, Sierra Leone

38 B 12 **Port Louis**, Mauritius 🏛

231 V 10 **Port Macquarie**, New South Wales, Australia

38 E 7 **Port Mathurin**, Rodrigues Island

87 T 4 **Port-Menier**, Québec, Canada

234 E 6 **Port Moresby**, Papua New Guinea 🏛

93 N 3 **Port Nelson**, The Bahamas

218 I 13 **Port Nolloth**, Republic of South Africa

124 F 8 **Port of Ness**, United Kingdom

93 Y 14 **Port of Spain**, Trinidad and Tobago 🏛

76 E 13 **Port Orford**, Oregon, U.S.A.

233 B 26 **Port Pegasus**, New Zealand ≈

231 P 11 **Port Pirie**, South Australia, Australia

61 P 15 **Port Royal**, South Carolina, U.S.A.

61 U 4 **Port Royal**, Virginia, U.S.A.

61 P 15 **Port Royal Sound**, South Carolina, U.S.A. ≈

212 F 7 **Port Said**, Egypt

64 M 13 **Port Sanilac**, Michigan, U.S.A.

219 P 13 **Port Shepstone**, Republic of South Africa

63 R 8 **Port St Joe**, Florida, U.S.A.

219 O 14 **Port St Johns**, Republic of South Africa

111 K 24 **Port Stephens**, Falkland Islands

213 H 14 **Port Sudan**, Sudan

62 M 9 **Port Sulphur**, Louisiana, U.S.A.

127 N 10 **Port Talbot**, United Kingdom

129 R 15 **Port-Vendres**, France

235 Q 11 **Port Vila**, Vanuatu 🏛

232 K 9 **Port Waikato**, New Zealand

231 P 11 **Port Wakefield**, South Australia, Australia

194 A 6 **Port Weld**, Malaysia

231 S 14 **Port Welshpool**, Victoria, Australia

125 E 16 **Portadown**, United Kingdom

64 F 13 **Portage**, Wisconsin, U.S.A.

84 I 10 **Portage la Praire**, Manitoba, Canada

130 I 9 **Portalegre**, Portugal ▣

130 I 8 **Portalegre**, Portugal

75 U 11 **Portales**, New Mexico, U.S.A.

131 Y 3 **Portbou**, Spain

127 T 13 **Portchester**, United Kingdom

109 L 16 **Porteirinha**, Brazil

108 I 10 **Portel**, Brazil

130 I 10 **Portel**, Portugal

77 J 22 **Porterville**, California, U.S.A.

127 O 10 **Porth**, United Kingdom

127 N 11 **Porthcawl**, United Kingdom

126 M 5 **Porthmadog**, United Kingdom

147 B 20 **Porthmos Zakynthou**, Greece ≈

131 W 9 **Portinatx**, Spain

127 P 10 **Portishead**, United Kingdom

231 Q 13 **Portland**, Victoria, Australia

59 P 7 **Portland**, Maine, U.S.A.

65 K 18 **Portland**, Indiana, U.S.A.

71 Q 13 **Portland**, Texas, U.S.A.

76 G 9 **Portland**, Oregon, U.S.A.

232 O 13 **Portland Island**, New Zealand 🏝

43 K 26 **Portland Point**, Ascension ▶

125 D 18 **Portlaoise**, Republic of Ireland

130 H 5 **Porto**, Portugal ▣

130 H 5 **Porto**, Portugal

108 I 11 **Porto Alegre**, Brazil

112 H 12 **Porto Alegre**, Brazil

218 G 3 **Porto Amboim**, Angola

109 H 15 **Porto Artur**, Brazil

112 J 10 **Porto Belo**, Brazil

108 I 10 **Pôrto de Moz**, Brazil

109 G 14 **Porto dos Gaúchos**, Brazil

141 I 23 **Porto Empedocle**, Italy

109 F 16 **Porto Esperidião**, Brazil

108 K 12 **Porto Franco**, Brazil

108 I 9 **Porto Grande**, Brazil

43 B 17 **Porto Inglês**, Cape Verde

109 G 16 **Porto Jofre**, Brazil

42 N 4 **Porto Moniz**, Madeira

109 G 18 **Porto Murtinho**, Brazil

43 A 15 **Porto Novo**, Cape Verde

215 O 13 **Porto-Novo**, Benin 🏛

140 I 11 **Porto Recanati**, Italy

43 B 17 **Porto Rincão**, Cape Verde

140 I 11 **Porto San Giorgio**, Italy

42 O 4 **Porto Santo**, Madeira

112 G 6 **Porto São José**, Brazil

109 N 16 **Porto Seguro**, Brazil

141 B 16 **Porto Torres**, Italy

129 Y 15 **Porto-Vecchio**, France

108 D 13 **Porto Velho**, Brazil

91 W 13 **Portobelo**, Panama

140 E 12 **Portoferraio**, Italy

77 H 17 **Portola**, California, U.S.A.

106 B 9 **Portoviejo**, Ecuador

124 F 10 **Portree**, United Kingdom

127 T 13 **Portsmouth**, United Kingdom

59 O 8 **Portsmouth**, New Hampshire, U.S.A.

61 V 7 **Portsmouth**, Virginia, U.S.A.

65 M 20 **Portsmouth**, Ohio, U.S.A.

93 Y 10 **Portsmouth**, Dominica

134 L 9 **Porttipahdan tekojärvi**, Finland 💧

130 G 12 **Portugal**, Europe ▣

104 M 3 **Portuguesa**, Venezuela ▣

111 H 25 **Porvenir**, Chile

135 M 19 **Porvoo**, Finland

187 K 20 **Poryŏng**, South Korea

112 E 10 **Posadas**, Argentina

138 J 10 **Poschiavo**, Switzerland

154 J 12 **Poshekhon'ye**, Russian Federation

176 L 8 **Posht-e Badam**, Iran

134 M 11 **Posio**, Finland

193 O 11 **Poso**, Indonesia

171 R 7 **Posof**, Turkey

187 L 22 **Posŏng**, South Korea

106 A 10 **Posorja**, Ecuador

109 K 15 **Posse**, Brazil

71 O 5 **Possum Kingdom Lake**, Texas, U.S.A. 💧

70 K 5 **Post**, Texas, U.S.A.

210 L 13 **Post Weygand**, Algeria

144 B 8 **Postojna**, Slovenia

67 U 10 **Postville**, Iowa, U.S.A.

144 G 13 **Posušje**, Bosnia and Herzegovina

197 I 17 **Potatan**, Philippines

69 R 11 **Poteau**, Oklahoma, U.S.A.

71 O 11 **Poteet**, Texas, U.S.A.

141 L 16 **Potenza**, Italy

131 N 1 **Potes**, Spain

171 Q 6 **P'ot'i**, Georgia

215 T 10 **Potiskum**, Nigeria

72 J 5 **Potlatch**, Idaho, U.S.A.

61 U 4 **Potomac**, Maryland, U.S.A. 〰

69 X 5 **Potosi**, Missouri, U.S.A.

107 J 21 **Potosí**, Bolivia

107 J 23 **Potosí**, Bolivia ▣

136 M 13 **Potsdam**, Germany

58 I 5 **Potsdam**, New York, U.S.A.

58 H 13 **Pottstown**, Pennsylvania, U.S.A.

58 G 12 **Pottsville**, Pennsylvania, U.S.A.

181 H 25 **Pottuvil**, Sri Lanka

177 W 8 **Potwar Plateau**, Pakistan ◇

58 J 10 **Poughkeepsie**, New York, U.S.A.

232 M 13 **Poukawa**, New Zealand

127 P 2 **Poulton-le-Fylde**, United Kingdom

235 O 13 **Poum**, New Caledonia

64 G 11 **Pound**, Wisconsin, U.S.A.

112 L 6 **Pouso Alegre**, Brazil

191 K 20 **Poŭthisăt**, Cambodia

232 O 12 **Poverty Bay**, New Zealand ≈

130 H 4 **Póvoa de Varzim**, Portugal

157 N 6 **Povorino**, Russian Federation

73 Y 6 **Powder**, Montana, U.S.A. 〰

73 W 11 **Powder River**, Wyoming, U.S.A.

73 X 8 **Powder River Basin**, Wyoming, U.S.A. ◇

73 T 9 **Powell**, Wyoming, U.S.A.

43 G 22 **Powell Basin**, Atlantic Ocean ◇

83 F 21 **Powell River**, British Columbia, Canada

64 H 10 **Powers**, Michigan, U.S.A.

61 S 6 **Powhatan**, Virginia, U.S.A.

65 O 18 **Powhatan Point**, Ohio, U.S.A.

188 K 4 **Powo**, China

194 A 14 **Poyan Reservoir**, Singapore 💧

189 V 7 **Poyang Hu**, China 💧

185 U 11 **PoyangHu**, China 💧

139 Y 2 **Poysdorf**, Austria

89 S 11 **Poza Rica**, Mexico

170 J 12 **Pozanti**, Turkey

144 M 10 **Požarevac**, Serbia and Montenegro

144 K 12 **Požega**, Serbia and Montenegro

142 G 12 **Poznań**, Poland

131 P 11 **Pozo Alcón**, Spain

109 G 19 **Pozo Colorado**, Paraguay

107 M 20 **Pozo del Tigre**, Bolivia

110 J 8 **Pozo Hondo**, Argentina

130 M 10 **Pozoblanco**, Spain

141 K 24 **Pozzallo**, Italy

192 F 12 **Prabumulih**, Indonesia

191 G 21 **Prachuap Khiri Khan**, Thailand

143 G 17 **Praděd**, Czech Republic ▲

129 Q 15 **Prades**, France

109 N 16 **Prado**, Brazil

139 O 7 **Prägraten**, Austria

143 C 17 **Prague**, Czech Republic 🏛

43 B 17 **Praia**, Cape Verde 🏛

108 H 10 **Prainha**, Brazil

76 J 11 **Prairie City**, Oregon, U.S.A.

191 J 18 **Prakhon Chai**, Thailand

148 G 5 **Prangli**, Estonia 🏝

192 D 9 **Prapat**, Indonesia

191 J 18 **Prasat**, Thailand

38 B 9 **Praslin**, Seychelles 🏝

112 J 4 **Prata**, Brazil

140 F 10 **Prato**, Italy

68 L 6 **Pratt**, Kansas, U.S.A.

41 S 2 **Pratt Seamount**, Pacific Ocean ▲

63 Q 4 **Prattville**, Alabama, U.S.A.

127 N 15 **Prawle Point**, United Kingdom ▶

192 L 15 **Praya**, Indonesia

149 J 14 **Prazaroki**, Belarus

139 S 7 **Predlitz**, Austria

139 T 3 **Pregarten**, Austria

148 I 12 **Preiļi**, Latvia

71 P 14 **Premont**, Texas, U.S.A.

64 E 10 **Prentice**, Wisconsin, U.S.A.

136 M 11 **Prenzlau**, Germany

191 B 18 **Preparis Island**, Myanmar 🏝

191 B 17 **Preparis North Channel**, Myanmar ≈

191 B 18 **Preparis South Channel**, Myanmar ≈

143 G 18 **Přerov**, Czech Republic

89 W 14 **Presa de la Angostura**, Mexico 💧

89 P 12 **Presa del Infiernillo**, Mexico 💧

89 T 13 **Presa Miguel Alemán**, Mexico 💧

Country ▣ Internal administrative region: State/Province/Territory/Dependent territory 🏛 Capital city ⛰ Mountain range/Undersea ridge ▲ Mountain peak/Volcano/Seamount ◇ Geographic feature ▶ Headland/Point/Cape/Peninsula ◓ Desert 🏝 Island/Island group ⁙ Antarctic base 🌀 Ocean 🌊 Sea ≈ Bay/Gulf/Channel/Strait 💧 Lake ▦ Salt pan/Dry/Intermittent lake 〰 River

⬚ Country   ⬚ Internal administrative region: State/Province/Territory/Dependent territory   ▲ Capital city   ◇ Mountain range/ Undersea ridge   ▲ Mountain peak/ Volcano/Seamount   ◇ Geographic feature   ▶ Headland/Point/ Cape/Peninsula   ⬚ Desert   ⌇ Island/Island group   ⬚ Antarctic base   ≋ Ocean   ≈ Sea   ≈ Bay/Gulf/Channel/Strait   ⌇ Lake   ∿ Salt pan/Dry/ Intermittent lake   ∿ River

C 12 Punxsutawney, Pennsylvania, U.S.A.
4 M 13 Puolanka, Finland
3 H 15 Puponga, New Zealand
5 T 11 Puqi, China
7 E 18 Puquio, Peru
0 G 8 Puquios, Chile
2 L 9 Puranpur, India
4 C 6 Puratu Island, Papua New Guinea 🏝
9 Y 4 Purbach, Austria
8 G 5 Purekkari neem, Estonia ▶
1 F 15 Purén, Chile
1 J 17 Puri, India
9 X 3 Purkersdorf, Austria
2 H 10 Purmerend, Netherlands
3 R 11 Purnia, India
1 E 17 Purranque, Chile
P 12 Puruarán, Mexico
2 L 11 Purukcahu, Indonesia
3 Q 13 Puruliya, India
8 D 12 Purus, Brazil ∿
5 O 16 Puruvesi, Finland ◡
6 J 10 Pŭrvomay, Bulgaria
2 H 14 Purwakarta, Indonesia
5 O 10 Pusa, Malaysia
7 N 21 Pusan, South Korea
7 O 22 Pusan Point, Philippines ▶
7 Q 6 Pushkino, Russian Federation
4 D 14 Pustoshka, Russian Federation
5 W 13 Putai, Taiwan
0 F 6 Putao, Myanmar
2 L 10 Putaruru, New Zealand
9 X 10 Putian, China
7 H 18 Putina, Peru
2 N 12 Putorino, New Zealand
0 G 2 Putre, Chile
1 F 24 Puttalam, Sri Lanka
2 J 11 Putten, Netherlands
6 I 8 Puttgarden, Germany
1 D 21 Puttur, India
1 H 9 Putumayo, Colombia ▣
4 J 11 Putumayo, Colombia ∿
2 K 10 Putusibau, Indonesia
1 T 2 Putyvl', Ukraine
5 M 17 Puula, Finland ◡
5 N 17 Puumala, Finland
P 5 Puvurnituq, Québec, Canada
9 R 2 Puxian, China
9 U 2 Puyang, China
1 F 16 Puyehue, Chile
6 C 9 Puyo, Ecuador
3 A 25 Puysegur Point, New Zealand ▶
5 R 8 Puzla, Russian Federation
7 W 12 Pwani, Tanzania ▣
7 Q 13 Pweto, Democratic Republic of Congo
6 M 5 Pwllheli, United Kingdom
4 K 5 Pyalitsa, Russian Federation
4 I 8 Pyal'ma, Russian Federation
1 D 17 Pyapon, Myanmar
3 O 6 Pyasinskiy Zaliv, Russian Federation ≈
7 O 13 Pyatigorsk, Russian Federation
1 T 6 P''yatykhatky, Ukraine
0 D 12 Pyawbwe, Myanmar
1 C 14 Pyè, Myanmar
9 K 21 Pyetrykaw, Belarus
5 L 14 Pyhäjoki, Finland ∿
5 M 15 Pyhasalmi, Finland
5 O 16 Pyhäselkä, Finland ◡
4 M 10 Pyhätunturin, Finland ▲
0 D 13 Pyinmana, Myanmar
7 D 22 Pylos, Greece
7 L 18 P'yŏnggang, North Korea
7 K 17 P'yŏngsong, North Korea
7 M 19 P'yŏngt'aek, South Korea
7 J 17 P'yŏngyang, North Korea ⌂
I 16 Pyramid Lake, Nevada, U.S.A. ◡
8 K 15 Pyrenees, France/Spain ⛰
7 E 15 Pyrgetos, Greece
147 K 19 Pyrgi, Greece
147 C 21 Pyrgos, Greece
151 R 4 Pyryatyn, Ukraine
142 D 11 Pyrzyce, Poland
149 J 15 Pyshna, Belarus
151 V 7 Pys'menne, Ukraine
154 D 13 Pytalovo, Russian Federation
135 C 16 Pyttegga, Norway ▲
191 D 14 Pyu, Myanmar

Q

174 L 7 Qaḏimah, Saudi Arabia
173 U 4 Qādir Karam, Iraq
186 F 8 Qagan, China
186 B 13 Qagan Nur, China
186 C 13 Qagan Nur, China ◡
186 J 11 Qagan Nur, China ◡
187 C 14 Qagan Nur, China
186 B 13 Qagan Teg, China
188 J 4 Qagca, China
177 R 6 Qaisar, Afghanistan
173 U 2 Qalā Diza, Iraq
179 S 13 Qal'aikhum, Tajikistan
175 W 14 Qalansīyah, Yemen
177 T 9 Qalāt, Afghanistan
173 W 12 Qal'at Abū Ghar, Iraq
174 J 4 Qal'at al Aẓlam, Saudi Arabia
172 H 4 Qal'at al Ḥiṣn, Syria
175 O 9 Qal'at Bishah, Saudi Arabia
173 Y 10 Qal'at Ṣāliḥ, Iraq
173 W 9 Qal'at Sukkār, Iraq
177 Q 7 Qal'eh-ye, Afghanistan
172 F 9 Qalqilya, Israel
82 M 9 Qamanittuaq, Nunavut, Canada
188 I 6 Qamdo, China
211 W 8 Qamīnis, Libya
213 O 18 Qandala, Somalia
171 V 10 Qapiciğ Dağl, Armenia ▲
173 U 5 Qara Tepe, Iraq
174 M 2 Qārah, Saudi Arabia
173 Q 1 Qaratshuk, Syria
213 N 20 Qardho, Somalia
179 U 13 Qarokŭl, Tajikistan ◡
186 H 10 Qarsan, China
179 P 13 Qashqadaryo Wiloyati, Uzbekistan ▣
187 A 16 Qasq, China
172 I 9 Qaṣr al Azraq, Jordan
172 H 10 Qaṣr al Kharānah, Jordan
175 S 2 Qaṣr aṣ Ṣabīyah, Kuwait
212 D 10 Qasr Farafra, Egypt
175 Q 8 Qaṣr Ḥimām, Saudi Arabia
211 S 11 Qaṣr Larocu, Libya
172 H 7 Qatanā, Syria
175 U 5 Qatar, Asia ▣
176 K 11 Qaṭrūyeh, Iran
212 C 9 Qattâra Depression, Egypt ◆
171 W 7 Qax, Azerbaijan
177 N 8 Qāyen, Iran
173 S 3 Qayyārah, Iraq
171 U 7 Qazax, Azerbaijan
171 Y 8 Qazimämmäd, Azerbaijan
176 H 5 Qazvīn, Iran
176 H 5 Qazvīn, Iran ▣
212 F 10 Qena, Egypt
45 N 12 Qeqertarsuaq, Greenland
176 L 13 Qeshm, Iran
176 L 13 Qeshm, Iran 🏝
188 K 6 Qêyi, China
176 J 13 Qeys, Iran 🏝
172 E 11 Qeẓi'ot, Israel
186 J 12 Qian'an, China
189 P 7 Qianjiang, China
189 T 6 Qianjiang, China
188 L 6 Qianning, China
188 K 10 Qiansuo, China
188 M 7 Qianwei, China
187 F 17 Qianxi, China
189 O 9 Qianxi, China
189 P 3 Qianxian, China
189 P 3 Qianyang, China
189 Q 2 Qiaozhen, China
189 V 7 Qichun, China
189 S 9 Qidong, China
189 Z 5 Qidong, China
185 N 9 Qidukou, China
184 J 7 Qiemo, China
189 O 7 Qijiang, China
184 M 5 Qijiaojing, China
177 Q 12 Qila Ladgasht, Pakistan
177 P 11 Qila Safed, Pakistan
177 U 10 Qila Saifullah, Pakistan
185 N 7 Qilian Shan, China ⛰
189 W 7 Qimen, China
189 P 4 Qin Ling, China ⛰
189 O 3 Qin'an, China
186 L 10 Qing'an, China
187 G 20 Qingdao, China
186 K 10 Qinggang, China
185 N 8 Qinghai, China ▣
185 O 8 Qinghai Hu, China ◡
189 R 1 Qingjian, China
187 F 16 Qinglong, China
187 B 16 Qingshuihe, China
189 Y 8 Qingtian, China
189 S 1 Qingxu, China
189 P 2 Qingyang, China
187 J 15 Qingyuan, China
189 T 12 Qingyuan, China
189 X 8 Qingyuan, China
187 F 20 Qingzhou, China
187 G 17 Qinhuangdao, China
189 S 1 Qinxian, China
189 T 3 Qinyang, China
189 S 2 Qinyuan, China
189 Q 13 Qinzhou, China
189 R 15 Qionghai, China
188 M 6 Qionglai, China
188 L 5 Qionglai Shan, China ⛰
186 G 5 Qiqian, China
186 I 10 Qiqihar, China
176 J 11 Qīr, Iran
172 F 10 Qiryat Gat, Israel
175 U 12 Qishn, Yemen
184 L 5 Qitai, China
186 N 10 Qitaihe, China
188 M 11 Qiubei, China
187 G 19 Qixia, China
189 S 1 Qixian, China
189 U 3 Qixian, China
186 G 4 Qiyahe, China
189 S 9 Qiyang, China
186 J 7 Qizhan, China
179 V 14 Qizilrabot, Tajikistan
176 J 5 Qolleh-ye Damāvand, Iran ▲
176 I 6 Qom, Iran
176 I 6 Qom, Iran ▣
213 O 21 Qooriga Neegro, Somalia ≈
178 L 10 Qoraqalpoghiston Respublikasi, Uzbekistan ▣
172 H 5 Qornet es Saouda, Lebanon ▲
173 T 2 Qosh Tepe, Iraq
58 M 9 Quabbin Reservoir, Massachusetts, U.S.A. ◡
136 E 12 Quakenbrück, Germany
191 K 23 Quân Đao Nam Du, Vietnam 🏝
189 S 4 Quanbao Shan, China ▲
191 O 17 Quang Ngai, Vietnam
191 N 16 Quang Tri, Vietnam
189 X 11 Quanzhou, China
189 S 10 Quanzhou, China
85 R 5 Quaqtaq, Québec, Canada
112 E 12 Quaraí, Brazil
39 Y 3 Quarantine Station, Cocos Islands
233 D 25 Quarry Hills, New Zealand
38 B 12 Quartier Militaire, Mauritius
141 C 19 Quartu Sant'Elena, Italy
77 M 20 Quartzite Mountain, Nevada, U.S.A. ▲
74 G 12 Quartzsite, Arizona, U.S.A.
171 X 7 Quba, Azerbaijan
177 N 5 Quchan, Iran
172 K 4 Qudaym, Syria
231 U 12 Queanbeyan, New South Wales, Australia
86 K 7 Québec, Canada ▣
87 N 8 Québec, Québec, Canada
137 I 15 Quedlinburg, Germany
83 C 19 Queen Charlotte, British Columbia, Canada
111 J 23 Queen Charlotte Bay, Falkland Islands ≈
83 B 19 Queen Charlotte Islands, British Columbia, Canada 🏝
83 D 20 Queen Charlotte Sound, British Columbia, Canada ≈
80 M 3 Queen Elizabeth Islands, Nunavut, Canada 🏝
241 W 8 Queen Mary Land, Antarctica ◆
43 O 15 Queen Mary's Peak, Tristan da Cunha ▲
84 J 1 Queen Maud Gulf, Nunavut, Canada ≈
241 O 3 Queen Maud Land, Antarctica ◆
241 O 9 Queen Maud Mountains, Antarctica ⛰
231 R 6 Queensland, Australia ▣
231 S 15 Queenstown, Tasmania, Australia
233 C 23 Queenstown, New Zealand
76 F 7 Queets, Washington, U.S.A.
218 I 2 Quela, Angola
219 S 7 Quelimane, Mozambique
111 F 18 Quellón, Chile
75 N 11 Quemado, New Mexico, U.S.A.
111 F 17 Quemchi, Chile
113 D 19 Quequén, Argentina
89 Q 11 Querétaro, Mexico
89 Q 11 Querétaro, Mexico ▣
137 J 16 Querfurt, Germany
131 P 11 Quesada, Spain
83 G 19 Quesnel, British Columbia, Canada
83 G 19 Quesnel Lake, British Columbia, Canada ◡
177 T 10 Quetta, Pakistan
111 F 16 Queule, Chile
106 A 9 Quevedo, Ecuador
90 F 5 Quezaltenango, Guatemala
90 J 6 Quezaltepeque, Guatemala
197 C 19 Quezon, Philippines
196 G 11 Quezon City, Philippines
210 I 6 Quezzane, Morocco
189 V 2 Qufu, China
190 L 13 Qui Châu, Vietnam
191 O 19 Qui Nhon, Vietnam
218 G 2 Quibaxe, Angola
104 G 6 Quibdó, Colombia
128 J 6 Quiberon, France
136 H 10 Quickborn, Germany
133 D 21 Quiévrechain, Belgium
109 G 20 Quiindy, Paraguay
218 G 5 Quilengues, Angola
83 N 18 Quill Lakes, Saskatchewan, Canada ◡
107 F 17 Quillabamba, Peru
110 G 4 Quillagua, Chile
129 Q 15 Quillan, France
113 D 16 Quilmes, Argentina
181 D 24 Quilon, India
231 S 8 Quilpie, Queensland, Australia
110 F 11 Quilpue, Chile
218 H 1 Quimbele, Angola
110 K 8 Quimilí, Argentina
128 H 6 Quimper, France
128 I 6 Quimperlé, France
76 F 7 Quinault, Washington, U.S.A.
107 G 17 Quince Mil, Peru
63 S 7 Quincy, Florida, U.S.A.
65 D 19 Quincy, Illinois, U.S.A.
77 H 17 Quincy, California, U.S.A.
110 I 11 Quines, Argentina
219 U 6 Quinga, Mozambique
78 M 10 Quinhagak, Alaska, U.S.A.
197 G 16 Quiniluban, Philippines 🏝
89 Z 11 Quintana Roo, Mexico ▣
131 P 8 Quintanar, Spain
218 F 1 Quinzau, Angola
219 U 3 Quionga, Mozambique
218 G 5 Quipungo, Angola
111 F 14 Quirihue, Chile
107 K 21 Quiroga, Bolivia
113 B 16 Quiroga, Argentina
218 I 3 Quitapa, Angola
218 H 6 Quiteve, Angola
63 N 5 Quitman, Mississippi, U.S.A.
63 T 7 Quitman, Georgia, U.S.A.
106 B 8 Quito, Ecuador ⌂
108 N 11 Quixadá, Brazil
188 M 10 Qujing, China
179 Q 13 Qullai Chimtarha, Tajikistan ▲
179 S 13 Qullai Garmo, Tajikistan ▲
179 T 14 Qullai Karl Marks, Tajikistan ▲
188 I 5 Qu'nyido, China
231 P 10 Quorn, South Australia, Australia
175 Z 6 Qurayat, Oman
179 R 14 Qŭrghonteppa, Tajikistan
112 I 7 Qurinhos, Brazil
171 X 7 Qusar, Azerbaijan
175 T 13 Qusāy'ir, Yemen
212 G 10 Quseir, Egypt
189 P 6 Quxian, China
189 X 7 Quzhou, China
189 U 2 Quzhou, China
189 P 2 Quzi, China
171 V 6 Qvareli, Georgia

R

139 V 2 Raabs an der Thaya, Austria
134 L 13 Raahe, Finland
132 L 11 Raalte, Netherlands
192 L 14 Raas, Indonesia 🏝
143 K 18 Raba, Poland ∿
193 N 15 Raba, Indonesia
143 G 23 Rába, Hungary ∿
213 F 18 Rabak, Sudan
210 H 7 Rabat, Morocco ⌂
141 J 26 Rabat, Malta
234 H 3 Rabaul, Papua New Guinea
230 L 5 Rabbit Flat Roadhouse, Northern Territory, Australia
235 Y 11 Rabi, Fiji 🏝
192 B 9 Rabi, Indonesia 🏝
174 L 7 Rābigh, Saudi Arabia
90 H 5 Rabinal, Guatemala
143 K 18 Rabka, Poland
62 L 8 Raceland, Louisiana, U.S.A.
191 L 23 Rach Gia, Vietnam
71 P 15 Rachal, Texas, U.S.A.
143 H 17 Racibórz, Poland
65 H 14 Racine, Wisconsin, U.S.A.
175 P 13 Radā', Yemen
149 I 17 Radashkovichy, Belarus
60 G 5 Radcliff, Kentucky, U.S.A.
150 J 4 Radekhiv, Ukraine
61 O 7 Radford, Virginia, U.S.A.
181 B 14 Radhanpur, India
157 R 4 Radishchevo, Russian Federation
85 P 9 Radisson, Québec, Canada
104 E 8 Rado de Tumaco, Colombia ≈
213 B 19 Radom, Sudan
143 L 14 Radom, Poland
146 F 9 Radomir, Bulgaria
143 J 15 Radomsko, Poland
146 L 11 Radovets, Bulgaria
146 E 11 Radoviš, Macedonia (F.Y.R.O.M.)
139 R 6 Radstadt, Austria
149 F 17 Radun', Belarus
148 E 13 Radviliškis, Lithuania
142 N 13 Radzyń Podlaski, Poland
182 M 11 Rae Bareli, India
82 H 12 Rae-Edzo, Northwest Territories, Canada
82 G 11 Rae Lakes, Northwest Territories, Canada
61 R 10 Raeford, North Carolina, U.S.A.
233 D 24 Raes Junction, New Zealand
232 K 13 Raetihi, New Zealand
112 B 13 Rafaela, Argentina
175 O 2 Rafḥā', Saudi Arabia
147 H 20 Rafina, Greece
176 L 10 Rafsanjān, Iran
213 B 20 Raga, Sudan
196 I 12 Ragay Gulf, Philippines ≈
232 K 10 Raglan, New Zealand
127 P 10 Raglan, United Kingdom
62 H 7 Ragley, Louisiana, U.S.A.
141 K 23 Ragusa, Italy
193 P 13 Raha, Indonesia
149 M 19 Rahachow, Belarus
213 F 17 Rahad Canal, Sudan ∿
215 S 11 Rahama, Nigeria
177 V 12 Rahimyar Khan, Pakistan
176 H 6 Rāhjerd, Iran
182 I 6 Rahon, India
181 E 19 Raichur, India
183 S 11 Raiganj, India
181 H 15 Raigarh, India
193 O 15 Raijua, Indonesia 🏝
83 G 15 Rainbow Lake, Alberta, Canada
67 R 2 Rainy Lake, Minnesota, U.S.A. ◡
135 J 15 Raippaluoto, Finland 🏝
181 G 16 Raipur, India
181 G 16 Raj-Nandgaon, India
181 I 15 Rajagangapur, India
181 H 18 Rajahmundry, India
195 P 10 Rajang, Malaysia ∿
177 V 11 Rajanpur, Pakistan
181 E 23 Rajapalaiyam, India
181 C 18 Rajapur, India
182 G 8 Rajasthan, India ▣
183 Q 12 Rajauli, India
183 R 10 Rajbiraj, Nepal
182 H 8 Rajgarh, India
181 B 15 Rajkot, India
181 D 15 Rajpur, India
183 T 12 Rajshahi, Bangladesh
183 T 12 Rajshahi, Bangladesh ▣
237 O 6 Rakahanga, Cook Islands 🏝
217 R 8 Rakai, Uganda
233 G 21 Rakaia, New Zealand
233 F 20 Rakaia, New Zealand ∿
179 P 6 Rakhmet, Kazakhstan
143 C 17 Rakovník, Czech Republic
148 H 6 Rakvere, Estonia
61 S 9 Raleigh, North Carolina, U.S.A.
61 V 11 Raleigh Bay, North Carolina, U.S.A. ≈
237 W 2 Ralik Chain, Marshall Islands 🏝
70 K 4 Ralls, Texas, U.S.A.
176 I 5 Rām-Sar, Iran
172 G 7 Rama, Israel
91 Q 9 Rama, Nicaragua
172 F 9 Ramallah, Israel
181 F 23 Ramanathapuram, India
181 H 14 Ramanuj Ganj, India
234 E 2 Rambutyo Island, Papua New Guinea 🏝
150 I 7 Rakhiv, Ukraine
126 L 15 Rame Head, United Kingdom ▶
183 Q 10 Ramechhap, Nepal
156 L 1 Ramenskoye, Russian Federation
154 H 13 Rameshki, Russian Federation
183 Q 13 Ramgarh, India
183 V 13 Ramgarh, Bangladesh
176 H 9 Rāmhormoz, Iran
231 O 1 Ramingining, Northern Territory, Australia
172 F 9 Ramla, Israel
175 Q 13 Ramlat as Sab'atayn, Yemen ☗
175 P 11 Ramlat Dahm, Yemen ☗
172 G 13 Ramm, Jordan
182 K 8 Ramnagar, India
150 L 11 Râmnicu Sărat, Romania
150 I 11 Râmnicu Vâlcea, Romania
91 P 12 Ramon, Costa Rica
77 L 26 Ramona, California, U.S.A.
182 K 8 Rampur, India
182 K 6 Rampur, India
183 S 12 Rampur Hat, India
191 B 14 Ramree Island, Myanmar 🏝
125 H 16 Ramsey, United Kingdom
86 C 7 Ramsey, Ontario, Canada

Country ▣ Internal administrative region: State/Province/Territory/Dependent territory ⌂ Capital city ⛰ Mountain range/Undersea ridge ▲ Mountain peak/Volcano/Seamount ◆ Geographic feature ▶ Headland/Point/Cape/Peninsula ☗ Desert 🏝 Island/Island group ⁂ Antarctic base 🌊 Ocean ∽ Sea ≈ Bay/Gulf/Channel/Strait ◡ Lake ⬚ Salt pan/Dry/Intermittent lake ∿ River

126	J 9	**Ramsey Island**, United Kingdom ⌘
86	C 8	**Ramsey Lake**, Ontario, Canada
127	Z 11	**Ramsgate**, United Kingdom
176	G 9	**Rāmshir**, Iran
135	G 17	**Ramsjö**, Sweden
234	C 4	**Ramu**, Papua New Guinea ⌁
183	W 15	**Ramu**, Bangladesh
180	D 13	**Rana Pratap Sagar**, India ⌁
110	G 12	**Rancagua**, Chile
133	F 23	**Rance**, Belgium
181	I 14	**Ranchi**, India
89	O 9	**Rancho Grande**, Mexico
141	K 22	**Randazzo**, Italy
135	C 24	**Randers**, Denmark
134	H 11	**Randijaure**, Sweden ⌁
214	F 8	**Ranérou**, Senegal
233	E 23	**Ranfurly**, New Zealand
191	I 26	**Rangae**, Thailand
183	V 14	**Rangamati**, Bangladesh
183	W 10	**Rangapara North**, India
232	I 5	**Rangaunu Bay**, New Zealand ≈
59	O 5	**Rangeley**, Maine, U.S.A.
75	N 3	**Rangely**, Colorado, U.S.A.
71	O 6	**Ranger**, Texas, U.S.A.
86	B 8	**Ranger**, Ontario, Canada
183	V 10	**Rangia**, India
232	L 12	**Rangipo**, New Zealand
232	K 9	**Rangiriri**, New Zealand
232	M 12	**Rangitaiki**, New Zealand
233	F 21	**Rangitata**, New Zealand
232	L 13	**Rangitikei**, New Zealand ⌁
191	E 16	**Rangoon**, Myanmar ⌖
183	T 11	**Rangpur**, Bangladesh
90	K 3	**Ranguana Cay**, Belize ⌘
181	D 20	**Ranibennur**, India
183	R 13	**Raniganj**, India
70	K 8	**Rankin**, Texas, U.S.A.
84	L 4	**Rankin Inlet**, Nunavut, Canada ≈
181	A 14	**Rann of Kachchh**, India ◇
157	U 5	**Ranneye**, Russian Federation
219	W 9	**Ranohira**, Madagascar
191	F 23	**Ranong**, Thailand
234	J 6	**Ranongga**, Solomon Islands ⌘
191	H 25	**Ranot**, Thailand
193	V 11	**Ransiki**, Indonesia
192	L 12	**Rantau**, Indonesia
65	G 18	**Rantoul**, Illinois, U.S.A.
134	M 12	**Ranua**, Finland
173	U 2	**Rānya**, Iraq
186	O 9	**Raohe**, China
140	C 9	**Rapallo**, Italy
181	A 14	**Rapar**, India
66	G 9	**Rapid City**, South Dakota, U.S.A.
64	H 9	**Rapid River**, Michigan, U.S.A.
148	I 8	**Räpina**, Estonia
148	G 6	**Rapla**, Estonia
138	H 7	**Rapperswil**, Switzerland
196	K 13	**Rapurapu**, Philippines
58	I 7	**Raquette Lake**, New York, U.S.A. ⌁
237	O 11	**Rarotonga**, Cook Islands ⌘
212	F 9	**Rās**, Egypt
174	K 6	**Rās Abū Madd**, Saudi Arabia ▶
212	H 13	**Rās Abu Shagara**, Sudan ▶
175	Z 9	**Rās ad Daqm**, Oman
173	N 1	**Ra's al ʿAyn**, Syria
172	H 3	**Rās al Basīṭ**, Syria
175	Z 7	**Rās al Ḩadd**, Oman
175	Z 7	**Rās al Ḩadd**, Oman ▶
159	Q 12	**Rās al Hilāl**, Mediterranean Sea ▶
175	S 13	**Rās al Kalb**, Yemen ▶
175	X 5	**Rās al Khaimah**, United Arab Emirates
175	Z 10	**Rās al Madrakah**, Oman ▶
175	S 3	**Rās al Mish'āb**, Saudi Arabia
211	Y 7	**Rās al Muraysah**, Libya ▶
212	B 7	**Rās al Muraysah**, Egypt ▶
159	R 12	**Rās al Tin**, Mediterranean Sea ▶
159	U 12	**Rās 'Alam el Rûm**, Mediterranean Sea ▶
172	G 12	**Rās an Naqb**, Jordan
174	I 3	**Rās ash Shaykh Humayd**, Saudi Arabia ▶
211	X 7	**Rās at Tin**, Libya ▶
175	S 4	**Rās az Zawr**, Saudi Arabia ▶
175	O 15	**Rās Bāb al Mandab**, Yemen ▶
212	G 12	**Rās Banās**, Egypt ▶
174	K 6	**Rās Baridī**, Saudi Arabia ▶
213	O 22	**Rās Cabaad**, Somalia ▶
213	O 18	**Rās Caluula**, Somalia ▶
213	O 18	**Rās Caseyr**, Somalia ▶
213	I 18	**Rās Dashen**, Ethiopia ▲
213	O 20	**Rās Durdura**, Somalia ▶
176	G 10	**Rās-e Barkan**, Iran ▶
176	H 11	**Rās-e Halīleh**, Iran ▶
177	N 14	**Rās-e Meydanī**, Iran ▶
212	D 7	**Rās el Kanāyis**, Egypt ▶
159	U 12	**Rās el Kanāyis**, Mediterranean Sea ▶
175	V 12	**Rās Fartak**, Yemen ▶
213	O 20	**Rās Gabbac**, Somalia ▶
212	H 13	**Rās Hardârba**, Sudan ▶
174	L 8	**Rās Ḩāṭibah**, Saudi Arabia ▶
213	O 21	**Rās Ilig**, Somalia ▶
175	O 13	**Rās 'Īsá**, Yemen ▶
177	Q 14	**Ras Jaddi**, Pakistan ▶
176	M 14	**Rās Jagīn**, Iran ▶
158	K 10	**Rās Kaboudia**, Mediterranean Sea ▶
174	K 5	**Rās Karkūmā**, Saudi Arabia ▶
213	I 15	**Rās Kasar**, Sudan/Eritrea ▶
213	M 19	**Rās Khansiir**, Somalia ▶
213	O 20	**Rās Macbar**, Somalia ▶
175	X 11	**Rās Mirbāṭ**, Oman ▶
175	X 14	**Rās Momi**, Yemen ▶
177	T 15	**Ras Muari**, Pakistan ▶
174	I 3	**Rās Muhammad**, Egypt ▶
175	X 11	**Rās Naws**, Oman ▶
210	A 14	**Rās Nouâdhibou**, Western Sahara ▶
214	E 5	**Rās Nouâdhibou**, Mauritania ▶
177	P 14	**Ras Nuh**, Pakistan ▶
177	R 14	**Ras Ormara**, Pakistan ▶
176	H 11	**Rās osh Shaṭṭ**, Iran ▶
175	W 11	**Rās Sājir**, Oman ▶
175	Y 10	**Rās Şawqirah**, Oman ▶
217	X 9	**Ras Shaka**, Kenya ▶
175	Y 10	**Rās Sharbithāt**, Oman ▶
175	V 14	**Rās Shu'ab**, Yemen ▶
175	Z 9	**Rās Şirāb**, Oman
213	N 19	**Rās Surud**, Somalia ▶
175	S 3	**Rās Tanāqib**, Saudi Arabia ▶
175	T 4	**Rās Tannūrah**, Saudi Arabia
214	E 6	**Rās Timirist**, Mauritania ▶
213	O 19	**Rās Xaafuun**, Somalia ▶
197	C 19	**Rasa**, Philippines ⌘
149	D 14	**Raseiniai**, Lithuania
213	E 19	**Rashad**, Sudan
151	T 4	**Rashivka**, Ukraine
176	K 6	**Rashm**, Iran
176	H 4	**Rasht**, Iran
191	K 17	**Rasi Salai**, Thailand
145	L 14	**Raška**, Serbia and Montenegro
177	Q 11	**Raskoh**, Pakistan ▲
84	L 1	**Rasmussen Basin**, Nunavut, Canada ≈
82	L 7	**Rasmussen Bay**, Nunavut, Canada ≈
149	L 16	**Rasna**, Belarus
150	J 11	**Râşnov**, Romania
43	A 16	**Raso**, Cape Verde ⌘
157	N 4	**Rasskazovo**, Russian Federation
137	E 22	**Rastatt**, Germany
134	L 6	**Rásttigáisa**, Norway ▲
191	G 19	**Rat Buri**, Thailand
78	C 13	**Rat Island**, Alaska, U.S.A. ⌘
78	C 12	**Rat Islands**, Alaska, U.S.A. ⌘
233	L 14	**Rata**, New Zealand
237	X 2	**Ratak Chain**, Marshall Islands ⌘
182	H 9	**Ratangarh**, India
135	F 16	**Rätansbyn**, Sweden
182	L 11	**Rath**, India
190	A 12	**Rathedaung**, Myanmar
136	K 13	**Rathenow**, Germany
181	D 14	**Ratlam**, India
181	C 18	**Ratnagiri**, India
181	G 25	**Ratnapura**, Sri Lanka
150	J 1	**Ratne**, Ukraine
177	U 12	**Rato Dero**, Pakistan
75	S 8	**Raton**, New Mexico, U.S.A.
139	N 6	**Rattenberg**, Austria
194	C 8	**Raub**, Malaysia
113	D 17	**Rauch**, Argentina
175	R 2	**Raudhatain**, Kuwait
232	O 11	**Raukumara Range**, New Zealand ▲
135	J 18	**Rauma**, Finland
181	I 15	**Raurkela**, India
198	M 3	**Rausu**, Japan
232	O 10	**Rautoria**, New Zealand
150	I 3	**Rava-Rus'ka**, Ukraine
72	M 4	**Ravalli**, Montana, U.S.A.
176	M 9	**Rāvar**, Iran
133	H 16	**Ravels**, Belgium
77	I 16	**Ravendale**, California, U.S.A.
140	G 9	**Ravenna**, Italy
137	G 25	**Ravensburg**, Germany
231	T 4	**Ravenshoe**, Queensland, Australia
230	H 11	**Ravensthorpe**, Western Australia, Australia
177	X 10	**Ravi**, Pakistan ⌁
179	N 14	**Ravnina**, Turkmenistan
173	Q 5	**Rāwah**, Iraq
177	W 8	**Rawalpindi**, Pakistan
173	T 1	**Rawāndiz**, Iraq
193	U 11	**Rawas**, Indonesia
182	G 8	**Rawatsar**, India
143	O 14	**Rawicz**, Poland
230	K 10	**Rawlinna**, Western Australia, Australia
73	V 13	**Rawlins**, Wyoming, U.S.A.
111	I 18	**Rawson**, Argentina
185	N 11	**Rawu**, China
66	H 3	**Ray**, North Dakota, U.S.A.
172	H 6	**Rayak**, Lebanon
153	U 14	**Raychikhinsk**, Russian Federation
175	P 12	**Raydah**, Yemen
157	V 2	**Rayevskiy**, Russian Federation
127	Y 10	**Rayleigh**, United Kingdom
76	F 8	**Raymond**, Washington, U.S.A.
71	P 15	**Raymondville**, Texas, U.S.A.
191	I 20	**Rayong**, Thailand
62	J 4	**Rayville**, Louisiana, U.S.A.
177	V 8	**Razani**, Pakistan
146	L 7	**Razgrad**, Bulgaria ⊡
146	L 7	**Razgrad**, Bulgaria
146	G 11	**Razlog**, Bulgaria
127	U 11	**Reading**, United Kingdom
58	H 13	**Reading**, Pennsylvania, U.S.A.
65	K 20	**Reading**, Ohio, U.S.A.
64	E 13	**Readstown**, Wisconsin, U.S.A.
110	J 13	**Realicó**, Argentina
191	J 20	**Reăng Kesei**, Cambodia
211	Q 8	**Rebaa**, Algeria
134	I 7	**Rebbenesøy**, Norway ⌘
211	W 12	**Rebiana Sand Sea**, Libya ◇
154	G 7	**Reboly**, Russian Federation
198	I 3	**Rebun-tō**, Japan ⌘
149	M 20	**Rechytsa**, Belarus
108	O 13	**Recife**, Brazil
111	F 14	**Recinto**, Chile
112	C 12	**Reconquista**, Argentina
110	I 9	**Recreo**, Argentina
190	K 11	**Red**, Asia ⌁
57	P 12	**Red**, Texas, U.S.A. ⌁
60	H 10	**Red Bank**, Tennessee, U.S.A.
63	O 2	**Red Bay**, Alabama, U.S.A.
85	X 8	**Red Bay**, Newfoundland and Labrador, Canada ⌁
77	G 16	**Red Bluff**, California, U.S.A.
66	M 15	**Red Cloud**, Nebraska, U.S.A.
83	J 19	**Red Deer**, Alberta, Canada
68	J 7	**Red Hills**, Kansas, U.S.A. ◇
74	H 9	**Red Lake**, Arizona, U.S.A. ⌁
84	J 10	**Red Lake**, Ontario, Canada
73	S 8	**Red Lodge**, Montana, U.S.A.
212	H 11	**Red Sea**, Africa/Asia ⌁
213	G 14	**Red Sea**, Sudan ⊡
67	T 8	**Red Wing**, Minnesota, U.S.A.
194	D 5	**Redang**, Malaysia ⌘
125	K 15	**Redcar**, United Kingdom
77	G 16	**Redding**, California, U.S.A.
127	R 8	**Redditch**, United Kingdom
108	J 12	**Redenção**, Brazil
108	L 13	**Redenção do Gurguéia**, Brazil
66	M 8	**Redfield**, South Dakota, U.S.A.
154	H 14	**Redkino**, Russian Federation
77	K 24	**Redlands**, California, U.S.A.
76	H 11	**Redmond**, Oregon, U.S.A.
65	L 20	**Redoak**, Ohio, U.S.A.
126	J 15	**Redruth**, United Kingdom
67	Q 8	**Redwood Falls**, Minnesota, U.S.A.
77	F 17	**Redwood Valley**, California, U.S.A.
64	J 13	**Reed City**, Michigan, U.S.A.
66	H 6	**Reeder**, North Dakota, U.S.A.
76	E 11	**Reedsport**, Oregon, U.S.A.
61	V 5	**Reedville**, Virginia, U.S.A.
233	G 17	**Reefton**, New Zealand
137	B 15	**Rees**, Germany
171	N 9	**Refahiye**, Turkey
63	O 3	**Reform**, Alabama, U.S.A.
71	Q 12	**Refugio**, Texas, U.S.A.
142	E 9	**Rega**, Poland ⌁
137	M 22	**Regen**, Germany
137	K 22	**Regensburg**, Germany
210	L 11	**Reggane**, Algeria
140	E 8	**Reggio**, Italy
141	L 21	**Reggio di Calabria**, Italy
150	J 9	**Reghin**, Romania
83	N 19	**Regina**, Saskatchewan, Canada
177	R 10	**Registan**, Afghanistan ◇
112	K 8	**Registro**, Brazil
183	X 8	**Regong**, India
130	I 10	**Reguengos de Monsaraz**, Portugal
218	I 10	**Rehoboth**, Namibia
61	X 3	**Rehoboth Beach**, Delaware, U.S.A.
61	Y 8	**Reidsville**, North Carolina, U.S.A.
127	V 11	**Reigate**, United Kingdom
129	S 3	**Reims**, France
138	F 7	**Reinach**, Switzerland
83	M 16	**Reindeer**, Saskatchewan, Canada ⌁
83	M 14	**Reindeer Lake**, Saskatchewan, Canada ⌁
131	N 2	**Reinosa**, Spain
139	Y 2	**Reinthal**, Austria
82	J 12	**Reliance**, Northwest Territories, Canada
210	L 6	**Relizane**, Algeria
211	N 12	**Remada**, Tunisia
137	C 18	**Remagen**, Germany
192	J 14	**Rembang**, Indonesia
211	Q 8	**Remel el Abiod**, Tunisia ▲
133	M 26	**Remich**, Luxembourg
65	H 17	**Remington**, Indiana, U.S.A.
129	V 6	**Remiremont**, France
157	O 10	**Remontnoye**, Russian Federation
137	C 16	**Remscheid**, Germany
190	F 6	**Renam**, Myanmar
65	F 21	**Rend Lake**, Illinois, U.S.A. ⌁
234	K 6	**Rendova**, Solomon Islands ⌘
136	G 8	**Rendsburg**, Germany
86	H 10	**Renfrew**, Ontario, Canada
192	E 11	**Rengat**, Indonesia
110	G 12	**Rengo**, Chile
189	T 10	**Renhua**, China
151	N 11	**Reni**, Ukraine
231	Q 11	**Renmark**, South Australia, Australia
129	P 1	**Rennes**, France
84	J 10	**Rennie**, Manitoba, Canada
234	L 8	**Rennell**, Solomon Islands ⌘
128	L 5	**Rennes**, France
77	I 17	**Reno**, Nevada, U.S.A.
58	E 11	**Renovo**, Pennsylvania, U.S.A.
187	D 18	**Renqiu**, China
189	N 7	**Renshou**, China
193	O 15	**Reo**, Indonesia
179	N 13	**Repetek**, Turkmenistan
108	F 10	**Represa de Balbina**, Brazil ⌁
112	H 9	**Represa de Foz de Areia**, Brazil ⌁
112	L 5	**Represa de Furnas**, Brazil ⌁
112	F 8	**Represa de Itaipu**, Brazil/Paraguay ⌁
112	G 7	**Represa de Salto Santiago**, Brazil ⌁
112	G 7	**Represa Ilha Grande**, Brazil ⌁
112	H 4	**Represa Porto Primavera**, Brazil ⌁
112	I 3	**Represa São Simão**, Brazil ⌁
109	J 15	**Represa Serra da Mesa**, Brazil ⌁
109	L 17	**Represa Três Marias**, Brazil ⌁
108	J 11	**Represa Tucuruí**, Brazil ⌁
90	L 5	**Represa el Cajón**, Honduras ⌁
64	G 9	**Republic**, Michigan, U.S.A.
76	J 6	**Republic**, Washington, U.S.A.
218	M 12	**Republic of South Africa**, Africa ◆
144	F 10	**Republica Srpska**, Bosnia and Herzegovina ⊡
85	N 2	**Repulse Bay**, Nunavut, Canada
106	E 12	**Requena**, Peru
131	S 8	**Requena**, Spain
129	Q 3	**Réquista**, France
170	M 9	**Reşadiye**, Turkey
171	S 11	**Reşadiye**, Turkey
146	C 12	**Resen**, Macedonia (F.Y.R.O.M.)
112	H 8	**Reserva**, Brazil
75	N 12	**Reserve**, New Mexico, U.S.A.
86	I 8	**Réservoir Baskatong**, Québec, Canada ⌁
86	I 8	**Réservoir Cabonga**, Québec, Canada ⌁
86	H 8	**Réservoir Dozois**, Québec, Canada ⌁
86	K 6	**Réservoir Gouin**, Québec, Canada ⌁
85	P 9	**Réservoir la Grande Deux**, Québec, Canada ⌁
85	Q 9	**Réservoir la Grande Trois**, Québec, Canada ⌁
87	P 4	**Réservoir Manic Trois**, Québec, Canada ⌁
87	P 2	**Réservoir Manicouagan**, Québec, Canada ⌁
85	Q 9	**Réservoir Opinaca**, Québec, Canada ⌁
87	O 4	**Réservoir Outardes Quatre**, Québec, Canada ⌁
87	N 4	**Réservoir Pipmuacan**, Québec, Canada ⌁
151	T 5	**Reshetylivka**, Ukraine
112	C 10	**Resistencia**, Argentina
150	F 11	**Reşiţa**, Romania
142	E 9	**Resko**, Poland
81	P 4	**Resolute Bay**, Nunavut, Canada
233	A 24	**Resolution Island**, New Zealand ⌘
85	T 4	**Resolution Island**, Nunavut, Canada ⌘
156	L 12	**Respublika Adygeya**, Russian Federation
152	M 13	**Respublika Altay**, Russian Federation ⊡
157	W 2	**Respublika Bashkortostan**, Russian Federation ⊡
153	R 13	**Respublika Buryatiya**, Russian Federation ⊡
157	R 15	**Respublika Dagestan**, Russian Federation ⊡
157	Q 10	**Respublika Kalmykiya**, Russian Federation ⊡
154	H 6	**Respublika Kareliya**, Russian Federation ⊡
153	N 13	**Respublika Khakasiya**, Russian Federation ⊡
155	R 7	**Respublika Komi**, Russian Federation ⊡
155	O 14	**Respublika Mariy El**, Russian Federation ⊡
157	O 3	**Respublika Mordoviya**, Russian Federation ⊡
153	R 10	**Respublika Sakha**, Russia Federation ⊡
157	O 14	**Respublika Severnaya Osetiya-Alaniya**, Russian Federation ⊡
157	S 1	**Respublika Tatarstan**, Russian Federation ⊡
153	O 13	**Respublika Tyva**, Russian Federation ⊡
90	F 6	**Retalhuleu**, Guatemala
110	F 13	**Retén Llico**, Chile
127	T 4	**Retford**, United Kingdom
129	S 3	**Rethel**, France
147	H 26	**Rethymno**, Greece
139	W 2	**Retz**, Austria
38	F 3	**Réunion**, France ⊡
137	G 23	**Reutlingen**, Germany
138	L 6	**Reutte**, Austria
66	H 7	**Reva**, South Dakota, U.S.A.
129	P 14	**Revel**, France
83	H 20	**Revelstoke**, British Columbia, Canada
106	A 12	**Reventazón**, Peru
41	V 5	**Revillagigedo Islands**, Mexico ⌘
172	E 11	**Revivim**, Israel
182	M 12	**Rewa**, India
182	I 9	**Rewari**, India
73	N 10	**Rexburg**, Idaho, U.S.A.
107	I 18	**Reyes**, Bolivia
134	A 11	**Reykanestá**, Iceland ▶
45	N 14	**Reykjanes Basin**, Arctic Ocean ⌁
45	N 15	**Reykjanes Ridge**, Arctic Ocean ▲
134	B 11	**Reykjavík**, Iceland ⌖
89	R 7	**Reynosa**, Mexico
148	I 12	**Rēzekne**, Latvia
151	N 8	**Rezina**, Moldova
144	N 12	**Rgotina**, Serbia and Montenegro
127	N 8	**Rhayader**, United Kingdom
136	D 13	**Rheine**, Germany
138	E 6	**Rheinfelden**, Switzerland
137	D 20	**Rheinland-Pfalz**, Germany ⊡
138	H 9	**Rheinwaldhorn**, Switzerland ▲
129	W 5	**Rhine**, Europe ⌁
64	F 10	**Rhinelander**, Wisconsin, U.S.A.
217	R 6	**Rhino Camp**, Uganda
136	K 12	**Rhinow**, Germany
133	H 21	**Rhisnes**, Belgium
59	N 11	**Rhode Island**, U.S.A. ⊡
59	O 11	**Rhode Island Sound**, Rhode Island, U.S.A. ≈
147	O 24	**Rhodes**, Greece ⌘
159	U 9	**Rhodes Basin**, Mediterranean Sea ◇
146	G 11	**Rhodope Mountains**, Bulgaria ▲

▣ Country | ▣ Internal administrative region: State/Province/Territory/Dependent territory | ♦ Capital city | ▲ Mountain range/Undersea ridge | ▲ Mountain peak/Volcano/Seamount | ◇ Geographic feature | ▶ Headland/Point/Cape/Peninsula | ▲ Desert | ⌀ Island/Island group | ⊞ Antarctic base | Ⓢ Ocean | ⊃ Sea | ≈ Bay/Gulf/Channel/Strait | ⌇ Lake | ⌇ Salt pan/Dry/Intermittent lake | ⌇ River

240 I 6 **Rothschild Island**, Antarctica 🏝
127 U 7 **Rothwell**, United Kingdom
193 P 15 **Roti**, Indonesia
233 G 19 **Rotomanu**, New Zealand
141 N 17 **Rotondella**, Italy
232 M 11 **Rotorua**, New Zealand
139 T 6 **Rottenmann**, Austria
132 G 13 **Rotterdam**, Netherlands
132 M 5 **Rottumeroog**, Netherlands 🏝
132 L 4 **Rottumerplaat**, Netherlands 🏝
137 F 24 **Rottweil**, Germany
235 W 8 **Rotuma**, Fiji 🏝
129 Q 1 **Roubaix**, France
129 O 3 **Rouen**, France
60 F 6 **Rough River Lake**, Kentucky, U.S.A. ◣
38 C 11 **Round Island**, Mauritius 🏝
71 P 9 **Round Rock**, Texas, U.S.A.
74 M 8 **Round Rock**, Arizona, U.S.A.
73 T 6 **Roundup**, Montana, U.S.A.
124 I 6 **Rousay**, United Kingdom 🏝
86 F 7 **Rouyn**, Québec, Canada
134 L 11 **Rovaniemi**, Finland
154 L 9 **Rovdino**, Russian Federation
151 Z 7 **Roven'ky**, Ukraine
138 H 10 **Roveredo**, Switzerland
140 F 6 **Rovereto**, Italy
191 L 19 **Rôvieng Tbong**, Cambodia
140 G 8 **Rovigo**, Italy
150 H 12 **Rovinari**, Romania
157 Q 6 **Rovnoye**, Russian Federation
61 R 11 **Rowland**, North Carolina, U.S.A.
85 O 1 **Rowley Island**, Nunavut, Canada 🏝
39 U 7 **Rowley Shoals**, Indian Ocean ◇
197 I 16 **Roxas**, Philippines
197 E 17 **Roxas**, Philippines
197 H 14 **Roxas**, Philippines
61 R 8 **Roxboro**, North Carolina, U.S.A.
231 P 10 **Roxby Downs**, South Australia, Australia
73 T 4 **Roy**, Montana, U.S.A.
75 S 9 **Roy**, New Mexico, U.S.A.
127 S 8 **Royal Leamington Spa**, United Kingdom
127 X 12 **Royal Tunbridge Wells**, United Kingdom
58 M 7 **Royalton**, Vermont, U.S.A.
128 L 10 **Royan**, France
129 Q 3 **Roye**, France
127 W 9 **Royston**, United Kingdom
63 U 2 **Royston**, Georgia, U.S.A.
145 L 15 **Rožaje**, Serbia and Montenegro
142 L 11 **Różan**, Poland
151 T 11 **Rozdol'ne**, Ukraine
150 K 20 **Rožňava**, Slovakia
132 F 13 **Rozenburg**, Netherlands
132 K 13 **Rozendaal**, Netherlands
150 K 3 **Rozhyshche**, Ukraine
145 K 17 **Rrëshen**, Albania
157 O 5 **Rtishchevo**, Russian Federation
127 P 5 **Ruabon**, United Kingdom
218 G 7 **Ruacana**, Namibia
233 L 14 **Ruahine Range**, New Zealand ⛰
232 J 6 **Ruakaka**, New Zealand
233 C 26 **Ruapuke Island**, New Zealand 🏝
232 M 11 **Ruatahuna**, New Zealand
232 J 7 **Ruawai**, New Zealand
175 Q 10 **Rub' al Khālī**, Saudi Arabia ◇
151 Y 5 **Rubizhne**, Ukraine
152 L 13 **Rubtsovsk**, Russian Federation
79 P 7 **Ruby**, Alaska, U.S.A.
77 M 17 **Ruby Mountains**, Nevada, U.S.A. ⛰
150 J 11 **Rucăr**, Romania
148 B 12 **Rucava**, Latvia
189 U 10 **Rucheng**, China
61 S 4 **Ruckersville**, Virginia, U.S.A.
177 Q 11 **Rudbar**, Afghanistan
156 G 1 **Rudnya**, Russian Federation
157 P 6 **Rudnya**, Russian Federation
179 O 3 **Rudnyy**, Kazakhstan
137 J 17 **Rudolstadt**, Germany
189 Z 5 **Rudong**, China
129 P 2 **Rue**, France
213 F 17 **Rufa'a**, Sudan
129 N 9 **Ruffec**, France
113 A 16 **Rufino**, Argentina
219 O 5 **Rufunsa**, Zambia
189 Y 5 **Rugao**, China
125 K 20 **Rugby**, United Kingdom
127 T 7 **Rugby**, United Kingdom
66 K 3 **Rugby**, North Dakota, U.S.A.
127 R 6 **Rugeley**, United Kingdom
136 L 8 **Rügen**, Germany 🏝
217 Q 8 **Ruhengeri**, Rwanda
148 E 9 **Ruhnu**, Estonia 🏝
189 Z 8 **Rui'an**, China
189 V 7 **Ruichang**, China
75 R 13 **Ruidoso**, New Mexico, U.S.A.
189 V 10 **Ruijin**, China
188 H 11 **Ruili**, China
217 U 12 **Ruipa**, Tanzania
88 M 10 **Ruiz**, Mexico
148 G 9 **Rūjiena**, Latvia
134 N 11 **Ruka**, Finland
217 R 12 **Rukwa**, Tanzania ◘
124 E 11 **Rum**, United Kingdom 🏝
93 N 3 **Rum Cay**, The Bahamas 🏝
144 K 10 **Ruma**, Serbia and Montenegro
175 R 5 **Rumāh**, Saudi Arabia
173 Y 12 **Rumaila**, Iraq
213 D 21 **Rumbek**, Sudan
234 A 4 **Rumginae**, Papua New Guinea
198 J 4 **Rumoi**, Japan
219 R 3 **Rumphi**, Malawi
189 U 4 **Runan**, China
127 P 4 **Runcorn**, United Kingdom
218 J 7 **Rundu**, Namibia
217 P 6 **Rungu**, Democratic Republic of Congo
217 T 12 **Rungwa**, Tanzania
188 L 4 **Ru'nying**, China
135 O 17 **Ruokolahti**, Finland
184 K 6 **Ruoqiang**, China
134 M 6 **Ruostefjelbma**, Norway
192 E 10 **Rupat**, Indonesia 🏝
150 J 10 **Rupea**, Romania
61 O 5 **Rupert**, West Virginia, U.S.A.
240 M 12 **Ruppert Coast**, Antarctica ◇
107 I 18 **Rurrenabaque**, Bolivia
219 Q 7 **Rusape**, Zimbabwe
150 I 7 **Ruscova**, Romania
146 K 6 **Ruse**, Bulgaria ◘
146 K 6 **Ruse**, Bulgaria
187 H 20 **Rushan**, China
127 U 8 **Rushden**, United Kingdom
65 D 18 **Rushville**, Illinois, U.S.A.
149 C 14 **Rusnė**, Lithuania
148 I 12 **Rušonu ezers**, Latvia ◣
60 L 4 **Russell**, Kentucky, U.S.A.
68 L 4 **Russell**, Kansas, U.S.A.
234 L 6 **Russell Islands**, Solomon Islands 🏝
60 H 7 **Russell Springs**, Kentucky, U.S.A.
60 F 7 **Russellville**, Kentucky, U.S.A.
63 O 2 **Russellville**, Alabama, U.S.A.
69 U 10 **Russellville**, Arkansas, U.S.A.
152 J 9 **Russian Federation**, Europe □
240 M 12 **Russkaya**, Antarctica ⁙
153 V 7 **Russkoye Ust'ye**, Russian Federation
171 U 7 **Rust'avi**, Georgia
219 N 11 **Rustenburg**, Republic of South Africa
62 I 4 **Ruston**, Louisiana, U.S.A.
135 C 17 **Ruten**, Norway ▲
193 O 15 **Ruteng**, Indonesia
77 M 18 **Ruth**, Nevada, U.S.A.
60 M 10 **Rutherfordton**, North Carolina, U.S.A.
58 L 7 **Rutland**, Vermont, U.S.A.
181 N 22 **Rutland Island**, India 🏝
184 H 8 **Rutog**, China
86 D 9 **Rutter**, Ontario, Canada
157 R 15 **Rutul**, Russian Federation
132 M 12 **Ruurlo**, Netherlands
217 U 14 **Ruvuma**, Tanzania ◘
219 S 3 **Ruvuma**, Mozambique/Tanzania ∫
175 V 6 **Ruweis**, United Arab Emirates
157 P 3 **Ruzayevka**, Russian Federation
149 F 19 **Ruzhany**, Belarus
143 J 19 **Ružomberok**, Slovakia
217 Q 9 **Rwanda**, Africa □
156 M 2 **Ryazan'**, Russian Federation
156 M 2 **Ryazanskaya Oblast'**, Russian Federation ◘
156 M 3 **Ryazhsk**, Russian Federation
240 J 7 **Ryberg Peninsula**, Antarctica ▶
154 J 13 **Rybinsk**, Russian Federation
154 I 12 **Rybinsk Reservoir**, Russian Federation ◣
143 I 17 **Rybnik**, Poland
127 T 13 **Ryde**, United Kingdom
231 S 13 **Rye**, Victoria, Australia
127 Y 12 **Rye**, United Kingdom
127 Y 13 **Rye Bay**, United Kingdom ≈
73 T 6 **Ryegate**, Montana, U.S.A.
143 M 14 **Ryki**, Poland
156 I 5 **Ryl'sk**, Russian Federation
198 I 13 **Ryōtsu**, Japan
142 J 11 **Rypin**, Poland
199 N 24 **Ryukyu Islands**, Japan 🏝
40 K 5 **Ryukyu Trench**, Pacific Ocean ◇
142 D 12 **Rzepin**, Poland
143 M 17 **Rzeszów**, Poland
154 G 14 **Rzhev**, Russian Federation

S

132 L 13 **'s-Heerenberg**, Netherlands
133 I 14 **'s-Hertogenbosch**, Netherlands
90 I 5 **Sa de las Minas**, Guatemala ⛰
191 M 22 **Sa Đec**, Vietnam
113 D 18 **Sa del Tandil**, Argentina ⛰
191 I 19 **Sa Kaeo**, Thailand
213 K 24 **Saacow**, Somalia
137 J 15 **Saale**, Germany ∫
137 J 18 **Saalfeld**, Germany
139 Q 6 **Saalfelden**, Austria
137 C 21 **Saarbrücken**, Germany
137 B 20 **Saarburg**, Germany
148 D 9 **Sääre**, Estonia
148 D 8 **Saaremaa**, Estonia 🏝
135 L 16 **Saarijärvi**, Finland
137 C 21 **Saarland**, Germany ◘
138 E 10 **Saas Fee**, Switzerland
172 J 6 **Sab' Ābār**, Syria
93 W 8 **Saba**, Netherlands Antilles 🏝
144 J 10 **Šabac**, Serbia and Montenegro
131 W 4 **Sabadell**, Spain
199 G 16 **Sabae**, Japan
195 W 6 **Sabah**, Malaysia ◘
180 E 12 **Sabalgarh**, India
90 M 7 **Sabamagrande**, Honduras
104 L 3 **Sabana Grande**, Venezuela
104 I 2 **Sabanalarga**, Colombia
104 L 3 **Sabaneta**, Venezuela
192 B 8 **Sabang**, Indonesia
196 G 7 **Sabangan**, Philippines
150 L 9 **Săbăoani**, Romania
181 G 25 **Sabaragamuwa**, Sri Lanka ◘
141 H 15 **Sabaudia**, Italy
107 I 21 **Sabaya**, Bolivia
172 H 9 **Şabḩā**, Jordan
211 T 11 **Sabhā**, Libya
71 N 11 **Sabinal**, Texas, U.S.A.
131 T 3 **Sabiñánigo**, Spain
89 Q 6 **Sabinas Hidalgo**, Mexico
62 H 6 **Sabine**, Louisiana, U.S.A. ∫
62 H 8 **Sabine Lake**, Louisiana, U.S.A. ◣
211 T 8 **Sabkhat al Hayshah**, Libya ◣
211 X 9 **Sabkhat al Qunayyin**, Libya ◣
211 W 9 **Sabkhat Ghuzayyil**, Libya ◣
197 F 14 **Sablayan**, Philippines
215 S 9 **Sabon Kafi**, Niger
128 M 13 **Sabres**, France
241 X 12 **Sabrina Coast**, Antarctica ◇
196 H 2 **Sabtang**, Philippines 🏝
130 J 6 **Sabugal**, Portugal
193 N 11 **Sabulu**, Indonesia
175 O 11 **Şabyā**, Saudi Arabia
176 M 6 **Sabzevār**, Iran
76 K 10 **Sacajawea Peak**, Oregon, U.S.A. ▲
131 Q 6 **Sacedón**, Spain
187 M 21 **Sach'ŏn**, South Korea
137 M 16 **Sachsen**, Germany ◘
136 J 12 **Sachsen-Anhalt**, Germany ◘
58 G 6 **Sackets Harbor**, New York, U.S.A.
73 V 2 **Saco**, Montana, U.S.A.
197 I 22 **Sacol**, Philippines 🏝
77 G 19 **Sacramento**, California, U.S.A.
77 G 17 **Sacramento**, California, U.S.A. ∫
75 R 13 **Sacramento Mountains**, New Mexico, U.S.A. ⛰
77 G 16 **Sacramento Valley**, California, U.S.A. ◇
172 I 5 **Şadad**, Syria
175 O 11 **Şa'dah**, Yemen
191 H 26 **Sadao**, Thailand
181 E 18 **Sadaseopet**, India
173 V 4 **Sadd Darband-i Khān**, Iraq ◣
173 T 8 **Saddat al Hindīyah**, Iraq
175 X 11 **Şadḩ**, Oman
213 G 20 **Sadi**, Ethiopia
177 V 12 **Sadiqabad**, Pakistan
183 Y 9 **Sadiya**, India
198 I 13 **Sadoga-shima**, Japan 🏝
151 U 11 **Sadove**, Ukraine
157 P 9 **Sadovoye**, Russian Federation
177 V 4 **Safed Khirs**, Afghanistan ⛰
177 P 7 **Safed Koh**, Afghanistan ⛰
135 E 21 **Säffle**, Sweden
74 L 13 **Safford**, Arizona, U.S.A.
127 X 8 **Saffron Walden**, United Kingdom
210 G 8 **Safi**, Morocco
177 O 10 **Safidabeh**, Iran
172 H 4 **Şāfītā**, Syria
156 I 1 **Safonovo**, Russian Federation
173 Z 12 **Safwān**, Iraq
234 E 4 **Sag Sag**, Papua New Guinea
184 I 10 **Saga**, China
199 B 21 **Saga**, Japan
199 E 21 **Saga**, Japan
198 K 12 **Sagae**, Japan
190 C 10 **Sagaing**, Myanmar ◘
190 D 11 **Sagaing**, Myanmar
199 K 17 **Sagami-nada**, Japan ≈
199 K 16 **Sagami-wan**, Japan ≈
67 U 2 **Saganaga Lake**, Minnesota, U.S.A. ◣
191 F 21 **Saganthif Kyun**, Myanmar 🏝
181 F 14 **Sagar**, India
153 S 7 **Sagastyr**, Russian Federation
183 P 10 **Sagauli**, India
176 L 8 **Saghand**, Iran
64 L 13 **Saginaw**, Michigan, U.S.A.
64 L 13 **Saginaw Bay**, Michigan, U.S.A. ≈
178 J 6 **Sagiz**, Kazakhstan
64 G 9 **Sagola**, Michigan, U.S.A.
131 P 11 **Sagra**, Spain ▲
130 G 12 **Sagres**, Portugal
190 C 13 **Sagu**, Myanmar
92 M 6 **Sagua de Tánamo**, Cuba
92 J 4 **Sagua la Grande**, Cuba
75 Q 6 **Saguache**, Colorado, U.S.A.
87 N 6 **Saguenay**, Québec, Canada
87 N 6 **Saguenay**, Québec, Canada ∫
131 T 8 **Sagunto**, Spain
79 R 3 **Sagwon**, Alaska, U.S.A.
172 H 9 **Saḩāb**, Jordan
210 I 13 **Sahara**, Algeria ◇
42 J 10 **Saharan Seamounts**, Atlantic Ocean ▲
182 J 7 **Saharanpur**, India
183 R 11 **Saharsa**, India
171 V 10 **Şahbuz**, Azerbaijan
183 S 12 **Sahibganj**, India
177 X 10 **Sahiwal**, Pakistan
177 W 9 **Sahiwal**, Pakistan
177 O 9 **Sahlābād**, Iran
173 T 12 **Şaḩrā' al Ḩijārā**, Iraq ◇
88 J 4 **Sahuaripa**, Mexico
89 O 11 **Sahuayo**, Mexico
39 V 6 **Sahul Shelf**, Indian Ocean ◇
213 B 20 **Sa'id Bundas**, Sudan
210 L 6 **Saïda**, Algeria
172 G 6 **Saïda**, Lebanon
234 D 4 **Saidor**, Papua New Guinea
183 T 11 **Saidpur**, Bangladesh
199 E 17 **Saigō**, Japan
183 X 14 **Saiha**, India
187 B 14 **Saihan Tal**, China
199 E 20 **Saijō**, Japan
199 D 21 **Saiki**, Japan
135 N 17 **Saimaa**, Finland ◣
177 P 11 **Saindak**, Pakistan
124 J 13 **St Abb's Head**, United Kingdom ▶
139 W 5 **St Aegyd am Neuwalde**, Austria
126 J 15 **St Agnes**, United Kingdom
129 O 7 **St-Aignan**, France
85 Y 10 **St Alban's**, Newfoundland and Labrador, Canada
127 V 10 **St Albans**, United Kingdom
60 M 4 **St Albans**, West Virginia, U.S.A.
127 R 14 **St Alban's Head**, United Kingdom ▶
129 Q 8 **St-Amand-Montrond**, France
129 U 9 **St-Amour**, France
139 U 8 **St Andrä**, Austria
38 B 14 **St-André**, Réunion
63 X 6 **St Andrew Sound**, Georgia, U.S.A. ≈
124 I 12 **St Andrews**, United Kingdom
38 B 9 **Ste Anne**, Seychelles 🏝
87 R 5 **Ste-Anne-des-Monts**, Québec, Canada
85 X 9 **St Anthony**, Newfoundland and Labrador, Canada
138 K 7 **St Anton am Arlberg**, Austria
231 R 13 **St Arnaud**, Victoria, Australia
233 H 17 **St Arnaud**, New Zealand
127 O 4 **St Asaph**, United Kingdom
85 W 9 **St-Augustin**, Québec, Canada
63 W 8 **St Augustine**, Florida, U.S.A.
126 K 15 **St Austell**, United Kingdom
126 K 15 **St Austell Bay**, United Kingdom ≈
93 X 8 **St Barthélémy**, France, France 🏝
129 N 15 **St-Béat**, France
38 B 14 **St-Benoit**, Réunion
126 J 9 **St Bride's Bay**, United Kingdom ≈
128 J 5 **St-Brieuc**, France
129 O 6 **St-Calais**, France
86 F 13 **St Catharines**, Ontario, Canada
42 B 6 **St Catherine Point**, Bermuda ▶
127 T 14 **St Catherine's Point**, United Kingdom ▶
129 P 12 **St-Céré**, France
73 Q 13 **Saint Charles**, Idaho, U.S.A.
69 X 4 **St Charles**, Missouri, U.S.A.
126 L 9 **St Clears**, United Kingdo
67 R 7 **St Cloud**, Minnesota, U.S.A.
93 V 8 **St Croix**, Virgin Islands, U.S.A. 🏝
64 C 10 **St Croix Falls**, Wisconsin, U.S.A.
87 O 9 **St-Damien-de-Buckland**, Québec, Canada
126 J 9 **St David's**, United Kingdom
126 J 9 **St David's Head**, United Kingdom ▶
42 B 7 **St David's Island**, Bermuda 🏝
38 A 14 **St-Denis**, Réunion ⌂
129 W 5 **St-Dié**, France
129 T 5 **St Dizier**, France
129 T 10 **St-Étienne**, France
93 X 8 **St Eusatius**, Netherlands Antilles 🏝
87 P 6 **St-Fabien**, Québec, Canada
86 M 6 **St-Félicien**, Québec, Canada
129 S 6 **St-Florentin**, France
129 R 11 **St-Flour**, France
68 G 2 **St Francis**, Kansas, U.S.A.
138 I 6 **St Gallen**, Switzerland
129 N 15 **St-Gaudens**, France
231 U 9 **St George**, Queensland, Australia
42 C 7 **St George**, Bermuda
61 P 14 **St George**, South Carolina, U.S.A.
74 H 7 **St George**, Utah, U.S.A.
87 S 10 **St George**, New Brunswick, Canada
63 S 8 **St George Island**, Florida, U.S.A. 🏝
78 J 11 **St George Island**, Alaska, U.S.A. 🏝
139 U 3 **St Georgen**, Austria
93 Y 13 **St George's**, Grenada ⌂
105 Y 7 **St Georges**, French Guiana
87 O 9 **St-Georges**, Québec, Canada
87 X 9 **St George's Bay**, Nova Scotia, Canada ≈
85 W 11 **St Georges Bay**, Newfoundland and Labrador, Canada ≈
125 E 21 **St George's Channel**, Republic of Ireland/United Kingdom ≈
234 H 3 **St George's Channel**, Papua New Guinea ≈
42 B 7 **St George's Island**, Bermuda 🏝
139 R 5 **St Gilgen**, Austria
133 F 17 **St-Gillis-Waas**, Belgium
129 O 15 **St-Girons**, France
126 K 10 **St Govan's Head**, United Kingdom ▶
64 K 12 **Saint Helen**, Michigan, U.S.A.
43 M 25 **St Helena**, U.K. ◘
218 J 14 **Saint Helena Bay**, Republic of South Africa ≈
43 J 16 **Saint Helena Fracture Zone**, Atlantic Ocean ◇
61 P 15 **St Helena Sound**, South Carolina, U.S.A. ≈

□ Country ◘ Internal administrative region: State/Province/Territory/Dependent territory ⌂ Capital city ⛰ Mountain range/Undersea ridge ▲ Mountain peak/Volcano/Seamount ◇ Geographic feature ▶ Headland/Point/Cape/Peninsula ◭ Desert 🏝 Island/Island group ⁙ Antarctic base ◎ Ocean ∿ Sea ≈ Bay/Gulf/Channel/Strait ◣ Lake ⚑ Salt pan/Dry/Intermittent lake ∫ River

■ Country ▣ Internal administrative region: State/Province/Territory/Dependent territory ▲ Capital city ▲ Mountain range/ Undersea ridge ▲ Mountain peak/ Volcano/Seamount ◇ Geographic feature ▶ Headland/Point/ Cape/Peninsula ▲ Desert ⤳ Island/Island group ▲ Antarctic base ⊚ Ocean ⤳ Sea ≈ Bay/Gulf/Channel/Strait ⤳ Lake ⤳ Salt pan/Dry/ Intermittent lake ⤳ River

331

□ Country   □ Internal administrative region: State/Province/Territory/Dependent territory   ▪ Capital city   ▲ Mountain range/ Undersea ridge   ▲ Mountain peak/ Volcano/Seamount   ◇ Geographic feature   ▶ Headland/Point/ Cape/Peninsula   ▬ Desert   ⌐ Island/Island group   ⊞ Antarctic base   ⌐ Ocean   ⌐ Sea   ≈ Bay/Gulf/Channel/Strait   ⌇ Lake   ⌇ Salt pan/Dry/ Intermittent lake   ⌇ River

333

▣ Country | ▣ Internal administrative region: State/Province/Territory/Dependent territory | ♦ Capital city | ▲ Mountain range/Undersea ridge | ▲ Mountain peak/Volcano/Seamount | ◇ Geographic feature | ▶ Headland/Point/Cape/Peninsula | Desert | ⇄ Island/Island group | Antarctic base | Ocean | Sea | ≈ Bay/Gulf/Channel/Strait | Lake | Salt pan/Dry/Intermittent lake | River

Sherbrooke – Sirajganj

5 M 10 Sherbrooke, Québec, Canada
X 10 Sherbrooke, Nova Scotia, Canada
13 F 15 Shereiq, Sudan
30 B 12 Shergarh, India
33 P 12 Sherghati, India
V 12 Sheridan, Arkansas, U.S.A.
V 9 Sheridan, Wyoming, U.S.A.
R 4 Sherman, Texas, U.S.A.
R 3 Sherman Mills, Maine, U.S.A.
33 U 11 Sherpur, Bangladesh
27 T 5 Sherwood Forest, United Kingdom
24 J 4 Shetland Islands, United Kingdom
78 H 9 Shetpe, Kazakhstan
13 G 21 Shewa Gīmīra, Ethiopia
39 X 7 Shexian, China
39 Y 4 Sheyang, China
5 M 4 Sheyenne, North Dakota, U.S.A.
76 J 13 Sheykh Sho'eyb, Iran
24 F 9 Shiant Islands, United Kingdom
75 S 12 Shibām, Yemen
98 J 13 Shibata, Japan
36 J 4 Shibazhan, China
98 M 4 Shibecha, Japan
98 K 4 Shibetsu, Japan
98 M 4 Shibetsu, Japan
12 E 8 Shibîn el Kôm, Egypt
37 I 17 Shicheng Dao, China
37 I 20 Shidao, China
38 J 9 Shigu, China
34 K 4 Shihezi, China
38 L 5 Shihoro, Japan
99 C 22 Shiiba, Japan
37 C 18 Shijiazhuang, China
98 J 7 Shikabe, Japan
7 U 12 Shikarpur, Pakistan
99 K 18 Shikine-shima, Japan
32 J 10 Shikohabad, India
99 E 20 Shikoku, Japan
L 4 Shikoku Basin, Pacific Ocean
99 E 21 Shikoku-sanchi, Japan
98 J 6 Shikotsu-ko, Japan
33 S 10 Shiliguri, India
33 V 11 Shillong, India
39 Q 12 Shilong, China
56 M 2 Shilovo, Russian Federation
99 B 22 Shimabara, Japan
53 U 13 Shimanovsk, Russian Federation
13 M 19 Shimbiris, Somalia
99 J 17 Shimizu, Japan
32 J 6 Shimla, India
99 B 24 Shimo-Koshiki-jima, Japan
99 K 17 Shimoda, Japan
31 C 20 Shimoga, India
38 J 8 Shimokita-hantō, Japan
99 B 20 Shimonoseki, Japan
77 Y 5 Shimshal, Pakistan
32 I 1 Shimshal, India
54 E 12 Shimsk, Russian Federation
77 Q 8 Shīndand, Afghanistan
90 E 7 Shingbwiyang, Myanmar
4 I 9 Shingleton, Michigan, U.S.A.
99 H 19 Shingū, Japan
98 K 12 Shinjō, Japan
98 K 5 Shintoku, Japan
17 T 10 Shinyanga, Tanzania
17 T 10 Shinyanga, Tanzania
98 K 12 Shiogama, Japan
99 I 16 Shiojiri, Japan
99 N 26 Shiokawa, Japan
99 H 20 Shiono-misaki, Japan
99 L 14 Shioya-zaki, Japan
88 L 11 Shiping, China
27 S 2 Shipley, United Kingdom
5 N 8 Shiprock, New Mexico, U.S.A.
5 N 8 Shiprock Peak, New Mexico, U.S.A.
89 Z 7 Shipu, China
189 Q 4 Shiquan, China
176 J 9 Shīr Kūh, Iran
198 J 8 Shirakami-misaki, Japan
199 K 14 Shirakawa, Japan
198 M 5 Shiranuka, Japan
241 N 11 Shirase Coast, Antarctica
176 I 10 Shīrāz, Iran
198 M 3 Shiretoko-hantō, Japan
198 M 3 Shiretoko-misaki, Japan
198 K 8 Shiriya-zaki, Japan
58 L 12 Shirley, New York, U.S.A.
198 K 12 Shiroishi, Japan
215 R 11 Shiroro Reservoir, Nigeria
177 N 5 Shīrvān, Iran
186 J 5 Shisanzhan, China
78 L 13 Shishaldin Volcano, Alaska, U.S.A.
78 M 5 Shishmaref, Alaska, U.S.A.
189 S 7 Shishou, China
186 J 5 Shisizhan, China
189 T 11 Shitan, China
180 B 12 Shiv, India
180 E 13 Shivpuri, India
186 G 6 Shiwei, China
189 R 5 Shiyan, China
186 J 6 Shiyizhan, China
188 M 11 Shizong, China
198 L 11 Shizugawa, Japan
185 R 7 Shizuishan, China
199 J 17 Shizuoka, Japan
149 M 16 Shklow, Belarus
145 J 16 Shkodër, Albania
145 J 19 Shkumbin, Albania
199 D 19 Shōbara, Japan
199 F 19 Shodo-shima, Japan
198 J 5 Shokanbetsu-dake, Japan
179 O 4 Sholaksay, Kazakhstan
179 R 9 Shollakorgan, Kazakhstan
43 M 20 Shona Ridge, Atlantic Ocean
177 S 14 Shorap, Pakistan
234 J 5 Shortland Island, Solomon Islands
198 J 4 Shosanbetsu, Japan
72 M 12 Shoshone, Idaho, U.S.A.
77 L 22 Shoshone, California, U.S.A.
77 K 18 Shoshone Mountains, Nevada, U.S.A.
73 U 11 Shoshoni, Wyoming, U.S.A.
151 S 1 Shostka, Ukraine
189 X 7 Shouchang, China
189 V 5 Shouxian, China
189 T 1 Shouyang, China
74 L 11 Show Low, Arizona, U.S.A.
213 G 17 Showak, Sudan
154 M 3 Shoyna, Russian Federation
154 K 9 Shozhma, Russian Federation
62 H 4 Shreveport, Louisiana, U.S.A.
127 P 6 Shrewsbury, United Kingdom
179 T 10 Shu, Kazakhstan
173 Y 11 Shu'aiba, Iraq
188 M 5 Shuajingsi, China
186 J 11 Shuangcheng, China
189 S 9 Shuangfeng, China
188 J 11 Shuangjiang, China
186 I 13 Shuangliao, China
186 N 10 Shuangyashan, China
178 L 6 Shubarkuduk, Kazakhstan
189 V 6 Shucheng, China
186 L 12 Shulan, China
151 Y 5 Shul'hynka, Ukraine
79 N 13 Shumagin Islands, Alaska, U.S.A.
178 L 10 Shumanay, Uzbekistan
146 M 7 Shumen, Bulgaria
146 L 8 Shumen, Bulgaria
157 Q 1 Shumerlya, Russian Federation
152 I 11 Shumikha, Russian Federation
149 L 14 Shumilina, Belarus
189 X 9 Shunchang, China
189 T 12 Shunde, China
79 O 5 Shungnak, Alaska, U.S.A.
187 B 17 Shuozhou, China
175 Q 14 Shuqrah, Yemen
176 I 7 Shūr Āb, Iran
177 N 11 Shūr Gaz, Iran
176 M 7 Shūrāb, Iran
219 P 7 Shurugwi, Zimbabwe
177 O 9 Shusf, Iran
176 G 8 Shūsh, Iran
176 G 8 Shushtar, Iran
90 I 5 Shutaque, Guatemala
154 K 14 Shuya, Russian Federation
189 X 3 Shuyang, China
190 D 11 Shwebo, Myanmar
179 R 11 Shymkent, Kazakhstan
182 K 3 Shyok, India
151 S 8 Shyroke, Ukraine
151 T 4 Shyshaky, Ukraine
149 J 19 Shyshchytsy, Belarus
191 G 18 Si Nakarin Reservoir, Thailand
191 H 20 Si Racha, Thailand
193 V 14 Sia, Indonesia
177 Q 13 Siahan Range, Pakistan
177 Y 8 Sialkot, Pakistan
234 E 5 Sialum, Papua New Guinea
192 G 9 Siantan, Indonesia
197 N 18 Siargao, Philippines
197 G 24 Siasi, Philippines
197 G 25 Siasi, Philippines
234 E 4 Siassi, Papua New Guinea
147 D 15 Siatista, Greece
197 J 19 Siaton, Philippines
193 Q 9 Siau, Indonesia
148 E 13 Šiaulėnai, Lithuania
148 E 13 Šiauliai, Lithuania
196 H 1 Siayan, Philippines
141 M 18 Sibari, Italy
197 G 15 Sibay, Philippines
153 N 9 Siberia, Russian Federation
192 C 11 Siberut, Indonesia
177 T 11 Sibi, Pakistan
234 B 6 Sibidiri, Papua New Guinea
216 G 10 Sibiti, Congo
150 I 10 Sibiu, Romania
67 P 10 Sibley, Iowa, U.S.A.
193 N 10 Siboa, Indonesia
192 C 10 Sibolga, Indonesia
183 Y 10 Sibsagar, India
127 W 5 Sibsey, United Kingdom
194 F 9 Sibu, Malaysia
195 P 9 Sibu, Malaysia
197 H 22 Sibuco, Philippines
197 H 22 Sibuco Bay, Philippines
197 J 21 Sibuguey, Philippines
197 I 22 Sibuguey Bay, Philippines
216 J 4 Sibut, Central African Republic
197 D 25 Sibutu, Philippines
197 D 26 Sibutu Group, Philippines
197 E 25 Sibutu Passage, Philippines
197 I 14 Sibuyan, Philippines
197 I 14 Sibuyan Sea, Philippines
107 I 20 Sicasica, Bolivia
191 G 24 Sichon, Thailand
188 M 6 Sichuan, China
189 O 7 Sichuan Basin, China
141 J 23 Sicilia, Italy
141 F 21 Sicilian Channel, Italy/Tunisia
141 I 22 Sicily, Italy
158 M 9 Sicily–Malta Escarpment, Mediterranean Sea
91 P 4 Sico, Honduras
91 O 5 Sico, Honduras
144 J 9 Šid, Serbia and Montenegro
210 L 6 Sid, Algeria
141 M 21 Siderno, Italy
183 N 12 Sidhi, India
210 L 6 Sidi Ali, Algeria
212 C 7 Sidi Barrani, Egypt
210 K 6 Sidi Bel Abbès, Algeria
210 G 7 Sidi-Bennour, Morocco
211 Q 6 Sidi Bouzid, Tunisia
210 F 9 Sidi Ifni, Morocco
210 I 6 Sidi Kacem, Morocco
210 G 7 Sidi-Smaïl, Morocco
192 C 9 Sidikalang, Indonesia
146 G 12 Sidirokastro, Greece
127 O 13 Sidmouth, United Kingdom
66 H 14 Sidney, Nebraska, U.S.A.
73 Z 3 Sidney, Montana, U.S.A.
109 H 18 Sidrolândia, Brazil
142 M 13 Siedlce, Poland
137 E 17 Siegen, Germany
191 K 19 Siem Reap, Cambodia
142 N 12 Siemiatycze, Poland
191 M 19 Siempang, Cambodia
140 F 11 Siena, Italy
143 I 14 Sieradz, Poland
142 J 11 Sierpc, Poland
70 F 8 Sierra Blanca, Texas, U.S.A.
70 F 8 Sierra Blanca, Texas, U.S.A.
111 H 16 Sierra Colorada, Argentina
90 M 6 Sierra de Agalta, Honduras
111 H 14 Sierra de Auca Mahuida, Argentina
88 G 5 Sierra de Camalli, Mexico
88 F 2 Sierra de Juárez, Mexico
90 M 6 Sierra de la Esperanza, Honduras
113 A 18 Sierra de la Ventana, Argentina
89 S 14 Sierra de Miahuatlán, Mexico
70 F 7 Sierra Diablo, Texas, U.S.A.
111 I 17 Sierra Grande, Argentina
214 G 11 Sierra Leone, Africa
42 K 13 Sierra Leone Basin, Atlantic Ocean
42 J 13 Sierra Leone Rise, Atlantic Ocean
196 G 9 Sierra Madre, Philippines
89 V 14 Sierra Madre, Mexico
89 P 13 Sierra Madre del Sur, Mexico
88 K 4 Sierra Madre Occidental, Mexico
89 P 5 Sierra Madre Oriental, Mexico
92 L 6 Sierra Maestra, Cuba
105 N 6 Sierra Maigualida, Venezuela
130 K 11 Sierra Morena, Spain
110 H 7 Sierra Nevada, Argentina
77 G 17 Sierra Nevada, California, U.S.A.
105 P 6 Sierra Parima, Venezuela
88 F 2 Sierra San Pedro Martir, Mexico
105 O 10 Sierra Tapirapecó, Venezuela
70 F 8 Sierra Vieja, Texas, U.S.A.
74 L 15 Sierra Vista, Arizona, U.S.A.
110 I 11 Sierras de Córdoba, Argentina
138 D 10 Sierre, Switzerland
135 L 14 Sievi, Finland
147 I 22 Sifnos, Greece
235 W 12 Sigatoka, Fiji
45 N 11 Sigguup Nunaa, Greenland
150 I 7 Sighetu Marmației, Romania
150 J 10 Sighișoara, Romania
192 B 8 Sigli, Indonesia
134 C 9 Siglufjörður, Iceland
197 I 16 Sigma, Philippines
137 F 24 Sigmaringen, Germany
133 L 20 Signal de Botrange, Belgium
74 H 7 Signal Peak, Utah, U.S.A.
240 H 1 Signy, Antarctica
90 L 6 Siguatepeque, Honduras
131 S 2 Sigüés, Spain
214 H 10 Siguiri, Guinea
148 G 10 Sigulda, Latvia
189 W 4 Sihong, China
181 G 14 Sihora, India
107 C 14 Sihuas, Peru
189 T 12 Sihui, China
135 N 15 Siilinjärvi, Finland
171 R 12 Siirt, Turkey
235 N 6 Sikaiana, Solomon Islands
182 G 9 Sikar, India
190 E 9 Sikaw, Myanmar
69 Z 7 Sikeston, Missouri, U.S.A.
153 W 15 Sikhote-Alin', Russian Federation
147 J 23 Sikinos, Greece
183 S 9 Sikkim, India
143 H 26 Siklós, Hungary
153 S 8 Siktyakh, Russian Federation
197 M 14 Sila Point, Philippines
140 E 5 Silandro, Italy
197 J 17 Silay, Philippines
183 W 12 Silchar, India
61 Q 9 Siler City, North Carolina, U.S.A.
143 D 14 Silesia, Poland
211 N 14 Silet, Algeria
182 M 8 Silgarhi, Nepal
38 A 9 Silhouette, Seychelles
170 I 14 Silifke, Turkey
180 K 12 Siliguri, India
189 P 12 Silin, China
184 K 9 Siling Co, China
146 M 6 Silistra, Bulgaria
146 M 6 Silistra, Bulgaria
170 D 7 Silivri, Turkey
135 F 18 Siljan, Sweden
131 T 8 Silla, Spain
148 J 6 Sillamäe, Estonia
139 P 9 Sillian, Austria
69 S 9 Siloam Springs, Arkansas, U.S.A.
71 U 9 Silsbee, Texas, U.S.A.
149 C 14 Šilutė, Lithuania
171 Q 11 Silvan, Turkey
171 Q 11 Silvan Baraji, Turkey
181 C 16 Silvassa, India
67 U 4 Silver Bay, Minnesota, U.S.A.
75 N 13 Silver City, New Mexico, U.S.A.
76 H 12 Silver Lake, Oregon, U.S.A.
232 K 8 Silverdale, New Zealand
127 T 8 Silverstone, United Kingdom
130 H 12 Silves, Portugal
89 Y 12 Silvituc, Mexico
138 J 8 Silvretta Gruppe, Switzerland
157 X 1 Sim, Russian Federation
188 J 12 Simao, China
197 H 14 Simara, Philippines
170 D 10 Simav, Turkey
216 M 7 Simba, Democratic Republic of Congo
234 C 4 Simbai, Papua New Guinea
86 D 14 Simcoe, Ontario, Canada
213 I 18 Simēn Mountains, Ethiopia
192 A 9 Simeuluë, Indonesia
151 U 12 Simferopol', Ukraine
181 H 15 Simga, India
77 J 24 Simi Valley, California, U.S.A.
183 N 7 Simikot, Nepal
62 J 6 Simmesport, Louisiana, U.S.A.
73 P 4 Simms, Montana, U.S.A.
149 E 16 Simnas, Lithuania
134 M 11 Simojärvi, Finland
108 M 13 Simplicio Mendes, Brazil
138 F 10 Simplon, Switzerland
73 R 2 Simpson, Montana, U.S.A.
231 P 7 Simpson Desert, Northern Territory, Australia
82 M 5 Simpson Peninsula, Nunavut, Canada
183 P 10 Simra, Nepal
135 F 25 Simrishamn, Sweden
195 N 10 Simunjan, Malaysia
197 E 25 Simunul, Philippines
213 M 22 Sina Dhaqa, Somalia
192 B 9 Sinabang, Indonesia
196 H 9 Sinadipan, Philippines
212 F 9 Sinai, Egypt
88 K 7 Sinaloa, Mexico
211 R 8 Sīnāwin, Libya
190 E 8 Sinbo, Myanmar
190 C 12 Sinbyugyun, Myanmar
170 M 10 Sincan, Turkey
104 H 3 Sincelejo, Colombia
177 U 13 Sind, Pakistan
180 E 13 Sind, India
177 W 10 Sind Sāgar Doāb, Pakistan
197 J 20 Sindañgan, Philippines
197 I 20 Sindangan Bay, Philippines
192 H 14 Sindangbarang, Indonesia
148 F 8 Sindi, Estonia
155 Q 8 Sindor, Russian Federation
130 G 10 Sines, Portugal
214 J 13 Sinfra, Côte d'Ivoire
191 H 18 Sing Buri, Thailand
213 F 18 Singa, Sudan
182 M 9 Singahi, India
194 B 14 Singapore, Singapore
194 B 15 Singapore, Asia
192 L 15 Singaraja, Indonesia
181 G 20 Singarāyakonda, India
137 F 25 Singen, Germany
151 N 8 Sîngerei, Moldova
217 T 12 Singida, Tanzania
217 T 10 Singida, Tanzania
190 D 7 Singkaling Hkamti, Myanmar
193 O 13 Singkang, Indonesia
192 I 10 Singkawang, Indonesia
192 F 11 Singkep, Indonesia
231 V 11 Singleton, New South Wales, Australia
183 V 11 Singra, India
141 D 16 Siniscola, Italy
193 O 13 Sinjai, Indonesia
173 P 2 Sinjār, Iraq
190 E 9 Sinkan, Myanmar
213 H 15 Sinkat, Sudan
187 J 17 Sinmi-do, North Korea
109 H 14 Sinop, Brazil
170 K 6 Sinop, Turkey
170 K 6 Sinop Burnu, Turkey
187 M 16 Sinp'o, North Korea
187 L 18 Sinp'yŏng, North Korea
192 J 10 Sintang, Indonesia
71 Q 13 Sinton, Texas, U.S.A.
130 F 9 Sintra, Portugal
187 J 16 Sinŭiju, North Korea
213 O 20 Sinujiif, Somalia
78 L 6 Sinuk, Alaska, U.S.A.
197 H 21 Siocon, Philippines
143 H 24 Siófok, Hungary
138 D 10 Sion, Switzerland
67 P 12 Sioux City, Iowa, U.S.A.
67 O 10 Sioux Falls, South Dakota, U.S.A.
84 K 10 Sioux Lookout, Ontario, Canada
90 G 7 Sipacate, Guatemala
195 Y 7 Sipadan, Malaysia
197 I 18 Sipalay, Philippines
186 J 13 Siping, China
195 U 6 Sipitang, Malaysia
84 J 7 Sipiwesk, Manitoba, Canada
241 O 11 Siple Coast, Antarctica
240 K 11 Siple Island, Antarctica
192 D 12 Sipura, Indonesia
91 P 8 Siquia, Nicaragua
91 P 9 Siquia, Nicaragua
197 K 19 Siquijor, Philippines
91 R 12 Siquirres, Costa Rica
231 P 2 Sir Edward Pellew Group, Northern Territory, Australia
135 A 21 Sira, Norway
181 E 20 Sira, India
183 T 12 Sirajganj, Bangladesh

Country | Internal administrative region: State/Province/Territory/Dependent territory | Capital city | Mountain range/Undersea ridge | Mountain peak/Volcano/Seamount | Geographic feature | Headland/Point/Cape/Peninsula | Desert | Island/Island group | Antarctic base | Ocean | Sea | Bay/Gulf/Channel/Strait | Lake | Salt pan/Dry/Intermittent lake | River

Sirdaryo Wiloyati – Souris

179 R 12 Sirdaryo Wiloyati, Uzbekistan
150 L 7 Siret, Romania
183 Q 10 Sirha, Nepal
176 L 13 Sīrīk, Iran
191 H 15 Sirikit Reservoir, Thailand
176 L 11 Sīrjān, Iran
171 R 12 Şirnak, Turkey
176 J 13 Sirrī, Iran
182 H 7 Sirsa, India
181 D 20 Sirsi, India
181 F 17 Sirsilla, India
211 U 8 Sirte, Libya
159 O 12 Sirte Rise, Mediterranean Sea
149 G 15 Širvintos, Lithuania
173 V 4 Sirwan, Iraq
191 K 18 Sisaket, Thailand
189 P 3 Sishilipu, China
171 V 9 Sisian, Armenia
191 J 19 Sisŏphŏn, Cambodia
234 B 3 Sissano, Papua New Guinea
67 O 7 Sisseton, South Dakota, U.S.A.
177 P 13 Sīstān Va Balūchestān, Iran
130 L 7 Sistema Central, Spain
131 O 4 Sistema Ibérico, Spain
131 N 12 Sistemas Béticos, Spain
129 V 13 Sisteron, France
181 N 22 Sisters, India
76 H 11 Sisters, Oregon, U.S.A.
183 V 14 Sitakunda, Bangladesh
182 L 9 Sitapur, India
147 K 26 Siteia, Greece
131 W 5 Sitges, Spain
79 W 11 Sitka, Alaska, U.S.A.
191 D 14 Sittang, Myanmar
133 K 18 Sittard, Netherlands
127 Y 11 Sittingbourne, United Kingdom
190 B 13 Sittwe, Myanmar
91 P 7 Siuna, Nicaragua
183 R 13 Siuri, India
181 F 23 Sivaganga, India
176 J 10 Sivand, Iran
170 M 9 Sivas, Turkey
171 O 12 Siverek, Turkey
151 Y 5 Sivers'k, Ukraine
154 E 11 Siverskiy, Russian Federation
170 G 10 Sivrihisar, Turkey
212 B 9 Siwa, Egypt
193 O 12 Siwa, Indonesia
212 B 8 Siwa Oasis, Egypt
182 J 6 Siwalik Range, India
183 P 11 Siwan, India
64 J 13 Six Lakes, Michigan, U.S.A.
91 S 13 Sixaola, Costa Rica
189 W 4 Sixian, China
189 W 4 Siyang, China
171 Y 7 Siyäzän, Azerbaijan
135 D 25 Sjaelland, Denmark
145 K 14 Sjenica, Serbia and Montenegro
151 S 10 Skadovs'k, Ukraine
135 C 22 Skagen, Denmark
135 B 23 Skagerrak, Denmark
79 W 9 Skagway, Alaska, U.S.A.
147 E 22 Skala, Greece
150 L 6 Skala-Podil's'ka, Ukraine
135 E 24 Skälderviken, Sweden
147 H 17 Skantzoura, Greece
177 Y 6 Skardu, Pakistan
182 I 2 Skardu, India
135 A 19 Skare, Norway
143 L 15 Skarżysko-Kamienna, Poland
210 C 12 Skaymat, Western Sahara
127 X 4 Skegness, United Kingdom
134 J 13 Skellefteå, Sweden
135 D 20 Ski, Norway
147 F 17 Skiathos, Greece
147 G 17 Skiathos, Greece
134 I 7 Skibotn, Norway
149 F 18 Skidal', Belarus
135 C 20 Skien, Norway
142 K 13 Skierniewice, Poland
211 O 5 Skikda, Algeria
127 V 2 Skipsea, United Kingdom
127 R 2 Skipton, United Kingdom
135 B 24 Skive, Denmark
147 F 16 Sklithro, Greece
126 J 10 Skokholm Island, United Kingdom
150 I 5 Skole, Ukraine
126 J 9 Skomer Island, United Kingdom
147 G 17 Skopelos, Greece
147 G 17 Skopelos, Greece
146 D 10 Skopje, Macedonia (F.Y.R.O.M.)
135 F 22 Skövde, Sweden
153 T 13 Skovorodino, Russian Federation
59 P 5 Skowhegan, Maine, U.S.A.
135 D 20 Skrimfjell, Norway
148 C 11 Skrunda, Latvia
135 A 20 Skudeneshavn, Norway
219 P 10 Skukuza, Republic of South Africa
148 C 12 Skuodas, Lithuania
151 O 5 Skvyra, Ukraine
142 E 12 Skwierzyna, Poland
124 F 10 Skye, United Kingdom
147 H 18 Skyropoula, Greece
147 I 18 Skyros, Greece
147 H 18 Skyros, Greece
135 D 25 Slagelse, Denmark
79 S 8 Slana, Alaska, U.S.A.
125 E 19 Slaney, Republic of Ireland
154 D 11 Slantsy, Russian Federation
150 I 13 Slatina, Romania
70 K 5 Slaton, Texas, U.S.A.
153 Y 8 Slautnoye, Russian Federation
80 M 9 Slave, Northwest Territories, Canada
215 O 13 Slave Coast, Nigeria
83 I 17 Slave Lake, Alberta, Canada
156 K 12 Slavyansk-na-Kubani, Russian Federation
149 N 18 Slawharad, Belarus
142 G 8 Sławno, Poland
127 V 5 Sleaford, United Kingdom
85 O 7 Sleeper Island, Ontario, Canada
81 S 9 Sleeper Islands, Nunavut, Canada
142 H 12 Ślesin, Poland
58 J 10 Slide Mountain, New York, U.S.A.
62 M 8 Slidell, Louisiana, U.S.A.
125 C 16 Sligo, Republic of Ireland
125 C 16 Sligo Bay, Republic of Ireland
146 L 9 Sliven, Bulgaria
146 K 9 Sliven, Bulgaria
146 K 6 Slivo Pole, Bulgaria
151 O 7 Slobidka, Ukraine
155 P 12 Slobodskoy, Russian Federation
150 M 13 Slobozia, Romania
132 N 6 Slochteren, Netherlands
135 B 16 Slogen, Norway
143 K 17 Słomniki, Poland
149 G 19 Slonim, Belarus
132 J 8 Slotermeer, Netherlands
127 U 10 Slough, United Kingdom
143 I 21 Slovak Ore Mountains, Slovakia
143 I 20 Slovakia, Europe
151 N 2 Slovechne, Ukraine
144 C 7 Slovenia, Europe
144 D 6 Slovenska Bistrica, Slovenia
151 X 5 Slov''yans'k, Ukraine
149 L 22 Slovyechna, Belarus
142 D 12 Słubice, Poland
150 L 2 Sluch, Ukraine
133 C 16 Sluis, Netherlands
142 H 13 Słupca, Poland
142 G 8 Słupsk, Poland
134 H 13 Slussfors, Sweden
149 J 19 Slutsk, Belarus
125 A 17 Slyne Head, Republic of Ireland
153 P 14 Slyudyanka, Russian Federation
59 P 7 Small Point, Maine, U.S.A.
85 U 8 Smallwood Reservoir, Newfoundland and Labrador, Canada
149 J 17 Smalyavichy, Belarus
149 H 16 Smarhon', Belarus
144 L 10 Smederevo, Serbia and Montenegro
144 M 11 Smederevska Palanka, Serbia and Montenegro
151 R 5 Smila, Ukraine
149 J 17 Smilavichy, Belarus
148 H 10 Smiltene, Latvia
68 L 2 Smith Center, Kansas, U.S.A.
85 P 5 Smith Island, Nunavut, Canada
77 E 14 Smith River, California, U.S.A.
81 Q 2 Smith Sound, Nunavut, Canada
86 I 11 Smiths Falls, Ontario, Canada
69 R 12 Smithville, Oklahoma, U.S.A.
68 L 4 Smoky Hill, Kansas, U.S.A.
68 K 3 Smoky Hills, Kansas, U.S.A.
135 C 15 Smøla, Norway
156 H 1 Smolensk, Russian Federation
156 I 1 Smolenskaya Oblast', Russian Federation
156 H 1 Smolensko-Moskovskaya Vozvyshennost', Russian Federation
147 C 15 Smolikas, Greece
146 I 11 Smolyan, Bulgaria
146 I 12 Smolyan, Bulgaria
73 Q 12 Smoot, Wyoming, U.S.A.
86 D 5 Smooth Rock Falls, Ontario, Canada
146 L 8 Smyadovo, Bulgaria
240 J 7 Smyley Island, Antarctica
61 W 2 Smyrna, Delaware, U.S.A.
134 D 10 Snaefell, Iceland
134 C 11 Snaekollur, Iceland
127 T 3 Snaith, United Kingdom
73 P 10 Snake, Idaho/Washington, U.S.A.
72 M 12 Snake River Plain, Idaho, U.S.A.
135 E 14 Snåsvatn, Norway
132 J 7 Sneek, Netherlands
132 K 7 Sneekermeer, Netherlands
134 A 11 Snæfellsjökull, Iceland
127 X 5 Snettisham, United Kingdom
153 O 8 Snezhnogorsk, Russian Federation
143 E 16 Sněžka, Czech Republic
151 S 9 Snihurivka, Ukraine
143 M 19 Snina, Slovakia
135 C 16 Snøhetta, Norway
135 B 20 Snønuten, Norway
135 C 16 Snota, Norway
61 W 4 Snow Hill, Maryland, U.S.A.
82 L 12 Snowbird Lake, Northwest Territories, Canada
126 M 5 Snowdon, United Kingdom
74 L 11 Snowflake, Arizona, U.S.A.
240 I 3 Snowhill Island, Antarctica
72 L 3 Snowshoe Peak, Montana, U.S.A.
74 J 1 Snowville, Utah, U.S.A.
93 O 4 Snug Corner, The Bahamas
85 X 8 Snug Harbour, Newfoundland and Labrador, Canada
191 M 20 Snuŏl, Cambodia
150 K 6 Snyatyn, Ukraine
68 K 12 Snyder, Oklahoma, U.S.A.
70 L 6 Snyder, Texas, U.S.A.
219 X 6 Soalala, Madgascar
187 L 22 Soan-kundo, South Korea
219 Z 6 Soanierana-Ivongo, Madgascar
187 M 21 Sobaek-sanmaek, South Korea
213 E 20 Sobat, Sudan
143 C 19 Soběslav, Czech Republic
108 M 11 Sobral, Brazil
191 M 23 Soc Trăng, Vietnam
142 K 13 Sochaczew, Poland
156 L 13 Sochi, Russian Federation
146 G 13 Sochos, Greece
41 R 9 Society Archipelago, French Polynesia
110 H 6 Socompa, Argentina
104 I 5 Socorro, Colombia
75 P 12 Socorro, New Mexico, U.S.A.
175 W 14 Socotra, Yemen
77 M 23 Soda Lake, California, U.S.A.
73 Q 12 Soda Springs, Idaho, U.S.A.
134 L 10 Sodankylä, Finland
135 H 18 Söderhamn, Sweden
213 D 17 Sodiri, Sudan
213 H 21 Sodo, Ethiopia
193 Q 15 Soë, Indonesia
219 P 9 Soekmekaar, Republic of South Africa
148 D 7 Soela Väin, Estonia
132 I 12 Soest, Netherlands
147 D 17 Sofades, Greece
219 R 7 Sofala, Mozambique
146 G 9 Sofia, Bulgaria
147 F 20 Sofiko, Greece
146 H 9 Sofiya, Bulgaria
151 T 7 Sofiyivka, Ukraine
184 M 10 Sog, China
104 J 6 Sogamoso, Colombia
135 A 17 Sognefjorden, Norway
197 L 17 Sogod, Philippines
187 L 23 Sŏgwip'o, South Korea
212 E 10 Sohâg, Egypt
127 W 7 Soham, United Kingdom
181 I 16 Sohapur, India
177 X 8 Sohawa, Pakistan
133 J 21 Soheit-Tinlot, Belgium
42 F 9 Sohm Abyssal Plain, Atlantic Ocean
133 F 20 Soignies, Belgium
129 R 3 Soissons, France
199 E 19 Sōja, Japan
197 I 18 Sojoton Point, Philippines
187 M 18 Sokch'o, South Korea
170 B 11 Söke, Turkey
179 S 12 Sokh, Uzbekistan
171 Q 5 Sokhumi, Georgia
144 N 13 Sokobanja, Serbia and Montenegro
215 N 12 Sokodé, Togo
154 K 11 Sokol, Russian Federation
144 I 12 Sokolac, Bosnia and Herzegovina
151 P 6 Sokolivka, Ukraine
142 O 10 Sokółka, Poland
151 U 9 Sokolohirne, Ukraine
142 M 12 Sokołów Podlaski, Poland
215 P 9 Sokoto, Nigeria
215 P 9 Sokoto, Nigeria
157 V 5 Sol'-Iletsk, Russian Federation
182 J 6 Solan, India
233 A 26 Solander Island, New Zealand
181 D 18 Solapur, India
151 N 7 Soldănești, Moldova
138 L 8 Sölden, Austria
104 I 2 Soledad, Colombia
77 G 21 Soledad, California, U.S.A.
112 H 11 Soledade, Brazil
129 Y 15 Solenzara, France
171 Q 10 Solhan, Turkey
154 L 12 Soligalich, Russian Federation
127 S 7 Solihull, United Kingdom
155 T 10 Solikamsk, Russian Federation
108 D 11 Solimões, Brazil
137 C 16 Solingen, Germany
171 Y 6 Şollar, Azerbaijan
135 H 15 Sollefteå, Sweden
131 Y 7 Soller, Spain
150 L 5 Soloblovtsi, Ukraine
192 D 11 Solok, Indonesia
90 G 5 Sololá, Guatemala
235 O 6 Solomon Islands, Oceania
234 G 6 Solomon Sea, Solomon Islands/Papua New Guinea
186 H 10 Solon, China
59 P 5 Solon, Maine, U.S.A.
64 D 9 Solon Springs, Wisconsin, U.S.A.
193 P 15 Solor, Indonesia
156 M 2 Solotcha, Russian Federation
138 E 7 Solothurn, Switzerland
154 I 6 Solovetskiy, Russian Federation
154 I 5 Solovetskiye Ostrova, Russian Federation
143 I 24 Solt, Hungary
176 I 6 Soltānābād, Iran
177 N 5 Soltānābād, Iran
136 G 12 Soltau, Germany
154 E 12 Sol'tsy, Russian Federation
125 H 15 Solway Firth, United Kingdom
219 N 4 Solwezi, Zambia
198 L 13 Sōma, Japan
170 C 9 Soma, Turkey
213 M 22 Somali, Ethiopia
38 J 5 Somali Basin, Indian Ocean
213 K 24 Somalia, Africa
218 K 2 Sombo, Angola
144 I 8 Sombor, Serbia and Montenegro
133 G 21 Sombreffe, Belgium
89 N 9 Sombrerete, Mexico
111 H 24 Sombrero, Chile
150 H 8 Şomcuta Mare, Romania
180 C 12 Somdari, India
133 K 16 Someren, Netherlands
72 M 3 Somers, Montana, U.S.A.
42 A 7 Somerset, Bermuda
60 I 7 Somerset, Kentucky, U.S.A.
65 N 19 Somerset, Ohio, U.S.A.
75 O 5 Somerset, Colorado, U.S.A.
42 A 7 Somerset Island, Bermuda
81 P 4 Somerset Island, Nunavut, Canada
58 H 11 Somersville, Pennsylvania, U.S.A.
58 J 13 Somerville, New Jersey, U.S.A.
71 R 9 Somerville, Texas, U.S.A.
71 Q 9 Somerville Lake, Texas, U.S.A.
173 Y 9 Sömeydeh, Iraq
137 I 16 Sömmerda, Germany
134 E 12 Sømna, Norway
235 Y 11 Somosomo, Fiji
90 M 8 Somotillo, Nicaragua
181 I 17 Sompeta, India
133 J 15 Son, Netherlands
183 N 12 Son, India
190 K 12 Son La, Vietnam
91 U 15 Soná, Panama
187 J 17 Sŏnch'ŏn, North Korea
135 C 26 Sønderborg, Denmark
137 I 16 Sonderhausen, Germany
140 D 5 Sondrio, Italy
195 Q 10 Song, Malaysia
191 O 19 Sông Cau, Vietnam
191 L 24 Sông Đôc, Vietnam
187 G 16 Song Range, China
189 T 9 Songbai, China
217 U 14 Songea, Tanzania
186 K 13 Songhua Hu, China
191 H 25 Songkhla, Thailand
186 G 9 Songling, China
188 L 10 Songming, China
187 K 18 Songnim, North Korea
218 G 1 Songo, Angola
219 Q 5 Songo, Mozambique
188 M 5 Songpan, China
183 U 11 Songsak, India
189 Y 9 Songxi, China
189 S 4 Songxian, China
186 J 11 Songyuan, China
189 S 7 Songzi, China
186 C 13 Sonid Zuoqi, China
182 J 8 Sonipat, India
177 T 14 Sonmiani, Pakistan
177 S 14 Sonmiani Bay, Pakistan
88 H 2 Sonoita, Mexico
70 L 9 Sonora, Texas, U.S.A.
77 H 19 Sonora, California, U.S.A.
88 I 4 Sonora, Mexico
88 I 4 Sonora, Mexico
74 G 13 Sonoran Desert, Arizona, U.S.A.
90 I 7 Sonsonate, El Salvador
236 I 15 Sonsorol Islands, Palau
153 Z 10 Sopka Klyuchevskaya, Russian Federation
153 Z 11 Sopka Koryakskaya, Russian Federation
153 Z 10 Sopka Shiveluch, Russian Federation
142 I 8 Sopot, Poland
143 F 22 Sopron, Hungary
151 T 1 Sopych, Ukraine
241 S 2 Sor Rondane Mountains, Antarctica
141 I 14 Sora, Italy
187 M 18 Sŏrak-san, South Korea
131 Q 13 Sorbas, Spain
86 L 10 Sorel, Québec, Canada
170 K 9 Sorgun, Turkey
131 Q 4 Soria, Spain
113 D 15 Soriano, Uruguay
181 J 16 Soro, India
112 K 7 Sorocaba, Brazil
157 U 4 Sorochinsk, Russian Federation
236 K 15 Sorol, Federated States of Micronesia
193 T 11 Sorong, Indonesia
217 T 7 Soroti, Uganda
134 J 6 Sørøya, Norway
134 J 6 Sørøysundet, Norway
141 J 16 Sorrento, Italy
134 N 9 Sorsatunturi, Finland
134 H 12 Sorsele, Sweden
196 K 13 Sorsogon, Philippines
154 F 8 Sortavala, Russian Federation
134 G 8 Sortland, Norway
134 F 9 Sørvågen, Norway
219 O 10 Soshanguve, Republic of South Africa
155 Q 7 Sosnogorsk, Russian Federation
154 H 6 Sosnovets, Russian Federation
154 K 4 Sosnovka, Russian Federation
154 F 10 Sosnovo, Russian Federation
154 E 10 Sosnovyy Bor, Russian Federation
143 J 17 Sosnowiec, Poland
151 R 2 Sosnytsya, Ukraine
152 J 10 Sos'va, Russian Federation
135 N 14 Sotkamo, Finland
110 I 10 Soto, Argentina
89 R 9 Soto la Marina, Mexico
135 A 18 Sotra, Norway
89 Y 10 Sotuta, Mexico
216 G 6 Souanké, Congo
214 J 13 Soubré, Côte d'Ivoire
147 H 26 Souda, Greece
146 K 12 Soufli, Greece
214 G 11 Souguéta, Guinea
38 B 13 Souillac, Mauritius
129 P 11 Souillac, France
211 P 5 Souk Ahras, Algeria
210 I 6 Souk el Arbaâ du Rharb, Morocco
128 L 10 Soulac-sur-Mer, France
172 F 7 Soûr, Lebanon
107 G 18 Source of the Amazon, Peru
108 J 10 Soure, Brazil
87 W 8 Souris, Prince Edward Island, Canada

Country · Internal administrative region: State/Province/Territory/Dependent territory · Capital city · Mountain range/Undersea ridge · Mountain peak/Volcano/Seamount · Geographic feature · Headland/Point/Cape/Peninsula · Desert · Island/Island group · Antarctic base · Ocean · Sea · Bay/Gulf/Channel/Strait · Lake · Salt pan/Dry/Intermittent lake · River

▣ Country ▣ Internal administrative region: State/Province/Territory/Dependent territory ▲ Capital city ▲▲ Mountain range/Undersea ridge ▲ Mountain peak/Volcano/Seamount ◇ Geographic feature ▶ Headland/Point/Cape/Peninsula ▲ Desert ☷ Island/Island group ⊞ Antarctic base ▩ Ocean ▩ Sea ≈ Bay/Gulf/Channel/Strait ☊ Lake ☷ Salt pan/Dry/Intermittent lake ☊ River

□ Country   □ Internal administrative region: State/Province/Territory/Dependent territory   ⚓ Capital city   ▲ Mountain range/Undersea ridge   ▲ Mountain peak/Volcano/Seamount   ◇ Geographic feature   ▶ Headland/Point/Cape/Peninsula   ▲ Desert   ⊞ Island/Island group   ⊞ Antarctic base   ◇ Ocean   ∿ Sea   ≈ Bay/Gulf/Channel/Strait   ∿ Lake   ∿ Salt pan/Dry/Intermittent lake   ∿ River

Svrljig – Taouz

44 N 13 **Svrljig**, Serbia and Montenegro
49 L 20 **Svyetlahorsk**, Belarus
37 F 24 **Swabian Alp**, Germany
27 X 6 **Swaffham**, United Kingdom
36 K 7 **Swains**, American Samoa
3 V 4 **Swainsboro**, Georgia, U.S.A.
18 H 9 **Swakopmund**, Namibia
27 S 1 **Swale**, United Kingdom
35 Q 7 **Swallow Islands**, Solomon Islands
31 R 12 **Swan Hill**, Victoria, Australia
4 H 9 **Swan River**, Manitoba, Canada
27 R 14 **Swanage**, United Kingdom
V 9 **Swanquarter**, North Carolina, U.S.A.
9 R 6 **Swans Island**, Maine, U.S.A.
31 T 15 **Swansea**, Tasmania, Australia
31 V 11 **Swansea**, New South Wales, Australia
26 M 10 **Swansea**, United Kingdom
42 G 12 **Swarzędz**, Poland
19 P 11 **Swaziland**, Africa
35 F 22 **Sweden**, Europe
5 G 11 **Sweet Home**, Oregon, U.S.A.
0 J 9 **Sweetwater**, Tennessee, U.S.A.
0 L 6 **Sweetwater**, Texas, U.S.A.
18 K 15 **Swellendam**, Republic of South Africa
43 N 15 **Świdnik**, Poland
42 E 9 **Świdwin**, Poland
42 E 13 **Świebodzin**, Poland
42 I 10 **Świecie**, Poland
3 M 20 **Swift Current**, Saskatchewan, Canada
27 S 10 **Swindon**, United Kingdom
27 V 5 **Swineshead**, United Kingdom
42 D 9 **Świnoujście**, Poland
38 B 8 **Switzerland**, Europe
54 K 11 **Syamzha**, Russian Federation
49 L 15 **Syanno**, Belarus
54 G 10 **Syas'troy**, Russian Federation
56 I 1 **Sychevka**, Russian Federation
43 H 15 **Syców**, Poland
31 V 11 **Sydney**, New South Wales, Australia
7 Y 8 **Sydney**, Nova Scotia, Canada
51 Y 5 **Syeverodonets'k**, Ukraine
36 F 12 **Syke**, Germany
55 P 9 **Syktyvkar**, Russian Federation
3 R 3 **Sylacauga**, Alabama, U.S.A.
83 W 12 **Sylhet**, Bangladesh
83 V 12 **Sylhet**, Bangladesh
36 E 7 **Sylt**, Germany
0 K 10 **Sylva**, North Carolina, U.S.A.
3 W 4 **Sylvania**, Georgia, U.S.A.
3 T 6 **Sylvester**, Georgia, U.S.A.
47 N 23 **Symi**, Greece
51 V 6 **Synel'nykove**, Ukraine
35 C 18 **Synnfjell**, Norway
55 S 5 **Synya**, Russian Federation
41 U 2 **Syowa**, Antarctica
41 L 23 **Syracuse**, Italy
8 G 8 **Syracuse**, New York, U.S.A.
8 G 5 **Syracuse**, Kansas, U.S.A.
79 Q 10 **Syrdar'ya**, Kazakhstan
72 K 4 **Syria**, Asia
91 D 16 **Syriam**, Myanmar
72 K 8 **Syrian Desert**, Jordan
47 L 24 **Syrna**, Greece
47 I 21 **Syros**, Greece
35 N 15 **Syväri**, Finland
157 R 3 **Syzran'**, Russian Federation
142 F 12 **Szamotuły**, Poland
142 D 10 **Szczecin**, Poland
142 F 9 **Szczecinek**, Poland
143 J 16 **Szczekociny**, Poland
142 M 10 **Szczuczyn**, Poland
142 L 10 **Szczytno**, Poland
143 K 25 **Szeged**, Hungary
143 L 24 **Szeghalom**, Hungary
143 I 23 **Székesfehérvár**, Hungary
143 I 25 **Szekszárd**, Hungary
143 K 24 **Szentes**, Hungary
143 H 26 **Szentőrinc**, Hungary
143 L 21 **Szerencs**, Hungary
143 K 23 **Szolnok**, Hungary
143 F 13 **Szombathely**, Hungary
143 E 14 **Szprotawa**, Poland
142 H 11 **Szubin**, Poland

T

190 F 12 **Ta-Kaw**, Myanmar
190 I 11 **Ta Loung San**, Laos
196 K 13 **Tabaco**, Philippines
234 H 3 **Tabar Islands**, Papua New Guinea
176 M 8 **Ţabas**, Iran
89 V 12 **Tabasco**, Mexico
176 M 10 **Tabāsīn**, Iran
108 B 11 **Tabatinga**, Brazil
210 J 10 **Tabelbala**, Algeria
83 K 20 **Taber**, Alberta, Canada
217 P 7 **Tabili**, Democratic Republic of Congo
236 E 3 **Tabiteuea**, Kiribati
197 H 14 **Tablas**, Philippines
197 H 15 **Tablas Strait**, Philippines
197 D 18 **Table Point**, Philippines
69 S 8 **Table Rock Reservoir**, Missouri, U.S.A.
143 D 19 **Tábor**, Czech Republic
217 S 11 **Tabora**, Tanzania
217 S 11 **Tabora**, Tanzania
179 R 12 **Taboshar**, Tajikistan
214 I 14 **Tabou**, Côte d'Ivoire
176 F 3 **Tabrīz**, Iran
237 P 1 **Tabuaeran**, Kiribati
234 A 4 **Tabubil**, Papua New Guinea
174 K 3 **Tabūk**, Saudi Arabia
196 G 7 **Tabuk**, Philippines
184 J 3 **Tacheng**, China
104 K 5 **Tachira**, Venezuela
197 L 16 **Tacloban**, Philippines
104 L 11 **Tacna**, Colombia
107 H 20 **Tacna**, Peru
107 H 20 **Tacna**, Peru
110 J 6 **Taco Pozo**, Argentina
76 G 7 **Tacoma**, Washington, U.S.A.
58 K 10 **Taconic Range**, New York, U.S.A.
90 H 5 **Tactic**, Guatemala
113 E 14 **Tacuarembo**, Uruguay
112 E 13 **Tacuarembó**, Uruguay
197 L 23 **Tacurong**, Philippines
127 T 2 **Tadcaster**, United Kingdom
235 Q 14 **Tadine**, New Caledonia
211 N 12 **Tadjmout**, Algeria
213 K 19 **Tadjoura**, Djibouti
210 M 7 **Tadjrouna**, Algeria
87 O 7 **Tadoussac**, Québec, Canada
181 E 20 **Tadpatri**, India
187 M 18 **T'aebaek-sanmaek**, North Korea/South Korea
187 J 19 **Taech'ŏng-do**, South Korea
187 M 20 **Taegu**, South Korea
187 K 22 **Taehŭksan-kundo**, South Korea
187 L 20 **Taejŏn**, South Korea
187 L 23 **Taejŏng**, South Korea
131 R 3 **Tafalla**, Spain
110 I 7 **Tafi Viejo**, Argentina
210 F 9 **Tafraoute**, Morocco
176 K 9 **Taft**, Iran
181 O 24 **Tafwap**, India
213 E 14 **Tagab**, Sudan
156 L 10 **Taganrog**, Russian Federation
214 H 6 **Tagant**, Mauritania
199 C 21 **Tagawa**, Japan
197 K 18 **Tagbilaran**, Philippines
210 K 9 **Taghit**, Algeria
83 B 15 **Tagish Lake**, British Columbia, Canada
179 O 15 **Tagtabazar**, Turkmenistan
109 K 14 **Taguatinga**, Brazil
234 H 8 **Tagula**, Papua New Guinea
234 H 8 **Tagula Island**, Papua New Guinea
197 M 22 **Tagum**, Philippines
42 K 9 **Tagus Abyssal Plain**, Atlantic Ocean
186 J 5 **Tahe**, China
77 I 18 **Tahoe City**, California, U.S.A.
70 K 5 **Tahoka**, Texas, U.S.A.
76 F 7 **Taholah**, Washington, U.S.A.
232 K 12 **Tahora**, New Zealand
215 Q 8 **Tahoua**, Niger
215 Q 8 **Tahoua**, Niger
173 V 9 **Taḩrīr**, Iraq
176 M 11 **Tahrūd**, Iran
212 E 10 **Tahta**, Egypt
170 K 13 **Tahtali Dağlari**, Turkey
107 I 16 **Tahuamanu**, Bolivia
193 Q 9 **Tahulandang**, Indonesia
232 L 9 **Tahuna**, New Zealand
193 Q 9 **Tahuna**, Indonesia
214 I 13 **Taï**, Côte d'Ivoire
189 Y 6 **Tai Hu**, China
189 V 2 **Tai'an**, China
189 P 4 **Taibai**, China
189 Q 2 **Taibai**, China
189 P 4 **Taibai Shan**, China
189 Y 11 **T'aichung**, Taiwan
233 E 24 **Taieri**, New Zealand
147 E 22 **Taigetos**, Greece
189 S 1 **Taigu**, China
189 T 2 **Taihang Shan**, China
232 L 13 **Taihape**, New Zealand
189 U 9 **Taihe**, China
189 V 4 **Taihe**, China
189 V 6 **Taihu**, China
189 U 4 **Taikang**, China
191 D 16 **Taikkyi**, Myanmar
186 I 10 **Tailai**, China
231 Q 12 **Tailem Bend**, South Australia, Australia
124 H 9 **Tain**, United Kingdom
189 Z 12 **T'ainan**, Taiwan
189 Z 10 **Taipei**, Taiwan
189 O 13 **Taiping**, China
189 U 12 **Taiping**, China
194 B 6 **Taiping**, Malaysia
186 G 9 **Taiping Ling**, China
199 B 26 **Taira-jima**, Japan
232 L 9 **Tairua**, New Zealand
176 E 6 **Tairuq**, Iran
192 E 13 **Tais**, Indonesia
189 T 13 **Taishan**, China
189 Z 12 **T'aitung**, Taiwan
134 M 12 **Taivalkoski**, Finland
189 Y 11 **Taiwan**, Asia
189 Y 12 **Taiwan Strait**, Taiwan/China
186 I 6 **Taiyanggou**, China
189 S 1 **Taiyuan**, China
189 Y 5 **Taizhou**, China
189 Z 7 **Taizhou**, China
175 P 14 **Ta'izz**, Yemen
211 T 12 **Tajarḩī**, Libya
179 S 13 **Tajikistan**, Asia
199 K 14 **Tajima**, Japan
88 I 3 **Tajitos**, Mexico
130 L 7 **Tajo**, Spain
191 G 16 **Tak**, Thailand
176 G 5 **Takāb**, Iran
217 X 6 **Takabba**, Kenya
233 I 15 **Takaka**, New Zealand
199 F 19 **Takamatsu**, Japan
199 D 23 **Takanabe**, Japan
199 H 15 **Takaoka**, Japan
232 J 8 **Takapuna**, New Zealand
199 B 26 **Takara-jima**, Japan
199 J 15 **Takasaki**, Japan
218 M 10 **Takatokwane**, Botswana
199 G 18 **Takatsuki**, Japan
199 E 21 **Takatsuki-yama**, Japan
199 H 16 **Takayama**, Japan
199 C 25 **Take-shima**, Japan
199 G 17 **Takefu**, Japan
192 B 8 **Takengon**, Indonesia
199 B 21 **Takeo**, Japan
176 H 5 **Tākestān**, Iran
199 C 22 **Taketa**, Japan
191 L 22 **Takêv**, Cambodia
177 V 6 **Takhār**, Afghanistan
177 S 10 **Takhta Pul Post**, Afghanistan
198 J 5 **Takikawa**, Japan
198 K 4 **Takinoue**, Japan
234 G 3 **Takis**, Papua New Guinea
83 E 18 **Takla Lake**, British Columbia, Canada
184 H 6 **Taklimakan Desert**, China
153 R 12 **Taksimo**, Russian Federation
191 F 24 **Takua Pa**, Thailand
215 S 12 **Takum**, Nigeria
237 P 10 **Takutea**, Cook Islands
234 K 4 **Takuu Islands**, Papua New Guinea
113 F 15 **Tala**, Uruguay
110 H 10 **Talacasto**, Argentina
149 L 16 **Talachyn**, Belarus
177 W 8 **Talagang**, Pakistan
181 F 23 **Talaimannar**, Sri Lanka
192 G 12 **Talangbatu**, Indonesia
106 A 11 **Talara**, Peru
179 T 10 **Talas**, Kyrgyzstan
234 F 4 **Talasea**, Papua New Guinea
179 T 11 **Talasskaya Oblast'**, Kyrgyzstan
130 M 7 **Talavera de la Reina**, Spain
110 F 13 **Talca**, Chile
111 E 14 **Talcahuano**, Chile
181 J 16 **Talcher**, India
179 W 8 **Taldykorgan**, Kazakhstan
179 V 10 **Talgar**, Kazakhstan
127 O 9 **Talgarth**, United Kingdom
213 E 22 **Tali Post**, Sudan
193 Q 11 **Taliabu**, Indonesia
197 K 18 **Talibon**, Philippines
181 D 19 **Talikota**, India
179 P 13 **Talimardzhan**, Uzbekistan
171 W 10 **Talish Mountains**, Azerbaijan
192 L 15 **Taliwang**, Indonesia
173 Q 2 **Tall 'Afar**, Iraq
172 K 1 **Tall al Aḩmar**, Syria
173 W 11 **Tall al Laḩm**, Iraq
173 O 1 **Tall Baydar**, Syria
172 J 7 **Tall Ghāb**, Syria
173 Q 2 **Tall Ḩuqnah**, Iraq
173 R 2 **Tall Kayf**, Iraq
173 Q 1 **Tall Kūjik**, Syria
172 L 7 **Tall Salāh**, Jordan
173 N 1 **Tall Tamir**, Syria
173 Q 1 **Tall 'Uwaynāt**, Iraq
63 S 7 **Tallahassee**, Florida, U.S.A.
148 F 5 **Tallinn**, Estonia
62 K 5 **Tallulah**, Louisiana, U.S.A.
150 I 11 **Tălmaciu**, Romania
210 G 8 **Talmest**, Morocco
151 P 6 **Tal'ne**, Ukraine
213 E 19 **Talodi**, Sudan
177 V 5 **Tāloqān**, Afghanistan
185 O 4 **Talshand**, Mongolia
148 D 10 **Talsi**, Latvia
110 F 7 **Taltal**, Chile
193 P 10 **Taludaa**, Indonesia
192 E 11 **Taluk**, Indonesia
191 O 17 **Tam Ky**, Vietnam
236 E 3 **Tamana**, Kiribati
210 F 8 **Tamanar**, Morocco
211 T 11 **Tamanhint**, Libya
211 O 14 **Tamanrasset**, Algeria
190 D 8 **Tamanthi**, Myanmar
126 L 14 **Tamar**, United Kingdom
143 H 25 **Tamási**, Hungary
89 R 9 **Tamaulipas**, Mexico
89 R 10 **Tamazunchale**, Mexico
214 F 9 **Tambacounda**, Senegal
192 H 10 **Tambelan Besar**, Indonesia
152 M 7 **Tambey**, Russian Federation
195 Z 6 **Tambisan**, Malaysia
231 T 7 **Tambo**, Queensland, Australia
107 G 20 **Tambo**, Peru
106 A 12 **Tambo Grande**, Peru
219 W 7 **Tambohorano**, Madgascar
217 N 4 **Tamboura**, Central African Republic
157 N 4 **Tambov**, Russian Federation
157 N 4 **Tambovskaya Oblast'**, Russian Federation
195 V 5 **Tambunan**, Malaysia
213 C 22 **Tambura**, Sudan
214 H 7 **Tāmchekket**, Mauritania
181 F 22 **Tamil Nadu**, India
138 I 8 **Tamins**, Switzerland
144 L 10 **Tamiš**, Serbia and Montenegro
135 L 20 **Tammisaari**, Finland
63 V 10 **Tampa**, Florida, U.S.A.
63 U 11 **Tampa Bay**, Florida, U.S.A.
135 L 17 **Tampere**, Finland
89 S 10 **Tampico**, Mexico
194 C 9 **Tampin**, Malaysia
194 B 14 **Tampines**, Singapore
175 Q 9 **Tamrah**, Saudi Arabia
106 F 11 **Tamshiyacu**, Peru
139 S 7 **Tamsweg**, Austria
231 U 10 **Tamworth**, New South Wales, Australia
127 S 6 **Tamworth**, United Kingdom
191 M 22 **Tân An**, Vietnam
210 E 10 **Tan-Tan**, Morocco
134 M 6 **Tana Bru**, Norway
199 G 20 **Tanabe**, Japan
78 E 13 **Tanaga Island**, Alaska, U.S.A.
194 C 5 **Tanah Merah**, Malaysia
192 C 11 **Tanahbala**, Indonesia
192 M 11 **Tanahgrogot**, Indonesia
193 O 14 **Tanahjampea**, Indonesia
192 C 11 **Tanahmasa**, Indonesia
182 L 8 **Tanakpur**, India
230 M 5 **Tanami Desert**, Northern Territory, Australia
79 Q 6 **Tanana**, Alaska, U.S.A.
187 M 16 **Tanch'ŏn**, North Korea
214 L 12 **Tanda**, Côte d'Ivoire
183 N 10 **Tanda**, India
197 N 19 **Tandag**, Philippines
150 M 12 **Tăndărei**, Romania
195 V 4 **Tandek**, Malaysia
113 D 18 **Tandil**, Argentina
215 W 11 **Tandjilé**, Chad
177 U 14 **Tando Adam**, Pakistan
199 C 25 **Tanega-shima**, Japan
143 N 16 **Tanew**, Poland
210 K 15 **Tanezrouft**, Algeria
217 W 11 **Tanga**, Tanzania
217 W 11 **Tanga**, Tanzania
234 H 3 **Tanga Islands**, Papua New Guinea
188 L 9 **Tangdan**, China
188 L 4 **Tanggor**, China
184 K 9 **Tanggula Shan**, China
189 S 5 **Tanghe**, China
210 I 6 **Tangier**, Morocco
61 W 5 **Tangier Island**, Virginia, U.S.A.
189 U 10 **Tangjiang**, China
194 B 14 **Tanglin**, Singapore
199 F 17 **Tango**, Japan
232 N 13 **Tangoio**, New Zealand
184 J 9 **Tangra Yumco**, China
192 B 8 **Tangse**, Indonesia
187 F 17 **Tangshan**, China
189 U 2 **Tangyin**, China
186 M 10 **Tangyuan**, China
219 V 9 **Tanjona Ankaboa**, Madgascar
219 Z 4 **Tanjona Bobaomby**, Madgascar
219 Z 6 **Tanjona Masoala**, Madgascar
219 W 6 **Tanjona Vilanandro**, Madgascar
219 W 11 **Tanjona Vohimena**, Madgascar
192 L 11 **Tanjung**, Indonesia
193 O 10 **Tanjung Arus**, Indonesia
194 A 7 **Tanjung Beras Basah**, Malaysia
195 X 5 **Tanjung Bidadari**, Malaysia
192 J 14 **Tanjung Bugel**, Indonesia
192 F 13 **Tanjung Cina**, Indonesia
194 M 10 **Tanjung Datu**, Malaysia
193 X 11 **Tanjung d'Urville**, Indonesia
194 E 7 **Tanjung Gelang**, Malaysia
192 G 14 **Tanjung Guhakolak**, Indonesia
195 O 9 **Tanjung Jerijih**, Malaysia
193 O 10 **Tanjung Kandi**, Indonesia
195 Q 8 **Tanjung Kidurong**, Malaysia
193 O 13 **Tanjung Koku**, Indonesia
192 L 13 **Tanjung Layar**, Indonesia
193 S 11 **Tanjung Libobo**, Indonesia
192 G 12 **Tanjung Lumut**, Indonesia
193 N 10 **Tanjung Mangkalihat**, Indonesia
192 L 15 **Tanjung Mebulu**, Indonesia
192 I 10 **Tanjung Mungguresak**, Indonesia
193 R 12 **Tanjung Palpetu**, Indonesia
195 R 8 **Tanjung Payung**, Malaysia
195 N 10 **Tanjung Po**, Malaysia
192 J 12 **Tanjung Puting**, Indonesia
194 E 9 **Tanjung Resang**, Malaysia
192 I 12 **Tanjung Sambar**, Indonesia
192 L 13 **Tanjung Selatan**, Indonesia
195 V 4 **Tanjung Simpang Mangayau**, Malaysia
195 N 10 **Tanjung Sipang**, Malaysia
195 O 9 **Tanjung Sirik**, Malaysia
193 S 9 **Tanjung Sopi**, Indonesia
195 W 4 **Tanjung Sugut**, Malaysia
195 W 4 **Tanjung Sumangat**, Malaysia
194 C 9 **Tanjung Tuan**, Malaysia
193 X 15 **Tanjung Vals**, Indonesia
193 R 12 **Tanjung Waka**, Indonesia
192 H 12 **Tanjungpandan**, Indonesia
192 F 10 **Tanjungpinang**, Indonesia
192 L 9 **Tanjungredeb**, Indonesia
192 M 9 **Tanjungselor**, Indonesia
177 V 9 **Tank**, Pakistan
182 K 3 **Tankse**, India
235 R 12 **Tanna**, Vanuatu
197 J 18 **Tañon Strait**, Philippines
215 S 8 **Tanout**, Niger
183 O 9 **Tansen**, Nepal
212 E 8 **Tanta**, Egypt
172 F 8 **Tantura**, Israel
78 L 9 **Tanunak**, Alaska, U.S.A.
217 S 11 **Tanzania**, Africa
189 S 8 **Taojiang**, China
186 I 11 **Taonan**, China
141 L 21 **Taormina**, Italy
75 R 8 **Taos**, New Mexico, U.S.A.
210 I 6 **Taounate**, Morocco
210 J 6 **Taourirt**, Morocco
210 J 9 **Taouz**, Morocco

Country · Internal administrative region: State/Province/Territory/Dependent territory · Capital city · Mountain range/Undersea ridge · Mountain peak/Volcano/Seamount · Geographic feature · Headland/Point/Cape/Peninsula · Desert · Island/Island group · Antarctic base · Ocean · Sea · Bay/Gulf/Channel/Strait · Lake · Salt pan/Dry/Intermittent lake · River

189 Z 10 **T'aoyüan**, Taiwan
189 S 8 **Taoyuan**, China
148 H 6 **Tapa**, Estonia
89 W 15 **Tapachula**, Mexico
108 G 11 **Tapajós**, Brazil ⌇
192 C 9 **Tapaktuan**, Indonesia
113 C 17 **Tapalqué**, Argentina
192 D 12 **Tapan**, Indonesia
233 D 24 **Tapanui**, New Zealand
108 E 12 **Tapauá**, Brazil
108 C 12 **Tapauá**, Brazil ⌇
112 G 11 **Tapera**, Brazil
112 H 12 **Tapes**, Brazil
214 H 13 **Tapeta**, Liberia
111 G 23 **Tapi Aike**, Argentina
130 K 1 **Tapia de Casariego**, Spain
183 R 9 **Taplejung**, Nepal
143 G 24 **Tapolca**, Hungary
61 U 5 **Tappahannock**, Virginia, U.S.A.
198 J 8 **Tappi-zaki**, Japan ▶
197 G 24 **Tapul**, Philippines
197 G 24 **Tapul Group**, Philippines 🏝
173 T 3 **Ţaqţaq**, Iraq
112 H 11 **Taquari**, Brazil ⌇
112 J 5 **Taquaritinga**, Brazil
215 T 12 **Taraba**, Nigeria ▣
173 W 9 **Tarād al Kahf**, Iraq
232 M 13 **Taradale**, New Zealand
211 T 11 **Tarāghin**, Libya
192 M 9 **Tarakan**, Indonesia
199 N 26 **Tarana-jima**, Japan 🏝
232 J 12 **Taranaki**, New Zealand ▣
131 P 7 **Tarancón**, Spain
124 E 9 **Taransay**, United Kingdom 🏝
141 N 17 **Taranto**, Italy
159 N 7 **Taranto Valley**, Mediterranean Sea ◇
104 M 12 **Tarapacá**, Colombia
110 G 3 **Tarapacá**, Chile ▣
106 D 13 **Tarapoto**, Peru
108 B 9 **Taraquá**, Brazil
129 T 9 **Tarare**, France
151 P 5 **Tarashcha**, Ukraine
211 Q 12 **Tarat**, Algeria
107 H 20 **Tarata**, Peru
108 B 13 **Tarauacá**, Brazil
108 B 13 **Tarauacá**, Brazil ⌇
236 D 2 **Tarawa**, Kiribati 🏝
232 M 12 **Tarawera**, New Zealand
179 S 10 **Taraz**, Kazakhstan
131 R 4 **Tarazona**, Spain
179 X 6 **Tarbagatay**, Kazakhstan
124 H 9 **Tarbat Ness**, United Kingdom ▶
177 X 7 **Tarbela Reservoir**, Pakistan ◢
124 E 9 **Tarbert**, United Kingdom
124 F 13 **Tarbert**, United Kingdom
125 B 19 **Tarbert**, Republic of Ireland
129 N 14 **Tarbes**, France
144 H 12 **Tarčin**, Bosnia and Herzegovina
231 O 10 **Tarcoola**, South Australia, Australia
231 V 11 **Taree**, New South Wales, Australia
153 O 7 **Tareya**, Russian Federation
210 D 10 **Tarfaya**, Morocco
150 J 12 **Târgovişte**, Romania
150 H 11 **Târgu Jiu**, Romania
150 J 9 **Târgu Mureş**, Romania
150 K 10 **Târgu Secuiesc**, Romania
211 S 8 **Tarhūnah**, Libya
175 W 6 **Tarif**, United Arab Emirates
130 L 14 **Tarifa**, Spain
196 I 8 **Tarigtig Point**, Philippines ▶
107 K 23 **Tarija**, Bolivia
107 K 23 **Tarija**, Bolivia ▣
107 K 23 **Tarija**, Bolivia ⌇
184 I 6 **Tarim Basin**, China ◇
184 I 5 **Tarim He**, China ⌇
217 T 8 **Tarime**, Tanzania
177 S 8 **Tarīn Kowt**, Afghanistan
193 X 12 **Taritatu**, Indonesia ⌇
152 M 9 **Tarko-Sale**, Russian Federation
196 F 10 **Tarlac**, Philippines
196 F 9 **Tarlac**, Philippines ⌇
143 M 16 **Tarnobrzeg**, Poland
143 N 16 **Tarnogród**, Poland
154 L 10 **Tarnogskiy Gorodok**, Russian Federation
143 L 17 **Tarnów**, Poland
135 H 19 **Tärnsjö**, Sweden
176 L 12 **Ţārom**, Iran
231 U 8 **Taroom**, Queensland, Australia
210 G 9 **Taroudannt**, Morocco
63 V 10 **Tarpon Springs**, Florida, U.S.A.
92 M 2 **Tarpum Bay**, The Bahamas
140 G 13 **Tarquinia**, Italy
231 N 4 **Tarrabool Lake**, Northern Territory, Australia ◢
131 V 5 **Tarragona**, Spain
215 X 5 **Tarso Emissi**, Chad ▲
170 J 13 **Tarsus**, Turkey
110 J 5 **Tartagal**, Argentina
112 C 11 **Tartagal**, Argentina
148 I 8 **Tartu**, Estonia
172 H 4 **Ţarţūs**, Syria
198 J 6 **Tarumae-san**, Japan ▲
199 C 24 **Tarumizu**, Japan
192 C 9 **Tarutung**, Indonesia
151 O 10 **Tarutyne**, Ukraine
140 I 5 **Tarvisio**, Italy
153 T 10 **Tas-Tumas**, Russian Federation
179 P 9 **Tasbuget**, Kazakhstan
179 T 11 **Tash-Kömür**, Kyrgyzstan
171 T 7 **Tashir**, Armenia
179 R 11 **Tashkent**, Uzbekistan ⌂
179 N 15 **Tashkepri**, Turkmenistan
194 D 6 **Tasik Kenyir**, Malaysia ◢
194 B 5 **Tasik Temengor**, Malaysia ◢
85 R 6 **Tasiujaq**, Québec, Canada
45 O 11 **Tasiusaq**, Greenland
215 T 8 **Tasker**, Niger
179 X 6 **Taskesken**, Kazakhstan
170 J 7 **Taşköprü**, Turkey
234 G 2 **Taskul**, Papua New Guinea
171 S 10 **Taşlişay**, Turkey
233 H 16 **Tasman**, New Zealand ▣
41 N 12 **Tasman Basin**, Pacific Ocean ◇
233 I 15 **Tasman Bay**, New Zealand ≈
231 T 15 **Tasman Peninsula**, Tasmania, Australia ▶
231 U 15 **Tasman Sea**, Australia/New Zealand ≋
231 R 15 **Tasmania**, Australia ▣
170 L 8 **Taşova**, Turkey
215 Q 7 **Tassara**, Niger
211 N 15 **Tassili du Hoggar**, Algeria ◇
211 O 11 **Tassili n'Ajjer**, Algeria ◇
108 L 13 **Tasso Fragoso**, Brazil
210 G 9 **Tata**, Morocco
143 I 22 **Tata**, Hungary
143 I 22 **Tatabánya**, Hungary
211 Q 7 **Tataouine**, Tunisia
151 O 11 **Tatarbunary**, Ukraine
152 L 12 **Tatarsk**, Russian Federation
153 W 13 **Tatarskiy Proliv**, Russian Federation ≈
195 Q 9 **Tatau**, Malaysia
199 L 17 **Tateyama**, Japan
83 H 14 **Tathlina Lake**, Northwest Territories, Canada ◢
175 O 9 **Tathlīth**, Saudi Arabia
190 D 13 **Tatkon**, Myanmar
83 F 20 **Tatla Lake**, British Columbia, Canada
170 I 15 **Tatlisu**, Cyprus
143 J 19 **Tatra Mountains**, Slovakia ⛰
177 U 15 **Tatta**, Pakistan
179 T 10 **Tatti**, Kazakhstan
75 U 12 **Tatum**, New Mexico, U.S.A.
171 R 11 **Tatvan**, Turkey
108 N 12 **Taua**, Brazil
112 L 7 **Taubaté**, Brazil
178 H 9 **Tauchik**, Kazakhstan
137 F 18 **Taufstein**, Germany ▲
69 X 6 **Taum Sauk Mountain**, Missouri, U.S.A. ▲
232 K 12 **Taumarunui**, New Zealand
190 E 12 **Taunggyi**, Myanmar
190 F 11 **Taunglau**, Myanmar
190 D 12 **Taungtha**, Myanmar
191 C 14 **Taunqup**, Myanmar
177 V 10 **Taunsa**, Pakistan
127 O 12 **Taunton**, United Kingdom
59 N 10 **Taunton**, Massachusetts, U.S.A.
137 D 19 **Taunus**, Germany ◇
232 K 10 **Taupiri**, New Zealand
232 M 11 **Taupo**, New Zealand
149 C 14 **Tauragė**, Lithuania
232 M 10 **Tauranga**, New Zealand
141 M 21 **Taurianova**, Italy
232 H 5 **Tauroa Point**, New Zealand ▶
170 F 13 **Taurus Mountains**, Turkey ⛰
131 S 4 **Tauste**, Spain
41 Y 15 **Tautama**, Pitcairn Island ▶
237 Z 8 **Tautira**, French Polynesia
153 X 10 **Tauyskaya Guba**, Russian Federation ≈
170 D 12 **Tavas**, Turkey
152 J 10 **Tavda**, Russian Federation
127 Z 6 **Taverham**, United Kingdom
131 T 9 **Tavernes de la Valldigna**, Spain
235 Y 11 **Taveuni**, Fiji 🏝
130 I 12 **Tavira**, Portugal
126 M 14 **Tavistock**, United Kingdom
191 F 19 **Tavoy**, Myanmar
191 F 19 **Tavoy Point**, Myanmar ▶
170 E 9 **Tavşanli**, Turkey
126 M 12 **Taw**, United Kingdom ⌇
181 E 15 **Tawa Reservoir**, India ◢
183 V 9 **Tawang**, India
64 L 12 **Tawas City**, Michigan, U.S.A.
195 X 7 **Tawau**, Malaysia
127 N 10 **Tawe**, United Kingdom ⌇
197 E 25 **Tawitawi**, Philippines 🏝
189 Z 12 **Tawu**, Taiwan
89 Q 12 **Taxco**, Mexico
184 G 6 **Taxkorgan**, China
124 H 12 **Tay**, United Kingdom ⌇
191 M 21 **Tây Ninh**, Vietnam
196 H 12 **Tayabas Bay**, Philippines ≈
213 L 23 **Tayeeglow**, Somalia
185 O 4 **Taygan**, Mongolia
66 L 13 **Taylor**, Nebraska, U.S.A.
71 Q 9 **Taylor**, Texas, U.S.A.
61 O 9 **Taylorsville**, North Carolina, U.S.A.
65 F 19 **Taylorville**, Illinois, U.S.A.
174 L 5 **Taymā'**, Saudi Arabia
178 I 5 **Taypak**, Kazakhstan
153 O 12 **Tayshet**, Russian Federation
197 E 17 **Taytay**, Philippines
197 E 17 **Taytay Bay**, Philippines ≈
197 M 17 **Taytay Point**, Philippines ▶
186 I 5 **Tayuan**, China
177 O 7 **Tayyebād**, Iran
179 R 2 **Tayynsha**, Kazakhstan
153 N 8 **Taz**, Russian Federation ⌇
210 J 7 **Taza**, Morocco
173 T 4 **Tāza Khurmātū**, Iraq
210 H 9 **Tazenakht**, Morocco
60 K 8 **Tazewell**, Tennessee, U.S.A.
211 X 11 **Tāzirbū**, Libya
152 M 8 **Tazovskiy**, Russian Federation
210 H 9 **Tazzarine**, Morocco
210 J 8 **Tazzouguert**, Morocco
171 U 7 **T'Bilisi**, Georgia ⌂
215 T 12 **Tchabal Mbabo**, Cameroon ▲
216 E 9 **Tchibanga**, Gabon
215 Q 8 **Tchin-Tabaradene**, Niger
215 V 12 **Tcholliré**, Cameroon
142 I 9 **Tczew**, Poland
233 B 24 **Te Anau**, New Zealand
232 O 10 **Te Araroa**, New Zealand
232 N 10 **Te Kaha**, New Zealand
232 H 4 **Te Kao**, New Zealand
232 O 12 **Te Kapu**, New Zealand ▲
232 O 11 **Te Karaka**, New Zealand
233 L 17 **Te Kaukau Point**, New Zealand ▶
232 K 11 **Te Kuiti**, New Zealand
232 M 12 **Te Pohue**, New Zealand
232 M 10 **Te Puke**, New Zealand
232 I 6 **Te Raupa**, New Zealand ▲
232 N 10 **Te Teko**, New Zealand
233 B 25 **Te Waewae**, New Zealand
233 A 25 **Te Waewae Bay**, New Zealand ≈
88 M 9 **Teacapán**, Mexico
237 Z 8 **Teahupoo**, French Polynesia
89 W 13 **Teapa**, Mexico
193 X 11 **Teba**, Indonesia
195 N 11 **Tebedu**, Malaysia
156 M 14 **Teberda**, Russian Federation
211 P 6 **Tébessa**, Algeria
171 U 6 **Tebulos Mt'a**, Georgia/Russian Federation ▲
88 F 2 **Tecate**, Mexico
151 N 13 **Techirghiol**, Romania
147 C 17 **Techniti Limni Kremaston**, Greece ◢
111 G 18 **Tecka**, Argentina
89 N 12 **Tecomán**, Mexico
88 J 5 **Tecoripa**, Mexico
89 Q 13 **Técpan**, Mexico
150 M 11 **Tecuci**, Romania
213 L 23 **Ted**, Somalia
178 M 14 **Tedzhen**, Turkmenistan
153 N 14 **Teeli**, Russian Federation
125 J 16 **Tees**, United Kingdom ⌇
108 D 11 **Tefé**, Brazil
192 I 14 **Tegal**, Indonesia
133 L 16 **Tegelen**, Netherlands
215 Q 11 **Tegina**, Nigeria
235 Q 9 **Tégua**, Vanuatu 🏝
90 L 6 **Tegucigalpa**, Honduras ⌂
77 J 23 **Tehachapi**, California, U.S.A.
176 I 5 **Tehrān**, Iran ▣
176 I 6 **Tehran**, Iran ⌂
182 K 7 **Tehri**, India
89 S 12 **Tehuacán**, Mexico
237 W 9 **Tehuata**, French Polynesia 🏝
213 B 16 **Teiga Plateau**, Sudan ◇
127 N 14 **Teignmouth**, United Kingdom
150 H 10 **Teiuş**, Romania
90 F 5 **Tejutla**, Guatemala
179 W 8 **Tekeli**, Kazakhstan
179 X 10 **Tekes**, Kazakhstan
184 H 7 **Tekilitag**, China ▲
146 N 13 **Tekirdağ**, Turkey ▣
170 C 7 **Tekirdağ**, Turkey
193 P 11 **Teku**, Indonesia
172 E 9 **Tel Aviv-Jaffa**, Israel
90 L 4 **Tela**, Honduras
210 K 6 **Télagh**, Algeria
171 U 6 **T'elavi**, Georgia
89 Y 10 **Telchac Puerto**, Mexico
150 I 8 **Telciu**, Romania
42 N 12 **Telde**, Canary Islands
234 A 4 **Telefomin**, Papua New Guinea
112 I 8 **Telêmaco Borba**, Brazil
151 N 8 **Teleneşti**, Moldova
108 G 13 **Teles Pires**, Brazil ⌇
77 K 22 **Telescope Peak**, California, U.S.A. ▲
230 I 6 **Telfer**, Western Australia, Australia
127 Q 6 **Telford**, United Kingdom
138 L 7 **Telfs**, Austria
78 L 6 **Teller**, Alaska, U.S.A.
173 W 10 **Telloh**, Iraq
75 O 6 **Telluride**, Colorado, U.S.A.
151 Y 8 **Tel'manove**, Ukraine
194 A 14 **Telok Blangah**, Singapore
111 I 17 **Telsen**, Argentina
148 C 13 **Telšiai**, Lithuania
194 B 7 **Teluk Anson**, Malaysia
193 U 12 **Teluk Beru**, Indonesia ≈
193 O 12 **Teluk Bone**, Indonesia ≈
193 W 12 **Teluk Cenderawasih**, Indonesia ≈
195 N 10 **Teluk Datu**, Malaysia ≈
193 V 12 **Teluk Kamrau**, Indonesia ≈
195 U 5 **Teluk Kimanis**, Malaysia ≈
192 J 12 **Teluk Kumai**, Indonesia ≈
195 X 5 **Teluk Labuk**, Malaysia ≈
195 X 6 **Teluk Lahad Datu**, Malaysia ≈
195 V 4 **Teluk Marudu**, Malaysia ≈
195 W 4 **Teluk Paitan**, Malaysia ≈
192 G 14 **Teluk Palabuhanratu**, Indonesia ≈
193 O 11 **Teluk Poso**, Indonesia ≈
192 K 12 **Teluk Sampit**, Indonesia ≈
192 I 11 **Teluk Sukadana**, Indonesia ≈
193 O 11 **Teluk Tomini**, Indonesia ≈
192 I 11 **Telukbatang**, Indonesia
192 C 10 **Telukdalam**, Indonesia
195 W 5 **Telupid**, Malaysia
86 E 8 **Temagami Lake**, Ontario, Canada ◢
237 W 11 **Tematangi**, French Polynesia 🏝
193 W 13 **Tembagapura**, Indonesia
192 F 11 **Tembilahan**, Indonesia
219 O 11 **Tembisa**, Republic of South Africa
131 O 8 **Tembleque**, Spain
218 H 2 **Tembo Aluma**, Angola
77 K 25 **Temecula**, California, U.S.A.
144 K 9 **Temerin**, Serbia and Montenegro
194 D 8 **Temerloh**, Malaysia
179 T 5 **Temirtau**, Kazakhstan
86 F 9 **Temiscaming**, Québec, Canada
157 O 2 **Temnikov**, Russian Federation
231 T 12 **Temora**, New South Wales, Australia
88 L 4 **Temósachic**, Mexico
235 Q 7 **Temotu**, Solomon Islands ▣
74 J 13 **Tempe**, Arizona, U.S.A.
71 Q 8 **Temple**, Texas, U.S.A.
126 M 8 **Temple Bar**, United Kingdom
126 K 9 **Templeton**, United Kingdom
218 I 5 **Tempué**, Angola
156 J 12 **Temryuk**, Russian Federation
151 X11 **Temryukskiy Zaliv**, Ukraine ≈
111 F 15 **Temuco**, Chile
233 F 21 **Temuka**, New Zealand
181 M 23 **Ten Degree Channel**, India ≈
63 W 13 **Ten Thousand Islands**, Florida, U.S.A. 🏝
106 C 9 **Tena**, Ecuador
71 U 7 **Tenaha**, Texas, U.S.A.
181 G 19 **Tenali**, India
237 Y 11 **Tenararo**, French Polynesia 🏝
191 F 20 **Tenasserim**, Myanmar ▣
127 Q 8 **Tenbury Wells**, United Kingdom
126 L 10 **Tenby**, United Kingdom
213 J 19 **Tendaho**, Ethiopia
213 E 18 **Tendelti**, Sudan
198 K 12 **Tendō**, Japan
73 N 8 **Tendoy**, Idaho, U.S.A.
210 K 7 **Tendrara**, Morocco
215 T 5 **Ténéré du Tafassâsset**, Niger ◇
42 M 12 **Tenerife**, Canary Islands 🏝
210 L 5 **Ténès**, Algeria
188 I 10 **Tengchong**, China
194 E 6 **Tenggul**, Malaysia 🏝
214 J 11 **Tengréla**, Côte d'Ivoire
189 R 12 **Tengxian**, China
189 W 3 **Tengzhou**, China
63 U 8 **Tenille**, Florida, U.S.A.
217 O 14 **Tenke**, Democratic Republic of Congo
231 O 5 **Tennant Creek**, Northern Territory, Australia
60 C 9 **Tennessee**, U.S.A. ▣
60 C 10 **Tennessee**, Tennessee, U.S.A. ⌇
133 J 23 **Tenneville**, Belgium
134 M 10 **Tenniöjoki**, Finland ⌇
134 L 7 **Tenojoki**, Finland ⌇
195 U 6 **Tenom**, Malaysia
89 X 13 **Tenosique**, Mexico
199 I 17 **Tenryū**, Japan
199 I 17 **Tenryū**, Japan ⌇
127 Y 12 **Tenterden**, United Kingdom
231 V 9 **Tenterfield**, New South Wales, Australia
112 H 6 **Teodoro Sampaio**, Brazil
109 M 17 **Teófilo Otôni**, Brazil
197 G 23 **Teomabal**, Philippines 🏝
193 T 14 **Tepa**, Indonesia
89 O 11 **Tepatitlán**, Mexico
145 K 21 **Tepelenë**, Albania
88 M 10 **Tepic**, Mexico
143 C 14 **Teplice**, Czech Republic
237 W 8 **Tepoto**, French Polynesia 🏝
89 N 11 **Tequila**, Mexico
132 O 8 **Ter Apel**, Netherlands
215 N 9 **Téra**, Niger
237 O 1 **Teraina**, Kiribati 🏝
140 I 12 **Teramo**, Italy
132 M 13 **Terborg-Silvolde**, Netherlands
171 P 9 **Tercan**, Turkey
42 O 1 **Terceira**, Azores 🏝
150 G 11 **Teregova**, Romania
157 Q 14 **Terek**, Russian Federation ⌇
179 Z 5 **Terekty**, Kazakhstan
194 E 6 **Terengganu**, Malaysia ▣
179 P 9 **Terenozek**, Kazakhstan
108 M 11 **Teresina**, Brazil
112 N 6 **Teresópolis**, Brazil
142 O 13 **Terespol**, Poland
181 N 24 **Teressa Island**, India 🏝
129 R 3 **Tergnier**, France
70 H 11 **Terlingua**, Texas, U.S.A.
170 M 8 **Terme**, Turkey
179 Q 14 **Termez**, Uzbekistan
141 I 21 **Termini Imerese**, Italy
215 T 8 **Termit-Kaoboul**, Niger
193 R 10 **Ternate**, Indonesia
133 E 16 **Terneuzen**, Netherlands
140 H 13 **Terni**, Italy
151 P 6 **Ternivka**, Ukraine
150 K 5 **Ternopil'**, Ukraine
151 T 2 **Terny**, Ukraine
218 L 11 **Terra Firma**, Republic of South Africa
241 R 13 **Terra Nova Bay**, Antarctica ⠿
83 E 18 **Terrace**, British Columbia, Canada
84 M 12 **Terrace Bay**, Ontario, Canada
141 H 15 **Terracina**, Italy
134 E 13 **Terråk**, Norway
141 B 18 **Terralba**, Italy
65 H 20 **Terre Haute**, Indiana, U.S.A.
71 R 6 **Terrell**, Texas, U.S.A.
73 P 10 **Terreton**, Idaho, U.S.A.
127 W 6 **Terrington St Clement**, United Kingdom
62 L 5 **Terry**, Mississippi, U.S.A.
73 X 5 **Terry**, Montana, U.S.A.
132 I 5 **Terschelling**, Netherlands 🏝
179 V 11 **Terskey Ala-Too**, Kyrgyzstan ⛰
154 J 5 **Terskiy Bereg**, Russian Federation ◇
141 D 18 **Tertenia**, Italy
131 S 7 **Teruel**, Spain
191 G 26 **Terutao**, Thailand 🏝
146 M 6 **Tervel**, Bulgaria
213 H 17 **Teseney**, Eritrea
198 M 4 **Teshikaga**, Japan
198 J 3 **Teshio**, Japan
198 J 3 **Teshio**, Japan ⌇
198 J 3 **Teshio-sanchi**, Japan ⛰

□ Country ▣ Internal administrative region: State/Province/Territory/Dependent territory ⌂ Capital city ⛰ Mountain range/Undersea ridge ▲ Mountain peak/Volcano/Seamount ◇ Geographic feature ▶ Headland/Point/Cape/Peninsula ◭ Desert 🏝 Island/Island group ⠿ Antarctic base ◎ Ocean ≋ Sea ≈ Bay/Gulf/Channel/Strait ◢ Lake ◪ Salt pan/Dry/Intermittent lake ⌇ River

3	C 15	**Teslin Lake**, British Columbia, Canada 💧
10	L 15	**Tessalit**, Algeria
15	R 9	**Tessaoua**, Niger
36	K 9	**Tessin**, Germany
27	S 12	**Test**, United Kingdom ∿
27	R 10	**Tetbury**, United Kingdom
19	R 6	**Tete**, Mozambique
19	Q 5	**Tete**, Mozambique ▣
3	G 19	**Tête Jaune Cache**, British Columbia, Canada
34	K 6	**Tetepare**, Solomon Islands 🏝
51	P 3	**Teteriv**, Ukraine ∿
36	K 9	**Teterow**, Germany
37	T 9	**Tetiaroa**, French Polynesia 🏝
31	Q 12	**Tetica de Becares**, Spain ▲
51	O 5	**Tetiyiv**, Ukraine
27	W 3	**Tetney**, United Kingdom
3	R 11	**Teton Range**, Wyoming, U.S.A. ⛰
10	I 6	**Tétouan**, Morocco
46	C 10	**Tetovo**, Macedonia (F.Y.R.O.M.)
37	Z 8	**Tetufera**, French Polynesia ▲
57	R 2	**Tetyushi**, Russian Federation
99	B 24	**Teuchi**, Japan
93	S 14	**Teun**, Indonesia 🏝
98	J 4	**Teuri-tō**, Japan 🏝
1	O 9	**Teustepe**, Nicaragua
88	M 3	**Têwo**, China
9	S 14	**Texarkana**, Arkansas, U.S.A.
1	U 4	**Texarkana**, Texas, U.S.A.
31	V 9	**Texas**, Queensland, Australia
0	L 8	**Texas**, U.S.A. ▣
1	T 10	**Texas City**, Texas, U.S.A.
32	H 7	**Texel**, Netherlands 🏝
3	G 8	**Texhoma**, Oklahoma, U.S.A.
0	I 6	**Texistepeque**, El Salvador
0	I 1	**Texline**, Texas, U.S.A.
54	K 14	**Teykovo**, Russian Federation
83	W 10	**Tezpur**, India
83	Z 9	**Tezu**, India
10	F 11	**Tfaritiy**, Western Sahara
91	K 18	**Tha Tum**, Thailand
19	O 12	**Thabana-Ntlenyana**, Lesotho ▲
19	N 10	**Thabazimbi**, Republic of South Africa
90	M 12	**Thai Binh**, Vietnam
90	L 11	**Thai Nguyên**, Vietnam
91	G 17	**Thailand**, Asia □
83	S 11	**Thakurgaon**, Bangladesh
77	V 8	**Thal**, Pakistan
91	H 25	**Thale Luang**, Thailand 💧
31	U 9	**Thallon**, Queensland, Australia
75	W 11	**Thamarīt**, Oman
27	T 10	**Thame**, United Kingdom
32	L 9	**Thames**, New Zealand
27	X 10	**Thames**, United Kingdom ∿
91	F 23	**Than Kyun**, Myanmar 🏝
91	F 17	**Thanbyuzayat**, Myanmar
81	B 17	**Thane**, India
82	I 7	**Thanesar**, India
90	M 13	**Thanh Hoa**, Vietnam
81	F 22	**Thanjavur**, India
91	G 21	**Thap Sakae**, Thailand
80	B 12	**Thar Desert**, India/Pakistan ◇
31	S 9	**Thargomindah**, Queensland, Australia
73	R 6	**Tharthar**, Iraq
75	W 7	**Tharwānīyyah**, United Arab Emirates
47	I 14	**Thasos**, Greece 🏝
46	I 13	**Thasos**, Greece
91	E 16	**Thaton**, Myanmar
91	F 20	**Thayawthadangyi Kyun**, Myanmar 🏝
91	C 14	**Thayetmyo**, Myanmar
3	Q 12	**Thayne**, Wyoming, U.S.A.
27	Z 6	**The Broads**, United Kingdom ◇
6	H 9	**The Dalles**, Oregon, U.S.A.
127	V 6	**The Fens**, United Kingdom ◇
212	E 11	**The Great Oasis**, Egypt ◇
93	Z 12	**The Grenadines**, St Vincent and the Grenadines 🏝
132	F 12	**The Hague**, Netherlands ⌂
233	E 21	**The Hunters Hills**, New Zealand ⛰
124	F 9	**The Minch**, United Kingdom ≈
126	M 10	**The Mumbles**, United Kingdom
127	Z 9	**The Naze**, United Kingdom ▶
127	S 14	**The Needles**, United Kingdom ▶
84	H 8	**The Pas**, Manitoba, Canada
43	L 26	**The Peak**, Ascension ▲
93	Y 11	**The Pitons**, St Lucia ▲
127	S 13	**The Solent**, United Kingdom ≈
190	F 7	**The Triangle**, Myanmar ◇
93	X 8	**The Valley**, Anguilla ⌂
127	W 5	**The Wash**, United Kingdom ≈
127	X 12	**The Weald**, United Kingdom ◇
71	S 9	**The Woodlands**, Texas, U.S.A.
66	K 13	**Thedford**, Nebraska, U.S.A.
191	F 21	**Theinkun**, Myanmar
74	K 12	**Theodore Roosevelt Lake**, Arizona, U.S.A. 💧
147	F 15	**Thermaïkos Kolpos**, Greece ≈
73	U 10	**Thermopolis**, Wyoming, U.S.A.
147	E 18	**Thermopyles**, Greece
82	E 6	**Thesiger Bay**, Northwest Territories, Canada ≈
147	E 17	**Thessalia**, Greece ▣
86	A 9	**Thessalon**, Ontario, Canada
0	F 14	**Thessaloniki**, Greece
127	Y 7	**Thetford**, United Kingdom
87	N 9	**Thetford Mines**, Québec, Canada
62	L 8	**Thibodaux**, Louisiana, U.S.A.
67	P 3	**Thief River Falls**, Minnesota, U.S.A.
129	R 10	**Thiers**, France
214	D 8	**Thiès**, Senegal
217	V 8	**Thika**, Kenya
181	L 16	**Thiladhunmathee Atoll**, Maldives 🏝
183	T 9	**Thimphu**, Bhutan ⌂
235	P 14	**Thio**, New Caledonia
129	V 3	**Thionville**, France
147	J 24	**Thira**, Greece 🏝
147	J 23	**Thira**, Greece
147	J 23	**Thirasia**, Greece 🏝
127	T 1	**Thirsk**, United Kingdom
135	B 23	**Thisted**, Denmark
147	G 19	**Thiva**, Greece
129	O 10	**Thiviers**, France
191	G 15	**Thoen**, Thailand
190	H 13	**Thoeng**, Thailand
219	P 9	**Thohoyandou**, Republic of South Africa
61	Q 3	**Thomas**, West Virginia, U.S.A.
63	S 4	**Thomaston**, Georgia, U.S.A.
63	P 5	**Thomasville**, Alabama, U.S.A.
63	T 7	**Thomasville**, Georgia, U.S.A.
133	L 22	**Thommen**, Belgium
74	M 5	**Thompson**, Utah, U.S.A.
84	J 7	**Thompson**, Manitoba, Canada
72	L 4	**Thompson Falls**, Montana, U.S.A.
231	R 7	**Thomson**, Queensland, Australia ∿
63	V 3	**Thomson**, Georgia, U.S.A.
129	V 9	**Thonon-les-Bains**, France
127	Q 10	**Thornbury**, United Kingdom
125	H 14	**Thornhill**, United Kingdom
241	R 2	**Thorshavnheiane**, Antarctica ⛰
128	M 8	**Thouars**, France
77	N 15	**Thousand Springs**, Nevada, U.S.A.
159	R 7	**Thracian Sea**, Europe 🌊
147	I 14	**Thrakiko Pelagos**, Greece 🌊
73	Q 7	**Three Forks**, Montana, U.S.A.
189	Q 6	**Three Gorges Dam**, China 💧
231	S 14	**Three Hummock Island**, Tasmania, Australia 🏝
232	G 3	**Three Kings Islands**, New Zealand 🏝
191	F 18	**Three Pagodas Pass**, Thailand ◇
65	J 16	**Three Rivers**, Michigan, U.S.A.
71	P 12	**Three Rivers**, Texas, U.S.A.
71	N 5	**Throckmorton**, Texas, U.S.A.
191	M 21	**Thu Dâu Môt**, Vietnam
133	F 21	**Thuin**, Belgium
45	P 9	**Thule**, Greenland
219	O 9	**Thuli**, Zimbabwe
138	E 8	**Thun**, Switzerland
64	M 11	**Thunder Bay**, Michigan, U.S.A. ≈
84	L 12	**Thunder Bay**, Ontario, Canada
138	E 8	**Thuner See**, Switzerland 💧
191	G 24	**Thung Song**, Thailand
137	J 17	**Thüringen**, Germany ▣
137	H 17	**Thüringer Wald**, Germany ◇
125	D 19	**Thurles**, Republic of Ireland
231	R 1	**Thursday Island**, Queensland, Australia
124	H 8	**Thurso**, United Kingdom
240	J 9	**Thurston Island**, Antarctica 🏝
138	I 9	**Thusis**, Switzerland
231	N 6	**Ti Tree**, Northern Territory, Australia
184	H 5	**Tian Shan**, China ⛰
189	X 5	**Tianchang**, China
189	P 12	**Tiandeng**, China
189	P 11	**Tian'e**, China
187	E 17	**Tianjin**, China
187	E 17	**Tianjin Shi**, China ▣
185	O 8	**Tianjun**, China
189	O 11	**Tianlin**, China
189	T 6	**Tianmen**, China
186	M 13	**Tianqiaoling**, China
188	L 7	**Tianquan**, China
186	G 13	**Tianshan**, China
189	O 3	**Tianshui**, China
189	Z 7	**Tiantai**, China
189	O 12	**Tianyang**, China
189	Q 9	**Tianzhu**, China
210	L 6	**Tiaret**, Algeria
235	O 13	**Tiari**, New Caledonia
214	K 13	**Tiassalé**, Côte d'Ivoire
112	I 7	**Tibagi**, Brazil ∿
215	U 13	**Tibati**, Cameroon
73	Q 3	**Tiber Reservoir**, Montana, U.S.A. 💧
172	G 8	**Tiberias**, Israel
215	W 5	**Tibesti**, Chad ⛰
184	J 8	**Tibet**, China ▣
197	H 16	**Tibiao**, Philippines
231	R 9	**Tibooburra**, New South Wales, Australia
183	O 8	**Tibrikot**, Nepal
197	K 14	**Ticao**, Philippines 🏝
214	I 6	**Tîchît**, Mauritania
210	C 14	**Tichla**, Western Sahara
138	G 10	**Ticino**, Switzerland ▣
58	K 7	**Ticonderoga**, New York, U.S.A.
89	Y 11	**Ticul**, Mexico
231	S 14	**Tidal River**, Victoria, Australia
190	B 10	**Tiddim**, Myanmar
181	O 24	**Tiden**, India
214	G 6	**Tidjikja**, Mauritania
187	I 14	**Tiefa**, China
138	I 9	**Tiefencastel**, Switzerland
132	J 13	**Tiel**, Netherlands
186	L 10	**Tieli**, China
187	J 14	**Tieling**, China
184	I 7	**Tielongtan**, China
190	N 11	**Tiên Yên**, Vietnam
133	H 19	**Tienen**, Belgium
137	E 25	**Tiengen**, Germany
135	H 19	**Tierp**, Sweden
75	P 8	**Tierra Amarilla**, New Mexico, U.S.A.
89	R 13	**Tierra Colorada**, Mexico
111	I 25	**Tierra del Fuego**, Argentina ▣
112	K 7	**Tietê**, Brazil
112	I 5	**Tietê**, Brazil ∿
65	M 17	**Tiffin**, Ohio, U.S.A.
193	R 10	**Tifore**, Indonesia 🏝
63	U 6	**Tifton**, Georgia, U.S.A.
193	R 12	**Tifu**, Indonesia
235	Q 13	**Tiga**, New Caledonia 🏝
195	U 5	**Tiga**, Malaysia 🏝
76	L 6	**Tiger**, Washington, U.S.A.
151	O 9	**Tighina**, Moldova
215	U 12	**Tignère**, Cameroon
87	U 7	**Tignish**, Prince Edward Island, Canada
213	H 17	**Tigray**, Ethiopia ▣
106	D 10	**Tigre**, Peru ∿
171	P 12	**Tigris**, Iraq/Turkey ∿
214	E 7	**Tiguent**, Mauritania
232	L 11	**Tihoi**, New Zealand
182	J 9	**Tijara**, India
211	R 8	**Tijī**, Libya
88	E 1	**Tijuana**, Mexico
90	I 2	**Tikal**, Guatemala
237	T 8	**Tikehau**, French Polynesia 🏝
237	V 8	**Tikei**, French Polynesia 🏝
156	L 11	**Tikhoretsk**, Russian Federation
154	G 11	**Tikhvin**, Russian Federation
41	T 9	**Tiki Basin**, Pacific Ocean ◇
232	O 10	**Tikitiki**, New Zealand
235	R 8	**Tikopia**, Solomon Islands 🏝
173	S 5	**Tikrīt**, Iraq
154	G 6	**Tiksha**, Russian Federation
153	S 7	**Tiksi**, Russian Federation
133	I 15	**Tilburg**, Netherlands
127	X 11	**Tilbury**, United Kingdom
110	I 5	**Tilcara**, Argentina
71	O 12	**Tilden**, Texas, U.S.A.
215	P 8	**Tilemsès**, Niger
215	O 9	**Tillabéri**, Niger
215	O 9	**Tillabéri**, Niger ▣
76	F 9	**Tillamook**, Oregon, U.S.A.
181	O 24	**Tillanchong Island**, India 🏝
83	K 20	**Tilley**, Alberta, Canada
215	P 8	**Tillia**, Niger
63	O 7	**Tillmans Corner**, Alabama, U.S.A.
86	D 14	**Tillsonburg**, Ontario, Canada
215	O 8	**Tiloa**, Niger
110	H 5	**Tilomonte**, Chile
147	N 23	**Tilos**, Greece 🏝
211	N 7	**Tilrhemt**, Algeria
156	K 5	**Tim**, Russian Federation
212	E 10	**Tima**, Egypt
42	O 11	**Timanfaya**, Canary Islands ▲
155	O 3	**Timanskiy Kryazh**, Russian Federation ◇
171	S 10	**Timar**, Turkey
233	F 22	**Timaru**, New Zealand
157	T 3	**Timashevo**, Russian Federation
156	K 11	**Timashevsk**, Russian Federation
62	L 9	**Timbalier Bay**, Louisiana, U.S.A.
214	I 8	**Timbedgha**, Mauritania
230	M 3	**Timber Creek**, Northern Territory, Australia
195	X 6	**Timbun Mata**, Malaysia 🏝
215	R 7	**Timia**, Niger
210	L 10	**Timimoun**, Algeria
179	P 2	**Timiryazevo**, Kazakhstan
150	G 11	**Timiș**, Romania ∿
150	F 10	**Timișoara**, Romania
41	X 15	**Timiti's Crack**, Pitcairn Island ▶
86	D 6	**Timmins**, Ontario, Canada
64	E 10	**Timms Hill**, Wisconsin, U.S.A. ▲
237	Z 12	**Timoé**, French Polynesia 🏝
61	U 2	**Timonium**, Maryland, U.S.A.
193	Q 15	**Timor**, Indonesia 🏝
230	K 1	**Timor Sea**, Australia/Indonesia 🌊
39	V 6	**Timor Trough**, Indian Ocean ◇
113	A 16	**Timote**, Argentina
210	K 10	**Timoudi**, Algeria
135	H 16	**Timrå**, Sweden
105	N 3	**Tinaco**, Venezuela
172	L 2	**Tinah**, Syria
196	J 12	**Tinambac**, Philippines
181	F 21	**Tindivanam**, India
210	G 10	**Tindouf**, Algeria
130	K 1	**Tineo**, Spain
210	I 8	**Tinerhir**, Morocco
210	H 10	**Tinfouchy**, Algeria
194	F 9	**Tinggi**, Malaysia 🏝
107	D 14	**Tingo Maria**, Peru
236	A 8	**Tinian**, Northern Mariana Islands 🏝
195	S 8	**Tinjar**, Malaysia ∿
110	H 8	**Tinogasta**, Argentina
147	J 21	**Tinos**, Greece 🏝
147	J 21	**Tinos**, Greece
183	Y 9	**Tinsukia**, India
126	K 13	**Tintagel**, United Kingdom
83	E 18	**Tintagel**, British Columbia, Canada
214	H 7	**Tîntâne**, Mauritania
110	K 7	**Tintina**, Argentina
66	H 3	**Tioga**, North Dakota, U.S.A.
194	F 9	**Tioman**, Malaysia 🏝
140	E 6	**Tione di Trento**, Italy
58	C 11	**Tionesta**, Pennsylvania, U.S.A.
84	M 12	**Tip Top Hill**, Ontario, Canada ▲
91	N 9	**Tipitapa**, Nicaragua
125	C 19	**Tipperary**, Republic of Ireland
69	U 4	**Tipton**, Missouri, U.S.A.
60	A 8	**Tiptonville**, Tennessee, U.S.A.
181	D 21	**Tiptur**, India
89	Q 12	**Tiquicheo**, Mexico
90	G 6	**Tiquisate**, Guatemala
145	K 18	**Tirana**, Albania ⌂
140	E 5	**Tirano**, Italy
151	O 9	**Tiraspol**, Moldova
232	L 10	**Tirau**, New Zealand
233	L 15	**Tiraumea**, New Zealand
171	N 8	**Tirebolu**, Turkey
124	E 12	**Tiree**, United Kingdom 🏝
214	I 3	**Tiris Zemmour**, Mauritania ▣
138	K 7	**Tirol**, Austria ▣
216	L 2	**Tiroungoulou**, Central African Republic
232	K 11	**Tirua Point**, New Zealand ▶
181	E 24	**Tiruchchendur**, India
181	F 22	**Tiruchchirappalli**, India
181	E 24	**Tirunelveli**, India
181	F 21	**Tirupati**, India
181	E 22	**Tiruppur**, India
181	E 22	**Tiruvannamalai**, India
181	G 21	**Tiruvottiyur**, India
144	K 8	**Tisa**, Serbia and Montenegro ∿
181	E 24	**Tisaiyanvilai**, India
210	M 6	**Tissemsilt**, Algeria
143	L 22	**Tiszafüred**, Hungary
143	L 22	**Tiszaújváros**, Hungary
143	M 21	**Tiszavasvári**, Hungary
211	O 13	**Tit**, Algeria
153	S 7	**Tit-Ary**, Russian Federation
181	H 16	**Titlagarh**, India
144	E 11	**Titov Drvar**, Bosnia and Herzegovina
137	L 24	**Tittmoning**, Germany
150	J 12	**Titu**, Romania
58	B 10	**Titusville**, Pennsylvania, U.S.A.
63	X 9	**Titusville**, Florida, U.S.A.
180	C 12	**Tivari**, India
127	N 13	**Tiverton**, United Kingdom
172	K 5	**Tiyās**, Syria
211	N 5	**Tizi Ouzou**, Algeria
89	Z 10	**Tizimín**, Mexico
210	F 9	**Tiznit**, Morocco
132	K 8	**Tjeukemeer**, Netherlands 💧
135	D 22	**Tjörn**, Sweden 🏝
134	E 12	**Tjøtta**, Norway
230	J 8	**Tjukayirla Roadhouse**, Western Australia, Australia
89	T 13	**Tlacolula**, Mexico
89	R 12	**Tlalnepantla**, Mexico
89	R 12	**Tlaxcala**, Mexico ▣
89	S 13	**Tlaxiaco**, Mexico
210	K 6	**Tlemcen**, Algeria
219	N 10	**Tlokweng**, Botswana
157	Q 15	**Tlyarata**, Russian Federation
211	U 11	**Tmassah**, Libya
214	F 5	**Tmeïmîchât**, Mauritania
199	K 17	**To-shima**, Japan 🏝
194	B 14	**Toa Payoh**, Singapore
219	Z 7	**Toamasina**, Madgascar
219	Y 7	**Toamasina**, Madgascar ▣
237	U 9	**Toau**, French Polynesia 🏝
188	I 5	**Toba**, China
177	T 10	**Toba and Kakar Ranges**, Pakistan ⛰
93	Z 13	**Tobago**, Trinidad and Tobago 🏝
131	R 10	**Tobarra**, Spain
231	P 6	**Tobermorey**, Northern Territory, Australia
124	E 11	**Tobermory**, United Kingdom
86	C 10	**Tobermory**, Ontario, Canada
83	M 17	**Tobin Lake**, Saskatchewan, Canada 💧
192	G 12	**Toboali**, Indonesia
179	N 3	**Tobol**, Kazakhstan
152	K 10	**Tobol'sk**, Russian Federation
211	Y 7	**Tobruk**, Libya
155	P 2	**Tobseda**, Russian Federation
109	J 14	**Tocantins**, Brazil ▣
108	J 11	**Tocantins**, Brazil ∿
60	L 11	**Toccoa**, South Carolina, U.S.A.
63	U 2	**Toccoa**, Georgia, U.S.A.
110	G 4	**Toco**, Chile
90	K 6	**Toco**, Honduras ∿
110	H 5	**Toconao**, Chile
110	F 4	**Tocopilla**, Chile
140	H 12	**Todi**, Italy
127	R 3	**Todmorden**, United Kingdom
198	J 7	**Todohokke**, Japan
107	K 19	**Todos Santos**, Bolivia
88	J 9	**Todos Santos**, Mexico
233	C 26	**Toetoes Bay**, New Zealand ≈
237	R 15	**Tofol**, Federated States of Micronesia
236	I 10	**Tofua**, Tonga 🏝
235	Q 9	**Toga**, Vanuatu 🏝
199	L 16	**Tōgane**, Japan
213	M 20	**Togdheer**, Somalia ▣
199	H 15	**Togi**, Japan
79	N 10	**Togiak**, Alaska, U.S.A.
193	P 11	**Togian**, Indonesia 🏝
215	N 12	**Togo**, Africa □
184	M 3	**Tögrög**, Mongolia
178	M 7	**Toguz**, Kazakhstan
75	N 9	**Tohatchi**, New Mexico, U.S.A.
237	Y 8	**Tohiea**, French Polynesia ▲
199	J 17	**Toi**, Japan
199	D 24	**Toi-misaki**, Japan ▶
199	E 18	**Tōjō**, Japan
79	T 7	**Tok**, Alaska, U.S.A.
199	I 18	**Tōkai**, Japan
199	J 14	**Tōkamachi**, Japan
213	H 15	**Tokar**, Sudan
199	B 26	**Tokara-rettō**, Japan 🏝

□ Country ▣ Internal administrative region: State/Province/Territory/Dependent territory ⌂ Capital city ⛰ Mountain range/Undersea ridge ▲ Mountain peak/Volcano/Seamount ◇ Geographic feature ▶ Headland/Point/Cape/Peninsula ◒ Desert 🏝 Island/Island group ⁙ Antarctic base ◎ Ocean 🌊 Sea ≈ Bay/Gulf/Channel/Strait 💧 Lake ◩ Salt pan/Dry/Intermittent lake ∿ River

Tokarahi – Ts'khinvali

233 F 23 Tokarahi, New Zealand
199 N 25 Tokasiki-jima, Japan
170 L 9 Tokat, Turkey
187 K 19 Tŏkchŏk-to, South Korea
236 J 5 Tokelau Islands, New Zealand
232 K 12 Tokirima, New Zealand
198 L 5 Tokkachi, Japan
151 V 8 Tokmak, Ukraine
232 O 11 Tokomaru Bay, New Zealand
198 L 4 Tokoro, Japan
232 L 11 Tokoroa, New Zealand
214 H 11 Tokounuo, Guinea
179 T 11 Toktogul, Kyrgyzstan
236 I 10 Toku, Tonga
199 N 22 Toku-no-shima, Japan
199 N 22 Tokunoshima, Japan
199 F 19 Tokushima, Japan
199 D 20 Tokuyama, Japan
199 K 16 Tokyo, Japan
199 K 16 Tōkyō-wan, Japan
177 S 6 Tokzār, Afghanistan
232 O 11 Tolaga Bay, New Zealand
219 X 11 Tōlanaro, Madgascar
157 W 2 Tolbazy, Russian Federation
184 M 3 Tolbo, Mongolia
91 U 14 Tolé, Panama
179 T 9 Tole Bi, Kazakhstan
112 G 8 Toledo, Brazil
131 O 7 Toledo, Spain
197 J 17 Toledo, Philippines
65 L 16 Toledo, Ohio, U.S.A.
76 F 10 Toledo, Oregon, U.S.A.
62 H 6 Toledo Bend Reservoir, Louisiana, U.S.A.
184 J 3 Toli, China
219 V 10 Toliara, Madgascar
219 W 9 Toliara, Madgascar
104 H 7 Tolima, Colombia
193 O 10 Tolitoli, Indonesia
179 U 10 Tolmak, Kyrgyzstan
140 H 5 Tolmezzo, Italy
144 A 7 Tolmin, Slovenia
143 I 25 Tolna, Hungary
216 J 9 Tolo, Democratic Republic of Congo
197 I 19 Tolong Bay, Philippines
131 R 1 Tolosa, Spain
89 Q 12 Toluca, Mexico
141 M 16 Tolve, Italy
157 R 3 Tol'yatti, Russian Federation
219 O 9 Tom Burke, Republic of South Africa
230 G 6 Tom Price, Western Australia, Australia
64 E 12 Tomah, Wisconsin, U.S.A.
198 K 6 Tomakomai, Japan
198 J 4 Tomamae, Japan
195 Y 6 Tomanggong, Malaysia
195 U 6 Tomani, Malaysia
179 U 7 Tomar, Kazakhstan
156 J 6 Tomarovka, Russian Federation
170 K 11 Tomarza, Turkey
143 O 16 Tomaszów Lubelski, Poland
143 K 14 Tomaszów Mazowiecki, Poland
88 M 11 Tomatlán, Mexico
63 O 5 Tombigbee, Alabama, U.S.A.
218 F 1 Tomboco, Angola
74 L 15 Tombstone, Arizona, U.S.A.
218 F 6 Tombua, Angola
111 F 14 Tomé, Chile
193 Q 13 Tomea, Indonesia
131 P 9 Tomelloso, Spain
179 Q 9 Tomenaryk, Kazakhstan
198 L 13 Tomioka, Japan
104 M 6 Tomo, Colombia
216 H 6 Tomori, Central African Republic
58 J 14 Toms River, New Jersey, U.S.A.
152 M 12 Tomsk, Russian Federation
153 V 9 Tomtor, Russian Federation
193 U 12 Tomu, Indonesia
199 N 25 Tonaki-jima, Japan
89 V 14 Tonalá, Mexico
108 C 11 Tonantins, Brazil
76 J 5 Tonasket, Washington, U.S.A.
58 D 8 Tonawanda, New York, U.S.A.
127 W 11 Tonbridge, United Kingdom
193 Q 10 Tondano, Indonesia
135 B 26 Tønder, Denmark
240 K 10 Toney Mountain, Antarctica
236 I 9 Tonga, Oceania
41 P 10 Tonga Trench, Pacific Ocean
189 X 11 Tong'an, China
237 P 6 Tongareva, Cook Islands
236 I 11 Tongatapu, Tonga
236 H 12 Tongatapu Group, Tonga
189 T 5 Tongbai, China
186 K 9 Tongbei, China
189 W 6 Tongcheng, China
187 M 17 T'ongch'ŏn, North Korea
189 Q 3 Tongchuan, China
189 R 10 Tongdao, China
133 J 19 Tongeren, Belgium
189 U 8 Tonggu, China
189 R 3 Tongguan, China
189 T 8 Tongguan, China
187 N 19 Tonghae, South Korea
188 L 11 Tonghai, China
186 L 10 Tonghe, China
187 K 15 Tonghua, China
186 O 9 Tongjiang, China
186 H 13 Tongliao, China
189 W 6 Tongling, China
235 R 11 Tongoa, Vanuatu
197 H 24 Tongquil, Philippines
189 Q 9 Tongren, China
189 Q 15 Tongshi, China
124 H 8 Tongue, United Kingdom
189 N 3 Tongwei, China
187 E 17 Tongxian, China
185 Q 8 Tongxin, China
186 E 13 Tongxing, China
186 I 12 Tongyu, China
189 O 8 Tongzi, China
88 J 5 Tónichi, Mexico
213 D 21 Tonj, Sudan
180 D 12 Tonk, India
176 I 5 Tonkābon, Iran
190 L 11 Tonkin, Vietnam
191 K 20 Tônlé Sab, Cambodia
129 S 6 Tonnerre, France
136 F 8 Tönning, Germany
77 K 19 Tonopah, Nevada, U.S.A.
91 V 15 Tonosí, Panama
135 D 20 Tønsberg, Norway
74 J 3 Tooele, Utah, U.S.A.
231 V 9 Toowoomba, Queensland, Australia
213 O 18 Tooxin, Somalia
230 M 3 Top Springs, Northern Territory, Australia
69 Q 4 Topeka, Kansas, U.S.A.
150 J 9 Toplița, Romania
42 N 1 Topo, Azores
77 N 24 Topock, California, U.S.A.
146 C 12 Topolčani, Macedonia (F.Y.R.O.M.)
88 K 7 Topolobampo, Mexico
146 K 10 Topolovgrad, Bulgaria
151 N 3 Toporyshche, Ukraine
127 N 13 Topsham, United Kingdom
232 J 7 Topuni, New Zealand
127 N 14 Tor Bay, United Kingdom
170 B 11 Torbali, Turkey
177 O 7 Torbat-e Heydarīyeh, Iran
177 O 6 Torbat-e Jām, Iran
130 M 4 Tordesillas, Spain
134 K 12 Töre, Sweden
151 Y 7 Torez, Ukraine
137 L 15 Torgau, Germany
136 N 10 Torgelow, Germany
179 O 5 Torghay, Kazakhstan
133 B 18 Torhout, Belgium
213 E 23 Torit, Sudan
154 E 11 Torkovichi, Russian Federation
134 I 9 Torneälven, Sweden
134 I 9 Torneträsk, Sweden
134 I 9 Torneträsk, Sweden
85 T 5 Torngat Mountains, Québec, Canada
70 E 8 Tornillo, Texas, U.S.A.
134 K 12 Tornio, Finland
113 B 18 Tornquist, Argentina
215 S 11 Toro, Nigeria
130 M 4 Toro, Spain
77 L 25 Toro Peak, California, U.S.A.
215 O 9 Torodi, Niger
234 J 5 Torokina, Papua New Guinea
143 K 23 Törökszentmiklós, Hungary
86 F 13 Toronto, Ontario, Canada
154 F 14 Toropets, Russian Federation
217 T 7 Tororo, Uganda
126 L 15 Torpoint, United Kingdom
127 N 14 Torquay, United Kingdom
131 N 3 Torquemada, Spain
77 J 25 Torrance, California, U.S.A.
130 H 10 Torrão, Portugal
131 V 3 Torre de Cadí, Spain
130 J 5 Torre de Moncorvo, Portugal
130 M 13 Torrecilla, Spain
131 O 1 Torrelavega, Spain
89 O 7 Torreón, Mexico
112 I 11 Torres, Brazil
235 P 9 Torres Islands, Vanuatu
130 H 8 Torres Novas, Portugal
193 Y 15 Torres Strait, Asia/Oceania
130 G 8 Torres Vedras, Portugal
131 T 11 Torrevieja, Spain
234 A 3 Torricelli Mountains, Papua New Guinea
140 C 9 Torriglia, Italy
58 L 10 Torrington, Connecticut, U.S.A.
73 Z 13 Torrington, Wyoming, U.S.A.
135 F 14 Torrön, Sweden
135 E 19 Torsby, Sweden
111 F 21 Tortel, Chile
179 T 4 Tortkuduk, Kazakhstan
93 V 8 Tortola, Virgin Islands, United Kingdom
171 Q 9 Tortum, Turkey
176 L 6 Ţorūd, Iran
171 O 8 Torul, Turkey
142 H 11 Toruń, Poland
148 H 9 Tõrva, Estonia
154 H 14 Torzhok, Russian Federation
199 E 20 Tosa, Japan
199 F 21 Tosa-wan, Japan
199 E 21 Tosashimizu, Japan
134 F 13 Tosbotn, Norway
218 M 11 Tosca, Republic of South Africa
140 F 11 Toscana, Italy
179 R 11 Toshkent Wiloyati, Uzbekistan
112 B 12 Tostado, Argentina
148 F 8 Tõstamaa, Estonia
136 G 11 Tostedt, Germany
170 J 8 Tosya, Turkey
131 R 11 Totana, Spain
154 L 11 Tot'ma, Russian Federation
127 N 14 Totnes, United Kingdom
105 V 6 Totness, Suriname
110 F 8 Totoral, Chile
235 Y 12 Totoya, Fiji
157 U 4 Totskoye, Russian Federation
199 F 17 Tottori, Japan
214 I 12 Touba, Côte d'Ivoire
214 E 8 Touba, Senegal
215 V 12 Touboro, Cameroon
211 O 7 Touggourt, Algeria
214 G 10 Tougué, Guinea
235 P 13 Touho, New Caledonia
214 H 8 Touil, Mauritania
129 U 4 Toul, France
129 V 15 Toulon, France
129 P 14 Toulouse, France
214 J 13 Toumodi, Côte d'Ivoire
215 U 12 Toungo, Nigeria
191 E 14 Toungoo, Myanmar
215 V 9 Tourba, Chad
133 C 20 Tournai, Belgium
107 E 14 Tournavista, Peru
129 T 11 Tournon-sur-Rhône, France
129 T 8 Tournus, France
108 O 12 Touros, Brazil
129 N 7 Tours, France
185 Q 3 Töv, Mongolia
156 J 2 Tovarkovo, Russian Federation
171 U 7 Tovuz, Azerbaijan
198 K 9 Towada, Japan
198 K 9 Towada-ko, Japan
58 G 10 Towanda, Pennsylvania, U.S.A.
127 T 8 Towcester, United Kingdom
66 J 3 Towner, North Dakota, U.S.A.
73 Q 6 Townsend, Montana, U.S.A.
231 T 4 Townsville, Queensland, Australia
213 G 22 Towot, Sudan
61 U 2 Towson, Maryland, U.S.A.
198 J 6 Tōya-ko, Japan
70 H 8 Toyah, Texas, U.S.A.
199 H 15 Toyama, Japan
199 H 14 Toyama-wan, Japan
155 N 9 Toyma, Russian Federation
199 I 18 Toyohashi, Japan
199 F 17 Toyooka, Japan
90 L 4 Toyós, Honduras
199 I 17 Toyota, Japan
211 P 7 Tozeur, Tunisia
171 S 6 Tqibuli, Georgia
171 Q 5 Tqvarch'eli, Georgia
191 M 23 Tra Vinh, Vietnam
130 K 4 Trabazos, Spain
171 O 8 Trabzon, Turkey
139 W 4 Traisen, Austria
125 B 20 Tralee, Republic of Ireland
135 F 22 Tranås, Sweden
110 I 7 Trancas, Argentina
191 G 25 Trang, Thailand
193 V 14 Trangan, Indonesia
112 E 13 Tranqueras, Uruguay
241 N 7 Transantarctic Mountains, Antarctica
38 H 9 Transkei Basin, Indian Ocean
150 G 10 Transylvania, Romania
150 G 11 Transylvanian Alps, Romania
150 H 8 Transylvanian Basin, Romania
141 H 21 Trapani, Italy
214 F 6 Trarza, Mauritania
183 V 9 Trashigang, Bhutan
191 J 20 Trat, Thailand
139 T 4 Traun, Austria
139 S 5 Traunsee, Austria
136 I 9 Travemünde, Germany
64 J 11 Traverse City, Michigan, U.S.A.
140 D 8 Travo, Italy
127 N 5 Trawsfynydd, United Kingdom
234 J 5 Treasury Islands, Solomon Islands
143 E 19 Třebíč, Czech Republic
145 H 15 Trebinje, Bosnia and Herzegovina
143 M 20 Trebišov, Slovakia
233 C 22 Treble Cone, New Zealand
144 C 8 Trebnje, Slovenia
181 B 22 Tree Island, India
126 K 15 Tregony, United Kingdom
113 G 14 Treinta y Tres, Uruguay
113 F 14 Treinta y Tres, Uruguay
111 I 18 Trelew, Argentina
135 E 26 Trelleborg, Sweden
126 M 6 Tremadog Bay, United Kingdom
38 B 15 Tremblet, Réunion
74 J 1 Tremonton, Utah, U.S.A.
64 I 9 Trenary, Michigan, U.S.A.
143 H 20 Trenčín, Slovakia
113 A 17 Trenque Lauquen, Argentina
127 U 5 Trent, United Kingdom
140 F 5 Trentino-Alto Adige, Italy
140 F 6 Trento, Italy
58 I 13 Trenton, New Jersey, U.S.A.
69 T 2 Trenton, Missouri, U.S.A.
86 H 12 Trenton, Ontario, Canada
85 Z 11 Trepassey, Newfoundland and Labrador, Canada
113 C 18 Tres Arroyos, Argentina
108 E 12 Três Casas, Brazil
111 H 21 Tres Cerros, Argentina
112 L 6 Tres Corações, Brazil
104 H 9 Tres Esquinas, Colombia
112 B 9 Tres Isletas, Argentina
112 H 5 Três Lagoas, Brazil
111 G 22 Tres Lagos, Argentina
89 V 14 Tres Picos, Mexico
75 Q 8 Tres Piedras, New Mexico, U.S.A.
90 K 4 Tres Puntas, Guatemala
112 N 6 Três Rios, Brazil
135 D 18 Tretten, Norway
140 D 7 Treviglio, Italy
140 G 6 Treviso, Italy
126 K 14 Trevose Head, United Kingdom
145 N 16 Trgovište, Serbia and Montenegro
147 M 24 Tria Nisia, Greece
68 G 4 Tribune, Kansas, U.S.A.
181 D 22 Trichur, India
139 T 6 Trieben, Austria
137 B 20 Trier, Germany
140 I 7 Trieste, Italy
144 A 6 Triglav, Slovenia
147 D 16 Trikala, Greece
181 G 24 Trincomalee, Sri Lanka
107 K 18 Trinidad, Bolivia
113 E 15 Trinidad, Uruguay
75 S 7 Trinidad, Colorado, U.S.A.
92 I 5 Trinidad, Cuba
93 Z 14 Trinidad, Trinidad and Tobago
93 Y 13 Trinidad and Tobago, North America
71 T 9 Trinity, Texas, U.S.A.
85 Z 10 Trinity Bay, Newfoundland and Labrador, Canada
79 P 12 Trinity Islands, Alaska, U.S.A.
38 B 11 Triolet, Mauritius
211 S 7 Tripoli, Libya
147 E 21 Tripoli, Greece
172 G 5 Tripoli, Lebanon
158 K 11 Tripolitanian Valley, Mediterranean Sea
183 V 13 Tripura, India
136 F 9 Trischen, Germany
43 O 15 Tristan da Cunha, Tristan da Cunha
43 N 15 Tristan da Cunha, U.K.
43 I 18 Tristan da Cunha Fracture Zone, Atlantic Ocean
90 M 8 Triunfo, Honduras
181 D 24 Trivandrum, India
141 K 14 Trivento, Italy
143 G 21 Trnava, Slovakia
234 G 6 Trobriand Islands, Papua New Guinea
179 P 2 Troebratskÿ, Kazakhstan
134 F 12 Trofors, Norway
144 E 12 Troglav, Bosnia and Herzegovina
141 L 15 Troia, Italy
87 P 7 Trois-Pistoles, Québec, Canada
133 K 21 Trois-Ponts, Belgium
86 L 9 Trois-Rivières, Québec, Canada
152 I 11 Troitsk, Russian Federation
155 S 8 Troitsko-Pechorsk, Russian Federation
135 E 22 Trollhättan, Sweden
108 G 9 Trombetas, Brazil
219 N 13 Trompsburg, Republic of South Africa
134 I 7 Tromsø, Norway
135 D 15 Trondheim, Norway
135 D 15 Trondheimsfjorden, Norway
183 U 9 Trongsa, Bhutan
125 G 14 Troon, United Kingdom
147 D 20 Tropaia, Greece
141 L 20 Tropea, Italy
42 J 11 Tropic Seamount, Atlantic Ocean
151 U 3 Trostyanets', Ukraine
64 K 9 Trout Lake, Michigan, U.S.A.
83 F 14 Trout Lake, Northwest Territories, Canada
84 K 10 Trout Lake, Ontario, Canada
73 S 9 Trout Peak, Wyoming, U.S.A.
127 R 11 Trowbridge, United Kingdom
58 K 9 Troy, New York, U.S.A.
63 Q 5 Troy, Alabama, U.S.A.
69 X 3 Troy, Missouri, U.S.A.
72 K 2 Troy, Montana, U.S.A.
77 M 19 Troy Peak, Nevada, U.S.A.
146 I 8 Troyan, Bulgaria
129 S 5 Troyes, France
151 Y 4 Troyits'ke, Ukraine
75 R 9 Truchas Peak, New Mexico, U.S.A.
77 I 17 Truckee, California, U.S.A.
104 L 3 Trujillo, Venezuela
107 B 14 Trujillo, Peru
130 L 8 Trujillo, Spain
91 N 4 Trujillo, Honduras
146 E 9 Trŭn, Bulgaria
126 J 15 Truro, United Kingdom
87 V 10 Truro, Nova Scotia, Canada
83 F 16 Trutch, British Columbia, Canada
75 P 13 Truth Or Consequences, New Mexico, U.S.A.
146 J 9 Tryavna, Bulgaria
66 J 13 Tryon, Nebraska, U.S.A.
144 D 10 Tržac, Bosnia and Herzegovina
142 F 11 Trzcianka, Poland
142 E 12 Trzciel, Poland
143 G 15 Trzebnica, Poland
144 B 6 Tržič, Slovenia
185 U 3 Tsagaannuur, Mongolia
157 Q 9 Tsagan Aman, Russian Federation
134 I 9 Tsåktso, Sweden
171 T 7 Ts'alka, Georgia
146 N 10 Tsarevo, Bulgaria
151 U 6 Tsarychanka, Ukraine
185 N 4 Tseel, Mongolia
156 M 10 Tselina, Russian Federation
218 J 11 Tses, Namibia
218 L 9 Tsetseng, Botswana
215 N 13 Tsévié, Togo
218 L 11 Tshabong, Botswana
218 L 10 Tshane, Botswana
216 F 11 Tshela, Democratic Republic of Congo
216 L 12 Tshibala, Democratic Republic of Congo
216 L 13 Tshibwika, Democratic Republic of Congo
216 K 11 Tshikapa, Democratic Republic of Congo
217 P 12 Tshimbo, Democratic Republic of Congo
219 Q 10 Tshokwane, Republic of South Africa
218 K 9 Tshootsha, Botswana
82 C 9 Tsiigehtchic, Northwest Territories, Canada
157 N 9 Tsimlyanskoye Reservoir, Russian Federation
218 L 11 Tsineng, Republic of South Africa
219 W 11 Tsiombe, Madgascar
219 W 7 Tsiroanomandidy, Madgascar
157 Q 1 Tsivil'sk, Russian Federation
171 T 6 Ts'khinvali, Georgia

Country · Internal administrative region: State/Province/Territory/Dependent territory · Capital city · Mountain range/Undersea ridge · Mountain peak/Volcano/Seamount · Geographic feature · Headland/Point/Cape/Peninsula · Desert · Island/Island group · Antarctic base · Ocean · Sea · Bay/Gulf/Channel/Strait · Lake · Salt pan/Dry/Intermittent lake · River

Tsnori – Ungwana Bay

71 V 7 Tsnori, Georgia
82 K 4 Tso Morari Lake, India
19 O 13 Tsolo, Republic of South Africa
71 R 6 Tsqaltubo, Georgia
99 H 18 Tsu, Japan
99 L 15 Tsuchiura, Japan
98 J 8 Tsugarū-kaikyō, Japan
99 D 21 Tsukumi, Japan
18 I 7 Tsumeb, Namibia
18 I 10 Tsumis Park, Namibia
18 J 8 Tsumkwe, Namibia
99 G 17 Tsuruga, Japan
99 F 20 Tsurugi-san, Japan
98 J 12 Tsuruoka, Japan
99 A 20 Tsushima, Japan
99 F 18 Tsuyama, Japan
19 N 11 Tswelelang, Republic of South Africa
49 N 20 Tsyerakhowka, Belarus
51 S 9 Tsyurupyns'k, Ukraine
3 F 14 Tthenaagoo, Northwest Territories, Canada
32 N 12 Tuai, New Zealand
32 K 9 Tuakau, New Zealand
25 C 17 Tuam, Republic of Ireland
37 T 8 Tuamotu Archipelago, French Polynesia
1 T 9 Tuamotu Fracture Zone, Pacific Ocean
90 J 11 Tuân Giao, Vietnam
96 G 6 Tuao, Philippines
56 L 13 Tuapse, Russian Federation
95 U 5 Tuaran, Malaysia
94 A 14 Tuas, Singapore
36 J 8 Tuasivi, Samoa
4 K 9 Tuba City, Arizona, U.S.A.
93 S 11 Tubalai, Indonesia
92 J 14 Tuban, Indonesia
12 J 11 Tubarão, Brazil
72 G 8 Tūbās, Israel
97 E 20 Tubbataha Reefs, Philippines
37 F 23 Tübingen, Germany
33 F 20 Tubize, Belgium
14 G 13 Tubmanburg, Liberia
37 T 12 Tubuai, French Polynesia
T 10 Tubuai Island, French Polynesia
07 O 21 Tucavaca, Bolivia
42 H 10 Tuchola, Poland
T 2 Tucker, Georgia, U.S.A.
B 7 Tucker's Town, Bermuda
K 14 Tucson, Arizona, U.S.A.
10 I 8 Tucumán, Argentina
T 10 Tucumcari, New Mexico, U.S.A.
10 H 10 Tucunuco, Argentina
8 J 11 Tucuruí, Brazil
31 R 3 Tudela, Spain
48 I 6 Tudu, Estonia
3 Y 10 Tuensang, India
75 S 4 Ţufayḩ, Saudi Arabia
34 F 6 Tufi, Papua New Guinea
S 2 Tufts Abyssal Plain, Pacific Ocean
97 M 16 Tugnug Point, Philippines
96 G 7 Tuguegarao, Philippines
3 V 13 Tugur, Russian Federation
32 K 12 Tuhua, New Zealand
30 H 3 Tui, Spain
N 12 Tuineje, Canary Islands
3 M 21 Tukayel, Ethiopia
50 H 6 Tukhol'ka, Ukraine
9 U 14 Tŭkhtamish, Tajikistan
1 W 7 Tūkrah, Libya
C 8 Tuktoyaktuk, Northwest Territories, Canada
48 E 11 Tukums, Latvia
7 T 13 Tukuyu, Tanzania
56 K 2 Tula, Russian Federation
Q 9 Tula, Mexico
34 M 6 Tulaghi, Solomon Islands
7 Q 8 Tulak, Afghanistan
R 11 Tulancingo, Mexico
I 22 Tulare, California, U.S.A.
H 22 Tulare Lake Bed, California, U.S.A.
06 B 8 Tulcán, Ecuador
151 N 12 Tulcea, Romania
70 K 3 Tulia, Texas, U.S.A.
186 H 6 Tulihe, China
82 E 11 Tulit'a, Northwest Territories, Canada
60 G 10 Tullahoma, Tennessee, U.S.A.
125 D 18 Tullamore, Republic of Ireland
129 P 11 Tulle, France
139 X 3 Tulln, Austria
62 J 5 Tullos, Louisiana, U.S.A.
231 T 4 Tully, Queensland, Australia
150 L 10 Tulnici, Romania
134 M 9 Tulppio, Finland
69 P 9 Tulsa, Oklahoma, U.S.A.
156 K 3 Tul'skaya Oblast', Russian Federation
153 P 13 Tulun, Russian Federation
234 J 4 Tulun Islands, Papua New Guinea
156 M 2 Tuma, Russian Federation
91 O 8 Tuma, Nicaragua
104 F 8 Tumaco, Colombia
216 M 9 Tumba, Democratic Republic of Congo
192 K 11 Tumbangsamba, Indonesia
106 A 11 Tumbes, Peru
83 G 18 Tumbler Ridge, British Columbia, Canada
231 O 11 Tumby Bay, South Australia, Australia
187 M 14 Tumen, China
105 S 5 Tumeremo, Venezuela
197 E 26 Tumindao, Philippines
181 E 21 Tumkur, India
194 C 5 Tumpat, Malaysia
105 V 8 Tumuc-Humac Mountains, Brazil/Suriname
171 O 10 Tunceli, Turkey
189 R 15 Tunchang, China
215 R 10 Tundun-Wada, Nigeria
217 V 14 Tunduru, Tanzania
146 J 9 Tundzha, Bulgaria
215 S 12 Tunga, Nigeria
181 D 20 Tungabhadra Reservoir, India
213 E 19 Tungaru, Sudan
197 I 22 Tungawan, Philippines
195 Z 6 Tungku, Malaysia
91 P 7 Tungla, Nicaragua
106 C 9 Tungurahua, Ecuador
181 H 18 Tuni, India
62 L 1 Tunica, Mississippi, U.S.A.
211 Q 5 Tunis, Tunisia
211 P 6 Tunisia, Africa
158 L 11 Tunisian Plateau, Mediterranean Sea
104 J 6 Tunja, Colombia
91 P 7 Tunki, Nicaragua
134 F 13 Tunnsjøen, Norway
127 W 2 Tunstall, United Kingdom
110 G 12 Tunuyán, Argentina
179 W 10 Tüp, Kyrgyzstan
112 I 6 Tupã, Brazil
237 R 9 Tupai, French Polynesia
112 G 11 Tupanciretã, Brazil
63 N 2 Tupelo, Mississippi, U.S.A.
108 J 13 Tupiratins, Brazil
107 J 23 Tupiza, Bolivia
58 I 6 Tupper Lake, New York, U.S.A.
186 H 11 Tuquan, China
153 P 10 Tura, Russian Federation
183 U 11 Tura, India
179 S 10 Tura-Ryskulova, Kazakhstan
175 N 8 Turabah, Saudi Arabia
233 K 14 Turakina, New Zealand
233 K 16 Turakirae Head, New Zealand
234 B 5 Turama, Papua New Guinea
178 K 13 Turan Lowland, Turkmenistan
232 L 12 Turangi, New Zealand
149 J 21 Turaw, Belarus
174 L 1 Turayf, Saudi Arabia
177 Q 14 Turbat, Pakistan
61 P 13 Turbeville, South Carolina, U.S.A.
104 G 4 Turbo, Colombia
150 I 9 Turda, Romania
237 X 11 Tureia, French Polynesia
142 I 13 Turek, Poland
179 T 4 Turgay, Kazakhstan
146 L 8 Tŭrgovishte, Bulgaria
146 L 8 Tŭrgovishte, Bulgaria
170 B 11 Turgutlu, Turkey
170 L 9 Turhal, Turkey
110 G 4 Turi, Chile
148 G 7 Türi, Estonia
131 S 8 Turia, Spain
108 L 10 Turiaçu, Brazil
140 A 7 Turin, Italy
150 J 2 Turiys'k, Ukraine
150 H 5 Turka, Ukraine
170 B 8 Türkeli, Turkey
179 Q 10 Turkestan, Kazakhstan
179 Q 12 Turkestan Range, Uzbekistan
170 M 10 Turkey, Asia/Europe
70 L 3 Turkey, Texas, U.S.A.
157 O 5 Turki, Russian Federation
178 H 12 Turkmenbashi, Turkmenistan
178 M 12 Turkmenistan, Asia
178 I 13 Turkmenskiy Zaliv, Turkmenistan
170 L 12 Türkoğlu, Turkey
93 Q 4 Turks and Caicos Islands, United Kingdom, United Kingdom
93 Q 5 Turks Islands, Turks and Caicos Islands
135 K 19 Turku, Finland
77 H 20 Turlock, California, U.S.A.
90 L 2 Turneffe Islands, Belize
133 H 16 Turnhout, Belgium
139 W 4 Türnitz, Austria
83 K 15 Turnor Lake, Saskatchewan, Canada
150 J 14 Turnu Măgurele, Romania
184 L 5 Turpan, China
184 L 5 Turpan Depression, China
139 S 8 Turrach, Austria
69 Y 10 Turrell, Arkansas, U.S.A.
91 R 12 Turrialba, Costa Rica
173 V 7 Tursāq, Iraq
178 M 11 Turtkul', Uzbekistan
197 C 23 Turtle Islands, Philippines
64 C 10 Turtle Lake, Wisconsin, U.S.A.
153 N 9 Turukhansk, Russian Federation
74 J 9 Tusayan, Arizona, U.S.A.
63 O 3 Tuscaloosa, Alabama, U.S.A.
140 D 9 Tuscan Archipelago, Italy
58 E 14 Tuscarora Mountains, Pennsylvania, U.S.A.
65 G 19 Tuscola, Illinois, U.S.A.
70 M 7 Tuscola, Texas, U.S.A.
171 S 10 Tutak, Turkey
181 E 24 Tuticorin, India
195 S 6 Tutong, Brunei
146 L 6 Tutrakan, Bulgaria
66 K 5 Tuttle, North Dakota, U.S.A.
69 O 3 Tuttle Creek Reservoir, Kansas, U.S.A.
137 F 24 Tuttlingen, Germany
193 R 15 Tutuala, East Timor
236 K 8 Tutuila, American Samoa
219 N 8 Tutume, Botswana
233 L 16 Tuturumuri, New Zealand
135 N 15 Tuusniemi, Finland
236 G 5 Tuvalu, Oceania
174 L 7 Tuwwal, Saudi Arabia
89 O 12 Tuxpan, Mexico
89 S 11 Tuxpan, Mexico
89 V 14 Tuxtla Gutiérrez, Mexico
191 N 20 Tuy Duc, Vietnam
191 O 19 Tuy Hoa, Vietnam
190 L 11 Tuyên Quang, Vietnam
170 I 11 Tuz Gölü, Turkey
173 U 4 Tūz Khurmātū, Iraq
144 I 11 Tuzla, Bosnia and Herzegovina
151 N 13 Tuzla, Romania
170 J 13 Tuzla, Turkey
154 H 14 Tver', Russian Federation
154 H 13 Tverskaya Oblast', Russian Federation
143 J 19 Tvrdošín, Slovakia
146 K 9 Tvŭrdista, Bulgaria
124 J 13 Tweed, United Kingdom
77 M 24 Twentynine Palms, California, U.S.A.
73 P 7 Twin Bridges, Montana, U.S.A.
63 V 4 Twin City, Georgia, U.S.A.
72 M 12 Twin Falls, Idaho, U.S.A.
72 M 9 Twin Peaks, Idaho, U.S.A.
76 I 6 Twisp, Washington, U.S.A.
233 E 21 Twizel, New Zealand
64 H 12 Two, Wisconsin, U.S.A.
43 L 26 Two Boats Village, Ascension
143 I 17 Tychy, Poland
71 S 6 Tyler, Texas, U.S.A.
62 L 6 Tylertown, Mississippi, U.S.A.
147 I 26 Tympaki, Greece
153 T 13 Tynda, Russian Federation
125 I 15 Tyne, United Kingdom
60 J 6 Tyner, Kentucky, U.S.A.
135 D 16 Tynset, Norway
135 D 19 Tyrifjorden, Norway
147 E 16 Tyrnavos, Greece
58 D 12 Tyrone, Pennsylvania, U.S.A.
158 L 7 Tyrrhenian Basin, Mediterranean Sea
141 E 15 Tyrrhenian Sea, Europe
152 K 11 Tyukalinsk, Russian Federation
157 W 4 Tyul'gan, Russian Federation
152 J 10 Tyumen', Russian Federation
126 M 9 Tywi, United Kingdom

U

237 X 6 Ua Huka, French Polynesia
237 W 6 Ua Pou, French Polynesia
108 D 11 Uarini, Brazil
108 F 10 Uatumã, Brazil
108 N 13 Uauá, Brazil
90 I 2 Uaxactún, Guatemala
109 L 18 Ubá, Brazil
112 N 5 Ubá, Brazil
109 N 15 Ubaitaba, Brazil
216 J 5 Ubangi, Central African Republic
173 N 7 Ubaylah, Iraq
199 C 20 Ube, Japan
131 O 11 Úbeda, Spain
112 K 4 Uberaba, Brazil
112 J 3 Uberlândia, Brazil
137 F 25 Überlingen, Germany
194 B 13 Ubin, Singapore
191 I 16 Ubolratna Reservoir, Thailand
219 Q 12 Ubombo, Republic of South Africa
191 L 17 Ubon Ratchathani, Thailand
217 N 8 Ubundu, Democratic Republic of Congo
107 E 14 Ucayali, Peru
107 E 14 Ucayali, Peru
133 F 19 Uccle, Belgium
153 P 10 Uchami, Russian Federation
179 X 7 Ucharal, Kazakhstan
199 C 24 Uchinoura, Japan
198 I 7 Uchiura-wan, Japan
179 O 11 Uchkuduk, Uzbekistan
127 W 12 Uckfield, United Kingdom
73 W 9 Ucross, Wyoming, U.S.A.
153 U 13 Uda, Russian Federation
153 R 9 Udachnyy, Russian Federation
182 H 9 Udaipur, India
151 S 3 Uday, Ukraine
135 D 22 Uddevalla, Sweden
134 H 12 Uddjaure, Sweden
133 J 15 Uden, Netherlands
140 I 6 Udine, Italy
41 S 13 Udintsev Fracture Zone, Pacific Ocean
181 C 21 Udipi, India
155 R 13 Udmurtskaya Respublika, Russian Federation
191 J 15 Udon Thani, Thailand
136 M 10 Uecker, Germany
199 I 15 Ueda, Japan
216 L 5 Uele, Democratic Republic of Congo
153 Z 5 Uelen, Russian Federation
153 Z 6 Uel'kal', Russian Federation
136 I 12 Uelzen, Germany
199 H 18 Ueno, Japan
157 W 1 Ufa, Russian Federation
157 W 1 Ufa, Russian Federation
148 D 10 Ugāle, Latvia
217 R 6 Uganda, Africa
141 O 18 Ugento, Italy
153 W 13 Uglegorsk, Russian Federation
154 J 13 Uglich, Russian Federation
153 Z 6 Ugol'nyye, Russian Federation
156 I 2 Ugra, Russian Federation
143 G 19 Uherské Hradiště, Czech Republic
65 O 18 Uhrichsville, Ohio, U.S.A.
124 F 10 Uig, United Kingdom
218 G 2 Uige, Angola
218 G 1 Uige, Angola
187 L 18 Uijongbu, South Korea
178 J 5 Uil, Kazakhstan
155 T 13 Uinskoye, Russian Federation
74 L 3 Uinta Mountains, Utah, U.S.A.
218 H 9 Uis, Namibia
132 H 11 Uithoorn, Netherlands
237 W 2 Ujae, Marshall Islands
143 M 22 Újfehértó, Hungary
199 G 18 Uji, Japan
199 B 24 Uji-guntō, Japan
199 K 14 Ujiie, Japan
181 D 14 Ujjain, India
193 N 13 Ujung Pandang, Indonesia
192 C 8 Ujung Tamiang, Indonesia
215 Q 11 Ukata, Nigeria
199 O 22 Uke-jima, Japan
217 S 9 Ukerewe Island, Tanzania
155 Q 7 Ukhta, Russian Federation
235 N 7 Uki, Solomon Islands
76 J 10 Ukiah, Oregon, U.S.A.
77 F 17 Ukiah, California, U.S.A.
149 F 14 Ukmergė, Lithuania
151 O 6 Ukraine, Europe
218 G 4 Uku, Angola
199 A 21 Uku-jima, Japan
185 R 3 Ulaanbaatar, Mongolia
184 M 2 Ulaangom, Mongolia
187 A 15 Ulan Hua, China
157 R 11 Ulan Khol, Russian Federation
153 Q 14 Ulan-Ude, Russian Federation
184 L 8 Ulan Ul Hu, China
179 S 9 Ulanbel', Kazakhstan
186 H 11 Ulanhot, China
170 C 7 Ulaş, Turkey
146 N 12 Ulaş, Turkey
170 M 10 Ulaş, Turkey
235 N 7 Ulawa, Solomon Islands
187 N 19 Ulchin, South Korea
145 J 17 Ulcinj, Serbia and Montenegro
185 T 2 Uldz, Mongolia
185 S 3 Uldz, Mongolia
181 C 17 Ulhasnagar, India
186 E 11 Uliastai, China
185 O 3 Uliastay, Mongolia
236 K 14 Ulithi, Federated States of Micronesia
179 N 5 Ul'kayak, Kazakhstan
231 U 12 Ulladulla, New South Wales, Australia
124 G 9 Ullapool, United Kingdom
187 O 19 Ullŭng-do, South Korea
137 H 24 Ulm, Germany
150 H 8 Ulmeni, Romania
144 H 13 Ulog, Bosnia and Herzegovina
219 R 5 Ulongue, Mozambique
187 N 20 Ulsan, South Korea
135 D 16 Ulsberg, Norway
125 D 15 ULSTER, United Kingdom
90 K 5 Ulúa, Honduras
170 D 8 Ulubat Gölü, Turkey
170 D 9 Uludağ, Turkey
184 G 5 Ulugqat, China
170 J 12 Ulukişla, Turkey
237 N 14 Ulul, Federated States of Micronesia
219 P 12 Ulundi, Republic of South Africa
184 L 3 Ulungur Hu, China
82 G 7 Uluqsaqtuuq, Northwest Territories, Canada
230 M 7 Uluru, Northern Territory, Australia
127 P 1 Ulverston, United Kingdom
151 P 7 Ul'yanovka, Ukraine
157 S 2 Ul'yanovsk, Russian Federation
157 S 3 Ul'yanovskaya Oblast', Russian Federation
179 T 5 Ul'yanovskiy, Kazakhstan
68 H 6 Ulysses, Kansas, U.S.A.
179 Q 6 Ulytau, Kazakhstan
151 P 6 Uman', Ukraine
177 V 14 Umarkot, Pakistan
76 J 9 Umatilla, Washington, U.S.A.
154 I 4 Umba, Russian Federation
140 G 11 Umbertide, Italy
234 E 4 Umboi Island, Papua New Guinea
140 H 12 Umbria, Italy
234 F 2 Umbukul, Papua New Guinea
135 J 15 Umeå, Sweden
135 I 14 Umeälven, Sweden
157 N 4 Umet, Russian Federation
175 R 3 Umgharah, Kuwait
79 Q 4 Umiat, Alaska, U.S.A.
82 I 8 Umingmaktok, Nunavut, Canada
219 P 13 Umlazi, Republic of South Africa
175 X 5 Umm al Qaiwain, United Arab Emirates
173 R 5 Umm al Ţūz, Iraq
213 C 17 Umm Bel, Sudan
174 K 5 Umm Lajj, Saudi Arabia
173 Z 12 Umm Qaşr, Iraq
213 E 18 Umm Ruwaba, Sudan
211 Y 7 Umm Sa'ad, Libya
175 U 6 Umm Sa'id, Qatar
213 E 17 Umm Saiyala, Sudan
174 J 5 Umm Urūmah, Saudi Arabia
45 O 9 Ummannaq, Greenland
78 J 14 Umnak Island, Alaska, U.S.A.
218 I 4 Umpulo, Angola
219 O 14 Umtata, Republic of South Africa
215 R 13 Umuahia, Nigeria
112 F 7 Umuarama, Brazil
109 N 16 Una, Brazil
144 E 10 Una, Bosnia and Herzegovina
78 K 14 Unalaska Island, Alaska, U.S.A.
134 L 10 Unari, Finland
134 L 10 Unari, Finland
193 O 11 Unauna, Indonesia
172 G 12 'Unayzah, Jordan
175 P 5 'Unayzah, Saudi Arabia
66 J 4 Underwood, North Dakota, U.S.A.
234 F 4 Unea Island, Papua New Guinea
156 H 3 Unecha, Russian Federation
85 S 5 Ungava Bay, Québec, Canada
217 X 9 Ungwana Bay, Kenya

Country · Internal administrative region: State/Province/Territory/Dependent territory · Capital city · Mountain range/Undersea ridge · Mountain peak/Volcano/Seamount · Geographic feature · Headland/Point/Cape/Peninsula · Desert · Island/Island group · Antarctic base · Ocean · Sea · Bay/Gulf/Channel/Strait · Lake · Salt pan/Dry/Intermittent lake · River

▫ Country ▫ Internal administrative region: State/Province/Territory/Dependent territory ◆ Capital city ▲ Mountain range/Undersea ridge ▲ Mountain peak/Volcano/Seamount ◇ Geographic feature ► Headland/Point/Cape/Peninsula ⬝ Desert ≈ Island/Island group ⊞ Antarctic base ≋ Ocean ≋ Sea ≈ Bay/Gulf/Channel/Strait ↳ Lake ↳ Salt pan/Dry/Intermittent lake ↳ River

Vella Lavella – Volgogradskoye Vodokhranilishche

4 J 5 **Vella Lavella**, Solomon Islands
1 F 21 **Vellore**, India
7 G 22 **Velopoula**, Greece
4 L 10 **Vel'sk**, Russian Federation
J 3 **Velva**, North Dakota, U.S.A.
1 R 9 **Velyka Korenykha**, Ukraine
1 T 8 **Velyka Lepetykha**, Ukraine
1 X 4 **Velykyy Burluk**, Ukraine
G 12 **Vema Fracture Zone**, Atlantic Ocean
M 17 **Vema Seamount**, Atlantic Ocean
3 B 15 **Venado Tuerto**, Argentina
0 H 9 **Vendas Novas**, Portugal
5 O 7 **Vendinga**, Russian Federation
9 O 6 **Vendôme**, France
0 G 7 **Veneto**, Italy
6 L 2 **Venev**, Russian Federation
5 N 5 **Venezuela**, Venezuela
E 12 **Venezuelan Basin**, Atlantic Ocean
0 G 7 **Venice**, Italy
M 9 **Venice**, Louisiana, U.S.A.
V 12 **Venice**, Florida, U.S.A.
3 L 16 **Venlo**, Netherlands
3 K 15 **Venray**, Netherlands
8 C 11 **Venta**, Latvia/Lithuania
9 N 13 **Venterstad**, Republic of South Africa
0 A 10 **Ventimiglia**, Italy
1 F 17 **Ventisquero**, Argentina
7 T 14 **Ventnor**, United Kingdom
8 C 10 **Ventspils**, Latvia
I 24 **Ventura**, California, U.S.A.
2 B 12 **Vera**, Argentina
1 R 12 **Vera**, Spain
T 12 **Veracruz**, Mexico
R 10 **Veracruz**, Mexico
1 A 16 **Veraval**, India
0 C 6 **Verbania**, Italy
0 B 7 **Vercelli**, Italy
5 E 14 **Verdalsøra**, Norway
J 11 **Verde**, Arizona, U.S.A.
6 F 12 **Verde Island Passage**, Philippines
9 T 4 **Verdun**, France
3 G 14 **Vergara**, Uruguay
3 L 6 **Vergennes**, Vermont, U.S.A.
1 U 8 **Verkhiniy Rohachyk**, Ukraine
5 N 12 **Verkhnespasskoye**, Russian Federation
4 G 2 **Verkhnetulomskoye Vodokhranilishche**, Russian Federation
6 K 4 **Verkhov'ye**, Russian Federation
3 T 7 **Verkhoyanskiy Khrebet**, Russian Federation
3 K 18 **Vermilion**, Alberta, Canada
2 J 8 **Vermilion Bay**, Louisiana, U.S.A.
7 T 3 **Vermilion Lake**, Minnesota, U.S.A.
7 O 11 **Vermillion**, South Dakota, U.S.A.
8 K 7 **Vermont**, U.S.A.
40 H 4 **Vernadsky**, Antarctica
4 M 3 **Vernal**, Utah, U.S.A.
6 E 9 **Verner**, Ontario, Canada
29 O 4 **Verneuil-sur-Avre**, France
3 O 3 **Vernon**, Alabama, U.S.A.
1 N 4 **Vernon**, Texas, U.S.A.
4 J 3 **Vernon**, Utah, U.S.A.
3 H 21 **Vernon**, British Columbia, Canada
3 Y 11 **Vero Beach**, Florida, U.S.A.
47 E 14 **Veroia**, Greece
40 F 7 **Verona**, Italy
13 E 16 **Verónica**, Argentina
29 P 4 **Versailles**, France
5 J 20 **Versailles**, Indiana, U.S.A.
9 U 5 **Versailles**, Missouri, U.S.A.
38 A 10 **Versoix**, Switzerland
2 K 5 **Vertientes**, Cuba
51 R 2 **Vertiyivka**, Ukraine
133 K 20 **Verviers**, Belgium
129 S 2 **Vervins**, France
83 M 20 **Verwood**, Saskatchewan, Canada
129 Z 14 **Vescovato**, France
151 U 9 **Vesele**, Ukraine
156 M 10 **Veselovskoye Vodokhranilishche**, Russian Federation
157 N 7 **Veshenskaya**, Russian Federation
129 V 6 **Vesoul**, France
63 Q 3 **Vestavia Hills**, Alabama, U.S.A.
135 A 21 **Vestbygd**, Norway
134 G 8 **Vesterålen**, Norway
134 G 9 **Vestfjorden**, Norway
134 G 9 **Vestvågøy**, Norway
141 J 16 **Vesuvius**, Italy
154 J 12 **Ves'yegonsk**, Russian Federation
143 H 24 **Veszprém**, Hungary
135 G 23 **Vetlanda**, Sweden
155 N 13 **Vetluga**, Russian Federation
154 M 14 **Vetluzhskiy**, Russian Federation
146 K 6 **Vetovo**, Bulgaria
140 G 13 **Vetralla**, Italy
146 M 9 **Vetren**, Bulgaria
133 A 17 **Veurne**, Belgium
138 C 9 **Vevey**, Switzerland
129 U 12 **Veynes**, France
170 K 8 **Vezirköprü**, Turkey
112 H 12 **Viamão**, Brazil
130 H 3 **Viana do Castelo**, Portugal
130 H 4 **Viana do Castelo**, Portugal
133 L 24 **Vianden**, Luxembourg
132 I 13 **Vianen**, Netherlands
190 H 12 **Viangphoukha**, Laos
140 E 10 **Viareggio**, Italy
141 M 20 **Vibo Valentia**, Italy
135 C 24 **Viborg**, Denmark
131 X 4 **Vic**, Spain
128 M 14 **Vic-en-Bigorre**, France
140 F 7 **Vicenza**, Italy
104 M 6 **Vichada**, Colombia
104 L 7 **Vichada**, Colombia
129 R 9 **Vichy**, France
68 K 9 **Vici**, Oklahoma, U.S.A.
62 K 5 **Vicksburg**, Mississippi, U.S.A.
112 N 5 **Viçosa**, Brazil
67 U 12 **Victor**, Iowa, U.S.A.
73 Q 11 **Victor**, Idaho, U.S.A.
231 P 12 **Victor Harbor**, South Australia, Australia
230 M 3 **Victoria**, Northern Territory, Australia
231 T 13 **Victoria**, Australia
38 A 9 **Victoria**, Seychelles
113 B 14 **Victoria**, Argentina
196 F 10 **Victoria**, Philippines
71 Q 11 **Victoria**, Texas, U.S.A.
83 F 22 **Victoria**, British Columbia, Canada
90 L 5 **Victoria**, Honduras
218 M 7 **Victoria Falls**, Zimbabwe
82 H 6 **Victoria Island**, Nunavut, Canada
241 R 12 **Victoria Land**, Antarctica
197 C 19 **Victoria Peak**, Philippines
90 J 3 **Victoria Peak**, Belize
230 M 3 **Victoria River**, Northern Territory, Australia
218 L 14 **Victoria West**, Republic of South Africa
86 M 10 **Victoriaville**, Québec, Canada
110 I 13 **Victorica**, Argentina
77 K 24 **Victorville**, California, U.S.A.
110 J 12 **Vicuña Mackenna**, Argentina
73 X 3 **Vida**, Montana, U.S.A.
77 N 24 **Vidal**, California, U.S.A.
150 J 13 **Videle**, Romania
130 I 10 **Vidigueira**, Portugal
146 E 6 **Vidin**, Bulgaria
146 F 6 **Vidin**, Bulgaria
145 H 14 **Viduša**, Bosnia and Herzegovina
149 H 14 **Vidzy**, Belarus
113 B 21 **Viedma**, Argentina
148 D 12 **Viekšniai**, Lithuania
131 V 2 **Vielha**, Spain
133 K 22 **Vielsalm**, Belgium
139 X 3 **Vienna**, Austria
61 N 3 **Vienna**, West Virginia, U.S.A.
65 F 23 **Vienna**, Illinois, U.S.A.
69 V 5 **Vienna**, Missouri, U.S.A.
129 T 10 **Vienne**, France
191 J 15 **Vientiane**, Laos
137 B 16 **Viersen**, Germany
138 F 8 **Vierwaldstätter See**, Switzerland
129 P 7 **Vierzon**, France
148 G 12 **Viesīte**, Latvia
141 M 14 **Vieste**, Italy
190 L 12 **Việt Tri**, Vietnam
134 I 10 **Vietas**, Sweden
190 L 13 **Vietnam**, Asia
93 Z 11 **Vieux Fort**, St Lucia
196 K 12 **Viga**, Philippines
196 F 7 **Vigan**, Philippines
140 C 7 **Vigevano**, Italy
89 Z 11 **Viga Chico**, Mexico
128 M 15 **Vignemale**, France/Spain
130 H 3 **Vigo**, Spain
177 X 10 **Vihari**, Pakistan
135 L 19 **Vihti**, Finland
148 I 10 **Viļaka**, Latvia
148 I 11 **Viļāni**, Latvia
135 M 15 **Viitasaari**, Finland
148 H 5
181 G 19 **Vijayawada**, India
134 E 13 **Vik**, Norway
134 C 12 **Vík**, Iceland
146 G 11 **Vikhren**, Bulgaria
83 K 18 **Viking**, Alberta, Canada
134 E 13 **Vikna**, Norway
109 F 15 **Vila Bela da Santíssima Trindade**, Brazil
108 B 10 **Vila Bittencourt**, Brazil
43 A 16 **Vila da Ribeira Brava**, Cape Verde
43 B 16 **Vila da Sal Rei**, Cape Verde
219 R 6 **Vila de Sena**, Mozambique
130 G 12 **Vila do Bispo**, Portugal
43 B 17 **Vila do Tarrafal**, Cape Verde
67 T 4 **Virginia**, Minnesota, U.S.A.
130 G 9 **Vila Franca de Xira**, Portugal
130 J 5 **Vila Nova de Foz Coa**, Portugal
130 H 5 **Vila Nova de Gaia**, Portugal
43 A 17 **Vila Nova Sintra**, Cape Verde
108 F 9 **Vila Novo Paraíso**, Brazil
130 I 5 **Vila Real**, Portugal
130 I 5 **Vila Real**, Portugal
112 O 5 **Vila Velha**, Brazil
107 K 22 **Vilacaya**, Bolivia
130 J 1 **Vilalba**, Spain
219 R 9 **Vilanculos**, Mozambique
181 E 23 **Vilatikkulam**, India
135 H 14 **Vilhelmina**, Sweden
109 F 14 **Vilhena**, Brazil
151 T 12 **Viline**, Ukraine
148 G 8 **Viljandi**, Estonia
149 D 15 **Vilkaviškis**, Lithuania
149 E 15 **Vilkija**, Lithuania
110 L 8 **Villa**, Argentina
107 K 22 **Villa Abecia**, Bolivia
88 M 3 **Villa Ahumada**, Mexico
112 B 10 **Villa Angela**, Argentina
112 B 10 **Villa Berthet**, Argentina
113 C 15 **Villa Constitución**, Argentina
110 J 10 **Villa del Rosario**, Argentina
110 I 11 **Villa Dolores**, Argentina
89 W 14 **Villa Flores**, Mexico
113 E 17 **Villa Gesell**, Argentina
88 I 7 **Villa Insurgentes**, Mexico
113 A 19 **Villa Iris**, Argentina
141 J 16 **Villa Literno**, Italy
113 A 14 **Villa María**, Argentina
107 I 22 **Villa Martín**, Bolivia
107 L 23 **Villa Montes**, Bolivia
112 C 11 **Villa Ocampo**, Argentina
88 M 6 **Villa Ocampo**, Mexico
110 J 9 **Villa Ojo de Agua**, Argentina
110 H 9 **Villa Unión**, Argentina
88 M 9 **Villa Unión**, Mexico
89 N 8 **Villa Unión**, Mexico
110 I 12 **Villa Valeria**, Argentina
130 K 2 **Villablino**, Spain
131 P 11 **Villacarrillo**, Spain
131 N 6 **Villacastín**, Spain
139 S 9 **Villach**, Austria
130 M 3 **Villada**, Spain
130 J 2 **Villafranca del Bierzo**, Spain
141 I 22 **Villafrati**, Italy
89 Q 8 **Villagrán**, Mexico
112 C 13 **Villaguay**, Argentina
89 W 13 **Villahermosa**, Mexico
131 T 10 **Villajoyosa**, Spain
113 B 20 **Villalonga**, Argentina
111 J 16 **Villálonga**, Argentina
130 M 4 **Villalpando**, Spain
141 B 16 **Villanova Monteleone**, Italy
131 P 10 **Villanueva de los Infantes**, Spain
143 I 26 **Villány**, Hungary
130 M 4 **Villardefrades**, Spain
111 F 15 **Villarrica**, Chile
131 Q 8 **Villarrobledo**, Spain
141 C 19 **Villasimius**, Italy
104 J 7 **Villavicencio**, Colombia
130 M 1 **Villaviciosa de Asturias**, Spain
107 K 23 **Villazon**, Bolivia
86 F 8 **Ville-Marie**, Québec, Canada
129 P 12 **Villefranche-de-Rouergue**, France
129 T 9 **Villefranche-sur-Saône**, France
131 S 10 **Villena**, Spain
67 R 14 **Villisca**, Iowa, U.S.A.
149 G 16 **Vilnius**, Lithuania
137 L 23 **Vilsbiburg**, Germany
137 M 23 **Vilshofen**, Germany
133 G 18 **Vilvoorde**, Belgium
149 I 16 **Vilyeyka**, Belarus
153 S 10 **Vilyuy**, Russian Federation
153 Q 10 **Vilyuyskoye Vodokhranilishche**, Russian Federation
130 G 1 **Vimianzo**, Spain
129 N 4 **Vimoutiers**, France
110 E 11 **Viña del Mar**, Chile
59 R 6 **Vinalhaven Island**, Maine, U.S.A.
219 Z 6 **Vinanivao**, Madgascar
131 U 6 **Vinarós**, Spain
65 H 21 **Vincennes**, Indiana, U.S.A.
241 Y 11 **Vincennes Bay**, Antarctica
181 C 15 **Vindhya Ranges**, India
150 F 10 **Vinga**, Romania
191 L 14 **Vinh**, Vietnam
191 N 16 **Vinh Linh**, Vietnam
191 M 22 **Vinh Long**, Vietnam
191 L 23 **Vinh Rach Gia**, Vietnam
130 J 4 **Vinhais**, Portugal
146 E 11 **Vinica**, Macedonia (F.Y.R.O.M.)
69 Q 8 **Vinita**, Oklahoma, U.S.A.
151 N 5 **Vinnytsya**, Ukraine
240 L 7 **Vinson Massif**, Antarctica
216 G 10 **Vinza**, Congo
140 F 4 **Vipiteno**, Italy
196 K 13 **Virac**, Philippines
181 B 14 **Viramgam**, India
171 P 13 **Viranşehir**, Turkey
177 W 15 **Virawah**, Pakistan
84 H 10 **Virden**, Manitoba, Canada
128 M 4 **Vire**, France
218 G 6 **Virei**, Angola
93 V 7 **Virgin Corda**, Virgin Islands, United Kingdom
93 V 7 **Virgin Islands**, United Kingdom, United Kingdom
93 V 8 **Virgin Islands, U.S.A.**, U.S.A.
219 N 12 **Virginia**, Republic of South Africa
57 R 5 **Virginia**, Minnesota, U.S.A.
61 Q 5 **Virginia**, U.S.A.
65 E 19 **Virginia**, Illinois, U.S.A.
61 W 7 **Virginia Beach**, Virginia, U.S.A.
73 P 8 **Virginia City**, Montana, U.S.A.
77 I 18 **Virginia City**, Nevada, U.S.A.
86 F 7 **Virginiatown**, Ontario, Canada
135 N 18 **Virojoki**, Finland
133 J 26 **Virton**, Belgium
148 E 7 **Virtsu**, Estonia
107 B 14 **Virú**, Peru
77 I 21 **Visalia**, California, U.S.A.
197 J 15 **Visayan Sea**, Philippines
135 H 23 **Visby**, Sweden
108 B 11 **Visconde do Rio Branco**, Brazil
45 O 7 **Viscount Melville Sound**, Arctic Ocean
81 N 4 **Viscount Melville Sound**, Nunavut, Canada
133 K 19 **Visé**, Belgium
144 J 12 **Višegrad**, Bosnia and Herzegovina
130 I 6 **Viseu**, Portugal
130 I 6 **Viseu**, Portugal
181 H 18 **Vishakhapatnam**, India
146 L 11 **Vishegrad**, Bulgaria
179 S 4 **Vishnevka**, Kazakhstan
138 E 10 **Visp**, Switzerland
142 J 12 **Vistula**, Poland
149 A 16 **Vistula Lagoon**, Russian Federation
151 S 8 **Visun'**, Ukraine
146 I 7 **Vit**, Bulgaria
140 G 13 **Viterbo**, Italy
235 W 11 **Viti Levu**, Fiji
130 K 5 **Vitigudino**, Spain
112 O 5 **Vitória**, Brazil
109 M 16 **Vitória da Conquista**, Brazil
108 I 10 **Vitória do Xingu**, Brazil
131 Q 2 **Vitoria-Gasteiz**, Spain
43 H 16 **Vitória Seamount**, Atlantic Ocean
146 F 9 **Vitosha**, Bulgaria
128 L 5 **Vitré**, France
129 T 4 **Vitry-le-François**, France
149 M 14 **Vitsyebsk**, Belarus
149 L 15 **Vitsyebskaya Voblasts'**, Belarus
134 J 10 **Vittangi**, Sweden
129 U 5 **Vittel**, France
141 J 23 **Vittoria**, Italy
41 P 6 **Vityaz Seamount**, Pacific Ocean
130 J 1 **Viveiro**, Spain
131 T 7 **Viver**, Spain
219 O 9 **Vivo**, Republic of South Africa
129 N 9 **Vivonne**, France
146 N 11 **Vize**, Turkey
181 H 18 **Vizianagaram**, India
155 P 10 **Vizinga**, Russian Federation
150 M 12 **Viziru**, Romania
145 K 20 **Vjosë**, Albania
133 I 19 **Vlaams Brabant**, Belgium
132 F 13 **Vlaardingen**, Netherlands
145 N 15 **Vladičin Han**, Serbia and Montenegro
157 P 14 **Vladikavkaz**, Russian Federation
156 M 1 **Vladimir**, Russian Federation
146 G 7 **Vladimirovo**, Bulgaria
153 V 15 **Vladivostok**, Russian Federation
132 O 7 **Vlagtwedde**, Netherlands
144 I 12 **Vlasenica**, Bosnia and Herzegovina
144 G 11 **Vlašić**, Bosnia and Herzegovina
143 D 18 **Vlašim**, Czech Republic
145 N 14 **Vlasotince**, Serbia and Montenegro
132 H 6 **Vlieland**, Netherlands
133 D 16 **Vlissingen**, Netherlands
145 J 20 **Vlorë**, Albania
143 C 18 **Vltava**, Czech Republic
139 R 4 **Vöcklabruck**, Austria
155 Q 7 **Vodnyy**, Russian Federation
215 T 12 **Vogel Peak**, Nigeria
137 F 18 **Vogelsberg**, Germany
219 Y 9 **Vohilava**, Madgascar
148 D 7 **Võhma**, Estonia
148 G 7 **Võhma**, Estonia
217 W 10 **Voi**, Kenya
150 I 11 **Voineasa**, Romania
214 H 12 **Voinjama**, Liberia
129 U 10 **Voiron**, France
139 V 7 **Voitsberg**, Austria
144 J 9 **Vojvodina**, Serbia and Montenegro
215 U 12 **Voko**, Cameroon
73 X 7 **Volborg**, Montana, U.S.A.
90 H 6 **Volcán Agua**, Guatemala
110 G 6 **Volcán Antofalla**, Argentina
110 H 4 **Volcán Apagado**, Chile
91 S 14 **Volcán Barú**, Panama
110 G 8 **Volcán Copiapó**, Chile
111 F 18 **Volcán Corcovado**, Chile
106 B 9 **Volcán Cotopaxi**, Ecuador
107 A 18 **Volcán Darwin**, Ecuador
90 I 7 **Volcán de Santa Ana**, El Salvador
89 W 15 **Volcán de Tacaná**, Mexico
111 G 14 **Volcán Domuyo**, Argentina
110 G 2 **Volcán Guallatiri**, Chile
91 R 12 **Volcán Irazu**, Costa Rica
107 A 18 **Volcán La Cumbre**, Ecuador
111 F 16 **Volcán Lanin**, Argentina
88 H 5 **Volcán Las Tres Vírgenes**, Mexico
110 H 5 **Volcán Licancábur**, Chile
110 G 6 **Volcán Llullaillaco**, Chile
91 P 11 **Volcán Miravalles**, Costa Rica
107 G 19 **Volcán Misti**, Peru
107 I 23 **Volcán Ollagüe**, Bolivia
91 Q 12 **Volcán Poás**, Costa Rica
110 G 12 **Volcán San José**, Chile
106 B 10 **Volcán Sangay**, Ecuador
104 G 8 **Volcán Sotará**, Colombia
107 H 20 **Volcán Tacora**, Chile/Peru
90 F 5 **Volcán Tajumulco**, Guatemala
111 G 14 **Volcán Tromen**, Argentina
111 F 16 **Volcán Villarrica**, Chile
107 A 18 **Volcán Wolf**, Ecuador
78 E 9 **Volcano**, Hawaii, U.S.A.
155 R 8 **Vol'dino**, Russian Federation
132 I 10 **Volendam**, Netherlands
152 F 10 **Volga**, Russian Federation
157 O 8 **Volga–Don Canal**, Russian Federation
157 N 9 **Volgodonsk**, Russian Federation
157 P 8 **Volgograd**, Russian Federation
157 O 7 **Volgogradskaya Oblast'**, Russian Federation
157 Q 7 **Volgogradskoye Vodokhranilishche**, Russian Federation

Country · Internal administrative region: State/Province/Territory/Dependent territory · Capital city · Mountain range/Undersea ridge · Mountain peak/Volcano/Seamount · Geographic feature · Headland/Point/Cape/Peninsula · Desert · Island/Island group · Antarctic base · Ocean · Sea · Bay/Gulf/Channel/Strait · Lake · Salt pan/Dry/Intermittent lake · River

▣ Country · ▣ Internal administrative region: State/Province/Territory/Dependent territory · ▪ Capital city · ▲ Mountain range/Undersea ridge · ▲ Mountain peak/Volcano/Seamount · ◆ Geographic feature · ▶ Headland/Point/Cape/Peninsula · ▲ Desert · ≊ Island/Island group · ▦ Antarctic base · ⊇ Ocean · ⊇ Sea · ≈ Bay/Gulf/Channel/Strait · ⌇ Lake · ⌇ Salt pan/Dry/Intermittent lake · ⌇ River

Watertown – Willamette

7 N 8 **Watertown**, South Dakota, U.S.A.
25 A 21 **Waterville**, Republic of Ireland
7 Z 5 **Waterville**, Maine, U.S.A.
9 N 2 **Waterville**, Kansas, U.S.A.
6 I 7 **Waterville**, Washington, U.S.A.
27 V 10 **Watford**, United Kingdom
6 G 3 **Watford City**, North Dakota, U.S.A.
8 G 9 **Watkins Glen**, New York, U.S.A.
8 L 9 **Watonga**, Oklahoma, U.S.A.
17 Q 6 **Watsa**, Democratic Republic of Congo
16 K 8 **Watsi Kengo**, Democratic Republic of Congo
3 M 18 **Watson**, Saskatchewan, Canada
3 D 14 **Watson Lake**, Yukon Territory, Canada
7 G 20 **Watsonville**, California, U.S.A.
0 I 9 **Watts Bar Lake**, Tennessee, U.S.A.
38 H 7 **Wattwil**, Switzerland
13 C 21 **Wau**, Sudan
34 E 5 **Wau**, Papua New Guinea
31 N 5 **Wauchope**, Northern Territory, Australia
3 W 11 **Wauchula**, Florida, U.S.A.
5 H 15 **Waukegan**, Illinois, U.S.A.
5 G 14 **Waukesha**, Wisconsin, U.S.A.
4 F 12 **Waupaca**, Wisconsin, U.S.A.
8 M 12 **Waurika**, Oklahoma, U.S.A.
4 F 11 **Wausau**, Wisconsin, U.S.A.
4 F 12 **Wautoma**, Wisconsin, U.S.A.
30 M 3 **Wave Hill**, Northern Territory, Australia
27 Z 7 **Waveney**, United Kingdom
8 G 10 **Waverly**, Pennsylvania, U.S.A.
0 D 8 **Waverly**, Tennessee, U.S.A.
7 P 14 **Waverly**, Nebraska, U.S.A.
33 G 20 **Wavre**, Belgium
11 U 11 **Wāw al Kabīr**, Libya
15 P 11 **Wawa**, Nigeria
6 A 6 **Wawa**, Ontario, Canada
1 Q 6 **Wawa**, Nicaragua
34 B 5 **Wawoi**, Papua New Guinea
1 Q 6 **Waxahachie**, Texas, U.S.A.
93 S 9 **Wayabula**, Indonesia
93 T 10 **Wayag**, Indonesia
3 V 6 **Waycross**, Georgia, U.S.A.
0 D 10 **Waynesboro**, Tennessee, U.S.A.
1 R 5 **Waynesboro**, Virginia, U.S.A.
3 N 6 **Waynesboro**, Mississippi, U.S.A.
3 V 3 **Waynesboro**, Georgia, U.S.A.
0 L 10 **Waynesville**, North Carolina, U.S.A.
8 L 8 **Waynoka**, Oklahoma, U.S.A.
15 V 10 **Waza**, Cameroon
77 T 9 **Wazi Khwa**, Afghanistan
77 Y 8 **Wazirabad**, Pakistan
42 H 10 **Wda**, Poland
35 Q 13 **Wé**, New Caledonia
8 K 10 **Weatherford**, Oklahoma, U.S.A.
7 F 15 **Weaverville**, California, U.S.A.
4 M 9 **Webequie**, Ontario, Canada
0 K 8 **Weber Basin**, Pacific Ocean
8 F 8 **Webster**, New York, U.S.A.
34 G 7 **Wedau**, Papua New Guinea
3 H 23 **Weddel Abyssal Plain**, Atlantic Ocean
11 K 24 **Weddell Island**, Falkland Islands
240 K 5 **Weddell Sea**, Antarctica
231 U 10 **Wee Waa**, New South Wales, Australia
77 G 15 **Weed**, California, U.S.A.
58 D 11 **Weedville**, Pennsylvania, U.S.A.
133 I 16 **Weelde**, Belgium
133 K 17 **Weert**, Netherlands
132 H 11 **Weesp**, Netherlands
142 L 8 **Wegorzewo**, Poland
142 M 12 **Węgrów**, Poland
192 B 8 **Weh**, Indonesia
189 N 3 **Wei**, China
187 E 15 **Weichang**, China
137 K 20 **Weiden**, Germany
187 G 20 **Weifang**, China
187 I 19 **Weihai**, China
137 J 17 **Weimar**, Germany
189 Q 3 **Weinan**, China
189 N 9 **Weining**, China
231 R 1 **Weipa**, Queensland, Australia
61 O 1 **Weirton**, West Virginia, U.S.A.
72 J 9 **Weiser**, Idaho, U.S.A.
188 K 10 **Weishan**, China
189 V 3 **Weishan Hu**, China
189 U 3 **Weishi**, China
63 R 2 **Weiss Lake**, Alabama, U.S.A.
137 I 22 **Weissenburg in Bayern**, Germany
137 N 15 **Weisswasser**, Germany
133 L 23 **Weiswampach**, Luxembourg
139 U 2 **Weitra**, Austria
188 J 9 **Weixi**, China
189 N 8 **Weixin**, China
139 W 7 **Weiz**, Austria
142 H 8 **Wejherowo**, Poland
233 G 15 **Wekakura Point**, New Zealand
61 N 6 **Welch**, West Virginia, U.S.A.
213 I 19 **Weldiya**, Ethiopia
77 J 22 **Weldon**, California, U.S.A.
41 T 2 **Welker Seamount**, Pacific Ocean
213 H 21 **Welk'īt'ē**, Ethiopia
219 N 12 **Welkom**, Republic of South Africa
86 F 14 **Welland Canal**, Ontario, Canada
181 G 25 **Wellawaya**, Sri Lanka
231 Q 3 **Wellesley Islands**, Queensland, Australia
133 I 23 **Wellin**, Belgium
127 V 8 **Wellingborough**, United Kingdom
231 U 11 **Wellington**, New South Wales, Australia
233 L 16 **Wellington**, New Zealand
233 L 16 **Wellington**, New Zealand
127 Q 6 **Wellington**, United Kingdom
127 P 12 **Wells**, United Kingdom
77 M 15 **Wells**, Nevada, U.S.A.
127 Y 5 **Wells-next-the-Sea**, United Kingdom
232 K 7 **Wellsford**, New Zealand
64 J 12 **Wellston**, Michigan, U.S.A.
139 S 4 **Wels**, Austria
127 O 6 **Welshpool**, United Kingdom
85 P 9 **Wemindji**, Québec, Canada
76 J 7 **Wenatchee**, Washington, U.S.A.
189 R 15 **Wenchang**, China
189 Y 8 **Wencheng**, China
188 M 6 **Wenchuan**, China
137 E 17 **Wenden**, Germany
74 H 12 **Wenden**, Arizona, U.S.A.
187 H 19 **Wendeng**, China
127 U 10 **Wendover**, United Kingdom
77 N 16 **Wendover**, Nevada, U.S.A.
138 E 9 **Wengen**, Switzerland
189 Z 8 **Wenling**, China
237 O 15 **Weno**, Federated States of Micronesia
65 F 17 **Wenona**, Illinois, U.S.A.
184 J 4 **Wenquan**, China
184 L 9 **Wenquan**, China
188 M 12 **Wenshan**, China
231 R 11 **Wentworth**, New South Wales, Australia
69 X 4 **Wentzville**, Missouri, U.S.A.
189 S 3 **Wenxi**, China
189 N 4 **Wenxian**, China
189 Y 8 **Wenzhou**, China
133 K 21 **Werbomont**, Belgium
218 L 10 **Werda**, Botswana
213 L 21 **Werdër**, Ethiopia
139 R 6 **Werfen**, Austria
137 E 15 **Werl**, Germany
137 K 21 **Wernberg-Köblitz**, Germany
137 I 15 **Wernigerode**, Germany
213 H 19 **Werota**, Ethiopia
137 H 16 **Werra**, Germany
137 G 20 **Wertheim**, Germany
132 I 9 **Wervershoof**, Netherlands
137 B 15 **Wesel**, Germany
137 G 15 **Weser**, Germany
59 S 4 **Wesley**, Maine, U.S.A.
231 O 1 **Wessel Islands**, Northern Territory, Australia
71 Q 7 **West**, Texas, U.S.A.
158 B 9 **West Alboran Basin**, Mediterranean Sea
240 L 7 **West Antarctica**, Antarctica
172 G 9 **West Bank**, Israel
62 M 9 **West Bay**, Louisiana, U.S.A.
63 Q 7 **West Bay**, Florida, U.S.A.
64 G 13 **West Bend**, Wisconsin, U.S.A.
183 R 14 **West Bengal**, India
127 T 5 **West Bridgford**, United Kingdom
127 R 7 **West Bromwich**, United Kingdom
73 Q 2 **West Butte**, Montana, U.S.A.
233 A 25 **West Cape**, New Zealand
40 K 7 **West Caroline Basin**, Pacific Ocean
233 E 19 **West Coast**, New Zealand
71 S 11 **West Columbia**, Texas, U.S.A.
111 J 23 **West Falkland**, Falkland Islands
236 M 15 **West Fayu**, Federated States of Micronesia
73 N 2 **West Glacier**, Montana, U.S.A.
59 S 4 **West Grand Lake**, Maine, U.S.A.
241 X 6 **West Ice Shelf**, Antarctica
39 Y 2 **West Island**, Cocos Islands
39 Y 3 **West Island Settlement**, Cocos Islands
65 I 18 **West Lafayette**, Indiana, U.S.A.
126 L 14 **West Looe**, United Kingdom
86 C 14 **West Lorne**, Ontario, Canada
40 K 6 **West Mariana Basin**, Pacific Ocean
69 Y 10 **West Memphis**, Arkansas, U.S.A.
234 F 5 **West New Britain**, Papua New Guinea
219 P 8 **West Nicholson**, Zimbabwe
63 Z 12 **West Palm Beach**, Florida, U.S.A.
69 V 8 **West Plains**, Missouri, U.S.A.
61 U 6 **West Point**, Virginia, U.S.A.
63 R 3 **West Point Lake**, Alabama, U.S.A.
43 E 22 **West Scotia Ridge**, Atlantic Ocean
38 J 2 **West Sheba Ridge**, Indian Ocean
152 L 9 **West Siberian Plain**, Russian Federation
132 I 6 **West-Terschelling**, Netherlands
67 U 10 **West Union**, Iowa, U.S.A.
61 O 3 **West Virginia**, U.S.A.
133 A 18 **West-Vlaanderen**, Belgium
231 T 11 **West Wyalong**, New South Wales, Australia
73 Q 9 **West Yellowstone**, Montana, U.S.A.
64 D 13 **Westby**, Wisconsin, U.S.A.
75 R 6 **Westcliffe**, Colorado, U.S.A.
132 M 8 **Westerbork**, Netherlands
217 T 7 **Western**, Kenya
218 L 6 **Western**, Zambia
234 B 5 **Western**, Papua New Guinea
234 J 6 **Western**, Solomon Islands
181 F 25 **Western**, Sri Lanka
183 O 9 **Western**, Nepal
214 F 12 **Western Area**, Sierra Leone
230 J 7 **Western Australia**, Australia
213 C 21 **Western Bahr el Ghazal**, Sudan
218 L 14 **Western Cape**, Republic of South Africa
213 A 17 **Western Darfur**, Sudan
212 C 9 **Western Desert**, Egypt
148 F 11 **Western Dvina**, Belarus/Latvia
213 D 22 **Western Equatoria**, Sudan
181 C 17 **Western Ghats**, India
41 X 14 **Western Harbour**, Pitcairn Island
234 C 4 **Western Highlands**, Papua New Guinea
213 D 19 **Western Kordofan**, Sudan
210 C 12 **Western Sahara**, Africa
133 D 16 **Westerschelde**, Netherlands
58 B 9 **Westfield**, New York, U.S.A.
132 K 5 **Westgat**, Netherlands
66 J 2 **Westhope**, North Dakota, U.S.A.
133 G 16 **Westmalle**, Belgium
61 T 2 **Westminster**, Maryland, U.S.A.
61 O 3 **Weston**, West Virginia, U.S.A.
127 O 11 **Weston-super-Mare**, United Kingdom
233 G 17 **Westport**, New Zealand
125 B 17 **Westport**, Republic of Ireland
76 E 7 **Westport**, Washington, U.S.A.
124 I 6 **Westray**, United Kingdom
84 H 8 **Westray**, Manitoba, Canada
86 D 7 **Westree**, Ontario, Canada
65 I 16 **Westville**, Indiana, U.S.A.
126 L 12 **Westward Ho!**, United Kingdom
193 R 14 **Wetar**, Indonesia
83 J 19 **Wetaskiwin**, Alberta, Canada
217 X 11 **Wete**, Tanzania
127 S 2 **Wetherby**, United Kingdom
137 E 18 **Wetzlar**, Germany
133 C 19 **Wevelgem**, Belgium
78 M 3 **Wevok**, Alaska, U.S.A.
63 S 8 **Wewahitchka**, Florida, U.S.A.
234 C 3 **Wewak**, Papua New Guinea
69 O 11 **Wewoka**, Oklahoma, U.S.A.
125 E 20 **Wexford**, Republic of Ireland
83 N 19 **Weyburn**, Saskatchewan, Canada
139 U 5 **Weyer Markt**, Austria
137 D 17 **Weyerbusch**, Germany
127 Q 14 **Weymouth**, United Kingdom
59 O 10 **Weymouth**, Massachusetts, U.S.A.
87 T 11 **Weymouth**, Nova Scotia, Canada
127 Q 14 **Weymouth Bay**, United Kingdom
82 G 12 **Wha Ti**, Northwest Territories, Canada
232 M 11 **Whakamaru**, New Zealand
232 J 6 **Whakapara**, New Zealand
233 M 15 **Whakataki**, New Zealand
232 N 10 **Whakatane**, New Zealand
232 N 13 **Whakatu**, New Zealand
84 L 4 **Whale Cove**, Nunavut, Canada
124 K 4 **Whalsay**, United Kingdom
232 M 9 **Whangamata**, New Zealand
232 K 12 **Whangamomona**, New Zealand
233 H 15 **Whanganui Inlet**, New Zealand
232 O 10 **Whangaparaoa**, New Zealand
232 O 11 **Whangara**, New Zealand
232 J 6 **Whangarei**, New Zealand
127 U 1 **Wharram le Street**, United Kingdom
39 R 7 **Wharton Basin**, Indian Ocean
70 M 2 **Wheeler**, Texas, U.S.A.
63 P 1 **Wheeler Lake**, Alabama, U.S.A.
75 R 8 **Wheeler Peak**, New Mexico, U.S.A.
77 N 18 **Wheeler Peak**, Nevada, U.S.A.
61 O 1 **Wheeling**, West Virginia, U.S.A.
65 G 15 **Wheeling**, Illinois, U.S.A.
232 L 8 **Whenuakite**, New Zealand
127 Q 1 **Whernside**, United Kingdom
127 N 13 **Whiddon Down**, United Kingdom
232 I 6 **Whirinaki**, New Zealand
83 G 21 **Whistler**, British Columbia, Canada
125 L 16 **Whitby**, United Kingdom
127 P 5 **Whitchurch**, United Kingdom
127 T 12 **Whitchurch**, United Kingdom
66 H 10 **White**, South Dakota, U.S.A.
85 X 10 **White Bay**, Newfoundland and Labrador, Canada
66 H 6 **White Butte**, North Dakota, U.S.A.
59 Q 3 **White Cap Mountain**, Maine, U.S.A.
76 G 13 **White City**, Oregon, U.S.A.
231 R 10 **White Cliffs**, New South Wales, Australia
87 X 8 **White Hill**, Nova Scotia, Canada
232 N 9 **White Island**, New Zealand
62 I 8 **White Lake**, Louisiana, U.S.A.
77 K 20 **White Mountain**, California, U.S.A.
59 N 6 **White Mountains**, New Hampshire, U.S.A.
213 F 18 **White Nile**, Sudan
213 D 21 **White Nile**, Sudan
76 I 9 **White Salmon**, Oregon, U.S.A.
45 W 13 **White Sea**, Arctic Ocean
154 I 5 **White Sea**, Russian Federation
61 P 5 **White Sulphur Springs**, West Virginia, U.S.A.
73 R 6 **White Sulphur Springs**, Montana, U.S.A.
83 J 18 **Whitecourt**, Alberta, Canada
58 K 6 **Whiteface Mountain**, New York, U.S.A.
72 M 2 **Whitefish**, Montana, U.S.A.
64 K 8 **Whitefish Bay**, Michigan, U.S.A.
64 J 8 **Whitefish Point**, Michigan, U.S.A.
58 K 7 **Whitehall**, New York, U.S.A.
64 D 12 **Whitehall**, Wisconsin, U.S.A.
125 H 15 **Whitehaven**, United Kingdom
83 B 14 **Whitehorse**, Yukon Territory, Canada
74 L 12 **Whiteriver**, Arizona, U.S.A.
60 A 10 **Whiteville**, Tennessee, U.S.A.
61 S 11 **Whiteville**, North Carolina, U.S.A.
75 N 13 **Whitewater Baldy**, New Mexico, U.S.A.
125 H 15 **Whithorn**, United Kingdom
61 N 11 **Whitmire**, South Carolina, U.S.A.
86 G 10 **Whitney**, Ontario, Canada
126 L 15 **Whitsand Bay**, United Kingdom
231 U 5 **Whitsunday Group**, Queensland, Australia
64 L 12 **Whittemore**, Michigan, U.S.A.
79 R 9 **Whittier**, Alaska, U.S.A.
127 V 7 **Whittlesey**, United Kingdom
82 K 12 **Wholdaia Lake**, Northwest Territories, Canada
231 P 11 **Whyalla**, South Australia, Australia
191 G 14 **Wiang Pa Pao**, Thailand
190 G 13 **Wiang Phran**, Thailand
86 D 11 **Wiarton**, Ontario, Canada
73 Z 5 **Wibaux**, Montana, U.S.A.
69 N 6 **Wichita**, Kansas, U.S.A.
71 N 4 **Wichita**, Texas, U.S.A.
71 O 4 **Wichita Falls**, Texas, U.S.A.
68 L 11 **Wichita Mountains**, Oklahoma, U.S.A.
124 I 8 **Wick**, United Kingdom
74 I 12 **Wickenburg**, Arizona, U.S.A.
127 Z 8 **Wickham Market**, United Kingdom
60 B 7 **Wickliffe**, Kentucky, U.S.A.
125 F 19 **Wicklow Head**, Republic of Ireland
127 P 4 **Widnes**, United Kingdom
137 E 15 **Wiedenbrück**, Germany
137 D 17 **Wiehl**, Germany
136 L 7 **Wiek**, Germany
142 L 10 **Wielbark**, Poland
143 I 15 **Wieluń**, Poland
139 X 5 **Wiener Neustadt**, Austria
143 M 14 **Wieprz**, Poland
137 E 19 **Wiesbaden**, Germany
137 C 18 **Wiesemscheid**, Germany
137 F 21 **Wiesloch**, Germany
127 P 3 **Wigan**, United Kingdom
75 S 3 **Wiggins**, Colorado, U.S.A.
127 T 7 **Wigston**, United Kingdom
133 K 14 **Wijchen**, Netherlands
132 J 13 **Wijk bij Duurstede**, Netherlands
213 I 17 **Wik'ro**, Ethiopia
138 H 6 **Wil**, Switzerland
76 J 7 **Wilbur**, Washington, U.S.A.
231 R 10 **Wilcannia**, New South Wales, Australia
136 E 12 **Wildeshausen**, Germany
138 D 9 **Wildhorn**, Switzerland
139 W 8 **Wildon**, Austria
138 L 8 **Wildspitze**, Austria
83 I 18 **Wildwood**, Alberta, Canada
105 V 7 **Wilhelmina Gebergte**, Suriname
136 E 10 **Wilhelmshaven**, Germany
58 H 11 **Wilkes Barre**, Pennsylvania, U.S.A.
241 W 13 **Wilkes Coast**, Antarctica
241 V 12 **Wilkes Land**, Antarctica
61 O 8 **Wilkesboro**, North Carolina, U.S.A.
76 F 11 **Willamette**, Oregon, U.S.A.

Country · Internal administrative region: State/Province/Territory/Dependent territory · Capital city · Mountain range/Undersea ridge · Mountain peak/Volcano/Seamount · Geographic feature · Headland/Point/Cape/Peninsula · Desert · Island/Island group · Antarctic base · Ocean · Sea · Bay/Gulf/Channel/Strait · Lake · Salt pan/Dry/Intermittent lake · River

▫ Country ▫ Internal administrative region: State/Province/Territory/Dependent territory ▪ Capital city ▲▲ Mountain range/ Undersea ridge ▲ Mountain peak/ Volcano/Seamount ◇ Geographic feature ▶ Headland/Point/ Cape/Peninsula ▲ Desert ⌑ Island/Island group ▪ Antarctic base ⌒ Ocean ⌒ Sea ≈ Bay/Gulf/Channel/Strait ⌇ Lake ⌇ Salt pan/Dry/ Intermittent lake ⌇ River

Xuanwei – Yunta

88 M 10 **Xuanwei**, China
89 X 6 **Xuanzhou**, China
89 T 4 **Xuchang**, China
13 L 23 **Xuddur**, Somalia
13 N 20 **Xudun**, Somalia
89 W 3 **Xuecheng**, China
89 X 3 **Xugou**, China
86 L 7 **Xunhe**, China
86 L 7 **Xunke**, China
89 V 11 **Xunwu**, China
89 Q 5 **Xunyang**, China
89 Q 3 **Xunyi**, China
89 R 8 **Xupu**, China
89 R 14 **Xuwen**, China
89 N 8 **Xuyong**, China
89 W 3 **Xuzhou**, China
47 F 20 **Xylokastro**, Greece

Y

88 L 7 **Ya'an**, China
213 I 23 **Yabēlo**, Ethiopia
46 H 8 **Yablanitsa**, Bulgaria
215 P 10 **Yabo**, Nigeria
72 I 6 **Yabrūd**, Syria
86 L 12 **Yabuli**, China
76 F 11 **Yachats**, Oregon, U.S.A.
89 Q 15 **Yacheng**, China
07 L 23 **Yacuiba**, Bolivia
07 J 18 **Yacuma**, Bolivia
86 I 8 **Yadong**, China
57 P 1 **Yadrin**, Russian Federation
99 M 26 **Yaeyama-rettō**, Japan
211 S 8 **Yafran**, Libya
43 E 21 **Yaghan Basin**, Atlantic Ocean
198 J 4 **Yagishiri-tō**, Japan
153 W 9 **Yagodnoye**, Russian Federation
83 I 21 **Yahk**, British Columbia, Canada
151 R 4 **Yahotyn**, Ukraine
216 M 7 **Yahuma**, Democratic Republic of Congo
199 J 17 **Yaizu**, Japan
188 K 6 **Yajiang**, China
216 J 5 **Yaka**, Central African Republic
186 G 8 **Yakeshi**, China
76 I 8 **Yakima**, Washington, U.S.A.
177 Q 12 **Yakmach**, Pakistan
146 G 11 **Yakoruda**, Bulgaria
199 D 25 **Yaku-shima**, Japan
198 I 7 **Yakumo**, Japan
79 U 10 **Yakutat**, Alaska, U.S.A.
153 T 10 **Yakutsk**, Russian Federation
151 V 9 **Yakymivka**, Ukraine
191 I 26 **Yala**, Thailand
217 N 8 **Yaleko**, Democratic Republic of Congo
216 M 4 **Yalinga**, Central African Republic
216 I 4 **Yaloké**, Central African Republic
170 E 8 **Yalova**, Turkey
151 U 13 **Yalta**, Ukraine
187 J 16 **Yalu**, China
152 J 11 **Yalutorovsk**, Russian Federation
170 F 11 **Yalvaş**, Turkey
198 L 10 **Yamada**, Japan
199 C 22 **Yamaga**, Japan
198 K 12 **Yamagata**, Japan
199 C 20 **Yamaguchi**, Japan
157 X 2 **Yamantau**, Russian Federation
199 N 22 **Yamato**, Japan
213 C 23 **Yambio**, Sudan
146 L 10 **Yambol**, Bulgaria
146 L 9 **Yambol**, Bulgaria
152 M 8 **Yamburg**, Russian Federation
193 T 14 **Yamdena**, Indonesia
196 H 1 **Y'ami**, Philippines
214 K 13 **Yamoussoukro**, Côte d'Ivoire
75 N 3 **Yampa**, Colorado, U.S.A.
151 N 7 **Yampil'**, Ukraine
151 T 1 **Yampil'**, Ukraine
182 L 11 **Yamuna**, India
184 L 11 **Yamzho Yumco**, China
187 E 16 **Yan Shan**, China
153 T 8 **Yana**, Russian Federation
234 H 7 **Yanaba Island**, Papua New Guinea
199 E 20 **Yanadani**, Japan
199 D 20 **Yanai**, Japan
181 H 19 **Yanam**, India
189 Q 2 **Yan'an**, China
155 S 14 **Yanaul**, Russian Federation
174 K 6 **Yanbu' al Baḩr**, Saudi Arabia
189 Y 4 **Yancheng**, China
185 N 7 **Yanchiwan**, China
189 R 1 **Yanchuan**, China
216 I 9 **Yandja**, Democratic Republic of Congo
216 K 3 **Yangalia**, Central African Republic
217 N 7 **Yangambi**, Democratic Republic of Congo
184 L 10 **Yangbajain**, China
188 J 10 **Yangbi**, China
189 S 3 **Yangcheng**, China
189 S 13 **Yangchun**, China
186 O 11 **Yanggang**, China
187 C 16 **Yanggao**, China
189 V 2 **Yanggu**, China
189 S 13 **Yangjiang**, China
189 T 1 **Yangquan**, China
189 T 11 **Yangshan**, China
189 R 11 **Yangshuo**, China
189 V 7 **Yangtze**, China
188 L 11 **Yangwu**, China
189 P 4 **Yangxian**, China
189 U 7 **Yangxin**, China
187 M 18 **Yangyang**, South Korea
187 C 16 **Yangyuan**, China
189 X 5 **Yangzhou**, China
189 Q 8 **Yanhe**, China
186 M 13 **Yanji**, China
188 M 8 **Yanjin**, China
188 J 7 **Yanjing**, China
67 N 11 **Yankton**, South Dakota, U.S.A.
188 J 8 **Yanmen**, China
187 D 16 **Yanqing**, China
187 E 19 **Yanshan**, China
188 M 12 **Yanshan**, China
189 R 11 **Yanshan**, China
189 W 8 **Yanshan**, China
153 T 7 **Yanskiy Zaliv**, Russian Federation
187 H 19 **Yantai**, China
149 A 15 **Yantarnyy**, Russian Federation
186 K 13 **Yantongshan**, China
189 Y 8 **Yantou**, China
146 J 6 **Yantra**, Bulgaria
189 X 3 **Yanweigang**, China
188 K 8 **Yanyuan**, China
189 V 2 **Yanzhou**, China
188 K 10 **Yao'an**, China
215 T 14 **Yaoundé**, Cameroon
189 Q 3 **Yaoxian**, China
236 K 14 **Yap**, Federated States of Micronesia
236 L 15 **Yap**, Federated States of Micronesia
40 K 7 **Yap Trench**, Pacific Ocean
193 W 11 **Yapen**, Indonesia
88 J 5 **Yaqui**, Mexico
104 M 3 **Yaracuy**, Venezuela
155 O 13 **Yaransk**, Russian Federation
170 E 14 **Yardimci Burnu**, Turkey
171 Y 10 **Yardimli**, Azerbaijan
127 Z 6 **Yare**, United Kingdom
237 U 1 **Yaren**, Nauru
155 P 9 **Yarensk**, Russian Federation
104 J 10 **Yari**, Colombia
175 P 13 **Yarīm**, Yemen
108 H 9 **Yaripo**, Brazil
184 H 6 **Yarkant He**, China
170 H 12 **Yarma**, Turkey
87 S 12 **Yarmouth**, Nova Scotia, Canada
154 J 13 **Yaroslavl'**, Russian Federation
154 J 12 **Yaroslavskaya Oblast'**, Russian Federation
156 H 1 **Yartsevo**, Russian Federation
104 H 5 **Yarumal**, Colombia
235 W 11 **Yasawa Group**, Fiji
157 N 11 **Yashalta**, Russian Federation
215 R 10 **Yashi**, Nigeria
215 P 11 **Yashikera**, Nigeria
157 P 11 **Yashkul'**, Russian Federation
150 I 7 **Yasinya**, Ukraine
149 C 14 **Yasnoye**, Russian Federation
191 K 17 **Yasothon**, Thailand
231 U 12 **Yass**, New South Wales, Australia
176 I 9 **Yāsūj**, Iran
170 M 7 **Yasun Burnu**, Turkey
170 C 12 **Yatağan**, Turkey
235 Q 14 **Yaté**, New Caledonia
69 P 6 **Yates Center**, Kansas, U.S.A.
84 K 3 **Yathkyed Lake**, Nunavut, Canada
217 N 7 **Yatolema**, Democratic Republic of Congo
199 C 22 **Yatsushiro**, Japan
172 F 10 **Yatta**, Israel
107 E 19 **Yauca**, Peru
107 G 18 **Yauri**, Peru
106 F 11 **Yavari**, Brazil/Peru
88 J 6 **Yávaros**, Mexico
181 F 16 **Yavatmal**, India
91 Z 14 **Yaviza**, Panama
179 Q 2 **Yavlenka**, Kazakhstan
150 I 4 **Yavoriv**, Ukraine
199 D 21 **Yawatahama**, Japan
176 K 9 **Yazd**, Iran
176 L 9 **Yazd**, Iran
176 I 9 **Yazd-e Khast**, Iran
177 O 8 **Yazdan**, Iran
171 N 11 **Yazihan**, Turkey
62 L 4 **Yazoo City**, Mississippi, U.S.A.
139 U 4 **Ybbs an der Donau**, Austria
147 G 22 **Ydra**, Greece
147 G 21 **Ydra**, Greece
191 F 18 **Ye**, Myanmar
215 X 5 **Yebbi-Bou**, Chad
184 H 6 **Yecheng**, China
131 S 10 **Yecla**, Spain
88 K 5 **Yécora**, Mexico
191 D 14 **Yedashe**, Myanmar
149 I 14 **Yedy**, Belarus
213 K 23 **Yeed**, Somalia
63 X 11 **Yeehaw Junction**, Florida, U.S.A.
154 H 11 **Yefimovskiy**, Russian Federation
156 K 4 **Yefremo**, Russian Federation
171 U 9 **Yeghegnadzor**, Armenia
179 V 5 **Yegindybulak**, Kazakhstan
215 N 12 **Yégué**, Togo
191 C 15 **Yegyi**, Myanmar
213 E 23 **Yei**, Sudan
213 D 22 **Yei**, Sudan
152 J 10 **Yekaterinburg**, Russian Federation
157 T 1 **Yelabuga**, Russian Federation
157 O 6 **Yelan'**, Russian Federation
151 R 8 **Yelanets'**, Ukraine
156 L 4 **Yelets**, Russian Federation
155 U 3 **Yeletskiy**, Russian Federation
157 T 3 **Yelkhovka**, Russian Federation
124 J 4 **Yell**, United Kingdom
189 R 2 **Yellow**, China
72 L 8 **Yellow Pine**, Idaho, U.S.A.
185 X 8 **Yellow Sea**, China
82 H 12 **Yellowknife**, Northwest Territories, Canada
73 U 7 **Yellowstone**, Montana, U.S.A.
73 S 9 **Yellowstone Lake**, Wyoming, U.S.A.
157 O 2 **Yel'niki**, Russian Federation
179 N 14 **Yeloten**, Turkmenistan
149 L 21 **Yel'sk**, Belarus
215 P 11 **Yelwa**, Nigeria
61 O 15 **Yemassee**, South Carolina, U.S.A.
175 T 12 **Yemen**, Asia
150 M 3 **Yemil'chyne**, Ukraine
154 K 8 **Yemtsa**, Russian Federation
155 P 8 **Yemva**, Russian Federation
190 L 11 **Yên Bai**, Vietnam
190 C 13 **Yenangyaung**, Myanmar
216 F 10 **Yénéganou**, Congo
184 G 6 **Yengisar**, China
216 H 7 **Yengo**, Congo
170 E 8 **Yenişehir**, Turkey
153 N 10 **Yenisey**, Russian Federation
45 X 9 **Yeniseykiy Zaliv**, Arctic Ocean
153 N 11 **Yeniseyskiy Kryazh**, Russian Federation
127 P 13 **Yeovil**, United Kingdom
88 K 5 **Yepachi**, Mexico
231 V 6 **Yeppoon**, Queensland, Australia
178 L 13 **Yerbent**, Turkmenistan
153 Q 11 **Yerbogachen**, Russian Federation
171 T 9 **Yerevan**, Armenia
179 T 4 **Yereymentau**, Kazakhstan
77 J 18 **Yerington**, Nevada, U.S.A.
170 J 9 **Yerköy**, Turkey
181 D 17 **Yermala**, India
153 T 13 **Yerofey**, Russian Federation
172 F 11 **Yeroham**, Israel
157 R 5 **Yershov**, Russian Federation
190 C 11 **Yesagyo**, Myanmar
179 P 4 **Yesil'**, Kazakhstan
170 J 11 **Yeşilhisar**, Turkey
170 E 12 **Yeşilova**, Turkey
157 N 13 **Yessentuki**, Russian Federation
171 W 8 **Yevlax**, Azerbaijan
151 T 12 **Yevpatoriya**, Ukraine
189 T 4 **Yexian**, China
156 K 10 **Yeysk**, Russian Federation
148 L 13 **Yezyaryshcha**, Belarus
186 J 9 **Yi'an**, China
189 N 8 **Yibin**, China
189 R 6 **Yichang**, China
189 S 6 **Yicheng**, China
189 R 2 **Yichuan**, China
186 L 9 **Yichun**, China
189 U 8 **Yichun**, China
188 J 6 **Yidun**, China
189 U 8 **Yifeng**, China
189 Q 3 **Yijun**, China
186 J 8 **Yilaha**, China
186 M 10 **Yilan**, China
170 L 9 **Yildizeli**, Turkey
186 I 6 **Yilehuli Shan**, China
188 M 11 **Yiliang**, China
188 M 9 **Yiliang**, China
188 L 9 **Yimen**, China
186 L 11 **Yimianpo**, China
186 G 4 **Yimuhe**, China
189 W 2 **Yinan**, China
185 Q 7 **Yinchuan**, China
189 T 6 **Yingcheng**, China
189 T 11 **Yingde**, China
188 I 11 **Yingjiang**, China
188 M 7 **Yingjing**, China
187 H 16 **Yingkou**, China
189 O 6 **Yingshan**, China
189 T 6 **Yingshan**, China
189 V 5 **Yingshang**, China
189 W 8 **Yingtan**, China
187 B 17 **Yingxian**, China
184 J 4 **Yining**, China
189 P 8 **Yinjiang**, China
188 L 10 **Yipinglang**, China
189 P 9 **Yiquan**, China
213 E 22 **Yirol**, Sudan
186 G 10 **Yirxie**, China
189 Q 11 **Yishan**, China
189 X 2 **Yishui**, China
194 B 13 **Yishun**, Singapore
186 H 6 **Yitulihe**, China
189 Y 7 **Yiwu**, China
187 H 15 **Yixian**, China
186 J 4 **Yixiken**, China
189 Y 6 **Yixing**, China
189 S 8 **Yiyang**, China
189 W 8 **Yiyang**, China
189 W 4 **Yiyuan**, China
189 T 10 **Yizhang**, China
148 C 12 **Ylakiai**, Lithuania
134 L 12 **Yli-Kärppä**, Finland
134 K 11 **Ylitornio**, Finland
45 Q 11 **Ymer Nunatak**, Greenland
153 V 11 **Ynykchanskiy**, Russian Federation
215 T 10 **Yobe**, Nigeria
198 I 6 **Yobetsu-dake**, Japan
213 K 19 **Yoboki**, Djibouti
196 K 12 **Yog Point**, Philippines
192 I 14 **Yogyakarta**, Indonesia
192 I 15 **Yogyakarta**, Indonesia
199 F 17 **Yōka**, Japan
215 V 14 **Yokadouma**, Cameroon
199 N 21 **Yokate-jima**, Japan
199 H 18 **Yokkaichi**, Japan
215 U 13 **Yoko**, Cameroon
199 K 16 **Yokohama**, Japan
199 K 16 **Yokosuka**, Japan
198 K 11 **Yokote**, Japan
215 U 12 **Yola**, Nigeria
216 M 9 **Yolombo**, Democratic Republic of Congo
199 E 18 **Yonago**, Japan
199 L 26 **Yonaguni-jima**, Japan
198 K 13 **Yonezawa**, Japan
194 E 10 **Yong Peng**, Malaysia
189 W 10 **Yong'an**, China
189 V 4 **Yongcheng**, China
187 N 20 **Yŏngch'ŏn**, South Korea
189 O 7 **Yongchuan**, China
189 V 9 **Yongfeng**, China
189 R 11 **Yongfu**, China
187 M 19 **Yŏngju**, South Korea
189 Y 7 **Yongkang**, China
188 J 10 **Yongping**, China
188 L 10 **Yongren**, China
188 M 8 **Yongshan**, China
188 K 9 **Yongsheng**, China
189 R 8 **Yongshun**, China
189 T 10 **Yongxing**, China
189 U 9 **Yongxing**, China
189 V 7 **Yongxiu**, China
189 S 10 **Yongzhou**, China
58 K 12 **Yonkers**, New York, U.S.A.
230 G 11 **York**, Western Australia, Australia
127 T 2 **York**, United Kingdom
58 F 14 **York**, Pennsylvania, U.S.A.
63 O 4 **York**, Alabama, U.S.A.
67 N 14 **York**, Nebraska, U.S.A.
86 E 13 **York**, Ontario, Canada
59 O 8 **York Harbor**, Maine, U.S.A.
231 P 11 **Yorke Peninsula**, South Australia, Australia
231 O 12 **Yorketown**, South Australia, Australia
127 R 1 **Yorkshire Dales**, United Kingdom
127 U 1 **Yorkshire Wolds**, United Kingdom
83 N 18 **Yorkton**, Saskatchewan, Canada
61 V 6 **Yorktown**, Virginia, U.S.A.
65 G 16 **Yorkville**, Illinois, U.S.A.
90 M 5 **Yoro**, Honduras
199 N 22 **Yoro-jima**, Japan
199 O 23 **Yoron-tō**, Japan
77 I 20 **Yosemite Village**, California, U.S.A.
155 O 14 **Yoshkar-Ola**, Russian Federation
187 M 21 **Yŏsu**, South Korea
172 F 12 **Yotvata**, Israel
125 C 20 **Youghal**, Republic of Ireland
125 D 21 **Youghal Bay**, Republic of Ireland
231 T 12 **Young**, New South Wales, Australia
110 M 11 **Young**, Uruguay
241 S 15 **Young Island**, Antarctica
41 X 14 **Young's Rock**, Pitcairn Island
65 O 17 **Youngstown**, Ohio, U.S.A.
210 G 7 **Youssoufia**, Morocco
189 Q 8 **Youyang**, China
152 M 14 **Youyi Feng**, Russian Federation
127 Z 8 **Yoxford**, United Kingdom
170 J 9 **Yozgat**, Turkey
77 G 14 **Yreka**, California, U.S.A.
234 F 2 **Ysabel Channel**, Papua New Guinea
135 E 26 **Ystad**, Sweden
127 N 9 **Ystalyfera**, United Kingdom
179 V 10 **Ysyk-Köl**, Kyrgyzstan
193 T 11 **Yu**, Indonesia
189 Z 11 **Yü Shan**, Taiwan
185 X 13 **Yü-Shan**, Taiwan
189 R 8 **Yuan**, China
189 Q 10 **Yuanbao Shan**, China
188 L 12 **Yuanjiang**, China
189 R 8 **Yuanling**, China
188 L 10 **Yuanmou**, China
187 B 18 **Yuanping**, China
189 S 3 **Yuanqu**, China
77 G 17 **Yuba City**, California, U.S.A.
198 K 5 **Yūbari-sanchi**, Japan
89 Y 10 **Yucatán**, Mexico
89 Y 9 **Yucatan Channel**, Mexico
89 Y 11 **Yucatan Peninsula**, Mexico
189 T 1 **Yuci**, China
187 E 14 **Yudaokou**, China
186 H 4 **Yudi Shan**, China
230 M 6 **Yuendumu**, Northern Territory, Australia
189 Z 8 **Yueqing**, China
188 L 8 **Yuexi**, China
189 V 6 **Yuexi**, China
189 T 7 **Yueyang**, China
189 W 8 **Yugan**, China
155 S 1 **Yugorskiy Poluostrov**, Russian Federation
189 R 1 **Yuhebu**, China
189 V 8 **Yujiang**, China
153 X 7 **Yukagirskoye Ploskogor'ye**, Russian Federation
148 K 13 **Yukhavichy**, Belarus
156 J 2 **Yukhnov**, Russian Federation
216 K 10 **Yuki**, Democratic Republic of Congo
80 I 6 **Yukon**, Yukon Territory, Canada
79 R 5 **Yukon Flats**, Alaska, U.S.A.
82 B 13 **Yukon Territory**, Canada
171 T 12 **Yüksekova**, Turkey
199 C 20 **Yukuhashi**, Japan
230 M 7 **Yulara**, Northern Territory, Australia
157 X 4 **Yuldybayevo**, Russian Federation
63 W 7 **Yulee**, Florida, U.S.A.
189 Z 12 **Yüli**, Taiwan
185 S 7 **Yulin**, China
189 R 13 **Yulin**, China
188 K 9 **Yulongxue Shan**, China
74 G 13 **Yuma**, Arizona, U.S.A.
216 I 9 **Yumbi**, Democratic Republic of Congo
217 O 8 **Yumbi**, Democratic Republic of Congo
185 O 7 **Yumen**, China
188 L 10 **Yun Gui Gaoyuan**, China
170 G 10 **Yunak**, Turkey
189 S 12 **Yunan**, China
78 I 14 **Yunaska Island**, Alaska, U.S.A.
189 R 3 **Yuncheng**, China
189 V 2 **Yuncheng**, China
189 S 12 **Yunfu**, China
107 J 20 **Yungas**, Bolivia
189 T 6 **Yunmeng**, China
188 K 11 **Yunnan**, China
231 Q 11 **Yunta**, South Australia, Australia

Country · Internal administrative region: State/Province/Territory/Dependent territory · Capital city · Mountain range/Undersea ridge · Mountain peak/Volcano/Seamount · Geographic feature · Headland/Point/Cape/Peninsula · Desert · Island/Island group · Antarctic base · Ocean · Sea · Bay/Gulf/Channel/Strait · Lake · Salt pan/Dry/Intermittent lake · River

▣ Country ▣ Internal administrative region: State/Province/Territory/Dependent territory ⚓ Capital city ▲ Mountain range/ Undersea ridge ▲ Mountain peak/ Volcano/Seamount ◇ Geographic feature ▶ Headland/Point/ Cape/Peninsula ▲ Desert ☷ Island/Island group ☷ Antarctic base ≋ Ocean ⤴ Sea ≈ Bay/Gulf/Channel/Strait ⤳ Lake ⬛ Salt pan/Dry/ Intermittent lake ⤳ River

CREDITS

PHOTO CREDITS

2t Craig Mahew & Robert Simmon/NASA/GSFC **5**bl Serg Andrefouet & Frank Muller-Karger/Institute for Marine Remote Sensing/University of South Florida; br DS **6**tc, tc AV HRR/NDVI/Seawifs/MODIS/NCEP/DMSP/Sky2000 star catalog/AVHRR & Seawifs/Reto Stockli/Marit Jentoft-Nilsen; tl PL; tr GI; Globes N_V **7**tc, tc, tl AVHRR/NDVI/Seawifs/ODIS/NCEP/DMSP/ Sky2000 star catalog/AVHRR & Seawifs/Reto Stockli/Marit Jentoft-Nilsen; tr Jerry Stebbins; Globes N_V **12**t PL **14**tc NASA/GSFC; c NASA/GSFC/METI/ ERSDAC/JAROS/US/ Japan ASTER Science Team; bc PL **17**b APL/Corbis; br, cr, tr GI **18**c NASA; cl APL/Corbis; tr DS **19**cr AAP/AFP; tr APL/Corbis **20**cr, tr APL/Corbis; tr PL **21**cr, br APL/Corbis **22**cr, br APL/ Corbis **23**tr REU **24**c, tr APL/Corbis **25**br, cr APL/Corbis **26**tr APL/Corbis **27**br, tc, tr APL/Corbis **28**t PL **32**bl APL/Corbis **33**br, tc, tl APL/Corbis **34**c METI/ERSDAC/JAROS/US/Japan ASTER Science Team/NASA/GSFC **36**bl Liam Gumley/MODIS Atmosphere Team/University of Wisconsin-Madison; cr COR **37**c APL/Corbis **38**cl APL/Corbis/AFP **39**tr APL/Corbis **40**bc, br, tc, tr APL/Corbis; c AAP **42**br, cl, tr APL/Corbis **43**c APL/Corbis **44**bc, br, c, cr, tr APL/Corbis **46**c Craig Mahew & Robert Simmon/NASA/GSFC **48**c NASA/GSFC/MITI/ERSDAC/JAROS/US/Japan ASTER Science Team; b APL/ Corbis; t Professor Stanley Herwitz/Clark University/NASA **49**c SRTM Team/NASA/JPL/NIMA **50**bl DS; br NASA/GSFC/LaRC/JPL/MISR Team; c Jacques Descloitres/ MODIS Land Rapid Response Team/NASA/GSFC **51**bl N_J; c Jeff Schmaltz/MODIS Rapid Response Team/NASA/GSFC **52**cl GI **55**br NASA; bc, c, cl, tc APL/Corbis **56**tc, tr APL/Corbis **57**br GI; tl APL/Corbis **58**tc PD; tr APL/Corbis **59**c, cl GI; cl APL/Corbis **61**bc, cr APL/Corbis **62**c GI; cl DS **63**cr GI; tr DS **64**cl APL/Corbis **65**br, cr, tr APL/Corbis **67**br, tr APL/Corbis; cr PD **68**cl APL/Corbis **69**bl, tr APL/Corbis **70**br APL/Corbis **71**bc, tc, tc, tr APL/Corbis; tl PD **72**bc, br APL/Corbis; tc GI **75**tc, tr APL/Corbis **76**bc GI; br COR **77**bc, bl PD; cr APL/ Corbis **78**bl, c, tc, tr GI; c PD **80**tc, tr APL/Corbis **81**br, cr APL/Corbis **82**cl GI; tl PD **83**bc, tc APL/Corbis **84**c GI; cl COR **85**br APL/Corbis; cr COR **86**br GI; tr APL/Corbis **87**tr GI **88**bc, br, cr APL/Corbis **89**tc, tl GI **90**br, cr APL/Corbis **91**c, tc, tl APL/Corbis **92**bl GI; cl APL/Corbis **94**c Craig Mahew & Robert Simmon/NASA/GSFC **96**bl, br, tr GI; **97**c Sea WiFS Project/NASA/Goddard Space Flight Centre/ORBIMAGE **98**br APL/Corbis; c NASA/GSFC/MITI/ERSDAC/JAROS/US/Japan Aster Science Team; cl GI **99**bl APL/ Corbis; c Sea WiFS Project/NASA/Goddard Space Flight Centre/ORBIMAGE; tr NASA/EFS **100**tl PD **103**br, c, cl, tr APL/Corbis; tl GI **104**bc APL/Corbis; br PD **105**bc, bl APL/ Corbis; c GI **106**c GI; cl APL/Corbis **107**tl, cr PD; tr PE **109**bc, cr, tc APL/Corbis; bc, bl PD **110**cr APL/Corbis; br GI **111**tl, tr GI **112**cl, cr, tl, tr APL/Corbis **113**c APL/Corbis **114**c Craig Mayhew & Robert Simmon/NASA/GSFC **116**bl NASA/GSFC/ MITI/ERSDAC/ JAROS/US/Japan ASTER Science Team; br, t NASA/GSFC/METI/ERSDAC/JAROS/US/Japan ASTER Science Team **117**c NASA/Our Earth as Art/USGC **118**bc APL/ Corbis; cl Jacques Descloitres/MODIS Rapid Response Team/NASA/GSFC tl PL **119**bl NASA/GSFC/LaRC/ JPL/MISR Team; c Earth Sciences and Image Analysis, NASA-Johnson Space Center **120**cr PL **123**c, cr APL/Corbis; tr AAP/Associated Press **124**bc APL/Corbis; br GI **125**tl GI **126**c, tc, tr APL/Corbis **127**br, tr APL/Corbis; tr GI **129**br, cr GI; tr APL/Corbis; tr PD **130**c COR; cl IOT **132**bl APL/Corbis; cl COR; tl GI **133**tc APL/Corbis; tl IOT **135**c PE; cr GI **136**br GI **137**br APL/Corbis; tr GI **138**tc, tr GI **139**tl GI **141**tc, tr APL/Corbis **142**bc Georg Gerster; br GI **143**tr PE **145**c, cl, tc, tr APL/Corbis; tl GI **147**tc APL/Corbis; tl Guido Alberto Rossi **149**bc, cr, APL/Corbis; tr GI **150**br APL/Corbis **151**tc, tr APL/ Corbis **152**tc GI; cl, tr APL/Corbis **154**bl, cl APL/Corbis **155**br, tc, tr APL/Corbis **156**c APL/Corbis **157**bc APL/Corbis; c GI **158**bc, br APL/Corbis; c PD **159**bl Guido Alberto Rossi; br APL/Corbis **160**c Craig Mahew & Robert Simmon/NASA/GSFC **162**b, c N_J cr NASA/ GSFC/METI/ERSDAC/JAROS/US/Japan Aster Science Team **163**br N_J **164**bc Jacques Descloitres /MODIS Land Rapid Response Team; bl APL/Corbis; cr Jeff Schmaltz/MODIS Rapid Response Team/NASA/GSFC **165**bl Jacques Descloitres/MODIS Land Rapid Response Team/ NASA/GSFC; cl Jacues Descloitres/MODIS Land Rapid Response Team/ NASA/GSFC **168**bl APL/Corbis **169**tc AAP/AFP; cl, tr APL/Corbis **170**bl APL/Corbis **171**bc, bl APL/Corbis **172**br, cr GI **173**br, tr APL/Corbis; cr GI **174**br APL/Corbis **175**br, tr APL/Corbis; tc GI **176**cl, c, tc, tr APL/Corbis **177**br APL/Corbis **178**tc, tr APL/ Corbis **179**tr APL/Corbis **180**bc AAP/EPA AFPI; c APL/Corbis **181**c APL/Corbis **182**c, cl, cr APL/Corbis **183**bl APL/Corbis **184**bc AAP/Associated Press/XINHUA NEWS AGENCY; br, cl APL/ Corbis; c PD **185**br PD **186**br, tl PD; cl, tc APL/Corbis **188**br AAP Image/EPA/Michael Reynolds; c, cl, cr APL/Corbis **189**br GI **190**c, cl, cr APL/Corbis **191**tr APL/Corbis; cr PD **192**bc GI bl AAP/Associated Press AP cr APL/Corbis **194**cr, tr APL/Corbis **195**bl, tr APL/Corbis **196**br, cr APL/Corbis **197**bl, cr APL/Corbis **198**tc GI; tr APL/Corbis **199**bl, tl GI; cr, tc APL/Corbis **200**c Craig Mahew & Robert Simmon/NASA/GSFC **202**bl, br, tr N_J **203**c Jacques Descloitres/MODIS Rapid Response Team/NASA/GSFC **204**br, cr APL/ Corbis; cl Jacques Descloitres/MODIS Land Science Team/NASA/GSFC; cl Jacques Descloitres/MODIS Land Rapid Response Team/NASA/GSFC **205**br, cl APL/Corbis; c Jacques Descloitres/ MODIS Land Rapid Response Team/ NASA/GSFC **206**cr GI **209**cr, tc, tr APL/Corbis **210**c, cl APL/Corbis **211**bc AAP/Associated Press; c APL/Corbis **212**cr APL/Corbis **213**cl, tl, tr APL/Corbis **214**cl APL/Corbis **215**br APL/ Corbis **216**cl PL **217**br, cr APL/Corbis **219**bc, bl, c, tr APL/Corbis **220**c Craig Mahew & Robert Simmon/NASA/GSFC **222**t Jacques Descloitres/MODIS Rapid Response Team/NASA/ GSFC; tl NASA/GSFC/MITI/ERSDAC/JAROS/US/Japan Aster Science Team **223**cr Jacques Descloitres/MODIS Land Science Team; tr GSFC/Landsat Team/Australian Ground Receiving Station Teams/NASA **224**bl APL/Corbis; br, c N_ES **225**c, cr N_ES **228**bl, br APL/Corbis **229**br PL; c Paul Hoehenberger/pacific-picture Bildagentur; cl, cr APL/Corbis **230**br APL/Corbis **231**bl, cr, tr APL/Corbis **232**c, cr APL/Corbis **233**bl, bc, c, cl APL/Corbis **234**bc, br, cr, tr APL/Corbis **236**br, cl, tr APL/Corbis **237**bl, tc APL/Corbis **238**c PL **240**c, cr, tr APL/Corbis **241**br, cr, tr APL/Corbis **242**c APL/Corbis; cr PL **243**c, br, tc APL/Corbis; cr N_T **244**t Jerry Stebbins

ILLUSTRATION CREDITS

Richard Bonson/Tom Connell/Wildlife Art: 18 **John Bull:** 1 **Andrew Davies/Creative Communication:** 16, 18, 20, 22, 23, 24, 26, 27, 36, 37, 44, 52, 54, 56, 59, 60, 62, 65, 66, 68, 71, 72, 75, 76, 79, 80, 83, 84, 87, 88, 90, 93, 99, 100, 102, 104, 106, 108, 110, 113, 120, 124, 126, 128, 130, 132, 134, 136, 138, 140, 142, 144, 146, 148, 150, 155, 157, 159, 166, 167, 168, 169, 170, 172, 174, 177, 178, 180, 182, 184, 187, 188, 190, 193, 194, 195, 196, 198, 206, 210, 211, 212, 215, 217, 218, 230, 231, 233, 235, 240, 242, 243, 248 **Chris Forsey:** 164 **Mark A. Garlick/space-art.co.uk:** 14, 15 **Rob Mancini** 21 **Map Illustrations:** 18, 30, 32, 33, 36, 37, 38, 39, 40, 41, 42, 43, 44, 50, 51, 52, 54, 55, 59, 74, 77, 79, 80, 81, 82, 84, 86, 88, 90, 92, 98, 99, 100, 102, 103, 104, 106, 108, 110, 112, 118, 119, 120, 121, 122, 123, 124, 126, 128, 130, 131, 132, 134, 135, 136, 138, 140, 142, 144, 146, 148, 150, 154, 156, 158, 164, 165, 167, 168, 169, 170, 172, 174, 176, 178, 180, 181, 182, 183, 184, 186, 188, 190, 192, 194, 196, 198, 204, 205, 206, 207, 208, 209, 210, 211, 212, 214, 216, 218, 224, 225, 226, 227, 228, 230, 232, 234, 236, 237, 240, 246, 247 **Map Illustrations/Creative Communication:** 56, 58, 60, 62, 64, 66, 68, 70, 72, 74, 76, 78 **Edwina Riddell:** 20, 21 **Suzanne Tawansi:** 10, 11, 31, 208, 209, 226, 229 **Richard Bonson/Wildlife Art:** 16 **Rod Westblade:** 50 **Murray Zanoni:** 39, 41, 44, 57, 63, 67, 68, 70, 74, 80, 84, 89, 91, 105, 109, 110, 113, 126, 127, 128, 132, 137, 138, 140, 142, 144, 146, 148, 151, 156, 159, 170, 172, 174, 179, 183, 191, 193, 195, 196, 210, 213, 214, 216, 219, 231, 232

FLAGS OF THE WORLD

Antigua and Barbuda

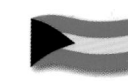

The Bahamas

Grenada

Guatemala

Haiti

Honduras

Jamaica

Mexico

Nicaragua

Panama

Brazil

Chile

Colombia

Ecuador

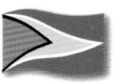

Guyana

Paraguay

Peru

Suriname

Bosnia and Herzegovina

Bulgaria

Croatia

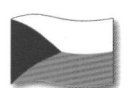

Czech Republic

Denmark

Estonia

Finland

France

Lithuania

Luxembourg

Macedonia

Malta

Moldova

Monaco

Netherlands

Norway

Spain

Sweden

Switzerland

Ukraine

United Kingdom

Vatican City

ASIA

Afghanistan

Cyprus

East Timor

Georgia

India

Indonesia

Iran

Iraq

Israel

Maldives

Mongolia

Myanmar (Burma)

Nepal

North Korea

Oman

Pakistan

Philippines

Thailand

Turkey

Turkmenistan

United Arab Emirates

Uzbekistan

Vietnam

Yemen

AFRICA

Central Africa Republic

Chad

Comoros

Congo

Côte d'Ivoire

Democratic Republic of Congo

Djibouti

Egypt

Kenya

Lesotho

Liberia

Libya

Madagascar

Malawi

Mali

Mauritania

Senegal

Seychelles

Sierra Leone

Somalia

South Africa, Republic of

Sudan

Swaziland

Tanzania

Kiribati

Marshall Islands

Micronesia, Federated States of

Nauru

New Zealand

Palau

Papua New Guinea

Samoa